EU LAW

EU LAW

TEXT, CASES, AND MATERIALS

Third Edition

PAUL CRAIG
AND
GRÁINNE DE BÚRCA

OXFORD
UNIVERSITY PRESS

OXFORD

UNIVERSITY PRESS

Great Clarendon Street, Oxford OX2 6DP

Oxford University Press is a department of the University of Oxford.
It furthers the University's objective of excellence in research, scholarship,
and education by publishing worldwide in

Oxford New York

Auckland Bangkok Buenos Aires Cape Town Chennai
Dar es Salaam Delhi Hong Kong Istanbul Karachi Kolkata
Kuala Lumpur Madrid Melbourne Mexico City Mumbai Nairobi
S„o Paulo Shanghai Taipei Tokyo Toronto

Oxford is a registered trade mark of Oxford University Press
in the UK and in certain other countries

Published in the United States
by Oxford University Press Inc., New York

© Text, Introductory Materials, Selection, and Notes
Paul Craig and Gr·inne de B'r ca, 2003

Database right Oxford University Press (maker)

First published 2003

British Library of Cataloguing in Publication Data

Data available

Library of Congress Cataloging in Publication Data

Data available

ISBN-13: 978–0–19–924943–5
ISBN-10: 0–19–924943–1

5 7 9 10 8 6

Typeset by RefineCatch Limited, Bungay, Suffolk
Printed in Great Britain by
Ashford Colour Press Ltd, Gosport, Hampshire

For Anita and Ciaran
P.P.C.

Do mo mháthair agus i gcuimhne m'athar
G. de B.

PREFACE TO THE THIRD EDITION

Four years is always a long time in the development of EU law. The period since the second edition has seen the passage, albeit not yet the ratification, of the Nice Treaty. The Community has approved a Charter of Fundamental Rights, the legal status of which is to be determined at the Inter-Governmental Conference 2004. The European Council established in 2002 a Convention to examine a broad range of matters that go to the heart of the EU, including its sphere of competence, the inter-institutional allocation of power, simplification of the Treaties, and the possibility of a European Constitution. Its conclusions will frame the deliberations of the Inter-Governmental Conference in 2004. There have, as ever, been important decisions from the Community courts, the enactment of significant Community legislation, and a vibrant secondary literature. These changes have been incorporated in the new edition. This has inevitably meant that material has been cut, and there have been some invidious choices as to what to include.

The structure of the chapters within the new edition has also been modified. The general aim has been to make what is often complex material more readily understandable. To this end, some chapters have been sub-divided. In more general terms, chapters now have sections setting out the central issues relating to a particular topic, summaries within the chapter of more difficult aspects of the discussion, and a concluding section.

We are indebted to Sophie Rogers, Jane Kavanagh, Miranda Vernon, and Angela Griffin at OUP, and to Maggie Shade for their professionalism and help in the preparation of this edition. Kate Elliott has, as always, done a wonderful job as copy-editor. Thanks also to Jo Aschenbrenner for excellent research assistance.

The book has been written on the basis of the law as it stood on 1 April 2002. We have, however, assumed that the Nice Treaty will be ratified.

Paul Craig
Gráinne de Búrca

OUTLINE TABLE OF CONTENTS

CONTENTS

TABLE OF ABBREVIATIONS

AC	Appeal Cases
All ER	All England Law Reports
Am. Econ. Rev.	*American Economic Review*
Am. J Comp. L	*American Journal of Comparative Law*
ANEC	European Association for the Co-ordination of Consumer Representation in Standardization
Antitrust B	*Antitrust Bulletin*
Antitrust LJ	*Antitrust Law Journal*
Bull. EC	Bulletin of the European Communities
BYIL	British Yearbook of International Law
CA	English Court of Appeal
CAP	Common Agricultural Policy
CDE	*Cahiers de Droit Européen*
CDP	Common Defence Policy
CEE	Charges of Equivalent Effect
CEN	European Committee for Standardization
CENELEC	European Committee for Technical Standardization
CFI	Court of First Instance
CFSP	Common Foreign and Security Policy
CLJ	*Cambridge Law Journal*
CLP	*Current Legal Problems*
CMLR	Common Market Law Reports
CMLRev.	*Common Market Law Review*
Col. JEL	*Columbia Journal of European Law*
Col. LR	*Columbia Law Review*
COREPER	Committee of the Permanent Representatives (of the Member States)
Cornell L Rev	*Cornell Law Review*
CYELS	*Cambridge Yearbook of European Legal Studies*
D & R	Decisions and Reports of the European Commission of Human Rights
Dec.	Decision
DG	Directorate General
Dir.	Directive
EAGGF	European Agricultural Guidance and Guarantee Fund
EC	European Community
ECB	European Central Bank
ECHR	European Convention on Human Rights
ECommHR	European Commission on Human Rights
ECtHR	European Court of Human Rights

ECJ	European Court of Justice
ECLR	*European Competition Law Review*
ECOSOC	Economic and Social Committee
ECR	European Court Reports
ECSC	European Coal and Steel Connunity
EC Treaty	European Community Treaty
ECU	European Currency Unit(s)
EDA	Exclusive Distribution Agreement
EDC	European Defence Community
EEA	European Economic Area
EEC	European Economic Community
EELR	*European Environmental Law Review*
EFTA	European Free Trade Association
EHRLR	European Human Rights Law Reports
EHRR	European Human Rights Reports
EIPR	*European Intellectual Property Review*
EJIL	*European Journal of International Law*
ELJ	*European Law Journal*
ELRev.	*European Law Review*
EMI	European Monetary Institute
EMU	Economic and Monetary Union
EP	European Parliament
EPA	Exclusive Purchasing Agreement
EPC	European Political Co-operation
EPL	European Public Law
ERPL	*European Review of Private Law*
ESCB	European System of Central Banks
EUP	*European Union Politics*
Euratom	European Atomic Energy Community
Europol	European Police Office
EU	European Union
Fordham Int. LJ	*Fordham International Law Journal*
GATT	General Agreement on Tariffs and Trade
GATS	General Agreement on Trade in Services
GNP	Gross national product
Harv. Int. LJ	*Harvard International Law Journal*
Harv. LR	*Harvard Law Review*
Hastings I & Comp. LJ	*Hastings International and Comparative Law Journal*
HL	House of Lords (England or Scotland)
HRLJ	*Human Rights Law Journal*
ICLQ	*International and Comparative Law Quarterly*
ICR	Industrial Cases Reports
IGC	Intergovernmental Conference
IJEL	*Irish Journal of European Law*

ILJ	*Industrial Law Journal*
IR	Irish Reports
JCMS	*Journal of Common Market Studies*
JEPP	*Journal of European Public Policy*
JHA	Justice and Home Affairs 'Pillar'
Jnl. Cons. Policy	*Journal of Consumer Policy*
J Pol. Econ.	*Journal of Political Economy*
JSWFL	*Journal of Social Welfare and Family Law*
JWTL	*Journal of World Trade Law*
LIEI	*Legal Issues of European Integration/Legal Issues of Economic Integration*
LQR	*Law Quarterly Review*
LS	*Legal Studies*
MCA, MCAs	Monetary Compensatory Amount(s)
MEQR	Measures having Equivalent Effect to a Quantitative Restriction
Mich. LR	*Michigan Law Review*
MJ	*Maastricht Journal of European and Comparative Law*
MLR	*Modern Law Review*
MTF	Mergers Task Force
NATO	North Atlantic Treaty Organization
Notre Dame LRev.	*Notre Dame Law Review*
NWJ Int. L and Bus.	*Northwestern Journal of International Law and Business*
NYULRev.	*New York University Law Review*
OECD	Organization for Economic Co-operation and Development
OEEC	Organization for European Economic Co-operation
OJ	Official Journal of the European Communities
OJLS	*Oxford Journal of Legal Studies*
PDB	Preliminary Draft Budget (of the Community)
PJCC	Police and Judicial Co-operation in Criminal Matters
PL	*Public Law*
QB	Queen's Bench Reports
Reg.	Regulation
SDA	Selective Distribution Agreement
SEA	Single European Act
SMEs	Small and Medium-sized Enterprises
So. Cal. L Rev.	*Southern California Law Review*
SPA	Social Policy Agreement
Summit	European Council Meeting

TBT	Technical Barriers to Trade
TEU	Treaty on European Union ('Maastricht Treaty')
TN	Treaty of Nice
ToA	Treaty of Amsterdam
TRIPS	Trade-Related Aspects of Intellectual Property Rights
U Chic. Legal Forum	*University of Chicago Legal Forum*
Vand. L Rev.	*Vanderbilt Law Review*
VAT	Value Added Tax
WEU	Western European Union
WLR	Weekly Law Reports
WTO	World Trade Organization
YaleLJ	*Yale Law Journal*
YBEL	*Yearbook of European Law*

ACKNOWLEDGEMENTS

Grateful acknowledgement is made to all the authors and publishers of copyright material which appears in this book, and in particular to the following for permission to reprint material from the sources indicated:

BASIC BOOKS, a member of Perseus Books LLC for extracts from R. H. Bork: *The Antitrust Paradox: A Policy at War with Itself* (1978), copyright © 1978 Basic Books, Inc.

BLACKWELL PUBLISHERS for extract from P. Dankert: 'The EC—Past, Present and Future' in L. Tsoukalis (ed.): *The EC—Past, Present and Future* (Basil Blackwell, 1983).

BLACKWELL SCIENCE LTD for extracts from *Modern Law Review*, A. Arnull: 'The use and abuse of Article 177', *MLR* 52 (1989); W. Bishop: 'Price discrimination under Article 86: Political economy in the European Court', *MLR* 44 (1981); A. McGee and S. Weatherill: 'The evolution of the single market-harmonization or liberalisation', *MLR* 53 (1990); and F. Snyder: 'The Effectiveness of European Community Law', *MLR* 56 (1993); extracts from *European Law Journal*, P. Kirchhof: 'The Balance of Powers between National and European Institutions' *ELJ* 5 (1999); and R. Rawlings: 'Engaged Elites: Citizen Action and Institutional Attitudes in Commission Enforcement', *ELJ* 6 (2000); and extract from J. Pelkmans: 'The new approach to technical harmonization and standardization', *JCMS* 25 (1987).

THE BUTTERWORTHS DIVISION OF REED ELSEVIER (UK) LTD for extracts from F. Jacobs: 'Is the Court of Justice of the European Communities a Constitutional Court?', and D. O'Keeffe: 'Judicial Interpretation of the Public Service Exception to the Free Movement of Workers', in D. Curtin & D. O'Keeffe (eds.): *Constitutional Adjudication in European Community and National Law* (Butterworths Ireland, 1992); M. Westlake: *The Commission and the Parliament: Partners and Rivals in the European Policy-Making Process* (Butterworths, 1994); and R. Whish: *Competition Law* (Butterworths, 2001).

CONTINUUM INTERNATIONAL PUBLISHING GROUP LTD, The Tower Building, 11 York Road, London for extracts from M. Holland: *European Integration from Community to Union* (Pinter, 1993); J. Lodge: introduction, and 'EC Policymaking: Insitutional Dynamics', and from S. Mazey & J. Richardson: 'Pressure Groups and Lobbying in the EC', in J. Lodge (ed): *The European Community and the Challenge of the Future* (Pinter, 1993); and W. Wessels: 'Administrative Interaction', in W. Wallace (ed.): *The Dynamics of European Integration* (RSIA/Pinter 1990).

FORDHAM UNIVERSITY SCHOOL OF LAW for extract from B. Hawk: 'Joint ventures under EEC Law', in B. Hawk (ed.): *Fordham Corporate Law Institute* (Fordham, 1991).

HART PUBLISHING LTD for extracts from A. Dashwood & A. Johnston (eds.): *The Future of the Judicial System of the European Union* (Hart, 2001); C. Harlow: 'A

Common European Law of Remedies?', in C. Kilpatrick, T. Novitz, and P. Skidmore (eds.): *The Future of Remedies in Europe* (Hart, 2000); M. P. Maduro: *We the Court, The European Court of Justice and the European Economic Constitution* (Hart, 1998); S. Peers: 'Fundamental Right or Political Whim? WTO Law and the ECJ', in G. de Búrca and J. Scott (eds.): *The EU and the WTO: Legal and Constitutional Issues* (Hart, 2001); and R. Wesseling: *The Modernisation of the EC Antitrust Law* (Hart, 1985).

HARVARD LAW REVIEW for extract from W. Comanor: 'Vertical price-fixing, vertical market restrictions, and the new antitrust policy', in *Harvard Law Review* 98 (1985), copyright © 1985 Harvard Law Review Association.

JOHNS HOPKINS UNIVERSITY PRESS for extract from Wayne Sandholz and John Zysman: '1992: Recasting the European Bargain', in *World Politics* 42:1 (1989), copyright © 1989 Center of International Studies, Princeton University.

KLUWER LAW INTERNATIONAL for extracts from *Common Market Law Review*, G. Bebr: 'The Existence of a genuine dispute: An indispensable precondition for the jurisdiction of the Court under Article 177 EEC Treaty?', *CMLR* 17 (1980); J. Coppel and A. O'Neill: The European Court of Justice: Taking Rights Seriously', *CMLR* 29 (1992); D. Curtin: 'Scalping the Community Legislator: Occupational Pensions and "Barber"', *CMLR* 27 (1990); C.-D. Ehlermann: 'The international market following the Single European Act', *CMLR* 24 (1987); J. Frowein: 'Solange II', *CMLR* 25 (1988); G. Gaja: 'New developments in the continuing story: The relationship between EEC Law and Italian Law', *CMLR* 27 (1990); B. Hawk: 'System Failure: Vertical restraints and the EC Competition Law', *CMLR* 32 (1995); H. Rasmussen: 'Remedying the crumbling EC Judicial system', *CMLR* 37 (2000); A. Rosas: 'Portugal v Council', *CMLR* 37 (2000); S. Weatherill: 'After Keck: Some thoughts on how to clarify the clarification', *CMLR* 33 (1996); and E. White: 'In search of the limits to Article 30 of the EEC Treaty', *CMLR* 26 (1989); for extracts from *Legal Issues of European Integration*, G. Davies: 'Welfare as a Service', *LIEI 27* (2002); and A. G. Toth: 'The law as it stands on the Appeal for Failure Act', in *LIEI* 2 (1975); and for extract from S. O'Leary: *The Evolving Concept of Community Citizenship* (Kluwer, 1996).

VALENTINE KORAH for extract from V. Korah: 'The Rise and Fall of Provisional Validity—The Need for a Rule of reason in EEC Antitrust', in *NWJ Int. L and Bus.*, 320 (Northwestern University School of Law, 1981).

MANCHESTER UNIVERSITY PRESS for extract from P. K. Armstrong and S. Bulmer: *The Governance of the Single European Market* (1998).

MIT PRESS JOURNALS for extract from Andrew Moravcsik: 'Negotiating the Single European Act: National interests and conventional Statecraft in the European Community', in *International Organization* 45:1 (Winter, 1991), copyright © 1991 the World Peace Foundation and the Massachusetts Institute of Technology.

NOMOS VERLAGSGESELLSCHAFT for extracts from R. Dehousse: 'Completing the Internal Market: Institutional constraints and challenges', in R. Bieber, R. Dehousse, J. Pinder, and J. Weiler (eds.): *One European Market?* (1988); and N. Fennelly:

'Preserving the Legal Coherence within the New Treaty: The ECJ after the Treaty of Amsterdam', in *Maastricht Journal of European & Comparative Law* 5 (1998).

OXFORD UNIVERSITY PRESS for extracts from P. P. Craig: 'Britain in the European Union', in J. Jowell & D. Oliver (eds.): *The Changing Constitution* (OUP, 4th edn., 2000); N. MacCormick: *Questioning Sovereignty* (OUP, 1999); F. Snyder: 'EMU Revisited: Are We Making a Constitution? What Constitution Are We Making?', in P. Craig and G. de Búrca (eds.) *The Evolution of EU Law* (OUP, 1999); J. H. H. Weiler: 'The Judicial Après-Nice', in G. de Búrca and J. H. H. Weiler (eds.): The *European Court of Justice* (OUP, 2001); and for extracts from *Year Book of European Law*, G. de Búrca: 'The Principles of Proportionality and its Application in EC Law', *YBEL* 13 (1993); C. Harding: 'The impact of Article 177 of the EEC Treaty on the Review of Community Action', *YBEL* 1 (1981); G. F. Mancini and D. T. Keeling: 'From CILFIT to ERT: The constitutional challenge facing the European Court', *YBEL* 11 (1991); J. Weiler: 'The Community System: the Dual Character of Supranationalism', *YBEL* 1 (1981); and R. Whish and B. Sufrin: 'Article 85 and the Rule of Reason', *YBEL* 7 (1987).

OXFORD UNIVERSITY PRESS JOURNALS for extracts from *Industrial Law Journal*, B. Fitzpatrick: 'Equality in Occupational Pension Schemes', *ILJ* 23 (1994), and S. Fredman: 'European Community Discrimination Law: A Critique', *ILJ* 21 (1992); and extract from N. Reich: 'Judge-made "Europe a la carte": Some remarks on recent conflicts between European and German Constitutional Law provoked by the Banana Litigation', *European Journal of International Law* 7 (1996).

PALGRAVE PUBLISHERS LTD for extract from N. Nugent: *The Government and Politics in the European Union* (Macmillan, 4th edn., 1999).

PEARSON EDUCATION LTD for extract from D. Curtin: 'The Constitutional Structure of the Union: A Europe of Bits and Pieces', in *The Common Market Law Review*, published by Kluwer.

PENGUIN BOOKS LTD for extracts from Christopher Johnson: *In with the Euro, Out with the Pound* (Penguin, 1996), copyright © Christopher Johnson 1969; Dennis Swann: *The Economics of the Common Market* (7th edn., Penguin, 1992), copyright © Dennis Swann 1970, 1992; and Stephen Weatherill and Paul Beaumont: *EU Law: The Essential Guide* (3rd edn., Penguin, 1999), copyright © Stephen Weatherill & Paul Beaumont 1993.

SAGE PUBLICATIONS, INC for extracts from K. J. Alter and S. Meunier-Aitsahalia: 'Judicial politics in the European Community: European integration and the pathbreaking Cassis de Dijon decision', in *Comparative Political Studies* 26 (1994), copyright © 1994 Sage Publications, Inc.

SWEET & MAXWELL LTD for extracts from W. R. Cornish: *Intellectual Property: Patents, Copyright, Trade Marks and Allied Rights* (4th edn., Sweet & Maxwell, 1999); from *Law Quarterly Review*, P. P. Craig: 'Compensation in Public Law', *LQR* 96 (1980), and F. G. Jacobs: 'When to refer to the European Court', *LQR* 90 (1974); from *European Competition Law Review*, D. Ridyard: 'Essential facilities and the obligation to supply competitors' (1996); and from *European Law Review*, C. Barnard: 'Fitting the remaining pieces into the Goods and Persons jigsaw', *ELR* 26 (2001); J. S. Chard: 'The economics of the application of Article 85 to selective distribution systems', *ELR* 7 (1982); L. Gormley and J. de Haan: 'The democratic deficit of the European Central Bank', *ELR* 21 (1996); C. Harding: 'The private interest in challenging community action', *ELR* 5 (1980); F. Jacobs: 'Human Rights in the EU: the Role of the Court of Justice', *ELR* 26 (2001); H.-C. Lasa and U. D. von Heydebrand: 'Free movement of foodstuffs, consumer protection and food standards in the European Community: Has the Court of Justice got it wrong?', *ELR* 16 (1991); J. F. M. Martin & On Stehmann: 'Product Market Integration versus Regional Cohesion in the Community', *ELR* 16 (1991); P. Pescatore: 'The Doctrine of "Direct Effect": An Infant Disease of Community Law', *ELR* 8 (1983); R. Petriccione: 'Italy: Supremacy of Community Law over National Law', *ELR* 11 (1986); D. Pollard: 'The Conseil d'Etat is European—Official', *ELR* 15 (1990); C. Quigley: 'The Notion of a State Aid in the EEC', *ELR* 13 (1988); H. Rasmussen: 'Why is Article 173 interpreted against Private Plaintiffs?', *ELR* 5 (1980); W. P. J. Wills: The search for the rule in Article 30 EEC: Much Ado About Nothing?', *ELR* 18 (1993); D. Wyatt: 'Foglia (No. 2): The Court denies it has jurisdiction to give advisory opinions', *ELR* 7 (1982; and G. Zonnekyn: 'The Status of WTO Law in the Community legal order: some comments in the light of the Portuguese Textiles Case', *ELR* 25 (2000).

TAYLOR & FRANCIS GROUP PLC (www.tandf.co.uk) for extracts from J. Fitzmaurice: 'The European Commission', in A. Duff, J. Pinder, and R. Pryce (eds.): *Maastricht and Beyond, Building the European Union* (Routledge, 1994); Lord Mackenzie Stewart: *The European Communities and the Rule of Law* (Stevens, 1977); and J. Sohrab: 'Women and Social Security Law: The limits of EEC Equality law', *Journal of Social Welfare and Family Law*, 5.

JOHN WILEY & SONS LTD: extracts from A. G. Toth: 'A Legal Analysis of Subsidiarity' and J. Steiner: 'Subsidiarity under the Maastricht Treaty', from D. O'Keeffe & P. M. Twomey (eds.): *Legal Issues of the Maastricht Treaty* (Chancery Press, 1994), copyright © 1994 John Wiley & Sons Ltd.

THE YALE UNIVERSITY LAW JOURNAL COMPANY and WILLIAM S. HEIN COMPANY for extracts from J. Weiler: 'The Transformation of Europe', *The YaleLJ* Vol. 100 (1991).

Every effort has been made to trace and contact copyright holders prior to publication. If notified, the publisher will undertake to rectify any errors or omissions at the earliest opportunity.

TABLE OF CASES

EUROPEAN COURT OF JUSTICE & COURT OF FIRST INSTANCE

A ALPHABETICAL

B NUMERICAL

EUROPEAN COURT OF FIRST INSTANCE

CASES FROM OTHER JURISDICTIONS

BELGIUM

EUROPEAN COURT & COMMISSION OF HUMAN RIGHTS

EUROPEAN PARLIAMENT

DENMARK

FRANCE

GERMANY

IRELAND

ITALY

TABLE OF TREATIES, EUROPEAN LEGISLATIVE INSTRUMENTS, AND NATIONAL LEGISLATION

TABLE OF EQUIVALENCES REFERRED TO IN ARTICLE 12 OF THE TREATY OF AMSTERDAM

A. TREATY ON EUROPEAN UNION

Previous numbering	New numbering	Previous numbering	New numbering
TITLE I	TITLE I	TITLE VI (***)	TITLE VI
Article A	Article 1	Article K.1	Article 29
Article B	Article 2	Article K.2	Article 30
Article C	Article 3	Article K.3	Article 31
Article D	Article 4	Article K.4	Article 32
Article E	Article 5	Article K.5	Article 33
Article F	Article 6	Article K.6	Article 34
Article F.1 (*)	Article 7	Article K.7	Article 35
		Article K.8	Article 36
TITLE II	TITLE II	Article K.9	Article 37
Article G	Article 8	Article K.10	Article 38
		Article K.11	Article 39
TITLE III	TITLE III	Article K.12	Article 40
Article H	Article 9	Article K.13	Article 41
		Article K.14	Article 42
TITLE IV	TITLE IV		
Article I	Article 10	TITLE VIA (**)	TITLE VII
		Article K.15 (*)	Article 43
TITLE V (***)	TITLE V	Article K.16 (*)	Article 44
Article J.1	Article 11	Article K.17 (*)	Article 45
Article J.2	Article 12		
Article J.3	Article 13	TITLE VII	TITLE VIII
Article J.4	Article 14	Article L	Article 46
Article J.5	Article 15	Article M	Article 47
Article J.6	Article 16	Article N	Article 48
Article J.7	Article 17	Article O	Article 49
Article J.8	Article 18	Article P	Article 50
Article J.9	Article 19	Article Q	Article 51
Article J.10	Article 20	Article R	Article 52
Article J.11	Article 21	Article S	Article 53
Article J.12	Article 22		
Article J.13	Article 23		
Article J.14	Article 24		
Article J.15	Article 25		
Article J.16	Article 26		
Article J.17	Article 27	(*) New Article introduced by the Treaty of Amsterdam	
Article J.18	Article 28	(**) New Title introduced by the Treaty of Amsterdam	
		(***) Title restructured by the Treaty of Amsterdam	

B. TREATY ESTABLISHING THE EUROPEAN COMMUNITY

Previous numbering	New numbering	Previous numbering	New numbering
PART ONE	PART ONE	Article 20 (repealed)	—
Article 1	Article 1	Article 21 (repealed)	—
Article 2	Article 2	Article 22 (repealed)	—
Article 3	Article 3	Article 23 (repealed)	—
Article 3a	Article 4	Article 24 (repealed)	—
Article 3b	Article 5	Article 25 (repealed)	—
Article 3c (*)	Article 6	Article 26 (repealed)	—
Article 4	Article 7	Article 27 (repealed)	—
Article 4a	Article 8	Article 28	Article 26
Article 4b	Article 9	Article 29	Article 27
Article 5	Article 10		
Article 5a (*)	Article 11	CHAPTER 2	CHAPTER 2
Article 6	Article 12	Article 30	Article 28
Article 6a (*)	Article 13	Article 31 (repealed)	—
Article 7 (repealed)	—	Article 32 (repealed)	—
Article 7a	Article 14	Article 33 (repealed)	—
Article 7b (repealed)	—	Article 34	Article 29
Article 7c	Article 15	Article 35 (repealed)	—
Article 7d (*)	Article 16	Article 36	Article 30
		Article 37	Article 31
PART TWO	PART TWO		
Article 8	Article 17	TITLE II	TITLE II
Article 8a	Article 18	Article 38	Article 32
Article 8b	Article 19	Article 39	Article 33
Article 8c	Article 20	Article 40	Article 34
Article 8d	Article 21	Article 41	Article 35
Article 8e	Article 22	Article 42	Article 36
		Article 43	Article 37
PART THREE	PART THREE	Article 44 (repealed)	—
TITLE I	TITLE I	Article 45 (repealed)	—
Article 9	Article 23	Article 46	Article 38
Article 10	Article 24	Article 47 (repealed)	—
Article 11 (repealed)	—		
		TITLE III	TITLE III
CHAPTER 1	CHAPTER 1	CHAPTER 1	CHAPTER 1
Section 1 (deleted)	—	Article 48	Article 39
Article 12	Article 25	Article 49	Article 40
Article 13 (repealed)	—	Article 50	Article 41
Article 14 (repealed)	—	Article 51	Article 42
Article 15 (repealed)	—		
Article 16 (repealed)	—		
Article 17 (repealed)	—		
Section 2 (deleted)	—		
Article 18 (repealed)	—	(*) New Article introduced by the Treaty of Amsterdam	
Article 19 (repealed)	—	(**) New Title introduced by the Treaty of Amsterdam	
		(***) Title restructured by the Treaty of Amsterdam	

Previous numbering	New numbering	Previous numbering	New numbering
CHAPTER 2	CHAPTER 2	TITLE IV	TITLE V
Article 52	Article 43	Article 74	Article 70
Article 53 (repealed)	—	Article 75	Article 71
Article 54	Article 44	Article 76	Article 72
Article 55	Article 45	Article 77	Article 73
Article 56	Article 46	Article 78	Article 74
Article 57	Article 47	Article 79	Article 75
Article 58	Article 48	Article 80	Article 76
		Article 81	Article 77
CHAPTER 3	CHAPTER 3	Article 82	Article 78
Article 59	Article 49	Article 83	Article 79
Article 60	Article 50	Article 84	Article 80
Article 61	Article 51		
Article 62 (repealed)	—	TITLE V	TITLE VI
Article 63	Article 52	CHAPTER 1	CHAPTER 1
Article 64	Article 53	SECTION 1	SECTION 1
Article 65	Article 54	Article 85	Article 81
Article 66	Article 55	Article 86	Article 82
		Article 87	Article 83
CHAPTER 4	CHAPTER 4	Article 88	Article 84
Article 67 (repealed)	—	Article 89	Article 85
Article 68 (repealed)	—	Article 90	Article 86
Article 69 (repealed)	—	Section 2 (deleted)	—
Article 70 (repealed)	—	Article 91 (repealed)	—
Article 71 (repealed)	—		
Article 72 (repealed)	—	SECTION 3	SECTION 2
Article 73 (repealed)	—	Article 92	Article 87
Article 73a (repealed)	—	Article 93	Article 88
Article 73b	Article 56	Article 94	Article 89
Article 73c	Article 57		
Article 73d	Article 58	CHAPTER 2	CHAPTER 2
Article 73e (repealed)	—	Article 95	Article 90
Article 73f	Article 59	Article 96	Article 91
Article 73g	Article 60	Article 97 (repealed)	—
Article 73h (repealed)	—	Article 98	Article 92
		Article 99	Article 93
TITLE IIIA	TITLE IV		
Article 73i (*)	Article 61	CHAPTER 3	CHAPTER 3
Article 73j (*)	Article 62	Article 100	Article 94
Article 73k (*)	Article 63	Article 100a	Article 95
Article 73l (*)	Article 64	Article 100b (repealed)	—
Article 73m (*)	Article 65	Article 100c (repealed)	—
Article 73n (*)	Article 66	Article 100d (repealed)	—
Article 73o (*)	Article 67	Article 101	Article 96
Article 73p (*)	Article 68	Article 102	Article 97
Article 73q (*)	Article 69		

Previous numbering	New numbering	Previous numbering	New numbering
TITLE VI	**TITLE VII**	**TITLE VII**	**TITLE IX**
CHAPTER 1	CHAPTER 1	Article 110	Article 131
Article 102a	Article 98	Article 111 (repealed)	—
Article 103	Article 99	Article 112	Article 132
Article 103a	Article 100	Article 113	Article 133
Article 104	Article 101	Article 114 (repealed)	—
Article 104a	Article 102	Article 115	Article 134
Article 104b	Article 103	Article 116 (repealed)	—
Article 104c	Article 104		
		TITLE VIIA (**)	**TITLE X**
CHAPTER 2	CHAPTER 2	Article 116 (*)	Article 135
Article 105	Article 105		
Article 105a	Article 106	**TITLE VIII**	**TITLE XI**
Article 106	Article 107	CHAPTER 1 (***)	CHAPTER 1
Article 107	Article 108	Article 117	Article 136
Article 108	Article 109	Article 118	Article 137
Article 108a	Article 110	Article 118a	Article 138
Article 109	Article 111	Article 118b	Article 139
		Article 118c	Article 140
CHAPTER 3	CHAPTER 3	Article 119	Article 141
Article 109a	Article 112	Article 119a	Article 142
Article 109b	Article 113	Article 120	Article 143
Article 109c	Article 114	Article 121	Article 144
Article 109d	Article 115	Article 122	Article 145
CHAPTER 4	CHAPTER 4	CHAPTER 2	CHAPTER 2
Article 109e	Article 116	Article 123	Article 146
Article 109f	Article 117	Article 124	Article 147
Article 109g	Article 118	Article 125	Article 148
Article 109h	Article 119		
Article 109i	Article 120	CHAPTER 3	CHAPTER 3
Article 109j	Article 121	Article 126	Article 149
Article 109k	Article 122	Article 127	Article 150
Article 109l	Article 123		
Article 109m	Article 124	**TITLE IX**	**TITLE XII**
		Article 128	Article 151
TITLE VIA (**)	**TITLE VIII**		
Article 109n (*)	Article 125	**TITLE X**	**TITLE XIII**
Article 109o (*)	Article 126	Article 129	Article 152
Article 109p (*)	Article 127		
Article 109q (*)	Article 128	**TITLE XI**	**TITLE XIV**
Article 109r (*)	Article 129	Article 129a	Article 153
Article 109s (*)	Article 130		
		TITLE XII	**TITLE XV**
		Article 129b	Article 154
		Article 129c	Article 155
		Article 129d	Article 156

(*) New Article introduced by the Treaty of Amsterdam
(**) New Title introduced by the Treaty of Amsterdam
(***) Title restructured by the Treaty of Amsterdam

Previous numbering	New numbering	Previous numbering	New numbering
TITLE XIII	TITLE XVI	PART FIVE	PART FIVE
Article 130	Article 157	TITLE I	TITLE I
		CHAPTER 1	CHAPTER 1
TITLE XIV	TITLE XVII	SECTION 1	SECTION 1
Article 130a	Article 158	Article 137	Article 189
Article 130b	Article 159	Article 138	Article 190
Article 130c	Article 160	Article 138a	Article 191
Article 130d	Article 161	Article 138b	Article 192
Article 130e	Article 162	Article 138c	Article 193
		Article 138d	Article 194
TITLE XV	TITLE XVIII	Article 138e	Article 195
Article 130f	Article 163	Article 139	Article 196
Article 130g	Article 164	Article 140	Article 197
Article 130h	Article 165	Article 141	Article 198
Article 130i	Article 166	Article 142	Article 199
Article 130j	Article 167	Article 143	Article 200
Article 130k	Article 168	Article 144	Article 201
Article 130l	Article 169		
Article 130m	Article 170	SECTION 2	SECTION 2
Article 130n	Article 171	Article 145	Article 202
Article 130o	Article 172	Article 146	Article 203
Article 130p	Article 173	Article 147	Article 204
Article 130q (repealed)	—	Article 148	Article 205
		Article 149 (repealed)	—
TITLE XVI	TITLE XIX	Article 150	Article 206
Article 130r	Article 174	Article 151	Article 207
Article 130s	Article 175	Article 152	Article 208
Article 130t	Article 176	Article 153	Article 209
		Article 154	Article 210
TITLE XVII	TITLE XX		
Article 130u	Article 177	SECTION 3	SECTION 3
Article 130v	Article 178	Article 155	Article 211
Article 130w	Article 179	Article 156	Article 212
Article 130x	Article 180	Article 157	Article 213
Article 130y	Article 181	Article 158	Article 214
		Article 159	Article 215
PART FOUR	PART FOUR	Article 160	Article 216
Article 131	Article 182	Article 161	Article 217
Article 132	Article 183	Article 162	Article 218
Article 133	Article 184	Article 163	Article 219
Article 134	Article 185		
Article 135	Article 186		
Article 136	Article 187		
Article 136a	Article 188		

Previous numbering	New numbering	Previous numbering	New numbering
SECTION 4	SECTION 4	CHAPTER 3	CHAPTER 3
Article 164	Article 220	Article 193	Article 257
Article 165	Article 221	Article 194	Article 258
Article 166	Article 222	Article 195	Article 259
Article 167	Article 223	Article 196	Article 260
Article 168	Article 224	Article 197	Article 261
Article 168a	Article 225	Article 198	Article 262
Article 169	Article 226		
Article 170	Article 227	CHAPTER 4	CHAPTER 4
Article 171	Article 228	Article 198a	Article 263
Article 172	Article 229	Article 198b	Article 264
Article 173	Article 230	Article 198c	Article 265
Article 174	Article 231		
Article 175	Article 232	CHAPTER 5	CHAPTER 5
Article 176	Article 233	Article 198d	Article 266
Article 177	Article 234	Article 198e	Article 267
Article 178	Article 235		
Article 179	Article 236	TITLE II	TITLE II
Article 180	Article 237	Article 199	Article 268
Article 181	Article 238	Article 200 (repealed)	—
Article 182	Article 239	Article 201	Article 269
Article 183	Article 240	Article 201a	Article 270
Article 184	Article 241	Article 202	Article 271
Article 185	Article 242	Article 203	Article 272
Article 186	Article 243	Article 204	Article 273
Article 187	Article 244	Article 205	Article 274
Article 188	Article 245	Article 205a	Article 275
		Article 206	Article 276
SECTION 5	SECTION 5	Article 206a (repealed)	—
Article 188a	Article 246	Article 207	Article 277
Article 188b	Article 247	Article 208	Article 278
Article 188c	Article 248	Article 209	Article 279
		Article 209a	Article 280
CHAPTER 2	CHAPTER 2		
Article 189	Article 249		
Article 189a	Article 250		
Article 189b	Article 251		
Article 189c	Article 252		
Article 190	Article 253		
Article 191	Article 254		
Article 191a (*)	Article 255		
Article 192	Article 256		

(*) New Article introduced by the Treaty of Amsterdam
(**) New Title introduced by the Treaty of Amsterdam
(***) Title restructured by the Treaty of Amsterdam

Previous numbering	New numbering	Previous numbering	New numbering
PART SIX	PART SIX	Article 231	Article 304
Article 210	Article 281	Article 232	Article 305
Article 211	Article 282	Article 233	Article 306
Article 212 (*)	Article 283	Article 234	Article 307
Article 213	Article 284	Article 235	Article 308
Article 213a (*)	Article 285	Article 236 (*)	Article 309
Article 213b (*)	Article 286	Article 237 (repealed)	—
Article 214	Article 287	Article 238	Article 310
Article 215	Article 288	Article 239	Article 311
Article 216	Article 289	Article 240	Article 312
Article 217	Article 290	Article 241 (repealed)	—
Article 218 (*)	Article 291	Article 242 (repealed)	—
Article 219	Article 292	Article 243 (repealed)	—
Article 220	Article 293	Article 244 (repealed)	—
Article 221	Article 294	Article 245 (repealed)	—
Article 222	Article 295	Article 246 (repealed)	—
Article 223	Article 296		
Article 224	Article 297	FINAL	FINAL
Article 225	Article 298	PROVISIONS	PROVISIONS
Article 226 (repealed)	—	Article 247	Article 313
Article 227	Article 299	Article 248	Article 314
Article 228	Article 300		
Article 228a	Article 301		
Article 229	Article 302		
Article 230	Article 303		

(*)   New Article introduced by the Treaty of Amsterdam
(**) New Title introduced by the Treaty of Amsterdam
(***) Title restructured by the Treaty of Amsterdam

PROLOGUE

This book is written on the basis that the Treaty of Nice (TN), signed in 2000 by all fifteen Member States, is in force. At the time of writing, the Treaty has not been ratified by the Member States, and indeed was rejected in June 2001 by the Irish people in a referendum. None the less, perhaps rashly, it is assumed that the Treaty will eventually be ratified and will enter into force in 2002 or thereafter. The TN makes a number of substantive changes to the Treaty on European Union (TEU) and to the European Community (EC) Treaty, as well as to the European Coal and Steel Community (ECSC) and the European Atomic Energy Community (Euratom) Treaties, but leaves in place the basic overarching three-pillar structure of the European Union, containing these three (soon to be two) Communities and two flanking 'pillars'. Four protocols, including an important protocol on enlargement, one on the functioning of the Court of Justice, and one on the expiry of the ECSC Treaty, were also annexed to the existing Treaties.

The book will continue to refer in parentheses, at appropriate points, to the 'old' numbering of provisions of the EC and EU Treaties as they existed prior to the renumbering effected by the Treaty of Amsterdam. The table of 'equivalences' or conversion table, which sets out the pre-Amsterdam number of each TEU and EC Treaty Article alongside its post-Amsterdam equivalent, which was introduced in the second edition of this textbook, is retained for explanatory purposes.

1

THE DEVELOPMENT OF
EUROPEAN INTEGRATION

1. INTRODUCTION

This Chapter briefly examines the history of the European Union, describing some of the major political events and decisions which contributed to shaping its legal and constitutional structure, and the various reforms which were proposed and implemented, beginning with a thumbnail sketch of some of the theories of integration offered to explain its evolution. The second half of the chapter deals with the four major Intergovernmental Conferences which have taken place since 1985—those which led to the Single European Act, and to the Maastricht, Amsterdam, and Nice Treaties—and explains the significant legal reforms brought about by each of the Treaties adopted.

EU law is a complex and fascinating subject of study. Given the recent origins of the economic and political order which is governed by this legal system, we tend to begin by seeking to understand how and why the EU was first created. What factors prompted the establishment of this dense and elaborate political organization with its complex legal system? How has it evolved into the entity we see today? What are its objectives and what role does law appear to play in furthering those objectives? This book aims to illuminate the EU legal and constitutional processes, and to depict some dimensions of the dynamic relationship between the substantive aims and policies of the European Community and Union, their institutions and procedures, and the constituent Member States. It also aims to illustrate the strongly dynamic nature of the EU polity, whose aims, policies, institutional structures, and membership have been in a continuous and vibrant process of development and expansion for several decades now. And despite the discussion in recent years of a *finalité politique*, this active, reflexive, and constantly changing polity seems unlikely to reach a firm settlement in the near future. None the less, at a time when the biggest and most dramatic enlargement in the history of the EU is imminent, an active European-wide debate is taking place for the first time since the failed European Political Community of the 1950s on the desirability of a constitutional settlement for the Union.

The European Union was created as recently as 1993. Since that time, when the Treaty of Maastricht came into force, the much longer-established European Community has formed only one of three 'pillars' constituting the overarching European Union entity. Initially the law of the other two pillars remained less defined, less powerful, and less distinctively 'supranational' in nature. However, since the coming into force of the Amsterdam Treaty in 1999, the scope and significance of the legal measures adopted under the so-called third pillar have developed considerably.

None the less, it is still the law of the supranational European Community pillar which occupies most of this book. The second and third pillars of the European Union concern important and sensitive areas of policy hitherto considered to be at the core of national sovereignty, and the legal nature of those provisions and of the instruments adopted under them continues to differ in various respects from those of the EC Treaties. Under the terms of the Maastricht Treaty on European Union (TEU), the second pillar on the Common Foreign and Security Policy (CFSP) and the third pillar on Justice and Home Affairs (JHA) were more like familiar creations of international law, not sharing the institutional structure, law-making processes, or legal instruments of the Community pillar, largely beyond the jurisdiction of the European Court of Justice, and lacking the key Community law characteristics of supremacy and direct effect. Under the terms of the 1997 Treaty of Amsterdam (ToA) amending the TEU, however, the provisions of the third pillar were changed and are now more closely linked with both the institutional structure and the legal nature of the Community pillar, while the second pillar remains largely unchanged in this respect. The structure and the nature of the second and third pillars were left largely intact by the Nice Treaty (TN) of 2000.[1]

A considerably more complex legal picture now exists than in the early years of the Community's history, when it developed certain key characteristics which distinguished it discernibly from international law. The Community pillar remains the most distinctively supranational in nature and the second pillar remains closer to traditional forms of international law, while the third pillar reflects a hybrid of the two. But even within the EC Treaty pillar there are now many different types of law, including since 1999 a title on immigration and visa policy containing residual and third-pillar characteristics. Further, it is difficult to know how to classify the kinds of EU law provided for under existing and newer Treaty provisions on flexibility and enhanced co-operation.

There have always been many different and contested views about the original aims and *raison d'être* of the EC and EU among its political actors, populace, and commentators. A complex range of historical, political, and economic forces and contingencies contributed to creating the entity which exists today. This history is partly reflected in the gradual legal shaping of the Community and Union: in the progressive and continuing enlargement of its membership; and in the series of Treaty amendments over the years dealing with all sorts of substantive and institutional issues. It is important for students of law to situate the legal doctrine of the EU in its historical and political context. EU law does not emerge in a vacuum, however devoid of context the legislative texts and judgments may at times appear. Periods of political change have significantly affected the nature of law-making within both the political institutions and the Court, as well as the reception of such law into the Member States.

In this book, reference will be made to the 'European Community' to describe the three Communities which were originally established in the 1950s, even though, until

---

[1] For a rather different analysis of the notion of the EU three-pillar structure see B. Laffan 'The European Union Polity: A Union of Regulative, Normative and Cognitive Pillars' (2001) 8 *JEPP* 709.

the amendments made by the TEU in 1993, the European Coal and Steel Community (ECSC, which expires in 2002), the Economic Community (EEC), and the Atomic Energy Community (Euratom) were, properly speaking, the 'Communities'. After the TEU, the EEC was renamed the European Community, whereas the ECSC and the Euratom retain their original titles, but it is likely that the title European Community will continue to be used to refer to all three collectively.

2. A BRIEF OVERVIEW OF ANALYSES OF INTEGRATION

The development of European integration has been broadly described in a simplified and linear way. A number of relatively distinct periods or phases of the integration process have been identified, and different theories have emerged to explain the various phases, beginning with the *functionalism* of the 1950s. At this stage there was a belief that European integration would best be furthered by focusing initially on discrete economic sectors which could be managed efficiently and technocratically by supranational institutions, away from the fray of politics. Following the move from the sectoral Coal and Steel Community to the broader Economic Community in the late 1950s, *neofunctionalist* theory emerged as an alternative way of explaining the developing integration process—perhaps most famously described by Ernest Haas in the 1960s.[2] Functionalist and neofunctionalist theory are briefly described in the following extract.

J. Lodge, The European Community and the Challenge of the Future[3]

Functionalism starts from the premise that by promoting functional cooperation among states it may be possible to deter them from settling disputes over competition for scarce resources aggressively. The logic behind the approach is to prevent war not negatively—by keeping states apart— but positively by engaging them in cooperative ventures . . . to establish functionally specific agencies, initially in what were then seen as non-contentious areas like welfare. These were to transcend national boundaries and be managed by rational technocrats (not swung by the vagaries of political ideology and power-hungry political parties) owing allegiance to a functionally specific organization not to a given nation state. . . . Their tasks will cover those areas of the economy essential to running military machines.

Neofunctionalists have a common starting point with functionalists in their attachment to the collective pursuit of mutually beneficial goals leading to enhanced economic prosperity. . . . They argue that competitive economic and political elites mediate in the process and not only become involved in it but become key players. . . . Neofunctional integration sees integration as a process based on spill-over from one initially non-controversial, technical sector to other sectors of possibly greater political salience, involving a gradual reduction in the power of national government and a commensurate increase in the ability of the centre to deal with sensitive, politically charged issues.

---

[2] E.B. Haas, *Beyond the Nation State* (Stanford University Press, CA, 1964).
[3] (Pinter, 1993), Introduction, p. xix.

The assumptions and predictions of neofunctionalism were in turn challenged by what has been described as the intergovernmentalist phase of the Community in the 1970s, during which the supranational political EC institutions appeared to lose initiative and influence, and the interests of individual Member States—most clearly symbolized by the so-called Luxembourg veto—dominated the process. Neofunctionalist arguments were challenged by *neorealist*[4] *and neorational* accounts—amongst which *liberal intergovernmentalism* emerged as a particularly prominent theory[5]—presenting States rather than supranational institutions as the key actors in the integration process, seeking essentially to pursue their own respective preferences and to protect their sphere of power. These theories were applied to the renewed dynamism and deepening of the integration process in the 1980s with the signature of the Single European Act (SEA)[6] and the Intergovernmental Conferences (IGCs) of the early 1990s leading to the Maastricht Treaty, although the events of this period also generated counter-claims of a *neofederalist* revival.

From the late 1980s on, the supranationalism–intergovernmentalism dichotomy which underpinned the debate between the two major integration theories of neofunctionalism and neorealism has been questioned by growing bodies of literature on the phenomenon of the EU as a system of multi-level or network governance.[7] Unlike the emphasis of earlier theories, this work has concentrated as much on examining the nature of the political entity which exists and how it is governed, as on seeking to explain the dynamics of the integration process. Rather than focusing debate principally on whether it is Member State governments or Europe's supranational institutions which drive the integration process, increasing attention has been paid to the wide range of actors and institutions involved at different levels in lawmaking and policy-making within the European Union. Thus we see a broader concept of institutions in use,[8] and a focus which goes beyond national and supranational actors and institutions to include the subnational, 'infra-national', public, and private entities which participate in the system of governance. A range of alternatives to or variants on the dominant integration theories is emerging,[9] and new debates and divisions are

---

[4] See R. Keohane, Neo-Realism and Its Critics (Columbia University Press, NY, 1986).

[5] See A. Moravcsik, 'Preferences and Power in the European Community: A Liberal Intergovernmental Approach' (1993) 31 *JCMS* 473 and *The Choice for Europe* (UCL Press, 1999).

[6] W. Sandholtz and J. Zysman, '1992: Recasting the European Bargain' (1989) 42 *World Politics* 1; G. Garrett, 'International Cooperation and Institutional Choice: The European Community's Internal Market' (1992) 46 *International Organization* 533.

[7] See, e.g., M. Jachtenfuchs, 'Theoretical Perspectives on European Governance' (1995) 1 *ELJ* 115 and 'The Governance Approach to European Integration' (2001) 39 *JCMS* 245; G. Marks, L. Hooghe, and K. Blank, 'European Integration since the 1980s: State-centric Versus Multi-level Governance' (1996) 34 *JCMS* 341; B. Kohler Koch (who uses the term 'penetrated governance' rather than multi-level governance), 'The Evolution and Transformation of European Governance' (Institute for Advanced Studies, Vienna: Political Science Series No. 58); K. Armstrong and S. Bulmer, *The Governance of the Single European Market* (Manchester, 1998); S. Hix, 'The Study of the European Union II. The 'New Governance' Agenda and its Rival' (1998) 5 *JEPP* 38. On networks see, e.g., T. Börzel, 'Policy Networks: A New Paradigm for European Governance?' and K. Ladeur, 'Towards a Legal Theory of Supranationality—The Viability of the Network Concept' (1997) 3 *ELJ* 33.

[8] On the relevance of institutionalist theory to the EU see K. Armstrong, 'The New Institutionalism', in P. Craig and C. Harlow (eds.), *Lawmaking in the European Union* (Kluwer, 1998), and G. Schneider and M. Aspinwall (eds.), *The Rules of Integration: Institutionalist Approaches to the Study of Europe* (Manchester University Press, 2001).

[9] See, e.g., T. Doleys, 'Member States and the European Commission: Theoretical Insights from the New Economics of Organization' (2000) 7 JEPP 532; A. Branch and J.C. Øhrgaard, 'Trapped in the Supranational-

replacing the traditional intergovernmental–supranational/neofunctionalist–neorealist polarities, such as those between 'rationalist' approaches which view decision-making as being driven by the pursuit of material interests by strategic actors, and 'constructivist' approaches which lay more emphasis on the influence of norms, ideas, and principles in the process of integration.[10]

3. THE BACKGROUND TO EUROPEAN INTEGRATION

Most contemporary accounts of European integration begin with the aftermath of the Second World War, and with the desire to secure a lasting peace between European nations. After the destruction and ruin of the war years, and the climate of nationalism which preceded them, many hoped for a new model of political co-operation in Europe. This important point in the story of modern European integration, however, should be considered in a much longer time-frame. Ideas of European unity were articulated long before the arrival of the twentieth century, including the call in 1693 by a prominent English Quaker, William Penn, for a European Parliament and the end of the state mosaic in Europe.[11]

During the war, the Resistance movement had strongly supported the idea of a united Europe, as a way of consolidating the spirit of co-operation and fellowship of the war years and replacing the destructive forces of national pride and chauvinism.[12] However, despite the urgings of federalists such as Altiero Spinelli, the movement for integration faltered after the war, especially after the electoral defeat in the UK of Churchill, who had been a strong proponent of European unity. Promptings towards greater European co-operation, however, came from other sources. Faced with the onset of the cold war and with Europe's severe post-war economic problems, the USA in 1947, the same year in which the General Agreement on Tariffs and Trade (GATT) was signed in an effort to liberalize world trade,[13] announced its so-called Marshall Plan. The Marshall Plan was a scheme to provide financial aid for Europe, and the USA required an organization to be established to administer the programme. This became, in 1948, the Organization for European Economic Co-operation (OEEC)

intergovernmental Dichotomy: A Reply to Reply to Stone Sweet and Sandholtz' (1999) 6 *JEPP* 123; and M. Pollack, 'International Relations Theory and European Integration' (2001) 39 *JCMS* 221. For an account of the relationship between theories of integration and discourses of democracy in the EU see P.P. Craig, 'The Nature of the Community: Integration, Democracy and Legitimacy', in P.P. Craig and G. de Búrca (eds.), *The Evolution of EU Law* (Oxford University Press, 1999), 1.

[10] See the introduction to the special issue of the Journal of European Public Policy on the subject by T. Christiansen, K.E. Jørgensen, and A. Wiener, 'The Social Construction of Europe' (1999) 6 *JEPP* 528, and more generally T. Checkel, 'The Constructivist Turn in International Relations Theory' (1998) 50 *World Politics* 324.

[11] See D. Urwin, *The Community of Europe: A History of European Integration* (Longman, 2nd edn., 1995), tracing many of the arguments for various forms of European co-operation and unity before the onset of the Second World War.

[12] See the collection of W. Lipgens (ed.), *Documents of the History of European Integration* (European University Institute, 1985).

[13] The GATT 1947 was replaced in 1994, after the very lengthy Uruguay Round negotiations, and the World Trade Organization came into force in 1995.

and in 1960, the Organization for Economic Co-operation and Development (OECD). Although essentially intergovernmental, the OEEC required a degree of institutionalized co-ordination and co-operation between the European States which received aid, and provided useful experience for the more developed forms of co-operation and integration to come.[14]

Further examples of early co-operation in defence and other matters are evident in the 1948 Brussels Treaty between France, the UK, and the three Benelux countries, the North Atlantic Treaty Organization (NATO), signed in 1949, and the Western European Union (WEU), created in 1954, which was itself based on the earlier Brussels Treaty. On the economic side, Belgium, The Netherlands, and Luxembourg had signed the Benelux Treaty in 1944, establishing a customs union between them. Developments in the direction of political union were stalled by the UK, when, after the 'Congress of Europe' was convened at The Hague in 1948 to draw up proposals for European unity, the UK insisted on an intergovernmental organization which would not compromise state sovereignty. What emerged was the Statute on the Council of Europe, signed in 1949, providing for a Committee of Ministers and a Parliamentary Assembly. The latter had few powers beyond making recommendations to the Committee of Ministers, a twice-yearly meeting of the foreign ministers of the signatory States. However, despite its limitations the Council of Europe became involved in many cultural, economic, and scientific activities, and collaborates with various other international organizations including the EU. Probably its best-known achievement was the adoption of the European Convention on Human Rights (ECHR), which was signed in 1950 and came into force in 1953. The Convention established a Commission and subsequently a Court of Human Rights, which were merged into a single court when the 11th Protocol to the ECHR was ratified by all of the Council of Europe Member States and came into force in 1998. Further, the Council of Europe's Social Charter was signed in 1961 and came into force in 1965, and although lacking the stronger legal enforcement mechanisms of the Human Rights Convention, it has been important in the field of social and economic rights, complementing the focus on civil and political rights in the ECHR.[15]

Given the failure to convince Britain to participate in more concrete moves towards European integration, the French foreign minister, Robert Schuman, who was a strong supporter of integration, proposed the pooling of Franco-German coal and steel resources under a single High Authority, with the option for other European States to participate. The plan had been drafted by Jean Monnet, a committed federalist. Although based on a belief in economic co-operation, the plan was clearly not only economically inspired, but represented an attempt to restabilize relations between France and Germany after the war, to allay French fears about any military threat which the defeated German State might represent, and to bind them within a limited framework of peaceful co-operation in order to avert emerging rivalry over the coal-producing regions of the Ruhr and the Saar.[16] The Schuman proposal led to the

[14] M. Holland, *European Integration From Community to Union* (Pinter, 1993), 23.
[15] See Ch. 8 for discussion of the way the ECJ has drawn on the provisions of both the Convention and the Charter in its case law.
[16] Holland, n. 14 above.

setting-up of the European Coal and Steel Community (ECSC), with a limited life-span of fifty years, to expire in 2002. This was the first significant step towards European integration going beyond intergovernmentalism, establishing a supra-national authority whose independent institutions had the power to bind its constituent member States.

The ECSC Treaty was signed in 1951 by France, Germany, Italy, and the three Benelux countries, to establish a common market in coal and steel. Four institutions were set up: a High Authority, made up of nine independent appointees of the six Member State governments, to be the main executive institution with decision-making power and responsibility for implementing the aims of the Treaty; an Assembly made up of national parliaments' delegates with mainly supervisory and advisory powers; a Council made up of one representative of each of the national governments, with a consultative role and some decision-making powers, and the task of harmonizing the activities of the States and the High Authority; and finally a Court of Justice of nine judges. Since the High Authority could adopt binding decisions by a majority, it was a supranational authority, but its influence was coun-tered in areas in which its decision was not final by the Council, which represented the Member States' interests. The balance of power between the High Authority (later named the Commission after the 1965 Merger Treaty) and the Council was different under the ECSC Treaty from under the later EEC Treaty, with a stronger supranational element and a weaker intergovernmental element. The greater level of detailed policy in the ECSC Treaty as compared with the EEC Treaty was another factor explaining the enhanced role of the High Authority. The self-financing capacity of the ECSC through levies on coal and steel production added to its independence and autonomy. The Assembly had relatively little power, although it could in extreme circumstances require the resignation of the High Authority, and Article 21 of the ECSC Treaty also provided for the future possibility of direct elections.

The ECSC was a significant development, as much because of what it symbolized as because of its actual achievements in the organization of the coal and steel market. It was clear from the outset that, for its architects and proponents, this Community was not merely about coal and steel, but represented a first step in the direction of the integration of Europe.[17] Many supporters of European unity identified themselves as federalists, in the sense of believing in the creation of a supranational political entity with constitutionally defined powers to take over many of the functions of individual nation States. By contrast, Monnet, who drew up the original plans for the ECSC and subsequently served as the first President of its High Authority, is generally seen as a functionalist, whose preferred approach to European integration was to proceed sector by sector, and who favoured elite supranational institutions over more political bodies such as the Assembly or the Council.

While the ECSC had some success in bringing about greater co-operation and trust between the Member States, in particular between France and Germany, the

---

[17] See F. Duchêne, *Jean Monnet: The First Statesman of Interdependence* (Norton, NY, 1994), 239, quoting Monnet's comments from 1952.

period between 1951 and 1957 was a mixed one from the point of view of European integration. The sensitive area of defence was next to be tackled, and rather than agree to German rearmament within NATO, as the USA had suggested, France proposed instead, in its 1950 Pleven plan, the setting-up of a European Defence Community (EDC) with a European army, a common budget, and joint institutions. The EDC Treaty was signed in 1952 by the six ECSC States, with Britain once again refusing to participate, but progress towards ratification was slow. It was argued that, if there was to be a European army, a common European foreign policy would also be needed, and accordingly plans for a European Political Community were drawn up. The 1953 draft statute which emerged represented a serious effort at designing a European federation, with a detailed institutional structure and ambitious aims, including a co-ordinated foreign policy and eventual economic integration. However, these developments were stopped in their tracks when France, which had been wary of German remilitarization, finally submitted the EDC Treaty to its national assembly, where the proposal to debate its ratification was rejected.[18] This resulted in a major setback for the integration process and the shelving of the plans for both defence and political union. It would be thirty-nine years before the Member States would ratify another Treaty—that signed at Maastricht in 1992—purporting to establish a 'European Union'.

4. THE EEC AND EURATOM TREATIES

Yet moves towards integration were not halted. After a conference of foreign ministers of the six States in Messina in Italy in 1955, agreement on moving in the direction of economic integration was reached. A committee chaired by Paul-Henri Spaak, then Belgian Prime Minister and another strong advocate of integration, in 1956 published its report which contained the basic plan for what became the European Atomic Energy Community (Euratom) and the European Economic Community (EEC). This time, although the Treaties may have been politically motivated, the focus was specifically economic. The peaceful development of atomic energy under the responsibility of a permanent institution was considered to be of great importance, and as a clearly defined sector it was an appropriate area of energy policy which could be placed under common authority.

The economic impetus for the 1957 Treaties was made clear. In accordance with the thrust of the Spaak report, the EEC Treaty avoided the explicit political objectives of the earlier draft European Political Co-operation (EPC) Treaty, and concentrated on the aims of economic integration in its preamble and in Article. These were to establish a common market, to approximate the economic policies of the Member States, to promote harmonious development of economic activities throughout the Community, to increase stability and raise the standard of living, and to promote closer relations between the Member States. Barriers to trade were to be abolished and a

---

[18] According to J. Pinder, *The Building of the European Union* (Oxford University Press, 3rd edn., 1998), this defeat was due to a combination of nationalists and Stalinists in the French National Assembly in 1954.

common customs tariff was to be set up, undistorted competition was to be ensured, national economic and monetary policies were to be progressively co-ordinated, and fiscal and social policies gradually harmonized. Unlike the ECSC there was to be no temporal limit on the existence of the Treaty. The Parliamentary Assembly and the Court of Justice were to be shared with the ECSC,[19] but there was to be a separate Council of Ministers and executive authority—this time called the Commission rather than the High Authority. It was not until the Merger Treaty of 1965 that these two institutions were also merged and shared by the three Communities.[20] An Economic and Social Committee with advisory status was set up, to be shared with the Euratom Community.

The location of the Community institutions, a task which under the Treaty fell to the Member States, was a matter of some dispute. The Assembly of the ECSC had been located in Strasbourg, with the High Authority, the Council, and the Court of Justice in Luxembourg. Now the Council, the Commission, their respective staffs, as well as the Economic and Social Committee and the Committee of the Regions are based in Brussels. Certain meetings of the Council are held, and certain departments of the Commission are based, however, along with the Court of Justice, the Court of First Instance, the Court of Auditors, and the European Investment Bank,[21] in Luxembourg. The Parliament continues to have its seat in Strasbourg, with its secretariat in Luxembourg and certain sessions and committee meetings in Brussels. These seats were finally formalized by a Protocol attached to the EC Treaty by the Treaty of Amsterdam, which also determines the seat of some newer institutions, assigning the European Monetary Institute and the European Central Bank to Frankfurt, and the European Police Office (Europol) to The Hague. Such weighty questions appear to remain a matter of great concern and interest to Member State governments, given the well-publicized wrangling over the seat of various new agencies which marked the ending of the European Council summit at Laeken in December 2001.

The common market was to be established over a transitional period of several stages, during which tariff barriers would be removed and a common external customs tariff set up. There were to be common policies in agriculture and transport, free movement of workers, companies, the self-employed, goods, and services, and strict control of anti-competitive practices in the various States. A European Social Fund was established to improve employment opportuntites, and an Investment Bank to give loans and guarantees and to help less developed regions or sectors. A European Development Fund for overseas countries and territories of some of the Member States was also established.

The Commission was not accorded the same degree of legislative autonomy under

---

[19] This was decided in the Convention on certain Institutions common to the European Communities, signed on the same day as the EEC and Euratom Treaties in 1957.

[20] This Treaty was repealed and replaced, without any substantive amendments, by Art. 9 of the Treaty of Amsterdam signed in 1997.

[21] The European Investment Bank was established under what was originally Art. 129 of the EEC Treaty to finance projects in less-developed regions of the Community, as a kind of early regional policy. After the Maastricht Treaty amendments the bank was mentioned in Arts. 4b and 198d–e, which, after the Treaty of Amsterdam, have been renumbered Arts. 9 and 266–267 of the EC Treaty respectively.

the EEC Treaty and Euratom Treaties[22] as it had under the ECSC Treaty, and the Council was given the power of approval of most Commission legislative proposals. However, the Commission was given a very important position as the initiator of all legislation and overall 'watchdog' of the Treaties, as well as having certain decision-making powers of its own and being the negotiator of international agreements on behalf of the Community.

Voting in the Council was weighted, but its voting procedure would vary according to the nature of the issue. In a very few instances voting was by simple majority, in many other matters by qualified majority, and in others unanimity was required. The issue of voting in Council is crucial to the nature and development of the Community, since, crudely speaking, it influences strongly whether intergovernmentalism—i.e. the interests of each of the Member States—or supranationalism— i.e. the overall interest of the Community—has greater sway. We will see also that the legislative process and the different voting procedures for different matters under the Treaty are frequently arbitrary, representing the result of political bargaining and compromise in the course of negotiating the terms of an amending Treaty, rather than anything intrinsic to the issue being decided. On the whole, the process of weighted qualified-majority voting was intended to give greater weight to the larger Member States than to the smaller, to reflect in part the difference in their population size. The fractious nature of the negotiations over changes to the voting weights at the Nice European Council, in preparation for the accession of up to twelve new members, testifies to the political significance of this issue.[23]

The Parliamentary Assembly which, although it called itself the Parliament, was not officially so named until the adoption of the Single European Act in 1986, had few powers under the original Treaty provisions. It had a consultative role in legislation, but was largely a supervisory body whose powers involved questioning the Commission and receiving its annual report. It also possessed, as under the ECSC Treaty, a strong but never-used power of censure, despite the tabling of many motions of censure over the years, including one shortly before the dramatic resignation of the Commission in 1999.[24]

---

[22] Many motions of censure have, however, been tabled over the years. See K. Bradley, 'Legal Developments in the European Parliament' (1992) 12 *YBEL* 505. The institutional provisions of the Euratom Treaty are essentially the same as those of the EC Treaty.

[23] See Art. 3 of the first protocol to the Nice Treaty and Declaration 21 on enlargement.

[24] See Ch. 2 for a fuller discussion of the circumstances of the resignation. For further accounts see K. Bradley, 'The Institutional Law of the EU in 1999' (1999/2000) 19 *YBEL* 547, 584 and D. Dinan, 'Governance and Institutions 1999: Resignation, Reform and Renewal' (2000) 38 *JCMS* 25; A. McMullan, 'Political Responsibility for the Administration of Europe: the Commission's Resignation' (1999) 54 *Parliamentary Affairs* 703.

5. 1966–86: FROM THE LUXEMBOURG ACCORDS TO THE SINGLE EUROPEAN ACT

Despite the EEC Treaty's concentration on economic integration, calls for political co-operation between the States continued throughout the early 1960s. President de Gaulle of France clearly favoured an intergovernmental rather than a supranational model of European co-operation, and proposed a regular forum for meetings of the heads of government of the six Member States. This proposal was not taken up seriously until the emergence of European Political Co-operation in 1970 and De Gaulle's view of the Community during these years was at odds with those of other Member States, and a source of tension between France and the Commission which, under Walter Hallstein as President, had adopted a dynamic and activist approach.

(a) CRISIS: THE LUXEMBOURG ACCORDS

This tension erupted into a crisis in 1965, when the time came under the transitional provisions of the Treaty for the Council of Ministers to move to qualified-majority voting rather than the unanimous voting which had been in force until then. De Gaulle objected to an important institutional reform proposal made by the Commission—which was combined with a proposal to resolve a conflict over agricultural policy—for the Community to raise its own resources from agricultural levies and external tariffs, instead of being funded by national contributions. He strenuously objected to the 'federalist logic' of the proposal[25] and, after a failure to reach a compromise in the Council, France refused to attend any further Council meetings and adopted what became known as the 'empty-chair' policy. This lasted for seven months, from June 1965 until January 1966, after which a settlement was reached, which became known as the Luxembourg Compromise or the Luxembourg Accords. These Accords, which were to have considerable impact on the direction and pace of Community development over the next two decades, were essentially an agreement to disagree over voting methods in the Council. While the French asserted that even in cases which provided for majority decision-making, discussion *must* continue until unanimity was reached whenever important national interests were at stake, the other five Member States declared instead that in such circumstances the Council would 'endeavour, within a reasonable time, to reach solutions which can be adopted by all'.[26] Each acknowledged that there was a divergence of views on how to proceed in the event of a total failure to reach agreement.

In practice, it seems that for many years the French view in effect prevailed. States endeavoured to reach agreement in their meetings, and the effect of pleading the 'very important interests' of a State was treated as a veto which the other Member States would respect. Recourse to qualified-majority voting became the exception rather than the norm. The 'return to intergovernmentalism', as some have termed it, with

---

[25] See Pinder, n. 18 above, 12.   [26] Bull. EC 3–1966, 9.

primacy being accorded to an individual Member State's wish even if against what was felt by the majority to be in the interests of the Community as a whole, affected the dynamics of decision-making in the following years. The shift of power away from the Commission towards the Council also diluted the role of the Parliament, which exercised supervisory powers over the Commission. It also emphasized the import- ance of COREPER, the Committee of Permanent Representatives established under Article 207 (ex Article 151) EC, which prepared the agenda for Council meetings, since it carried out most of the negotiation between the Commission and the Council on the various initiatives to be put forward by the Commission.

While the Community was experiencing internal crises, on the other hand, it began to find its voice on the international stage as a single entity rather than as six Member States. This could be seen in the GATT negotiations of 1967, and in the signing of the Yaoundé Convention between the EEC and eighteen African States in 1963 which was intended to offer preferential treatment in importation to developing countries.

(b) COMMUNITY ENLARGEMENT IN THE 1970S AND 1980S

The next boost to the Community came with the first enlargement in 1973. The UK in the 1950s had chosen to remain outside the EEC, and instead in 1960 set up the European Free Trade Association (EFTA) with six other States: Norway, Sweden, Austria, Switzerland, Denmark, and Portugal. In 1961, after a change of policy, the UK made its first application for Community membership. De Gaulle, who viewed Britain's place as being within the Commonwealth rather than as part of continental Europe, vetoed the application on this occasion and again after a second application in 1967. It was not until after De Gaulle's resignation that Britain's application for membership was finally accepted, together with those of Ireland and Denmark in 1973. At the same time Norway, whose application had also been accepted, delivered its first blow to Community morale when it failed to ratify the Treaty of Accesssion after a national referendum yielded a majority opposing Community membership. In 1981 the Community expanded again when Greece became a member. Greenland, however, finally left the Community in 1985 after obtaining a degree of internal legislative independence from Denmark, and Spain and Portugal became members in 1986.

(c) POLITICAL CO-OPERATION

Moves towards co-operation in political matters had begun again in 1970, when the Davignon Report recommended the holding of quarterly meetings of the foreign ministers of the Member States, as well as the establishment of a permanent political secretariat. This became an essentially intergovernmental forum for co-operation in foreign policy, without any developed institutional structure. A second report in 1973 recommended its continuation as a form of co-operation, and it became known as European Political Co-operation (EPC). EPC was successful in enabling the Community to be represented as one voice in other international organizations in which all of the Member States participated, but also represented a move towards intergovernmentalism. In 1974 the European Council was established to regularize the practice of holding summits. This body consisted of the heads of governments of the Member States, with the President of the Commission attending its bi-annual meetings. The European Council's 'summitry' provided the Community with much-needed direction which its internal structure did not provide, but represented to some a weakening in the supranational elements of the Community. The European Council was not within the framework created by the Treaties, and it was not until the Single European Act was passed that it was actually recognized in a formal instrument. Even after the TEU enshrined the crucial leadership role of the European Council, it continues to operate largely outside the institutional structure of the EC Treaties (and hence the supervision of the Parliament or Court), although reference is now made to it in several EC Treaty provisions, such as those on the economic policy and employment policy guidelines.

This trend within the Community from early supranationalism towards greater intergovernmentalism from the time of the Luxembourg Compromise until the adoption of the Single European Act in 1986 has been the subject of much comment. The following extract reflects on the way the Luxembourg Accords affected institutional dynamics and the Community's pace of progress from 1966 until the early 1980s.

P. Dankert, The EC—Past, Present and Future[27]

The dialectics of co-operation or integration have also continued to dominate the process of European unification—to an increasing extent—ever since 25th March 1957. It has been a continuous 'to and fro' for years, as can be seen from the course of development of the Community institutions. The Council of Ministers, which was originally intended to be a Community body, has now become largely an intergovernmental institution thanks to the famous Luxembourg Agreement, which, under French pressure, put an end to the majority decisions which the Council was supposed to take according to the Treaty on proposals submitted by the European Commission. This rule that decisions could only be taken unanimously had the effect of gradually transforming the Commission into a kind of secretariat for the Council which carefully checked its proposals with national officials before deciding whether or not to submit them. This in turn has a negative effect on the European Parliament which can only reach for power, under the Treaty, via the Commission. The move towards intergovernmental solutions for Community problems reached its peak—after frustrated attempts such as the Fouchet plan at the beginning of the 60s—in the creation of the European Council, the EPC and the EMS.

But there were trends too in the other direction: the Community's autonomy through its own resources, the related extension of the European Parliament's budgetary powers and, in 1979, the direct election of that Parliament.

During the 1960s and 1970s—often referred to as a period of political stagnation in the Community—various reports on reforming the Community's institutional structure and strengthening the integration process were commissioned. After the

---

[27] L. Tsoukalis (ed.), *The EC: Past, Present and Future* (Basil Blackwell, 1983), 7.

1974 Paris summit, the Belgian Prime Minister, Leo Tindemans, was asked to produce a report on the Community's future. He proposed some far-reaching institutional reforms, including strengthening the Commission and the Parliament, establishing direct elections to the Parliament, and reforming the European Council. Economic and monetary integration, citizenship rights, and development of social and regional policy were also suggested. However, this report, like various others, was not acted upon at the time, although we can see that many of the ideas surfaced in later reforms. In 1976, direct elections to the Parliament were finally agreed by the Member States, and the first elections took place in 1979. This event ought to have represented a significant development for the Community since the Parliament would become the first Community institution with a direct democratic mandate of sorts, but the elections were not an unqualified success.

M. Holland, European Integration From Community to Union[28]

Transnational party cooperation was at a rudimentary level and the decision to run each of the nine European elections independently and according to national electoral rules did little to persuade voters that the elections were any different from their respective national elections. The election issues were not European ones, but reflected national concerns and parochialism: as a result, turnout was disappointingly low, averaging just 62 per cent . . . the United Kingdom having the lowest figure at 32.6 per cent. . . . . Faced with this apparent popular disinterest, the first direct elections failed to provide the anticipated springboard for accelerated integration; rather, as the Community entered the 1980s, the popular legitimacy and future development of the Community came into question and a renewed trend towards more modest intergovernmental cooperation emerged.

In 1978, after the European Council summit in Brussels, the (first of many) so-called 'Three Wise Men' Committee was established to consider again the question of greater political integration. This Committee proposed similar reforms to strengthen the Commission and to dilute intergovernmentalism by introducing more qualified-majority voting in the Council,[29] but no action was taken. Since institutional reform is inextricably bound up with the power relationship between the States and the Community and with perceptions about the appropriate pace of political integration, it is perhaps unsurprising that such change was slow to come. None the less, it provides an interesting contrast with the hectic pace of reform and change which we have seen during the 1990s and into the beginning of the twenty-first century.

During the period of 'political stagnation' and 'decisional malaise' from the mid-1970s into the 1980s, however, less noticeable but important constitutional changes were taking place in the gradual erosion of the limits to Community competences—in other words, the substantive areas in which the Community had jurisdiction to act were expanding through the use of Article 308 (ex Article 235) EC, with the sanction

---

[28] N. 14 above, 42.
[29] For an official summary of the report see Bull. EC 11–1979, 1.5.2.

of the Court of Justice.[30] We shall see later that the Court, often at times when the Community's political processes were less active or in crisis, contributed to its legal development and to the process of integration in certain ways. Thus the doctrine of direct effect which was developed in the early 1960s was utilized in the 1970s to make more effective Community policies which were provided for under the Treaty but which either the Member States or the Community institutions were failing to implement.[31] It was in the 1970s, too, that the Court triggered a policy of 'negative integration' and influenced the Commission in its subsequent single-market strategy by interpreting very broadly Article 28 (ex Article 30) of the Treaty, on the abolition of non-tariff barriers to the free movement of goods.[32]

The next major political initiative for change, brought forward by the German and the Italian foreign ministers and known as the Genscher–Colombo plan, covered institutional reform, but also budgetary reform and expansion of competence into new policy areas. This prompted the European Council to issue a 'Solemn Declaration on European Union' in 1983.[33] In 1984, on the basis of a report put together by Altiero Spinelli, an Italian MEP and a committed federalist, the European Parliament overwhelmingly approved a 'Draft Treaty on European Union'. This again suggested radical institutional reform with a strengthened Commission, a Council sharing joint legislative and budgetary powers with the Parliament, and increased qualified-majority voting in the Council. Yet no concrete action resulted from any of these initiatives. Finally, however, after the Fontainebleu European Council summit of 1984, two committees were set up to look at the question of Treaty revision and further political integration. One was the Adonnino Committee on a people's Europe, to consider the issue of furthering a European identity,[34] and the second was the Dooge Committee to look at questions of political reform. Although the Dooge Report, which again included strong reform proposals, was not itself acted upon, the 1985 European Council meeting in Milan agreed, voting for the first time by majority only, to convene an intergovernmental conference under what was then Article 236 of the EEC Treaty, now Article 48 TEU, to discuss treaty amendment.[35] What emerged from the meetings of the working parties within the inter-governmental conference became the Single European Act (SEA).

(d) DEVELOPMENTS IN THE BUDGETARY AND MONETARY SPHERES

Before examining the changes made by the SEA, a brief account of important developments in Community budgetary policy, and of those towards economic and monetary union (EMU) in the interim years, will be given. In 1969, agreement on the

---

[30] J. Weiler, 'The Transformation of Europe' (1991) 100 *Yale LJ* 2403, 2431–53. For further discussion of Art. 308, see Ch. 3.

[31] See Ch. 5.

[32] See the discussion of the 'Cassis' case: Case 120/78, *Rewe-Zentral AG* v. *Bundesmonopolverwaltung für Branntwein* [1979] ECR 649, in Ch. 15.

[33] See Bull. EC. 6–1983, 1.6.1.

[34] See COM(84)446 Final.

[35] See P. Pescatore, 'Some Critical Remarks on the Single European Act' (1987) 24 *CMLRev.* 9, 14, criticizing the outvoting of Denmark, Greece, and the UK in the European Council meeting, given the need for consensus in any revision of the Treaties.

principle of monetary union was reached, as well as an agreement on funding from the Community's own resources rather than from national contributions, and on the expansion of the Parliament's role in the budgetary process. The political significance of these last two issues, which were brought about in the first budgetary Treaty of 1970 and the Own-Resources Decision of the same date, lies in the financial independence achieved by the Community and in the strengthening of the Parliament's desired role as a decision-maker. The Community's own resources would hence come from agricultural levies, from customs duties on products from outside the Community, and from a maximum of 1 per cent Value Added Tax (VAT) as applied to an assessment basis determined uniformly for the Member States. The then Articles 203–202 EEC (now Articles 272–273 EC) were amended to reflect the Parliament's increased budgetary powers, which also shifted from Council to Parliament the symbolically important task of adopting the budget. By 1975, the date by which the Community budget was required to be financed entirely from its own resources, a second budgetary treaty had been agreed, with further increases in the Parliament's budgetary role. A Joint Declaration of the three institutions on a 'conciliation procedure' agreement was also made in 1975, followed in 1982 by a second declaration intended to reconcile the views of Parliament and Council concerning legislation with considerable financial implications. An Inter-institutional Agreement on Budgetary Discipline and Improvement of the Budgetary Procedure was adopted in 1993 and again in 1999, to provide for better institutional collaboration. A Court of Auditors had also been established by the 1975 Treaty to oversee Community revenue and expenditure and to report at the end of each financial year, and in 1992, following amendments made by the TEU, it acquired official status as the fifth Community institution. Little progress, however, was made towards economic and monetary union until the setting-up in 1979 of the European Monetary System, with an Exchange Rate Mechanism and a European Currency Unit. These developments are discussed further in Chapter 16.

One of the continuing problems which had faced the Community during the 1970s and 1980s was its serious financial situation. Part of the reason for the Community's increasing levels of expenditure was the cost of one of its central policies—the common agricultural policy (CAP). This was also a controversial policy, given its protectionism and the enormous and expanding costs of guaranteeing fixed prices for farmers. It was also a source of great divisiveness between Britain and the rest of the Community, which came to a climax in 1982 when the Council, despite the Luxembourg compromise, overrode the British veto, adopting an agricultural prices agreement by qualified majority over British opposition. The other Member States considered that Britain was objecting not to the agricultural prices agreement itself, but to the separate issue of what Britain considered to be its excessive contributions to the Community budget. However, at the 1984 Fontainebleu summit, a formula for budget contributions which was acceptable to Britain at the time was agreed. On the other hand, spending continued to rise, and in 1988 a second 'own-resources' decision was adopted to increase Community resources.[36] At the same time a more

---

[36] [1988] OJ L185/24.

thorough budgetary reform was agreed, based on an increase in Member States' contributions in proportion to each State's share of the Community's gross national product, and a further own-resources decision was agreed by the European Council and subsequently enacted as Community legislation after the TEU.[37]

6. THE SINGLE EUROPEAN ACT

In 1985 the British Commissioner, Lord Cockfield, drew up on behalf of the Commission a precise timetable for the completion of the internal market—known as the 'White Paper'—setting out a long list of the barriers which would have to be removed before a deadline of 1992.[38] The Single European Act represented a political commitment to this deadline, and, despite the delay occasioned by a constitutional challenge to the Act in Ireland, the support of all Member States, including Thatcher's Britain, can be explained by the centrality of the 'market project' to the SEA.

Undoubtedly, when it was signed in 1986, the Single European Act represented the most important revision of the Treaties since they were first adopted. Despite criticisms targeted at its limited and even regressive effects,[39] there is no doubt that it heralded a revival of the Community momentum towards integration which has continued at a breathless pace since then, with the signing of the TEU in 1992, the Treaty of Amsterdam in 1997, and the Nice Treaty in 2000, and yet another IGC on constitutional reform scheduled for 2004.[40]

Even if it did not go as far as any of the committees or reports presented during the 1970s and 1980s had proposed, the Single European Act made a number of significant institutional and substantive reforms. It gave a legal basis to European Political Co-operation and formal recognition to the European Council, although not within the Community treaties. A Court of First Instance (CFI) was provided for to assist the Court of Justice, and a new legislative 'cooperation' procedure was introduced into various policy fields under the EEC Treaty, with an enhanced consultative role for the European Parliament. The Parliament was also given a veto over the accession of new Member States and over the conclusion of agreements with associate States. Lastly, the so-called 'comitology' procedure, under which the Council delegates powers to the Commission on certain conditions, was formally included within Article 202 (ex Article 145) of the Treaty.[41]

Then followed the substantive changes. First, Article 18 (ex Article 8a) EC set out the internal market aim of 'progressively establishing the internal market over a period expiring on 31 December 1992', and defined the internal market as 'an area without internal frontiers in which the free movement of goods, persons, services and capital is ensured'. Secondly, qualified-majority voting by the Council was introduced into a range of areas which had previously provided for unanimity, and a new Article

---

[37] Council Regs. 2729/94 and 2730/94, [1994] OJ L293 5–6 and 7–8.
[38] COM(85)310.
[39] Pescatore, n. 35 above.
[40] See Declaration No. 23 attached to the Nice Treaty.
[41] For further discussion of the committee procedures see Ch. 4.

95 (ex Article 100a) was added by way of derogation from the 'harmonizing' provision of Article 94 (ex Article 100). Article 94 required unanimity in the Council when adopting directives to approximate national measures affecting the establishment or functioning of the common market, while Article 95 instead allows for qualified majority when adopting measures to achieve the internal market objectives of Article 18.

The SEA also added new substantive areas of Community competence, some of which had already in fact been asserted by the institutions and supported by the Court, without any express Treaty basis. The additions covered co-operation in economic and monetary union, social policy, economic and social cohesion,[42] research and technological development, and environmental policy.[43] Title III of the SEA, which governed European Political Co-operation outside the Community framework, was subsequently repealed and replaced by the TEU.

Responses to the SEA were mixed, some seeing it as an important and a positive step forward for the Community after a period of sluggishness, while others saw it as a serious setback for the integration process. The additions to the Parliament's powers were minor, the Commission gained no new powers, many of the 'new' areas of competence already existed in practice, and there had been no formal abolition of the 'Luxembourg veto'. Pierre Pescatore, formerly a judge on the Court of Justice, argued that the Act was fundamentally deceptive, that it ignored all the Community's achievements to date, and implied that the common market project begun in 1957 had to be started all over again.[44] Others, however, having observed the Act in operation for some years, compared the apparent weakness of its provisions with a more optimistic assessment of what it, together with the Commission's White Paper,[45] actually brought about.

J. Weiler, The Transformation of Europe[46]

Clearly, the new European Parliament and the Commission were far from thrilled with the new act.

And yet, with the hindsight of just three years, it has become clear that 1992 and the SEA do constitute an eruption of significant proportions. Some of the evidence is very transparent. First, for the first time since the very early years of the Community, if ever, the Commission plays the political role clearly intended for it by the Treaty of Rome. In stark contrast to its nature during the foundational period in the 1970s and early 1980s, the Commission in large measure both sets the Community agenda and acts as a power broker in the legislative process.

---

[42] This policy concerned reducing the disparities between various parts of the EU. Apart from the original provisions of Arts. 129 and 130 EEC (after the TEU and the ToA: see now Arts. 9 and 179 EC) establishing a European Investment Bank, and the setting up of a European Regional Development Fund in 1975 (see Bull. EC 3–1975, 1201), regional policy had not been very developed within the Treaty framework.

[43] Various Community environmental measures were passed on the basis of Art. 100 (now Art. 94) before the adoption of the Single European Act, and the Council had adopted Environmental Action Programmes since 1973.

[44] Pescatore, n. 35 above, 11.

[45] See the *White Paper on the Completion of the Internal Market*, COM(85)310.

[46] N. 30 above, 2454.

Second, the decisionmaking process takes much less time. Dossiers that would have languished and in some cases did languish in impotence for years in the Brussels corridors now emerge as legislation often in a matter of months.

For the first time, the interdependence of the policy areas at the new-found focal point of power in Brussels creates a dynamic resembling the almost forgotten predictions of neo-functionalist spillover. The ever-widening scope of the legislative and policy agenda of the Community manifests this dynamic.

The SEA was characterized essentially and crucially by its 'single market' aims. The provisions on regional policy, the environment, and research, and even on institutional reform, seemed secondary to or merely supportive of the central aim of freeing the internal market from inter-State barriers. Yet although some saw the Single Act as an economic charter, others saw the social and environmental policy amendments as a significant recognition of autonomous Community competence in these fields, and not merely as side-effects of its market-integration goals. As we will see of later Treaty revisions also, this ambiguity or perhaps complexity in its aims no doubt accounts for the broad support it gained, and reminds us again of the contested nature of the European entity. It signifies very different things to different observers, and constitutes a political forum in which competing and conflicting aims and goals must be negotiated and mediated.

In 1988, the Conservative British Prime Minister Margaret Thatcher, who, after signing the SEA, became displeased with the dynamism of the Commission under Jacques Delors, gave her famous Bruges speech setting out her vision of the Community, claiming that the original EEC Treaty was intended as a charter for economic liberty. This market-based vision of the origins of European integration was and still is of course a highly contested and challenged one, and, as Weiler has argued, the single-market project even at the time represented quite opposite ideological conceptions to different people so that to others 'it represented the realization of the old dream of a true common marketplace, which, because of the inevitable connection between the social and the economic in modern political economies, would ultimately yield the much vaunted 'ever closer union of the peoples of Europe'.[47] The debate between those on different sides of the political spectrum, between a neo-liberal conception of the EU and the 'European social model', indeed remains as lively today as ever.

Whatever the criticisms of the SEA at the time however, the Community momentum had undoubtedly been revived, and the renewal of qualified-majority voting affected not just the practice of the Council towards a greater degree of supranationalism in decision-making, but also the influence of the Commission and the Parliament in this process. Member States continued to assert the existence of the veto, even if not to invoke it, but it did not have its previously restraining effect on decision-making and qualified-majority voting became commonplace in the Council.

[47] *Ibid.*, 2458.

7. THE BIRTH OF THE EUROPEAN UNION: THE MAASTRICHT TREATY

The momentum which gave rise to and which was generated by the SEA continued after its adoption. The committee chaired by Jacques Delors on Economic and Monetary Union had presented a report in 1989 setting out a three-stage plan for reaching EMU. The European Council decided to hold an intergovernmental conference on the subject, and, significantly, to hold at the same time a second intergovernmental conference (IGC) on political union, apparently in order to balance economic integration with political integration.

On the basis of the IGC negotiations, a draft Treaty was presented by the Luxembourg presidency of the European Council in 1991. After various revisions, the Treaty on European Union (TEU) was eventually agreed and signed by the States in Maastricht in February 1992.[48] After vigorous debates leading up to the ratification process in the various Member States, which revealed considerable public disquiet and dissatisfaction with the Treaty and with the process of its negotiation, it was rejected by the Danish population in a national referendum. However, after several 'concessions' were secured by the Danish Government and formalized in a decision of the Heads of State at the Edinburgh European Council in 1992, including the right not to participate in the third and final stage of EMU and not to take on the Presidency of the European Council when defence issues were involved, a second referendum yielded a narrow majority in favour of ratification. When the last obstacle—in the shape of a challenge before the German Federal Supreme Court to the constitutionality of ratification[49]—was cleared, the Treaty entered into force in November 1993.

Undoubtedly, the popular profile of the Community was raised more by the 'Maastricht' debate than by any previous development in the Community's history. Apart from the detailed commitment to full economic and monetary union, the most striking feature of the TEU was the institutional change it brought about, establishing the 'three-pillar' structure for what was henceforth to be the European Union, with the Communities as the first of these pillars and the EEC Treaty being officially renamed the European Community (EC) Treaty.

Despite the enormous significance of the institutional and constitutional changes wrought by the TEU, what emerged from the IGCs on Monetary and Political Union was none the less more of a mixed bag and more of a compromise than those two Conferences had initially appeared to promise, in particular in the wake of the success of the SEA and the renewed enthusiasm for integration which that had appeared to generate. The ambiguities and tensions inherent in the European Community project from its earliest days, far from being resolved by the new Treaty, were positively enshrined in its provisions. These ambiguities were reflected in features such as the

---

[48] For a commentary on the Treaty 'From Conception to Ratification' see R. Corbett, *The Treaty of Maastricht* (Longman, 1993).

[49] See Cases 2 BvR 2134/92 and 2159/92, *Brunner v. The European Union Treaty* [1994] 1 CMLR 57, discussed in Ch. 7.

curious pillar structure with its overlapping mix of intergovernmental and supranational features, and the inclusion of new titles in the EC Treaty conferring substantive competence in potentially controversial non-economic fields such as culture, education, and health, while simultaneously severely circumscribing these new powers. One significant indicator of the mixed feelings about the TEU which was ultimately adopted was the fact that the Treaty provided for a further IGC to be convened in 1996—only four years after its signature and three years after its coming into force—in order to consider 'to what extent the policies and forms of cooperation introduced by this Treaty may need to be revised'. This was the IGC which resulted in the signing of the Treaty of Amsterdam in 1997.

There were originally seven titles in the TEU: Title I included the 'common provisions' which set out the basic objectives of the TEU. Titles II, III, and IV covered the 'first pillar' amendments to the EEC, ECSC, and Euratom Treaties respectively. Title V created the second pillar of the Common Foreign and Security Policy (CFSP), Title VI the third pillar of Justice and Home Affairs (JHA), and Title VII contained the final provisions. In addition there were various protocols to the Treaty and declarations adopted by the Member States. The Amsterdam and Nice Treaties leave this basic Union edifice largely as it was, despite the amendment and restructuring of the second and third pillars, and the addition of a new Title VII to allow for closer/enhanced co-operation between Member States (the final provisions thus becoming Title VIII). The Amsterdam and Nice Treaty changes will be discussed further below.

(a) TITLE I: THE COMMON PROVISIONS

The common provisions of the TEU set out the basic aims and principles of the newly created 'Union' and, although made expressly non-justiciable, they contained some high rhetoric on solidarity between States, closeness to the citizen, respect for national identities and for human rights, as well as a provision to safeguard the *acquis communautaire*—the body of Community law built up over the years.[50]

The objectives of the Union, which were to be achieved 'while respecting the principle of subsidiarity as defined in Article 3b' of the EC Treaty, included the promotion of 'balanced and sustainable' economic and social progress, through the creation of an area without internal frontiers, the strengthening of economic and social cohesion, and the establishment of EMU including a single currency. The Union's international identity was to be asserted 'through the implementation of a common foreign and security policy including the eventual framing of a common defence policy, which might in time lead to a common defence'. Citizenship of the Union was to be established and close co-operation on justice and home affairs was to be developed. These common provisions were not subject to the jurisdiction of the European Court of Justice (ECJ), although the Court in its subsequent judgments did expressly cite several of the common and final provisions, and some of these have since been rendered justiciable by the Amsterdam Treaty.

---

[50] See C. Delcourt, 'The Acquis Communautaire: Has the Concept had its Day?' (2001) 38 *CMLRev.* 829. See also the Commission's communication on *Codification of the Acquis Communautaire*, COM(2001)645.

(b) TITLES II–IV: CHANGES TO THE COMMUNITY TREATIES

The TEU brought about not only institutional and legislative changes to the EC Treaties, but also a concrete timetable for EMU with provision for a European Monetary Institute and a European Central Bank. New areas of competence were added and existing areas expanded, a concept of European citizenship was introduced, a Parliamentary Ombudsman was provided for, the principle of 'subsidiarity' was formalized, and a 'Committee of the Regions' was established. A Social Protocol with an Agreement on Social Policy was annexed to the EC Treaty, although the UK did not at the time sign the Agreement. Many other protocols were signed, including one which preserved the right of Denmark and the UK to opt out of (or rather, in the case of the UK, to opt into) the third and final stage of EMU.[51] Fewer changes—principally some of the institutional amendments and the citizenship amendments—were made to the ECSC and Euratom Treaties. The amendments made to the European Community by the TEU signed at Maastricht were numerous and complex and will not be discussed in detail here, although some, together with some of the important changes brought about by the subsequent Treaty of Amsterdam (ToA), will be discussed throughout the book in the chapters to which they are relevant.

Broadly speaking, the aims of the Community as defined in Article 2 EC were amended to include reference to EMU, as well as environmental concerns, convergence of economic policies, social protection, economic and social cohesion, and to emphasize not just balanced expansion but also 'sustainable' growth and 'quality of life' in addition to a raised standard of living. Article 3 EC, which set out the range of Community activities, in addition to listing some of these new aims and expanding on some existing activities, also included policies on research and technological development, trans-European networks, health protection, education, 'the flowering of cultures', development co-operation, consumer protection, energy, civil protection, and tourism.

Article 7 (ex Article 4) EC placed the Court of Auditors on a footing equal to that of the other four institutions (Council, Commission, Parliament, and Court of Justice) and Article 8 (ex Article 4a) provided for both a European System of Central Banks (ESCB) and a European Central Bank (ECB). A new timetable for free movement of capital was established by Articles 56–60 (ex Articles 73a–73h), and the provisions on economic and monetary policy, which provide for closer co-ordination of economic policies, set strict 'convergence criteria' relating to the size of government deficits, and set out detailed provisions relating to the operation and powers of the ESCB and the ECB, appeared in Articles 98–124 (ex Articles 102a–109m).[52] The timetable for the different stages of monetary union were set out in Articles 116–124 (ex Articles

---

[51] For criticism of some of the Protocols, including the Irish 'abortion' Protocol, the Danish 'acquisition of second homes' Protocol, and the 'Barber' Protocol, for 'tearing holes, of varying sizes, in the acquis communautaire veil' see D. Curtin, 'The Constitutional Structure of the Union: A Europe of Bits and Pieces' (1993) 30 *CMLRev*. 17.

[52] See also the various protocols on the ECB, ESCB, and EMI, as well as on the 'excessive deficit' procedure and the 'convergence criteria'. For further discussion see Ch. 16.

109e–109m).[53] The provisions on EMU were not touched in the subsequent ToA amendments.

The most significant change made by the Maastricht Treaty to the Community institutions was the increase in the Parliament's legislative involvement, by introducing the so-called co-decision procedure. The Parliament was also given the right to request the Commission to initiate legislation and the power to block the appointment of the new Commission.

(c) THE TWO INTERGOVERNMENTAL PILLARS

The second and third pillars of the Union created by the TEU remained apart from the Community institutional and legal structure. The second pillar concerned the 'Common Foreign and Security Policy' and the third pillar, prior to the ToA, concerned co-operation in 'Justice and Home Affairs'. However, these pillars were not entirely disconnected from the Community, since they involved the Community institutions and, in particular, the Council to a certain extent.

(I) PILLAR 2, TITLE V: COMMON FOREIGN AND SECURITY POLICY (CFSP)

The field of Common Foreign and Security Policy is covered by Articles 11–28 (ex Articles J.1–J.11) of the TEU. The Council was to define 'common positions' based on the agreement of the Member States, to which the States had to then ensure their national policies conformed. On the basis of guidelines from the European Council, the Council of Ministers could decide that a certain matter should be the subject of a 'joint action' and, in a departure from the consensus-based intergovernmental approach of the two new pillars, it could specify which matters were to be decided by qualified majority. This was significant because, with certain limited exceptions, Member States are committed to joint actions in the conduct of their activities. Qualified-majority voting was to apply to procedural matters too, but otherwise the Council was to act unanimously. The Council of Ministers was also given a role in the area of a possible future common defence policy, with a form of safeguard for the position of Member States which are neutral or which were not at the time full members of the WEU. The Commission was to be 'fully associated' with the work carried out in CFSP and could, as could any Member State, refer any question or submit proposals to the Council or request the convening of an extraordinary Council meeting. And it was to be fully associated with the Presidency of the European Council in representing 'the Union' and implementing any common measures adopted, as well as in keeping the European Parliament informed of developments. The Parliament was to be consulted by the Presidency 'on the main aspects and the basic choices' of the CFSP and its views to be taken into consideration. The Parliament could ask questions of the Council and make recommendations, as well as hold an annual debate on progress in these areas of policy. A Political Committee was

---

[53] See J. Pipkorn, 'Legal Arrangements in the Treaty of Maastricht for the Effectiveness of the Economic and Monetary Union' (1994) 31 *CMLRev.* 263.

established to assist the Council by monitoring the international situation, delivering opinions, and monitoring the implementation of agreed policies.

(II) PILLAR 3, TITLE VI: JUSTICE AND HOME AFFAIRS (JHA)

What was then established as the Justice and Home Affairs Pillar under Articles K.1 to K.9 of the TEU governed policies such as asylum, immigration, and 'third country' nationals, which have, since the ToA, been integrated into the EC Treaty instead. However, it also included and still today covers co-operation on a range of international crime issues and various forms of judicial, customs, and police co-operation, including the establishment of a European Police Office (Europol) for exchanging information. The Council of Ministers again was given the role of adopting joint positions and drawing up agreements on the basis of Member State or Commission initiatives, acting unanimously except on matters of procedure or when implementing joint actions or agreed conventions.

Again, the Commission was to be 'fully associated' and the Parliament was to be informed, its views to be 'duly taken into consideration', and it could question or recommend matters to the Council. A Co-ordinating Committee (which became the notorious and secretive K-4 committee) was set up to help the Council, which, like the Political Committee under CFSP, had a role similar to that of COREPER under the EC Treaty. The European Council did not have the same powerful leadership role under the JHA pillar as under the CFSP pillar.

(d) ENLARGEMENT OF THE COMMUNITY AFTER THE TEU

On the event of German reunification, the European Council decided that it was unnecessary for there to be any revision of the Treaties to facilitate the integration of the German Democratic Republic into the Community.[54] Two of the EFTA countries, Austria and Sweden, applied for membership of the Community in 1989 and 1991 respectively. At the same time, in 1991 an Agreement on the European Economic Area (EEA) between the EC and EFTA was made, providing for free-movement provisions similar to those in the EC Treaty, similar competition policy and rules, as well as 'close co-operation' in a range of other policy fields. The EFTA members who signed the amended Agreement in May 1992 with the Community were Austria, Sweden, Finland, Iceland, Liechtenstein, Norway, and Switzerland, although the last did not ratify the Agreement after it was rejected in a subsequent national referendum. The Agreement came into force at the beginning of 1994. Initially, the establishment of an EEA court led the Court of Justice (ECJ) to rule that the first EEA Agreement was incompatible with the EC Treaty,[55] but after various amendments establishing instead an EFTA Court without any connection with the ECJ, the ECJ upheld its compatibility with the EC Treaty.[56]

---

[54] See Bull. EC, Supp. 4–1990.   [55] *Opinion 1/91* [1991] ECR 6079.
[56] *Opinion 1/92* [1992] ECR I–2821. For an assessment of the operation of the EFTA court see J. Forman, 'The EEA Agreement Five Years On: Dynamic Homogeneity in Practice and its Implementation by the Two EEA Courts' (1999) 36 *CMLRev.* 751.

After Austria and Sweden had applied to join the EC, Finland and Norway also applied for membership in 1992 (as did Switzerland, but before that country's rejection by referendum of the EEA). The Acts of Accession of Norway, Austria, Sweden, and Finland to the European Union were signed at the European Council meeting in Corfu in 1994, but only the latter three acceded in 1995 when, for the second time in just over twenty years, a national referendum in Norway yielded a majority opposed to accession.

Since then, substantial progress towards a very significant eastwards expansion of the Union has been made, with a view to a membership of twenty-seven rather than the current fifteen. The scale and nature—in historical, political, and economic terms—of the impending enlargement sets it apart from all previous extensions of Community and Union membership, and the pre-accession process has been an intensive and often contentious one. The policy of conditionality pursued by the EU has meant that candidate States have been required to adapt their laws and institutions in very significant ways long before any date for accession is set, at a time when—despite the suggestion implicit in the language of accession 'partnerships'— they have little or no influence on the making of European laws and policies and are excluded from most of its processes.[57] The requirement to comply with the 'Copenhagen criteria' which were set by the European Council in 1993 and to adopt the entirety of the Community *acquis* has been a very considerable burden for the candidate countries, and an unprecedented one in terms of previous accession processes.[58] The Commission has, since the publication in 1997 of its Agenda 2000 document and opinions on each of the then candidate countries, produced annual 'country reports' on the progress of the various applicants.

Following the Laeken European Council meeting in December 2001, it was agreed that accession treaties would be drafted during 2002 and that negotiations on accession would be concluded by the end of that year with any of the candidate countries which were ready. Ten of the twelve candidates were identified as being potentially ready: Cyprus, Estonia, Hungary, Latvia, Lithuania, Malta, Poland, the Slovak Republic, the Czech Republic, and Slovenia. The remaining two, Bulgaria and Romania, were 'encouraged' to continue their efforts, with a view to opening negotiations with them on all chapters in 2002. The position of Cyprus has been complicated by the deep dispute between Greece and Turkey over the status of the north of the island since 1974, but the fact that, after so many years in a state of 'limbo', agreement has been reached in principle on the acceptability of opening negotiations for accession with Turkey, subject in particular to its compliance with political and human rights criteria, has made the accession prospects of both Cyprus and eventually of Turkey more realistic.

Although the 1996 IGC was intended to address the major institutional issues which needed to be agreed before the next wave of enlargement, these politically

---

[57] See H. Grabbe, 'A Partnership for Accession? The Implications of EU Conditionality for the Central and East European Applicants', EUI Robert Schuman Centre Working Paper 12/99, and 'How does Europeanization affect CEE Governance? Conditionality, Diffusion and Diversity' (2001) 8 *JEPP* 1013; and A. Williams, 'Enlargement of the Union and Human Rights Conditionality: A Policy of Distinction?' (2000) 25 *ELRev.* 601.
[58] See www.europa.eu.int/comm/enlargement/intro/criteria.htm#Accession criteria.

difficult issues were left largely unresolved by the Amsterdam Treaty and summit, and were postponed again until the Nice IGC in December 2000, at which political agreement on some of the key institutional questions was eventually reached.

8. FROM MAASTRICHT TO AMSTERDAM

For all its significance, the TEU, like the SEA before it, was extensively analysed and criticized. The obscurity and secrecy of the negotiation processes, the complexity of the new 'Union' structure, the mixed bag of institutional reforms, the borrowing of Community institutions for the intergovernmental pillar policy-making, and the many opt-outs and exceptions (the 'variable geometry') attracted much critical comment. The imminence of another IGC specifically to review the progress of policies and provisions introduced by the Maastricht Treaty also concentrated attention on the areas in need of reform. The perceived loss of unity and coherence of the Community legal order and the likely effect on the *acquis communautaire* which had been built up over many years, and which had bound all Member States to the same body of legal rules and principles, is addressed in the following extract.

D. Curtin, The Constitutional Structure of the Union: A Europe of Bits and Pieces[59]

The result of the Maastricht summit is an umbrella Union threatening to lead to constitutional chaos; the potential victims are the cohesiveness and the unity and the concomitant power of a legal system painstakingly constructed over the course of some 30 odd years. . . . And, of course, it does contain some elements of real *progress* (co-decision and powers of control for the European Parliament, increased Community competences, sanctions against recalcitrant Member States, Community 'citizenship', EMU etc.) but a *process* of integration, if it has any meaning at all, implies that you can't take one step forward and two steps backwards at the same time. Built into the principle of an 'ever closer union among the peoples of Europe' is the notion that integration should only be one way.

It must be said, at the heart of all this chaos and fragmentation, the unique *sui generis* nature of the European Community, its true world-historical significance, is being destroyed. The whole future and credibility of the Communities as a cohesive legal unit which confers rights on individuals and which enters into their national legal systems as an integral part of those systems, is at stake.

With hindsight, it is evident that the 'variable geometry', differentiation, or flexibility which appeared in several forms in the TEU and which was perceived as undermining the cohesiveness and unity of the Community order, is no merely temporary or transitional feature of European integration. The attraction of flexible or differentiated integration has grown, and both the Amsterdam and the Nice Treaties have firmly consolidated this trend in the variety of provisions on 'closer cooperation' and

---

[59] N. 51 above, 67.

'enhanced cooperation' adopted.[60] The variety of labels describes a range of related ideas, including the possibility that some States may participate in certain policies while other do not, or that some will participate only partially, or possibly at a later date than others.[61] Examples of differentiated integration introduced by the Maastricht Treaty were the UK's opt-out from what was then the Social Policy Chapter, the exemption from defence policy provisions of Member States which are neutral or were not full WEU members, and the option for the UK and Denmark to decide later whether or not to join in the arrangements for Economic and Monetary Union. While the disadvantages of variable geometry may be a perceived lack of unity and increasing fragmentation (the dangers of '*à la carte*' integration), the advantages of providing a means for accommodating difference and reaching consensus in the face of strong divergence, for permitting progress—even if qualified—in crucial areas such as EMU or foreign policy which might otherwise be deadlocked, are evidently considered sufficient to outweigh the former.[62] The ideas of variable geometry or different speeds were not new at Maastricht and had surfaced during earlier episodes in the Community's history,[63] but they are clearly now a confirmed part of EU strategy (at least in formal terms, even if they have hardly yet been operationalized) following the Amsterdam and Nice Treaties.

9. THE TREATY OF AMSTERDAM

Unlike the TEU, for which there were high hopes and bold plans after the dynamism of the 1980s, and which almost foundered on its own ambitions, the mood leading up to the Amsterdam intergovernmental conference (IGC) was considerably more cautious, certain lessons having been learned from the popular opposition to Maastricht and from the difficult ratification process. The aims of the 1996 IGC were more modestly stated and the Amsterdam Treaty was declared to be about consolidation rather than extension of Community powers, about enhancing effectiveness rather than expanding competence. The most important matter originally intended for the IGC agenda—that of preparing the Union for its enlargement eastwards—was ultimately postponed, being addressed only briefly in one of the Protocols and a number of declarations to the Amsterdam Treaty (ToA). The two major features of

---

[60] C.D. Ehlermann, 'Differentiation, Flexibility, Closer Cooperation: The New Provisions of the Amsterdam Treaty' (1998) 4 *ELJ* 246; J. Shaw, 'The Treaty of Amsterdam: Challenges of Flexibility and Legitimacy' (1998) 4 *ELJ* 63; E. Philippart and G. Edwards, 'The Provisions on Closer Co-operation in the Treaty of Amsterdam : The Politics of Flexibility in the European Union' (1998)37 *JCHS* 87; H. Bribosia, 'Les coopérations renforcées au lendemain du traité de Nice' [2001] *Revue du droit de l'Union européenne* 111.

[61] For some typologies see J. Usher, 'Variable Geometry or Concentric Circles: Patterns for the EU' (1997) 46 *ICLQ* 243; and A. Stubb, 'Differentiated Integration' (1996) 34 *JCMS* 283. More generally see G. de Búrca and J. Scott (eds.), *Constitutional Change in the EU: From Uniformity to Flexibility* (Hart, 2000) and B. de Witte, D. Hanf, and E. Vos (eds.), *The Many Faces of Differentiation in EU Law* (Intersentia, 2001).

[62] For an examination of the likely centripetal or centrifugal effects on the Union see A. Kolliker, 'Bringing Together or Driving Apart the Union?: Towards a Theory of Differentiated Integration' (2001) 24 West European Politics 125.

[63] B. Laffan, 'The Governance of the Union' in P. Keatinge (ed.), *Political Union*, (Institute of European Affairs, 1991), 3, 56. For a piece written in the early 1980s see C.-D. Ehlermann, 'How Flexible is Community Law? An Unusual Approach to the Concept of "Two Speeds"' (1984) 82 *Mich. LR* 1274.

the ToA—apart from the confusion generated by its renumbering of the existing Treaties—were the integration of parts of the former third pillar on JHA into the EC Treaty, and the introduction of the provisions on 'closer cooperation'. The ToA, known as a 'vanishing Treaty' since its provisions existed only to make amendments to the other existing Treaties and disappeared in effect once these changes were made, was signed in 1997 and came into effect on 1 May 1999.

(a) THE COMMON PROVISIONS

The common provisions of the TEU were changed slightly by adding the principle of openness to Article 1 TEU (ex Article A) so that decisions within the EU are be taken 'as openly as possible' and as closely as possible to the citizen. New objectives were listed in Article 2 TEU (ex Article B), including the promotion of a high level of employment and the establishment of the rather intriguingly, if somewhat ambiguously, entitled area of 'freedom, security and justice'. This new area was to be the result of the integration of parts of the former third pillar on justice and home affairs into the EC Treaty. In a move designed to enhance the image and assert the normative foundations of the Union, Article 6 (ex Article F) TEU was changed to declare that the Union is founded on respect for human rights, democracy, and the rule of law. Respect for these principles was also made a condition of application for membership of the Union under Article 49 (ex Article O) TEU. Article 6(2) (ex Article F) TEU, which declares that the Union shall respect the fundamental rights protected in the European Convention on Human Rights (ECHR) and in national constitutions, was rendered justiciable by an amendment to Article 46 (ex Article L) TEU.[64] A new Article 7 provided that if the Council finds a 'serious and persistent breach' by a Member State of principles set out in Article 6, it may suspend some of that State's rights under the Treaty. During the IGC the expulsion of the offending State in such circumstances had been proposed, but this was not accepted. A parallel provision now appears in the body of the EC Treaty, in Article 309, permitting the Council, where action has been taken under Article 7 TEU, to suspend other Treaty rights of the Member State in question, voting rights being automatically suspended.

(b) THE COMMUNITY PILLAR

The major substantive change made to the Community treaties—the incorporation of a large part of the former third pillar—is now to be found in Title IV (Articles 61–69) of the EC Treaty on the free movement of persons, covering visas, asylum, immigration, and judicial co-operation in civil matters.[65] This title, in respect of which the UK and Ireland have an opt-out with certain possibilities for subsequently opting in[66] and Denmark has a complex partial opt-out, will be further discussed in Chapter 17. The

---

[64] See Ch. 8 for a more detailed discussion.

[65] A new title on customs co-operation was also added in Art. 135 EC.

[66] These provisions are set out in a separate Protocol on the position of the UK and Ireland. See, for discussion, the UK House of Lords Select Committee *Report on UK Participation in the Schengen Acquis*, 9 Mar. 2000.

aim of this title and that of the amended third pillar, which now covers only police and judicial co-operation in criminal matters (PJCC), are similarly described, both being intended to establish 'an area of freedom, justice and security'.[67] Further, the *acquis*[68] of the 1985 Schengen Treaty on the gradual abolition of common border checks, which has now been signed (though not necessarily brought into force) by all Member States apart from the UK and Ireland, was integrated by a Protocol to the ToA into the EU framework, and the thirteen Member States are effectively authorized to engage in future 'closer co-operation' in this field. The UK and Ireland are not bound by the *acquis* as long as they wish not to be,[69] and special, rather complicated provision is also made for Denmark, in the Schengen Protocol and another separate Protocol. Norway and Iceland, two countries which participate in the Nordic passport union with Sweden, Denmark and Finland, but which are not themselves EU members, also participate on a different basis in the Schengen system.[70]

The various parts of the Schengen *acquis* were, as provided for by the Amsterdam Treaty, assigned by the Council, under the jurisdiction of the Court, to the appropriate EC or EU Treaty basis.[71] In the absence of such assignment, they are to be regarded as being based on the third pillar on Police and Judicial Co-operation in Criminal Matters (PJCC). Indeed, although the new Title IV on the free movement of persons is a part of Community law, the close legal and institutional connection between Community policies and those of the two other Union pillars is increasingly evident. The Court of Justice (ECJ) and the European Parliament now have a role, albeit still restricted, under the third pillar, and indeed the role of the ECJ and the Parliament under EC Title IV was deliberately more than under most of the rest of the EC Treaty. The Court's preliminary rulings jurisdiction over Title IV was, at least for the initial transitional period, limited to national courts from which there is no judicial remedy and, more significantly, it has no jurisdiction over certain free movement measures concerning law and order and internal security.[72] In the case of the Parliament, the consultation procedure—the most minimal in that respect of all the legislative procedures available under the Treaty—was applied at least for the transitional five-year period in most areas of decision-making, and in certain emergency situations no

[67] Protocols on the issues of asylum and the crossing of external borders were also annexed to the Treaty, and a number of Declarations on provisions of the new title were adopted.

[68] This *acquis*—roughly meaning the accumulated body of law—includes the Schengen Treaty itself and its implementing Convention, as well as decisions and declarations adopted by its Executive Committee (which is now to be taken over by the Council), and other acts of implementation. See P.J. Kuijper, 'Some Legal Problems Associated with the Communitarization of Policy on Visas, Asylum and Immigration under the Amsterdam Treaty and Incorporation of the Schengen Acquis' (2000) 37 *CMLRev.* 345 and S. Peers, 'Caveat Emptor: Integrating the Schengen Acquis into the European Union Legal Order' (1999) 2 *Cambridge Yearbook of European Legal Studies* 87.

[69] See, since the adoption of the ToA, the Commission's opinion on Ireland's request to take part in some of the provisions of the Schengen *acquis*: SEC(2000)1439, and the Council's decision 2000(356)EC on the earlier request of the UK [2000] OJ L131/43. The position of the UK and Ireland with regard to border controls is also protected by another Protocol on the application of Art. 14 (formerly Art. 7a) of the EC Treaty.

[70] See Council Decision 2000(29)EC [2000] OJ L1/51 and Council Decision 2000(777)EC [2000] OJ L309/29.

[71] As far as the ECSC and Euratom Treaties are concerned, similar amendments to the relevant institutional provisions of these treaties are made by the ToA. See Council Decision 1999(435)EC [1999] OJ L176/1, [2000] OJ L9/32, [2000] OJ L239/1 and all the subsequently published acts in the Official Journal. The Schengen secretariat was also incorporated into the Council's own secretariat: see [1999] OJ L119.

[72] See Art. 68 EC. For the Court's preliminary ruling jurisdiction in general see Ch. 11.

consultation of Parliament is required before action can be taken. This infiltration of the Community Treaty by certain third-pillar features together with the semi-communautairization of the third pillar highlight the increasing complexity and mixity of the EU constitutional order, and the continuing move away from the clarity and simplicity of the Community legal order of the past.

Paradoxically, one of the key concerns articulated by the European institutions themselves and by the Reflection Group which was established to prepare the agenda for the 1996 IGC was that of *simplification*: bringing the EU closer to the ordinary person and making it more comprehensible. Indeed, Part Two of the ToA contained a tidying-up section which deleted obsolete provisions from the EC Treaty and adapted others appropriately.[73] The final provisions of the ToA then, in a move which caused a good deal of confusion at the time but with the hope of ushering greater clarity at a later stage, renumbered all of the Articles, titles, and sections of the TEU and the EC Treaty. Obviously, these attempts at presentational clarification are largely superficial and have not reduced the overall complexity and entanglement of the constitutional structure of the European Union. However, the goal of simplification has not been abandoned yet by the EU institutions or the political elite, and following the signature of the Nice Treaty in 2000 it was expressly placed on the so-called 'post-Nice' agenda for the 2004 Intergovernmental Conference.

Apart from the introduction of Title IV, other noteworthy changes to the EC Treaty made by the ToA included new tasks in Article 2 EC: promotion of equality between men and women is now mentioned as a task, as is the promotion of a high degree of competitiveness, and the promotion of 'a high level of protection and improvement of the quality of the environment' was listed as an independent goal rather than an incidental requirement of economic growth. Complementing this change, an environmental 'integration clause' was added to Article 6 EC, requiring environmental protection to be integrated into the definition and implementation of all the Community policies and activities. And completing the strong environmental emphasis of these early Treaty provisions, economic development was henceforth required to be 'sustainable' as well as balanced and harmonious. Article 5 (ex Article 3b) EC on subsidiarity was not amended but a Protocol fleshing out the application of the principles of subsidiarity and proportionality, in line with an existing Inter-institutional Agreement and the European Council's 1992 guidelines, was annexed to the EC Treaty.

The second major innovation of the ToA, the closer co-operation provisions, is set out for the Community pillar in Article 11 EC. Article 11 refers back to the enabling provision on differentiated integration in Title VII of the TEU,[74] and provides that the Council may authorize 'closer cooperation' between Member States. In granting authorization, the Council acts by qualified majority on a Commission proposal after consulting the Parliament, following a request from the Member States wishing to establish such closer co-operation. The Commission must give reasons where it refuses to make a proposal. Article 11 has now been amended in this respect by the

---

[73] The General Secretariat of the Council issued an explanatory report on these provisions: see [1997] OJ C353/1.
[74] See further 11(d) below.

Nice Treaty, but when it was first introduced a version of the infamous 'Luxembourg veto' was included for any Member State which opposed the grant for important national policy reasons. The Amsterdam Treaty version of Article 11 contained a range of conditions restricting the circumstances under which closer co-operation could be established, including a bar on closer co-operation in relation to EU citizenship or wherever it would 'affect Community policies, actions or programmes', but these have since been relaxed by the Nice Treaty amendments and moved from Article 11 into the general conditions for enhanced co-operation in Title VII of the TEU. Despite being one of the most noteworthy changes introduced into EC law by the ToA, perhaps the most striking feature of the closer co-operation provision was the fact that it was never actually used before being amended by the Nice Treaty. However, although part of the explanation for this might be found in the restrictive conditions which were attached by Article 11 to its use, at least part of the reason must be found in the very short time—not much more than eighteen months—which elapsed between the coming into force of the Amsterdam Treaty and the conclusion of the Nice Treaty. Attempts to use it in the field of tax harmonization were made but apparently resisted strongly by Spain, and the need to invoke it to adopt a number of far-reaching anti-terrorism measures after the 11 September attacks in 2001, including a European arrest warrant, was averted at the last minute when the Italian Prime Minister, Silvio Berlusconi, agreed to abandon his vehement opposition to the measure.

Other notable changes to the Community pillar made by the ToA included a broad anti-discrimination provision in Article 13 EC, conferring legislative competence on the Community to combat discrimination based on sex, racial or ethnic origin, religion or belief, disability, age, or sexual orientation.[75] But despite the concern repeatedly voiced since the near-crisis of the Maastricht Treaty about the importance of the citizen's support for the EU project, the only amendments to the citizenship provisions at Amsterdam were the insertion of the qualification that Union citizenship was to complement and not replace national citizenship,[76] and a provision in Article 21(3) guaranteeing citizens who write to the European Parliament or the Ombudsman a reply in any one of the twelve Community languages in which they write. Amendments to a number of other Treaty provisions, however, did confer various additional rights on EU citizens, such as the provisions on consumer protection and that on access to documents in Article 255.[77] Other changes designed to enhance the legitimacy and transparency of the Union included the provision on data protection in Article 285 and that in Article 248 requiring the publication in the Official Journal of the Court of Auditors' statement as to the reliability of Community accounts.

Another significant addition made by the ToA was the title on Employment in Articles 125–130 EC. The measures provided for under this title were not the usual

---

[75] See Chs. 8 and 9 for further discussion.
[76] A longer version of this had appeared in the Edinburgh European Council decision which was adopted in Dec. 1992 to address Denmark's concerns after the ratification of the Maastricht Treaty had been rejected in a popular referendum.
[77] See, further, Ch. 9 on transparency.

'hard' Community legal instruments, but a range of soft-law measures largely complementary to national employment policies, with Article 127 specifically asserting the importance of respect for Member State competences. This title of the EC Treaty is now seen as the prototype for an experimental form of governance and policy-making, usually referred to as the 'open method of coordination' (OMC), which is increasingly being promoted across a range of EC and EU policy areas from education to immigration to social exclusion and others. Inspired by ideas of benchmarking, mutual learning, and revisability, this title charges the Council with drawing up, on the basis of European Council conclusions, annual employment *guidelines* which the Member States are to take into account in their national employment policies. A new Employment Committee was established to assist and advise the Council and, having examined how Member State policies have been implemented in the light of the guidelines, the Council may make *recommendations* to them. *Incentive measures*—excluding any harmonization measures—may also be adopted by the Council to support the policies of Member States and encourage co-operation between them. Further, following a change of government in Britain in 1997, the UK social policy opt-out was no longer necessary,[78] and consequently the Maastricht 'Social Protocol' was repealed. In its place, an amended version of the Social Policy Agreement, which strengthened the consultative role of the Committee of the Regions, provided an express basis for legislation on gender equality in employment, and enhanced the provisions on affirmative action, was incorporated into Articles 136–143 EC.[79]

The EC Treaty title on public health in Article 152 was replaced and enhanced, establishing more detailed aims and power for the Council to enact standard-setting measures, while simultaneously claiming to 'fully respect the responsibility of the member States for the organisation and delivery of health services and medical care'. The title on consumer protection in Article 153 was also slightly amended, to include the promotion of consumers' 'right to information, education and to organise themselves in order to safeguard their interests'. The absence of any specific legal provision for animal welfare in the context of EU policies has been criticized, and although the EC Treaty has not been amended to include such provision, a somewhat ambivalent Protocol was annexed to it by the ToA. This states that the EC and the Member States 'shall pay full regard to the welfare requirements of animals', while apparently also respecting the law and customs of Member States 'relating in particular to religious rites, cultural traditions and regional heritage'. Bull-fighting in Spain remains safe, it seems!

Other changes include the conferral of competence in Article 133 to conclude international agreements on services and intellectual property within the scope of the common commercial policy, and a more structured procedure for Member States to seek a derogation from a harmonization measure under Article 95(4). Special provisions for certain overseas departments and territories were made, replacing the previous Treaty provisions, and the procedures governing the making of international agreements in Article 300 (ex Article 228) were amended.

---

[78] See C. Barnard, 'The United Kingdom, the Social Chapter and the Amsterdam Treaty' (1997) 26 *ILJ* 275.
[79] See Ch. 20.

A very significant change in the institutional context was the amendment and considerable extension of the co-decision procedure, thus consolidating the role of the Parliament in the decision-making process and virtually eliminating the co-operation procedure apart from in the provisions on EMU.[80] The changes made to the co-decision procedure itself streamline and strengthen the Parliament's position within it. The consultation procedure remains in use, and indeed was introduced into some of the new provisions added by the ToA, such as those on closer co-operation and on discrimination. An upper limit of 700 on the number of European Parliament members was set, and the consultative role of the Committee of the Regions was extended to some further policy areas, including within the employment chapter and in environmental policy. The Treaty was also changed to provide that both the Committee of the Regions and the Economic and Social Committee may be consulted by the European Parliament as well as by the Council and Commission. The procedure for appointing the Commission President was slightly amended in Article 214(2) to require Parliamentary assent, and Article 207 provided that the Council's secretariat should include a Deputy Secretary-General to assist the Secretary General, who would henceforth act as High Representative for the Common Foreign and Security Policy. The Court of Auditors was granted *locus standi* under Article 230 similar to that given to the Parliament and the European Central Bank (ECB), and the Treaty provisions on combating fraud in Article 280 (ex Article 209a) were fortified with the conferral of legislative power on the Community.

(c) PILLAR 2, TITLE V: THE COMMON FOREIGN AND SECURITY POLICY (CFSP)

A number of changes were made to the second pillar by the Amsterdam Treaty, although without greatly changing its structure or the nature of institutional involvement since the Maastricht Treaty. The European Parliament's role did not alter and the jurisdiction of the ECJ remained excluded, and only a small change in the role of the Commission permitting it to submit implementation proposals was introduced. However, a variety of criticisms of the Title as established by the Maastricht Treaty had been voiced, and some of these were addressed by the ToA. One was that the CFSP lacked an identity on the international stage, and lacked a single individual to personify and represent this important policy area to the outside world. A second was that the instruments available under the pillar—common positions and joint actions—were obscure and ill-defined, and in practice the Council resorted frequently to the use of declarations, which were familiar from the CFSP's precursor, European Political Co-operation (EPC). A third criticism was that the decision-making procedures were ineffective—the perceived inadequacy of the EU's response to the crisis in the former Yugoslavia being a particular target—and that the general requirement of unanimity made progress difficult. Fourthly, it was argued that the provisions on financing of action under the CFSP were unsatisfactory, since although administrative

---

[80] As far as the ECSC and Euratom Treaties are concerned, similar amendments to the relevant institutional provisions of these Treaties were made by the ToA.

expenditure was to be charged to the Community budget and operational expenditure could be charged either to this or to the Member States, the Member States frequently did not finance operations which were charged to them. The fact that Community expenditure on the CFSP is categorized as non-compulsory expenditure and thus involves the European Parliament was considered to raise two problems: a lack of clarity about which expenditure is charged to the Community and which to national budgets, and the fact that the Parliament could have budgetary control over an area in which the Council was expressly given ultimate operational control. The responses of the ToA to these criticisms will be examined in turn.

The first criticism concerned the lack of an international identity for the CFSP. The Union itself was not formally accorded legal personality by the ToA, as this was firmly opposed by certain States. Following the suggestions made during the IGC to appoint a 'Monsieur or Madame PESC', to use the French acronym, the ToA nominated the Secretary-General of the Council as 'High Representative' for the CFSP (a post to which Javier Solana received the first appointment in October 1999) to assist the Council Presidency, which would remain the primary representative of the Union. The Secretary-General would assist by contributing in the formulation and implementation of policy decisions and, 'when appropriate and acting on behalf of the Council at the request of the Presidency, through conducting political dialogue with third parties'. The Council was also formally given power to appoint a 'special representative' with a mandate in relation to particular policy issues, and such appointments have so far been made in the context of political situations such as the African Great Lakes, the Yugoslav republic, Kosovo, Macedonia, South Eastern Europe, and the Middle East. The position of the monitoring and advisory Political Committee which was established by the TEU (with its permanent structure based in Brussels) remained unchanged, although it has since been renamed the Political and Security Committee by the Nice Treaty. However, the establishment of a new policy-planning and early-warning unit for CFSP—subsequently renamed the Policy Unit—to assist with longer-term planning was provided for in a Declaration annexed to the ToA. This unit, whose staff is drawn from the Council Secretariat, the Member States, the Commission, and the WEU, works under the High Representative.

In a significant amendment, Article 24 conferred power on the Council to 'conclude' international agreements, whenever the conclusion of such is necessary in implementing the CFSP, and these provisions were deemed also to apply to issues falling under the Third Pillar on Police and Judicial Co-operation in Criminal Matters (PJCC). Such agreements would be negotiated by the Presidency on the authorization of the Council, assisted 'as appropriate' by the Commission, and the agreements would be concluded by the Council acting unanimously on a recommendation of the Presidency. The Nice Treaty, more recently, has amended this by introducing qualified-majority voting where the Council acts to conclude certain kinds of second and third pillar agreement. Account is taken of the fact that Member States may have their own internal constitutional requirements for ratification to comply with before they can be bound by an agreement concluded by the Council, but the agreement in the meantime may be provisionally binding and applicable. Another amendment made by the TN is to omit the words 'to them', so that such provisionally applicable agreements appear henceforth to be binding on the *Union*, and not just on the States. The significance of these changes is that, although the Union is not expressly said to have legal personality or capacity (such as the Community has under Article 281 and 282 EC), it is now represented in the conclusion of an international agreement not by the Member States individually but by the Council of Ministers.[81] A Declaration which clearly reflected Member State concern over this provision at the time was adopted, stating that Article 24, along with the parallel Article under the third pillar, did not imply any 'transfer of competence' from the Member States to the Union. None the less, it is undeniable that the Council can now conclude international agreements on behalf of the Union under the CFSP, as evidenced by its decisions in 2001 concluding Agreements between the EU and the Federal Republic of Yugoslavia (FRY) and between the EU and Macedonia (FYROM) on the activities of the EU Monitoring Missions there.[82]

The second criticism mentioned above was the lack of clarity of the various policy instruments available. Following the ToA amendments, *joint actions* are defined (Article 14(1)) as addressing 'specific situations where operational action by the Union is deemed to be required', whereas *common positions* 'shall define the approach of the Union to a particular matter of a geographical or thematic nature' (Article 15). In addition to defining the principles and general guidelines of the CFSP, the European Council—which is the clearly designated legislator and policy leader under the second pillar—is also required by Article 13 TEU to decide on '*common strategies*', setting out specific objectives, duration, and means available, in areas where the Member States have important interests in common. Common strategies are then to be implemented by the Council by common position or by joint action. Finally, *systematic co-operation* between the Member States, the form of action which is least defined, is also required to be strengthened. In all, these provisions attempt to identify more precisely and to clarify the different instruments for developing and implementing the CFSP, and the relationship between them. However, other instruments which are not listed in the Treaty, such as declarations and contact with third countries (political dialogue and *démarches*), continue to be used, and the Council also adopts decisions in the context of the CFSP, albeit that these are not of the same legal character as the 'decisions' under the Community pillar which are defined in Article 249 EC.

Thirdly, the provisions on voting were changed, representing a partial compromise between those calling for more qualified majority voting and those arguing for a maintenance of the primarily intergovernmental, consensual approach. The compromise in Article 23 attempted to prevent the unanimity rule from blocking action which most of the States want, while at the same time not entirely overriding the interests of Member States in the minority. The default position is that decisions are to be taken by unanimity in the Council. However, a member of the Council can abstain from a vote and make a formal declaration, so that that Member State is not obliged to

---

[81] See J.W. de Zwaan, 'Legal Personality of the European Communities and the European Union' (1999) 30 *Netherlands Yearbook of International Law* 75; K. Lenaerts and E. de Smijter 'The European Union as an Actor under International Law' (1999/2000) 19 *YBEL* 95; and the editorial comment 'The European Union: A New International Actor' (2001) 38 *CMLRev.* 825.

[82] See Decision 2001/352/CFSP [2001] OJ L125 and Decision 2001/682/CFSP [2001] OJ L241/1.

apply the decision even while accepting that it commits the Union, and the State must not obstruct Union action based on that decision. Further, if the number of such abstentions amounts to over one third of weighted votes, the decision will not be adopted at all. By derogation from the default unanimity provision, the next paragraph specifies that the Council shall act by 'reinforced' qualified majority (votes being weighted in accordance with the EC Treaty but requiring sixty-two votes in favour cast by at least ten Member States) when joint actions, common positions, or any other decision based on an already agreed 'common strategy' are being adopted, or when a joint action or common position is being implemented. Under this considerable extension of the qualified-majority voting in CFSP, the position of dissenting Member States is protected as follows: in a Treaty expression of a Luxembourg-type veto, Article 23(2) provides that if a member of the Council declares that for 'important and stated reasons of national policy', it intends to oppose the adoption of a qualified-majority decision, a vote will not be taken, but the Council may vote, by qualified majority, to refer the matter to the European Council for a unanimous decision. For ordinary procedural questions, the Council is to act by a simple majority. This complex and differentiated decision-making process within a single title again reflects the different interests which had to be balanced in the process of negotiating the provisions on this sensitive policy area. The interests of the Union in being able to take effective action even if one State is opposed are protected by the 'unanimity with declared abstention' provision, and the important national interests of individual Member States are protected by the 'qualified majority with veto' provision.

The fourth criticism concerned the financing of the CFSP. The provisions governing budgetary arrangements were amended by the ToA to provide more guidance on which expenditure was to be charged to the Community rather than Member State budgets. Under Article 28 TEU, all administrative and operational expenditure to which the implementation of CFSP provisions gives rise must be charged to the Community budget, with the exception of operational expenditure from activities with military and defence implications or where the Council unanimously decides otherwise. In the latter situation, it is to be charged to the Member States in accordance with the gross domestic product scale, whereas in the case of military and defence operations, any Member States which abstained from a Council vote while making a formal declaration under Article 23 as described above is not obliged to contribute. An inter-institutional agreement on the budgetary procedures for the CFSP was also agreed.[83]

A final important amendment made by the ToA was the revision of the provisions on defence, which have since been significantly amended again by the Nice Treaty. At Amsterdam, the 'eventual' framing of a common defence policy was replaced in Article 17 TEU by the 'progressive' framing, and the words 'in time' were removed from the phrase 'which might (in time) lead to a common defence'. It was stated that policy of the Union in this respect 'shall not prejudice the specific character of the

[83] See Bull. EC 7/8–1997, 2.3.1. See also the subsequent Interinstitutional Agreement in 1999 on budgetary discipline and improvement of the budgetary procedure [1999] OJ C172/1, which deals in part with the CFSP.

security and defence policy of certain Member States' and that it is compatible with policy conducted in the framework of NATO obligations.[84] The decision on a common defence and the decision whether to integrate the WEU into the Union were explicitly placed in the hands of the European Council, and the relationship between the CFSP and the WEU was further elaborated, although these parts of Article 17 have since been repealed by the Nice Treaty. Article 17 placed 'tasks of combat forces in crisis management', peacemaking, peacekeeping, and humanitarian and rescue tasks—the so-called Petersberg tasks—firmly within the remit of CFSP.

(d) PILLAR 3, TITLE VI: POLICE AND JUDICIAL CO-OPERATION IN CRIMINAL MATTERS (PJCC)

As we have seen, one of the major criticisms of the third pillar on Justice and Home Affairs (JHA) under the Maastricht Treaty was partly addressed by the incorporation of much of its subject matter into Title IV of the EC Treaty. The essence of the criticism was that many of the policies under the JHA pillar called for institutional provisions and legal controls which were quite different from the intergovernmental processes established under its terms.[85] Unlike the foreign and security policy matters under the second pillar, JHA subjects such as immigration, asylum, border controls, and constraints on movement touch on fundamental human rights, and raise issues similar to those arising under the free movement provisions of the EC Treaty.[86] Consequently, it was argued that the need for openness and accountability in this policy field was much greater, requiring a full role for the European Parliament and review jurisdiction for the Court of Justice. Arguments for reform ranged from improving the institutional provisions under JHA as it stood to absorbing the third pillar entirely into the Community pillar. Predictably, what emerged in the ToA lay between these two, with parts of JHA being incorporated into the new EC title, and the remaining third pillar provisions being expanded and subjected to a range of institutional controls closer to those under the Community pillar.

The overall aim of the third pillar was declared to be the creation of an area of freedom, security, and justice, by developing 'common action' in three areas: police co-operation in criminal matters, judicial co-operation in criminal matters, and the prevention and combating of racism and xenophobia. Particular targets mentioned were terrorism, drug and arms trafficking, trafficking in persons, and offences against children, corruption, and fraud. The pillar in Article 29 set out three methods of addressing its aims: first through closer co-operation between police forces and customs and other Member State authorities, with the help of Europol; secondly through closer co-operation between judicial and other relevant Member State authorities; and thirdly through the approximation of certain criminal laws in the Member States.

---

[84] See also Art. 6 of the Protocol on the position of Denmark.

[85] For a very useful informative and critical website which discusses the impact of these and related EU policies on civil liberties, see **www.statewatch.org**.

[86] For some of the first academic works dealing with these new and growing areas of EU and EC law since the ToA see S. Peers, *EU Justice and Home Affairs Law* (Longman, 2000); K. Hailbronner, *Immigration and Asylum Law and Policy of the European Union* (Kluwer, 2000); and E. Guild and C. Harlow (eds.), *Implementing Amsterdam: Immigration and Asylum Rights in EC Law* (Hart, 2001).

Four areas of action—broadly (i) prevention and detection, (ii) storage and exchange of information, (iii) training, research, and equipment, and (iv) investigation of organized crime—in the field of police co-operation were identified in Article 30. The Council was charged with promoting co-operation in these areas through Europol, the European Police Office which was introduced by the Maastricht TEU and finally formally established in 1999 after the Europol Convention was ratified by all Member States in 1998.[87] The areas of judicial co-operation identified in Article 31 were (i) facilitating proceedings and enforcement of decisions, (ii) extradition, (iii) compatibility of rules, (iv) conflicts of jurisdiction, and (v) the establishment of minimum rules on substantive criminal laws and penalties in certain fields. These provisions have since been supplemented by the Nice Treaty's formal establishment of the institution of Eurojust (European Judicial Co-operation Unit).

Article 34 set out the range of legal instruments which the Council may adopt. These include *common positions*, which define the Union's approach to a given matter, *framework decisions* on harmonization (which are in character like first pillar directives which lack direct effect), *decisions* on other matters excluding harmonization (which seem like first pillar regulations or decisions which lack direct effect), and *conventions*, which are to be adopted by Member States in accordance with their constitutional requirements. All measures are to be adopted by the Council on an initiative from the Commission or a Member State, but the significant change introduced was that, with the exception of common positions, the European Parliament in Article 39 was given a consultative role in decision-making. The second significant institutional change was that the Court of Justice (ECJ) was given jurisdiction over certain measures adopted under this pillar. Article 35 established a preliminary reference procedure similar though not identical to that of Article 234 EC (ex Article 177), which is applicable only to the courts of a Member State which has expressly declared that it accepts such jurisdiction in relation to specified national courts. Further, the ECJ was given jurisdiction to review the legality of framework decisions and decisions at the suit of a Member State or the Commission, on the same grounds as those in Article 230 (ex Article 173) EC. However, in a somewhat similar provision to that under Article 68 EC, the Court's review jurisdiction was restricted, in that it cannot review the legality or proportionality of 'operations carried out by the police or other law enforcement services of a Member State or the exercise of the responsibilities incumbent upon Member States with regard to the maintenance of law and order and the safeguarding of internal security'. Finally, the Court was given jurisdiction in disputes between Member States concerning the interpretation or application of any legal acts adopted under Article 34(2), or between the Commission and a Member State concerning the interpretation or application of a Convention adopted under Article 34, if the Council cannot first resolve the dispute.

The Co-ordinating Committee remained unchanged, and the provisions of the amended CFSP pillar on the respective positions of the Council Presidency, the Secretary-General, the Council, and the Commission in relation to the representation of the Union, particularly in international fora, were applied also to the third pillar by

---

[87] For the Europol Convention see [1995] OJ C316/2.

Article 37. The same amendments with regard to the financing of this pillar were made as under the CFSP by Article 41, and the provision of the CFSP under which the Council is given the power to conclude international agreements negotiated by the Presidency was also applied to this title by Article 38. The final Article of the title, Article 42, contains the amended 'passarelle' provision linking the title with the new EC Treaty title on the free movement of persons, and providing a procedure whereby issues under the former may be dealt with under the latter.

Finally, anticipating the general provisions in the newly created Title VII TEU governing 'closer cooperation' on specific policies between groups of Member States (see the next paragraph below), Article 40 TEU provided for such co-operation with a view to achieving the objectives of the third pillar. As this Article has since been substantially amended by the Nice Treaty, the procedural provisions originally established will not be discussed here in any detail. Suffice it to say that those procedures differed slightly from those established for closer co-operation under the EC Treaty, with a lesser role for the Commission and Parliament, and a stronger role for the Council, European Council, and the Member States. The ECJ was given full jurisdiction over the terms of the Article, and the provisions of the rest of the third pillar were to apply so that the various legal instruments provided for under Article 34 could be adopted, with the same slightly circumscribed review jurisdiction and conditional preliminary rulings jurisdiction in this respect for the ECJ.

(e) TITLE VII: CLOSER CO-OPERATION

This title, which was introduced by the ToA, while not establishing a 'fourth pillar' set out the general conditions under which Member States could seek to establish closer co-operation between them, using the institutions and mechanisms of the TEU and the EC Treaty alike. Like the provisions on closer co-operation under the third pillar and those in Article 11 EC for the first pillar, it has been replaced and amended in certain respects by the Nice Treaty, and therefore will not be analysed here, but will be discussed further at 11(d) below in considering the changes introduced at Nice.

However, together with Article 40 TEU of the third pillar and Article 11 EC of the first pillar (and to some extent the Schengen protocols for the UK, Ireland, and Denmark), the new title introduced by the Amsterdam Treaty clearly demonstrated that differentiated integration should no longer be thought of as an aberration within the EC and EU legal order, nor as a temporary solution or a means of gradually easing all Member States into a uniform system. Along with the Nice Treaty amendments which followed, these sets of provisions constitutionalize and legitimate a mechanism for allowing different degrees of integration and co-operation between different groups of States, and provide a general legal basis for the sorts of situations—such as the Social Protocol and the EMU opt-outs—which had been individually negotiated in response to various political deadlocks in the past.

(f) TITLE VIII: FINAL PROVISIONS

Article 46 defines the scope of the ECJ's jurisdiction, which henceforth would extend not only to provisions of the EC Treaties but also, under specified conditions, to third pillar measures, to Title VII, to all of the final provisions (Articles 46–53), and to Article 6(2) of the TEU.

Article 49 provides the procedure for new states to become Members of the Union, replacing previous provisions of the EC, Euratom, and ECSC Treaties, and subjecting applicant States to the requirement of respect for the fundamental principles in Article 6 TEU, on which the European Union is now said to be based. This provision requires the Council to act unanimously after receiving the opinion of the Commission and the assent of the Parliament.[88]

10. FROM AMSTERDAM TO NICE

Given that one of the main tasks which the 1996 IGC was intended to address—that of preparing the institutional structure of the Union for the forthcoming enlargement—had been left largely unresolved by the Amsterdam Treaty, the next Intergovernmental Conference was not far around the corner. When we consider that the European Communities existed from 1957 until 1985 without a single IGC, the breathtaking pace of Treaty revision since the Single European Act and the virtually continuous process of amendment since that time is all the more striking.[89] Three IGCs have taken place since the Single Act was signed, with a fourth scheduled for 2004. And while the Maastricht Treaty may have represented a big bang moment creating the European Union, with the subsequent Amsterdam and Nice Treaties being deliberately more restrained and modest in scope, a sense of anticipation once again surrounds the 2004 IGC, given the agenda set by the post-Nice Declaration on the Future of the Union and the Laeken Declaration of December 2001.[90]

The failure to deal adequately with the institutional implications of enlargement at Amsterdam, however, and the limited nature of the Protocol on institutional reform which was annexed to the ToA resulted in the Intergovernmental Conference which followed being labelled as the 'Amsterdam leftovers'. The IGC was called by the European Council at its Cologne summit in 1999, only two months after the Amsterdam Treaty entered into force, with a mandate to address the questions of the size and composition of the Commission, the weighting of votes in the Council, the extension of qualified majority voting. Despite this relatively modest agenda, however, the deeper legitimacy issues which had surfaced during the Maastricht IGC, and which

---

[88] Art. 48 TEU would henceforth govern amendments to the Treaties, replacing Arts. 236 EC, 204 Euratom, and 96 ECSC.

[89] See B. de Witte, 'The Closest Thing to a Constitutional Conversation in Europe: The Semi-Permanent Treaty Revision Process', in P. Beaumont, C. Lyons, and N. Walker (eds.), *Convergence and Divergence in European Public Law* (Hart, 2002).

[90] See the collection of papers published in 2001 by the European Commission in *Europe 2004—Le Grand Débat: Setting the Agenda and Outlining the Options*, available online at **www.europa.eu.int/comm/ governance/whats_new/europe2004_en.pdf**.

have never since then been far from the forefront of debate, were considered by many to be challenges which could not be avoided—particularly after a period of crisis leading to the resignation of the entire Commission—when issues of institutional reform were on the table. Thus the questions of 'simplifying' the complex Treaty structure and establishing a basic constitutional text, of enhancing the transparency and accountability of the EU institutions and their functioning, and of clarifying the powers of the Union vis-à-vis the Member States were also discussed during this particular period.[91] At the same time and in parallel with the more bureacratic workings of the Intergovernmental Conference, the beginnings of a broader constitutional debate were taking place in the political sphere, stoked by the speech of Joschka Fischer in mid-2000 to the Humboldt University.[92] The process of the Nice IGC, following on from the practice begun during the Amsterdam IGC, unfolded in a considerably more transparent way than before, with many of the documents and position papers considered during the negotiations being posted on an official IGC website on the EU's Europa server. A debate had taken place about whether the agenda should be widened to other institutional and substantive questions or should remain narrow,[93] and this was partly resolved by the European Council at Feira in mid-2000, which added the issue of enhanced co-operation to the institutional questions already on the agenda.

In the meantime, the European Council at Cologne in 1999 had launched another initiative of major constitutional significance, in establishing a 'body' which included national parliamentarians, European parliamentarians, and national government representatives to draft a Charter of fundamental rights for the EU.[94] This body, which renamed itself a 'Convention', began work early in 2000 and drew up a Charter before the end of the same year. The Convention worked in an unusually open and transparent way, posting all of its documents and all of the materials submitted to it and the drafts discussed by it on a specially dedicated website, and holding its meetings openly. The Charter was 'solemnly proclaimed' by the Commission, Parliament, and Council and received the political approval of the Member States at the European Council meeting in Nice in December 2000,[95] but a decision on its legal status and specifically the question of its possible integration into the Treaties was placed on the so-called 'post-Nice agenda' and postponed until the 2004 IGC. The Charter was a significant development for the EU in a number of ways. In the first place, despite

[91] Two special reports had also been requested and received by the Commission during this period—one on the *Institutional Implications of Enlargement* presented by a high-level group chaired by Jean-Luc Dehaene: see **www.europa.eu.int/igc2000/repoct99_en.pdf**, and the other a study prepared by the European University Institute at Florence on the reorganization of the Treaties: see **www.europa.eu.int/comm/archives/igc2000/offdoc/repoflo_en.pdf**. See also *Commission Communication on a Basic Treaty for the European Union*, COM(2000)434 and *Adapting the Institutions to Make a Success of Enlargement*, COM(2000)34. At the same time, the Commission was preparing its own *White Paper on European Governance*: see COM(2001)428.

[92] For further discussion of the subject and implications of Fischer's speech see *Symposium: Responses to Joschka Fischer*, **www.iue.it/RSC/symposium/**.

[93] See P. De Schoutheete, 'The Intergovernmental Conference' (2000) 37 *CMLRev*. 845 and X. Yataganas, 'The Treaty of Nice: The Sharing of Power and the Institutional Balance in the European Union—A Continental Perspective' (2001) 7 *ELJ* 242.

[94] For an account of the origins of the Charter initiative see G. de Búrca, 'The Drafting of the EU Charter of Fundamental Rights' (2001) 26 *ELRev*. 126.

[95] See [2000] OJ C364/1.

criticisms of its content—for example, of the ambiguity and weakness of many of its provisions, the rights which were not included, the relationship with other constitutional and international human rights instruments, and the numerous questions left unresolved—the document was largely well received and welcomed as a step forward for the legitimacy, identity, and human rights commitment of the EU. Secondly, the process by which it was adopted also attracted positive comment as a considerable improvement on the typically secretive and intransparent processes—including Intergovernmental Conferences—by which treaties and other agreements have traditionally been negotiated and drawn up at EU level. So much so that, without actually agreeing to abandon the government-dominated IGC process, the European Council at Laeken in 2001 established a similar Convention (including the participation of members from the candidate countries) to 'prepare' for the 2004 IGC, alongside a Forum to structure a public debate on the constitutional future of Europe. How these constitutional innovations will function and whether they lead to an eventual change in the IGC method for Treaty revision remains, at the time of writing this book, to be seen.

11. THE NICE TREATY

The Nice Treaty (TN) was concluded in December 2000 after a notoriously fractious, unprecedentedly lengthy, and badly run European Council summit. The Treaty consists of two parts—the first part containing the substantive amendments to the EU and EC Treaties[96] and the second part containing the transitional and final provisions—and of four protocols: one on enlargement, the second on the statute of the Court of Justice, the third on the financial consequences of expiry of the ECSC Treaty, and the fourth on Article 67 of the EC Treaty (concerning the transitional provisions of Title IV on the free movement of persons). Twenty-four declarations, including the important declarations on Enlargement and on the Future of the Union, were also adopted and annexed to the final act of the IGC.

The major political achievement of the Nice summit was considered to be the agreement reached on the institutional questions relevant to enlargement: settling the weighting of votes in the Council, the composition of the Commission, the Economic and Social Committee, and the Committee of the Regions, and the distribution of seats in the European Parliament. Some of these changes—the ceiling of 732 on European Parliament members, the calculation of a qualified majority in the Council, and the cap on the total number of commissioners together with a system of rotation—were introduced as legal amendments in the Protocol on enlargement, while others—in particular the figures relevant to the candidate States for the future—were simply the subject of political agreement in the Declaration on enlargement, and will not be legally enshrined until the various accession treaties are signed.

---

[96] The relevant provisions of the Euratom Treaty are amended by Art. 3 of the Nice Treaty and those of the ECSC Treaty by Art. 4 TN. For some of the commentaries on the changes introduced by the Nice Treaty see K. Bradley, 'Institutional Design in the Treaty of Nice' (2001) 38 *CMLRev.* 1095 and R. Barents, 'Some Observations on the Treaty of Nice' (2001) 8 *MJ 121*.

The other major legal changes made by the Treaty are the extension of the co-decision procedure and of qualified majority voting, the reform of the judicial system of the Union, and the amendment of the provisions on what is now termed 'enhanced cooperation'. Various other less significant changes to the EU and the EC Treaties were made. However, the adverse media attention attracted by the ill-tempered exchanges and the late-night wrangling undoubtedly added to the pressure to be seen to reform the Treaty revision process, and formed part of the impetus for the decision of the European Council later in 2001 to establish a more open and representative Convention to prepare for the next IGC.

The principal changes to each of the Treaties will be briefly discussed, although some, such as the reform of the judicial system, will be treated in more detail in the later relevant chapters of this book.

(a) THE COMMON PROVISIONS

The single change made by the TN to this part of the TEU was in Article 7, where the provision on suspending the rights of a Member State found to be in serious and persistent breach of the principles of respect for democracy, human rights, and the rule of law is amended. One of the Member States which proposed this amendment was Austria, following its own less than satisfactory experience in 2000 when, after the coming into government of the right-wing FPÖ, the other fourteen Member States adopted *ad hoc* political sanctions against the country, which were not lifted until a three-person committee chaired by a judge of the ECHR issued a positive report. Article 7 as amended provides for more detailed procedures to be followed before a negative determination against a Member State is made, including an opportunity for the Member State to be heard and for an independent report to be made, and it also provides for the possibility of acting where there is a clear *risk* of breach. The Court of Justice is given jurisdiction over the procedural stipulations of Article 7 by Article 46 TEU.

(b) PILLAR 2: THE CFSP

The principal changes made are in relation to security and defence policy in Article 17. Most of the provisions referring to the WEU are repealed, leaving its remaining status somewhat unclear, but emphasizing the operational capability of the EU itself. Further, although not part of the actual Treaty amendments, the Nice European Council in its conclusions also adopted a declaration on the operational capability of the common European Security and Defence Policy (ESDP), and the strengthening in particular of its military and police capabilities. Qualified-majority voting by the Council is extended to the issue of the appointment of special representatives under Article 23(2), and to the conclusion of international agreements under Article 24 where the agreement is made in order to implement a joint action or common position, or when the issue is not one for which unanimity would be required for the adoption of internal decisions. This same extension of majority voting in the conclusion of international agreements is also applied to the parallel provisions of the third pillar. Under Article 25 the Political and Security Committee is given an enhanced strategic role in crisis-management operations.

Finally, a new and important provision permitting enhanced co-operation under the second pillar was adopted in Article 27a, although military and defence matters (apparently due to pressure during the IGC from the UK) are excluded by Article 27b. Instead, enhanced co-operation is available in other areas of the CFSP in relation to the implementation of a joint action or common position. The substantive conditions under which it may be established are set out, followed by the procedure, which remains largely in the hands of the Council at the request of the Member States in question, with the Commission and Parliament being informed and the Commission having an advisory role as regards its consistency with Union policies. The Council decides in accordance with the provisions of Article 23(2) by qualified majority, with a protective Luxembourg-style veto for any Member State which wishes to refer the matter to the European Council instead for a unanimous decision. The general provisions of the enhanced co-operation Title in Articles 43–45 TEU also apply to these specific CFSP provisions, and the Council must act by qualified majority and give reasons where it decides against a Member State which has requested permission to participate in an established instance of enhanced co-operation, and it must under Article 27e later re-examine the request. It is evident that, in view of the sensitive nature of second pillar policy, the institutional involvement of the Commission and Parliament in enhanced co-operation is considerably reduced and that of the Member States and the Council is paramount.

(c) PILLAR 3: PJCC

Few changes were made to the third pillar by the TN. A formal Treaty basis is given to Eurojust, the European judicial co-operation unit, and its role is elaborated in Article 31(2), but otherwise the principal change is to the provisions on enhanced co-operation in Articles 40, 40a, and 40b. Like the enhanced co-operation provisions of the second pillar, these are also subject to the general substantive conditions of the umbrella enhanced co-operation provisions in Articles 43–45. The main effect of the amendments to the third pillar is to strengthen the role of the Commission, to which Member States must first direct their request to establish enhanced co-operation, and only if it refuses to direct a proposal to the Council for authorization may the States submit their initiative directly to the Council. The Parliament is also given a consultative role. The Luxembourg-style veto has been repealed and replaced by a softer protection for Member States which may request that a matter be referred to the European Council. The procedure for deciding on a request by a Member State to participate in an established instance of enhanced co-operation are much the same as under the second pillar, except that the Commission is empowered to make specific recommendations if a Member State is to become such a party.

(d) TITLE VII ON ENHANCED CO-OPERATION

The provisions of Article 43, which were first established by the Amsterdam Treaty, have been replaced and (at least in the English version of the TEU) been renamed 'enhanced' rather than 'closer' co-operation. The Article, which deserves citation in full, now provides:

Member States which intend to establish enhanced cooperation between themselves may make use of the institutions, procedures and mechanisms laid down by this Treaty and by the Treaty establishing the European Community provided that the proposed cooperation:

(a) is aimed at furthering the objectives of the Union and of the Community, at protecting and serving their interests and at reinforcing their process of integration;

(b) respects the said Treaties and the single institutional framework of the Union;

(c) respects the acquis communautaire and the measures adopted under the other provisions of the said Treaties;

(d) remains within the limits of the powers of the Union or of the Community and does not concern the areas which fall within the exclusive competence of the Community;

(e) does not undermine the internal market as defined in Article 14(2) of the Treaty establishing the European Community, or the economic and social cohesion established in accordance with Title XVII of that Treaty;

(f) does not constitute a barrier to or discrimination in trade between the Member States and does not distort competition between them;

(g) involves a minimum of eight Member States;

(h) respects the competences, rights and obligations of those Member States which do not participate therein;

(i) does not affect the provisions of the Protocol integrating the Schengen acquis into the framework of the European Union;

(j) is open to all the Member States, in accordance with Article 43b.

This is followed by Articles 43a and 43b which provide respectively that enhanced co-operation should be used only as a last resort when it has been established that the same objectives cannot otherwise be attained within a reasonable period, and that enhanced co-operation should be open to all Member States at any stage under the conditions provided in the Treaty, and that as many States as possible should be encouraged to take part. Article 44 indicates the relevant institutional provisions to be used in the actual adoption of decisions within a field of enhanced co-operation, and explains the decision-making procedures and obligations in relation to participating and non-participating States. Such decisions are declared not to be part of the Union *acquis*. Article 44a (ex Article 44(2)) specifies that expenditure other than administrative costs is in principle to be borne by the participating states unless the Council unanimously—and after consulting the Parliament, which is a new requirement—decides otherwise.

The most significant change brought about by the TN is that only a minimum of eight Member States is necessary to establish enhanced co-operation (so that a majority of Member States will not be necessary in an EU of more than fifteen members, unless this number is changed consequent on future enlargement). Further, some of the conditions (part of conditions (d) and (f)) which are particularly applicable to enhanced co-operation under the Community Treaty have been included here in the umbrella title rather than in Article 11 EC only, and some of the stricter conditions of the previous Amsterdam provisions have been relaxed. Thus, enhanced co-operation is no longer prohibited where it may *affect* the *acquis communautaire* or the competences and rights of non-participating States; rather—in a more positive vein—any enhanced co-operation is required to *respect* the acquis and the competences and rights of non-participating States. The requirement that enhanced co-operation must not undermine the internal market or economic and social cohesion is, however, a newly added restrictive condition.

Given that the Amsterdam provisions on closer co-operation were never actually put into effect, it is difficult to assess the likely impact of the amendments made by the NT. However, it seems clear that they are intended to make the use of enhanced co-operation somewhat more feasible and operational, by relaxing some of the substantive conditions and softening the veto provisions under the third pillar.

(e) THE COMMUNITY PILLAR

The most significant changes to the EC Treaty, apart from those already discussed in relation to the weighting of votes and the institutional changes necessitated by enlargement, are those concerning the judicial system, and the extension of the co-decision procedure and of qualified majority voting.

The changes to the Court system will be discussed in more detail in Chapter 3. Suffice it for now to say that the powers of the Court of First Instance (CFI) are significantly strengthened, with provision being made for it to exercise preliminary rulings jurisdiction—the most important of all the judicial procedures in the EU—in certain circumstances. Such cases may be referred by the CFI to the Court of Justice (ECJ) or, in exceptional circumstances, preliminary rulings by the CFI may be subject to review by the ECJ under Article 225(3). In addition, the CFI's jurisdiction in direct actions is expanded and it gains appellate jurisdiction from new judicial panels which may be set up in accordance with Articles 220 and 225a. The ECJ under Article 225(2) will have review jurisdiction over such decisions of the CFI in exceptional cases. Thus the new panels, once established, will form a layer of judicial authority under the CFI, with the ECJ at the apex of the hierarchy looking more like a supreme appellate court than it ever has before. Less significant changes include the possibility for the Council under Articles 223 and 225a to amend the rules of procedure of the Court by qualified majority instead of unanimity, and for a separate Protocol containing the Statute of the ECJ to be capable of amendment for the most part by the Council following particular procedures, in accordance with Article 245, rather than by the cumbersome IGC process.[97] In another significant amendment, the European Parliament is finally given full *locus standi* to bring actions before the Court of Justice under Article 230,

---

[97] A somewhat similar power is provided in Art. 266 for the Council under certain circumstances to amend provisions of the Statute of the European Investment Bank.

and to request an opinion under Article 300(6) from the Court on the compatibility of an envisaged international agreement with the Treaty. In terms of composition, both the Court of Justice and the Court of Auditors are to have one member from each Member State—in the case of the Court of Auditors this is expressed as a requirement in Article 247(1) that there be one *national* from each Member State, whereas for the ECJ in Article 221 it is simply 'one judge per Member State'.

The closer co-operation provisions of Article 11 are amended and (in the English version, at least) renamed 'enhanced cooperation', in line with the amendments to the umbrella provision in Article 43 TEU. The substantive conditions for the establishment of enhanced co-operation under Article 11 EC are those set out in Article 43 TEU as amended, but the procedure for authorizing such co-operation is specific to the Community pillar with a stronger role for the Commission and Parliament. The Commission makes a proposal to the Council, on the request of the Member States, and the Council will grant authorization by qualified majority after consulting the European Parliament, or—following a TN innovation—where the area is one covered by the co-decision procedure, only after obtaining the assent of the Parliament. The Luxembourg-style veto has, as under the third pillar provisions, been removed, and a Member State which opposes the authorization can instead request that the matter first be referred to the European Council. Unlike under the second or third pillar, the Commission has the power to decide whether and under which arrangements a requesting Member State may join an established instance of enhanced co-operation.

Further EC Treaty changes include an amendment to the anti-discrimination provision of Article 13 which establishes a power to adopt non-harmonizing incentive measures using the co-decision procedure. But while the previous requirement of unanimity was removed from the Council's power to adopt measures to ensure free movement and residence under the citizenship provision of Article 18, the Nice Treaty has added a restrictive paragraph to this Article—once again, partly under pressure from the UK—which excludes provisions on passports, identity cards, residence permits, and social security and social protection measures from the scope of the power.

The co-decision procedure and qualified-majority voting are extended to a considerable range of Treaty provisions,[98] though not, given firm opposition from certain Member States, to certain areas including taxation or social security, a range of social policy provisions under Article 137, the cohesion policy provisions at least until 2007, and parts of Title IV concerning immigration and asylum, where the introduction of qualified-majority voting was also deferred for many provisions. The provisions of Article 133 on the common commercial policy in relation to the negotiation and conclusion of international agreements in the field of trade in services and the commercial aspects of intellectual property are also changed, specifying that such agreements are to be concluded by qualified majority, except when they include provisions for which unanimity is required for the adoption of internal rules, or when the agreement concerns an area on which the Community has not yet exercised its internal powers. Paragraph 6 of Article 133 provides that agreements related to the

---

[98] See A. Dashwood, 'The Constitution of the European Union after Nice: Law-making Procedures' (2001) 26 *ELRev.* 215.

politically sensitive areas of trade in cultural and audio-visual services, education services, and social and human health services continue to fall within the shared competence of the Member States and the Community, thus requiring the common accord of the Member States.

Other institutional changes include the establishment of a Social Protection Committee in Article 144, and following the Treaty title on Development Co-operation a new title on economic, financial, and technical co-operation with third countries was adopted in Article 181a. A provision in Article 191 empowering the Council to adopt regulations governing the funding of political parties at European level is also an interesting change, given the often-lamented absence of an active European public and political sphere. Another important institutional change is in the fact that the Commission President and the list of Commission members can now be nominated and appointed by qualified majority rather than by common accord, and the President's powers of organization within the Commission have been strengthened. The provisions concerning the Economic and Social Committee and the Committee of the Regions are amended by capping the number of their members at 350 by Articles 258 and 263 EC respectively.

The crucial institutional changes are those contained in the Protocol on Enlargement, relating to the weighting of votes and the calculation of a qualified-majority vote in the Council, the number of representatives in the Parliament, and the number of Commission members. As far as weighted voting is concerned, the main questions were whether a qualified majority must include a majority of Member States, what the size of a 'blocking minority' should be, and more generally what the specific figures and the system should be. Ultimately, what has been called a 'triple majority'[99] was agreed upon: a decision must command the agreement of a majority of the overall number of Member States (but it must command the agreement of two-thirds of the members where the Council is not acting on a proposal from the Commission), it must have 169 out of 237 weighted votes (or 258 out of 345 after enlargement), and, finally, where a Member State so requests, the votes in favour must represent 62 per cent of the total population of the EU. The provisions, together with the weighting of votes agreed for the candidate States in Declaration no. 20 to the Nice Treaty, are immensely complicated in mathematical terms, but it seems that for a time after a certain number of accessions, three large Member States and one small State will be able to form a blocking minority against a proposal which commands the support of all others.

In relation to the European Parliament, the overall ceiling of 700 established by the ToA was raised to 732, and reductions were made to the number of seats for most Member States except Germany and Luxembourg from the time of the next European elections in 2004. Article 2(4) of the Protocol allows for the new ceiling to be temporarily exceeded in certain circumstances in the event of accession. In relation to reform of the Commission, pressure from the smaller Member States resulted in a compromise whereby the position that there would be at least one Commissioner per Member State was retained from 2005 onwards, at least until the membership of the Union

---

[99] See X. Yataganas, 'The Treaty of Nice: The Sharing of Power and the Institutional Balance in the European Union—A Continental Perspective' (2001) 7 *ELJ* 242.

reaches twenty-seven. Whether this ceiling of twenty-seven overall will remain after that time is not clear, but it seems that the larger Member States will lose their second Commissioner and Article 4 of the Protocol provides that after that time the number of members of the Commission will be smaller than the number of Member States, and members will be chosen according to a rotation system on the basis of equality rather than size.

Unexpectedly, the Nice Treaty was rejected by the Irish population in a referendum held in June 2001, but, despite the objections of the successful 'No' campaigners, who have argued that enlargement could proceed without the Nice Treaty and that the legitimate democratic voice of the people voting no should be respected, both the Irish government and the EU institutions and political leaders seem determined that the Treaty shall enter into force, presumably after a second referendum in Ireland is held and when all other Member States have ratified the text.[100]

12. CONCLUSION

As we have seen, no sooner was the Nice Treaty agreed in 2000 but a Declaration on the Future of the Union was adopted, calling for a 'deeper and wider debate about the future of the European Union', involving wide-ranging discussions to include 'all those reflecting public opinion, namely political, economic and university circles, representatives of civil society' and also involving the candidate States. The four key issues identified by the Declaration for the 2004 IGC are the so-called 'delimitation of powers' between the EU and the Member States, the status of the Charter of Fundamental Rights, simplification of the Treaties, and the role of the national parliaments. However, the broader and more general question of Europe's constitutional future is also now firmly on the table since the Laeken summit of December 2001.

Already the academic literature on the subject is burgeoning, lectures, working groups, and conferences are proliferating, and the EU's dedicated Futurum website testifies to the Europe-wide nature of the debate, even if it still remains more of an elite debate than a popular discussion.[101] None the less, the series of high-profile speeches given by virtually all of Europe's political leaders—Blair, Verhofstadt, Rau, Amato, Prodi, Schroeder, Chirac, Jospin, and others—since Joschka Fischer's foray outlining his vision for Europe have also directed media and public attention to the otherwise unglamorous subject of the EU's constitutional future. For the first time since the 1950s, as the Declaration from the Laeken European Council summit even more clearly shows, the question of a constitution or a constitutional settlement for Europe has been placed explicitly on the political agenda and is not just a subject for discussion by lawyers and academics.[102]

---

[100] For an analysis of the reasons for the Irish No vote see the study by R. Sinnott requested by the European Commission, 'Attitudes and Behaviour of the Irish Electorate in the Referendum on the Treaty of Nice' available online at **www.europa.eu.int/comm/dg10/epo/flash/fl108_v2_en.pdf**. More generally see the publication of the Centre for Economic Policy Research, *Nice Try: Should the Treaty of Nice be Ratified?* (CEPR, 2001).

[101] See **www.europa.eu.int/futurum/index_en.htm**.

[102] See P.P. Craig, 'Constitutions, Constitutionalism and the European Union' (2001) 7 *ELJ* 125.

Paradoxically, at a time when the language of *finalité* is in frequent use, the EU finds itself in a period of dramatic political and constitutional activism and dynamism. The grand questions of legitimacy, democracy, and the very *raison d'être* of the EU are no longer hiding beneath the surface of 'technical' treaties or functionally limited market-oriented reforms, but are being vigorously aired and debated. A single currency is operating in most Member States, a Bill of Rights has recently been introduced, the EU's military capacity is being enhanced, as is its identity on the international scene; a dramatic phase of enlargement is imminent, the IGC method for reforming the polity is under serious strain, and most of Europe's leaders are openly engaged in debating the desirability of a European constitution. For the EU, these are interesting times indeed.

13. FURTHER READING

(a) *Books*

BOND, M., and FEUS, K., *The Treaty of Nice Explained* (Federal Trust, 2001)

CORBETT, R., *The Treaty of Maastricht* (Longman, 1993)

DUFF, A. (ed.), *The Treaty of Amsterdam* (Sweet & Maxwell, 1997)

EUROPEAN COMMISSION, *The Amsterdam Treaty: A Comprehensive Guide* (Office for Official Publications of the EC, 1999)

—— *Europe 2004: Le Grand Débat* www.europa.eu.int/comm/governance/whats_new/europe2004_en.pdf

HOLLAND, M., *European Integration from Community to Union* (Pinter, 1993)

LODGE, J., *The European Community and the Challenge of the Future* (Pinter, 1993)

MONAR, J., and WESSELS, W., *The European Union after the Treaty of Amsterdam* (Continuum, 2001)

MORAVCSIK, A., *The Choice for Europe* (University College London Press, 1999).

O'KEEFFE, D., and TWOMEY, P., *Legal Issues of the Amsterdam Treaty* (Hart, 1999)

PINDER, J., *The Building of the European Union* (Oxford University Press, 3rd edn., 1998)

URWIN, D., *The Community of Europe: A History of European Integration* (Longman, 2nd edn., 1995)

WINTER, J., CURTIN, D., KELLEMANN, A., DE WITTE, B., *Reforming the Treaty on European Union: The Legal Debate* (Kluwer, 1996)

(b) *Articles*

CURTIN, D., 'The Constitutional Structure of the Union: A Europe of Bits and Pieces' (1993) 30 *CMLRev.* 17

DANKERT, P., 'The EC—Past, Present and Future', in L. Tsoukalis (ed.) *The EC: Past, Present and Future* (Blackwell, 1983)

EVERLING, U., 'Reflections on the Structure of the European Union' (1992) 29 *CMLRev.* 1053

WEILER, J., 'The Transformation of Europe' (1991) 100 *Yale LJ* 2403

WOUTERS, J., 'Institutional and Constitutional Challenges for the European Union: Some Reflections in the Light of the Treaty of Nice' (2001) 26 *ELRev.* 342

YATAGANAS, X., 'The Treaty of Nice: The Sharing of Power and the Institutional Balance in the European Union—A Continental Perspective' (2001) 7 *ELJ* 242

2

THE INSTITUTIONS

1. CENTRAL ISSUES

i. There are five principal institutions mentioned in Article 7 (ex Article 4) EC which are entrusted with carrying out the tasks of the Community: the Council, the Commission, the European Parliament, the Court of Auditors, and the Court of Justice. This Chapter will describe the role each of these institutions plays in the Community and the way in which they interrelate. We shall also be considering other important institutions such as the European Council, the Economic and Social Committee, and the Committee of the Regions as well as some of the significant agencies and other bodies that play a role within the institutional system. The EC's monetary institutions will, however, be discussed later.[1]

ii. This Chapter should not be approached with any preconceptions about the traditional division of governmental functions into categories of legislative, executive, administrative, and judicial. Do not seek to pigeon-hole each of the institutions into one category as if it *only* undertook tasks of, for example, a legislative or executive nature. Many of these duties are shared between different institutions in a manner that renders it impossible to describe any one of them as the sole legislator, or the sole executive. In this sense the Community does not conform to any rigid separation-of-powers principle of the sort which has shaped certain domestic political systems.

iii. The pattern of institutional competence within the Community has not remained static. It has altered both as a consequence of subsequent Treaty revisions and as a result of organic change in the political balance of power between the institutions over time, including through the emergence of a web of committees and institutional actors beyond the original 'canonical' institutions.

iv. The Nice Treaty (TN) was designed specifically to modify the institutions in readiness for the enlargement of the EU from fifteen to twenty-seven Member States.

2. THE COMMISSION

(a) THE COLLEGE OF COMMISSIONERS: APPOINTMENT AND REMOVAL

The method of choosing Commissioners has been altered, with the consequence that the Parliament has more say in the process than hitherto. Under Article 214(2) (ex Article 158), as amended by the Treaty of Nice (TN), the Council, meeting as the Heads of State and acting by qualified majority, nominates the person intended to be appointed as President of the Commission. This nomination must be approved by the

---

[1] See Ch. 16.

European Parliament (EP). The Council, acting by qualified majority and by common accord with the nominee for President, adopts a list of proposed Commissioners, drawn up in accordance with the proposals made by each Member State. The President and the other Commissioners are then subject to a vote of approval by the EP. Prospective Commissioners will now be subject to scrutiny and questioning by the relevant parliamentary committee before being approved by the EP. Once this approval has been secured the Council, acting by qualified majority, appoints the President and Commissioners. The main amendment introduced by the TN is that the operative Council decisions are reached by qualified majority. This is in contrast to the position hitherto when they were made by common accord. The change was made because of the prospective enlargement of the EU: to require common accord in a Community with twenty-seven States could well be impossible.

Prior to the TN an individual Commissioner could be compulsorily retired if he or she no longer fulfilled the conditions for the performance of his or her duties, or in the event of serious misconduct. This decision was made by the ECJ on application by the Council: Article 216 (ex Article 160). The difficulty of removing individual Commissioners was, as we shall see, part of the problem leading to the downfall of the Santer Commission. Article 216 has now been supplemented by Article 217(4) (ex Article 161), introduced by the TN. It provides that a Commissioner shall resign if the President so requests, after obtaining the approval of the College of Commissioners. This gives formal effect to a power that Romano Prodi, the Commission President, exercised *de facto* when he came into office.

(b) THE COLLEGE OF COMMISSIONERS: COMPOSITION

There are, at present, twenty Commissioners, and the number can be increased by the Council: Article 213(1) (ex Article 157(1)) EC. They are to be persons whose 'independence is beyond doubt', and they 'shall neither seek nor take instructions from any government or from any other body': Article 213. Overt and excessive partisanship is therefore precluded, but one should not necessarily expect total neutrality.[2] The Commissioners meet collectively as the College of Commissioners. Their term of office is five years, and this term may be renewed.[3] The Commission operates under the guidance of its President, whose organizational powers have been strengthened by the TN reforms, and the Commissioners take decisions by majority vote.[4]

Article 213 provides that the Commission must include at least one, and no more than two, Commissioners from each State. In fact, the five larger countries (France, Germany, Italy, Spain, and the United Kingdom) have two Commissioners, while the other countries have one Commissioner each.

This is set to change as a result of the TN. In the Intergovernmental Conference (IGC) leading to the TN much consideration was given to the size of the Commission. Opinion was divided on whether there should continue to be one Commissioner from each State, or whether there should be an upper limit combined with a system of

---

[2] N. Nugent, *The Government and Politics of the European Union* (Macmillan, 4th edn., 1999), 105.
[3] Art. 214(1) (ex Art. 158(1)) EC.   [4] Art. 219(2) (ex Art. 163(1)) EC.

rotation.[5] The argument for the latter view was that Commissioners do not represent their State, and that the operation of a Commission with twenty-seven or twenty-eight Commissioners could cross the line between a collegiate body and a deliberative assembly. The TN embodied a compromise. The Protocol on Enlargement provided that from 1 January 2005 Article 213(1) should be amended to provide that the Commission should consist of one national from each State. The Council, acting unanimously, may alter the number of members of the Commission. When the Union has twenty-seven Member States Article 213(1) will be further modified, such that the number of Commissioners will be less than the number of Member States. The Council, acting on the principle of equality, will adopt a rotation system. It will also be for the Council to decide on the number of Commissioners.

The Commissioners will have their personal staffs (or *cabinets*), consisting partly of national and partly of Community officials.[6] There will normally be six or seven officials in these teams, although the President of the Commission will have a larger *cabinet* of about twelve. The members of the *cabinet* perform a variety of functions. They will liaise with other parts of the Commission and with the country from which the Commissioner was appointed. They will have a role in the legislative process, scrutinizing draft regulations and directives. They will keep the Commissioner informed about developments in other connected areas; and they can undertake research initiatives for the Commissioner.

(c) THE COLLEGE OF COMMISSIONERS: DECISION-MAKING

The College of Commissioners operates in three different ways.[7] There is the *delegation or habilitation procedure*, which allows for certain matters to be dealt with by individual Commissioners under powers delegated to them by the College. This procedure is used for routine business. The *written procedure* is used where 'deliberations in College do not seem to be necessary because all points have been agreed by the relevant DGs and approval has been given by the Legal Service'.[8] The proposal is sent to the Commissioners' *cabinets*, and if there is no objection within a specified period the decision is made. Any Commissioner can raise objections and request that the measure be considered at a College meeting. This procedure is used for routine and uncontroversial matters. All other matters are dealt with through *College meetings*. These occur weekly, normally on Wednesdays, and the agenda is prepared by the Secretariat-General. These meetings will be preceded by discussion held by the Commissioners' *chefs de cabinet*, who will try to resolve differences in advance of the College meeting. Matters on which the *chefs de cabinet* have agreed will be designated as 'A points', and will not normally require discussion within the College. There may also be meetings of Commission groups, designed to co-ordinate the activities of the Commission. Romano Prodi established five such groups, dealing with growth, competitiveness and employment, equal opportunities, external relations, reform, and inter-institutional relations.

---

[5] Presidency Note, CONFER 4813/00, 1 Dec. 2000.
[6] N. Nugent, *The European Commission* (Palgrave, 2001), ch. 5.
[7] *Ibid.*, 94–101.   [8] *Ibid.*, 94.

(d) THE PRESIDENCY OF THE COMMISSION

The Presidency of the Commission is a position of real significance. The holder of this post is clearly *primus inter pares* as compared with the other Commissioners. The President's powers have been increased as a result of the TN: Article 217 (ex Article 161). It provides that the Commission shall work under the political guidance of its President, who shall decide on its internal organization in order to ensure that it acts consistently, efficiently, and on the basis of collegiality. The responsibilities incumbent on the Commission shall be structured and allocated among the Commissioners by the President, who has power to reshuffle the portfolios. The President can also, after obtaining the approval of the College, appoint Vice-Presidents from among the Commissioners. We have also seen that the President has been given power to remove individual Commissioners.

The President will play an important role in shaping overall Commission policy, in negotiating with the Council and the Parliament, and in determining the future direction of the Community.[9] How much is made of the post, over and beyond this, will depend on the personality and vision of the incumbent.[10] Jacques Delors had a strong personality and a vision for the Community's development. Many of the broader Community initiatives were in no small measure the result of his leadership within the Commission.[11]

The President will, pursuant to Article 217 (ex Article 161), decide upon portfolios within the Commission, but there will be negotiations, often intense, between the Commissioners, the President, and the Member States about 'who gets what'. Commissioners who have seniority will press strongly for the high-profile portfolios, although Sir Leon Brittan's disappointment at not being assigned the portfolio of his choice in 1994 attests to the fact even senior Commissioners will not always be successful in securing their number one priority. This will be especially so as the Community becomes larger.

(e) THE COMMISSION BUREAUCRACY

The permanent officials who work in the Commission, and who form the Brussels bureaucracy, are organized as follows.

Directorates General (DG) cover the major internal areas over which the Commission has responsibility. There are now DGs for: Agriculture, Competition, Economic and Financial Affairs, Education and Culture, Employment and Social Affairs, Energy and Transport, Enterprise, Environment, Fisheries, Health and Consumer Protection, Internal Market, Joint Research, Justice and Home Affairs, Regional Policy, Research, and Taxation and the Customs Union. Financial matters are dealt with by the DGs for Budget, Financial Control, and the Internal Audit Service. There are DGs dealing with external relations, including: Development,

[9] *Ibid.*, ch. 3.

[10] J. Peterson, 'The Santer Era: The European Commission in Normative, Historical and Theoretical Perspective' (1999) 6 *JEPP* 46.

[11] N. Nugent, 'The Leadership Capacity of the European Commission' (1995) 2 *JEPP* 603.

Enlargement, EuropeAid-Co-operation Office, External Relations, Humanitarian Aid, and Trade.

There are also units which provide *General Services* across the spectrum of Commission activities. These include: the European Anti-Fraud Office (OLAF),[12] Eurostat, Press and Communication, Publications, Translation Service, the Legal Service, Personnel and Administration, the Policy Advisors' Group, the Joint Research Centre, and the Secretariat General of the Commission.

There are essentially four layers of hierarchical division within the Commission bureaucracy.[13] There is the Commissioner who has the portfolio for that area. Then there is the Director General who is the head of a particular DG. There are Directors. Each DG will have a number of Directorates within it, commonly somewhere between four and six, and each of these Directorates will normally be headed by a Director who is responsible to the Director General. The final part of the administrative organization is the Head of Division or Unit. These are parts of Directorates. Each Division or Unit will have a Head who will be responsible to the relevant Director.

Decisions and draft legislative proposals will normally emanate from a lower part of this hierarchy, upwards towards the College of Commissioners. There will be detailed discussion of the legislative process later.[14] Suffice it to say for the present that within the Commission a proposal will usually have its origins within the relevant DG. Outside experts will often be used at this formative stage, and there will be consultation with national civil servants. The draft proposal will then pass up through the DGs to the *cabinets* of the relevant Commissioners, and on to the weekly meeting held by the *chefs de cabinet*. From there it will proceed to the College of Commissioners, which may accept it, reject it, or suggest amendments. Matters are obviously more complex when a proposed measure affects more than one area, and hence more than one DG may be involved. It is, moreover, not uncommon for the different DGs which are involved with a measure to have a 'different angle' on the problem. The term 'multi-organization' has been used to describe the priorities of different parts of the administration.[15] It is for this reason that consultations within the Commission will precede the meeting of the College of Commissioners. Formal meetings will be held by the *chefs de cabinet*, the object being to try to reach agreement before the College itself convenes. The meeting of the *chefs de cabinet* will receive input from discussion sessions held by the particular member of a *cabinet* who specializes in the relevant area. In addition there will be informal exchanges between opposite numbers within the bureaucracy at all levels, including the Commissioners themselves, members of differing *cabinets*, and officials who work in DGs with an interest in a measure. The Secretariat-General will also play an important role in co-ordinating the drafting of legislative initiatives within the Commission as a whole.

[12] This office is still at present part of the Commission, although it has an individual independent status for its investigative functions and is significantly more independent than the anti-fraud unit which it replaced. See Commission Decision 99/352/EC, ECSC, Euratom establishing the European Anti-fraud Office (OLAF) [1999] OJ L136/20.

[13] Nugent, n. 6 above, 138–42; A. Stevens with H. Stevens, *Brussels Bureaucrats? The Administration of the European Union* (Palgrave, 2001), ch. 8.

[14] See Ch. 4 below.

[15] L. Cram, 'The European Commission as a Multi-Organisation: Social Policy and IT Policy in the EU' (1994) 1 *JEPP* 194.

The basic principle within the Commission is for positions and promotions to be based upon merit, determined by competitive examination. In this way a career structure is open to those who work in the bureaucracy. This meritocratic principle is, however, qualified by the fact that Member States will take a keen interest to ensure that their own nationals are properly represented, particularly in the senior posts. For this reason it has been traditional for an informal quota regime to operate in the allocation of such jobs.[16] Whether this can still survive is more doubtful, given that the Court has held that job allocation should not be predetermined and should be decided on merit.[17] We shall return to this issue when considering reform of the Commission.

There has been much carping over the years about the size of the Brussels bureaucracy. This is largely based on ignorance of the facts. In 2000 the Commission employed 21,703 people. 17,087 were administrators, the remainder being translators, interpreters, or researchers. This is far fewer than many individual ministries within Member States.

(f) THE POWERS OF THE COMMISSION

The powers of the Commission are set out in Article 211 (ex Article 155) EC:

In order to ensure the proper functioning and development of the common market, the Commission shall:

— ensure that the provisions of this Treaty and measures taken by the institutions pursuant thereto are applied;

— formulate recommendations or deliver opinions on matters dealt with in this Treaty, if it expressly so provides or if the Commission considers it necessary;

— have its own power of decision and participate in the shaping of measures taken by the Council and by the European Parliament in the manner provided for in this Treaty;

— exercise the powers conferred on it by the Council for the implementation of the rules laid down by the latter.

A 'bare' reading of Article 211 (ex Article 155) does little to convey the role played by the Commission in all aspects of the Community's life. The Community institutional structure is not characterized by any rigid doctrine of separation of powers, and the Commission is at the heart of many Community initiatives. It is important to realize that the Commission has legislative, administrative, executive, and judicial powers. These will be considered in turn.

The Commission plays a central part in the *legislative* process of the Community, the details of which will be discussed below.[18] An outline of the Commission's legislative powers will be given here. The most important is the Commission's right of legislative initiative. It has this right because the common format is for the Treaties to stipulate that the Council and European Parliament will act on a proposal from the

---

[16] Nugent, n. 6 above, 174–6.   [17] Case 105/75, *Giuffrida* v. *Council* [1976] ECR 1395.
[18] See Ch. 4 below.

Commission when making legislation.[19] This right of initiative places it in the forefront of the development of policy. Although legislative proposals will have to be approved by the Council and, in most circumstances, by the European Parliament, the Commission's right of initiative has enabled it to act as a 'motor of integration' for the Community as a whole. Furthermore, the Commission may exercise influence over the Council in diverse ways.[20] It should be noted, however, that the Council can be the *de facto* source of legislative initiatives, even if the details of these suggestions are then given more concrete form by the Commission.[21]

The capacity of the Commission to act as motor of integration for the Community is also evident in a second role which it plays in the legislative process. The Commission will develop the Community's overall legislative plan for any single year. Planning of this nature has become of increasing importance in recent years, and the agenda-setting aspect of the Commission's work is of real significance in shaping the Community's priorities for the forthcoming year.[22]

The Commission also affects Community policy in a third way, by developing general policy strategies for the Community. This is exemplified by the Commission's White Paper on the *Completion of the Internal Market*,[23] which shaped the Single European Act. Commission initiatives under the Presidency of Jacques Delors contributed to the development of Economic and Monetary Union. The Commission's *Community Charter of the Fundamental Social Rights of Workers*[24] (the Social Charter) was important in the debates about Community social policy. More recently, the Commission has initiated and involved itself in broader debates about the reform of European Union governance, publishing its White Paper on *European Governance* in 2001 shortly after the launching of the post-Nice debate on constitutional reform.[25]

A fourth way in which the Commission exercises legislative power is through its capacity, in certain limited areas, to enact Community norms without the formal involvement of any other Community institution.[26]

Finally, the Commission exercises delegated legislative power.[27] This is expressly contemplated by the fourth indent of Article 211 (ex Article 155). The Council will delegate power to the Commission to make further regulations within particular areas, such as agriculture, technical harmonization, and competition.

In addition to its legislative powers the Commission also has significant *administrative responsibilities*. Policies, once made, have to be administered. Legislation, once

---

[19] The major qualification to this right of initiative is to be found in Art. 67 (ex Art. 73(0)) EC dealing with visas, asylum, immigration, etc., where the Commission's right of initiative is shared with the Member States. The other important qualification is in the provisions dealing with foreign policy and co-operation and the provisions on police and judicial co-operation in criminal matters to be found in the TEU, Titles V and VI. The revised Title VI, Art. 34 (ex Art. K. 6) TEU does however give the Commission and any Member State the right to initiate the measures specified in Art. 34(2).

[20] S. Schmidt, 'Only an Agenda Setter?: the European Commission's Power over the Council of Ministers' (2000) 1 *EUP* 37.

[21] See 69 below.   [22] See 159–61 below.   [23] COM(85)310.   [24] See 349 below.

[25] See *European Governance: A White Paper*, COM(2001)428, and *Communication from the Commission on the Future of European Union—European Governance: Renewing the Community Method*, COM(2001)727. These are discussed at 174–5 below.

[26] See 140 below.   [27] See 150–3 below.

enacted, must be implemented. This will commonly be through shared administration, using national agencies.[28] The Commission will maintain a general supervisory overview, in order to ensure that the rules are uniformly and properly applied within the Member States. There can be difficulties in executing this supervisory role successfully, as will be seen below.[29] It has also become increasingly common for the Commission to exercise direct administrative responsibility for the implementation of certain Community policy.

The Commission possesses responsibilities of an *executive* nature. Two are of particular importance: those relating to finance and those concerning external relations.

The Commission plays an important role in the establishment of the Community's budget. It also has significant powers over expenditure, particularly in relation to agricultural support, which takes a substantial share of the Community's annual budget, and structural policy, which is designed, *inter alia*, to assist poorer regions to convert or adjust declining industries, and combat long-term unemployment.

The Commission also exercises executive powers in the sphere of external relations. Nugent explains.

N. Nugent, The Government and Politics of the European Union[30]

First, the Commission is centrally involved in determining and conducting the EU's external trade relations. On the basis of Article 113[31] of the EC Treaty, and with its actions always subject to Council approval, the Commission represents and acts on behalf of the EU both in formal negotiations, such as those which are conducted under the auspices of the World Trade Organisation (WTO), and in the more informal and explanatory exchanges such as are common between, for example, the EU and the United States over world trade, and between the EU and Japan over access to each other's markets.

Second, the Commission has important negotiating and managing responsibilities in respect of the various external agreements which the EU has with many countries and groups of countries. . . .

Third, the Commission represents the EU at, and participates in the work of, a number of important international organizations. Three of these are specifically mentioned in the TEC: the United Nations and its specialized agencies (Article 302); the Council of Europe (Article 303); and the Organization for Economic Cooperation and Development (Article 304).

Fourth, the Commission has responsibilities for acting as a key point of contact between the EU and non-member States. Over 160 countries have diplomatic missions accredited to the EU. . . . The EU, for its part, maintains an extensive network of diplomatic missions abroad, numbering 120 delegations and offices, and these are staffed by Commission employees.

Fifth, the Commission is entrusted with important responsibilities in regard to applications for EU membership. Upon receipt of an application the Council normally asks the Commission to

---

[28] Thus many agricultural regulations will be executed at the grass-roots level by *national* Agricultural Intervention Boards, and many rules concerning the free movement of goods will be the responsibility of bodies such as Customs and Excise Authorities or Veterinary Inspection Teams, which check the quality of foodstuffs.

[29] See 62–4 below.   [30] N. 2 above, 138–9.   [31] Now Art. 133.

carry out a detailed investigation of the implications and to submit an opinion (an opinion that the Council need not, of course, accept . . .). If and when negotiations begin, the Commission, operating within Council-approved guidelines, acts as the EU's main negotiator, except on showpiece ministerial occasions or when particularly sensitive or difficult matters call for an inter-ministerial resolution of differences. . . .

Finally, the Commission is 'fully associated' with the work carried out under the CFSP pillar of the TEU.

The Commission possesses two kinds of *judicial* powers, which are based on the first indent to Article 211 (ex Article 155).

It will, on the one hand, be the Commission that will bring actions against Member States when they are in breach of Community law.[32] The actions will be brought under Article 226 (ex Article 169) EC and will assume the form of *Commission* v. *Germany* etc. Recourse to formal legal action will be a last resort and will be preceded by Commission efforts to resolve the matter through negotiation. None the less Article 226 (ex Article 169) actions form a steady part of the Court's diet.

The Commission, on the other hand, acts in certain areas as investigator and initial judge of a Treaty violation, whether by private firms or by Member States. The two most important areas are competition policy[33] and state aids.[34] The Commission's decision will be reviewable by the Community's judiciary, and this will now normally be by the Court of First Instance (CFI). Notwithstanding the existence of judicial review, the Commission's investigative and adjudicative powers provide it with a significant tool for the development of Community policy. It allows the Commission to devise new strategies in relation to particular aspects of competition policy or state aids. The Commission can use selective prosecution to take cases which raise significant issues. The Commission can, moreover, give guidance to national courts on the more precise meaning of broadly framed Treaty Articles.

(g) THE DOWNFALL OF THE SANTER COMMISSION AND SUBSEQUENT REFORMS

There had been concern in the EC for some considerable time about fraud and mismanagement, particularly in areas such as the Common Agricultural Policy. The European Parliament repeatedly expressed its dissatisfaction with the management of the Community's financial resources.[35] This culminated in the setting up of a Committee of Independent Experts, under the auspices of the European Parliament and the Commission, with a mandate to deal with fraud, mismanagement, and nepotism. The Committee produced its first report within two months, by 15 March 1999.[36] The

---

[32] See Ch. 10 below.   [33] See Ch. 25 below.   [34] See Ch. 27 below.

[35] D. Spence, 'Plus Ça Change, Plus C'est La Meme Chose? Attempting to Reform the European Commission' (2000) 7 *JEPP* 1.

[36] Committee of Independent Experts, *First Report on Allegations regarding Fraud, Mismanagement and Nepotism in the European Commission*, 15 Mar. 1999, para. 1.4.2.

concluding paragraph of the Committee's Report spoke in terms of it 'becoming difficult to find anyone who has even the slightest sense of responsibility' within the Commission.[37] The Report had an immediate, dramatic effect: the Commission resigned *en bloc*. The resulting crisis was the dominant headline in newspapers across Europe, being the focus of attention in quality papers and the tabloid press alike.

The problem revealed by the Committee's Report was not however fraud by the Commission. It was the difficulty of maintaining control over those to whom power had been contracted out. The Commission was given direct management responsibility in a number of areas. It became necessary to contract out some of this work, and there proved to be insufficient control over the recipient private firms.[38] This is an endemic problem for all systems of public administration.[39]

Romano Prodi, the new Commission President, sought to restore faith in the institution. He introduced a new Code of Conduct for Commissioners, with strict rules about the declaration of interests and the outside activities that Commissioners could pursue.[40] This was followed by the creation, in September 1999, of the Task Force for Administrative Reform (TFRA), for which Neil Kinnock was given responsibility. The TFRA produced a White Paper,[41] which was heavily influenced by the Second Report of the Committee of Independent Experts.[42]

This Second Report dealt, *inter alia*, with the different ways in which services are delivered within the Community, the division being between those areas where the Commission has a direct management responsibility and those instances where this responsibility is shared between the Commission and the Member States. It contained a wealth of valuable analysis and recommendations. In relation to direct management, the Committee accepted that the 'Commission will in future have a huge number of tasks to perform, the temporary and specialized nature of which requires them to be contracted-out—subcontracting being justified on the grounds of efficiency, expediency and cost'.[43] The Committee was equally firm in its belief that the existing arrangements were imperfect. The way forward favoured by the Committee was the establishment of a new type of implementing agency. These should not be permanent, nor should they contain Member State representatives.[44] They should exist solely for the duration of the particular project. Such agencies would facilitate the working together of Community officials seconded to the agency, with staff from the private sector who would have responsibilities for particular aspects of the Community programme.[45] In relation to shared management, the Committee pointed to a number of areas where effective control had passed to the Member States, while a number

[37] *Ibid.*, para. 9.4.25.

[38] P. Craig, 'The Fall and Renewal of the Commission: Accountability, Contract and Administrative Organization' (2000) 6 *ELJ* 98.

[39] P. Craig, *Administrative Law* (Sweet & Maxwell, 4th edn., 1999), ch. 5; M. Freedland, 'Government by Contract and Private Law' [1994] *PL* 86.

[40] *The Formation of the Commission*, 12 July 1999. See also *Operation of the Commission*, 12 July 1999.

[41] *Reforming the Commission*, COM(2000)200.

[42] Committee of Independent Experts, *Second Report on Reform of the Commission, Analysis of Current Practice and Proposals for Tackling Mismanagement, Irregularities and Fraud*, 10 Sept. 1999.

[43] *Ibid.*, i, para. 2.3.1. See also paras. 2.0.1 and 2.3.8.   [44] *Ibid.*, i, para. 2.3.27.

[45] *Ibid.*, i, paras. 2.3.27–2.3.31.

of factors tended to divest them of responsibility.[46] The Commission's White Paper acknowledged the contributions made by the Reports of the Committee of Independent Experts[47] and the DECODE exercise.[48] The general theme of the White Paper was the need for the Commission to concentrate more on core functions such as policy conception, political initiative, and enforcing Community law. Steps were to be taken to ensure greater linkage between priorities and resources, and to ensure also that the requisite resources existed when new tasks were given to the Commission. Activities would be delegated to other bodies, so as to enable the Commission to concentrate on its core activities. This could mean assigning tasks to other Community bodies, decentralization to national public bodies, and contracting-out to the private sector.[49] 'Externalisation' was to be used only where it was the most efficient option; it would not be pursued at the expense of accountability; and there would have to be sufficient internal resources to ensure proper control. 'Externalisation' should not therefore be used for the administration of ill-defined activities, nor where real discretionary power was involved.[50] There was to be a new type of implementing body to be headed by Community staff.[51] Important recommendations were also made about staffing and financial control. The Commission hopes to implement the reforms detailed in the White Paper on reform by the second half of 2002, although action by the Council and European Parliament may be required on certain issues.[52] There are already proposals for a new type of agency to oversee work that has been contracted out.[53]

(h) THE ROLE OF THE COMMISSION: CONCLUSION

The preceding discussion reveals the centrality of the Commission to the Community and to the aspirations which underlie it. The Commission has always been the single most important political force for integration, ever seeking to press forward to attain the Community's objectives.[54] The institutional structure within the Community means that the Commission must work with the Council and the Parliament. The pace of Community development has not always been steady because of this inter-institutional dimension. What the Member States have been willing to accept, on what conditions, and how quickly has varied over the Community's brief history. We have already touched on this when considering the history of the Community,[55] and we shall return to this issue when discussing the Community's decision-making

---

[46] *Ibid.*, i, para. 3.22.3.   [47] *Reforming the Commission*, n. 41 above, Part I, 2.

[48] *Designing Tomorrow's Commission, A Review of the Commission's Organisation and Operation*, 7 July 1999. The exercise was begun by the Commission in 1997. The principal objective was to determine what work was being done, why it was being done, who did it, and how the work was being carried out.

[49] *Reforming the Commission*, n. 41 above, Part I, 6.

[50] *Ibid.*, Part I, 7.   [51] *Ibid.*

[52] See Commission Planning and Co-ordination Group on Externalisation, *Externalisation and the Management of Community Programmes* (May 2000); *The Reform of Financial Management and Control in the Commission*, SEC(2000)560/5.

[53] See 106 below.

[54] See, e.g., the Commission's communication prior to the Laeken European Council, *The Future of European Union—European Governance: Renewing the Community Method*, COM(2001)727.

[55] See Ch. 1 above.

structure.[56] That the power of the Commission relative to the other institutions, particularly the Council, has altered over time is undeniable. But it is equally undeniable that the general thrust of the Commission's vision for the Community has remained constant, and it remains a powerful force for the achievement of that objective in the present day.

There have, inevitably, been various attempts to model the relationship between Commission and Council. Rometsch and Wessels[57] have elaborated four such models. These are the Commission as a dynamic technocracy, with the Council as the body required to ratify Commission action. The second model sees the Commission as a form of federal government, with the Council as the second chamber. The third model posits the Commission as an expert secretariat, and the fourth views the Commission as a broker and negotiator within the Council. However, as Westlake notes,[58] all four models are of relevance, depending on the context and on the time in the Community's history. This is also apparent from the following extract.

J. Fitzmaurice, The European Commission[59]

The Commission's role within the Community can be defined as that of animator, impressario and manager. The Commission plays for the largest stakes. Member States and citizens have a largely instrumental view of the Community. It is one way, perhaps the best, but not the only way to achieve their policy objectives. The Commission, however, stands or falls by demonstrating that the Community and only the Community can deliver. This contrast creates a constructive dialectic. . . . The Commission has to be proactive; it has to bring together the component parts of the EC system and manage constructively both their cooperation and their conflicts. The Commission has to turn political principles into real and effective policy. The Commission is the 'player-manager' of the Community system.

3. THE COUNCIL

(a) COMPOSITION OF THE COUNCIL

Article 203 (ex Article 146) EC states that the Council shall consist of a representative of each Member State at ministerial level who is authorized to commit the government of that State. The members of the Council are, therefore, politicians as opposed to civil servants, but the politician can be a member of a regional government where this is appropriate. By a decision made in 1993 the Council decided that it should henceforth be known as the Council of the European Union.[60] Article 204 (ex Article

---

[56] See Ch. 4 below.

[57] 'The Commission and the Council of Ministers', in G. Edwards and D. Spence (eds.), *The European Commission* (Longman, 1994), 203.

[58] M. Westlake, *The Council of the European Union* (Cartermill, 1995), 336.

[59] A. Duff, J. Pinder, and R. Pryce, *Maastricht and Beyond, Building the European Union* (Routledge, 1994), 181.

[60] [1993] OJ L281/18. This change in title was motivated by the tasks which the Council now has under the second and third pillars of the EU.

147) states that the Council shall meet when convened by the President of the Council on his or her own initiative, or at the request of one of its members, or at the request of the Commission. There are approximately eighty to one hundred Council meetings per year, most of which take place in Brussels, although some are held in Luxembourg.

It is common for meetings of the Council to be arranged by subject-matter with different ministers attending from the Member States. Thus there is a General Affairs Council, attended by foreign ministers, which deals with external relations and also many matters concerning general Community policy. The Economics and Finance Council (Ecofin), by way of contrast, is concerned with matters such as the implementation of the programme for the completion of the Single Market and matters relating to Economic and Monetary Union. Sectoral issues will be dealt with in the various 'Technical Councils': Transport and Telecommunications, Internal Market, Consumer Affairs and Tourism, Fisheries, Agriculture, Justice, Home Affairs and Civil Protection, Research, Budget, Culture, Development, Employment and Social Policy, Health, Education and Youth Affairs, Industry and Energy, and the Environment. The ministers responsible for these matters within the Member States will attend such meetings. They will be supported by their own delegations of national officials who have expertise in the relevant area.

The Helsinki European Council approved guidelines for reform of the Council.[61] These guidelines were adopted in the light of the pending enlargement of the EU. They emphasize, *inter alia*, the need for proper co-ordination of the Council's work, policy leadership, the role of the President, the role of COREPER, and the need to limit the number of Council formations. Some of these matters have been addressed in the revised Council procedures,[62] including an enumeration of the sectoral or technical Councils, which have been reduced in number.

(b) THE PRESIDENCY OF THE COUNCIL[63]

Article 203 (ex Article 146) EC provides for the Presidency of the Council to be held by each Member State in turn for six months. It establishes two six-year cycles, the purpose being to ensure that the same States do not have the Presidency always during the same period of the Community's affairs.

The position of President of the Council has assumed greater importance in recent years, for a number of reasons.[64] Strong central management has become more necessary in order to combat the centrifugal tendencies within the Council. The growing complexity of the Community's decision-making structure has necessitated more co-ordination between the institutions. The scope of EU power has increased, demanding greater leadership in the Council. The Council's wish to take a more proactive role in the development of Community policy has required initiatives which the President can help to organize. Westlake captures the importance of the position when he states

---

[61] 10–11 Dec. 1999.   [62] Council Dec. 2000/396 [2000] OJ L149/21, Annex.
[63] E. Kirchner, *Decision-Making in the European Community: The Council Presidency and European Integration* (Manchester University Press, 1992).
[64] Westlake, n. 58 above, ch. V.

that 'the Presidency is neither an institution nor a body, but a function and an office which has become vital to the good workings of the Council'.[65]

In more concrete terms the President will perform a number of functions. The President will normally arrange Council meetings, and set the agenda for them, as stipulated by the Council's rules of procedure.[66] He or she may develop policy initiatives within areas which are of particular concern either to the Council as a whole or to the Member State which currently holds the Presidency. The President will have an important liaison role to play with the Presidents of the Commission and the Parliament, and will represent the Council in discussions with institutions outside the Community. The Treaty imposes certain more particular obligations on the President, in relation to matters as diverse as the Common Foreign and Security Policy and the operation of the European Central Bank. It should moreover be noted that the President of the Council also holds the Presidency of the European Council, the importance of which will be considered below.

While the Presidency therefore gives considerable power to the incumbent, the office is not without its stresses and pitfalls. Presidencies must since 1989 draw up their programmes and present them to the Commission and the EP. Six months is a short time within which to get things done. The eyes of the other Member States will be focused, often critically and sharply, on the incumbent to determine the use to which the office has been put during that period. If a country tries to use its Presidency to achieve goals which are felt not to accord with the majority sentiment in the Council and which are too narrowly nationalistic, then the criticism is likely to be particularly harsh.[67]

(c) THE COMMITTEE OF PERMANENT REPRESENTATIVES[68]

Article 207(1) (ex Article 151(1)) EC states that the work of the Council is to be prepared by the Committee of Permanent Representatives (COREPER), and that COREPER shall carry out the tasks assigned to it by the Council. COREPER is also empowered to adopt procedural decisions in cases provided for in the Council's rules of procedure. It does not, however, have the power to take substantive decisions in its own right, and must operate as an auxiliary to the Council.[69]

COREPER is staffed by senior national officials and it operates at two levels. COREPER II is the more important and consists of permanent representatives who are of ambassadorial rank. It deals with the more contentious matters such as economic and financial affairs, and external relations. It also performs an important liaison role with the national governments. COREPER I is composed of deputy permanent representatives and is responsible for issues such as the environment, social affairs, the internal market, and transport.

COREPER plays an important part in EC decision-making,[70] in part because it will

---

[65] *Ibid.*, 36. [66] Council Dec. 2000/396, n. 62 above, Art. 1.

[67] Westlake, n. 58 above, 49–50. [68] *Ibid.*, ch. X.

[69] Case C–25/94, *Commission* v. *Council* [1996] ECR I–1469.

[70] J. Lewis, 'The Methods of Community in EU Decision-Making and Administrative Rivalry in the Council's Infrastructure' (2000) 7 *JEPP* 261.

consider and digest draft legislative proposals that emanate from the Commission, and in part because it helps to set the agenda for Council meetings. The agenda is divided into Parts A and B: the former includes those items which COREPER has agreed can be adopted by the Council without discussion; the latter will cover topics which do require discussion.

A large number of working groups, recently about 150 to 250, will feed into COREPER. They have been described as the lifeblood of the Council.[71] These groups will examine legislative proposals from the Commission. They will be composed of national experts from the Member States or from the Permanent Representations. Their role in the policy-making process will be examined more fully below.[72] In addition to these working groups the Council and COREPER will receive input from specialist committees established under the Treaty and from committees created by Community legislation.

(d) THE COUNCIL SECRETARIAT

In addition to COREPER the Council also has its own General Secretariat, under the responsibility of a Secretary-General, which provides direct administrative support to it.[73] The Secretariat has a staff of about 2,500, and of these roughly 250 are 'A' grade, diplomatic level. This body will furnish administrative service to the Council itself and also to COREPER and the working parties. It will prepare documentation, give legal advice, undertake translation, process decisions, and take part in the preparation of agendas. It will also work closely with the staff of the President of the Council, helping to smooth conflicts and providing valuable information on the way in which such conflicts may best be resolved. The Secretary-General is an important figure— and also now, since the Amsterdam Treaty amendments, high representative for the EU's foreign and security policy—who will endeavour to smooth the way to agreement in the Council itself and in COREPER.

(e) THE POWERS OF THE COUNCIL

The powers of the Council are described in Article 202 (ex Article 145) EC, albeit in a rather vague manner:

To ensure that the objectives set out in the Treaty are attained, the Council shall, in accordance with the provisions of this Treaty:

— ensure co-ordination of the general economic policies of the Member States;

— have power to take decisions;

— confer on the Commission, in the acts which the Council adopts, powers for the implementation of the rules which the Council lays down. The Council may impose certain requirements in respect of the exercise of these powers. The Council may also reserve the right, in specific cases, to exercise directly implementing powers itself. The procedures referred to above must

---

[71] Westlake, n. 58 above, 312.   [72] See 165–6 below.

[73] Art. 207(2). This has been amended by the TN: the appointment of the Secretary General is to be made by qualified majority, not unanimity.

be consonant with principles and rules to be laid down in advance by the Council, acting unanimously on a proposal from the Commission and after obtaining the opinion of the European Parliament.

Some Treaty Articles convey a clear impression of the powers accorded to a particular institution. Some do not. Article 202 comes within the latter category. A simple reading of this provision does little to convey the reality of the Council's powers, nor does it explain their provenance. Explanation is therefore required. The Council exercises an important role in the legislative process in four ways.

First and foremost, the Council will have to vote its approval of Commission legislative initiatives before they become law. The Treaty Articles which give the Commission the right to propose legislation impose the condition of Council approval, whether by unanimity, qualified, or simple majority depending upon the requirements stipulated in the particular Treaty Article.[74] Moreover, the draft proposal from the Commission will often be subject to considerable modification as a result of scrutiny by COREPER and the working parties.[75] The modifications made by the TN to the Council voting rules to cope with enlargement will be considered below.[76]

Secondly, the Council has become more proactive in the legislative process through the use of Article 208 (ex Article 152). This states that the 'Council may request the Commission to undertake any studies which the Council considers desirable for the attainment of the common objectives, and to submit to it any appropriate proposals'. While the wording of this Article may indicate that the Council's requests would be couched in general terms, this is not always so. The Council has used this power to frame very specific proposals which it wishes the Commission to shape into concrete legislation.[77] The Council has also increasingly made use of opinions and resolutions as a way of pressuring the Commission into generating legislative proposals.[78] The Council's ability to trigger policy initiatives in this way is due in part to the more sophisticated back-up machinery that it now possesses, in the form of COREPER and the plethora of working parties, etc. which feed into it. It is also in part the result of the greater importance of the Council Presidency and the fact that the incumbent of this Office will often have an 'agenda' which he or she wishes to see achieved.

Thirdly, the Council can delegate power to the Commission, enabling the latter to pass further regulations within a particular area. It is now common for such delegations of power to be subject to the condition that the Commission action is acceptable to committees staffed by national representatives. This operates as a mechanism whereby the Council can ensure that the detail of the delegated legislation is in conformity with its own wishes.[79]

Finally, the increasing complexity of the Community's decision-making process, as a result of the changes introduced by the SEA and the TEU, has necessitated greater inter-institutional collaboration between the Commission, the Parliament, and the

---

[74] For a discussion of the Council's voting requirements see 153–6 below.
[75] See 162–7 below.   [76] See 155–6 below.
[77] Sir Leon Brittan, 'Institutional Development of the European Community' [1992] PL 567.
[78] Nugent, n. 2 above, 144–5.
[79] See the revised so-called 'Comitology decision' of 1999: Council Decision 1999/468/EC laying down the procedures for the exercise of implementing powers conferred on the Commission. See further 150–3 below.

Council. This assumes various guises, from informal discussions concerning the shape of the legislative agenda to the use of Inter-institutional Agreements. Such agreements are important as a way of fleshing out principles such as subsidiarity; as a mechanism for developing principles of good governance, such as transparency; and as a method of mediating difficult inter-institutional issues, such as the budget.[80]

The discussion thus far has considered the Council's powers under Pillar 1, the EC Treaty. The Council also has significant powers under Pillars 2 and 3. Thus, it will be the Council which takes the necessary decisions for defining and implementing the Common Foreign and Security Policy (CFSP) in the light of the guidelines laid down by the European Council,[81] and it is for the Council to adopt joint actions.[82] The Council also has important powers under the re-modelled Pillar 3, concerned with police and judicial co-operation in criminal matters.[83]

(f) THE ROLE OF THE COUNCIL: CONCLUSION

The Council represents national interests and always has. Whether the framers of the original Rome Treaty would have been surprised by the way in which the Commission and Council have interrelated since the inception of the Community is unclear. They hoped that the formation of the EEC would herald an era of greater collaboration in which sectional, national interests would diminish in relation to the collective interests of the Community as a whole. The original decision-making structure of the Community certainly bore testimony to the central role accorded to the Commission. The range of its powers is readily apparent from the preceding discussion. To be sure, the Council had to approve legislation, but the Commission was in the driving seat. This was because of the Commission's power to set the legislative agenda, and because of its institutional resources for the development of Community policy. Moreover, the message from the original Treaty was clear: while Council consent was required for the passage of legislation, unanimity was required for Council amendments to the Commission's proposals. It was then not to be easy for the Council to tinker with Community initiatives.

It would be wrong to depict the Commission and the Council as perpetually at odds with each other throughout the Community's history.[84] But it would be equally mistaken to view the two institutions as co-existing in perfect harmony. There have been real tensions between the federal pro-integration perspective of the Commission, and the more cautious, intergovernmental perspective of the Council. The Treaty framers might have hoped that these tensions would be short-lived.[85] If this was so it was too optimistic a forecast. The history of the Community has witnessed a series of institutional changes, often initially outside the strict letter of the Treaty, whereby the

---

[80] For a discussion of these agreements see 161–2 below.
[81] Art. 13(3) TEU.   [82] Art. 14(1) TEU.   [83] Art. 34 TEU.
[84] For an analysis of the evolution of relations between the Commission and the Council, and more specifically in the internal workings of the Commission and Council Secretariat, see T. Christiansen, 'Intra-institutional Politics and Inter-institutional Relations in the EU: Towards Coherent Governance?' (2001) 8 JEPP 747.
[85] See Ch. 1 above.

Council strengthened its own position in relation to that of the Commission. This 'temporal' perspective on decision-making will be charted more fully below.[86] Suffice it to say for the present that the development of a veto power in the Council, the growing importance of COREPER, the creation of committees to oversee the delegation of power to the Commission, and the evolution of the European Council all played a part in this process.

The balance of power within the Community is however dynamic, not static. The institutions' formal powers and the actual way in which they interrelate have altered across time. The SEA was the catalyst for a change of attitude on the part of the Member States as represented in the Council. There was a growing recognition that the threat of the veto, if a measure did not conform to a State's interests, was too negative. The SEA also made the European Parliament a more active force in Community decision-making than it had been hitherto. These developments do not mean that relationships between the Council and the Commission, or for that matter between the Council and the Parliament, will always be smooth. It does mean that the inter-institutional relationships that prevail within the Community have moved on.

4. THE EUROPEAN COUNCIL[87]

(a) COMPOSITION

The European Council now consists of the Heads of State or Government of the fifteen Member States, plus the President of the Commission. They will be assisted by their foreign ministers and by another member of the Commission, thus bringing the number to thirty-two.

The institution has evolved during the last twenty-five years. Meetings of Heads of Government took place during the 1960s, but the decision to institutionalize these meetings came in 1974 at the Paris summit. Meetings of the European Council continued to be held during the 1970s and 1980s, even though there was no formal remit in the Treaty for an institution of this nature. The first mention of the European Council within a Treaty came in the SEA. Its position is now set out in Article 4 (ex Article D) TEU:[88]

The European Council shall provide the Union with the necessary impetus for its development and shall define the general political guidelines thereof.

The European Council shall bring together the Heads of State or of Government of the Member States and the President of the Commission. They shall be assisted by the Ministers for Foreign Affairs of the Member States and by a Member of the Commission. The European Council shall meet at least twice a year, under the chairmanship of the Head of State or of Government of the Member State which holds the Presidency of the Council.

---

[86] See 157–9 below.

[87] S. Bulmer and W. Wessels, *The European Council* (Macmillan, 1987).

[88] In this technical sense the European Council is an institution of the Union, although, as we shall see, it plays a vital role in shaping the development of the Community.

The European Council shall submit to the European Parliament a report after each of its meetings and a yearly written report on the progress achieved by the Union.

The European Council is mentioned on other occasions within the TEU. Thus, for example, Article 13 TEU (ex Article J.3) provides that the European Council shall define the principles of and guidelines for the Common Foreign and Security Policy (CFSP). It shall decide on common strategies to be implemented by the Union in areas where the Member States have important interests in common.[89]

Mention of the European Council is also to be found in certain provisions of the EC Treaty itself. Not surprisingly this is in the context of politically sensitive matters. Thus, under Article 99(2) (ex Article 103(2)) EC it is accorded a role in relation to the co-ordination of the economic policies of the Member States, while under Article 113 (ex Article 109b) it is to be presented with a report by the European Central Bank.[90]

Although Article 4 (ex Article D) TEU mentions that the European Council will meet twice a year, the Lisbon European Council in 2000 decided that a third meeting would be held each Spring, in the context of the EU's newly articulated economic, employment, and cohesion strategy.[91] Meetings of the European Council have in the past been held in the country holding the Presidency of the Council at that time. However Declaration 22 attached to the TN specified that, as from 2002, one European Council meeting per Presidency would be held in Brussels, and when the Union comprises eighteen members, that all meetings would be held in Brussels.

(b) RATIONALE

Member States are represented in the Council. The emergence of another institution within which Member State interests are represented can be explained on a number of grounds. It was in part due to disagreements between the Member States themselves. These would normally be resolved through the ordinary Council mechanisms, but if the disagreements were particularly severe or on important issues, then resolution might be possible only by intervention at the highest level, through the Heads of Government themselves. Thus, one common item which has featured on European Council agendas has been the budget and the respective contributions which should be paid by each Member State. The evolution of the European Council was also due to the need for a focus of authority at the highest political level. This was in order that the general strategy for the Community's development could be properly planned, and in order that the EU's response to broader world problems could be properly focused.

---

[89] See also Art. 17 as amended by the ToA and the TN.

[90] Mention of Heads of Government, independently of the European Council, is also to be found in connection with appointment of members of the European Central Bank: Arts. 112 and 117 (ex Arts. 109a and 109f), and the final stages of the transition to Economic and Monetary Union: Arts. 121 and 122 (ex Arts. 109j and 109k).

[91] See point 7 of the Lisbon European Council conclusions, 24 Mar. 2000.

(c) ROLE

The paucity of Treaty references to the European Council should not lead one to doubt its importance. It plays a central role in setting the pace and shape of Community policy, establishing the parameters within which the other institutions operate. The issues which are commonly considered by the European Council vary, but can be grouped into the following categories.

One of the most significant issues to be discussed at the European Council is the very *development of the Community and Union itself.* Major changes in the Treaties will be preceded by an Intergovernmental Conference (IGC). The catalyst for the establishment of such conferences will normally come from a summit meeting of the European Council. Thus the IGC which laid the groundwork for the SEA was initiated by the summit held in Milan in June 1985. The European Council will not only initiate the IGC. It will also affirm the consequential Treaty changes, as exemplified by the Nice European Council[92] that approved the Nice Treaty, subject to ratification by the Member States. The European Council will, moreover, be central to the debates about the future of the European Union in the period prior to the next IGC in 2004.[93]

The European Council will often confirm important changes in the *institutional structure of the Community.* The final decision on the enlargement of the Parliament following German unification was taken by a summit of the European Council.

The European Council can provide the focus for significant *constitutional initiatives* that affect the operation of the Community and Union. We have already had occasion to mention Inter-institutional Agreements, and we shall return to this topic in the next chapter. Agreements of this nature between the three major institutions will often be made or finalized at a summit meeting. The Inter-institutional Agreement on Subsidiarity and the Declaration on Democracy, Transparency, and Subsidiarity were made at, or on the fringes of, such European Council meetings.

Not surprisingly, another item that frequently appears on the European Council's agenda is the *state of the European economy* as a whole.[94] This is in part because of Treaty provisions concerning closer social and economic union, which demand growing convergence between national economic policies. It is also because of the centrality of economic issues to the very health and vitality of the Community. For this reason the European Council may, for example, take initiatives that are designed to combat unemployment, promote growth, and increase competitiveness.

Conflict resolution is another issue addressed by the European Council. This was one of the rationales for its evolution, and it continues to be of importance. For example, budgetary matters, 'who contributes how much, and who gets what financial benefits', continued to cause conflict between the Member States in the early 1980s, and then once again in the later 1980s.

---

[92] 8 Dec. 2000.   [93] Goteborg European Council, 16 June 2001.
[94] See, e.g., Luxembourg Extraordinary European Council, 20 Nov. 1997; Stockholm European Council, 24 Mar. 2001.

While the European Council will normally focus on broad strategies for the Community, it can also play a role in the *initiation or development of particular policy strategies*. Examples of this include the adoption of the Social Charter in 1989, and policies aimed to combat problems concerning drugs, terrorism,[95] the extension of the so-called 'open method of coordination' to a range of social and economic policies,[96] and the like.

External relations form part of the European Council's focus. The European Council will, for example, consider important international negotiations, such as those with the World Trade Organisation (WTO). It will be the European Council which will issue declarations relating to more general international affairs, whether they be in relation to South Africa or the civil war in what was Yugoslavia. And it will be the European Council that sets the guidelines for the relationship between the EU and the former Soviet-bloc countries.

The European Council will also consider *new accessions* to the Community. Thus it was, for example, the summit held in late 1991 in Maastricht which requested the Commission to produce a report on the applications for membership by the EFTA countries, while the Edinburgh summit of late 1992 authorized the formal opening of negotiations.

(d) THE ROLE OF THE EUROPEAN COUNCIL: CONCLUSION

The European Council is a classic example of a change in the original institutional structure of the Treaty to accommodate political reality. This body evolved from a series of *ad hoc* meetings outside the letter of the Treaty to a more structured pattern of summits. Treaty-recognition was originally accorded in the SEA and has been modified by later Treaty amendments. Yet, as we have also seen, the brief mention of the European Council in the TEU does little to convey its real importance in the decision-making process of the Community. The reality is that no developments of genuine importance for the Community's internal structure, or for its external relations, will occur without having been considered by the European Council. The concluding resolutions of such meetings do not themselves have the force of law. When this is required legislation will have to be drafted in accordance with one of the procedures to be discussed below.[97] None the less the conclusions reached by the European Council will provide the framework within which the other institutions will consider more specific policy issues.

It should, moreover, be recognized that the relations between the European Council and other Community institutions have themselves evolved across time. Summits held by Heads of State were originally viewed with suspicion by bodies such as the Commission, since the meetings were often held in secret and the Commission was normally excluded. Matters are very different today. The increase in the number of its yearly meetings and the stabilization of its venue confirm the development of its role and profile. The Commission President is a member of the European Council, and

---

[95] Brussels Extraordinary European Council, 21 Sept. 2001.
[96] Cologne European Council, 4 June 1999 and Lisbon European Council, 24 Mar. 2000.
[97] See Ch. 4 below.

many of the European Council's initiatives are themselves the result of Commission initiatives. The President of the European Parliament has, since 1988, addressed a plenary session of the European Council. The European Council is, in the words of Westlake, 'no longer an unwelcome guest but a valued colleague'.[98]

5. THE EUROPEAN PARLIAMENT

The story of the European Parliament is one of gradual transformation from a relatively powerless Assembly under the 1952 ECSC Treaty to the considerably strengthened institution it represents today. The history of its development is touched upon in Chapter 1, and its role in the legislative processes is examined in Chapter 4. We have already seen that the Assembly, to give the Parliament its original title, was given few powers under the ECSC Treaty and under the original EEC and Euratom Treaties. It was intended to exercise consultative and supervisory powers, but not to play any substantial legislative role.

However, although the elite 'government of technocrats' established under the ECSC Treaty was not replicated in the provisions of the EEC Treaty, the institutions set up by the latter were not a model of democratic organization. We saw in Chapter 1 how the influence of the Parliament grew, first with the two budgetary treaties of 1970 and 1975, and subsequently—after the transition to direct elections—with the 'cooperation' and 'assent' procedures under the Single European Act of 1986 and the 'co-decision' procedure under the TEU in 1992,[99] which was strengthened and extended under the Amsterdam Treaty and the Nice Treaty.[100] Today, the European Parliament exercises substantial powers of a *legislative, budgetary*, and *supervisory* nature.

However, while the changes in the legislative process have enhanced the power of the only directly elected European institution, the problems of the EU's democratic legitimacy are certainly not thereby resolved.[101] The problems of secrecy, impenetrability, accountability, and representativeness, which have long been a focus for concern within the Community,[102] are not addressed simply by giving added powers to the European Parliament. The 'demos' question is a complex one,[103] and many would argue that national parliaments remain the proper democratic focus of the Community, whatever the powers of the European Parliament may be.[104] The question of

[98] Westlake, n. 58 above, 31.

[99] See P. Raworth, 'A Timid Step Forwards: Maastricht and the Democratisation of the European Community' (1994) 19 *ELRev.* 16.

[100] See A. Dashwood, 'The Constitution of the European Union after Nice: Law-making Procedures' (2001) 26 *ELRev.* 215.

[101] On the legitimacy of the EU more generally see D. Beetham and C. Lord, *Legitimacy and the EU* (Longman, 1998) and C. Lord, *Democracy in the European Union* (Sheffield University Press, 1998). On the political legitimacy of the Parliament see A. Muntean, 'The European Parliament's Political Legitimacy and the Commission's "Misleading Management": Towards a "Parliamentarian" European Union?', European Integration online Papers (EIoP) Vol. 4 (2000) No. 5; www. eiop.or.at/eiop/texte/2000–005a.htm.

[102] On transparency see Ch. 9, and on democratic legitimacy see Ch. 4, 163–73.

[103] For reflection on this question see several of the essays in J. Weiler's *The Constitution of Europe* (Cambridge University Press, 1999). For a provocative set of proposals for enhancing EU democracy see P. Schmitter, *How to Democratize the European Union . . . And Why Bother?* (Rowman & Littlefield, 2000).

[104] See Brittan, n. 77 above; and see M. Westlake, *A Modern Guide to the European Parliament* (Pinter, 1994), 53–63, and E. Smith, *National Parliaments as Cornerstones of European Integration* (Kluwer, 1996).

an enhanced role for national parliaments within the EU has been highlighted in
recent years and placed firmly on the agenda for the 2004 IGC by the Nice and Laeken
Declarations.

(a) COMPOSITION AND FUNCTIONING

Until recently, with a membership of fifteen States, there have been 626 Members of
the European Parliament. Article 189 (ex Article 137) EC was amended by the ToA, in
contemplation of the likelihood of enlargment, to provide that the overall number of
Parliament members should not exceed 700. This provision has been amended again
by the TN, which raised the ceiling to 732, with the possibility for this ceiling to be
temporarily exceeded in the case of accession of new Member States during 2004–9
(pursuant to Article 2 of the Protocol to the Nice Treaty). One of the serious criticisms
of the 'representativeness' of the European Parliament is the fact that the number of
MEPs for each State is far from proportionate to population size, and that smaller
countries are disproportionately over-represented. Article 190 (ex Article 138) EC was
amended at Amsterdam to provide that if future changes are to be made regarding the
number of MEPs, 'the number of representatives elected in each Member State must
ensure appropriate representation of the peoples of the States brought together in the
Community'. However not everyone would accept that the numbers agreed at the Nice
IGC to be elected from current and future Member States constitute such appropriate
representation. The present number of European Parliament seats held by each Member State is set out in the second column of Table 2.1 below, and the third column
contains the revised number agreed in the TN for the parliamentary term 2004–9. It
will be seen that the number of representatives is reduced for every current Member
State except Germany and Luxembourg, which are at present the biggest and the
smallest respectively. The third column also contains the numbers which have been
agreed for future Member States (Turkey not being included). These numbers do not
themselves bind the candidate States but represent a political agreement made
amongst the current EU Member States during the Nice European Council, in hotly
contested circumstances and when many candidate States were not present or
represented.

A further cause for complaint concerning the composition of the Parliament has
been the fact that, despite the holding of direct elections since 1979 in accordance
with a Council decision in 1976,[105] the uniform electoral procedure originally envisaged under the former Article 190 (ex Article 138) never came into existence. In 1993
following the instigation of litigation against it before the ECJ for failure to act,[106] the
Parliament finally adopted a resolution on a uniform electoral procedure, but the
Council did not agree on it. Subsequently Article 190(4) was amended by the ToA to
provide for the possibility of an electoral procedure based on *common principles*
rather than uniformity. In 1998 even before the ToA came into effect, the Parliament
adopted another resolution proposing an electoral procedure based on ten common

---

[105] Dec. 76/787 [1976] OJ L278/1. This Decision was amended by Art. 5 of the ToA.
[106] Case C–41/92, *Liberal Democrats* v. *Parliament* [1993] ECR I–3153.

Table 2.1 Composition of the Parliament

Current Member States	Current Seats	Seats in 2004–9
Austria	21	17
Belgium	25	22
Denmark	16	13
Finland	16	13
France	87	72
Germany	99	99
Greece	25	22
Ireland	15	12
Italy	87	72
Luxembourg	6	6
The Netherlands	31	25
Portugal	25	22
Spain	64	50
Sweden	22	18
United Kingdom	87	72
Future Member States		
Poland		50
Romania		33
Czech Republic		20
Hungary		20
Bulgaria		17
Slovakia		13
Lithuania		12
Latvia		8
Slovenia		7
Estonia		6
Cyprus		6
Malta		5

principles.[107] However, the Council's unanimous consent is required under Article 190(4), and the diversity of Member State electoral and constitutional traditions appears to be a major stumbling block to any further progress on this matter.[108]

[107] Resolution A4–0212/1998 based on the report by Giorgios Anastassopoulos [1998] OJ C210/7 and C292/45, 66.

[108] In Dec. 1999 the Council considered the Parliament's draft act, but there were apparently a number of 'sticking points' including the status of Gibraltar and the ECHR judgment in *Matthews* v. *UK* no. 24833/94 of 29 Feb. 1999; see *Agence Europe* No. 7607, 14 Dec. 1999. See also the Commissioner's reply to Written Question E–435/00 [2000] OJ C280/214.

Like the Commission's, the Parliament's term is five years. Prior to the first elections, MEPs had been delegates of their national parliaments. After the first direct elections, the practice of 'double-jobbing', i.e. the holding of a dual mandate by MEPs, became the exception.[109] Following the TEU provisions on citizenship, citizens of the Union who were resident in any Member State gained the right to vote and to stand as candidates in European Parliament elections, although the rate of participation so far has been very low indeed.[110] Given that traditional EU discourse on democracy relies very much on the democratic legitimacy of the European Parliament, such a low turnout is troubling.

MEPs sit in the Parliament according to political grouping, rather than nationality, although national parties generally remain together within the larger Parliamentary groupings. There are currently eight political groups, the largest three being, respectively, the centre-right European People's Party (Christian Democrats and European Democrats) with 233 seats after the 1999 elections, the Party of European Socialists with 180, and the Group of the European Liberal, Democrat and Reform Party with fifty-one. Others include the Greens/Free Alliance, and some more critical or Euro-sceptical groupings, the Union for Europe of the Nations, and the Group for Europe of Democracies and Diversities. There are also non-attached members. Article 191 (ex Article 138a) EC deals with the question of European political parties. This Article was amended by the TN to provide a concrete legal base in Article 191(4) for the Council to 'lay down the regulations governing political parties at European level and in particular the rules regarding their funding'. While the absence of properly constituted European-wide political parties has long been regretted by advocates of a genuine European political space, even this small step towards their establishment was not uncontentious.[111] Its enactment was prompted by criticism from the Court of Auditors of the practice of funding such parties without a proper legal base but, given the likely delay in the coming into force of the TN, a proposal for their funding has already been made under the more slippery 'residual powers' clause of Article 308 (ex Article 235) EC.[112]

The Parliament elects its own President, together with fourteen Vice-Presidents, for two-and-a-half-year terms, and collectively they form the Bureau of Parliament. The Bureau is the regulatory body responsible for the Parliament's budget and for administrative, organizational and staff matters. There are also five 'Quaestors', responsible for administrative and financial matters directly concerning members,

---

[109] See the recent Napolitano report arguing for an end to the practice: A5–0023/2002.

[110] See the Commission's evaluation report on the application of Council Dir. 93/109, [1993] OJ L329/34 on the 1994 EP elections and its communication on the 1999 EP elections: COM(2000)843. Turnout in the EU as a whole apparently dropped from 56.5% in the 1994 elections to 49.7% in 1999, whereas at the first elections held in 1979, it was 63%. See also J. Lodge (ed.), *The 1999 Elections to the European Parliament* (Palgrave, 2001).

[111] Declaration 11 attached to the TN rather nervously affirms that Art. 191 does not 'imply any transfer of powers to the EC' nor affect national constitutional rules. It also specifies that such European funding may not be used to fund political parties at national level and that it should apply on the same basis to all the political forces represented in the European Parliament.

[112] See COM(2000)898 [2001] OJ C154/283.

who assist the Bureau in an advisory capacity.[113] The 'Conference of Presidents' consists of the President together with the leaders of the various political groups. It is the political governing body of the Parliament and meets twice a month. It draws up the agenda for plenary sessions, fixes the timetable for the work of parliamentary bodies, and establishes the terms of reference and size of parliamentary committees and delegations.

The Parliament has seventeen standing committees on matters including foreign affairs, human rights, and CFSP; legal affairs and the internal market; citizens' freedom and rights and justice and home affairs; budgets; budgetary control, women's rights, and equal opportunities; and petitions,[114] which prepare the work for its plenary sessions and which are crucial to its functioning.[115] There are in addition a range of sub-committees, and temporary committees or committees of inquiry can also be established. The Parliament is helped by a large secretariat of approximately 3,500 staff, headed by a Secretary-General.

Article 199 (ex Article 142) states that the Parliament is to adopt its own rules of procedure,[116] and Article 190(5) requires it to lay down the regulations and general conditions governing the performance of its Members' duties. These regulations previously required unanimous Council approval, but the TN amended this to permit approval by qualified majority except where the rules concern taxation of MEPs. After years of wrangling between Member States over the seat of the Parliament, they finally decided in 1992, as required by Article 289 (ex Article 216) EC,[117] confirming practice over the years, that the Parliament would sit in Strasbourg. However, it has two other regular places of work, with a secretariat based in Luxembourg and certain sessions and committee meetings taking place in Brussels in order to facilitate contact with the Commission and Council.[118]

(b) THE PARLIAMENT'S DECISION-MAKING ROLE

We have already noted that from the original weakly consultative part it played in the EU legislative process, the Parliament has incrementally acquired a substantial decision-making role. Its position alongside the Council as one of the two arms of the budgetary authority, with the symbolic task of actually adopting the Budget, was for some years the Parliament's most significant power. Its wider legislative functions have since been greatly enhanced through successive Treaty amendments, most

---

[113] A complaint made by a Quaestor to the Ombudsman alleging maladminstration on the Bureau's part in transferring part of the Quaestor's powers to the Bureau was held inadmissible: See Case 1243/2000/PB, on **www.europarl.eu.int/ombudsman/**.

[114] See the Parliament's decision under its rules of procedure on the number, powers, and responsibilities of parliamentary committees [1999] OJ C219/374.

[115] See C. Neuhold, 'The "Legislative Backbone" Keeping the Institution Upright? The Role of the European Parliament Committees in the EU Policy-Making Process', European Integration online Papers, Vol. 5 (2001) No. 10.

[116] Most recently [1999] OJ L202/1.

[117] See Art. 77 ECSC and Art. 189 Euratom.

[118] See Case C–345/95, *France v. Parliament* [1997] ECR I–5215, on the holding of plenary sessions in Strasbourg.

recently in the ToA (and to a lesser extent the TN) which reformed and extended the application of the co-decision procedure.[119]

After the TEU however, some saw the requirement of a simple rather than an absolute majority for the assent procedure in a number of areas, including Article 300(3) (ex Article 228(3)) EC on certain international agreements, as a reduction in the Parliament's influence.[120] Further, certain international agreements, such as those in the common commercial policy field under Article 133(3) (ex Article 113(3)), provide no role for the Parliament at all.[121] Finally, under Article 300(2) (ex Article 228(2)), the Parliament does not participate in, but is merely to be informed about, certain decisions such as the provisional application or the suspension of an international agreement.

We have also seen in Chapter 1 that the Parliament's involvement under the second and third pillars of the TEU was originally limited, consisting principally in being consulted by the Presidency on the main choices within those areas, its views being 'duly taken into consideration', being informed of developments, and having the right to ask questions and hold an annual debate. This remains essentially true still of the Common Foreign and Security Policy (CFSP) pillar, but under the reformed third pillar on Police and Judicial Co-operation in Criminal Matters (PJCC) the Council must consult the Parliament before adopting measures, and provided the Parliament delivers its opinion within the time limit set, the Council may not act until the opinion is received. The Parliament also gains a consultative role, following the TN, in the authorization of enhanced co-operation under the third pillar, and in the allocation of expenditure under Article 44a of the general TEU title on enhanced co-operation.

Outside the formal legislative process and the conciliation procedures and 'trialogues' within this process, however, the Parliament, Council, and Commission regularly meet together in inter-institutional conferences, devoted either to particular topics or to general common problems.[122] The increasing number of occasions on which Parliament and Council meet together in the course of various procedures of this kind can only improve the dialogue and relationship between these two previously antagonistic institutions. Since the Council essentially represents Member State interests, it is often seen by the other institutions as a hindrance to more dynamic Community goals. However, the Parliament's increasing familiarity with the Council and with its workings, not only through the budgetary process but also through its increased legislative powers, may draw these two institutions closer.[123] The following

---

[119] See A. Kreppel, 'What Affects the European Parliament's Legislative Influence? An Analysis of the Success of EP Amendments' (1999) 37 *JCMS* 521.

[120] For litigation on the scope of the obligation under Art. 300(3) to gain the Parliament's assent, see Case C–189/97 *Parliament v. Council* [1999] ECR I–4741.

[121] While para. 7 of Art. 133, as amended by the TN, provides that the Parliament is to be consulted if the Council decides to extend paras. 1–4 of that Art. to international agreements on intellectual property (apart from those concerning commercial aspects), it is to be consulted only on the initial extension of competence, and not on the subsequent negotiation and conclusion of specific agreements.

[122] Westlake, n. 104 above, 37. For a post-Nice analysis of the relationships between the three primary institutions see S. Gozi, 'Does the EU Institutional Triangle Have a Future?' (2001) XXXVI *The International Spectator* 39.

[123] Westlake, n. 104 above, 150.

extract from a European Parliament delegation report comments on the gradual changes which the conciliation procedure has brought about in their relations.

Activity Report of the Delegations to the Conciliation Committee, 1 November 1993–30 April 1999[124]

When the Treaty of Maastricht was ratified in 1993 the Council had developed a legislative culture unused to sharing political decisions or legislative and administrative responsibilities, such as for legal and linguistic revision, preparation of texts, informing Parliament, co-chairing meetings and so on. This culture, combined with Parliament's new powers, led to a period of extremely strained relations between the two institutions, at the administrative as well as the political level. At the beginning of the conciliation procedure, every innovation in working methods, even when it was essential for effective management, required a determined effort by Parliament to gain acceptance. Council scepticism as to Parliament's ability to handle a full-scale codecision process was widespread.

. . .

The potential and dynamic of the codecision and conciliation procedures are illustrated by the development of relations between Parliament and the Council. It has been a long and gradual process, but apart from a few extremely formal encounters we have reached the point of almost weekly informal meetings. *Confidence and respect*, building on reliable and technically unassailable behaviour, were the factors that coaxed the Council out of its isolation.

Concerning legislative relations with the Commission, although the Parliament enjoys no power of legislative initiative, it has the right under Article 192 (ex Article 138b) to request the Commission to submit a proposal on any matter on which the Parliament thinks a Community act is necessary. While the Treaty imposes no express obligation on the Commission to respond or to provide reasons for rejecting a request, a Framework Agreement on relations between the Parliament and Commission signed in 2000 included a provision under which the Commission committed itself to undertake 'a prompt and sufficiently detailed response' to Article 192 requests.[125]

The Commission's accountability to the Parliament has also gradually been strengthened. Having had the power to censure the Commission and require its resignation ever since the ECSC Treaty was signed,[126] the Parliament has also since the Maastricht Treaty had the right to participate in the Commission's appointment. Initially this was by consultation, and by vote of approval of the Commission *en bloc*, but since the ToA, Article 214(2) (ex Article 158(2)) EC has provided that the

---

[124] DOC_EN\DV\377\377982 of 6 May 1999.

[125] See C 349/2000 [2000] OJ C121/122. An action for interim measures brought by 22 MEPs before the CFI for the annulment of the Framework Agreement was deemed inadmissible: Case T–236/00 *Stauner et al.* v. *Parliament and Commission*, order of the president of the CFI of 15 Jan. 2001. See also R. White, *Editorial* (2000) 25 *ELRev.* 333.

[126] See Art. 144 (now Art. 201) EC and Art. 114 Euratom. An absolute majority of the Parliament, with a two-thirds majority of the votes cast, is required to carry the motion of censure.

Parliament must also be consulted on the nomination of the Commission President, and its approval obtained. Together with the TN amendments to the nomination procedure, which specify that this is no longer by unanimity but by a qualified majority of the European Council, this alters the political nature of the Commission and the Commission President's appointment.[127]

The Parliament's powers of appointment are greatest in the context of the Commission, where it has an effective veto over both the President's appointment and that of the Commission as a whole. In the case of members of the Court of Auditors, the President of the European Monetary Institute, and the President, Vice-President, and Executive Board of the European Central Bank, the Parliament is to be consulted by the Council and the Member States, but its approval is not required.[128]

(c) THE PARLIAMENT'S SUPERVISORY ROLE

The European Parliament monitors the activities of the other institutions—principally the Commission—through the asking of oral and written questions[129] and the establishment of committees of inquiry. The longstanding practices permitting the setting-up of committees of inquiry and the right to petition the European Parliament were finally given Treaty status at Maastricht, and are now provided for under Articles 193 and 194 (ex Articles 138c and 138d) EC.[130] The Parliament's power of censure has never actually been used, though various motions of censure have been tabled and debated, including during the period prior to the resignation of the Santer Commission in 1999. Interestingly, the Parliament did not at that time set up a committee of inquiry to investigate the allegations of nepotism and mismanagement in the Commission, but instead established a committee of external independent experts.[131]

The Maastricht TEU also provided for the appointment by the Parliament of an Ombudsman.[132] The function of the Ombudsman is to receive complaints from Union citizens or resident third-country nationals or legal persons, concerning 'instances of maladministration in the activities of the Community institutions or bodies' as well as to 'conduct inquiries for which he finds grounds, either on his own initiative or on the basis of complaints submitted to him direct or through a member of the European Parliament'. The regulations governing the office provide that the

---

[127] See S. Hix, 'Executive Selection in the European Union: Does the Commission President Investiture Procedure Reduce the Democratic Deficit?', in K. Neunreither and A. Wiener (eds.), *European Integration After Amsterdam* (Oxford University Press, 2000), 95.

[128] See M. Westlake, 'The European Parliament's Emerging Powers of Appointment' (1998) 36 *JCMS* 431.

[129] Art. 197 (ex Art. 140) EC, Art. 23 ECSC, and Art. 110 Euratom.

[130] On the petition procedure see E. Marias, 'The Right to Petition the European Parliament after Maastricht' (1994) 19 *ELRev.* 169. See also the Lambert report of the Parliament's Committee on Petitions for 1999–2000, A5 2000/162.

[131] See n. 36 above.

[132] See Art. 138e (now Art. 195) EC, Art. 20d ECSC, and Art. 107d Euratom. For two of the first major works on the Ombudsman see K. Heede, *The European Ombudsman: Redress and Control at Union Level* (Kluwer, 2000) and P. Bonnor, *The European Ombudsman: A Novel Rule-source in Community Law* (PhD, Florence EUI, 2001).

Parliament is to elect as an Ombudsman a Union citizen, who must have 'full civil and political rights, offer every guarantee of independence, and meet the conditions required for the exercise of the highest judicial office in their country or have the acknowledged competence and experience to undertake the duties of Ombudsman'.[133] The Ombudsman is appointed for the duration of the mandate of the Parliament, and in the case of serious misconduct or non-fulfilment of the conditions of office the Court of Justice (ECJ), at the request of the Parliament, may dismiss her or him. The ECJ and the Court of First Instance (CFI) acting in their judicial role are excluded by Article 195 (ex Article 138e) from the Ombudsman's jurisdiction, and the regulations further prohibit intervention in cases before courts or questioning the soundness of a court's ruling.

The major limitation on the Ombudsman's jurisdiction is that only EU and not national institutions are subject thereto, although a large number of complaints outside mandate regarding national maladministration continue to be made.[134] The EU bodies which are subject to Ombudsman jurisdiction must supply information requested and give access to files, except where grounds of secrecy are pleaded. Pursuant to his power under the Treaty, Jacob Söderman, who was the first Ombudsman to be appointed and has since been re-appointed for a second term,[135] has held a number of own-initiative inquiries. One such initiative was his inquiry into public access to documents held by a number of Community institutions and bodies in 1996.[136] At the conclusion of an investigation the Ombudsman sends a report to the Parliament and to the institution under investigation, and the complainant is informed of the outcome. The Ombudsman has also adopted a number of special reports following the responses of the institutions to his draft recommendation on a complaint, and has advised that his recommendations be adopted by Parliament as resolutions, or on occasion, such as in relation to the need for a Code of Good Administration, that an administrative regulation should be enacted.[137] Under Article 41 TEU after Amsterdam (Article K.13 before), the Ombudsman gained jurisdiction over matters falling within the reformed third pillar.

The office of Ombudsman is considered to have been a significant success since its introduction and, despite some unsuccessful litigation[138] and challenges from the Commission over his jurisdiction in relation to its interpretation of European law,[139] his office is increasingly seen as a source of administrative norms rather than simply a

---

[133] See Art. 6(2) of the Parliament's regulations and conditions governing the performance of the Ombudsman's duties, approved by the Council in 1994 [1993] OJ C329/136 and Council Dec. 94/114 [1994] OJ L54/25.

[134] See the Ombudsman's annual reports for 1999 and 2000, listing the substantial proportion of complaints outside the mandate: [2000] OJ C/ 260 and [2001] OJ C218/1.

[135] See Parliament Decision 1999/780 [1999] OJ L306/32.

[136] See 1998 OJ C44/1.

[137] See the website of the Ombudsman for full details of these special reports and recommendations: www.euro-ombudsman.eu.int/special/en/default.htm.

[138] Cases T–209/00, *Lamberts* v. *European Ombudsman and Parliament* [2001] ECR II–765 and T–103/99, *Associazione delle Cantine Sociali Venete* v. *European Ombudsman and Parliament* [2000] ECR II–4165.

[139] See the Annual Report for 1999 [2000] OJ C260/1, in which the Ombudsman dismisses the Commission's claim that such questions can only be dealt with by the ECJ.

mediation facility for individual complaints.[140] Reference is made to the Ombudsman in Article 43 of the EU Charter of Fundamental Rights which was proclaimed at Nice in 2000. And the current Ombudsman has not been deterred by the ambivalent legal status of the Charter, but has referred frequently to the fundamental right to good administration contained in Article 41 of the Charter.

In this extract from his Report for 2000, the Ombudsman makes some general suggestions for reform.

The European Ombudsman Annual Report 2000[141]

The future

There have been many proposals debated about the future development of the European Ombudsman institution. Dealing only with complaints concerning possible maladministration by the institutions and bodies of the EU is indeed a limited mandate. This is demonstrated by the constant flow of complaints (up to 70%) which are outside our mandate even though many concern Community law. In order to deal with this situation, my Office has established a close co-operation with the national ombudsmen and similar bodies in the Member States. This co-operation is carried out through a network of liaison officers and involves regular seminars on Community law issues, the publication of a liaison newsletter and, since September 2000, a new Website and Summit. . . . This type of co-operation is now being extended to equivalent regional organizations and will soon even be offered to the municipal ones that are interested.

All these measures have been taken to achieve an efficient handling of complaints concerning Community law in the Member States. The institutions in the Member States have shown a good spirit of co-operation. It is my view that more can be achieved by this kind of co-operation than by extending the mandate of the European Ombudsman to all administrative levels of the Union where Community law is applied. . . . We have to put the important principle of subsidiarity into practice whenever possible and must respect it, not just talk about it.

(d) THE PARLIAMENT AS A LITIGANT

Apart from the gradual extension of the Parliament's legislative powers, a further significant development in its status and influence has occurred through progressive recognition of its right to litigate, initially through the judicial activism of the ECJ from 1980 to 1990, and subsequently by political agreement enshrined in a series of Treaty amendments.

At first in the 1980s in the *Roquette* and *Maizena* cases, the ECJ confirmed that the Parliament had the same right as the other institutions to intervene in any case, and ruled that where consultation of the Parliament was required, its opinion had actually

---

[140] See P. Bonnor, 'The European Ombudsman: A Novel Source of Soft Law in the EU' (2000) 25 *ELRev.* 39 and *Bonnor.* n. 132 above. For a defence of the less formal, non-juridical, and flexible nature of his role and procedures, however, see I. Harden, 'A l'écoute des griefs des citoyens de l'Union européenne: la mission du Médiateur européen' [2001] *RTDE* 573.

[141] [2001] OJ C218/1.

to be obtained.[142] Then in 1985, the Parliament successfully brought proceedings against the Council under Article 232 (ex Article 175) for failure to act.[143] The Court also famously included the Parliament as a respondent in annulment proceedings under Article 230 (ex Article 173) even though only the Council and the Commission were mentioned, declaring that: 'an interpretation of Article 173 which excluded measures adopted by the European Parliament from those which could be contested would lead to a result contrary both to the spirit of the Treaty . . . and to its system'.[144]

Many actions under Article 230 (ex Article 173) have been brought against the Parliament since then,[145] and the Court has ruled that acts which have no legal effects[146] or which have 'internal' legal effects only, such as a reorganization of the Parliament's workplace and practices,[147] cannot be the subject of annulment proceedings. However, the ECJ has admitted challenges to decisions of the Parliament in relation to its seat, no doubt on account of the Member States' strongly held views on such matters.[148]

Initially the court was reluctant to recognize the Parliament as a plaintiff in annulment proceedings[149] but subsequently ruled that it could indeed bring such an action, although only where its prerogatives had been infringed in the adoption of the contested act.[150] The Parliament made active use of this partial *locus standi* on many occasions and with a measure of success,[151] given the differing degrees of its participation under various Treaty procedures.[152] And despite the moves under the ToA and the TN to reduce the number of legislative procedures, there remains a multiplicity of different legislative processes which leave scope for institutional conflict.[153] In addition to the 'legal basis litigation' the Parliament also uses its standing as a litigant

---

[142] Cases 138/79, *Roquette Frères* v. *Council* [1980] ECR 3333 and 139/79, *Maizena* v. *Council* [1980] ECR 3393. See later Case C–65/93, *Parliament* v. *Council* [1995] ECR I–643 where the Council was permitted to adopt a measure even where the Parliament's required opinion had not been received.

[143] Case 13/83, *Parliament* v. *Council* [1985] ECR 1513, para. 17; and see Case 377/87, *Parliament* v. *Council* (*Draft Budget*) [1988] ECR 4017.

[144] Case 294/83, *Parti Ecologiste 'Les Verts'* v. *Parliament* [1986] ECR 1339, paras. 23, 25. See for an annulment action brought under all three Treaties, Case 230/81, *Luxembourg* v. *Parliament* [1983] ECR 255, para. 20. See also Case 108/83, *Luxembourg* v. *Parliament* [1984] ECR 1945 and Cases C–213/88 & 39/89, *Luxembourg* v. *Parliament* [1991] ECR I–5643.

[145] See, e.g., Cases 34/86, *Council* v. *Parliament* (Budget) [1986] ECR 2155 and C–284/90, *Council* v. *Parliament* (*Supplementary Budget*) [1992] ECR I–2277.

[146] See, e.g., Case 78/85, *Group of the European Right* v. *Parliament* [1986] ECR 1753.

[147] See Cases 358/85 & 51/85, *France* v. *Parliament* [1988] ECR 4821; C–314/91, *Weber* v. *Parliament* [1993] ECR I–1093; and T–329/99, *Martinez and De Gaulle* v. *Parliament*, judgment of 2 Oct. 2001.

[148] Case C–345/95, *France* v. *Parliament* [1997] ECR I–5215.

[149] Case 302/87, *Parliament* v. *Council* (Comitology) [1988] ECR 5616.

[150] Case C–70/88, *Parliament* v. *Council* (Chernobyl) [1990] ECR I–2041. No ground could be pleaded by the Parliament other than infringement of its prerogatives: Case C–187/93, *Parliament* v. *Council* (Transfer of Waste) [1994] ECR I–2857; Case C–360/93, *Parliament* v. *Council* (External Competence—GATT) [1996] ECR I–1195.

[151] See Case 295/90, *Parliament* v. *Council* [1992] ECR I–4193 on the students' residence directive.

[152] See Case C–300/89, *Commission* v. *Council* (Titanium Dioxide) [1991] ECR I–2867 and C–155/91, *Commission* v. *Council* (Waste Directive) [1993] ECR I–939; and also Case C–187/93, n. 150 above, and C–271/94, *European Parliament* v. *Council* (Trans-European Networks) [1996] ECR I–1689. See further Ch. 4, and also H. Cullen and A. Charlesworth, 'Diplomacy by Other Means: The Use of Legal Basis Litigation as a Political Strategy by the European Parliament and Member States' (1999) 36 *CMLRev.* 1243.

[153] See more recently Cases C–22/96, *European Parliament* v. *Council* (*Telephonic Networks*) [1998] ECR I–3231; C–42/97, *European Parliament* v. *Council* (*Linguistic Diversity*) [1999] ECR I–869; and C–164–165/97, *European Parliament* v. *Council* (*Forest Fires*) [1999] ECR I–1139, brought before the ToA came into effect.

to strengthen its right of consultation, for example in relation to comitology procedures and implementing measures,[154] and to ensure that the Council adequately re-consults it where the substance of the Commission's proposal changes after the first consultation of the Parliament.[155]

The various judicial developments were gradually incorporated into the relevant provisions of the EC Treaty following successive Treaty amendments. Thus Article 230 (ex Article 173) EC was amended to provide that the Parliament could bring proceedings challenging the legality of an act where necessary to protect its prerogatives, and that any of its acts which were intended to produce legal effects *vis-à-vis* third parties could be challenged. It was also listed as a potential defendant under the Article 232 (ex Article 175) action for failure to act. Following the TN, two further significant changes going beyond the Court's rulings were made: first, the Parliament was granted full *locus standi* alongside the Commission, the Council, and the Member States to bring annulment proceedings under Article 230 EC. And, secondly, the Parliament was granted the right alongside the Member States, Council, and Commission under Article 300(6) (ex Article 228(6)) EC to seek the Court's advisory opinion on the compatibility of a proposed international agreement with the EC Treaty. This political willingness not simply to follow the jurisprudence of the Court, as previous Treaty amendments had done, but to grant the Parliament new and co-equal institutional status as a litigant are clearly significant in symbolic and constitutional terms.

6. THE EUROPEAN COURT OF JUSTICE AND THE COURT OF FIRST INSTANCE

(a) INTRODUCTION

The Court of Justice (ECJ) and the Court of First Instance (CFI) together constitute the Community's judicial branch. Until the TN, the most significant change to the structure and functioning of the EC judicial system was the establishment of the CFI in 1988. The ToA had been expected to bring about judicial reform, but that Treaty in fact made few changes to the structure and powers of the Court, apart from the provisions governing the reformed third pillar and the new EC Treaty Title IV, which will be discussed below.

However, the amendments made by the TN introduced a number of potentially far-reaching provisions which cleared the way for altering the division of functions between the ECJ and the CFI, and which increasingly seek to concentrate the ECJ's jurisdiction and energies on litigation 'concerning essential Community issues'.[156]

---

154 See Case C–303/94, *European Parliament* v. *Council* [1996] ECR I–2943.

155 See Cases C–65/90, *European Parliament* v. *Council* [1992] ECR I–4953; C–388/92, *European Parliament* v. *Council* [1994] ECR I–2067; and C–21/94, *European Parliament* v. *Council* [1995] ECR I–1827 concerning transport policy measures. See also Case C–316/91, *European Parliament* v. *Council* (*Lomé Convention*) [1994] ECR I–625, paras. 16–18, and on reconsultation C–417/93, *European Parliament* v. *Council* (TACIS Programme) [1995] ECR I–1185 and Case C–392/95, *European Parliament* v. *Council* (*Visa Directive*) [1997] ECR I–3213.

156 Memorandum of the Commission's Secretary-General to members of the Commission, *Summary of the Treaty of Nice*, SEC(2001)99. See P. Dyrberg, 'What Should the Court of Justice be Doing' (2001) 26 *ELRev.* 291.

The debate on reform of the EU judicial system has run for a long time, fuelled largely by the mushrooming case-load of both the ECJ and the CFI, but it was joined in earnest during the negotiations on the Nice IGC by the judicial organs themselves, which produced various reports and options for reform.[157] The most striking changes are the provision for the establishment of a third layer of specialized 'judicial panels' under the CFI and the ECJ (Article 225a), and the provision clearing the way for the CFI to exercise the constitutionally cherished 'preliminary rulings' jurisdiction (Article 225(3)).

The ECJ is generally perceived to have pursued a vigorous policy of legal integration over the years, and in particular in the earlier decades of the Community's history. It is seen as having undertaken the task of giving flesh and substance to an 'outline' Treaty, and as having developed a particular vision of the kind of Europe it sought to promote. The primary concern of the Court has probably been to enhance the effectiveness of Community law and to promote its integration into national legal systems. The Court has been reactive to events during certain periods and in certain fields of law, proactive during other periods and in other fields of law, and at times a mixture of both. Like any institutional actor, albeit with its particular role, training, and judicial identity, the Court is influenced by many factors, and any simple theory or explanation of its role should be avoided. Further, the Court is not a single unitary actor, but a collection of individual judges, Advocates General, and other influential legal personnel. It has grown from a relatively small and cohesive Court of seven judges and two Advocates General to a Court of fifteen judges and eight Advocates General, sitting increasingly in chambers. The Court has a wide jurisdiction covering many matters and causes of action, and these will be examined further in later chapters of the book.

It has been said that the ECJ is the 'European lawyer's hobbyhorse'[158] and that 'legal scholars portray the Court as a hero who has greatly advanced the cause of integration'.[159] Certainly there has been a tendency in the study of Community law to focus heavily on the Court as an institution, and on case law as a source of law.[160] And while there can be no denying their importance, excessive concentration on courts and on case law results in the neglect of other central lawmaking processes.

(b) COMPOSITION AND STRUCTURE OF THE COURT OF JUSTICE

Following the TN amendments, the composition of the ECJ and the CFI is governed by Articles 221–225a (ex Articles 164–168a) of the EC Treaty.[161] A protocol on the

---

[157] For accounts of these developments see P.P. Craig, 'The Jurisdiction of the Community Courts Reconsidered', in G. de Búrca and J.H.H. Weiler (eds.), *The European Court of Justice*, 177; H. Rasmussen, 'Remedying the Crumbling EC Judicial System' (2000) 37 *CMLRev.* 1071; A. Arnull, 'Judicial Architecture or Judicial Folly? The Challenge Facing the European Union' (1999) 24 *ELRev.* 316; and the essays in A. Dashwood and A. Johnston (eds.), *The Future of the Judicial System of the EU* (Hart, 2001).

[158] T. Koopmans, 'The Future of the Court of Justice of the European Communities' (1991) 11 *YBEL* 15. See also 'The Role of Law in the Next Stage of European Integration' (1986) 35 *ICLQ* 925, 930.

[159] K. Alter and S. Meunier-Aitsahalia, 'Judicial Politics in the European Community' (1994) 26 *Comparative Political Studies* 535, 536.

[160] For more recent commentaries on academic perspectives on the Court see R. Dehousse, *The European Court of Justice* (Macmillan, 1998), 'Introduction' and ch. 3; de Búrca and Weiler (eds.), n. 157 above, 'Introduction'; and A. Arnull, *The European Union and its Court of Justice* (Oxford University Press, 1999).

[161] See also Arts. 137–140a Euratom. The ECSC Treaty expires in 2002.

Statute of the Court of Justice added by the TN, which will replace the former protocols, deals with the organization and procedure of the Court. Henceforth the Statute
will be capable of amendment by a unanimous act of the Council rather than by the
cumbersome Treaty amendment procedure (see Article 245 (ex Article 188) EC),
except for certain fundamental provisions on the status of judges and Advocates
General. The Rules of Procedure, which build on the provisions of the Statute, are
adopted by the ECJ under Article 223 (ex Article 167) EC. Following the TN changes
they no longer require the unanimous approval of the Council, but can be adopted by
qualified majority.

The Treaty provisions on the number of judges are amended upon the accession of
each new Member State. There are currently fifteen judges, and the TN amendment to
Article 221 (ex Article 165) specifies that there shall be one judge per Member State.
In the past, an additional judge was selected by the five large Member States,[162] but
from now on the number of judges on the ECJ (though not necessarily the CFI) will
be restricted to the number of Member States. The appointment of all judges is
required by Article 223 (ex Article 167) to be 'by common accord of the Governments
of the Member States'.[163] The term of office is six years, and the appointment of new
judges or reappointment of the existing judges is staggered so that there will be a
partial replacement of judges every three years.

Article 222 (ex Article 166) provides that the ECJ is to be assisted by eight Advocates General, and that the number can be raised by unanimous decision of the
Council. The qualifications for selection, method of appointment, and conditions of
office of the Advocate General (AG) are the same as for the ECJ judges. His or her
duty is set out in Article 222 EC, and is principally 'to make, in open court, reasoned
submissions on cases'. Before the TN, the AG's duty applied to all cases brought
before the ECJ, but this provision has now been amended and the conditions under
which an AG's opinion may or may not be required are left to be determined in
accordance with the Statute.[164]

The dangers of a fixed-term appointment for the independence of the judiciary have
been noted, but no change has been proposed to this and, in practice, most judges have
been reappointed. The secrecy of the Court's deliberations may be a protection against
perceived political appointments or refusals to renew, although this would not apply
to the Advocates General, whose individual opinions are made public.

The qualifications for selection as a judge or AG of the ECJ require 'persons whose
independence is beyond doubt and who possess the qualifications required for
appointment to the highest judicial offices in their respective countries or who are
jurisconsults of recognized competence'.[165] The Court elects its President from

---

[162] In 1993, to avoid an even number of judges on the Court, the European Council decided that the 'extra
acting judge' could become an AG: Bull. EC 12–1993, 1.18. Accordingly, after the accession of Austria,
Sweden, and Finland in 1995, the 16th judge became an AG from 1995–2000, leaving 15 judges on the Court.
Such situations will henceforth have to be resolved more flexibly by the quorum rules: see Art. 17 of the
amended Statute of the Court.

[163] Art. 224 now provides similarly for the CFI.

[164] Art. 20 of the revised Statute of the Court provides that the Court may dispense with the need for an
AG where the case raises no new point of law.

[165] Art. 167 (ex Art. 223) EC.

amongst its own judges and appoints its own Registrar.[166] In accordance with their respective traditions, certain Member States have appointed academics as judges of the ECJ, whereas others, such as the UK and Ireland, have nominated prominent practising advocates or existing domestic judges. For many decades there was no female presence on the ECJ apart from a brief period in the 1980s when there was one female Advocate General. The Scandinavian accessions in 1995 brought a welcome breath of gender awareness with the appointment of two women to the CFI, but the first female judge of the ECJ was appointed by Ireland only in 1999, followed by Germany's appointment of a female judge in 2000, and by Austria's of a female AG later that year.[167]

Although States normally select their own nationals (something which is not required by the TN 'one judge per Member State' formulation), the EC Treaty requires that the judges be entirely independent of the government which chose them or indeed of any other interest group. Judging from the nature of much of the ECJ's jurisprudence, the specific wishes of individual Member States have had little influence on its decision-making.[168] On the other hand, the Court is not immune from political pressures, and undoubtedly does not ignore the general wishes and interests of the Member States in its decision-making. It is certainly aware of the political environment in which it acts and its judgments are at times influenced by relatively 'non-legal' arguments made by Member States before the Court, particularly when they relate to the potential financial impact of a ruling, or on the other hand by critical responses from the public or from national and Community sources.[169]

Judges may not hold any other political or administrative office while they are members of the Court and, apart from their normal replacement, their period of office may terminate on death, resignation, or on removal from office. The Statute of the Court (Article 6) provides that a judge or AG who, in the unanimous opinion of the other judges and Advocates General, no longer fulfils the requisite conditions and obligations of office may be removed from office.

Article 221 (ex Article 165) provides that the ECJ may sit in chambers, or, in a provision added by the TN, in a 'Grand Chamber'. Prior to the Nice amendments, Article 221 had provided that the Court would sit in plenary session, and had specified the size of the chambers (then three, five, or seven members) which could be set up. Given the TN changes, however, plenary sittings are likely to be rare, and the Treaty henceforth leaves it to the Statute to determine the circumstances in which chambers can be established, and when the Grand Chamber or the plenary Court

---

[166] *Ibid.*

[167] For a broader analysis see J. Shaw, 'Gender and the Court of Justice', in de Búrca and Weiler (eds.), n. 157 above (Oxford University Press, 2001), ch. 4.

[168] Not all international relations theorists would agree with this: G. Garrett, 'The Politics of Legal Integration in the EU' (1995) 49 *International Organization* 171. Compare K. Alter, *Establishing the Supremacy of European Law* (Oxford University Press, 2001), ch. 2.

[169] The Court's decision in Case C–262/88, *Barber* v. *Guardian Royal Exchange Assurance Group* [1990] ECR I–1889, and the relationship between the '*Barber* Protocol' of the Maastricht Treaty and the Court's subsequent case law is a commonly cited example of the former; and the Court's reversal of its approach to positive action in the field of gender equality between Cases C–450/93, *Kalanke* v. *Freie Hansestadt Bremen* [1995] ECR I–3051 and C–409/95, *Hellmut Marschall* v. *Land Nordrhein Westfalen* [1997] ECR I–6363 as an example of the latter kind of responsiveness to external critique.

should sit.[170] The ability to sit in chambers is obviously vital to the Court's functioning, given its enormous and growing case-load, and it is a facility which has been used
extensively. The TN changes above all increase flexibility and the procedural room for
manœuvre of the Court, by reducing the number of stipulations in the Treaty relating
to its organization and functioning, and moving these instead to the more easily
amended Statute.

(c) THE COURT OF FIRST INSTANCE

The Court of First Instance (CFI)[171] was established in 1988 pursuant to a Treaty
amendment introduced by the Single European Act.[172] Initially the CFI had a clearly
derivative and secondary institutional status, and was described in the EC Treaty as
being 'attached to the Court of Justice'. Following the TN amendments, however,
Article 220 (ex Article 164) describes the ECJ and the CFI alongside one another, each
charged within their respective jurisdictions with the same fundamental task of ensuring that the law is observed in the interpretation and application of the Treaty.

The original reason for the establishment of the CFI was to relieve the burden on
the ECJ. It had been long argued that staff cases, which were numerous but usually
involved issues of individual rather than of general importance, could be transferred
to a tribunal to decide. And after more than twelve years in operation, a similar need
to relieve the overburdening of the CFI has been identified, resulting in the decision of
the TN (see Articles 220 and 225a EC) to provide for the establishment of a third
judicial layer ('judicial panels') to take on specialized cases. The first source of jurisdiction suggested for these new panels has been precisely those staff cases which in
turn had constituted the largest part of the CFI's own jurisdiction in the first years of
its operation.[173]

There are currently fifteen judges of the CFI. Following the TN amendments,
Article 224 (ex Article 168) provides that it shall comprise 'at least' one judge per
Member State, thus distinguishing it from the ECJ where there will henceforth be only
one judge per Member State. There are no separate Advocates General on the CFI,
although any judge may be called upon to perform the task of an AG.[174] The qualifications required for appointment as a judge of the CFI, which were amended slightly by
the TN, are only marginally less exalted than those required for appointment to
the ECJ. Together with the revised articulation of the role and function of the CFI
alongside that of the ECJ in Article 220 (ex Article 168), these changes confirm the
gradual enhancement of the CFI's status and significance over the years.

Like the ECJ, the CFI elects its own President from amongst its judges, and appoints
its Registrar (see Article 224). Similarly, it sits in chambers of three and five, sitting in

---

[170] See Arts. 16 and 17 of the Statute, as amended by the TN, which specify that a Grand Chamber shall
consist of 11 judges and that at least 9 must sit. A plenary Court can be constituted by 11 judges. No mention
is made under the amended Statute of a chamber of 7, only of 3 and 5 members.

[171] Known in French as the *Tribunal de Première Instance*, which explains the T used before the case
number when a case is registered with the CFI.

[172] Council Decision 88/591 [1988] OJ L319/1.   [173] See Declaration no. 16 adopted by the Nice IGC.

[174] See Art. 49 of the Statute.

plenary session with one judge acting as AG only rarely and in cases of legal difficulty.[175] In a further move to facilitate the Court in dealing with its heavy caseload, the Council in 1999 adopted a decision enabling the CFI to sit and take decisions as a single-judge court.[176] There is an appeal to the ECJ, on a point of law only, within two months from the date of the decision of the CFI.[177] This is set out in Article 58 of the amended Statute, which provides that 'it shall lie on the grounds of lack of competence of the Court of First Instance, a breach of procedure before it which adversely affects the interests of the appellant as well as the infringement of Community law by the Court of First Instance'. An appeal is not to have suspensory effect (Article 60 of the Statute), except where the CFI has declared a regulation void, in which case the decision of the Court will take effect only after the two-month period for appeal has expired or when the appeal has been dismissed.

Initially staff cases, competition cases brought by individuals against the Community institutions (because of their heavy and often complex factual content), and cases under the ECSC Treaty were dealt with by the CFI. Gradually the Council transferred to it other categories of case, until eventually it had jurisdiction over all actions brought by 'non-privileged' parties, and over other actions such as appeals from decisions concerning the Community trade mark.[178] After the TN, the CFI's jurisdiction is widened still further by Article 225 (ex Article 168a) EC, so that it gains jurisdiction over most direct actions[179] with the exception of those to be allocated to the new judicial panels, and the actions listed in Article 51 of the Statute. Those listed in Article 51, which can later be amended, currently include direct actions brought by a Community institution, by the ECB, or by a Member State. Enforcement actions under Articles 226 (ex Article 169) and 227 (ex Article 170) remain for the present under the jurisdiction of the ECJ, although again this can be amended for the future through the Statute. A new jurisdiction is given to the CFI by the TN amendments of Article 225 in proceedings against decisions of the new judicial panels, and such rulings of the CFI are to be subject to a further layer of review by the ECJ only in exceptional circumstances, 'where there is a serious risk of the unity or consistency of Community law being affected'.

One of the highly significant changes made by the TN to the jurisdiction of the CFI is that, for the first time, Article 225 (ex Article 168a) provides that the CFI may give preliminary rulings under Article 234 (ex Article 177) 'in specific areas laid down by the Statute'. The TN itself did not amend the Statute to provide for such areas, but the Nice IGC specified in Declarations numbers 12 and 13 that attention should be

---

[175] This was principally in cases decided not long after the CFI's establishment, e.g., Cases T–1–15/89, *Rhône-Poulenc et al* v. *Commission* [1990] ECR II–867; T–51/89, *Tetra Pak Rausing SA* v. *Commission* [1990] ECR II–309; T–24/90, *Automec Srl* v. *Commission* [1992] ECR II–2223; and T–28/90, *Asia Motor France SA* v. *Commission* [1992] ECR II–2285.

[176] Council Decision 1999/291, [1999] OJ L114/52. See also Art. 50 of the amended Statute of the Court.

[177] See, e.g., Case C–53/92P, *Hilti* v. *Commission* [1994] ECR I–667. For an interesting recent case see Cases C–302 and –308/99, *Commission* v. *TFI*, judgment of 12 July 2001.

[178] These come on appeal from the Office for Harmonization of the Internal Market. See Art. 63 of Reg. 40/94 on the Community Trade Mark [1994] OJ L/11.

[179] These are: annulment actions under Art. 230 (ex Art. 173), actions for failure to act under Art. 232 (ex Art. 175), damages actions under Arts. 235 (ex Art. 178) and 288 (ex Art. 215), staff cases under Art. 236 (ex Art. 179), and proceedings under contractual arbitration clauses in Art. 238 (ex Art. 181).

given as soon as possible to such questions. According to Article 225(3), there are two situations in which the ECJ may decide on a preliminary rulings case which initially came under the CFI's jurisdiction. In the first place, the CFI itself may, where it considers that the case requires 'a decision of principle likely to affect the unity or consistency of Community law', refer the case to the ECJ for a ruling. Secondly, paragraph 3 specifies that CFI decisions on a preliminary ruling may exceptionally be subject to review by the ECJ, under conditions and limits laid down by the Statute 'where there is a serious risk of the unity or consistency of Community law being affected'.[180]

It seems that the exceptional nature of the ECJ review jurisdiction over CFI decisions in the field of both preliminary rulings and appeals from judicial panels is intended to prevent a major rationale for the new panels and for CFI preliminary rulings jurisdiction, *viz.* to ease the burden on the ECJ, from being undermined. But at the same time the exceptional procedures underline the fact that the ECJ remains the supreme judicial tribunal of the EU, whose jurisdiction is particularly required when major questions of EC law and the unity of the legal order are raised.

As for the new judicial panels mentioned in Article 220 (ex Article 164) and 225 (ex Article 168a), their establishment is governed by Article 225a which was added by the TN. Article 225a provides that specialized judicial panels to determine at first instance 'certain classes of action' or 'proceedings brought in specific areas' may be established by decision of the Council, under a novel decision-making procedure. Decisions of such panels are to be subject to an appeal to the CFI on point of law, or also on matters of fact where so specified in the decision establishing the panel. The qualifications required for appointment to one of these panels are similar to but lower than those for the CFI. Mirroring the new flexibility introduced by the TN for amendment of the ECJ's rules of procedure, Article 225a provides that the rules of procedure of the judicial panels can also be adopted by a qualified majority of the Council.

Another interesting jurisdictional novelty introduced by the TN is the new provision in Article 229a EC, concerning disputes relating to acts which create Community industrial property rights.[181] The creation of new jurisdiction of this kind, particularly in a growth area, seems to move in the opposite direction from that of most of the other reforms, which seek to reduce the burden on the European Court system. None the less, it is evidently hoped that such judicial panels could address the case-load problem in a significant way. The older and often-mooted proposal to create a system of decentralized or regional community courts was not taken up,[182] but the creation of a third jurisdictional level below the ECJ and the CFI is undoubtedly one of the

---

[180] Declaration no. 13 of the Nice IGC also calls for definition of these conditions and limits in the Statute, and Declarations nos. 14 and 15 make further suggestions in relation to expediting and evaluating the ECJ's review procedure. Further, Art. 62 of the amended Statute provides that it is for the First AG to propose to the ECJ, where he considers that there is a serious risk of the kind mentioned in Art. 225, that it should review the decision of the CFI.

[181] Declaration no. 17 of the Nice IGC suggests that the new jurisdiction might also be exercised by the CFI or the judicial panels.

[182] For more recent debate on such see H. Rasmussen, 'Remedying the Crumbling EC Judicial System' (2000) 37 *CMLRev.* 1071, and for fuller argument in the earlier context of the Maastricht IGC see J.P. Jacqué and J. Weiler, 'On the Road to European Union: A New Judicial Architecture: An Agenda for the Intergovernmental Conference' (1990) 27 *CMLRev.* 185.

most significant steps taken to reform the EU judicial system since the establishment of the CFI itself.

Reform of the EU Court system was long-awaited and oft-proposed, but reactions to the Nice amendments to the 'judicial architecture' have been rather muted, as the following extracts suggest.

J.H.H. Weiler, The Judicial Après-Nice[183]

The actual outcome of the Conference in this area too, as with the political institutions, is an inability to break away from the scheme of the original Treaties. At the core of this architecture, and its most important feature by any perspective one may care to adopt, is the Preliminary Reference and the Preliminary Ruling. This procedure has remained substantially unchanged for half a century. A Court of First Instance with new-found dignity, Judicial Panels and all the rest notwithstanding, Europe continues to drive in its rusty and trusted 1950 model with the steering wheel firmly in the hands of the Court of Justice.

Put differently, the IGC was not willing to engage in either profound rethinking or profound re-engineering of the judicial function in view of a much changed polity to the one in which the current system was set. . . . And yet the context in which the judicial system is situated has changed radically in the last fifty years. The increase of size from six Member States to a potential of twenty-six is really only part of the problem, and possibly not even the most important part. Not a limited jurisdiction over some technical areas but a complex polity with jurisdiction ranging from human rights to monetary policy to difficult aspects of immigration and even citizenship. . . . And then the Court itself: no longer an instance for dispute settlement, but a judicial giant which has successfully positioned itself at the constitutional centre of Europe, a Europe in which national legal orders suddenly feel under threat.

A. Dashwood and A. Johnston, The Outcome at Nice: An Overview[184]

Perhaps the best overall assessment of the contribution of the Nice IGC to the reform of the European judicial system is provided in the title of the editorial of the Common Market Law Review when commenting on the Amsterdam Treaty as a whole: 'neither a bang nor a whimper'. In many respects, given the early scepticism at the potential for change at the Nice IGC, this assessment must be seen as something of a victory for those who argued in favour of the need for judicial reform. The serious attention paid to these issues by the Courts and the Commission has proved difficult to ignore and while the changes actually introduced do not make many fundamental changes to the system, they do put in place a framework within which further progress can undoubtedly be made.

(d) THE ROLE OF THE ADVOCATE GENERAL

The decision-making task of the ECJ is assisted by the existence of the office of AG. The AG is a full member of the Court and participates at the oral stage of the judicial

---

[183] Epilogue, in G. de Búrca and J.H.H. Weiler (eds.), n. 157 above (Oxford University Press, 2001), 217–18.

[184] In A. Dashwood and A. Johnston (eds.), *The Future of the Judicial System of the European Union* (Hart, 2001), 231.

hearing. His or her most important task is to produce a written opinion (the 'reasoned submissions' mentioned in Article 222 (ex Article 166) EC) for the Court. This opinion is produced by the AG who has been assigned to a given case, before the Court makes its decision. Since the TN amendment to Article 222, it has no longer been necessary for an AG to be involved in every case before the ECJ, and it is left to the Statute of the Court to determine when the AG's involvement is required.[185] The written opinion sets out the AG's understanding of the law applicable to the case, and recommends to the Court how the case ought to be decided. This opinion does not bind the Court, but is very influential, and in fact is followed by the ECJ in a majority of cases. The AG's opinion is intended to constitute impartial and independent advice, and in practice it tends to be a comprehensive and thoroughly reasoned account of the law governing all aspects of the case. The style and content of the AG's opinion are virtually always more readable than those of the Court's judgments, and often shed light on the meaning of an obscure judgment.

Another significant function which the AG has been allocated following the TN reforms to the Statute of the Court is to propose when the ECJ should, exceptionally, review a decision of the CFI given either under the lower court's new preliminary rulings jurisdiction or in its capacity as appellate court from one of the judicial panels established under Article 225a.[186]

(e) PROCEDURE BEFORE THE COURT

Procedure before the ECJ and CFI is governed by their respective rules of procedure.[187] The procedure before the ECJ takes place in two stages, the written and the oral stages.[188] The written part of the proceedings before the ECJ is far more thorough and more important than the oral. At the written stage, all applications, statements of case, defences, and any submissions or relevant documents are communicated to the parties to the case and to the institutions whose decisions are being contested. The oral stage, by contrast, is limited and short. The *juge-rapporteur*, the judge assigned in a given case, prepares and presents to the Court the 'report for the hearing', which summarizes the facts of the case and the arguments of the parties. Then the legal representatives of the various parties may make oral submissions to the Court, followed by submissions of the AG and the hearing of any necessary witnesses or experts. The Court has adopted the practice of asking questions of the legal representatives before it. This has become an important part of the oral stage of proceedings, since it focuses attention on and clarifies the issues which the Court considers of particular significance in the case.

---

[185] At present, Art. 20 of the revised Statute of the Court provides that where the ECJ 'considers that the case raises no new point of law, the Court may decide, after hearing the Advocate-General, that the case shall be determined without a submission from the Advocate-General'.

[186] See Art. 62 of the Statute, discussed at n. 180 above.

[187] For some of the differences between procedure before the ECJ and the CFI see N. Brown and T. Kennedy, *The Court of Justice of the European Communities* (Sweet & Maxwell, 5th edn., 2000). See also K. Lenaerts, 'The European Court of First Instance: Ten Years of Interaction with the Court of Justice' in D. O'Keeffe and A. Bavasso (eds.), *Judicial Review in EU Law* (Kluwer, 2000), 97.

[188] See Art. 20 of the revised Statute of the Court.

While there is an appeal from judicial panels to the CFI and appeals on points of law from decisions of the CFI to the ECJ, there is no further appeal from the judgments of the ECJ, which is the ultimate or supreme court of the European Union. However, Member States, Community institutions, and parties may under certain conditions contest a judgment rendered without their being heard, where it is prejudicial to their rights.[189] There is also a mechanism whereby any party with an interest in a particular judgment may apply to the Court to construe the meaning or scope of a judgment which is in doubt,[190] and a method for seeking revision of a judgment within ten years of its being given 'on discovery of a fact which is of such nature as to be a decisive factor' and which was unknown at the time the judgment was given.[191] It is also clear that the Court, although it generally builds on its own case law and follows the pattern and reasoning of its previous case law, does not consider itself bound by a strict system of precedent.[192] Occasionally, however, where it has clearly departed from the reasoning or result of a previous case, the ECJ has referred to the earlier ruling and explained the reason for its change.[193]

(f) STYLE OF THE COURT'S JUDGMENTS

The style of the ECJ's judgments contrasts considerably with the style and content of the opinions of the Advocates General. Article 36 of the revised Statute provides that judgments are to state the reasons on which they are based. But by way of contrast with the individual and less institutionally constrained opinions of the Advocates General, the ECJ's and the CFI's judgments are collegiate, representing the single and final ruling of all of the judges hearing the case. The fact that decisions of the ECJ may not often be unanimous and will require a vote is indicated by Article 15 of the Statute, which provides that decisions of the Court will be valid only when an uneven number of its members sits in deliberations. Since there are no dissents or separately concurring judgments, the divergent views of a number of different judges may be contained within the language of the judgment. This can result in obscurity or in a ruling which is ambiguous on matters of importance. Other explanations for the occasionally scanty reasoning or the less than thorough legal analysis in the Court's judgments have been suggested. For example, although the AG's opinion generally considers exhaustively all the legal arguments potentially relevant to the case, the

[189] See Art. 42 of the revised Statute and Art. 97 of the Rules of Procedure.

[190] Art. 43 of the Statute and Art. 102 of the Rules of Procedure. See also Case 69/85, *Re Wünsche* [1986] ECR 947, where the ECJ ruled that, although a national court cannot, in a reference under Art. 234 (ex Art. 177), question the validity of a previous preliminary ruling of the Court, it can ask for clarification of a previous ruling which is unclear.

[191] Art. 44 of the revised Statute and Arts. 98–100 of the Rules of Procedure. See, e.g., Case 115/73, *Serio* v. *Commission* [1974] ECR 671 on the requirement of 'new facts'. An application for revision of a judgment can also be brought before the CFI, and in turn an appeal against a decision of the CFI refusing such revision can be brought before the ECJ: see, e.g., Case C–5/93P, *DSM NV* v. *Commission* [1999] ECR I–4695.

[192] See, e.g., Case 302/87, *Parliament* v. *Council* (Comitology), n. 149 above, followed a year later by Case C–70/88, *European Parliament* v. *Council* (*Chernobyl*), n. 150 above. See in general A. Arnull, 'Owning up to Fallibility: Precedent and the Court of Justice' (1993) 30 *CMLRev.* 247.

[193] See, e.g., Case C–10/89, *SA CNL-SUCAL NV* v. *Hag GF AG* [1990] ECR I–3711, which followed Case 192/73, *Van Zuylen Frères* v. *Hag AG* [1974] ECR 731. In Cases 267–268/91, *Keck and Mithouard* [1993] ECR I–6097, however, although the Court was evidently departing from some of its past case law, it did not specify which decisions were 'overruled'.

Court may prefer not to commit itself on a specific legal issue until another case arises where the resolution of that issue is directly necessary for a decision.

A further reason for the inelegance or obscurity of judgments may be the fact that they are translated into all the official languages of the Community.[194] The working language which the ECJ has adopted for its secret deliberations is French, but the 'language of the case' depends on the kind of proceeding before the Court.

(g) ROLE AND METHODOLOGY OF THE COURT

The specific tasks to be performed by the Court are described in the Treaties. The main provisions governing its jurisdiction are Articles 226–243 (ex Articles 169–186) of the EC Treaty, and Article 46 (ex Articles L) of the TEU. The TEU enhanced the Court's jurisdiction under Article 228 (ex Article 171) EC, by giving it power to impose a pecuniary penalty on a Member State which failed to comply with a previous judgment against it. In accordance with Article 238 (ex Article 181), the Court can be given jurisdiction under an arbitration clause in a contract concluded by the Community, and under Article 239 (ex Article 182) ToA it is to have jurisdiction in any dispute between Member States where the subject matter is covered by the Treaty and the dispute is submitted to it by agreement of the parties. A number of international agreements concluded between the Member States also confer jurisdiction on the ECJ, such as the Convention on Jurisdiction and the Enforcement of Judgments in Civil and Commercial Matters made pursuant to Article 293 (ex Article 220) of the Treaty,[195] and the Convention on Jurisdiction and the Recognition and Enforcement of Judgments in Matrimonial Matters pursuant to what was then Article K.3 of the TEU,[196] which give the Court jurisdiction to give preliminary rulings. Under the European Economic Area (EEA) Agreement, too, the national courts of EFTA States may, if those States permit, make references on the interpretation of provisions of the Agreement to the ECJ.

However, it is Article 220 (ex Article 164) which perhaps figured most prominently in the Court's shaping of its own sphere of influence. The ECJ used this provision over the years to define its role broadly. This Article, which was amended by the TN to include the CFI, provides that 'the Court of Justice and the Court of First Instance, each within its jurisdiction, shall ensure that in the interpretation and application of this Treaty the law is observed'. It will be seen in subsequent chapters how the Court has utilized this provision to extend its review jurisdiction to cover bodies which were not expressly subject to it,[197] and measures which were not listed in the Treaty.[198] In

---

[194] See Arts. 29–31 of the Rules of Procedure of the ECJ and 35–37 of the Rules of the CFI. Following the TN amendments, Art. 64 of the Statute provides that the rules governing language will in the future be adopted under the Statute. This is obviously designed to preserve the requirement of unanimity in the Council for the sensitive language question, rather than the new provision for qualified-majority voting under the Rules of Procedure.

[195] [1972] OJ L299/32 and [1983] OJ C97/23.   [196] [1998] OJ C221/1.

[197] It subjected the Parliament to judicial review under Art. 230 (ex Art. 173) in Case 294/83, n. 144 above, although it was not included in the Treaty as a body subject to review. Conversely, in Case 70/88, the *Parliament v. Council* [1990] ECR 2041 it allowed Parliament to bring such an action despite not being covered by the Treaty.

[198] Case 22/70, *Commission v. Council (ERTA)* [1971] ECR 263.

the name of preserving 'the rule of law' in the Community, the Court has extended its functions beyond those expressly outlined in the Treaty under which it was established.[199] Since the competence of the Community, and hence of its institutions, is an attributed competence, limited by Article 5 (ex Article 3b) EC to what is given by the Treaty[200] an inherent jurisdiction for the Court could be considered problematic, despite its distinctive judicial role.[201]

In addition to extending its own review jurisdiction under Article 220 (ex Article 164), the 'gap-filling' role of the Court has also extended to developing principles of a constitutional nature as part of Community law, to which it then holds both the institutions and the Member States bound when they act within the Community sphere.[202] As interpreter of the Treaties and their limits, the Court also has to adjudicate not just among the EC institutions in disputes over their respective powers, but also, and more contentiously, in questions concerning the proper sphere of the Community as against that of the Member States.[203] These issues arise in many guises, either in direct challenges to Community action by Member States,[204] in actions between the institutions,[205] in preliminary references which may relate to the scope of areas of substantive Community law,[206] or in non-contentious advisory proceedings involving the compatibility of an international agreement with the Treaties.[207]

In the years of so-called institutional malaise or stagnation, the Court arguably played a 'political' role through law, attempting to render the Treaty effective when its provisions had not been implemented as required by the Community, and to render secondary legislation effective when it had not been properly implemented by the Member States.[208] It took an active part in the creation of the internal market through the litigation which came before it, by requiring the 'negative' removal of national barriers to trade, at a time when progress towards completing the Single Market through positive legislative harmonization was hindered by institutional inaction.[209]

The Court has achieved the hobby-horse status which it occupies amongst European lawyers as much on account of its reasoning and methodology as on account of the

[199] See Case C–2/88, *Zwartveld* [1990] ECR I–3365. The ECJ also uses Art. 220 (ex Art. 164) when defending the scope and nature of its review powers, as for e.g. in Case C–376/98, *Germany v. European Parliament and Council (Tobacco Advertising)* [2000] ECR I–8419, para 84. See also *Opinion 1/92 on the draft EEA agreement* [1992] ECR I–2821.

[200] In Case 26/62, *Van Gend en Loos* [1963] ECR 1, the Court said that the Member States had limited their sovereign rights in favour of the Community 'albeit within limited fields'. This limitation was subsequently omitted when the famous phrase was repeated in the Court's *Opinion 1/91 on the Draft EEA Agreement*, n. 199 above.

[201] See A. Arnull, 'Does the Court of Justice have Inherent Jurisdiction? (1990) 27 *CMLRev.* 684, 707.

[202] See Chs. 8 and 9.

[203] See J.H.H. Weiler, 'The Transformation of Europe' (1991) 100 *Yale LJ* 2403 on the ECJ's approach to Art. 308. More recently see *Opinion 2/94 on Accession by the Community to the ECHR* [1996] ECR I–1759, *Opinion 1/94 on the World Trade Organization* [1994] ECR I–5267, and Case C–376/98, *Germany v. European Parliament and Council (Tobacco Advertising)*, n. 199 above.

[204] Cases 281, 283–285, 287/85, *Germany v. Commission (Non-Community Workers)* [1987] ECR 3203 and Case C–376/98, n. 199 above.

[205] Case 22/70, n. 198 above.

[206] Case C–159/90, *SPUC v. Grogan* [1991] ECR 4685, and Cases 267–268/91, n. 193 above.

[207] See, e.g., *Opinion 1/94* and *Opinion 2/94*, n. 203 above.

[208] For further discussion see Ch. 5.

[209] Case 8/74, *Procureur du Roi v. Dassonville* [1974] ECR 837, and Case 120/78, *Rewe-Zentrale AG v. Bundesmonopolverwaltung für Branntwein (Cassis de Dijon)* [1979] ECR 649.

impact of its decisions. Its approach to interpretation is generally described as purposive or teleological, although not in the sense of seeking the purpose or aim of the authors of a text.[210] The fact that the *travaux préparatoires* to the original Treaties were never published meant these were never used as a source, and this is reflected in the Court's case law.[211] In the case of secondary legislation, although the discussions at Council and Commission meetings are not published, declarations and extracts from the minutes have occasionally been relied on as aids to interpretation before the Court. Occasionally the ECJ has referred to such material for assistance,[212] but in most cases it has denied its relevance if it does not appear in the text of the legislation itself.[213]

Rather than adopting a narrower historical-purposive approach, the Court tends to examine the whole context in which a particular provision is situated, and gives the interpretation most likely to further what the Court considers that provision in its context sought to achieve. Often this is far from a literal interpretation of the Treaty or of legislation in question, even to the extent of flying in the face of the express language. This aspect of the Court's methodology has attracted considerable criticism, although it has also had robust defenders from amongst the academic community, from its former personnel, and from amongst practitioners.

Probably the most famous of the Court's earlier critics was Hjalte Rasmussen, whose 1986 critique of the Court's policy-making role was one of the earliest sustained attacks on what the author viewed as its illegitimate practices. His thesis was that the Court has sought 'inspiration in guidelines which are essentially political of nature and hence, not judicially applicable. This is the root of judicial activism which may be an usurpation of power'.[214] He did not criticize all 'activism', but rather that which he believed to have lost popular legitimacy. In discussing Judge Pescatore's celebrated comment about the judges of the early ECJ having '*une certaine idée de l'Europe*' of their own, Rasmussen's book, using terms which, although written more than fifteen years ago, could equally well be used today, referred to 'society's declining taste for a precipitated process of integration'.[215]

There were mixed reactions to Rasmussen's strongly argued and polemical work from an academic community which had largely been supportive of the Court's strategy.[216] Mauro Cappelletti in particular argued that Rasmussen's critique lacked a historical dimension, that any constitutional court should have the courage to enforce

---

[210] For some of the few works on the reasoning of the Court see A. Bredimas, *Methods of Interpretation and Community Law* (North Holland, 1978); J. Bengoetxea, *The Legal Reasoning of the European Court of Justice* (Oxford University Press, 1993); and, more recently, T. Koopmans, 'The Theory of Interpretation and the Court of Justice', in D. O'Keeffe and A. Bavasso (eds.), n. 187 above, 45.

[211] See Case 149/79, *Commission* v. *Belgium* [1980] ECR 3881, 3890, and also the discussion of the use of *travaux préparatoires* and of 'declarations' by Member States by Mayras AG in Case 2/74, *Reyners* v. *Belgium* [1974] ECR 631, 666.

[212] See Case 136/78, *Ministère Public* v. *Auer* [1979] ECR 437, paras. 25–26 and Case 131/86, *UK* v. *Council* [1988] ECR 905, paras. 26–27.

[213] See, e.g., Case 38/69, *Commission* v. *Italy* [1970] ECR 47, para. 12; Case 143/83, *Commission* v. *Denmark* [1985] ECR 427; Case 237/84, *Commission* v. *Belgium* [1986] ECR 1247; Case 306/89, *Commission* v. *Greece* [1991] ECR 5863, paras. 6 and 8; Case C–292/89, *Antonissen* [1991] ECR I–745.

[214] H. Rasmussen, On Law and Policy in the European Court of Justice (Nijhoff, 1986), 62.

[215] *Ibid.*, 14.

[216] See the book reviews by M. Cappelletti (1987) 12 *ELRev.* 3; J. Weiler (1987) 24 *CMLRev.* 555; and A. Toth (1987) 7 *YBEL* 411.

its 'higher law' against temporary pressures, and that the ECJ's vision 'far from being arbitrary, is fully legitimate, for it is rooted in the text, most particularly in the Preamble and the first articles of the EEC Treaty'.[217] Some years ago a high-profile and more political attack on the methodology of the ECJ was made by Sir Patrick Neill, in his 'case study in judicial activism', in which he argued that the Court was a danger-ous institution, skewed by its own policy considerations and driven by an elite mission.[218]

In defence of the Court's 'constitutional' role,[219] however, Advocate General Jacobs has argued that it plays an essential role in preserving the balance between the Community and the Member States, and in developing constitutional principles of judicial review.

F. Jacobs, Is the Court of Justice of the European Communities a Constitutional Court?[220]

If then, the Court sometimes performs the task of a Constitutional Court, and if it has developed constitutional principles in its case law, we can understand why, in some quarters, the Court's activities have been misunderstood. The Court has sometimes been criticized as a 'political' Court. Such criticisms are probably based on unfamiliarity with the very notion of constitutional juris-prudence, which, as we have seen, is not familiar in all the Member States, and which requires what may seem novel judicial techniques, different approaches to interpretation, even a different conception of the law. Yet, in the Community system, which is based on the notion of a division of powers, some form of constitutional adjudication is inescapable, if indeed the Community is to be based, as its founders intended, on the rule of law.

Two former legal secretaries to Advocate General Jacobs at the ECJ, who are now academics, have also addressed the Court's critics, arguing that the Community is 'by its nature a dynamic organization', that 'the Treaties are imbued by teleology',[221] and that it is essential to preserve the central role of the Court.[222]

It is of course true that all constitutional courts must engage with political issues, but, given the unaccountability of courts, the nature and origin of the 'unwritten' values which they promote should undoubtedly be critically scrutinized, as should the *extent* to which their decisions seem to depart from what their express powers would

---

[217] *The Judicial Process in Comparative Perspective* (Clarendon Press, 1989), 390–1.

[218] *The European Court of Justice: A Case Study in Judicial Activism* (European Policy Forum, 1995). See also the critique by T. Hartley, 'The European Court, Judicial Objectivity and the Constitution of the European Union' (1996) 112 *LQR* 95.

[219] See the ECJ's view of its constitutional role and its ultimate interpretive authority in *Opinion 1/91* n. 199 above, paras. 21, 46. See also Case 294/83, n. 144 above, para. 23.

[220] D. Curtin and D. O'Keeffe (eds.), *Constitutional Adjudication in European Community and National Law*, (Butterworths (Ireland), 1992), 25, 32.

[221] T. Tridimas, 'The Court of Justice and Judicial Activism' (1997) 22 *ELRev.* 199, 205, 209. For a more recent discussion see A. Albors-Llorens, 'The European Court of Justice: More than a Teleological Court' (1999) 2 *CYELS* 373.

[222] A. Arnull, 'The European Court and Judicial Objectivity: A Reply to Professor Hartley' (1996) 112 *LQR* 95, and *The European Union and its Court of Justice* (Oxford University Press, 1999). See also G. Howe, 'Euro-Justice: Yes or No?' (1996) 21 *ELRev.* 187, 191.

appear to allow. Perhaps more importantly, such judicial decision-making requires full and thorough justification, whereas the reasoning of the ECJ tends to be rather thin.[223]

We have noted, with regard to the other political institutions, the dynamic character of their powers and functions. Each institution has had varying periods of strength and weakness, and the position and powers of each are linked to those of the others. This is true also of the ECJ, which has played its role in mediating between the institutions and defining the scope and limits of their powers, as well as mediating in the sensitive sphere between the Community and the Member States. It had been suggested, after the revival of the political processes of integration leading to the Single European Act, that the Court should thereafter adopt a 'minimalist' role.[224] However, as was noted earlier, the ECJ has not been a consistently 'activist' court at all times or in all policy spheres. It may for example simultaneously play a creative role in the creation of new remedies and methods of enforcement,[225] while reducing its intervention in an area of substantive law in which the legislative institutions have become more active.

The notion that the ECJ has played a less proactive role in its adjudication in the decade and a half since the SEA than before that time has gained credibility. In its famous 'Maastricht decision' on the constitutionality of Germany's ratification of the TEU, the Federal Constitutional Court sounded a warning note to the ECJ about its over-expansive methods of interpretation.[226] It has been suggested that this warning was unnecessary, and that the ECJ's dynamic approach to integration had already been replaced 'by the more static notion of subsidiarity' and 'the integrationist train had already come to a halt'.[227] The idea that the ECJ's own decision-making and methodology have been influenced by the concept of subsidiarity since the TEU was also voiced by a number of other commentators,[228] although the evidence for this is perhaps rather mixed.[229] On the other hand, the Court's review jurisdiction requires it to adjudicate in difficult political disputes concerning the proper sphere of Community competence and the observance of the subsidiarity principle by the other institutions. To date, the ECJ has not used this principle in an interventionist manner. Of the four major cases so far to invoke the subsidiarity principle in challenging Community measures, those concerning the Working Time Directive,[230] the

---

[223] For arguments in favour of better reasoning by the ECJ see U. Everling, 'The ECJ as a Decisionmaking Authority' (1994) 82 Mich. LR 1294.

[224] T. Koopmans, 'The Role of Law in the Next Stage of European Integration' (1986) 35 ICLQ 925.

[225] See, e.g., Cases C–6 & 9/90, Francovich and Bonifaci v. Italy [1991] ECR I–5357 and C–46 & /93, Brasserie du Pêcheur SA v. Germany and R. v. Secretary of State for Transport, ex p. Factortame Ltd. and others [1996] ECR I–1029. See below, Ch. 6.

[226] Brunner v. The European Union Treaty [1994] 1 CMLR 57. See Ch. 7.

[227] K. Meessen, 'Hedging European Integration: The Maastricht Judgment of the Federal Constitutional Court of Germany' [1994] Fordham Int. LJ 511, 529–30.

[228] V. Harrison, 'Subsidiarity in Article 3b of the EC Treaty: Gobbledegook or Justiciable Principle?' (1996) 45 ICLQ 431; G. Bermann, 'Taking Subsidiarity Seriously: Federalism in the EC and the US' (1994) 94 Col. LR 331; A. Dashwood, 'The Limits of European Community Powers' (1996) 21 ELRev. 113; J. Coppel (1996) 25 ILJ 153; D. Curtin (1994) 31 CMLRev. 631.

[229] See G. de Búrca, 'The Principle of Subsidiarity and the Court of Justice as an Institutional Actor' (1998) 38 JCMS 217.

[230] Case C–84/94, United Kingdom v. Council [1996] ECR I–5755.

Deposit-Guarantee Directive,[231] the Tobacco Advertising Directive,[232] and the Bio-technology Patents Directive,[233] only the tobacco advertising directive was annulled, and that because its legal basis was inadequate. Further, the Court has given a more cautious reading to the scope of Article 308 (ex Article 235) in recent years, as we will see in the next chapter.

To conclude on the role of the European Court within the EU legal system, we have seen that although the TN reforms restructured the judicial system somewhat in an attempt to address the problems of case-load, the substantive scope and coverage of the Court's jurisdiction were not significantly changed.[234] Similarly, the ToA had largely preserved the Court's existing role and powers, and had actually extended ECJ jurisdiction to cover 'fundamental rights' review in Article 6(2) (ex Article F(2)) TEU, and measures adopted under the third pillar on Police and Judicial Co-operation in Criminal Matters (PJCC). None the less, its jurisdiction over this pillar was circum-scribed in certain ways and its preliminary rulings jurisdiction covers only references from certain national courts whose States have expressly accepted such jurisdiction. More significantly, its preliminary rulings jurisdiction under the EC Treaty Title IV on the free movement of persons was limited to national courts from which there is no judicial remedy and was excluded, at least for five years, in relation to certain free movement measures concerning the maintenance of law and order and internal secur-ity. The possible impact of these ToA changes, and of the complex and partial system of the Court's jurisdiction in particular in the policy fields of the third pillar and of EC Title IV, has drawn a good deal of adverse comment.[235]

On the other hand, one of the Court's Advocates General has argued that its jurisdictional strength and its crucial role within the EU legal system have not only survived a number of IGCs in a politically challenging climate, but have emerged with its authority arguably strengthened.

N. Fennelly, Preserving the Legal Coherence within the New Treaty:
The ECJ after the Treaty of Amsterdam[236]

It is right to remark on the extent to which the existing jurisdictions of the Court have withstood the determined assaults upon its position so widely expressed and disseminated prior to and during the Intergovernmental process. It will be recalled that proposals seriously advanced included the possibility that certain decisions could be subjected to a type of political appeal and fast-track amendment to the relevant provisions of Community law in the event that a Member State

---

[231] Case C–233/94, Germany v. European Parliament and Council [1997] ECR I–2304.

[232] Case C–376/98, Germany v. European Parliament and Council [2000] ECR I–8419.

[233] Case C–377/98 Netherlands v. Parliament and Council, judgment of the ECJ of 9 Oct. 2001, not yet reported.

[234] The Court now has slightly wider jurisdiction in Arts. 230 (ex Art. 173) and 300(6) (ex Art. 228(6)) proceedings brought by the Parliament, and it has an increased role under the amended Article 7 (ex Art. F.1) TEU.

[235] S. Peers, 'Who's Judging the Watchmen? The Judicial System of the "Area of Freedom, Security and Justice"' (1998) 18 YBEL 337. See also P. Eeckhout, 'The ECJ and the "Area of Freedom, Security and Justice": Challenges and Problems', in O'Keeffe and Bavasso, n. 187 above, 153; and A. Albors-Llorens, 'Changes in the Jurisdiction of the ECJ under the Treaty of Amsterdam' (1998) 35 CMLRev. 1273.

[236] (1998) 5 MJ 185, 198.

considered that the Court had interpreted a provison in a manner not intended by its framers. The fact that, over a number of years, even following what were at the time considered to be extremely far-reaching decisions, the Member States have again and again unanimously both explicitly and implicitly given retrospective approbation to the Court's case law cannot fail to be a matter for satisfaction.

7. THE COURT OF AUDITORS

The Court of Auditors was established by the second Budgetary Treaty of 1975, and came into operation in 1977, replacing the previously existing Auditor of the ECSC and the Audit Board of the Communities. Since the enactment of the TEU, the Court of Auditors has occupied the status of the fifth Community institution in Article 7 (ex Article 4) of the EC Treaty. Its composition and functions are now governed by Articles 246–248 (ex Articles 188a–188c) EC.

Since the TN amendments, the Court of Auditors is to consist of one national from each Member State. Further, under the TN changes, they are no longer to be appointed unanimously by the Council but instead by qualified majority after consulting the Parliament. The Parliament has actively exercised its right of consultation, examining each of the proposed candidates thoroughly and not hesitating to express its disapproval of any candidate considered unsuitable.[237] The term of office is for six years, renewable, and appointments are staggered. The auditors' qualifications are simply stated: they must belong or have belonged in their country to an external audit body, or they must be 'especially qualified for this office'. In practice their professional backgrounds tend to be rather diverse, necessitating extensive training upon appointment. A crucial feature, emphasized in Article 247(2) and (4) (ex Article 188b(2) and (4)), is that their independence must be beyond doubt, and the tone of the Court's annual reports has undoubtedly often been extremely critical. It has been noted that it is sometimes difficult to show that the Court of Auditors and the Commission are 'on the same side', and that it could easily be accused of being 'anti-Communautaire'.[238] On the other hand, while its relations with the Parliament have been described as 'stable and cooperative',[239] there has been strong criticism of the 'indifference displayed at the Council's highest level to the auditing functions and findings of the European Court of Auditors'.[240]

The conditions of office are strict: members may not engage in any other occupation, paid or unpaid, and even after leaving office they must 'behave with integrity and discretion as regards the acceptance ... of certain appointments or benefits'.[241] A member of the Court of Auditors can be removed from office only by decision of the

[237] Westlake, n. 104 above, 118–19.
[238] I. Harden, F. While, and K. Donnelly, 'The Court of Auditors and Financial Control and Accountability in the European Community' (1995) 1 *European Public Law* 599.
[239] B. Laffan, 'Becoming a "Living Institution": The Evolution of the European Court of Auditors' (1999) 37 *JCMS* 251, 261.
[240] House of Lords Select Committee on the EU, Report no. 12 2000/2001 on 'The European Court of Auditors: The Case for Reform'.
[241] Art. 247(5) (now Art. 188b(5)).

ECJ. The task of the Court of Auditors is to scrutinize the finances of the Community and to ensure sound financial management, assisting the Parliament and the Council in their exercise of powers of control over the implementation of the budget. However, it has been pointed out that the scope of its functions is somewhat ambiguous and that the Court of Auditors and the Commission do not always agree on this issue.[242]

The Treaty provides that the Court is to 'examine the accounts of all revenue and expenditure of the Community' and of bodies set up by the Community, where that is permitted.[243] The Parliament and the Council are to be provided by the Court of Auditors with a statement of assurance (SoA) as to the reliability of the accounts and the legality of transactions and, following the ToA, any cases of irregularity are particularly to be reported. The TN also added a provision in Article 248(1) (ex Article 188c(1)), responding to dissatisfaction with the quality of the annual SoA, specifying that it may be supplemented by sectoral assessments on major areas of Community activity. The Court's audit is to be based on records, but also, if necessary, it can be performed on the spot in the Community institutions and in the Member States, in liaison with the competent national audit body. The ToA supplemented this to provide for the audit of other bodies which manage Community expenditure and parties receiving payments from the budget. Such institutions, bodies, and other parties must forward, at the Court's request, any necessary documentation. Article 248(3) governs the Court's right of access to information held by the European Investment Bank, and encourages trust and co-operation between the Court of Auditors and national audit bodies. Following the ToA, the Court was given *locus standi* to bring annulment actions under Article 230 (ex Article 173) EC, similar to that given the European Central Bank.

The Court of Auditors may submit observations on specific questions or deliver opinions at the request of one of the other institutions, as for example when it is consulted under the Treaty on specific legislative proposals (see Articles 279 (ex Article 209) and 280(4) (ex Article 209a)). At the end of each financial year, it issues an annual report, which is adopted by a majority of its members. The report is sent to the other Community institutions and published in the Official Journal together with the replies of the institutions. In an amendment introduced by the TN, Article 248(4) provides that internal chambers may be established in order to adopt certain categories of reports or opinions. This amendment has been criticized by a UK parliamentary report as being insufficiently radical to cope with the likely problems generated by an expanded membership of the Court consequent on enlargement.[244]

By comparison with the other institutions the Court of Auditors has been a relatively low-key institutional player. Indeed, one study suggests that it has an uneasy relationship with the Commission, has come into conflict with the Parliament's budgetary control committee, has been largely ignored by the Council, and remains virtually unknown to most national parliaments, although there have been other more recent and more positive appraisals of its evolving institutional role.[245]

---

[242] Harden *et al.*, n. 238 above.   [243] Art. 248(1) (ex Art. 188c(1)).
[244] House of Lords Select Committee Report, n. 240 above.
[245] Contrast Harden *et al.*, n. 238 above, with B. Laffan, n. 239 above.

8. OTHER COMMUNITY INSTITUTIONS

(a) THE ECONOMIC AND SOCIAL COMMITTEE

Article 7(2) (ex Article 4(2)) of the EC Treaty makes provision for an Economic and Social Committee (ECOSOC) to assist the Council and Commission. It is an advisory body representing various sectional or functional interests. Article 257 (ex Article 193) has been modified by the TN. In what may be a merely cosmetic amendment, but none the less one which acknowledges the increasing salience of 'civil society' in European and national discourse, it now provides that ECOSOC is to consist of the various components of organized civil society, in particular representatives of producers, farmers, carriers, workers, dealers, craftsmen, professional occupations, consumers, and the general interest.[246] The main members have been workers, who are principally represented by trade unions, employers, and others, such as farmers, consumer groups, and the professions. ECOSOC has 224 members.[247] Each country has a specified number of members, the largest being twenty-four and the smallest six. The Council appoints members of ECOSOC for four years, on the basis of proposals from the Member States, this term being renewable. Prior to the TN, the Council acted unanimously when making these appointments; it now acts by qualified majority.[248]

The members of ECOSOC may not be bound by any mandatory instructions, must be completely independent in the performance of their duties, and must act in the general interest of the Community.[249] ECOSOC operates via a number of different committees. In certain instances the Treaty stipulates that ECOSOC must be consulted, and the Commission or Council may consult it on other matters. ECOSOC may also be consulted by the European Parliament.[250] The Council or Commission may set a time limit, of not less than one month, within which ECOSOC has to act, and if it does not do so then matters can proceed without its input.

ECOSOC has not, traditionally, been a particularly influential institution, but its status could be enhanced by the increased institutional attention being paid to the importance of 'civil society' in enhancing EU legitimacy, and by the TN's express recognition of the role of civil society in its composition.[251]

(b) THE COMMITTEE OF THE REGIONS

This Committee was established by the TEU to represent regional and local bodies,[252] in part to counter the idea that the Community was becoming too centralized.[253] The total number of members is the same as for ECOSOC, as is the allocation between

---

[246] See S. Smismans, writing before the Nice Treaty, 'An Economic and Social Committee for the Citizen, or a Citizen for the Economic and Social Committee?' (1999) 5 *EPL* 557.
[247] Art. 258.   [248] Art. 259(1).   [249] Art. 258.   [250] Art. 262.
[251] See ECOSOC's own paper on 'The ESC: A Bridge between Europe and Civil Society' (Brussels, 2001).
[252] Art. 263 (ex Art. 198a) EC.
[253] See N. Roht-Arriaza, 'The Committee of the Regions and the Role of Regional Governments in the European Union' (1997) 20 *Hastings I & Comp. LJ* 413.

each Member State. The Council appoints the members for a renewable four-year term. Prior to the TN the Council made these appointments by unanimity; it now acts by qualified majority. No member of the Committee can at the same time be an MEP, but following an amendment by the TN, Article 263 (ex Article 198a) specifies that members must be 'representatives of regional and local bodies' with electoral accountability. They also must, like the members of ECOSOC, be independent and act in the Community's general interest. The Council and Commission must consult the Committee of the Regions where the Treaty so specifies. It may be consulted in other instances, in particular where a measure concerns cross-border co-operation; it can also be consulted by the European Parliament.[254] Time limits, like those appertaining to ECOSOC, can be set within which the Committee of the Regions must function.

Initially, according to a Protocol attached by the TEU to the EC Treaty, ECOSOC and the Committee of the Regions shared a common organizational structure. The ToA repealed this Protocol so that they no longer share the same structures. This amendment was desired by both bodies, but it falls considerably short of their call, during the 1996–7 IGC, for formal institutional status to be conferred on them. Like ECOSOC, although it is a much younger institution, the Committee of the Regions also perceives the possibility of enhancing its institutional status by virtue of the increasing calls for greater sub-national and local involvement in EU policy-making as a way of enhancing the overall legitimacy of the EU. The development of alternative forms of EU governance and policy-making such as those within the Employment Strategy[255] offer new possibilities for the involvement of the Committee of the Regions as a particular form of institutionalized representation of the local dimension.[256]

(c) AGENCIES

In addition to the major institutions and secondary bodies which have been discussed, the role of agencies within the EU institutional structure is one of growing importance. Apart from the EU's reliance on a range of national agencies in specialized fields for the proper implementation and execution of European law,[257] there are also at present twelve EU agencies. They have no formal basis in the Treaty but are creatures of secondary legislation, enacted mostly under Article 308 (ex Article 235) EC. The first two were created in 1975, the other ten in the 1990s, coming into operation at different stages. At present, they function in a range of areas including vocational training, working and living conditions, health and safety at work, the environment, drugs, medicines, plant varieties, internal market harmonization, translation, anti-racism, and reconstruction in the former Yugoslavia.[258]

---

[254] Art. 265 (ex Art. 198c) EC.   [255] See pp. 33–4 above.

[256] See the Opinion of the Committee of the Regions on the Commission's Communication COM(2000)196, 'Acting Locally for Employment—a Local Dimension for the European Employment Strategy' [2001] OJ C22/13.

[257] See also the Commission Communication COM(2001)648 on management of Community programmes by networks of national agencies.

[258] See www.europa.eu.int/agencies/carte_en.htm.

In its White Paper on European Governance, the Commission, while arguing against the need for 'comitology' committees which constrain its implementing functions, spoke in favour of the establishment of a greater number of 'autonomous regulatory agencies' with decision-making power in the application of regulatory rules.[259] However, although the Commission has made proposals for the creation of three new European agencies which should be established in 2002 having been approved by the European Council at Laeken,[260] only the aviation safety agency is to have clear decision-making powers. In addition to these new European agencies, the Commission has also recently proposed that some of its (non-discretionary) functions and programmes be externally managed by a new kind of 'executive agency', to enable it to concentrate on its 'core tasks' and to avoid the kind of outsourcing and inadequate accountability and control by the Commission which has occurred over the years.[261]

The existing EU agencies are relatively independent of the other institutions, although the Council and the Commission play differing parts in the appointment of the head of the respective agencies, and they enjoy varying degrees of financial autonomy.[262] In terms of composition, the administrative boards of the agencies are made up of national representatives and sometimes representatives of relevant organizations, of Commission representatives, and of European Parliament appointees also.

However, although they are relatively autonomous bodies, the agencies do not have a direct input into the legislative process, and their powers are fairly circumscribed. A significant part of their role involves the gathering and provision of specialized information, or, in the case of certain agencies such as the Community Plant Variety Office, the Office for Internal Market Harmonization, and the Agency for Evaluation of Medicinal Products, the implementation of a Community regime which has been established. The existing agencies presently do not have direct regulatory functions, although the technical advice and expertise they provide is used by the principal policy-making institutions and actors and affects the implementation process, partly through their co-ordination of the existing networks of national administrations which implement Community policy.[263] Further, their informational role is far from minor, given the crucial part played by information and expertise in controversial aspects of the policy process.[264]

---

[259] COM(2001)428, n. 25 above.

[260] On the European Food Authority see COM(2000)716 [2001] OJ C 96/247, on the European Aviation Safety Agency, COM(2000)595 [2001] OJ C154/1 and the European Maritime Safety Agency, COM(2000)802 [2001] OJ C120/183. A fourth on railway safety is also soon to be proposed. See the report of the UK House of Lords EU Committee, 7th Report, Session 1999–2000, *A European Food Authority*, and its 10th Report, Session 2000–01.

[261] See *Externalisation of the Management of Community programmes*, COM(2000)788 final [2001] OJ C120/140 and COM(2001)808 [2001] OJ C120/140. For earlier stages see *Guidelines for a policy of externalisation*, SEC(1999)2051/7 and the White Paper on Reforming the Commission, COM(2000)200.

[262] A. Kreher, 'Agencies in the European Community: A Step Towards Administrative Integration in Europe' (1997) 4 *JEPP* 225 and E. Chiti, 'The Emergence of a Community Administration: The Case of European Agencies' (2000) 37 *CMLRev*. 309.

[263] R. Dehousse, 'Regulation by Networks in the European Community: The Role of Agencies' (1997) 4 *JEPP* 246, 255.

[264] M. Shapiro, 'The Problems of Independent Agencies in the US and the EU' (1997) 4 *JEPP* 276. More generally on the possibilities and problems of agencies see E. Vos, 'Reforming the European Commission: What Role to Play for EU Agencies?' (2000) 37 *CMLRev*. 1113.

9. THE BUDGETARY PROCEDURE

Before concluding this Chapter, which has focused on the separate roles of the respective Community institutions, we will look briefly at the respective roles of the institutions within the EU budgetary procedure. As we saw in Chapter 1, the Community has been financed by its own resources since 1970.[265]

The Community's budgetary procedure is complex, and while Council and Parliament are generally referred to as the 'two arms' of the budgetary process, the EC Treaty in fact accords the three principal institutions a carefully balanced role. Article 272 (ex Article 203) EC provides the outline for the procedure under which the Commission prepares the Preliminary Draft Budget (PDB).[266] The Inter-institutional Agreement on Budgetary Discipline and Improvement of the Budgetary Procedure which was intended to improve institutional collaboration provides for three-way 'trialogue' discussions between delegations from Commission, Council, and Parliament before the PDB is approved by the Commission.[267] The PDB is then considered by the Council, where voting is by qualified majority.[268] If it appears to be likely that there will be conflict between the Council and the Parliament over the division between compulsory and non-compulsory expenditure (the Parliament having the last word on the latter and the Council on the former), the Inter-institutional Agreement makes provision for a conciliation procedure involving representatives of both institutions plus the Commission.

When the Council approves the PDB it passes to the Parliament for a first formal reading.[269] After the budgetary committee has done the preparatory work, the plenary session of the Parliament can then either: accept the PDB; propose amendments to non-compulsory expenditure;[270] or propose modifications to compulsory expenditure. Once again the financial perspectives will constrain the changes which the Parliament can suggest, but, other things being equal, the Parliament has persistently sought to increase non-compulsory expenditure relative to compulsory expenditure.

The PDB then goes back to the Council for a second reading.[271] It has three options, each of which requires a qualified majority: it can reject the Parliament's amendments;[272] it can reject modifications to compulsory expenditure proposed by the Parliament which do not have the effect of increasing total expenditure, but if it does not do so then the modifications stand;[273] it can accept the Parliament's proposed modifications to compulsory expenditure where these do increase total expenditure, but if it does not do so then the modifications fall.[274] If within fifteen days of receipt of the PDB the Council has not modified the Parliament's amendments and has

---

[265] For the most recent 'own resources' decision see Council Decision 2000/597/EC [2000] OJ L253/42.
[266] Art. 272(2).
[267] [1999] OJ C172/1. This Agreement was adopted in 1999 to replace the previous 1993 Agreement and also sets a financial perspective for 2000–6.
[268] Art. 272(3) (ex Art. 203) EC.   [269] Art. 272(4).   [270] Ibid.
[271] Art. 272(5).   [272] Art. 272(5)(a).   [273] Art. 272(5)(b).
[274] Art. 272(5)(c).

accepted the latter's proposed modifications, then the budget will be deemed to be finally adopted.[275]

If this does not occur, the next step is for the Parliament to have its second reading of the budget.[276] It then has fifteen days in which to exercise its options. It can, acting by a majority of its members and three-fifths of the votes cast, amend or reject the modifications to its amendments made by the Council. If it does not act within this period then the budget is deemed to have been adopted. The most potent weapon which the Parliament has is to reject the entire budget and request a new PDB.[277] If matters appear to be heading in this direction then there will normally be feverish negotiations between the institutions at all levels.

It is clear that both the Council and the Parliament have a real say in the budget. It is equally clear that the former is still pre-eminent, although developments since the late 1980s have redressed this balance of power to some extent by, for example, increasing the proportion of the budget devoted to non-compulsory expenditure and through the procedures provided for by Inter-institutional Agreements. The budgetary process clearly cannot be separated from more general issues of institutional power within the Community. As Nugent states, with 'the EP dissatisfied with its overall position in the EU system, it is only natural that it should have sought to use the budget to maximum advantage'.[278] To this end it has, on occasion, rejected the entire budget; interpreted the dividing line between compulsory and non-compulsory expenditure to the benefit of the latter; and attempted to exploit differences of opinion within the Council itself.[279] The conflicts which this has produced have sometimes ended up in the Court.[280] While the introduction of Inter-institutional Agreements and financial perspectives is likely to reduce the incidence of conflicts of this nature, one can still expect the Parliament to continue to use its budgetary powers to press for policies which it favours and to improve its own position in the Community's constitutional hierarchy.

10. CONCLUSION

i. No one of the EU institutions should be seen as a unitary actor. Although each has its own distinctive identity and role, it should be remembered that the internal structure and composition of each are varied and complex.

ii. The powers of the institutions are formally governed by Treaty provisions, but their actual functioning and interaction are determined by a range of inter-institutional agreements and practices, as well as by significant political developments.

iii. Recent years have witnessed a period of institutional flux, with proposals for

---

[275] Art. 272(5).   [276] Art. 272(6).
[277] Art. 272(8). This requires a majority of its members and two-thirds of the votes cast.
[278] N. 2 above, 359.   [279] *Ibid.*, 359–60.
[280] See, e.g., Case 34/86, *Council* v. *European Parliament* [1986] ECR 2155; Case 377/87, *European Parliament* v. *Council* [1988] ECR 4017; and Case C–284/90, *Council* v. *European Parliament* [1992] ECR I–2277.

reform of the internal working and governance structures of the EU administration, following the resignation of the Santer Commission.

iv. The role of the Court of Justice remains central within the EU institutional
framework and in the European legal system more generally. Its jurisdiction
remains wide and strong, despite flexible geometry and the pillar structure, and
recent structural reforms of the judicial system have enhanced the status and
powers of the Court of First Instance.

11. FURTHER READING

ARNULL, A., *The European Union and its Court of Justice* (Oxford University Press, 1999)

BACHE, I., and GEORGE, S., *Politics in the European Union* (Oxford University Press, 2000)

BROWN, N., and KENNEDY, T., *The Court of Justice of the European Communities* (Sweet &
Maxwell, 5th edn., 2000)

BULMER, S., and WESSELS, W., *The European Council* (Macmillan, 1987)

DASHWOOD, A., and JOHNSTON, A., *The Future of the Judicial System of the European Union*
(Hart, 2001)

DE BÚRCA, G., and WEILER, J.H.H., *The European Court of Justice* (Oxford University Press,
2001)

DEHOUSSE, R., *The European Court of Justice* (Macmillan, 1998)

DUFF, A., PINDER, J., and PRYCE, R. (eds.), *Maastricht and Beyond, Building the European
Union* (Routledge, 1994)

EDWARDS, G., and SPENCE, D. (eds.), *The European Commission* (Longman, 2nd edn.,
1997)

HAYES-RENSHAW, F., and WALLACE, H., *The Council of Ministers* (Macmillan, 1997)

KIRCHNER, E., *Decision-Making in the European Community: The Council Presidency and
European Integration* (Manchester University Press, 1992)

JACOBS, F., CORBETT, R., and SHACKLETON, M., *The European Parliament* (Harper, 4th edn.,
2000)

NUGENT, N., *The Government and Politics of the European Union* (Macmillan, 4th edn., 1999)

—— *The European Commission* (Palgrave, 2001)

O'KEEFFE, D., and BAVASSO, A. (eds.), *Judicial Review in EU Law* (Kluwer, 2000)

—— and TWOMEY, P.M. (eds.), *Legal Issues of the Maastricht Treaty* (Chancery, 1994)

SHACKLETON, M., *Financing the European Community* (Pinter, 1990)

STEVENS, A., with STEVENS, H., *Brussels Bureaucrats? The Administration of the European
Union* (Palgrave, 2001)

TSOUKALIS, L., *The New European Economy Revisited: The Politics and Economics of
Integration* (Oxford University Press, 3rd edn., 1997)

WALLACE, H., and WALLACE, W. (eds.), *Policy-Making in the European Union* (Oxford
University Press, 4th edn., 2000)

WESTLAKE, M., *A Modern Guide to the European Parliament* (Pinter, 1994)

—— *The Parliament and the Commission: Partners and Rivals in the European Policy-Making Process* (Butterworths, 1994)

—— *The Council of the European Union* (Harper, rev. edn., 1999)

3

THE SCOPE OF COMMUNITY POWERS: INSTRUMENTS, FORM, AND LEGAL BASIS

1. INTRODUCTION

In the previous chapter we examined the different institutional actors within the Union and their respective powers. In this Chapter, we shall be considering the existence and scope of Community powers and the basic requirements for their lawful exercise. In Chapter 1 we looked also at the powers of the Union under the second and third pillars, and at the forms of action available for their exercise. This Chapter, however, will concentrate on the various forms of Community action available, and on the fundamental substantive and procedural conditions which must be satisfied if their exercise is to be lawful. We will use the terms 'competences' and 'powers' interchangeably, although not everyone would agree that they have the same precise meaning.

2. CENTRAL ISSUES

i. The EC has a number of *formal legal methods* for developing Community policy: principally regulations, directives, and decisions. These will often be used in conjunction with each other. The foundational provision in an area may, for example, be a directive, and regulations and decisions may supplement it.

ii. The EC also has numerous *soft law methods* for developing Community policy. These include guidelines, policy statements, and declarations by the European Council.

iii. There are a range of *other legal and policy instruments* available under the second and third pillars, which differ in form and nature from those under the Community pillar. In addition, both the EC and the EU use *international treaties* and agreements in pursuit of their external policies and aims.

iv. *Formal and informal law will be used together* to attain EC and EU goals in any particular area.

v. Community action must satisfy a number of *procedural conditions* in order to be lawful. Community measures must be published, reasons must be given, and there are rights of access to documents.

vi. The fundamental principle of the legality of Community action is outlined in Article 5 EC. This provision indicates that the Community does not have general or inherent competence by stipulating that the Community must act within the *limits of its powers*. It must have a *legal basis* within the Treaties for every legal act it adopts. The application of these basic propositions can be problematic, both in relation to the EC's internal and in relation to its external competence. The search for a clearer delimitation of Community powers and competences is to be a central issue at the IGC in 2004.

vii. Closely related to the question of the *existence* of Community competence and the adequacy of the legal basis for action is the question of when such competence is properly *exercised*. This issue is governed by the principle of *subsidiarity*, which is set out in Article 2 (ex Art. B) TEU, Article 5 EC, and in a protocol to the Treaties. The meaning and application of this concept give rise to problems.

3. FORMS AND INSTRUMENTS OF COMMUNITY LAWMAKING

It is important to understand the different types of Community legislation. Article 249 (ex Article 189, see Prologue) EC is the foundational provision:

In order to carry out their task and in accordance with the provisions of this Treaty, the European Parliament acting jointly with the Council, the Council and the Commission shall make regulations and issue directives, take decisions, make recommendations or deliver opinions.

A regulation shall have general application. It shall be binding in its entirety and directly applicable in all Member States.

A directive shall be binding, as to the result to be achieved, upon each Member State to which it is addressed, but shall leave to the national authorities the choice of form and methods.

A decision shall be binding in its entirety upon those to whom it is addressed. Recommendations and opinions shall have no binding force.

There is no formal hierarchy between these provisions. It should not therefore be thought that regulations are somehow 'superior' to directives, or vice-versa. It is equally important to understand that regulations, directives, and decisions will often be connected in the development of Community policy in a particular area. There may, for example, be a 'foundational' regulation, and directives or decisions may be made pursuant to this. The 'foundational' provision may equally be a directive or a decision.

(a) REGULATIONS

Regulations are binding upon all the Member States and are directly applicable within all such States. They have to be published in the Official Journal and come into force on the date specified in the particular regulation or, if no such date is specified, on the twentieth day following publication.[1] The power to make regulations may be conferred on the Commission by a Council regulation. This issue will be considered more fully below.[2] In most instances the Treaty leaves open the choice whether to proceed by way of regulation, directive, or decision. Only rarely does it prescribe the necessity of legislating by way of regulation.[3]

---

[1] Art. 254 (ex Art. 191) EC. Regs. which are made under the Art. 251 (ex Art. 189b) procedure must also be signed by the President of the European Parliament and by the President of the Council: Art. 254(1).

[2] See 150–3 below.

[3] See, e.g., Art. 39(3)(d) (ex Art. 48(3)(d)) EC, Art. 89 (ex Art. 94) EC, concerning workers and state aids respectively.

It is quite common for an individual to allege that a measure which is called a regulation is really a decision. This arises most commonly in the context of challenges by individuals to annul a measure, because Article 230 (ex Article 173) limits the ability of individuals to challenge measures which are in the form of regulations. The test of whether a measure really is a regulation is one of substance and not form. The fact that the contested act is called a regulation will not therefore be conclusive. This issue will be examined below.[4]

It is common to think of regulations as akin to either primary or secondary legislation made by Member States. In some respects this analogy has force. Regulations are measures of general application, applicable to all Member States. Moreover, as will be seen,[5] the Court has held that regulations are abstract normative measures, which are not directed towards a particular named person or persons. While this reinforces the sense that regulations are analogous to domestic legislation, either primary or secondary, one should be cautious about pressing this analogy too far. Many regulations, for example in the agricultural sphere, affect only a very small group of people, and may be operative for only a short period of time. Such regulations may, in this sense, be indistinguishable from measures that would be regarded as administrative or executive acts within national legal systems.

Regulations are said by Article 249 (ex Article 189) to be 'directly applicable'. Commentators have debated the precise meaning of this term.[6] We cannot know the intent of those who drafted the Treaty in the absence of any available *travaux préparatoires*. It is unclear whether the Treaty framers meant the phrase 'directly applicable' to connote the idea that individuals have rights which they can enforce in their own name through national courts. We shall see that the ECJ has interpreted directly applicable in this manner.[7] It is however important to understand that the term has another meaning, which is concerned with the way in which international norms enter national legal systems. This can be explained in the following manner. Regulations are norms made by an international body, the EC. Under general principles of international law it is necessary for such norms to enter a national legal system. In some Member States, this must be done either by the national system transforming the measure into national law, or by a shorter national act adopting the relevant international act. A moment's thought will indicate that either of these will be very cumbersome when there is a large number of international measures to be transferred into national legal systems. The Community passes thousands of regulations. If each one had to be separately incorporated into each national legal system before it could be legally effective then the Community would grind to a halt. The phrase 'directly applicable' within Article 249 obviates this difficulty. It signifies that regulations are taken to be part of the national legal systems automatically, without the need for separate national legal measures.

Member States may need to modify their own law in order to comply with a regulation. This may be the case where a regulation has implications for different

---

[4] See Ch. 12 below.   [5] *Ibid.*

[6] See, e.g., J. Steiner, 'Direct Applicability in EEC Law—A Chameleon Concept' (1982) 98 *LQR* 229; A. Dashwood, 'The Principle of Direct Effect in European Community Law' (1978) 16 *JCMS* 229.

[7] See Ch. 5 below.

parts of national law. However this does not alter the fact that the regulation itself has legal effect in the Member States independently of any national law, and that the Member States should not pass measures that conceal the nature of the Community regulation.

Case 34/73, Variola v. Amministrazione delle Finanze
[1973] ECR 981

The ECJ was asked by a national court whether the provisions of a regulation could be introduced into the legal order of a Member State by internal measures which reproduced the contents of the Community provision 'in such a way that the subject-matter is brought under national law'.

THE ECJ

10. The direct application of a Regulation means that its entry into force and its application in favour of those subject to it are independent of any measure of reception into national law.

By virtue of the obligations arising from the Treaty and assumed on ratification, Member States are under a duty not to obstruct the direct applicability inherent in Regulations and other rules of Community law.

Strict compliance with this obligation is an indispensable condition of simultaneous and uniform application of Community Regulations throughout the Community.

11. More particularly, Member States are under an obligation not to introduce any measure which might affect the jurisdiction of the Court to pronounce on any question involving the interpretation of Community law or the validity of an act of the institutions of the Community, which means that no procedure is permissible whereby the Community nature of a legal rule is concealed from those subject to it.

Under Article 177 of the Treaty in particular the jurisdiction of the Court is unaffected by any provisions of national legislation which purport to convert a rule of Community law into national law.

(b) DIRECTIVES

Directives differ from regulations in two important ways. They do not have to be addressed to all Member States; and they are binding as to the end to be achieved while leaving some choice as to form and method open to the Member States. The Community institutions generally have considerable choice whether to legislate by means of regulations or directives. There are however a number of Treaty Articles which stipulate that directives must be used.[8]

Directives must be notified to the person to whom they are addressed.[9] There was, prior to the TEU, no duty to publish directives in the Official Journal, even though in practice many were published. It is now the case that directives which apply to all Member States and those passed pursuant to the co-decision procedure have to be published in the Official Journal.[10] The date of entry into force of directives is the

---

[8] See, e.g., Arts. 44, 46(2), 52, 94, 96, 132(1), and 137(2) (ex Arts. 54, 56(2), 63, 100, 101, 112(1), and 118(2)) EC.

[9] Art. 254(3) EC.   [10] Art. 254 EC.

same as that for regulations: either the date specified in the directive or, in the absence of any such date, the twentieth day following that of publication.[11]

The ability to legislate through directives as well as regulations gives the Community valuable flexibility. Regulations have the most direct impact, since they are directly applicable within the national legal systems. This does, however, serve to limit the utility of regulation. The direct applicability of regulations means that they have to be capable of being 'parachuted' into the legal systems of all the Member States just as they are. Normally every 't' must be crossed, and every 'i' must be dotted in regulations, since Member States must not tamper with them. If this were the only way to develop Community policy, the legislative process would work very slowly. There might be areas where it was difficult to devise regulations with the requisite specificity, which were suited to immediate impact in the Member States. It should be remembered that the Member States have differing legal systems, some being common law, some civil law, and that there are considerable differences between civil law regimes. There are, in addition, variations in the existing political, administrative, and social arrangements within the Member States.

Directives are particularly useful when the aim is to harmonize the laws within a certain area or to introduce complex legislative change. This is because discretion is left to Member States as to how the directive is to be implemented. It should not however be thought that directives are vague. They are not. The ends which Member States have to meet will be set out in considerable detail. The force of directives has been increased by ECJ decisions. The Court held that directives have direct effect, enabling individuals to rely on them, at least in actions against the State,[12] and that a Member State can be liable in damages for non-implementation of a directive.[13]

(c) DECISIONS

Decisions are, as stipulated by Article 249 (ex Article 189) EC, binding in their entirety on those to whom they are addressed. They must be notified to the addressee and take effect when notified to those to whom they are addressed.[14] Decisions which are adopted pursuant to Article 251 (ex Article 189b) must be published in the Official Journal. They take effect from the date specified therein or, in the absence of any such date, on the twentieth day following that of their publication.[15]

The Community institutions remain free to proceed by way of decision in many areas.[16] There are, however, areas where the Treaty stipulates that decisions should be used, as, for example, with breach of the competition rules[17] or the rules on state aids.[18]

The paradigm of a Community decision may well be one made in the context of competition or state aids, whereby the Commission expresses the formal conclusion

---

[11] Art. 254(1) and (2) EC. [12] See 202–27 below. [13] See 257–70 below.
[14] Art. 254(3) EC. [15] Art. 254(1).
[16] It is, e.g., common for the Commission to respond to requests concerning the detailed application of the CAP by issuing a decision on the matter.
[17] Art. 85(2) (ex Art. 89(2)) EC. [18] Art. 88(2) (ex Art. 93(2)) EC.

of its inquiry in relation to a particular undertaking or Member State. It must however also be recognized that there are a number of Community decisions that do not
fit this paradigm and which do not have a specific addressee or addressees. Decisions
may be the chosen method for introducing a new policy area, such as the Socrates
programme,[19] or for establishing general procedures, as in the context of the
Comitology Decision.[20]

It is open to the Council to delegate power to the Commission to take decisions that
are within the competence of the Council itself.[21]

We have already noted that the ECJ will determine whether a measure in the
form of a regulation is in substance to be classified in this way. The corollary is
that measures which are labelled as regulations but which the Court finds not to
be regulations in substance will be regarded as decisions. This issue is of
particular importance in relation to actions for annulment under Article 230 (ex
Article 173).[22]

(d) RECOMMENDATIONS AND OPINIONS

Article 249 (ex Article 189) EC states clearly that recommendations and opinions are
to have no binding force. While this precludes such measures from having direct
effect, it does not immunize them from the judicial process. It is, for example, open to
a national court to make a reference to the ECJ concerning the interpretation or
validity of such a measure.[23]

Article 211 (ex Article 155) gives the Commission a general power to formulate
recommendations or deliver opinions on matters dealt with in the Treaty, either where
it expressly so provides[24] or where the Commission believes that it is necessary to
do so.

(e) OTHER METHODS OF DEVELOPING POLICY

The four categories considered above constitute the principal ways in which policy is
developed within the Community. This list is not however exhaustive. The Commission has, for example, issued policy guidelines in the area of state aids to indicate how
it will exercise its discretion.[25]

There are also other ways in which the institutions can develop policy, such as
Inter-institutional Agreements. The place of such agreements within the Community
scheme will be examined more fully below.[26] Suffice it to say for the present that these
are agreements between the Council, Commission, and the Parliament, and that
they have been made on topics of constitutional significance such as subsidiarity,
transparency, and participation rights.

---

[19] Dec. 819/95, [1995] L87/10.   [20] Dec. 99/468, [1999] OJ L184/23.
[21] Art. 202 (ex Art. 145) EC.   [22] See Ch. 12 below.
[23] Case C–322/88, *Grimaldi* v. *Fonds des Maladies Professionelles* [1989] ECR 4407.
[24] Express provision for making recommendations or opinions is to be found in e.g. Arts. 77, 97, 105,
133(3), and 151(5) (ex Arts. 81, 102, 105, 113(3), and 128(5)) EC.
[25] See Ch. 27 below.   [26] See 161–2 below.

There is a connection between these methods of developing Community policy and recommendations and opinions. These measures taken as a whole constitute 'soft law',[27] as opposed to the more formal measures such as regulations, decisions, and directives. The admixture of formal and informal law is a common feature of any legal order. The difference in the late 1990s is that this feature has been positively lauded, rather than seen as a cause for apology or criticism. Thus the Commission in its *2000 Review of the Internal Market Strategy* included a neat checklist of the legislative and non-legislative measures it intended to take in order to attain the single market.[28] The same readiness to use the full range of policy instruments was apparent in the Nice European Council. In the implementation of the Social Agenda 'all existing Community instruments bar none must be used: the open method of co-ordination, legislation, the social dialogue, the Structural Funds, the support programmes, the integrated policy approach, analysis and research'.[29] It should none the less be recognized that the admixture of formal and informal law, while inevitable, can give rise to problems. It may be difficult for those affected to understand what the 'law' actually is in a particular area. Recourse to informal law may also prevent the Council and EP from having effective input into the content of the resulting norms.

4. THE REQUIREMENT TO GIVE REASONS

In addition to the duty to publish and notify Community measures, Article 253 (ex Article 190) EC establishes another important procedural condition for the lawful exercise of Community powers, *the giving of reasons*:

Regulations, directives and decisions adopted jointly by the European Parliament and the Council, and such acts adopted by the Council or the Commission, shall state the reasons on which they are based and shall refer to any proposals or opinions which were required to be obtained pursuant to the Treaty.

The *scope* of Article 253 is broad: it applies to regulations, decisions, and directives adopted either by the Council, Commission, and Parliament, or by the Council and Commission alone. This is noteworthy in itself. The duty to give reasons varies in the domestic law of the Member States,[30] but in most countries it is narrower than that in EC law. Thus Article 253 imposes a duty to give reasons not only for administrative decisions, but also for legislative norms, such as regulations or directives. Many national legal systems do not impose an obligation to furnish reasons for legislative acts, or do so only in limited circumstances. This should be borne in mind when assessing complaints about 'Brussels bureaucracy'.

---

[27] K. Wellens and G. Borchardt, 'Soft Law in European Community Law' (1989) 14 *ELRev.* 267; J. Klabbers, 'Informal Instruments before the European Court of Justice' (1994) 31 *CMLRev.* 997.

[28] COM(2000) 257 final.

[29] Nice European Council, 7–9 Dec. 2000, Annex 1, para. 28.

[30] For a discussion of the position in the UK see P.P. Craig, 'The Common Law, Reasons and Administrative Justice' (1994) 53 *CLJ* 282.

There are a number of *policy rationales* for the duty to provide reasons. From the perspective of affected parties, it makes the decision-making process more transparent, so that they can know why a measure has been adopted. From the perspective of the decision-maker itself, an obligation to give reasons will help to ensure that the rationale for the action has been thought through. Having to explain oneself, and defend the rationality of one's choice, is always a salutary exercise. From the perspective of the ECJ, the existence of reasons facilitates judicial review by, for example, enabling the Court to determine whether a decision was disproportionate.[31] In the words of the ECJ:[32]

In imposing upon the Commission the obligation to state reasons for its decisions, Article 190 is not taking mere formal considerations into account but seeks to give an opportunity to the parties defending their rights, to the court of exercising its supervisory functions and to Member States and to all interested nationals of ascertaining the circumstances in which the Commission has applied the Treaty.

The *content* of the obligation to give reasons will be shaped by two considerations, the policy rationales for the duty and the subject-matter covered by Article 253 (ex Article 190).

The policy rationale for the duty to supply reasons will affect the content of that duty. It will normally require specification of the Treaty Article on which the measure was based; the factual background to the measure; and the purposes behind it. This is exemplified by the *Tariff Preferences* case.[33] The ECJ annulled a Council measure in part because the legal basis of the measure had not been specified. In *Germany* v. *Commission*[34] the Court held that it was sufficient to set out in a concise, clear, and relevant manner the principal issues of law and fact upon which the action was based, such that the reasoning which led the Commission to its decision could be understood. Where a decision is establishing a new principle, or applying it in a novel fashion, there will have to be sufficient reasons in the decision itself,[35] but on some occasions the Court will sanction the incorporation of reasons from another instrument.[36]

The content of the duty will also be affected by the very scope of Article 253, applying as it does both to general legislative norms and to individualized decisions. The degree of specificity will, therefore, depend upon the nature of the contested measure, as was recognized by the Court in the *Beus* case, speaking of Article 190 (now Article 253):[37]

The extent of the requirement laid down by Article 190 of the Treaty to state the reasons on which measures are based, depends on the nature of the measure in question.

[31] For a more detailed discussion, see Ch. 12 below.
[32] Case 24/62, *Germany* v. *Commission* [1963] ECR 63, 69.
[33] Case 45/86, *Commission* v. *Council* [1987] ECR 1493.   [34] Case 24/62, n. 32 above.
[35] See, e.g., Case 73/74, *Papiers Peints de Belgique* v. *Commission* [1975] ECR 1491.
[36] This will occur not infrequently in areas such as the CAP, where the Commission may have to make numerous decisions or pass many regs. within a short space of time. Where this is so the Court has accepted that the Commission can refer back to a previous decision or regulation setting out the considerations which shaped the Commission's action: see, e.g., Case 16/65, *Schwarze* [1965] ECR 877.
[37] Case 5/67, *Beus* [1968] ECR 83, 95; Case C–205/94, *Binder GmbH* v. *Hauptzollamt Stuttgart-West* [1996] ECR I–2871.

It is a question in the present case of a regulation, that is to say, of a measure intended to have general application, the preamble to which may be confined to indicating the general situation which led to its adoption, on the one hand, and the general objectives which it intended to achieve on the other.

Consequently, it is not possible to require that it should set out the various facts, which are often very numerous and complex, on the basis of which the regulation was adopted, or *a fortiori* that it should provide a more or less complete evaluation of those facts.

Where a measure is of a general legislative nature it will be necessary for the Community authority to show the reasoning which led to its adoption, but it will not be necessary for it to go into every point of fact and law. Where the essential objective of the measure has been clearly disclosed there is no need for a specific statement of the reasons for each of the technical choices that have been made.[38]

The Court may well demand greater particularity where the measure being challenged is of an individual, rather than legislative, nature. Thus in *Germany* v. *Commission*[39] Germany produced an alcoholic drink called Brenwein, which was made from wine much of which was imported from outside the Community. The establishment of the common external tariff resulted in significant cost increases, and therefore the German Government asked the Commission for permission to import 450,000 hectolitres of this wine at the old, lower rate of duty. The Commission acceded to this request in principle, but for only 100,000 hectolitres. The Commission justified this decision on the grounds that there was ample production of wine in the EC, and that the grant of the requested quota would lead to serious disturbances on the relevant product market. The ECJ found the Commission's reasoning to be insufficiently specific concerning the size of any Community surplus, and that it was unclear why there would be serious disturbances in the market.

The content of the duty to provide reasons will also be affected by the extent to which the Court requires the Community institutions to respond to arguments advanced by the parties, what has been termed the dialogue dimension.[40] The ECJ has been cautious in this respect. In the *Sigarettenindustrie* case[41] the Court held that, although Article 253 (ex Article 190) required the Commission to state its reasons, it was not required to discuss all the issues of fact and law raised by every party during the administrative proceedings. It therefore dismissed the claim that the Commission had ignored the applicants' arguments, none of which had featured in the decision.[42] Shapiro explains why the ECJ has been reluctant to move in this direction, and also why, none the less, it might be pushed to do so. The references to Article 190 should now be read as referring to Article 253.

---

[38] Case C–122/94, *Commission* v. *Council* [1996] ECR I–881, para. 29; Case C–84/94, *United Kingdom* v. *Council* [1996] ECR I–5755, paras. 74, 79.

[39] Case 24/62, *Commission* v. *Germany*, n. 32 above; Case T–5/93, *Tremblay* v. *Commission* [1995] ECR II–185.

[40] M. Shapiro, 'The Giving Reasons Requirement' (1992) *U Chic. Legal Forum* 179, 203–4.

[41] Cases 240–242, 261–262, 268–269/82, *Stichting Sigarettenindustrie* v. *Commission* [1985] ECR 3831, para. 88.

[42] See also Case 42/84, *Remia BV and Nutricia BV* v. *Commission* [1985] ECR 2545.

M. Shapiro, The Giving Reasons Requirement[43]

The basic reason that the parties push and the ECJ resists dialogue lies in the difference between transparency and participation. Courts are likely to be initially hostile to demands for dialogue. Such requests are the last resort of regulated parties who have no substantive arguments left. Moreover, if dialogue claims are judicially accepted, they lead to a more and more cumbersome administrative process because the regulated parties will be encouraged to raise more and more arguments to which the agency will have to respond. If the only instrumental value for giving reasons is transparency, the courts will resist dialogue demands. One can discover an agency's actions and purposes without the agency rebutting every opposing argument.

. . .

If the ECJ sticks closely to transparency as the sole goal of Article 190, the ECJ is unlikely to move towards a dialogue requirement. Yet participation in government by interests affected by government decisions presents an increasingly compelling value in contemporary society, particularly where environmental matters are involved. The ECJ has already, however unintentionally, opened one avenue for linking participation to Article 190 by stating that the Council need not give full reasons to the Member States where they have participated in the decisions. To be sure, these ECJ opinions are transparency-based. They require that those Member States already know what was going on because they were there. Nevertheless they create an opening for counter-arguments from complainants who were not present and claim that, therefore, they need the Commission to be responsive. In short, full transparency can only be achieved through participation or through dialogue as a form of participation.

There has been some indication of movement in this direction. The CFI deals, *inter alia*, with cases within specialized fields, such as competition, where the facts are often complex. It has given a number of judgments on Article 253 (ex Article 190) EC. In one respect, its decisions simply apply existing orthodoxy, by confirming that, for example, the Commission is under no obligation to respond to all the arguments adduced by the parties in support of their application. In another respect, however, these decisions signal a more intensive species of review. The CFI has emphasized that the reasons that have been given must be sufficient to enable it to exercise its judicial review function, *and* it will scrutinize the Commission's reasoning, annulling the decision if it does not withstand examination.[44]

In more general terms, however, earlier indications of movement towards greater participation rights have not borne fruit. The 1993 Inter-institutional Declaration on Democracy, Transparency, and Subsidiarity indicated that the EC might be moving towards something akin to the notice and comment procedures, which govern rule-making in the USA.[45] The Declaration stated that the Commission was to introduce

---

[43] N. 40 above, 204–5.

[44] See, e.g., Case T–44/90, *La Cinq SA* v. *Commission* [1992] ECR II-1; Case T–7/92, *Asia Motor France SA* v. *Commission* [1993] ECR II–669.

[45] P.P. Craig, 'Democracy and Rule-making in the EC: An Empirical and Normative Assessment', in P. Craig and C. Harlow (eds.), *Lawmaking in the European Union* (Kluwer, 1998), ch. 2. For further discussion, see 516–18 below.

a notification procedure, consisting of the publication in the Official Journal of a brief summary of the measure proposed by the Commission, combined with a deadline by which interested parties were invited to submit their comments. While the Commission has done this on an *ad hoc* basis, it has not developed any more general structure of *participation rights* akin to the Administrative Procedure Act in the USA.[46] More recently, the Commission stated in its White Paper on *European Governance* that it was against the idea of enshrining consultation rights in legal rules, preferring instead a code of conduct that set minimum standards.[47]

A procedural right that emerged from the 1993 Declaration was that of *transparency and access to documents.* Access to the relevant documentation is crucial for understanding the reasons behind a measure. It facilitates construction of a reasoned argument by those opposed to a measure in its present form. Access to documentation is moreover of the essence of democracy. The 1993 Declaration stressed the importance of openness in government as a way of rendering the EC more legitimate to its citizens. The principles laid down in the Declaration were taken further by, for example, a Council Decision that set out the circumstances in which access to Council documents was to be available.[48] The CFI stressed in *Carvel*[49] that when the Council exercised its discretion whether to release documents pursuant to this Decision it must genuinely balance the interests of citizens in gaining access to documents with the need to maintain confidentiality of its deliberations. It could not simply adopt a general blanket denial of access to a class of documents. The ToA subsequently enshrined access to documents as a Treaty right. Article 1 (ex Article A) of the TEU, as amended by the ToA, states that decisions should be taken as openly and as closely as possible to the citizen, and Article 255(1) (introduced by the ToA) EC provides that:

Any citizen of the Union, and any natural or legal person residing or having their registered office in a Member State, shall have a right of access to European Parliament, Council and Commission documents, subject to the principles and the conditions to be defined in accordance with paragraphs 2 and 3.

Article 255(2) stipulated that the general principles concerning such access and the limits thereto should be determined by the Council, acting in accordance with the Article 251 (ex Article 189b) procedure, within two years of the entry into force of the ToA Article 255(3) (ex Article 131a(3)) instructed each institution to adopt Rules of Procedure regarding access to documents, a point reinforced in relation to the Council by Article 207(3) (ex Article 151 (3)). There is discussion of these and other aspects of transparency in Chapter 9 below.[50]

---

[46] *Ibid.*   [47] COM(2001)428 final, 17.

[48] For a discussion of Council practice and the relevant Council decisions see M. Westlake, *The Council of the European Union* (Cartermill, 1995), 144–62.

[49] Case T–194/94, *Carvel and Guardian Newspapers Ltd* v. *Council* [1995] ECR II–2765. The same reasoning was applied in relation to the Commission in Case T–105/95, *WWF UK (World Wide Fund for Nature)* v. *Commission* [1997] ECR II–313.

[50] See 392–4 below.

5. INTERNAL COMMUNITY COMPETENCE

Judicial review of Community action will be considered below.[51] We shall see that binding acts and acts which produce legal effects are capable of being reviewed by the ECJ or the CFI. The present discussion is related, but more limited. It is to examine the fundamental requirement that Community legislation should have a proper legal basis in the Treaty. The requirement that legislation must be properly based upon a Treaty Article may sound obvious, and so indeed it is. Normally this requirement will be unproblematic: the particular regulation will stipulate the Treaty Article on which it is based. Matters can, however, be more difficult for four reasons.

(a) DISAGREEMENT ABOUT THE AMBIT OF A TREATY ARTICLE

Disagreement about the ambit of a Treaty Article is exemplified by the *Working Time Directive* case.[52] The UK sought the annulment of a directive concerned with the organization of working time. The directive had been adopted by qualified majority pursuant to what was Article 118a of the Treaty,[53] concerned with health and safety. The UK argued that the measure should have been made under either Article 100 or 235 (now Article 94 or 308), which required unanimity in the Council. Article 118a was, the UK contended, not suitable for measures of broad social policy, and provisions concerning working time were insufficiently related to health and safety. The ECJ, save for one small point, rejected the argument and concluded that Article 118a was a sound legal basis for the measure.

(b) SHARED COMPETENCE

It is common for competence to be divided between the EC and the Member States, and in fact the great majority of Community powers are shared rather than exclusive. However, it is mostly in relation to the newer competences granted to the EC by the Treaties that the non-exclusive nature of these powers is made express. It is equally important to recognize that the precise division of competence between the EC and the Member States varies in different subject matter areas,[54] and that it is often drawn in rather imprecise terms. It may therefore be contestable whether a measure falls within the sphere allocated to the Community or to the Member States, and normally this question falls ultimately to the Court of Justice to decide.

---

[51] See Ch. 12 below.

[52] Case C–84/94, *United Kingdom* v. *Council* [1996] ECR I–5755. For a similar argument in the context of Art. 47 (ex Art. 57) see Case C–233/94, *Germany* v. *European Parliament and Council* [1997] ECR I–2405. See also Case C–377/98, *Netherlands* v. *Parliament and Council* [2001] ECR I–7079.

[53] The ToA has now substantially amended this and related Arts. of the EC Treaty: see Arts. 137 and 138 EC.

[54] Compare, e.g., the different formulations in Art. 152 (health), Art. 153 (consumer protection), Art. 157 (industry), Arts. 163–73 (research and technological development).

(c) IMPLIED POWERS

The institutions may claim that a particular Treaty Article contains an implied power to make the particular regulation. The notion of implied powers is well known in both domestic and international legal systems. The precise meaning of the phrase 'implied power' is more contestable. It can, as Hartley notes, be given a narrow or a wide formulation:[55]

According to the narrow formulation, the existence of a given power implies also the existence of any other power which is reasonably necessary for the exercise of the former; according to the wide formulation, the existence of a given *objective* or *function* implies the existence of any power reasonably necessary to attain it.

The narrow sense of implied power has been long accepted within the Community.[56] The ECJ is also willing to embrace the wider formulation. This is exemplified by the following case.

Cases 281, 283–285, 287/85, Germany v. Commission
[1987] ECR 3203

[Note ToA renumbering: Art. 118 is now Art. 137]

The Commission made a decision pursuant to Article 118 which established a prior communication and consultation process in relation to migration policies affecting workers from non-EC countries. The Member States were to inform the Commission and other Member States of their draft measures concerning entry, residence, equality of treatment, and the integration of such workers into the social and cultural life of the country. After notification to the Commission of such draft measures there would then be consultation with the Commission and other Member States. A number of States challenged this measure as being *ultra vires* the Commission. Article 118, which concerns collaboration in the social field, did not expressly give the Commission power to make binding decisions.

THE ECJ

15. The essence of the arguments put forward by the applicant Member States is that migration policy in relation to non-Member countries is not part of the social field envisaged by Article 118, or, alternatively, that it falls only partly within that field.

16. As regards the applicants' main argument it must be observed that the employment situation and, more generally, the improvement of living and working conditions within the Community are liable to be affected by the policies pursued by the Member States with regard to workers from non-Member countries. . . .

. . .

18. It must therefore be held that the argument that migration policy in relation to

---

[55] T.C. Hartley, *The Foundations of European Community Law* (Oxford University Press, 4th edn., 1998), 102. Italics in the original.
[56] Case 8/55, *Fédération Charbonnière de Belgique* v. *High Authority* [1956] ECR 245, 280.

non-Member States falls entirely outside the social field, in respect of which Article 118 provides for co-operation between the Member States, cannot be accepted.

[*The ECJ found that the Decision was partly* ultra vires *in so far as it sought to promote consultation in relation to cultural matters. It then proceeded to consider whether Article 118 could be construed to include a power to make binding decisions.*]

27. . . . it must be considered whether the second paragraph of Article 118, which provides that the Commission is to act, *inter alia,* by arranging consultations, gives it the power to adopt a binding decision with a view to the arrangement of such consultations.

28. In that connection it must be emphasised that where an Article of the EEC Treaty . . . confers a specific task on the Commission it must be accepted, if that provision is not to be rendered wholly ineffective, that it confers on the Commission necessarily and *per se* the powers which are indispensable in order to carry out that task. Accordingly, the second paragraph of Article 118 must be interpreted as conferring on the Commission all the powers which are necessary in order to arrange the consultations. In order to perform that task of arranging consultation the Commission must necessarily be able to require the Member States to notify essential information, in the first place to identify the problems and in the second place in order to pinpoint the possible guidelines for any future joint action on the part of the Member States; likewise it must be able to require them to take part in consultation.

The ECJ has, in the past, been disinclined to place limits on broadly worded Treaty Articles. It can however do so. In the *Tobacco Advertising* case the ECJ held that a directive relating to tobacco advertising could not be based on Article 95 (ex Article 100a).[57]

Case C–376/98, Germany v. European Parliament and Council
[2000] ECR I-8419

[Note ToA renumbering: Arts. 3b, 3(c), 7a, 57(2), 66, 100a, 164 are now Arts. 5, 3(1)(c), 14, 47(2), 55, 95, 220]

Germany sought the annulment of a Directive designed to harmonize the law relating to the advertising and sponsorship of tobacco. The Directive had been based on Articles 57(2), 66, and 100a. Article 100a allows the adoption of harmonization measures for the functioning of the internal market. The ECJ cited Articles 100a, 3(c), and 7a of the Treaty. It then continued as follows.

THE ECJ

83. Those provisions, read together, make it clear that the measures referred to in Article 100a(1) . . . are intended to improve the conditions for the establishment and functioning of the internal market. To construe that article as meaning that it vests in the Community legislature a general power to regulate the internal market would not only be contrary to the express wording of the provisions cited above, but would also be incompatible with the principle embodied in Article 3b . . . that the powers of the Community are limited to those specifically conferred on it.

84. Moreover, a measure adopted on the basis of Article 100a . . . must genuinely have as its

---

[57] T. Hervey, 'Up in Smoke? Community (Anti)-Tobacco Law and Policy' (2001) 26 *ELRev.* 101.

object the improvement of the conditions for the establishment and functioning of the internal market. If a mere finding of disparities between national rules and of the abstract risk of obstacles to the exercise of fundamental freedoms or of distortions of competition liable to result therefrom were sufficient to justify the choice of Article 100a as a legal base, judicial review of compliance with the proper legal basis might be nugatory. The Court would then be prevented from discharging the function entrusted to it by Article 164 . . . of ensuring that the law is observed in the interpretation and application of the Treaty.

85. So, in considering whether Article 100a was the proper legal basis, the Court must verify whether the measure whose validity is at issue in fact pursues the objectives stated by the Community legislature . . .

(d) ARTICLE 308 (EX ARTICLE 235)

The final reason there can be difficulties concerning the basis for legislation relates to Article 308 (ex Article 235) EC. Most Treaty Articles relate to a specific subject-matter area, such as workers or goods. The Treaty also contains broader legislative provisions, such as Articles 94 and 95 (ex Articles 100 and 100a), concerning harmonization of laws. Article 308 is broader still. It provides that:

If action by the Community should prove necessary to attain, in the course of the operation of the common market, one of the objectives of the Community and this Treaty has not provided the necessary powers, the Council shall, acting unanimously on a proposal from the Commission and after consulting the European Parliament, take the appropriate measures.

Article 308 has been a valuable legislative power, particularly when the Community did not possess more specific legislative authority in certain areas. Thus the Article was used to legitimate legislation on areas such as the environment and regional policy, before these matters were dealt with through later Treaty amendments. Weiler captures the importance of this provision and the manner in which it was interpreted.

J. Weiler, The Transformation of Europe[58]

In a variety of fields, including, for example, conclusion of international agreements, the granting of emergency food aid to third countries, and creation of new institutions, the Community made use of Article 235 in a manner that was simply not consistent with the narrow interpretation of the Article as a codification of implied powers doctrine in its instrumental sense. Only a truly radical and 'creative' reading of the Article could explain and justify its usage as, for example, the legal basis for granting emergency food aid to non-associated states. But this wide reading, in which all the institutions partook, meant that it would become virtually impossible to find an activity which could not be brought within the objectives of the Treaty.

Article 308 requires that the power should be used to attain a Community objective. Given, however, the breadth of the Treaty objectives, and given also the ECJ's purposive mode of interpreting Community aims, these 'conditions' have not placed

---

[58] (1991) 100 *Yale LJ* 2403, 2445–6.

a severe constraint on the Council. They are not however entirely devoid of meaning, as exemplified by *Opinion 2/94*.[59] The case was concerned with the legality of the EC's possible accession to the European Convention on Human Rights (ECHR). The ECJ held that Article 308 could not be used to widen the scope of Community powers beyond the framework created by the EC Treaty taken as a whole. Nor could it be used as the foundation for the adoption of provisions which would, in substance, amend the Treaty without following the necessary amendment procedures. It should also be acknowledged that the ECJ was probably content to reach this conclusion in the instant case, thereby avoiding subjecting itself to the ultimate authority of the European Court of Human Rights.

The most problematic aspect of Article 308 is the condition that the Treaty has not 'provided the necessary powers'. The mere fact that another, more specific, Treaty provision has given a power to make recommendations will not preclude the use of Article 308 to enact binding measures.[60] Nor, it seems, will Article 308 be excluded by the fact that the particular Treaty provisions could be interpreted broadly by using the implied-powers doctrine discussed above.[61] Whether the Treaty has provided necessary powers elsewhere can, however, be of particular significance in two situations.

One is where specific Treaty Articles provide for more extensive involvement of the European Parliament than does Article 308. Article 308 only requires the Council to consult the Parliament, whereas other Treaty Articles give the Parliament greater rights in the legislative process. If the Council is able to proceed via Article 308, there is a danger that this will diminish the European Parliament's role. The ECJ has, therefore, stressed that Article 308 can be used only where no other provision of the Treaty gives the Community institutions the necessary power to adopt the relevant measure. The Court will closely scrutinize the use of Article 308 where it is argued that another more specific Treaty Article would afford the European Parliament a greater role in the legislative process.[62]

The other situation in which the choice between Article 308 and a more specific Treaty Article can be of significance is where there are differences in the voting rules under the respective Articles. Article 308 requires unanimity in the Council, whereas many other Treaty provisions demand only a qualified majority.

Cases involving the appropriate boundaries of Article 308 have not infrequently been litigated before the ECJ. Thus in the *Tariff Preferences* case[63] the Commission sought the annulment of a Council regulation concerning tariff preferences for goods from developing countries. The Council argued that, since the purpose of the measures was in reality development aid, they could be adopted only by using Article 308. The Commission contended that Article 113 (now Article 133), which concerned the

---

[59] *Opinion 2/94 (Re the Accession of the Community to the European Human Rights Convention)* [1996] ECR I–1759. Cf. *Opinion 2/91 (Re the ILO Convention 170 on Chemicals at Work)* [1993] ECR I–1061.
[60] Case 8/73, *Hauptzollamt Bremerhaven v. Massey-Ferguson* [1973] ECR 897.
[61] *Ibid.*, para. 4.
[62] Case 45/86, *Commission v. Council* [1987] ECR 1493; Case C–350/92, *Spain v. Council* [1995] ECR I–1985; Case C–271/94, *European Parliament v. Council (Re the Edicom Decision)* [1996] ECR I–1689.
[63] Case 45/86, [1987] ECR 1493. See also Case 165/87, *Commission v. Council* [1988] ECR 5545; Case C–295/90, *European Parliament v. Council* [1992] ECR I–4193.

common commercial policy, could be used, and that this required only qualified-majority voting. In fact the Council did not specify any particular Article of the Treaty in the measures. The ECJ annulled the regulations because of failure to state the legal basis of the measures, and because they could have been adopted under Article 113.More recently in the *Biotechnology Directive* case, the ECJ ruled that a directive concerning patent protection for such inventions was properly adopted under Article 95 (ex Article 100) and did not require Article 308 as an additional legal basis.[64] By contrast, in a case concerning a regulation on mutual assistance between national administrative authorities to deal with EC agricultural and customs fraud, the Court upheld the use of Article 308, ruling that Article 95 would be inappropriate in this context.[65]

Article 308 (ex Article 235) has long been viewed with suspicion by those calling for a clearer delimitation of Community competences and in particular by the German *Länder*. Various calls for reform have been made before and during recent Inter-governmental Conferences.[66] This question was placed explicitly on the post-Nice and post-Laeken agenda for future reform of the Union. The Laeken Declaration, adopted by the Member States in December 2001, expressly asks whether Article 308 ought to be reviewed, in light of the twin challenges of preventing the 'creeping expansion of competences' from encroaching on national and regional powers, and yet allowing the EU to 'continue to be able to react to fresh challenges and developments and . . . to explore new policy areas'.

6. EXTERNAL COMMUNITY COMPETENCE

In Chapter 1, the changing legal personality of the Union was discussed. Here, a brief summary of the nature and scope of the Community's external competence will be provided.

(a) EXPRESS EXTERNAL COMPETENCES

Whereas the Community has always had a range of express 'internal' powers, the same is not true of its external competence: the Community's power to engage in relations with other States and international associations outside the EU.[67]

---

[64] See Case C–377/98, *Netherlands* v. *Council*, n. 52 above.

[65] See Case C–209/97, *Commission* v. *Council* [1999] ECR I–8067.

[66] See A. von Bogdandy and J. Bast, 'The Union's Powers: A Question of Competence. The Vertical Order of Competences and Proposals for its Reform' (2002) 38 *CMLRev.*, forthcoming, and G. de Búrca 'Setting Limits to EU Competences', Francisco Lucas Pires Working paper 2001/02, www.fd.unl.pt/je/wpflp02a.doc. There is a substantial German academic literature on the question of competences, including at least one monograph on Art. 308: M. Bungenberg, *Art. 235 EGV nach Maastricht: Die Auswirkungen der Einheitlichen Europäischen Akte und des Vertrages ueber die Europäische Union auf die Handlungsbefugnis des Art. 235 EGV (Art. 308 EGV)* (Nomos, 1999).

[67] For general texts see D. McGoldrick, *International Relations Law of the European Union* (Longman, 1997); I. Macleod, I. Hendry, and S. Hyett, *The External Relations of the European Communities: A Manual of Law and Practice* (Oxford University Press, 1996). See also M. Koskenniemi (ed.), *International Law Aspects of the European Union* (Kluwer, 1998), and A. Dashwood and C. Hillion (eds.), *The General Law of EC External Relations* (Sweet & Maxwell, 2000).

The express powers conferred on the Community to act in the international sphere were limited under the original EEC Treaty to commercial policy in Article 133 (ex Article 113), the scope of which was broadly construed and much debated,[68] and to association agreements, which generally establish a close relationship between the Community and a third country, in Article 310 (ex Article 238).[69] International activity on the part of the Community may be autonomous or unilateral, such as the adoption of an anti-dumping measure, or it may be contractual, involving the entry of an agreement with another party, State, or organization. Article 310 provides only for the adoption of contractual measures, unlike Article 133, which constitutes a legal basis for both types of external action. Articles 302–304 (ex Articles 229–231) govern the 'maintenance of relations' between the Community and international organizations such as the UN, the GATT, the Council of Europe, and the OECD.

Alongside the express Treaty bases granting external competence, the ECJ however developed a broad, controversial, and complex theory of implied external powers for the Community. The development of the concept of 'implied power' by the Court in the field of external powers, unlike in the internal sphere, led to a very substantial competence on the part of the Community, which is more or less parallel with its internal competence. Unlike the EU, which has only recently developed the capacity to enter international agreements, the Community has always had international legal personality.[70]

The ECJ's gradual extension of the Community's international competence was supplemented by the series of Treaty amendments made at successive IGCs, which conferred on the Community express (though usually not exclusive) competence across a range of policy areas. Those introduced by the Single European Act included development policy (Article 181 EC, ex Article 130y), environmental policy (Article 174 EC, ex Article 130r), and research and technology (Article 170 EC, ex Article 130m). The Maastricht TEU created external powers in monetary and foreign exchange matters, and co-operation powers with third countries in a range of areas such as education, culture, health, and trans-European networks. The Amsterdam Treaty (ToA) and the Nice Treaty (TN) subsequently provided for the extension of the scope of the CCP. The TN also introduced a new provision in Article 181a EC governing economic, financial, and technical co-operation with third countries, thus providing a separate Treaty basis for activities which were previously pursued under Article 308 (ex Article 235).

---

[68] See however *Opinion 1/94 on the WTO Agreement* [1994] ECR I–5267. See P. Eeckhout and T. Tridimas, 'The External Competence of the Community and the Case-Law of the Court of Justice: Principle Versus Pragmatism' (1994) 14 *YBEL* 143; N. Emiliou, 'The Death of Exclusive Competence' (1996) 20 *ELRev.* 294. See also Case C–383/93, *Polo/Lauren Company LP* v. *PT. Dwidua Langgeng Pratama IFF* [2000] ECR I–2519, and *Opinion 2/00 on the Biosafety Protocol*, judgment of 6 Dec. 2001.

[69] Limited express external powers were also conferred on the two other Communities under the Euratom and ECSC Treaties respectively.

[70] See Arts. 281 (ex 210) EC, and 101 Euratom. For discussion of the legal personality and capacity of the European Union, see 36–7 above, and 131–2 below.

(b) IMPLIED EXTERNAL COMPETENCES

For those policy areas in respect of which the Treaty does not expressly confer external competence, the case law of the Court concerning implied external powers applies. Articles 308, 94, and 95 (ex Articles 235, 100, and 100a) may be used, along with a range of other Treaty Articles (such as those on transport, social policy, and competition) which expressly establish competence in the internal sphere, as legal bases for the Community's entry into international relations.

In a series of cases beginning with the *ERTA* case[71] and leading on to the *Kramer*[72] and *Inland Waterways*[73] cases, the ECJ developed the theory of implied external competence. Such competence may flow either directly from the existence of Treaty provisions giving express power in the internal sphere or from the actual adoption of internal measures under the Treaty.

(c) EXCLUSIVITY AND ITS LIMITS

While such implied external competence could be shared between the Member States and the Community, the ECJ in *ERTA* went on to outline the concept of exclusive competence. It declared that whenever the Community acted to implement a common policy under the Treaty, the Member States would no longer have the right to take external action in an area which would affect that common policy. Subsequently in *Kramer* the ECJ ruled that while implied external powers could exist even though no internal measures had been adopted, the Member States, until such time as Community competence had been exercised, retained transitional competence to act so long as their actions were compatible with Community objectives. However, in *Opinion 1/76 on the Inland Waterways Scheme*, the Court seemed to rule that exclusive external competence could arise when exercised, without any prior exercise of internal powers, if external action by the Member States would jeopardize the objective in question. On the other hand, this was a very particular case in which it was apparently necessary to adopt international action in order to achieve the internal Community objective.[74] The relationship between the existence of external competence and the exclusivity of such external competence, however, remains complex.

The principal existing areas of exclusive external EC competence are those of the CCP (in part) and fisheries conservation. Exclusive external competence can arise, as we have seen, (a) where there are provisions of the Treaty or other internal measures to this express effect; (b) where such competence flows implicitly from the scope of

---

71 Case 22/70, *Commission* v. *Council* [1971] ECR 263.

72 Cases 3, 4, & 6/76, *Kramer* [1976] ECR 1279.

73 *Opinion 1/76 on the Draft Agreement Establishing a Laying-up Fund for Inland Waterway Vessels* [1977] ECR 741.

74 See also *Opinion 2/91*, n. 59 above. For discussion of these cases, see M. Cremona, 'External Relations and External Competence: The Emergence of an Integrated Policy', in P. Craig and G. de Búrca (eds.), *The Evolution of EU Law* (Oxford University Press, 1999), 137, and A. Dashwood and J. Heliskoski, 'The Classic Authorities Revisited', in Dashwood and Hillion (eds.), n. 67 above, 3.

internal measures adopted; or (c) where internal action can only effectively be adopted at the same time as external action.[75]

Following *Opinion 1/94 on the WTO Agreement*, a less expansive approach to the Community's exclusive external competence emerged.[76] The ECJ declared that several matters covered by the General Agreement on Trade in Services or the Agreement on Trade Related Intellectual Property Rights did not fall within the scope of the CCP and the Community did not have *exclusive* competence, since this was a field where the international action envisaged was not necessary for the attainment of some internal Community objective,[77] nor would it further the aims of some internal Community measures.[78]

Further, Article 133 (ex Article 113) was amended by the ToA after *Opinion 1/94* to empower the Council expressly to bring agreements on services and intellectual property (IP) within the scope of application of the Article. It was amended again by the TN so as to subject agreements on commercial aspects of IP and trade in services to the qualified-majority rule applicable to the CCP, but retaining the unanimity rule for certain aspects of these, including 'where an agreement includes provisions for which unanimity is required for the adoption of internal rules or where it relates to a field in which the Community has not yet exercised the powers conferred upon it by this Treaty by adopting internal rules'. Paragraph 6 of the amended Article contains two further limitations. In the first place it makes clear that the Community *lacks* external competence altogether to conclude an agreement if the agreement includes provisions which go beyond the EC's internal competence—for example by harmonizing national provisions whose harmonization is ruled out by the Treaty's rules on internal powers. In other words, there is a parallel limitation on the existence and not just the nature of EC competence in both the internal and the external spheres in this respect. Secondly, while most of the CCP—including those commercial aspects of IP and trade in services which have been included by the amendments to Article 133 (ex Article 113)—is an exclusive external competence of the Community, paragraph 6 specifies that agreements on trade relating to cultural, educational, social, and health services are a matter of shared competence and that such agreements *must* be concluded both by the Member States and by the Community.

(d) SHARED EXTERNAL COMPETENCE AND MIXED AGREEMENTS

For the most part, indeed, the external powers of the Community are shared with the Member States rather than being exclusive. Sometimes this is expressed in the Treaty and sometimes it is not.[79] When competence is shared, and where both the Community and the Member States are party to an international agreement, it is known as

---

[75] See McGoldrick, n. 67 above, ch. 4.   [76] *Opinion 1/94*, n. 68 above.
[77] See also on this point the ECJ in its *Opinion 2/00*, n. 68 above, at paras. 45–46.
[78] See more generally N. Emiliou and D. O'Keeffe (eds.), *The European Union and World Trade Law—After the GATT Uruguay Round* (Wiley, 1996); Dashwood and Hillion (eds.), n. 67 above, chs. 4, 9, and 10.
[79] On the sharing of competence in development aid, see Cases C–181 & 248/91, *European Parliament* v. *Council and Commission (Bangladesh Aid)* [1993] ECR I–3685.

a 'mixed agreement'.[80] An agreement in an area of shared competence may in some cases be signed only by the Member States,[81] or in other cases of shared competence it may be signed only by the Community.[82] However, there are areas of shared competence where an agreement involves separate and distinct obligations and responsibilities on the part of the Community and the Member States, and in such cases a mixed agreement is mandatory.[83] In either case, however, the Member States and Community must co-operate closely together in the negotiation and conclusion of agreements in fields where competence is shared.[84] Mixed agreements are legally complex and often politically controversial. They are disliked in particular by the Commission, on account of the more complex negotiation and conclusion procedures involved and the difficulties and delays in their ratification, but it is clear that mixed agreements remain an important feature of the EC's external relations.[85]

(e) THE PROCEDURAL BASIS FOR EXTERNAL ACTION

The standard procedure for negotiating and concluding international agreements is set out in Article 300(1) (ex Article 228(1)) EC.[86] The main negotiating role is played by the Commission, while the Council concludes the agreement on the basis of the Commission's proposal, having consulted the European Parliament. This basic procedure varies both in terms of the voting rules within Council, and the extent of the Parliament's involvement, which depends on the subject matter of the agreement and the procedures applicable to the adoption of internal measures.

(f) THE LEGAL BASIS FOR EXTERNAL ACTION BY THE UNION

While the focus on the Community's external powers for a long time was mainly on trade matters, we have seen that the Community has increasingly enjoyed international relations across an ever-widening sphere. Furthermore, as we saw in Chapter 1, although the EU was not expressly given legal personality on its creation, the effect of Article 24 TEU added by the ToA was to confer upon it the capacity to enter international agreements.[87] This provision applies to the conclusion of agreements under the second Common Foreign and Security Policy Pillar,[88] and also, in

---

[80] For an early account see M. Cremona, 'The Doctrine of Exclusivity and the Position of Mixed Agreements in the External Relations of the European Community' (1982) 2 *OJLS* 393.

[81] *Opinion 2/91*, n. 59 above.

[82] See, e.g., on development policy Case C–268/94, *Portugal* v. *Council* [1996] ECR I–6177.

[83] See the distinction drawn by A. Rosas between 'obligatory' and 'facultative' mixity: 'The EU and Mixed Agreements', in Dashwood and Hillion (eds.), n. 67 above, 200.

[84] *Opinion 1/78* [1979] ECR 2871. See C. Timmermans, 'Organising Joint Particiation of EC and Member States' and S. Hyett 'The Duty of Co-operation: A Flexible Concept', in Dashwood and Hillion (eds.), n. 67 above, 239 and 248 respectively.

[85] See A. Rosas, n. 83 above, and more generally D. O'Keeffe and H. Schermers (eds.), *Mixed Agreements* (Martinus Nijhoff, 1983).

[86] This Art. was amended by the ToA in various ways.

[87] See Ch. 1 and text accompanying n. 82.

[88] On the overlap between the CCP and CFSP see Case C–124/95, *R. ex parte Centro-Com* v. *HM Treasury and Bank of England* [1997] ECR 81. Also on dual-use goods see Case C–70/94, *Werner* v. *Germany* [1995] ECR I–3189 and Case C–83/94, *Leifer* [1995] ECR I–3231, noted by Govaere (1997) 34 *CMLRev.* 1019. See also P. Koutrakos, *Trade, Foreign Policy and Defence in EU Constitutional Law* (Hart, 2001).

accordance with Article 38 TEU, to those under the third pillar on Police and Judicial Co-operation in Criminal Matters (PJCC). External action under the third pillar has certainly come to prominence since 11 September 2001. More generally, the consistency and coherence of EU and EC external relations, and the compatibility of the respective bases for action under the different pillars is likely to become increasingly salient following the recognition of the international capacity of the Union.[89]

7. THE PRINCIPLE OF SUBSIDIARITY

Closely linked to the question of the *existence* of Community competence, and the identification of an adequate Treaty basis for action, is the principle of subsidiarity, which is intended to regulate the lawfulness of the *exercise* of Community competence. We shall see, however, that these two are not conceptually as distinct as they may at first appear. The centrality of subsidiarity to the Maastricht negotiations is well known. For those who feared further movement to some species of federalist Community the concept of subsidiarity was the panacea designed to halt such centralizing initiatives. The 'S' concept was to be used to defeat those who hoped to increase the federalist leanings of the Community under the TEU. It was one of the symbols used to placate the Tory right wing during those long nights spent debating the TEU at Westminster. The meaning of subsidiarity is, however, far from clear. We can at least be clear about the wording of Article 5 EC (ex Article 3b):

The Community shall act within the limits of the powers conferred upon it by this Treaty and of the objectives assigned to it therein.

In areas which do not fall within its exclusive competence, the Community shall take action, in accordance with the principle of subsidiarity, only if and in so far as the objectives of the proposed action cannot be sufficiently achieved by the Member States and can therefore, by reason of the scale or effects of the proposed action, be better achieved by the Community.

Any action by the Community shall not go beyond what is necessary to achieve the objectives of this Treaty.

(a) THE COMMUNITY MUST ACT WITHIN THE LIMITS OF ITS POWERS

This requirement, in the first paragraph of Article 5, need not detain us for long. It has always been recognized that the Community only has competence within the limited areas in which it has been given power. The extent to which this serves as a limit has, however, been reduced by the expansion of the areas over which the Community has competence. Thus the SEA, the TEU, and the ToA have added significantly to the subject-matter competence of the Community. The ECJ has moreover interpreted the Community's legislative competence broadly through recognition of the implied-powers doctrine, and through the use of Article 308 (ex Article 235).

---

[89] See R. Wessel, 'The Inside Looking Out: Consistency and Delimitation in EU External Relations' (2000) 37 *CMLRev*. 1135.

(b) THE EXCLUSIVE COMPETENCE OF THE COMMUNITY

The second point of our inquiry is, in some ways, the most crucial. Article 5 (ex Article 3b) makes it clear that subsidiarity will have to be considered only in relation to areas which do *not* fall within the exclusive competence of the Community. If an area is within the Community's exclusive competence then there is no legal obligation to apply subsidiarity, although it is in fact taken into account.

The problem is that there is no ready criterion for distinguishing between those areas which are, and those which are not, within the Community's exclusive competence. The Treaty itself is not explicitly framed in these terms, and thus the meaning of this phrase is contestable. The Commission has taken the view that an area falls within the exclusive competence of the Community if the Treaties impose on the Community a duty to act, in the sense that it has sole responsibility for the performance of a particular task.[90] It has argued that there is a 'block' of exclusive powers which are joined by the thread of the internal market, including: free movement of goods, persons, services, and capital; the Common Commercial Policy; competition; the Common Agricultural Policy (CAP); the conservation of fisheries; and transport policy.

Commentators who have examined the problem differ considerably, and there are both broad and narrow constructions of the term 'exclusive competence'. Toth provides the argument in favour of the broad view.

A.G. Toth, A Legal Analysis of Subsidiarity[91]

The Court has confirmed time and again . . . that in all matters transferred to the Community from the Member States, the Community's competence is, in principle, exclusive and leaves no room for concurrent competence on the part of the Member States. Therefore, where the competence of the Community begins, that of the Member States ends. From then on, Member States no longer have the power unilaterally to introduce legislation. They can act only within the limits of strictly defined management/implementing powers delegated back to the national authorities by the Community institutions. As the Court of Justice has stated: 'The existence of Community powers excludes the possibility of concurrent powers on the part of the Member States.'[92] Even the fact that during a certain period the Community fails to exercise a competence which has been transferred to it, does not create concurrent competence for the Member States during that period. This principle also follows from, or is closely related to, the doctrine of the supremacy of Community law, which of course is a basic tenet of Community law.

The central feature of this broad view is that the Community's exclusive competence exists in those areas in which the Member States have transferred power to the

---

[90] Bull. EC 10–1992, 116. See *1st Report of Commission on Subsidiarity*, COM(94)533. A similar view is taken in Wyatt and Dashwood's *European Union Law* (Sweet & Maxwell, 4th edn., 2000), 158–9.

[91] D. O'Keeffe and P.M. Twomey (eds.), *Legal Issues of the Maastricht Treaty* (Chancery, 1994), 39–40.

[92] The quotation comes from the *ERTA* case: Case 22/70, *Commission* v. *Council* [1971] ECR 263, 276.

Community, *irrespective* of whether the Community has actually exercised this power. From this premise Toth concluded that subsidiarity could not apply to any matter covered by the original EEC Treaty, including: the free movement of goods, services, persons, and capital; the Common Commercial Policy; competition; the Common Agricultural Policy; Transport Policy; and the common organization of the fisheries. Toth accepted that the Community did not possess exclusive competence within many of the newer areas in which it had been given some power, such as the environment, economic and social cohesion, education and vocational training, consumer protection, and Social Policy. This was because the relevant Treaty Articles were framed so as to give the Community more limited powers in these spheres. Community legislation on, for example, the environment or health could however also facilitate the completion of the internal market. This would, for Toth, take such matters outside the remit of subsidiarity.[93]

This view of the term 'exclusive competence' has not gone unchallenged. Steiner adopts a narrower construction.

J. Steiner, Subsidiarity under the Maastricht Treaty[94]

The EC, even at its beginnings, was not concerned with dividing competence between the Community and the Member States, but with sharing powers over a wide range of activity in order to achieve certain common and mutually beneficial objectives. Whilst it was clear that in some areas there would be little scope for action by Member States if the desired goal was to be achieved—a customs union is a necessary prerequisite to a single market—in most areas competence was concurrent. This did not mean that States and the Community could legislate on the same issue at the same time, nor that States' competence in these matters was unrestrained (since they are bound to comply with the rules of the EC Treaty), but that their action would be complementary or supplementary. Once the Community has exercised its powers under the Treaty, to regulate a particular matter within a certain area of activity, clearly States are not free to enact measures which conflict with those rules. As the volume and scope of Community law increase, so will States' powers diminish. But there are few areas of activity in which Member States do not retain some degree of competence. Thus it is not surprising that commentators have had difficulty in identifying areas in which the Community has exclusive competence, nor that the Heads of State refrained from doing so at Maastricht.

One is forced to the conclusion that the only areas in which the Community has exclusive competence for the purposes of Article 3b are those in which it *has already legislated*. . . . Surely the competence of Member States ends, not as Toth suggests, where the competence of the Community begins, but where its powers have been exercised. . . . The fact that the competence to act, even to act comprehensively, has been granted to the Community by the Treaty does not, and surely cannot mean that its competence to act in these areas cannot be subject to the subsidiarity principle. To allow whole areas of activity to escape scrutiny under paragraph 2, simply because the Community has potential competence in these areas, would surely undermine the very purpose for which this provision was intended.

---

[93] A.G. Toth, 'A Legal Analysis of Subsidiarity', 41.
[94] O'Keeffe and Twomey (eds.), n. 91 above, 57–8. Italics in the original.

The difference between this view and that advanced by Toth is readily apparent. Steiner's hypothesis is that subsidiarity will be excluded only where the Community has actually exercised its power; only in such areas will the Community have exclusive competence. Time will tell which of these formulations most accurately captures the meaning of Article 5 (ex Article 3b) EC. A decision of the ECJ will be required before the matter can be settled.

There is, none the less, one crucial respect in which the Steiner formulation needs clarification. For Steiner the key idea is that the Community must have exercised the power in the relevant area. Community power can, however, be exercised through the passage of formal regulations, directives, etc., or through the ECJ's decisions. The principles relating to the free movement of goods have, for example, been implemented in part by Community legislation, and in part by seminal Court decisions which have shaped the EC legislation.[95] It is clear that Steiner's approach would have to be construed so as to capture both modes of exercising Community power, and thus even the narrow formulation of the phrase 'exclusive competence' might not be as narrow as initially thought. This is particularly important, given the ECJ's contribution to many areas of EC law, and given also that legislative and judicial power so often interact.[96]

(c) THE SUBSIDIARITY PRINCIPLE ITSELF

We can now examine the subsidiarity principle itself. The Community is to take action 'only if and in so far as the objectives of the proposed action cannot be sufficiently achieved by the Member States and can therefore by reason of the scale or effects of the proposed action, be better achieved by the Community'. Article 5(3) adds the further condition that 'any action by the Community shall not go beyond what is necessary to achieve the objectives of this Treaty'. It seems clear that the drafting of Article 5 was influenced by the experience of German law concerning the relationship of the Federal authorities and the *Länder*.[97]

Subsidiarity embraces three separate, albeit related, ideas. The Community is to take action only if the objectives of that action cannot be sufficiently achieved by the Member States. The Community can better achieve the action, because of its scale or effects. If the Community does take action then this should not go beyond what is necessary to achieve the Treaty objectives. The first two parts of this formulation entail what the Commission has termed a test of comparative efficiency:[98] is it better for the action to be taken by the Community or the Member States? The third part of the formulation brings in a proportionality test.

The 1993 Inter-institutional Agreement on Procedures for Implementing the Principle of Subsidiarity required all three institutions to have regard to the principle when devising Community legislation. This was re-confirmed by the Protocol on

---

[95] See Ch. 15 below. [96] See Chs. 2, 4, 5, and 26.
[97] N. Emiliou, 'Subsidiarity: An Effective Barrier Against the "Enterprises of Ambition"?' (1992) 17 *ELRev.* 383 and 'Subsidiarity: Panacea or Fig Leaf?', in *Legal Issues of the Maastricht Treaty*, n. 91 above, ch. 5.
[98] Commission Communication to the Council and the European Parliament, Bull. EC 10–1992, 116.

the Application of the Principles of Subsidiarity and Proportionality attached to the ToA.[99] The Commission must provide in its explanatory memorandum concerning proposed legislation a justification for the measure in terms of the subsidiarity principle (paragraphs 4, 5, and 9 of the Protocol), and submit an annual report on the application of Article 5 (paragraph 9). Amendments by the Council or the European Parliament must likewise be accompanied by a justification in terms of subsidiarity, if they entail more extensive Community intervention (paragraph 11). The form of the Community legislation should be as simple as possible, with a preference for framework directives over regulations (paragraph 6). The Protocol none the less confirmed that subsidiarity applied only where the Community did not have exclusive competence, and that the subsidiarity principle did not call into question the powers conferred on the EC, as interpreted by the ECJ (paragraph 3). Time will tell how subsidiarity in practice affects the scope and nature of Community legislation. Two comments are in order at this juncture.

On the one hand, it is clear that there will be many areas in which the comparative efficiency calculus comes out in favour of Community action. The idea that matters should be dealt with at the level closest to those affected is fine in principle. The very *raison d'être* of the Community will, however, often demand Community action to ensure the uniformity of *general approach* which is of central importance to the realization of a common market. This is confirmed by the Commission's reports made pursuant to Article 9 of the Protocol.[100]

On the other hand, the very existence of Article 5, and in particular paragraph 3 thereof, will, as is apparent from paragraph 6 of the Protocol, have an impact on the existence and form of Community action. The Commission will consider whether action really is required at Community level, and its reasoning will be found in the recitals or explanatory memorandum.[101] If Community action is required, the Commission will proceed through directives rather than regulations. There will be a greater use of guidelines and codes of conduct. The idea of Community control with a 'lighter touch' fits with changes which pre-date the TEU. Thus, as we shall see when considering the completion of the Single Market,[102] the new approach to harmonization entails a less detailed and less rigid form of Community oversight. Minimum, rather than total, harmonization is now more the norm.

(d) THE ROLE OF THE COURT

It is clear that questions concerning the interpretation of Article 5 (ex Article 3b) can be adjudicated by the ECJ. The real issue is, therefore, as to the intensity of the judicial review process. We shall see that the Court reviews Community action with varying degrees of intensity.[103] Much will depend upon the intensity with which it decides to

---

[99] See G. de Búrca, 'Reappraising Subsidiarity's Significance after Amsterdam', Jean Monnet Working Paper 7/1999, www.jeanmonnetprogram.org/.

[100] Commission Report to the European Council, *Better Lawmaking 1999*, COM(1999)562 final, 2.

[101] Commission Report to the European Council, *Better Lawmaking 2000*, COM(2000)772 final, 4–8, 15–21.

[102] See Ch. 28 below.   [103] See 537–40 below.

review, for example, a Commission assertion that, on grounds of comparative efficiency, Community action was required in a particular area. The ECJ may well be faced with difficulties in this regard. If it takes a detailed look at the evidence underlying the Commission's claim it will have to adjudicate on what may be a complex socio-economic calculus concerning the most effective level of government for different regulatory tasks. If, by way of contrast, the ECJ decides to be less intensive, and only to intervene if there is some manifest error, it may be open to the critique from Member States that it is effectively denuding the obligation in Article 5 of all content. There is clearly a danger that the judicial process will become politicized.

The indications are that the ECJ will not lightly overturn Community action on the ground that it does not comply with Article 5. This is apparent in *procedural* terms from *Germany v. European Parliament and Council*.[104] The ECJ held that Article 190 (now Article 253) EC did not require that Community measures contain an express reference to the subsidiarity principle. It was sufficient that the recitals to the measure made it clear why the Community institutions believed that the aims of the measure could best be attained by Community action. The difficulty of overturning a measure because of subsidiarity is equally apparent in *substantive* terms from the *Working Time Directive* case.[105] The UK argued that the contested Directive infringed the principle of subsidiarity, since it had not been shown that action at Community level would provide clear benefits compared with action at national level. The ECJ disposed of the argument briskly. It was, said the Court, the responsibility of the Council under Article 118a (now Article 138) to adopt minimum requirements so as to contribute to the improvement of health and safety. Once the Council had found it necessary to improve the existing level of protection and to harmonize the law in this area while maintaining the improvements already made, achievement of that objective necessarily presupposed Community-wide action. A similarly 'light' judicial approach to subsidiarity review is evident in the *Biotechnology Directive* case.[106]

A range of suggestions has been made in recent years, by the UK Prime Minister Tony Blair, amongst others, for the establishment of a non-judicial forum to consider the compatibility of proposed Community action with the subsidiarity principle. Proposals have ranged from a specially constituted 'subsidiarity committee' to a second chamber of the European Parliament, to the COSAC (conference of EC and European Affairs committees of national parliaments). However difficult the concept of subsidiarity may be to define, it seems certain that the Court and possibly, in the future, another designated institution will be called to interpret it in various practical contexts.

---

[104] Case C–233/94, n. 52 above, paras. 26–28.   [105] Case C–84/94, n. 38 above, paras. 46–7, 55.
[106] Case C–377/98, *Netherlands v. Council*, n. 52 above.

8. CONCLUSION

i.   It is important to stress, as noted at the outset, that EC policy in any particular area will be made by various formal legal norms. A basic regulation can be made more concrete through directives or decisions. The foundational provision may equally well be a directive or even a decision. These formal legal norms will be supplemented by a plethora of soft-law devices.

ii. The conditions for the legality of Community action raise the fundamental issue as to the limits of Community competence. It is axiomatic that the EC has only the powers ascribed to it, but defining those so as to impose meaningful limits on Community competence is difficult to say the least. This is a task to be dealt with at the IGC in 2004. Experience from other polities where legislative competence is divided between the centre and state authorities indicates that a neat formulaic solution will not be possible.

iii. The ECJ is often cast as the 'villain' in this regard, by construing Articles 308 (ex Article 235) and 95 (ex Article 100a) very broadly. It should none the less be recognized that the greatest expansion of Community competence has been through successive Treaty revisions. It has been the Member States themselves that have been willing to accord new competences to the EC. The fact that the EC may only have been given limited competence over these areas does not change the substance of this point. In some ways, it reinforces it. The very fact that EC competence is shared, in differing ways in different areas, makes the task of 'limiting' or 'defining' Community competence even more problematic.

9. FURTHER READING

DASHWOOD, A., and HILLION, C. (eds.), *The General Law of EC External Relations* (Sweet & Maxwell, 2000)

O'KEEFFE, D., and TWOMEY, P.M. (eds.), *Legal Issues of the Maastricht Treaty* (Chancery, 1994)

SNYDER, F. (ed.), *Constitutional Dimensions of European Economic Integration* (Kluwer, 1996)

TRIDIMAS, T., *The General Principles of EC Law* (Oxford University Press, 1999)

WEATHERILL, S., *Law and Integration in the European Union* (Clarendon, 1995)

4

COMMUNITY LEGISLATION AND POLICY-MAKING

1. CENTRAL ISSUES

i. The previous Chapter focused on the forms of Community action, and the scope of Community powers. The present Chapter will consider the *process by which the Community enacts legislation*.

ii. The *legislative procedures under the Community pillar are complex*. They are however becoming simpler, although more could still be done in this respect.

iii. There are *issues of principle concerning the way in which the Community makes delegated legislation*. There is the perennial problem of reconciling the need for the expeditious passage of detailed regulatory norms, with some measure of legislative oversight.

iv. It is also necessary to consider in outline the *legislative process that applies under the second and third pillars*.

v. *It is important to understand the way in which legislation is made in practice*. The planning of the overall legislative agenda, and the passage of particular regulations or directives, involves interaction between Community institutions, interest groups, national Parliaments, and national bureaucracies.

vi. There is a *rich debate about democracy and legitimacy within the EU*. An understanding of the issues involved in this discourse is, as we shall see, a condition precedent for having something meaningful to say about it.

2. THE LEGISLATIVE PROCESS UNDER THE COMMUNITY PILLAR: SIX PROCEDURES

The distinguishing characteristic of the different legislative procedures is, principally, the degree of power afforded to the European Parliament. The European Parliament was given the smallest part to play in the legislative process in the original Rome Treaty. All subsequent Treaty modifications have increased its role, in ways politically acceptable to the other major players. There are three keys to preserving sanity when seeking to understand the Community's legislative procedures and their evolution.

First, one should dispel any thought of identifying a single body as the 'legislature' for the Community as a whole. The players which comprise the legislature vary in the different procedures described below.

The second key to emerging mentally intact is to realize that there is no magic formula determining which of these procedures applies in any area of the Treaty. Do not search for one. Which legislative procedure applies is dependent, in *formal* terms, upon what is specified under any particular Treaty Article. In so far as there is any *substantive* criterion which has determined this allocation it has been political: the European Parliament has sought to maximize the application of the procedures which give it most power.

Finally, while it is easy to lose sight of the wood for the trees, it should be recognized that 'some' measure of order is now being instilled into the legislative process as a result of the ToA. The Community institutions were mindful of the complexity of the legislative procedures and its damaging effect on the overall legitimacy of the EC. This is readily apparent from their respective reports for the 1996 IGC that led to the ToA.[1] While the number of legislative procedures has not in itself been altered by the ToA, this should not mask the fact that most important legislation made under the EC Treaty will now be governed by the co-decision procedure contained in Article 251 EC. The discussion should be read with this firmly in mind.

(a) COMMISSION ACTING ALONE

This is quite rare. The Treaty does, however, accord the Commission a power to make legislation without intervention from the other institutions in some areas. For example,[2] the Commission has power under Article 86(3) (ex Article 90(3)) to promulgate directives or decisions to ensure the application of this Article, which is concerned with the role of the State in relation to public undertakings. The Commission has exercised this power to enact a directive on the transparency of financial relations between Member States and public undertakings,[3] and a directive on competition as it relates to the telecommunications terminal market.[4] Member States challenged both directives, in part because Commission legislation made under Article 86(3) excludes the States, as represented in the Council, from any formal role in the legislative process. The Member States argued that a different Article of the Treaty should have been used, which would have given them such a role.[5]

(b) COUNCIL AND COMMISSION ACTING ALONE

There are a number of areas where the Council and the Commission can take action without any intervention by the European Parliament at all. The Council will act on a proposal from the Commission and take the decision in accordance with the voting requirement laid down in the relevant Treaty Article.[6] The Council may choose to consult the Parliament, but does not have to do so. This legislative procedure is used, for example, in relation to aspects of free movement of workers and of capital, economic policy, and the common commercial policy.

---

[1] P. Craig, 'Democracy and Rulemaking within the EC: An Empirical and Normative Assessment' (1997) 3 *ELJ* 105.

[2] The Commission can, e.g., act on its own initiative under Art. 39(3)(d) (ex Art. 48(3)(d)) EC.

[3] Dir. 80/723 [1980] OJ L195/35.

[4] Dir. 88/301 [1988] OJ L131/73.

[5] For discussion of these cases, see Ch. 27 below.

[6] See, e.g., Arts. 26, 45, 49, 55, 57, 60, 96, 99, 104, 133(2) (ex Arts. 28, 55, 59, 66, 73c, 73g, 101, 103, 104c, 113(2)) EC.

(c) COUNCIL, COMMISSION, AND CONSULTATION WITH PARLIAMENT

The original Rome Treaty concentrated power in the Commission and the Council: the former would propose a measure and the latter would vote upon it. The only role for the European Parliament was a consultative one. This existed only where specified by a particular Treaty Article.

There are still a number of areas in which the Parliament is limited in this manner. The Council must wait for the Parliament's opinion. If it does not the measure may be annulled.[7] The Parliament may have to be reconsulted where there are important changes to the measure, not prompted by the Parliament itself, after the initial consultation and prior to its adoption by the Council.[8] None the less, a bare requirement to consult with the European Parliament is all that is required. The Council is not bound to adopt the Parliament's opinion. The legislative process is still dominated by the Council and the Commission in these areas. Particular Treaty Articles can also stipulate that the Committee of the Regions or the Economic and Social Committee should be consulted.

The topics on which the Parliament has only a bare right to be consulted include, after the ToA: Article 19 (ex Article 8b), concerning rights to vote and stand in municipal elections; Article 22 (ex Article 8e), reinforcing citizenship rights; Article 89 (ex Article 94), State aids; Article 93 (ex Article 99), harmonization of indirect taxation; Article 94 (ex Article 100), approximation of laws for the functioning of the common market; Article 107(6) (ex Article 106(6)), provisions relating to the Statute of the European System of Central Banks; Article 175(2) (ex Article 130s(2)), fiscal measures etc. relating to the environment; Article 67(1), concerning visas, asylum etc.; the new Article 13, dealing with measures to combat various forms of discrimination; the new Article 128, dealing with guidelines for Member States in relation to their employment policies; Article 21 TEU, concerning the general direction of common foreign and security policy; and Article 39 TEU dealing with police and judicial co-operation in criminal matters.

(d) COUNCIL, COMMISSION, AND THE CO-OPERATION PROCEDURE WITH THE EUROPEAN PARLIAMENT

It was to be nearly thirty years before there was any real modification to allow the European Parliament a greater say in the legislative process. In so far as there was any attempted justification for the limited role accorded to the Parliament it was based on the claim that, since this body was at the inception of the Community only indirectly

---

[7] Case 138/79, *Roquette Frères* v. *Council* [1980] ECR 3333; Case C–65/93, *European Parliament* v. *Council (Re Generalized Tariff Preferences)* [1995] ECR I–643; Case C–156/93, *European Parliament* v. *Commission (Re Genetically Modified Micro-organisms in Organic Products)* [1995] 3 CMLR 707.

[8] Case C–388/92, *European Parliament* v. *Council* [1994] ECR I–2067; Case C–417/93, *European Parliament* v. *Council (Re Continuation of the TACIS Programme)* [1995] ECR I–1185; Case C–21/94, *European Parliament* v. *Council (Re Road Taxes)* [1996] 1 CMLR 94. Where the changes are either technical or in accordance with the Parliament's wishes reconsultation may not be necessary: Case 41/69, *ACF Chemiefarma* v. *Commission* [1970] ECR 661; Case 817/79, *Buyl* v. *Commission* [1982] ECR 245; Case C–331/88, *R.* v. *Minister of Agriculture, Fisheries and Food and Secretary of State for Health, ex p. FEDESA* [1990] ECR I–4023.

elected, its claim to participate in the legislative process was thereby weakened. This argument was palpably flawed. The indirectly elected Parliament had as strong, or stronger, a democratic claim to participate in the legislative process as any of the other Community institutions. In any event the argument failed even in its own terms after the advent of direct elections. Notwithstanding this obvious fact there was no rush by the other institutions to accord a greater democratic role to the Parliament. Quite the contrary. The attempts by the Parliament to secure for itself an equal role with the Council in the legislative process were studiously ignored or sidelined in the negotiations which led up to the SEA. What did emerge was a good deal less than equal status, although it did at least give the Parliament more power than it had hitherto.

The change brought about by the SEA is now, after the ToA, Article 252 EC (ex Article 189c). This procedure applies whenever the Treaty provides that the adoption of an act is to be in accordance with Article 252.

(1) The Council acting on a proposal from the Commission, and after obtaining an Opinion from the European Parliament, adopts a common position.[9]

(2) This is then communicated to the European Parliament (EP). The Council and the Commission are to inform the EP fully of the reasons that led the Council to adopt its common position, and also the Commission's position. If within three months the EP has either approved the common position or has not taken a decision then the Council shall definitively adopt the act in accord with the common position.[10]

(3) If the Parliament rejects the common position by an absolute majority of its component members then the Council can adopt the act only by unanimity. The Parliament may, alternatively, within three months propose amendments by an absolute majority of its component members.[11]

(4) If the latter occurs, it is then for the Commission within one month to re-examine the original proposal in the light of the EP's amendments. The Commission then forwards the re-examined proposal to the Council, together with the amendments of the EP which it has not accepted, and must express an opinion on these amendments. The Council may then adopt such amendments by unanimity.[12]

(5) The Council, acting by qualified majority, shall then adopt the proposal as re-examined by the Commission. Unanimity is required in the Council to amend the proposal as re-examined by the Commission.[13]

(6) The Council must act within three months in the situations covered by 3, 4, and 5 above. If no decision is made within this period then the Commission proposal will be deemed not to have been adopted.[14]

(7) The periods referred to in 2 and 6 may be extended by a maximum of one month by common accord between the Council and the EP.[15]

---

[9] Art. 252(a).   [10] Art. 252(b).   [11] Art. 252(c).
[12] Art. 252(d).   [13] Art. 252(e).   [14] Art. 252(f).
[15] Art. 252(g).

The co-operation procedure gave the European Parliament a greater role in the legislative process than hitherto. It gave the EP two readings for any proposed measure. The first, as identified in paragraph 1, occurred when the EP gave an opinion on the measure before the Council adopted its common position. The second reading takes place after the Council adopted its common position. The EP then has the options set out in paragraphs 2 and 5. The EP has rejected the Council's common position on only a limited number of occasions.[16] It has, however, tabled a large number of amendments, both at the first and the second reading stage, and has had a reasonably good success rate in getting its amendments accepted.[17]

When it was originally introduced by the SEA what is now Article 252 EC was used for many of the measures to implement the single market. For example, measures to achieve the internal market passed under Article 95 (hitherto Article 100a) required the use of the co-operation procedure. So too did directives to facilitate the mutual recognition of diplomas under Article 47 (ex Article 57). The TEU changed this, upgrading the EP's participation, by stipulating the stronger procedure of Article 251 (ex Article 189b) described below.[18] The ToA has continued this process of upgrading,[19] and hence the areas to which Article 252 now applies are mainly concerned with Economic and Monetary Union.[20]

While the range of application of Article 252 EC has therefore diminished this should not serve to mask the importance of its introduction in the SEA. It had an important effect on the entire legislative process as is brought out in the following extract.

M. Westlake, The Commission and the Parliament: Partners and Rivals in the European Policy-Making Process[21]

The Single European Act in general, and the co-operation procedure in particular, represented a major constitutional innovation in the Community system. . . .

First, it was immediately apparent that a badly-administered co-operation procedure could lead to blockages and delays. The Commission considered the potential stalling or loss of legislation to be the major risk of the new procedure, particularly in the field of the internal market, where the Single European Act had also introduced a 31 December 1992 deadline. The Commission's reaction was two-fold: internal reform, and increased inter-institutional co-operation, particularly with the Parliament.

---

[16] D. Earnshaw and D. Judge, 'The European Parliament and the Sweeteners Directive: From Footnote to Inter-institutional Conflict' (1993) 31 *JCMS* 1; R. Corbett, 'Testing the New Procedures: The European Parliament's First Experience with its New "Single Act" Powers' (1989) 27 *JCMS* 4.

[17] M. Westlake, *The Commission and the Parliament: Partners and Rivals in the European Policy-Making Process* (Butterworths, 1994), 39.

[18] The TEU also upgraded the legislative process which is required in certain areas from the ordinary consultation procedure to the co-operation procedure of Art. 252 EC.

[19] See, e.g., the upgrading to the Art. 251 procedure in the context of: transport, Art. 71 (ex Art. 75) EC; social policy, Art. 137 (ex Art. 118); the European Social Fund, Art. 148 (ex Art. 125); European Regional Fund, Art. 162 (ex Art. 130e); the environment, Art. 175 (ex Art. 130s).

[20] See, e.g., Arts. 102 and 103 (ex Arts. 104a and b) EC.

[21] N. 17 above, 37–8.

Second, the procedure accords the Commission important gate-keeping functions at various stages in the procedure which frequently involve it in delicate political arbitration. It must draft its proposals with an eye to what will 'play' in Parliament, as well as in the Council. It is involved in the Council deliberations leading to the Common Position. . . . It must give Parliament its opinion on the Common Position. It must assist Parliament in its deliberations on the Common Position. Should amendments be carried, the Commission must decide whether to accept them (and which). The Commission frequently finds itself in the invidious position of regretfully refusing parliamentary amendments because they may upset the delicate balance of a Common Position qualified majority in the Council.

Third, both the Commission and the Parliament immediately recognised the fundamental importance of the first reading stage. At this point there is no majority requirement, nor any deadline, and Parliament can still hope to influence Council deliberations before a Common Position has coalesced. From the Commission's point of view, parliamentary emphasis on the first reading diminishes the risk of blockage at the second stage and reduces the number of situations where the Commission has to arbitrate between conflicting institutional desires. Clearly, emphasis on the first reading has given Parliament's power of delay fresh significance.

Fourth, and more generally, the co-operation procedure entailed a general change in institutional attitudes, particularly in the Commission and the Council. Parliament's powers in the legislative process were transformed from the weak and essentially unconstructive power of delay to a stronger and potentially constructive role in the drafting of legislation.

(e) COUNCIL, COMMISSION, AND EUROPEAN PARLIAMENT: THE ARTICLE 251 PROCEDURE[22]

The TEU introduced another procedure, which bolstered still further the powers of the European Parliament. It is known as the 'co-decision' procedure. It is designed to prevent a measure being adopted without the approval of the Council and the European Parliament, and it places emphasis on the reaching of a jointly approved text. The procedure has been modified by the ToA and is now contained in Article 251 EC (ex Article 189b). It applies whenever the Treaty refers to it for the adoption of an act.

    (1) The Commission's proposal is sent to both the Council and the European Parliament (EP). The Council, acting by qualified majority, after obtaining the opinion of the EP, can adopt the act if it approves of the amendments contained in the EP's opinion or if the EP does not propose any amendments.[23]

    (2) If neither of the above occurs the Council shall adopt a common position which is communicated to the EP. The Council must inform the EP fully of the reasons which led it to adopt that position. The Commission is also obliged to inform the EP fully of its position.[24]

    (3) If within three months of the common position being communicated to the EP it either approves of the common position or does not take a decision,

---

[22] A. Dashwood, 'Community Legislative Procedures in the Era of the Treaty on European Union' (1994) 19 *ELRev.* 343.

[23] Art. 251(2).   [24] Art. 251(2).

then the act will be deemed to have been adopted in accordance with the common position.[25]

(4) If the Parliament rejects by an absolute majority of its component members the common position, the proposed act will be deemed not to have been adopted.[26]

(5) If the EP proposes amendments to the common position by an absolute majority of its component members, the amended text is then forwarded to the Council and Commission, which shall deliver an opinion on the amendments.[27]

(6) If, within three months of the matter being referred to it, the Council, acting by a qualified majority, approves of all the EP's amendments, the act will be deemed to have been adopted in the form of the common position thus amended. This is subject to the qualification that the Council must act unanimously in relation to any amendments on which the Commission has delivered a negative opinion. If the Council does not approve of all the amendments then the President of the Council, in agreement with the President of the EP, shall convene a meeting of the Conciliation Committee within six weeks.[28]

(7) The Conciliation Committee has an equal number of representatives from the Council and the European Parliament. Its task is to reach agreement on a joint text by a qualified majority of those representing the Council and a majority of those representing the EP. The Commission takes part in the Committee's work and will attempt to reconcile the disagreements between Council and the EP. The discussion starts from the common position together with the EP's proposed amendments.[29]

(8) If within six weeks the Conciliation Committee approves a joint text, then there is a further period of six weeks in which the EP, by absolute majority of the votes cast, and the Council, by qualified majority, can adopt the act in accordance with the joint text. If one of the two institutions fails to do so then the act is deemed not to have been adopted.[30]

(9) Where the Conciliation Committee does not approve a joint text, the proposed act shall be deemed not to have been adopted.[31]

(10) The periods of three months and six weeks referred to above can be extended by a maximum of one month and two weeks respectively at the initiative of the EP or the Council. However Declaration 34 attached to the ToA stated that the institutions should strictly respect the deadlines, and have recourse to these time extensions only where strictly necessary.

Article 251 has become the method for the making of most Community legislation. It applies to the preponderance of important legislation produced under the EC

---

[25] Art. 251(2)(a).   [26] Art. 251(2)(b).   [27] Art. 251(2)(c).
[28] Art. 251(3).   [29] Art. 251(4).   [30] Art. 251(5).
[31] Art. 251(6).

Treaty, and its application has been extended by the TN.[32] It is therefore important to understand the procedure.[33]

We can begin by making clear *the structure of Article 251*. The EP has two readings, the first of which occurs when the EP gives its opinion to the Council before the latter adopts a common position. The second reading takes place on the assumption that the Council has not approved all the EP's first-reading amendments, or if it has other amendments of its own, which must be passed unanimously in the Council.[34] If this happens then the Council communicates its common position to the EP, which then has the option to approve, reject, or propose amendments to the measure. If the EP suggests amendments, not all of which are acceptable to the Council, then the Conciliation Committee comes into operation. The EP and Council must approve the joint text from the Conciliation Committee.

The *ToA modified Article 251 so as to expedite the procedure and to strengthen further the position of the EP.*[35] The procedure was *expedited* because an act can now be adopted after the EP's first reading, provided that the Council agrees with any EP proposals. The Council will adopt a common position only if it disagrees with the EP's views. The modified procedure has also been expedited by the removal of what was in effect a further stage, which occurred if the Conciliation Committee was unable to agree a joint text. The procedure has further *strengthened* the position of the EP. The bottom line under the co-decision procedure has always been that the EP can actually veto legislation of which it disapproves, although it cannot actually force the Council to accept its amendments. The changes made by the ToA have improved the EP's role in this process. A rejection by the EP of the Council's common position now means that the proposed act will be deemed not to have been adopted, whereas previously it would have led to a meeting of the Conciliation Committee unless the EP reconfirmed that rejection.[36] Moreover, the co-decision procedure as modified by the ToA does not allow the Council to press forward with a measure after failure to reach agreement on a joint text in the Conciliation Committee.[37]

The *co-decision procedure has been modified in practice through the institutionaliza-tion of trialogues.*[38] These are informal meetings that precede, and can exist alongside, formal meetings of the Conciliation Committee. They have been common since

[32] See, e.g., Arts. 13(2), 65, 157(3), 159 third para., 191 third para.

[33] Particular Treaty Arts. may add to the Art. 251 procedure by requiring consultation with the Committee of the Regions and/or the Economic and Social Committee.

[34] Art. 250(1) (ex Art. 189a(1)).

[35] The practical implementation of these reforms were dealt with in the *Joint Declaration On Practical Arrangements for the New Co-Decision Procedure* [1999] OJ C148/1.

[36] Moreover, if the Conciliation Committee is unable to agree on a joint text the proposed measure is deemed not to have been adopted, whereas previously the EP might, if the Council re-confirmed its common position, have had to reject the measure once again in what was in effect a third reading.

[37] Under the co-decision procedure as introduced by the TEU the Council could, after failure to reach agreement in the Conciliation Committee, confirm its common position, in which case the measure would be adopted, unless the EP rejected the text by an absolute majority of its component members. Rule 78 of the EP's Rules of Procedure however signalled that the EP would vote against the measure, should the Council attempt to press forward with it in these circumstances. The changes to co-decision made by the ToA have formally removed this power from the Council.

[38] *European Parliament Conciliations Handbook*, 446191EN.doc (3rd. edn., European Parliament 2001), 12–13.

the mid-1990s. The trialogue contains representatives from the Council, EP, and Commission. It consists of a select number, normally no more than ten, from each institution. The aim is to facilitate compromise.

The *co-decision procedure in Article 251 has been successful in practice*. It has proven to be successful in accommodating the differing interests that have a stake in the legislative process.[39] There has been an increase by a factor of 2.5 over a year in the number of files dealt with by co-decision. Not all the stages of Article 251 will be gone through for any particular Community measure. Approximately 25 per cent of measures have been adopted at first reading, and more than 50 per cent at second reading. This has left only 25 per cent of measures to be dealt with by the conciliation procedure. This procedure has been effective. 20 per cent of the Parliament's second reading amendments to the Council's common position have been accepted in their entirety during the conciliation procedure, 70 per cent have been the subject of a compromise, and only 12 per cent have been rejected.[40]

Article 251 has a secure normative foundation. The EP has long been pressing for a co-equal role in the legislative process with the Council. The modifications introduced by the ToA go a considerable way to achieving this goal. The fact that the Article 251 procedure applies to most EC legislation is in accord with the proposals of the key players which made submissions to the 1996 IGC, including the EP, the Commission, and the Reflection Group.[41] Many of the points made in the extract from Westlake apply equally to the Article 251 procedure. Institutional attitudes have changed markedly since the early 1980s. The attention placed on democracy and legitimacy in the 1990s has helped to secure a more equal and constructive role for the EP in the legislative process.[42]

(f) COUNCIL, COMMISSION, AND THE EUROPEAN PARLIAMENT: ASSENT

The assent procedure is simplicity itself as compared with those considered above. The Council acts after obtaining the assent of the European Parliament: the act can be

---

[39] A. Dashwood, 'Community Legislative Procedures in the Era of the TEU' (1994) 19 *ELRev*. 343; D. Earnshaw and D. Judge, 'From Co-operation to Co-decision: The European Parliament's Path to Legislative Power', in J. Richardson (ed.), *European Union, Power and Policy-Making* (Routledge, 1996), ch. 6; S. Boyron, 'The Co-Decision Procedure: Rethinking the Constitutional Fundamentals', in P. Craig and C. Harlow (eds.), *Lawmaking in the European Union* (Kluwer, 1998), ch. 7; A. Dashwood, 'European Community Legislative Procedures after Amsterdam' (1998) 1 *CYELS* 25; A. Maurer, *Co-Governing after Maastricht: The European Parliament's Institutional Performance 1994–99*, EP Working Paper, POLI 104, 1999.

[40] A. Dashwood, 'The Constitution of the European Union after Nice: Law-Making Procedures' (2001) 26 *ELRev*. 215, 219.

[41] Craig, n. 1 above.

[42] There is an extensive literature in political science that attempts to model the operation of the different legislative procedures. There is, not surprisingly, considerable disagreement about the foundational assumptions and the conclusions: see, e.g., G. Tsebelis and G. Garrett, 'Legislative Politics and the European Union' (2000) 1 *EUP* 9; C. Crombez, 'Co-decision: Towards a Bicameral European Union' (2000) 1 *EUP* 363; B. Steunenberg, 'Seeing What you Want to See: The Limits of Current Modelling on the European Union' (2000) 1 *EUP* 368; R. Corbett, 'Academic Modelling of the Co-decision Procedure: A Practitioner's Puzzled Reaction' (2000) 1 *EUP* 373; G. Garrett and G. Tsebelis, 'Understanding Better the EU Legislative Process' (2001) 2 *EUP* 353; R. Corbett, 'A Response to a Reply to a Reaction (I Hope Someone is Still Interested)' (2001) 2 *EUP* 361.

adopted only if it has been approved by both the Council and the European Parliament. The assent procedure therefore 'grants Parliament an infinite power of delay and an absolute power of rejection',[43] albeit no formal mechanism for making amendments. In order to render this power more discriminating the Parliament's rules provide for the possibility of an interim report with a draft resolution containing recommendations for modification or implementation of the proposal.[44] The Parliament has also unilaterally introduced a conciliation procedure with the Council.[45]

The assent procedure was introduced by the SEA for important matters such as the expansion of Community membership and association agreements. The areas in which it now applies after the ToA include the following: Article 49 of the TEU (ex Article O of the TEU), concerning membership of the European Union; Article 105(6) EC (ex the same Treaty number), concerning various aspects of the functioning of a European Central Bank; Article 107(5) (ex Article 106(5)), amendment to the Statute of the European System of Central Banks (ESCB); and Article 161 (ex Article 130d), certain measures relating to economic and social cohesion.

(g) LEGISLATIVE INITIATIVE AND THE COUNCIL'S USE OF ARTICLE 208

The discussion of the legislative procedures within the Community would be incomplete if it did not take account of Article 208 EC (ex Article 152). This is not a procedure for the enactment of legislation as such, but it is a mechanism whereby the Council can adopt a more proactive role in the initiation of the legislative process. Under this Article the Council may request the Commission to undertake any studies which the Council considers desirable for the attainment of the common objectives, and to submit to it any appropriate proposals. The wording of this Article might suggest that the requests from Council to Commission would be couched in rather general terms, but this has not always proven to be so. The Council has not infrequently made use of this Article to give very specific instructions to the Commission concerning action which it, the Council, believes to be desirable. When this occurs the Commission will, at the very least, feel a strong pressure to bring forward legislation of the type suggested by the Council. The legislative procedure which is used for this purpose will depend upon the subject-matter of the proposed norm.

(h) THE SEEDS OF LEGISLATIVE INITIATIVE FOR THE PARLIAMENT: ARTICLE 192

The procedures outlined above encapsulate the existing ways in which measures can be enacted in the Community. It should, however, be noted that the European Parliament can be the catalyst for the initiation of the legislative process by virtue of

---

[43] Westlake, n. 17 above, 96.
[44] *Ibid.* See *Rules of Procedure of the European Parliament* (14th edn., European Parliament 1999), rule 86.
[45] Westlake, n. 17 above, 96.

Article 192 EC (ex Article 138b). This provides that the European Parliament may, acting by a majority of its members, request the Commission to submit any appropriate proposal on matters on which it considers that a Community act is required for the purpose of implementing the Treaty. The proposal will then take the legislative route that is appropriate for measures of that kind as identified in the Treaty. While Article 192 does not vest the Parliament with any right of initiative as such, it does provide a means whereby it can be 'proactive' rather than simply 'reactive'. The Commission, for its part, does not accept that it must automatically pursue a matter referred to it under Article 192. However the Code of Conduct it concluded with the Parliament does State that the Commission will take 'the greatest possible account' of any such request. The Parliament has also accepted that it must be cautious in its use of the Article.[46]

Parliament recognises that resort to this right must be sparing and realistic. To this end, it has introduced a series of filtering mechanisms into its rules. Such a resolution must result from an own-initiative report from the committee responsible, authorised by the Conference of Presidents. Before requesting authorisation, the committee must establish that no such proposal is under preparation. The resolution must indicate the appropriate legal basis and be accompanied by detailed recommendations and must respect the principle of subsidiarity and the fundamental rights of citizens.

The Parliament none the less pressed in its 1996 IGC report for Article 192 to be modified so that the Commission would have a duty to respond to such Parliamentary initiatives. It was, however, unsuccessful in this respect.

(i) SUMMARY

i. The changes introduced by the ToA are to be welcomed. Co-decision has become the general mode of decision-making for most Community legislation. The co-decision procedure works well in practice, and has a secure normative foundation. It facilitates a discourse between the Commission, EP, and Council, allowing the views of each to be taken into account when fashioning legislation.

ii. It would have been desirable to abolish the co-operation procedure. It now applies only to a very few areas, each of which could be subject to co-decision.

iii. If the co-operation procedure were to be abolished, then Community legislation could be rationalized in the following manner. The co-decision procedure would be the general method for the making of legislation. In areas of major importance the assent procedure would apply. In areas where Member State interests were particularly strong, the EP would be limited to a consultative role.

iv. It should not however be forgotten that, although the co-decision procedure is now dominant, there are still variables that can affect the legislative strategy in any particular area. There is the choice between regulations and directives,

---

[46] *Ibid.* See *Rules of Procedure*, n. 44 above, rule 59.

between detailed and framework legislation, and the balance between formal law and informal law.

3. THE COMMUNITY PILLAR: DELEGATED LEGISLATIVE POWER

A moment's thought will indicate why delegation of power to make regulations has been necessary. There are certain areas of Community policy, such as agriculture, which require numerous regulations, often passed quickly to cope with changing market circumstances. If the standard methods of enacting Community measures were to be applied the process would grind to a halt, since the large number of such norms could not be enacted with sufficient speed. This explains why the Council, through a 'parent' regulation, has authorized the Commission to enact more specific regulations within a particular area, such as agriculture and competition.

The Council was not, however, willing to give the Commission *carte blanche* to legislate in this manner. It made the exercise of delegated legislative power subject to institutional constraints, in the form of committees through which Member State interests could be represented. This was so for two complementary reasons.

On the one hand, there might be disagreements between the States themselves as to the content of the more detailed norms that should be made. It is common to think that Member States only ever disagree on points of general principle. This is quite mistaken. Often they agree on the general strategy, but disagree on its detailed application. The committee structure to be described below gave the Member States the opportunity for input into the making of the detailed norms.

On the other hand, the Council imposed conditions on the delegation of power to the Commission because of the inter-institutional tensions when the committee structure was created. The Council was wary of the federalizing tendencies of the Commission. It was unsurprising, at a time when the Council perceived the Community in intergovernmental terms, that it should be unwilling to delegate power to the Commission without institutional checks to ensure the *formal* representation of Member State interests.

The Council's 'solution' was to condition the exercise of delegated power on the approval of a committee composed of Member State representatives. This system came to be known as Comitology. There was no express warrant for such committees in the original Treaty, and their legality was challenged before the Court. The ECJ upheld the constitutional validity of the committee system, reasoning that if the Treaty gave power to the Council to delegate to the Commission, then it could do so on terms.[47]

The SEA modified Article 202 (ex Article 145) in order to provide a secure

---

[47] Case 25/70, *Koster* [1970] ECR 1161. It is questionable whether this argument is sound in the context of the general allocation of power within the Community. The ECJ's decision may well have been influenced by the realization that to find the committee structure unconstitutional would have caused a major upset in the evolving pattern of Community decision-making.

foundation for the existence of this delegation, and an impetus for the more orderly organization of the committee structure. The third indent of Article 202 states that the Council can confer on the Commission, in the acts which the Council adopts, powers for the implementation of the rules which the Council lays down. It further stipulates that the Council may impose certain requirements on the exercise of these powers, and that it may reserve the right, in specific cases, to exercise implementing powers itself. The procedures are to be consonant with principles and rules laid down in advance by the Council, acting unanimously on a proposal from the Commission after consulting the European Parliament. The Comitology decision establishing the principles and rules to be followed was adopted by the Council in 1987.[48] This Decision rationalized the committee structure.

The European Parliament was unhappy with the 1987 Decision, because it was excluded from the committee system. This discontent increased as the European Parliament gained a greater say in the passage of 'primary' Community legislation, through extension of the co-decision procedure. The Parliament argued that the committee structure was inconsistent with co-decision, legally and in terms of principle. Primary legislation will, as we have seen, now normally be made under co-decision. This includes the primary legislation pursuant to which power is then delegated to the Commission, subject to the committee system. The exclusion of the Parliament from the passage of this delegated legislation served therefore to undermine the gains that the Parliament had made through the extension of co-decision.[49]

Declaration 31 appended to the ToA called on the Commission to submit to the Council by the end of 1998 proposals to amend the 1987 Comitology Decision. A new Decision was adopted in 1999,[50] and the recitals specified four objectives. There should be greater consistency in the choice of committee procedure; greater involvement of the European Parliament; improvement in the information given to the Parliament; and the committees should be more accessible to the public.

Article 1 of the Decision provides that, except in cases where the basic instrument reserves to the Council the right to exercise implementing powers, these powers shall be conferred on the Commission in accordance with the provisions in the basic instrument.

Article 2 sets out criteria for the choice of committee procedure. The management procedure is to be used for management measures, such as agricultural policy, and for the implementation of programmes with substantial budgetary implications. The regulatory procedure is to be used for measures of general scope designed to apply essential provisions of basic instruments, such as those concerned with health and safety. The advisory procedure is to be used whenever it is felt to be most appropriate.

Article 3 lays down the advisory procedure. A committee of an advisory nature

---

[48] Dec. 87/373, [1987] OJ L197/33.

[49] The Parliament challenged the 1987 Decision, but the action was held to be inadmissible: Case 302/87, *European Parliament* v. *Council* [1988] ECR 5615. See K. St. C. Bradley, 'The European Parliament and Comitology: On the Road to Nowhere?' (1997) 3 *ELJ* 230.

[50] *Council Decision laying down the Procedures for the Exercise of Implementing Powers Conferred on the Commission*, Dec. 99/468, [1999] OJ L184/23.

assists the Commission. It is composed of representatives of the Member States and chaired by the Commission. The Commission submits a draft of the proposed measure to the committee, and the committee then delivers its opinion. The Commission is not bound by this opinion, although it shall take the 'utmost account' of it.

The management procedure is laid down in Article 4. The composition of the committee is the same as above. The Commission submits a proposal, and the committee then delivers an opinion within a time limit set by the Commission chairman. The committee votes in the same manner as the Council itself,[51] but the Commission itself has no vote. Under this procedure the Commission adopts measures which 'shall apply immediately'. However, if the measure *is not in accordance* with the opinion of the committee, the Commission must communicate this to the Council. The Commission then *may* defer application of the measure for a maximum period of three months. The Council, acting by qualified majority, can take a different decision within this period. The nub of the management procedure is that the committee, composed of national representatives, must vote against the measure in order for it to be 'kicked back' to the Council.

The regulatory procedure is covered by Article 5. The composition of the committee is the same as above, and the voting is in accordance with that in the Council. The sting in the tail is that the Commission can adopt a measure only *if it is in accord* with the opinion of the committee. If *it is not in accord* with the committee's opinion, or *if no opinion* is delivered, then the Commission *must* submit to the Council a proposal relating to the measures to be taken, and *must* inform the EP. The nub of the regulatory procedure is that the measure must be referred back to the Council unless the committee votes in favour of it. If the EP considers that the Commission's proposal, made pursuant to a basic instrument under the co-decision procedure, exceeds the implementing powers provided in that instrument, it shall inform the Council. The Council can, within three months of the date of referral, make clear its opposition to the proposal, in which case the Commission must re-examine it. The Commission can then re-submit the proposal, amend it, or present a (new) proposal. Where the Council, within three months, neither adopts the proposed measure nor indicates its opposition, the Commission shall adopt the proposed act.

The objective of making the committee system more accessible to the public is dealt with in Article 7.[52] The principles and conditions on access to documents apply to the committees, and the Commission must publish a list of all the committees which assist it in the exercise of implementing powers. It has now done so.[53] The Commission must, from 2000 onwards, publish an annual report on the working of the committees. Moreover, the references of documents sent to the European Parliament are to be made public.

We have already seen that the EP has a role under the regulatory procedure. It is, in addition, given a right by Article 7(3) to be informed by the Commission of

---

[51] See 153–5 below.

[52] Art. 6 of Dec. 99/468, n. 50 above deals with procedures to be followed in the case of safeguard measures.

[53] *Information from the Commission—List of Committees which Assist the Commission in the Exercise of its Implementing Powers* [2000] OJ C225/2.

committee proceedings. It is to receive committee agendas, voting records, and draft measures submitted to the committees for implementation of primary law made under the co-decision procedure. The EP must also be kept informed when the Commission transmits proposals to the Council. In an agreement made between the EP and the Commission,[54] the latter stated that it will also forward to the EP, at its request, specific draft measures for implementing basic instruments even if they were not adopted under co-decision, where they are of particular importance to the EP. The EP can moreover request access to minutes of committee meetings.[55]

Article 8 allows the EP to indicate by resolution that draft implementing measures, which have been submitted to a committee pursuant to a basic instrument adopted by co-decision, would exceed the implementing powers in that instrument. The Commission *must* re-examine the draft measure. It *may* submit new draft measures, continue with the procedure, or submit a (new) proposal. The Commission must inform the Parliament of what it has done, and provide reasons. The agreement between the EP and the Commission provides that the resolution must be made within one month of the EP receiving the final draft of the implementing measures. It must also be made in plenary session.[56]

The committee structure provides a means whereby Member States can have influence even when power has been delegated to the Commission. There has been a considerable literature on the Comitology regime,[57] some of which pre-dates the 1999 Council Decision. Concerns were rightly voiced about the exclusion of the EP, the undemocratic nature of the process, the lack of accountability and transparency, and the corporatist nature of the process. The 1999 Council Decision is undoubtedly an improvement in this regard.[58] It will be evaluated when considering the broader issues of democracy and legitimacy within the EU.[59]

4. THE COMMUNITY PILLAR: THE VOTING REQUIREMENTS IN THE COUNCIL

(a) THE POSITION PRIOR TO 2005

The general principle is, unless the Treaty specifies to the contrary, that voting in the Council is to be by majority.[60] The Treaty provides for three different rules on voting: on some occasions unanimity is required;[61] in some instances a simple majority; and in most circumstances a qualified majority is stipulated. Which of these voting rules

---

[54] *Agreement between the European Parliament and the Commission on Procedures for Implementing Council Decision 99/468* [2000] OJ L256/19, para. 2.
[55] Case T–188/97, *Rothmans v. Commission* [1999] ECR II–2463.
[56] N. 54 above, paras. 6–7. The time limit can be shorter in urgent cases.
[57] C. Joerges and E. Vos (eds.), *EU Committees: Social Regulation, Law and Politics* (Hart, 1999); M. Andenas and A. Turk (eds.), *Delegated Legislation and the Role of Committees in the EC* (Kluwer, 2000).
[58] K. Lenaerts and A. Verhoeven, 'Towards a Legal Framework for Executive Rule-Making in the EU? The Contribution of the New Comitology Decision' (2000) 37 *CMLRev.* 645.
[59] See 167–75 below. [60] Art. 205(1) (ex Art. 148(1)) EC.
[61] Abstentions do not prevent the adoption of acts for which unanimity is required: Art. 205(3) EC.

applies will be specified in the particular Treaty Article under which a measure is enacted. The figure required for a qualified majority is sixty-two votes out of a possible eighty-seven. Where the Treaty provides for acts to be made by qualified majority on a proposal from the Commission sixty-two votes will therefore be needed. In cases where the Council decides by qualified majority, but does not act on a Commission proposal, there must be sixty-two votes in favour cast by at least ten States.[62] France, Germany, Italy, and the United Kingdom each have ten votes; Spain has eight; Greece, Belgium, Portugal, and the Netherlands have five; Austria and Sweden have four; Denmark, Finland, and Ireland each have three; and Luxembourg has two. There is provision for the voting rights of a State to be suspended if it seriously and persistently breaches the principles of liberty, democracy, etc. contained in Article 6(1) TEU.[63]

Qualified-majority voting has been the formal legal norm in many areas since the end of the second stage of the transitional period in 1965. The range of issues which can be decided in this way was extended by the SEA, particularly through the addition of Article 95 (ex Article 100a), which deals with completion of the internal market. A requirement of unanimity now generally applies only to politically sensitive topics,[64] to decisions which are of particular importance for the character of the Community,[65] or in circumstances where the Council is seeking to depart from a proposal from one of the other Community institutions, as described above.

For some considerable time these formal legal powers were overshadowed by the Luxembourg Compromise. This was the result of a political crisis in the Community in the mid-1960s, and coincided with the shift to qualified-majority voting in the Council.[66] In essence the Compromise provided that when majority voting applied to a topic which concerned the important interests of States, they should attempt to reach a solution acceptable to all, and France added the rider that discussion should continue until unanimity was attained. The Compromise fostered a climate in which majority voting prejudicial to the interests of a particular State tended to be avoided. The 'threat' that a Member State would exercise a *de facto* veto power did not enhance the speed of Community decision-making. The Luxembourg Compromise has not been formally abolished, because it never formally existed in legal terms. However, the climate in the Community after the SEA, the TEU, the ToA, and the TN renders it less likely that States will attempt to use any explicit veto power.[67] These Treaty amendments require a greater use of qualified-majority voting in order to achieve the Community's goals.[68] Moreover, these Treaty amendments reflected a shift in Member State perceptions about the nature of the Community, which renders it less likely that

---

[62] Art. 205(2) (ex Art. 148(2)) EC. A political compromise, known as the Ionninna Compromise, provides that if Members of the Council representing a total of 23 to 25 votes indicate their intention to oppose the adoption of an act by qualified majority, the Council will do all in its power to reach a satisfactory solution that could be adopted by at least 65 votes: see M. Westlake, *The Council of the European Union* (Cartermill, 1995), 94–5.

[63] Art. 7 TEU, 309 EC (Art. 236).

[64] E.g. some matters concerned with employment: Art. 137(2) EC as modified by the TN.

[65] E.g. accession of new Member States: Art. 49 (ex Art. O) TEU.

[66] See 13–14 above.   [67] Westlake, n. 62 above, 91–111.

[68] A form of veto was enshrined in Arts. 23 and 40 TEU, and Art. 11 EC. However the TN has modified Art. 40 TEU and Art. 11 EC to reduce the power of a Member State that is opposed to closer co-operation.

exclusively national interests will be regarded as a valid rationale for the exercise of a veto.[69] The ability to invoke the veto will be further dependent on the perceptions of other States as to whether the State invoking it really does have important interests at stake. The very fact that use of the veto is now less readily accepted[70] than hitherto means, however, that Member States will exert more pressure at other parts of the decision-making system so as to ensure that the measure which emerges is acceptable to them. It should also be acknowledged that the Council *will* search for consensus even where the formal voting rules do provide for a qualified majority.[71]

(b) THE NICE TREATY

Institutional reform of the Council occupied more of the IGC's time than any other topic. The negotiation centred on the extension of qualified-majority voting, on the weighting of votes, and the number required for a qualified majority.

All States acknowledged that there had to be an extension of qualified-majority voting in an expanded Union. Unanimity would often be synonymous with inaction, since one State out of twenty-seven would almost certainly object. Forging agreement on the areas where there should be a shift to qualified majority proved more difficult. Discussions in the IGC were akin to a series of individual skirmishes about whether another bastion of unanimity should be given up. The fact that the veto was always a double-edged sword was rarely acknowledged: it can protect State autonomy, but it can equally prevent Union action. Much then depended on whether States felt that they would be more 'vetoed against' than 'exercisers of veto power' themselves.

The options canvassed as to weighting of votes approached the byzantine in terms of complexity. The issue cast into sharp relief the relative power of large, medium, and small States in the Council. The solution embodied in the Nice Treaty is to be found in the Protocol on Enlargement of the Union, coupled with Declaration 20 on Enlargement, and is posited on a Union with twenty-seven States. The Protocol comes into effect on 1 January 2005, at which date Article 205(2) is modified as follows. The votes accorded to each of the States have been 'stretched' to accommodate the new, smaller States. The largest States have twenty-nine votes each, the smallest three, with gradations in between for others. Prior to enlargement a qualified majority will be 169 out of 237 in cases where the Council acts on a proposal from the Commission. Where it does not do so, there is the additional requirement that the votes must be cast by at least two-thirds of the States. After enlargement a qualified majority will be 258 out of 345. The other rules are the same. The wishes of the larger States have been further reinforced by the addition of Article 205(4). This allows a member of the Council to request verification that the States constituting the qualified majority

[69] The approach of the Conservative Government to the beef crisis which consisted, in part, of refusing to agree to any measure on which unanimity was required under the Treaty, itself provoked a very unfavourable response from other States: M. Westlake, 'Mad Cows and Englishmen—The Institutional Consequences of the BSE Crisis', in N. Nugent (ed.), *The European Union 1996*, 15–27.

[70] The Luxembourg Compromise has, however, been invoked by Germany in 1985, by Ireland in 1986, and by Greece in 1988, in the context of the CAP.

[71] W. Nicoll, 'Representing the States', in A. Duff, J. Pinder, and R. Pryce (eds.), *Maastricht and Beyond, Building the European Union* (Routledge, 1994), 193–4.

represent at least 62 per cent of the population. If this condition is not met then the relevant decision cannot be adopted.

5. DECISION-MAKING PROCESS UNDER PILLARS 2 AND 3

Space precludes a detailed examination of decision-making under the second and third pillars. It is however important to have a bare outline of the relevant provisions, since an increasing number of decisions are adopted in this manner.

(a) PILLAR 2: COMMON FOREIGN AND SECURITY POLICY (CFSP)

The European Council and the Council dominate decision-making under Pillar 2, which remains very largely intergovernmental in nature. This is unsurprising, given the nature of the subject matter. The range of instruments that can be used under Pillar 2 includes defining the principles and general guidelines for the CFSP; deciding on common strategies; adopting joint actions; adopting common positions; and strengthening systematic co-operation between Member States in the conduct of policy.[72] The meaning of each form of action has been considered above, and reference should be made to that discussion.[73]

(b) PILLAR 3: POLICE AND JUDICIAL CO-OPERATION IN CRIMINAL MATTERS (PJCC)

The changes made to PJCC by the TN were primarily concerned with the conditions for closer co-operation and have been considered above.[74] The present discussion will focus on decision-making in the general PJCC area.[75] The key provision is Article 34 (ex K.6 TEU). It establishes four principal mechanisms for attaining the Union's objectives in this area. The Council acts unanimously on the initiative of any Member State or the Commission.

The Council can adopt a *common position* defining the approach of the Union to a particular matter. It can adopt a *framework decision* for the purpose of approximating the laws and regulations of the Member States. These are like directives: they are binding as to the result to be achieved, but leave choice of form and method to the Member States. They are however expressly stipulated not to entail direct effect. The Council can adopt *decisions* for any purpose consistent with the objectives of this Title.[76] These decisions are binding but do not have direct effect.[77] The Council may also establish *conventions*, which it can recommend for adoption by the Member

---

[72] Art. 12 TEU.   [73] See Ch. 1 above.   [74] *Ibid.*
[75] S. Peers, *EU Justice and Home Affairs Law* (Longman, 2000), ch. 3.
[76] Excluding any approximation of the laws and regulations of the Member States: Art. 34(2)(c) TEU.
[77] The Council, acting by qualified majority, adopts the implementing measures needed at the Union level: Art. 34(2)(c).

States in accordance with their national constitutions. The European Parliament has the right to be consulted in the making of framework decisions, decisions, and conventions.[78]

6. THE REALITY OF COMMUNITY DECISION-MAKING: THE TEMPORAL DIMENSION

The discussion thus far has focused on the legislative procedures. To stop there would, however, give only an imperfect grasp of the Community legislative process. We need to press further to understand the way in which Community decision-making actually works. There are different dimensions to this inquiry, one of which is temporal in nature.

By the temporal dimension we mean the way in which EC decision-making has unfolded since its inception. By concentrating exclusively on the current position we miss significant aspects in the evolution of the Community institutions. The earlier discussion of the history of the Community has provided a framework within which to understand the development of the EC. We need now to consider more specifically the respective roles played by the Community institutions in the decision-making process and their evolution. What follows does not purport to be a thorough historical analysis, but rather a thematic one.

A central theme is the development of institutional structures outside the strict letter of the Treaty, as a response to tensions that existed between the Council and Commission. We have already seen that, prior to the SEA, the EP played only a minor role in Community decision-making. The Commission and the Council were the dominant forces. There were, however, tensions between these institutions, since they embodied differing conceptions of the Community.

The Council perceived it principally in intergovernmental terms, and this had both a substantive and a procedural dimension. In substantive terms, the Council was unclear precisely how far it really did wish to travel down the road of European integration. In procedural terms, intergovernmentalism connoted the idea that Member State interests should not readily be sacrificed to the Community good, and that the Council, as representative of those interests, should retain control over the development of Community policy.

The Commission had a more federalist conception of the Community. This, too, had a substantive and a procedural component. In substantive terms, it manifested itself in a commitment to proceed with the attainment of the Community goals as expeditiously as possible, and to move beyond these to other matters that would further the process of integration. In procedural terms, the Commission's vision naturally inclined to the use of majority voting, as dictated by the Treaty itself in many areas, with the necessary consequence that the interests of a Member State might have to be sacrificed to achieve the greater Community good.

---

[78] Art. 39(1) TEU. The Council Presidency and the Commission must regularly inform the EP of discussions in areas covered by this Title, Art. 39(2) TEU. The EP may ask questions of the Council, and make recommendations to it, Art. 39(3).

The original Rome Treaty divided power between Council and Commission. In many respects it did, however, place the Commission in the driving seat as regards the development of Community policy. This is evident from the Commission's right of legislative initiative; from the plethora of other functions which it was given; and from the fact that the voting rules, while requiring Council consent to a measure, also required unanimity for any Council amendment.[79] The message was that, while the Council had to consent to a proposed norm, it was not easy for it to alter the measure drafted by the Commission.

The first twenty years or so of the Community were marked by *de facto* changes in the nature of Community decision-making. The unifying theme was the increased dominance of the Council over the Commission, and the limiting of the federalist tendencies within the Commission by the intergovernmental impulses of the Council. Institutional developments outside the strict letter of the Treaty were the vehicle through which this was achieved.

The Luxembourg Accords were one such development. They were the prime example of negative intergovernmentalism: they gave the Member States the power to block measures they disliked which they felt touched their vital interests. Statistics on the number of occasions on which this power was actually used are, of course, only part of the story, since the threat of the veto shaped the very policies which the Commission would put forward.[80] The Council's intergovernmental orientation also had a more positive side to it. The Luxembourg Accords were fine if the ultimate objective was to veto a measure. But the Member States also desired more finely tuned tools through which to influence legislation which they wished to be enacted. The growing influence of COREPER, the establishment of management and regulatory committees, the increased use of Article 208 (ex Article 152) EC, and the evolution of the European Council were all features of positive intergovernmentalism. They increased Member State influence over Community legislation, and did so in complementary ways. COREPER and the management/regulatory committees enabled the Council to have a more formalized input into the detail of the emergent legislation. Article 208 became a useful vehicle whereby the Council could suggest Community action in particular areas, while the European Council became a mechanism which enabled Member States to discuss general issues of Community concern, outside the framework of the Council itself. The results of their deliberations were often 'binding', in the sense of laying down the parameters of future Community action, whether in relation to the size of the CAP budget or the timetable for moves towards closer economic union.

These developments contributed to the Euro-sclerosis that beset the Community during much of the 1970s. This had reverberations for the ECJ's role. This story has been told most fully in the important work of Joseph Weiler.[81] He explains how the

---

[79] Art. 250(1) (ex 189a(1)).

[80] See the important analysis by K. Neunreither, 'Transformation of a Political Role: Reconsidering the Case of the Commission of the European Communities' (1971–2) 10 *JCMS* 233.

[81] J. Weiler, 'The Community System: The Dual Character of Supranationalism' (1981) 1 *YBEL* 267, and 'The Transformation of Europe' (1991) 100 *Yale LJ* 2403, 2412–31.

impediments to the attainment of Community objectives through the political process led to the growing importance of normative supranationalism. This is the relationship between Community policies and measures on the one hand, and competing policies and legal measures of the Member States on the other. The doctrines of direct effect, the supremacy of Community law, and pre-emption were central in this respect. They allowed the ECJ to develop EC law, notwithstanding the difficulties of securing the passage of the required regulations and directives through the legislative process.[82]

Many of the institutional developments which occurred outside the strict letter of the Treaty have now been accorded *de jure* status by their inclusion in Treaty revisions. Thus we have seen how the management and regulatory committee structure attained a more secure footing by the revisions to Article 145 in the SEA, now Article 202 EC. The European Council was also recognized by the SEA, and now has its foundations in what is, after the ToA, Article 4 of the TEU. COREPER was accorded a more formal status in Article 207.

Community decision-making process is dynamic, not static. To concentrate wholly on the current Treaty provisions, and to 'freeze' them, means losing sight of the institutional dynamics that have shaped the present regime. The temporal dimension is therefore of crucial importance in enriching our understanding of the reality of Community decision-making across time, and in helping us to comprehend the existing pattern of institutional competence.

7. THE REALITY OF COMMUNITY DECISION-MAKING: INTER-INSTITUTIONAL DIMENSION

(a) INSTITUTIONAL CO-OPERATION: PLANNING THE GENERAL LEGISLATIVE STRATEGY

The institutional reforms in the SEA had a mixed impact on Community decision-making. In one respect they expedited decision-making, by extending qualified-majority voting, as exemplified by Article 95 (ex Article 100a) EC. The climate when the SEA was passed meant, moreover, that it was less likely that Member States would be able to employ the veto. In another respect however the SEA served to make the legislative process more complex. The Parliament now had power through the co-operation procedure. It was another institutional player whose views had to be accommodated. This has already been touched upon in the previous quotation from Westlake.[83] It became clear that there would have to be more inter-institutional co-operation in planning the overall legislative programme.

---

[82] P.P. Craig, 'Once Upon a Time in the West: Direct Effect and the Federalization of EEC Law' (1992) 12 *OJLS* 453.

[83] See 143–4 above.

M. Westlake, The Commission and the Parliament: Partners and Rivals in the European Policy-Making Process[84]

Although only recently instigated, and still evolving procedurally, the annual legislative programming exercise has already become a centre-piece of Commission–Parliament relations. The Single European Act greatly enhanced the importance of collaborative planning. It was in the Commission's interest first, to give Parliament advanced warning of its general intent in particular policy areas, enabling any general debate to precede specific proposals and, second, to give Parliament an overall view of the legislative calendar, enabling it to programme its work efficiently. Planning has taken on further practical importance with the implementation of the Maastricht Treaty, and political importance in the light of the Treaty's provisions on the nomination of the Commission and its President. As the procedure is still evolving, the schematic description given here is necessarily tentative, although the basic trend is clear.

In the autumn preceding each legislative year, the Commission President presents the Commission's Programme to the Parliament, and a debate then ensues. The Programme is not an exhaustive document but is intended to set out the main themes and political priorities of the Commission for the coming legislative year. Parliament is constantly considering ways of organising its work so as to gain maximum influence over the Programme, in particular by setting out its political priorities in advance, and continues to seek to exert influence thereafter, concluding with a plenary debate. Parliament has attempted to provide an additional dimension by drawing in the work programme of the Council Presidency-in-office. The December 1992 Edinburgh Council endorsed a Commission proposal that the annual work programme be produced in October of the preceding year, thereby providing Parliament (and, of course, public opinion) with more time to exert policy influence. . . .

Together with its Programme, the Commission submits to Parliament a copy of its indicative legislative timetable. Although it cannot be exhaustive, the timetable sets out all major and important proposals for the forthcoming year. It includes all proposals related to the political priorities established in the Commission's Programme, but has in the past rarely extended beyond these to the broader range of Commission competences. However, at the December 1992 Edinburgh Council the Commission undertook, in line with a greater desire for transparency and broader consultation, to resort more frequently to green papers, and the 1993 legislative programme subsequently annexed a list of those topics where it was intending to draft green papers during the year in question.

A document of hybrid status, the Commission's indicative legislative timetable is divided into quarterly rolling programmes and is constantly updated. It serves as a concretisation of the Commission's Programme, is designed to involve the other Community institutions, and serves as the basis for co-ordination between them. Indeed, the indicative legislative timetable is the subject of considerable co-operation and co-ordination between Parliament and Commission services, and although the Commission retains some rights of authorship, the result is nevertheless a jointly-agreed programme.

The Commission publishes its work programme for a particular year. Thus the *Commission Work Programme for 2001*[85] listed four legislative priorities. New forms of governance would be promoted. Europe's place in the world would be strengthened. A

---

[84] N. 17 above, 19–21.   [85] COM(2001)28 final.

new social and economic agenda would be launched. Measures in areas such as consumer protection, health, and food safety would be enacted to improve the quality of life. The Commission will also set out more far-reaching strategic objectives.[86]

Inter-institutional co-operation directed to the general legislative programme has been modified more recently as part of the strategy for reform of the Commission. An important aim is to ensure a better fit between the Community's objectives and the resources needed to fulfil them. In the past decisions about priorities and resource allocation occurred at different times. The new planning cycle is designed to integrate these decisions more closely together. The following decision-making cycle is beginning to emerge. In December the Commission will make initial decisions on the political orientation of policies for two years hence. Thus decisions made in December 2001 will be for 2003. Guidelines will be set for the various Directorates General within the Commission, which will develop them by the following February. This will result in the Annual Policy Strategy (APS). There will then be a dialogue between Commission, Council, and the EP about the APS. The Preliminary Draft Budget is set in April, and there will be discussion between the Commission, Council, and EP. The 'stability' of legislative planning is, however, subject to the changing policy priorities of different Presidencies of the Council.

Inter-institutional co-operation also occurs through the Conference of Presidents.[87] This is chaired by the President of the Parliament in a non-voting capacity, and composed of the leaders of the political groups, each of which has a vote weighted in accordance with the numerical strength of that group in the Parliament. This body meets twice or three times per month, and, *inter alia*, prepares the agenda for the EP. The Commission will normally attend, and it, as well as the Council, will have the opportunity to make suggestions about the agenda.

(b) INSTITUTIONAL CO-OPERATION: INTER-INSTITUTIONAL AGREEMENTS

An important vehicle through which more formal inter-institutional co-operation occurs is the Inter-institutional Agreement or Declaration.[88] Such agreements or declarations form what has been termed 'a sort of constitutional glue'[89] for the Community. Important examples are the 1993 Inter-institutional Agreement on Subsidiarity, and the 1993 Inter-institutional Declaration on Democracy, Transparency, and Subsidiarity. Such agreements have also been made in relation to, for example, budgetary discipline, codification, implementation of the budget, and comitology. We have already considered the agreement concerning subsidiarity itself. The Agreement on Democracy, Transparency, and Subsidiarity may be taken as an example of the role of such agreements in developing Community constitutional principles.

---

[86] *Strategic Objectives 2000–2005, "Shaping the New Europe"*, COM(2000)154 final.

[87] R. Corbett, F. Jacobs, and M. Shackleton, *The European Parliament* (Harper, 4th edn., 2000), 102–3.

[88] Such agreements can be found at various stages of the Community's development: J. Monar, 'Interinstitutional Agreements: The Phenomenon and its Dynamics after Maastricht' (1994) 31 *CMLRev.* 693.

[89] Westlake, n. 17 above, 101.

The 1993 Inter-institutional Declaration on Democracy, Transparency, and Sub-sidiarity was agreed to by the three institutions on the margins of the 1993 Brussels European Council. Article 1 affirmed the attachment of the institutions to principles of democracy and transparency, within the framework of the existing legislative procedures. Article 3 brought together steps that the institutions had taken, or were taking, in order to increase transparency.

For the EP this meant confirmation of the fact that its plenary sessions and its committee meetings were to be in public. For the Council, it entailed opening some of its debates to the public, publishing records and explanations of its voting, and pub-lishing the common positions adopted under Articles 251 and 252. It also entailed simplification of legislation, and provision of access to archives.

For the Commission it meant, *inter alia*, making wider consultations before pre-senting proposals, in particular through Green or White Papers. The Commission was, in addition, to introduce a notification procedure. Proposed measures would be published in the Official Journal, with a deadline for interested parties to comment. It was to publish legislative programmes in the Official Journal, including those for legislative consolidation. There was to be easier access to Commission documents, and faster publication of Commission documents in all Community languages. Measures were to be taken to facilitate the public's understanding of Commission business.

This particular Declaration is clearly of importance in itself, and is also of signifi-cance for the insights which it provides on the evolution of Community consti-tutional principles. Such agreements or declarations serve as the foundation for the development of more specific rules to attain the agreed principles. The Council and the Commission made decisions on access to information.[90] The ToA took matters further by, for example, enshrining a right of access to documents in Article 255. This reflected the concerns with democracy, legitimacy, and transparency, found in the reports leading to the 1996 IGC. It would, however, be mistaken to conclude that all the principles mentioned in the 1993 Declaration were safely secured, and this a matter to which we shall return when considering the broader issues of democracy within the EC.

(c) INTER-INSTITUTIONAL CO-OPERATION AND CONFLICT-RESOLUTION: THE MAKING OF PARTICULAR POLICIES

The discussion within this section has focused on the differing ways in which the institutions interact in the formulation of *general* legislative policy choices. It is now time to consider the ways in which the institutions interact in the making of a *particular* legislative norm.

Legislative proposals do not emerge from the Commission out of thin air. They will be the result of a Commission initiative. If the issue is of any importance then it will normally have been flagged in the Commission's outline of legislation submitted to the EP. Although the Commission has the right of initiative, the Council has made

---

[90] Council Dec. 93/731, [1993] OJ L340/43; Commission Dec. 94/90, [1994] OJ L46/58.

increasing use of Article 208 to request the Commission to submit legislative proposals.[91]

The *content of the Commission proposal* will be the result of interaction between the Commission, interest groups, national experts, and senior civil servants. The Commissioner will assume overall responsibility for a proposal within his or her area. It will have been fashioned by the relevant Directorate-General, and by the appropriate Directorates and Divisions which are part of that bureaucracy. When those directly involved with the proposed measure have given their approval, the draft will be sent to the *cabinet* of the Commissioner. When the Commissioner is satisfied with the draft it will then be submitted to the College of Commissioners. Legislative proposals, once formulated, require the endorsement of the whole Commission. The College of Commissioners will normally meet weekly. Legislative drafts which have been framed by those lower within the Commission hierarchy will pass up to higher levels, to be accepted, amended, or rejected as the case may be. One should not, however, assume that the process works in only one way.[92]

There is no single way in which decisions are taken. In practice teams of relevant commissioners can be delegated to act on behalf of the College; brain storming can be used; or a written procedure adopted whereby urgent and/or uncontroversial proposals are deemed adopted if no objection is lodged within a specified time to the dossier and draft proposal, normally a week.... Only routine matters are delegated to individual commissioners who are then empowered to act within the confines of a very narrow remit on the Commission's behalf: recurrent agricultural regulations are adopted in this way.

The *role of groups of national experts, civil servants, and interest groups in this process of policy-formation* is an interesting one. The framing of the proposal will, as indicated, involve close collaboration and consultation with a wide variety of groups. It should be emphasized that this will occur *before* the proposal begins its journey on one of the legislative routes considered above. The following extract embodies one view about the relationship between national civil servants and the Community bureaucracy. It expresses the idea that bureaucracies at the national and the Community level may become more interlocked, or *engrenagé*. A discourse takes place between the two bureaucratic levels.

W. Wessels, Administrative Interaction[93]

By participating in Community decision-making the national civil servants gain 'access' to and 'influence' on EC decision-making and implementation, thus also increasing their weight inside their respective national systems. The same general cost–benefit calculation applies to Community officials who gain access and influence on 'national' domains by opening their policy cycles to the national colleagues – although traditional federalists and supranationalists would argue that this is an unacceptable loss in autonomy and independence of the EC bureaucracy. This cost–benefit

[91] Sir Leon Brittan, 'Institutional Development of the European Community' [1992] *PL* 567.

[92] J. Lodge, 'EC Policymaking: Institutional Dynamics', in J. Lodge (ed.), *The European Community and the Challenge of the Future* (Pinter, 2nd edn., 1993), 11.

[93] W. Wallace (ed.), *The Dynamics of European Integration* (RISIA/Pinter, 1990), 230.

analysis by civil servants (*mutatis mutandis* by heads of State, ministers and interest groups, but not by national parliamentarians) creates a major dynamic for European integration leading not to a transfer of loyalty by national officials to a new centre but to cooperation of officials into a new system of shared government. This stage of State evolution is characterized by an increasing degree of cooperation, in vertical terms between different governmental levels, and in horizontal terms, among several groups of actors. The 'multi-level' interactions of civil servants of several national and international administrations thus reinforce trends towards specific forms of the 'sharing' or 'fusion' of powers between 'bureaucrats and politicians' which non-EC-related studies have identified.

National civil servants are not the only group that has input into policy-formation. Interest groups have, not surprisingly, concentrated increasing resources on the Community. Given that the maxim of lobbyists is to 'shoot where the ducks are' we should therefore expect interest groups to organize themselves at a European level. There is a considerable literature documenting the way in which such groups operate within the Community.[94] Certain matters are reasonably clear. Successful lobbying is dependent upon developing good advance intelligence; watching the national agenda; maintaining good links with national administrations; maintaining close contacts with Commission officials; presenting rational arguments; being co-operative; developing a European perspective; not gloating when successful; and not ignoring the implementation process.[95] Many Euro-associations have been formed to foster this process. The attitude of the Commission to such associations is, however, somewhat ambivalent, as the following extract demonstrates.

S. Mazey and J. Richardson, Pressure Groups and Lobbying in the EC[96]

There are many examples of the Commission helping to resource these associations and of individual officials 'massaging' the developmental process within the associations (via direct funding and via 'soft' money, for example financing conferences etc.). Thus much of the Commission's activity—particularly at the service level—is very supportive of Euro-associations. Yet, when faced with the day-to-day pressures of initiating and formulating policy proposals which will actually work in the twelve Member States, Commission officials regularly by-pass the Euro-associations. The reasons for this are two-fold. First . . . the associations are of necessity broad in their interests. Commonly, the national industries being represented by the associations have quite different traditions, different structures, and above all, different and *competing* interests. For example, the financial services sector is quite different in Britain and Germany. This means that a European-level regulatory regime which would suit the British would probably not suit the Germans. As with governmental coalitions, the associations have to devise compromise policies—

---

[94] See, e. g., S.P. Mazey and J.J. Richardson, *Lobbying in the EC* (Oxford University Press, 1992); R.H. Pedler and M.P.C.M. Van Schendelen (eds.), *Lobbying the European Union: Companies, Trade Associations and Issue Groups* (Dartmouth, 1994).

[95] S.P. Mazey and J.J. Richardson, 'Pressure Groups and Lobbying in the EC', in Lodge (ed.), n. 92 above, 44.

[96] *Ibid*. 38–9. Italics in the original.

often referred to by the Commission as 'lowest common denominator policies'—which are so general as to be of little practical use to officials. Moreover, the associations often lack the necessary expertise so needed by Commission officials. Thus, it is very common for officials to develop links with individual national associations . . . and to develop links with individual firms as a means of securing reliable technical information quickly.

The Commission has developed its own principles to govern its dealings with interest groups. It distinguishes between profit and non-profit organizations. It may consult such groups on an *ad hoc* basis, or through an advisory committee. It uses Green Papers and the like as a mechanism for eliciting the views of such groups. The Commission also demands certain standards from such groups, relating to their dissemination of EC information, their behaviour, and the way in which they represent themselves.

Interest-group pressure at the Community level is to be expected. This does not mean we should be complacent about the problems it entails. Profit-making groups outnumber non-profit groups by a very significant margin, and their resources are much larger. The costs of organizing at the European level may be especially onerous for the voluntary/non-profit sector. Powerful groups are likely to make their voices heard irrespective of whether formal participatory rights exist. This is less obviously so for those with less financial muscle.

Once a Commission proposal has been formulated *it will make its way to the Council, and normally to the European Parliament,* where the latter has a legislative role in the particular area. We shall begin by considering the way in which the Council deals with the proposal.

COREPER is of crucial importance in this respect. The structure of this body has been considered in a previous chapter.[97] We are concerned here with the role played by COREPER in the legislative process. Before any measure is actually seen by the Council itself, it will have been thoroughly examined by one or more working groups that assist COREPER, as well as by COREPER I or II. These working groups are composed of national officials and experts from the Member States, plus a member of the Commission. They may be permanent or *ad hoc*. There may be 250 such groups at any one time.[98] These working groups will examine the Commission proposal and prepare a report. This will indicate the areas on which agreement has been reached ('Roman I points') and all other points ('Roman II points'). The latter will then be discussed within COREPER. Points agreed by the working group will normally be accepted by COREPER, with debate focusing on those issues where consensus has not yet been attained. Reference back to the working group may occur.

COREPER continues to be important once proposed measures have been tabled before the Council. This is because of its agenda-setting function. Issues on which there is agreement within COREPER will be placed on the 'A list' and will be adopted without discussion. If agreement within COREPER has not been possible then such

[97] See 67–8 above.
[98] F. Hayes-Renshaw, C. Lequesne, and P. Mayor Lopez, 'The Permanent Representations of the Member States to the European Communities' (1989) 27 *JCMS* 119, 132.

issues will be placed on the 'B list', indicating that debate and decision by the Council are required. Members of COREPER will attend Council meetings as advisers to their national ministerial representatives.

The modifications in the decision-making process since the SEA have increased the importance of the Council Presidency. The Office of the Presidency will co-ordinate the meetings of the differing Councils. It should be remembered that the Council is fragmented. The participants will vary depending upon the subject-matter: on some occasions foreign ministers will attend, on others it will be the minister responsible for a particular sectoral problem. The President will also mediate conflicts between the Member States themselves, between the Member States and the Commission, and between the Council and the Parliament. The necessity for conflict mediation, both by the Council President and by the Commission, is particularly important in those areas in which the European Parliament has a greater say in the legislative process.

Amendments to Commission proposals normally require unanimity in the Council.[99] This requirement is applicable when the Council adopts a common position at first reading under the co-decision procedure. It gives the Commission considerable leverage in the passage of legislation.[100] This is because if the Council wishes to make changes to legislation, the only way that it can avoid the unanimity requirement is to negotiate with the Commission. The compromise can then take the form of an amended proposal that can pass by qualified majority.

Decisions within the Council will normally be reached by consensus. We should not, however, underestimate the importance of the shift to majority voting brought about by the SEA. Weiler captures this when stating that 'reaching consensus under the shadow of the vote is altogether different from reaching it under the shadow of the veto'.[101]

It is to the *role of the Parliament* in the passage of legislation that we should now turn. The main part of the Parliament's legislative work is, not surprisingly, undertaken by standing committees, which are normally subject-matter based.[102] The appropriate committee will make the initial draft report on legislation submitted to the Parliament pursuant to Article 251 or 252 (ex Article 189b or 189c) EC. The responsibility for drawing up the committee report is given to a *rapporteur*. The *rapporteur* can seek assistance from the Parliament's secretariat, from the secretariat of his or her own political group, from the research services which each MEP possesses, and from research institutes. The *rapporteur* will present the draft report to the committee. It will normally have four parts: any amendments to the Commission proposal; a Draft Legislative Resolution; an Explanatory Statement; and any relevant Annexes. The committee will advise the MEPs as a whole how to vote in the plenary session, and the *rapporteur* will usually act as the committee's spokesperson. The same committee will examine the proposed legislation in the light of the common position adopted by the Council under Article 251.

The Commission will, as indicated earlier, often have an important arbitral role to

---

[99] Art. 250(1) (ex 189a(1)).
[100] Wyatt and Dashwood's *European Union Law* (Sweet & Maxwell, 4th edn., 2000), 53.
[101] N. 81 above, 2461.   [102] See 78–9 above.

play. It will often have to 'juggle' matters in the attempt to find a legislative package acceptable to Parliament, the Council and itself.

It should not be forgotten that the Commission may well have *resort to soft law* where it is impossible to secure the passage of a regulation or directive, or where it believes that this is a better way to reach a particular policy goal. Thus, for example, the Commission has resorted to the use of a Communication to achieve goals on pension funds, which it had been unable to attain through the passage of a directive because of deadlock in the Council.[103] It has used circulars in the place of formal decisions where Council approval was not forthcoming.[104]

8. DEMOCRACY WITHIN THE COMMUNITY[105]

The democratic legitimacy of the decision-making structure within the EC has long been a subject of debate. This has been particularly so since the TEU, as reflected in the institutional reports which led up to the 1996 IGC[106] and the rich vein of academic literature.[107] A significant part of this literature is concerned with the EC's 'democratic deficit'. While views undoubtedly differ on this issue, the following account, developed from Joseph Weiler's summary of the democratic deficit,[108] is reasonably representative. It is important to understand that the phrase 'democratic deficit' has a number of different features which must be distinguished.

---

[103] Case C–57/95, *France v. Commission (Re Pension Funds Communication)* [1997] ECR I–1627.

[104] Cases 239–240/96R, *United Kingdom v. Commission (Re Measures to Assist the Elderly)* [1996] ECR I–4475.

[105] The discussion within this section draws in part on P. Craig, 'The Nature of the Community: Integration, Democracy and Legitimacy', in P. Craig and G. de Búrca (eds.), *The Evolution of EU Law* (Oxford University Press, 1999), ch. 1.

[106] Craig, n. 1 above; G. de Búrca, 'The Quest for Legitimacy in the European Union' (1996) 59 *MLR* 349.

[107] See, e.g., just in terms of books, S. Garcia (ed.), *European Identity and the Search for Legitimacy* (Pinter, 1993); J. Hayward (ed.), *The Crisis of Representation in Europe* (Frank Cass, 1995); A. Rosas and E. Antola (eds.), *A Citizens' Europe, In Search of a New Order* (Sage, 1995); R. Bellamy, V. Bufacchi, and D. Castiglione (eds.), *Democracy and Constitutional Culture in the Union of Europe* (Lothian Foundation Press, 1995); S. Andersen and K. Eliassen (eds.), *The European Union: How Democratic Is It?* (Sage, 1996); R. Bellamy and D. Castiglione (eds.), *Constitutionalism in Transformation: European and Theoretical Perspectives* (Blackwell, 1996); R. Bellamy (ed.), *Constitutionalism, Democracy and Sovereignty: American and European Perspectives* (Avebury, 1996); F. Snyder (ed.), *Constitutional Dimensions of European Economic Integration* (Kluwer, 1996); R. Dehousse (ed.), *Europe: The Impossible Status Quo* (Macmillan, 1997); D. Curtin, *Postnational Democracy, The European Union in Search of a Political Philosophy* (Kluwer, 1997); Craig and Harlow (eds.), n. 39 above; R. Corbett, *The European Parliament's Role in Closer EU Integration* (Palgrave, 1998); J. Weiler, *The Constitution of Europe* (Cambridge University Press, 1999); C. Hoskyns and M. Newman (eds.), *Democratizing the European Union* (Manchester University Press, 2000); B. Laffan, R. O'Donnell, and M. Smith, *Europe's Experimental Union: Rethinking Integration* (Routledge, 2000); F. Mancini, *Democracy and Constitutionalism in the European Union* (Hart, 2000); K. Neunreither and A. Wiener (eds.), *European Integration after Amsterdam, Institutional Dynamics and Prospects for Democracy* (OUP, 2000); R. Prodi, *Europe As I See It* (Polity, 2000).

[108] J. Weiler, U. Haltern, and F. Mayer, 'European Democracy and its Critique', in J. Hayward (ed.), *The Crisis of Representation in Europe*, (Frank Cass, 1995), 32–3; J. Weiler, 'European Models: Polity, People and System', in *Lawmaking in the European Union*, n. 39 above, ch. 1.

(a) THE NATURE OF THE ARGUMENT

An important critique of Community decision-making is that it is 'unresponsive to democratic pressures'. It is a cardinal feature of democratic regimes that voters at the ballot box can change the government. This is not the case within the EU. Legislative power is divided between the Council, Commission, and Parliament. It is only the Parliament that is elected. A change in the Parliament's composition through European elections will not, therefore, necessarily lead to any major shift in EU policy, precisely because it is only one component in the legislative process.

A second facet of the democracy deficit argument concerns 'executive dominance'. The transfer of competence to the Community enhances the power of the executive at the expense of parliaments. This is because of the dominance of the Council and European Council in the EC's decision-making process, and the difficulty experienced by national parliamentary bodies in exercising any real control over the decisions made in the EC. While the existence of the EP alleviates this problem, by providing a directly elected forum at the European level, it does not remove it. This is in part because of its limited powers; it is in part because of lack of voter interest in elections to the EP; and it is in part because of the absence of any developed party system within the EC.

A third feature of the democracy deficit argument is the 'by-passing of democracy argument'. This is applied most frequently to the operation of the EC's complex committee structure known generally as Comitology. We have seen that many technical, but important, regulations are made by committees established pursuant to a delegation of power to the Commission. Technocrats and national interest groups have dominated this sphere of decision-making to the exclusion of the more regular channels of democratic decision-making, such as the European Parliament and even the Council.

There is, fourthly, what may be termed the 'distance issue'. The existence of the Community has involved the transfer of competence on many issues to Brussels and away from the nation State. This has meant that, in a literal sense, matters are further removed from the citizen.

A fifth aspect of democracy deficit can be termed the 'transparency and complexity issue'. Traditionally much of the decision-making of the Community, particularly that of the Council, has taken place behind closed doors. In addition the very complexity of the legislative procedures has meant that it is virtually impossible for any one, other than an expert, to understand them.

There is, sixthly, the less known 'substantive imbalance issue'. Writers from the left argue that the democratic deficit should also encompass the imbalance between labour and capital, which they claim has been exacerbated by the freeing up of the European market.

There is, finally, the 'weakening of judicial control issue'. A number of legal systems possess courts which have powers, either *ex ante* or *ex post*, over the constitutionality of primary legislation. The transfer of competence to the Community means that such powers are thereby reduced in scope.

(b) EVALUATION OF THE ARGUMENT: THE EMPIRICAL
FRAME OF REFERENCE

We live by and through language. The very language of democratic deficit is powerful in its imagery. It speaks to some base point from which we are deviating, an impression reinforced by the analogy with budget deficit. Democracy cannot however be measured or calibrated in the same way as a budget. Any assessment of the democratic deficit argument must necessarily be partly empirical and partly theoretical. These aspects of the argument will be addressed in turn. The discussion that follows does not mean that democracy within the EU is incapable of improvement. It does mean that we must be realistic and fair when assessing democracy within the EU in comparison to national regimes, and in comparison to what would be the case if the EU did not exist.

The empirical frame of reference is the *status quo ante*. The Community's democratic deficit of democracy is adjudged to be so by way of comparison with the position as it would be if matters were still dealt with at the national level. In order to assess the accuracy of this argument we must examine the reality of decision-making within national polities *and* postulate what the locus of decision-making would be if there were no EU.

The *first step of the argument* takes us into familiar territory. Executives tend to be dominant in most modern domestic polities. The degree of dominance varies, but the general proposition none the less holds true. The idea that national parliaments really control the emergence or content of legislative norms no longer comports with reality. The force of the 'executive dominance' critique of Community decision-making appears weaker when viewed in this light.[109] It is, moreover, by no means self-evident that the EP has less power over the content of legislation than do national parliaments. It is common to read general statements that the EP has little real power even now. Empirical evidence for such propositions is wanting. Most Community legislation is now subject to the co-decision procedure. Statistics show that the EP has had a pretty good strike rate at getting its amendments included in the final regulation or directive.[110] It might be argued that these amendments were minor, or ones that the Council was willing to accept. The former can only be tested by a detailed study of the various legislative acts in question. The latter is simply reductionist: of course the Council has to accept the amendments since otherwise the norm will not become law, but this does not prove that the EP exercised no power. The matter can, in any event, be put differently. How many changes which were not executive-sponsored did the legislature in, for example, the UK manage to have incorporated in statutes in any one year?

An understanding of the reality of national decision-making is also of importance

---

[109] It is not fortuitous that the thesis advanced by Andersen and Burns, about the erosion of parliamentary democracy, applies a theory about that erosion as it operates *within* nation States to the Community: S. Andersen and T. Burns, 'The European Union and the Erosion of Parliamentary Democracy: A Study of Post-Parliamentary Governance', in *The European Union: How Democratic Is It?*, n. 107 above, ch. 13.

[110] Westlake, n. 17 above, 39; S. Boyron, 'The Co-decision Procedure: Rethinking the Constitutional Fundamentals', in *Lawmaking in the European Union*, n. 39 above, ch. 8; Maurer, n. 39 above, 21–9.

when considering the Comitology problem and the 'bypassing of the normal democratic process'. There is a real problem here for the Community. We should, however, be mindful of the fact that the legitimation of secondary norms is an endemic problem for all domestic political systems. The UK, for example, has not satisfactorily resolved the need for the expeditious passage of secondary norms and the need to ensure effective legislative oversight. Indeed, many norms of a legislative nature are not seen by the legislature at all. The Community has moreover endeavoured to alleviate this problem through the reform of the Comitology decision considered above. These reforms have sought to make the committee procedure more transparent, and have brought the Parliament more fully into the process than hitherto.

The *second step of the argument* takes us into less familiar terrain. The assumption commonly made is that if the EU did not exist then the matters currently within its competence would be dealt with at national level. Decisions would then be made closer to the people, hence alleviating the 'distance problem', and parliaments would have greater control, hence mitigating the 'executive dominance' problem. The conclusion does not follow from the premise. The pressures for some form of international co-ordination would still be present, even if the EU never existed. An enduring insight from integration theory is that cross-border flows of goods create international policy externalities, which in turn create incentives for policy co-ordination.[111] The key issue then becomes not whether States interact, but how. They can do so by *ad hoc* international agreements, involving two or more parties. Some more permanent form of international co-operation will often be preferred in order to reduce the bargaining and transaction costs of *ad hoc* co-ordination. This is especially so when the number of parties becomes larger, and the issues on which they seek to co-ordinate become broader.

The real contrast must, therefore, be between how issues such as 'distance', 'executive dominance', 'transparency', and the like play out as between these differing forms of international co-ordination. There is little room for doubt here: if we apply these criteria then the people fare less well when matters are regulated through a series of *ad hoc* international agreements than they do when they are regulated through a body such as the EU. This is so for a number of reasons. International agreements normally include no forum such as the EP at all. Such agreements are made by the executives, they are run by the executives, and terminated by the executives. National parliaments can exercise only minimal control. They may have to give their approval to the agreement, but any parliamentary supervision thereafter will usually be interstitial and marginal at best.[112]

---

[111] A. Moravcsik, 'Preferences and Power in the European Community: A Liberal Intergovernmentalist Approach' (1993) 31 *JCMS* 473, 485. See also W. Wessels, 'The Modern West-European State and the European Union: Democratic Erosion or a New Kind of Polity?', in *The European Union: How Democratic Is It?*, n. 107 above, ch. 4; G. Majone, 'The European Community Between Social Policy and Social Regulation' (1993) 31 *JCMS* 153 and 'The Rise of the Regulatory State in Europe' (1994) *West European Politics* 1; Craig, n. 105 above.

[112] This is so even in those countries where national legislation is required to transform rules made pursuant to such international agreements into national law, since executive control over the legislature will mean that this is often unproblematic. The very fact that a large number of such agreements may exist renders it more difficult for parliaments to keep track, and takes such matters out of the purview of the ordinary citizen entirely.

(c) EVALUATION OF THE ARGUMENT: THE NORMATIVE FRAME OF REFERENCE

We must now consider the theoretical aspect of the democracy deficit argument. The theory is vital, because of the differing meanings of democracy. It is therefore axiomatic that discussion of the deficits of a particular system must be grounded in some more particular conception of democracy. If this is not done then we are testing the system against a criterion which is either not stated, or is at best only implicit.

Thus one strand of the democracy deficit critique is based implicitly on the assumption that the EU must be judged by the same normative criteria that are applied to ordinary nation States. It is common to see the argument develop in the following way: national parliaments have certain types of power, and the decision-making structure of the EU is deficient in not according the European Parliament the same degree of power. This will not withstand examination. The EU may not conform to the stereotype of the traditional international agreement, but nor is it a super State in the traditional sense of the term.[113] To reason unthinkingly from the division of power within nation States to the EU is therefore unwarranted.

A more promising approach is to develop the line of argument advanced by Joseph Weiler,[114] and to recognize that different aspects of the EU may best reflect different modes of governance. There are international/intergovernmental facets of Community governance, dealing with fundamental rules of the system and issues of high politics, in which the Member States are the prominent players. There are supra-national aspects of the EU, which best capture governance and legislation under the EC Treaty itself. Member States, combined with the Community institutions, are the main actors in this arena. There are, finally, those aspects of the Community, primarily the making of detailed regulatory norms implementing Community policy, which are best explained in terms of infranationalism. Here the main players tend to be interest groups, and bureaucrats, both national and European, which often bypass traditional forms of democratic governance. Weiler argues that these differing forms of Community governance can best be captured through different models of democracy. He contends that the international facets can be explained through a consociational model of democracy; the supranational aspects of Community governance through some version of Schumpeterian elite democracy or pluralist democracy; and the infranational elements through a neo-corporatist model.

Commentators will undoubtedly have different views on which model of democracy best fits the different aspects of EU governance.[115] This is to be expected. Weiler's general methodology does, none the less, free us when thinking about EU democracy from the confines of what is an inappropriate, rigid paradigm of the traditional nation State. If we pursue this general approach then the division of power as it currently exists within the EC itself can be more readily understood and justified.

---

[113] For an interesting discussion of different forms of State and their application to the EU see J. Caporaso, 'The European Union and Forms of State: Westphalian, Regulatory and Post-Modern' (1996) 34 *JCMS* 29.

[114] N. 108 above.

[115] Compare Weiler, n. 108 above, and Craig, n. 105 above.

The Community is built on an institutional balance between the Council, European Parliament, and the Commission, as is evident from, *inter alia*, all the institutional reports leading to the 1996 IGC.[116] It rests on the twinfold legitimacy of the Member States, as represented in the Council, and their peoples, as represented in the European Parliament.

The role accorded to the Council in this institutional balance can be defended, most fundamentally, because the democratic legitimacy of the Community is founded upon the Member States as well as its peoples. The Council does, in any event, have an indirect democratic mandate, flowing from the fact that those who sit on the Council will normally be elected members of their own national executive. The Council's powers can also be sustained on the ground that the Community is based on an international agreement. While it can be accepted that it no longer fits within the paradigm of the standard international agreement, it is a *non sequitur* to conclude that elements of State control are normatively unjustified within such a system.

It is accepted that the European Parliament is deserving of power within the system, by virtue of being directly elected. The gradual extension of the EP's powers in the legislative process bears testimony to this, notwithstanding the fact that it has had to struggle for its powers: the EP 'was born hungry and frustrated and has developed into an habitual struggler'.[117] The generalization of the co-decision procedure to cover most important Community legislation means that the EP has come close to attaining co-equal status in the legislative process with the Council. This is, as the Commission has stated, a natural step in the process of enhancing the democratic legitimacy of the Union, and establishes 'the twofold legitimacy on which the Community is founded, its States and its peoples'.[118] The failure of the EP to obtain a power of legislative initiative *and* its decision not to press for this power at the 1996 IGC are indicative of the limited consequences flowing from the direct democratic mandate. The reasons for this limitation are eclectic. They are in part a reflection of the fact that the EC is not perceived as a State. It is in part because to accord the EP such a power would unbalance the system in its favour *vis-à-vis* the Council. It is in part also because of the perceived need to preserve the unique position of the Commission, so as not to compromise its role as guardian of the Treaties and 'engine room' of the Community.

The Commission's powers, and its right of legislative initiative, can be seen as helping to ensure that Community policies are directed towards the advancement of the general good laid down in the constituent Treaties, as opposed to narrow sectional self-interests. It is for this reason that the Commission has always opposed any inroad into its right of legislative initiative, believing its 'sole right of initiative to be a fundamental constitutional prerogative vital to the good functioning of the Community's institutional balance and its legislative machinery'.[119] This does not mean that the detailed interpretations of general Community principles or their

---

[116] Craig, n. 1 above.
[117] M. Westlake, *A Modern Guide to the European Parliament* (Pinter, 1994), 28.
[118] *Scope of the Codecision Procedure*, SEC(96) 1225/4, July 1996, Pt. IIA, para. 1.
[119] Westlake, n. 17 above, 79. See also, J. Fitzmaurice, 'The European Commission', in *Maastricht and Beyond, Building the European Union*, n. 71 above (Routledge, 1994), 183–4.

prioritization are value-free, or that the Commission is free from interest-group pressure. It does mean that the Commission is well placed to consider legislation to attain the general good as laid down in the Treaties. It also means that it conceives of its role in this manner and, at the present stage of the Community's development, that it can fulfil this role better than either the Council or the EP. The members of the Council will often be swayed by relatively short-term considerations relating to the needs of their own Member State. This is less of a problem with the EP, which has not, thus far, divided along generally nationalistic lines. It is, however, not yet institutionally well suited to the generation of a coherent, general legislative strategy to attain the objectives laid down in the constituent Treaties. When considered from this perspective the retention of the Commission's right of legislative initiative appears more defensible in normative terms. This is particularly so given the fact that the Commission will engage in detailed negotiations with both the Council and the EP on the annual legislative plan, as well as on specific legislative proposals; and given also the greater control exercized by the EP over the appointment of the Commission.

We can, in the light of this, return to the very first aspect of the democracy deficit argument, which we have not evaluated thus far. This is, as will be recalled, the argument that EU democracy is deficient because those who make the decisions cannot be voted from office. The very fact that legislative power is divided between Council, Commission, and the EP precludes this. There is some force in this argument. We must however think through the consequences of this critique. EU decision-making is posited on institutional balance. If it were felt that the EU could only be properly democratic if the citizens were able to vote out *the body* that exercized legislative power, then this would involve a radical restructuring of the EU. It would not be sufficient for the EP to have some control over the Commission, as it does at present. Nor would it suffice for the President of the Commission and the Commissioners to be elected. Nor would it even be sufficient for an elected Commission to become the EU's executive and control the EP. These changes would be highly contentious. They would not meet the critique, because the voters could still not 'vote out' the Member State representatives in the Council. It is doubtful whether the Member States would accede to a system in which their representatives were directly elected, and where they functioned as a 'second chamber' under the control of a directly elected Commission.

(d) THE CONVENTION AND THE GOVERNANCE WHITE PAPER

The Laeken European Council and the Commission's White Paper on *European Governance* both address issues that are central to democracy and legitimacy in the EU.

The Laeken European Council[120] laid the institutional foundations for the next round of Treaty reform. It established a Convention, headed by Giscard d'Estaing, with two vice-chairmen, a representative from each State, two national members of Parliament from each country, sixteen MEPs, and two Commission representatives. The accession candidate countries are involved in the Convention proceedings.

---

[120] 14–15 Dec. 2001.

The Convention began its deliberations in March 2002, with the object of completing them within one year. The Convention will consider the division of competence between the EU and Member States, simplification of the Union Treaties, the status to be given to the Charter of Rights, the possibility of a European Constitution, and moves to enhance democracy, efficiency, and transparency in the EU. Each of these areas was given a broad reading in the Laeken Declaration. We shall therefore have to await the outcome of the Convention, to determine the conclusions reached on these topics, being mindful that the final Convention document will be the 'starting point' for discussion in the IGC, which will take the ultimate decisions.

The Convention will draw on a wide range of sources, and it is intended that civil society will be involved through a Forum. The views of the Commission are however likely to be especially influential, given its status within the Community and given that it produced a White Paper on *European Governance*,[121] which was welcomed by the Laeken European Council.[122] A brief look at the Commission White Paper is therefore timely, especially since it addresses matters that are central to the debate about democracy and legitimacy in the EU.[123]

The key to the Commission's document is its conception of the 'Community method'.[124] On this view, the Commission represents the general interest and has the monopoly over legislative initiation. It also executes agreed policy and acts as guardian of the Treaty. The Council and the EP are seen as the joint legislature, representing the Member States and national citizens respectively. This is in itself unexceptionable. It is the implications that the Commission draws from it that are contentious. It is, said the Commission, necessary to revitalize the Community method.[125] There should, for example, be greater consistency in the work of the sectoral Council. The Council and the EP should limit their involvement in primary Community legislation to defining the essential elements.[126] This legislation would define the conditions and limits within which the Commission performed its executive role. It would, in the Commission's view, make it possible to do away with the Comitology committees. There would instead be a simple legal mechanism allowing the Council and EP to control the actions of the Commission against the principles adopted in the legislation. The Commission would promote openness, transparency, and consultation when making initial legislative proposals and when implementing agreed policy. The centrality accorded by the Commission to the 'Community method' is further apparent in its submission to the Laeken European Council.[127]

The revitalization of the Community method as given expression in the White Paper is, however, problematic. The combination of greater use of framework legislation, informal law, and increased Commission control over implementing

---

[121] COM(2001)428 final.   [122] Laeken European Council, para. 4.
[123] The White Paper provoked a variety of critical comment: see the *Symposium: Responses to the European Commission's White Paper on Governance*, www.jeanmonnetprogram.org/papers/01.
[124] COM(2001)428 final, 8.   [125] *Ibid.*, 29.   [126] *Ibid.*, 20.
[127] *Communication from the Commission on the Future of the European Union, Renewing the Community Method*, COM(2001)727 final.

norms would in reality alter significantly the institutional balance of power in the Community. It would reduce the power of the Council and EP, and increase that of the Commission. The Community method has never allowed the Commission full autonomy over the execution of delegated norms. Comitology-type committees were created as soon as the need to delegate extensive powers to the Commission became a reality. They have been part of the institutional landscape for over thirty years. They were created precisely to accord Member States an institutionalized method for input into the content of delegated legislation. It is true that the Comitology committees have been much criticized. They have however survived and expanded into new areas. On the view proposed by the Commission, the Member States would give up input into the content of delegated legislation, the substitute being a legal action allowing the Council and EP to control the exercise of delegated legislative power. Generalized *ex ante* input through the political process accords more power than does individualized *ex post facto* control through the legal process.

This issue will, like many others, be debated in the Convention created by the Laeken European Council. The Convention's final document will then be the starting point for the IGC that is to follow.

9. CONCLUSION

i. Institutional balance between the Commission, Council, and European Parliament has always characterized decision-making within the EU. That balance is dynamic, not static, and it has changed over time.

ii. The increase in the power of the EP has been the principal feature in that institutional dynamic. The EP has struggled for power and has used gains that it has made to further its claim for a co-equal status in the legislative process.[128] The generalization of the co-decision procedure has gone a considerable way to affording the EP this co-equal status. The 1999 Comitology Decision has also improved the position of the EP in relation to delegated legislation.

iii. The legitimacy of EU decision-making is now founded on the Council, as representing State interests, and the EP as representing the interests of the peoples of Europe. The Commission, which is increasingly accountable to the EP, seeks to ensure that the goals laid down in the Treaties are met.

iv. The fact that the general distribution of legislative authority as it operates in the supranational arena of EC governance can be defended does not mean that the system could not be improved.

v. There is room for improvement in many areas. These include the quality of EU

---

[128] R. Corbett, *The European Parliament's Role in Closer EU Integration* (Palgrave, 1998).

legislation,[129] the role of national parliaments,[130] and citizen participation in EU decision-making.[131]

vi. It should also be recognized that 'differentiation' and 'variable geometry' have implications for the governance of the EU, and for the conception of democracy that it embodies.[132] There are, moreover, newer forms of governance emerging.[133]

10. FURTHER READING[134]

ANDENAS, M., and TURK, A. (eds.), *Delegated Legislation and the Role of Committees in the EC* (Kluwer, 2000)

ANDERSON, S., and ELIASSEN, K. (eds.), *The European Union: How Democratic Is It?* (Sage, 1996)

BELLAMY, R. (ed.), *Constitutionalism, Democracy and Sovereignty: American and European Perspectives* (Avebury, 1996)

—— and CASTIGLIONE, D. (eds.), *Constitutionalism in Transformation: European and Theoretical Perspectives* (Blackwell, 1996)

—— BUFACCHI, V., and CASTIGLIONE, D. (eds.), *Democracy and Constitutional Culture in the Union of Europe* (Lothian Foundation Press, 1995)

CHRISTIANSEN, T., and KIRCHNER, E., *Committee Governance in the European Union* (Manchester University Press, 2000)

CORBETT, R., *The European Parliament's Role in Closer EU Integration* (Palgrave, 1998)

CRAIG, P., and HARLOW, C. (eds.), *Lawmaking in the European Union* (Kluwer, 1998)

CURTIN, D., *Postnational Democracy, The European Union in Search of a Political Philosophy* (Kluwer, 1997)

DEHOUSSE, R. (ed.), *Europe: The Impossible Status Quo* (Macmillan, 1997)

DUFF, A., PINDER, J., and PRYCE, R. (eds.), *Maastricht and Beyond, Building the European Union* (Routledge, 1994)

GARCIA, S. (ed.), *European Identity and the Search for Legitimacy* (Pinter, 1993)

GEORGE, S. and BACHE, I., *Politics in the European Union* (Oxford, 2001)

---

[129] T. Burns, 'Better Lawmaking? An Evaluation of Lawmaking in the European Community', in *Lawmaking in the European Union*, n. 39 above, ch. 21. See also Declaration 39 appended to the ToA on the Quality of the Drafting of Community Legislation.

[130] P. Norton (ed.), *National Parliaments and the Role of the European Union* (Frank Cass, 1996); E. Smith (ed.), *National Parliaments as Cornerstones of European Integration* (Kluwer, 1996); H. Schmitt and J. Thomassen (eds.), *Political Representation and Legitimacy in the European Union* (Oxford University Press, 1999); R. Katz and B. Wessels (eds.), *The European Parliament, the National Parliaments and European Integration* (Oxford University Press, 1999). See Protocol on the Role of National Parliaments in the European Union, attached to the ToA, which provides, *inter alia*, for Commission Consultation documents to be forwarded promptly to such parliaments, and for a six-week period in which national parliaments can consider proposed Community legislation before it is declared upon by the Community institutions.

[131] Craig, n. 1 above; Curtin, n. 107 above.

[132] J. Shaw, 'Constitutionalism and Flexibility in the EU: Developing a Relational Approach', in G. de Búrca and J. Scott (eds.), *Constitutional Change in the EU, From Uniformity to Flexibility?*, (Hart, 2000), ch. 15.

[133] J. Scott and D. Trubek, 'Mind the Gap: Law and New Approaches to Governance in the European Union' (2002) 8 *ELJ* 1.

[134] The volume of material on this topic means that only books have been listed here.

HAYWARD, J. (ed.), *The Crisis of Representation in Europe* (Frank Cass, 1995)

HOSKYNS, C., and NEWMAN, M. (eds.), *Democratizing the European Union* (Manchester University Press, 2000)

JACOBS, F., CORBETT, R., and SHACKLETON, M., *The European Parliament* (Harper, 4th edn., 2000)

JOERGES, C. and VOS, E. (eds.), *EU Committees: Social Regulation, Law and Politics* (Hart, 1999)

KEOHANE, R., and HOFFMANN, S. (eds.), *The New European Community, Decisionmaking and Institutional Change* (Westview Press, 1991)

LAFFAN, B., *Integration and Co-operation in Europe* (Routledge, 1992)

—— O'DONNELL, R., and SMITH, M., *Europe's Experimental Union: Rethinking Integration* (Routledge, 2000)

LODGE, J. (ed.), *The European Community and the Challenge of the Future* (Pinter, 2nd edn., 1993)

MANCINI, F., *Democracy and Constitutionalism in the European Union* (Hart, 2000)

NEUNREITHER, K., and WIENER, A., (eds.), *European Integration after Amsterdam, Institutional Dynamics and Prospects for Democracy* (Oxford University Press, 2000)

NUGENT, N., *The Government and Politics of the European Union* (Macmillan, 4th edn., 1999)

O'KEEFFE, D., and TWOMEY, P.M. (eds.), *Legal Issues of the Maastricht Treaty* (Chancery, 1994)

PEERS, S., *EU Justice and Home Affairs Law* (Longman, 2000)

PRODI, R., *Europe As I See It* (Polity, 2000)

RICHARDSON, J. (ed.), *European Union: Power and Policy-Making* (Routledge, 2nd edn., 2001)

ROSAS, A., and ANTOLA, E. (eds.), *A Citizens' Europe, In Search of a New Order* (Sage, 1995)

SNYDER, F. (ed.), *Constitutional Dimensions of European Economic Integration* (Kluwer, 1996)

WALLACE, W. (ed.), *The Dynamics of European Integration* (RIIA/Pinter, 1990)

—— and WALLACE, H. (eds.), *Policy-making in the European Union* (Oxford University Press, 4th edn., 2000)

WEILER, J., *The Constitution of Europe* (Cambridge University Press, 1999)

WESTLAKE, M., *The Commission and the Parliament: Partners and Rivals in the European Policy-Making Process* (Butterworths, 1994)

—— *A Modern Guide to the European Parliament* (Pinter, 1994)

—— *The Council of the European Union* (Harper, rev. edn., 1999)

—— (ed.), *The European Union Beyond Amsterdam: New Concepts of European Integration* (Routledge, 1998)

5

THE NATURE AND EFFECT OF EC LAW

1. CENTRAL ISSUES

i. The doctrine of 'direct effect' of EC law is applicable at least in principle to all binding Community law including the EC Treaties, secondary legislation, and international agreements. The most problematic issues concern international agreements and EC directives.

ii. The precise meaning of direct effect remains contested. In a broad sense it means that provisions of binding EC law which are clear, precise, and unconditional enough to be considered justiciable can be invoked and relied on by individuals before national courts. There is also a 'narrower' or classical concept of direct effect which is defined in terms of the capacity of a provision of EC law to *confer rights* on individuals.

iii. Although most international agreements entered into by the EC can be invoked and enforced by individuals in national courts if they satisfy the criteria of justiciability, the ECJ has ruled that this is not true of the World Trade Organization Agreements. However, they can under certain circumstances be invoked as a standard of legality for reviewing EC legislation. Further, secondary EC law must, in principle, be interpreted as far as possible in conformity with international agreements.

iv. While directives can be enforced directly by individuals against the State after the time limit for their implementation has expired (vertical direct effect), the ECJ has ruled that they cannot of themselves impose obligations on individuals (no horizontal direct effect).

v. However, the Court has developed other legal mechanisms for giving greater effect to directives which have not properly been implemented. First, there is a broad obligation on national courts to interpret domestic law, as far as possible, in the light of and in conformity with directives (indirect effect). Secondly, a directive can in certain cases be legally invoked in proceedings between private parties (incidental effect) so long as the directive does not in itself impose a legal obligation on one of the parties. These are complex legal developments which will be discussed further below.

2. INTRODUCTION: THE AMBIGUOUS CONCEPT OF DIRECT EFFECT

In the first decades of the Community's existence, the most striking feature of EC law was the impact it claimed to have on the legal systems of the Member States. In distinguishing EC law from the law of other international organizations, the Court of Justice asserted the autonomy and original nature of the Community legal system. In a series of judgments, the Court not only declared Community laws to be binding but also required them to be internalized—often without any national implementing measures—within the domestic legal systems of the Member States. The Court developed a bold theory of the nature of EC law, attributing to it the characteristics and force which the Court considered necessary to promote a set of dynamic and far-reaching common goals within a group of distinct and sovereign States. This became clear in its early case law in which the Court outlined what has become known as the 'direct effect' of Community law.

In contrast to the ECJ's approach of *stipulating* the domestic effect which EC law and the EC Treaties were to have, the domestic effect of an international treaty has traditionally been a matter to be determined in accordance with the constitutional law of each of the States which is party to that treaty. In countries which adopt a largely dualist approach to international law, international agreements do not of themselves give rise to rights or interests which citizens can invoke and enforce before national courts. Instead, the provisions of such treaties bind only the States at an intergovern-mental level and, in the absence of implementation, cannot be directly domestically invoked or enforced by citizens.[1] Since the texts of the EC Treaties made no reference to the effect which their provisions were to have, it is possible that some of the original Member States did not envisage that the provisions of these Treaties were to be treated any differently, in domestic terms, from other international treaties.

The doctrine of direct effect has been relevant primarily to the *Community* legal system rather than that of the European Union as a whole. This is because the ECJ lacks jurisdiction over the provisions of the second pillar and cannot therefore in the same way determine the legal effect of those provisions or of measures adopted under them, and because, despite the changes made to the third pillar by the Amsterdam Treaty, it is unlikely that the Court will find its provisions to have direct effect, particularly since Article 34 TEU stipulates that the legislative decisions which may be adopted under those provisions shall not entail direct effect.[2]

We shall see in this Chapter that the concept of direct effect is not straightforward. Academic and even judicial uncertainty remains about the exact meaning and scope of the term. There are many different ways of giving effect to EC law and not all of these necessarily involve 'direct effect' in what we may call its strict or original sense.[3] In recent years, for example, debate has arisen over whether the 'conferral of rights on individuals' is a necessary precondition for the existence of direct effect, or whether on the other hand it is merely a normal but not inevitable consequence of direct effect. To put the matter differently, it is possible on the basis of the ECJ's case law to adopt either a broad or a narrow definition of direct effect.[4] The broader definition, which can arguably be derived from the classic *Van Gend en Loos* judgment, can be

---

[1] See D. Wyatt, 'New Legal Order or Old' (1982) 7 *ELRev.* 14.

[2] However, although this is said of decisions and framework decisions, the Art. does not say that imple-menting measures may not entail direct effect, and it remains to be seen how the ECJ will construe such measures.

[3] See also the earlier discussion of the differences in meaning of the terms 'direct applicability' and 'direct effect', which the ECJ seemed to use interchangeably: T. Winter, 'Direct Applicability and Direct Effects' (1972) 9 *CMLRev.* 425; Warner AG in Case 131/79, *Santillo* [1980] ECR 1585, 1608–9, [1980] 2 CMLR 308; and more recently P. Eleftheriadis, 'The Direct Effect of Community Law: Conceptual Issues' (1996) 16 *YBEL* 205, and the opinion of Geelhoed AG in Case C–253/00, *Antonio Muñoz v. Frumar Ltd.*, 13 Dec. 2001.

[4] For various analyses see S. Prechal, 'Does Direct Effect Still Matter?' (2000) 37 *CMLRev.* 1047 and also in her longer work *Directives in EC Law* (Oxford University Press, 1995); M. Lenz, D.S. Tynes, and L. Young, 'Horizontal What? Back to Basics' (2000) 25 *ELRev.* 509, and C. Hilson and T. Downes, 'Making Sense of Rights: Community Rights in EC Law' (1999) 24 *ELRev.* 121.

expressed as *the capacity of a provision of EC law to be invoked before a national court.*[5] This is sometimes referred to as 'objective' direct effect.[6] And while it is true that the normal consequence of a legal provision being invoked, as indeed in *Van Gend en Loos* itself, is that it confers a legal right of some kind on the individual who invokes it, this is not, on the broader definition, an essential component of the notion of direct effect. If on the other hand the narrower (and arguably the 'classical') definition of direct effect is adopted, it is usually expressed in terms of the *capacity of a provision of EC law to confer rights on individuals which they may enforce before national courts.* This is sometimes referred to as 'subjective' direct effect.

Much, however, depends on the definition of 'rights' which is being used. If what is meant is simply the *right to invoke* EC law in a national court to assist one's case, then there is little difference between the narrow and the broad notions of direct effect.[7] In a series of recent cases in which the ECJ declared the 'establishment' provisions of the various Europe Association Agreements to be directly effective, the Court began by stating that the provisions in question had established:

a precise and unconditional principle which is sufficiently operational to be applied by a national court and which is therefore capable of governing the legal position of individuals.[8]

Here we see clarity and precision mentioned as the conditions of justiciability and of direct applicability of EC law in national courts. But do these justiciable provisions automatically confer rights upon individuals? The ECJ in each of the cases concerning these provisions of the Europe Agreements went to say that:

the direct effect which those provisions must therefore be recognised as having means that . . . nationals relying on them have the right to invoke them before the courts of the host Member State.

The ECJ thus did not specify *how* the national courts should respond to the invocation of the provisions on freedom of establishment in the various Europe Agreements nor what substance it should give to them, but defined the 'right' conferred on the individuals simply in terms of a right to invoke those provisions. This approach seems to bring together the narrow and the broad notions of direct effect, by conflating 'invocability' with the 'conferral of a right'.

---

[5] In Case 26/62, *Van Gend en Loos* the ECJ ruled that Art. 12 should be interpreted 'as producing direct effects and creating individual rights', thus implying that the latter followed from, but was not necessarily a condition for, the former: [1963] ECR 13.

[6] W. van Gerven, 'Of Rights, Remedies and Procedures' (2000) 37 *CMLRev.* 501 and D. Edward, 'Direct Effect, the Separation of Powers and the Judicial Enforcement of Obligations', in *Scritti in Onore di Giuseppe Federico Mancini, II, Diritto dell' Unione Europea* (Guiffré, 1998) 423.

[7] A related question, if the narrower 'subjective' definition is adopted, concerns *who* can invoke the rights conferred by a directly effective provision of law. In Cases C–87–89/90, *Verholen* [1991] ECR I–3757 the ECJ ruled that someone other than an affected party could plead the direct effect of a Community provision on the other's behalf, whereas in Case C–72/95, *Kraaijeveld* [1996] ECR I–5403 paras. 57–60 the ECJ ruled that the direct effect of Community provisions could be raised by the national court even where none of the parties to the case had done so; and see also Cases C–240–244/98, *Océano Grupo Editorial* v. *Rocio Murciano Quintero* [2000] ECR I–4491, discussed below at n. 112 and text. Case C–230/97, *Awoyemi* [1998] ECR I–6781 established that a non-EU national could invoke the directly effective provisions of Dir. 80/1263 on driving licences since he fell within the scope of the measure, even while he could not invoke more fundamental and directly effective EC Treaty provisions on free movement of persons since they did not apply to him.

[8] Cases–C–63/99, *Gloszczuk* [2001] ECR I–nyr; C–257/99, *Barkoci and Malik* [2001] ECR I–nyr; C–235/99, *Kondova* [2001] ECR I–nyr, C–268/99, *Jany* [2001] ECR I–nyr.

In many other cases, however, the ECJ has gone beyond the simple reference to a right to invoke, and has indicated that an individual litigant can rely before a national court on the substantive right—such as the right to be free from discrimination based on nationality—which is contained in a clear and precise provision of EC law.[9] And if, indeed, the 'conferral of rights on individuals' necessarily involves something more specific and substantive than the bare right to invoke a legal provision—if for example it involves the entitlement to a particular remedy[10] or it entails the imposition of a corresponding duty or liability on another party[11]—then there may well be a relevant difference between the broad and the narrow definitions. The reality of the situation in EC law, however, is that the ECJ seems to use the language of conferral of rights in the context of direct effect in several different senses: in some cases, the Court spells out quite a specific substantive right to which the individual is entitled, and even indicates the kind of remedy required for its enforcement. In others, it goes no further than to mention a 'right to invoke' such as that in the Europe Agreement cases. Thus even the narrow definition of direct effect in subjective terms as 'the conferral of individual rights' is not particularly precise, given the ambiguity in the notion of 'rights'.

This discussion is not of purely academic interest, because it has arisen in a practical way in a number of different contexts in recent years. Three contexts in particular will be mentioned briefly here. The *first* concerns the so-called horizontality problem, namely the question of the legal effects which unimplemented EC directives may have in cases between private partices. This will be discussed in further detail below.[12] Although the ECJ has appeared to rule out the direct effect of directives between private litigants, it has none the less permitted individuals in certain circumstances to invoke and rely on provisions of directives in proceedings against other individuals. The *second* practical context in which a distinction between a broader and a narrower definition of direct effect has come to light concerns the legal effects which certain international agreements—and in particular the World Trade Organization agreements—may have in litigation before EC and national courts.[13] While the ECJ ruled out the possibility of individual litigants deriving substantive rights from the provisions of the WTO agreements, it has allowed for the possibility that provisions of such agreements may, under specified circumstances, be invoked to challenge the legality of a Community act. The *third* context in which the debate over a narrower or a broader conception of direct effect has had practical relevance concerns the legal effect of certain provisions of EC law, such as environmental law, which appear to impose legal obligations, but where the existence of an individual right or interest which could be invoked by a litigant is less clear.[14]

---

[9] For an early example see Case 57/65, *Lütticke* v. *Hauptzollamt Sarrelouis* [1966] ECR (Sp.Ed.) 205 on Art. 90 (ex Art. 95) of the then EEC Treaty.

[10] See for discussion Prechal, n. 4 above; M. Ruffert, 'Rights and Remedies in European Community Law: A Comparative View' (1997) 34 *CMLRev*. 307; and W. Van Gerven, n. 6 above.

[11] See the arguments of Hilson and Downes, n. 4 above, who attempt to apply a Hohfeldian analysis to the language and judgments of the ECJ in this field.

[12] See below at 220–7.

[13] See Cases C–280/93, *Germany* v. *Commission* [1994] ECR I–4873 and C–149/96, *Portugal* v. *Council* [1999] ECR I–8395.

[14] See Cases C–72/95, *Kraaijeveld* [1996] ECR I–5403 and C–287/98, *Linster* [2000] ECR I–6917. The ECJ stated that where a Community measure imposes a clear obligation on a Member State, a national court must

In each of these three contexts, direct effect in the narrow sense seems to have been ruled out by the Court. However, we will see that the legal provisions in question can none the less be invoked to the advantage of an individual litigant under certain circumstances in all three contexts. Whether we call such cases instances of a broadly conceived direct effect or whether instead they should be labelled as some kind of 'other legal effect' remains a matter for academic and judicial debate. However, it could reasonably be argued that if the narrower doctrine (the conferral of particular substantive rights) is properly labelled 'direct effect', then, for the avoidance of confusion and uncertainty, a different conceptual label should be found for the broader doctrine of invocability. Alternatively and more radically, if we accept that the broader notion of invocability is simply the basic requirement of justiciability, and that the narrower notion of 'conferral of rights' is too ambiguous and multi-faceted in practice to have a distinctive meaning, it could be argued that the language of direct effect as a 'special feature' of EC law should be abandoned entirely.[15] Instead, we could simply focus on the range of different legal effects triggered or enjoyed by various types of EC law in different contexts and circumstances, at the suit of different types of litigant. For the moment, however, the proposal to abandon the language of direct effect entirely seems unlikely to be accepted and so we must continue to live with the concept and with its ambiguities for some time yet.

3. THE FIRST STEPS: THE DIRECT EFFECT OF TREATY PROVISIONS

The ECJ first articulated its doctrine of direct effect in 1963 in what is probably the most famous of all of its rulings.

Case 26/62, NV Algemene Transporten Expeditie Onderneming van Gend en Loos v.
Nederlandse Administratie der Belastingen
[1963] ECR 1

[Note ToA renumbering: Art. 12 is now Art. 25, and Art. 177 is now Art. 234 EC]

The Van Gend en Loos company imported a quantity of a chemical substance from Germany into the Netherlands. It was charged by Customs and Excise with an import duty which the company alleged had been increased (by changing the tariff classification of the substance from one with a lower to a higher tariff-heading) since the coming into force of the EEC Treaty, contrary to Article

---

not be prevented 'from taking it into consideration as an element of Community law', e.g. in reviewing compliance by that Member State with the obligation. In Cases C–431/92, *Commission* v. *Germany* [1995] ECR I–2189 and C–365/97, *Commission* v. *Italy* [1999] ECR I–7773, the ECJ ruled (albeit in the context of infringement proceedings) that the question whether a sufficiently clear and precise obligation has been imposed by a Community provision was different from the question whether an individual can derive rights from those provisions.

[15] See Prechal, n. 4 above. For a contrary view see B. de Witte, 'Direct Effect, Supremacy and the Nature of the Legal Order', in P. Craig and G. de Búrca (eds.), *The Evolution of EU Law* (Oxford University Press, 1999) 177, 188.

12 of that Treaty. An appeal against payment of the duty was brought before the Dutch Tarief-commissie, and Article 12 was raised in argument. The Tariefcommissie referred two questions to the ECJ under Article 177 of the Treaty, and asked 'whether Article 12 of the EEC Treaty has direct application within the territory of a Member State; in other words, whether nationals of such a State can, on the basis of the Article in question, lay claim to individual rights which the courts must protect'.

Observations were submitted to the ECJ by the Belgian, German, and Netherlands governments. Belgium argued that the question was whether a national law ratifying an international Treaty would prevail over another law, and that this was a question of national constitutional law which lay within the exclusive jurisdiction of the Netherlands court. The Netherlands government also argued that the EEC Treaty was no different from a standard international Treaty, and that the concept of direct effect would contradict the intentions of those who had created the Treaty.

THE ECJ[16]

To ascertain whether the provisions of an international treaty extend so far in their effects it is necessary to consider the spirit, the general scheme and the wording of those provisions.

The objective of the EEC Treaty, which is to establish a Common Market, the functioning of which is of direct concern to interested parties in the Community, implies that this Treaty is more than an agreement which merely creates mutual obligations between the contracting states. This view is confirmed by the preamble to the Treaty which refers not only to governments but to peoples. It is also confirmed more specifically by the establishment of institutions endowed with sovereign rights, the exercise of which affects Member States and also their citizens. Furthermore, it must be noted that the nationals of the states brought together in the Community are called upon to cooperate in the functioning of this Community through the intermediary of the European Parliament and the Economic and Social Committee. . . .

The conclusion to be drawn from this is that the Community constitutes a new legal order of international law for the benefit of which the states have limited their sovereign rights, albeit within limited fields, and the subjects of which comprise not only Member States but also their nationals. Independently of the legislation of Member States, Community law therefore not only imposes obligations on individuals but is also intended to confer upon them rights which become part of their legal heritage. These rights arise not only where they are expressly granted by the Treaty, but also by reason of obligations which the Treaty imposes in a clearly defined way upon individuals as well as upon the Member States and upon the institutions of the Community. . . .

The wording of Article 12 contains a clear and unconditional prohibition which is not a positive but a negative obligation. This obligation, moreover, is not qualified by any reservation on the part of states which would make its implementation conditional upon a positive legislative measure enacted under national law. The very nature of this prohibition makes it ideally adapted to produce direct effects in the legal relationship between Member States and their subjects.

The implementation of Article 12 does not require any legislative intervention on the part of the states. The fact that under this Article it is the Member States who are made the subject of the negative obligation does not imply that their nationals cannot benefit from this obligation. . . .

It follows from the foregoing considerations that, according to the spirit, the general scheme

[16] [1963] ECR 1, 12–13.

and the wording of the Treaty, Article 12 must be interpreted as producing direct effects and creating individual rights which national courts must protect.

Van Gend en Loos was a ground-breaking judgment. The strong submissions made on behalf of the three governments (half of the total number of Member States at the time) which intervened in the case indicate that the concept of direct effect of Treaty provisions—understood as the *immediate enforceability by individual applicants of those provisions in national courts*—probably did not accord with the understanding of those States of the obligations they had assumed when they became parties to the EEC Treaty. It is clear also that Advocate General Roemer, although he agreed that certain Treaty provisions could produce direct effects, considered that Article 25 (ex Article 12) was not one of these, and that to hold it to be directly effective could lead to a non-uniform application of that Article by different courts amongst the Member States.[17]

The ECJ reasoned partly by reference to the text of the Treaty itself, but most markedly by reference to a vision of the kind of legal community that the Treaties seemed designed to create. *Van Gend en Loos* provides an early example of the ECJ's distinctive interpretive approach and methodology. Variously referred to as instrumentalist, purposive, or teleological, this often controversial method of interpretation involves the Court reading the text—and the gaps in the text—of the Treaty in such a way as to further what it determines to be the underlying and evolving aims of the Community enterprise as a whole.[18]

In *Van Gend en Loos*, the Court developed the concept of direct effect principally in view of the kind of legal system which it considered necessary to carry through the ambitious economic and political programme outlined in the Treaties. Pierre Pescatore, a former judge of the Court, commented as follows.

P. Pescatore, The Doctrine of 'Direct Effect': An Infant Disease of Community Law[19]

It appears from these considerations that in the opinion of the Court, the Treaty has created a Community not only of States but also of peoples and persons and that therefore not only Member States but also individuals must be visualised as being subjects of Community law. This is the consequence of a democratic ideal, meaning that in the Community, as well as in a modern constitutional State, Governments may not say any more what they are used to doing in international law: *L'Etat, c'est moi.* Far from it; the Community calls for participation of everybody, with the result that private individuals are not only liable to burdens and obligations, but that they have also prerogatives and rights which must be legally protected. It was thus a highly political idea, drawn from a perception of the constitutional system of the Community, which is at the basis of *Van Gend en Loos* and which continues to inspire the whole doctrine flowing from it.

[17] *Ibid.*, 19, 20, 24.   [18] See Ch. 2, n. 210 and text.
[19] (1983) 8 *ELRev.* 155, 158.

Apart from invoking the 'spirit' of the Treaties, the Court in *Van Gend en Loos* also drew on the text in support of the concept of direct effect. It pointed to the Preamble which makes reference to citizens as well as to States, and argued that the preliminary-ruling procedure established in Article 234 (ex Article 177) envisaged that parties before national courts could plead and rely on points of EC law. The ECJ pointed also to the fact that citizens were envisaged as having a role to play under the Treaties through the medium of the European Parliament. None of this textual 'evidence' for direct effect is particularly strong, however, and the Court's elaboration of the aims of the Treaties provides a better explanation (if not a justification) of its decision to conclude that Article 25 (ex Article 12) could be invoked and enforced by the applicant before the Dutch courts. The ECJ evidently considered a strong enforcement method was needed to ensure that Member States did in practice comply with the provisions to which they had agreed. Automatic internalization of Treaty rules within national legal systems would clearly strengthen the effectiveness of Community norms as well as aiding the Commission in its Article 226 (ex Article 169) enforcement function by involving individuals and all levels of the national court system directly in their implementation.[20] The various drawbacks of the public enforcement mechanism of the Community, and in particular in so far as the vindication of individual rights or interests is concerned, are considered further in Chapter 10.

4. THE CONDITIONS FOR DIRECT EFFECT

It seems that legal integration, effectiveness, and uniform application of EC law across Member States were among the principal motivating factors behind the ECJ's attribution of direct effect to provisions of the EC Treaty. Yet, unlike much of national law which is specifically drafted with a view to its immediate operability and judicial enforcement, international treaties are frequently drafted in general terms, and not all of their provisions may be designed for immediate application by local courts and tribunals. Even if national courts were willing to attempt this task, they might reach rather different results in different States, thus undermining the aim of uniform application. Secondly, if national courts were themselves to flesh out an EC Treaty provision which was broadly phrased and which required further elaboration, those courts would arguably be usurping the political discretion of whichever authority— be it the Member States or one of the Community institutions—was entrusted with the role of implementing that provision.

Perhaps in view of these concerns, and also to introduce the idea of the direct effect of Treaty provisions to reluctant Member States in a more gradual manner, the ECJ in *Van Gend en Loos* established the requirement that a provision be essentially 'self-executing'. Thus the criteria which were met by Article 25 (ex Article 12) of the Treaty and which enabled it to have direct effect were that it was: *clear, negative, unconditional, containing no reservation on the part of the Member State, and not dependent on any national implementing measure.* Although these criteria were

[20] P.P. Craig, 'Once upon a Time in the West: Direct Effect and the Federalization of EEC Law (1992) 12 *OJLS* 453.

expressed in *Van Gend en Loos* in fairly strong terms, their application since then suggests that they are little more than conditions of justiciability, articulated in order to ensure that national courts can apply the law (and in particular, at the time, the new and unfamiliar Treaty law) without undue uncertainty or complexity in cases arising before them.[21]

Indeed, the Court's elaboration of what initially appeared to be specific and strong criteria for direct effect did not hinder the application of the doctrine to a wide range of Treaty provisions, nor to various other forms of Community law. Where Treaty provisions seemed overly broad or general, the ECJ suggested ways of considering separately the more precise and the 'unconditional' parts, and enabling those deemed sufficiently clear and exact to be applied directly by the national court. In other words, the ECJ sought to assist the national courts in rendering provisions of EC law operable and justiciable. This strategy is apparent in the early *Costa* v. *ENEL* case, in which the Court ruled that whereas Article 31(1) (ex Article 37(1)) of the EC Treaty imposed a positive and ongoing obligation on Member States to 'progressively adjust any State monopolies of a commercial character', the second paragraph of that same Article contained 'an absolute prohibition . . . an obligation to refrain from doing something'.[22] Since the latter obligation was unconditional and not dependent on any implementing national act, it was capable, unlike the first paragraph, of having direct effect.[23]

The apparently strict original criteria did not prevent the emergence in practice of a more general and commonsense notion of justicability. Article 43 (ex Article 52) of the EC Treaty, for example, provides that restrictions on freedom of establishment of Community nationals in States other than that of their nationality are to be abolished 'within the framework of the provisions set out below'. The framework in question was to have included a general programme and a set of directives adopted under Articles 44(2) (ex Article 54(2)) and 47(1) (ex Article 57(1)) to liberalize the activities of employed and self-employed persons, but few of these had been adopted by the time the *Reyners* case arose in 1973.

Case 2/74, Reyners v. Belgium
[1974] ECR 631

[Note ToA renumbering: Arts. 52, 54, and 57 are now Arts. 43, 44, and 47 respectively]

Jean Reyners was a Dutch national who obtained his legal education in Belgium, but was refused admission to the Belgian Bar (as *avocat*) solely on the ground that he lacked Belgian nationality. He challenged the relevant Belgian legislation before the Conseil d'Etat, which referred several questions to the ECJ, including the question whether Article 52 was directly effective in the absence of implementing directives under Articles 54 and 57.

---

[21] Pescatore, n. 19 above, 176–7. Van Gerven AG suggested that the test for direct effect is whether a provision of Community law is 'sufficiently operational' to be applied by a court: Case C–128/92, *Banks* v. *British Coal* [1994] ECR I–1209, 1237.

[22] Case 6/64, *Flaminio Costa* v. *ENEL* [1964] ECR 585.

[23] See also Case C–390/98, *H.J. Banks & Co. Ltd* v. *The Coal Authority*, 20 Sept. 2001, paras. 72 and 93, where parts of Art. 4 of the ECSC Treaty were held to be directly effective while other parts were not.

24. The rule on equal treatment with nationals is one of the fundamental legal provisions of the Community.

25. As a reference to a set of legislative provisions effectively applied by the country of establishment to its own nationals, this rule is, by its essence, capable of being directly invoked by nationals of all the other Member States.

26. In laying down that freedom of establishment shall be attained at the end of the transitional period, Article 52 thus imposes an obligation to attain a precise result, the fulfilment of which had to be made easier by, but not made dependent on, the implementation of a programme of progressive measures.

27. The fact that this progression has not been adhered to leaves the obligation itself intact beyond the end of the period provided for its fulfilment. . . .

. . .

29. It is not possible to invoke against such an effect the fact that the Council has failed to issue the directive provided for by Articles 54 and 57 or the fact that certain of the directives actually issued have not fully attained the objective of non-discrimination required by Article 52.

30. After the expiry of the transitional period the directives provided for by the Chapter on the right of establishment have become superfluous with regard to implementing the rule on nationality, since this is henceforth sanctioned by the Treaty itself with direct effect.

In this case the Court appeared determined that, despite the slow pace of harmonization of national laws in the field of free movement and establishment of self-employed persons, the Treaty could be directly invoked by individuals in order to challenge obvious instances of nationality discrimination against them. The basic principle of non-discrimination was deemed to be directly effective, even though the conditions for genuine freedom of establishment were far from being achieved. Whereas many cases on direct effect concern the enforcement of obligations against a Member State which has failed properly to implement Community requirements (*Van Gend*, *Costa* v. *ENEL*, and *Defrenne II*[24]), the *Reyners* case shows the Court employing the direct-effect concept to compensate for insufficient action on the part of the *Community* legislative institutions. Four of the Member States had argued to the Court in *Reyners* that it should not ignore the absence of any harmonizing directives and should not declare Article 43 (ex Article 52) to be directly effective, since it was not 'for the courts to exercise a discretionary power reserved to the legislative institutions of the Community and the Member States'. However, since in this case there were no relevant disparities between the laws of two Member States, and yet one of the States specifically treated non-nationals less favourably purely on grounds of nationality, the principle of Article 43 could be directly invoked by the individual regardless of the absence of implementing directives.

A similar use of direct effect to 'trigger' the proper implementation of a Treaty provision can be seen in the second *Defrenne* judgment,[25] which relaxed further the

[24] Case 43/75, *Defrenne* v. *Société Anonyme Belge de Navigation Aérienne* [1976] ECR 455.
[25] *Ibid.*

original *Van Gend en Loos* criteria for direct effect. While in *Reyners*, Article 43 (ex Article 52) seemed expressly to envisage further implementing measures, Article 141 (ex Article 119) in *Defrenne* appeared to lack sufficient precision to be invoked by an individual and directly enforced by a national court. Article 141 (ex Article 119) at that time required States to ensure 'the application of the principle that men and women should receive equal pay for equal work'.[26] Unlike the Treaty provisions in *Van Gend* and *Costa*, Article 141 did not impose a very precise negative obligation on the Member States. The term 'principle', for example, is not very specific, nor were the terms 'pay' and 'equal work' defined. It was also evident from a Commission recommendation of 20 July 1960 and a resolution of the Member States of 30 December 1961 concerning Article 141, that neither the Commission nor the States considered that provision to be directly effective or legally complete.[27] What the Court did, however, was to identify and isolate the principle of Article 141 at the time—that of equal pay for equal work—and to ignore the fact that there might be cases involving complex factual questions regarding 'work of equal value' concerning jobs which were different in nature. In the latter sort of case the Court seemed to suggest that there might not be sufficient precision or clarity to enable the national court to apply the Article directly nor to afford a remedy to the worker in question, but that would not affect the direct effectiveness of the core principle of Article 119 in cases such as the present one, where the factual issues were clearly determined.

The Court's concern in such cases seems to have been to ensure that the Community's aims were not ignored either by reluctant Member States or by sluggish Community institutions, during the years of so-called legislative sclerosis which followed the Luxembourg Accords.[28] If a national court was unsure of the exact meaning of the relevant provision, the ECJ was more than willing to clarify its scope in a preliminary ruling under Article 234 (ex Article 177).

There have, however, been cases in which the ECJ has ruled that a particularly aspirational Treaty provision such as Article 2, or a provision which clearly required further implementation in order to be capable of precise judicial application such as Article 255 (ex Article 191a) could not have direct effect.[29] Apart from the lack of uniformity to which its domestic judicial application could give rise, the requirement of direct enforceability could, in the absence of more specific implementing measures at Community level, involve too great a transfer of political discretion and legislative-type power to the national courts. In the following case a Spanish national sought to rely before a national tribunal on Article 2 of the Treaty, which provides *inter alia* that 'the Community shall have as its task . . . an accelerated raising of the standard of

[26] See further Ch. 20 on Equal Treatment of Women and Men for the inclusion of 'work of equal value' with the amended Art. 141.

[27] See Trabucchi AG in Case 43/75, n. 24 above, 485.

[28] See Ch. 1.

[29] In Case T–191/99, *Petrie* v. *ALLS I/CDFL*, judgment of 11 Dec. 2001, paras. 34–35, the CFI ruled that the principle of access to documents in Art. 255 (ex Art. 191a) was not unconditional and required further implementation before it could be relied upon for a precise result.

In Case C–236/92, *Comitato di Coordinamento per la Difesa della Cava* v. *Regione Lombardia* [1994] ECR I–483 the ECJ ruled that provisions of a dir. on waste disposal were insufficiently precise or unconditional to give rise to direct effect. See later however Case C–365/97, *Commission* v. *Italy* [1999] ECR I–7773 the ECJ ruled that the same provision was sufficiently clear to impose an obligation on the Member State.

living', to challenge a rule of national law which prohibited the overlapping of a retirement pension with his employment in the public service.

Case 126/86, Zaera v. Institutio Nacionale de la Seguridad Social
[1987] ECR 3697

THE ECJ

10. Article 2 of the Treaty describes the task of the European Economic Community. The aims laid down in that provision are concerned with the existence and functioning of the Community; they are to be achieved through the establishment of the Common Market and the progressive approximation of the economic policies of Member States, which are also aims whose implementation is the essential object of the Treaty.

11. With regard to the promotion of an accelerated raising of the standard of living, in particular, it should therefore be stated that this was one of the aims which inspired the creation of the European Economic Community and which, owing to its general terms and its systematic dependence on the establishment of the Common Market and progressive approximation of economic policies, cannot impose legal obligations on Member States or confer rights on individuals.

The Treaty provision in question, to quote from Advocate General Mancini's opinion, 'contains expressions of intent, purpose and motive, rather than rules that are of direct operative effect'.

5. THE LEGAL EFFECTS OF OTHER MEASURES: REGULATIONS AND DECISIONS

Apart from the provisions of the Treaties, which are seen by the ECJ as the constitutional basis of the Community,[30] the principal forms of legislative action which the Community may adopt are set out in Article 249 (ex Article 189) of the EC Treaty. In legal terms, the most important of these are regulations and directives, although there are also many softer forms of law which are provided for in the Treaty or which have evolved in practice. The Community, as we saw in Chapter 2, also has external competence to enter into agreements with countries outside the EU. A further important source of Community law is what the Court refers to as the 'general principles' of law deriving from the common traditions and constitutional rules shared by the Member States,[31] and from international agreements and conventions to which all are party.[32] The Court has also ruled that the Community and its institutions 'must respect' international law and are 'required to comply with the rules of customary

---

[30] See para. 3 of the judgment in Case 294/83, *Parti Ecologiste 'Les Verts' v. Parliament* [1986] ECR 1339, and para. 21 of *Opinion 1/91 (Draft Treaty on a European Economic Area)* [1991] ECR 6079.
[31] See Chs. 8 and 9.
[32] See in particular Case 11/70, *Internationale Handelsgesellschaft* [1970] ECR 1125.

international law' in the exercise of their powers, although the Court did not go so far as to say that those rules were sufficiently precise to be directly effective in the narrow sense.[33] It will be seen in the discussion which follows, however, that most binding forms of Community law have been deemed by the ECJ to be capable of direct effect, and that while other types of non-binding or soft law are not said to have direct effect, they are influential in other ways and may have what has become known as indirect or interpretative effect.[34]

We have seen that the textual basis in the EC Treaty for the conclusion that Treaty provisions could have direct effect was not compelling. However, Article 249 (ex Article 189) of the Treaty provides that a regulation 'shall be binding in its entirety and directly applicable in all Member States'. Policy considerations aside, this language seems to envisage that regulations, at least, will immediately become part of the domestic law of Member States, without needing transposition. And if they are immediately part of the domestic law of Member States there is no reason why—so long as their provisions are sufficiently clear, precise, and relevant to the situation of an individual litigant[35]—they should not be capable of being relied upon and enforced by individuals before their national courts.[36]

Case 39/72, Commission v. Italy
[1973] ECR 101

[ToA renumbering: Arts. 43, 169, 189, and 191 are now Arts. 37, 226, 249, and 254 respectively]

The Commission by a series of regulations instituted a system of premiums for slaughtering cows and withholding milk products from the market. Taking the view that Italy had not complied with these, the Commission brought infringement proceedings under Article 169, claiming that the delay and the eventual manner of giving effect to the system were in breach of the Commission Regulations.

THE ECJ

17. By following this procedure, the Italian Government has brought into doubt both the legal nature of the applicable provisions and the date of their coming into force.

According to the terms of Articles 189 and 191 of the Treaty, Regulations are, as such, directly

---

[33] Case C–162/96, *Racke* v. *Hauptzollamt Mainz* [1998] ECR I–3655. The ECJ however ruled that 'an individual relying in legal proceedings on rights which he derives directly from an agreement with a non-member country may not be denied the possibility of . . . invoking, in order to challenge the validity of [an EC] regulation, obligations deriving from rules of customary international law'.

[34] See, e.g., Case 322/88, *Salvatore Grimaldi* v. *Fonds des Maladies Professionelles* [1989] ECR 4407, on the indirect effect of non-binding Community recommendations.

[35] See Case C–403/98, *Azienda Agricola Monte Arcosu* v. *Regione Autonoma della Sardegna* [2001] ECR I–103 in which the provisions of a reg. were not sufficiently precise and therefore could not be directly relied upon.

[36] See Geelhoed AG's recent discussion of the relationship between the direct applicability of provisions of a reg. and their direct effect in terms of the capacity of individuals to invoke and derive rights from those provisions, in Case C–253/00, *Antonio Muñoz* v. *Frumar Ltd.*, 13 Dec. 2001.

applicable in all Member States and come into force solely by virtue of their publication in the *Official Journal* of the Communities, as from the date specified in them, or in the absence thereof, as from the date provided in the Treaty.

Consequently, all methods of implementation are contrary to the Treaty which would have the result of creating an obstacle to the direct effect of Community Regulations and of jeopardizing their simultaneous and uniform application in the whole of the Community. . . .

20. According to the third paragraph of Article 43(2) of the Treaty, on which Regulation No 1975/69 is founded, Regulations are validly enacted by the Council as soon as the conditions contained in the Article are fulfilled.

Under the terms of Article 189, the Regulation is binding 'in its entirety' for Member States.

In consequence, it cannot be accepted that a Member State should apply in an incomplete or selective manner provisions of a Community Regulation so as to render abortive certain aspects of Community legislation which it has opposed or which it considers contrary to its national interests.

In this case the Court emphatically confirmed the direct effect of regulations and criticized any attempt by a Member State to alter or dilute the requirements of a Community regulation. This does not necessarily mean, however, that any national measure enacted with the intention of giving effect to a regulation will be invalid. In the following case the ECJ indicated that it is only if a national measure alters, obstructs, or obscures the nature of the Community regulation that it will constitute a breach of Community law.

Case 50/76, Amsterdam Bulb BV v. Produktschap voor Siergewassen
[1977] ECR 137

THE ECJ

4. As the Court has already stated in other contexts, in particular in its judgment of 10 October 1973 (*Variola SpA* v. *Amministrazione Italiana delle Finanze* [1973] ECR 981), the direct application of a Community Regulation means that its entry into force and its application in favour of or against those subject to it are independent of any measure of reception into national law.

5. By virtue of the obligations arising from the Treaty the Member States are under a duty not to obstruct the direct effect inherent in regulations and other rules of Community law.

6. Strict compliance with this obligation is an indispensable condition of simultaneous and uniform application of Community regulations throughout the Community.

7. Therefore, the Member States may neither adopt nor allow national organizations having legislative power to adopt any measure which would conceal the Community nature and effects of any legal provision from the person to whom it applies.

The Court's concern here seems to be that, by taking steps to transpose a regulation into national law, a Member State may obscure the fact that the provision was one of

Community law. This could have adverse consequences for the Community, since the particular qualities of Community law—that it takes priority over conflicting national law, that there must be adequate remedies for breach, that it may be subject to different methods of interpretation from those traditionally used in the national context, etc.—may be ignored. Further, the Court was clearly concerned that Member States might alter or adversely affect the content of the regulation by adopting measures to transpose it into national law in a slightly different form. However, in the *Amsterdam Bulb* case itself the ECJ accepted that Member States could provide in national legislation for appropriate sanctions which were not provided for in the Regulation, and could legitimately continue to regulate various related issues which were not covered in the Regulation. Indeed, in some cases a Regulation may positively *require* implementing measures to be adopted by the State. As the ECJ ruled in *Azienda Agricola Monte Arcosu*:

although, by virtue of the very nature of regulations and of their function in the system of sources of Community law, the provisions of those regulations generally have immediate effect in the national legal systems without its being necessary for the national authorities to adopt measures of application, some of their provisions may none the less necessitate, for their implementation, the adoption of measures of application by the Member States.[37]

Another of the forms of Community act listed under Article 249 (ex Article 189) is the decision, which is to be 'binding in its entirety upon those to whom it is addressed'. Unlike a regulation, a decision will not normally be a general measure but an individual one which is directed to a specific addressee or addressees.[38] The ECJ had little hesitation in holding that decisions, too, could be directly effective, despite the fact that Article 249 (ex Article 189), unlike in the case of regulations, made no reference to their 'direct applicability'.

Case 9/70, Franz Grad v. Finanzamt Traunstein
[1970] ECR 825

[Note ToA renumbering: Articles 177 and 189 are now Articles 234 and 249]

THE ECJ

4. The German Government in its observations defends the view that by distinguishing between the effects of regulations on the one hand and of decisions and directives on the other, Article 189 precludes the possibility of decisions and directives producing the effects mentioned in the question, which are reserved to regulations.

5. However, although it is true that by virtue of Article 189, regulations are directly applicable and therefore by virtue of their nature capable of producing direct effects, it does not follow

---

[37] Case C–403/98, *Azienda Agricola Monte Arcosu v. Regione Autonoma della Sardegna* [2001] ECR I–103, para. 26.

[38] See the discussion in Ch. 3, 115–16, indicating the various types of EC dec. which are used, some of which are individual in nature and addressed to particular parties, but others of which are general in nature and without addressees.

from this that other categories of legal measures mentioned in that article can never produce similar effects. In particular, the provision according to which decisions are binding in their entirety on those to whom they are addressed enables the question to be put whether the obligation created by the decision can only be invoked by the Community institutions against the addressee or whether such a right may possibly be exercised by all those who have an interest in the fulfilment of this obligation. It would be incompatible with the binding effect attributed to decisions by Article 189 to exclude in principle the possibility that persons affected may invoke the obligation imposed by a decision. Particularly in cases where, for example, the Community authorities by means of a decision have imposed an obligation on a Member State or all the Member States to act in a certain way, the effectiveness (*l'effet utile*) of such a measure would be weakened if the nationals of that State could not invoke it in the courts and the national courts could not take it into consideration as part of Community law. Although the effects of a decision may not be identical with those of a provision contained in a regulation, this difference does not exclude the possibility that the end result, namely the right of the individual to invoke the measure before the courts, may be the same as that of a directly applicable provision of a regulation.

In that case the Court held that the obligation imposed in the decision in question was sufficiently unconditional, clear, and precise to be capable of giving rise to direct effect. Returning to our earlier discussion of the narrower and the broader conceptions of direct effect, the ECJ in this judgment discusses direct effect in terms of the right of an individual to 'invoke the obligation' created by a decision before a national court (the broad notion of invocability), but also spells out in some detail the substance of that obligation which the individual can invoke and have enforced (the more precise notion of conferral of rights).

6. THE LEGAL EFFECTS OF INTERNATIONAL AGREEMENTS IN EC LAW

By virtue of Articles 281 (ex Article 210) and 300 (ex Article 228) of the EC Treaty, the Community has legal personality and is empowered to enter into contractual relations with other persons and organizations. The question arising within the current discussion concerns the legal effect of international agreements entered into by the EC. We shall see that in this context the 'direct effect' of international agreements concerns the capacity for such agreements to be directly invoked and enforced not only within the legal orders and courts of the Member States, but also within the legal order of the EU before the Court of Justice.

On the one hand, as treaties concluded with other States or international organizations, these could be seen as traditional international agreements binding only the States or organizations which signed them and having no specific effect upon individuals. On the other hand, as agreements entered by the Community, they could share some of the key characteristics of EC law, and in particular could be capable of direct effect and enforcement by individuals whenever sufficiently precise and unconditional. Opting broadly for the approach which would integrate agreements made by the Community into the law of the Member States, the Court held that international agreements can, *under certain circumstances*, be directly effective. We shall see, however, that in the field of international agreements, a range of more political considerations comes into play, and the question whether or not the provisions of a particular kind of agreement have direct effect is not determined by reference only to the legal criteria first developed in *Van Gend en Loos*. The issue which has dominated this area of law in recent years and which has generated a vast academic literature, namely whether the provisions of the General Agreement on Trade and Tariffs (GATT) 1947 and the successor World Trade Organization (WTO) agreements can have direct effect, was first raised several decades ago. In the *International Fruit Company* case, a Dutch court made a preliminary reference to the ECJ, asking whether it had jurisdiction to rule on the validity of Community regulations in relation to a provision of international law and if so whether the regulations in question were contrary to the GATT.

Cases 21–24/72, International Fruit Company v. Produktschap voor
Groenten en Fruit
[1972] ECR 1219

THE ECJ

7. Before the incompatibility of a Community measure with a provision of international law can affect the validity of that measure, the Community must first of all be bound by that provision.

8. Before invalidity can be relied upon before a national court, that provision of international law must also be capable of conferring rights on citizens of the Community which they can invoke before the courts. . . .

18. It therefore appears that, in so far as under the EEC Treaty the Community has assumed the powers previously exercised by Member States in the area governed by the General Agreement, the provisions of that agreement have the effect of binding the Community.

19. It is also necessary to examine whether the provisions of the General Agreement confer rights on citizens of the Community on which they can rely before the courts in contesting the validity of a Community measure.

20. For this purpose, the spirit, the general scheme and the terms of the General Agreement must be considered.

The Court concluded from various aspects of the GATT, including the 'great flexibility of its provisions', the possibilities of derogation, and the power of unilateral withdrawal from its obligations, that it was 'not capable of conferring on citizens of the Community rights which they can invoke before the courts'. In other words, in terms of the criteria for direct effect laid down in earlier cases, the provisions of GATT were insufficiently precise and unconditional in the sense that they permitted the obligations contained therein to be modified, and they allowed for too great a degree of flexibility. The ECJ was unwilling to accord direct effect to international obligations of this nature, in particular since they were normally invoked to challenge the legality of EC legislation.[39]

In *Polydor*, the Court was confronted with a provision not of the GATT, but of a free trade agreement between the Community and Portugal before Portugal had joined the Community.[40] Here the ECJ ruled that a provision of the trade agreement on free movement of goods, although it was worded identically to a provision of the then EEC Treaty (Article 28, ex Article 30), was not to be interpreted in the same way and should not be given direct effect, since the agreement with Portugal did not have the same aim or purpose as the EEC Treaty of establishing a single market. In *Hauptzollamt Mainz* v. *Kupferberg*,[41] however, the ECJ ruled that a different provision of the Portugeuse free trade agreement did have direct effect, since the provision was unconditional, sufficiently precise, and its direct application was within the *purpose* of the agreement. It is worth noting that, unlike in the GATT cases, the effect of declaring the trade agreement in *Kupferberg* to be directly effective was to extend the scope of Community rules rather than challenging or invalidating them. Similarly, the ECJ has held that provisions of the earlier Lomé Convention governing relations between the EC and the African, Caribbean, and Pacific States were directly effective, and this again was in a case in which national rather than Community legislation was being challenged for incompatibility with the Convention.[42]

It should be noted that in paragraph 8 of its *International Fruit* judgment (above), the Court appeared to equate direct effect with the possibility of review of legality, and to rule out the latter unless the former were present. However, in the later *Nakajima* case, the Court distinguished between the 'direct effect' of the provisions of an international trade agreement and the possibility of invoking those provisions to claim that EC legislation was incompatible with them.[43] Here we see the distinction once again between a narrower conception of direct effect and a broader conception of invocability (for the purposes of review). However, in the case of *Germany* v. *Commission*, the ECJ made clear that a GATT provision could be invoked for the purposes of alleging the incompatibility of an EC measure in only two circumstances: (1) where the Community *intended* to implement that particular obligation, or (2) where the Community measure being challenged expressly referred to the particular GATT provision.[44] None the less, despite this restrictive approach, the ECJ in other cases has applied the 'obligation of harmonious interpretation'—i.e. the principle that EC law should be interpreted in the light of international law and of binding international

[39] This was confirmed in various cases after *Kupferberg* including cases 9/73, *Schluter* v. *Hauptzollamt Lörrach* [1973] ECR 1135, and C–469/93 *Amministrazione delle Finanze dello Stato Chiquita Italia* [1995] ECR I–4533.

[40] Case 270/80, *Polydor Ltd. and RSO Records Inc.* v. *Harlequin Record Shops Ltd. and Simons Records Ltd.* [1982] ECR 329.

[41] Case 104/81, [1982] ECR 3641. See G. Bebr, 'Agreements Concluded by the Community and their Possible Direct Effect: From International Fruit Company to Kupferberg' (1983) 20 *CMLRev*. 35.

[42] See Case C–469/93, *Amministrazione delle Finanze dello Stato* v. *Chiquita Italia* [1995] ECR I–4533.

[43] Case C–69/89, *Nakajima* v. *Council* [1991] ECR 2069, paras. 28–29. For this purpose, according to the Court, the provisions need only be binding on the Community. However, in the case in question the ECJ ruled that the Community anti-dumping rules in issue did not conflict with the Anti-Dumping Code adopted under the GATT. See also Case 70/87, *Fediol* v. *Commission* [1989] ECR 1781.

[44] Case C–280/93, *Germany* v. *Commission* [1994] ECR I–4873.

agreements,[45] to the provisions of GATT and other WTO agreements.[46] This has the consequence of enhancing their effectiveness in certain circumstances, albeit not normally when they are being invoked to challenge EC measures.

Following the establishment of the WTO and the adoption of the new GATT in 1994, however, it was argued that in view of the changed provisions and the more effective means of dispute settlement and enforcement under the new system, the premises on which the GATT 1947 had been held to lack direct effect no longer applied.[47] Having avoided addressing the question of the legal effect and enforceability of the WTO agreements in a series of cases before the ECJ and the CFI, the ECJ finally confronted it directly.

Case C–149/96, Portugal v. Council
[1999] ECR I–8395

Portugal brought an action for annulment of a 1996 Council Decision which concluded a memorandum of understanding on market access for textiles with Pakistan and with India respectively. Portugal argued *inter alia* that the Decision was in breach of the WTO rules, including provisions of GATT 1994. Portugal argued that the case did not raise the problem of direct effect but rather 'the circumstances in which a Member State may rely on the WTO agreements before the Court for the purpose of reviewing the legality of a Council measure'. The ECJ began by indicating that it was only where an international agreement did not itself settle the question of the effects which its provisions would have within the legal orders of the contracting parties that it would fall to be decided by the courts.

THE ECJ

36. While it is true that the WTO agreements, as the Portuguese Government observes, differ significantly from the provisions of GATT 1947, in particular by reason of the strengthening of the system of safeguards and the mechanism for resolving disputes, the system resulting from those agreements nevertheless accords considerable importance to negotiation between the parties.

The ECJ then went on to examine the dispute-settlement rules under Articles 2, 3, and 22 of the Dispute Settlement Understanding (DSU) of the WTO, and noted that although they provided for withdrawal of any measures found to be incompatible

---

[45] See Cases C–61/94, *Commission v. Germany* [1996] ECR I–3989, para. 52 and C–341/95, *Safety Hi-Tech v. S & T srl* [1998] ECR I–4355, para. 20. See also Case C–286/90, *Anklagemyndigheden v. Poulsen and Diva Navigation* [1992] ECR I–6019, para. 9.

[46] Cases C–53/96 *Hermès International v. FHT Marketing Choice* [1998] ECR I–3603 and C–300 & 392/98, *Dior v. Tuk Consultancy,* judgment of 14 Dec. 2001.

[47] See, e.g., Case T–228/95R, *S. Lehrfreund Ltd. v. Council and Commission* [1996] ECR II–111, para. 28, and many cases which followed. There is also a vast academic literature on this subject. For a small sample see J. Scott, 'The GATT and Community Law: Rethinking the Regulatory Gap', in J. Shaw and G. More (eds.), *New Legal Dynamics of European Union* (Oxford University Press, 1995) and P. Lee and B. Kennedy, 'The Potential Direct Effect of GATT 1994 in EC Law' (1996) 30 *Journal of World Trade* 67; P. Eeckhout, 'The Domestic Legal Status of the WTO Agreement: Interconnecting Legal Systems' (1997) 34 *CMLRev.* 11; J. Berkey, 'The European Court of Justice and Direct Effect for the GATT: A Question Worth Revisiting' (1998) 9 *EJIL* 626.

with WTO rules, they also allowed for compensation to be paid instead as a temporary measure where withdrawal would be impracticable. And if a member of the WTO failed to comply with a recommendation made by the dispute resolution body, that member would be requested to enter negotiations with the other party to the dispute 'with a view to finding mutually acceptable compensation'. The Court continued:

40. Consequently, to require the judicial organs to refrain from applying the rules of domestic law which are inconsistent with the WTO agreements would have the consequence of depriving the legislative or executive organs of the contracting parties of the possibility afforded by Article 22 of that memorandum of entering into negotiated arrangements even on a temporary basis.

41. It follows that the WTO agreements, interpreted in the light of their subject-matter and purpose, do not determine the appropriate legal means of ensuring that they are applied in good faith in the legal order of the contracting parties.

42. As regards, more particularly, the application of the WTO agreements in the Community legal order, it must be noted that, according to its preamble, the agreement establishing the WTO, including the annexes, is still founded, like GATT 1947, on the principle of negotiations with a view to 'entering into reciprocal and mutually advantageous arrangements and is thus distinguished, from the viewpoint of the Community, from the agreements concluded between the Community and non-member countries which introduce a certain asymmetry of obligations, or create special relations of integration with the Community, such as the agreement which the Court was required to interpret in *Kupferberg*.

43. It is common ground, moreover, that some of the contracting parties, which are among the most important commercial partners of the Community, have concluded from the subject-matter and purpose of the WTO agreements that they are not among the rules applicable by their judicial organs when reviewing the legality of their rules of domestic law.

44. Admittedly, the fact that the courts of one of the parties consider that some of the provisions of the agreement concluded by the Community are of direct application whereas the courts of the other party do not recognise such direct application is not in itself such as to constitute a lack of reciprocity in the implementation of the agreement (*Kupferberg*, paragraph 18).

45. However, the lack of reciprocity in that regard on the part of the Community's trading partners, in relation to the WTO agreements which are based on 'reciprocal and mutually advantageous arrangements and which must *ipso facto* be distinguished from agreements concluded by the Community, referred to in paragraph 42 of the present judgment, may lead to disuniform application of the WTO rules.

46. To accept that the role of ensuring that those rules comply with Community law devolves directly on the Community judicature would deprive the legislative or executive organs of the Community of the scope for manoeuvre enjoyed by their counterparts in the Community's trading partners.

47. It follows from all those considerations that, having regard to their nature and structure, the WTO agreements are not in principle among the rules in the light of which the Court is to review the legality of measures adopted by the Community institutions.

The ECJ then went on to rule that the neither of the two conditions established in the *Nakajima* and *Germany* cases[48] was fulfilled and so it could not review the legality of the Council Decision in the light of the WTO rules.

[48] See nn. 43 and 44 above.

Here we see a number of factors cited by the ECJ as arguments against the direct judicial enforceability of the WTO agreements. In the first place, the Court ruled that the terms of the Agreements themselves do not specify precisely what their own methods of enforcement are to be, given that compensation is permitted in certain circumstances as an alternative to direct enforcement, and that there is scope for negotiation over the recommendations of the WTO dispute-settlement bodies. In the second place, and contrary to the arguments which had been made in the academic literature and before the Court about the differences between GATT 47 on the one hand and the new GATT 94 in the context of the WTO on the other, the ECJ took the view that the WTO was still founded on the principle of mutually advantageous negotiations, rather than on clearly and precisely binding legal commitments of the kind apparently to be found in other international agreements entered by the Community. Such other agreements according to the Court include those involving an 'asymmetry of obligations', where a guarantee of clear legal enforcement by the EC is given regardless of the lack of direct reciprocity in the relationship with the other party—for example, agreements such as the previous Lomé agreements with the ACP States—as well as those involving special relationships of integration with the Community—for example, the Portugal free trade agreement in *Kupferberg*, or the Europe Association agreements.[49] In other words, lack of reciprocity in obligations and commitments under an international agreement has not in itself been sufficient reason for the ECJ to deny the direct applicability of such an agreement. However, the ECJ declared itself unwilling to accord such legal effect within the EC legal order to the WTO agreements, given the particular kind of lack of reciprocity in *enforcement* which this would involve—i.e. the Community's courts giving effect to the obligations contained in these broad-ranging multilateral trade agreements while the other trading partners could enjoy the full 'scope for manœuvre' expressly permitted under them. The ECJ also commented that the lack of reciprocity in terms of willingness to recognize the direct applicability of the WTO agreements could lead to 'disuniform application of WTO rules'.

The Court's judgment has generated another avalanche of academic commentary, much of which concedes that while the legal reasoning is less than convincing, the political motivation for the ruling is relatively obvious.

S. Peers, Fundamental Right or Political Whim? WTO Law and the ECJ[50] [footnotes omitted]

What about the Court's new arguments for rejecting the direct effect of the WTO? As regards the first argument (the nature of the WTO dispute settlement system), it is true that the Community has the discretion, according to WTO rules, to negotiate compensation with aggrieved parties after an adverse WTO panel report. The Court's argument on this point did not make any comparison with bilateral agreements agreed by the Community, but such a comparison cannot be avoided as long as the latter can confer direct effect but EC rules cannot. . . . Whatever the

---

[49] See n. 8 above.
[50] In G. de Búrca and J. Scott (eds.), *The EU and the WTO: Legal and Constitutional Issues* (Hart, 2001), 111, 120–2.

position on paper, the WTO system is far more 'judicial' and less political in practice than the Community's special relationships.

What about the Court's second argument, concerning the difference between the WTO rules and 'special relationships'? There are really two heads to this argument: the assertion that the WTO rules are distinct in nature from the Community's bilateral treaties and the conclusion that the Community should not grant direct effect to WTO rules as long as its trading partners do not.

The first head is not a credible argument. As noted above, the Community's bilateral treaties were always closely connected to the GATT rules allowing for further economic integration . . . [And] for *the majority of WTO Members*, the WTO *does* contain a 'certain asymmetry of obligations', just like the Community's bilateral non-reciprocal treaties.

The second, more political, head is the Court's strongest argument for refusing direct effect of WTO rules. Even so, its conclusion is problematic for two reasons. First, the argument is not applied consistently. Does the Court know whether the Community's main trading partners also apply an 'implementation exception'? If not, there will still be a risk of non-uniform application of sorts, because the trading partners' implementation will not be subject to potential invalidity under domestic law. . . .

Second, several of the Community's largest trading partners already have bilateral agreements with the Community, most notably Switzerland (its second largest partner) and Norway. These bilateral agreements confer direct effect. Why does the lack of guaranteed reciprocity of enforcement of the Community's bilateral agreements with these countries not bother the Court? . . .

Since both arguments of the Court are unconvincing, its underlying concern must therefore be that the Community's other large trading partners, lacking any general preferential agreement with the Community and accounting for much of its external trade, would take advantage of the 'scope for manoeuvre' which the lack of domestic direct effect affords them if the WTO rules were directly effective in the Community. Put very bluntly, the Americans and the Japanese (and likely soon the Chinese and Taiwanese) could reap huge commercial advantages from one-sided direct effect of WTO rules.

Some have been critical of the political motivation of the Court.[51]

G. Zonnekeyn, The Status of WTO Law in the Community Legal Order: Some Comments in the Light of the Portugese Textiles Case[52]

The implications of the Court of Justice's judgment cannot be understimated . . .

The non-recognition of direct effect linked to the impossibility of legality control of Community acts on the basis of the WTO Agreements must be regretted. However, one should not be desperate since the Court has developed an alternative in its caselaw. The *Hermès* case has shown that the

---

[51] For one of the particularly trenchant critiques see S. Griller, 'Judicial Enforceability of WTO Law in the EU' (2000) 3 *JIEL* 441. Another longstanding advocate of the justiciability and direct effect of the GATT/ WTO Agreements has been E.-U. Petersmann: see 'The Dispute Settlement System of the World Trade Organization and the Evolution of the GATT Dispute Settlement System since 1948' (1994) 31 *CMLRev.* 1157 and 'Proposals for a New Constitution for the European Union: Building Blocks for a Constitutional Theory and Constitutional Law of the EU' (1995) 32 *CMLRev.* 1123.

[52] (2000) 25 *ELRev.* 293, 302.

principle of consistent interpretation is a valuable substitute for direct effect but not for legality control.

It is clear that the Court's ruling is to a large extent inspired by political motives, which is regrettable but probably unavoidable. The 'separation of powers' or *trias politica*, a well known principle on the continent, has been sacrificed to give leeway to the political institutions of the Community.

while others have defended the political deference shown by the judgment.

A. Rosas, Portugal v Council[53]

[I]t can be surmised that one of the criticisms will be that the judgment undermines the relevance of the WTO Agreements as restraints on the conduct of the EU institutions and bases for individuals and Member States to challenge that conduct.

But in the aftermath of the riots of Seattle, it is perhaps permitted to recall that a 'strict' application of existing WTO rules is the opposite of what the increasingly vocal critics of the WTO have in mind. They assert that the WTO is a system to favour multinational corporations, and narrow commercial interests at the expense of health, environmental, human rights and other societal concerns. Granting direct effect to WTO rules would certainly not meet those concerns, but could instead deprive the democratic institutions of the EU and other WTO members of the margin of maneouvre they currently possess so as to strike a balance between trade and societal values.

Since the *Portugal* case, the ECJ has resisted attempts to narrow the potential scope of its judgment. Not only has it clearly ruled out the direct effect of provisions of the GATT,[54] but it has confirmed the application of the *Portugal* ruling in this respect to the other WTO agreements such as that Agreement on Trade Related Intellectual Property Rights (TRIPS),[55] and the Agreement on Technical Barriers to Trade (TBT).[56] It has also rejected a series of creative attempts to use the *Nakajima* doctrine and to rely on the effects of the ruling of a panel within the WTO dispute-settlement system,[57] to rely on Article 307 (ex Article 234) of the EC Treaty,[58] and to invoke the provisions of the WTO agreements in the context of actions for damages.[59]

---

[53] (2000) 37 *CMLRev.* 797, 815–16.

[54] Case C–307/99, *OGT v. Hauptzollamt Hamburg-St. Annen* [2001] ECR I–3159.

[55] Cases C–300 & 392/98, *Dior v. Tuk Consultancy* [2000] ECR I–1307 and C–89/99, *Schieving-Nijstad v. Groeneveld*, judgment of 13 Sept. 2001, paras. 51–55.

[56] See the AG's Opinion in Case C–27/ & 122/00, *Omega Air Ltd*, 12 Mar. 2002, paras. 89–94.

[57] Cases T–18/99, *Cordis Obst und Gemüse Großhandel v. Commission* [2001] ECR II–913; T–30/99, *Bocchi Food Trade International v. Commission* [2001] ECR II–943; and T–52/99, *T. Port GmbH v. Commission* [2001] ECR II–981.

[58] Cases T–2/99, *T-Port GmbH v. Council*, 12 July 2001 and T–3/99, *Bananatrading GmbH v. Council* [2001] ECR II–2093. For pre-*Portugal v. Council* cases attempting to use Art. 307 EC in the context of the GATT see Cases C–364 & 365/95, *T-Port v. Hauptzollamt Hamburg-Jonas* [1998] ECR I–1023.

[59] Cases T–18/99, T–30/99 & 52/99, n. 57 above.

In contrast to its refusal to permit the judicial enforceability of the WTO agreements, the ECJ has more readily recognized the enforceability of other international agreements, even broad multilateral agreements, which do not involve special relations of integration with the EU. In the *Biotechnology* case, the ECJ declined to rule on whether the Rio Convention on Biological Diversity had created directly effective individual rights in the narrow sense, but went on to confirm its broader 'invocability' by declaring that, unlike the WTO Agreement, the Biodiversity Convention was 'not strictly based on reciprocal and mutually advantageous arrangements' and that courts could therefore review the Community's compliance with the obligations contained therein.[60]

The ECJ in *Racke* ruled that provisions of the EEC–Yugoslavia co-operation agreement of 1980 were directly effective, and could be invoked along with provisions of customary international law to challenge the legality of an EC Regulation.[61] Further, in a recent series of cases involving some of the Europe Association Agreements, the ECJ declared their provisions on freedom of establishment to be directly effective and capable of being invoked before national courts to challenge national law.[62] These judgments follow the pattern of similar rulings in which the Court has recognized the direct effect of various provisions of association or co-operation agreements with third countries,[63] as well as the provisions of secondary decisions adopted by association councils or bodies set up under those agreements.[64] Agreements of this sort fall within the category of those setting up 'special relations of integration' with the EC of the kind referred to by the ECJ in paragraph 42 of its ruling in *Portugal* v. *Council*. None the less, while it is certainly true that the ECJ has recognized the direct effect of an increasing range of provisions of such agreements, these have not always translated into concrete benefits for the third-country nationals seeking to rely on those provisions before national courts.[65]

[60] Cases C–377/98, *Netherlands* v. *Council*, judgment of 9 Oct. 2001.

[61] Case C–162/96, n. 33 above.

[62] Cases C–63/99, *Gloszczuk*, C–257/99, *Barkoci and Malik*, C–235/99, *Kondova*, and C–268/99, *Jany*, n. 8 above.

[63] See Cases C–18/90, *Onem* v. *Kziber* [1991] ECR I–199; C–58/93; *Yousfi* v. *Belgium* [1994] ECR I–1353; C–126/95, *Hallouzi-Choho* v. *Bestuur van Sociale* [1996] ECR I–4807; C–416/96, *El-Yassini* v. *Home Secretary* [1999] ECR I–1209; and C–179/98, *Belgium* v. *Mesbah* [1999] ECR I–7955 on the EEC–Morocco Co-operation Agreement; Case C–103/94, *Krid* v. *WAVTS* [1995] ECR I–719 and C–113/97, *Babahenini* v. *Belgium* [1998] ECR I–813 on the EEC–Algeria Co-operation Agreement. For cases on the EC–Turkey association agreement see C–37/98, *Savas* [2000] ECR I–2927.

[64] See Cases 12/86, *Demirel* v. *Stadt Schwäbisch Gmünd* [1987] ECR 3719; C–192/89, *Sevince* v. *Staatsecretaris van Justitie* [1990] ECR I–3461. See also Cases C–237/91, *Kus* [1992] ECR I–6781; C–355/93, *Eroglu* v. *Land Baden-Württemberg* [1994] ECR I–5113; C–277/94, *Taflan-Met* v. *Bestuur van de Sociale Verzekerings-bank* [1996] ECR I–4085; C–262/96, *Sürül* [1999] ECR I–2685; C–285/95, *Suat Kol* [1997] ECR I–3069; C–351/95, *Kadiman* [1997] ECR I–2133; C–36/96, *Günaydin* [1997] ECR I–5143; C–1/97, *Birden* [1998] ECR I–7747; C–210/97, *Akman* [1998] ECR I–7519; C–329/97, *Ergat* [1999] ECR I–1487; C–102/98, *Kocak* [2000] ECR I–1287; C–340/97, *Nazli* [2000] ECR I–957; and Case C–65/98, *Eyup* [2000] ECR I–4747.

[65] For an analysis of much of this case law and of other developments in relation to resident third-country nationals within EC law see M. Hedemann Robinson, (2001) 38 *CMLRev.* 525.

7. THE LEGAL EFFECTS OF DIRECTIVES

(a) DIRECT EFFECT AND THE VERTICAL/HORIZONTAL DISTINCTION

The key reason given by the Court for the direct effect of Treaty provisions was that the fundamental aims of the Treaty and the nature of the system it was designed to create would be seriously hampered if its clear provisions could not be domestically enforced by those it affected. In the case of international agreements, the explanation was that direct effect was important in order to ensure respect in every Member State for the commitments of the Community arising from agreements concluded with non-member countries. The explanation for the direct effect of regulations was more straightforwardly textual: Article 249 (ex Article 189) specifically provided for their direct applicability, from which the Court deduced that they had the capacity to be invoked by individuals before national courts and to confer rights on them. In the case of decisions, the ECJ took the view that, since they were intended to be binding upon addressees, there was no reason why they should not be directly enforced before a national court where their provisions were sufficiently clear.

The position of directives under the Treaty is somewhat different. Under Article 249 (ex Article 189), a directive 'shall be binding as to the result to be achieved, upon each Member State to which it is addressed, but shall leave to the national authorities the choice of form and methods'. Unlike that of regulations or decisions, national implementation of directives is specifically envisaged by the Treaty. Its rationale may be explained as follows. The directive is one of the main 'instruments of harmoniza-tion' used by the Community institutions to bring together or co-ordinate the dispar-ate laws of the Member States in various fields. In that context, the provisions of a directive sometimes represent a compromise between Member States on a complex or sensitive matter and in respect of which certain discretionary options are left open to States. Eventual implementation need not be uniform in every Member State, although the actual aim of the directive must be properly secured in each. From this description, it appears that some of the criteria for direct effect laid down in the early case law are missing. A directive may well leave some discretion to the Member States; it will always require further implementing measures, and if it sets out its aim only in general terms, it may not be sufficiently precise to allow for proper national judicial enforcement.

On the other hand, the aims of legal integration and effectiveness which under-pinned the ECJ's original articulation of the notion of the direct effect of Treaty provisions can be equally applied to the case of directives. Many important areas of Community policy rely, in accordance with the Treaty, for their practical realization on the proper implementation of Community directives. If States fail or refuse to implement such measures properly, those Community policies will suffer. The ECJ therefore sought to promote the legal effectiveness of directives even in the absence of their implementation.

The problem of reconciling the original criteria for direct effect—the requirements of precision, unconditionality, the absence of discretion, and the absence of a need for implementing measures—with the particular nature of directives arose in the following case, in which the Court adapted many of the arguments from its judgment concerning the direct effect of decisions in *Grad*, above.[66]

Case 41/74, Van Duyn v. Home Office
[1974] ECR 1337

[Note ToA renumbering: Arts. 48, 177, and 189 are now Arts. 39, 234, and 249 respectively]

Van Duyn was a Dutch national who had come to the UK to work for the Church of Scientology. She was refused leave to enter the UK since Scientology was officially regarded by the British Government as socially harmful, although no legal restrictions were placed upon its practice. She challenged this refusal on the basis of Article 48 of the Treaty, Regulation 1612/68, and Directive 64/221, which regulate the free movement of workers within the Community. The High Court asked the ECJ whether the provisions of Directive 64/221 could have direct effect.

THE ECJ

12. . . . It would be incompatible with the binding effect attributed to a directive by Article 189 to exclude, in principle, the possibility that the obligation which it imposes may be invoked by those concerned. In particular, where the Community authorities have, by directive, imposed on Member States the obligation to pursue a particular course of conduct, the useful effect of such an act would be weakened if individuals were prevented from relying on it before their national courts and if the latter were prevented from taking it into consideration as an element of Community law. Article 177, which empowers national courts to refer to the Court questions concerning the validity and interpretation of all acts of the Community institutions, without distinction, implies furthermore that these acts may be invoked by individuals in the national courts. It is necessary to examine, in every case, whether the nature, general scheme and wording of the provision in question are capable of having direct effects on the relations between Member States and individuals.

The thrust of the Court's argument in this passage is that, if directives are *binding*, then the possibility of relying on them directly before national courts cannot be ruled out. Each provision must be examined in its context to see whether the obligation imposed is sufficiently clear and exact to be capable of being applied directly by a national court. Directive 64/221 allowed Member States to take measures restricting the movement of non-nationals on grounds such as public policy, without defining the permissible range of public-policy concerns. Was this degree of discretion too great to permit a national court to say that the Directive prohibited a given State from adopting a particular restrictive measure? The ECJ ruled that it was not, and that, by providing that measures taken on public-policy grounds had to be based on the personal conduct of the individual, the directive had limited the discretionary power

---

[66] Case 9/70, *Franz Grad* v. *Finanzamt Traunstein* [1970] ECR 825, para. 5.

conferred on States. The obligation imposed was clear, precise, and legally complete.[67] In later cases the ECJ ruled that the existence of discretion would not prevent a directive from being directly relied upon by an individual where the Member State had fully exercised its discretion on implementation,[68] or had chosen not to exercize a particular discretionary option,[69] or where a clear and precise obligation could be severed from other parts of a directive.[70] More controversially, in *Kortas*, the ECJ ruled that the possibility for a Member State to derogate from a harmonizing directive under Article 95(4) (ex Article 100a(4)) of the Treaty did not affect the direct effect of the directive nor preclude an individual from relying directly on its provisions, *even in the situation where* a Member State had sought permission for such a derogation and the Commission had unreasonably failed to respond to its request.[71]

Immediately after the *Van Duyn* judgment, however, some Member States felt the Court had gone too far in advancing its conception of Community law at the expense of the clear language of the Treaty, and the obvious limitations on directives as a form of legislation: if directives were specifically intended to leave Member States with choices of how to enact a particular Community obligation, the Court should not allow this to be overridden by individuals invoking the directive directly.

Perhaps in response to such criticisms, the Court in later cases added a more specific line of reasoning to its general argument in *Van Duyn*. This was the so-called 'estoppel' reasoning: that Member States were precluded by their failure (in breach of the Treaty) to implement a directive properly from refusing to recognize its binding effect in cases where it was pleaded against them.

Case 148/78, Pubblico Ministero v. Tullio Ratti
[1979] ECR 1629

Ratti's Italian company had begun packaging and labelling its containers of solvents in accordance with the requirements of two Council directives. These directives had not yet been implemented in Italy, and the Italian legislation on the matter contained more stringent requirements than the Directive, with penalties for failure to comply. In criminal proceedings brought against Ratti under the domestic legislation, he relied in his defence on the direct effect of the two directives.

---

[67] See also Cases C–72/95, *Kraaijeveld* [1996] ECR I–5403, para. 59; and C–287/98, *Linster* [2000] ECR I–6917, paras. 37–39, where the existence of discretion in a dir. did not preclude a national court from examining whether the discretion had been exceeded. Contrast Case C–365/98, *Brinkmann* [2000] ECR I–4619.

[68] Case C–441/99, *Riksskatteverket* v. *Gharehveran*, 18 Oct. 2001.

[69] Case C–303/98, *SIMAP* v. *Valencia Sindicatode Médicos Asistencia Pública*, 31 Oct. 2001. See also Cases C–76/97, *Tögel* [1998] ECR I–5357 and C–241/97, *Försäkringsaktiebolaget Skandia* [1999] ECR I–1951, where the existence of exceptions did not prevent the provisions of a dir. from being directly effective.

[70] Case C–346/97, *Braathens Sverige AB* v. *Riksskatteverket* [1999] ECR I–3419.

[71] Case C–319/97, *Kortas* [1999] ECR I–3143. Action against the Commission for breach of its obligations under Art. 232 (ex Art. 175) of the Treaty was the appropriate remedy in the Court's view.

However, it is clear from the Treaty and has also been emphasized again and again in the case-law that a clear distinction must be drawn between regulations and directives, the latter creating obligations only for the Member States. So under no circumstances can one say—as the defendant in the main action has said—that directives may also have the content and effects of a regulation; at most directives may produce *similar* effects. . . . The essence of such effects is that in certain cases, which however constitute the exception to the rule, Member States which do not comply with their obligations under the directive are unable to rely on provisions of the internal legal order which are illegal from the point of view of Community law, so that individuals become entitled to rely on the directives as against the defaulting State and acquire rights thereunder which national courts must protect.

The Court repeated what it ruled in *Van Duyn* about the possibility of direct effect for directives, and continued:

THE ECJ

22. Consequently a Member State which has not adopted the implementing measures required by the directive in the prescribed periods may not rely, as against individuals, on its own failure to perform the obligations which the directive entails.

23. It follows that a national court requested by a person who has complied with the provisions of a directive not to apply a national provision incompatible with the directive not incorporated into the internal legal order of a defaulting Member State, must uphold that request if the obligation in question is unconditional and sufficiently precise.

The Italian court had also asked whether the Directive could be relied upon by an individual before the time limit for its implementation had expired. The Court answered:

43. It follows that, for the reasons expounded in the grounds of the answer to the national court's first question, it is only at the end of the prescribed period and in the event of the Member State's default that the directive . . . will be able to have the effects described in the answer to the first question.

44. Until that date the Member States remain free in that field.

In other words, since the terms of each directive give Member States a specific date by which implementation must be assured, the provisions of the directive cannot be pleaded directly by individuals before that date. After that date, however, the Member State forfeits its discretion on the 'choice of form and methods' under Article 249 (ex Article 189) by its failure to implement, and is then estopped from relying on conflicting provisions of national law against individuals.

Ratti involved a situation in which the direct effect of a directive was pleaded as a

---

[72] [1979] ECR 1629, 1650.

'shield', in defence of an individual who had been prosecuted by the State. In *Becker*, the Court permitted the provisions of a directive to be used actively as a 'sword' against the State by an individual who sought to calculate her tax returns in accordance with those provisions.[73] The date for implementation of the directive had expired without it having been implemented in Germany, and the ECJ responded sharply to the German government's argument that to permit direct enforcement would allow the court to usurp the political discretion of the Member State, and would demand too much of administrative authorities and courts in requiring them to disregard domestic law. If any such administrative or other difficulties were to arise, according to the Court, 'they would be the consequence of the Member State's failure to implement the Directive in question within the period prescribed for that purpose. The consequences of that situation must be borne by the administrative authorities and may not be passed on to the tax-payers who rely on the fulfillment of a precise obligation which has been incumbent on the State under Community law since 1 January 1979'.[74]

This quotation emphasizes the 'punitive' reasoning developed by the Court for the direct effect of directives. Article 249 (ex Article 189) does not declare directives to be directly applicable, therefore they do not automatically become part of national law upon adoption, but they may produce 'similar effects' to regulations when the time limit for their implementation has expired and the State has not properly implemented them.

The expansion of direct effect did not, however, continue unchecked. The Court continued to emphasize the distinction between regulations and directives, repeating that the 'direct applicability' of directives was not provided for under Article 249 (ex Article 189) and that a directive could have direct effect only when a Member State failed to implement. The distinction was sharpened after the 1986 judgment in which the Court decided that the direct effect of a directive could not be pleaded against an individual but only against the State.

Case 152/84, Marshall v. Southampton and South-West Hampshire Area
Health Authority (Teaching)
[1986] ECR 723

[Note ToA renumbering: Arts. 189 and 191 are now Arts. 249 and 254 respectively]

Helen Marshall was dismissed after 14 years' employment by the respondent health authority on the ground that she had passed the normal retiring age applicable to women. The Authority's policy required female employees to retire at 60 and male employees at 65. National legislation did not impose any obligation on women to retire at 60 and the UK Sex Discrimination Act 1975 appeared to exclude retirement matters from its scope, but Marshall argued that her dismissal

---

[73] Case 8/81, *Becker* v. *Finanzamt Münster-Innenstadt* [1982] ECR 53.

[74] *Ibid.*, para. 47. Although Member States are not obliged to implement before the period for transposition of a dir. has expired, the ECJ ruled in Case C–129/96, *Inter-Environnement Wallonie ASBL* v. *Région Wallone* [1997] ECR I–7411, that they must, during that period, refrain from adopting any measures liable to compromise seriously the result prescribed by the dir.

violated the the 1976 Equal Treatment Directive. The Court of Appeal asked the ECJ whether she could rely on the provisions of the Directive notwithstanding the apparent conflict with the Sex Discrimination Act.

ADVOCATE GENERAL SLYNN[75]

I remain . . . of the view expressed in my opinion in *Becker* that a directive not addressed to an individual cannot of itself impose obligations on him. It is, in cases like the present, addressed to Member States and not to the individual. . . .

  To give what is called 'horizontal effect' to directives would totally blur the distinction between regulations and directives which the Treaty establishes in Articles 189 and 191. . . .

THE ECJ

48. With regard to the argument that a directive may not be relied upon against an individual, it must be emphasized that according to Article 189 of the EEC Treaty, the binding nature of a directive, which constitutes the basis for the possibility of relying on the directive before a national court, exists only in relation to 'each Member State to which it is addressed'. It follows that a directive may not of itself impose obligations on an individual and that a provision of a directive may not be relied upon as such against such a person.

The Advocate General reached the same conclusion as the Court by slightly different reasoning. Slynn AG had two concerns: first, that to accord full direct effect to directives would destroy the distinction between directives and regulations, and thus perhaps also the advantages and flexibility permitted by the 'looser' legislative instrument. He also expressed what was at the time a 'rule of law' concern: that directives were not formally required, before the Maastricht Treaty amendments, to be notified or published in the Official Journal.[76]

It should be noted that the problems of legal certainty which could be created by the so-called 'horizontal' application of directives are problems which the Court has surmounted in the case of other kinds of directly effective Community law. Directives contain a time limit for their implementation, and the requirement of publication now contained in Article 254 (ex Article 191) EC ensures that knowledge of this time limit is accessible to all those affected. Another argument sometimes made is that directives, even if their core aim or principle is clear and thus can be directly enforced, often leave much to be fleshed out in national implementing measures. However, this is equally true of the 'vertical' direct effect of directives, and it has not prevented the Court from pursuing its quest for effectiveness of Treaty Articles which share similar characteristics.

The principal reason offered by the ECJ against according horizontal direct effect to directives was based upon the text of Article 249 (ex Article 189), under which the binding effect of a directive is said to exist only as against the State(s) to which it is addressed. The Court's unusual textual faithfulness in this context and its emphasis

---

[75] [1986] ECR 723, 734.
[76] See also the Court in Case C–192/89, *Sevince* v. *Staatssecretaris van Justitie* [1990] ECR I–3461, para. 24.

on the addressee of directives contrasts with its approach to the direct effectiveness
of certain Treaty Articles which, like directives, are also explicitly addressed only to
the Member State. Article 141 (ex Article 119), for example, is addressed only to the
Member States, providing that States are to ensure the application of the principle of
equal pay for male and female workers. In the first *Defrenne* case, however, the ECJ
dismissed the argument that Article 141 could be relied upon only as against the State:

Since Article 119 is mandatory in nature, the prohibition on discrimination between men and
women applies not only to the action of public authorities, but also extends to all agreements
which are intended to regulate paid labour collectively, as well as to contracts between
individuals.[77]

This ruling undermines some of the force of the ECJ's textual argument in *Marshall*.
The Advocate General in the case also pointed to the unacceptable discrimination
between the private and the public sectors which would ensue from such a limitation.[78]

(b) EXPANDING VERTICAL DIRECT EFFECT: A BROAD CONCEPT
OF THE STATE

However, having imposed this 'horizontal' limitation on the direct effect of directives,
the ECJ began to develop other strategies to advance the domestic enforcement of
these measures. The first strategy was to expand the notion of a 'public body' against
which directives could be enforced. In *Marshall* itself, having ruled out the direct
enforcement of a directive against an individual, the Court concluded that the
complainant could nevertheless rely on the provisions of this Directive as against
the Health Authority, since it could be regarded as an organ of the State:[79]

THE ECJ

49. In that respect it must be pointed out that where a person involved in legal proceedings is
able to rely on a directive as against the State he may do so regardless of the capacity in which the
latter is acting, whether employer or public authority. In either case it is necessary to prevent the
State from taking advantage of its own failure to comply with Community law. . . .

51. The argument submitted by the United Kingdom that the possibility of relying on provisions
of the directive against the respondent *qua* organ of the State would give rise to an arbitrary and
unfair distinction between the rights of State employees and those of private employees does
not justify any other conclusion. Such a distinction may easily be avoided if the Member State
concerned has correctly implemented the directive into national law.

It is clear from decisions of the Court that the justification for allowing the 'vertical' direct effect of directives against organs of the State is not based upon the

---

[77] Case 43/75, *Defrenne* v. *Sabena* [1976] ECR 455. See also Case C–281/93, *Angonese* v. *Cassa di Risparmio
di Bologna* [2000] ECR I–4134, paras. 32–36 on the horizontal direct effect of Art. 39 (ex Art. 48) EC.

[78] See also R. Mastroianni, 'On the Distinction Between Vertical and Horizontal Direct Effect of
Directives: What Role for the Principle of Equality?' (1999) 5 *EPL* 417.

[79] See also Case C–438/99, *Jiménez Melgar* v. *Ayuntamiento de Los Barrios*, 4 Oct. 2001, paras. 32–33.

responsibility of the particular state organ (such as a Health Authority) in question for failure to implement the directive pleaded, which weakens somewhat the 'punitive' estoppel basis for vertical effect.

Nevertheless, the Court has held that not only courts but even state organs and domestic administrations which play no part in the formal implementation of European legislation are bound to apply the provisions of directives in practice, something which has been referred to as 'administrative direct effect'.[80] The extent to which this takes place in practice is difficult to determine, since the relative paucity of litigation on the question could be interpreted as evidence in either direction.

Case 103/88, Fratelli Costanzo SpA v. Comune di Milano
[1989] ECR 1839

Costanzo challenged the procedure for the award of a public works contract in preparation for the 1990 World Cup for football in Italy. After its bid was excluded by the Municipality of Milan from the tendering procedure under a provision of Italian law, Costanzo claimed that the Italian legislation, which was intended to implement a 1971 Council Directive on the award of public-works contracts, was incompatible with that Directive. The Tribunale Amministrativo asked the ECJ whether the municipal authority was bound by the provisions of the Directive itself.

THE ECJ

30. It is important to note that the reason for which an individual may, in the circumstances described above, rely on the provisions of a directive in proceedings before the national courts is that the obligations arising under those provisions are binding upon all the authorities of the Member States.

31. It would, moreover, be contradictory to rule that an individual may rely upon the provisions of a directive which fulfil the conditions defined above in proceedings before the national courts seeking an order against the administrative authorities, and yet to hold that those authorities are under no obligation to apply the provisions of the directive and refrain from applying provisions of national law which conflict with them. It follows that when the conditions under which the Court has held that individuals may rely on the provisions of a directive before the national courts are met, all organs of the administration, including decentralized authorities such as municipalities, are obliged to apply those provisions.

The broad interpretation of what constitutes an organ of the State for the purposes of enforcement of directives seems at odds with the refusal to extend their direct enforceability to relations between non-state entities and individuals. Yet the *Marshall* ruling, despite widespread academic criticism and numerous opinions given by Advocates General in favour of full horizontal direct effect, was confirmed ten years

---

[80] See de Witte, n. 15 above. See also Cases C–246–249/94 *Cooperativa Agricola Zootecnica S. Antonio* v. *Amministrazione delle finanze dello Stato* [1996] ECR I–4373.

later in the *Dori* case.[81] None the less, it is significant to note that all but one of the Member States supported the *Dori* ruling in this respect. However, although it has elaborated somewhat on the Community meaning of the State or public body for the purposes of the enforceability of directives, the ECJ has been criticized for failing in key decisions to provide adequate guidance on a complex issue.[82] The following case, decided in 1990, remains the primary ruling on the matter.

Case C–188/89, A. Foster and Others v. British Gas plc
[1990] ECR I–3313

The plaintiffs were employed by British Gas, whose policy it was to require women to retire at 60 and men at 65. British Gas was, at the time relevant to these proceedings, a nationalized industry with responsibility for and a monopoly of the gas-supply system in Great Britain. The plaintiffs sought to rely on the provisions of the 1976 Equal Treatment Directive and the House of Lords asked the ECJ whether British Gas was a body of the kind against which the provisions of the Directive could be invoked.

THE ECJ

18. On the basis of those considerations, the Court has held in a series of cases that unconditional and sufficiently precise provisions of a directive could be relied on against organizations or bodies which were subject to the authority or control of the State or had special powers beyond those which result from the normal rules applicable between individuals.

19. The Court has accordingly held that provisions of a directive could be relied on against tax authorities (the judgments in Case 8/81 *Becker* [1982] ECR 53, Case 221/88 *ECSC* v. *Busseni* [1990] ECR I–495), local or regional authorities (judgment in Case 103/88 *Costanzo* [1989] ECR 1839), constitutionally independent authorities responsible for the maintenance of public order and safety (judgment in Case 222/84 *Johnston* v. *Chief Constable of the RUC* [1986] ECR 1651), and public authorities providing public health services (judgment in Case 152/84 *Marshall* [1986] ECR 723).

20. It follows from the foregoing that a body, whatever its legal form, which has been made responsible, pursuant to a measure adopted by the State, for providing a public service under the control of the State and has for that purpose special powers beyond those which result from the normal rules applicable in relations between individuals, is included in any event among the bodies against which the provisions of a directive capable of having direct effect may be relied upon.

It is evident from paragraph 20 of *Foster* that the Court considered a company in the position of British Gas to be an organ of the State. It remains unclear, however, what kind of control over a body the State must have in order for it to be a body

---

[81] See Case C–91/92, *Dori* v. *Recreb Srl* [1994] ECR I–3325. For a strong critique see J. Coppel, 'Rights, Duties and the End of Marshall' (1994) 57 *MLR* 859.

[82] D. Curtin, 'The Province of Government: Delimiting the Direct Effect of Directives in the Common Law Context' (1990) 15 *ELRev*. 195 and E. Szyszczak, 'Foster v. British Gas' (1990) 27 *CMLRev*. 859.

which, constitutionally speaking, represents the power of the State.[83] Certainly the estoppel argument for vertical effect is rather weak in this context, since British Gas could hardly have affected the State's decision on how and when to implement the Equal Treatment Directive. *Foster* provides no authoritative definition but merely indicates that a body which has been made responsible for providing a public service under the control of the State is *included* within the Community definition of a public body. Case law since then has not notably clarified the situation but has left it to the national courts to apply the loose criteria.[84]

(c) 'INDIRECT EFFECT': DEVELOPMENT OF THE PRINCIPLE OF INTERPRETATION

The second way in which the Court of Justice encouraged the application and effectiveness of directives, despite denying the possibility of direct horizontal enforcement, was by developing a principle of harmonious interpretation which requires national law to be interpreted 'in the light of' directives. We have seen a similar principle used in the context of international law and international agreements, whereby the Community is required to interpret secondary EC legislation in their light.[85] By urging national courts to read domestic law in such a way as to conform to the provisions of directives, the Court sought to ensure that directives would be given some effect despite the absence of proper implementation. In this case, the ECJ ruled that the Equal Treatment Directive on which the plaintiffs were relying in their claim for unlawful sex discrimination was not sufficiently precise to guarantee them a specific remedy of appointment to a post, but it went on to rule on what effect the directive's aims might none the less have on the interpretation of national law.

Case 14/83, Von Colson and Kamann v. Land Nordrhein-Westfalen
[1984] ECR 1891

[Note ToA renumbering: Art. 189 is now Art. 249]

THE ECJ

26. However, the Member States' obligation arising from a directive to achieve the result envisaged by the directive and their duty under Article 5 of the Treaty to take all appropriate measures, whether general or particular, to ensure the fulfillment of that obligation, is binding on

---

[83] In Case C–419/92, *Scholz* v. *Opera Universitaria di Cagliari* [1994] ECR I–505, the case proceeded on the 'common ground' that the University of Cagliari was an emanation of the State. See R. White, 'Equality in the Canteen' (1994) 19 *ELRev.* 308.

[84] See Case C–343/98, *Collino & Chiappero* v. *Telecom Italia* [2000] ECR I–6659; Cases C–253/–258/96, *Kampelmann* v. *Landschaftsverband Westfalen-Lippe* [1997] ECR I–6907, para. 47 and the dicta of the CFI in Cases T–172 and 175–177/98, *Salamander* v. *Parliament & Council* [2000] ECR II–2487, para. 60.

[85] See the cases at n. 45 above and text. Further, the requirement that national law should be interpreted in the light of EC law so as to give effect to the aims of the latter is not restricted to directives or to non-directly effective law: see Case C–165/91, *Van Munster* v. *Rijksdienst voor Pensionen* [1994] ECR I–4661.

all the authorities of Member States including, for matters within their jurisdiction, the courts. It follows that, in applying the national law and in particular the provisions of a national law specifically introduced in order to implement Directive No 76/207, national courts are required to interpret their national law in the light of the wording and the purpose of the Directive in order to achieve the result referred to in the third paragraph of Article 189.

. . .

28. . . . It is for the national court to interpret and apply the legislation adopted for the implementation of the directive in conformity with the requirements of Community law, in so far as it is given discretion to do so under national law.

The Court here expressly identified the national courts as organs of the State which are responsible for the fulfillment of Community obligations, and paragraph 26 did not seem to restrict this responsibility specifically to the interpretation of national *implementing* legislation. The judgment was significant from the point of view of enhancing the effectiveness of unimplemented or misimplemented directives, since the ECJ called on the national court to supplement the domestic legislation (which did not on its face seem to provide an adequate remedy) by reading it in conformity with the Directive's requirement to provide a real and effective remedy. Further, the doctrine of harmonious interpretation or 'indirect effect' does not require the provisions of a Directive to satisfy the more restrictive justiciability conditions for direct effect.

The *Von Colson* case concerned a Directive which had been inadequately implemented,[86] and it concerned an attempt by an individual litigant to rely on the provisions of the Directive against a *state* employer. But could the State ask a national court to interpret national law in the light of a misimplemented Directive, in proceedings against an individual? Could the provisions of a Directive be *indirectly* enforced by the State against an individual in this way, even if Marshall had ruled out the direct enforcement of a directive against an individual? In *Kolpinghuis Nijmegen*, the ECJ firmly denied this possibility in the context of criminal proceedings brought against an individual, where the Dutch prosecution authorities sought to use the provisions of a non-implemented EC Directive against the defendant.[87] The ECJ, after reiterating the principle of interpretation in paragraph 26 of *Von Colson*, delared that:

'the obligation on the national court to refer to the content of the directive when interpreting the relevant rules of its national law is limited by the general principles of law which form part of Community law and in particular the principles of legal certainty and non-retroactivity. . . .
a directive cannot, of itself and independently of a law adopted for its implementation, have the effect of determining or aggravating the liability in criminal law of persons who act in contravention of the provisions of that directive.'[88]

---

[86] See also Case C–421/92, *Habermann-Beltermann* v. *Arbeiterwohlfahrt, Bezirksverband* [1994] ECR I–1657.

[87] Case 80/86, *Criminal proceedings against Kolpinghuis Nijmegen BV* [1987] ECR 3969.

[88] *Ibid.*, paras. 13–14. The ruling was confirmed in subsequent cases including Cases C–74/129/95, *Criminal Proceedings against X* [1996] ECR I–6609.

This ruling indicated that there were limits to the *Von Colson* requirement of harmonious or sympathetic interpretation. But it remained unclear exactly what these limits were, and whether the interpretation requirement could apply in a case between individuals, when the enforcement of criminal law was not concerned, and when the State was not attempting to remedy its own default in failing to implement a directive. The opportunity to address some of these issues arose in *Marleasing*,[89] which concerned a 'horizontal' situation involving two private parties before a domestic court, where the interpretation of national law in the light of an unimplemented Directive would not impose penal liability on one party, but would affect its legal position in a disadvantageous way. There was no domestic implementing legislation which could be interpreted in the light of the Directive, but only domestic law which pre-dated the Directive and was not intended to implement it.

Case C–106/89, Marleasing SA v. La Comercial Internacionale de Alimentacion SA [1990] ECR I–4135

[Note ToA renumbering: Articles 5 and 189 EC are now Articles 10 and 249]

The plaintiff company brought proceedings against La Comercial to have the defendant company's articles of association declared void as the company was created for the sole purpose of defrauding and evading creditors, which included Marleasing. The provisions of the relevant Council Directive did not include this 'lack of cause' as a ground for the nullity of a company, whereas certain provisions of the Spanish Civil Code provided for the ineffectiveness of contracts for lack of cause. The Spanish court referred the case to the ECJ, asking whether the Council Directive could have direct effect between individuals so as to preclude the declaration of nullity of a company on grounds other than those set out in the Directive.

THE ECJ

7. However, it is apparent from the documents before the Court that the national court seeks in substance to ascertain whether a national court hearing a case which falls within the scope of Directive 68/151 is required to interpret its national law in the light of the wording and the purpose of that directive in order to preclude a declaration of nullity of a public limited company on a ground other than those listed in Article 11 of the directive.

8. In order to reply to that question, it should be observed that, as the Court pointed out in its judgment in Case 14/83 *Von Colson and Kamann* v. *Land Nordrhein-Westfalen* [1984] ECR 1891, paragraph 26, the Member States' obligation arising from a directive to achieve the result envisaged by the directive and their duty under Article 5 of the Treaty to take all appropriate measures, whether general or particular, to ensure the fulfilment of that obligation, is binding on all the authorities of Member States including, for matters within their jurisdiction, the courts. It follows that, in applying national law, whether the provisions in question were adopted before or after the directive, the national court called upon to interpret it is required to do so, as far as possible, in the light of the wording and the purpose of the directive in order to

---

[89] See Case C–106/89, *Marleasing SA* v. *La Comercial de Alimentacion SA* [1990] ECR I–4135, confirmed in many subsequent cases. See G. Betlem, 'The Principle of Indirect Effect of Community Law' (1995) 3 *ERPL* 1.

achieve the result pursued by the latter and thereby comply with the third paragraph of Article 189 of the Treaty.

ADVOCATE GENERAL VAN GERVEN[90]

8. The obligation to interpret a provision of national law in conformity with a directive arises whenever the provision in question is to any extent open to interpretation. In those circumstances the national court must, having regard to the usual methods of interpretation in its legal system, give precedence to the method which enables it to construe the national provision concerned in a manner consistent with the directive.

This judgment confirmed that an unimplemented directive could indeed be relied on to influence the interpretation of national law in a case between individuals, and that this was so even where the national law predated the directive. What remained unclear was how strongly were national courts being encouraged to read otherwise clear provisions of national law so as to comply with the terms of a directive?[91] Even if, as the Advocate General suggested, it is essentially a matter for resolution in accordance with national principles of interpretation, the Treaty-derived obligation on national courts to take all measures possible to comply with Community law clearly constrains the interpretative discretion they would otherwise have under national law alone.

The Advocate General had also argued that an interpretation of national law in the light of a directive which would impose a 'civil penalty' upon an individual would contravene the principles of legal certainty and non-retroactivity. In *Marleasing* itself, although the Directive was not being used to penalize or declare void the statute establishing the defendant company, the interpretation of Spanish contract law in the light of the unimplemented Directive operated to the disadvantage of Marleasing, which was a creditor of the defendant company. As a result of the 'interpretative influence' of the Directive, Marleasing could not base an argument on Spanish contract law which might enable it to recover its money more easily.[92] The Court, however, did not discuss the question whether the indirect application of the Directive would impose any legal obligation or detriment on one of the parties,[93] and despite declaring that national courts must read national law in conformity with a relevant directive only 'in so far as possible', it went on to rule that that Spanish court was *precluded* from interpreting national law in a way which did not comply with the provisions of the Directive.

[90] At 4146.

[91] See Van Gerven AG in Cases 262/88, *Barber* v. *Guardian Royal Exchange* [1990] ECR 1889; 1937, and 63–64/91, *Jackson* v. *Chief Adjudication Officer* [1992] ECR I–4737, para. 29 of his Opinion; and C–271/91, *Marshall (No. 2)* [1993] ECR I–4367, para. 10 of his Opinion, that EC law could not compel the national court to give an interpretation *contra legem*. See also Case C–168/95, *Luciano Arcaro* [1996] ECR I–4705, discussed in more detail below.

[92] See, for a contrary view, N. Maltby, 'Marleasing: What is All the Fuss About?' (1993) 109 *LQR* 301.

[93] Hilson and Downes, n. 4 above, use Hohfeld's category of immunity/disability in analysing *Marleasing* and other judgments of the ECJ in this area, although acknowledging that while it may help to clarify loose language, it cannot explain the different rulings and results of the case law.

After *Marleasing*, the ECJ did not noticeably retreat from the strong encouragement to national courts to interpret domestic law in conformity with directives. In general, the ECJ left it essentially to the national court to decide whether an interpretation in conformity with a Directive was possible.[94] In *Wagner-Miret*, the Court accepted that the Spanish legislation in question could not be interpreted in such a way as to give effect to the result sought by the applicants.[95] Similarly in *Dori*,[96] *El Corte Inglés*,[97] *Evobus Austria*[98] and *Alcatel Austria*[99] the limits of interpretation which were articulated by the national court or which were evident in the terms of the law were readily accepted by the ECJ.

The other main limit to the interpetation obligation was the principle of non-retroactivity of penal liability articulated by the ECJ in *Kolpinghuis*,[100] However, in the later case of *Arcaro*, in which criminal proceedings were brought against the defendant under Italian law, this limit was restated by the ECJ in rather broader terms, which initially suggested a possible retreat from the implications of a strong interpretative obligation.[101] The Italian law was designed to implement two Council Directives but the national magistrate felt that there was an incompatibility between domestic law and the Directives, and asked the ECJ whether any procedure could be adopted to 'achieve the elimination from national legislation of provisions which are incompatible with those of Community law', even though the application of the Directive's provisions would worsen the defendant's legal position. The ECJ, having confirmed that a directive could not be directly effective as against an individual and having reiterated the obligation of harmonious interpretation, ruled:

However, that obligation of the national court to refer to the content of the directive when interpreting the relevant rules of its own national law reaches a limit where such an interpretation leads to the imposition on an individual of an obligation laid down by a directive which has not been transposed, or, more especially, where it has the effect of determining or aggravating, on the basis of the Directive and in the absence of a law enacted for its implementation, the liability in

---

94 See for a recent example Case C–365/98, *Brinkmann* [2000] ECR I–4619, para. 41: Betlem, n. 89 above, suggests that the ECJ gave a *Marleasing*-style mandatory ruling also in Case C–177/88, *Dekker* v. *Stichting Vormingscentrum voor Jong Volwassenen* [1990] ECR I–3941 which came close to requiring an interpretation of national law *contra legem*. See also the ECJ's comment in Case C–300/95, *Commission* v. *UK* [1997] ECR I–2649, effectively dismissing the Commission's argument that the UK courts should not interpret domestic law *contra legem* in order to comply with Community law.

95 See Case C–334/92, *Wagner Miret* v. *Fondo de Garantía Salarial* [1993] ECR I–6911, para. 22. See also C–131/97, *Carbonari* v. *Università degli Studi di Bologna* [1999] ECR I–1103, paras. 48–50.

96 Case C–91/92, n. 81 above, para. 27.

97 Case C–192/94, *El Corte Inglés* v. *Cristina Blázques Rivero* [1996] ECR I–1281, para. 22.

98 Case C–111/97, *Evobus Austria* v. *Niederösterreichischer Verkehrsorgination* [1998] ECR I–5411, paras. 18–21.

99 Case C–81/98, *Alcatel Austria* v. *Bundesministerium für Wissenschaft und Verkehr* [1999] ECR I–7671, paras. 49–50. Contrast Case C–76/97, *Tögel* v. *Niederösterreichische Gebietskrankenkasse* [1998] ECR I–5357, para. 28.

100 An unresolved question concerns whether national courts should interpret national law in the light of a dir. even before the time limit for its implementation has expired This is ambiguous in the judgment in *Kolpinghuis* (see para. 32). However, it seems likely, given that the Member States have discretion to choose the manner of implementation before the expiry of the period, that a national court would not be so obliged. See the AG's opinion in Case C–156/91, *Hansa Fleisch Ernst Mundt* [1992] ECR I–5567, para. 23, concerning a Dec. with a time limit for implementation. See also Betlem, n. 89 above, 11–12 and the AG Case in, C–106/89, *Marleasing* [1990] ECR I–4135, para. 9.

101 Case C–168/95, *Luciano Arcaro* [1996] ECR I–4705.

criminal law of persons who act in contravention of that directive's provisions (see *Kolpinghuis Nijmegen,* cited above).[102]

The Court's statement that the limit to the interpretative obligation is reached 'where such an interpretation leads to the imposition on an individual of an obligation laid down by a directive which has not been transposed' seemed to suggest a narrowing of the principle of interpretation.[103] The limit suggested by the Court seemed less like a *contra legem* limit based on what the language of the domestic legislation could bear,[104] and more like a limit based on the possible impact of an interpretation which conformed with the directive. Yet the whole point of seeking an interpretation of national law in the light of Community law, and specifically in the light of a directive, would be to give national law a different meaning from that which it might otherwise have been given, and in a way which is legally disadvantageous to the other party.[105] If the limit placed on the interpretation requirement in *Luciano Arcaro* were not to be read as a virtual reversal of the interpretation obligation articulated in *Von Colson* and *Marleasing* by the ECJ, then it seemed that a relevant distinction would have to be found between the 'imposition of an obligation' on an individual party and the creation of other kinds of legal disadvantage or detriment for that party which fall short of a legal obligation.[106]

In the later case of *Centrosteel,* Advocate General Jacobs denied that *Arcaro* had in any way affected the well-established *Von Colson/Marleasing* interpretation obligation, and suggested that the words of the Court in *Arcaro* should be read in the context of the criminal proceedings in which they had arisen.[107] His synopsis of the relevant line of case law was as follows:

35. In summary, I am of the opinion that the Court's case law establishes two rules: (1) a directive cannot *of itself* impose obligations on individuals in the absence of proper implementation in national law; (2) the national courts must nevertheless interpret national law, as far as possible, in the light of the wording and purpose of relevant directives. While that process of interpretation cannot, of itself and independently of a national law implementing the directive, have the effect of determining or aggravating criminal liability, it may well lead to the imposition upon an individual of civil liability or a civil obligation which would not otherwise have existed.

His first point reiterates the ban on direct horizontal effect, and the second point, while ruling out the interpretation of non-implementing national law in such a way as

---

[102] *Ibid.,* para. 42.

[103] For various possible interpretations of this phrase see P. Craig, 'Directives: Direct Effect, Indirect Effect and the Construction of National Legislation' (1997) 22 *ELRev.* 519.

[104] Elmer AG, n. 101 above, at para. 39 of his Opinion in *Arcaro* had stated that the principle of interpretation could not be applied 'so as to undertake an actual redrafting of the provisions of national law. That would be tantamount to introducing the direct effect of provisions of a directive . . . by the back door'.

[105] See, e.g., the response of the UK House of Lords to the ECJ ruling on the meaning of the Equal Treatment Dir. in Case C–32/93, *Webb* v. *EMO Cargo* [1994] ECR I–3567, where it interpreted the domestic Sex Discrimination Act in conformity with the Dir. in a manner which the Court of Appeal had previously deemed to be a distortion of the meaning of the Act: [1995] 4 All ER 577, and which imposed on an employer a legal obligation not to dismiss an employee on grounds of pregnancy.

[106] Hilson and Downes, n. 4 above, prefer to use Hohfeld's conceptual scheme, and they contrast the notion of legal obligation with that of legal disability. Others suggest a notion of 'passive' horizontal direct effect which does not amount to a 'positive obligation': J. Stuyck and P. Wytinck in their early comment on *Marleasing:* (1991) 28 *CMLRev.* 205.

[107] Case C–456/98, *Centrosteel* v. *Adipol* [2000] ECR I–6007, paras. 31–35 of his Opinion.

to aggravate or determine an individual's criminal liability, does not rule out an obligation on national courts to interpret non-implementing national law in such a way as to aggravate or determine an individual's *civil* liability, or to impose a legal obligation on such an individual.

While the ECJ in *Centrosteel* did not refer to *Arcaro* or to the debate about the limits of the obligation of interpretation, it gave a strong ruling clearly directing the Italian court to interpret national law in conformity the directive. The case concerned a contractual action brought by Centrosteel (an Italian company) for payment of money under a commercial agency contract with the defendant Adipol (an Austrian company), which claimed that the agency contract was void under Italian law because of Centrosteel's failure to comply with the requirement of compulsory registration of commercial agents. Centrosteel sought to rely on EC Directive 86/653 on self-employed commercial agents, whose only requirement for the validity of an agency contract was that a written document be drawn up, and which had been interpreted by the ECJ in the earlier *Bellone* case[108] as precluding a law such as the Italian measure in question. Since Centrosteel and Adipol were private parties, and the directive had not been implemented at the time their dispute arose, to permit Centrosteel to rely directly on the Directive against Adipol would have amounted to giving it a form of horizontal effect. Interestingly, although the ECJ could have decided the case also on the basis of the direct effect of the Treaty provisions on freedom of establishment and services, it chose not to do so and based its reasoning on the directive instead. After noting that certain Italian courts already had, following the *Bellone* ruling, begun to change their case law relating to the invalidity of agency contracts in the light of the EC Directive and in order to conform with the Directive's requirements, the ECJ continued:

18. In view of the considerations set out above, it is likewise unnecessary, as the Italian government and the Commission have rightly submitted, to answer the national court's questions concerning the Treaty provisions on freedom of establishment and freedom to provide services, since the case pending before that court may be resolved on the basis of the Directive and the case law of the Court of Justice on the effects of directives.

19. In those circumstances, the answer to be given to the questions referred must be that the Directive precludes national legislation which makes the validity of an agency contract conditional upon the commercial agent being entered in the appropriate register. The national court is bound, when applying the provisions of domestic law predating or post-dating the said Directive, to interpret those provisions, so far as possible, in the light of the wording and purpose of the Directive, so that those provisions are applied in a manner consistent with the result pursued by the Directive, so that those provisions are applied in a manner consistent with the result pursued by the Directive.[109]

Thus, although the ECJ did not engage in explicit discussion about whether a civil obligation could be imposed on a private party by reason of the interpretation of national law in the light of an unimplemented directive, the result of the Court's clear indication to the Italian court on how it should interpret national law was (presumably) that Adipol would be under a legal obligation to pay the amount due under

---

[108] Case C–215/97, *Bellone* v. *Yokohama* [1998] ECR I–2191.
[109] Case C–456/98, n. 107 above.

the contract with Centrosteel. If Italian law were not to be read in the light of the Directive and if the agency contract were rendered void, Adipol would not be under this contractual obligation. A crucial factor in the case, however, seems to have been that the Italian courts had already begun to read the Italian law in question in such a way as to conform to the requirements of the EC directive, without this being considered *contra legem*, so that it was not contentious for the ECJ to require such an interpretation in the case at hand.

The ruling in *Coote*,[110] too, demonstrates the ECJ's readiness to articulate a strong interpretation obligation and to provide firm guidance to the national court in this respect. While the ECJ in *Coote* did not specify exactly how the British court should interpret domestic sex discrimination legislation, it gave a clear indication that when interpreting that law in the light of the Equal Treatment Directive, the national court should read it in the light of the obligation imposed by the Directive to introduce measures to protect workers who are victimized after the employment relationship has ended, by the refusal of the employer to provide a reference.[111]

The *Océano* judgment provides further evidence of the continued significance of the interpretation obligation, although the Court did not follow the more radical suggestion of the Advocate General.[112] Saggio AG's opinion proposes something close to horizontal direct effect (which he argues is already implicit in the ECJ's case law such as *CIA Security* and *Ruiz Bernaldéz*, discussed below), namely a duty on national courts to give effect to unimplemented directives by refusing to apply any conflicting rules of national law, even in cases concerning disputes between individuals. He refers to this as the 'exclusionary effect' of unimplemented directives—i.e. the fact that they are a superior source of EC law means that national courts are obliged to give them precedence over conflicting national law.[113] By focusing on the duty of the national courts and their obligation to 'invoke' unimplemented directives, and their duty to 'disapply' conflicting national law without necessarily substituting provisions of EC law, he avoids declaring that individuals can rely directly on the provisions of unimplemented directives against one another. But it is evident that he is advocating the horizontal use of directives by national courts in situations which will involve legal liabilities and obligations for individuals to which they would not have been subject had only the provisions of national law been applied to them without the intervention of the Directive.

The case involved proceedings brought by Océano before a Barcelona court for payment owed to it under a contract for the sale of encyclopædias to the defendant Murciano Quintero. The national court was unsure whether it had jurisdiction over the case, since the term in the contract which specified that the Barcelona courts

---

[110] Case C–185/97, *Coote* v. *Granada Hospital* [1998] ECR I–5199. See also Tizzano AG in Case C–168/00, *Leitner* v. *TUI Deutschland*, not yet reported, at para. 46 of his Opinion of 20 Sept. 2001, and Stix Hackl AG in Case C–60/00, *Carpenter* v. *Home Secretary*, not yet reported at para 41. of her Opinion of 13 Sept. 2001.

[111] *Ibid.*, paras. 18–27. Note that the Sex Discrimination Act in question, although it predated the Dir., was none the less intended to implement it, although the industrial tribunal had ruled that the provisions of the Act did not regulate behaviour after the contract of employment had ended.

[112] Cases C–240–244/98, *Océano Grupo Editorial* v. *Rocio Murciano Quintero* [2000] ECR I–4491. See J. Stuyck, (2001) 38 *CMLRev.* 719.

[113] *Ibid.*, para. 37 of his Opinion. For similar arguments see Lenz, Tynes, and Young, n. 4 above.

should have jurisdiction was of a kind which had on several occasions been judicially deemed to be unfair. While Spanish contract law provided in general that unfair terms in consumer contracts were automatically void, this law was amended to incorporate the list of terms which, according to the EC Unfair Contract Terms Directive, are to be regarded as unfair (and which include a jurisdiction term) only *after* the events which were the subject of this litigation had taken place. The question therefore was whether the Spanish court should, of its own motion, determine whether the jurisdiction clause of the contract was unfair by reference to the Directive. The case therefore touched on two separate issues: first whether the national court (rather than one of the parties) ought to raise the issue of the unfairness of the term of its own motion, and, secondly, the implications of this for the litigation, which concerned a dispute between two private parties which had taken place before the Directive had been implemented. Having ruled that the term was indeed unfair and that the Directive would entail a national court being able to raise and determine that of its own motion, the ECJ cited *Marleasing* and *Dori* and continued:

Cases C–240–244/98, Océano Grupo Editorial v. Rocio Murciano Quintero
[2000] ECR I–4491

31. Since the court making the reference is seised of a case falling within the scope of the Directive and the facts giving rise to the case postdate the expiry of the period allowed for transposing the Directive, it therefore falls to that court, when it applies the provisions of national law outlined in paragraphs 10 and 11 above which were in force at the material time, to interpret them, as far as possible, in accordance with the Directive and in such a way that they are applied of the court's own motion.

32. It is apparent from the above considerations that the national court is obliged, when it applies national law provisions predating or postdating the said Directive, to interpret those provisions, so far as possible, in the light of the wording and purpose of the Directive. The requirement for an interpretation in conformity with the Directive requires the national court, in particular, to favour the interpretation that would allow it to decline of its own motion the jurisdiction conferred on it by virtue of an unfair term.

This ruling does not declare that the Spanish court *must* decline jurisdiction by reading national law in the light of the Directive's requirements, but it certainly encourages the national court to do this, by indicating that it should 'favour' that interpretation if it is possible. And while such an interpretation of national law would not impose any legal obligation on Océano, it would deprive that company of any possible existing right under national law to enforce the consumer contract before the Barcelona court. While the defendant would not himself or herself have to 'invoke' the right (since a defendant might well not appear before a court outside his or her domicile) that party would benefit from the terms of the directive even though it was not implemented, and the plaintiff company would suffer a legal disadvantage.

Certainly it seems to be the case, after the rulings in *Coote*, *Océano*, and *Centrosteel*, that the harmonious interpretation requirement is alive and well, despite the brief tremor suggested by the ambiguous *Arcaro* judgment. *Contra legem* interpretation is not required, and often the ECJ will leave it to the discretion of the national court to determine whether harmonious interpretation is possible. However, this trio of cases demonstrates that when the circumstances are suitable, the ECJ will not hesitate to give firm guidance to a national court on how it should 'harmoniously' interpret national law even when, as in *Centrosteel*, this results in the imposition on a private party of civil liability which would not otherwise have been imposed.

(d) 'INCIDENTAL' HORIZONTAL EFFECTS

The third recent development which has lessened the impact of the *Marshall/Dori* prohibition on the horizontal direct effect of directives is a line of case law which permits the use of unimplemented directives in certain cases between private parties. This development, which is most strikingly evident in the *CIA Security*[114] and *Unilever Italia*[115] cases, is complex and confusing and it is difficult to distinguish, in convincing conceptual terms, from direct horizontal effect. It brings us back also to the distinction suggested at the outset of the Chapter between the broader concept of direct effect which entails the invocability of EC law, and a narrower concept which relates to the conferral of subjective rights on individuals. The following cases suggest that directives can have a limited form of horizontal effect when they do not directly impose legal obligations on individuals.

Case C–194/94, CIA Security International SA v. Signalson SA and Securitel SPRL [1996] ECR I–2201

CIA Security brought proceedings against the defendants before the Belgian commercial courts asking for orders requiring them to cease unfair trading practices. CIA argued that the two companies had libelled it by claiming that the alarm system which it marketed had not been approved as required under Belgian legislation. CIA agreed that it had not sought approval but argued that the Belgian legislation was in breach of Article 28 (ex Article 30) EC and had not been notified to the Commission as required by Directive 83/189 on technical standards and regulations. The national court asked the ECJ whether the Directive was sufficiently clear and precise to be directly effective before the national court, and whether a national court should refuse to apply a national regulation which had not been communicated as required by the Directive. The ECJ began by ruling that the national regulation should indeed have been notified under the Directive.

THE ECJ

44. ... Articles 8 and 9 of Directive 83/189 lay down a precise obligation on Member States to notify draft technical regulations to the Commission before they are adopted. Being,

---

114 Case C–194/94, *CIA Security International SA v. Signalson SA and Securitel SPRL* [1996] ECR I–2201.
115 Case C–443/98, *Unilever Italia SpA v. Central Food SpA* [2000] ECR I–7535.

accordingly, unconditional and sufficiently precise in their content, those articles may be relied on by individuals before national courts.

45. It remains to examine the legal consequences to be drawn from a breach by Member States of their obligation to notify and, more precisely, whether Directive 83/189 is to be interpreted as meaning that a breach of the obligation to notify, constituting a procedural defect in the adoption of the technical regulations concerned, renders such technical regulations inapplicable so that they may not be enforced against individuals.

The Court went on to rule that part of the aim of the Directive was to protect the free movement of goods by preventive control, and that it would enhance the effectiveness of that control to provide that a breach of the obligation to notify would render the unnotified domestic regulation inapplicable to individuals.[116] The ECJ did not mention *Dori* or *Marshall* and did not (unlike the Advocate General) directly advert to the fact that this was a case between private parties. However, although CIA would rely on the Directive primarily as against the application of the State's technical regulation on the requirement of approval of alarm systems,[117] the outcome of such reliance in the proceedings against the two defendants before the national court could presumably be that the defendants may be found liable for unfair trading. Thus, the case gives some effect to the provisions of a Directive in proceedings between individuals, and it may relieve the plaintiff from a domestic legal obligation. Further, although it does not of itself impose a legal obligation on the defendants, it removes from them the protection of the national technical regulation and exposes them to potential liability under other provisions of national law. In other words, this is the kind of 'exclusionary' effect referred to by Saggio AG in the *Océano* case: the directive is invoked in a case between individuals to preclude the application of a conflicting provision of national law, and the result is that one of the parties to the case is subject to a legal liability or disadvantage to which it would not have been subject had the offending national law been applied.[118]

The issue of indirect horizontal reliance on directives in disputes involving private parties had also emerged in some noteworthy earlier cases, such as *Ruiz Bernáldez*,[119] *Panagis Pafitis*,[120] and *Smithkline Beecham*.[121] *Ruiz Bernáldez* concerned criminal proceedings against the defendant for causing an accident while driving drunk, in

---

[116] Contrast Cases C–235/95, *AGS Assedic Pas-de-Calais* v. *François Dumon* [1998] ECR I–4531, paras. 32–33, and 280/87, *Enichem Base* v. *Comune di Cinisello Balsamo* [1989] ECR 2491, paras. 22–24 in which the obligation imposed on Member States by various dirs. to notify the Commission of national rules could not be invoked by individuals in order to challenge national legislation.

[117] See Elmer AG's view, paras. 68–74, that it was effectively against the State's rules on marketing and commercial practices that the dir. was being pleaded, and that it was immaterial that the issue arose in the context of an action between private parties, since it did not, in his opinion, impose any obligations on Signalson or Securitel.

[118] One explanation offered for what was at the time a surprising outcome in the case was that it concerned an action to enforce a public-law obligation under Belgian trade practices legislation, to prevent a breach of statutory duty by the defendants, rather than merely resolving a private-law dispute. See J. Stuyck, (1996) 33 *CMLRev.* 1261 and J. Coppel, (1997) 26 *ILJ* 69. See also P.J. Slot (1996) 33 *CMLRev.* 1035, 1049, suggesting something similar to Saggio AG's 'exclusionary effect' distinction.

[119] Case C–129/94, *Criminal Proceedings Against Rafael Ruiz Bernáldez* [1996] ECR I–1829.

[120] Case C–441/93, *Panagis Pafitis* v. *Trapeza Kentrikis Ellados AE* [1996] ECR I–1347.

[121] Case C–77/97, *Österreichische Unilever GmbH* v. *Smithkline Beecham* [1999] ECR I–431.

which he was ordered to pay reparation for the damage to property caused. Taking the view that Spanish law governing drunken driving absolved his insurance company from the obligation to pay, the Spanish criminal court referred to the ECJ the question whether the national insurance rules were compatible with EC Directive 72/166 on motor vehicle insurance. The ECJ ruled that the Directive did require an insurer to compensate third-party victims of car accidents, and that an insurer was precluded from being able to rely on national statutory provisions or contractual clauses to refuse to compensate such victims. Thus a legal obligation to compensate the third party, which may not have existed under domestic law alone, could be derived from the Directive and imposed directly on the insurer.[122] As in *CIA Security*, one possible way which has been suggested to understand the case and to distinguish it from the impermissible 'horizontal direct effect' is that it involved the enforcement of a public-law obligation, rather than the purely private-law contractual obligations whose horizontal direct effect was prohibited in *Dori*[123] or in *El Corte Inglés*.[124] Further, it might be argued that the enforcement of the Directive simply removed or 'excluded' the exemption provided under national law for the insurance company, and that the Directive did not in itself impose any direct obligation.

Panagis Pafitis concerned an action brought against a Greek bank and its new shareholders by its old shareholders who objected to certain increases in capital.[125] The increases had been ratified pursuant to a Presidential Decree, on the basis of Greek legislation. The plaintiffs argued that the provisions of Council Directive 77/91 required a general meeting of shareholders to decide on any such increase in capital, that these provisions were directly effective, and that the Presidential Decree was incompatible with them. The ECJ agreed and ruled that the directive in question precluded national legislation of the kind being challenged. Again, it might be argued here that the Directive was being enforced to prevent the application of a provision of national law, and that although the effect of invoking the Directive would change the legal position of the defendant bank and the new shareholders by invalidating the capital increase, the Directive did not in itself impose new legal obligations (but merely a legal disadvantage) on them.

In the case of *Smithkline Beecham*, in which a private party sought an injunction under national law to restrain the defendant from marketing its toothpaste, the ECJ ruled that Directive 76/768 on cosmetics precluded the application of national law restricting certain forms of toothpaste marketing.[126] This resulted in the enforcement

---

[122] Note that the insurer was not actually party to the case: Stuyck, n. 118 above, 1272 argues that, because proceedings were brought by the State, the Court permitted a dir. to confer rights on an individual which would generate obligations for other individuals.

[123] Case C–91/92, *Faccini Dori* v. *Recreb* [1994] ECR I–3325, in which Dori sought unsuccessfully to rely on a right contained an unimplemented dir., to resist the enforcement against her of a contract she had entered into with Recreb. The ECJ confirmed its *Marshall I* (Case C–152/84 [1986] ECR 723) ruling that dir. could not be relied on to impose obligations on individuals.

[124] See Case C–192/94, *El Corte Inglés* v. *Cristina Blázquez Rivero* [1996] ECR I–1281, a contractual dispute in which the defendant sought to rely in a Spanish court as against the plaintiff finance company on the provisions of a dir. which would have given her a right to resist the enforcement of a contract against the company, but in which the ECJ ruled that since the dir. had not been implemented in Spain its provisions could not be given horizontal direct effect.

[125] Case C–441/93, *Panagis Pafitis* v. *Trapeza Kentrikis Ellados AE* [1996] ECR I–1347.

[126] Case C–77/97, n. 121 above.

between private parties of a Directive containing substantive rules on the marketing of cosmetics so as to remove a conflicting national law. No new legal obligation was imposed on either party, but the plaintiff would be disabled from relying on national law and the defendant would thereby gain the benefit of the prohibition in the directive. To use the term suggested by a recent commentator, one way of understanding the *Pagagis Pafitis* and *Smithkline Beecham* cases might be to see them as instances of 'disguised vertical direct effect' in which a private party is precluded from benefiting from the State's substantive breach of an EC Directive.[127] None the less, these are 'horizontal' cases in the sense that one party certainly suffers a legal detriment and the other party gains a legal advantage from the terms of an unimplemented directive.

Apart from the apparent erosion of the 'no horizontal direct effect' principle which these cases seemed to suggest, the potentially more serious implications of the *CIA Security* ruling became evident when a number of other cases concerning the direct enforceability of Directive 83/189 arose.[128] The *Lemmens* case—although not involving litigation between invididuals—demonstrated the limits to the kind of reliance which an individual could place on a directive in challenging national law. A Dutch driver who had been prosecuted for drunken driving challenged the use of the results of a breathalyser test as evidence against him, on the basis that the national regulation on breath analysis under which the breathalysing equipment was approved had not been notified to the Commission as required under Directive 83/189.[129] The argument based on *CIA Security* was in essence that, since the Dutch regulation had not been notified under the Directive, it was invalid, therefore the breathalysing equipment used to provide evidence against the defendant was not approved as required by Dutch law, and so the evidence could not be used against him. The ECJ ruled that although the notification requirements of Directive 83/189 were sufficiently clear and precise, they could be relied on by an individual only where such reliance would promote the aim of the Directive. This aim was to promote free movement of goods by the preventive control of unjustified technical obstacles to trade, and enabling individuals to invoke its provisions so as to prevent the enforcement of unnotified national regulations would further that aim. Thus, while a plaintiff could invoke provisions of the Directive so as to prevent the enforcement of a regulation which restricted the marketing or trade in goods (as in *CIA Security*), the only regulations at issue in the *Lemmens* case were the criminal law on drunk driving and the regulation providing for the introduction of breathalyser test results in evidence. Disapplying either of these would have no connection with and would not advance the free movement of goods. *Lemmens* was thus less about the capacity of an individual to *invoke* the provisions of a directive, especially since these provisions were clear and precise and there was no question in the circumstances of horizontal effect, and more about the kind of use or reliance which could be placed on specific provisions of EC law.

---

[127] M. Dougan, 'The "Disguised" Vertical Direct Effect of Directives' (2000) 59 *CLJ* 586.

[128] See S. Weatherill, 'A Case Study in Judicial Activism in the 1990s: the Status before National Courts of Measures Wrongfully Un-notified to the Commission', in D. O'Keeffe and A. Bavasso (eds.), *Judicial Review in EU Law* (Kulwer, 2000), i, 481. For an extensive earlier analysis of Dir. 83/189 by the same author see 'Compulsory Notification of Draft Technical Regulations: the Contribution of Directive 83/189 to the Management of the Internal Market' (1996) 16 *YBEL* 129.

[129] Case C–226/97, *Lemmens* [2000] ECR I–3711.

The *Unilever Italia* v. *Central Foods* case, which also involved Directive 83/189, demonstrates more dramatically the successful reliance of an individual on the terms of that Directive in a contractual dispute with another individual. The Directive was invoked to prevent the enforcement of a national regulation which, although it had been properly notified, had then been adopted in breach of a standstill clause under the Directive.[130] The contract was for delivery of a quantity of olive oil, and the olive oil delivered by the plaintiff was labelled in a way which complied with EC law, but not with the contested Italian labelling legislation. Thus it was a case where reliance by one party on the terms of the Directive in order to have national law disapplied would result in the imposition of contractual obligations on the defendant, which would not have been imposed had the national law been applied. Jacobs AG, having discussed the *CIA Security* ruling, argued that the Court should not conclude that the offending national legislation would be unenforceable in private contractual proceedings of this kind. He contended that such unenforceability would give rise to considerable legal uncertainty, and that it would be unjust since it would penalize individuals for the State's failure. He argued further that breach of the Directive's standstill clause was different from a breach of the notification requirement and should not lead to the unenforceability of national regulations. It seems likely that the AG had his doubts even about the *CIA Security* ruling itself, and was seeking to distinguish it so as to narrow the relevance and applicability of the ruling.[131] The Court, however, did not agree and did not address the arguments of the Advocate General.[132] Having recalled in paragraphs 40–43 its reasoning in *CIA Security* about the aim of Directive 83/189 and why it should render unenforceable any national regulations adopted in breach thereof, the Court continued:

Case C–443/98, Unilever Italia SpA v. Central Food SpA
[2000] ECR I–7535

THE ECJ

45. It is therefore necessary to consider, secondly, whether the inapplicability of technical regulations adopted in breach of Article 9 of Directive 83/189 can be invoked in civil proceedings between private individuals concerning contractual rights and obligations.

46. First, in civil proceedings of that nature, application of technical regulations adopted in breach of Article 9 of Directive 83/189 may have the effect of hindering the use or marketing of a product which does not conform to those regulations.

47. That is the case in the main proceedings, since application of the Italian rules is liable to hinder Unilever in marketing the extra virgin olive oil which it offers for sale.

48. Next, it must be borne in mind that, in *CIA Security*, the finding of inapplicability as a legal consequence of breach of the obligation of notification was made in response to a request for a

---

[130] Case C–443/98, n 115 above.

[131] See his subsequent Opinion in Case C–159/00, *Sapod Audic* v. *Eco Emballages SA*, given on 17 Jan. 2002, at para. 62.

[132] For comment on the case see S. Weatherill, 'Breach of Directives and Breach of Contract' (2001) 26 *ELRev.* 177.

preliminary ruling arising from proceedings between competing undertakings based on national provisions prohibiting unfair trading.

49. Thus, it follows from the case-law of the Court that the inapplicability of a technical regulation which has not been notified in accordance with Article 8 of Directive 83/189 can be invoked in proceedings between individuals for the reasons set out in paragraphs 40 to 43 of this judgment. The same applies to non-compliance with the obligations laid down by Article 9 of the same directive, and there is no reason, in that connection, to treat disputes between individuals relating to unfair competition, as in the *CIA Security* case, differently from disputes between individuals concerning contractual rights and obligations, as in the main proceedings.

50. Whilst it is true, as observed by the Italian and Danish Governments, that a directive cannot of itself impose obligations on an individual and cannot therefore be relied on as such against an individual (see Case C–91/92 *Faccini Dori* [1994] ECR I–3325, paragraph 20), that case-law does not apply where non-compliance with Article 8 or Article 9 of Directive 83/189, which constitutes a substantial procedural defect, renders a technical regulation adopted in breach of either of those articles inapplicable.

51. In such circumstances, and unlike the case of non-transposition of directives with which the case-law cited by those two Governments is concerned, Directive 83/189 does not in any way define the substantive scope of the legal rule on the basis of which the national court must decide the case before it. It creates neither rights nor obligations for individuals.

52. In view of all the foregoing considerations, the answer to the question submitted must be that a national court is required, in civil proceedings between individuals concerning contractual rights and obligations, to refuse to apply a national technical regulation which was adopted during a period of postponement of adoption prescribed in Article 9 of Directive 83/189.

The 'public law' rationale suggested to explain earlier cases does not help in this case, which concerned a dispute between private parties where one sought to impose contractual obligations on another, rather than public-law requirements such as unfair trading law (as in *CIA Security*) or compulsory insurance law (as in *Ruiz Bernáldez*). True, the labelling legislation challenged here was a public regulation, but the plaintiff was seeking to have that set aside rather than enforced against the defendant. The ECJ attempted in two ways to distinguish this case from the prohibited 'horizontal direct effect' cases such as *Dori* and *Marshall*. The first was by emphasizing the particular nature and aims of Directive 83/189 and the rationale outlined in *CIA Security* for declaring national rules which breach this Directive to be unenforceable.[133] The second was to argue that the Directive itself creates no individual rights and imposes no obligations on individuals.[134] This is the now familiar 'exclusionary effect' argument: that the Directive can be invoked by individuals in order to have national law disapplied, but it does not create new law, new rights or new obligations

[133] For other post-*CIA Security* cases in which various attempts to invoke Dir. 83/189 [1983] OJ L109/8 were made, but without success for the applicants, see Cases C–425–427/97, *Albers* [1999] ECR I–2947; C–37/99, *Donkersteeg* [2000] ECR I–10223; C–314/98, *Sneller's Autos* v. *Algemeen Directeur van de Dienst Wegverkeer* [2000] ECR I–8633; C–278/99, *Van der Burg* [2001] ECR I–2015; and C–159/00, *Sapod Audic* v. *Eco Emballages SA*, Opinion of 17 Jan. 2002.

[134] The ECJ here may have been seeking to avoid acknowledging rights for individuals which they could use in seeking damages from the State under the *Francovich* doctrine. See n. 140 below and Ch. 6 for further discussion.

to be applied. Rather it leaves a 'void' which will be filled by other provisions of national law—and, in this case, of national contract law. It might well be said in response, however, that such distinctions between rights and obligations on the one hand and legal advantages and disadvantages on the other, or between the use of a directive merely to 'exclude' national law as opposed to substituting its provisions for those of national law, are a form of legal sophistry which provide no convincing explanation for apparently contradictory lines of case law.

How are we to understand this series of cases in relation to the ECJ's refusal to depart from the clear *Marshall/Dori* rulings that a directive cannot be invoked by an individual so as to impose a direct obligation on another individual?[135] A *first* answer is to say that Directive 83/189 is an unusual directive in that it imposes procedural obligations only on a Member State, so that its enforcement against national law can never of itself impose direct obligations on individuals.[136] This however does not account for cases such as *Panagis Pafitis* or *Smithkline Beecham*, where the directives in question contain substantive rules and requirements which directly affect the legal position of the parties and the outcome of the litigation even if they do not impose 'obligations' in a strict sense. A *second* answer is to say that the enforcement of the directives in these cases between private parties, including *Panagis Pafitis*, *Smithkline Beecham*, *CIA Security*, and *Unilever Italia* have 'exclusionary effect' only. In other words, they remove the applicability of an offending national law but do not substitute any substantive EC obligations for either party. Although the invocation of the directives in these cases normally entails indirect disadvantages and disabilities for one of the parties, the directives do not *directly* impose obligations on either party (other than perhaps in the *Panagis Pafitis* case), since those obligations flow instead from other existing national legal provisions when the offending provision has been disapplied.

However, rather like the strong interpretative obligation in cases such as *Centrosteel*, which is supposedly distinguishable from the 'no horizontal direct effect' rule of *Marshall/Dori* on the basis that an unimplemented directive does not directly impose a legal obligation on the parties, but only indirectly through a change in the meaning of pre-existing settled national law, these rationalizations rely on highly refined and often confusing distinctions. The 'direct effect in the strict sense'[137] which is still prohibited under *Marshall/Dori* seems to have shrunk to a fairly narrow exception which lacks normative coherence. Directives are being used in litigation to govern the legal relations between private parties in all sorts of contexts. Legal uncertainty about the effectiveness and applicability of an unimplemented directive—and correspondingly about the validity of conflicting national law—in any given situation is extremely high. The clear message for individuals is that they need to be firmly aware of the existence of directives and of how they may affect their legal position even when the directives have not been implemented and when existing national law conflicts with them. They are a source of law, they can be invoked indirectly and directly by individuals in litigation, although it is extremely difficult to predict to what use

---

[135] See, for a nuanced attempt to provide possible answers to the confusion, Dougan, n. 127 above.

[136] This is the tenor of Jacob AG's argument in *Unilever Italia*, n. 115 above at paras. 79–81 of his Opinion.

[137] See Editorial (1999) 24 *ELRev.* 1.

they may be put by a national court. A 'sympathetic' provision of national law will almost always ensure the indirect enforceability of the obligations contained in a directive; and even in the absence of such a provision, a directive can be used to exclude other provisions of national law and to change the nature of the legal rights and obligations which would otherwise govern the parties under domestic law.

If the ECJ is serious about the importance of textual fidelity to the Treaty and respect for the specificity of directives as distinct legal instruments which seem to inspire adherence to the *Marshall/Dori* rulings, then it ought to reconsider some of its tangled legal rulings on incidental horizontal effects. If, on the other hand, it is determined to promote the effectiveness of directives in a variety of complex legal ways regardless of their proper domestic implementation, then the prohibition on horizontal direct effect looks increasingly hollow and intellectually incoherent.[138] Directives however remain important and flexible legal intruments which are seen in part as an embodiment of the principle of subsidiarity,[139] and the distinction between directives and regulations remains salient in political terms even while the legal consequences of their use are complex and confused.

(e) STATE LIABILITY IN DAMAGES FOR NON-IMPLEMENTATION OF A DIRECTIVE

One final and increasingly important way for an individual to enforce the provisions of a directive when the prohibition on horizontal direct effect is encountered is to sue the State in damages, pursuant to the famous *Francovich* ruling of the ECJ, for loss caused by its failure to implement a directive.[140] Rather than attempting to enforce the directive against the private party on whom the obligation contained therein would be imposed if the directive were properly implemented, the individual instead can bring proceedings for damages against the State. The significance of the *Francovich* ruling will be discussed in fuller detail in the next chapter. Suffice it to say in this context that the ruling has provided a further sharp incentive for Member States to implement directives properly and on time.

8. CONCLUSION

i. While some have argued that EC law should simply be applicable law, capable of use in national courts as the 'law of the land', it remains the case that different kinds of EC law enjoy different kinds of legal effects.

ii. Most provisions of EC law can be invoked before national courts when they satisfy basic conditions of justiciability. Normally, but not always, this means

---

[138] Dougan, n. 127 above, and Weatherill, n. 132 above.

[139] See Art. 6 of the Protocol on Subsidiarity and Proportionality added by the Amsterdam Treaty, which states that 'other things being equal, directives should be preferred to regulations and framework directives to detailed measures'.

[140] Cases C–6 & 9/90, *Francovich and Bonifaci* v. *Italy* [1991] ECR I–5357.

that they are capable of conferring rights on individuals, but the difference between legal rights and other legal interests is sometimes difficult to discern.

iii. The position of international agreements to which the EC is a party is more complex. Certain international agreements, even when clear and precise enough to be justiciable, cannot be invoked before national or EC courts because of the non-reciprocal nature of their provisions.

iv. The position of directives is most complex of all. They can be directly invoked by individuals before national courts against a state body, or indirectly invoked against any party in order to influence the interpretation of national law in their light. However, they can be directly invoked in proceedings against other individuals (horizontally) only in circumstances where they do not of themselves impose an obligation on a private party.

v. The principle that national law should be interpreted in the light of EC law is a broad one. It applies not only to directives, but also to EC Treaty provisions, to general principles of EC law, to international agreements entered by the EC, and to other forms of non-binding EC law.

9. FURTHER READING

(a) *Books*

PRECHAL, S., *Directives in European Community Law: A Study on EC Directives and their Enforcement by National Courts* (Oxford University Press, 1995)

(b) *Articles*

BETLEM, G., 'The Principle of Indirect Effect of Community Law' (1995) 3 *ERPL* 1

COPPEL, J., 'Rights, Duties and the End of Marshall' (1994) 57 *MLR* 859

—— 'Horizontal Direct Effect of Directives' (1997) 28 *ILJ* 69

CRAIG, P.P., 'Once upon a Time in the West: Direct Effect and the Federalization of EEC Law' (1992) 12 *OJLS* 453

—— 'Directives: Direct Effect, Indirect Effect and the Construction of National Legislation' (1997) 22 *ELRev.* 519

CURTIN, D., 'The Province of Government: Delimiting the Direct Effect of Directives in the Common Law Context' (1990) 15 *ELRev.* 195

DE WITTE, B., 'Direct Effect, Supremacy and the Nature of the Legal Order', in P. Craig and G. de Búrca (eds.), *The Evolution of EU Law* (Oxford University Press, 1999) 177

DOUGAN, M., 'The "Disguised" Vertical Direct Effect of Directives' (2000) 59 *CLJ* 586

ELEFTHERIADIS, P., 'The Direct Effect of Community Law: Conceptual Issues' (1996) 16 *YBEL* 205

GRILLER, S., 'Judicial Enforceability of WTO Law in the EU' (2000) 3 *JIEL* 441

HILSON, C., and DOWNES, T., 'Making Sense of Rights: Community Rights in EC Law' (1999) 24 *ELRev.* 121

Lenz, M., Tynes, D.S., and Young, L., 'Horizontal What? Back to Basics' (2000) 25 *ELRev.* 509

Mastroianni, R., 'On the Distinction Between Vertical and Horizontal Direct Effect of Directives: What Role for the Principle of Equality?' (1999) 5 *EPL* 417

Peers, S., 'Fundamental Rights or Political Whim? WTO Law and the ECJ', in G. de Búrca and J. Scott (eds.), *The EU and the WTO: Legal and Constitutional Issues* (Hart, 2001) 111

Pescatore, P., 'The Doctrine of "Direct Effect": An Infant Disease of Community Law' (1983) 8 *ELRev.* 155

Prechal, S., 'Does Direct Effect Still Matter?' (2000) 37 *CMLRev.* 1047

Ruffert, M., 'Rights and Remedies in European Community Law: A Comparative View' (1997) 34 *CMLRev.* 307

Van Gerven, W., 'The Horizontal Direct Effect of Directive Provisions Revisited: the Reality of Catchwords', in T. Heukels and D. Curtin (eds.), *Institutional Dynamics of European Integration, Liber Amicorum for Henry Schermers* (Martinus Nijhoff, 1994)

—— 'Of Rights, Remedies and Procedures' (2000) 37 *CMLRev.* 501

Weatherill, S., 'Breach of Directives and Breach of Contract' (2001) 26 *ELRev.* 177

Winter, T., 'Direct Applicability and Direct Effects' (1972) 9 *CMLRev.* 425

Wyatt, D., 'New Legal Order or Old' (1982) 7 *ELRev.* 147

6

THE APPLICATION OF EC LAW: REMEDIES IN NATIONAL COURTS

1. CENTRAL ISSUES

i. The notion of the effectiveness of EC law has been developed by the ECJ into an obligation on national courts to ensure that they give adequate effect to EC law in cases arising before them.

ii. Neither the EC Treaty nor Community legislation lays down a general scheme of substantive or procedural law governing remedies for the enforcement of EC law, although sectoral legislation exists in some fields, and there have been moves towards more ambitious harmonization and co-ordination projects.[1]

iii. The ECJ's early case law emphasized a principle of national autonomy in the field of remedies, whereby EC law would be given effect at domestic level in accordance with the procedures and conditions laid down by national law, and in accordance with which the Treaty did not require national courts to provide new remedies. This principle was qualified by two requirements: that these conditions should be applied to national law and to EC law in the same way (equivalence) and that they should not render the exercise of EC rights impossible in practice (practical possibility).

iv. Over time the ECJ, drawing on the obligations of Member States under Article 10 (ex Article 5) EC, began to emphasize stronger notions of adequacy and effectiveness, rather

than merely practical possibility, in the domestic enforcement of EC law. Initially this seemed to be in particular sectors such as sex discrimination, but the doctrine was gradually expanded. The Court also sometimes required national courts to make available a particular type of remedy (reparation, interim relief etc.), regardless of whether or not this would be available under national law.

v. The most famous ruling in which the ECJ indicated that EC law requires national courts to provide a *specific* form of remedy is *Francovich*, where the principle of state liability to provide compensation for breach of EC law was introduced. It remains to be seen whether this develops into a general principle of individual liability to compensate for breaches of EC law.

vi. A synthesis of the case law indicates that while the principle of national procedural and remedial autonomy remains important, the qualifications of equivalence and effectiveness have become powerful doctrinal tools directing national courts to undertake a case-by-case appraisal of national rules. National courts are expected to engage in a context-specific proportionality analysis of any restrictive provisions of national law and to disapply these whenever necessary to give effect to EC law.

---

[1] Art. 65 EC added by the Amsterdam Treaty governs the adoption of measures concerning 'judicial co-operation in civil matters', and suggests promoting the compatibility of the rules on civil procedure in the various Member States 'if necessary' for the good functioning of civil proceedings. More recently, in the field of private law, the Commission has issued a communication which asks 'whether problems result from divergences in contract law between Member States' and which raises the question of possible alternatives to 'the existing approach of sectoral harmonisation of contract law': COM(2001)398.

2. THE BASIC PRINCIPLE OF NATIONAL PROCEDURAL AUTONOMY

(a) IN THE ABSENCE OF RELEVANT COMMUNITY RULES

Early in its case law, the ECJ ruled that it was for the national legal system to determine how the interests of a person adversely affected by an infringement of Community law were to be protected. Only a very basic degree of guidance was provided in these cases.[2]

Case 33/76, Rewe-Zentralfinanz eG and Rewe-Zentral AG v. Landwirtschaftskammer für das Saarland [1976] ECR 1989

[Note: Art. 5 EC is now Art. 10]

The applicant companies applied for a refund, including interest, of charges they had paid in Germany for import inspection costs, when these charges were found to be in breach of the Treaty. The national time limit for contesting the validity of national administrative measures had passed, and the case was referred to the ECJ to see whether Community law required that the applicants be granted the remedy sought.

THE ECJ[3]

Applying the principle of cooperation laid down in Article 5 of the Treaty, it is the national courts which are entrusted with ensuring the legal protection which citizens derive from the direct effect of the provisions of Community law.

Accordingly, in the absence of Community rules on this subject, it is for the domestic legal system of each Member State to designate the courts having jurisdiction and to determine the procedural conditions governing actions at law intended to ensure the protection of the rights which citizens have from the direct effect of Community law, it being understood that such conditions cannot be less favourable than those relating to similar actions of a domestic nature. . . .

In the absence of such measures of harmonisation the right conferred by Community law must be exercised before the national courts in accordance with the conditions laid down by national rules.

The position would be different only if the conditions and time-limits made it impossible in practice to exercise the rights which the national courts are obliged to protect.

This is not the case where reasonable periods of limitation of actions are fixed.

---

[2] Case 6/60, *Humblot v. Belgium* [1960] ECR 559; Case 13/68, *Salgoil v. Italian Ministry for Foreign Trade* [1973] ECR 453, [1969] CMLR 181.
[3] [1976] ECR 1989, 1997.

Despite emphasizing the responsibility of the Member State, where there are no relevant Community rules, for determining the procedural conditions under which Community rights are to be protected,[4] the Court imposed two 'Community' requirements on any national conditions.[5] These were the principle of *equivalence* or non-discrimination, which provides that the remedies and forms of action available to ensure the observance of national law must be made available in the same way to ensure the observance of Community law, and the principle of *practical possibility*, which provides that national conditions and procedures should not make the exercise of the right impossible in practice.

(b) NO CREATION OF 'NEW' REMEDIES

Thus the procedures and remedies for breach of Community law were primarily a matter for the Member States. In the absence of harmonization or the creation of Community rules, EC law did not require the States to supply remedies which would not be available under national law.

Case 158/80, Rewe-Handelsgesellschaft Nord mbH v. Hauptzollamt Kiel
[1981] ECR 1805

[Note ToA renumbering: Art. 177 is now Art. 234]

The applicants argued that 'butter-buying cruises' which were permitted under German law and allowed for the purchase of tax-free butter, were contrary to Community taxation and customs law. They argued that their economic interests were adversely affected by the Member State's failure to apply Community rules to third party competitors, and sought a remedy from the national court to compel the national authorities to apply those Community rules.

THE ECJ

44. With regard to the right of a trader to request the courts to require the authorities of a Member State to compel a third party to comply with obligations arising from Community rules in a given legal situation in which that trader is not involved but is economically adversely affected by the failure to observe Community law, it must be remarked first of all that, although the Treaty has made it possible in a number of instances for private persons to bring a direct action, where appropriate, before the Court of Justice, it was not intended to create new remedies in the national courts to ensure the observance of Community law other than those already laid down by national law. On the other hand the system of legal protection established by the Treaty, as set out in Article 177 in particular, implies that it must be possible for every type of action provided for by national

---

[4] See also Case 45/76, *Comet BV* v. *Produktschap voor Siergewassen* [1976] ECR 2043, and Case 179/84, *Bozetti* v. *Invernizzi* [1985] ECR 2301.

[5] See, for criticism of the conflation of 'procedures' and 'remedies' in discussion of this subject and for a query whether the appropriate term should be national *remedial* autonomy rather than national *procedural* autonomy, C. Kilpatrick, 'The Future of Remedies in Europe', in C. Kilpatrick, T. Novitz, and P. Skidmore (eds.), *The Future of Remedies in Europe* (Hart, 2000) 1, 4.

law to be available for the purpose of ensuring observance of Community provisions having direct effect, on the same conditions concerning the admissibility and procedure as would apply were it a question of ensuring observance of national law.

Thus Member States could apply their own procedural rules and conditions without being required to create new national remedies, although these rules remained subject to the twin principles of equivalence and practical possibility.[6]

In one particular branch of case law, however, concerning the repayment of charges levied in breach of EC law, the Court effectively insisted that a right to repayment must in principle be available under national law,[7] on the basis that this flowed directly from the nature of the substantive provisions of EC law in question. Thus in *San Giorgio* the Court ruled:

12. In that connection it must be pointed out in the first place that entitlement to the repayment of charges levied by a member state contrary to the rules of Community law is a consequence of, and an adjunct to, the rights conferred on individuals by the Community provisions prohibiting charges having an effect equivalent to customs duties or, as the case may be, the discriminatory application of internal taxes. Whilst it is true that repayment may be sought only within the framework of the conditions as to both substance and form, laid down by the various national laws applicable thereto, the fact nevertheless remains, as the court has consistently held that those conditions may not be less favourable than those relating to similar claims regarding national charges and they may not be so framed as to render virtually impossible the exercise of rights conferred by Community law.[8]

It has been argued that this line of case law concerning unlawfully levied charges actually involved the ECJ imposing a particular remedy,[9] or perhaps rather insisting upon the availability in principle of a specific remedy within national legal systems, as a matter of Community law.

At the same time, even in these cases the Court continued to emphasize the primary role of the national legal system in laying down the conditions governing the grant of such a remedy, so long as they satisfied the principles of equivalence and practical possibility. As Advocate General Warner said in the case of *Ferwerda*:[10]

To that one might object that, if so, there will be a lack of uniformity in the consequences of the application of Community law in the different Member States. The answer to that objection is . . . that this Court cannot create Community law where none exists: that must be left to the Community's legislative organs.

---

[6] In Case 309/85, *Barra* v. *Belgium* [1988] ECR 355 the Court considered that national legislation restricting repayment of a fee which had been charged in breach of Community law would render the exercise of Community rights impossible in practice. More recently in a similar factual context to that in *Barra*, see the AG's Opinion in Case C–62/00, *Marks & Spencer* v. *Commissioners of Customs and Excise*, 24 Jan. 2002.

[7] See, e.g., Cases 199/82, *Amministrazione delle Finanze dello Stato* v. *San Giorgio* [1983] ECR 3595, and C–192/95, *Comateb* v. *Directeur Général des Douanes et Droits Indirects* [1997] ECR I–165.

[8] Case 199/82, n. 7 above.

[9] See M. Dougan, 'Cutting your Losses in the Enforcement Deficit: A Community Right to the Recovery of Unlawfully Levied Charges?' (1998) 1 *CYELS* 233.

[10] See Case 265/78, *Ferwerda* v. *Produktschap voor Vee en Vlees* [1980] ECR 617, 640. In this case the Court accepted that the systematic application of the principle of legal certainty could make it practically impossible for the authorities to recover money granted in breach of an EC Reg.

3. THE REQUIREMENTS IMPOSED BY COMMUNITY LAW

(a) THE BASIC REQUIREMENTS OF PROPORTIONALITY, ADEQUACY, AND EFFECTIVENESS OF NATIONAL RESPONSES TO A BREACH OF COMMUNITY LAW

The 'recovery of charges' cases generally involve either an individual seeking to recover from the State the cost of charges which it has imposed in breach of EC law, or the State's attempt to recover money which it has wrongfully paid in breach of EC law. The issue of national rules and enforcement procedures has also arisen in the context of domestic remedies for the breach of EC law by *individuals*. Some of these cases, such as *Sagulo* and *Heylens* below, raise questions of the compatibility with Community law of heavy penalties imposed by a Member State for relatively minor administrative breaches by persons enjoying rights under Community law. Others, such as *Von Colson*, concern the adequacy and deterrent effect of national penalties for serious breaches by companies or individuals of fundamental rules of Community law.[11]

In *Sagulo*, the applicants were French and Italian nationals resident in Germany who had failed to comply with the necessary administrative formalities to obtain residence permits to which they were entitled under EC law. They were therefore penalized under German law, and the question of the compatibility of these penalties with EC law was referred to the ECJ.

Case 8/77, Sagulo, Brenca, and Bakhouche
[1977] ECR 1495

[ToA renumbering: Art. 7 EEC is now Art. 12 EC]

12. . . . In the absence of a criterion which in the present case might be based on the principle of national treatment contained in Article 7 of the Treaty it is nevertheless to be observed that although Member States are entitled to impose reasonable penalties for infringement by persons subject to Community law of the obligation to obtain a valid identity card or passport, such penalties should by no means be so severe as to cause an obstacle to the freedom of entry and residence provided for in the Treaty. . . .

13. The answer to the question raised must therefore be that it is for the competent authorities of each Member State to impose penalties where appropriate on a person subject to the provisions of Community law who has failed to provide himself with one of the documents of identity referred to in Article 3 of Directive No 68/360 but that the penalties imposed must not be disproportionate to the nature of the offence committed.

---

[11] See also Case 68/88, *Commission* v. *Greece* [1989] ECR 2965.

Thus national penalties imposed for breach of EC law must not be disproportionate,[12] and must not undermine a basic Community right such as freedom of movement. More recently the ECJ ruled that Member States are *required* by EC law—more specifically by Article 10 EC—to take 'all effective measures to sanction conduct which affects the financial interests of the Community'.[13] Further, the States may impose criminal penalties even where Community legislation provides only for civil sanctions, so long as any sanctions imposed satisfy the principle of equivalence and are 'effective, proportionate and dissuasive'.[14]

In *Von Colson*, the Court was asked to rule on the compatibility with EC law of national sanctions designed to remedy breaches by an employer (or by the State) of fundamental Community rights enjoyed by individuals under the Equal Treatment Directive 76/207.

Case 14/83, Von Colson and Kamann v. Land Nordrhein-Westfalen
[1984] ECR 1891

The female plaintiffs had applied for posts as social workers at a German prison. When two male candidates were appointed, the plaintiffs successfully brought legal proceedings against the prison administrators, claiming that they had been discriminated against on grounds of sex. They sought by way of remedy to be appointed to a post in the prison, or to be awarded six months' salary in the alternative. The Arbeitsgericht considered that under German law it could allow only the claim for 'reliance loss'—i.e the reimbursement of one of the plaintiffs' travelling expenses. A preliminary reference was made to discover whether the Directive specifically required that discrimination be remedied by the appointment of the complainant to a post.

THE ECJ

23. Although . . . full implementation of the directive does not require any specific form of sanction for unlawful discrimination, it does entail that that sanction be such as to guarantee real and effective judicial protection.

. . .

28. It should, however, be pointed out to the national court that although Directive No 76/207/EEC, for the purpose of imposing a sanction for the breach of the prohibition of discrimination, leaves the Member States free to choose between the different solutions suitable for achieving its objective, it nevertheless requires that if a Member State chooses to penalize breaches of that prohibition by the award of compensation, then in order to ensure that it is effective and that it has a deterrent effect, that compensation must in any event be adequate in relation to the damage sustained and must therefore amount to more than purely nominal compensation such as, for example, the reimbursement only of the expenses incurred in connection with the application.

---

[12] See also Case 77/81, *Zuckerfabrik Franken* [1982] ECR 681.
[13] C–186/98, *Nunes and de Matos* [1999] ECR I–4883.   [14] *Ibid.*

Consequently, in addition to the established principles of practical possibility and equivalence/non-discrimination[15] and to the requirement of proportionality of penalties, the issue of *adequacy and effectiveness* of national remedies in securing Community rights was given central importance in *Von Colson*. This was emphasized also in later decisions, such as *Johnston*[16] and *Heylens*.[17] In the latter case, the applicant was a Belgian national employed as a football trainer in France by the Lille Olympic Sporting Club. His Belgian trainer's diploma was refused recognition by the relevant French authorities, and the ECJ, drawing on the right to an effective judicial remedy in Articles 6 and 13 of the European Convention on Human Rights (ECHR), ruled:

[S]ince free access to employment is a fundamental right which the Treaty confers individually on each worker in the Community, the existence of a remedy of a judicial nature against any decision of a national authority refusing the benefit of that right is essential in order to secure for the individual effective protection for his right.[18]

According to the Court, the right to effective judicial review also generally required the giving of reasons for decisions which curtailed or denied a Community right, and must enable the person affected 'to defend that right under the best possible conditions'.[19] More recently in *Coote* v. *Granada*,[20] the Court underscored again the fundamental nature of the right of access to court, and ruled that the principle of access to judicial control must extend also to retaliatory measures adopted by an employer in reaction to legal proceedings brought against it under the Equal Treatment Directive.[21] In a different factual context,[22] in *Upjohn*, the ECJ ruled also on the standard of review which might be required, indicating that EC law did not oblige the national legal system to provide a judicial review procedure under which national courts would be competent to substitute their assessment of the facts and the scientific evidence found for that of the national decision-making body, provided that those courts were empowered effectively to apply the principles of EC law when conducting judicial review.[23]

---

[15] For cases in which national procedural rules on security for costs were found to be indirectly discriminatory, not as compared with equivalent Community law claims, but in relation to traders from other Member States, see Case C–43/95, *Data Delecta* [1996] ECR I–4661, para. 12 and Case C–323/95, *Hayes* v. *Kronenberger* [1996] ECR I–1711, para. 13.

[16] Case 222/84, *Johnston* v. *Chief Constable of the RUC* [1986] ECR 1651. See also Cases C–87–89/90, *Verholen* v. *Sociale Verzekeringsbank* [1991] ECR I–3757, para. 24, concerning national rules on standing.

[17] Case 222/86, *UNECTEF* v. *Heylens* [1987] ECR 4097, [1989] 1 CMLR 901.

[18] *Ibid.*, para. 14. See Chs. 8 and 17 for further discussion of the case.

[19] *Ibid.*, para. 15. See also, on the right to judicial review, Case C–228/98, *Dounias* v *Ypourgio Oikonomikon* [2000] ECR I–577, paras. 64–66; C–424/99 *Commission* v. *Austria* [2001] ECR I–9285, C–1/99 *Kofisa Italia* [2001] ECR I–207; and C–226/99 *Siples* [2001] ECR I–277.

[20] See Case C–185/97, *Coote* v. *Granada Hospitality Ltd.* [1998] ECR I–5199, in which an employer had refused to provide references for an employee, in retaliation for proceedings brought against it under the Dir.

[21] See also Case C–253/00, *Muñoz*, opinion of Geelhoed AG of 13 Dec. 2001, where the AG concluded that breach of a Reg. gave a party the right as a matter of EC law to enforce its provisions in civil proceedings before a national court.

[22] The relevance of the varying factual contexts and the different substantive sectors in which the ECJ has ruled on the remedial requirements of national law is a dimension which clearly merits further analysis: see C. Kilpatrick *et al.*, n. 5 above, Part II, 'Sectoral Approaches to EC Remedies'.

[23] Case C–120/97, *Upjohn* v. *The Licensing Authority* [1999] ECR I–223, paras. 33–36.

(b) EARLY TENSIONS BETWEEN THE PRINCIPLE OF EFFECTIVENESS AND THE 'NO NEW REMEDIES' STATEMENT

The shift in focus from the *non-discriminatory* application of national rules, and from the minimal-sounding requirement that EC rights should not be rendered *impossible in practice* to the more positive requirement that they be given *adequate and effective* protection, brought certain tensions to the fore. In *Rewe-Handelsgesellschaft Nord* v. *Hauptzollamt Kiel*[24] the Court had declared that the Treaty had not intended to create new remedies in national courts nor to require those courts to create new remedies, and that national provisions could be applied so long as they complied with the principles of equivalence and practical possibility. However, in the recovery-of-charges cases, the provision of a certain type of remedy was held to be inherent in or an adjunct to the substantive EC right. Further, when a national rule or principle rendered the exercise of a Community right impossible in practice, that rule would have to be set aside. These developments had already begun to undermine the significance of the Court's 'no new remedies' statement.

Such developments were vividly highlighted in *Factortame I*, in which the ECJ, drawing on the earlier constitutional case of *Simmenthal*,[25] strongly emphasized the requirement of effectiveness, and insisted on its priority over rules and principles of UK law. And although, legally speaking, this went no further than previous rulings of the Court, the results in *Factortame I* were rather dramatic. The national rule in question was a principle which, according to the House of Lords, prohibited absolutely the grant of the particular remedy sought. Therefore, the impact of requiring the principle of effectiveness of Community law to be given priority over the national rule was to require the grant of a remedy in novel circumstances, where it had not previously been available in a comparable situation involving purely national law.

Case C–213/89, R. v. Secretary of State for Transport, ex parte Factortame Ltd. and Others [1990] ECR I–2433

[Note ToA renumbering: Art. 5 is now Art. 10]

Factortame Ltd. and other companies, most of the directors and shareholders of which were Spanish nationals, were incorporated under UK law and owned or operated fishing vessels registered as British vessels under the Merchant Shipping Act 1894. The 1988 Merchant Shipping Act was adopted to require all fishing vessels to register anew, and the applicants did not satisfy the new registration conditions. In the High Court they argued that these conditions, including a 75 per cent nationality requirement for directors and shareholders, breached Community law. They also sought interim relief until final judgment was given. The House of Lords held that the grant of interim relief was precluded both by the common law rule prohibiting the grant of an interim

---

[24] Case 158/80, *Rewe–Handelsgesellschaft Nord mbH* v. *Hauptzollamt Kiel* [1981] ECR 1805, para. 44.

[25] Case 106/77, *Amministrazione delle Finanze dello Stato* v. *Simmenthal SpA* [1978] ECR 629, [1978] 3 CMLR 263. See Ch. 7, 280–3 for further discussion of this case.

injunction against the Crown and by the presumption that an Act of Parliament is in conformity with Community law until a decision on its compatibility with Community law has been given, but referred the case to the ECJ to see if interim relief was none the less required as a matter of EC law.

THE ECJ

13. The House of Lords . . . found in the first place that the claims by the appellants in the main proceedings that they would suffer irreparable damage if the interim relief which they sought were not granted and they were successful in the main proceedings were well founded. However, it held that, under national law, the English courts had no power to grant interim relief in a case such as the one before it. . . .

. . .

17. . . . [T]he preliminary question raised by the House of Lords seeks essentially to ascertain whether a national court which, in a case before it concerning Community law, considers that the sole obstacle which precludes it from granting interim relief is a rule of national law, must disapply that rule.

. . .

19. In accordance with the case-law of the Court, it is for the national courts, in application of the principle of cooperation laid down in Article 5 of the EEC Treaty, to ensure the legal protection which persons derive from the direct effect of provisions of Community law. . . .

20. The Court has also held that any provision of a national legal system and any legislative, administrative or judicial practice which might impair the effectiveness of Community law by withholding from the national court having jurisdiction to apply such law the power to do everything necessary at the moment of its application to set aside national legislative provisions which might prevent, even temporarily, Community rules from having full force and effect are incompatible with those requirements, which are the very essence of Community law (judgment of 9 March 1978 in Case 106/77 *Simmenthal* [1978] ECR 629).

21. It must be added that the full effectiveness of Community law would be just as much impaired if a rule of national law could prevent a court seised of a dispute governed by Community law from granting interim relief in order to ensure the full effectiveness of the judgment to be given on the existence of the rights claimed under Community law. It follows that a court which in those circumstances would grant interim relief, if it were not for a rule of national law, is obliged to set aside that rule.

The Court concentrated here on the issue of effectiveness, rather than—as it had in earlier judgments—reiterating that it is for the Member States to lay down the rules governing the enforcement of EC law. Thus it articulated a clear obligation on national courts under Article 10 (ex Article 5) EC to set aside obstructive national rules which preclude the grant of an appropriate remedy. The Court left it to the House of Lords to specify the conditions under which a national remedy such as interim relief should be granted in a given case,[26] but made clear that a rule which

---

[26] The precise conditions under which interim relief against a provision of national law which implemented Community law should be available were later specified by the ECJ in Cases C–143/88 & C–92/89, *Zuckerfabrik Süderdithmarschen* [1991] ECR I–415, and C–334/95, *Kruger GmbH* [1997] ECR I–4517.

prohibited absolutely the grant of interim relief would contradict the principle of effectiveness. Thus *Factortame I* weakens the force of the Court's previous statement that, in the absence of harmonization, EC law does not oblige national courts to create new remedies which would not be available under national law.[27] We will see below that later cases involving a strong 'effectiveness' ruling by the ECJ have further reduced the significance and scope of the 'no new remedies' rule.[28]

(c) DEVELOPMENT OF THE REQUIREMENT OF EFFECTIVENESS

(i) A STRONG SERIES OF RULINGS

A growing stream of cases from the early 1990s onwards highlighted the tension between the principle that national courts may apply all domestic rules which comply with the conditions of equivalence and practical possibility, and the more positive principle that national remedies—particularly in the context of EC directives whose provisions require the availability of adequate judicial remedies—must secure the effectiveness of Community rights.

Case C–177/88, Dekker v. Stichting voor Jong Volwassenen (VJV) Plus
[1990] I–ECR 3941

The applicant sought damages before the Dutch courts for the defendant's refusal to employ her on grounds of her pregnancy. On a preliminary reference, the ECJ ruled that such refusal constituted unlawful sex discrimination.

THE ECJ

23. Article 6 of the Directive recognizes the existence of rights vesting in the victims of discrimination which can be pleaded in legal proceedings. Although full implementation of the Directive does not require any specific form of sanction for unlawful discrimination, it does entail that that sanction be such as to guarantee real and effective judicial protection (judgment in Case 14/03 *Von Colson* [1984] ECR 1891, paragraph 23). It must, furthermore, have a real deterrent effect on the employer.

24. It must be observed that, if the employer's liability for infringement of the principle of equal treatment were made subject to proof of a fault attributable to him and also to there being no ground of exemption recognized by the applicable national law, the practical effect of those principles would be weakened considerably.

. . .

26. Accordingly, the answer must be that, although Directive 76/207 gives the Member State, in penalizing infringements of the prohibition of discrimination, freedom to choose between the various solutions appropriate for achieving its purpose, it nevertheless requires that, where a

---

[27] See J. Temple Lang, 'The Duties of National Courts under Community Constitutional Law' (1997) 22 *ELRev.* 3, 6; also W. van Gerven (1995) 32 *CMLRev.* 679, and M. Ross, 'Refining Effective Enjoyment' (1990) 15 *ELRev.* 476, 478.

[28] See nn. 50–52 below, and accompanying text.

Member State opts for a sanction forming part of the rules on civil liability, any infringement of the prohibition of discrimination suffices in itself to make the person guilty of it fully liable, and no regard may be had to the grounds of exemption envisaged by national law.

Thus, although the remedy was to be determined in accordance with national law, the Court ruled that the national provisions governing civil liability could not be applied where they would subject the claim for redress to a requirement of fault or to a defence of justification. The provisions of the Equal Treatment Directive requiring access to a judicial remedy[29] may account in part for the strength of the ruling.[30] None the less, the judgment marked a further dilution of the principle of national procedural autonomy, especially since the national rule did not discriminate between situations involving Community law and those involving purely domestic law, and the requirement of fault would probably not render the exercise of the Community right 'impossible' in practice.

Shortly after *Dekker*, the Irish Supreme Court in *Cotter and McDermott* considered that the payment to married women of social welfare benefits for dependents which had previously been paid to married men but denied to married women in breach of EC sex discrimination law would offend against the national legal principle prohibiting unjust enrichment.[31] On a reference to the ECJ, however, the Court ruled that:

21. To permit reliance on that prohibition would enable the national authorities to use their own unlawful conduct as a ground for depriving Article 4(1) of the directive of its full effect.

22. The reply to the first question must therefore be that Article 4(1) of the directive must be interpreted as meaning that if, after the expiry of the period allowed for implementation of the directive, married men have automatically received increases in social security benefits in respect of a spouse and children deemed to be dependents without having to prove actual dependency, married women without actual dependents are entitled to those increases even if in some circumstances that will result in double payment of the increases.

The fact that the national legal principle prohibiting unjust enrichment would have enabled the State to profit from its own wrong played a clear part in the Court's reasoning, rather than merely the fact that it would have undermined the effectiveness of the Directive.[32]

---

[29] See however Case C–188/95, *Fantask A/S* v. *Industriministeriet* [1997] ECR I–6783, which was a 'recovery of charges', where the ECJ ruled that a general principle of national law under which a claim for the recovery of charges levied in breach of EC law should be dismissed where they were levied for a long time and neither the national authorities nor the applicants were aware of their unlawfulness would make it excessively difficult to obtain a remedy for the breach.

[30] For further discussion of remedies in the specific context of sex discrimination, see Ch. 20.

[31] Case C–377/89, *Cotter and McDermott* v. *Minister for Social Welfare and Attorney General* [1991] ECR I–1155.

[32] Contrast Case 68/79, *Hans Just I/S* v. *Danish Ministry for Fiscal Affairs* [1980] ECR 501, in which the State was not obliged to repay taxes it had imposed in breach of Community law, if that would unjustly enrich a trader who had passed on the cost of the tax to third parties. See also Cases C–192–218/95, *Comateb* v. *Directeur Général des Douanes et Droits Indirects* [1997] ECR I–165 and C–453/99, *Courage Ltd* v. *Crehan* [2001] ECR I–6297, para 30. The difference in the way the unjust enrichment argument was treated in these cases on the one hand and in *Cotter* on the other is not easy to understand.

In *Emmott*, the applicant sought retrospective payment of a disability benefit for the period of time during which Council Directive 79/7 had remained unimplemented in Ireland, during which time she had been discriminated against on grounds of sex. She had been told by the relevant government department that no decision could be made in her case pending the ECJ's ruling in *Cotter and McDermott*, but when she finally applied for judicial review of the decisions relating to her social security benefit the department pleaded that her delay in initiating proceedings constituted a bar to the action.

Case C–208/90, Emmott v. Minister for Social Welfare
[1991] ECR I–4269

The Court began by setting out the principle of national procedural autonomy, as qualified by the conditions of equivalence and practical possibility.

THE ECJ

17. Whilst the laying down of reasonable time-limits which, if unobserved, bar proceedings, in principle satisfies the two conditions mentioned above, account must nevertheless be taken of the particular nature of directives.

. . .

21. So long as a directive has not been properly transposed into national law, individuals are unable to ascertain the full extent of their rights. That state of uncertainty for individuals subsists even after the Court has delivered a judgment finding that the Member State in question has not fulfilled its obligations under the directive and even if the Court has held that a particular provision or provisions of the directive are sufficiently precise and unconditional to be relied upon before a national court.

. . .

23. It follows that, until such time as a directive has been properly transposed, a defaulting Member State may not rely on an individual's delay in initiating proceedings against it in order to protect rights conferred upon him by the provisions of the directive and that a period laid down by national law within which proceedings must be initiated cannot begin to run before that time.

The Court's reasoning suggests that although the national time limit for bringing proceedings was not discriminatory, and did not *per se* render the exercise of the right impossible, it could nevertheless not be applied against an applicant seeking to rely on the provisions of a directive until that directive had been properly implemented.[33] As in *Cotter*, the Court relied to a considerable extent on the concept of 'estoppel', i.e., of

---

[33] Further, in a number of discrimination cases, the ECJ has specified that following the disapplication of an offending national law and pending the adoption of non-discriminatory rules, the appropriate interim remedy would be to level upwards to the existing EC rule. See, e.g., Cases 286/85 *McDermott and Cotter* v. *Minister for Social Welfare and Attorney-General* [1987] ECR 1453, Case C–33/89, *Kowalska* v. *Freie und Hansestadt Hamburg* [1990] ECR I–2591, para. 20, and Case C–18/95, *Terhoeve* v. *Inspecteur van de Belastingdienst Particulieren* [1999] ECR I–345, para. 57.

preventing the State from relying upon its own default. The contested national rule did not have to yield to the principle of effectiveness, but instead to the prior obligation of the State to implement directives before time could start running to bar the rights arising under them. This broad ruling, however, has since been confined closely to the facts of the case, with particular emphasis on the misleading conduct of the national authorities.

In the initial period after *Factortame I*, *Cotter*, and *Emmott*, it seemed that the requirement that remedies for breach of Community law should be effective had become stronger and had modified considerably the basic notion of national procedural autonomy. The requirement of 'practical possibility' had mutated into a requirement of effectiveness, as the Court's formulation changed from requiring that the national rule would not render the exercise of the Community right 'impossible in practice' to requiring that it would not render the right 'excessively difficult' to exercise.[34] The deference to national substantive rules and procedures implicit in earlier rulings was replaced by an expectation that national courts would be creative in deciding which national rules should be disapplied in order to enforce EC law more effectively.

One consequence of this creativity was a greater degree of uncertainty for both national courts and litigants. In the following case, the complainant was faced with a domestic statutory ceiling on awards of compensation for discrimination in breach of EC law. The question was whether the national court should ignore or override the statutory limit even though it did not render the exercise of her right 'practically impossible'.

Case C–271/91, Marshall v. Southampton and South West Area Health Authority II
[1993] ECR I–4367

Following the ECJ ruling in Case 152/84 *Marshall (No. 1)*,[35] the case was remitted to the Industrial Tribunal, which assessed compensation at £18,405 including a sum of £7,710 by way of interest. Under UK legislation, however, the maximum amount of compensation which could be awarded was £6,250, and it was unclear whether the Industrial Tribunal had power to award interest here. The House of Lords asked the ECJ whether such an applicant was entitled to full reparation for the loss sustained, and whether Article 6 of Directive 76/207 could be relied on to challenge national legislation which which limited the amount of compensation which could be awarded.

THE ECJ

22. Article 6 of the Directive puts Member States under a duty to take the necessary measures to enable all persons who consider themselves wronged by discrimination to pursue their claims by

---

[34] See Cases C–312/93, *Peterbroeck, Van Campenhout & Cie* v. *Belgian State* [1995] ECR I–4599, para. 12, and C–430–431/93, *Van Schijndel & Van Veen* v. *Stichting Pensioenfonds voor Fysiotherapeuten* [1995] ECR I–4705, para. 17.

[35] See Ch. 5.

judicial process. Such obligation implies that the measures in question should be sufficiently effective to achieve the objective of the directive and should be capable of being effectively relied upon by the persons concerned before national courts.

23. As the Court held in Case 14/83, *Von Colson and Kamann* v. *Land Nordrhein-Westfalen* [1984] ECR 1891, paragraph 18, Article 6 does not prescribe a specific measure to be taken in the event of a breach of the prohibition of discrimination but leaves Member States free to choose between the different solutions suitable for achieving the objective of the Directive, depending on the different situations which may arise.

24. However, the objective is to arrive at real equality of opportunity and cannot therefore be attained in the absence of measures appropriate to restore such equality when it has not been observed. As the Court stated in paragraph 23 in *Von Colson*, cited above, those measures must be such as to guarantee real and effective judicial protection and have a real deterrent effect on the employer.

25. Such requirements necessarily entail that the particular circumstances of each breach of the principle of equal treatment should be taken into account. In the event of discriminatory dismissal contrary to Article 5(1) of the Directive, a situation of equality could not be restored without either reinstating the victim of discrimination or, in the alternative, granting financial compensation for the loss and damage sustained.

26. When financial compensation is the measure adopted in order to achieve the objective indicated above, it must be adequate, in that it must enable the loss and damage actually sustained as a result of the discriminatory dismissal to be made good in full in accordance with the applicable national rules.

. . .

30. It also follows from that interpretation that the fixing of an upper limit of the kind at issue in the main proceedings cannot, by definition, constitute proper implementation of Article 6 of the directive, since it limits the amount of compensation *a priori* to a level which is not necessarily consistent with the requirement of ensuring real equality of opportunity through adequate reparation for the loss and damage sustained as a result of discriminatory dismissal.

31. With regard to the second part of the second question relating to the award of interest, suffice it to say that full compensation for the loss and damage sustained as a result of discriminatory dismissal cannot leave out of account factors, such as the effluxion of time, which may in fact reduce its value. The award of interest, in accordance with the applicable national rules, must therefore be regarded as an essential component of compensation for the purposes of restoring real equality of treatment.

Thus in this case, two more national rules governing remedies, the one substantive (the ceiling on damages) and the other jurisdictional (the lack of power to award interest), had to be overridden or disapplied by the national court in order to provide an effective remedy for breach of Community law. *Marshall II* contrasts with earlier case law of the Court, in particular the decisions in *Humblet*[36] and *Roquette*.[37] In those cases the ECJ had ruled that it was for the Member States to decide whether or not to award interest on the reimbursement of sums wrongly levied under Community law,

---

[36] Case 6/60, n. 2 above.
[37] Case 26/74, *Société Roquette Frères* v. *Commission* [1976] ECR 677.

whereas in *Marshall II*, it was not open to the Member State to refuse interest. We shall see below, however, that later case law has narrowed the scope of the *Marshall II* ruling, and possibly even confined its application to the situation of discriminatory dismissal.

(II) JUDICIAL RETREAT

Subsequent developments began to suggest that *Dekker*, *Factortame I*, *Emmott*, and *Marshall II* represented a particularly interventionist phase in the Court's elaboration of the remedial obligations of national courts.

A first noticeable brake on the progressive strengthening of the 'effective national remedy' requirement came in the case of *Steenhorst-Neerings*, which concerned an action for retrospective payment of disability benefits which had been denied for several years to the applicant, at a time when the EC Social Security Directive had not been properly implemented into Dutch law. The Dutch law governing her claim however provided that such benefits should not be payable retroactively for more than one year.

Case C–338/91, Steenhorst-Neerings v. Bestuur van de Bedrijfsvereniging voor Detailhandel, Ambachten en Huisvrouwen
[1993] ECR I–5475

THE ECJ

15. The right to claim benefits for incapacity for work under the same conditions as men, conferred on married women by the direct effect of Article 4(1) of Directive 79/7, must be exercised under the conditions determined by national law, provided that, as the Court has consistently held, those conditions are no less favourable than those relating to similar domestic actions and that they are not framed so as to render virtually impossible the exercise of rights conferred by Community law (see, *inter alia,* Case C–208/90 *Emmott* [1991] ECR I–4269, paragraph 16).

16. The national rule restricting the retroactive effect of a claim for benefits for incapacity for work satisfies the two conditions set out above.

17. However, the Commission considers that according to the judgment in *Emmott* (paragraphs 21, 22 and 23) the time-limits for proceedings brought by individuals seeking to avail themselves of their rights are applicable only when a Member State has properly transposed the Directive and that that principle applies in this case.

18. That argument cannot be upheld.

. . .

21. It should be noted first that, unlike the rule of domestic law fixing time-limits for bringing actions, the rule described in the question referred for a preliminary ruling in this case does not affect the right of individuals to rely on Directive 79/7 in proceedings before the national courts against a defaulting Member State. It merely limits the retroactive effect of claims made for the purpose of obtaining the relevant benefits.

22. The time-bar resulting from the expiry of the time-limit for bringing proceedings serves to ensure that the legality of administrative decisions cannot be challenged indefinitely. The judgment

in *Emmott* indicates that that requirement cannot prevail over the need to protect the rights conferred on individuals by the direct effect of provisions in a directive so long as the defaulting Member State responsible for those decisions has not properly transposed the provisions into national law.

23. On the other hand, the aim of the rule restricting the retroactive effect of claims for benefits for incapacity for work is quite different from that of a rule imposing mandatory time-limits for bringing proceedings. As the Government of the Netherlands and the defendant in the main proceedings explained in their written observations, the first type of rule, of which examples can be found in other social security laws in the Netherlands, serves to ensure sound administration, most importantly so that it may be ascertained whether the claimant satisfied the conditions for eligibility and so that the degree of incapacity, which may well vary over time, may be fixed. It also reflects the need to preserve financial balance in a scheme in which claims submitted by insured persons in the course of a year must in principle be covered by the contributions collected during that same year.

The domestic rule restricting the retroactivity of a claim for benefit clearly weakened the effectiveness of the Directive. The applicant had been unlawfully prevented from claiming benefits to which she had been entitled at the time, on account of the State's failure to implement the Directive properly, and she was now prevented from claiming that benefit retroactively. The legal circumstances in *Steenhorst-Neerings* were similar to those in *Emmott*, given the existence of a plaintiff who had in the past been prevented from claiming a right under Community law, and who now confronted a restriction which substantially reduced the effectiveness and extent of the available remedy. While not barring her claim entirely, as was the case in *Emmott*, the rule substantially restricted her remedy to one year's benefit only. The broader principle articulated in *Emmott*, that a Member State could not rely on domestic procedural restrictions to inhibit an applicant's claim to rights under a directive until that directive had been properly implemented, was abandoned.

Since *Steenhorst-Neerings*, the *Emmott* ruling has been further confined. In *Johnson II*, the ECJ ruled that 'the solution adopted in *Emmott* was justified by the particular circumstances of that case, in which a time-bar had the result of depriving the applicant of any opportunity whatever to rely on her right to equal treatment under the directive'.[38] Advocate General Jacobs in his opinions in *BP Supergas*[39] and *Denkavit International*[40] went further in suggesting that the fact that the State itself was at fault and led the applicant to make the error in question was highly significant.[41] Such reasoning may be implicit in the Court's restriction of the scope of *Emmott* in

---

[38] Case C–410/92, *Johnson* v. *Chief Adjudication Officer* [1994] ECR I–5483, para. 26. See also Cases C–114–5/95, *Texaco A/S* v. *Havn*, 17 July 1997, para. 48, and Case C–90/94, *Haahr Petroleum* v. *Havn* [1997] ECR I–4085, paras. 51–52.

[39] Case C–62/93, *BP Supergas* v. *Greece* [1995] ECR I–1883, paras. 55–9 of his Opinion.

[40] Case C–2/94, *Denkavit International BV* v. *Kamer van Koophandel en Fabrieken voor Midden-Gelderland* [1996] ECR I–2827, at para. 74 of his Opinion.

[41] See also, in his extra-judicial capacity, F. Jacobs, 'Enforcing Community Rights and Obligations in National Courts: Striking the Balance' in J. Lonbay and A. Biondi (eds.), *Remedies for Breach of EC Law* (Wiley, 1997) 25, 29, and see M. Hoskins, 'Tilting the Balance: Remedies and National Procedural Rules' (1996) 21 *ELRev.* 365.

Johnston II, *Texaco A/S*,[42] and *Fantask A/S*,[43] in the actual effect of its ruling in *BP Supergas*,[44] and more explicitly in part of its ruling in *Spac*.[45] The later *Levez* ruling also lends support to this reasoning, since the Court in that case acknowledged that an otherwise reasonable legislative limit on the retroactivity of a claim for damages could be rendered inapplicable by the improper conduct of the defendant (in this case a private employer rather than the State).[46]

Steenhorst-Neerings also seemed to represent a retreat, however, not only from *Emmott*, but also from the strong principle of adequacy of compensation for sex discrimination established in *Marshall II*. If a ceiling on compensation or a lack of power to award interest was contrary to the principle of effectiveness in *Marshall II*, why was the restriction of the retroactive effect of a claim for a benefit in *Steenhorst-Neerings* not equally contrary thereto? Yet *Steenhorst-Neerings* was reinforced in this respect by *Johnson II*, in which the Court ruled that, even where the concerns of the State to ensure administrative convenience and financial balance were not in issue, a provision restricting to one year the retroactive effect of a claim for a non-contributory incapacity benefit was compatible with Community law.[47]

In the later *Sutton* case concerning social security benefits, the ECJ had to deal more directly with the scope of its ruling in *Marshall II*, and appeared to confine it even further.

Case C–66/95 R. v. Secretary of State for Social Security, ex parte Eunice Sutton [1997] ECR I–2163

The applicant successfully challenged the refusal to grant her an invalid care allowance under national law, arguing that this refusal contravened Directive 79/7 on equal treatment in social security. She was awarded arrears of benefit, but was refused interest on the basis that national law did not provide for the payment of interest on social security benefits. On a reference to the ECJ, she argued that Article 6 of Directive 79/7 was almost identically worded to Article 6 of Directive 76/207 in *Marshall II*, both being concerned with equal treatment, and that interest should therefore be awarded just as in the earlier case.

THE ECJ

23. That interpretation cannot be adopted. The judgment in *Marshall II* concerns the award of interest on amounts payable by way of reparation for loss and damage sustained as a result

[42] Cases C–114–115/95, *Texaco A/S* v. *Havn* [1997] ECR I–4263.

[43] Case C–188/95, *Fantask A/S* v. *Industriministeriet* [1997] ECR I–6783. See also Case C–88/99 *Roquette Frères* v. *Direction des Services Fiscaux du Pas-de-Calais* [2000] ECR I–10465.

[44] See J. Coppel, 'Time up for Emmott?' (1996) 25 *ILJ* 153.

[45] Case C–260/96, *Ministero delle Finanze* v. *Spac* [1998] ECR I–4997, para 31.

[46] Case C–326/96, *Levez* v. *Jennings Ltd.* [1998] ECR I–7835, para. 34.

[47] Case C–410/92, *Johnson* v. *Chief Adjudication Officer* [1994] ECR I–5483. For further discussion, see Ch. 20. See also Case C–394/93, *Alonso-Pérez* v. *Bundesanstalt für Arbeit* [1995] ECR I–4101. Contrast Case C–246/96, *Magorrian and Cunningham* v. *Eastern Health and Social Services Board* [1997] ECR I–7153 discussed in Ch. 20 below, and Case C–78/98, *Preston* v. *Wolverhampton Healthcare NHS Trust* [1999] ECR I–3201.

of discriminatory dismissal. As the Court observed in paragraph 31 of that judgment, in such a context full compensation for the loss and damage sustained cannot leave out of account factors, such as the effluxion of time, which may in fact reduce its value. The award of interest, in accordance with the applicable national rules, must therefore be regarded as an essential component of compensation for the purposes of restoring real equality of treatment.

24. By contrast, the main proceedings concern the right to receive interest on amounts payable by way of social security benefits. Those benefits are paid to the person concerned by the competent bodies, which must, in particular, examine whether the conditions laid down in the relevant legislation are fulfilled. Consequently, the amounts paid in no way constitute reparation for loss or damage sustained and the reasoning of the Court in its judgment in *Marshall II* cannot be applied to a situation of that kind.

...

27. ... Amounts paid by way of social security benefit are not compensatory in nature, with the result that payment of interest cannot be required on the basis either of Article 6 of Directive 76/207 or of Article 6 of Directive 79/7.

Just as the originally broad principle in *Emmott* was subsequently confined to the circumstances of that case, the strong requirement that national law must provide adequate compensation in *Marshall II* seemed later to be confined to discriminatory dismissal under Directive 76/207. *Sutton* suggests that the requirements imposed by EC law on the availability of national remedies may not be universally applicable, but may depend on the nature of the right at stake and on the kind of Community measure which has been breached.[48] Thus payment of arrears of social security benefits was distinguished from compensation for loss or damage, so that there is no requirement of full or adequate compensation under national law. Further, even if, according to *Marshall II*, there is a requirement of adequate compensation for damage caused by a breach of the Equal Treatment Directive, this does not mean that a ceiling on damages will always be impermissible. Thus in *Draehmpaehl*, the ECJ ruled that a maximum compensatory award of three months' salary could be adequate in the case of a candidate who had been deemed ineligible for a job on grounds of sex, where that candidate would not have obtained the job because the person appointed had superior qualifications, and where the loss sustained was therefore more limited.[49]

(iii) regrouping after the retreat?

More recently in *Metallgesellschaft & Hoechst*, in which the plaintiffs challenged the discriminatory imposition of advance corporation tax (ACT) on subsidiaries whose parent companies were not resident within the Member State, the ECJ ruled that it was for the national court to classify the nature of an action brought, whether as an

---

[48] The cases concerning repayment of sums wrongly paid are also instructive in this respect, since we see that not all repayment cases are subject to the same analysis. Contrast some of the cases concerning unduly paid agricultural subsidies with those concerning improperly paid state aid: compare, e.g., Case C–24/95 *Land Rheinland-Pfalz* v. *Alcan Deutschland* [1997] ECR I–1591 on state aid with Case C–298/96, *Oelmühle Hamburg* v. *Bundesanstalt für Landwirtschaft und Ernährung* [1998] ECR I–4767 and Case C–366/95, *Landbrugsministeriet—EF-Direktoratet* v. *Steff-Houlberg Export* [1998] ECR I–2661 on agricultural subsidies.

[49] Case C–180/95, *Draehmpaehl* v. *Urania Immobilienservice* [1997] ECR I–2195. See, now, however, the proposed amendment to Dir. 76/207, which would limit the cases in which a prior ceiling on damages can be fixed: COM (2000) 334 and COM (2001) 321.

action for restitution or an action for compensation for damage.[50] In this case, the substance of the plaintiffs' claim was precisely the interest which would have accrued had they not been subject to discriminatory advance taxation.

Case C–410/98, Metallgesellschaft & Hoechst v. Inland Revenue
[2001] ECR I–1727

86. It is likewise for national law to settle all ancillary questions relating to the reimbursement of charges improperly levied, such as the payment of interest, including the rate of interest and the date from which it must be calculated. . . .

87. In the main proceedings, however, the claim for payment of interest covering the cost of loss of the use of the sums paid by way of ACT is not ancillary, but is the very objective sought by the plaintiffs' actions in the main proceedings. In such circumstances, where the breach of Community law arises, not from the payment of the tax itself but from its being levied prematurely, the award of interest represents the 'reimbursement' of that which was improperly paid and would appear to be essential in restoring the equal treatment guaranteed by Article 52 of the Treaty.

88. The national court has said that it is in dispute whether English law provides for restitution in respect of damage arising from loss of the use of sums of money where no principal sum is due. It must be stressed that in an action for restitution the principal sum due is none other than the amount of interest which would have been generated by the sum, use of which was lost as a result of the premature levy of the tax.

89. Consequently, Article 52 of the Treaty entitles a subsidiary resident in the United Kingdom and/or its parent company having its seat in another Member State to obtain interest accrued on the ACT paid by the subsidiary during the period between the payment of ACT and the date on which MCT became payable, and that sum may be claimed by way of restitution.

This passage, and paragraph 88 in particular, suggests a further *Factortame*-type erosion of the 'no new remedies' rule since, although restitution is not a remedy unknown to the English legal system, the national court's argument that restitution might not be available in these circumstances under English law was brushed aside by the Court's characterization of the claim as damage flowing directly from the breach of Article 43 (ex Article 52). And on the question whether full compensation equal to the sum claimed by the plaintiffs had to be paid, the ECJ continued:

92. In this regard, the United Kingdom Government's argument that the plaintiffs could not be awarded interest if they sought compensation in a claim for damages cannot be accepted.

93. Admittedly, the Court ruled in *Sutton* that the Community directive at issue in that case conferred only the right to obtain the benefits to which the person concerned would have been entitled in the absence of discrimination and that the payment of interest on arrears of benefits could not be regarded as an essential component of the right as so defined. However, in the present cases, it is precisely the interest itself which represents what would have been available to the plaintiffs, had it not been for the inequality of treatment, and which constitutes the essential component of the right conferred on them.

---

[50] Case C–410/98, [2001] ECR I–4727.

94. Moreover, in paragraphs 23 to 25 of *Sutton*, the Court distinguished the circumstances of that case from those of Case C–271/91 *Marshall* [1993] ECR I-4367 (*'Marshall II'*). In the latter case, which concerned the award of interest on amounts payable by way of reparation for loss and damage sustained as a result of discriminatory dismissal, the Court ruled that full compensation for the loss and damage sustained cannot leave out of account factors, such as the effluxion of time, which may in fact reduce its value, and that the award of interest is an essential component of compensation for the purposes of restoring real equality of treatment (*Marshall II*, cited above, paragraphs 24 to 32). The award of interest was held in that case to be an essential component of the compensation which Community law required to be paid in the event of discriminatory dismissal.

95. In circumstances such as those in the cases in the main proceedings, the award of interest would therefore seem to be essential if the damage caused by the breach of Article 52 of the Treaty is to be repaired.

Metallgesellschaft is a robust ruling in the tradition of *Johnston I* and *Marshall II*, and is joined in that respect by the more recent judgment in *Courage*, in which the ECJ ruled that a right of action in damages against another party for breach of Article 81 (ex Article 85) EC must be available in principle to an individual before national courts.[51] In these cases, the Court focused primarily not on the procedural autonomy of the national legal system, but instead on the nature and importance of the substantive Community right in issue (for example, non-discrimination under Article 43 (ex Article 52) EC in *Factortame* and *Metallgesellschaft*, equal treatment in employment in *Marshall II*, competition law rules in *Courage* and *Eco Swiss China Time*[52]). The emphasis on the substantive Community right at issue seems to increase the likelihood that the ECJ's ruling will point to the need to override or disapply a restrictive national rule, whereas in cases which begin by emphasizing the presumptive legitimacy of national remedial systems (such as *Steenhorst-Neerings*, *Sutton*, and *Johnston II*), we see that such an outcome is less likely.

(IV) FINDING A BALANCE

Putting these trends in a broader context, what we have seen after the initial retreat in *Steenhorst-Neerings*, *Johnson II*, and *Sutton* from the rather strongly interventionist approach suggested by *Factortame*, *Marshall II*, and *Emmott* is the emergence of a more balanced approach in the case law. The principles of effectiveness and equivalence must be applied by national courts in order to ascertain whether a national rule or principle may undermine the exercise of a Community right. This approach is well outlined in the cases of *Peterbroeck*[53] and *Van Schijndel*[54] which concerned the capacity of national courts to consider points of Community law of their own motion.

---

[51] Case C–453/99, *Courage Ltd* v. *Crehan* [2001] ECR I–6297, paras. 25–28.
[52] See Case C–126/97, *Eco Swiss China Time Ltd* v. *Benetton International NV* [1999] ECR I–3055, n. 61 below, and text.
[53] Case C–312/93, *Peterbroeck, Van Campenhout & Cie* v. *Belgian State* [1995] ECR I–4599.
[54] Cases C–430–431/93, *Van Schijndel & Van Veen* v. *Stichting Pensioenfonds voor Fysiotherapeuten* [1995] ECR I–4705.

Cases C–430–431/93 Van Schijndel & Van Veen v. Stichting
Pensioenfonds voor Fysiotherapeuten
[1995] ECR I–4705

The applicants argued that the appeal court whose ruling they sought to challenge ought to have considered, if necessary of its own motion, the compatibility of a compulsory Pension Fund provision with EC competition law. They had not themselves previously raised any point of EC law. Under Dutch law, such a plea involving a new argument could only be made where no examination of facts was required, and the court could not raise such points of law of its own motion. On a reference, the ECJ was asked whether the national court must apply provisions of EC law even where the party to the proceedings had not relied on them. The ECJ began by setting out the basic notion of national procedural autonomy, qualified by the principles of equivalence and practical effectiveness.

THE ECJ

19. For the purposes of applying those principles, each case which raises the question whether a national procedural provision renders application of Community law impossible or excessively difficult must be analysed by reference to the role of that provision in the procedure, its progress and its special features, viewed as a whole, before the various national instances. In the light of that analysis the basic principles of the domestic judicial system, such as the protection of the rights of the defence, the principle of legal certainty and the proper conduct of procedure must, where appropriate, be taken into consideration.

20. In the present case, the domestic law principle that in civil proceedings a court must or may raise points of its own motion is limited by its obligation to keep to the subject matter of the dispute and to base its decision on the facts put before it.

21. That limitation is justified by the principle that, in a civil suit, it is for the parties to take the initiative, the court being able to act of its own motion only in exceptional cases where the public interest requires its intervention. That principle reflects conceptions prevailing in most of the Member States as to the relations between the State and the individual; it safeguards the rights of the defence; and it ensures proper conduct of proceedings by, in particular, protecting them from the delays inherent in examination of new pleas.

22. In those circumstances, the answer to the second question must be that Community law does not require national courts to raise of their own motion an issue concerning the breach of provisions of Community law where examination of that issue would oblige them to abandon the passive role assigned to them by going beyond the ambit of the dispute defined by the parties themselves and relying on facts and circumstances other than those on which the party with an interest in application of those provisions bases his claim.

Thus each national provision (in this case the principle of judicial passivity) which governs the enforcement of a Community right before national courts must be examined not in the abstract, but in the specific circumstances of each case, in order to see whether it renders the exercise of that right excessively difficult. The purpose of the national rule must be examined and weighed against the degree of restriction on the enforcement of the Community right. In *Van Schijndel*, the ECJ considered the national principle to be compatible with the exercise of the Community right. By contrast, in the Belgian case of *Peterbroeck*, where similar aims of legal certainty and the proper conduct of procedure underpinned a procedural provision of the national Tax Code preventing both the parties and the court from raising a point of EC law after a sixty-day time period, the application of the rule was found in the particular circumstances of the case to render the exercise of the Community right excessively difficult.[55] While the sixty-day period for raising new pleas was itself reasonable, the particular circumstances of the case were deemed by the ECJ to render the rule objectionable.[56]

The reasoning in the case is somewhat strained,[57] but, together with a number of later cases concerning the role of national courts in raising points of EC law of their own motion, it illustrates well that the determination of the compatibility of a national procedural rule with the Community requirement of effectiveness depends on the precise circumstances of each case. In *Kraaijeveld*, the ECJ appeared to indicate that EC law does not confer a *general* power on national courts to consider points of EC law of their own motion, but that if they have a discretion or obligation to raise points of national law of their own motion they must also apply such discretion or obligation in relation to Community law.[58] In *Fazenda Pública*, the Court linked the power and 'in certain cases' the obligation on national courts to make a reference to the ECJ with their power or obligation to raise points of EC law of their own motion.[59] In *Océano*, the ECJ went further still in declaring that the aims of the Unfair Contract Terms Directive would not be ensured if the consumer were obliged to raise the unfair nature of such terms, and that the national court must acknowledge that it had 'power to evaluate terms of this kind of its own motion'.[60] While not actually specifying that national courts *must raise* a specific point of EC law of their own motion, the ECJ ruled that they *must have the power to raise* such a point of their own motion. This rather stronger formulation—that a national court must have power to raise rather than simply that it *may* raise a point of its own motion—was clearly linked to the facts of the case, and particularly to the nature of the EC law in question which was intended for the protection of consumers. The strongest ruling on this 'own motion' issue seems to be that in *Eco Swiss China Time*, where the ECJ indicated that, in the circumstances of that case concerning review of an arbitration award, the national court *must* actually raise a point based on breach of Article 81 (ex Article 85) EC.[61] Once again, the nature of the substantive EC right in question—in this case the

---

[55] N. 53 above.

[56] This was apparently because no court or tribunal in the proceedings had had an opportunity to raise the point of EC law so as to make a reference to the ECJ.

[57] G. de Búrca, 'National Remedies for Breach of EC Law: The Changing Approach of the ECJ', in Lonbay and Biondi (eds.), n. 41 above.

[58] Case C–72/95, *Aannemersbedrijf P.K. Kraaijeveld BV* v. *Gedeputeerde Staten van Zuid-Holland* [1996] ECR I–5403.

[59] Case C–446/98, *Fazenda Pública* v. *Camara Municipal do Porto* [2000] ECR I–11435, para. 48.

[60] Cases C–240–244/98, *Océano Grupo Editorial* v. *Rocio Murciano Quintero* [2000] ECR I–4491, para. 26.

[61] Case C–126/97, *Eco Swiss China Time Ltd* v. *Benetton International NV* [1999] ECR I–3055, paras. 36–37. This judgment might be understood, however, as being simply based on the principle of equivalence, since national courts were required to permit an application for annulment of an arbitration award on grounds of failure to observe national public policy rules, and Art. 81 EC was deemed by the ECJ to have at least the same status as those national public policy rules. None the less, the ECJ usually leaves the question of equivalence to be determined by the national court, whereas here that decision was taken out of the national court's hands.

fundamental competition rules of the Treaty—was very relevant to the Court's conclusion.

The 'balancing' approach to the relationship between the requirements of equivalence and effectiveness and the *prima facie* principle of national procedural autonomy thus introduces a kind of proportionality test for weighing the impact of a national rule on a particular Community right against the legitimate aim served by that rule, and consequently also introduces a considerable degree of uncertainty from case to case.[62] Whether a national remedial rule will be lawful or not will depend not just on the intrinsic nature, aim, and effects of that rule, but also on its application to a particular factual set of circumstances, when weighed against the aim and importance of the Community right in question.

(V) CAN THE PLAINTIFF'S CONDUCT AFFECT THE RIGHT TO AN EFFECTIVE REMEDY?

The ECJ on several occasions has addressed the compatibility with EC law of national rules which limit the availability of a remedy by reference to the plaintiff's conduct. In *Dionysios Diamantis*, the ECJ ruled that a national court may refuse to permit a plaintiff to rely on EC rights if such reliance constitutes an abuse of those rights.[63] The ECJ in *Rechberger* rejected an argument raised by Austria as a defence to an action for damages brought against it for breach of EC law, where the argument was based on the misconduct not of the plaintiff but of a relevant third party.[64] In *Banks*, it ruled that the failure to take legal action under Article 35 of the ECSC Treaty could not deprive an applicant, under domestic law, of the right to plead the infringement of another directly effective provision of that Treaty.[65] Finally, in *Courage v. Crehan*, the Court ruled that an individual could not be prohibited from relying on Article 81 (ex Article 85) simply because he had been party to an anticompetitive agreement within the meaning of that provision, but that EC law did not prohibit a national rule preventing such a party from relying on his own unlawful actions to obtain damages where he bears significant responsibility for the distortion of competition.[66]

The impact of a plaintiff's alleged failure to mitigate losses on the avaibiilty and extent of national remedies has also been considered by the ECJ. In *Metallgesellschaft* the Court dismissed the argument made by the UK that the plaintiffs should have refused to comply with the national tax rule which infringed their EC rights and should have relied on the direct effect of EC rights, rather than paying the tax and challenging it afterwards.[67] However, reasonable national rules governing the responsibility of parties to show due diligence in mitigating their losses are quite

---

[62] See Hoskins, n. 41 above. And see, e.g., Case C–54/96, *Dorsch Consult Ingenieurgesellschaft mbH* v. *Bundesbaugesellschaft Berlin mbH* [1997] ECR I–4961.

[63] See Case C–373/97, *Dionysios Diamantis* v. *Elliniko Dimosio* [1999] ECR I–1705, paras. 42–44, in which the ECJ however ruled that some of the impugned conduct would not amount to an abuse of rights under the second company Dir.

[64] Case C–140/97, *Rechberger* v. *Austria* [1999] ECR I–3499. See further, n. 107 below.

[65] Case C–390/98, *H.J. Banks & Co. Ltd* v. *The Coal Authority* [2001] ECR I–6117, paras. 122–123.

[66] Case C–453/99, *Courage Ltd* v. *Crehan* [2001] ECR I–6297, paras. 24 and 36 in particular.

[67] Case C–397/98, *Metallgesellschaft Ltd* v. *Inland Revenue* [2001] ECR I–1727, paras. 99–107.

compatible with EC law so long as they are applied equally to claims based on EC law.[68]

(d) DEVELOPMENT OF THE PRINCIPLE OF EQUIVALENCE

While much of the ECJ's case law since *Von Colson* has thus focused on the concrete · implications of the effectiveness principle, attention has also been given more recently to the principle of equivalence.

This is well illustrated by the case law concerning national time limits. Reasonable time limits had on several occasions been held by the Court to be compatible with the effectiveness principle,[69] whereas the exact meaning of the equivalence principle remained unclear. The *Edis* case concerned the repayment of charges which had been paid but were not due under Community law, where national law imposed a time limit of three years for bringing proceedings for repayment for charges of this kind. This was less favourable than the ordinary time limits governing actions between individuals for repayment of sums paid but not due.

Case C–231/96 Edis v Ministero delle Finanze
[1998] ECR I–4951

36. Observance of the principle of equivalence implies, for its part, that the procedural rule at issue applies without distinction to actions alleging infringements of Community law and to those alleging infringements of national law, with respect to the same kind of charges or dues (see, to that effect, Joined Cases 66/79, 127/79 and 128/79 *Amministrazione delle Finanze dello Stato* v. *Salumi* [1980] ECR 1237, paragraph 21). That principle cannot, however, be interpreted as obliging a Member State to extend its most favourable rules governing recovery under national law to all actions for repayment of charges or dues levied in breach of Community law.

37. Thus, Community law does not preclude the legislation of a Member State from laying down, alongside a limitation period applicable under the ordinary law to actions between private individuals for the recovery of sums paid but not due, special detailed rules, which are less favourable, governing claims and legal proceedings to challenge the imposition of charges and other levies. The position would be different only if those detailed rules applied solely to actions based on Community law for the repayment of such charges or levies.

Similar rulings were given in the cases of *Spac*,[70] *Aprile*,[71] *Dilexport*,[72] and *Roquette*,[73] affirming the acceptability of national time limits which were not the most favourable

[68] This indeed is the case for claims against the Community institutions before the ECJ: see Case T–178/98, *Fresh Marine Company* v. *Commission* [2000] ECR II–3331, para. 121.

[69] On the reasonableness of a 3-month time limit to challenge an interim arbitration award see Case C–126/97, *Eco Swiss China Time Ltd* v. *Benetton International NV* [1999] ECR I–3055.

[70] Case C–260/96, *Ministero delle Finanze* v. *Spac* [1998] ECR I–4997.

[71] Case C–229/96, *Aprile* v. *Amminstrazione delle Finanze dello Stato* [1998] ECR I–7141.

[72] Case C–343/96, *Dilexport* v. *Amministrazione delle Finanze dello Stato* [1999] ECR I–579.

[73] Case C–88/99, *Roquette Frères* v. *Direction des Services Fiscaux du Pas-de-Calais* [2000] ECR I–10465.

within the national remedial system, but which applied equally to actions based on Community law and 'similar' actions based on national law. While the ECJ has frequently stated that it is in principle for the national court to determine the question of equivalence,[74] it has also intervened at times to indicate that the application of a particular national rule does not satisfy the principle of equivalence. In *Levez*, an employee was seeking damages for arrears in payment which had been denied to her in breach of the equal pay provision of the Treaty. The ECJ had ruled that the two-year limit on arrears of damages in Industrial Tribunal proceedings could not be applied to her on account of the role played by her employer's deception in the delay.[75] However, the UK argued that the time limit should none the less apply to her case, because an alternative full remedy before the county court in an action for deceit against her employer and in an action based on the Equal Pay Act had been open to her, meaning that the exercise of her right was not rendered ineffective in practice. The ECJ accepted the effectiveness point, but went on to consider the requirement of equivalence and gave very firm guidance to the national court on how to apply this.

Case C–326/96 Levez v Jennings Ltd
[1998] ECR I–7835

43. In order to determine whether the principle of equivalence has been complied with in the present case, the national court—which alone has direct knowledge of the procedural rules governing actions in the field of employment law—must consider both the purpose and the essential characteristics of allegedly similar domestic actions (see *Palmisani*, paragraphs 34 to 38).

44. Furthermore, whenever it falls to be determined whether a procedural rule of national law is less favourable than those governing similar domestic actions, the national court must take into account the role played by that provision in the procedure as a whole, as well as the operation and any special features of that procedure before the different national courts (see, *mutatis mutandis, Van Schijndel and Van Veen*, paragraph 19).

After rejecting the UK's argument that the equivalence requirement was satisfied by the fact that a claim under the Equal Pay Act (which was specifically intended to implement EC law) was comparable to a claim based directly on Article 141 (ex Article 119) EC, the Court went on to consider the other arguments of equivalence which had been made:

49. Secondly, it is necessary to consider the possibilities contemplated by the order for reference. It is there suggested that claims similar to those based on the Act may include those linked to breach of a contract of employment, to discrimination in terms of pay on grounds of race, to unlawful deductions from wages or to sex discrimination in matters other than pay.

---

[74] Case C–261/95, *Palmisani* v. *INPS* [1997] ECR I–4025, para. 33: Case C–326/96, *Levez* v. *Jennings Ltd*. [1998] ECR I–7835, para. 39.
[75] See n. 46 above.

50. If it transpires, on the basis of the principles set out in paragraphs 41 to 44 of this judgment, that a claim under the Act which is brought before the County Court is similar to one or more of the forms of action listed by the national court, it would remain for that court to determine whether the first-mentioned form of action is governed by procedural rules or other requirements which are less favourable.

51. On that point, it is appropriate to consider whether, in order fully to assert rights conferred by Community law before the County Court, an employee in circumstances such as those of Mrs Levez will incur additional costs and delay by comparison with a claimant who, because he is relying on what may be regarded as a similar right under domestic law, may bring an action before the Industrial Tribunal, which is simpler and, in principle, less costly.

52. Also of relevance here is the fact mentioned by the national court that the rule at issue applies solely to claims for equal pay without discrimination on grounds of sex, whereas claims based on 'similar' rights under domestic law are not limited by the operation of such a rule, which means that such rights may be adequately protected by actions brought before Industrial Tribunals.

53. In view of the foregoing, the answer must be that Community law precludes the application of a rule of national law which limits an employee's entitlement to arrears of remuneration or damages for breach of the principle of equal pay to a period of two years prior to the date on which the proceedings were instituted, even when another remedy is available, if the latter is likely to entail procedural rules or other conditions which are less favourable than those applicable to similar domestic actions. It is for the national court to determine whether that is the case.

The ECJ followed this ruling closely in the later case of *Preston*, in which it was also asked by the UK House of Lords for more precise guidance on the EC law criteria for identifying a 'similar' cause of action in domestic law.[76] We see that in both *Levez* and *Preston*, the Court outlined the same context-specific balancing approach for assessing the 'equivalence' of domestic rules as it did for assesssing their 'effectiveness' in *Peterbroeck* and *Van Schijndel*. After citing paragraphs 44 and 51 of *Levez* (above), the Court continued.

Case C–78/98 Preston v Wolverhampton Healthcare NHS Trust
[2000] ECR I–3201

62. It follows that the various aspects of the procedural rules cannot be examined in isolation but must be placed in their general context. Moreover, such an examination may not be carried out subjectively by reference to circumstances of fact but must involve an objective comparison, in the abstract, of the procedural rules at issue.

63. In view of the foregoing, the answer to the third part of the second question must be that, in order to decide whether procedural rules are equivalent, the national court must verify objectively, in the abstract, whether the rules at issue are similar taking into account the role played by those rules in the procedure as a whole, as well as the operation of that procedure and any special features of those rules.

---

[76] Case C–78/98, *Preston* v. *Wolverhampton Healthcare NHS Trust* [2000] ECR I–3201.

Similarly in *Dounias*, the ECJ ruled that it was for the national court to scrutinize the domestic procedures to determine not only whether they were comparable, but also to detect whether there was any inherent discrimination in their application in favour of domestic claims.[77]

Indeed, some have argued that an excessive emphasis on the need for effectiveness of EC rights rather than on the principle of equivalence could lead to a reverse form of discrimination in favour of EC law.[78] This notion of equality of domestic remedies for EC rights and for national law rights is also mirrored by another development in ECJ case law which points towards the need for parity between national-level and EC-level remedies for the enforcement of EC rights. In other words, EC law should not demand better enforcement of EC law from the national legal orders than it is prepared to provide itself at European level. Thus in *Upjohn*, the ECJ ruled that Community law did not require the Member States to establish a procedure for judicial review of national decisions revoking marketing authorizations for medicinal products, which involved a more extensive review than that carried out by the ECJ in similar cases.[79] And in *Bergaderm*, in an action for damages brought against the Community before the ECJ, the Court ruled that the conditions under which Member States may incur liability for damage to individuals caused by a breach of Community law could not. in principle, differ from those governing the liability of the Community in similar circumstances.[80]

(e) SUMMARY

i. While the early position of the Court emphasized the primacy of the national legal system in the absence of Community harmonization of remedies, this approach gave way to a stronger insistence on the effectiveness of Community law in the early 1990s, before the retreat in cases like *Steenhorst-Neerings*, *Johnston II*, and *Sutton*.

ii. Since then, a more intensive balancing approach has been articulated, which provides for the importance of the Community right to be weighed against the scope and purpose of the national rule in the particular circumstances of the case.

iii. Although its guidelines on the requirements of adequacy, effectiveness, and equivalence are relatively strong, the ECJ has also clearly acknowledged the legitimacy of restrictive domestic rules and the primary role of the national court in assessing these.

iv. Some recent examples demonstrate the latter point: in *Clean Car*, where the question of costs was not governed by EC law, it was fully permissible for

---

[77] Case C–228/98, *Dounias v. Ypourgio Oikonomikon* [2000] ECR I–577, para. 65. In this case the Court seemed to suggest that the equivalence principle should be considered first, and only then the effectiveness principle: see para. 60.

[78] See, e.g., Jacobs AG in Cases C–430–431/93, *Van Schijndel* [1995] ECR I–4705, and Léger AG in Case C–66/95, *Sutton* [1997] ECR I–2163.

[79] See Case C–120/97 n. 23 above, para. 33.

[80] Case C–352/98P, *Bergaderm v. Commission* [2000] ECR I–5291, para. 41, drawing on Cases C–46 & 48/93 *Brasserie du Pêcheur SA v. Germany* [1996] ECR I–1029, para. 42.

the national court to apply existing national rules on costs to the preliminary reference procedure.[81] In *Eco Swiss China Time* the compatibility in principle of a national *res judicata* rule which rendered an interim arbitration award final and unchallengeable after a three-month period was acceptable, even where fundamental rules of EC law were in question.[82] In *IN.CO.GE. '90*, concerning recovery of charges, the ECJ rejected the Commission's argument that the national rule imposing unlawful charges should be treated as invalid rather than merely inapplicable, so that the full sum paid would be recoverable, on the basis that such an argument would totally undermine the freedom of the national legal system to lay down its own rules governing the grant of the repayment remedy:[83]

4. THE PRINCIPLE OF (STATE) LIABILITY FOR BREACH OF EC LAW

(a) THE ORIGINS OF THE PRINCIPLE OF STATE LIABILITY

We have seen that while the ECJ declared that the Treaty in general does not require national courts to provide 'new' remedies for breach of EC law, several of its rulings had none the less in effect dictated to the national court that a particular kind of remedy must be made available. Thus cases such as *San Giorgio* and others on the repayment of charges,[84] *Factortame I* on interim relief,[85] *Heylens* on access to judicial review,[86] and *Courage* on damages,[87] have effectively required national courts to ensure the availability of particular remedies in certain circumstances, although leaving the more specific conditions governing the grant of such remedies for the national legal system to lay down.

However, the most dramatic and distinctive of the Court's interventionist rulings, and that which is most commonly seen as creating or demanding the availability of a particular remedy as a matter of EC law, is the *Francovich* judgment. This ruling established the principle of state liability in damages for breach of EC law.

Cases C–6 & 9/90, Francovich and Bonifaci v. Italy
[1991] ECR I–5357

[Note ToA renumbering: Art. 5 is now Art. 10]

The applicants brought proceedings against the Italian State arising out of the government's failure to implement Directive 80/987 on the protection of employees in the event of their

---

[81] Case C–472/99, *Clean Car Autoservice GmbH* v. *Stadt Wien* [2001] ECR I–nyr, paras. 27–31.
[82] See n. 61 above, paras. 43–47.
[83] Cases C–10–22/97, *Ministero delle Finanze* v. *IN.CO.GE.'90 Srl* [1998] ECR I–6307, para. 28.
[84] N. 7 above.   [85] See Case C–213/89, n. 140 below.
[86] N. 17 above.   [87] N. 51 above.

employer's insolvency. Both were owed wages from their employers, but since no steps had been taken pursuant to the Directive to guarantee payment of wages, they argued that the State was liable to pay them the sums owed. The ECJ ruled that although the provisions of the Directive lacked sufficient precision to be directly effective or to make the State directly liable as guarantor, they nevertheless clearly intended to confer rights of which these individuals had been deprived through the State's failure to implement it.

THE ECJ

29. The national court thus raises the issue of the existence and scope of a State's liability for harm resulting from the breach of its obligations under Community law. . . .

(a) The existence of State liability as a matter of principle
30. It must be recalled first of all that the EEC Treaty has created its own legal system which is an integral part of the legal systems of the Member States and which their courts are bound to apply; the subjects of that legal system are not only the Member States but also their nationals. Just as it imposes obligations on individuals, Community law is also intended to create rights which become part of their legal patrimony; those rights arise not only where they are expressly granted by the Treaty but also by virtue of obligations which the Treaty imposes in a clearly defined manner both on individuals and on the Member States and the Community institutions: see Case 26/62 *Van Gend en Loos* and Case 6/64 *Costa* v. *ENEL*.
. . .
32. Furthermore, it has been consistently held that the national courts whose task it is to apply the provisions of Community law in cases within their jurisdiction must ensure that those rules have full effect and protect the rights which they confer on individuals: see in particular Case 106/77 *Simmenthal* and Case C–213/89 *Factortame*.
33. It must be held that the full effectiveness of Community rules would be impaired and the protection of the rights which they grant would be weakened if individuals were unable to obtain compensation when their rights are infringed by a breach of Community law for which a Member State can be held responsible.
34. The possibility of compensation by the Member State is particularly indispensable where, as in this case, the full effectiveness of Community rules is subject to prior action on the part of the State and consequently individuals cannot, in the absence of such action, enforce the rights granted to them by Community law before the national courts.
35. It follows that the principle of State liability for harm caused to individuals by breaches of Community law for which the State can be held responsible is inherent in the system of the Treaty.
36. Further foundation for the obligation on the part of Member States to pay compensation for such harm is to be found in Article 5 EEC, under which the Member States are required to take all appropriate measures, whether general or particular, to ensure fulfilment of their obligations under Community law. Among these is the obligation to nullify the unlawful consequences of a breach of Community law. . . .
37. It follows from all the foregoing that it is a principle of Community law that the Member States are obliged to pay compensation for harm caused to individuals by breaches of Community law for which they can be held responsible.

Thus the judgment appeared to contrast directly with the early *Rewe-Handelsgesellschaft* statement that the Treaty did not intend to create new remedies by declaring that the principle of state liability is inherent in the EC Treaty.[88] While, as we have already noted, several of the Court's previous cases could be understood as requiring national courts to make remedies available in novel situations, the *Francovich* case asserted the principle of state liability, and thus the availability in principle of an action for compensation against the State, as a general requirement of Community law.[89]

Another significant feature of *Francovich* at the time was that it required the provision by national courts of a damages remedy for breach of Community measures which lacked direct effect.[90] The judgment thus represented an important additional move in the direction of enhancing the effectiveness of unimplemented directives which we have seen in the preceding chapter with the development of the notions of indirect and incidental effects,[91] presenting an alternative remedy for cases where national law could not otherwise be construed compatibly with a non-implemented directive.[92]

(b) CONDITIONS FOR LIABILITY UNDER *FRANCOVICH*

Despite the importance of the principle established therein, *Francovich* gave only minimal guidance for the future. Three basic conditions were established for breaches involving a State's non-implementation of a directive, but no guidance was given in relation to other breaches of EC law.[93] Instead, the Court fell back on the familiar principle of national procedural autonomy:

38. Although State liability is thus required by Community law, the conditions under which that liability gives rise to a right to compensation depend on the nature of the breach of Community law giving rise to the harm.

39. Where, as in this case, a Member State fails to fulfil its obligations under Article 189(3) EEC to take all measures necessary to achieve the result prescribed by a directive, the full effectiveness of that rule of Community law requires that there should be a right to compensation where three conditions are met.

40. The first of those conditions is that the result prescribed by the directive should entail the

---

[88] M. Dougan has argued that while the Court clearly intended to develop a Community system of liability of public authorities and a right to reparation, it did not necessarily intend to create a specific 'Community remedy in damages': see 'The Francovich Right to Reparation: Reshaping the Contours of Community Remedial Competence' (2000) 6 *EPL* 103.

[89] See M. Ross, 'Beyond Francovich' (1993) 56 *MLR* 55, and P. Craig, 'Francovich, Remedies and the Scope of Damages Liability' (1993) 109 *LQR* 595.

[90] D. Curtin, 'State Liability under Private Law: A New Remedy for Private Parties' (1992) 21 *ILJ* 74.

[91] See 211–27.

[92] See, e.g., Cases C–334/92, *Wagner Miret* v. *Fondo de Garantía Salarial* [1993] ECR I–6911; C–54/96, *Dorsch Consult Ingenieurgesellschaft mbH* v. *Bundesbaugesellschaft Berlin mbH* [1997] ECR I–4961; C–81/98, *Alcatel Austria* v. *Bundesministerium für Wissenschaft und Verkehr* [1999] ECR I–7671; C–111/97, *Evobus Austria* [1998] ECR I–5411; C–258/97. *Hospital Ingenieure Krankenhaustechnik Planungs-Gesellschaft mbH (HI)* v. *Landeskrankenanstalten-Betriebsgesellschaft* [1999] ECR I–1405; and C–131/97, *Carbonari* v. *Università degli Studi di Bologna* [1999] ECR I–1103.

[93] For speculation on this point see G. Bebr (1992) 29 *CMLRev.* 557. And for a more fundamental challenge to the basic concept of state liability see C. Harlow, '*Francovich* and the Problem of the Disobedient State' (1996) 2 *ELJ* 199.

grant of rights to individuals. The second condition is that it should be possible to identify the content of those rights on the basis of the provisions of the directive. Finally, the third condition is the existence of a causal link between the breach of the State's obligation and the harm suffered by the injured parties.

. . .

42. Subject to that reservation, it is in accordance with the rules of national law on liability that the State must make reparation for the consequences of the harm caused. In the absence of any Community legislation, it is a matter for the internal legal order of each Member State to determine the competent courts and lay down the detailed procedural rules for legal proceedings intended fully to safeguard the rights which individuals derive from Community law: see Case 60/75, *Russo* v. *Aima*, Case 33/76, *Rewe* v. *Landwirtschaftskammer Saarland* and Case 158/80, *Rewe* v. *Hauptzollamt Kiel*.

43. It must also be pointed out that the substantive and procedural conditions laid down by the national law of the various Member States on compensation for harm may not be less favourable than those relating to similar internal claims and may not be so framed as to make it virtually impossible or excessively difficult to obtain compensation.

(c) *BRASSERIE DU PÊCHEUR/FACTORTAME III*: CLARIFYING THE BASIS OF THE PRINCIPLE OF STATE LIABILITY

The opportunity for many questions to be clarified came, however, in the joined cases of *Brasserie du Pêcheur* and *Factortame III*, in which a series of questions was referred from the German Bundesgerichtshof and the English High Court respectively. Over two years after the references were received, the ECJ finally delivered its ruling. It is a long and detailed judgment, less opaque than many of the Court's typical rulings, and deserves close reading.[94]

Cases C–46/93 & C–48/93 Brasserie du Pêcheur SA v. Germany, and R. v. Secretary of State for Transport, ex parte Factortame Ltd. and others
[1996] ECR I–1029

[ToA renumbering: Arts. 5, 30, 52, 164, 189, & 215 are now Arts. 10, 28, 43, 220, 249, & 288 respectively]

The *Factortame* reference arose out of the same factual background as *Factortame I*, above, in which Spanish fishermen had invoked Article 52 EC to challenge the UK's conditions for registration as a British vessel, and succeeded on the substantive point in a second ECJ ruling.[95] Here they sought damages for losses caused by the UK's breach of the Treaty. At the same time, in a case arising from litigation over Germany's beer purity laws, in which Germany had been found to be in

---

[94] For some of the many commentaries on the case see N. Emiliou (1996) 21 *ELRev*. 399; C. Harlow, 'The Problem of the Disobedient State' (1996) 2 *ELJ* 199; J. Convery, 'State Liability in the UK after *Brasserie du Pêcheur*' (1997) 34 *CMLRev*. 603; P. Craig, 'Once More unto the Breach: The Community, the State and Damages Liability' (1997) 105 *LQR* 67; P. Oliver (1997) 34 *CMLRev*. 635.

[95] Case C–221/89, *R.* v. *Secretary of State for Transport, ex p. Factortame* [1991] ECR I–3905, known as *Factortame II*.

breach of Article 30 EC, a French brewery which suffered losses when it was forced to cease exports to Germany sought compensation from the German State. A wide variety of questions was referred to the ECJ from both courts. The first argument made was that compensation should not be available for breach of directly effective EC law, since national remedies would already be available for such.

THE ECJ

19. That argument cannot be accepted.

20. The Court has consistently held that the right of individuals to rely on the directly effective provisions of the Treaty before national courts is only a minimum guarantee and is not sufficient in itself to ensure the full and complete implementation of the Treaty. . . . The purpose of that right is to ensure that provisions of Community law prevail over national provisions. It cannot, in every case, secure for individuals the benefit of rights conferred on them by Community law and, in particular, avoid their sustaining damage as a result of a breach of Community law attributable to a Member State. As appears from paragraph 33 of the judgment in *Francovich*, the full effectiveness of Community law would be impaired if individuals were unable to obtain redress when their rights were infringed by a breach of Community law.

. . .

22. It is all the more so in the event of an infringement of a right directly conferred by a Community provision upon which individuals are entitled to rely before the national courts. In that event, the right to reparation is the necessary corollary of the direct effect of the Community provision whose breach caused the damage sustained.

The Court ruled that breaches of both Articles 28 (ex Article 30) and 43 (ex Article 52) could give rise to reparation, and rejected the German government's argument that a general right to reparation under Community law could be created only by legislation. Instead, the Court asserted forcefully that this was a matter of Treaty interpretation within its jurisdiction:

27. Since the Treaty contains no provisions expressly and specifically governing the consequences of breaches of Community law by Member States, it is for the Court, in pursuance of the task conferred on it by Article 164 of the Treaty of ensuring that in the interpretation and application of the Treaty, the law is observed, to rule on such a question in accordance with generally accepted methods of interpretation, in particular by reference to the fundamental principles of the Community legal system and, where necessary, general principles common to the legal systems of the Member States.

28. Indeed it is to the general principles common to the laws of the Member States that the second paragraph of Article 215 of the Treaty refers as the basis of the non-contractual liability of the Community for damage caused by its institutions or by its servants in the performance of their duties.

29. The principle of non-contractual liability of the Community expressly laid down in Article 215 of the Treaty is simply an expression of the general principle familiar to the legal systems of the member states that an unlawful act or omission gives rise to an obligation to make good the damage caused. That provision also reflects the obligation on public authorities to make good damage caused in the performance of their duties.

Here, the ECJ did not base the principle of state liability only on the principle of effectiveness or on Article 10 (ex Article 5) EC, which had been the foundation for the *Francovich* ruling. Instead, the principle of state liability was located also in the context of the Treaty provisions on the *Community's* liability under Article 288 (ex Article 215), which in turn are expressly based on the general principles common to the Member States. This reasoning seems intended to legitimate the development of the principle of state liability, so that it is seen to derive from well-established principles of the national legal orders rather than from the imagination of the ECJ. The Court went on to rule, as in its case law under Article 226 (ex Article 169) EC,[96] that the State will be liable whichever organ of the State is responsible for the breach and regardless of the internal division of powers between constitutional authorities.[97] In subsequent rulings the Court has indicated that Member States are not required to change the distribution of powers and responsibilities between public bodies on their territory, and that in States with a federal structure, reparation for damage does not necessarily have to be provided by the federal State.[98] Equally, in States without a federal structure, reparation for damage caused to individuals could properly be made by a public law body legally distinct from the State, or an autonomous territorial body to which legislative or administrative tasks have been delegated.[99]

The possible extension of the action for compensation following *Brasserie du Pêcheur* to cover damage caused through a breach of EC law by *private* rather than state parties was the subject of some speculation,[100] due in particular to the reasoning in paragraph 22 of that case, before the ECJ was directly confronted with that question in the *Courage* case. Here the Court first reiterated the famous 'new legal order' reasoning in *Van Gend en Loos*, and secondly it emphasized the fundamental nature of the prohibition on anti-competitive agreements in Article 81 (ex Article 85) EC, breach of which would render any such agreement automatically void.

Case C–453/99 Courage Ltd. v. Crehan
[2001] ECR I–6297

23. Thirdly, it should be borne in mind that the Court has held that Article 85(1) of the Treaty and Article 86 of the EC Treaty (now Article 82 EC) produce direct effects in relations between individuals and create rights for the individuals concerned which the national courts must safeguard . . .

---

[96] See Ch. 10.
[97] Whether the State could be liable for a breach of Community law by the national judiciary remains an open question, which was addressed by Léger AG in Case C–5/94, *Lomas* [1996] ECR I–2553. See the recent reference made in Case C–224/01, *Kobler* [2001] OJ 212/18. See also S. Prechal, 'EC Requirements for an Effective Remedy' in n. 41 above; H. Toner, 'Thinking the Unthinkable? State Liability for Judicial Acts after *Factortame (III)* ' (1997) 17 *YBEL* 165; and G. Anagnostaras, 'The Principle of State Liability for Judicial Breaches: The Impact of European Community Law' (2001) 7 EPL 281.
[98] See Case C–302/97, *Konle* v. *Austria* [1999] ECR I–3099, paras. 61–64.
[99] Case C–424/97, *Haim* v. *Kassenzahnärtztliche Vereinigung Nordrhein* [2000] ECR I–5123, paras. 31–32.
[100] See Van Gerven AG in Case C–128/92, *Banks* v. *British Coal* [1994] ECR I–1209, and again extra-judicially in 'Bridging the Unbridgeable: Comunity and National Tort Laws after *Francovich* and *Brasserie*' (1996) 45 *ICLQ* 507, 530–2.

24. It follows from the foregoing considerations that any individual can rely on a breach of Article 85(1) of the Treaty before a national court even where he is a party to a contract that is liable to restrict or distort competition within the meaning of that provision.

25. As regards the possibility of seeking compensation for loss caused by a contract or by conduct liable to restrict or distort competition, it should be remembered from the outset that, in accordance with settled case-law, the national courts whose task it is to apply the provisions of Community law in areas within their jurisdiction must ensure that those rules take full effect and must protect the rights which they confer on individuals (see *inter alia* the judgments in Case 106/77 *Simmenthal* [1978] ECR 629, paragraph 16, and in Case C–213/89 *Factortame* [1990] ECR I–2433, paragraph 19).

26. The full effectiveness of Article 85 of the Treaty and, in particular, the practical effect of the prohibition laid down in Article 85(1) would be put at risk if it were not open to any individual to claim damages for loss caused to him by a contract or by conduct liable to restrict or distort competition.

27. Indeed, the existence of such a right strengthens the working of the Community competition rules and discourages agreements or practices, which are frequently covert, which are liable to restrict or distort competition. From that point of view, actions for damages before the national courts can make a significant contribution to the maintenance of effective competition in the Community.

28. There should not therefore be any absolute bar to such an action being brought by a party to a contract which would be held to violate the competition rules.

The Court went on to reiterate the principle of national procedural autonomy, subject to the requirements of equivalence and effectiveness. The *Courage* ruling is certainly significant, in requiring that national law must provide in principle for an action for damages against a private party for breach of a particular provision of EC law, but it remains to be seen whether its implications extend beyond breach of the competition law rules of the Treaty to breaches of other directly effective EC law. Certainly the Court chose to emphasise the fundamental place occupied within the EC legal order by the competition rules, but paragraph 22 of *Brasserie du Pêcheur* hints at the development of a broader principle for the future.

(d) CLARIFYING THE CONDITIONS FOR STATE LIABILITY IN *BRASSERIE DU PÊCHEUR/FACTORTAME III*

Taking its cue from the submissions of many of the governments before it, and from the proposal of Advocate General Tesauro, the Court in *Brasserie du Pêcheur* also emphasized the relevance of Article 288 (ex Article 215), as a basis for developing the conditions for state liability.

Cases C–46 & 48/93 Brasserie du Pêcheur SA v. Germany
[1996] ECR I–1029

41. First, the second paragraph of Article 215 of the Treaty refers, as regards the non-contractual liability of the Community, to the general principles common to the laws of the Member States, from which, in the absence of written rules, the Court also draws inspiration in other areas of Community law.

42. Second, the conditions under which the State may incur liability for damage caused to individuals by a breach of Community law cannot, in the absence of particular justification, differ from those governing the liability of the Community in like circumstances. The protection of the rights which individuals derive from Community law cannot vary depending on whether a national authority or a Community authority is responsible for the damage.

43. The system of rules which the Court has worked out with regard to Article 215 of the Treaty, particularly in relation to liability for legislative measures, takes into account, inter alia, the complexity of the situations to be regulated, difficulties in the application or interpretation of the texts and, more particularly, the margin of discretion available to the author of the act in question.

44. Thus, in developing its case-law on the non-contractual liability of the Community, in particular as regards legislative measures involving choices of economic policy, the Court has had regard to the wide discretion available to the institutions in implementing Community policies.

45. The strict approach taken towards the liability of the Community in the exercise of its legislative activities is due to two considerations. First, even when the legality of measures is subject to judicial review, exercise of the legislative function must not be hindered by the prospect of actions for damages whenever the general interest of the Community requires legislative measures to be adopted which may adversely affect individual interests. Second, in a legislative context characterized by the exercise of a wide discretion, which is essential for implementing a Community policy, the Community cannot incur liability unless the institution concerned has manifestly and gravely disregarded the limits on the exercise of its powers.

Basing Member State liability for breach of EC law on the same conditions as those established for EC liability under Article 288 did not establish a strict form of liability,[101] but rather one depending on factors such as the degree of discretion open to the institution and the clarity or ambiguity of the law which is said to have been breached.[102]

46. That said, the national legislature—like the Community institutions—does not systematically have a wide discretion when it acts in a field governed by Community law. Community law may impose upon it obligations to achieve a particular result or obligations to act or refrain from acting which reduce its margin of discretion, sometimes to a considerable degree. This is so, for

[101] Further, although the ECJ specified the basic conditions under which a Member State must be held liable to an individual for breach of EC law, it also ruled that national law could, if so desired, set stricter conditions for liability: see para. 66.

[102] Whether the Court really did apply the same principles in these joined cases as it does to the Community institutions under Art. 215 (now Art. 228) has been questioned: see P. Oliver, n. & 94 above, 651 and E. Deards, 'Curioser and Curioser? The Development of Member State Liability in the Court of Justice' (1997) 3 *EPL* 117.

instance, where, as in the circumstances to which the judgment in *Francovich* relates, Article 189 of the Treaty places the Member State under an obligation to take, within a given period, all the measures needed in order to achieve the result required by a directive. In such a case, the fact that it is for the national legislature to take the necessary measures has no bearing on the Member State's liability for failing to transpose the directive.

47. In contrast, where a Member State acts in a field where it has no wide discretion, comparable to that of the Community institutions in implementing Community policies, the conditions under which it may incur liability must, in principle, be the same as those under which the Community institutions incur liability in the comparable situation.

. . .

51. In such circumstances, Community law confers a right to reparation where three conditions are met: the rule of law infringed must be intended to confer rights on individuals; the breach must be sufficiently serious; and there must be a direct causal link between the breach of the obligation resting on the State and the damage sustained by the injured parties.

. . .

53. . . . Those conditions correspond in substance to those defined by the Court in relation to Article 215 in its case-law on liability of the Community for damage caused to individuals by unlawful legislative measures adopted by its institutions.

The Court then ruled that both Articles 28 (ex Article 30) and 48 (ex Article 52) satisfied the first condition:

55. As to the second condition, as regards both Community liability under Article 215 and Member State liability for breaches of Community law, the decisive test for finding that a breach of Community law is sufficiently serious is whether the Member State or the Community institution concerned manifestly and gravely disregarded the limits on its discretion.

56. The factors which the competent court may take into consideration include the clarity and precision of the rule breached, the measure of discretion left by that rule to the national or Community authorities, whether the infringement and the damage caused was intentional or involuntary, whether any error of law was excusable or inexcusable, the fact that the position taken by a Community institution may have contributed towards the omission, and the adoption or retention of national measures or practices contrary to Community law.

57. On any view, a breach of Community law will clearly be sufficiently serious if it has persisted despite a judgment finding the infringement in question to be established, or a preliminary ruling or settled case law of the Court on the matter from which it is clear that the conduct in question constituted an infringement.

Although emphasizing the primary responsibility of the national courts for applying these principles to the facts of the cases, the ECJ also gave them a certain amount of guidance in this case. Although the national legislature in each case had possessed a measure of discretion, the ECJ suggested that the authorities must have known that the German rules on the designation 'bier' were in breach of Community law given the earlier ECJ rulings to this effect, whereas the legality of other rules concerning additives was less clear.[103] The Court also indicated that while the existence of a prior

---

[103] The referring German court, upon receiving the ECJ's ruling in *Brasserie du Pêcheur*, ultimately awarded no damages at all to the plaintiffs even as regards the provisions governing the designation 'bier', on the basis that there had been no direct causal connection between Germany's sufficiently serious breach and the damage suffered: see [1997] 1 CMLR 971. See Oliver, n. 94 above, 657; E. Deards, (1997) 22 *ELRev.* 620.

ECJ ruling finding an infringement of EC law would determine the fact that a subsequent similar infringement constitutes a sufficiently serious breach, such a ruling would not be *necessary* to establish a sufficiently serious breach.[104] Similarly, parts of the Merchant Shipping Act 1988's conditions for registration were *prima facie* incompatible with EC law, whereas others might have appeared to the UK to be capable of justification.[105] In assessing the question of 'sufficient seriousness' the national court was encouraged to consider the existing legal disputes over the common fisheries policy, the fact that the Commission had made its attitude known in good time to the UK, and 'the assessments as to the state of certainty of Community law made by the national courts in the interim proceedings brought'.[106] Causation of damage was ultimately a question for the national courts to decide,[107] and while later rulings have confirmed this position, the ECJ has none the less given legal guidance on the causation question.[108]

On the crucial question of the standard of liability, while the ECJ did not engage directly with the meaning of 'fault' in response to a question from the German government, it made clear that the concept of 'sufficiently serious breach' (which arguably carries connotations of fault) was as much as could be required by domestic law:[109]

76. As is clear from the case-file, the concept of fault does not have the same content in the various legal systems.

77. Next, it follows from the reply to the preceding question that, where a breach of Community law is attributable to a Member State acting in a field in which it has a wide discretion to make legislative choices, a finding of a right to reparation on the basis of Community law will be conditional, inter alia, upon the breach having been sufficiently serious.

78. So, certain objective and subjective factors connected with the concept of fault under a national legal system may well be relevant for the purpose of determining whether or not a given breach of Community law is serious [*The ECJ here referred back to the criteria which it set out in paragraphs 56–57*].

79. The obligation to make reparation for loss or damage caused to individuals cannot, however, depend upon a condition based on any concept of fault going beyond that of a sufficiently serious breach of Community law. Imposition of such a supplementary condition would be tantamount to calling in question the right to reparation founded on the Community legal order.

Cases following *Brasserie du Pêcheur* gave further indication of what could constitute a 'sufficiently serious breach'. In *British Telecom*[110] and *Denkavit*,[111] the ECJ effectively itself applied the criteria to the facts of the national cases. In *British*

---

104 Paras. 91–95.

105 The House of Lords ultimately upheld the finding of the Divisional Court and Court of Appeal that the breach was sufficiently serious to give rise to liability in damages. For the series of domestic judgments on this issue, see [1997] *Eu LR* 475, [1998] 1 All ER 736, [1999] All ER 640(C4), [2000] 1 AC 524(HL), and finally the Div. Ct. ruling in [2001] 1 WLR 942.

106 Para. 63 of the judgment.

107 Para. 65. See also Cases C–140/97, *Rechberger* v. *Austria* [1999] ECR I–3499, paras. 72–73 and C–127/95, *Norbrook Laboratories Ltd* v. *Ministry of Agriculture Fisheries and Food* [1998] ECR I–1531.

108 See Case C–319/96, *Brinkmann Tabakfabriken GmbH* v. *Skatteministeriet* [1998] ECR I–5255 para. 29.

109 On this point see also Case C–424/97, *Haim* v. *Kassenzahnärztliche Vereinigung Nordrhein* [2000] ECR I–5123.

110 Case C–392/93, *R.* v. *HM Treasury, ex p. British Telecommunications plc* [1996] ECR I–1631.

111 Cases C–283, 291, & 292/94, *Denkavit International* v. *Bundesamt für Finanzen* [1996] ECR I–5063.

Telecom, BT sought the annulment of part of the UK regulations implementing Directive 90/351 on procurement procedures of entities in certain utilities sectors. An annex to the domestic measure had excluded BT from an exemption provided in Article 8 the Directive, and BT argued that it was entitled to compensation for loss caused by this. The ECJ agreed that the UK had misimplemented the Directive, but concluded that it did not amount to a sufficiently serious breach. The provision of EC law breached was not clear and precise, the UK's interpretation had been made in good faith and was in keeping with the aims and wording of the Directive, and no guidance had been available from past rulings of the Court or the Commission.[112] Similarly in *Denkavit*, an incorrect transposition by Germany of Directive 90/435 on the taxation of parent companies and subsidiaries in different States was deemed by the ECJ not to amount to a sufficiently serious breach, since almost all other Member States had adopted the same interpretation of the Directive as Germany and there was no existing case law on the provision in question.[113] A similar ruling was given by the ECJ in the case of *Brinkmann*, concerning the second tobacco Directive.[114]

By contrast, in *Dillenkofer*,[115] which concerned Germany's failure to implement Directive 90/314 on package holidays, the ECJ ruled that the judgment in *Francovich* had established that non-transposition of a directive within the prescribed time limit *of itself* amounted to a sufficiently serious breach.[116] Another finding of sufficiently serious breach was in *Lomas*,[117] where the UK had refused to grant licences for the export of live sheep to Spain, on the ground that Spanish slaughterhouses were not complying with the terms of an EC Directive. The UK government conceded a breach of Article 29 (ex Article 34) EC on export restrictions but argued it was justified under Article 30 (ex Article 36) for the protection of animal welfare. The Court ruled that the lack of discretion left to Member States following the adoption of the Directive, the clarity of the Treaty provision breached, and the absence of a properly verified ground of justification pointed to the existence of a sufficiently serious breach.[118] Similarly detailed guidance was given by the Court on the question of a sufficiently serious breach in the cases of *Larsy*,[119] and *Stockholm Lindöpark*.[120]

---

[112] Paras. 43–45 of the ruling.

[113] Paras. 51–52 of the ruling.

[114] Case C–319/96, *Brinkmann Tabakfabriken GmbH* v. *Skatteministeriet* [1998] ECR I–5255, paras 30–32. See also Case C–127/95, *Norbrook Laboratories Ltd* v. *Ministry of Agriculture Fisheries and Food* [1998] ECR I–1531.

[115] Cases C–178–9/94, 188–190/94, Dillenkofer and others v. *Federal Republic of Germany* [1996] ECR I–4845. For a misimplementation, rather than non-implementation, of the package holiday Dir. which also constituted a sufficiently serious breach see Case C–140/97, *Rechberger* v. *Austria* [1999] ECR I–3499, paras. 51–53.

[116] Paras. 21–23 of the ruling in *Dillenkofer*, n. 115 above.

[117] Case C–5/94 R. v. *Ministry of Agriculture, Fisheries and Food, ex p. Hedley Lomas* [1996] ECR I–2553.

[118] Case C–5/94, n 117 above, paras. 28–29.

[119] Case C–118/00, *Larsy* v. *INASTI* [2001] ECR I–5063.

[120] Case C–150/99, *Stockholm Lindöpark Aktiebolag* v. *Sweden* [2001] ECR I–493.

(e) THE RELATIONSHIP BETWEEN THE COMMUNITY PRINCIPLE OF STATE LIABILITY AND THE NATIONAL REMEDIAL FRAMEWORK

Although the *Brasserie du Pêcheur/Factortame* judgment gave more detailed guidelines than *Francovich* on the conditions governing state liability, many issues were not addressed in the ruling, but were left to be governed by national law subject to the familiar principles of equivalence and effectiveness.[121] In the two cases in question, the ECJ ruled that German legal provisions limiting the State's liability in exercising its legislative function, and certain conditions of English law such as the requirement of abuse of power or proof of misfeasance in public office, fell foul of these principles, since they would make it 'excessively difficult' to obtain effective reparation.

As regards the extent of reparation, the Court ruled that, in order to constitute effective protection, 'reparation for loss or damage caused to individuals as result of breaches of Community law must be commensurate with the loss or damage sustained'.[122] The requirement of commensurability is a strong one, recalling the Court's earlier ruling in *Marshall II*, above. However, the ruling in *Brasserie du Pêcheur* does not state that *no* restrictions on the extent of damages are permissible, but rather that any restrictions must satisfy the conditions of equivalence and effectiveness. Rules on mitigation of loss would be acceptable, but the total exclusion of loss of profits, or the restriction of damages to certain specific interests only such as property, would fall foul of the latter principle.[123] Given the generality of these two principles and the difficulty of prediction, however, the German government was clearly concerned about the possible scale of its liability and asked for a temporal limitation on the effects of the ruling to be imposed. The ECJ in response, while it did not impose such a limit, indicated that Germany could take account, within the framework of its domestic law on liability, of such temporal concerns as the principle of legal certainty.[124]

In the final paragraphs of the ruling the duality in the nature of the principle of state liability for breach of EC law is very evident. The right to reparation on the one hand is required by Community law, and its core principles and conditions have been established by the ECJ. Yet it remains a set of principles which must be provided within the framework of domestic legal systems, with their varying procedural and substantive rules on matters such as time limits, causation, mitigation of loss, and assessment of damages.[125]

---

[121] These two principles appear repeatedly throughout the judgment: see paras. 67, 70, 71, 73, 83, 87, 90, and 99.

[122] Para. 82.

[123] Paras. 84–88. On mitigation of loss and economic loss see also Case C–410/98, *Metallgesellschaft & Hoechst* v. *Inland Revenue* [2001] ECR I–1727, para. 91, and see n. 67 above and text. As regards exemplary damages in English law, the ECJ in *Brasserie du Pêcheur* ruled that such an award could not be ruled out in the case of the State's breach of EC law in similar circumstances to those which would give rise to an award in an action founded on domestic law: para. 89.

[124] Para. 98.

[125] For some recent cases see Cases C–228/98, *Dounias* v. *Ypourgou Oikonomikon* [2000] ECR I–577, where the exceptional availability of witness evidence in proceedings to establish state liability was held to be compatible with the principles of equivalence and effectiveness, and C–118/00, *Larsy* v. *INASTI* [2001] ECR I–5063.

Many such questions have been raised since the *Brasserie du Pêcheur* ruling. In a trilogy of Italian cases concerning claims arising out of the original *Francovich* litigation, the compatibility of national provisions restricting the availability of compensation for the State's prior breach of EC law was in issue.[126] This breach was the failure to implement Directive 80/987 on the protection of employees in the event of their employer's insolvency. Following the first *Francovich* ruling, legislation was passed to implement the Directive, and also to establish a compensation scheme for those who had suffered loss as a result of the earlier failure to implement. In *Bonifaci and Berto*, the national court questioned the compatibility with EC law of provisions of that scheme which specified that the guarantee of protection for employees' wages would cover only certain wage claims relating to a particular period prior to the insolvency declaration. The ECJ ruled that the period in question must run not from the date the employer was declared insolvent, but from the date on which a request to open proceedings was made, since otherwise the employees' claims would be defeated through no fault of their own. The Court also ruled that while retroactive application of the measures which had since been adopted should, in principle, be sufficient to ensure adequacy of reparation, this would not necsesarily be so if employees could demonstrate otherwise.[127]

The ruling in *Palmisani* provides an example of the application of the requirements of effectiveness and equivalence to the conditions governing the grant of a domestic remedy which was established in order to provide reparation for the loss caused by the State.[128] The applicant had been refused compensation under the Italian scheme, because she had not brought her claim for compensation until after the time limit set in the Italian legislation, which was one year from the date of entry into force of that legislation. The national court had doubts about the general compatibility of the one-year time limit with Community law and asked whether it breached the principle of equivalence with domestic remedies, since the general time limit for cases of non-contractual liability brought under the Italian Civil Code was five years. The ECJ ruled that while a one-year time limit from the date of entry into force of the measure implementing the directive would not breach the principle of effectiveness, since it would not make it excessively difficult for an applicant to obtain reparation, the position in relation to the principle of equivalence was less clear. The Court then distinguished between claims for wages under the national measure actually implementing the Directive and claims for damages for loss caused by the late implementation of the Directive which were governed by the compensation scheme set up by the later measure. The latter had been established precisely to satisfy the *Francovich* requirement of ensuring a system of state liability, and so its aim was to compensate individuals for loss caused by the State's failure to implement a directive, whereas the

---

[126] Cases C–94–95/95, *Bonifaci and Berto* v. *Istituto Nazionale della Previdenza Sociale (IPNS)* [1997] ECR I–3969; C–261/95, *Palmisani* v. *INPS* [1997] ECR I–4025; and C–373/95, *Maso and Gazzetta* v. *IPNS* [1997] ECR I–4051. For further discussion of these cases, see Dougan, n. 88 above.

[127] Paras. 51–53 of the ruling. See also Case C–373/95, *Maso and Gazzetta*, n. 126 above, paras. 58–59, in which the Court ruled that although national rules against aggregation of benefits were in principle permissible, they could not cover benefits such as jobseekers' allowances which arose after termination of employment and would not have overlapped with the unpaid wages.

[128] Case C–261/95, n. 126 above.

former was intended to provide a particular social security benefit. For this reason, it might be inappropriate to compare the time limit for actions under the compensation scheme with the time limit for social-security claims in national law, rather than with the ordinary system of non-contractual liability. The latter system, like the *Francovich* right of reparation, was 'intended to guarantee reparation of the loss or damage sustained as a result of the conduct of the perpetrator'. Ultimately, the ECJ left the appropriateness of the comparison for the Italian court to decide, even while clearly suggesting that it *might* be contrary to the principle of equivalence for there to be a five-year time limit for domestic actions for non-contractual liability and a one-year limit for actions for compensation due to the State's non-implementation of a directive.[129]

(f) THE RELATIONSHIP BETWEEN EXISTING NATIONAL REMEDIES AND THE COMMUNITY DAMAGES REMEDY

Given that the action for compensation is available for breach of directly effective as well as non-directly effective Community rights, what advantages may there be for an individual to choose the EC-mandated action for compensation rather than another existing national remedy?[130] There has been some suggestion in the Court's case law that where a national remedy is not satisfactory, due to the existence of a legitimate national procedural restriction, an action in damages against the State may provide an alternative remedy which is not affected by that particular restrictive national rule. In *Société Comateb*, a repayment of charges case, the ECJ considered the compatibility with Community law of a national rule whereby traders who had been required to pay charges in breach of EC law were denied the possibility of reimbursement, on the ground that they would be unjustly enriched, since national legislation had already required them to pass on the cost of the charges to purchasers of their goods.[131] The ECJ ruled that the national provision denying reimbursement might be compatible with EC law if it could be established that the charge had actually been passed on in its entirety and that reimbursement of the trader would in fact constitute unjust enrichment. In such circumstances, the national rule would not fall foul of the principle of effectiveness. However, the Court then ruled that another way for traders to obtain reparation, rather than seeking *reimbursement* of sums paid in accordance with national law, would be to apply for *compensation* for loss caused by the State under the principles in *Brasserie du Pêcheur* 'irrespective of whether those charges have been passed on'. This seems to imply that even if the fact that charges have been passed on may be used to justify the denial of a *national* remedy of reimbursement, it may not be used to justify a refusal of damages for loss in an action under the *Francovich/Brasserie*

---

[129] See in particular para. 39. See also Cases C–52 & 53/99, *ONP* v. *Camarotto* [2001] ECR I–1395, for a similar kind of ruling.

[130] See Oliver, n. 94 above, and Deards, n. 103 above, who question whether the action for damages may be made subsidiary to other national remedies.

[131] Cases C–192–218/95, *Société Comateb* v. *Directeur Général des Douanes et Droits Indirects* [1997] ECR I–165. There is an extensive case law on repayment of charges and the defence of passing on. For further discussion, see Dougan, n. 9 above.

du Pêcheur principles.[132] So long as the three criteria of a clear right conferred, a sufficiently serious breach, and causation of loss are established, the fact of a charge having been passed on seems, from *Comateb*, to be irrelevant, thus making the *Francovich* action a potentially more attractive and less restricted remedy than other domestic remedies.

Secondly, in *Sutton*, after ruling that a national provision denying the availability of interest on arrears of social security owed under Directive 79/7 was compatible with the principles of equivalence and effectiveness, the ECJ went on to consider whether the State might be liable to the applicant for loss caused through its breach of the Directive.[133] The possibility that an action for damages against the State for loss caused by the misimplementation of the Directive would also have to include any loss caused by the effluxion of time, even where such loss could not be recovered as interest on the payment of arrears under national law, is given support also by *Palmisani*.[134] There the ECJ distinguished between the purpose of an action for compensation against the State for breach of EC law, and the purpose of a claim for social security under domestic or EC law.[135] The assumption underlying these rulings may be thought to be that an action for compensation under *Francovich* principles may prove to be a more effective remedy than others which are available under national law. This suggestion has, however, been criticized on the basis that an action based on *Francovich* requires the establishment of additional onerous conditions, such as a sufficiently serious breach and causation of loss.[136]

The ECJ has considered the opposite argument in the *Stockholm Lindöpark* case, namely that the fact that an action could be brought under national law in direct reliance on the direct effect of Community law should be a barrier to the availability of a *Francovich*-style action for damages.[137] The Court rejected this argument, ruling that the principle of state liability was inherent in the scheme of the Treaty, and thus arguably affirming the fact that the right to reparation flowing from this principle is not a residual remedy which exists only when no other remedy is available under national law.

---

[132] On the other hand, the Court ruled that the national remedy of reimbursement could legitimately be denied where reimbursement would lead to the unjust enrichment of the applicant, and the ruling does not make clear whether the State could equally legitimately deny an action for damages for breach of EC law where compensation for loss could be seen as an unjust enrichment of the trader.

[133] Case C–66/95, *R. v. Secretary of State for Social Security, ex p. Eunice Sutton* [1997] ECR I–2163, paras. 33–34. Similarly in Case C–90/96, *Petrie v. Università degli Studi di Verona et Camilla Bettoni* [1997] ECR I–6525, the ECJ ruled that although applicants for teaching posts who had been subject to an unlawful discriminatory condition could not insist that they must be eligible for appointment to these posts under national law, that did not mean that they could not seek compensation under the conditions laid down in *Brasserie du Pêcheur*.

[134] Case C–261/95, n. 126 above.

[135] It is also given some support by the distinction made by the ECJ in *Sutton* between the compensation for loss or damage in *Marshall II* and the payment of social security arrears which arose in *Sutton*.

[136] Dougan, n. 88 above.

[137] Case C–150/99, *Stockholm Lindöpark Aktiebolag v. Sweden* [2001] ECR I–493, para. 35.

5. CONCLUSION

i. The response of the ECJ to the lack of legislation at Community level to create a system of harmonized remedies for breach of Community law, in intervening to bring about a more incremental judicial harmonization, has prompted a number of different reactions.

ii. Some have applauded the Court for treading a difficult path between respect for the autonomy of the national legal systems and the competing need to promote adequate enforcement of EC law.[138] The reliance on national courts to scrutinize the compatibility of national procedural rules with Community requirements, and to provide a detailed framework for implementing the principle of state liability or the provision of ECJ-mandated remedies such as the right to reparation, has been described as an example of the principles of subsidiarity and proportionality at work in the judicial sphere.[139]

iii. Others have cautioned against the effects of such reactive, *ad hoc*, and inevitably haphazard judicial lawmaking and have argued for a more systematic, politically legitimate, and carefully considered legislative approach to the effectiveness of EC law and the creation of a system of Community remedies and procedures.[140]

iv. Others still have argued that since it is now over two decades since the Court and its Advocates General regretted the absence of Community legislation to harmonize remedial procedures, and given that no such action is currently on the political agenda, incremental reform through the Court's case law may be in certain ways desirable.[141]

v. The Community's lack of legislative activity can be interpreted in different ways. In the first place, it may be seen to reflect a clear political wish on the part of the Member States and the Council not to co-ordinate or harmonize domestic rules in this respect. Secondly it may be seen to reflect the lower priority of EU procedural/remedial rather than substantive policy measures. Thirdly, it may be seen as reflecting the difficulty and complexity of the task which would be involved.[142]

vi. Different reasons have also been given for resistance to remedial harmonization by the Community. It has been pointed out that Member States may be particularly resistant to the prospect of Community interference—be it legislative or

---

[138] E.g., Jacobs, n. 41 above, and D. Curtin (1994) 31 *CMLRev.* 631, 649.

[139] See *ibid.*, 650, and Jacobs AG in Cases C–430–31/93, *Van Schijndel*, n. 54 above, para. 27 of his Opinion.

[140] See F. Snyder, 'The Effectiveness of European Community Law' (1993) 56 *MLR* 19, 50–53, and, e.g., the submission of the Irish Government to the ECJ in Case C–213/89, *Factortame Ltd. v. Secretary of State for Transport* [1990] ECR I–2433, at paras. 37 and 39 of the report for the hearing.

[141] C. Himsworth, 'Things Fall Apart: The Harmonisation of Community Judicial Protection Revisited' (1997) 22 *ELRev.* 291, 307.

[142] See C. Harding, 'Member State Enforcement of European Community Measures: The Chimera of "Effective" Enforcement' (1997) 4 *Maastricht Journal of European and Comparative Law* 5.

    judicial—with their systems of private law, which reflect implicit but funda-
    mental social and cultural choices.[143]

vii. Finally, it has been argued that the impulse towards harmonization of national
    remedies, whether of administrative procedure or more fundamental provi-
    sions of public and of private law, can be understood as a matter of political
    choice, rather than of judicial or legal necessity.[144]

C. Harlow, A Common European Law of Remedies?[145]

The general lesson of this chapter is that the 'level playing field' of procedural rights is illusory.
Limited competence and limited interest combine to inhibit harmonisation through codification.
The curious structure of the EC legal order prevents sensible judicial approximation. Uniformity is
largely a symbolic concept, part of a wider integrationist project to 'make Europe more relevant
to its citizens'. . . .

    The way forward is to trust national courts, best fitted to understand the national context, to
decide routine points of EC law for themselves, as the ECJ is currently encouraging them to do.
The more radical suggestion of allowing national courts to give judgment on points of EC law
before reference to the ECJ is also worth considering. This would enhance judicial cooperation,
providing an opening for national courts to indicate the potential impact of decisions on the
national legal system; forcing them to articulate their reasoning in the language of that system;
reinforcing domestic accountability by submitting judgments to scrutiny in the national arena
where their impact needs to be weighed and tested. The basic *Saarland* rule of national procedural
autonomy must be reinstated and incursions subjected to a formal proportionality test, rigorously
applied, requiring them to be overwhelmingly justified.

6. FURTHER READING

(a) *Books*

BEATSON, J., and TRIDIMAS, T. (eds.), *European Public Law* (Hart, 1998)

BEAUMONT, P., LYONS, C., and WALKER, N., *Convergence and Divergence in European Public
    Law* (Hart, 2002)

KILPATRICK, C., NOVITZ, T., and SKIDMORE, P., *The Future of Remedies in Europe*
    (Hart, 2000)

LADEUR, K.-H., *The Europeanisation of Administrative Law* (Ashgate, 2002)

LONBAY, J., and BIONDI, A. (eds.), *Remedies for Breach of EC Law* (Wylie, 1997)

(b) *Articles*

ANAGNOSTARAS, G., 'The Allocation of Responsibility in State Liability Actions for Breach of
    Community Law' (2001) 26 *ELRev.* 139

---

[143] D. Caruso, 'The Missing View of the Cathedral: The Private law Paradigm of European Legal Integration' (1997) 3 *ELJ* 3 and H. Collins, 'European Private Law and the Cultural Identity of States' (1995) 3
European Review of Private Law 353.
[144] See, e.g., n. 1 above on moves towards harmonization of contract law.
[145] N. 5 above, 69, 81–3.

CARANTA, R., 'Judicial Protection Against Member States: A New Jus Commune Takes Shape' (1995) 32 *CMLRev.* 703

—— 'Learning from our neighbours: Public Law Remedies—Homogenization from Bottom Up' (1997) 4 *MJ* 220

CRAIG, P.P., '*Francovich*, Remedies and the Scope of Damages Liability' (1993) 109 *LQR* 595

—— 'Once More unto the Breach: The Community, the State and Damages Liability' (1997) 105 *LQR* 67

DEARDS, E., 'Curioser and Curioser? The Development of Member State Liability in the Court of Justice' (1997) 3 *EPL* 117

DOUGAN, M., 'Cutting your Losses in the Enforcement Deficit: A Community Right to the Recovery of Unlawfully Levied Charges?' (1998) 1 *CYELS* 233

—— 'The *Francovich* Right to Reparation: Reshaping the Contours of Community Remedial Competence' (2000) 6 *EPL* 103

HARLOW, C., '*Francovich* and the Problem of the Disobedient State' (1996) 2 *ELJ* 199

HIMSWORTH, C., 'Things Fall Apart: The Harmonisation of Community Judicial Procedural Protection Revisited' (1997) 22 *ELRev.* 291

HOSKINS, M., 'Tilting the Balance: Supremacy and National Procedural Rules' (1996) 21 *ELRev.* 365

ROSS, M., 'Beyond *Francovich*' (1993) 56 *MLR* 55

SNYDER, F., 'The Effectiveness of European Community Law' (1993) 56 *MLR* 19

TEMPLE LANG, J., 'The Duties of National Courts under Community Constitutional Law' (1997) 22 *ELRev.* 3

TRIDIMAS, T., 'Liability for Breach of Community Law: Growing Up and Mellowing Down?' (2001) 38 *CMLRev.* 301

—— 'Bridging the Unbridgeable: Community and National Tort laws after *Francovich* and *Brasserie*' (1996) 45 *ICLQ* 507

VAN GERVEN, W., 'Bridging the Gap between Community and National Laws: Towards a Principle of Homogeneity in the Field of Legal Remedies?' (1995) 32 *CMLRev.* 679

7

THE RELATIONSHIP BETWEEN EC LAW AND NATIONAL LAW: SUPREMACY

1. CENTRAL ISSUES

i. Like the doctrine of direct effect, the doctrine of supremacy of Community law[1] had no basis in the EC Treaty but was developed by the ECJ on the basis of its conception of how the 'new legal order' should operate. EC law was autonomous rather than derivative on the basis that Member States had voluntarily chosen to transfer their sovereignty.

ii. More pragmatically, the ECJ ruled that the aim of creating a uniform common market between different States would be undermined if Community laws could be made subordinate to the national laws of the various States.[2]

iii. Accordingly, the validity of EC law can never be assessed by reference to national law. National courts are required to give immediate effect to the provisions of directly effective EC law (of whatever rank) in cases which arise before them, and to ignore or to set aside any national law (of whatever rank) which could impede the application of EC law.

iv. The requirement to 'set aside' conflicting national law does not entail an obligation to nullify national law, which may continue to apply in any situation which is not covered by a conflicting provision of Community law.

v. Most national courts do not accept the unconditionally monist view of the ECJ as regards the supremacy of EC law. While they accept the requirements of supremacy in practice, most regard this as flowing from their national constitutions rather than from the authority of the EC Treaties or the ECJ, and they retain a power of ultimate constitutional review over measures of EC law.

---

[1] The extent to which the principle of supremacy may apply to the second and third pillars of EU law remains to be seen, when the ECJ has an opportunity to rule on these questions.

[2] See the statement in Case 44/79, *Hauer* v. *Land Rheinland-Pfalz* [1979] ECR 3727, para. 14, that this would 'lead inevitably to the destruction of the unity of the Common Market'.

2. THE FIRST DIMENSION: SUPREMACY OF COMMUNITY LAW FROM THE COURT OF JUSTICE'S PERSPECTIVE

Case 26/62, NV. Algemene Transporten Expeditie Onderneming van Gend en Loos v. Nederlandse Administratie der Belastingen
[1963] ECR 1

The facts are set out in Chapter 5.[3] The Belgian Government submitted in its observations that the ECJ should not answer the first question submitted, since the matter fell exclusively within the jurisdiction of the referring Dutch court:

> That court is confronted with two international treaties both of which are part of national law. It must decide under national law . . . which Treaty prevails over the other or more exactly whether a prior national law of ratification prevails over a subsequent one. This is a typical question of national constitutional law which has nothing to do with the interpretation of an Article of the EEC Treaty. . . .

THE ECJ[4]

The objective of the EEC Treaty, which is to establish a Common Market, the functioning of which is of direct concern to interested parties in the Community, implies that this Treaty is more than an agreement which merely creates mutual obligations between the contracting states. . . . It is also confirmed more specifically by the establishment of institutions endowed with sovereign rights. . . .

The conclusion to be drawn from this is that the Community constitutes a new legal order of international law for the benefit of which the states have limited their sovereign rights, albeit within limited fields, and the subjects of which comprise not only Member States but also their nationals.

The reasoning of the Court in the case is brief, and apart from elaborating the concept of direct effect and emphasizing the need for direct enforcement by national courts of Community norms, little more is said about the need for national courts to accord *primacy* to such norms over conflicting national law. The Court's focus was on whether Article 25 (ex Article 12) EC could give rise to direct effect, and no express consideration was given to the problem this might create for a domestic court faced with a clearly conflicting provision of national law. However, Advocate General Roemer, who considered that the Treaty Article in question did not have direct effect, drew attention to the constitutional difficulties which national courts could face,[5] and pointed to the fact that the constitutional laws of Belgium, Italy, and Germany did not accord primacy to international treaties over national law.

---

[3] At 182.   [4] [1963] ECR 1, 12.   [5] *Ibid.*, 23.

The ECJ however sidestepped the problem of differing national constitutional approaches to international treaties by describing the legal order created by the States under the Treaty as an entirely new system which was different in nature from international law. The novel nature of the Treaty and of the legal order it had created derived, on the Court's analysis, from a voluntary limitation of their sovereign rights by the Member States, which had chosen to create and endow new political institutions with such sovereign rights. Beyond this major and controversial constitutional claim, which includes a claim to sovereignty on behalf of the Community, the Court concentrated in *Van Gend* on the specific legal nature of Article 25 (ex Article 12) and whether it could have direct effect.

Two years later, however, the Court affirmed and developed its constitutional theory of the Community, spelling out this time the precise implications (from the Community's perspective) for a provision of national law which was in conflict with a provision of EC law.

Case 6/64, Flaminio Costa v. ENEL
[1964] ECR 585, 593

[Note ToA renumbering: Arts. 5, 7, 177, and 189 are now Arts. 10, 12, 234, and 249 respectively]

THE ECJ

By contrast with ordinary international treaties, the EEC Treaty has created its own legal system which, on the entry into force of the Treaty, became an integral part of the legal systems of the Member States and which their courts are bound to apply.

By creating a Community of unlimited duration, having its own institutions, its own personality, its own legal capacity and capacity of representation on the international plane and, more particularly, real powers stemming from a limitation of sovereignty or a transfer of powers from the States to the Community, the Member States have limited their sovereign rights, albeit within limited fields, and have thus created a body of law which binds both their nationals and themselves.

The integration into the laws of each Member State of provisions which derive from the Community, and more generally the terms and the spirit of the Treaty, make it impossible for the states, as a corollary, to accord precedence to a unilateral and subsequent measure over a legal system accepted by them on the basis of reciprocity. Such a measure cannot therefore be inconsistent with that legal system. The executive force of Community law cannot vary from one State to another in deference to subsequent domestic laws, without jeopardizing the attainment of the objectives of the Treaty set out in Article 5(2) and giving rise to the discrimination prohibited by Article 7.

The obligations undertaken under the Treaty establishing the Community would not be unconditional, but merely contingent, if they could be called into question by subsequent legislative acts of the signatories. . . .

The precedence of Community law is confirmed by Article 189, whereby a regulation 'shall be binding' and 'directly applicable in all Member States'. This provision, which is subject to no reservation, would be quite meaningless if a State could unilaterally nullify its effects by means of a legislative measure which could prevail over Community law.

It follows from all these observations that the law stemming from the Treaty, an independent source of law, could not, because of its special and original nature, be overridden by domestic legal provisions, however framed, without being deprived of its character as Community law and without the legal basis of the Community itself being called into question.

The transfer by the states from their domestic legal system to the Community legal system of the rights and obligations arising under the Treaty carries with it a permanent limitation of their sovereign rights, against which a subsequent unilateral act incompatible with the concept of the Community cannot prevail.

It is worth looking individually at each of the arguments made by the Court in support of its conclusion that Community law must be given primacy by national courts over any incompatible national law.[6] Just as in the case of the principle of direct effect, the EC Treaty is silent on the relationship between national law and Community law, and makes no reference to the supremacy of Community law. The first two arguments are in fact assertions by the Court, giving its own interpretation of what the spirit and aims of the Treaty require and of how the Member States brought this about.

First is the statement that the Treaty created its own legal order which immediately became 'an integral part' of the legal systems of the Member States. *Second*, and perhaps more contentious, is the Court's statement of how, in constitutional terms, the Member States created this legal order. This was done, said the Court, by the States transferring to the new Community institutions 'real powers stemming from a limitation of sovereignty', a limitation furthermore declared in the judgment to be *permanent*. As in the case of *Van Gend*, the Court made no reference to the constitution of any particular Member State to see whether such a transfer or limitation of sovereignty was contemplated or was possible in accordance with that constitution.

In its *third* argument, the Court drew on the spirit and the aims of the Treaty to conclude that it was 'impossible' for the Member States to accord primacy to domestic laws. The 'spirit' of the Treaty required that they all act with equal diligence to give full effect to Community laws which they had accepted on the basis of 'reciprocity'. Since the 'aims' of the Treaty were those of integration and co-operation, their achievement would be undermined by one Member State refusing to give effect to a Community law which, as they had agreed, should uniformly and equally bind all. This, again, was a pragmatic and purposive argument rather than a textual one, and an argument which is to be seen repeatedly in the case law of the Court: that securing the uniformity and effectiveness of Community law is necessary if the concrete aims set out in the Treaties are to be realized.

---

[6] Several of these arguments were later used by the Procureur Général before the Belgian Cour de Cassation in *Minister for Economic Affairs* v. *SA Fromagerie Franco-Suisse 'Le Ski'* [1972] 2 CMLR 330, where he successfully persuaded the court that the supremacy of Community law over Belgian law should be acknowledged.

The *fourth* argument was again a practical one—that the obligations undertaken by the Member States in the Treaty would be 'merely contingent' rather than unconditional if they were to be subject to later legislative acts on the part of the States. The only genuinely textual evidence used by the Court was in its *fifth* argument: that the language of direct applicability in Article 189 (now Article 249) would be meaningless if States could negate the effect of Community law by passing subsequent inconsistent legislation. Yet this textual argument is weak, since Article 249 (ex Article 189) refers only to the direct applicability of regulations, while the Court in *Costa* v. *ENEL* was seeking to establish a general principle of the supremacy of *all* binding Community law, and specifically of a Treaty Article. Further, direct applicability refers to the way in which Community law becomes part of the national legal system without the need for implementing measures, but it does not resolve the question of priority between this law and other forms of national law.

What comes across most strongly in the judgment is the teleological rather than textual approach of the Court. The aims of the Community and the spirit of the Treaties are constantly emphasized, and there is little support in the text of the Treaties for the proposition that Community law has a 'special and original nature' of which it would be deprived if subsequent domestic laws were to prevail. The Court's ruling was clearly a bold step to support its own conception of the Community legal order by asserting that the States had permanently limited their powers and had transferred sovereignty to the Community institutions. And while the conceptual basis for the principle of supremacy of Community law was set out by the Court in *Van Gend* and *Costa* v. *ENEL*, the force and practical application of the principle became clearer still in its later decisions. In the following case, the Court ruled that the legal status of a conflicting national measure was not relevant to the question whether Community law should take precedence.[7] Not even a fundamental rule of national constitutional law could be invoked to challenge the supremacy of a directly applicable Community law.

Case 11/70, Internationale Handelsgesellschaft mbH v. Einfuhr- und Vorratsstelle für
Getreide und Futtermittel
[1970] ECR 1125

The facts are set out in Chapter 8.[8]

THE ECJ

3. Recourse to the legal rules or concepts of national law in order to judge the validity of measures adopted by the institutions of the Community would have an adverse effect on the uniformity and efficacy of Community law. The validity of such measures can only be judged in the light of Community law. In fact, the law stemming from the Treaty, an independent source of law,

---

[7] See also Case C–473/93, *Commission* v. *Luxembourg* [1996] ECR I–3207, para. 38.   [8] At 322.

cannot because of its very nature be overridden by rules of national law, however framed, without being deprived of its character as Community law and without the legal basis of the Community itself being called into question. Therefore the validity of a Community measure or its effect within a Member State cannot be affected by allegations that it runs counter to either fundamental rights as formulated by the constitution of that State or the principles of a national constitutional structure.

More recently, the ECJ faced the opposite kind of argument in the *Ciola* case where the Austrian government sought to argue that the principle of primacy should not automatically apply 'to specific individual administrative acts'.[9] The Court readily dismissed this argument, reaffirming that any provision of national law which conflicted with directly effective Community law should not be applied. Thus the principle of primacy is equally asserted and required by the ECJ whenever directly effective EC law is concerned,[10] and regardless of whether fundamental national constitutional norms or minor administrative acts are at issue.

As will be seen below, the *Internationale Handelsgesellschaft* ruling gave rise for some time to a potentially serious conflict in the relationship between the German Constitutional Court and the Court of Justice. And although it has demonstrated caution on occasions by seeking to avoid a direct constitutional conflict with a national court,[11] the ECJ has never retreated from its claims, but rather continued to emphasize the importance of ensuring that the supremacy of Community law was not simply a matter of theory, but was given practical effect by all national courts in cases arising before them.

Case 106/77, Amministrazione delle Finanze dello Stato v. Simmenthal SpA
[1978] ECR 629

The respondent company, which had imported beef from France into Italy, brought an action before the Pretore claiming repayment of the fees which had been charged to it for a veterinary inspection at the frontier, on the basis that the charge was incompatible with EC law. The ECJ, on a preliminary reference, ruled that such charges were indeed contrary to the Treaty. When the Pretore therefore ordered repayment of the amounts with interest, the Italian fiscal authorities objected that the national court could not simply refuse to apply a national law which conflicted with Community law, but must first bring the matter before the Italian Constitutional Court to have the Italian law declared unconstitutional. The Pretore therefore referred the case again

---

[9] Case C–224/97, *Ciola* v. *Land Vorarlberg* [1999] ECR I–2517, para. 24. The government claimed that such automatic application to all administrative acts would undermine the principles of legal certainty and legitimate expectations.

[10] For the application of the *Simmenthal* reasoning and the principle of primacy to the decisions of Association Councils see Case C–65/98, *Eyup* v. *Landesgeschäftstelle* [2000] ECR I–4747, at para. 41.

[11] See, e.g., Case C–446/98, *Fazenda Pública* v. *Câmara* [2000] ECR I–11435, paras. 36–38 where the ECJ avoided declaring to a Portugese court that it must apply a provision of national law necessitated by EC law where such provision would be unconstitutional under Portugese law, by interpreting away any conflict of the kind alleged between EC law and the Portugese constitution.

to the ECJ, asking whether in these circumstances the national law must be disregarded forthwith without waiting until it was set aside by the appropriate constitutional authority.

THE ECJ

17. Furthermore, in accordance with the principle of the precedence of Community law, the relationship between provisions of the Treaty and directly applicable measures of the institutions on the one hand and the national law of the Member States on the other is such that those provisions and measures not only by their entry into force render automatically inapplicable any conflicting provision of current national law but—in so far as they are an integral part of, and take precedence in, the legal order applicable in the territory of each of the Member States—also preclude the valid adoption of new national legislative measures to the extent to which they would be incompatible with Community provisions.

18. Indeed any recognition that national legislative measures which encroach upon the field within which the Community exercises its legislative power or which are otherwise incompatible with the provisions of Community law had any legal effect would amount to a corresponding denial of the effectiveness of obligations undertaken unconditionally and irrevocably by Member States pursuant to the Treaty and would thus imperil the very foundations of the Community.

. . .

21. It follows from the foregoing that every national court must, in a case within its jurisdiction, apply Community law in its entirety and protect rights which the latter confers on individuals and must accordingly set aside any provision of national law which may conflict with it, whether prior or subsequent to the Community rule.

22. Accordingly any provision of a national legal system and any legislative, administrative or judicial practice which might impair the effectiveness of Community law by withholding from the national court having jurisdiction to apply such law the power to do everything necessary at the moment of its application to set aside national legislative provisions which might prevent Community rules from having full force and effect are incompatible with those requirements which are the very essence of Community law.

23. This would be the case in the event of a conflict between a provision of Community law and a subsequent national law if the solution of the conflict were to be reserved for an authority with a discretion of its own, other than the court called upon to apply Community law, even if such an impediment to the full effectiveness of Community law were only temporary.

24. The first question should therefore be answered to the effect that a national court which is called upon, within the limits of its jurisdiction, to apply provisions of Community law is under a duty to give full effect to those provisions, if necessary refusing of its own motion to apply any conflicting provision of national legislation, even if adopted subsequently, and it is not necessary for the court to request or await the prior setting aside of such provision by legislative or other constitutional means.

Simmenthal was a very important case, which spelt out in stark terms the practical implications for the Community legal order of the principles of supremacy and direct effect. All national courts must directly and immediately enforce a clear and unconditional provision of Community law, even where there is a directly conflicting national law of constitutional or other elevated status. Although this much had emerged from the rulings in *Costa* v. *ENEL* and *Internationale Handelsgesellschaft*, the facts of *Simmenthal* highlighted a further problem. What if the national court had no domestic jurisdiction to question or to set aside national legislative acts? In the Italian legal system, this is the function of the Constitutional Court, which is why the Italian tax authorities in *Simmenthal* questioned the Pretore's order awarding the repayment of fees which had been charged under an existing national law. The clear message of the ECJ's response was that, even if the Constitutional Court is the only national court empowered to pronounce on the constitutionality of a national law, where a conflict between national law and Community law arises before another national court, that court must give immediate effect to the Community law without awaiting the prior ruling of the constitutional court. This ruling has been affirmed many times, as indicated in the previous chapter concerning remedies in national courts. Further, in *Larsy* the ECJ ruled that not only national courts but also the relevant administrative agencies—in this case a national social insurance institution—should disapply conflicting national laws in order to give effect to the primacy of Community law.[12]

Simmenthal was thus an early example of what we have seen in the previous chapter, i.e., how Community law has sometimes required domestic courts to exercise powers and jurisdiction which they would not have under national law. The emphasis in such rulings is on the principle of effectiveness. The Court apparently does not wish to be seen to create new areas of jurisdiction for national courts, and its rulings often appear to be deliberately negatively worded. Thus national courts 'must not apply' national rules which form an obstacle to the immediate applicability or effectiveness of Community law. It is clear, however, that such rulings nevertheless do sometimes lead to an increase or change in the jurisdiction or functions of particular national courts. This became evident in quite a dramatic way in the UK after the *Factortame* ruling on the question of interim relief against a provision of national law which appeared to conflict with Community law. Having repeated much of the *Simmenthal* ruling on the need for effectiveness and for the automatic precedence of directly effective Community law over national law, the ECJ continued.

Case C–213/89, R. v. Secretary of State for Transport, ex parte Factortame Ltd. and Others [1990] ECR I–2433

21. It must be added that the full effectiveness of Community law would be just as much impaired if a rule of national law could prevent a court seised of a dispute governed by Community law from granting interim relief in order to ensure the full effectiveness of the judgment to be given on the existence of the rights claimed under Community law. It follows that a court which in those circumstances would grant interim relief, if it were not for a rule of national law, is obliged to set aside that rule.

---

[12] Case C–118/00, *Larsy* v. *INASTI* [2001] ECR I–nyr, paras. 52–53. See the similar discussion of what has been termed 'administrative direct effect' in Ch. 5, at n. 80 and text.

The overriding requirement that priority be given to directly effective Community law over conflicting national law meant that, even if the Community provision were only putatively directly effective, a national rule which absolutely barred domestic courts from giving interim relief in any such circumstance should be set aside or ignored by those domestic courts. In the UK, in which the principle of parliamentary sovereignty is a fundamental tenet of constitutional law, this ruling—despite being based on the same reasoning as the well-established *Simmenthal* judgment—had quite an impact. The ECJ however did not repeat the basis for the principle of supremacy, but simply spelt out the practical consequences for the national judicial system.

One of the ways in which the ECJ has avoided appearing to interfere too directly in the functioning and jurisdiction of national courts within their domestic legal systems has been to emphasize the limit to what the principle of primacy entails. Thus the supremacy principle does not necessarily require national courts to rule on the general validity of a provision of national law nor to annul conflicting provisions, but rather simply to refuse to apply such provisions in the case in question, and to refuse to apply them whenever a directly effective provision of EC law is at issue. This distinction between disapplying as opposed to actually nullifying national law was emphasized in the *IN.CO.GE '90* case in which the ECJ rejected the Commission's argument that the incompatibility of EC law with a subsequently adopted rule of national law must render the national rule non-existent. Having recalled the terms of its ruling in *Simmenthal*, the ECJ continued:

It cannot therefore, contrary to the Commission's contention, be inferred from the judgment in *Simmenthal* that the incompatibility with Community law of a subsequently adopted rule of national law has the effect of rendering that rule of national law non-existent. Faced with such a situation, the national court is, however, obliged to disapply that rule, provided always that this obligation does not restrict the power of the competent national courts to apply, from among the various procedures available under national law, those which are appropriate for protecting the individual rights conferred by Community law.[13]

The supremacy of Community law and the requirement that national courts must ensure its practical effectiveness were thus, as far as the ECJ was concerned, established beyond question in a consistent line of case law.

There are a number of provisions of the EC Treaty which some may view as a partial dilution of the supremacy principle, such as Article 307 (ex Article 234) which relieves Member States of the obligation to ensure the primacy of EC law in certain circumstances,[14] or Article 297 (ex Article 224) which appears to carve out an area

---

[13] Cases C–10–22/97, *Ministero delle Finanze* v. *IN.CO.GE.'90 Srl* [1998] ECR I–6307, para. 21.

[14] Art. 307 (ex Art. 234) EC, e.g., provides a limited exception to the obligation of Member States to ensure the supremacy of EC law, where conflicting state obligations arise from agreements concluded with non-Member States before the entry into force of the EC Treaty: see, e.g., Cases C–158/91, *Ministère Public and Direction du Travail et de l'Emploi* v. *Levy* [1993] ECR I–4287; C–13/93, *Office Nationale de l'Emploi* v. *Minne* [1994] ECR I–371; and C–124/95, *R., ex p. Centro-Com Srl* v. *HM Treasury and Bank of England* [1997] ECR I–81. More recently, see Cases C–364/95 and T–2/99, n. 51 below on the GATT in this context. For a comment on Art. 307 in the context of two recent cases concerning Portugal see J. Klabbers, 'Moribund on the Fourth of July? The Court of Justice on the prior Agreements of the Member States' (2001) 26 *ELRev.* 187 and C. Hillion (2001) 38 *CMLRev.* 1269. Most recently see Case C–55/00, *Gottardo* v. *INPS* ruling of 15 Jan. 2002.

within which the Member States retain a degree of sovereignty.[15] None the less, these are provisions of limited scope, and the basic principle of supremacy articulated by the ECJ is a broad and general one.

Nevertheless, this constitutes only one part of the supremacy story. Ultimately, the acceptance and practical application of the primacy of EC law are dependent on the adaptation and acquiescence of the legal and constitutional orders of the Member States.

J. Weiler, The Community System: the Dual Character of Supranationalism[16]

As in the case of 'direct effect' the derivation of supremacy from the Treaty depended on a 'constitutional' rather than international law interpretation. The Court's reasoning that supremacy was enshrined in the Treaty was contested by the governments of Member States in this case and others. Acceptance of this view amounts in effect to a quiet revolution in the legal orders of the Member States. . . .

It follows that the evolutionary nature of the doctrine of supremacy is necessarily bi-dimensional. One dimension is the elaboration of the parameters of the doctrine by the European Court. But its full reception, the second dimension, depends on its incorporation into the constitutional orders of the Member States and its affirmation by their supreme courts. It is relatively easy to trace the evolution of the Community dimension of the doctrine. . . .

As regards the second dimension, the evolutionary character of the process is more complicated. It should be remembered that in respect of the original Member States there was no specific constitutional preparation for this European Court-inspired development.

This evolutionary nature of the process of acceptance of supremacy remains fully evident today. The tension between national accounts of the character of Community law and the ECJ's account persists, and not only in Member States which have more recently joined the EU. Constitutional conflicts continue to arise in specific cases, and it remains ultimately for national courts to resolve particular cases arising before them involving a conflict between Community law and national law. Even if a national court fully accepts that, within its proper sphere, EC law should take precedence over national law, agreement may be lacking on the question of competence—on whether or not this is in fact the proper sphere of Community law. Given the uncertain boundaries of Community powers under the Treaties, the question of *Kompetenz-Kompetenz*—of who has ultimate authority to define the allocation of competence as between the Community and the Member States, and whether in particular the Community possesses the autonomy to define the limits of its own competence—remains contested. The ECJ under Article 220 (ex Article 164) of the EC Treaty takes this to be its task, whereas virtually all national constitutional or supreme courts determine such questions ultimately by reference to their own national constitutional

---

[15] See, e.g., P. Koutrakos, 'Is Article 297 EC a "Reserve of Sovereignty"' (2000) 37 *CMLRev.* 1339.

[16] (1981) 1 *YBEL* 267, 275–6.

provisions.[17] As we have seen in Chapter 3, the principle of subsidiarity in Article 5 (ex Article 3b) EC, although it purports to set some sort of standard for judging the appropriateness of Community action in a given field, does not provide much concrete guidance. Further, it was only recently that the ECJ in the tobacco advertising case gave its first major ruling which could be seen as reflecting a more rigorous approach to the 'creeping competences' issue.[18] And, finally, the fact that the question of a better 'delimitation of powers' has been placed at the centre of the political and constitutional reform agenda by the Nice and Laeken European Council summits demonstrates the continuing debate over this question.

The accommodation so far reached by the courts of various Member States on the issue of the primacy of Community law will now be examined. For reasons of space, only a small number of the Member States are selected for discussion, although each State has its own interesting constitutional perspective to offer,[19] as indeed do the many candidate States.

3. THE SECOND DIMENSION: SUPREMACY OF COMMUNITY LAW FROM THE PERSPECTIVE OF THE MEMBER STATES

(a) FRANCE

The French judicial system is divided between the administrative courts and the ordinary courts, and a doctrinal 'split' occurred when the supremacy of Community law over French law was accepted in 1975 by the Cour de Cassation,[20] the highest of the ordinary judicial courts, but was rejected in practice by the Conseil d'Etat, the supreme administrative court, until as late as 1989.[21] In the case of *Semoules*,[22] the problem was expressed as a jurisdictional one: the Conseil d'Etat ruled that, since it had no jurisdiction to review the validity of French legislation, it could not find such legislation to be incompatible with Community law, nor could it accord priority to the latter. And although the French Constitution provided for the primacy of certain international treaties over domestic law, in the view of the Conseil d'Etat, decisions

---

[17] It has been pointed out that in the Netherlands the status of Community law is largely acknowledged to be based not on the national Constitution but on the Community legal order itself—i.e. the ECJ's unitary or monist conception is accepted: see L. Besselink, 'Curing a "Childhood Sickness"'? On Direct Effect, Internal Effect, Primacy and Derogation from Civil Rights' (1996) 3 *MJ* 165 and M. Claes and B. de Witte, n. 119 below.

[18] Case C–376/98, *Germany* v. *Parliament and Council* [2000] ECR I–8419.

[19] For a number of books containing surveys of certain national perspectives on the questions of sovereignty and supremacy see A. Slaughter, A. Stone Sweet, and J. Weiler (eds.), *The ECJ and National Courts: Doctrine and Jurisprudence* (Hart, 1998); K. Alter, *Establishing the Supremacy of European Law: The Making of an International Rule of Law in Europe* (Oxford University Press, 2001); and N. Walker (ed.), *Sovereignty in Transition* (Hart, 2003).

[20] Decision of 24 May 1975 in *Administration des Douanes* v. *Société 'Cafés Jacques Vabre' et SARL Weigel et Cie* [1975] 2 CMLR 336.

[21] See D. Pollard (1990) 15 *ELRev.* 267, 268–70 and 'European Community Law and the French Conseil d'Etat' (1992–5) 30 *Irish Jurist* 79.

[22] Decision of 1 Mar. 1968 in *Syndicat Général de Fabricants de Semoules de France* [1970] CMLR 395.

on the constitutionality of legislation were for the Conseil Constitutionnel—the Constitutional Council—to make before the legislation was promulgated.

However, in the *Café Jacques Vabres* case in 1975, when faced with a conflict between Article 90 (ex Article 95) of the EC Treaty and a later provision of the French Customs Code, the Cour de Cassation took a different view of its jurisdiction. Following the suggestion of the Procureur Général, the Cour held that the question was not whether it could review the constitutionality of a French law. Instead, when a conflict existed between an 'internal law' and a properly ratified 'international act' which had thus entered the internal legal order, the Constitution itself accorded priority to the latter. Respect for the principle of the primacy of international treaties should not be left to the Conseil Constitutionnel to secure, since it was the duty of the ordinary courts before which such problems actually arose to do justice in the case. However, the Cour based its decision on Article 55 of the French Constitution, rather than adopting the *communautaire* or global approach which was urged by Procureur Général Adolphe Touffait, '*pour encourager les autres*', as it were:

It would be possible for you to give precedence to the application of Article 95 of the Rome Treaty over the subsequent statute by relying on Article 55 of our Constitution, but personally I would ask you not to mention it and instead to base your reasoning on the very nature of the legal order instituted by the Rome Treaty.

Indeed, so far as you restricted yourselves to deriving from Article 55 of our Constitution the primacy in the French internal system of Community law over national law you would be explaining and justifying that action as regards our country, but such reasoning would let it be accepted that it is on our Constitution and on it alone that depends the ranking of Community law in our internal legal system.

In doing so you would impliedly be supplying a far from negligible argument to the courts of the Member States which, lacking any affirmation in their constitutions of the primacy of the Treaty would be tempted to deduce therefrom the opposite solution, as the Italian Constitutional Court did in 1962 when it claimed that it was for internal constitutional law to fix the ranking of Community law in the internal order of each Member State.[23]

It was not until 1989, however, that the Conseil d'Etat finally abandoned its so-called 'splendid isolation' and decided, in its capacity as an electoral court, to adopt the same position as the Conseil Constitutionnel and the Cour de Cassation.[24]

Raoul Georges Nicolo
[1990] 1 CMLR 173

The applicants were French citizens who brought an action for the annulment of the European Parliament elections in France in 1989, on the ground that the right to vote and to stand had been

---

[23] N. 14 above, 363–4.

[24] Decision of 20 Oct. 1989 in *Nicolo*. It has been suggested that earlier decisions of the Conseil Constitutionnel, which indicated that it was for the other French courts to ensure that international treaties were applied, acted as a spur to the Conseil d'Etat to reverse its original position. See P. Oliver, 'The French Constitution and the Treaty of Maastricht' (1994) 43 *ICLQ* 1, 10.

given to French citizens in the non-European overseas departments and territories of France. It was argued that the French statutory rule under challenge—Act 77–729—was contrary to the EEC Treaty.

COMMISSAIRE FRYDMAN[25]

However, the whole difficulty is then to decide whether, in conformity with your settled case law, you should dismiss this second argument by relying on the 1977 Act alone, without even having to verify whether it is compatible with the Treaty of Rome, or whether you should break fresh ground today by deciding that the Act is applicable only because it is compatible precisely with the Treaty.

In this connection we know that you held, in the famous divisional decision of 1 March 1968, *Syndicat Général des Fabricants de Semoules de France* that an administrative court cannot accord treaties precedence over subsequent legislation which conflicts with them and that this case law applies to Community rules just as much as to ordinary international conventions. . . .

The theoretical foundation of these decisions, which clearly does not take the form of an objection to the principle of the superiority of treaties over statutes, which is expressly stated by Article 55, should rather be sought in your wish to uphold the principle that it is not for the administrative courts to review the validity of legislation. . . .

On the other hand I believe it is possible to take the view that . . . Article 55 of itself necessarily enables the courts, by implication, to review the compatibility of statutes with treaties. Indeed, we must attribute to the authors of the Constitution an intention to provide for actual implementation of the supremacy of treaties which they embodied in that provision. . . .

On this basis, therefore, I propose that you should agree to give treaties precedence over later statutes.

. . . I am aware that the Court of Justice of the European Communities—which, as we know, gives the Community law absolute supremacy over the rules of national law, even if they are constitutional—has not hesitated for its part to affirm the obligation to refuse to apply in any situation laws which are contrary to Community measures.

I do not think you can follow the European Court in this judge-made law which, in truth, seems to me at least open to objection. Were you to do so, you would tie yourself to a supranational way of thinking which is quite difficult to justify, to which the Treaty of Rome does not subscribe expressly and which would quite certainly render the Treaty unconstitutional, however it may be regarded in the political context. . . .

I therefore suggest that you should base your decision on Article 55 of the Constitution and extend its ambit to all international agreements.

Although it did not expressly adopt the view expressed by the Commissaire, the Conseil d'Etat appeared to accept the premises on which that view was based. It ruled that the French statutory rules were not invalid on the ground that they were 'not incompatible with the clear stipulations of the abovementioned Article 227(1) of the Treaty of Rome'.

[25] [1990] 1 CMLR 173, 177, 178.

D. Pollard, The Conseil d'Etat is European—Official[26]

The *Semoules* decision and subsequent case law resulted in treaties repudiated by subsequent statutes having no force within the French internal legal system while at the same time continuing to bind France on the international legal plane; the existence of two lines of case law, one by the Conseil d'Etat and one by the Cour de Cassation, led to absurd practical consequences for the citizen and there was no logic in one jurisdiction applying the treaty and one the statute; . . .

The [Nicolo] decision's legal basis is significant. The Conseil d'Etat could have rejected M. Nicolo's action simply on the combination of the electoral statute and Articles 2 and 72 of the Constitution. In one sense it was unnecessary to invoke the compatibility of the electoral statute with the EEC Treaty.

It should be noted, however, that *Commissaire* Frydman discouraged the Conseil d'Etat from subscribing entirely to the 'supranational way of thinking' of the ECJ. *Nicolo* did not represent an unqualified acceptance by the Conseil d'Etat of the supremacy of EC law on the Court's terms. Instead the ruling rests on the interpretation of Article 55 of the French Constitution, which provides for the superiority of international treaties over national law. The Conseil d'Etat has also, since *Nicolo*, recognized the primacy of both Community regulations and directives over French statutes, without discussing the theoretical basis for that supremacy,[27] but it has not recognized the primacy of EC law over the Constitution itself.[28]

The French Constitution was amended in 1992, pursuant to a decision of the Conseil Constitutionnel, in order to give effect to changes made by the Maastricht Treaty, and this resulted in the insertion of Article 88–3 into the Constitution concerning the right to vote and stand in municipal elections. In 1999 the Constitution was again revised, once again pursuant to a decision of the Conseil Constitutionnel, in order to facilitate ratification of the Amsterdam Treaty.[29] According to the Conseil, in order for the transfer of competences required by ratification of the Maastricht and Amsterdam Treaties to be compatible with the French Constitution, the 'essential

---

[26] Pollard, n. 21 above, 271, 273–4.

[27] See *Boisdet* [1991] 1 CMLR 3, on a reg. which was adopted after the French law, and *Rothmans and Philip Morris* and *Arizona Tobacco and Philip Morris* [1993] 1 CMLR 253 on a dir. adopted before the French law. For comment on *Boisdet* see H. Cohen, (1991) 16 *ELRev.* 144. See also P. Roseren, 'The Application of Community Law by French Courts From 1982 to 1993' (1994) 31 *CMLRev.* 315, 342, who argues that Art. 55 cannot explain the primacy of Community *secondary* legislation over French law in cases such as *Boisdet* and *Rothmans*.

[28] In *Sarran and Levacher*, Decision of 30 Oct. 1998 the Conseil d'Etat declared that Art. 55 does not give international treaties a position of precedence over the Constitution itself or over provisions of a constitutional nature. Although the case did not concern EC law, see the discussion of its implications for the relationship between EC law and French *constitutional* law by C. Richards, 'Sarran et Levacher: Ranking Legal Norms in the French Republic' (2000) 25 *ELRev.* 192. The Cour de Cassation gave a similar ruling in the *Fraisse* case on 2 June 2000: for discussion of both cases see V. Kronenberger 'A New Approach to the Interpretation of the French Constitution in Respect of International Conventions' (2000) 47 *NILR* 323.

[29] For discussion of both the substance and the procedure of this constitutional revision, including the decision not to put the matter to a popular referendum following the near crisis over the narrow referendum result on the Maastricht Treaty see S. Millns, 'The Treaty of Amsterdam and the Constitutional Revision in France' (1999) 5 *EPL* 61.

conditions for the exercise of national sovereignty' must not be affected.[30] Following the Maastricht Treaty amendment to the Constitution in 1992, the Conseil Constitutionnel had also indicated that French law would also have to comply not only with the EC Treaty but also with secondary EC law implementing the Treaty voting rights. Therefore, although the Constitutional Council will not normally review the conformity of French legislation with treaties since this is a function of the ordinary and administrative courts under Article 55 of the Constitution, it did so exceptionally in a 1998 case in which it declared that the French organic law on voting, in order to be considered in conformity with Article 88–3 of the Constitution, would also have to conform to Article 18 (ex Article 8(b)) EC and to the relevant EC Directive.[31]

SUMMARY

i. The caution displayed for many years by the French Conseil d'Etat concerning the supremacy of Community law is mirrored in the case law of other States.

ii. The ECJ's view that national law can never take precedence over directly effective EC law due to the transfer of sovereignty made by the Member States is not unconditionally accepted by Member State courts, which recognize the primacy of Community law 'not by virtue of the inherent nature of Community law as the Court of Justice would have it, but under the authority of their own national legal order'.[32]

iii. In France, the main obstacle to the recognition of supremacy of EC law has been the jurisdictional limitation of the French courts under the Constitution, rather than, as in other Member States, difficulties concerning the fundamental constitutional status of the norms which appeared to conflict with Community law.

(b) GERMANY

Article 24 of the German Constitution allows for the transfer of legislative power to international organizations, but the question raised in the following case was whether Article 24 permitted the transfer, to an organization outside the German constitutional structure such as the European Community, of a power to contravene certain basic principles protected under the Constitution itself.

---

[30] The criteria for determining what these essential conditions may be, however, remain unclear. For further discussion see A. Bonnie, 'The Constitutionality of Transfers of Sovereignty: The French Approach' (1998) 4 *EPL* 517. See also J. Plötner, 'Report on France' in Slaughter *et al.*, n. 19 above.

[31] Decision no. 98–400 of 20 May 1998. For further discussion see S. Wright, 'The French Conseil Constitutionnel: International Concerns' (2000) 5 *EPL* 199.

[32] See B. De Witte, 'Community Law and National Constitutional Values' (1991) 2 *LIEI* 1, 4 and also 'Direct Effect, Supremacy and the Nature of the Legal Order', in P. Craig and G. de Búrca (eds.), *The Evolution of EU Law* (Oxford University Press, 1999).

Internationale Handelsgesellschaft mbH v. Einfuhr- und Vorratstelle für
Getreide und Futtermittel
[1972] CMLR 177

The facts are those as set out in Case 11/70 before the European Court of Justice.[33] On receiving
the ECJ's ruling in that case, the German Administrative Court decided as follows.

VERWALTUNGSGERICHT (Administrative Court)[34]

This Chamber agrees with those who wish to test Community law against the fundamental
principles of the Constitution, since a critical appraisal of the views set out above shows that the
view that Community law takes precedence cannot be based on any legal foundation. The integration powers contained in Article 24 enable the Federal legislature to alienate its legislative
monopoly in certain spheres in favour of international institutions. The Community organs have
thereby obtained the power to enact law directly effective within the territorial scope of the
Constitution without a separate writ of enforcement. However, since the effect of Article 24
cannot be equated with an amendment of the Constitution the Federal legislature could not, when
ratifying the EEC Treaty, disclaim the observance of elementary basic rights in the Constitution,
within the scope of Article 24.

. . .

[I]f Community law . . . is given precedence over any divergent constitutional provisions, and
this European legal system is exempt from the obligations contained in Articles 19(2) and 79(3)
of the Constitution, it would lead to a constitutional and legal vacuum. For constitutional law
would be eliminated as the highest national check on a European legislation that is becoming
increasingly more expansive without the institution of equivalent legal safeguards. The democratic
constitutional state guaranteed by the Constitution will itself only be able with difficulty to remain
faithful to its basic decisions in constitutional law if as a result of particular advancing integration
processes crucial spheres are withdrawn from its jurisdiction and, with the constant decline in the
standing of the national legislature, placed under a supranational 'purely executive regime' which
does not have to observe the fundamental principles laid down in Articles 19(2) and 79(3) of the
Constitution in its measures.

A number of concerns were expressed by the Administrative Court here. First, it
was concerned that the German State would be deemed by Community law to have
transferred greater powers to the Community than it was constitutionally permitted
to exercise, let alone to transfer. Secondly it was concerned that the continuing
integration process might gradually withdraw crucial spheres of competence from
national jurisdiction, simultaneously empowering a supranational executive which
was not bound by the fundamental guarantees of the German Constitution. Consequently the Administrative Court ruled, in the face of the ECJ's conflicting
judgment, that the Community's deposit system breached basic principles of German
constitutional law, and it requested a ruling on the matter from the Federal

---

[33] See n. 8 above and text.   [34] [1972] CMLR 177, 184.

Constitutional Court, the Bundesverfassungsgericht (BVerfG). This judgment, known as the 'Solange I' decision, was given by the BVerfG in 1974:[35]

Article 24 of the Constitution deals with the transfer of sovereign rights to inter-state institutions. This . . . does not open the way to amending the basic structure of the Constitution, which forms the basis of its identity, without a formal amendment to the Constitution, that is, it does not open any such way through the legislation of the inter-state institution. Certainly, the competent Community organs can make law which the competent German constitutional organs could not make under the law of the Constitution and which is none the less valid and is to be applied directly in the Federal Republic of Germany. But Article 24 of the Constitution limits this possibility in that it nullifies any amendment of the Treaty which would destroy the identity of the valid constitutional structure of the Federal Republic of Germany by encroaching on the structures which go to make it up. . . .

The part of the Constitution dealing with fundamental rights is an inalienable essential feature of the valid Constitution of the Federal Republic of Germany and one which forms part of the constitutional structure of the Constitution. Article 24 of the Constitution does not without reservation allow it to be subjected to qualifications. In this, the present state of integration of the Community is of crucial importance. The Community still lacks a democratically legitimated Parliament directly elected by general suffrage which possesses legislative powers and to which the Community organs empowered to legislate are fully responsible on a political level. It still lacks in particular a codified catalogue of fundamental rights, the substance of which is reliably and unambiguously fixed for the future in the same way as the substance of the Constitution. . . .

Provisionally, therefore, in the hypothetical case of a conflict between Community law and . . . the guarantees of fundamental rights in the Constitution . . . the guarantee of fundamental rights in the Constitution prevails as long as the competent organs of the Community have not removed the conflict of norms in accordance with the Treaty mechanism.

This refusal by the highest German court to recognize the unconditional supremacy of Community law challenged the smooth development by the ECJ of the relationship between national law and Community law and of its own relationship with national courts. The major objection of the BVerfG to recognizing the supremacy of Community law was not just, as in the case of the French Conseil d'Etat, a jurisdictional concern, but a concern over the possible impact of EC law on basic rights enshrined in the German Constitution. For this reason it ruled that Article 24 of the Constitution could not cover a transfer of power to amend an 'inalienable essential feature' of the German constitutional structure, such as its protection for fundamental rights. The BVerfG would not abandon its jurisdiction to decide which legislative transfers would purport to alter an unalterable feature of the Constitution, and the protection of fundamental rights in the German Constitution would prevail over Community law in the event of conflict.

By 1986, however, in a case in which an EC import licensing system was challenged despite an ECJ ruling on its validity,[36] the BVerfG delivered its so-called *Solange II* judgment which qualified the 1974 *Solange I* judgment to a considerable extent. Literally translated, Solange means the 'so long as' case, and it refers to the statement of the BVerfG that so long as the Community had not removed the possible 'conflict

---

[35] [1974] 2 CMLR 540, 549–50.
[36] See Case 345/82, *Wünsche Handelsgesellschaft v. Germany* [1984] ECR 1995.

of norms' between provisions of Community law and national constitutional rights, the German court would ensure that those rights took precedence. Having considered various changes in Community law since the 1974 decision, however, including the ECJ's development of a doctrine of protection for fundamental rights, the adoption of various declarations on rights and democracy by the Community institutions,[37] and the fact that all EC Member States had acceded to the European Convention on Human Rights, the BVerfG in *Solange II* ruled:[38]

In view of these developments, it must be held that, *so long as* the European Communities, and in particular the case law of the European Court, generally ensure an effective protection of fundamental rights as against the sovereign powers of the Communities which is to be regarded as substantially similar to the protection of fundamental rights required unconditionally by the Constitution, and in so far as they generally safeguard the essential content of fundamental rights, the Federal Constitutional Court will no longer exercise its jurisdiction to decide on the applicability of secondary Community legislation cited as the legal basis for any acts of German courts or authorities within the sovereign jurisdiction of the Federal Republic of Germany, and it will no longer review such legislation by the standard of the fundamental rights contained in the Constitution.

J. Frowein, Solange II[39]

As the Court points out, its finding leads to the result that the Federal Constitutional Court will no longer exercise jurisdiction over the applicability of secondary Community law in the Federal Republic of Germany and will no longer control such law on the basis of the fundamental rights in the basic law. It is clear that the Federal Constitutional Court did not give up its jurisdiction or come to the conclusion that no such jurisdiction exists. It only states that it will not exercise the jurisdiction as long as the present conditions as to the protection of fundamental rights by the European Court of Justice prevail.

. . . It seems doubtful whether one should not accept the great wisdom which exists in constructing a rather careful balance with eventual safeguards on the national level. There is no dispute under British constitutional law that the House of Commons could, by an Act of Parliament, immediately stop the applicability of European Community law on British soil. The Italian Constitutional Court has reserved a final position for extreme cases. Under German law the legislature cannot intervene in Community matters because of the acceptance of the priority of Community law. The Federal Constitutional Court wanted to preserve its final authority to intervene where real problems concerning the protection of fundamental rights in Community law could arise. As long as the Community system has not developed into a federal structure, questions of sovereignty or final priority as to sources of law have to be kept in suspense.[40]

The most dramatic stage in the story, however, came with the so-called 'Maastricht judgment' of the BVerfG, when the constitutionality of the State's ratification of the

---

[37] See Ch. 8.

[38] *Re Wünsche Handelsgesellschaft*, Decision of 22 Oct. 1986, [1987] 3 CMLR 225, 265.

[39] (1988) 25 *CMLRev.* 201, 203–4. See also W. Roth, 'The Application of Community law in West Germany: 1980–1990' (1991) 28 *CMLRev.* 137.

[40] See further the cases discussed by Roth, *ibid.*, 144–5.

Treaty on European Union was challenged. Germany had completed the legislative part of the TEU ratification process in 1992, amending its Constitution, but before the Federal President signed the formal instrument of ratification, constitutional complaints were made to the BVerfG. That Court decided in 1993 that ratification was compatible with the Constitution and it ruled not just on Germany's constitutional competence at that time to ratify the Treaty, but also on what the future position would be if the Community attempted to exercise powers which were not clearly provided for in the Treaties.[41] The judgment is a fascinating and highly political one which provoked a great deal of comment.[42] Affirming the sovereignty of the German State, the Constitutional Court made clear that it would not relinquish its power to decide on the compatibility of Community law with the fundamentals of the German Constitution and would continue to exercise a power of review over the scope of Community competence.

Brunner v. The European Union Treaty
[1994] 1 CMLR 57

THE FEDERAL CONSTITUTIONAL COURT

13. . . . The Federal Constitutional Court by its jurisdiction guarantees that an effective protection of basic rights for the inhabitants of Germany will also generally be maintained as against the sovereign powers of the Communities and will be accorded the same respect as the protection of basic rights acquired unconditionally by the Constitution, and in particular the Court provides a general safeguard of the essential content of the basic rights. The Court thus guarantees this essential content as against the sovereign powers of the Community as well. . . .

48. There is . . . a breach of Article 38 of the Constitution if an Act that opens up the German legal system to the direct validity and application of the law of the (supranational) European Communities does not establish with sufficient certainty the intended programme of integration. If it is not clear to what extent and degree the German legislature has assented to the transfer of the exercise of sovereign powers, then it will be possible for the European Community to claim functions and powers that were not specified. That would be equivalent to a general enablement and would therefore be a surrender of powers, something against which Article 38 of the Constitution provides protection.

. . .

---

[41] In a ruling which may well have been inspired partly by the warning contained in para. 99 of the *Maastricht* decision, the ECJ at para. 30 of its *Opinion 2/94 on accession of the EC to the ECHR* [1996] ECR I–1759, declared that 'Article 235 cannot be used as a basis for the adoption of provisions whose effect would, in substance, be to amend the Treaty without following the procedure which it provides for that purpose'.

[42] For some of the English-language commentaries see M. Herdegen, 'Maastricht and the German Constitutional Court: Constitutional Restraints for an Ever Closer Union' (1994) 31 *CMLRev.* 235; U. Everling, 'The Maastricht Judgment of the German Federal Constitutional Court and its Significance for the Development of the European Union' (1994) 14 *YBEL* 1; M. Zulegg, 'The European Constitution under Constitutional Constraints: The German Scenario' (1997) 22 *ELRev.* 19; J.H.H. Weiler, 'Does Europe Need a Constitution? Reflections on Demos, Telos and the German Maastricht Decision' (1995) 1 *ELJ* 219; N. MacCormick, 'The Maastricht-Urteil: Sovereignty Now' (1995) 1 *ELJ* 259; J. Kokott, 'German Constitutional Jurisprudence and European Integration' (1996) 2 *EPL* 237 and 413.

55. The Federal Republic of Germany, therefore, even after the Union Treaty comes into force, will remain a member of a federation of States, the common authority of which is derived from the Member States and can only have binding effects within the German sovereign sphere by virtue of the German instruction that its law be applied. Germany is one of the 'Masters of the Treaties' which have established their adherence to the Union Treaty concluded 'for an unlimited period' with the intention of long-term membership, but could ultimately revoke that adherence by a contrary act. The validity and application of European law in Germany depends on the application-of-law instruction of the Accession Act. Germany thus preserves the quality of a sovereign state in its own right.

. . .

99. Inasmuch as the Treaties establishing the European Communities, on the one hand, confer sovereign rights applicable to limited factual circumstances and, on the other hand, provide for Treaty amendments . . . this distinction is also important for the future treatment of the individual powers. Whereas a dynamic extension of the existing Treaties has so far been supported on the basis of an open-handed treatment of Article 235 of the EEC Treaty as a 'competence to round off the Treaty' as a whole, and on the basis of considerations relating to the 'implied powers' of the Communities, and of Treaty interpretation as allowing maximum exploitation of Community powers (*effet utile*), in future it will have to be noted as regards interpretation of enabling provisions by Community institutions and agencies that the Union Treaty as a matter of principle distinguishes between the exercise of a sovereign power conferred for limited purposes and the amending of the Treaty, so that its interpretation may not have effects that are equivalent to an extension of the Treaty. Such an interpretation of enabling rules would not produce any binding effects for Germany.

This was a long and powerful judgment, which provided a warning to the Community institutions and the ECJ that Germany's acceptance of the supremacy of Community law is conditional. In particular, the BVerfG emphasized its intention to ensure that the Community does not stray beyond the powers expressly conferred upon it in the Treaties by the Member States. Even if German courts have accepted that, within its proper sphere of application, Community law should be given precedence over national law, the BVerfG asserted its jurisdiction to review the actions of European 'institutions and agencies'—which presumably includes the Court—to ensure first that they remain within the limits of their powers (*ultra vires* control) and secondly do not transgress the basic constitutional rights of German inhabitants.

In addition to its ruling on the need for adequate delimitation and predictability of the powers transferred, some of the more contentious aspects of the judgment concerned the BVerfG's comments about the nature of national democracy, and about the need for national democratic legitimation to express the 'spiritual, social and political' homogeneity of a people.[43] However, other sections of the judgment appear more open to the possibility that the EU could develop the conditions of political openness and the 'free interaction of social forces, interests and ideas' necessary for full democratic legitimation,[44] so that, presumably, a wider range of powers and competences

---

[43] See in particular paras. 44–46 of the judgment, and the comments of Weiler about the *volkish* nature of this view of the demos, n. 42 above.

[44] Paras 41–42.

could be transferred by Germany to the EU without breaching the basic principle of democracy guaranteed by the Constitution.

Since the drama of the Maastricht decision, some more concrete challenges to the supremacy of EC law and to the rulings of the ECJ arose before the German courts in a lengthy, contentious, and much-litigated dispute over the Community's banana import regime.[45] The ECJ dismissed an action brought by Germany for the annulment of Council Regulation 404/93,[46] which established a common organization of the banana market and gave preferential treatment to ACP producers over the Central American producers,[47] from whom German importers traditionally obtained supplies of bananas at reduced tariff rates. The ECJ rejected the argument that the Regulation violated the principles of non-discrimination and proportionality as well as fundamental EC law rights to trade and to property, or that it had illegally infringed provisions of the GATT.[48] The judgment prompted a further spate of litigation in the German administrative and tax courts,[49] in which importers argued, notwithstanding the ECJ ruling, that the Regulation infringed their constitutional rights to private property and breached provisions of the GATT, which as a prior international obligation should take primacy over Community law under Article 307 (ex Article 234) of the Treaty. The Federal Tax Court in 1996 upheld a regional court decision granting interim relief to banana importers against the customs authorities, and, relying on the BVerfG's *Maastricht* judgment, ruled that the European banana regime may violate the GATT and the WTO Agreement and that German courts must not apply *ultra vires* acts of the Community.[50]

In the meantime, the regional tax court which had granted interim relief referred the case back to the ECJ to rule again on the substantive questions.[51] One of the main questions again concerned the compatibility of provisions of the GATT with Council Regulation 404/93, the very question on which the ECJ had already ruled in the action brought by Germany. The case raised the question of the primacy of international

[45] For discussion see U. Everling, 'Will Europe Slip on Bananas? The Bananas Judgment of the Court of Justice and National Courts' (1996) 33 *CMLRev.* 401; N. Reich, 'Judge-made Europe à la Carte' (1996) 7 *EJIL* 103.

[46] Case C–280/93, *Germany* v. *Commission* [1994] ECR I–4873. This decision was confirmed in a preliminary ruling in Case C–466/93, *Atlanta Fruchthandelsgesellschaft* v. *Bundesamt für Ernährung* [1995] ECR I–3799, and in the accompanying Case C–465/93, the ECJ ruled on the capacity of the national court to give interim relief pending a decision on the validity of the Reg.: see [1995] ECR I–3761.

[47] The EC had a longstanding development policy in relation to the African-Caribbean-Pacific (ACP) States under the terms of the Lomé Convention.

[48] See Ch. 5, nn. 47–58 and text for the ECJ's ruling that GATT provisions were not directly effective, nor could they be pleaded as grounds for the annulment of Community acts since they were not intended by the Community to have such effect.

[49] For an account of the litigation which, apart from the many proceedings before German courts, led to numerous direct actions and preliminary references before the ECJ and the CFI see U. Everling, 'Will Europe Slip on Bananas? The Bananas Judgment of the Court of Justice and National Courts' (1996) 33 *CMLRev.* 401. Germany also sought in different ways to challenge the EC's conclusion of the framework agreement on bananas within the WTO agreement: see *Opinion 3/94* of the ECJ [1995] ECR I–4577, and Case C–122/95, *Germany* v. *Council* [1998] ECR I–973 in which the ECJ annulled part of the Council's decision concluding this agreement for violation of the non-discrimination principle.

[50] Order of the Federal Tax Court, 9 Jan. 1996, 7 *EuZW* 126 (1996). For a very critical comment see Reich, n. 54 below,

[51] Cases C–364 & 365/95, *T. Port GmbH* v. *Hauptzollamt Hamburg-Jonas* [1998] ECR I–1023 and see also the unsuccessful direct actions in Cases T–2/99, *T. Port* v. *Council* [2001] ECR II–2093, paras. 73–85 and T–3/99, *Bananatrading* v. *Council* [2001] ECR II–2093.

trade law over Community law under Article 307 (ex Article 234) EC as well as the legality under Community law of a national court's grant of interim relief against a Community measure in circumstances where the ECJ has already upheld the legality of that measure. The ECJ dismissed the argument based on Article 234 (now Article 307) and declined to rule on the direct effect of GATT, but it did partly annul Regulation 478/95, which supplemented Regulation 404/93, for violation of the non-discrimination principle. A number of German commentators cautioned against the judicial defiance shown by the German courts, in particular the judgment of the Federal Tax Court, and warned against the effect it could have in stimulating other national constitutional courts to similar defiance,[52] although virtually all have been sharply critical of the Community's banana regime.[53]

N. Reich, Judge-made 'Europe à la carte': Some Remarks on Recent Conflicts between European and German Constitutional law Provoked by the Banana Litigation[54]

[Note ToA renumbering: Arts. 164 and 234 are now Arts. 220 and 307 respectively]

The judgment, if other jurisdictions follow suit, could encourage Member States to proclaim supremacy of their specific theories on fundamental rights and on the relationship between international and European law over Community action. The idea of fundamental rights protection risks being transformed into a tool for the protection of the property rights of special groups, whose interests take priority over 'the objectives of general interest pursued by the Community'. The control of Community jurisdiction by the ECJ under its general mandate of Article 164, namely to guarantee the observance of 'the law' would be seriously impaired if national courts could install a parallel jurisdiction controlling the legality of Community acts under fundamental rights theory or international law according to Article 234.

At the same time as the litigation in the tax courts was ongoing, the Frankfurt Administrative Court which had made the preliminary reference on the question of interim relief was dissatisfied with the ECJ's response,[55] and referred the case to the Federal Constitutional Court, taking the view that the intereferences with the right to pursue a trade and the right to property were disproportionate and fell below the level of protection guaranteed by the German Constitution. A full four years later, the BverfG finally gave its ruling and deemed the reference inadmissible.[56] The Constitutional Court stated that it had already declared itself satisfied, in its *Solange II* and

---

[52] See Everling, n. 45 above to the effect that 'chaotic consequences would ensue if national courts decided on the application of Community law according to their own criteria'.

[53] See also C. Schmid, 'All Bark and No Bite: Notes on the Federal Constitutional Court's "Banana Decision"' (2001) 7 *ELJ* 95.

[54] (1996) 7 *EJIL* 103, 110–11.

[55] See Cases C–465 & 466/93, n. 46 above.

[56] Decision of 7 June 2000. For commentaries see A. Peters, 'The Bananas Decision 2000 of the German Federal Constitutional Court: Towards Reconciliation with the ECJ as regards Fundamental Rights Protection in Europe' (2000) 43 *German Yearbook of International Law* 276; Schmid n. 53 above; F. Hoffmeister (2001) 38 *CMLRev.* 791; M. Aziz, 'Sovereignty Lost, Sovereignty Regained: the European Integration Project and the BVerfG', Robert Schuman Centre Working Paper, EUI 2001/31.

Maastricht decisions, with the fact that human rights protection within the EC legal order was generally comparable to the level of human rights protection under the German Basic law. Consequently, referrals and constitutional complaints attacking secondary Community law on the basis of German fundamental rights would be inadmissible *ab initio* if they did not argue that the general level of European human rights protection, including ECJ case law since *Solange II*, fell below the necessary level, on the basis of a comparison with German levels of protection. The Frankfurt court in this case had not pointed to any general decline in the standards of EC human rights protection since *Solange*.[57]

To sum up first the more particular banana saga: the legal challenges to the EC's contested import regime finally met with some success when the WTO dispute settlement body ruled in 1997 that the regime violated provisions of the WTO Agreement. The EU legislature eventually amended the contested measures,[58] and although the ECJ has consistently refused to rule that the provisions of the GATT/ WTO were directly effective or could have primacy over EC law,[59] part of the related Community banana regime was nevertheless subsequently annulled by the Court on more limited grounds of discrimination.[60]

As far as the broader question of the continuing relationship between German constitutional law and EU law is concerned, and between the Bundesverfassungs- gericht and the ECJ in particular, the June 2000 decision of the Bundesverfas- sungsgericht has been hailed as evidence of a renewed co-operative relationship between the two courts,[61] and as an indication that the threat to the supremacy of EC law posed by the terms of the Maastricht judgment has subsided. Some consider that the Maastricht ruling has in effect been partly repealed and the '*ultra vires*' aspect of that judgment abandoned.[62] One commentator, looking at the bananas decision together with another recent decision of the BVerfG in a case concerning an alleged violation of legitimate expectations following a ruling of the ECJ in the state aid context, suggests that the BVerfG has erected such high hurdles that 'it has become very improbable that the Constitutional Court will exercise its reserve control',[63] or its 'subsidiary emergency jurisdiction'[64] over the compatibility of EC law with the German constitution. Others have been more sharply critical of the BVerfG's failure to articulate a proper test for what the required general guarantee of fundamental rights is, and regret the reduction of the Bundesverfassungsgericht's power of review in this

---

[57] The BVerfG also ruled that the Frankfurt court had not taken into account the ruling of the ECJ in Case C–68/95, T. Port [1996] ECR I–6055, in which the Court had required the Commission to take the necessary transitional measures to provide for cases of serious hardship for companies affected by the new banana regime. For criticism of this and other aspects of the Constitutional Court's judgment, see Schmid, n. 53 above.

[58] See Reg. 216/2001 and 2587/2001, amending Reg. 404/93, [2001] OJ L31/2 and L345/13.

[59] See in further detail Ch. 5, 196–200.

[60] See Cases C–122/95, n. 49 above, and C–364 & 365/95, n. 51 above.

[61] Albeit a co-operative relationship over which the BVerfG seeks to retain a degree of control: see Aziz, n. 56 above.

[62] U. Elbers and N. Urban, 'The Order of the German Federal Constitutional Court of 7 June 2000 and the Kompetenz-Kompetenz in the European Judicial System' (2001) 7 *EPL* 21, 32.

[63] F. Hoffmeister (2001) 38 *CMLRev.* 791, commenting also on the *Alcan* decision of the BVerfG on 17 Feb. 2000, (2000) *EuZW* 445.

[64] Peters, n. 56 above 281.

context 'to a largely symbolic political significance'.[65] What is clear, however, is that direct conflict in a concrete case between the ECJ and the BVerfG has been successfully avoided, and that, at least for the present, the Constitutional Court has greatly reduced the likelihood of a serious judicial challenge to the supremacy of EC law in Germany.[66]

(c) ITALY

Article 11 of the Italian Constitution permits such limitations of sovereignty as are necessary to an organization which ensures peace and justice between nations. This has formed the basis for the Italian courts' acceptance of the supremacy of Community law, although, as in the case of other Member States, this acceptance has not been unconditional.

Frontini v. Ministero delle Finanze
[1974] 2 CMLR 372

The plaintiff was a trader who brought proceedings to challenge the applicability of increased agricultural levies, which had been imposed by EC Regulation, on the import of meat into Italy. Frontini argued that the Regulation was inapplicable in Italy, and the case was transmitted to the Italian Constitutional Court to determine the constitutional legitimacy of the Italian EEC Treaty Ratification Act 1957. That Act made Article 249 (ex Article 189) of the EEC Treaty, providing for the direct applicability of Community regulations, effective in Italy.

THE COURT[67]

The EEC Treaty Ratification Act 1957, whereby the Italian Parliament gave full and complete execution to the Treaty instituting the EEC, has a sure basis of validity in Article 11 of the Constitution whereby Italy 'consents, on condition of reciprocity with other states, to limitations of sovereignty necessary for an arrangement which may ensure peace and justice between the nations' and then 'promotes and favours the international organizations directed to such an aim'. . . .

. . . It is hardly necessary to add that by Article 11 of the Constitution limitations of sovereignty are allowed solely for the purpose of the ends indicated therein, and it should therefore be excluded that such limitations of sovereignty, concretely laid out in the Rome Treaty, signed by countries whose systems are based on the principle of the rule of law and guarantee the essential liberties of citizens, can nevertheless give the organs of the EEC an unacceptable power to violate the fundamental principles of our constitutional order or the inalienable rights of man. And it is obvious that if ever Article 189 had to be given such an aberrant interpretation, in such a case the

---

[65] Schmid, n. 53 above, 106.

[66] For some other suggestions which have been made for addressing these deep questions of constitutional conflict see C. Schmid, 'From Pont d'Avignon to Ponte Vecchio: The Resolution of Constitutional Conflicts between the EU and the Member States through Principles of Public International Law' (1998) 18 *YBEL* 415 and M. Kumm, 'Who is the Final Arbiter of Constitutionality in Europe?' (1999) 36 *CMLRev.* 251.

[67] [1974] 2 CMLR 372, 384.

guarantee would always be assured that this Court would control the continuing compatibility of the Treaty with the above mentioned fundamental principles.

While accepting the direct effect of Community law and confirming Italy's constitutional competence to ratify the EC Treaties, the Constitutional Court in *Frontini* expressed similar reservations to those of the German BVerfG. In particular, although it accepted the effectiveness of Community law within its proper field of application, the Italian court confirmed that it would continue to review the exercise of power by the 'organs of the EEC' to ensure that there was no infringement of fundamental rights or of the basic principles of the Italian constitutional order.

Frontini was followed in 1984 by the case of *Granital*,[68] in which the Italian Constitutional Court accepted that, in order to give effect to the supremacy of Community law, Italian courts must be prepared where necessary to disregard conflicting national law and to apply Community law directly. However, this acceptance was subject to several reservations concerning the supremacy of Community law in Italy.

R. Petriccione, Italy: Supremacy of Community Law over National Law[69]

In *Granital* the Constitutional Court restates its firm belief that Community law and national law must be kept conceptually distinct. . . . Given the separation between the two legal systems, Community rules and national ones have separate fields of application, so that no problem of temporal order arises between them. Since the division of competence between Community institutions and the national legislature has been given a constitutional foundation, the result is that once a matter is governed by a Community regulation, that regulation alone applies as it must under Article 189 EEC. In this way there is no question of the abrogation, or nullity, of national law: it must simply be ignored, because the field in which it is supposed to operate has been preempted by the intervention of Community institutions, whose competence, in the areas provided for by the Treaty, prevails over that of the national legislature. The national provisions survive, and they still govern the subject-matter in all the aspects which are beyond the scope of the relevant Community act. . . .

However, the problems which the *Granital* case has left unsolved are of no little relevance. First, the Constitutional Court has reserved to itself not only the question of conflicts between Community provisions and basic constitutional principles or the inalienable rights of the human being, but also the question of national law which challenges the very division of competence established by the Treaties, on the grounds, obviously, that such a division draws constitutional force from Article 11 of the Constitution. Should this be the case, an ordinary judge is not allowed to disregard the national legislation but is bound to refer it to the Constitutional Court. More generally, this is a consequence of the markedly different approach to the issue of the supremacy of Community law adopted by the Court when contrasted with the view taken by the European Court: a difference which could still lead, in the future, to further conflicts.

---

[68] Dec. 170 of 8 June 1984 in *SpA Granital* v. *Amministrazione delle Finanze*. For an unofficial translation see G. Gaja (1984) 21 *CMLRev.* 756.

[69] (1986) 11 *ELRev.* 320.

Such a conflict was demonstrated in the case of *Fragd*,[70] in which the Italian Constitutional Court stated that even where the ECJ had upheld the validity under EC law of a Community measure, that measure would not be applied in Italy if it contravened a fundamental principle of the Italian Constitution concerning human rights protection.

G. Gaja, New Developments in a Continuing Story: The Relationship between EEC Law and Italian Law[71]

While the *Frontini* decision by the Constitutional Court has often been viewed as a significant example of the willingness on the part of national courts to subject EEC legislation to constitutional rules concerning the protection of fundamental rights, little has happened so far to justify this evaluation. . . .

In *Spa Fragd* v. *Amministrazione delle Finanze*, the Court examined whether a system, such as that applying to preliminary rulings on validity of Community acts, whereby a declaration of invalidity may not produce any effect in the proceedings before the referring court, is consistent with the constitutional principles on judicial protection . . . The Constitutional Court's main aim was to try and support the view that, as a matter of Community law, rulings should always have some effects in those proceedings. Possibly as a way of persuading the Court of Justice of the need to accept this solution, the Constitutional Court also viewed the problem from the perspective of the constitutional protection of fundamental rights. The Court said:

> If a judgment (by the Court of Justice) went as far as ruling out that the effects of a declaration of invalidity cover the act or acts which are the object of the dispute that led to the preliminary reference by the national court, serious doubts would arise about the consistency of the rule that allows this type of judgment with the essential elements of the right to judicial protection. . . .

> In substance, everyone's right to have a court and judicial proceedings for each dispute would be emptied of its essential content if, when a court doubts the validity of a rule which should be applied, the answer came from the court to whom the question has to be referred that the rule is in fact void, but that this should not be relevant for the dispute before the referring court, which should nevertheless apply the rule that is declared to be void.

> Contrary to the State Attorney's view, one could not invoke the primary need for the uniform application of Community law and for certainty of law against the possible violation of a fundamental right.

> . . .

Unlike *Frontini*, the *Fragd* decision shows that the Constitutional Court is willing to test the consistency of individual rules of Community law with the fundamental principles for the protection of human rights that are contained in the Italian Constitution. This significantly widens the way for the exercise by the Constitutional Court of a control which has hitherto been only theoretical.

---

[70] *Spa Fragd* v. *Amministrazione delle Finanze*, Dec. 232 of 21 Apr. 1989 (1989) 72 RDI.
[71] (1990) 27 *CMLRev.* 83, 93–4.

As Frowein observed above in his comment on the German *Solange II* case, while this does not accord with the ECJ's approach to the unconditional primacy of Community law, most national constitutional courts see the wisdom of maintaining, in the EU context, ultimate safeguards with regard to fundamental constitutional norms. Further, as Petriccione notes, the Italian Constitutional Court in *Granital* was prepared to adjudicate not simply on questions of conflict between specific Community measures and fundamental Italian constitutional rights, but also on the basic question of the division of competence between national law and Community law.[72] While we saw that the German Bundesverfassungsgericht in its 2000 bananas decision moved away somewhat from this aspect of its earlier Maastricht decision, the Italian Constitutional Court in *Fragd* was not prepared to accept the final word of the Community institutions or the ECJ on the question of competence. Further, the Constitutional Court in 1995 took a restrictive view of its own position as a national 'court or tribunal' for the purposes of making references to the ECJ under Article 234 (ex Article 177).[73] Similar and less direct challenges to the authority of the European Court to determine the applicability of EC law in a Member State are frequently made by higher national courts, which refuse to make references to the ECJ on particular points of law where it seems likely that EC law would lead to a conflict with national constitutional law which the domestic courts do not wish to countenance.[74] None the less, the Italian jurisprudence suggests a relatively smooth relationship—certainly in practice—between the two legal orders, while ultimate or residual constitutional control over the domestic applicability of EC law is in theory retained by the Italian judiciary.

(d) THE UNITED KINGDOM

The acceptance of the supremacy of Community law within the UK has not been unproblematic. Since the British Constitution is largely unwritten it is difficult to speak of 'amending' it. Constitutional conventions in UK law cannot be formally created, but rather evolve or emerge over time. No special mechanism exists for amending rules or conventions of a constitutional nature, in the way the written constitutions of other Member States have been amended, other than by an ordinary Act of Parliament. The central obstacle to acceptance by the UK of the supremacy of EC law is the fundamental constitutional principle of Parliamentary sovereignty, which in its traditional formulation holds that Parliament has the power to do

[72] See P. Ruggeri Laderchi, 'Report on Italy' in A. Slaughter *et al.*, n. 19 above, ch. 5, who points out the procedural problems for Italian courts wishing to exercise a form of *ultra vires* review of Community acts. See also on this point and on related questions A. Adinolfi, 'The Judicial Application of Community Law in Italy (1981–1997)' (1998) 35 *CMLRev.* 1313, 1314–25.

[73] See Constitutional Court order of 29 Dec. 1995, no. 536, discussed by Ruggeri Laderchi, *ibid.* at 167–8. For a reminder that national courts may also fail to apply Community law properly, even while not expressly challenging its supremacy, see A. Biondi, 'The Corte di Cassazione and the Proper Implementation of Community Law' (1996) 21 *ELRev.* 485.

[74] The Greek Council of State, in a ruling concerning recognition of degrees awarded by foreign educational establishments, refused to make a preliminary reference to the ECJ on grounds which were quite clearly contrary to EC law: see E. Maganaris, 'The Principle of Supremacy of Community law in Greece: From Direct Challenge to Non-application' (1999) 24 *ELRev.* 426.

anything other than to bind itself for the future.[75] A basic principle of this nature clearly made it very difficult, constitutionally, for the UK to transfer (on a permanent basis, according to the ECJ in *Costa* v. *ENEL* above) to the European Community institutions a sphere of exclusive legislative power.

Further, on its dualist approach to international law—which in contrast to a monist approach treats domestic law and international law as two different and separate systems of law—international treaties signed and ratified by the United Kingdom are not part of the domestic law of the UK. Consequently, in order to be enforceable and binding at the domestic level, such treaties must be domestically incorporated by an Act of Parliament. But the principle of absolute Parliamentary sovereignty then seems to make it very difficult for the supremacy of Community law over later Parliamentary legislation to be guaranteed, since the Act of Parliament which incorporates EC law and makes it domestically binding and enforceable seems vulnerable to any later Act of Parliament which contravenes or contradicts it. The traditional principle of Parliamentary sovereignty would not permit the earlier statute to constrain Parliament, which may wish to contradict its earlier measure in a later statute. According to the doctrine of implied repeal, the courts would be obliged to give effect to the latest expression of Parliament's legislative will and to treat the earlier Act as having been implicitly repealed.

It was nevertheless decided, after the EC Treaties were signed and ratified by the UK in 1972, to give internal legal effect to Community law by means of an Act of Parliament: the European Communities Act 1972. The central provision of the Act is section 2(1), which provides:

All such rights, powers, liabilities, obligations and restrictions from time to time created or arising by or under the Treaties, and all such remedies and procedures from time to time provided for by or under the Treaties, as in accordance with the Treaties are without further enactment to be given legal effect or used in the United Kingdom shall be recognised and available in law, and be enforced, allowed and followed accordingly; and the expression 'enforceable Community right' and similar expressions shall be read as referring to one to which this subsection applies.

Section 2(2) provides for the implementation of Community obligations—even when they are intended to replace national legislation and Acts of Parliament—by means of Order in Council or statutory instrument rather than by primary legislation only. Section 2(4) then provides:

The provision that may be made under subsection (2) above includes, subject to Schedule 2 to this Act, any such provision (of any such extent) as might be made by Act of Parliament, and any enactment passed or to be passed, other than one contained in this Part of this Act, shall be construed and have effect subject to the foregoing provisions of this section; . . .

The Schedule to which the provision refers sets out a number of powers—such as increasing taxation or legislating retroactively—which cannot be exercised by Order

---

[75] For a discussion of the meaning of Parliamentary sovereignty see P. P. Craig, 'United Kingdom Sovereignty after *Factortame*' (1991) 11 *YBEL* 221, and, for a more recent overview of the effects of EU membership on UK constitutional law, 'Britain in the European Union' in J. Jowell and D. Oliver (eds.), *The Changing Constitution* (Oxford University Press, 4th edn., 2000), ch. 3.

in Council or by delegated legislation, even if they are necessary to comply with a Community obligation. For these powers it seems an Act of Parliament will be needed. But the part of section 2(4) which has received most attention is the clause beginning 'any enactment passed or to be passed', which became prominent when the courts sought a way to reconcile new obligations under Community law with the traditional approach to statutory interpretation.

Section 3 of the Act then provides:

For the purposes of all legal proceedings any question as to the meaning or effect of any of the Treaties, or as to the validity, meaning or effect of any Community instrument, shall be treated as a question of law (and, if not referred to the European Court, be for determination as such in accordance with the principles laid down by and any relevant decision of the European Court or any court attached thereto).

What this provision appears to do is to make the decisions of the ECJ on the meaning and effect of EC law authoritative in UK courts—giving them, to use domestic legal language, the force of precedent.

Section 2(1) is the provision of the Act which aims to make the concept of direct effect a part of the UK legal system. It deems law which under the EC Treaties is to be given immediate legal effect to be directly enforceable in the UK. Accordingly UK courts, which on the orthodox domestic approach to international law may not directly enforce a provision of an international treaty or a measure passed thereunder, are directed by section 2(1) to enforce any directly effective EC measures. There is no need for a fresh act of incorporation to enable UK courts to enforce each EC Treaty provision, regulation, or directive which according to EC law has direct effect. Just as in the cases of France, Germany, and Italy, the supremacy of EC law is recognized in the UK by virtue of *domestic* legal processes and legal theory—albeit by an apparently simple Act of Parliament[76] rather than a special constitutional provision—and not by what has been called the monist view urged by the ECJ.

Again, however, just as in the case of other Member States, the existence of a domestic channel for the incorporation of EC law did not prevent judicial difficulties from arising over the practical recognition of the primacy of EC law. As in the case of the French Conseil d'Etat, which for many years held that it had no jurisdiction to rule upon the constitutionality or validity of domestic legislation, the English courts traditionally have no constitutional jurisdiction to review Acts of Parliament, their role in relation to such primary legislation being limited to its interpretation and enforcement. Initially, however, and despite earlier judicial comments to the contrary,[77] Lord Denning, in the case of *Shields* v. *Coomes*, seemed willing to accept the principle of supremacy of Community law, declaring that Parliament clearly intended, when it enacted the 1972 European Communities Act, to abide by the principles of direct effect and supremacy.[78] As a consequence, in his view, national courts should resolve any ambiguity or inconsistency with EC law in national statutes so as to give primacy

---

[76] See however the view of the European Communities Act as a special constitutional statute in the recent comments of Laws LJ in the *Metric Martyrs* case, nn. 110–111 below and text.

[77] *Felixstowe Dock and Railway Company* v. *British Transport and Docks Board* [1976] 2 CMLR 655.

[78] See *Shields* v. *E. Coomes (Holdings) Ltd.* [1979] 1 All ER 456, 461.

to EC law. Lord Denning avoided the problem of implied repeal by giving such weight to the 1972 Act, and to Parliament's presumed intention in enacting it, that a UK court should not enforce a later conflicting Act of Parliament if the domestic statute was ambiguous or if it was inconsistent with Community law. He did not, however, say that national courts should give primacy to Community law even if the statute *expressly* showed that Parliament intended to contradict Community law on that matter. One of the first genuine conflicts between national law and Community law which arose before a domestic courts was in the case of *Macarthys* v. *Smith* concerning Article 119 (now Article 141) of the EC Treaty and section 1 of the UK Equal Pay Act 1970. Lord Denning's celebrated dictum in the case still retains its relevance:

In construing our statute, we are entitled to look to the EC Treaty as an aid to its construction; but not only as an aid but as an overriding force. If on close investigation it should appear that our legislation is deficient or is inconsistent with Community law by some oversight of our draftsmen then it is our bounden duty to give priority to Community law. . . .

Thus far I have assumed that our Parliament, whenever it passes legislation, intends to fulfil its obligations under the Treaty. If the time should come when our Parliament deliberately passes an Act with the intention of repudiating the Treaty or any provision in it or intentionally of acting inconsistently with it and says so in express terms then I should have thought that it would be the duty of our courts to follow the statute of our Parliament.[79]

Here was the judicial reconciliation of Parliamentary sovereignty with the supremacy of EC law.[80] A provision of domestic legislation which appears to contravene Community law is presumed to be an accidental contravention, and in such circumstances section 2(1) and (4) direct the courts to construe the domestic law in conformity with EC law or, if necessary, to override the conflicting domestic provision. Such overriding of the Act of Parliament is to be seen as a fulfilment of true Parliamentary intention—the intention to comply with directly effective Community law—whereas if it is clear that the legislative contravention of Community law was intentional, then domestic law must prevail.[81] The other two judges in *Macarthys*, however, disagreed on the 'construction' route. They felt that the meaning of the English statute was clear, and that if there was a conflict between the Treaty provision and the Act, they would have to choose between the two provisions, rather than 'construing' the Equal Pay Act in the light of the Treaty provision. When the case returned from the ECJ, confirming that there was a conflict, the Court ruled that the Treaty Article should be directly applied.[82]

Shortly afterwards, in *Garland* v. *British Rail* before the House of Lords, Lord Diplock cited section 2(4) of the European Communities Act and reverted to Lord Denning's approach in *Macarthys*, stating that, where an apparently conflicting provision of English law was capable of being read in conformity with Community

---

[79] [1979] 3 All ER 325, 329.

[80] See T. Allan, 'Parliamentary Sovereignty: Lord Denning's Dexterous Revolution' (1983) 3 *OJLS* 22.

[81] An example of a clearly expressed intention of Parliament that a later statute should prevail despite the terms of the 1972 Act was given by the district judge in the famous *Metric Martyrs* prosecution, where he cites the Fisheries Limits Act 1976 which states that the Act 'shall have effect regardless of the European Communities Act 1972'. See District Judge Morgan in *R.* v. *Thoburn*, Sunderland Magistrates Court, 9 Apr. 2001.

[82] [1981] 1 QB 180, 199.

law, this was the proper approach to take.[83] Referring to Section 2(4), Diplock also drew on an already well-established principle of construction of English statutes:

it Is a principle of construction of United Kingdom statutes, now too well established to call for citation of authority, that the words of a statute passed after the treaty has been signed and dealing with the subject matter of the international obligation of the United Kingdom are to be construed, if they are reasonably capable of bearing such a meaning, as intended to carry out the obligation and not to be inconsistent with it.[84]

However, the *Garland* 'harmonious construction' approach to securing the supremacy of Community law led to some later difficulties. This approach advocates the interpretation of national law in conformity with EC law, rather than the direct application of the latter.[85] However, the *Simmenthal* ruling of the ECJ requires national courts to ensure the immediate and direct enforcement of directly effective EC law. This does not mean that they should not also strive to interpret domestic law in conformity with directly effective EC law,[86] but national courts are required to go further and to override a conflicting domestic provision when harmonious interpretation is not possible.

The situation became more complex when the ECJ began to direct its attention not only to the supremacy and immediate enforcement of directly effective Community law by national courts, but also to the role of national courts in remedying the failure of Member States to implement non-directly effective Community law.[87] As we have seen in Chapter 5, directives require national implementation, and are directly effective only as against public bodies. Consequently, in cases between two non-state parties, national courts are under no obligation to accord supremacy over national law to an EC directive by enforcing it directly.[88] However, in the cases of *Von Colson*[89] and *Marleasing*,[90] the ECJ ruled that Article 10 (ex Article 5) of the EC Treaty instead imposed an obligation on national courts to ensure the effectiveness of EC law by interpreting national law in the light of the wording and purpose of directives. This encountered initial problems before the UK courts which had adopted the interpretation approach to section 2(4) of the European Communities Act in relation to directly effective EC law. The ECJ's rulings, on the other hand, require national courts to ensure the supremacy of directly effective Community law by directly enforcing it where necessary, and require them to give some effect to *non-directly effective* Community law (mainly directives[91]) by interpreting national law in conformity with it.

[83] [1983] 2 AC 751.   [84] *Ibid.*, 771.
[85] Contrast the ruling of the CA in *Pickstone* v. *Freemans plc* [1989] AC 66, where Art. 119 EC was applied directly in preference over s. 1(2)(c) of the Equal Pay Act 1970, with the ruling of the HL on appeal in the same case [1989] AC 66, 109, that s.1(2)(c) should be construed in conformity with Art. 119 (now Art. 141).
[86] See, e.g., Case C–165/91, *Van Munster* v. *Rijksdienst voor Pensionen* [1994] ECR I–4661.
[87] Although the ECJ has developed the doctrine of supremacy in relation to directly effective Community law, interestingly, the Netherlands, Raad van State in a 1995 judgment ruled that Community law took precedence over national law regardless of whether it was directly effective or not: see Besselink, n. 17 above.
[88] Case 152/84, *Marshall* v. *Southampton and South West Hampshire Area Health Authority (Teaching)* [1986] ECR 723.
[89] Case 14/83, *Von Colson* v. *Land Nordrhein-Westfalen* [1984] ECR 1891.
[90] Case C–106/89, *Marleasing SA* v. *La Comercial Internacional de Alimentacion SA* [1990] ECR I–4135.
[91] See also Case 322/88, *Salvatore Grimaldi* v. *Fonds des Maladies Professionelles* [1989] ECR 4407 for the obligation on national courts to take into account other non-directly effective EC laws such as recommendations, when interpreting national implementing laws.

The difference between the EC and the UK approaches were evident in the case of *Duke* v. *GEC Reliance*, concerning the apparent inconsistency between the provisions of the UK Sex Discrimination Act 1975 and the EC Equal Treatment Directive 1976 in relation to retirement.[92] According to Lord Templeman in the House of Lords:

[T]he Sex Discrimination Act 1975 was not intended to give effect to the equal treatment directive as subsequently construed in *Marshall's case* and . . . the words of s. 6(4) are not reasonably capable of being limited to the meaning ascribed to them by the appellant. Section 2(4) of the European Communities Act 1972 does not in my opinion enable or constrain a British court to distort the meaning of a British statute in order to enforce against an individual a Community directive which has no direct effect between individuals. Section 2(4) applies and only applies where Community provisions are directly applicable. . . .[93]

Duke was initially followed in other cases,[94] but a different approach was then adopted in *Litster* v. *Forth Dry Dock Co. Ltd.*[95] and *Pickstone* v. *Freemans.*[96] In these cases, the House of Lords demonstrated that it was prepared to construe domestic statutes in conformity with EC law which was not directly effective, even where that construction was not in accordance with the literal or *prima facie* meaning of the statutes. The difference between *Litster* and *Pickstone* on the one hand, and *Duke* on the other, was that the domestic statutes in the former two cases were introduced specifically in order to give effect to non-directly effective EC law. Thus the UK courts could abide by the *Von Colson* ruling (as section 3 of the 1972 Act requires them to do) and at the same time could more comfortably claim to be carrying out the intention of Parliament in reading an undeniably 'implementing' domestic measure in compliance with the Community directive in question.

After the *Marleasing* ruling, however, the ECJ made clear that the obligation on national courts to construe domestic legislation in accordance with directives was *not* restricted to legislation designed to implement those directives. Thus to follow *Marleasing*, although UK courts would be acting in accordance with Parliament's intention by complying with section 3 of the 1972 Act, they might have to ignore a more specific intention of Parliament represented by the particular statute which they were construing against its *prima facie* interpretation, and in accordance with a later Community directive. While the courts were prepared to do this in relation to directly effective Community law (as shown in *Macarthys* and *Factortame*), they seemed reluctant to ensure the enforcement of non-directly effective directives. The 1972 Act appeared to provide in section 2(1) and (4) for the primacy of directly effective Community law, which was all the ECJ in 1972 had required. But by the 1990s the ECJ had also required national courts to ensure, in so far as possible by means of interpretation of any relevant national law, the effectiveness of non-directly effective EC law. And since section 3 of the 1972 Act directs UK courts to accept the rulings of the ECJ on the meaning and effect of EC law, the courts were for a time pulled in two different directions.

---

[92]   *Duke* v. *GEC Reliance Ltd.* [1988] AC 618.   [93]   *Ibid.*, 638–41.
[94]   See the HL decision in *Finnegan* v. *Clowney Youth Training Programme Ltd.* [1990] 2 AC 407, the CA in *Marshall* v. *Southampton and South West Hampshire Area Health Authority (Teaching)* [1991] ICR 136, and in *Webb* v. *EMO Cargo* [1992] 2 All ER 43.
[95]   [1990] 1 AC 546.   [96]   N. 85 above.

This dilemma was faced by the Court of Appeal in *Webb* v. *EMO*,[97] where the provisions of the Sex Discrimination Act 1975 were alleged by the applicant to conflict with the ECJ's interpretation of the 1976 Equal Treatment Directive. The Court of Appeal accepted that it should interpret domestic legislation in the light of a non-directly effective directive even where the domestic measure was not designed to implement the directive, but it ruled, citing *Duke*, that to read the 1975 Act in the manner contended for by the applicant would distort its natural meaning and that *Marleasing* did not require national courts to do this. The House of Lords on appeal agreed that national courts were not required by *Marleasing* to 'distort' the meaning of a domestic statute, but none the less referred the case to the ECJ for a ruling on the meaning of the Equal Treatment Directive.[98] The ECJ's ruling supported the applicant's claim, so that her dismissal on grounds of unavailability for work due to pregnancy constituted direct sex discrimination in breach of the Directive.[99] When the ruling was received by the House of Lords, Lord Keith gave a short judgment in which the Sex Discrimination Act was interpreted so as to conform with the ECJ's interpretation of the Directive, despite the fact that the Court of Appeal had considered that such an interpretation would amount to a distortion.[100] Lord Keith made no reference to this, even though the interpretation which he gave the relevant provisions of the Sex Discrimination Act was different from that which had previously been given by the House of Lords.[101] It is clear that a strong obligation to construe in conformity with the ECJ's ruling was ultimately accepted.

The UK courts have evidently changed their approach considerably over the time since the enactment of the European Communities Act 1972. The 'construction' approach to section 2(4) has been supplemented by a willingness to enforce directly effective provisions of Community law directly, even where this involves suspending or setting aside an inconsistent Act of Parliament (and, as we have seen from the *IN.CO.GE. '90* ruling above, the ECJ does not require more than this, and in particular does not require conflicting domestic law to be declared void[102]). Further, the interpretation approach has been extended, in accordance with the ECJ's rulings, so that national statutes which were not introduced in order to implement a non-directly effective directive should nevertheless be read in conformity with it, even where that does not conform with the *prima facie* interpretation favoured by the national court—although EC law does not require national courts to read domestic legislation in a way which is patently *contra legem*.[103]

As far as directly effective Community law is concerned, Lord Bridge's speech in the course of the lengthy *Factortame* litigation demonstrates that, although an equilibrium may have been reached in the relationship between the ECJ and the UK courts as to the requirements of supremacy of EC law, the national courts certainly do not accept the view that those obligations stem directly from the Treaties but

---

[97] [1992] 2 All ER 43.   [98] [1993] 1 WLR 49.

[99] Case C–32/93, *Webb* v. *EMO Cargo* [1994] ECR I–3567.

[100] *Webb* v. *EMO Cargo (No. 2)* [1996] 2 CMLR 990.

[101] [1996] 2 CMLR 990, 995. For commentaries see E. Deards, 'Indirect Effect After Webb v. EMO Cargo UK' (1996) 2 *EPL* 71; C. Boch, (1996) 33 *CMLRev.* 547.

[102] See n. 13 above.   [103] See Ch. 5, 215 above.

rather from the express will of the UK Parliament, and their responsibility is not to the ECJ but to Parliament. The first excerpt below is from Lord Bridge's judgment before the case was referred to the ECJ, and the second is from his judgment after its return.

Factortame Ltd. v. Secretary of State for Transport
[1990] 2 AC 85

LORD BRIDGE[104]

If the applicants fail to establish the rights they claim before the European Court, the effect of the interim relief granted would be to have conferred on them rights directly contrary to Parliament's sovereign will and correspondingly to have deprived British fishing vessels, as defined by Parliament, of the enjoyment of a substantial proportion of the United Kingdom quota of stocks of fish protected by the common fisheries policy. I am clearly of the opinion that, as a matter of English law, the court has no power to make an order which has these consequences.

It follows that this appeal must fall to be dismissed unless there is, as the applicants contend, some overriding principle derived from the jurisprudence of the European Court which compels national courts of Member States, whatever their own law may provide, to assert, and in appropriate cases to exercise, a power to provide an effective interlocutory remedy to protect putative rights in Community law.

After the ECJ's ruling to the effect that a national rule which was the sole obstacle to the national court's grant of interim relief in a case concerning directly effective Community rights should be set aside by the national court, Lord Bridge summarized what he understood to be the constitutional position of the UK:[105]

Factortame Ltd. v. Secretary of State for Transport (No. 2)
[1991] 1 AC 603

LORD BRIDGE[106]

Some public comments on the decision of the Court of Justice, affirming the jurisdiction of the courts of member states to override national legislation if necessary to enable interim relief to be

---

[104] [1990] 2 AC 85, 143.

[105] For commentaries on the implications of the *Factortame* case for UK constitutional law see Craig, n. 75 above, 252; W. Wade, 'Sovereignty—Revolution or Evolution?' (1996) 112 *LQR* 568; T. Allan, 'Parliamentary Sovereignty: Law, Politics and Revolution' (1997) 113 *LQR* 443. See also D. Nicol, *EC Membership and the Judicialization of British Politics* (Oxford University Press, 2001), ch. 7.

[106] [1991] 1 AC 603, 658. For the remainder of the 'soap opera' saga of the *Factortame* litigation in the UK following the action for damages brought against the State by the fishermen concerned see [1997] *Eu LR* 1475, [1998] 1 All ER 736, [1999] 2 All ER 640, [2000] 1 AC 524, and finally the latest Div. Ct. ruling at [2001] 1 WLR 942.

granted in protection of rights under Community law, have suggested that this was a novel and dangerous invasion by a Community institution of the sovereignty of the United Kingdom Parliament. But such comments are based on a misconception. If the supremacy within the European Community of Community law over the national law of member states was not always inherent in the EEC Treaty it was certainly well established in the jurisprudence of the Court of Justice long before the United Kingdom joined the Community. Thus, whatever limitation of its sovereignty Parliament accepted when it enacted the European Communities Act 1972 was entirely voluntary. Under the terms of the 1972 Act it has always been clear that it was the duty of a United Kingdom court, when delivering final judgment, to override any rule of national law found to be in conflict with any directly enforceable rule of Community law. Similarly, when decisions of the Court of Justice have exposed areas of United Kingdom statute law which failed to implement Council directives, Parliament has always loyally accepted the obligation to make appropriate and prompt amendments. Thus there is nothing in any way novel in according supremacy to rules of Community law in those areas to which they apply and to insist that, in the protection of rights under Community law, national courts must not be inhibited by rules of national law from granting interim relief in appropriate cases is no more than a logical recognition of that supremacy.

In a further phase of its acceptance of the primacy of Community law, the House of Lords in the *EOC* case stated that there is no constitutional barrier to an applicant before a UK court—and not only before the House of Lords—directly seeking judicial review of primary legislation which is alleged to be in breach of Community law. As was the case in the *Factortame* judgment of the Lords, while this is presented by Lord Keith as a natural extension of earlier case law and, by implication, as based on the will of Parliament as expressed in the 1972 Act, the symbolic impact of the ruling was none the less powerful.

Equal Opportunities Commission v. Secretary of State for Employment
[1994] 1 WLR 409

[Note ToA renumbering: Arts. 7, 52, and 177 are now Arts. 12, 43, and 234 respectively]

The Equal Opportunities Commission (EOC) considered that the Employment Protection (Consolidation) Act of 1978 on part-time workers was contrary to Community law. In a letter from the Secretary of State for Employment to the EOC, the Secretary refused to accept that the UK was in breach of EC law. The EOC sought judicial review of the Secretary of State's decision, and also sought a declaration and an order of mandamus requiring the Secretary to introduce legislation to provide equal pay for equal work for men and women, and to amend the 1978 Act so as to provide protection for part-time workers. The Secretary of State argued that the English court had no jurisdiction to declare that the UK or the Secretary of State was in breach of any obligations under Community law.

LORD KEITH[107]

The question is whether judicial review is available for the purpose of securing a declaration that certain United Kingdom primary legislation is incompatible with Community law. . . . In the *Factortame* series of cases . . . the applicants for judicial review sought a declaration that the provisions of Part II of the Merchant Shipping Act 1988 should not apply to them on the ground that such application would be contrary to Community law, in particular Articles 7 and 52 of the EEC Treaty. . . . The Divisional Court, under Article 177 of the Treaty, referred to the Court of Justice of the European Communities a number of questions, including the question whether these restrictive conditions were compatible with Articles 7 and 52 of the Treaty. The European Court . . . answered that question in the negative, and although the final result is not reported, no doubt the Divisional Court in due course granted a declaration accordingly. The effect was that certain provisions of United Kingdom primary legislation were held to be invalid in their purported application to nationals of Member States of the European Community, but without any prerogative order being available to strike down the legislation in question, which of course remained valid as regards nationals of non-member States. At no stage in the course of the litigation, which included two visits to this House, was it suggested that judicial review of legislation was not available for obtaining an adjudication upon the validity of the legislation in so far as it affected the applicants.

The *Factortame* case is thus a precedent in favour of the EOC's recourse to judicial review for the purpose of challenging as incompatible with Community law the relevant provisions of the 1978 Act.

P.P. Craig, Britain in the European Union[108]

The substantive impact of *Factortame* and *EOC* may be described as follows.

First, in doctrinal terms these decisions mean that the concept of *implied repeal,* or *implied disapplication,* under which inconsistencies between later and earlier norms were resolved in favour of the former, will, subject to what is said below, no longer apply to clashes concerning Community and national law.

Secondly, if Parliament ever does wish to derogate from its Community obligations then it will have to do so *expressly and unequivocally*. The reaction of our national courts to such an unlikely eventuality remains to be seen. In principle two options would be open to the national judiciary. Either they could choose to follow the latest will of Parliament, thereby preserving some remnant of traditional orthodoxy on sovereignty. Or they could argue that it is not open to our legislature to pick and choose which obligations to subscribe to while still remaining within the Community. . . .

Thirdly, the supremacy of EC law over national law *operates in areas where EC law is applicable,* as is made clear from the dictum of Lord Bridge set out above . . . The problem being addressed here is often referred to as *Kompetenz-Kompetenz*: who has the ultimate authority to decide whether a matter is within the competence of the EC? The ECJ may well believe that it is the ultimate determinor of this issue. However a moment's reflection will reveal that national courts may not always be content with this arrogation of authority.

. . .

---

[107] [1994] 1 WLR 409, 418–19.   [108] Ch. 3 of Jowell and Oliver (eds.), n. 75 above.

Commentators have been divided as to how best to conceptualise the impact of the courts' jurisprudence.

It is possible to rationalise what the courts have done as a species of *statutory construction*. . . . All would agree that if a statute can be reconciled with a Community norm through construing the statutory words without thereby unduly distorting them then this should be done, more especially when the statute was passed to effectuate a directive. However the species of statutory construction being considered here is more far-reaching. On this view accommodation between national law and EC law is attained through a rule of construction to the effect that inconsistencies *will* be resolved in favour of the latter *unless* Parliament has indicated clearly and ambiguously that it intends to derogate from Community law. The degree of linguistic inconsistency between the statute and the Community norm is not the essential point of the inquiry. Provided that there is no unequivocal derogation from Community law then it will apply, rather than any conflicting domestic statute. . . . The construction view is said to leave the essential core of the traditional view of legal sovereignty intact, in the sense that it is always open to a later Parliament to make it unequivocally clear that it wishes to derogate from EC law. . . . This approach is, however, problematic. . . .[109]

A second way in which it is possible to conceptualise what the courts have done is to regard it as a *technical legal revolution*. This is the preferred explanation of Sir William Wade who sees the courts' decisions as modifying the ultimate legal principle or rule of recognition on which the legal system is based. On this view the 'rule of recognition is itself a political fact which the judges themselves are able to change when they are confronted with a new situation which so demands'. Such choices are made by the judiciary at the point where the law 'stops'.

There is however a third way in which to regard the courts' jurisprudence. This is to regard decisions about supremacy as being based on *normative arguments of legal principle the content of which can and will vary across time*. . . . On this view there is no *a priori* inexorable reason why Parliament, merely because of its very existence, must be regarded as legally omnipotent. The existence of such power, like all power, must be justified by arguments of principle which are normatively convincing. Possible constraints on Parliamentary omnipotence must similarly be reasoned through and defended on normative grounds. This approach fits well with the reasoning of Lord Bridge in the second *Factortame* case.

While the *Factortame* and *EOC* cases remain the most recent authoritative statements of the House of Lords on the constitutional relationship between UK and EC law, another much publicized legal controversy in the so-called 'metric martyrs' case has given rise more recently to some interesting judicial comments in the lower courts. The judgment in question, which touches not only on the issue of implied repeal, but also on more fundamental questions concerning the constitutional relationship between UK and EU law, could indeed be seen as Britain's parallel to the German Constitutional Court's *Maastricht* decision, albeit that it is not the House of Lords but as yet only a division of the High Court which has ruled on the matter. The case arose out of appeals by four traders against their conviction for breach of various

---

[109] The section of the extract which has been omitted here sets out three specific problems with the 'statutory construction' view, and indicates also that this particular view of the reconciliation of UK parliamentary sovereignty with the supremacy of EC law in the UK has been expressed extrajudicially by Lord Hoffmann, and by Laws, LJ (who gave the judgment in the *Metric Martyrs* case discussed at n. 110 and text below).

UK legislative requirements, including the Weights and Measures Act 1985 and a number of statutory instruments, by reason of the appellants' apparent refusal to use metric measurements alongside imperial pounds and ounces in their trade.[110] Their argument, which centred around a challenge to the power created by the 1972 Act to amend Acts of Parliament by means of a statutory instrument or Order, was that Section 1 of the 1985 Act had impliedly repealed Section 2(2) of the 1972 Act. The judgment in the case was given by Sir John Laws, and the reasoning reflects views which he had previously expressed extra-judicially on the general matter.[111] Although he rejected the appeal on the basis that the 1985 Act was not in fact inconsistent with the 1972 Act, he went on to give his view that the 1972 Act was 'by force of the common law' a 'constitutional statute' which could not be subject to implied repeal by a later inconsistent statute. He emphasized further that the fundamental legal basis of the UK's relationship with the EU 'rests with the domestic, not the European, legal powers'. In other words, this special constitutional status, which protects the 1972 Act against implied repeal and gives it an enhanced status within the UK legal order, exists by reason of the common law and not as a result of EU law.[112] And in a further sentence which also reflects the stance taken on the same issue by the Bundesverfassungsgericht, by the Italian Constitutional Court, and also by the Danish Supreme Court, but which has particular significance in the British context given the absence of an 'entrenched rights' tradition in British constitutional law, he stated:

In the event, which no doubt would never happen in the real world, that a European measure was seen to be repugnant to a fundamental or constitutional right guaranteed by the law of England, a question would arise whether the general words of the ECA were sufficient to incorporate the measure and give it overriding effect in domestic law.

If the ruling of the High Court in the metric martyrs case is appealed, the views of the higher courts on these central constitutional questions will be awaited with considerable interest.

(e) OTHER RECENT DEVELOPMENTS

Some years after the *Brunner* challenge, the Danish Supreme Court delivered its own 'Maastricht' ruling in the *Carlsen* case, many aspects of which echo dimensions of the Bundesverfassungsgericht's *Maastricht* judgment.[113] The *Carlsen* court ruled that it was for the Danish Supreme Court to determine whether a given measure of Community law has exceeded the boundaries of the transfer of sovereignty brought about by the Danish Act of Accession (for example, an EC law which would infringe

---

[110] See *Thoburn v. Sunderland County Council, Hunt v. London Borough of Hackney, Harman and Dove v. Cornwall County Council* and *Collins v. London Borough of Sutton*, QBD, 18 Feb. 2002. For the judgment of the district judge, which also comments extensively on questions of UK constitutional law and the basis for the supremacy of EC law in the UK, see n. 81 above.

[111] J. Laws, 'Law and Democracy' [1995] *PL* 72. See n. 109 above.

[112] For an analysis of the *Thoburn* judgment in the broader context of UK sovereignty in relation to the impact of both EU law and the Human Rights Act 1998 see K. Armstrong, 'United Kingdom, Divided Sovereignty?' in N. Walker (ed.), *Sovereignty in Transition* (Hart, 2003).

[113] *Carlsen v. Prime Minister*, judgment of the Højesteret, 6 April 1998; for English language translation see [1999] 3 CMLR 854, and for comment see K. Høegh, 'The Danish Maastricht Judgment' (1999) 24 *ELRev.* 80.

basic rights protected under the Danish constitution) and that, if it did, the Danish courts could refuse to apply any such EC act in Denmark. A similar concern with the problem of 'creeping competences' and with the danger of improper use of Article 308 (ex Article 235) EC is evident in the ruling, and the ultimate power of constitutional review of EC acts is reserved to the Supreme Court.

Further, it seems that Member States which have enacted specific constitutional amendments in order to provide for the supremacy and applicability of EC law within their national legal systems are not necessarily any more likely to abandon the power of ultimate constitutional review of EC law. In Ireland, for example, Article 29.4.7 of the Constitution, which ensures the applicability of EC law and protects it from constitutional review, was questioned in the *Grogan* abortion information case by a member of the Supreme Court, who suggested that a subsequent constitutional amendment guaranteeing the right to life might have qualified it.[114] In a move of more practical significance, however, despite the constitutional protection given by Article 29.4.7 to acts which are 'necessitated' by EC membership, the Irish Supreme Court in the *Crotty* case ruled that this provision would not cover all further transfers of sovereignty away from the State, and would not cover any amendments to the EC Treaties which alter the essential objectives or scope of the Community.[115] Any Treaty amendment of this kind requires a further constitutional amendment, which in Ireland necessitates approval by popular referendum. And, as we saw in Chapter 1, the negative outcome of the Irish Nice Treaty referendum in June 2001 has so far stalled the coming into force of that Treaty, thus highlighting the importance for the EU as a whole—and also for its future members—of each Member State's particular constitutional relationship with the EU.[116]

While the debate over whether there is or can be a final judicial arbiter in Europe remains a live one, different versions of constitutional pluralism are increasingly being proposed as a more attractive alternative to the stalemate of nation-State-centred versus EU-centred monism. The following extracts are from the writings of two commentators whose approaches to the constitutional relationship between national law and European law have altered somewhat in recent years. Paul Kirchhof, former judge of the Bundesverfassungsgericht and one of the main architects of the *Maastricht* judgment at the time, expresses a more co-operative and pluralist vision of this relationship than some of his earlier views suggested; while Neil MacCormick's proposed analysis is one of 'legal pluralism under international law', in place of his earlier radically pluralist perspective which saw the answer to fundamental constitutional conflict lying in politics rather than in law.

---

[114] *Society for the Protection of the Unborn Child* v. *Grogan* [1989] IR 753, 768. On Ireland's position in relation to the supremacy of EC law see D. Rossa Phelan and A. Whelan, 'National Constitutional Law and European Integration' (1997) 6 *IJEL* 24.
[115] *Crotty* v. *An Taoiseach* [1987] IR 713.
[116] See G. Hogan, 'The Nice Treaty and the Irish Constitution' (2001) 7 *EPL* 565.

N. MacCormick, Questioning Sovereignty[117]

The doctrine of supremacy of Community law is not to be confused with any kind of all purpose subordination of Member State law to Community law. Rather, the case is that these are interacting systems, one of which constitutes in its own context and over the relevant range of topics a source of valid law superior to other sources recognised in each of the Member State systems. . . .

On the whole therefore, the most appropriate analysis of the relations of legal systems is pluralistic rather than monistic, and interactive rather than hierarchical. The legal systems of Member States and their common legal system of EC law are distinct but inter-acting systems of law, and hierarchical relationships of validity within criteria of validity proper to distinct systems do not add up to any sort of all-purpose superiority of one system over another. It follows also that the interpretative power of the highest decisionmaking authorities of the different systems must be, as to each system, ultimate. It is for the ECJ to interpret in the last resort and in a finally authoritative way the norms of Community law. But equally, it must be for the highest constitutional tribunal of each member State to interpret its constitutional and other norms, and hence to interpret the interaction of the validity of EC law with higher level norms of validity in the given state system. . . .

. . . The potential conflicts and collisions of systems that can in principle occur as between Community and member States do not occur in a legal vacuum, but in a space to which international law is also relevant. Indeed, it is decisively relevant, given the origin of the Community in Treaties and the continuing normative significance of *pacta sunt servanda*, to say nothing of the fact that in respect of their Community membership and otherwise the states owe each other obligations under international law. . . . What that signals is that state Courts have no right to assume an absolute superiority of state constitution over international good order, including the European dimension of that good order. This is not the same as saying that they must simply defer to whatever the ECJ considers to be mandated by the European constitution. . . . But in the event of an apparently irresoluble conflict arising between one or more national courts and the ECJ, there would always on- this thesis be a possibility of recourse to international arbitration or adjudication to resolve the matter.

P. Kirchhof, The Balance of Powers between National and European Institutions[118]

European law would lose its roots and its power to grow by being made autonomous and separate from the Member States, whereas in the close interweaving with Member States' constitutions it gains its identity in a unitary origin and a unitary future.. [C]onflicts of norms that may arise are not to be avoided or resolved by a conflict of laws provision whereby one takes primacy over the other and norms are rendered non-legal, but through mutual respect and through 'cooperation'. . . . The ECJ and the constitutional courts each have adjudicatory responsibility of their own for the success of the European legal community. . . . Accordingly, it is not just 'open skies' that are above these courts of last instance; a system of balance of powers between the European and Member State courts is developing. Whoever seeks to interpret this system of balance and cooperation as a hierarchy is closing off the way laid down in European integration towards a balance of powers within the judicature. . . . Adjudicating means establishing the culture of measure, of balance, of co-operation, not dominance, subordination and rejection.

---

[117] (Oxford University Press, 1999), 117–21.   [118] (1999) 5 *ELJ* 225, 227–8, 241.

4. CONCLUSIONS

i. The supremacy of EC law still clearly retains its 'bidimensional' character, despite the monist view of supremacy asserted by the ECJ in the *Simmenthal* and *Internationale Handelsgesellschaft* cases.

ii. While there are exceptions, most notably in the Netherlands,[119] most Member State courts continue to locate the authority of EU law in the national legal order centrally within the national constitution, and not in the jurisprudence of the Court of Justice or in the sovereignty of the EU.

iii. Further, many higher national courts have asserted the ultimate (albeit residual) role of national courts in ensuring that the proper boundaries of EC competence are respected and in protecting rights which are fundamental within the national legal order.

iv. Thus far, while the residual control of national courts has been firmly asserted as a matter of constitutional theory, it has rarely materialized in practice. None the less, it remains as a clear counterpoint to the ECJ's assertion of the autonomy of Community law, and it may influence the ECJ in showing greater sensitivity to national constitutional concerns.[120]

5. FURTHER READING

(a) *Books*

ALTER, K., *Establishing the Supremacy of European Law: The Making of an International Rule of Law in Europe* (Oxford University Press, 2001)

MACCORMICK, N., *Questioning Sovereignty* (Oxford University Press, 1999)

NICOL, D., *EC Membership and the Judicialization of British Politics* (Oxford University Press, 2001)

PHELAN, D.R., *Revolt or Revolution: The Constitutional Boundaries of the European Community* (Roundhall, 1997)

SLAUGHTER, A.-M., STONE SWEET, A., and WEILER, J.H.H. (eds.), *The European Court of Justice and National Courts: Doctrine and Jurisprudence* (Hart, 1998)

WALKER, N. (ed.), *Sovereignty in Transition* (Hart, 2003)

(b) *Articles*

CRAIG, P.P., 'Britain in the European Union', in J. Jowell and D. Oliver (eds.), *The Changing Constitution* (4th edn., Oxford University Press, 2000)

---

[119] See M. Claes and B. de Witte, 'Report on the Netherlands', in A. Slaughter *et al.*, n. 19 above, ch. 6, and B. de Witte, 'Do Not Mention the Word: Sovereignty in two Europhile Countries', in Walker (ed.), n. 19 above.

[120] Various commentators have suggested that the ECJ has responded to the challenges posed by national courts by adapting its case law in subsequent rulings. See, e.g., De Witte, 'Community Law and National Constitutional Values', n. 32 above, and also the notion of 'contrapunctual law' in M. Maduro, 'The Forms of European Power', in Walker, n. 19 above.

CRAIG, P.P., 'National Courts and Community Law', in J. Hayward and A. Menon (eds.), *Governing Europe* (Oxford University Press, 2003)

DE WITTE, B., 'Community Law and National Constitutional Values' (1991) 2 *LIEI* 1

—— 'Direct Effect, Supremacy and the Nature of the Legal Order', in P. Craig and G. de Búrca (eds.), *The Evolution of EU Law* (Oxford University Press, 1999)

ELBERS, U., and URBAN, N., 'The Order of the German Gederal Constitutional Court of 7 June 2000 and the Kompetenz-Kompetenz in the European Judicial System' (2001) 7 *EPL* 21

EVERLING, U., 'The Maastricht Judgment of the German Federal Constitutional Court and its Significance for the Development of the European Union' (1994) 14 *YBEL* 1

—— 'Will Europe Slip on Bananas? The Bananas Judgment of the Court of Justice and National Courts' (1996) 33 *CMLRev.* 401

GAJA, G., 'New Developments in a Continuing Story: The Relationship between EEC Law and Italian Law' (1990) 27 *CMLRev.* 83

KUMM, M., 'Who is the Final Arbiter of Constitutionality in Europe?' (1999) 36 *CMLRev.* 251

MILLNS, S., 'The Treaty of Amsterdam and the Constitutional Revision in France' (1999) 5 *EPL* 61

OLIVER, P., 'The French Constitution and the Treaty of Maastricht' (1994) 43 *ICLQ* 1

PETRICCIONE, R., 'Italy: Supremacy of Community Law over National Law' (1986) 11 *ELRev.* 320

POLLARD, D., 'European Community Law and the French Conseil d'Etat' (1992–95) 30 *Irish Jurist* 79

REICH, N., 'Judge-made "Europe à la carte": Some Remarks on Recent Conflicts between European and German Constitutional Law Provoked by the Banana Litigation' (1996) 7 *EJIL* 103

ROSERN, P., 'The Application of Community Law by French Courts From 1982 to 1993' (1994) 31 *CMLRev.* 315

SCHMID, C., 'All Bark and No Bite: Notes on the Federal Constitutional Court's "Banana Decision"' (2001) 7 *ELJ* 95

WEILER, J., 'The Community System: the Dual Character of Supranationalism' (1981) 1 *YBEL* 267

ZULEGG, M., 'The European Constitution under Constitutional Constraints: The German Scenario' (1997) 22 *ELRev.* 19

8

GENERAL PRINCIPLES I: FUNDAMENTAL RIGHTS

1. CENTRAL ISSUES

i. When the original three European Community Treaties were signed in the 1950s, they contained no provisions concerning the protection of human rights in the conduct of Community affairs. More than fifty years since the ECSC was founded, the position has changed considerably in this respect.

ii. The Court of Justice over the years has declared that the 'general principles of EC law' include protection for fundamental rights which are part of the common constitutional traditions of the Member States and contained in international human rights treaties on which they have collaborated or which they have signed.

iii. There is currently a lively debate on the significance of human rights for the EU and the appropriate scope of an EU human rights policy.[1] At the same time, the Community has begun to exercise the competence created by the Treaty of Amsterdam to enact anti-discrimination policies in fields such as race, sexual orientation, age, and religion.

iv. A Charter of Fundamental Rights for the EU was drafted and officially 'proclaimed' in 2000, and the proposal to give it full legal effect by incorporating it into the Treaties has been placed on the post-Nice and post-Laeken reform agenda, to be considered at the Intergovernmental Conference in 2004.[2]

v. This development has rekindled rather than quashed the debate over accession by the EC to the European Convention on Human Rights (ECHR), which had abated for a time after the ECJ ruled in 1996 that the Community lacked competence under the Treaties to accede to the Convention,[3] but which has now been placed on the political agenda by the Laeken Declaration.

---

[1] See P. Alston, J. Heenan, and M. Bustelo (eds.), *The EU and Human Rights* (OUP, 1999), in particular ch. 1; A. von Bogdandy, 'The European Union as a Human Rights Organization: Human Rights and the Core of the European Union' (2000) 37 *CMLRev.* 1307; D. McGoldrick, 'The EU after Amsterdam: An Organisation with General Human Rights Competence?', in D. O'Keeffe and P. Twomey (eds.), *Legal Issues of the Amsterdam Treaty* (Hart, 1999); and G. de Búrca, 'The Case for an EU Human Rights Policy' in P. Beaumont, C. Lyons, and N. Walker (eds.), *Convergence and Divergence in European Public Law* (Hart, 2002).

[2] The literature on the Charter is already vast. For some early collections see (2001)8(1) *Maastricht Journal of European and Comparative Law*; E. Eriksen, J.E. Fossum, and A. Menéndez (eds.), *The Chartering of Europe* (Arena Report No. 8/2001); K. Feus (ed.), *An EU Charter of Fundamental Rights: Text and Commentaries* (Federal Trust, 2000); and K. Lenaerts and E. de Smijter, 'A Bill of Rights for the EU' (2001) 38 *CMLRev.* 273.

[3] *Opinion 2/94 on Accession of the Community to the ECHR* [1996] ECR I–1759. For some of the comments on the Opinion see G. Gaja, (1996) 33 *CMLRev.* 973; A. Toth, (1997) 34 *CMLRev.* 491; N. Burrows, (1997) 22 *ELRev.* 594; S. O' Leary, [1997] *EHRLR* 362; P. Allott (1996) 55 *CLJ* 409; C. Vedder, [1996] *Europarecht* 309.

2. THE BACKGROUND

This high political profile in recent years of human rights issues in the EU context has not been a sudden development. The ECJ's progressive development over many years of a kind of unwritten bill of rights for the Community was gradually given express recognition within the Treaties. In particular, Article 6 of the TEU declares that respect for fundamental rights and freedoms constitutes one of the basic principles on which the Union is founded, and Article 7 provides a mechanism for sanctioning Member States who violate these principles in a grave or persistent manner.[4] Nevertheless, these and other provisions were grafted on to a set of Treaties which, despite the broad range of powers and policies covered, were for a long time very largely focused on economic aims and objectives with little reference to other values. This legacy remains significant since, despite its constantly changing and expanding nature, the European Union's dominant focus remains an economic one, and the debate over the appropriate scope of its 'human rights role' remains lively and contested even after the adoption of the Charter.

The omission of any reference to basic human rights and values in the original Treaties has been explained in various ways. To put it in historical context, the Treaty establishing a European Defence Community had been signed by the six original Member States in 1952, at a time when there were great hopes for European integration.[5] More ambitious proposals for a European Political Community were drawn up in 1953, and presented in a new draft Treaty,[6] one of whose primary aims was declared to be the protection of human rights and fundamental freedoms. The rights provisions of the ECHR were to be incorporated into this new Treaty. In 1954, however, the proposals for Political Union were abandoned after the French National Assembly failed to ratify the European Defence Treaty.[7] It seems likely that considerable restraint was exercised when it came to the drafting of the EEC Treaty, lest this, too, would suffer the same fate as the earlier draft treaties. The 1957 EEC Treaty was restricted essentially to the aims of economic integration, and no mention of political union or of human rights was included,[8] although the preambles to the various treaties, including the limited ECSC Treaty, included idealistic rhetoric and posited economic integration as a means to better ends rather than as an end in itself. Drawing further on this historical explanation, it is also conceivable that the drafters assumed that a functionally limited economic organization would be unlikely to encroach on traditionally protected fundamental human rights, and that powerful economic actors rather than individual citizens or other vulnerable beneficiaries of human rights protection would be the most directly affected.

---

[4] This provision has not yet been used, although it has been amended by the Nice Treaty. See however, the discussion of the related 'Haider affair' at n. 112 below and text.

[5] See Ch. 1.

[6] See for a discussion A.H. Robertson, 'The European Political Community' (1952) XXIX *BYIL* 383.

[7] See A.H. Robertson, *European Institutions* (Stevens & Sons, 2nd edn., 1966), 19–21.

[8] M. Dauses, 'The Protection of Fundamental Rights in the Community Legal Order' (1985) 10 *ELRev.* 398, 399. See also P. Pescatore, 'The Context and Significance of Fundamental Rights in the Law of the European Communities' (1981) 2 HRLJ 295.

However, the Community before long established itself as a powerful entity whose actions had considerable impact on many broader political and social issues, and its express policy competences were extended into areas such as the environment, consumer protection, culture, health, and education. Further, Community action through the doctrine of direct effect often had a direct legal impact on private economic and commercial interests. These interests began to claim legal protection for fundamental property and commercial rights which were given specific protection within certain Member State constitutions. Thus the first steps taken by the ECJ in the field of fundamental rights protection concerned economic rights such as the right to property and the freedom to pursue a trade or profession.

The initial trigger for the Court's declaration that fundamental rights formed part of the EC legal order was the challenge posed to the supremacy of Community law by Member State jurisdictions which felt that EC legislation was encroaching upon important rights protected under national law. The ECJ's development initially gained the support of the Member States, since protection for these rights was being introduced by the ECJ into Community law as a restraint upon the powers of the Community institutions rather than as a restraint upon Member States. Since then, however, there has been a considerable expansion of both judicial and legislative activity in the area of human rights protection, including the extension by the ECJ of fundamental rights review in certain circumstances to acts of the Member States. Some of these developments have given rise to misgivings that the EU is overreaching itself and assuming tasks properly performed by national constitutions and by the ECHR. The drafting of the Charter of Fundamental Rights and the debate surrounding it have also illustrated these tensions, with some calling for a stronger and more extensive role for the EU and the ECJ in human rights protection, while others favour a more limited supplementary role for the EU and view the Charter as being primarily relevant to the EU institutions rather than the Member States.[9] We will return to this subject further below.

3. FUNDAMENTAL RIGHTS AND GENERAL PRINCIPLES AS STANDARDS BINDING ON THE COMMUNITY

(a) THE COURT'S INITIAL RESISTANCE

One national jurisdiction in particular played a strong role in persuading the Court of Justice to acknowledge the existence and the relevance for the EC legal order of unwritten general principles of law, including protection for certain fundamental rights. The Court initially resisted attempts by litigants to invoke principles and rights which were recognized in domestic law, as part of the Community's legal order. Only after refusing in several cases to consider the applicability of rights or principles which

---

[9] For an example of the latter view see, e.g., the comments of the UK representative who participated in the drafting of the Charter, Lord Goldsmith, 'A Charter of Rights, Freedoms and Principles' (2001) 38 *CMLRev.* 1201.

were not specifically set out in the Treaties did the Court change its approach. It seems likely that one of the main ECJ objections was to the domestic *source* of the principles invoked, and to the danger of subordinating EC law to national constitutional law, rather than to the general idea of giving judicial recognition within EC law to fundamental constitutional principles. Most litigants relied on principles recognized in their domestic law such as protection for legitimate expectations, proportionality, and natural justice.

In *Stork*,[10] in which a coal wholesaler complained of a decision of the High Authority governing the sale of coal, the ECJ declared that 'the High Authority is not empowered to examine a ground of complaint which maintains that, when it adopted its decision, it infringed principles of German constitutional law'.[11] The applicant's concern in *Stork* was that Community law was riding roughshod over rights which had a central place in national constitutional law, and despite the potential supremacy conflict which was brewing, the ECJ persisted in its refusal to consider such rights. In *Geitling*,[12] another coal-wholesaler case, the Court not only rejected the relevance to the dispute of a German constitutional principle, but also dismissed the suggestion that Community law might give similar protection: 'Community law, as it arises under the ECSC Treaty, does not contain any general principle, express or otherwise, guaranteeing the maintenance of vested rights'.[13] And in *Sgarlata*,[14] some five years later, the Court ruled that the express provisions of the Treaty could not be overridden by a plea founded on other principles, even if those were fundamental principles common to the legal systems of all the Member States.[15]

(b) A MORE RECEPTIVE APPROACH

Some years later, the Court's attitude began to change, and in the *Stauder* case it responded more positively to a claim that the implementation of a Community scheme constituted an infringement of the applicant's right to dignity.[16] The applicant before the German courts challenged a Community scheme to reduce the surplus of butter, in accordance with which social security recipients would be eligible to receive subsidized butter from national traders. He argued that the requirement that beneficiaries must reveal their names and addresses constituted an infringement of basic rights protected under German constitutional law, and a reference was made to the ECJ. Unlike in the *Stork, Sgarlata*, and *Geitling* cases, the ECJ did not reject the applicability of principles of this nature, but neither did it accept the claim that the Commission's butter scheme infringed such a right. Instead, the Court interpreted

---

[10] Case 1/ 58, *Stork* v. *High Authority* [1959] ECR 17.
[11] *Ibid.*, para. 4 of the judgment.
[12] Cases 36, 37, 38, & 40/ 59, *Geitling* v. *High Authority* [1960] ECR 423.
[13] *Ibid.*, 438.
[14] Case 40/ 64, *Sgarlata and others* v. *Commission* [1965] ECR 215, [1966] CMLR 314.
[15] The Court did not, however, deny the existence in EC law of any general legal principles other than those written in the Treaty: see in Case 35/67, *Van Eick* v. *Commission* [1968] ECR 329, 342, that the Disciplinary Board under the Community staff regulations was bound to exercise its powers in accordance with 'the fundamental principles of the law of procedure'. However, unlike in the case of *Sgarlata*, there was no question of these general principles overriding specific Treaty provisions.
[16] Case 29/ 69, *Stauder* v. *City of Ulm* [1969] ECR 419.

the Commission decision by looking at different language versions of the text and concluding that it was unnecessary for a recipient of subsidized butter to be identified by name, so that any potential infringement of the right to human dignity could be avoided. The assertion that protection for fundamental human rights is part of the general principles of EC law appeared in the final paragraph of the judgment, and no reference was made to the previous and apparently contradictory case law:

7. Interpreted in this way the provision at issue contains nothing capable of prejudicing the fundamental human rights enshrined in the general principles of Community law and protected by the Court.

The Court provided no further comment in the case on the nature, identity, or extent of these general principles. However, Advocate General Roemer argued that the Commission decision was not being reviewed for compatibility with *national* constitutional rights, but rather that the general principles of EC law were informed by a 'comparative evaluation' of national constitutional concepts and fundamental rights.[17]

Indeed, the change of approach in *Stauder* might not have been quite the u-turn which is suggested in some of the academic literature, since the ECJ had already paid some attention to the development of general principles of individual protection, drawing not just on Treaty provisions but also on principles of domestic origin such as legal certainty, proportionality, and due process.[18] None the less, it is indisputable that the Court responded negatively in its early case law to the attempts of applicants to plead particular principles of law other than those expressed in the Treaties, and to this extent *Stauder* represented a notable change in approach.[19]

(c) FUNDAMENTAL RIGHTS AS GROUNDS FOR ANNULMENT OF COMMUNITY LAWS

Stauder was a relatively easy case to decide, since the impugned Community measure was capable of being interpreted in conformity with the principle which had been invoked. But before long the ECJ was confronted with an apparent conflict between a Community measure and a right protected within a Member State's law which could not so easily be resolved through interpretation. In the following case, the applicant effectively wanted the German Constitutional Court to disapply or to 'strike down' a Community provision.

[17] [1969] ECR 419, 428.
[18] U. Scheuner, 'Fundamental Rights in European Community law and in National Constitutional Law' (1975) 12 *CMLRev.* 171.
[19] For a discussion of the early 'fundamental rights' implicit within the Treaty itself which were developed by the ECJ as general principles of law see D. Shachor-Landau, 'Reflections on the Two European Courts of Justice', in Y. Dinstein *et al.* (eds.), *International Law at a Time of Perplexity* (Martinus Nijhoff, 1989), 792.

Case 11/70, Internationale Handelsgesellschaft v. Einfuhr und Vorratstelle
für Getreide und Futtermittel
[1970] ECR 1125

The applicant company obtained an export licence for a quantity of maize, the validity of which expired on 31 December 1967. Under Council Regulation 120/67 such a licence could be obtained by lodging a deposit, and the deposit would be forfeit if the goods were not exported within the period of time set. The applicant company brought legal proceedings challenging the validity of the deposit system under which a portion of his deposit had been forfeit upon failure to export the full quantity of maize. The national court considered that the deposit system was contrary to principles of national constitutional law, including freedom of action and of disposition, economic liberty and proportionality, and referred the question of the system's validity to the ECJ.

THE ECJ

3. Recourse to the legal rules or concepts of national law in order to judge the validity of measures adopted by the institutions of the Community would have an adverse effect on the uniformity and efficacy of Community law. The validity of such measures can only be judged in the light of Community law. In fact, the law stemming from the Treaty, an independent source of law, cannot because of its very nature be overridden by rules of national law, however framed, without being deprived of its character as Community law and without the legal basis of the Community itself being called into question. Therefore the validity of a Community measure or its effect within a Member State cannot be affected by allegations that it runs counter to either fundamental rights as formulated by the constitution of that State or the principles of a national constitutional structure.

4. However, an examination should be made as to whether or not any analagous guarantee inherent in Community law has been disregarded. In fact, respect for fundamental rights forms an integral part of the general principles of Community law protected by the Court of Justice. The protection of such rights, whilst inspired by the constitutional traditions common to the Member states, must be ensured within the framework of the structure and objectives of the Community. It must therefore be ascertained, in the light of the doubts expressed by the Verwaltungsgericht, whether the system of deposits has infringed rights of a fundamental nature, respect for which must be ensured in the Community legal system.

The ECJ then concluded that there had been no infringement of the rights claimed, since the restriction on the freedom to trade etc. was not disproportionate to the general interest advanced by the deposit system. When the case returned to the German court, however, a different conclusion was reached, to the effect that the principle of proportionality enshrined in German constitutional law had indeed been violated by the Community deposit system. The effect of this and of subsequent cases on the constitutional relationship between Community law and German law is discussed in Chapter 7, but the case also provides an interesting illustration of the difficulty facing the ECJ if it seeks to assimilate the 'common constitutional principles' of the Member States as part of the Community legal order. If the ECJ's interpretation of the requirements of these principles differs significantly from the interpretation of the

Member States which also claim to guarantee their protection, the legitimacy of the Court's adjudication may be called into question.[20]

4. THE SOURCES OF FUNDAMENTAL RIGHTS DERIVED BY THE COURT

Following the *Handelsgesellschaft* litigation, the ECJ continued to emphasize the autonomy of Community 'general principles' of law, while simultaneously stressing that the source of these general principles was not entirely independent of the legal cultures and traditions of the Member States.[21]

Case 4/73, Nold v. Commission
[1974] ECR 491

The applicant company had been a coal wholesaler and sought the annulment of a Commission decision authorizing the Ruhr coal-selling agency to adopt certain restrictive criteria for its supply of coal, which had the effect of withdrawing from Nold its status as a direct wholesaler. Nold claimed that the Commission Decision discriminated against it and breached its fundamental rights.

THE ECJ

13. As the Court has already stated, fundamental rights form an integral part of the general principles of law, the observance of which it ensures.

In safeguarding these rights, the Court is bound to draw inspiration from constitutional traditions common to the Member States, and it cannot therefore uphold measures which are incompatible with fundamental rights recognized and protected by the Constitutions of those States.

Similarly, international treaties for the protection of human rights on which the Member States have collaborated or of which they are signatories, can supply guidelines which should be followed within the framework of Community law.

In subsequent cases, the Court continued to refer to particular 'sources of inspiration' for the general principles of EC law, thereby giving a more positivistic foundation to the development. In *Rutili*, for example, even though the rights invoked

---

[20] See the discussion in Ch. 7, 295–7, of the recent banana litigation in Germany, and the conviction of many commentators that the EU banana regime was fundamentally flawed and violated many basic principles of German administrative and constitutional law.

[21] See Case 17/74, *Transocean Marine Paint* v. *Commission* [1974] ECR 1063, para. 17, where the Court, after a survey of the administrative law of several of the Member States by the AG, gave recognition to 'the general rule that a person whose interests are perceptibly affected by a decision taken by a public authority, must be given the opportunity to make his point of view known'.

by the applicant were expressed in provisions of Community legislation, the Court nevertheless described them as specific manifestations of more general fundamental principles of Community law which could be found in the European Convention on Human Rights (ECHR).[22] In reasoning that the restrictions imposed by the Community legislation on the powers of Member State authorities to limit the free movement and residence of Community nationals were specific manifestations of general principles contained in the ECHR, the ECJ was linking the fundamental rules of Community law and the law of the ECHR, as it had earlier done in *Nold*. More recent examples of this strategy can be seen in *Johnston*,[23] *P* v. *S*,[24] and *Coote*,[25] in which particular Community legislative provisions on the right to pursue a claim by judicial process and on sex discrimination were declared by the ECJ to constitute specific expressions of the ECHR requirement of judicial control and of the fundamental principle of equality. The early reference to the ECHR in *Rutili* prompted comments at the time about whether the Convention had been incorporated into Community law as a direct formal source of law. However, Advocate General Trabucchi in the case of *Watson and Belmann* argued that such comments were misconceived:

On the basis of this analogy between rules of Community law and rules of international law accepted by all the Member States, some learned writers have felt justified in concluding that the provisions of the said Convention must be treated as forming an integral part of the Community legal order, whereas it seems clear to me that the spirit of the judgment did not involve any substantive reference to the provisions themselves but merely to the general principles of which, like the Community rules with which the judgment drew an analogy, they are a specific expression.

. . .

The extra-Community instruments under which those [Member] States have undertaken international obligations in order to ensure better protection for those rights can, without any question of their being incorporated as such in the Community order, be used to establish principles which are common to the States themselves.[26]

This passage effectively summarizes the ECJ's continuing approach to the source of 'Community fundamental rights', by stressing that the importance of international declarations of rights such as the ECHR lies not in their character as direct sources of Community law, but in the fact that they represent basic principles and common values to which all of the Member State signatories to the Convention have committed themselves. In this way the Court can maintain the autonomy and supremacy of Community law, and while avoiding the charge of having judicially incorporated the Convention and other international agreements into Community law without Member State consent, it can at the same time point to a strong consensus among the States as regards the foundations of the general principles of Community law. The Court's approach was given official legitimacy by a joint declaration of the Parliament, Council,

[22] Case 36/75, *Rutili* v. *Minister for the Interior* [1975] ECR 1219.
[23] Case 222/84, [1986] ECR 1651, para. 18. See further on the right to judicial review Case C–424/99, *Commission* v. *Austria* [2001] ECR I–nyr, paras. 45–47.
[24] Case C–13/94, [1996] ECR I–2143, para. 18.
[25] C–185/97, *Coote* v. *Granada Hospitality* [1998] ECR I–5199, paras. 21–23.
[26] Case 118/75, *Watson and Belmann* [1976] ECR 1185, 1207.

and Commission in 1977, which affirmed the development of general principles of EC law by the ECJ, and in which the three institutions formally committed themselves to ensuring respect for fundamental rights in the exercise of their powers.[27] This joint declaration, although not legally binding, was symbolically important in indicating that the Community's political institutions supported the Court's derivation of rights from the ECHR and from national constitutional principles.

A good example of the ECJ's 'comparative constitutional approach' to the sources of Community fundamental rights is in the *Hauer* case, in which it referred not only to the ECHR, but also to specific provisions of particular national constitutions.

Case 44/79, Hauer v. Land Rheinland-Pfalz
[1979] ECR 3727

The applicant was refused national authorization to undertake the new planting of vines on a plot of land which she owned. When she objected, she was told that the EC Council had passed a regulation prohibiting the new planting of vines in that region. She appealed to the German court against the refusal, pleading the incompatibility of the Council Regulation with the German Constitution. The *Verwaltungsgericht* referred the case to the ECJ, stating that if it were incompatible with fundamental German constitutional rights, the Regulation might be inapplicable in Germany.

THE ECJ

14. As the Court declared in its judgment of 17 December 1970, *Internationale Handelsgesellschaft* [1970] ECR 1125, the question of a possible infringement of fundamental rights by a measure of the Community institutions can only be judged in the light of Community law itself. The introduction of special criteria for assessment stemming from the legislation or constitutional law of a particular Member State would, by damaging the substantive unity and efficacy of Community law, lead inevitably to the destruction of the unity of the Common Market and the jeopardizing of the cohesion of the Community.

15. The Court also emphasized in the judgment cited, and later in the judgment of 14 May 1974, *Nold* [1974] ECR 491, that fundamental rights form an integral part of the general principles of the law, the observance of which it ensures; that in safeguarding those rights, the Court is bound to draw inspiration from constitutional traditions common to the Member States, so that measures which are incompatible with the fundamental rights recognized by the Constitutions of those States are unacceptable in the Community, and that, similarly, international treaties for the protection of human rights on which the Member States have collaborated or of which they are signatories, can supply guidelines which should be followed within the framework of Community law. That conception was later recognized by the joint declaration of the European Parliament, the Council and the Commission of 5 April 1977, which, after recalling the case law of the Court, refers on the one hand to the European Convention for the Protection of Human Rights and Fundamental Freedoms of 4 November 1950.

---

[27] [1977] OJ C103/1.

The Court then referred to the right to property protected within the First Protocol to the ECHR, and to the restrictions on the exercise of the right which that provision envisaged. It also made specific reference, mirroring the opinion of Advocate General Capotorti, to provisions of the German, Italian, and Irish Constitutions, and to the fact that in all Member States there were legislative provisions restricting the use of real property in order to promote various public interests. Similarly in *Bosphorous*, which concerned the effects on the applicant's rights of an EC regulation implementing UN-mandated sanctions against Yugoslavia, the ECJ ruled that the fundamental interests of the international community could justify restrictions of property or trade rights caused by the impounding of a Yugoslav-owned aircraft leased by the applicant.[28]

Apart from the ECHR and national constitutional provisions, the Court has also occasionally drawn on other international instruments. In *Defrenne v. Sabena III*,[29] the Court, deeming the elimination of sex discrimination to be a fundamental Community right, supported its conclusion by noting that 'the same concepts are recognized by the European Social Charter of 18 November 1961 and by Convention No. 111 of the International Labour Organization of 25 June 1958 concerning discrimination in respect of employment and occupation'.[30] In a number of cases, the International Covenant on Civil and Political Rights (ICCPR) has been identified as a source of inspiration for the general principles of EC law, although the ECJ in the case of *Grant* was surprisingly dismissive of an opinion given by the ICCPR Human Rights Committee.[31]

The fact that the Court so frequently draws on the ECHR in identifying the fundamental rights protected within Community law has not, however, led it to refuse legal status to a right which is not expressly protected under these. In the *AM & S* case concerning the production of documents in competition law proceedings, Advocate General Warner noted that the ECHR made no mention of a principle of lawyer/client confidentiality, yet the Court held that it was a part of Community law.

Case 155/79, AM & S Europe Ltd. v. Commission
[1982] ECR 1575

THE ECJ

18. . . . Community law, which derives from not only the economic but also the legal interpenetration of the Member States, must take into account the principles and concepts common to the laws of those States concerning the observance of confidentiality, in particular, as regards

---

[28] See Case C–84/95, *Bosphorous v. Minister for Transport* [1996] ECR I–3953 and also the first instance judgment in Case T–184/95, *Dorsch Consult v. Council* [1998] ECR II–667, paras. 87–88.

[29] Case 149/77, *Defrenne v. Sabena* [1978] ECR 1365.

[30] [1978] ECR 1365, para. 26 of the judgment. See also Case 6/75, *Horst v. Bundesknappschaft* [1975] ECR 823, 836, where Reischl AG drew on an 'internationally recognized principle of social security as set out in Art. 22(2) of International Labour Convention No. 48 on the Maintenance of Migrants' Pension Rights of 1935'.

[31] See Case C–249/96, *Grant v. South West Trains Ltd.* [1998] ECR I–621, paras. 44–47. For a case involving criminal penalties where the ICCPR was discussed by the CFI, see Case T–48/96, *Acme Industry v. Council* [1999] ECR II–3089.

certain communications between lawyer and client. That confidentiality serves the requirements, the importance of which is recognized in all the Member States, that any person must be able, without constraint, to consult a lawyer whose profession entails the giving of independent legal advice to all those in need of it.

19. As far as the protection of written communications between lawyer and client is concerned, it is apparent from the legal systems of the Member States that, although the principle of such protection is generally recognized, its scope and the criteria for applying it vary.

. . .

21. Apart from these differences, however, there are to be found in the national laws of the Member States common criteria inasmuch as those laws protect, in similar circumstances, the confidentiality of written communications between lawyer and client provided that, on the one hand, such communications are made for the purposes and in the interests of the client's rights of defence, and on the other hand, they emanate from independent lawyers, that is to say, lawyers who are not bound to the client by a relationship of employment.

22. Viewed in that context Regulation No 17 must be interpreted as protecting, in its turn, the confidentiality of written communications between lawyer and client subject to those two conditions, and thus incorporating such elements of that protection as are common to the laws of the Member States.

5. THE STANDARD OF PROTECTION FOR EU FUNDAMENTAL RIGHTS

There are two aspects to the question of what standard of protection for fundamental rights is applied by the ECJ. The first derives from what we have discussed above, namely how exactly those general principles are drawn from other sources, and the second concerns the way in which the ECJ approaches the question whether or not a breach of a fundamental right has occurred.

(a) DERIVING RIGHTS FROM THE 'SOURCES OF INSPIRATION'

Beginning with the first aspect, we have seen how the ECJ endeavoured to legitimate its development of unwritten general principles of EC law by grounding them in positive legal sources: in national constitutional laws and in international human rights instruments. Such identification of shared underpinnings is, however, only a first step. Sometimes, the international agreements to which all Member States are party represent a lowest common denominator, and may not necessarily provide a satisfactory standard of protection for rights which are particularly important to certain Member States. It was argued some decades ago that the ECHR would not provide a suitable charter for the Community in protecting fundamental rights and general principles of law, on the ground that it provided too low a standard of protection.[32] A certain amount of support for this view may be detected in the comments of Advocate General Lenz in the case of *Mutsch*,[33] concerning the right of Community workers in a Member State other than that of their nationality to require

---

[32] Scheuner, n. 18 above, 181.   [33] Case 137/84, *Ministère Public* v. *Mutsch* [1985] ECR 2681.

that criminal proceedings against them take place in a language other than that normally used in the Court in question, if nationals of the host Member State had that right:

Nor can I agree with the view that it is sufficient to place an interpreter at the disposal of the accused, as is required by the European Convention on Human Rights. In the area of fundamental rights the Court has certainly drawn guidelines from the Convention, in the sense that it has treated the Convention as supplying common minimum standards.

It is not contrary to the European Convention on Human Rights for Community law to grant more extensive protection to individual rights. Indeed the Court has held that Community law takes precedence over other agreements concluded within the framework of the Council of Europe in so far as it is more favourable for individuals.[34]

And as regards the comparative derivation of common principles from Member State constitutional traditions, it has recently been argued that the ECJ, far from applying a lowest common denominator standard, should apply a 'univeral maximum standard', which would involve the recognition of any right protected by any single Member State or in any relevant international agreement as a fundamental right in EC law.[35] This approach is unlikely to be adopted, since although the Court will normally be careful to affirm protection within EC law for any principle which is important in the constitutional law of a number of Member States (given the potential supremacy threat underlying fundamental rights challenges), the opposite risk that it may be accused of exporting a very specific fundamental principle recognized within only one or very few Member States into all the others in the guise of a commonly shared EC law principle is equally present.

Indeed, in the recent case of *Mannesmannröhren-Werke*, in relation to the right to remain silent in the context of competition proceedings the CFI appeared to dismiss the 'universal maximum standard' approach:

In the field of competition law, the national laws of the Member States do not, in general, recognise a right not to incriminate oneself. It is, therefore, immaterial to the result of the present case whether or not, as the applicant claims, there is such a principle in German law.[36]

Further, we saw in *AM & S* that the ECJ derived a principle of confidentiality between lawyer and client from a comparative survey of the laws of the Member States. Yet not all of the Member States were happy with the Court's conclusion, and the French government in particular argued that the case represented 'an attempt to foist on the Community what was no more than a domestic rule of English law'.[37] Nevertheless, the Advocate General took the view that a general principle could be distilled from among the various States even if the 'conceptual origin' of the principle and 'the scope of its application in detail' differed as between Member States.[38] Ultimately, neither he nor the Court considered these differences to constitute a barrier to

---

[34] *Ibid.*, 2690.

[35] L. Besselink, 'Entrapped by the Maximum Standard: on Fundamental Rights, Pluralism and Subsidiarity in the European Union' (1998) 35 *CMLRev*. 629. See for a different view J. Weiler, 'Fundamental Rights and Fundamental Boundaries', in his *The Constitution of Europe* (CUP, 1999), ch. 3.

[36] T–112/98, *Mannesmannröhren-Werke* v. *Commission* [2001] ECR II–729, para. 84.

[37] See Warner AG in Case 155/79, *AM & S Europe Ltd.* v. *Commission* [1982] ECR 1575, 1631.

[38] *Ibid.*

the derivation of a common principle which would represent the appropriate level of Community protection. The case however clearly highlights the difficulty inherent in attempting to ascertain the degree of protection for a particular right or principle amongst twelve or fifteen different Member States.[39]

In *Martinez et al.*, the applicants drew unsuccessfully on the common parliamentary traditions of the Member States, as well as on the principle of freedom of association,[40] in order to challenge the refusal to permit them, as a group of non-aligned MEPs, to register as a political party in order to gain certain privileges, although the CFI did not deny the possibility in principle that 'common parliamentary traditions' could form a source of inspiration for the general principles of EC law.[41] And in the case of *Al-Jubail*, concerning protection of the right to a fair hearing, the ECJ demonstrated its awareness of the dangers of falling below the level of protection provided for a right which is important within the legal systems of various Member States:

It should be added that, with regard to the right to a fair hearing, any action taken by the Community institutions must be all the more scrupulous in view of the fact that, as they stand at present, the rules in question do not provide all the procedural guarantees for the protection of the individual which may exist in certain national legal systems.[42]

The Advocate General in the same case was concerned that the level of protection given should also not be seen to fall below that which was guaranteed by the ECHR.[43] Interestingly this seems to suggest that, rather than providing too low a level of protection, as was argued by others above, the ECHR as interpreted by the European Court of Human Rights in fact represents a standard against which the Community institutions and the ECJ should measure their 'fundamental rights' performance. However, the Convention is not formally part of EC law, and indeed in *Mayr-Melnhof Kartongesellschaft*, we see the CFI declaring that 'the Court of First Instance has no jurisdiction to apply the ECHR when reviewing an investigation under competition law, because the ECHR is not itself part of Community law'.[44] Nevertheless, the CFI's insistence on the formal 'externality' of the ECHR and the autonomy of EC fundamental rights law needs to be placed alongside the fact that Article 6 TEU expressly refers to the ECHR and, more practically, that the ECJ and the CFI routinely refer to the 'special significance' of the Convention as a key source of inspiration for the general principles of EC law.[45]

---

[39] Case 17/74, *Transocean Marine Paint*, n. 21 above, provides another example of the recognition by the Court of a general principle of Community law where some but not all of the Member States afford protection to the particular right or principle.

[40] For other cases on freedom of association see Cases C–415/93, *Union Royal Belge des Sociétés de Football Association* v. *Bosman* [1995] ECR I–4921 and C–325/92, *Montecatini* v. *Commission* [1999] ECR I–4539.

[41] Joined Cases T–222/99, T–327/99, & T–329/99, *Martinez, Gaulle, Front national and Bonino* v. *European Parliament*, judgment of the CFI of 2 Oct. 2001, para. 240.

[42] Case C–49/88, *Al-Jubail Fertilizer Co. and Saudi Arabian Fertilizer Co.* v. *Council* [1991] ECR I–3187, para. 16.

[43] *Ibid.*, 3230–1.

[44] Case T–347/94, *Mayr-Melnhof Kartongesellschaft mbH* v. *Commission* [1998] ECR II–1751, para. 311. See also Case T–112/98, *Mannesmannröhren-Werke* v. *Commission* [2001] ECR II–729, para. 59.

[45] See, e.g., Case C–260/89, *ERT* v. *DEP* [1991] ECR I–2925, para. 41; *Opinion 2/94 on Accession by the Community to the ECHR* [1996] ECR I–1759, para. 33; and Case C–299/95, *Kremzow* v. *Austria* [1997] ECR I–2629, para. 14.

The debate on the adequacy or otherwise of the standards reflected in the ECHR as the basis for EC human rights protection surfaced actively again during the recent drafting of the EU Charter of Fundamental Rights. It seems that a long and heated debate on the proper relationship of the Charter to the Convention was held, and on whether a right contained in the Charter should necessarily be interpreted in the same way as a similar or identical right contained in the ECHR, as well as on the proper relationship of the Court of Justice and the European Court of Human Rights.[46] This question, which was highlighted also by the litigation in the *Emesa Sugar* case in which the ECJ's interpretation of the right to adversarial proceedings in the context of the role of the Advocate General sits uneasily with ECHR jurisprudence, will be returned to below.[47]

(b) ADJUDICATING RIGHTS CLAIMS

(I) DIFFERENT DEGREES OF PROTECTION FOR DIFFERENT RIGHTS

Let us now turn to the second aspect of the standard of protection applied by the ECJ. It seems likely that even if all of the Member States were agreed on *which* specific rights should be recognized, they may well differ on *how* those rights should be protected. For instance, all Member States agree that there should be protection for freedom of expression, yet they may have rather different views on how, in a particular context, it should be protected. National legal systems vary widely, for example, in the degree to which they regulate the nature and content of broadcasting.[48] Some States accept greater restrictions than others on the scope of individual rights and freedoms in the pursuit of other public interests. And while all Member States recognize the right to life, for example, Ireland is alone amongst the current fifteen Member States in maintaining extremely restrictive national abortion laws, which reflect the current, albeit contested, scope of that right under the constitution. Germany's *GrundGesetz*, as we saw in Chapter 7, gives strong protection to economic rights and to the freedom to pursue a trade or profession, while the constitutions of other States may reflect different social priorities. In *Grant* and *D v. Council*, the ECJ relied in part on different national legal conceptions of marriage to deny that there had been any breach of the applicants' rights under the general principles of EC law.[49] The current controversy over the introduction of an EU arrest warrant[50] following the events of 11 September 2001 has also highlighted the differing constitutional traditions and human rights concerns of various Member States.

(II) EXCEPTIONS AND LIMITATIONS ON THE SCOPE OF RIGHTS

Even if the ECJ accepts the argument of a particular party that a given right should be recognized as part of Community law, the way in which the Court determines the

---

[46] See the account of Goldsmith, n. 9 above.

[47] Case C–17/98, *Emesa Sugar v. Aruba* [2000] ECR I–665.

[48] See R. Craufurd-Smith, *Broadcasting Law and Fundamental Rights* (Oxford University Press, 1997).

[49] Case C–249/96, *Grant v. South West Trains Ltd* [1998] ECR I–621 and C–122 & 125/99P *D v. Council* [2001] ECR I–4319.

[50] See COM(2001)521 and COM(2001)522 [2001] OJ C332/300.

legal scope of that right and applies it in the context of the case at hand may well differ from the way it would be applied in a national context, and may disappoint the applicant, as we saw in *Hauer*[51] and *Handelsgesellschaft*.[52] Despite the fact that the ECJ in *Nold*[53] declared that 'general principles of law' would take precedence, in the event of conflict, over specific Community measures, the cases in which Community legislative action has been impeded by human rights claims are few.

Nold in fact provides a good illustration of the general approach taken by the Court in many cases:

14. If rights of ownership are protected by the constitutional laws of all the Member States and if similar guarantees are given in respect of their right freely to choose and practise their trade or profession, the rights thereby guaranteed, far from constituting unfettered prerogatives, must be viewed in the light of the social function of the property and activities protected thereunder.

For this reason, rights of this nature are protected by law subject always to limitations laid down in accordance with the public interest.

Within the Community legal order it likewise seems legitimate that these rights should, if necessary, be subject to certain limits justified by the overall objectives pursued by the Community, on condition that the substance of these rights is left untouched.

As regards the guarantees accorded to a particular undertaking, they can in no respect be extended to protect mere commercial interests or opportunities, the uncertainties of which are part of the very essence of economic activity.

15. The disadvantages claimed by the applicant are in fact the result of economic change and not of the contested decision.[54]

Cases such as these suggest that despite the Court's recognition of fundamental rights as part of Community law and as grounds for annulment, the impact of this development on the outcome of cases claiming a breach of fundamental rights may be minimal,[55] even though such claims are regularly made. In *Prais*, the applicant relied on Article 9 of the ECHR concerning freedom of religion as a ground for the annulment of a Council decision setting the date of a job competition on a Jewish feastday,[56] and, although the case was ultimately unsuccessful, the ruling indicated that the Council should 'take steps' to respect the requirements of a candidate's religion.[57] Similarly in *Hauer*, where the applicant claimed that the refusal of permission to grow vines on her land infringed her rights to trade and to property, the Court simultaneously acknowledged these rights as part of Community law, but denied that the restriction imposed upon them was disproportionate to the objectives of the Community's structural policy in this area.[58]

---

[51] Case 44/79, *Hauer* v. *Land Rheinland-Pfalz* [1979] ECR 3727.

[52] Case 11/70, *Internationale Handelsgesellschaft* v. *Einfuhr und Vorratstelle für Getreide und Futtermittel* [1970] ECR 1125.

[53] Case 4/73, Nold v. *Commission* [1974] ECR 491.   [54] *Ibid.*

[55] See, e.g., A. Clapham, 'A Human Rights Policy for the European Community' (1990) 10 *YBEL* 309, 331, and J. Coppel and A. O'Neill, 'The European Court of Justice: Taking Rights Seriously?' (1992) 29 *CMLRev.* 669.

[56] Case 130/75, *Prais* v. *Council* [1976] ECR 1589.   [57] *Ibid.*, para. 18.

[58] [1979] ECR 3727, para. 22. See also the *Bosphorous* case, n. 28 above.

More recently, one of the grounds relied on by the Dutch government in challenging the legality of the Biotechnology Directive, which required Member States to provide patent protection for biotechnological inventions, was that its provisions concerning the patentability of isolated parts of the body violated the right to human dignity and to human integrity.[59] In a judgment which will certainly not convince opponents of the directive, the ECJ did not acknowledge any infringement of these rights, and therefore did not consider the question of justification. Instead, the Court side-stepped the connection between the genetic manipulation of the human body and the subsequent industrial use and exploitation of inventions, and claimed that the legislative provisions ensured full respect for human dignity and integrity:

71. As regards respect for human dignity, this is guaranteed in principle by Article 5(1) of the Directive which provides that the human body at the various stages of its formation and development cannot constitute a patentable invention.

And after a brief discussion of particular provisions of the Directive, such as those concerning the sequence of human genes, the cloning of human beings, and the commercial use of embryos, the ECJ concluded that:

77. It is clear from those provisions that, as regards living matter of human origin, the Directive frames the law on patents in a manner sufficiently rigorous to ensure that the human body effectively remains unavailable and inalienable and that human dignity is thus safeguarded.

The strong objection of the Dutch government (and, apparently, of Dutch public and political opinion) and the strength of conviction concerning the importance of respect for human dignity did not appear to influence the Court. In fact, the ECJ normally shows great deference to general legislative measures adopted by the Community, only very rarely annulling such measures, whether for breach of fundamental rights or otherwise.

(iii) CHALLENGING ADMINISTRATIVE ACTS FOR VIOLATION OF FUNDAMENTAL RIGHTS

Staff Cases

A greater degree of success has been achieved in cases challenging specific administrative acts, rather than broad legislative measures, for breach of fundamental rights. Challenges in the field of competition law and in staff cases[60] have been more readily entertained by the Court of First Instance and, on occasion, by the ECJ. In *Oyowe and Traore*, the ECJ required the Commission to change its employment practice in relation to journalists from the African, Caribbean, and Pacific (ACP) States who were working for the Community's European Co-operation Agency, in such a way as to respect their freedom of expression.[61] The Court took the view that the Commission

---

[59] Case C–377/98, *Netherlands v. Council and Parliament* [2001] ECR I–7079.

[60] For some examples see Cases C–404/92P, *X v. Commission* [1994] ECR I–4737; C–122 & 125/99P, *D v. Council* [2001] ECR I–4319; C–191/98P, *Tzoanos v. Commission* [1999] ECR I–8223; C–252/97, *N v. Commission* [1998] ECR I–4871.

[61] Case 100/88, *Oyowe and Traore v. Commission* [1989] ECR 4285. The Court chose to emphasize the restriction on the applicants' freedom of expression, which they did not expressly raise, but did not address the principles of equality and non-discrimination which they specifically pleaded.

was imposing the duty of allegiance in a way which would infringe the fundamental right to freedom of expression of employees. In the rather fascinating case of *Connolly* v. *Commission*, however, both the CFI and the ECJ concluded that a reasonable balance between the requirement of allegiance and the freedom of expression of employees had been struck by the Commission when it dismissed one of its senior officials following the publication of his highly publicized and controversial book on economic and monetary union, entitled *The Rotten Heart of Europe*, without obtaining the permission required under the staff regulations.[62] The case is very interesting in many respects, not least because of the extensive discussion by the ECJ of ECHR jurisprudence concerning Article 10 on freedom of expression,[63] but also because of the far more detailed judicial treatment of the human rights claim than is usual for the ECJ.

In *X* v. *Commission*, proceedings were successfully brought against the Commission by a staff member who argued that an AIDS test had effectively been carried out without his consent, when the ECJ, annulling the contrary decision of the CFI, ruled that there had in fact been a breach of the applicant's right to respect for private life which was 'embodied in Article 8 of the ECHR and deriving from the common constitutional traditions of the Member States'.[64] As against this, the ECJ gave a rather weaker ruling in *D* v. *Council*, in which it ruled that neither the principle of equal treatment, non-discrimination on grounds of sex, nor respect for private and family life had been breached by the Council's refusal to recognize a Swedish employee's registered partnership with a same-sex partner (which had a civil status comparable to marriage in Sweden) as equivalent to marriage for the purposes of obtaining an EU staff household allowance.[65] Unlike the CFI, however, the ECJ did not actually rule that that the right to family life under ECHR and EC law did not cover same-sex relationships, but rather simply ruled that on the facts of the case, there had been no actual interference with family life.

Competition Proceedings

The area of the Commission's enforcement powers in competition proceedings has been a fertile source of litigation, in which general principles of law and fundamental rights have frequently been invoked to challenge EC action.[66] Complaints in this context, like those of staff cases discussed above, normally concern individual administrative or executive action rather than discretionary powers in the creation of legislative policy. The Commission's powers in competition proceedings are very wide, including the authority to investigate and make searches, as well as to impose severe financial penalties, and affected parties have repeatedly called upon the Court to limit and control their exercise by reference to fundamental legal principles.[67]

---

[62] Case C–274/99P, *Connolly* v. *Commission* [2001] ECR I–1611.

[63] Ibid., paras. 39–51 of the judgment.

[64] Case C–404/92P, *X* v. *Commission* [1994] ECR I–4737, para. 17, annulling the judgment in Cases T–121/89 & 13/90.

[65] Case C–122 & 125/99P, *D* v. *Council* [2001] ECR I–4319.   [66] See Ch. 25.

[67] For a few examples from a long list see Cases 17/74, n. 21 above; 209–215/78, *Van Landewyck* v. *Commission* [1980] ECR 3125; 136/79, *National Panasonic* v. *Commission* [1980] ECR 2033; 100–103/80, *Musique Diffusion Française* v. *Commission* [1983] ECR 1825; 322/81, *Michelin* v. *Commission* [1983] ECR 3461; 5/85, *AKZO Chemie* v. *Commission* [1986] ECR 2585; 374/87, *Orkem* v. *Commission* [1989] ECR 3283;

Cases 46/87 and 227/88, Hoechst AG v. Commission
[1989] ECR 2859

Hoechst brought an action for the annulment of various Commission decisions which had ordered an investigation into its affairs, in the context of suspected anti-competitive practices, and which had subsequently imposed periodic penalty payments upon it for refusing to permit the carrying out of this investigation. The applicant argued that the decisions in question had violated fundamental rights protected within Community law, including various procedural rights and the right to inviolability of the home.

THE ECJ

12. It should be noted, before the nature and scope of the Commission's powers of investigation under Article 14 of Regulation No 17 are examined, that that article cannot be interpreted in such a way as to give rise to results which are incompatible with the general principles of Community law and in particular with fundamental rights.

. . .

14. In interpreting Article 14 of Regulation No 17, regard must be had in particular to the rights of the defence, a principle whose fundamental nature has been stressed on numerous occasions in the Court's decisions (see in particular the judgment of 9 November 1983 in Case 322/81 *Michelin* v. *Commission* [1983] ECR 3461 paragraph 7).

. . .

17. Since the applicant has also relied on the requirements stemming from the fundamental right to the inviolability of the home, it should be observed that, although the existence of such a right must be recognized in the Community legal order as a principle common to the laws of the Member States in regard to the private dwellings of natural persons, the same is not true in regard to undertakings, because there are not inconsiderable divergences between the legal systems of the Member States in regard to the nature and degree of protection afforded to business premises against intervention by the public authorities.

18. No other inference is to be drawn from Article 8(1) of the European Convention on Human Rights which provides that: 'Everyone has the right to respect for his private and family life, his home and his correspondence'. The protective scope of that article is concerned with the development of man's personal freedom and may not therefore be extended to business premises. Furthermore, it should be noted that there is no case law of the European Convention on Human Rights on that subject.

19. None the less, in all the legal systems of the Member States, any intervention by the public authorities in the sphere of private activities of any person, whether natural or legal, must have a legal basis and be justified on the grounds laid down by law, and, consequently, those systems provide, albeit in different forms, protection against arbitrary or disproportionate intervention. The need for such protection must be recognized as a general principle of Community law.

T–11/89; *Shell* v. *Commission* [1992] ECR II–757; T–347/94, *Mayr-Melnhof Kartongesellschaft* v. *Commission* [1998] ECR II–1751; T–348/94, *Enso Española SA* v. *Commission* [1998] ECR II–1875; C–185/95P *Baustahlgewebe* v. *Commission* [1998] ECR I–8417; Joined Cases T–305/94 *et seq.*, *Limburgse Vinyl Maatschappij NV* v. *Commission* [1999] ECR II–931; T–112/98, *Mannesmannröhren-Werke* v. *Commission* [2001] ECR II–729.

The Court found on the facts of the case that there had been no breach by the Commission of any of the principles invoked by the applicants. The judgment was criticized on the ground that the Court too rapidly dismissed the argument that the Commission's power of search contravened the right to privacy of the dwelling which is protected in the ECHR. It was pointed out that later case law of the Court of Human Rights (ECtHR) had suggested that Article 8 of the Convention could apply to business premises.[68] Various commentators had expressed concern that the Community should ensure the Commission's wide powers in competition proceedings should remain within acceptable limits, respecting the rights of other parties.[69] Shortly afterwards, it became clear that the ruling of the ECJ on the matter did not correspond exactly with the view of the ECtHR. In *Niemietz*,[70] the ECtHR ruled that the right to respect for private life in Article 8 of the Convention did extend to business premises, stating that 'to interpret the words "private life" and "home" as including certain professional or business activities or premises would be consonant with the essential object and purpose of Article 8, namely to protect the individual against arbitrary interference by the public authorities'.[71] The scope of protection afforded by Article 8 in accordance with that judgment is broader than the ECJ in its ruling in *Hoechst* specified, although of course the right protected in Article 8 is by no means absolute.[72]

Similarly, in relation to the right to a fair trial in Article 6(1) of the ECHR, the decision of the ECJ in *Orkem*,[73] in which it ruled that Article 6 did not confer the right 'not to give evidence against oneself', was at odds with the subsequent ruling of the ECtHR in the case of *Funke*, in which that court indicated that Article 6 protected the right 'to remain silent and not to contribute to incriminating [oneself]'.[74] However in *Hüls*, another EC competition law case, the significance of the ECHR and of the case law of the ECtHR is evident in the ECJ's reasoning:

149. The Court observes first of all that the presumption of innocence resulting in particular from Article 6(2) of the ECHR is one of the fundamental rights which, according to the Court's settled case-law, reaffirmed in the preamble to the Single European Act and in Article F(2) of the Treaty on European Union, are protected in the Community legal order.

150. It must also be accepted that, given the nature of the infringements in question and the nature and degree of severity of the ensuing penalties, the principle of the presumption of

---

[68] See Clapham, n. 55 above, 337–8, referring to the European Commission on Human Rights Report in the *Chappell* case, App. no. 10461/83. The judgment of the ECHR in the case did not directly resolve the issue: Series A, No 152A.

[69] Clapham, n. 55 above, 335–8. See also M. Lauwaars, (1990) 27 *CMLRev.* 355 and J. Shaw, (1990) 15 *ELRev.* 326.

[70] *Niemietz* v. *Germany*, Series A, No 251.

[71] *Ibid.*, para. 31.

[72] See the Opinion of Mischo AG in *Hoechst* [1989] ECR 2859, para. 112.

[73] Case 374/87, n. 67 above, para. 30 of the judgment. However, the Court did go on to rule that by virtue of the 'rights of the defence' in investigative procedures, the Commission could not compel a company to provide it with answers which might involve an admission of a breach which it was incumbent on the Commission to prove. See also Case C–60/92, *Otto* v. *Postbank* [1993] ECR I–5683. For a case dealing with alleged pressure imposed by the Commission on an applicant to admit to particular allegations in order to have the potential fine reduced, see Case T–347/94, *Mayr-Melnhof Kartongesellschaft mbH* v. *Commission* [1998] ECR II–1751.

[74] *Funke* v. *France*, Series A, No 256A, para. 44 of the judgment. See W. van Overbeek, 'The Right to Remain Silent in Competition Investigations' (1994) 15 *ECLR* 127.

innocence applies to the procedures relating to infringements of the competition rules applicable to undertakings that may result in the imposition of fines or periodic penalty payments (see, to that effect, in particular the judgments of the European Court of Human Rights of 21 February 1984, ztürk, Series A No 73, and of 25 August 1987 Lutz, Series A No 123-A).[75]

In *Mannesmannröhren-Werke*, where the applicant contested the Commission's insistence, on pain of penalty, that it must answer certain questions posed in the course of a competition investigation, the CFI denied the direct applicability of ECHR provisions, while at the same time insisting that the general principles of EC law provide equivalent protection:

66. To acknowledge the existence of an absolute right to silence, as claimed by the applicant, would go beyond what is necessary in order to preserve the rights of defence of undertakings, and would constitute an unjustified hindrance to the Commission's performance of its duty under Article 89 of the EC Treaty (now, after amendment, Article 85 EC) to ensure that the rules on competition within the common market are observed.

. . .

75. As regards the arguments to the effect that Article 6(1) and (2) of the Convention enables a person in receipt of a request for information to refrain from answering the questions asked, even if they are purely factual in nature, and to refuse to produce documents to the Commission, suffice it to repeat that the applicant cannot directly invoke the Convention before the Community courts.

. . .

77. However, it must be emphasised that Community law does recognise as fundamental principles both the rights of defence and the right to fair legal process (see *Baustahlgewebe* v *Commission*, cited above, paragraph 21, and Case C–7/98 *Krombach* [2000] ECR I–1935, paragraph 26). It is in application of those principles, which offer, in the specific field of competition law, at issue in the present case, protection equivalent to that guaranteed by Article 6 of the Convention, that the Court of Justice and the Court of First Instance have consistently held that the recipient of requests sent by the Commission pursuant to Article 11(5) of Regulation No 17 is entitled to confine himself to answering questions of a purely factual nature and to producing only the pre-existing documents and materials sought and, moreover, is so entitled as from the very first stage of an investigation initiated by the Commission.[76]

None the less, in both *Hüls* and *Mannesmannröhren-Werke*, the Court found no infringement on the facts of the case.

Finally, apart from challenges to individual administrative acts, the ECJ has been somewhat more willing to protect a specific legal right when to guarantee respect for that right would not interfere with the substance of a Community policy, but e.g. would simply require the observance of procedural protection within the implementation of a substantive Community policy.[77] In *Al-Jubail*, the Court was asked to declare provisions of an anti-dumping regulation void in its application to the plaintiffs, who argued that they had been denied the right to a fair hearing in

---

[75] Case C–199/92P, *Hüls* v. *Commission* [1999] ECR I–4287.
[76] Case T–112/98, *Mannesmannröhren-Werke* v. *Commission* [2001] ECR II–729.
[77] For discussion of successful claims invoking fundamental rights against the Community see J.H.H. Weiler and N. Lockhart, ' "Taking Rights Seriously" Seriously: The European Court and its Fundamental Rights Jurisprudence' (1995) 32 *CMLRev.* 51 and 579.

the process leading to the adoption of the measure.[78] The ECJ stressed the importance of the right to a fair hearing and ruled that it should be taken into account in interpreting the regulation in question. Ultimately, the Court found that there had been an infringement of the right to a fair hearing in the case at hand, and declared certain aspects of the impugned provision of the regulation to be void. Indeed, in a number of other prominent cases such as *Krombach* and *Baustahlgewebe*, claims based on the right to a fair hearing as a general principle of EC law have met with a degree of success.[79]

(c) SUMMARY

i. Although the 'sources of inspiration' for the general principles of EC law in national constitutional traditions and international agreements are relatively clear, the way in which the ECJ has derived particular concrete rights from these sources is more difficult to conceptualize.

ii. Some have argued for the ECJ to develop a 'maximum universal standard' while others have warned against the risk of a lowest common denominator. While the Court is clearly very reluctant to refuse EC law recognition to a principle which is important in a number of Member States, it has never expressly endorsed either a maximalist or a minimalist approach. Instead it seems to develop relatively autonomous EC law principles on a case-by-case basis.

iii. Similarly, while the European Convention on Human Rights is not a formal part of EC law, it is the most common source of reference for fundamental EC rights. The CFI and the ECJ regularly draw on the provisions of the ECHR and in recent years have made extensive reference to the case law of the Court of Human Rights. The relationship between the two systems, however, remains legally ambiguous.

iv. While fundamental rights claims are increasingly frequently made, they have been more successful in disputes involving individual administrative acts such as in staff cases or competition proceedings, than in challenges to legislative policy.

6. DO THE GENERAL PRINCIPLES OF COMMUNITY LAW BIND THE MEMBER STATES?

In most of the cases so far considered, the ECJ was asked to assess measures of EC law in the light of particular fundamental rights or general principles of law. A more unexpected development, however, was the ECJ's application of these requirements to

[78] Case C–49/88, n. 42 above.
[79] Case C–7/98, *Krombach* v. *Bamberski* [2000] ECR II–1935 (in the context of the Brussels Convention), and for comment see A. van Hoek (2001) 37 *CMLRev.* 1011; Case C–185/95P, *Baustahlgewebe* v. *Commission* [1998] ECR I–8417 (on the length of time of proceedings), and for a similar but unsuccessful claim, Cases T–213/95 & 18/96, *SCK & FNK* v. *Commission* [1997] ECR II–1739. See also Case T–83/96, *van der Wal* v. *Commission* [1998] ECR II–545 (on the right of access to documents used in judicial proceedings).

acts of the Member States in certain contexts. While the first step of developing fundamental rights as a constraint on EC action was welcomed by most States, the second step—in subjecting Member State action, even within the field of EC law, to an unwritten and uncertain cluster of legal rights—was rather a different matter. It might, of course, be argued that since these rights and principles really are derived from the constitutional traditions of the Member States and from international agreements signed by them all, there should be little objection to the requirement that Member States also comply with those shared legal values. However, as we have seen, not only does the interpretation of the meaning and scope of such rights vary from State to State, but not all general principles of Community law will be shared by all States. Further, even if it were possible to reach agreement on the exact substance of these rights and principles, the Member States would not necessarily want the ECJ to have a role in assessing their compliance with such principles. The Community 'law' with which Member States have bound themselves to comply and the Community 'obligations' which they must fulfil were probably understood by the States to be those specific obligations expressly set out in the Treaties and in the legislation adopted by the Community institutions in which the States participate. Indeed, the extension of a form of 'human rights review' by the ECJ to Member State action came about gradually, and the exact scope of this development remains unclear. Further, Article 51 of the Charter of Fundamental Rights, which is the provision governing this matter, is expressed in rather more restrictive terms than the case law of the ECJ on the issue, although the explanatory memorandum to the Charter (whose legal status is even less clear, at present, than that of the Charter itself) suggests a more expansive reading in conformity with ECJ case law.

(a) MEMBER STATES APPLYING PROVISIONS OF COMMUNITY LAW WHICH ARE BASED ON PROTECTION FOR HUMAN RIGHTS

In the *Rutili* case in 1975, discussed above, the ECJ had described provisions of Directive 64/221, which set limits on the restrictions which Member States could apply to the free movement of workers, as specific expressions of the more general principles enshrined in the ECHR. The restrictive measures adopted by France in that case had to be examined for compliance with the provisions of the Directive, which in turn reflected provisions of the ECHR.[80] Subsequently, in *Johnston* v. *RUC*, the UK sought to rely on a derogation contained in the Equal Treatment Directive, 76/207, to justify terminating the employment of a female reserve member of the police force on the ground that female reserves could no longer be armed. Her attempt to challenge this decision was blocked by a certificate, which constituted conclusive evidence under national law, that the decision had been adopted for the purposes of safeguarding national security and protecting public safety and order. Johnston relied on the remedial provision in Article 6 of the EC Directive, and the case was eventually referred to the ECJ.

---

[80] For comment on this aspect of the case see Trabucchi AG in Case 118/75, n. 26 above, 1207–8 (ECR).

Case 222/84, Johnston v. Chief Constable of the Royal Ulster Constabulary
[1986] ECR 1651

THE ECJ

18. The requirement of judicial control stipulated by that article [Article 6 of the Directive] reflects a general principle of law which underlies the constitutional traditions common to the Member States. That principle is also laid down in Articles 6 and 13 of the European Convention for the Protection of Human Rights and Fundamental Freedoms of 4 November 1950. As the European Parliament, Council and Commission recognized in their joint Declaration of 5 April 1977 and as the Court has recognized in its decisions, the principles on which that Convention is based must be taken into consideration in Community law.

19. By virtue of Article 6 interpreted in the light of the general principle stated above, all persons have the right to obtain an effective remedy in a competent court against measures which they consider to be contrary to the principle of equal treatment for men and women laid down in the directive. It is for the Member States to ensure effective judicial control as regards compliance with the applicable provisions of Community law and of national legislation intended to give effect to the rights for which the directive provides.

The Court ruled ultimately that the national measure deeming such a certificate to be conclusive evidence was an infringement of the principle of effective judicial control. As in *Rutili*, the ECJ treated the provision of EC law as a specific manifestation of a recognized general principle of law, and therefore was to be read 'in the light of' the corresponding principle in the ECHR, which in turn was said to underlie the constitutional traditions of the Member States, dealing with access to court and an effective judicial remedy.[81] Thus the ECJ's indirect method of requiring a rule of national law to be reviewed for conformity with a principle embodied in the ECHR was presented as no more than the application of a principle which was part of the Member State's own constitutional tradition.

(b) MEMBER STATES AS AGENTS OF COMMUNITY LAW: ENFORCING EC POLICIES AND INTERPRETING EC RULES

In a subsequent case, the Commission brought enforcement proceedings against Germany, claiming that the State was in breach of Community law on account of its implementation of Regulation 1612/68 on migrant workers.[82] Article 10 of Regulation 1612/68 permits members of a migrant Community worker's family to install themselves with the worker in the host Member State, provided that the worker has available for the family housing 'considered as normal for national workers' in that region. Germany had implemented this provision in a way which made renewal of a family member's residence permit conditional upon the family living in appropriate

---

[81] See also Cases 222/86, *UNECTEF* v. *Heylens* [1987] ECR 4097 and C–185/97, *Coote* v. *Granada Hospitality* [1998] ECR I–5199. Also on access to court and the ECHR, see Case T–111/96, *ITT Promedia NV* v. *Commission* [1998] ECR II–2937.

[82] Case 249/86, *Commission* v. *Germany* [1989] ECR 1263.

housing, not merely at the time of their arrival in Germany, but for the entire period of residence. The ECJ ruled that the German legislation in question was incompatible with Community law:

Regulation No 1612/68 must also be interpreted in the light of the requirement of respect for family life set out in Article 8 of the Convention for the Protection of Human Rights and Fundamental Freedoms. That requirement is one of the fundamental rights which, according to the Court's settled case-law, restated in the preamble to the Single European Act, are recognized by Community law.[83]

Thus it seems that Member States, when interpreting and implementing Community law, are required to act and to legislate in a way which would respect the rights set out in the ECHR,[84] even when the Community measures do not themselves embody the particular right claimed, as was the case in *Rutili* and *Johnston*. In the case of *Kent Kirk*, the ECJ ruled that the domestic effect of applying a retroactive provision of an EC fisheries regulation to a UK statutory instrument was impermissible, since it would violate the principle of non-retroactivity of penal liability enshrined in Article 7 of the ECHR. Such an application of the regulation would approve a breach by the UK of the principle of non-retroactivity of penal liability.[85]

In *Klensch*,[86] the ECJ ruled that where provisions relating to the CAP leave Member States to choose between various methods of implementation, the Member States must comply with the principle of non-discrimination stated in Article 40(3) (now Article 34(2)) EC, which 'is merely a specific enunciation of the general principle of equality which is one of the fundamental principles of Community law'.[87] However, it was in *Wachauf* that the Court first made clear that Member States were bound, in implementing Community law, by all of the same principles and rights which bound the Community in its actions.

Case 5/88, Wachauf v. Germany
[1989] ECR 2609

The applicant was a tenant farmer who, upon the expiry of his tenancy, requested compensation under German law for the discontinuance of milk production. The German law was based on a power contained in Council Regulation 857/84, and it provided for compensation for the discontinuance of milk production, on condition that where the application was made by a tenant farmer, the lessor must give written consent. Wachauf was refused compensation since his landlord, who had never engaged in milk production nor contributed to the setting up of a dairy farm,

[83] *Ibid.*, para. 10.

[84] See also Case C–219/91, *Criminal Proceedings against Ter Voort* [1992] ECR I–5495, paras. 33–38 on compliance by a Member State with Art. 10 of the ECHR when giving effect to EC Dir. 65/65 on the categorization of medicinal products.

[85] Case 63/83, *R. v. Kent Kirk* [1984] ECR 2689, paras. 21–23. More recently on Art. 7 ECHR see Cases C–74/ & 129/95, *Criminal Proceedings against X* [1996] ECR I–6609.

[86] See also Cases 201 & 202/85, *Klensch v. Secrétaire d'Etat à l'Agriculture et à la Viticulture* [1986] ECR 3477.

[87] *Ibid.*, para. 9.

had withdrawn consent. He challenged the refusal before the German administrative courts and a reference was made to the ECJ.

17. The Court has consistently held, in particular in its judgment in Case 44/79 *Hauer*, that fundamental rights form an integral part of the general principles of law, the observance of which is ensured by the Court. In safeguarding those rights, the Court has to look to the constitutional traditions common to the Member States, so that measures which are incompatible with the fundamental rights recognized by the constitutions of those states may not find acceptance in the Community. International treaties concerning the protection of human rights on which the Member States have collaborated or to which they have acceded can also supply guidelines to which regard should be had in the context of Community law.

. . .

19. Having regard to those criteria, it must be observed that Community rules which, upon the expiry of the lease, had the effect of depriving the lessee, without compensation, of the fruits of his labour and of his investments in the tenanted holding would be incompatible with the requirements of the protection of fundamental rights in the Community legal order. Since those requirements are also binding on the Member States when they implement Community rules, the Member States must, as far as possible, apply those rules in accordance with those requirements.

A similar formulation to the *Wachauf* case was used also in a more recent agricultural policy case, *Karlsson*, where the ECJ ruled that the requirements flowing from the protection of fundamental rights in the Community legal order 'are also binding on Member States when they implement Community rules'.[88] Thus the ECJ has been prepared to assess the compatibility of Member States' laws with fundamental rights in two contexts: first, when considering the compatibility of national laws with provisions of Community law which reflect certain fundamental principles or rights; and, secondly, where the States are implementing a Community law or scheme, and thus in some sense acting as agents on the Community's behalf.[89] But there is also a third possible (and more contentious) context in which the ECJ claims it will assess the compatability of national law with EC fundamental rights, which we will now examine.

(c) MEMBER STATES DEROGATING FROM COMMUNITY LAW REQUIREMENTS

Consider the situation in which a Member State, far from implementing Community law, seeks to derogate from its provisions or to justify a restriction on Community rules in the interests of some conflicting national policy. *Rutili* provides one example

---

[88] Case C–292/97, *Karlsson* [2000] ECR I–2737, para. 37.
[89] See J. Temple Lang, 'The Sphere in which Member States are Obliged to Comply with the General Principles of Law and Community Fundamental Rights Principles' (1991) 18 *LIEI* 23.

of such a situation, but in that case an EC directive, which defined the scope of the derogation, actually required the Member States to protect certain rights which happen also to be included within the ECHR. It was subsequently argued, however, that whenever they created an exception to the operation of Community rules, the Member States were acting within the field of Community law and thus should be bound to respect such rights. It seemed at first as though the ECJ would not accept this argument. *Cinéthèque* concerned an alleged restriction on the free movement of goods created by French law which prohibited the exploitation of films shown in cinemas in the form of videos until the expiration of a twelve-month period.[90] The ECJ ruled that any barriers to inter-state trade caused by this rule were justified since it was non-discriminatory in nature and was intended to prioritise cinematic exploitation, and it continued:

25. The plaintiffs and the interveners in the main action also raised the question whether Article 89 of the French law on audio-visual communication was in breach of the principle of freedom of expression recognized by Article 10 of the European Convention for the Protection of Human Rights and Fundamental Freedoms and was therefore incompatible with Community law.

26. Although it is true that it is the duty of this Court to ensure observance of fundamental rights in the field of Community law, it has no power to examine the compatibility with the European Convention of national law which concerns, as in this case, an area which falls within the jurisdiction of the national legislator.

ADVOCATE GENERAL SLYNN[91]

It is clear from Case 4/73 *Nold*, and Case 44/79 *Hauer* that the Convention provides guidelines for the Court in laying down those fundamental rules of law which are part of Community law, though the Convention does not bind, and is not part of the law of the Community as such . . .

In my opinion it is right, as the Commission contends, that the exceptions in Article 36 and the scope of 'mandatory requirements' taking a measure outside Article 30 should be construed in the light of the Convention.

The ECJ rejected the Advocate General's proposal that it should subject any national measures which would breach Article 28 (ex Article 30) were it not for the existence of an exception in Article 30 (ex Article 36) or in the ECJ's case law on 'mandatory requirements',[92] to scrutiny in the light of the ECHR. Instead, the ECJ ruled that although the French law constituted a *prima facie* restriction on the free movement of goods, the fact that it could be justified as a 'mandatory requirement' of the public interest (the promotion of the cinematographic industry in France) brought it 'within the jurisdiction of the national legislator'.

In *Demirel*,[93] the Court restated this point in a different way, ruling that it would not examine the compatibility of national law with fundamental rights or general

---

[90] Cases 60 & 61/84, *Cinéthèque v. Fédération Nationale des Cinémas Français* [1985] ECR 2605.
[91] [1985] ECR 2605, 2616.
[92] See Case 120/78, *Cassis de Dijon* [1979] ECR 649, discussed in Ch. 14.
[93] Case 12/86, *Demirel v. Stadt Schwäbisch Gmünd* [1987] ECR 3719.

principles of law where the national law lay outside the jurisdiction of the Community. The case involved a Turkish woman who had come to Germany and who was ordered to leave the country when her visa expired. The ECJ ruled that rights to family reunification were not at that time covered by the provisions of the EC–Turkey Assocation Agreement, and it responded to the invocation of Article 8 of the ECHR on the right to family life as follows:

As to the point whether Article 8 of the European Convention on Human Rights has any bearing on the answer to that question, it must be observed that, as the Court ruled in its judgment of 11 July 1985 in Joined Cases 60 and 61/84 *Cinéthèque* v. *Fédération Nationale des Cinémas Français* [1985] ECR 2605 at 2618 although it is the duty of the Court to ensure observance of fundamental rights in the field of Community law, it has no power to examine the compatibility with the ECHR of national legislation lying outside the scope of Community law . . . . In those circumstances, the Court does not have jurisdiction to determine whether national rules such as those at issue are compatible with the principles enshrined in Article 8 of the ECHR.[94]

The ECJ's indication that it would not examine the compatibility with the ECHR of national measures 'lying outside the scope of Community law' suggests a willingness to examine the compatibility of national measures which lie *within* the scope of EC law. None the less, the meaning of these words is ambiguous. The *Demirel* judgment prompted certain commentators to suggest with dismay that the ECJ was seeking to increase its jurisdiction to promote its own conception of Community fundamental rights in the face of conflicting Member State conceptions of national fundamental principles and rights.[95]

Some years later, in a case involving the invocation by a Member State of a derogation in the Treaty from the principle of free movement, the ECJ took a different approach from that in *Cinéthèque*, declaring that it had a duty to ensure that the Member State had adequately respected the fundamental rights which were part of Community law.

Case C–260/89, Elliniki Radiophonia Tileorassi AE v. Dimotiki Etairia Pliroforissis and Sotirios Kouvelas [1991] ECR I–2925

[Note ToA renumbering: Arts. 56 and 66 are now Arts. 46 and 55 respectively]

ERT was a Greek radio and television company to which the Greek State had granted exclusive rights under statute. ERT sought an injunction from a domestic court against the two respondents who had set up a television station and had begun to broadcast programmes in defiance of the applicants' exclusive statutory rights. The defence relied mainly on the provisions of Community law relating to the free movement of goods and to the rules on competition and monopolies, as well as on the provisions of the ECHR concerning freedom of expression. The ECJ began by

[94] N. 74 above, para. 28.
[95] See the views of J. Coppel and A. O'Neill, 'The European Court of Justice: Taking Rights Seriously?' (1992) 29 *CMLRev.* 669. For a response see J. Weiler and N. Lockhart, ' "Taking Rights Seriously" Seriously?' (1995) 32 *CMLRev.* 51 and 579.

repeating its traditional sentences on the sources of inspiration for fundamental rights in EC law, and cited its judgments in *Nold* and *Wachauf*.

THE ECJ

42. As the Court has held (see Cases C–60 & 61/84 *Cinéthèque*, paragraph 25 and Case C–12/86 *Demirel* v. *Stadt Schwäbisch Gmünd*, paragraph 28), it has no power to examine the compatibility with the European Convention on Human Rights of national rules which do not fall within the scope of Community law. On the other hand, where such rules do fall within the scope of Community law, and reference is made to the Court for a preliminary ruling, it must provide all the criteria of interpretation needed by the national court to determine whether those rules are compatible with the fundamental rights the observance of which the Court ensures and which derive in particular from the European Convention on Human Rights.

43. In particular, where a Member State relies on the combined provisions of Articles 56 and 66 in order to justify rules which are likely to obstruct the exercise of the freedom to provide services, such justification, provided for by Community law, must be interpreted in the light of the general principles of law and in particular of fundamental rights. Thus the national rules in question can fall under the exceptions provided for by the combined provisions of Article 56 and 66 only if they are compatible with the fundamental rights, the observance of which is ensured by the Court.

44. It follows that in such a case it is for the national court, and if necessary, the Court of Justice to appraise the application of those provisions having regard to all the rules of Community law, including freedom of expression, as embodied in Article 10 of the European Convention on Human Rights, as a general principle of law the observance of which is ensured by the Court.

45. The reply to the national court must therefore be that the limitations imposed on the power of the Member States to apply the provisions referred to in Articles 66 and 56 of the Treaty on grounds of public policy, public security and public health must be appraised in the light of the general principle of freedom of expression embodied in Article 10 of the European Convention on Human Rights.

The ruling, in which the ECJ disregarded the advice of the Advocate General, represented a further extension of the Court's jurisdiction to review compliance with fundamental rights by the Member States when they rely upon derogations from basic Treaty rules, and a further encroachment by the general principles of law into the legal systems of the Member States. It has been observed, in the context of the *ERT* ruling, that 'some of those derogations are bound up with fundamental notions governing the relationship between States and their citizens cannot fail to appreciate the potential incidence of that judgment on national sovereignty'.[96] The later case of *Vereinigte Familiapress Zeitungsverlags* seems also to suggest that the *ERT* judgment marked a departure from part of the earlier *Cinéthèque* judgment, in so far as the latter indicated that when a non-discriminatory restriction on the free movement of goods was justified by a public interest requirement, that measure would fall within the scope of national law and not EC law, and so would not be considered for compatibility with

---

[96] D. Mancini and D. Keeling, 'From *CILFIT* to *ERT*: The Constitutional Challenge Facing the European Court' (1991) 11 *YBEL* 1, 11–12.

EC general prinicples or fundamental rights.[97] But the ECJ ruled in *Familiapress* that the mandatory or 'overriding' requirements (promoting press diversity) relied on by a Member State to justify non-discriminatory national legislation which obstructed the free movement of goods (by prohibiting the distribution of a magazine containing competitions for prizes) had to be interpreted in the light of general principles and fundamental rights, including in this case the freedom of expression of the publisher under Article 10 ECHR. The case thus suggests that the 'scope of Community law' is being given a wider meaning than it was given in *Cinéthèque*, and that the scope of application of fundamental rights to Member State action was correspondingly widened.

It seems, however, that not all members of the Court are comfortable with the *ERT/Familiapress* development, and certain suggestions to confine this line of case law have been made.[98]

(d) LIMITS TO THE 'SCOPE OF COMMUNITY LAW' AND TO THE DOMESTIC APPLICABILITY OF COMMUNITY FUNDAMENTAL RIGHTS

Given the developments in *ERT* and *Familiapress*, it is necessary to consider what is the current scope of Community law, and to ask which situations lie outside the 'fundamental rights' jurisdiction of the Court.[99]

In the case of *Konstantinidis*, a self-employed Greek masseur working in Germany complained that the German authorities were infringing his Community rights in their official mistranslation of his name. The referring court considered that there might be an infringement of the applicant's right of personal identity and of the principle of non-discrimination on the ground of nationality in the employment context.[100] Having surveyed various national laws and the ECHR, Advocate General Jacobs in the case concluded that Article 8 of the Convention protected an individual's right to oppose unjustified interference with his name, and went on to argue that the action of the German authorities should be considered to fall within the scope of Community law, so that the ECJ could examine its compatibility with the ECHR.

46. In my opinion, a Community national who goes to another Member State as a worker or self-employed person under Articles 48, 52 or 59 of the Treaty is entitled not just to pursue his trade or profession and to enjoy the same living and working conditions as nationals of the host State; he is in addition entitled to assume that, wherever he goes to earn his living in the European Community, he will be treated in accordance with a common code of fundamental values, in particular those laid down in the European Convention on Human Rights. In other words, he is entitled to say 'civis europeus sum' and to invoke that status in order to oppose any violation of his fundamental rights.[101]

---

[97] Case C–368/95, *Vereinigte Familiapress Zeitungsverlags- und Vertriebs GmbH v. Heinrich Bauer Verlag*, [1997] ECR I–3689.

[98] F. Jacobs, 'Human Rights in the European Union: The Role of the Court of Justice' (2001) 26 *ELRev.* 331, 337–9.

[99] See, e.g., Case C–309/96, *Annibaldi v. Sindaco del Commune di Guidoma* [1997] ECR I–7493.

[100] Case C–168/91, *Konstantinidis v. Stadt Altensteig, Standesamt, and Landratsamt Calw, Ordnungsamt* [1993] ECR I–1191.

[101] [1993] ECR I–1191, 1211–12.

The position argued for here was novel and broad, suggesting that whenever an EC national goes to another Member State in reliance on one of the rights of free movement in the Treaty, any failure to respect a fundamental human right of that national, whether or not it is connected with his or her work, should constitute an infringement of EC law. Implicit in the Advocate General's reasoning is the argument that such failure might dissuade the national from exercising Community rights of movement, so that whenever an EC national is lawfully present in another Member State and exercising Community rights, he or she should be entitled under Community law to protection against any infringement of his or her human rights, regardless of whether that protection is provided for nationals of the Member State. The Court, however, made no reference to fundamental rights in the case, basing its reasoning instead on settled EC law relating to the right of self-employed people to establish themselves in a Member State, without being disadvantaged in their business on account of their nationality.[102] The failure to address, let alone to adopt, the Advocate General's proposal certainly suggests that the ECJ was not in favour of such an extension of its human rights jurisdiction over Member State law, and this seems to be confirmed by the rulings such as *Grado and Bashir*.[103]

Further, in *Maurin*, criminal proceedings were brought against the defendant under national law for selling food products after the expiry of their use-by date.[104] He argued that procedural unfairnesses in his trial breached his rights of the defence as protected under the ECHR, and when the case was referred to the ECJ, the French and UK governments argued that the national legislation fell outside the scope of EC law. While there was a directive requiring food products to indicate a sell-by date on their label, there was no Community measure governing the sale of properly labelled food products after the sell-by date, which was the situation in this case. The ECJ ruled that since Community law imposed no obligation on the Member States in relation to the sale of products whose use-by date had expired, the offence with which Maurin was charged concerned national legislation falling 'outside the scope of Community law', so that the ECJ had no jurisdiction to determine whether there had been a breach of the rights of the defence. A similar conclusion was reached in *Kremzow*, which concerned an Austrian national who had been convicted of murder but whose appeal on sentence had been found by the ECtHR to violate Article 6 of the Convention on the right to a fair trial.[105] He subsequently sought compensation in the domestic courts for unlawful detention, and a reference was made to the ECJ asking whether the provisions of the ECHR were part of Community law and whether the ECJ had jurisdiction to give preliminary rulings on the interpretation of these provisions. In

[102] See Gulman AG in Case C–2/92, *R. v. Ministry of Fisheries, Agriculture and Food, ex p. Bostock* [1994] ECR I–955, 971, expressing disagreement with the arguments of Jacobs AG in *Konstantinidis* and noting that the ECJ did not adopt the same reasoning.

[103] Without mentioning the *Konstantinidis* case, the ECJ in Case C–291/96, *Criminal Proceedings Against Grado and Bashir* [1997] ECR I–5531, ruled that the position of a national of a Member State in criminal proceedings within another Member State did not of itself raise an issue of Community law, so that the ECJ could not consider whether the right to dignity and equality of the non-national had been respected. See also Case C–177/94, *Criminal Proceedings against Perfili* [1996] ECR I–161.

[104] Case C–144/95, *Maurin* [1996] ECR I–2909.

[105] Case C–299/95, *Kremzow v. Austria* [1997] ECR I–2629.

order to bring himself within 'the scope of Community law', Kremzow argued that, as a citizen of the EU, his right to free movement under Article 18 (ex Article 8a) EC had been infringed by the Austrian court's unlawful sentence of imprisonment. The ECJ, however, rejected his argument:

16. The appellant in the main proceedings is an Austrian national whose situation is not connected in any way with any of the situations contemplated by the Treaty provisions on free movement of persons. Whilst any deprivation of liberty may impede the person concerned from exercising his right to free movement, the Court has held that a purely hypothetical prospect of exercising that right does not establish a sufficient connection with Community law to justify the application of Community provisions (see in particular Case 180/83 *Moser* [1984] ECR 2539, para 18).

17. Moreover, Mr Kremzow was sentenced for murder and for illegal possession of a firearm under provisions of national law which were not designed to secure compliance with rules of Community law (see in particular case C–144/95 *Maurin* [1996] ECR I–2909).

18. It follows that the national legislation applicable in the main proceedings relates to a situation which does not fall within the field of application of Community law.

The Court gives two reasons why Kremzow's case did not fall within the scope of EC law. First, his situation did not fall within the Treaty provisions on the free movement of persons, since he was not seeking to exercise a right to move between Member States. This seems to give a negative answer to the question whether Article 18 (ex Article 8a) introduced into the EC Treaty by the TEU gave EU citizens a right to move freely within the territory of a single Member State, rather than only from one Member State to another.[106] Secondly, Kremzow's situation was not brought within the scope of EC law by virtue of the national legislation under which he was convicted and imprisoned, since that legislation, like the legislation in *Maurin*, was not in any way implementing EC law or securing compliance with it.

Despite the rulings in *ERT* and *Vereinigte Familiapress* on the scope of EC law for the purposes of 'fundamental rights review' by the ECJ, and the indications in *Kremzow* and *Maurin* that those situations lie outside the jurisdiction of the ECJ, various doubts remain about the exact boundaries of the sphere of action within which Member States can be held to account by the ECJ for their observance of human rights and general principles of law. As indicated above, the formulation adopted in Article 51 of the EU Charter on Fundamental Rights on this matter is a rather restrictive one which seems to omit the *ERT* jurisprudence:

The provisions of this Charter are addressed to the institutions and bodies of the Union . . . and to the Member States only when they are implementing Union law.

The explanatory memorandum to the Charter clearly endeavours to read the wording of Article 51 more broadly by emphasizing the unambiguous nature of the *ERT* ruling, and placing the *Wachauf and Karlsson* cases,[107] which seem to have influenced

---

[106] This question had been raised in the case of *R. v. Secretary of State for the Home Department, ex p. Adams* [1995] All ER (EC) 177, from which a reference was made as Case C–229/94 to the ECJ, before being withdrawn in 1995.

[107] See n. 88 above. The *Karlsson* case involved a relatively simple example of a Member State implementing EU law, and has little or nothing to say about whether other situations fall within the scope of EC or EU law for the purposes of the applicability of the general principles of EC law.

the choice of wording in the Charter, in that context.[108] Further, there were strong political voices raised in support of limiting the Charter's applicability as much as possible to the EU and its institutions, and to limiting its relevance for the Member States as much as possible.[109]

Finally, in a recent extra-judicial publication, Advocate General Jacobs takes a rather different position from that expressed in his Opinion in *Konstantinidis*, criticizing the *Familiapress* case and arguing for a narrowing of the potential scope of the *ERT* ruling.

F. Jacobs, Human Rights in the EU: the Role of the Court of Justice[110]

It is now the accepted case law that Member States measures must be subject to fundamental rights review wherever they derogate from the Treaty or wherever such measures restrict the exercise of a 'common market freedom'. We are now perhaps better placed to assess the implications.

. . .

The difficulty arises I think from the apparent suggestion that, even after the Court of Justice has held that a derogation is in principle applicable, there is a further question: is the exercise compatible with human rights—and that this further question is also a question of Community law. As it seems to me, the position is as follows: if a Member State seeks to justify a restriction in the interest of human rights—eg to preseve plurality of the press—then that is to be examined as part of the public policy derogation under the Treaty. Once that question has been answered, there is no further question of Community law.

. . .

It seems to me that, when acting under such derogations, the Member States are subject to some constraints imposed by Community law but not by others.

The Advocate General goes on to say that the Member States should be bound by the principles of proportionality and non-discrimination on grounds of nationality when availing of a derogation under Community law, but that they should not be bound by other general principles such as, e.g., the fundamental right to freedom of expression or religion. In other words, his view is that the ECJ should not review acts of the Member States adopted in derogation from Community rules for compliance with fundamental rights other than proportionality and nationality non-discrimination, unless the aim of derogation in question is precisely to promote a particular fundamental right. In the latter case, he considers that the ECJ, in adjudicating on the availability of the derogation under EC law, should assess the compatibility of the measure with that particular right. This is undoubtedly a narrower view than that expressed in *ERT* and *Familiapress*, but there is no evidence at present that it is a view held by other members of the Court. Nevertheless, the reservations expressed by

---

[108] For further discussion on this point see G. de Búrca, 'The Drafting of the EU Charter of Fundamental Rights' (2000) 25 *ELRev*. 331.

[109] See Lord Goldsmith's comments, n. 9 above.

[110] N. 98 above, 337–8.

the Advocate General about the scope of fundamental rights review by the ECJ of Member State action is evidently shared by some other political actors and possibly by Member States, to judge from the drafting of Article 51 of the Charter.

However, until the legal fate of the Charter becomes clearer and the ECJ begins to interpret its provisions, it will be difficult to know whether the general scope of review of national action in the field of EC law has been reduced, at least in so far as the rights contained within the Charter are concerned. And that, in turn, may well affect the situation as far as other existing general principles of EC law are concerned, depending on the relationship which is established between the Charter and such other pre-existing sources of fundamental rights and general principles of EC law, something which is partly dealt with in Articles 52(3) and 53 of the Charter. For now, the *ERT* and *Familiapress* jurisprudence remains in place, but the future scope of the ECJ's jurisdiction to assess the compatibility of Member State action with fundamental rights remains uncertain.

7. FUNDAMENTAL RIGHTS AND THE ROLE OF THE POLITICAL INSTITUTIONS

(a) POLITICAL APPROVAL OF THE ECJ'S DEVELOPMENTS

We have seen that in 1977 the Council, Commission, and Parliament issued a Joint Declaration effectively approving the ECJ's development of general principles as part of EC law, and affirming their commitment to respect fundamental rights in their activities. After this declaration, several other non-binding political initiatives were taken, including a Joint Declaration of the three institutions in 1986, various Declarations and Resolutions on Racism and Xenophobia by the European Council, a Declaration of Fundamental Rights and Freedoms by the European Parliament in 1989, a Community Charter of Fundamental Social Rights, signed by eleven of the then twelve Member States in 1989, as well as lofty references in the preamble of the SEA to the ECHR, the European Social Charter, and to 'equality and social justice'. These statements and resolutions remained a relatively 'soft' form of response to the jurisprudential initiatives, although in legal terms they did add weight to the ECJ's development of unwritten Community law, and could be relied upon for support when other provisions of EC law were being interpreted.

'Hard' legal approval came with the amendments introduced by the Treaty on European Union and the Treaty of Amsterdam. But while the TEU initially referred to fundamental rights in a number of its provisions, the only provision of the EC Treaty to be amended in this way at that time was Article 177 (ex Article 130u), which provides that Community policy in the area of development co-operation:

shall contribute to the general objective of developing and consolidating democracy and the rule of law, and to that of respecting human rights and fundamental freedoms.

Article 6(2) (ex Article F(2)) of the TEU, which was not at that stage justiciable, provided that the Union would respect the fundamental rights guaranteed by the

ECHR and by national constitutional traditions, and respect for human rights and fundamental freedoms was also mentioned in the two other 'pillars' of the TEU. Following the changes made by the Amsterdam Treaty, much of the third pillar was integrated in Title IV of the EC Treaty, and references to the rights of non-Community nationals and the Geneva Convention on refugees now appear in this Title.

The major change introduced by the Amsterdam Treaty, was to amend Article 6 (ex Article F) TEU, and to add a new Article 7. Whereas the old Article F stated that the Union would respect fundamental rights etc., Article 6 now declares that the Union 'is founded on' the principles of liberty, democracy, and respect for human rights and fundamental freedoms. The most legally significant feature is that this provision was finally rendered justiciable, so that the ECJ has jurisdiction not only under the EC Treaty, but under any provision of the other two pillars over which it has been given jurisdiction (primarily pillar three), to review the conduct of the European institutions for compliance with these principles. The Amsterdam amendment strengthened and expressly legitimated what the Court in practice had been doing for many years, at least in relation to the EU institutions. Further, the new Article 7 empowered the Council to suspend some of the voting rights and other rights of a Member State which is found to be responsible for a serious and persistent breach of the fundamental principles in Article 6.[111] Following the Amsterdam Treaty, respect for these fundamental principles was also made a condition of application for membership of the European Union. These evidently represented significant political moves to assert the role of fundamental human rights within the European Union.

In 2000, a series of rather controversial diplomatic sanctions was adopted by fourteen of the Member States against the fifteenth, in protest against the entry of the very right-wing Freedom Party into coalition government in Austria in 2000.[112] The sanctions were ultimately lifted after a positive report on the situation in Austria was issued following an *ad hoc* procedure carried out by a three-person committee appointed by the President of the ECtHR, and composed of Martti Ahtisaari, Jochen Frowein, and Marcelino Oreja. However, in part as a result of unease over the way the Austrian situation had been handled, amendments to Article 7 TEU were introduced in the Nice Treaty. These provide for more detailed and fairer procedures to be followed before a negative determination against a Member State is made, they include the possibility of acting before a breach has occurred, and the ECJ has jurisdiction over the procedural provisions.[113]

Finally, it is clear that the most important recent development has been the approval of the EU Charter of Fundamental Rights at the Nice European Council in 2000. Before assessing this development, however, the evolution of EU human rights policies to date will briefly be considered.

---

[111] See Art. 309 (ex Art. 236) EC as amended.

[112] See M. Merlingen, C. Muddle, and U. Sedelmeier, 'The Right and the Righteous?: European Norms, Domestic Politics and the Sanctions against Austria' (2001) 39 *JCMS* 59.

[113] See Ch. 1, 45.

(b) FUNDAMENTAL RIGHTS AS A SOURCE OF POLICY COMPETENCE?

Thus far, the discussion has focused primarily on the jurisprudence of the Court, which established fundamental rights and general principles as a constraint on Community and Member State action, as values they must respect in the course of their activities. But what of promotion and protection of human rights as an objective of the EU, and thus as a source of Community competence?

(i) OPINION 2/94 AND THE LIMITS TO THE EC'S 'HUMAN RIGHTS' POWERS

In its Opinion on accession of the Community to the European Convention on Human Rights, the ECJ made a number of statements on the extent of the Community's then existing powers to take positive action in the field of protecting human rights. This Opinion was requested by the Council of Ministers under Article 300 (ex Article 228) EC in order to clarify whether the Community could become a party to the ECHR. Since, as we have seen, the Community already effectively declares itself bound to respect the rights contained in the Convention and the ECJ exercises review jurisdiction in that context, one of the main differences which accession would bring is that the Community institutions would be made subject to the review jurisdiction of the Court of Human Rights, and the ECJ would no longer be the final arbiter of the lawfulness of EC action. Having declared in its Opinion that it could not rule on the *compatibility* of accession with the EC Treaty in the absence of sufficient information about the institutional arrangements envisaged, the ECJ, however, stated that the Community in any case lacked *competence* under the Treaty to accede.

Opinion 2/94 on Accession by the Community to the ECHR
[1996] ECR I–1759

[ToA renumbering: Arts. 3b, 130u, and 235 EC are now Arts. 5, 177, and 308 EC respectively. Arts. F and J. 1 TEU are now Arts. 6 and 11 respectively, and Art. K. 2 has been replaced]

23. It follows from Article 3b of the Treaty, which states that the Community is to act within the limits of the powers conferred upon it by the Treaty and of the objectives assigned to it therein, that it has only those powers which have been conferred upon it.

24. That principle of conferred powers must be respected in both the internal action and the international action of the Community.

25. The Community acts ordinarily on the basis of specific powers which, as the Court has held, are not necessarily the express consequence of specific provisions of the Treaties, but may also be implied from them.

26. Thus, in the field of international relations, at issue in this request for an Opinion, it is settled case-law that the competence of the Community to enter into international commitments may not only flow from express provisions of the Treaty but also be implied from those provisions. The Court has held, in particular, that whenever Community law has created for the institutions

of the Community powers within its internal system for the purpose of attaining a specific objective, the Community is empowered to enter into the international commitments necessary for attainment of that objective even in the absence of an express provision to that effect. (Opinion 2/91 [1993] ECR I–1061).

27. No Treaty provision confers on the Community institutions any general power to enact rules on human rights or to conclude international conventions in this field.

28. In the absence of express or implied powers for this purpose, it is necessary to consider whether Article 235 of the Treaty may constitute a legal basis for accession.

29. Article 235 is designed to fill the gap where no specific provisions of the Treaty confer on the Community institutions express or implied powers to act, if such powers appear none the less to be necessary to enable the Community to carry out its functions with a view to attaining one of the objectives laid down by the Treaty.

30. That provision, being an integral part of an institutional system based on the principle of conferred powers, cannot serve as a basis for widening the scope of Community powers beyond the general framework created by the provisions of the Treaty as a whole and, in particular, by those that define the activities and tasks of the community. On any view, Article 235 cannot be used as a basis for the adoption of provisions whose effect would, in substance, be to amend the Treaty without following the procedure which it provides for that purpose.

31. It is in the light of those considerations that the question whether accession by the Community to the Convention may be based on Article 235 must be assessed.

32. It should first be noted that the importance of respect for human rights has been emphasized in various declarations of the Member States and of the Community institutions. Reference is also made to respect for human rights in the preamble to the Single European Act and in the preamble to, and in Article F(2), the fifth indent of Article J. 1.(2) and Article K. 2 (1) of, the Treaty on European Union. Article F provides that the Union is to respect fundamental rights, as guaranteed, in particular, by the Convention. Article 130u(2) of the EU Treaty provides that Community policy in the area of development cooperation is to contribute to the objective of respecting human rights and fundamental freedoms.

33. Furthermore, it is well settled that fundamental rights form an integral part of the general principles of law whose observance the Court ensures. For that purpose, the Court draws inspiration from the constitutional traditions common to the Member States and from the guidelines supplied by international treaties for the protection of human rights on which the Member States have collaborated or of which they are signatories. In that regard, the Court has stated that the Convention has special significance (see in particular *ERT*).

34. Respect for human rights is therefore a condition of the lawfulness of Community acts. Accession to the Convention would, however, entail a substantial change in the present Community system for the protection of human rights in that it would entail the entry of the Community into a distinct international institutional system as well as the integration of all the provisions of the Convention into the Community legal order.

35. Such a modification of the system for the protection of human rights in the Community, with equally fundamental institutional implications for the Community and for the Member States, would be of constitutional significance and would therefore be such as to go beyond the scope of Article 235. It could be brought about only by way of Treaty amendment.

In ruling that the Community lacked legislative competence under the Treaties to become a party to the Convention, the ECJ gave some indication of the limits of human rights as a legislative foundation for Community action, although without ruling more specifically on the issue of what other, less fundamental kinds of legislation the Community might be competent to adopt in the human rights field. Paragraph 27 is particularly relevant in this respect, although it merely denies that the Community has any jurisdiction under specific Treaty provisions to enact *general* rules on human rights. The opinion however can be read as agreeing that Article 308 (ex Article 235) may form the basis for the adoption of specific Community measures for the protection of human rights,[114] so long as they do not amount to an amendment of the Treaty by going beyond the scope of the Community's defined aims and activities. Ensuring respect for human rights is not actually described by the Court as an independent objective of the Community, but rather as a 'condition for the lawfulness of Community acts'.[115] What appeared to place accession to the ECHR beyond the scope of Community competence was not the fact that it would entail concluding an agreement for the protection of fundamental rights, but the fact that the agreement envisaged would bring with it fundamental institutional and constitutional changes which would actually require a Treaty amendment, with the associated national ratification processes, rather than merely a piece of Community legislation under Article 235 (now Article 308).[116]

In a subsequent decision concerning the external competence of the Community relating to human rights issues, the Portuguese government challenged the legal basis of the Community's competence to conclude a Co-operation Agreement with India.[117] Portugal argued to the ECJ that the fact that respect for human rights 'ranks among the general principles whose observance is mandatory in the Community legal order does not justify the conclusion that the Community is competent to adopt measures in that field, whether external or internal'. The Agreement was based on Articles 133 and 181 (ex Articles 113 and 130y) EC. Portugal objected to the provision in Article 1(1) of the Agreement that respect for human rights and democratic principles was 'the basis for the cooperation between the contracting parties' and 'constitutes an essential element of the ingredient', arguing that the Community should have had recourse to Article 308 (ex Article 235) as a legal basis if it wished to adopt such human rights provisions.[118] The Court disagreed and referred to the provision in Article 177 (ex Article 130u) EC which specifies that Community development co-operation policy shall contribute to respecting human rights and fundamental freedoms.[119] Although the Court did not address the issue of EC competence to legislate in the field of human rights more generally, it upheld the legal basis which the Council had used for the human rights clause in the Co-operation Agreement,

[114] See, e.g., the 1999 Regulations on human rights and democratization in development and co-operation policy, n. 123 below and text.

[115] See also the subsequent Resolution of the European Parliament on Respect for Human Rights in the EU [1996] OJ C320/36.

[116] For a discussion of various aspects of *Opinion 2/94*, see *The Human Rights Opinion of the ECJ and its Constitutional Implications* (Cambridge University CELS, Occasional Paper No. 1, Cambridge University Press, 1996).

[117] Case C–268/94, *Portuguese Republic* v. *Council* [1996] ECR I–6177.

[118] See for a comment on the case and on Portugal's motives for the challenge see N. Burrows (1997) 22 *ELRev.* 594. See also E. Fierro, 'Legal Basis and Scope of the Human Rights Clasues in EC Bilateral Agreements: Any Room for Positive Interpretation' (2001) 7 *ELJ* 41.

[119] *Ibid.*, para. 23.

noting that respect for human rights was an 'essential element' of the Agreement rather than a specific field of co-operation within it. The implication is that the Community would not have had competence under Article 181 (ex Article 130y) to conclude a co-operation agreement principally on the subject of human rights, although it does have the power under its development policy provisions to insert a clause such as this one, making respect for human rights an essential element and basis for co-operation. The Nice Treaty has since added Article 181a to provide an express basis for human rights clauses in co-operation policy, mirroring that which already existed for development policy under Article 177.

(ii) EXTERNAL AND INTERNAL COMPETENCE

The EU has frequently been criticized for its apparently greater willingness to promote and enforce human rights—often through negative sanction clauses[120]—in its external policies than in its internal policies.[121] There seems to have been greater willingness to present human rights as an actual objective of EU foreign policy, and a wider range of instruments has been used in this context, such as the regular practice since 1995 of including human rights clauses in external agreements dealing with trade, development, and association relationships. None the less, criticism has also been voiced at the fact that, in the external sphere, human rights policy was largely confined to projects funded under the 'human rights and democratization' initiative provided for in the so-called B7–70 heading of the EU budget, and that it was not integrated across the pillars and across the different dimensions of foreign policy.

As far as internal policy is concerned, one of the few areas of what could be called internal human rights policy, which was the practice of funding significant 'non-pilot' projects including those of NGOs working in areas of social exclusion and poverty, was condemned by the ECJ in 1998 for lack of a legal basis.[122] This judgment also had implications for the external 'human rights and democratization' funding, which had been introduced in 1994 under an EU budget heading but without any legal basis in the Treaty or in legislation. One consequence of this was the adoption of one of the first 'hard' pieces of EC human rights legislation in the form of two regulations on human rights and democratization in development policy and co-operation policy, which were based on Articles 177 (ex Article 130) and 308 (ex Article 235) EC respectively.[123] Since then, the newly added Article 181a EC provides an independent legal basis for measures in the field of co-operation policy which contribute to respect for human rights and fundamental freedoms, so that recourse to Article 308 will not be necessary for such measures in the future. Further, the Council since 1999 has begun to publish an EU Annual Report on Human Rights, and the trend within these reports has been to move from an initially much greater emphasis on foreign and

---

[120] Fierro, n. 118 above, and B. Brandtner and A. Rosas, 'Human Rights and the External Relations of the EC: An Analysis of Doctrine and Practice' (1998) 9 *EJIL* 468.

[121] See, e.g., P. Alston and J. Weiler, 'A Human Rights Agenda for the Year 2000', in *The EU and Human Rights*, n. 1 above and A. Williams, 'Enlargement of the Union and Human Rights Conditionality: A Policy of Distinction?' (2000) 25 *ELRev.* 601. The Council itself has referred to this criticism in its second and third Annual Reports on Human Rights in the EU for 2000 and 2001.

[122] Case C–106/96, *UK v. Commission* [1998] ECR I–2729.

[123] See Regulations 975/1999 and 976/1999 [1999] OJ L120/1 and 8.

external policy towards a gradually more extensive consideration of the human rights aspects of internal EU policies also, including anti-discrimination policy, social exclusion, combating human trafficking, and gender mainstreaming. The two main reasons usually given for this difference in emphasis are that there are more severe and more fundamental human rights problems occurring outside the EU than within, and that the EU has only a very limited competence to address human rights issues within its boundaries. None the less, in its most recent Annual Report for 2001, the Council declared that 'the Union is committed to intensifying the process of "mainstreaming" human rights and democratisation objectives into all aspects of EU external and internal policies'.

(III) ANTI-DISCRIMINATION LAW

Undoubtedly the main 'hard' source of EC competence in the field of human rights protection within the EU, apart from the last-resort provision in Article 7 TEU, has been that introduced by the Amsterdam Treaty into Article 13 of the EC Treaty, supplementing the existing range of EU gender equality policies. Article 13 provides that the Community legislature may, within the limits of the Community's powers, take 'appropriate action to combat discrimination based on sex, racial or ethnic origin, religion or belief, disability, age or sexual orientation'. Hitherto, discrimination on grounds of sex and nationality was expressly prohibited by Community law, even though the basis for adopting general legislation in these fields was unclear.[124] And while the case of *P* v. *S*[125] appeared to suggest that a more general prohibition on discrimination extending beyond sex and nationality to embrace transsexuality and other grounds were already part of the 'great value of equality' and one of the fundamental principles underlying EC law, the ECJ in *Grant* v. *South West Trains* beat a hasty retreat from that position.[126] In *Grant* the Court ruled, in a case concerning an employee who had been refused travel benefits for her same-sex partner, that EC law did not currently cover discrimination on the basis of sexual orientation. The Court confined its ruling in *P* v. *S* to discrimination based essentially on the sex of the person, which did not, in its view, apply to discrimination on the grounds of sexual orientation of the kind at issue in *Grant*. In making reference to Article 13 EC concerning sexual orientation which was not yet in force at that time, the ECJ argued that it was not for it to extend Community law beyond the scope provided for in the Treaty.[127]

This judicial restraint was reinforced in the case of *D* v. *Council*, which also concerned unequal benefits for an EU employee whose relationship with a same-sex partner had been granted formal status as a registered partnership under Swedish law.[128] While the case on its facts clearly concerns an indirect form of discrimination on grounds of sexual orientation, the ECJ's reasoning turned on the non-equivalence

---

[124] See Ch. 20 for discussion of the legislative basis for some of the equal treatment legislation between men and women, and Case C–295/90, *European Parliament* v. *Council* [1992] ECR I–4193 on the appropriate legal basis for legislation concerning nationality discrimination in the field of vocational training.

[125] Case C–13/94, *P* v. *S and Cornwall County Council* [1996] ECR I–2143, especially paras. 18–22 of the ruling.

[126] Case C–249/96, *Grant* v. *South West Trains* [1998] ECR I–621. Contrast the Opinion of the AG.

[127] *Ibid.*, paras. 47–48.   [128] N. 49 above.

of a traditional marriage and a nationally recognized registered partnership. Further, just as in the *Grant* case, the ECJ emphasized its own unfitness, as a judicial institution, to bring about a positive change which was more properly to be enacted by legislation. This clearly represents a retreat from the strong principle of equality as a fundamental right,[129] and a deferential judicial stance in a situation where the exercise of positive legislative competence has been made possible under the Treaty and under staff regulations, but not yet exercised. Further, although no legislative move had been made to give registered partnerships a position equivalent to marriage, an amendment to the Staff Regulations which had not come into force at the time of the case provided for equal treatment of officials irrespective of their sexual orientation.

Cases C–122 and C–125/99P D v. Council
[2001] ECR I–4319

36. It is clear, however, that apart from their great diversity, such arrangements for registering relationships between couples not previously recognised in law are regarded in the Member States concerned as being distinct from marriage.

37. In such circumstances the Community judicature cannot interpret the Staff Regulations in such a way that legal situations distinct from marriage are treated in the same way as marriage. The intention of the Community legislature was to grant entitlement to the household allowance under Article 1(2)(a) of Annex VII to the Staff Regulations only to married couples.

38. Only the legislature can, where appropriate, adopt measures to alter that situation, for example by amending the provisions of the Staff Regulations. However, not only has the Community legislature not shown any intention of adopting such measures, it has even (see paragraph 32 above) ruled out at this stage any idea of other forms of partnership being assimilated to marriage for the purposes of granting the benefits reserved under the Staff Regulations for married officials, choosing instead to maintain the existing arrangement until the various consequences of such assimilation become clearer.

Thus we can see that the introduction of positive legislative competence to promote fundamental rights such as the right to be free from arbitrary discrimination has led the Court to limit the judicial development of such rights as general principles of EC law.

Article 13 EC is not in itself a prohibition on discrimination on grounds of race, disability, sexual orientation, etc., and, unlike the equal pay provision in Article 141 EC on sex discrimination, it is not directly effective. Rather it enables the Community to adopt measures to combat discrimination on the grounds listed within the scope of the policies and powers otherwise granted in the Treaty. Prior to the coming into force of Article 13, the European Monitoring Centre for Racism and Xenophobia had been established by a regulation based on Articles 284 and 308 (ex Articles 213 and 235)

---

[129] The ECJ seems to be more comfortable in promoting a stronger notion of equality as a fundamental right in more conventionally accepted spheres of anti-discrimination such as gender equality: see, e.g., the judgment in Case C–50/96, *Deutsche Telekom* v. *Schröder* [2000] ECR I–743.

EC,[130] but, Article 13 has since facilitated stronger law-making in this field.[131] Two directives were adopted in 2000, the first being a directive to prohibit discrimination on grounds of race and ethnic origin,[132] and the second being the so-called framework employment directive, covering discrimination in the field of employment on the grounds listed in Article 13 (other than race, ethnic origin, or sex, which are already covered by other legislation): religion, belief, disability, age, and sexual orientation.[133] While the jurisdictional limitation in Article 13 specifies that the EC can act only within the limits of the Community's powers, Article 3 of the anti-racism directive gives it an apparently wide scope, including a prohibition on discrimination in relation to social protection, health care, housing, and education. An action plan to combat racism had been adopted in 1998, and in 2000 a broader action programme to combat discrimination on all the grounds listed in Article 13 (other than sex, which is already covered by an action programme) was adopted.[134] Further, the Commission has begun to promote 'mainstreaming' policies in the areas of gender, race, and disability in particular, to integrate anti-discrimination considerations into other areas of EC policy formation. Finally, Article 13 was amended by the Nice Treaty, which added a power for the Council to adopt non-harmonizaing 'incentive measures' under the co-decision legislative procedure.

(IV) A CAUTIOUS APPROACH

The institutional response to Opinion 2/94 of the Court was a cautious one, emphasizing the limits to the Community's competence in the human rights field, and warning against any attempts to erode the constitutional limits to its powers. This was evident in the opinion given by the Council legal service on the original Commission proposal for a regulation on democratization and human rights in 1997.[135] It is apparent also in Article 13 of the Treaty, which, although creating a new EC power to combat discrimination on the one hand, can be adopted only within the limits of the powers already conferred on the Community by the Treaty.

Significantly, this cautious approach is particularly clear in Article 51 of the new EU Charter on Fundamental Rights, which proclaims due regard for the principle of subsidiarity, and states that the Charter does not establish any new power or task for the Community or the Union, or modify any of the powers and tasks defined by the Treaties. The explanatory memorandum to the Charter emphasizes this fact further.[136] In other words, the Charter is presented not as any source of or basis for positive

---

[130] Council Reg. 1035/97 [1997] OJ L151.

[131] See M. Bell, *Anti-Discrimination Law and the EU* (OUP, 2002).

[132] Council Dir. 2000/43 [2000] OJ L180/22.

[133] Council Dir. 2000/78 [2000] OJ L303/16.

[134] Council Dec. 2000/750 [2000] OJ L303/23.

[135] See the discussion of this opinion in J.H.H. Weiler and S. Fries, 'A Human Rights Policy for the European Community and Union: the Question of Competences' in Alston *et al.* (eds.), n. 1 above. The proposal ultimately resulted in 1999 in the adoption of two separate regs. on development co-operation and on other forms of co-operation: see n. 123 above.

[136] The relevant explanatory note to Art. 51 reads '[p]aragraph 2 confirms that the Charter may not have the effect of extending the competences and tasks which the Treaties confer on the Community and the Union. Explicit mention is made here of the logical consequences of the principle of subsidiarity and of the fact that the Union only has those powers which have been conferred upon it. The fundamental rights as guaranteed in the Union do not have any effect other than in the context of the powers determined by the Treaty.'

legislative action, but simply as a codified or supplemented form of what already exists under ECJ jurisprudence: i.e. a broad set of standards against which EU and Member State action within the scope of existing EU policies and powers is to be judged.[137]

8. THE CHARTER OF FUNDAMENTAL RIGHTS

(a) BACKGROUND

We have seen in Chapter 1 that the European Council in 1999 launched an initiative to draft a Charter of Fundamental Rights for the EU.[138] This development came after many years of discussion of whether the EU should accede to the ECHR or should have its own Bill of Rights. The novel 'Convention' process by which the Charter was adopted, which became a model for the subsequent Convention on the Future of Europe, produced a draft Charter in less than a year, following a more open and relatively more participative procedure than almost any previous EC or EU initiative.[139] The Charter was solemnly proclaimed by the Commission, Parliament, and Council and was politically approved by the Member States at the Nice European Council summit in December 2000.[140] Although the Charter was drafted 'as if' it were to have full legal effect,[141] the question of its legal status and its possible integration into the Treaties was postponed and placed on the political agenda by the Nice and Laeken Declarations, to be decided ultimately by the IGC in 2004.[142] Although the mandate given by the European Council to the body drafting the Charter was to consolidate and render visible the EU's existing 'obligation to respect fundamental rights' rather than to create anything new, and although this mandate actually indicated the sources on which the drafting body was to draw,[143] the Charter none the less contains a number of innovations (e.g., prohibition on reproductive human cloning) and notable omissions (e.g., protection for the rights of minorities). And while the preamble declares that the EU *recognizes* the rights, freedoms, and principles set out

---

[137] Contrast the speech of Commissioner Vitorino to the European Parliament on 17 Apr. 2002, 'The Future of Fundamental Rights in the EU', in which he argues that the Charter should not be limited by a negative approach but should have a proactive effect in the promoting of human rights by creating policies related to them.

[138] See 43–4.

[139] G. de Búrca, 'The Drafting of the EU Charter of Fundamental Rights' (2001) 26 *ELRev.* 126; J. Schönlau, 'Drafting Europe's Value Foundation: Deliberation and Arm-twisting in Formulating the Preamble to the EU Charter of Fundamental Rights', in Eriksen *et al.* (eds.), n. 2 above.

[140] See [2000] OJ C364/1.

[141] Commission Communication on the legal nature of the Charter: COM(2000)644. See also L. Betten 'The EU Charter of Fundamental Rights: A Trojan Horse or a Mouse?' [2001] *Int'l Journal of Comparative Labour Law and Industrial Relations* 151, and Lenaerts and de Smijter, n. 2 above.

[142] B. de Witte, 'The Legal Status of the Charter: Vital Question or Non-Issue?' (2001) 8 *MJ* 81; C. McCrudden, 'The Future of the EU Charter of Fundamental Rights', J. Dutheil de la Rochere 'Droits de l'homme: La Charte des droits fondamentaux et au dela' and G. de Búrca, 'Human Rights: The Charter and Beyond', all forming Jean Monnet Working Paper 10/01, www.jeanmonnetprogram.org/papers.

[143] These were specified as the rights contained in the ECHR, and those derived from the common constitutional traditions of the Member States, as well as from provisions of the European Social Charter and the Community Charter of Fundamental Social Rights of Workers 'which go beyond mere objectives'. See Conclusions of the Cologne European Council, June 1999.

therein, the Charter could perhaps best be described as a creative distillation of the rights contained in the various European and international agreements and national constitutions on which the ECJ had for some years already been drawing.

(b) CONTENT

After a lofty preamble in the name of the 'peoples of Europe',[144] which refers amongst other things to the common and indivisible universal values on which the Union is founded, and to the diversity of cultures, traditions, and identities in Europe, the Charter is divided into seven chapters. The various rights are grouped into six distinct chapters, and the final chapter contains the so-called horiontal clauses or general provisions. The first six chapters are headed: I. Dignity, II. Freedoms, III. Equality, IV. Solidarity, V. Citizens Rights, VI. Justice.

While the foundational rights contained in the first Chapter, such as the right to life, freedom from torture, slavery, and execution, appear to sit oddly within a Charter which is primarily directed towards the institutions of the EU, given that EU powers to infringe such rights remain very limited, the gradual moves in the direction of a European defence policy and the incipient policing, criminal law, and now 'anti-terrorism' policies suggest that this may not always be true. The second Chapter on freedoms also concentrates on basic civil and political liberties to be found in the ECHR, such as liberty, association, expression, property, private and family life,[145] but contains in addition certain fundamental social rights such as the right to education, the right to engage in work, and the right to asylum, as well as some provisions which have gained more particular prominence in the EU context, such as the right to protection of data and the freedom to conduct a business. Chapter III on equality contains a basic equality-before-the-law guarantee, as well as a provision similar (though not identical) to that in Article 13 EC, a reference to positive action provisions in the field of gender equality, protection for children's rights, and some weaker provisions guaranteeing 'respect' for cultural diversity, for the rights of the elderly, and for persons with disabilities. Chapter IV on solidarity contains certain labour rights and reflects some of the provisions of the European Social Charter which have already been integrated into EC law.[146] This Chapter contains a mixture of fundamental provisions such as the prohibition on child labour, and the right to fair and just working conditions, as well as others which have been criticized as insufficiently fundamental to have a place in this Charter, such as the right to a free placement service. Further, this Chapter of the Charter has been particularly criticized because of the weak formulation of many of the rights contained (including some, such as environmental and consumer protection, which are not formulated as rights or freedoms at all), and because of the phrase 'in accordance with Community law and national laws and practices' which follows them and which seems to undermine the content of the guarantee.

---

[144] For an analysis see Schönlau, n. 139 above.

[145] See C. McGlynn, 'Families and the EU Charter of Fundamental Rights: Progressive Change or Entrenching the Status Quo?' (2001) 26 *ELRev.* 582.

[146] M. Gijzen, 'The Charter: A Milestone for Social Protection in Europe?' (2001) 8 *MJ* 33.

Chapter V contains 'citizens' rights', many of which, unlike the other provisions of the Charter, are not universal but are guaranteed only to EU citizens. These include the rights of EU citizenship in Articles 18–22 of the EC Treaty, while the more broad applicable rights include the right of access to documents and the right to good administration, which is the first to have been judicially cited by the CFI.[147] Chapter VI, entitled Justice, includes several of the so-called rights of the defence, such as the right to a fair trial, the presumption of innocence, the principle of legality and proportionality of penalties, and the familiar EC right to an effective remedy.

(c) THE 'HORIZONTAL CLAUSES'

The final Chapter VII contains the general clauses which relate to the scope and applicability of the Charter, its addressees, its relationship to other legal instruments, and the 'standard' of protection.

Article 51(1), which is discussed at 5(d) above, indicates that the Charter is addressed to the institutions and bodies of the EU, and to the Member States, only when they are implementing Union law. A cursory mention of the principle of subsidiarity is made in this context, although its meaning is rather difficult to discern. Article 51 goes on to specify that the EU and the Member States 'respect the rights, observe the principles and promote the application thereof in accordance with their respective powers'. This obligation to 'promote' the rights in the Charter arguably counters the rather more negative phrasing of the sentence which follows in Article 51(2), and which asserts that no new power or task for the EC or EU is created by the Charter.

Article 52(1), which draws on the jurisprudence both of the ECHR and of the ECJ, contains a general 'derogation' clause, indicating the nature of the restrictions on Charter rights which will be acceptable.[148] Any limitation on the exercise of rights and freedoms contained in the Charter must be 'provided for by law' and must respect the *essence* of those rights and freedoms. Limitations must meet the requirements of proportionality and must be 'necessary and genuinely meet objectives of general interest recognised by the Union or the need to protect the rights and freedoms of others'. Article 52(2) then addresses the question of overlap between existing provisions of EC law and the new provisions of the Charter, providing that rights recognized by the Charter which are 'based on' the EC or EU Treaties 'shall be exercised under the conditions and within the limits defined by those Treaties'. This seems intended to avoid any potential differences in the interpretation of similarly worded provisions of the Charter and of the EC/EU Treaties, although the phrase 'based on' is perhaps somewhat ambiguous. The explanatory memorandum refers instead to a right which 'results from' the Treaties, and states that the Charter does not alter the system of rights conferred by the Treaties.

---

[147] Case T–54/99, *max.mobil Telekommunikation Service GmbH* v. *Commission,* ruling of 31 Jan. 2002, para. 48.

[148] For criticism see D. Triantafyllou, 'The European Charter of Fundamental Rights and the "Rule of Law": Restricting Fundamental Rights by Reference' (2002) 39 *CMLRev.* 53.

The tricky relationship between the ECHR,[149] other international human rights instruments, national constitutional provisions, and the new Charter is addressed in Articles 52(3) and 53. Article 52(3) relates specifically to the ECHR and is evidently intended to promote harmony between the the provisions of the European Convention and those of the Charter, while not preventing the EU from developing more extensive protection than is provided for under the Convention:

In so far as this Charter contains rights which correspond to rights guaranteed by the Convention for the Protection of Human Rights and Fundamental Freedoms, the meaning and scope of those rights shall be the same as those laid down by the said Convention. This provision shall not prevent Union law providing more extensive protection.

This provision does not address more specifically the question of the relationship between the two European Courts, the ECtHR and the ECJ, although it seems likely to be intended to promote deference on the part of the ECJ to the ECtHR. The explanatory memorandum declares that the EU legislator must comply with the standards laid down in the ECHR 'without thereby adversely affecting the autonomy of Community and that of the Court of Justice', but it also indicates that the meaning of the rights are determined in part by the ECtHR.

Article 53 of the Charter on the other hand is a more general clause, which is similar in ways to that in Article 53 of the ECHR, and which refers not only to the ECHR but also to national constitutions and international agreements:

Nothing in this Charter shall be interpreted as restricting or adversely affecting human rights and fundamental freedoms as recognised, in their respective fields of application, by Union law and international law and by international agreements to which the Union, the Community or all the Member States are party, including the European Convention for the Protection of Human Rights and Fundamental Freedoms, and by the Member States' constitutions.

It has been queried whether the presence of this clause and the absence of a 'supremacy' clause in the Charter guaranteeing the primacy of EC law could call into question the long-established supremacy doctrine.[150] Such a concession however seems highly unlikely, even if the general wording of Article 53(3) preserves the existing tension between the autonomy of the EU/EC legal order on the one hand, and the claims of Member States to the authority of their fundamental constitutional provisions (which we saw in Chapter 7) on the other. Finally, Article 54 contains a clause modelled on Article 17 of the ECHR, which provides that no provision of the Charter shall imply the right to engage in any activity aimed at the destruction or excessive limitation of any of the rights contained therein.

---

[149] See P. Lemmens, 'The Relationship between the Charter of Fundamental Rights of the EU and the ECHR: Substantive Aspects' (2001) 8 *MJ* 49; K. Lenaerts and E. de Smijter, 'The Charter and the Role of the European Courts' (2001) 8 *MJ* 49; and F. Tulkens, 'Towards a Greater Normative Coherence in Europe: The Implications of the Draft Charter of Fundamental Rights of the European Union' (2000) 21 *HRLJ* 329. S. Parmar, 'International Human Rights Law and the EU Charter' (2001) 8 *MJ* 351.

[150] J. Liisberg, 'Does the EU Charter of Fundamental Rights Threaten the Supremacy of Community Law?' (2001) 38 *CMLRev.* 1171.

(d) CURRENT STATUS

Pending the decision on the legal status of the Charter to be taken by the IGC in 2004, possibly following the recommendation of the Convention on the Future of Europe, the Charter may be in something of a legal limbo, but it is certainly not without any legal influence or effect.[151]

A range of institutional actors has already made use of its provisions. The Commission decided by an internal decision of 13 March 2001 to conduct a form of compatibility review with regard to the Charter. Any legislative proposal connected with the protection of fundamental rights would be considered by the Commission for its compatibility with the provisions of the Charter. As an expression of that control, the legislative proposal would henceforth contain a recital mentioning respect for the rights and principles contained in the Charter. The Commission has so far followed this practice fairly extensively in its legislative proposals, although it is of course difficult to tell from such references and recitals whether the Charter is actually having any substantive influence on the content of the measures in question.

The European Ombudsman has also made frequent reference to the Charter, to various aspects of the right to good administration, and to the right of access to the Ombudsman in Articles 41–43 thereof, in his speeches and his annual report. Indeed, in a speech to the European Parliament on 8 April 2002. he criticized the EU institutions for their failure to observe many of the rights contained in the Charter, in particular in relation to their own recruitment and staff regulations:

High officials tell me that the Charter is only a political declaration. I understand from such statements that citizens should not expect political promises to be kept. To me this seems like a way to undermine democracy. I would like to stress that European citizens have the right to expect the Charter to be followed by those institutions whose presidents solemnly proclaimed it in Nice in December 2000, that is the Council, the Parliament and the Commission.

Finally, the Charter was for the first time mentioned in an EU judicial decision when the Court of First Instance, in *max.mobil Telekommunikation Service* referred to Articles 41 and 47 of the Charter as an affirmation of the general principles of law common to the Member States,[152] and more significantly in *Jégo-Quéré*, in which it relied on Article 47 to move away from the restrictive case law on individual *locus standi* to challenge EC regulations.[153] Numerous references to provisions of the Charter have also been made by various Advocates General,[154] although the ECJ in early 2002 has not yet mentioned it in a judgment. Whether or not the Court will do

---

[151] See nn. 141–142 above.

[152] Case T–54/99, *max.mobil Telekommunikation Service GmbH* v. *Commission*, ruling of 31 Jan. 2002, paras. 48, 57. In Case T–112/98, *Mannesmannroehren-Werke AG* v. *Commission* 2001 ECR II–729, the plaintiff invoked the Charter but the CFI dismissed the argument on the basis that the contested measure had been adopted before the Charter was proclaimed: paras. 15, 76.

[153] Case T–177/01, *Jégo-Quéré et Cie SA* v. *Commission*, judgment of 3 May 2002.

[154] Some of the better known Opinions (which at the time of writing amount to 17 in number) are those of Tizzano AG in Case C–173/99, *BECTU*, 8 Feb. 2001; Mischo AG in Cases C–122P & 125/99P, *D* v. *Council* [2000] ECR I–4319; Jacobs AG in Case C–270/99P, *Z* v. *Parliament*, 22 Mar. 2001 and C–50/00P, *Unión de Pequeños Agricultores* v. *Council*, 21 Mar. 2002 ; Geelhoed AG in Case C–413/99, *Baumbast*, 5 July 2001; Léger AG in Case C–353/99P, *Council* v. *Hautala*, 10 July 2001; Stix-Hackl AG in Case C–60/00, *Carpenter*, 13 Sept. 2001.

so before a further decision is taken on the legal status of the Charter remains to be seen, but it is clear even from this brief survey that the Charter is already beginning to enter into the 'constitutional practice' of the EU.

9. SOME QUESTIONS ON THE FUTURE OF HUMAN RIGHTS IN EU LAW

Despite the changing and gradually enhanced status of human rights within EC and EU law, the development of the general principles and fundamental rights of EC law, and in particular their development over the years by the ECJ, has been subject to a number of criticisms, not all of which are likely to be assuaged by the recent adoption of the Charter. A first concern is that the Court has attempted to extend the influence of Community law over areas which remain the primary concern of the Member States, given their considerable political, cultural, and ideological diversity. A second concern is that the Court has manipulated the rhetorical force of the language of rights, while in reality merely advancing the commercial goals of the common market, being biased towards 'market rights' instead of protecting values which are genuinely fundamental to the human condition. A third concern is that the ECJ has attempted to act as another European Human Rights Court, when its primary purpose and function under the Treaties have been quite different, and when another European Court was specifically entrusted by the Member States of the Council of Europe with that jurisdiction and role. Related to this concern is the view that the EC/EU and its institutions should in fact be subject to the ECHR system, including to the jurisdiction of the Strasbourg institutions.

All three concerns are to some extent related, and reflect a degree of scepticism in particular about the ECJ's ability to enforce a satisfactory system of human rights protection for the EU. This concern has been voiced by some who have felt that the Court over the years has manipulated the language of human rights to pursue economic integration goals. Some of the most critical comments were prompted by *Grogan*,[155] in which the Advocate General suggested that the prohibition in Ireland on the provision of information about abortion facilities in other Member States should be tested for compliance with other human rights, including freedom of information and expression. Although the Court did not follow his opinion and ruled that the restriction on information did not fall within the scope of Community law, the ruling was narrowly based on the fact that there was no commercial link between the providers of the medical service (abortion) in one Member State, and the providers of the information in the other Member State.[156]

---

[155] Case C–159/90, *SPUC* v. *Grogan* [1991] ECR I–4685.

[156] For an attempt by the Irish government (which it subsequently sought to qualify by means of a Declaration) to insulate the Irish constitutional prohibition on abortion, and on information and referral services, from the possible impact of Community law: see Protocol 17 of the TEU.

J. Coppel and A. O'Neill, The European Court of Justice: Taking Rights Seriously?[157]

From the terms of the *Heylens* decision it appears that the four freedoms of workers, services, goods and capital enshrined in the Treaties can be translated into individuals' fundamental rights. It would seem, then, that there is no distinction and hence no hierarchical relationship being posited by the European Court between the basic human rights outlined, for example, in the European Convention on Human Rights and the free market rights arising out of the Treaties of the European Community.

. . . Such a procedure can be seen in the opinion of the Advocate General in *Grogan*. Ultimately, he balances freedom of information (seen as a corollary of the Community freedom to provide services) against the right to life of the unborn child. The result of this equality in practical terms can only be that the court will find it easier to subordinate a fundamental human right to a Community economic freedom. . . .

Evidently it is economic integration, to be achieved through the acts of Community institutions, which the court sees as its fundamental priority. In adopting and adapting the slogan of protection of human rights the court has seized the moral high ground. However, the high rhetoric of human rights protection can be seen as no more than a vehicle for the court to extend the scope and impact of European law.

Others have taken a less sceptical view of the Court's strategy in expanding the field of application of human rights within EC law,[158] and the Court indeed has been criticized not because the rights which it favours are essentially market rights rather than human rights, but rather because it has at times been too deferential, and has sometimes stopped short of requiring Member States to observe human rights principles in areas covered by Community law.[159]

Certainly it would be difficult to detect a consistent strategic design on the ECJ's part to promote Community economic goals over conflicting national interests, and the pattern of case law is varied and complex. Although it has certainly promoted 'market rights' in some cases at the expense of important national concerns, there is also evidence of recognition by the Court of the moral rather than the purely economic dimension of the fundamental rights it may be called on by an applicant to protect.[160] Rather than always elevating every economic right into a fundamental legal right capable of 'trumping' competing rights protected under national law, the Court in some of its case law has recognized that rights created by the Treaty do not attach only to individuals as 'factors of production', but to individuals as human beings. And these human rights—to family life, or to freedom from discrimination—at times have been required to prevail even over a Member State's conception of the public interest

[157] (1992) 29 *CMLRev.* 669.

[158] J.H.H. Weiler and N.J.S. Lockhart, ' "Taking Rights Seriously" Seriously: The European Court and its Fundamental Rights Jurisprudence' (1995) 32 *CMLRev.* 51 and 579.

[159] See J.H.H. Weiler, 'The European Court at a Crossroads: Community Human Rights and Member State Action' in F. Capotorti *et al.* (eds.), *Du Droit International au Droit de l'Intégration* (Nomos, 1987), 839–41. Contrast Jacobs, n. 98 above.

[160] For a recent case in which the ECJ declared that the economic goals of Art. 141 (ex Art. 119) EC are secondary to the social goals, which constitute the expression of a fundamental human right: see Case C–50/99, *Deutsche Telekom* v. *Schröder* [2000] ECR I–743, para. 57.

or the competing human right. Even if Community aims and freedoms derived initially from a Treaty which was primarily concerned with economic integration, they may also have moral and social importance beyond their economic significance.[161] Such reasoning is also to be found in the opinion of Advocate General Tesauro and the judgment of the ECJ in *P* v. *S*,[162] and the judgment in *Schröder*,[163] which focus not on the economic aims and origins of the prohibition on sex discrimination at work, but rather on the dignity of the individual and the value of equality as a fundamental human right.

Against the background of these concerns, some have argued that a fuller commitment to ensure respect for fundamental human rights could provide the EU with the ethical foundation which it has lacked, on account of its origins as a common market and the constant emphasis on economic goals.[164] Further, such a shared commitment to human rights has been presented as a potentially unifying force and a common foundation for the EC legal system.[165] It is certainly clear that the desire for the kind of polity legitimacy associated with such an explicit commitment was one of the many factors motivating the drafting of an EU Charter of Rights, as indeed the European Council's mandate at the Cologne summit demonstrates.

None the less, the third of the issues mentioned above, concerning the comparative suitability of the ECJ as the final EU forum for human rights review, remains salient. Quite apart from any history of market integration bias in the jurisprudence of the ECJ, the very existence of the European Court of Human Rights in Strasbourg, which was established precisely to monitor compliance by the member states of the Council of Europe with the commitments of the Convention on Human Rights, has led some to question the appropriateness of a parallel jurisdiction being exercised by the ECJ.[166] The ECtHR was not only established with an express human rights jurisdiction, but has acquired expertise and a moral stature which the ECJ does not share. The ECJ's extension of the Community's competence to require national laws to comply with fundamental rights has also highlighted the possibility of conflict between the pronouncements of the two European Courts. And in the absence of accession by the EC (or the EU, if it is recognized as having international legal capacity for that purpose) to the ECHR, there is no final arbiter on such questions. The problem of overlap or conflict has been discussed by several commentators,[167] with some taking the view that any serious conflict of interpretation between the two courts is unlikely,[168] but

[161] See G. de Búrca, 'Fundamental Human Rights and the Reach of EC Law' (1993) 13 *OJLS* 283.

[162] Case C–13/94, n. 24 above.

[163] N. 160 above.

[164] E.g., P. Alston and J. Weiler 'Leading by Example: A Human Rights Agenda for the Year 2000', in Alston *et al.* (eds.), n. 1 above.

[165] See, e.g., M. Cappelletti, *The Judicial Process in Comparative Perspective* (Clarendon, 1989), 175, 381; and J. Fröwein, 'The ECHR as the Public Order of Europe', in A. Clapham and F. Emmert (eds.), *Collected Courses of the Academy of European Law* (Martinus Nijhoff, 1990), pp. i–ii, 357–8.

[166] See, e.g., the argument of the UK Government in Case 118/75, n. 26 above, 1191 (ECR).

[167] See R. Lawson, 'Confusion and Conflict? Diverging Interpretations of the ECHR in Strasbourg and Luxembourg', in R. Lawson and M. de Bloijs (eds.), *The Dynamics of the Protection of Human Rights in Europe* (Kluwer, 1994), and D. Spielman, 'Human Rights Case Law in the Strasbourg and Luxembourg Courts: Inconsistencies and Complementarities', in Alston *et al.* (eds.), n. 1 above.

[168] P. van Dijk and G. van Hoof, *Theory and Practice of the European Convention on Human Rights* (Kluwer, 3rd edn., 1998), 21.

many have none the less recommended that accession by the EC to the ECHR, and indeed to the Council of Europe, should take place.[169]

While the Strasbourg Court will not actually hear complaints brought directly against the EC since the latter is not a party to the Convention,[170] the ECtHR held in 1999 in the *Matthews* case that, while the Convention did not preclude the transfer of national competences to an international organization such as the EC, the responsibility of the Member States for violations of the ECHR would continue even after such a transfer.[171] The case concerned the UK's denial of voting rights in Gibraltar for elections to the European Parliament, but the actual denial and therefore the violation of Article 3 of Protocol No. 1 to the ECHR stemmed from a treaty signed by all the Member States of the EU, the 1976 Act Concerning the Election of the Representatives of the European Parliament by Direct Universal Suffrage. In other words, the violation resulted from an atyptical piece of primary EU law rather than from a British law. According to the ECtHR, however, this did not absolve the UK from responsibility for the violation, since that responsibility derived from the UK having entered EC Treaty commitments. The Court ruled ultimately that there was a violation of the essence of the right to vote. The case is interesting not only in its outcome, but also in the indication that acts will not escape the review of the ECtHR simply because they are adopted by the EC or EU, since the Member States retain responsibility for securing the rights protected by the Convention. [172]

More recently a number of cases concerning EC competition law have been brought before the ECtHR, with the complaint being made against all fifteen EU Member States in order to avoid the inadmissibility of complaints against the EC before the ECtHR.[173] One of these was brought by a German company, Senator Lines, complaining of a fine imposed upon it by the EC Commission for breach of competition law.[174] A challenge to the Commission's decision had already been brought before the CFI, but both the CFI and the ECJ had rejected an application for interim relief,[175] and the essence of its consequent complaint to the ECtHR was of a violation of the presumption of innocence and the right to a fair trial. The outcome of this case will be awaited with considerable interest, since it represents the closest the ECtHR has come,

---

[169] A. Clapham, 'Where is the EU's Human Rights Common Foreign Policy?', in Alston *et al.* (eds.), n. 1 above.

[170] For decisions of the previously existing Commission on Human Rights on a number of related questions see App. no 13258/87, *Melcher (M) v. Germany*, 64 D & R 138; App. no. 21090/92, *Heinz v. Contracting States and Parties to the European Patent Convention*, 76 AD & R 125; and App. no. 21072/92, *Gestra v. Italy*, 80 BD & R 93.

[171] App. no. 24833/94, *Matthews v. UK*, judgment of 18 Feb. 1999, esp. paras. 34–35. See R. Harmsen, 'National Responsibility for EC Acts under the ECHR: Recasting the Accession Debate' (2001) 7 *EPL* 625.

[172] See also App. No 43844/98, *TI v. UK*, decision of 7 Mar. 2000, on the UK's responsibility under the Dublin Convention, an agreement signed between all EU Member States concerning asylum procedures, for continuing to secure ECHR rights.

[173] App. no. 51717/99, *Guérin Automobiles v. 15 Etats Membres de l'UE*, Decision of 4 July 2000 (inadmissible) and App. no. 38837/97. *Lenz v. Germany and the other EC Member States*.

[174] App. no. 56672/00, *DSR-Senator Lines GmbH v. 15 EU Member States*.

[175] Cases T–191/98R, *DSR Senator Lines v. Commission* [1999] ECR II–2531 and, on appeal, C–364/99P R [1999] ECR I–8733.

other than in the *Matthews* case, to ruling on the compatiblity of EC action with the Convention.[176]

Undoubtedly, similar cases and similar issues are increasingly likely to arise before the ECtHR and the ECJ/CFI, given the expansion of the scope of EC law and EC human rights law, and given the likely influence of the Charter of Fundamental Rights. The issue of AIDS testing has already arisen before both the CFI and the ECJ in the form of privacy claims against the Community institutions under Article 8 of the ECHR. And although the CFI has shown itself ready to dismiss these claims quickly,[177] the ECJ has been more cautious and has found a breach of the right to privacy in one case.[178] The potential for differences in interpretation as between the two sets of European courts, and different conclusions on the same issues has already been seen by contrasting decisions like that of the Court of Human Rights in *Open Door Counselling*[179] with the Opinion of the Advocate General in *Grogan*[180], the approach of the ECJ in *ERT*[181] with that of the ECtHR in *Lentia* v. *Austria*[182], the decision of the ECJ in *Hoechst*[183] with that of the ECtHR in *Niemietz*[184]; the ECJ in *Orkem*[185] with the ECtHR in *Funke*,[186] and the subsequent series of ECJ and CFI cases concerning various rights of the defence in EC competition proceedings in *SKC*,[187] *Limburgse Vinyl Maatschappij*,[188] and *Baustahlgewebe*.[189]

Tension between the rulings of the ECtHR and the ECJ on very closely related issues arose most recently in one of the cases in the lengthy *Emesa Sugar*

[176] For previous cases in which the Convention organs heard applications concerning the adverse effects of the implementation of Community policies by Member States see App. no. 17862/91, *Cantoni* v. *France*, Decision of 22 Oct. 1996; App. no. 20323/92, *Pafitis* v. *Greece*, Decision of 26 Feb. 1998; App. no. 14561/89, *J. S.* v. *Netherlands* (1995) 20 EHRR CD 41 on EC milk quotas; App. no. 24581/94, *Gialouris* v. *Greece*, 81B D & R 123 on the impact of the Single European Act on customs employees; and App. no. 21072/92, *Gestra* v. *Italy* 80B D & R 89 on compliance with the Brussels Convention; and the ECHR in *Procola* v. *Luxembourg* (1995) Series A no. 326 considered the implementation of EC milk quotas in Luxembourg.

[177] See Cases T–121/89 & T–13/90, *X* v. *Commission* [1992] ECR II–2195 and T–10/93, *A* v. *Commission* [1994] ECR II–179, [1994] 3 CMLR 242. For similarly unsuccessful challenges see Cases T–11/90, *H. S.* v. *Council* [1992] ECR II–1869 and T–176/94, *K* v. *Commission* [1995] ECR SC IA–203, II–261.

[178] Case C–404/92P, *X* v. *Commission* [1994] ECR I–4737, n. 60 above. For an earlier unsuccessful challenge see, however, Case C–206/89R, *S* v. *Commission* [1989] ECR 2841.

[179] *Open Door Counselling Ltd. and Dublin Well Woman Centre* v. *Ireland*, Series A no. 246.

[180] Case C–159/90, n. 155 above.

[181] Case C–260/89, *Elliniki Radiophonia Tileorassi AE* v. *Dimotiki Etairia Pliroforissis and Sotirios Kouvelas*, n. 45 above.

[182] *Informationsverein Lentia* v. *Austria*, Series A no 276. In this case the ECtHR found that the radio and television monopoly of the Austrian Broadcasting Corporation constituted a violation of Art. 10 of the Convention, whereas the ECJ in Case C–260/89, n. 181 above left the Art. 10 issue to be decided by the national court. See also Case C–23/93, *TV10 SA* v. *Commissariaat voor de Media*, [1994] ECR I–4795, concerning Dutch broadcasting restrictions, in which the ECJ referred to its conclusion in an earlier case, Case C–353/89, *Commission* v. *Netherlands* [1991] ECR I–4069, that the maintenance of the pluralism which the broadcasting policy sought to safeguard was precisely what the ECHR was designed to protect. See the similar conclusion of the Commission on Human Rights in its Dec. of 11 Jan. 1994, App. no. 21472/93, *X* v. *The Netherlands*, 76A D & R 129.

[183] Cases 46/87 & 227/88, *Hoechst AG* v. *Commission* [1989] ECR 2859.

[184] *Niemietz* v. *Germany*, n. 70 above.

[185] Case 374/87, n. 67 above.

[186] *Funke* v. *France*, n. 74 above.

[187] Cases T–213/95 & 18/96, *SCK & FNK* v. *Commission* [1997] ECR II–1739, esp. paras. 56–57.

[188] Joined Cases T–305/94–T–335/94, *Limburgse Vinyl Maatschappij NV* v. *Commission* [1999] ECR II–931, esp. para. 420.

[189] Case C–185/95 P, *Baustahlgewebe* v. *Commission* [1998] ECR I–8417. For discussion of some of these issues see K. Lenaerts and E. de Smijter, 'The Charter and the Role of the European Courts' (2001) 8 *MJ* 90.

litigation,[190] in which Emesa relied before the ECJ on the *Vermeulen* judgment of the ECtHR[191] in order to argue that the lack of opportunity to reply to the Advocate General's Opinion constituted a violation of the right to adversarial proceedings in Article 6(1) of the ECHR. The ECtHR in *Vermeulen* had condemned the lack of opportunity to reply to the submissions of the Procureur Général before the Belgian Cour de Cassation under Article 6(1), but the ECJ ruled that the role of the Advocate General in the context of EC proceedings was different in key respects, so that there was no violation of Article 6(1).

C–17/98 Emesa Sugar v. Aruba
[2000] ECR I–665

14. Under Article 18 of the EC Statute of the Court of Justice and Article 59 of the Rules of Procedure of the Court, the Opinion of the Advocate General brings the oral procedure to an end. It does not form part of the proceedings between the parties, but rather opens the stage of deliberation by the Court. It is not therefore an opinion addressed to the judges or to the parties which stems from an authority outside the Court or which derives its authority from that of the Procureur Général's department [in the French version, 'ministère public'] (judgment in Vermeulen v Belgium, cited above, paragraph 31). Rather, it constitutes the individual reasoned opinion, expressed in open court, of a Member of the Court of Justice itself.

15. The Advocate General thus takes part, publicly and individually, in the process by which the Court reaches its judgment, and therefore in carrying out the judicial function entrusted to it. Furthermore, the Opinion is published together with the Court's judgment.

16. Having regard to both the organic and the functional link between the Advocate General and the Court, referred to in paragraphs 10 to 15 of this order, the aforesaid case-law of the European Court of Human Rights does not appear to be transposable to the Opinion of the Court's Advocates General.

Not all commentators are convinced by this judgment, however, or by the assertion of compatibility with the ECHR of the role of the Advocate General in ECJ proceedings.[192] None the less, it has been argued that the real importance of this controversy lies not so much in the question whether Emesa might eventually succeed if its case is brought before the ECtHR, as it does in 'offering telling testimony to the growing intensity of the interconnections between the Strasbourg and the Luxembourg Courts' and in the more general relationship between the two systems.[193] Further, it has been argued that cases such as *Matthews* and potentially *Senator Lines* demonstrate that a *de facto* accession of the EC to the ECHR is already taking place.[194]

---

[190] Case C–17/98, *Emesa Sugar* v. *Aruba* [2000] ECR I–665. For comment see R. Lawson (2000) 37 *CMLRev.* 983.

[191] *Vermeulen* v. *Belgium* [1996] I, Reports of Judgments and Decisions 224.

[192] Lawson, n 190 above.

[193] Harmson, n. 171 above, 640.

[194] *Ibid.*, 641–2.

10. CONCLUSIONS

i. Human rights issues occupy an increasingly high profile within EU law and policy, in particular following the introduction of anti-discrimination powers in Article 13 EC, and following the adoption of the Charter of Fundamental Rights. The Council in its annual Human Rights Report also now asserts a commitment to mainstreaming human rights into all aspects of EU external and internal policies.

ii. While the Charter applies mainly to the EU and its institutions, it is addressed also to the Member States 'when implementing Union law', and it declares that no new power or task for the EU is created by its provisions. None the less, all addressees are expressly required to promote the rights contained therein. The scope of application and impact of the Charter on the Member States as well as on the policy competence of the EU therefore remains to be seen.

iii. While its legal status remains unresolved pending the IGC in 2004, the Charter is already being invoked in the institutional practice of the Commission, Parliament, Ombudsman, Court of First Instance, Advocates General, and others.

iv. The complex but co-operative relationship between the ECJ and the European Court of Human Rights is increasingly highlighted both by the number of cases before the CFI and the ECJ in which ECHR jurisprudence is cited and used, and by the cases being brought before the ECtHR against the Member States to challenge EC laws. The provisions of the Charter endeavour to promote harmony between the two systems but do not resolve all of the issues which may arise, and the question of accession by the EC to the ECHR remains a live one.

11. FURTHER READING

(a) *Books and Collections*

Alston, P., Bustelo, M., and Heenan, J. (eds.), *The EU and Human Rights* (Oxford University Press, 1999)

Cassese, A., Clapham, A., and Weiler, J. (eds.), *European Union: The Human Rights Challenge* (Nomos, 1991)

Eriksen, E., Fossum, J.E., and Menéndez, A. (eds.), *The Chartering of Europe* (Arena Report No. 8, 2001)

Feus, K. (ed.), *An EU Charter of Fundamental Rights: Text and Commentaries* (Federal Trust, 2000)

Maastricht Journal of European and Comparative Law (2001) Volume 8, Issue 1

Neuwahl, N., and Rosas, A. (eds.), *The European Union and Human Rights* (Kluwer, 1995)

(b) *Articles*

Besselink, L., 'Entrapped by the Maximum Standard: On Fundamental Rights, Pluralism and Subsidiarity in the European Union' (1998) 35 *CMLRev.* 629

COPPELL, J., and O'NEILL, A., 'The European Court of Justice: Taking Rights Seriously?' (1992) 12 *Legal Studies* 227

DE BÚRCA, G., 'The Drafting of the EU Charter of Fundamental Rights' (2001) 26 *ELRev.* 126

DE WITTE, B., 'The Past and Future Role of the ECJ in the Protection of Human Rights', in P. Alston, M. Bustelo, and J. Heenan (eds.), *The EU and Human Rights* (Oxford University Press, 1999)

GOLDSMITH, T., 'A Charter of Rights, Freedoms and Principles' (2001) 38 *CMLRev.* 1201

HARMSEN, R., 'National Responsibility for EC Acts under the ECHR: Recasting the Accession Debate' (2001) 7 *EPL* 625

JACOBS, F., 'Human Rights in the EU: the Role of the Court of Justice' (2001) 26 *ELRev.* 331

LIISBERG, J., 'Does the EU Charter of Fundamental Rights Threaten the Supremacy of Community Law?' (2001) 38 *CMLRev.* 1171

LENAERTS, K., and DE SMIJTER, E., 'A Bill of Rights for the EU' (2001) 38 *CMLRev.* 273

McGOLDRICK, D., 'The EU after Amsterdam: An Organisation with General Human Rights Competence?', in D. O'Keeffe and P. Twomey (eds.), *Legal Issues of the Amsterdam Treaty* (Hart, 1999)

McCRUDDEN, C., 'The Future of the EU Charter of Fundamental Rights', Jean Monnet Working Paper 10/2001, **www.jeanmonnetprogram.org/papers/01/013001**

VON BOGDANDY, A., 'The EU as a Human Rights Organization' (2000) 37 *CMLRev.* 1307

WEILER, J., 'Fundamental Rights and Fundamental Boundaries', in N. Neuwahl and A. Rosas (eds.), *The EU and Human Rights* (Kluwer, 1995)

—— 'Does the EU Truly Need a Charter of Rights?' (2000) 6 *ELJ* 95

—— and LOCKHART, N., '"Taking Rights Seriously" Seriously: The European Court and its Fundamental Rights Jurisprudence' (1995) 32 *CMLRev.* 51, 579

9

GENERAL PRINCIPLES II: PROPORTIONALITY, LEGITIMATE EXPECTATIONS, NON-DISCRIMINATION, AND TRANSPARENCY

1. CENTRAL ISSUES

i. In the previous chapter we analysed the role played by fundamental rights in Community law. We now consider a number of other general principles that have featured prominently within the Court's jurisprudence: proportionality, legitimate expectations, non-discrimination, and the more recently developed principle of transparency. The dividing line between these two chapters is far from absolute: there are certain principles, such as the right to a fair hearing, or legal and professional privilege, which some might classify as fundamental rights,[1] while others would characterize them as principles of administrative legality.[2] Moreover, when reading this chapter the earlier discussion of subsidiarity should not be forgotten.[3] This is in certain respects a general principle of Community law, albeit one

which goes principally to the initial legality of Community conduct.

ii. Some of the principles, such as non-discrimination, have a textual foundation in the Treaty, while others have been developed in Community legislation. However, the ECJ has played a key role in developing the general principles considered in this chapter, drawing on principles to be found in national law but fashioning these to the Community's own objectives.

iii. The principles serve as an interpretative guide, and also form part of the principles of judicial review. They can be used when evaluating Community norms, and national norms in the areas covered by Community law.

2. PROPORTIONALITY

(a) PROPORTIONALITY: MEANING

The EC Treaty does not possess an explicit, detailed set of principles against which to test the legality of Community or state action within the sphere covered by Community law. It has therefore largely fallen to the ECJ to fashion principles of

---

[1] Both of these principles have been considered in Ch. 8.
[2] The treatment afforded to the principles considered within this chapter will be somewhat briefer than the discussion of fundamental rights. This should not be taken to signify that these principles are somehow less important in absolute terms. It is rather because they will also be considered in other parts of the book, see Chs. 17, 18, 19, and 20.
[3] See Ch. 3 above.

administrative legality. In undertaking this task it has reasoned partly from specific Treaty provisions, which justify Community action only where it is 'necessary' or 'required' in order to reach a certain end. It has also inevitably drawn upon principles from the legal systems of the Member States[4] and, as in many other contexts, it has then fashioned these principles to suit the needs of the Community itself.

The concept of proportionality is most fully developed within German law. It appeared initially in the context of policing, as a ground for challenging measures on the basis that they were excessive or unnecessary in relation to the objective being pursued.[5] In its modern formulation within Germany the consensus appears to be that proportionality involves the evaluation of three factors. The suitability of the measure for the attainment of the desired objective; the necessity of the disputed measure, in the sense that the agency has no other option at its disposal which is less restrictive of the individual's freedom; the proportionality of the measure to the restrictions which are thereby involved. Some notion of proportionality also features within the legal systems of other Member States such as France, although one should be cautious about ascribing the same meaning to the concept whenever the word 'proportionality' is to be found in any guise within differing legal systems.[6]

Proportionality is now well established as a general principle of Community law. A version of the principle is now also enshrined in Article 5 EC, which provides that action by the Community shall not go beyond what is necessary to achieve the objectives of the Treaty, and its requirements are further fleshed out in a protocol to the Treaty. Proportionality can thus be used to challenge Community action itself, and also to challenge the legality of state action which falls within the sphere of application of Community law. In any proportionality inquiry the relevant interests must be identified, and there will be some ascription of weight or value to those interests, since this is a necessary condition precedent to any balancing operation. A decision must be made on whether the public body's decision was indeed proportionate or not in the light of the above considerations. This will normally require us to decide:

(1) Whether the measure was suitable to achieve the desired end;

(2) Whether it was necessary to achieve the desired end;

(3) Whether the measure imposed a burden on the individual that was excessive in relation to the objective sought to be achieved (proportionality *stricto sensu*).

On some occasions the ECJ will articulate and apply all three steps of the inquiry. It will not do so where the case can be resolved at one of the earlier stages. Moreover, in some cases the ECJ may distinguish stages two and three of the inquiry, in others it may in effect 'fold' stage three of the inquiry back into stage two.

The court will have to decide how intensively it is going to apply the test set out above. In any system of administrative law the courts will have to decide not only which tests to apply to determine the legality of administrative action, but also the rigour or intensity with which to apply them. In some legal systems this is worked

---

[4] For a recent unusual example of a 'general principle of labour law common to the Member States' see Case T–192/99, *Dunnett v. European Investment Bank* [2001] ECR II–813, para. 89.

[5] J. Schwarze, *European Administrative Law* (Sweet & Maxwell, 1992), 685–6.

[6] *Ibid.*, 680–5.

out to a high degree, but it is present to varying degrees in all systems. The relative intensity of judicial review is just as much a live question in relation to proportionality as it is in relation to any other tool of judicial oversight.

We can distinguish at least three broad types of cases, which may be subject to challenge on grounds of proportionality. The intensity of review may well differ in these types of cases.

First, there are cases where an individual argues that her rights have been unduly restricted by administrative action. The courts are likely to engage in vigorous scrutiny. Society may well accept that these rights cannot be regarded as absolute, but the very denomination of certain interests as Community rights means that any interference should be kept to a minimum. In this sense proportionality is a natural and necessary adjunct to the recognition of such rights. Moreover, courts regard it as a natural and proper part of their legitimate function to adjudicate on the boundary lines between state action and individual rights, even though this line may be controversial.

A second type of case is where the attack is on the penalty imposed, the claim being that it is excessive. Courts are likely to be reasonably searching in this type of case. This is in part because penalties can impinge on personal liberties. It is in part also because a court can normally strike down a particular penalty without thereby undermining the entirety of the administrative policy with which it is connected.

A third type of case is where the individual argues that the very policy choice made by the administration is disproportionate, because, for example, the costs are excessive in relation to the benefits, or because the measure is not suitable or necessary to achieve the end in view. The judiciary is likely to be more circumspect in this type of case. The reasons are not hard to find. The administrative/political arm of government makes policy choices, and it is generally recognized that the courts should not overturn these merely because they believe that a different way of doing things would have been better. They should not substitute their judgment for that of the administration. This does not mean that proportionality is ruled out in such instances. It does mean that the courts are likely to apply the concept less intensively than in the previous two categories of case, and will overturn the policy choice only if it is clearly or manifestly disproportionate.

The crucial issue in reality will, therefore, often be the intensity with which the Court applies the proportionality test, as the following extract reveals.

G. de Búrca, The Principle of Proportionality and its Application in EC Law[7]

It becomes apparent that in reaching decisions, the Court of Justice is influenced not only by what it considers to be the nature and the importance of the interest or right claimed by the applicant, and the nature and importance of the objective alleged to be served by the measure, but by the relative expertise, position and overall competence of the Court as against the decision-making authority in assessing those factors. It becomes apparent that the way the proportionality

---

[7] (1993) 13 *YBEL* 105, 111–12.

principle is applied by the Court of Justice covers a spectrum ranging from a very deferential approach, to quite a rigorous and searching examination of the justification for a measure which has been challenged.

. . . Courts are generally prepared to adjudicate on issues involving traditionally categorized individual rights, where interference with a discretionary policy decision can be explained not on the ground that it is not the most sensible or effective measure, but on the ground that it unjustifiably restricts an important legally recognized right, the protection of which is entrusted to the court. Courts are accepted as having a legitimate role in deciding on civil liberties and personal rights even in controversial contexts such as euthanasia, abortion and freedom of speech. But in certain specific political contexts, in the case of measures involving, for example, national security, economic policy or national expenditure concerns, courts tend to be considerably more deferential in their review. They are more reluctant to adjudicate if the interest affected is seen as a collective or general public interest rather than an individual right, and if the interest of the State is a mixed and complex one, e.g. in an area involving national economic and social policy choices. Where a measure of this nature is challenged, it may be that it does not appear to affect any traditionally characterized right, but rather indirectly affects the interests and welfare of many people. Or even if it does affect a recognized right, it also concerns many other interests, both individual and general, over which the policy-maker has presumably deliberated at length in coming to a deci-sion. . . . The ways in which a court may defer in such circumstances range from deeming the measure to be non-justiciable, to refusing to look closely at the justification for the restrictive effects of the measure, to placing the onus of proof on the challenger who is claiming that the measure is disproportionate. Courts tend to be deferential in their review in cases which highlight the non-representative nature of the judiciary, the limited evidentiary and procedural processes of adjudication, and the difficulty of providing a defined individual remedy in contexts which involve complex political and economic policies.

(b) PROPORTIONALITY AND CHALLENGES TO COMMUNITY ACTION

The differing ways in which proportionality is applied, depending upon the type of case before the Court, can be demonstrated by considering challenges to Community action.[8]

The general interrelationship between proportionality and fundamental rights was considered in the previous chapter. The *Hauer* case[9] provides a good example of the way in which the Court applies proportionality in this type of case. It will be remem-bered that the applicant sought to challenge a Community regulation that placed limitations on the planting of new vines. The Court found that this did not, in itself, constitute an invalid restriction on property rights. It then proceeded to determine whether the planting restrictions were disproportionate, 'impinging upon the very substance of the right to property'.[10] The Court found that they were not, but in reaching this conclusion it did, however, carefully examine the purpose of the general scheme within which the contested regulation fell. The objects of this scheme were to attain a balanced wine market, with fair prices for consumers and a fair return for producers; the eradication of surpluses; and an improvement in the quality of wine.

---

[8] T. Tridimas, *The General Principles of EC Law* (Oxford University Press, 1999), ch. 3.
[9] Case 44/79, *Hauer* v. *Land Rheinland-Pfalz* [1979] ECR 3727.
[10] *Ibid.*, para. 23.

The disputed regulation, which prohibited new plantings, was part of this overall plan. It was not disproportionate in the light of the legitimate, general Community policy for this area. This policy was designed to deal with an immediate problem of surpluses, while at the same time laying the foundation for more permanent measures to facilitate a balanced wine market. The *Hautala* case[11] provides a more recent example of proportionality and rights. The action was brought by Ms Hautala, an MEP, who sought access to a Council document concerning arms exports. The Council refused to grant access, on the ground that this could be harmful to the EU's relations with third countries, and sought to justify this under Article 4(1) of Decision 93/731,[12] governing access to Council documentation. The ECJ held that the right of access to documents was to be broadly construed so as to include access to information contained in the document, not just the document itself. The principle of proportionality required the Council to consider partial access to a document that contained information the disclosure of which could endanger one of the interests protected by Article 4(1). Proportionality also required that derogation from the right of access be limited to what was appropriate and necessary for achieving the aim in view.[13]

Many of the second and third types of cases concerning proportionality arise from the Common Agricultural Policy (CAP). The objectives of the CAP are set out at a high level of generality in Article 33 (ex Article 39) EC. It is clear, moreover, that these objectives can clash *inter se*, with the result that the Commission and Council will have to make difficult discretionary choices, often under fairly extreme exigencies of time, in order to decide how best to balance and attain these aims. Actions seeking the annulment of CAP regulations etc. have been very common and provide insights into how the Court applies the principles of substantive review in particular subject-matter areas.[14]

There has been a regular stream of such cases, in which the essence of the proportionality argument is that a penalty is excessive in relation to the aim of the measure. The Court has found in favour of the individual on a number of occasions. In *Man (Sugar)*[15] the applicant was required to give a security deposit to the Board when seeking a licence to export sugar outside the Community. The applicant was then late, but only by four hours, in completing the relevant paperwork. The Board, acting pursuant to a Community regulation, declared the entire deposit of £1,670,370 to be forfeit. Not surprisingly the company was aggrieved. The Court held that the automatic forfeiture of the entire deposit in the event of any failure to fulfil the time requirement was too drastic, given the function performed by the system of export licences.[16] In addition to cases dealing with penalties *stricto sensu*

---

[11] Case C–353/99P, *Council* v. *Hautala*, 6 Dec. 2001.

[12] [1993] OJ L340/43.

[13] Cases T–222, 327, & 329/99, *Martinez, de Gaulle and Bonino* v. *European Parliament*, 2 Oct. 2001, reveal how proportionality might be used to challenge internal rules as to the organization of political parties within the EP. The challenge failed on the facts.

[14] See Ch. 12 below.

[15] Case 181/84, *R.* v. *Intervention Board, ex parte E. D. & F. Man (Sugar) Ltd.* [1985] ECR 2889.

[16] Case 181/84, [1985] ECR 2889, para. 29; Case 240/78, *Atalanta Amsterdam BV* v. *Produktschap voor Vee en Vlees* [1979] ECR 2137; Case 122/78, *Buitoni SA* v. *Fonds d'Orientation et de Régularisation des Marchés Agricoles* [1979] ECR 677.

the Court has applied proportionality in the field of economic regulation, scrutinizing the level of charges imposed by the Community institutions. Thus in *Bela-Mühle*[17] the Court held that a scheme whereby producers of animal feed were forced to use skimmed milk, rather than soya, in their product in order to reduce a milk surplus was unlawful. Skimmed milk was three times more expensive than soya: the obligation to purchase the milk, therefore, imposed a disproportionate burden on the animal-feed producers. There have been other, more recent, cases in which the essence of the argument was that the burden imposed by a Community norm was excessive. 'Mad cow' disease, and the Community response thereto, generated a number of such cases. Thus in *Portugal v. Commission*[18] Portugal argued that an export ban on meat products, imposed in response to mad cow disease, was disproportionate. This was because Portugal was not a significant meat exporter, and it was therefore easier to regulate low-volume exports as compared to the large-volume exports from the UK. The ECJ rejected the argument. Beef exports from the UK had not been allowed until the UK had put in place export arrangements of a kind advocated by a certain health code. This had not been done at the time when the ban was imposed on Portugal.

The *Fedesa* case provides a good example of a challenge to a more general Community policy choice made under the CAP. The Court has frequently emphasized that the Community institutions possess a wide discretion in the operation of the CAP, and that review will not therefore be intensive.[19] This more deferential approach is likely to carry across to challenges based on proportionality.

Case C–331/88, R. v. Minister for Agriculture, Fisheries and Food, ex parte Fedesa
[1990] ECR 4023

Council Directive 81/602 provided that the Council would take a decision as soon as possible on the prohibition of certain hormone substances for administration to animals, but that in the meantime any arrangements made by Member States in relation to such substances would continue to apply. In 1988 Council Directive 88/146 was adopted as an approximating measure, prohibiting the use in livestock farming of certain of these hormonal substances. An earlier identical directive adopted in 1985 had been declared void by the ECJ on grounds of an infringement by the Council of an essential procedural requirement. The applicants were manufacturers and distributors of veterinary medicine who challenged the validity of the national legislative measure implementing the 1988 Directive, on the ground that the Directive itself was invalid. They argued that the Directive infringed the principles of legal certainty, proportionality, equality, and non-retrospectivity. The following extract considers the ECJ's reasoning on proportionality.

---

[17] Case 114/76, *Bela-Mühle Josef Bergman KG v. Grows-Farm GmbH & Co. KG* [1977] ECR 1211.
[18] Case C–365/99, [2001] ECR I–5645.
[19] See, e.g., Case 138/78, *Stolting v. Hauptzollamt Hamburg-Jonas* [1979] ECR 713; Case 265/87, *Schräder v. Hauptzollamt Gronau* [1989] ECR 2237.

THE ECJ

12. It was argued that the Directive infringes the principle of proportionality in three respects. In the first place, the outright prohibition on the administration of the five hormones in question is inappropriate in order to attain the declared objectives, since it is impossible to apply in practice and leads to the creation of a dangerous black market. In the second place, outright prohibition is not necessary because consumer anxieties can be allayed simply by the dissemination of information and advice. Finally, the prohibition in question entails excessive disadvantages, in particular considerable financial losses on the part of the traders concerned, in relation to the alleged benefits accruing to the general interest.

13. The Court has consistently held that the principle of proportionality is one of the general principles of Community law. By virtue of that principle, the lawfulness of the prohibition of an economic activity is subject to the condition that the prohibitory measures are appropriate and necessary in order to achieve the objectives legitimately pursued by the legislation in question; when there is a choice between several appropriate measures recourse must be had to the least onerous, and the disadvantages caused must not be disproportionate to the aims pursued.

14. However, with regard to judicial review of compliance with those conditions it must be stated that in matters concerning the common agricultural policy the Community legislature has a discretionary power which corresponds to the political responsibilities given to it by . . . the Treaty. Consequently, the legality of a measure adopted in that sphere can be affected only if the measure is manifestly inappropriate having regard to the objective which the competent institution is seeking to pursue. (See in particular the judgment in Case 265/87, *Schräder* [1989] ECR 2237, paras. 21 and 22).

The applicants had therefore to show that the measure was manifestly inappropriate, and the Court concluded that they had not discharged this burden.[20] The prohibition, even though it might have caused financial loss to some traders, could not be regarded as manifestly inappropriate. The Court's application of the proportionality principle in this case contrasts with the more rigorous application of the principle in other cases, in which it is not Community action but Member State action that is being challenged.[21]

(c) PROPORTIONALITY AND CHALLENGES TO MEMBER STATE ACTION

There have been many cases dealing with proportionality in the context of Community rights and Member State action which seek to restrict the ambit of those rights.[22] In these types of cases the Court tends to engage in fairly intensive review, in

[20] See also, e.g., Case T–30/99, *Bocchi Food Trade International GmbH* v. *Commission* [2001] ECR II–943, para. 92.

[21] See, e.g., Case 5/88, *Wachauf* v. *Germany* [1989] ECR 2609. See further the case law involving state restrictions on freedom of movement in the Community, where the proportionality test applied by the Court to such measures generally involves a search for less restrictive alternatives: Case 104/75, *Officier van Justitie* v. *de Peijper* [1976] ECR 613; Case 261/81, *Walter Rau Lebensmittelwerke* v. *De Smedt, Pvba* [1982] ECR 3961; Case 33/74, *Van Binsbergen* v. *Bestuur van de Bedrijfsvereniging Metaalnijverheid* [1974] ECR 1299.

[22] Tridimas, n. 8 above, ch. 4.

order to determine whether the restriction which the Member State has imposed on an important right granted by the Treaties really is necessary or warranted. This same theme can be seen throughout the Court's case law when dealing with free movement, whether of persons, services, or goods. These cases will commonly arise when Member States seek to argue that a restriction on the Community right is justified on grounds of public policy, public health, or one of the other limits which are, in principle, recognized by the Treaty.

Thus the ECJ has insisted that derogation from the principle of free movement of workers can be sanctioned only in cases which pose a genuine and serious threat to public policy, and even then the measure must be the least restrictive possible in the circumstances.[23] The same principle is evident in cases on freedom to provide services. In *Van Binsbergen*[24] the Court held that residence requirements limiting this freedom might be justified, but only where they were strictly necessary to prevent the evasion, by those outside the territory, of professional rules applicable to the activity in question. In *Canal*[25] the ECJ considered the legality of national legislation requiring operators of certain television services to register details of their equipment in a national register. It held that such a measure could not satisfy the necessity requirement of the proportionality test if the registration requirement duplicated controls which had already been carried out, either in the same state or in another Member State. We can see the same approach at work in cases concerned with the free movement of goods. Thus in the famous *Cassis de Dijon* case[26] the Court decided that a German rule which prescribed the minimum alcohol content for a certain alcoholic beverage could constitute an impediment to the free movement of goods. The Court then considered whether the rule was necessary in order to protect consumers from being misled. It rejected the defence, because the interests of consumers could be safeguarded in other, less restrictive ways, by displaying the alcohol content on the packaging of the drinks.[27] Proportionality will also often be of relevance in equality cases. Thus in *Kreil*[28] it was held that a German rule, requiring that all armed units in the Bundeswehr be male, contravened the principle of proportionality. Four variables appear to affect the intensity of the Court's review in this type of case.

First, other things being equal, the Court has tended to be more intensive in its review as time has gone on. Cases which have come before the Court involving similar facts or raising similar principles have tended to be subject to more rigorous scrutiny, with the result that Member State action which was regarded as lawful in the earlier case has been held not to be so in a later action.[29]

---

[23] Case 36/75, *Rutili* v. *Ministre de l'Intérieur* [1975] ECR 1219; Case 30/77, *R.* v. *Bouchereau* [1977] ECR 1999.

[24] Case 33/74, *Van Binsbergen*, n. 21 above; Case 39/75, *Coenen* v. *Social Economische Raad* [1975] ECR 1547.

[25] Case C–390/99, *Canal Satelite Digital SL* v. *Aministacion General del Estado and Distribuidora de Television Gigital SA (DTS)*, 22 Jan. 2002.

[26] Case 120/78, *Rewe-Zentrale AG* v. *Bundesmonopolverwaltung für Branntwein* [1979] ECR 649.

[27] Recent examples of the same principle are Case C–217/99, *Commission* v. *Belgium* [2000] ECR I–10251; Case C–473/98, *Kemikalieinspektionen* v. *Toolex Alpha AB* [2000] ECR I–5681.

[28] Case C–285/98, *Kreil* v. *Bundesrepublik Deutschland* [2000] ECR I–69.

[29] Compare, e.g., Case 41/74, *Van Duyn* v. *Home Office* [1974] ECR 1337, with Cases 115 & 116/81, *Adoui and Cornuaille* v. *Belgian State* [1982] ECR 1665. Compare Case 34/79, *R.* v. *Henn and Darby* [1979] ECR 3795, with Case 121/85, *Conegate* v. *Customs and Excise Commissioners* [1986] ECR 1007.

Secondly, the intensity of the Court's review will also be a function of how seriously it takes the Member State's argument that measures really were necessary in order to protect, for example, public health. If the Court feels that these measures were really a 'front' for a national protective policy, designed to insulate its own producers from foreign competition, then it will be inclined to subject the Member State's argument to close scrutiny. This is exemplified by *Commission v. United Kingdom*.[30] The Court considered a claim by the United Kingdom Government that a ban on the import of poultry could be justified on grounds of public health under what is now Article 30 (ex Article 36) EC. A reading of the Court's judgment leaves one in little doubt that it was suspicious, to say the least, of the motives for the United Kingdom action. The Court felt that the measures were, in reality, aimed at protecting United Kingdom poultry producers from the effects of French imports in the run up to Christmas. The Court accordingly rejected the United Kingdom's defence.

A third factor, which will influence the intensity of review, will be the nature of the subject-matter. Where a Member State raises genuine concerns relating to public health,[31] and there is scientific uncertainty about the effects of certain foodstuffs, the Court has been more willing to accept that limitations on free movement are warranted.[32] However, one should be cautious about characterizing such cases as involving less intensive review.[33] They may equally well be regarded as instances where the Court, *having surveyed the evidence*, believed that the Member State's action was warranted. There are, moreover, examples of public-health claims where the Court, while accepting that there was some scientific uncertainty, none the less concluded that there was a less restrictive way of achieving the Member State's aim.[34]

The final variable affecting the intensity of the proportionality inquiry is rather different from those considered above. In some instances the Court has passed the application of proportionality back to the national courts, as in the context of the free movement of goods.[35] This should not, however, be taken to mean that the Court is necessarily being more deferential in the application of proportionality. This can only be determined by considering the conditions, or guidelines, which the ECJ lays down for national courts on how the proportionality inquiry should be decided in a particular area.[36] There is, moreover, justifiable concern about the complexity of the issues that are sent back to national courts to be resolved through a proportionality inquiry.[37]

---

[30] Case 40/82, [1982] ECR 2793.
[31] See 632–4 below.
[32] Case 174/82, *Officier van Justitie v. Sandoz BV* [1983] ECR 2445; Case 97/83, *Melkunie* [1984] ECR 2367.
[33] See the different views expressed by Schwarze, n. 5 above, 790 and Lord Slynn, 'The Concept of Free Movement of Goods and the Reservation for National Action under Art. 36 EEC', in J. Schwarze (ed.), *Discretionary Powers of the Member States in the Field of Economic Policies and their Limits under the EEC Treaty* (Nomos 1988).
[34] Case 178/84, *Commission v. Germany* [1987] ECR 1227.
[35] See 644–5 below.
[36] G. de Búrca, 'The Principle of Proportionality and its Application in EC Law' (1993) 13 *YBEL* 105.
[37] W. van Gerven, 'The Effect of Proportionality on the Actions of Member States of the European Community: National Viewpoints from Continental Europe', in E. Ellis (ed.), *The Principle of Proportionality in the Laws of Europe* (Hart, 1999), 37–64.

3. LEGAL CERTAINTY AND LEGITIMATE EXPECTATIONS

The connected concepts of legal certainty and legitimate expectations are to be found in many legal systems, although their precise legal content may vary from one system to another.[38] These concepts are applied in a number of different ways and it is important to distinguish them in order to avoid confusion.

(a) LEGAL CERTAINTY AND ACTUAL RETROACTIVITY

The most obvious application of legal certainty is in the context of rules with an actual retroactive effect. Following Schwarze,[39] 'actual retroactivity' covers the situation where a rule is introduced and applied to events which have already been concluded. Retroactivity of this nature may occur either where the date of entry into force precedes the date of publication, or where the regulation applies to circumstances which have actually been concluded before the entry into force of the measure.

The arguments against allowing such measures to have legal effect are simple and compelling. A basic tenet of the rule of law is that people ought to be able to plan their lives, secure in the knowledge of the legal consequences of their actions. This fundamental aspect of the rule of law is violated by the application of measures which were not in force at the time that the actual events took place. Our concerns about retrospective norms are particularly marked in the context of criminal penalties, where the effect of the norm may be to criminalize activity that was lawful when it was undertaken. The application of retrospective rules may also be extremely damaging in commercial circumstances, upsetting the presuppositions on which important transactions have been based.

It is therefore unsurprising that national legal systems take a very dim view of attempts to apply rules in this manner. The Community is no different in this respect. The basic principle was enunciated in *Racke*.[40] The Commission had introduced monetary compensatory amounts for a certain product by a regulation, and then in two further regulations altered the amounts. Each of the relevant regulations provided that they would apply fourteen days before they were published. The Court held that it was a fundamental principle of the Community legal order that a measure should not be applicable to those concerned before they had the opportunity to make themselves acquainted with it.[41] The Court then drew out the implications for retroactive measures, stating that:[42]

Although in general the principle of legal certainty precludes a Community measure from taking effect from a point in time before its publication, it may exceptionally be otherwise where the

---

[38] S. Schonberg, *Legitimate Expectations in Administrative Law* (Oxford University Press, 2000); Schwarze, n. 5 above, ch. 6; Tridimas, n. 8 above, ch. 5.

[39] Schwarze, n. 5 above, 1120.

[40] Case 98/78, *Firma A. Racke* v. *Hauptzollamt Mainz* [1979] ECR 69. See also Case 99/78, *Weingut Gustav Decker KG* v. *Hauptzollamt Landau* [1979] ECR 101; Case T–115/94, *Opel Austria GmbH* v. *Council* [1997] ECR II–2739.

[41] *Ibid.*, 84.   [42] *Ibid.*, 86.

purpose to be achieved so demands and where the legitimate expectations of those concerned are duly respected.

The Court has, in accordance with this proviso, upheld the validity of retroactive measures, particularly in the agricultural sphere where they were necessary to ensure market stability, or where the retroactivity places the individual in a more favourable position.[43] The normal presumption is, however, against the validity of retroactive measures. This manifests itself in both procedural and substantive terms.

In procedural terms, the Court has made it clear that it will interpret norms as having retroactive effect only if this clearly follows from their terms, or from the objectives of the general scheme of which they are a part. The general principle of construction is, therefore, against giving rules any retroactive impact.[44]

In substantive terms, the Court will strike down measures that have a retroactive effect where there is no pressing Community objective which demands this temporal dimension, or where the legitimate expectations of those affected by the measure cannot be duly respected,[45] as the following case shows.

Case 63/83, Regina v. Kent Kirk
[1984] ECR 2689

Criminal proceedings were brought in the United Kingdom for infringement of fisheries legislation. During the course of these proceedings the question arose whether Council Regulation 170/83 of 25 January 1983, by which, with retroactive effect from 1 January 1983, national measures contravening Community law prohibitions on discrimination were approved by way of transitional arrangements, could also retroactively validate national penal provisions. The ECJ said no, firmly.

THE ECJ

20. The Commission . . . contends that the Member States were empowered to adopt measures such as the Sea Fish Order 1982 by Article 6(1) of Regulation 170/83 of 25 January 1983 which authorises retroactively, as from 1 January 1983, the retention of the derogation regime defined in Article 100 of the 1972 Act of Accession for a further ten years, and which extends the coastal zones from six to twelve nautical miles. . . .·

21. Without embarking upon an examination of the general legality of the retroactivity of Article 6(1) of that Regulation, it is sufficient to point out that such retroactivity may not, in any event, have the effect of validating ex post facto national measures of a penal nature which impose penalties for an act which, in fact, was not punishable at the time at which it was committed. That would be the case where at the time of the act entailing a criminal penalty, the national measure was invalid because it was incompatible with Community law.

22. The principle that penal provisions may not have retroactive effect is one which is common to all the legal orders of the Member States and is enshrined in Article 7 of the European Convention for the Protection of Human Rights and Fundamental Freedoms as a fundamental

---

[43] Case T–7/99, *Medici Grimm KG* v. *Council* [2000] ECR II–2671.
[44] Cases 212–217/80, *Salumi* [1981] ECR 2735.
[45] Case 224/82, *Meiko-Konservenfabrik* v. *Federal Republic of Germany* [1983] ECR 2539.

right; it takes its place among the general principles of law whose observance is ensured by the Court of Justice.

23. Consequently the retroactivity provided for in Article 6(1) of Regulation 170/83 cannot be regarded as validating ex post facto national measures which imposed criminal penalties, at the time of the conduct at issue, if those measures were not valid.

Where there is a pressing Community objective and where the legitimate expectations of those concerned are duly respected, then retroactivity may, *exceptionally*, be accepted by the Court in the non-criminal context. This is exemplified by *Fedesa*.[46] The applicants argued that the Directive was in breach of the principle of non-retroactivity, on the ground that it was adopted on 7 March 1988 and stipulated that it was to be implemented by 1 January 1988 at the latest. The Court drew a distinction between the retroactive effect of penal provisions and retroactive effect outside the criminal sphere. As to the former, the Court affirmed *Kent Kirk*, but held that the Directive in the *Fedesa* case would not impose any criminal liability as such. As to the latter, the Court ruled that the Directive did not contravene the principle of non-retroactivity. It had been adopted to replace an earlier Directive which had been annulled. The time frame of the challenged Directive was necessary in order to avoid a temporary legal vacuum where there would be no Community legislation to back up the Member States' existing implementing provisions. It was for this reason that the Council had maintained the date of the earlier Directive when it passed the later Directive.[47]

(b) LEGAL CERTAINTY, LEGITIMATE EXPECTATIONS, AND APPARENT RETROACTIVITY

Apparent retroactivity covers the situation where legislative acts are applied to events which occurred in the past, but which have not yet been definitively concluded.[48] These cases can be particularly difficult.[49] The moral arguments against allowing laws to have actual retroactive effect are powerful and straightforward. Cases involving apparent retroactivity are more problematic because the administration must obviously have the power to alter its policy for the future, even though this may have implications for the conduct of private parties which has been planned on the basis of the pre-existing legal regime.[50] The ECJ's approach can be described as follows.

First, the protection of legitimate expectations in EC law developed initially in

---

[46] Case C–331/88, [1990] ECR 4023.

[47] The Court held that there was no infringement of the legitimate expectations of any individual, because the earlier dir. was clearly only annulled because of a procedural defect, and people affected by the national implementing legislation could not expect the Council to change its attitude on the substance of the matter in the dir. during the short time between the annulment of the first dir. and the notification of the second dir.: *ibid.*, para. 47.

[48] It may sometimes be difficult to decide whether the case, in legal terms, concerns actual or apparent retroactivity: Case C–162/00, *Land Nordrhein-Westfalen* v. *Beata Pokrzeptowicz-Meyer*, 29 Jan. 2002.

[49] Schwarze, n. 5 above, 1121.

[50] A valuable analysis of the justifications for protecting legitimate expectations can be found in Schonberg, n. 38 above, ch. 1.

relation to revocation of administrative decisions. It has however been extended to representations, as opposed to formal decisions.[51] The applicant will have to show that the representation gave rise to a legitimate expectation, but such an expectation can, in principle, be based on a representation as well as a formal decision. This is especially important since Community policy may be developed through various 'soft-law' devices, such as guidelines, notices, and the like.[52] Whether a Commission guideline or notice has generated an expectation will depend upon its nature and wording, but the Community courts have been willing to treat guidelines and notices in this manner. This is exemplified by case law on state aids. In *CIRFS*[53] the ECJ was willing to accept that in the instant case the Commission was bound by the terms of its policy framework, and in *Ijssel-Vliet*[54] it held that Commission guidelines which had been built into a Dutch aid scheme were binding upon the Dutch government. Moreover, in *Vlaams Gewest*[55] the CFI held that the guidelines adopted by the Commission had to be applied in accord with the principle of equal treatment, with the implication that like cases, as defined in the guidelines, had to be treated alike.

Secondly, the mere fact that a trader is disadvantaged by a change in the law will not, in and of itself, give any cause for complaint based upon disappointment of legitimate expectations. A trader will not be held to have a legitimate expectation that an existing situation, which is capable of being altered by decisions taken by the institutions within the limits of their discretionary powers, will be maintained.[56] This is particularly so in the context of the CAP, where constant adjustments to meet new market circumstances are required.[57] It may also be so in other areas, such as competition policy, where the CFI emphasized that the Commission has discretion to alter the level of fines.[58]

Thirdly, the claim will fail where the Court adjudges that the applicant's expectations were not legitimate. This will be so where, for example, the challenged Community activity was designed to close a legal gap in order to prevent traders from making a speculative profit.[59] Or where the expectations were not reasonable, because the contested measure should have been foreseen.[60] Or where the applicant has not met the conditions attached to a grant of funding.[61] Or because the Court simply

[51] Case 54/65, *Chatillon* v. *High Authority* [1966] ECR 185, 196; Case 81/72, *Commission* v. *Council (Staff Salaries)* [1973] ECR 575, 584–5; Case 148/73, *Louwage* v. *Commission* [1974] ECR 81, para. 12.

[52] See Ch. 3 above.

[53] Case C–313/90, *CIRFS* v. *Commission* [1993] ECR I–1125, paras. 34–36.

[54] Case C–311/94, *Ijssel-Vliet Combinatie BV* v. *Minister van Economische Zaken* [1996] ECR I–5023.

[55] Case T–214/95, *Vlaams Gewest* v. *Commission* [1998] ECR II–717.

[56] Case C–110/97, *Netherlands* v. *Council*, 22 Nov. 22 2001; Case C–402/98, *ATB* v. *Ministero per le Politiche Agricole* [2000] ECR I–5501; Case T–18/99, *Cordis Obst und Gemüse GrossHandel GmbH* v. *Commission* [2001] ECR II–913; Case C–104/97P, *Atlanta AG* v. *Commission and Council* [1999] ECR I–6983.

[57] See n. 56 above, and Case C–63/93, *Duff* v. *Minister for Agriculture and Food Ireland and the Attorney General* [1996] ECR I–569; Case C–22/94, *Irish Farmers Association* v. *Minister for Agriculture, Food and Forestry (Ireland) and the Attorney General* [1997] 2 CMLR 621; Case 52/81, *W. Faust* v. *Commission* [1982] ECR 3745, 3762; Case 245/81, *Edeka* v. *Federal Republic of Germany* [1982] ECR 2745, 2758.

[58] Case T–31/99, *ABB Asea Brown Boveri Ltd* v. *Commission*, 20 Mar. 2002.

[59] Case 2/75, *Einfuhr und Vorratsstelle für Getreide und Futtermittel* v. *Firma C. Mackprang* [1975] ECR 607; Case C–179/00, *Weidacher* v. *Bundesminister für Land- und Forstwirtschaft*, 15 Jan. 2002.

[60] Case 265/85, *Van den Bergh en Jurgens and Van Dijk Food Products* v. *Commission* [1987] ECR 1155; Case C–350/88, *Delacre* v. *Commission* [1990] ECR I–395; Case T–489/93, *Unifruit Hellas EPE* v. *Commission* [1994] ECR II–1201; Cases T–466, 469, 473, 474, & 477/93, *O'Dwyer* v. *Council* [1996] ECR II–2071; E. Sharpston, 'Legitimate Expectations and Economic Reality' (1990) 15 *ELRev.* 103.

[61] Case T–126/97, *Sonasa—Sociedade Nacional de Seguranca Ld* v. *Commission* [1999] ECR II–2793.

disagreed with the reason the applicants claimed that their expectations had been disappointed. Thus in the *Fedesa* case, the Court felt that the traders could not have had a reasonable expectation that the substances in question would not be banned in the absence of conclusive scientific findings as to their dangers.[62]

Fourthly, the protection of legitimate expectations extends to any individual who is in a situation from which it is clear that, in giving specific assurances,[63] the Community institutions caused that person to entertain justified hopes.[64] The individual must be able to point either to a bargain of some form between the individual and the authorities, or to a course of conduct or assurance on the part of the authorities which can be said to generate the legitimate expectation. The *Mulder* case illustrates the first of these situations.

Case 120/86, Mulder v. Minister van Landbouw en Visserij
[1988] ECR 2321

The Community had an excess of milk. In order to reduce this excess it passed Regulation 1078/77, under which producers could cease milk production for a certain period in exchange for a premium for non-marketing of the milk. The applicant made such an arrangement in 1979 for five years. In 1984 he began to plan a resumption of his production and applied to the relevant Dutch authorities for a reference quantity of milk which he would be allowed to produce without incurring the payment of any additional levy. He was refused on the ground that he could not prove milk production during the relevant reference year, which was 1983. This was of course impossible for Mulder since he did not produce at all during that period, because of the bargain struck in 1979. He challenged Regulation 857/84, which was the basis of the Dutch authorities' denial of his quota, arguing, *inter alia*, that it infringed his legitimate expectations. The Court found in his favour.

THE ECJ

23. It must be conceded . . . that a producer who has voluntarily ceased production for a certain period cannot legitimately expect to be able to resume production under the same conditions as those which previously applied and not to be subject to any rules of market or structural policy adopted in the meantime.

24. The fact remains that where such a producer, as in the present case, has been encouraged by a Community measure to suspend marketing for a limited period in the general interest and against payment of a premium he may legitimately expect not to be subject, upon the expiry of his undertaking, to restrictions which specifically affect him precisely because he availed himself of the possibilities offered by the Community provisions.

25. However, the regulations on the additional levy on milk give rise to such restrictions for producers who, pursuant to an undertaking entered into under Regulation 1078/77, did not deliver milk during the reference year. . . . Those producers may in fact be denied a reference quantity

---

[62] Case C–331/88, n. 46 above, para. 10.

[63] Case T–72/99, *Meyer v. Commission* [2000] ECR II–2521; Case T–290/97, *Mehibas Dordtselaan BV v. Commission* [2000] ECR II–15.

[64] Case T–534/93, *Grynberg and Hall v. Commission* [1994] ECR II–595; Case T–456/93, *Consorzio Gruppo di Azioni Locale Murgia Messapica v. Commission* [1994] ECR II–361.

under the new system precisely because of that undertaking if they do not fulfil the specific conditions laid down in Regulation 857/84 or if the Member States have no reference quantity available.

26. ... There is nothing in the provisions of Regulation 1078/77 or in its Preamble to show that the non-marketing undertaking entered into under that Regulation might, upon its expiry, entail a bar to resumption of the activity in question. Such an effect therefore frustrates those producers' legitimate expectations that the effect of the system to which they had rendered themselves would be limited.

The following cases illustrate the second type of situation, where the legitimacy of the applicant's expectation is based upon some course of conduct by the administration, or an assurance it has given. In *Embassy Limousines*[65] it was held that there could be a breach of legitimate expectations where a company submitting a tender was encouraged to make irreversible investments in advance of the contract being awarded, and thereby to go beyond the risks inherent in making a bid. In *CEMR*[66] it was held that the Commission could not, without infringing the principle of legitimate expectations, reduce the budgetary allocation for a project where the relevant work had been included in the original bid that had been accepted by the Commission. In the *Sofrimport* case[67] the applicant sought to import apples from Chile into the Community. A licence was required in accordance with Regulation 346/88. By a later Regulation, 962/88, the Commission took protective measures and suspended all such licences for Chilean apples. The parent Regulation, 2707/72, which gave the Commission power to adopt protective measures, specifically stated in Article 3 that account should be taken of the special position of goods in transit, for the obvious reason that such measures could have a particularly harmful effect on traders. The applicant's goods were already in transit when Regulation 962/88 was introduced, but they were refused entry to the Community. In an action for annulment the Court held that the failure of the Commission to make any special provision for goods in transit as required by the parent Regulation was an infringement of the applicant's legitimate expectations.[68] A similar theme is apparent in the *CNTA* case.[69] The case centred on monetary compensation amounts (mcas), which were payments designed to compensate for fluctuations in exchange rates. The applicant was a firm which had made export contracts on the supposition that mcas would be payable. After these contracts had been made, but before they were to be performed, the Commission passed a regulation abolishing mcas in that sector. The applicant suffered loss, since it had made the contracts on the assumption that the mcas would be payable. The Court held that, while mcas could not be said to insulate exporters from all fluctuations in exchange rates, they did have the effect of shielding them from such risks, with the

[65] Case T–203/96, *Embassy Limousines & Services* v. *European Parliament* [1998] ECR II–4239.

[66] Cases 46 & 151/98, *Council of European Municipalities and Regions* v. *Commission* [2000] ECR II–167.

[67] Case C–152/88, *Sofrimport Sàrl* v. *Commission* [1990] ECR I–2477. *Cf.* Case T–336/94, *Efisol SA* v. *Commission* [1997] ECR II–1343.

[68] *Cf.* Case C–110/97, n. 56 above.

[69] Case 74/74, *CNTA SA* v. *Commission* [1975] ECR 533.

consequence that even a prudent exporter might choose not to cover himself against it. The Court then stated:[70]

In these circumstances, a trader might legitimately expect that for transactions irrevocably undertaken by him because he has obtained, subject to a deposit, export licences fixing the amount of the refund in advance, no unforeseeable alteration will occur which could have the effect of causing him inevitable loss, by re-exposing him to the exchange risk.

In the absence of some overriding public interest, the Commission should have adopted transitional measures to protect those in the position of the applicant.[71] There may, however, be cases, such as *Dieckmann*,[72] where there is an overriding public interest to protect consumers, which means that transitional measures should *not* be adopted.

The Court has, therefore, sought to balance the need of the Community to alter its policy for the future with the impact that such alteration might have on traders who based their commercial bargains on pre-existing norms. This is a problem all legal systems have to face.[73] It is important to note that the Court is willing to accept that legitimate expectations can have a substantive and not just a procedural impact.[74] Thus in the cases considered above in which the Court has found in favour of the applicant, the result is that the applicant obtains the substantive benefit sought, in the absence of any overriding public interest to the contrary. This does not always mean that the applicant will succeed in a damages action against the Community.[75] It does mean, for example, in *Mulder* that the Community regulation denying the applicant his milk quota was struck down, and the Court made it clear that it was invalid for the Community institutions to deny him the opportunity to re-enter the milk market.

(c) LEGAL CERTAINTY, LEGITIMATE EXPECTATIONS, AND REVOCATION OF UNLAWFUL ACTS

The preceding cases were all concerned with changes of policy which caused loss to an individual. The policy choice in these cases was, however, not itself unlawful, on a ground separate from breach of legitimate expectations. We must now consider the situation where the Community has passed an illegal act and then seeks to revoke it. For students of administrative law in the United Kingdom the appropriate analogy is with the problem of representations or decisions made by public bodies which are *ultra vires*, and the extent to which they may none the less be relied on by the individual.

The Community's case law on this issue is complex, being mainly derived from decisions concerning the functioning of the ECSC. This case law is, however, instructive. Detailed treatment can be found elsewhere,[76] but two of the central aspects of the Court's approach can be sketched briefly here.

---

[70] *Ibid.*, para. 42.   [71] *Ibid.*, para. 43.

[72] Case T–155/99, *Dieckmann & Hansen GmbH* v. *Commission*, 23 Oct. 2001.

[73] For the analogous problem in UK law see P. Craig, *Administrative Law* (Sweet & Maxwell, 4th edn., 1999), ch. 19.

[74] P. Craig, 'Substantive Legitimate Expectations in Domestic and Community Law' [1996] *CLJ* 289.

[75] See Ch. 13 below.

[76] Schwarze, n. 5 above, 991–1025; T.C. Hartley, *The Foundations of European Community Law* (Clarendon Press, 4th edn., 1998), 435–9.

First, unreasonable delay by the administration can operate as a bar to the revocation of an unlawful administrative act.[77] Secondly, in deciding whether to allow retroactive revocation at all it may be necessary to balance the public interest in legality and the private interest in legal certainty. The former does not always trump the latter.[78] This point is of particular interest in the United Kingdom where we are still generally wedded to the idea that the illegal nature of a decision or representation precludes any reliance on it by an individual. We could have much to learn from the more nuanced approach of the Court.[79]

4. NON-DISCRIMINATION

Although equality and non-discrimination (which are often treated as synonymous) are universally recognized principles,[80] the legal concept of discrimination is not unproblematic. Identifying a difference in treatment between two people who appear to be similarly placed is only a first step in considering whether a breach of the principle of non-discrimination has occurred. The second step is to determine whether that apparent difference in treatment was justified on any ground. We shall see some of the difficulties in identifying what constitutes impermissible discrimination in later chapters dealing with the free movement of persons, services, and goods, as well as with sex discrimination.[81]

(a) NON-DISCRIMINATION AS A 'GENERAL' PRINCIPLE OF EC LAW

The principle of non-discrimination, although a general principle and therefore binding on both the Community and the Member States within the scope of application of EC law, is also expressly mentioned in a number of distinct contexts in the Treaty. Before the insertion by the Amsterdam Treaty of Article 13 (ex Article 6a) EC, the three main areas were: (a) the field of non-discrimination on grounds of nationality as expressed in Article 12 (ex Article 6), and in the free movement context as expressed in Articles 39, 43, and 49–50 (ex Articles 48, 52, and 59–60) of the EC Treaty;[82] (b) equal treatment of men and women as set out now in the amended

[77] Case 15/85, *Consorzio Cooperative d'Abruzzo* v. *Commission* [1987] ECR 1005.
[78] Cases 42, 49/59, *SNUPAT* v. *High Authority* [1961] ECR 53; Case 14/61, *Hoogovens* v. *High Authority* [1962] ECR 253.
[79] For suggestions of a similar balancing approach in the UK see Craig, n. 73 above, ch. 19.
[80] On equality in EC law see G. More, 'The Principle of Equal Treatment: from Market Unifier to Fundamental Right', in P. Craig and G. de Búrca (eds.), *The Evolution of EU Law* (Oxford University Press, 1999).
[81] See Chs. 15, 17–20. See, e.g., Case C–132/92, *Roberts* v. *Birds Eye Walls Ltd.* [1993] ECR I–5579, and on goods see Case 2/90, *Commission* v. *Belgium (Walloon Waste)* [1992] ECR I–4431, later criticized by Jacobs AG in Case C–379/98, *PreussenElektra AG* v. *Schleswag AG* [2001] ECR I–2099 for the ECJ's reasoning on the discrimination point.
[82] National rules requiring non-residents to provide security for costs in litigation were potentially indirectly discriminatory according to the ECJ in Cases C–43/95, *Data Delecta and Forsberg* v. *MSL Dynamics* [1996] ECR I–4661; C–323/95, *Hayes* v. *Kronenberger* [1996] ECR I–1711; and C–122/96, *Saldanha and MTS Securities Corporation* v. *Hiross Holdings* [1997] ECR I–5325. Contrast Case C–177/94, *Perfili* [1996] ECR I–161. For a recent case on Art. 6 (ex Art. 12) EC and nationality discrimination in the treatment of traffic offences see Case C–224/00, *Commission* v. *Italy* [2002] ECR I–nyr.

Articles 2 and 3, and in Articles 137 and 141 (ex Articles 118 and 119) EC;[83] and (c) non-discrimination as between producers or consumers in the field of agriculture, in accordance with Article 34(2) (ex Article 40(3)). There are also specific provisions such as Article 90 (ex Article 95), prohibiting discriminatory taxation. However, the non-discrimination principle has also been applied more generally by the ECJ where there was arbitrarily or unjustifiably unequal treatment of two persons within an area of Community competence, such as in the context of Community staff policy.[84]

The Advocates General in *P* v. *S*[85] and *Grant*[86] had argued, prior to the enactment of Article 13, that the general principles of Community law imposed a requirement on the EC institutions and the Member States not to discriminate within the areas covered by Community law on arbitrary grounds such as sexual orientation or having undergone gender reassignment. The Court, however, has been more conservative. Although in *P* v. *S* it declared that Directive 76/207 on equal treatment of men and women in employment was 'simply the expression, in the relevant field, of the principle of equality', which is one of the fundamental principles of Community law', the Court, in its subsequent ruling in *Grant* concerning travel benefits for the same-sex partners of employees, retreated from this broad principle of equality and decided that discrimination on grounds of sex in EC law did *not* cover discrimination on grounds of sexual orientation.[87] The Court ruled that ensuring respect for fundamental rights could not have the effect of extending the scope of the Treaty provisions (which at the time required Member States only to ensure *sex* equality in employment) beyond the competences of the Community.

It might have been hoped in view of the earlier ruling in *P* v. *S* that discrimination on grounds of gender reassignment would be 'tantamount . . . to a failure to respect the dignity and freedom' of the individual, that the ECJ would articulate a broad principle of non-discrimination on *any* arbitrary ground within fields covered by EC law, but the case of *D* v. *Council*[88] appeared to reinforce the cautious approach taken in *Grant*. In *D* there was no possible doubt about Community competence, as there may have been in *Grant*, since the former case concerned the EU's treatment of its own employees rather than regulation of the employment relationship within Member States. The facts concerned the EU's refusal to pay a staff household allowance, which would have been payable to a married employee, to a homosexual employee who was in a stable partnership registered under Swedish law. The Court first denied that there had been any discrimination on grounds of sex, and then gave rather an odd response to the argument that there had been discrimination on grounds of sexual orientation:

[83] In Case C–50/99, *Deutsche Telekom* v. *Schröder* [2000] ECR I–743, the ECJ ruled that the economic aims of the sex equality principle in Art. 141 (ex Art. 119) EC were secondary to its social aims as a fundamental human right.

[84] Cases 75, 117/82, *Razzouk and Beydoun* v. *Commission* [1984] ECR 1509, paras. 16–17. See also Case 20/71, *Sabbatini* [1972] ECR 345, para. 3, and Case 149/77, *Defrenne* v. *Sabena* [1978] ECR 1365, paras. 26–27.

[85] See Tesauro AG in Case C–13/94, *P* v. *S and Cornwall County Council* [1996] ECR I–2143.

[86] Elmer AG in Case C–249/96, *Grant* v. *South-West Trains Ltd* [1998] ECR I–621.

[87] *Ibid.*, para. 42.

[88] Case C–125/99P, *D* v. *Council* [2001] ECR I–4319.

47. [A]s regards infringement of the principle of equal treatment of officials irrespective of their sexual orientation, it is clear that it is not the sex of the partner which determines whether the household allowance is granted, but the legal nature of the ties between the official and the partner.

Thus, while ruling that there had been no unequal treatment on grounds of sexual orientation the Court did not actually deny the possible existence of a general principle of EC law prohibiting discrimination on grounds of sexual orientation within its field of application. So, despite the rulings in *Grant* and *D*, it remains arguable that within the proper scope of application of EC law, there exists a general principle of non-discrimination on the basis of sexual orientation, race, and other arbitrary grounds.

More significantly, Article 21(1) of the Charter of Fundamental Rights now declares that:

Any discrimination based on any ground such as sex, race, colour, ethnic or social origin, genetic features, language, religion or belief, political or any other opinion, membership of a national minority, property, birth, disability, age or sexual orientation shall be prohibited.

This provision, which by virtue of Article 51 of the Charter is to be binding on the EU institutions and on the Member States when implementing EU law, clearly establishes a broad general principle of non-discrimination with an open-ended list of prohibited grounds. Further, as we have seen in the previous chapter, even though its legal status remains unresolved until at least 2004, the Charter is already beginning to have legal effects through the practice of various institutional actors.

(b) NON-DISCRIMINATION AS A COMMUNITY GOAL AND A BASIS FOR COMMUNITY ACTION

Apart from the Charter, the major development in the area of non-discrimination came with the addition of Article 13 EC by the Amsterdam Treaty.[89] Paragraph one of this Article provides:

Without prejudice to the other provisions of this Treaty and within the limits of the powers conferred by it upon the Community, the Council, acting unanimously on a proposal from the Commission and after consulting the European Parliament, may take appropriate action to combat discrimination based on sex, racial or ethnic origin, religion or belief, disability, age or sexual orientation.

Unlike Article 21 of the Charter, or Article 12 (ex Article 6) EC, Article 13 is not a direct prohibition against discrimination, but rather an empowering provision which enables the Community to take action against the forms of discrimination listed. The Nice Treaty has added a second paragraph to Article 13, providing for a power to adopt non-harmonizing 'incentive measures' by co-decision. And while action under Paragraph one can only be taken 'within the limits of the powers conferred' on the Community under the Treaty, the Community's objectives and aims are broadly

---

[89] See M. Bell, 'The New Article 13 EC Treaty: a Sound Basis for European Anti-discrimination Law?' (1999) 6 *MJ* 5 and L. Waddington, 'Testing the Limits of the EC Treaty Article on Non-Discrimination' (1999) 28 *ILJ* 133.

expressed and its powers quite widespread, so that this limiting clause may not be a particularly serious restraint.

Before the enactment of Article 13 the Community's legal competence to act directly to combat discrimination of this kind was contested.[90] None the less, a number of non-discrimination clauses were inserted into various pieces of Community legislation such as Broadcasting Directive 89/552,[91] and the European Monitoring Centre on Racism and Xenophobia was established by Regulation under Articles 284 (ex Article 213) and 308 (ex Article 235) EC.[92] However, Article 13 EC represents an unambiguous conferral of power on the Community which, although it is not clear prohibition and lacks direct effect, has undoubtedly facilitated stronger law-making in this field.[93] A general directive prohibiting discrimination on grounds of race or ethnic origin,[94] and a directive prohibiting discrimination on grounds of religion, belief, disability, age, or sexual orientation in the field of employment,[95] were adopted in 2000. In the same year, an action programme to combat discrimination on all the grounds listed in Article 13 (other than sex) was adopted,[96] and the Commission has announced a policy of 'mainstreaming' so as to integrate anti-discrimination considerations such as race and disability in particular into other areas of EC policy formation.[97]

None the less, it has been argued that the action taken so far does not reflect a single undifferentiated equality principle, but rather demonstrates a clear hierarchy within the Article 13 grounds of discrimination, with race currently at the top, and age at the bottom.[98] How the additional grounds listed in Article 21 of the Charter—such as social origin, genetic features, political opinion or membership of a national minority—may fit within this hierarchy remains to be seen. However the Ombudsman, who, as we saw in Chapter 8, has treated the Charter of Rights as a source of binding law for the institutions ever since its proclamation, has adopted a strong stance on a range of non-discrimination issues. Most recently he refused to sign a decision establishing the European Recruitment Office until the provision allowing age discrimination was deleted.

(c) JUSTIFYING DISCRIMINATION

To discriminate means to differentiate or to treat differently, which in itself seems innocuous. In Community law it is however impermissible when done without adequate justification on the basis of one of the prohibited grounds, or when there is no relevant difference between two persons or situations which would justify a difference in their treatment. These are not necessarily easy criteria to apply, since it is

---

[90] For a history of EC anti-discrimination policy in the fields of race and sexual orientation see M. Bell, *Anti-Discrimination Law and the EU* (Oxford University Press, 2002).

[91] [1989] OJ L298/23.   [92] Council Reg. 1035/97, [1997] OJ L151/1.

[93] See Bell, n. 90 above.   [94] Council Dir. 2000/43, [2000] OJ L180/22.

[95] Council Dir. 2000/78, [2000] OJ L303/16.

[96] Council Dec. 2000/750, [2000] OJ L303/23.

[97] For a comment on the implications of mainstreaming for one particular policy area see M. Bell 'Mainstreaming Equality Norms into EU Asylum Law' (2001) 26 *ELRev*. 20.

[98] L. Waddington and M. Bell, 'More Equal than Others: Distinguishing European Union Equality Directives' (2001) 38 *CMLRev*. 587.

not always clear which factors may be taken into account in determining whether two persons are 'similarly situated'. Nor is it clear whether, if differences in situation are taken into account to justify discriminatory treatment, this should be seen as a form of justified 'positive discrimination' or should in fact be seen as not discriminatory at all.[99]

A straightforward example of discrimination on grounds of sex would be where a woman was paid a lower wage than a man for doing exactly the same job, and a simple example of discrimination on grounds of nationality would be where a UK employer refused to hire any employee who was not British. The more difficult situations arise where the discrimination is neither clear nor direct, but is either indirect and disguised or is entirely unintentional but none the less discriminatory in its impact. Indirect and disguised discrimination would occur if, for example, a UK employer claimed to hire workers of any nationality so long as they had received their education in the UK, since in practice this requirement would not be fulfilled by most non-UK nationals.[100] A form of unintentional and indirect sex discrimination may occur where an employer pays part-time workers less per hour than full-time workers, where the overwhelming majority of part-time workers are women.[101]

In Community law, direct or deliberate disguised discrimination on grounds of sex or nationality is prohibited, subject to fairly limited grounds of exception,[102] wheras indirect and unitentional discrimination may be justified on a variety of non-exhaustive grounds.[103] Thus in the context of nationality discrimination, a language requirement which is indirectly discriminatory may be justified if it is proportionate and genuinely required for the job to be undertaken.[104] Similarly in the context of sex discrimination, the payment of a higher hourly wage to full-time than to part-time workers may, even where it indirectly discriminates against women, be 'objectively justified' on grounds relating to the needs of the employer.[105] Discrimination on grounds of nationality and sex will be discussed in fuller detail in Chapters 17 to 20. Indirect discrimination was expressly defined for the first time (in the context of sex discrimination) in the Burden of Proof Directive in 1997,[106] and differently again in the recent anti-discrimination directives adopted under Article 13 EC.[107] In addition to the 'objective justification' requirements, these directives permit other specific exceptions to the general non-discrimination principle.

---

[99] See Case C–132/92, *Roberts* v. *Birds Eye Walls Ltd.* [1993] ECR I–5579 and also the discussion on positive action in cases such as Cases C–450/93, *Kalanke* v. *Freie Hansestadt Bremen* [1995] ECR I–3051; C–409/95, *Hellmut Marschall* v. *Land Nordrhein-Westfalen* [1997] ECR I–6363 and others in Ch. 20.

[100] For an example of indirect discrimination see Case 152/73, *Sotgiu* v. *Deutsche Bundespost* [1974] ECR 153, where the pay differential was based on the country or place of recruitment, rather than the nationality of the worker.

[101] See further Ch. 20.

[102] See Chs. 17 and 18 on the subject of justifications for direct discrimination in the context of free movement of persons and services. See Ch. 20 on the subject of direct sex discrimination, for which limited grounds of exception are provided in some of the secondary legislation.

[103] See Chs. 17–20.

[104] See Ch. 17 and Art. 3(1) of Reg. 1612/68 on freedom of movement for workers.

[105] E.g. Case 96/80, *Jenkins* v. *Kingsgate (Clothing Productions) Ltd.* [1981] ECR 911. See further Ch. 20.

[106] Dir. 97/80.

[107] For discussions of the various provisions of the Race Dir., n. 94 above, see the ch. by S. Fredman, D. Chalmers, and C. McCrudden in S. Fredman (ed.), *Discrimination and Human Rights: The Case of Racism* (Oxford University Press, 2001).

5. TRANSPARENCY

(a) TREATY PROVISIONS

Whether or not transparency can be counted as a general principle of EC law has been a matter for debate for some years. The notion of transparency in a constitutional context encompasses a number of different features, such as the holding of meetings in public, the provision of information, and the right of access to documents. This latter right forms the most developed legal dimension of the principle of transparency in the EU context, and it is on this that the discussion below will focus. However, even though this right of access to documents is now enshrined in Article 42 of the Charter of Fundamental Rights, it is not yet clear what added status this may give the legal entitlement which was included in Article 254 (ex Article 190) EC by the Amsterdam Treaty in 1999. A related amendment introduced at Amsterdam was the rhetorical declaration in Article 1 (ex Article A) TEU that all EU decisions are to be taken 'as openly as possible'.

(b) BACKGROUND

Undoubtedly transparency is a value whose status and importance within EU law have increased considerably since the time of the Maastricht Treaty.[108] The early Communities, as we saw in Chapter 1, were weak in terms of democracy, account-ability, and accessibility to public scrutiny. Meetings of the Council were secretive and minutes were not published; the Commission was perceived as a distant and remote bureaucracy and the Community processes as labyrinthine and opaque, peopled by a bewildering number of committees. Not least as a result of the near failure to have the Treaty on European Union ratified in Denmark and in France, which highlighted in a dramatic and effective way an undeniable degree of popular antipathy towards the Community, there was a greater focus thereafter, and particularly during the Inter-governmental Conference preceding the Amsterdam Treaty, on the need to improve matters of the openness and transparency of the Union and its institutions, and to make them more accessible to the public.[109] Further, a number of the Member States, notably the Netherlands and Denmark and also the two newer Scandinavian Member States after 1995, increasingly objected to the secrecy surrounding the Council of Ministers, and were dissatisfied with the steps which the Council had taken.[110] The Council and Commission had adopted a joint Code of Conduct in 1993,[111] and each had immediately implemented it into their rules of procedure by decision.[112]

---

[108] For an excellent and comprehensive account of the origins and development of transparency in the EU see S. Peers, 'From Maastricht to Laeken: The Political Agenda of Openness and Transparency in the EU', in V. Deckmyn (ed.), *Increasing Transparency in the European Union* (Maastricht EIPA, 2002). See also A. Tomkins, 'Transparency and the Emergence of a European Administrative Law' (1999–2000) 19 *YBEL* 217.

[109] G. de Búrca, 'The Quest for Legitimacy in the European Union' (1996) 59 *MLR* 359. For an analysis of the transparency debate around the time of the TEU see J. Lodge, 'Transparency and Democratic Legitimacy' (1994) 32 *JCMS* 343. Also Peers, n. 108 above.

[110] See D. Curtin, 'Betwixt and Between: Democracy and Transparency in the Governance of the European Union', in J. Winter *et al.* (eds.), *Reforming the Treaty on European Union: The Legal Debate* (Kluwer, 1996), 95.

[111] [1993] OJ L340/41.

[112] See Council Dec. 93/731, [1993] OJ L340/43 and Commission Dec. 94/90, [1994] OJ L46/58.

(c) THE CASE LAW

Transparency in itself has not been accorded the legal status of a general principle of Community law by the Court. The initial response of the CFI and the ECJ to the challenges brought in the cases of *Carvel*[113] and *The Netherlands*,[114] although supportive of the values of transparency and access, did not require the adoption of secondary legislation by the Council, declaring instead that Council decisions on access to documents could properly be based on its Rules of Procedure. In the latter case brought by the Netherlands against the Council, the Dutch government argued that the principle of openness of the legislative process was an essential requirement of democracy, and that the right of access to information was an internationally recognized fundamental human right. Yet while the ECJ confirmed the importance of the right of public access to information, and its relationship to the democratic nature of the institutions, it rejected the argument that such a fundamental right should not be dealt with purely as a matter of the Council's own internal rules of procedure.[115] The CFI ruled in *Carvel*, however, that the institutions' rules of procedure are not a purely internal matter, but give rise to expectations and rights on the part of individuals who seek access to documents. More recently in the *Hautala* case, despite upholding the CFI's decision to annul the Council's refusal to consider granting partial access to politically sensitive documents, the ECJ declared that it was not necessary for it to pronounce on whether or not EC law recognizes a general 'principle of the right to information'.[116]

None the less, despite the failure to articulate a general principle of transparency or a general right of access to information, the two European Courts have played a significant role in elaborating on the nature and content of the right of access to information contained in the procedural rules and legislative decisions of the institutions. In a series of cases, the CFI and the ECJ have annulled quite a number of decisions of the Council and Commission refusing access to their documents, not on the ground that the institutions had breached a 'general principle of transparency' but on other grounds, such as the automatic application of non-mandatory exceptions, the inappropriate use of the authorship rule, the refusal to consider partial access, or the inadequacy of the reasons given for refusal.[117] And while many other judicial challenges have been unsuccessful on their facts,[118] a significant and substantial body

---

[113] Case T–194/94, Carvel v. *Council* [1995] ECR II–2765, in which an action of the Council was held to be in breach of the guarantees on access to documents it had made in a decision implementing its own Rules of Procedure.

[114] Case C–58/94, Netherlands v. *Council* [1996] ECR I–2169.   [115] *Ibid.*, paras. 31–36.

[116] Case C–353/99P, *Council* v. *Hautala* [2001] ECR I–nyr, para 31.

[117] See, e.g., Cases T–105/95 *Worldwide Fund for Nature* v. *Commission* [1997] ECR II–313; T–124/96, *Interporc Im- und Export GmbH* v. *Commission* [1998] ECR II–231; T–92/98, *Interporc* v. *Commission* [1999] ECR II–3521; T–188/97, *Rothmans International* v. *Commission* [1999] ECR II–2463; T–174/95, *Svenska Journalistförbundet* [1998] ECR II–2289; C–353/99P, *Hautala* v. *Council* [2001] ECR I–nyr; T–123/99, *JT's Corporation* v. *Commission* [2000] ECR II–3269, T–188/98, *Kuijer* v. *Council* [2000] ECR II–1959.

[118] See, e.g., Case T–610/97, *Carlsen et al.* v. *Council* [1998] ECR II–0485—denial of interim relief against Council refusal to supply documents; Case T–309/97, *Bavarian Lager Company* v. *Commission* [1999] ECR II–3217—refusal to grant access was justified to protect proper conduct of infringement procedure; Case T–106/99, *Meyer* v. *Commission* [1999] ECR II–3273—right of access to documents does not mean that Commission must answer any request for information; Case T–20/99, *Denkavit Nederland* v. *Commission*

of law relating to the right of access to documents has evolved. The general trend of this case law has been to give a broad reading to the right of access as an important value connected to the democratic nature of the EU, and to interpret the exceptions narrowly.[119]

(d) LEGISLATIVE DEVELOPMENT

As far as the legislative foundation for the right of access to information is concerned, Article 255 of the EC Treaty, which was recently held in the *Petrie* case to lack direct effect,[120] was added by the Amsterdam Treaty some years after the Code of Conduct had been adopted and implemented by the institutions. Article 255 provides:

Any citizen of the Union, and any natural or legal person residing or having their registered office in a Member State, shall have a right of access to European Parliament, Council and Commission documents, subject to the principles and the conditions to be defined in accordance with paragraphs 2 and 3.

The legislation setting out the principles and limits 'on grounds of public or private interest' had to be adopted under the co-decision procedure, with each institution being required to make provision for access to its own documents in its rules of procedure. The amended Article 207 (ex Article 151) EC also imposed additional requirements on the Council in this respect, specifying that access to documents, explanations and results of votes, and statements of minutes are particularly important when the Council is acting in its legislative capacity.

The legislation required by Article 255 was eventually adopted in the form of a regulation late in 2001,[121] following a number of earlier more specific decisions, including the much-criticized 'Solana' decision of the Council in 2000 which had excluded certain types of foreign-policy document entirely from the scope of the access-to-information rules.[122] This and the other previous legislation was however replaced by Regulation 1049/2001, which improves the position governing access to documents in several respects (e.g. by abolishing the authorship rule, softening the nature of some of the exceptions, and requiring a register of documents to be kept), while narrowing it in others.[123] The new legislation was again implemented by the three EU institutions into their own rules of procedure.

[2000] ECR II–3011—refusal to grant access to investigation report prepared by the Commission in an ongoing investigation was justified; Case T–191/99, *Petrie* v. *Commission* [2001] ECR I–nyr—refusal to produce documents relating to Commission procedure under Art. 226 upheld; and Case T–204/99, *Mattila* v. *Council and Commission* [2001] ECR II–2265.

[119] For a helpful summary of the case law see Peers, n. 108 above.

[120] Case T–191/99, *Petrie* v. *Commission* [2001] ECR I–nyr.

[121] Reg. 1049/2001, [2001] OJ L145/43.

[122] Dec. 2000/527, [2000] OJ L212/9. For a discussion of the applicability of the transparency rules to the second and third pillars of the EU see S. Peers, 'Access to Information on EU External Relations and Justice and Home Affairs', in Deckmyn, n. 108 above.

[123] See Peers, n. 108 above, and 'The New Regulation on Access to Documents: A Critical Analysis' (2002) 21 *YBEL*, forthcoming.

(e) THE OMBUDSMAN

Apart from the activity of the Courts and the legislative branches, the Ombudsman has also been a key player in the development of openness and transparency as broader principles of law.[124] He undertook an own-initiative inquiry into public access to documents addressed to fifteen Community institutions other than the Council and Commission.[125] In his decision subsequently based on this inquiry, he concluded that failure to adopt rules governing public access to documents and to make those rules easily available to the public constituted maladministration. As a result most of the other important EU bodies including the Court of Auditors and ECB have now adopted rules governing access to documents. Further, although Article 255 applies only to the Council, Commission, and Parliament, the preamble to Regulation 1049/2001 declares that all agencies established by the institutions should apply the same principles.

Nevertheless, it remains uncertain whether transparency can be counted yet among the general principles of EC law. While it is undoubtedly a value which the Community institutions purport to uphold, and a term which can be applied to describe the growing collection of Treaty provisions, institutional rules, and practices governing access to information and openness, it remains uncertain whether 'transparency' has actually become a fundamental and justiciable principle which the ECJ will protect.[126]

6. CONCLUSIONS

i. While the category of general principles of EC law is broad and non-exhaustive, the most familiar are drawn from national constitutional and administrative traditions and are developed and adapted by the ECJ to the EC context.

ii. A key characteristic of the general principles of EC law is that they are justiciable both as aids to interpretation and as grounds for judicial review.

iii. Some principles which have not always been fully recognized in EC law, such as the emergent transparency principle, and the principle of non-discrimination on grounds such as sexual orientation, race, and age, have been implemented and concretized in detailed secondary legislation, and their legal status has been gradually enhanced in this way.

iv. While the Charter of Fundamental Rights articulates rights such as access to documents and freedom from discrimination in reasonably strong terms, their contribution to the creation and strengthening of justiciable general principles of EC law remains speculative as long as the Charter's legal status is not settled.

---

[124] The Ombudsman in 2002 criticized the institutions for using new data-protection rules to impose more confidentiality on their activities instead of concentrating on the protection of citizens' rights.

[125] (616/PUBAC/F/IJH) [1998] OJ C44/9. This included the ECJ in so far as administrative documents were concerned, since the ECJ is only outside the mandate of the Ombudsman in so far as its judicial role is concerned.

[126] On a related matter, the right to be given reasons for a decision did not seem to be accorded the status of a general principle in Case C–70/95, *Sodemare v. Regione Lombardia* [1997] ECR I–3395.

7. FURTHER READING

ARNULL, A., *General Principles of EEC Law and the Individual* (Leicester University Press/ Pinter, 1990)

BELL, M., *Anti-Discrimination Law and the European Union* (Oxford University Press, 2002)

BERNITZ, U., and NERGELIUS, J., *General Principles of European Community Law* (Kluwer, 2000)

BUNYAN, T., *Secrecy and Openness in the EU* (Kogan Page, 1999)

DASHWOOD, A., and O'LEARY, S. (eds.), *The Principle of Equal Treatment in EC Law* (Sweet & Maxwell, 1997)

DECKMYN, V. (ed.), *Increasing Transparency in the European Union* (Maastricht EIPA, 2002)

ELLIS, E. (ed.), *The Principle of Proportionality in the Laws of Europe* (Hart, 1999)

EMILIOU, N., *The Principle of Proportionality in European Law* (Kluwer, 1996)

EUROPEAN OMBUDSMAN WEBSITE *Bibliography*, **www.euro-ombudsman.eu.int/bibliog/en/ default.htm**

GERAPETRITIS, G., *Proportionality in Administrative Law* (Sakkoulas, 1997)

NEHL, A., *Principles of Administrative Procedure in EC Law* (Hart, 1999)

SCHONBERG, S., *Legitimate Expectations in Administrative Law* (Oxford University Press, 2000)

SCHWARZE, J., *European Administrative Law* (Office for Official Publications of the European Communities/Sweet and Maxwell, 1992)

TRIDIMAS, T., *The General Principles of EC Law* (Oxford University Press, 1999)

USHER, J., *General Principles of EC Law* (Longman, 1998)

10

ENFORCEMENT ACTIONS AGAINST MEMBER STATES

1. CENTRAL ISSUES

i. Amongst the tasks entrusted to the Commission by Article 211 (ex Article 155) EC is that of ensuring the proper application of Community law. The main component of the Commission's task in ensuring the application of Community law is to monitor Member State compliance and to respond to non-compliance.

ii. The Treaty provides for various enforcement mechanisms involving judicial proceedings against the Member States, which are brought either by the Commission or by a Member State.[1] Article 226 (ex Article 169) establishes the general enforcement procedure, giving the Commission broad power to bring enforcement proceedings against Member States which it considers to be in breach of their obligations under Community law.[2]

iii. The nature of this enforcement procedure is mixed. It functions in part as a diplomatic means for resolving disputes amicably without recourse to litigation,[3] in part as a channel for individuals to complain to the Commission about breaches of EC law, and in part as an 'objective' law enforcement tool by the Commission.[4]

iv. A mechanism allowing the Commission to request the ECJ to impose a penalty payment on a Member State which has failed to comply with a previous judgment in Article 226 proceedings was introduced under Article 228 (ex Article 171) in 1993, and is now actively used by the Commission.

---

[1] Some of these apart from the general procedure in Art. 226 (ex Art. 169) are dealt with elsewhere: see Ch. 26 on Art. 88(2) (ex Art. 93(2)) and Ch. 27 on Art. 95(4) (ex Art. 100a(4)). Under Art. 237 (ex Art. 180) the Board of the European Investment Bank and the Council of the European Central Bank have powers similar to those of the Commission under Art. 226 (ex Art. 169). Art. 298 (ex Art. 225) provides for an enforcement procedure where Member States have relied on Art. 297 (ex Art. 224) to derogate from fundamental Community rules: see, e.g., Case C–120/94, R *Commission* v. *Greece* [1994] ECR I–3037.

[2] Under the similar enforcement provision of Art. 88 ECSC, the High Authority is empowered to record the failure of a state to fulfil its obligations, without first bringing the case before the ECJ. Following such a finding, however, the state affected may itself bring the matter before the Court. The parallel Euratom provisions are Arts. 141–142, which mirror Arts. 226–227(formerly Arts. 169–170) of the EC Treaty.

[3] See the *8th Annual Report* on Commission Monitoring of the Application of Community Law, 1990 [1991] OJ C338/6–7.

[4] For a discussion of the tensions between all three dimensions, see R. Rawlings, 'Engaged Elites: Citizen Action and Institutional Attitudes in Commisison Enforcement' (2000) 6 *ELJ* 4.

2. THE FUNCTION AND OPERATION OF THE INFRINGEMENT PROCEDURE

Article 226 provides:

If the Commission considers that a Member State has failed to fulfil an obligation under this Treaty, it shall deliver a reasoned opinion on the matter after giving the State concerned the opportunity to submit its observations.

If the State concerned does not comply with the opinion within the period laid down by the Commission, the latter may bring the matter before the Court.

(a) FUNCTION OF THE PROCEDURE

The Commission initiates Article 226 (ex Article 169) proceedings either in response to a complaint from someone in a Member State, or on its own initiative. Since it has no investigation service, complaints are brought on the basis of information gained, for example, through the press, from European Parliament questions or petitions, or increasingly from 'modernized' means such as databases indicating when Member States have failed to notify their implementation of a Directive.

The Commission has repeatedly stated in its annual reports over the past ten years that complaints from citizens constitute a significant source for the detection of infringements, and has suggested that the Article 226 (ex Article169) procedure thus contributes towards creating a more participatory Community in which citizens can play a role in law enforcement.[5] As against this, it has equally emphasized the fact that the enforcement procedure is not intended primarily to provide individuals with a means of redress, but rather an 'objective' mechanism for ensuring state compliance with EC law.[6] In its eighteenth annual report for 2000, after asserting once against the importance of the individual complainant for the infringement procedure, the Commission goes on to caution against over-reading the role of individuals:

But the primary objective of the infringement procedure is still, as before, to cause the offending Member State to come into line with Community law. Nor does it have any effect on the discretionary power that the Commission is acknowledged to have by the ECJ as regards commencing infringement proceedings.

This is all the more important as the nature of the procedure may sometimes leave complainants feeling frustrated; they of course, are aiming for a different result—the satisfaction of their individual interests which they see as threatened by the Member State's alleged unlawful conduct.[7]

After the Commission, in its fourteenth report in 1996, noted a gradual decline in the number of complaints, a complaint form for individuals to use was designed and published, ostensibly in the interests of transparency.[8]

---

[5] See the comments in its *10th Annual Report* (1992) [1993] OJ C233/7, and also the *11th Annual Report* (1993) [1994] OJ C154/6.
[6] See, e.g., *13th Annual Report* [1996] OJ C303/8.
[7] *18th Annual Report*, COM(2001)309.   [8] [1997] OJ C332/12.

Given this ambivalence in the Commission's attitude, it is not surprising to find that the role actually played by individual complainants is imprecise and varying. On the one hand, the individual has no say in determining whether or not the Commission actually initiates proceedings against a Member State.[9] On the other hand, since the establishment of the Ombudsman's office, individuals have regularly made complaints about the Commission's procedures, and this has led to certain changes and improvements being introduced by the Commission.[10] In 1996 the Ombudsman conducted an own-initiative investigation into the Commission's enforcement procedures, following which the Commission ceased its previous practice of failing to inform complainants when a case had been terminated.[11] The Commission also now makes more frequent use of press releases, and places considerably more information about the various formal stages of the infringement procedure on the internet.[12]

In his 1999 report, the Ombudsman noted that the Article 226 investigation procedure 'is not yet organised as a normal administrative procedure, in which the complainant is treated as a party' with the result that the Commission does not supply complainants with all of the documents relevant to a complaint.[13] However, the Commission claimed in 2001 to have 'embarked on the codification of the current administrative rules to ease contacts with complainants'.[14] Until now, as we shall see below, various attempts by individuals to obtain documents pertaining to Article 226 proceedings through the European courts have been frustrated by confidentiality and public interest exceptions.[15] Commenting on the role of individuals in infringement proceedings in the *Petrie* case, the CFI ruled:

So far as concerns the applicants' argument that proceedings under Article 226 EC seeking to establish the facts relating to the infringements of Community law complained of must respect the audi alteram partem principle, it must be noted that individuals are not party to proceedings concerning failure to fulfil obligations and for that reason cannot invoke rights to a fair hearing involving application of the audi alteram partem principle.[16]

However, the Commission's attitude towards citizen complainants in the infringement procedure, and also the Ombudsman's response both to individual complaints and in his own-initiative inquiry, have been criticized sharply by Rawlings, who argues that the Commission and its legal service tend to be aloof, unresponsive, and negative

---

[9] See Case 247/87, *Star Fruit* v. *Commission* [1989] ECR 291; Case T–182/97 *Smanor* v. *Commission* [1998] ECR II– 271.

[10] For some recent examples see decision on complaints nos. 1060/97/OV and 1140/97/IJH discussed in the Ombudsman's 1999 Annual Report, and complaint no. 813/98/(PD)/GG discussed in his 2000 Annual Report. All reports are available on the Ombudsman website, www.euro-ombudsman.eu.int/.

[11] For the Ombudsman's own-initiative inquiry, 303/97/PD, reported in Ombudsman Annual Report for 1997. For the Commission's announcement of changes consequently introduced into its procedures, see *14th Annual Report on Monitoring the Application of EC Law for 1996* [1997] OJ C332/16. Also R. Mastroianni, 'The Enforcement Procedure under Article 169 of the EC Treaty and the Powers of the European Commission: Quis Custodiet Custodes?' (1995) 1 *European Public Law* 535, and P. Kunzlik, 'The Enforcement of EU Environmental Law: Article 169, the Ombudsman and the Parliament' (1997) 6 *EELR* 46.

[12] See the *18th Annual Report* for 2000, COM(2001)309.

[13] See the discussion of complaint no. 749/97/IJH in the 1999 Ombudsman's Report.

[14] *18th Annual Report*, n. 12 above.   [15] See nn. 76, 78, and 79 below and text.

[16] Case T–191/99, *Petrie* v. *Commission*, judgment of 12 Dec. 2001, para. 70. See also Case T–105/95, *WWF* v. *Commission* [1997] ECR II–313 and Case T–309/97, *Bavarian Lager Company* v. *Commission* [1999] ECR II–3217.

to citizens, while the Ombudsman is criticized for having adopted an excessively legalistic approach and wasting the opportunity to push for stronger administrative reforms.[17] Rawlings identifies three competing paradigms or dimensions of the Article 226 procedure: first, that of elite international co-operation and regulatory bargaining (which can be seen in the preference for diplomatic resolution through negotiation between the Commission and individual states), secondly that of citizen participation (which is emphasized in much of the Commission's rhetoric), and thirdly that of effective technocratic law enforcement. (which fits with the description of the procedure as 'objective'). His essential argument is that a rebalancing between the Commission's discretion and the procedural recognition of complainants is necessary in view of the increasing emphasis on democratic involvement in EU affairs and the mounting challenges to the legitimacy of elite-led practices.

R. Rawlings, Engaged Elites: Citizen Action and Institutional Attitudes in Commisison Enforcement[18]

Fons et origo of Commission enforcement, the general procedure is an exception today. In other areas where the Commission is directly responsible for administration, the procedures are commonly well established and have been formulated in regulations. In fact, the recent reform of the supervision of state aids provides a possible role model. By this is meant an insistence via Council Regulation on time limits for Commission decisions; on additional information gathering to enable better verification of compliance; and on notice and comment rights for third parties, which does not burden the Commission with full contradictory procedure at each stage of the process . . . Urgent consideration should thus be given to applying to the general procedure the kind of soft law techniques that previously have characterised state aids policy and practice. Open and flexible guidelines furnish the means to an appropriate balance of regulatory choice for the Commission, proper procedural protections, and more rational forms of decision-making. . . .

Practical steps to improve the procedural position of complainants could usefully begin with acceptance of a general administrative obligation of advice and assistance. Complainant interviews and visits; in difficult cases, professional aid to formulate grievance; such measures ought not to pose problems if resources are properly targeted, and are vital if the role of the 'guardian of the treaties' is to be taken seriously. Attention should further be given to enabling complainants to make timely representations as the procedure unfolds, including detailed representations in cases of complex and disputed facts. The role of active citizenship would be amply demonstrated, without having to afford complainants full legal party status.

(b) OPERATION OF THE PROCEDURE

The infringement procedure can be divided into four distinct stages:

1. Negotiations at the initial *pre-contentious stage* give the Member State the occasion to explain its position and the opportunity to reach an accommodation with the Commission.

---

[17] Rawlings, n. 4 above.   [18] *Ibid.*, 26–7.

2. If the matter is not clarified or resolved informally between the two at this stage, the state will be *formally notified* of the specific infringement alleged by means of a letter from the Commission. The state is usually given two months to reply, except in cases of urgency, and the Commission normally decides within a year either to close a case or to proceed.

3. If, after negotiation with the State, the matter has not been resolved, the Commission may proceed to the stage of issuing a *reasoned opinion*. The reasoned opinion sets out clearly the grounds on which the alleged infringement rests, and marks the beginning of the time period within which the Member State must comply, if it is to avoid the final stage.

4. which is *referral* of the matter by the Commission *to the Court of Justice*.

In 1990 the Commission adopted a stricter practice than before in issuing letters of formal notice, which in turn led to a greater number of reasoned opinions. None the less, for a few years subsequently there was a reduction in the number of cases actually referred to the ECJ, which the Commission took to be evidence of satisfactory settlement on the basis of the reasoned opinions which had been issued. The Commission makes much of, and clearly values, this 'elite co-operation' dimension of the infringement procedure which enables disputes over enforcement to be resolved without actual recourse to the Court. In 1994, 1995, and 1996, however, the number of referrals to the Court rose again, and the figure for 1996 was described by the Commission as a 'historic record'.[19] More recently, the number of referrals has stabilized again and even dropped in 1999 and 2000, and the Commission has remarked on the increased speed and efficiency with which it now handles cases.[20]

It is clear that the public, centralized Community enforcement mechanism provided by Article 226 (ex Article 169) is simply one mechanism for ensuring the application of EC law, and that it is not necessarily the most effective method. In the first place, as we have noted, the Commission has neither the time nor the resources to detect and pursue every instance of national infringement of Community law. Secondly, there are pragmatic and political reasons why the Commission, even if it possessed the capacity to monitor all such infringements, might wish to exercise political discretion and not to pursue to judgment every Member State breach. As Rawlings has noted: 'Commission discretion allows, and scarce resources dictate, an ordered policy of selective enforcement', for example by focusing on the category of breaches where private enforcement actions at national level are unlikely.[21]

Thirdly, enforcement actions successfully brought before the ECJ do not necessarily lead to compliance, even with the cumbersome procedure introduced into Article 228 (ex Article 171) EC by the Maastricht Treaty which provides for the imposition on a Member State which has failed to comply with a judgment of the Court in infringement proceedings against it of a penalty payment.

[19] See the *13th* and *14th Annual Reports* for 1995 and 1996 [1996] OJ C303 and [1997] OJ C332 respectively.
[20] See the *16th, 17th*, and *18th Annual Reports* for 1998, 1999, and 2000, COM(1999)301, COM(2000)92, and COM(2001)309 respectively.
[21] Rawlings, n. 17 above, 26.

(c) SHARPENING THE ENFORCEMENT PROCEDURE:
THE PECUNIARY PENALTY

Article 228 (ex Article 171) provides:

1. If the Court of Justice finds that a Member State has failed to fulfil an obligation under this Treaty, the State shall be required to take the necessary measures to comply with the judgment of the Court of Justice.

2. If the Commission considers that the Member State concerned has not taken such measures it shall, after giving that State the opportunity to submit its observations, issue a reasoned opinion specifying the points on which the Member State concerned has not complied with the judgment of the Court of Justice.

If the Member State concerned fails to take the necessary measures to comply with the Court's judgment within the time-limit laid down by the Commission, the latter may bring the case before the Court of Justice. In so doing it shall specify the amount of the lump sum or penalty payment to be paid by the Member State concerned which it considers appropriate in the circumstances.

If the Court of Justice finds that the Member State concerned has not complied with its judgment it may impose a lump sum or penalty payment on it.

This procedure shall be without prejudice to Article 227.

Under this provision the ECJ has jurisdiction to impose a pecuniary penalty on a Member State which has failed to comply with a previous judgment establishing a breach by that state of the Treaty. No upper limit is specified,[22] and the ECJ is not bound by the Commission's recommendation or guidelines. The efficiency and effectiveness of this new power under Article 228 (ex Article 171) have been questioned on the basis that there is no mechanism for 'collection' should a Member State refuse to comply, and that there is no power to seek an injunction or to order a Member State to take action.[23] The ECJ has also indicated that, in addition to the lack of jurisdiction to order specific remedial measures, it has no jurisdiction under Article 228 to require Member States to comply with its judgment within a specified period of time.[24]

The Commission, after a slow start, has made active use of the procedure for proposing pecuniary penalties. It began in 1996 by adopting a memorandum on the application of the Treaty provision, followed by a method of calculation for penalties.[25] According to the Commission, the amount must reflect the aim of

---

[22] Art. 229 (ex Art. 172), which provides for the imposition of penalties by the Court under regulations adopted by the Council and the Parliament, also specifies that the Court's jurisdiction under such legislation may be unlimited.

[23] D. Curtin, 'The Constitutional Structure of the Union: A Europe of Bits and Pieces' (1993) 30 *CMLRev.* 17, 33. Although the Court has power to order injunctive measures in interim proceedings under Art. 243 (ex Art. 186), it does not have these powers under Art. 228 (ex Art. 171) when giving judgment in Art. 226 (ex Art. 169) proceedings.

[24] See Case C–473/93, *Commission* v. *Luxembourg* [1996] ECR I–3207, paras. 51–52. However, in Case C–291/93, *Commission* v. *Italy* [1994] ECR I–859, para. 6, the ECJ ruled that, although Art. 228 (ex Art. 171) did not specify the period within which a judgment must be complied with, the interest in the immediate and uniform application of Community law required compliance as soon as possible.

[25] See [1996] OJ C242/6 and [1997] OJ C63/2. Penalties are only to be imposed in respect of periods of non-compliance subsequent to the entry into force of the TEU, which was 1 Nov. 1993.

the sanction, which is to secure effective compliance with EC law as quickly as possible, and in its view the most appropriate means of achieving this aim is a periodic penalty running from the date of service of the ECJ's judgment. The daily penalty should, according to the Commission, be calculated on the basis of three criteria: the seriousness of the infringement, its duration, and the need to ensure that the penalty itself is a deterrent to further infringements. Apart from the seriousness of failure to comply with the ECJ's ruling, the penalty should, in the Commission's view, reflect the individual seriousness of the original infringement, both in terms of the importance of the Community rules infringed and the effects of the infringement. Penalties should be deterrent and never purely symbolic. The method of calculation should involve a uniform flat-rate amount per day of delay to penalize the violation of the principle of legality, multiplied by factors reflecting the seriousness of the infringement and its duration, and then by a factor representing the ability of the Member State to pay and the number of votes it has in the Council.

During 1996 and 1997, the first set of proceedings were initiated by the Commission under Article 228(2), with a view to proposing financial penalties to the Court, against Germany, Italy, France, Spain, Belgium, and Greece in respect of environmental breaches, and against each of these states and Portugal in respect of a variety of other breaches. By early 2002, only one judgment under Article 228(2) had been handed down by the ECJ, in a case against Greece concerning disposal of toxic waste,[26] although several other cases have been referred to the Court, and some of these subsequently withdrawn, while many other proceedings are still underway.[27]

In the first substantive Article 228(2) ruling against Greece, the ECJ outlined its view of the penalty payment and of the Commission's guidelines in that respect:

Case C–387/97, Commission v. Greece
[2000] ECR I–5047

87. Those guidelines, setting out the approach which the Commission proposes to follow, help to ensure that it acts in a manner which is transparent, foreseeable and consistent with legal certainty and are designed to achieve proportionality in the amounts of the penalty payments to be proposed by it.

88. The Commission's suggestion that account should be taken both of the gross domestic product of the Member State concerned and of the number of its votes in the Council appears appropriate in that it enables that Member State's ability to pay to be reflected while keeping the variation between Member States within a reasonable range.

89. It should be stressed that these suggestions of the Commission cannot bind the Court. It is

---

[26] Case C–387/97, *Commission* v. *Greece* [2000] ECR I–5047. For comment see L. Borszak, 'Punishing Member States or Influencing Their Behaviour or *Iudex (non)* calculat?' (2001) 13 *JEL* 235 and C. Hilson (2001) 3 *Env. LR* 131. In a separate case, Case C–197/98, *Commission* v. *Greece* [2000] ECR I–8609 also brought under Art. 228, the ECJ ordered its removal from the register after late compliance by the state.

[27] The Commission now publishes, with its annual reports on monitoring the application of EC law, a list of ECJ judgments under Art. 226 proceedings with which individual Member States have not yet complied, and an indication of what action it is taking under Art. 228 or otherwise against those states.

expressly stated in the third paragraph of Article 171(2) of the Treaty that the Court, if it 'finds that the Member State concerned has not complied with its judgment . . . may impose a lump sum or a penalty payment on it. However, the suggestions are a useful point of reference.

90. First, since the principal aim of penalty payments is that the Member State should remedy the breach of obligations as soon as possible, a penalty payment must be set that will be appropriate to the circumstances and proportionate both to the breach which has been found and to the ability to pay of the Member State concerned.

91. Second, the degree of urgency that the Member State concerned should fulfil its obligations may vary in accordance with the breach.

92. In that light, and as the Commission has suggested, the basic criteria which must be taken into account in order to ensure that penalty payments have coercive force and Community law is applied uniformly and effectively are, in principle, the duration of the infringement, its degree of seriousness and the ability of the Member State to pay. In applying those criteria, regard should be had in particular to the effects of failure to comply on private and public interests and to the urgency of getting the Member State concerned to fulfil its obligations.

The Court went on to rule that the breaches committed by Greece had been very serious, but it reduced the penalty payment proposed by the Commission from 24,600 to 20,000 Euros daily (from the date of service of the judgment), to take account of the failure to prove certain allegations, while rejecting other mitigating factors suggested by the Commission.

The Commission has predictably hailed the success and efficacy of the Article 228(2) procedure in its reports,[28] but others have criticized it for its simultaneously convoluted and limited nature, and have questioned its efficacy.[29]

3. THE RELATIONSHIP BETWEEN THE 'PUBLIC' AND THE 'PRIVATE' ENFORCEMENT MECHANISMS

It is apparent from the early rulings of the ECJ which established the principle of direct effect that the public enforcement procedures under Articles 226 and 227 (ex Articles 169 and 170) are but one mode provided for ensuring the application of Community law. That other means of monitoring the enforcement of Community law exist was made clear by the Court in the case of *Van Gend en Loos*:

Case 26/62, Van Gend en Loos
[1963] ECR 1

[ToA renumbering: Arts. 169, 170, and 177 are now Arts. 226, 227, and 234]

The facts of the case are set out in Chapter 7.[30]

---

[28] See *16th*, *17th*, and *18th Reports*, n. 20 above.
[29] Rawlings, n. 17 above, at 23.   [30] At 276.

THE ECJ[31]

In addition the argument based on Articles 169 and 170 of the Treaty put forward by the three Governments which have submitted observations to the Court in their statements of case is misconceived. The fact that these Articles of the Treaty enable the Commission and the Member States to bring before the Court a State which has not fulfilled its obligations does not mean that individuals cannot plead these obligations, should the occasion arise, before a national court, any more than the fact that the Treaty places at the disposal of the Commission ways of ensuring that obligations imposed upon those subject to the Treaty are observed, precludes the possibility, in action between individuals before a national court, of pleading infringements of these obligations. . . .

The vigilance of individuals concerned to protect their rights amounts to an effective supervision in addition to the supervision entrusted by Articles 169 and 170 to the diligence of the Commission and of the Member States.

Advocate General Roemer in the case also argued that the preliminary rulings procedure and the infringement procedure are fundamentally distinguished by the fact that in a preliminary reference from a national court under Article 234 (ex Article 177), the ECJ will give only a ruling on the interpretation of Community law, leaving it for the national court to spell out the implications of that ruling in the particular case; whereas in proceedings under Article 226 or 227 (ex Article 169 or 170) the ECJ will pronounce directly on the compatibility of a Member State's conduct with Community law.[32] In *Mölkerei-Zentrale* the ECJ ruled that proceedings brought by an individual were intended to protect individual rights in a specific case, whereas Commission enforcement proceedings were intended to ensure the general and uniform observance of Community law.[33] This meant that the two kinds of proceedings 'have different objects, aims and effects, and a parallel may not be drawn between them'.[34]

The importance of the distinction between the different kinds of proceedings was also strongly emphasized by Advocate General Lagrange in *Costa* v. *Enel* where the Italian Government argued that to allow an individual to plead the direct effect of Community law through the mechanism of Article 234 (ex Article 177) would circumvent the fact that individuals had no right to bring an enforcement action under Article 226 (ex Article 169).[35] The Italian government evidently preferred the safeguards of an action under Article 226 with its pre-litigation procedure, where the ECJ's ruling would have declaratory effect only, and where national law would not change until the Italian legislature adopted measures to comply. If an individual succeeded in pleading the direct effect of the Community provision and having the national court refer it to the ECJ under Article 177 (ex Article 234), on the other hand, the Community provision would have to be given immediate effect over national law by the national court which had referred the case. The Advocate General rejected this view and distinguished the two procedures on the basis that the enforcement action

---

[31] [1963] ECR 1, 13.   [32] *Ibid.*, 25.
[33] Case 28/67, *Mölkerei-Zentrale Westfalen* v. *Hauptzollamt Paderborn* [1968] ECR 143, 153.
[34] *Ibid.*   [35] Case 6/64, *Costa* v. *ENEL* [1964] ECR 585.

was not open to individuals and an ECJ ruling could not affect the validity of the impugned law.[36]

Despite these attempts to maintain the strong distinction between the outcome of a preliminary ruling and an enforcement action, however, it is clear from *Van Gend en Loos* and from many subsequent decisions that the ECJ under its preliminary rulings interpretative jurisdiction does often effectively declare whether a Member State is in breach of EC law.[37]

The most common complaint in enforcement proceedings against Member States concerns their failure to implement directives correctly or at all. This helps to explain the ECJ's development of the direct-effect doctrine, since the result was in part to bypass the problem of national non-implementation of directives by encouraging their direct enforcement at the national judicial level. In this way it forms a supplementary and frequently more effective method of enforcement than the action provided for in Article 226 (ex Article 169).

In *Van Gend* and *Costa* v. *ENEL*, the Member States were seeking to resist an ECJ ruling on the direct effect of Community law, and they argued that the proper method of seeking compliance by a state with Community law was for the Commission to bring public enforcement proceedings. Conversely, over two decades later, the German government made effectively the opposite argument by way of defence to an enforcement action, arguing that principles of German constitutional law were adequate to implement a directive without need for specific legislative enactment.

Case 29/84, Commission v. Germany
[1985] ECR 1661

THE ECJ

21. Even if it is conceded that the administration is bound by its own practice to the extent indicated by the German Government, the Commission denies that that is sufficient to provide the legal certainty, clarity and transparency sought by the directives. In particular a Member State cannot rely on the direct effect of the principle of non-discrimination on grounds of nationality in order to evade the obligation to incorporate into domestic law a directive which is intended precisely to give that principle practical effect.

. . .

29. . . . As the Commission has pointed out, the direct effect of that Community principle may not be used in order to evade the obligation to implement a directive providing for specific measures to facilitate and secure the full application of that principle in the Member States.

Thus the direct effect of a Community provision, and hence the ability of individuals to enforce it before national courts, was no defence to a Commission action under Article 226 (ex Article 169) for failure to implement that provision.[38]

---

[36] [1964] ECR 585, 601–2.   [37] See Ch. 11.
[38] See also Cases 102/79, *Commission* v. *Belgium* [1980] ECR 1473 and 168/85, *Commission* v. *Italy* [1986] ECR 2945.

4. THE COMMISSION'S DISCRETION

There has been considerable debate over the extent of the Commission's discretion to bring proceedings under Article 226. On the one hand, this discretion may be problematic if it leads the Commission to be too lenient with defaulting Member States. But on the other hand, the breadth of its discretion could equally lead to an unfair or oppressive use of enforcement proceedings, if there are too few constraints of time and procedure on the Commission.

To begin with the first concern, given the role the Commission plays within the Community and the various functions it exercises, it has been argued that there may be political and other reasons leading it to exercise its discretion against bringing proceedings, even where it is clear that a Member State is in breach of the Treaty.[39] Certainly it seems clear from the terms of paragraph 2 of Article 226 (ex Article 169) that, once it has issued a reasoned opinion indicating a breach by a Member State, the Commission has broad discretion whether or not to bring the matter before the ECJ. However, there has been some debate over whether the same discretion exists in respect of the decision to issue a reasoned opinion in the first place. In other words, if the Commission considers that a Member State has failed to fulfil a Treaty obligation, is it *obliged* to issue a reasoned opinion to that effect? Whereas paragraph 2 states that the Commission 'may' bring the matter before the Court, paragraph 1 states that the Commission 'shall' deliver a reasoned opinion where it considers that a state has failed to fulfil a Treaty obligation. There seems nevertheless to be agreement on the fact that this language (especially the subjective term 'considers') leaves the Commission with discretion whether and when to issue a reasoned opinion.[40]

The second concern mentioned above was that the Commission may not be sufficiently constrained in the *manner* in which it exercises its discretion under Article 226 (ex Article 169) in bringing proceedings. It has been argued before the ECJ that, despite the relatively open language of the Article, the Commission's discretion is not unlimited, and that in particular the Commission's decision as to whether and why an action should be brought, as well as its decision concerning the time at which proceedings should be brought, are subject to certain constraints.

However, as far as the reasons for bringing enforcement proceedings are concerned, the ECJ has declared that the proceedings are entirely 'objective'. This apparently means that the Court will examine only whether the infringement alleged by the Commission does in fact exist, and will not look into the Commission's motives for bringing the action.[41]

---

[39] P.P. Craig, 'Once Upon a Time in the West: Direct Effect and the Federalization of EEC Law' (1992) 12 *OJLS* 453, 456.

[40] A. Evans, 'The Enforcement Procedure of Article 169 EEC: Commission Discretion' (1979) 4 *ELRev.* 442, 445.

[41] See, e.g., Case C–200/88, *Commission* v. *Greece* [1990] ECR I–4299, para. 9, where the Court repeated that it would not consider whether the Commission's discretion under Art. 226 (ex Art. 169) had been 'wisely exercised'. See also the AG's opinion in the Open Skies case, dismissing the argument that the Commission's action should be inadmissible on the ground of misuse of procedure, since it had brought this set of infringement proceedings against 8 Member States primarily in order to pressurize the Council to open negotiations with the USA: Case C–466–476/98, *Commission* v. *UK et al.*, Opinion of 31 Jan. 2002, para. 29.

Case 416/85, Commission v. United Kingdom
[1988] ECR 3127

THE ECJ

8. The United Kingdom contends that there is a political motive behind the Commission's application to the Court and that such a motive is not a proper basis for an action pursuant to Article 169 EEC. The Commission's action is intended in fact to attain by means of judicial proceedings an objective which can be achieved only by a decision of the Community legislature. It is clear from the Commission's reply that its intention in bringing these proceedings is to bypass the procedural requirements of Article 28 of the Sixth Directive, under which it is for the Council, acting unanimously, to decide to abolish the exemptions permitted by that article. The United Kingdom therefore submits that it is not the task of the Court 'to substitute itself for the political procedures envisaged by Article 28 of the Sixth Directive and to substitute an immediate obligation upon a Member State for the progressive compliance envisaged by Article 28'.

9. That argument cannot be upheld. In the context of the balance of powers between the institutions laid down in the Treaty, it is not for the Court to consider what objectives are pursued in an action brought under Article 169 of the Treaty. Its role is to decide whether or not the Member State in question has failed to fulfil its obligations as alleged. As the Court held in Case 7/68 *Commission* v. *Italy* [1968] ECR 423, an action against a Member-State for failure to fulfil its obligations, the bringing of which is a matter for the Commission in its entire discretion, is objective in nature.

Conversely, the ECJ has also ruled that the *absence* of a specific motive or interest on the Commission's part in bringing proceedings against a Member State will not affect the admissibility of the enforcement proceedings.[42]

It has also been argued that there are restrictions on the time at which proceedings should be brought, and limits to the length of time the Commission can take in bringing proceedings against a Member State on the basis of a specific infringement. An early attempt to make the first of these arguments was rejected by the Court, which declared that the Commission's choice of time could not affect the admissibility of the proceedings.[43] As far as the length of time taken by the Commission to bring proceedings in respect of a particular infringement was concerned, while the ECJ initially seemed reluctant to interfere,[44] it ruled subsequently that the Treaty could impose certain constraints on the Commission's discretion in this respect.

---

[42] Case C–431/92, *Commission* v. *Germany* [1995] ECR I–2189, paras. 19–22.
[43] Case 7/68, *Commission* v. *Italy* [1968] ECR 423, 428.
[44] Case 7/71, *Commission* v. *France* [1971] ECR 1003, paras. 5–6.

Case C–96/89, Commission v. Netherlands
[1991] ECR 2461

[ToA renumbering: Arts. 93 and 169 are now Arts. 88 and 226]

THE ECJ

14. The Netherlands Government considers, in the first place, that the application is inadmissible owing to the delays attributable to the Commission in these proceedings. While the first letter sent by the Commission to The Netherlands Government regarding the matters in question dates from 1 February 1984, the Commission did not bring its action until 21 March 1989, that is to say, more than five years later. . . .

15. In that regard, it is sufficient to point out that, as the Court ruled in its judgment of 10 April 1984 in Case 324/82 *Commission* v. *Belgium* [1984] ECR 1861, the rules of Article 169 of the Treaty, unlike those of Article 93 which derogate expressly therefrom, must be applied and the Commission is not obliged to act within a specific period. In the present case, the Commission has explained that it had decided to await the Court's judgment . . . in the *Krohn* case, as well as the reactions of the Netherlands Government to that judgment before bringing this action. In doing that the Commission has not exercised the discretion which it has under Article 169 in a way that is contrary to the Treaty.

16. It is true that in certain cases the excessive duration of the pre-litigation procedure laid down by Article 169 is capable of making it more difficult for the Member State concerned to refute the Commission's arguments and of thus infringing the rights of the defence. However, in the instant case, the Netherlands Government has not proved that the unusual length of the procedure had any effect on the way in which it conducted its defence.

It is clear from this ruling that, although there are no specific rules requiring the Commission to act within a given period of time under Article 226 (ex Article 169), an excessive delay in the period before bringing a case before the Court might prejudice the rights of the Member State's defence to such an extent that the action could be deemed inadmissible.

Restrictions are also imposed on the Commission's discretion regarding when to refer a matter to the Court after the issuing of a reasoned opinion, rather than on its discretion in commencing the infringement proceedings in the first place. Clearly, requiring a response to a reasoned opinion within an excessively short period of time is just as likely to affect the ability of a Member State to exercise its rights of defence as is delay in commencing proceedings. In an action against Ireland, the ECJ referred to the Commission's 'regrettable behaviour' and reprimanded it for the short length of time it allowed the State for compliance with the reasoned opinion. However, the Commission's action was nevertheless admissible since, despite the short time period, the Commission had in fact awaited Ireland's reply before referring the matter to the Court:

The Court is compelled to state its disapproval of the Commission's behaviour in this regard. It is indeed unreasonable, as Ireland has pointed out, to allow a Member State five days to amend legislation which has been applied for more than 40 years and which, moreover, has not give rise to any action on the part of the Commission over the period which has elapsed since the accession of the Member State in question. Furthermore, it is clear that there was no particular urgency.[45]

In subsequent proceedings against Belgium, the ECJ declared the Commission's action inadmissible on account of the shortness of the time allowed for responding to the letter of formal notice and the reasoned opinion.[46] It ruled that a reasonable period must be allowed, although very short periods could be justified in circumstances of urgency or where the Member State was fully aware of the Commission's views long before the procedure started.[47] A period of four months to respond to a reasoned opinion was adequate where a Member State had three years' prior notice of the Commission's view.[48] And in a case against Austria the ECJ rejected the argument that a period of seven days for responding to a formal letter and fourteen days for responding to a reasoned opinion were too short, accepting that these periods were justified by the urgency of the complaint and the particular circumstances of the case.[49]

However, the ECJ's unwillingness to require the Commission, apart from a case in which the rights of the defence may be prejudiced, to initiate Article 226 proceedings within a reasonable time contrasts with its approach to the action under Article 232 (ex Article 175) of the EC Treaty.[50] Proceedings under Articles 232 are the converse of the action under Article 226 (ex Article 169), in that they are brought against one of the Community institutions for failure to take action required by the Treaty, rather than against a Member State. In the case of proceedings against a Community institution, the ECJ has held that the party bringing the action is required to do so within a reasonable period, even though Article 232 makes no mention of any time limit. In an early action, The Netherlands attempted to require the Commission to bring enforcement proceedings against France, but failed on the ground that the action under the corresponding provision of the ECSC Treaty had not been brought within a reasonable period of time,[51] and this reasoning would be equally applicable to Article 232.

The desire of the ECJ not to place too many fetters on the Commission's discretion under Article 226 (ex Article 169) is further revealed by the Court's response to actions for 'failure to act' brought by *non-privileged* parties against the Commission under Article 232 (ex Article 175) EC, which have attempted to require the Commission to initiate infringement proceedings under Article 226. The Court has consistently refused to admit such actions. In *Star Fruit* v. *Commission*, the Court rejected an attempt by the company to use Article 232 to require the Commission to commence infringement proceedings against France:

---

[45] Case 74/82, *Commission* v. *Ireland* [1984] ECR 317, para. 12.
[46] Case 293/85, *Commission* v. *Belgium* [1988] ECR 305.
[47] *Ibid.*, para. 14 of the judgment. See also Cases C–56/90, *Commission* v. *UK* [1993] ECR I–4109 and C–333/99, *Commission* v. *France* [2000] ECR I–1025.
[48] Case C–473/93, *Commission* v. *Luxembourg* [1996] ECR I–3207.
[49] Case C–328/96, *Commission* v *Austria* [1999] ECR I–7479.
[50] See also Art. 148 Euratom.
[51] Case 59/70, *Netherlands* v. *Commission* [1971] ECR 639, paras. 14–18 of the judgment.

It is clear from the scheme of Article 169 of the Treaty that the Commission is not bound to commence the proceedings provided for in that provision but in this regard has a discretion which excludes the right for individuals to require that institution to adopt a specific position.[52]

Further, the Court has dismissed actions for annulment directed by an individual litigant against a 'decision' by the Commission not to commence proceedings against a Member State, again on the basis that this was a matter within the Commission's discretion and that the action sought—the adoption of a reasoned opinion—would not be susceptible in any case to an action for annulment.[53]

Although the lack of a role for individuals in the initiation and conduct of enforcement proceedings has provoked adverse comment,[54] we have seen above that the Commission's discretion in this respect is not at all unjustified.[55]

F. Snyder, The Effectiveness of European Community Law[56]

The main form of dispute settlement used by the Commission is negotiation, and litigation is simply a part, sometimes inevitable but nevertheless generally a minor part, of this process. The Commission's view of litigation thus differs substantially from that of the European Court. In order to understand why this is so, we need to consider the role of the Commission in the Community litigation system.

Put simply, it is a distinctive role. The Commission has complete discretion in bringing infringement proceedings against Member States under Article 169; it is a necessary intermediary in actions by one Member State against another under Article 170; it will . . . be entitled under the amended Article 171 to request the Court to impose a lump sum or penalty payment on Member States which have failed to comply with a previous judgment by the Court; . . . Consequently the Commission can use litigation as an element in developing longer-term strategies. Instead of simply winning individual cases, it is able to concentrate on establishing basic principles or playing for rules.

Notwithstanding this discretion, the Commission in 1989 stated that its approach to monitoring compliance with EC law would henceforth entail the bringing of immediate infringement proceedings against a defaulting state as soon as the time limit for implementation of directives had passed.[57] A year later, the Commission adopted the practice of routinely issuing letters of formal notice whenever Member

---

[52] Case 247/87, n. 9 above, para. 11. Compare Case C–107/95P, *Bundesverband der Bilanzbuchalter* v. *Commission* [1997] ECR I–947.

[53] Case C–87/89, *Sonito* v. *Commission* 1990 ECR I–1981; Case T–201/96, *Smanor and Others* v. *Commission* [1997] ECR II–1081; and Case T–182/97, *Smanor* v. *Commission* [1998] ECR II–271. In the latter two cases the applicant wanted the Commission to bring infringement proceedings against France as a basis for its own *Francovich* action against the State, having already failed before the French courts in an action for damages.

[54] See E. Szyszczak, 'L'Espace Sociale Européenne: Reality, Dreams or Nightmares?' [1990] *German Yearbook of International Law* 284, 300.

[55] See n. 21 above and text, and also J. Weiler, 'The Community System: The Dual Character of Supranationalism' (1981) 1 *YBEL* 267, 299.

[56] (1993) 56 *MLR* 19, 30.

[57] *7th Annual Report* [1990] OJ C232/6.

States had not 'notified national measures implementing Directives which are due for implementation'.[58] As noted earlier, however, the effect of these letters is not necessarily to increase the number of infringement proceedings brought before the Court, since the Commission uses the procedure, where possible, as a tool to secure state compliance rather than as a means of bringing them to Court.

Finally, another 'constraint' on Commission discretion in the conduct of infringement proceedings is the supervisory role of the Ombudsman, who has not only undertaken an own-initiative inquiry into Commission enforcement proceedings, but also considers many individual complaints from citizens objecting to the Commissions conduct of or failure to bring infringement proceedings.[59] The extent to which this administrative supervision by the Ombudsman operates as a significant constraint or influence on the Commission is open to debate, but it seems difficult to deny that it has had some effects.

5. THE REASONED OPINION

The reasoned opinion which the Commission is required to issue and to notify to a Member State forms an important part of the pre-judicial procedure under Article 226 (ex Article 169), and provides the Member State concerned with a measure of protection. Together with the letter of formal notice the reasoned opinion (sometimes followed by a supplementary reasoned opinion[60]) is the official means by which the Commission communicates to the state the substance of the complaint against it, and specifies a time period within which the violation of Community law must be remedied. Effectively, it is aimed to provide the Member State with a clear statement of the case against it, and to 'ensure respect for the principles of natural justice'.[61]

(a) CHALLENGING THE REASONED OPINION

We have seen in Chapter 3 that the obligation to provide reasons is one of general importance in Community law, and that Article 254 (ex Article 191) of the Treaty expressly requires regulations, directives, and decisions to state the reasons on which they are based. Article 226 (ex Article 169) extends this requirement to opinions issued by the Commission under the enforcement procedure. Although the reasoning requirement in EC law constitutes an 'essential procedural requirement', breach of which constitutes a ground for annulment of a measure under Article 230 (ex Article 173), the Commission's opinion under Article 226 is not subject to an action for annulment because it does not have binding effect.[62] According to Advocate General Lagrange in an early case:

---

[58] *8th Annual Report*, n. 3 above, at 7(e).   [59] See nn. 10 and 11 above.

[60] See, e.g., Cases C–354/99, *Commission* v. *Ireland* [2001] ECR I–7657, and C–155/99, *Commission* v. *Italy* [2001] ECR I–4007.

[61] A. Evans, 'The Enforcement Procedure of Article 169 EEC: Commission Discretion' (1979) 4 *ELRev.* 442, 446.

[62] Case 48/65, *First Lütticke Case* (*Alfons Lütticke GmbH* v. *Commission*) [1966] ECR 19.

No formalism must be demanded of this document, since, as I have said, the reasoned opinion is not an administrative act subject to review by the Court of its legality.[63]

However, although a reasoned opinion may not be the subject of a direct action for annulment, a Member State which is the subject of such an opinion may contest the lack of adequate reasoning in a different way, by raising the matter before the ECJ if and when the enforcement proceedings reach that stage. In an early case in which Italy claimed that the reasoned opinion lacked adequate reasoning and was not in due legal form, the ECJ replied that:

The opinion referred to in Article 169 of the Treaty must be considered to contain a sufficient statement of reasons to satisfy the law when it contains—as it does in this case—a coherent statement of the reasons which led the Commission to believe that the State in question has failed to fulfil an obligation under the Treaty.[64]

This means that the Commission is not obliged in its reasoned opinion to address or to answer every argument made by the Member State at the pre-litigation stage, nor to indicate what steps should be taken by the state to remedy the alleged breach.[65] Further, the initial letter of formal notice need not meet particularly strict requirements, since the reasoned opinion is the crucial document which sets out the complaint to which the Member State must respond. None the less, the essence of the complaint must be the same in the formal letter, the reasoned opinion, and in the Commission's application to bring the case before the ECJ.[66] But so long as the Commission sets out clearly in the reasoned opinion the grounds on which it has relied in concluding that the state has violated Community law, and the particular complaints which will form the subject matter of the proceedings,[67] the reasoning requirement will be satisfied.

Recently Germany sought in a number of cases to challenge the reasoned opinion on the basis that it had been adopted in violation of the principle of Commission collegiality, since the Commissioners took the decision to issue a reasoned opinion against Germany without having the text of that opinion before them.[68] The ECJ, while accepting that the collegiality principle required the decision to bring enforcement proceedings to be the subject of collective deliberation by the College of Commissioners, none the less dismissed Germany's argument on the basis that it had been sufficient for the Commissioners to have available to it at the time the information on which the decision to commence proceedings had been based.

---

[63] Case 7/61, *Commission* v. *Italy* [1961] ECR 317, 334, 336.

[64] Case 7/61, *Commission* v. *Italy* [1961] ECR 317, 327.

[65] See Case C–247/89, *Commission* v. *Portugal* [1991] ECR I–3659, para. 22.

[66] See Cases C–191/95, *Commission* v. *Germany* [1998] ECR I–5449, para. 54, and C–365/97, *Commission* v. *Italy* [1999] ECR I–7773, para. 26.

[67] See Case C–328/96, *Commission* v. *Austria* [1999] ECR I–7479, paras. 39–41, where part of the Commission's complaint was ruled inadmissible for failure to specify this.

[68] Cases C–191/95, *Commission* v. *Germany* [1998] ECR I–5449; C–272/97, *Commission* v. *Germany* [1999] ECR I–2175; and C–198/97, *Commission* v. *Germany* [1999] ECR I–3257.

(b) CAN THE COMMISSION CHANGE THE SUBJECT MATTER OF ITS ACTION AFTER IT HAS ISSUED A REASONED OPINION?

If the reasoned opinion is intended to operate as a procedural protection for the Member State, by containing a precise statement of the Commission's case against the state, it seems that the Commission should not be entitled to change or amend the content of its submission when the case comes to be heard before the Court. But what if both the Commission and the Member State in question wish the Court to consider other aspects of the state's conduct which took place after the date of the reasoned opinion?

Case 7/69, Commission v. Italy
[1970] ECR 111

[ToA renumbering: Arts. 169 and 171 are now Arts. 226 and 228]

After the date of a reasoned opinion issued by the Commission, informing Italy that it was considered to be in breach of Community law, the Italian Government enacted a law to remedy the alleged violation. The Commission was not satisfied that the new law had entirely cured the violation, and so did not withdraw proceedings from before the Court. Both parties now wished the Court to take the impact of this new law into account in its judgment.

THE ECJ

5. Because of the importance which the Treaty attaches to the action available to the Community against Member States for failure to fulfil obligations, this procedure in Article 169 is surrounded by guarantees which must not be ignored, particularly in view of the obligation imposed by Article 171 on Member States to take as a consequence of this action the necessary measures to comply with the judgment of the Court. Accordingly the Court cannot give judgment in the present case on the failure to fulfil an obligation occurring after legislation has been amended during the course of the proceedings without thereby adversely affecting the rights of the Member State to put forward its arguments in defence based on complaints formulated according to the procedure laid down by Article 169.

The Court therefore refused to consider whether Italy was in breach of Community law after it had taken remedial action in response to the Commission's reasoned opinion, and declared the Commission's action to be inadmissible. Its reason for doing so was that the subject matter of the Commission's complaint had changed significantly since it had issued the reasoned opinion, which is a compulsory part of the preliminary procedure set up under the Treaty. In the ECJ's view, there are guarantees inherent in this procedure for the protection of the Member State in question. If the subject matter of the Commission's allegation against a Member State changes after the reasoned opinion is issued, then, in order to provide procedural safeguards for the state, the entire process under Article 226 must be initiated again.

The requirement that the content of the reasoned opinion be essentially the same as the submissions in the Commission's application to the Court has been reiterated many times.[69] However, it will not be sufficient for the Commission when the matter comes before the Court simply to refer in its application to 'all the reasons set out in the letter of formal notice and the reasoned opinion'. Rather the application itself must contain a statement of the grounds on which it is based.[70] On the other hand, where enforcement proceedings brought by the Commission have been found by the ECJ to be inadmissible on the ground that the Commission's application is based on an objection different from that in the reasoned opinion, the Commission is not obliged to recommence the entire pre-litigation procedure but may lodge a fresh application before the Court based on the same objections as the reasoned opinion originally issued.[71] And where EC legislation on which the reasoned opinion was based has been amended prior to the case coming before the ECJ, this does not necessarily mean the Commission has to withdraw the action or issue a new reasoned opinion, so long as the obligations under the amended measure correspond to those arising under the original legislation.[72] Finally, where the application made by the Commission is not the same as it was under the reasoned opinion, this may acceptable so long as the change *limits* what is contained in the reasoned opinion rather than expanding it in a way which could disadvantage the respondent state.[73]

Further, the Commission is not prohibited from responding, during the hearing before the Court, to arguments and defences raised by the respondent Member State, even where it has not made those points in the reasoned opinion itself.[74] And the Member State cannot complain of breach of the right to a fair hearing by the fact that the Commission, in its application to the ECJ, does not take account of facts or defences put forward by the Member State after the expiry of the period set by the reasoned opinion.[75]

(c) CONFIDENTIALITY OF THE REASONED OPINION

In a number of cases where individual complainants who had sought to persuade the Commission to bring proceedings against a Member State were disappointed by the Commission's ultimate failure or refusal to do so, they subsequently sought to obtain disclosure of the reasoned opinion and of other documentation relevant to the investigative proceedings. However, despite an initial setback for the Commission in the *WWF* case,[76] neither the CFI nor the ECJ has been prepared to require disclosure

---

[69] See, e.g., Cases 232/78, *Commission* v. *France* [1979] ECR 2729; 193/80, *Commission* v. *Italy* [1981] ECR 3019; 211/81, *Commission* v. *Denmark* [1982] ECR 4547; 124/81, *Commission* v. *UK* [1983] ECR 203; 166/82, *Commission* v. *Italy* [1984] ECR 459.

[70] Case C–43/90, *Commission* v. *Germany* [1992] ECR I–1909, paras. 7–8. See also Case C–52/90, *Commission* v. *Denmark* [1992] ECR I–2187.

[71] Case C–57/94, *Commission* v. *Italy* [1995] ECR I–1249.

[72] Case C–365/97, *Commission* v. *Italy* [1999] ECR I–7773.

[73] Case C–191/95, *Commission* v. *Germany* [1998] ECR I–5449.

[74] Case 211/81, *Commission* v. *Denmark* [1982] ECR I–4547, para 16.

[75] Case C–3/96 *Commission* v. *Netherlands* [1998] ECR I–3931.

[76] See Case T–105/95, *WWF* v. *Commission* [1997] ECR II–313, in which the CFI restricted the Commission's ability to rely on a particular exception to the obligation to provide access to documents as a mandatory general exception rather than an individual discretionary one.

of a reasoned opinion, a draft reasoned opinion, or indeed of any documents relating to the investigative stage of the infringement procedure.

Thus in *WWF*, the CFI ruled, in relation to an investigation into possible breaches of EC law, that:

In this regard, the Court considers that the confidentiality which the Member States are entitled to expect of the Commission in such circumstances warrants, under the heading of protection of the public interest, a refusal of access to documents relating to investigations which may lead to an infringement procedure, even where a period of time has elapsed since the closure of the investigation.[77]

Similarly, in the *Bavarian Lager* case the Court ruled, in the context of a draft reasoned opinion which was not ultimately sent by the Commission to the Member State under investigation, that since the procedure was still at the stage of investigation at the time, the Member States were entitled to expect confidentiality from the Commission.[78] Finally, in *Petrie*, which concerned a request for access to a range of documents including letters of formal notice and reasoned opinions, the CFI ruled:

This requirement of confidentiality remains even after the matter has been brought before the Court of Justice, on the ground that it cannot be ruled out that the discussions between the Commission and the Member State in question regarding the latter's voluntary compliance with the Treaty requirements may continue during the court proceedings and up to the delivery of the judgment of the Court of Justice. The preservation of that objective, namely an amicable resolution of the dispute between the Commission and the Member State concerned before the Court of Justice has delivered judgment, justifies refusal of access to the letters of formal notice and reasoned opinions drawn up in connection with the Article 226 EC proceedings on the ground of protection of the public interest relating to inspections, investigations and court proceedings, which comes within the first category of exceptions in Decision 94/90.[79]

6. WHY IS AN ENFORCEMENT ACTION ADMISSIBLE AFTER THE BREACH IS REMEDIED?

Article 226 (ex Article 169) sets out the conditions which must be satisfied before the Commission may initiate enforcement proceedings in the Court. If the Commission has not issued a reasoned opinion nor given the Member State concerned a period of time within which to cure the alleged infringement, the action will not be admissible. On the other hand, once those conditions have been fulfilled and the period laid down by the Commission for compliance has expired without any action being taken by the Member State, it is no answer for that state to assert, when the case is heard before the ECJ, that the breach has since been remedied. The issue for the ECJ is whether the Member State was in breach at the time the Commission found it necessary to initiate proceedings before the Court. As with its attitude to delay in initiating proceedings,[80]

---

[77] *Ibid.*, para. 62.
[78] Case T–309/97, *Bavarian Lager Company* v. *Commission* [1999] ECR II–3217, para. 46.
[79] Case T–191/99, *Petrie* v. *Commission*, 12 Dec. 2001, para. 68.
[80] N. 50 above and text.

the Court's approach here contrasts with its approach to actions brought against a Community institution for failure to act. In a case where proceedings were brought against the European Parliament under Article 232 (ex Article 175) for failure to act, the ECJ held that the action was devoid of purpose once the institution in question had acted to remedy its default.[81] Where proceedings have been brought under Article 226 by the Commission against Member States on the other hand, such actions have been declared admissible by the Court even though the state in question had remedied its breach by that time. Several reasons have been offered to explain why enforcement actions may be admissible after the infringement has been cured.

(a) THE COMMISSION'S CONTINUED INTEREST IN BRINGING THE ACTION

Case 7/61, Commission v. Italy
[1961] ECR 317

ADVOCATE GENERAL LAGRANGE[82]

The purpose of the action is to obtain the Court's finding that a Member State has failed to fulfil an obligation under the Treaty . . . I. If, subsequent to the making of the application, the State concerned took the measures necessary to bring the infringement to an end, it is possible that the action may no longer have very much practical effect, but, so the Commission argues, it still has the highest interest in having the Court settle the issue whether the failure indeed occurred . . . the opposite argument would allow a State which so desired to denude the action of its purpose by bringing its illegal conduct to an end just before the judgment, thereafter remaining safe to carry on with its improper conduct in the absence of any judgment finding that it was in breach of its obligations.

(b) THE NEED TO RULE ON THE LEGALITY OF SHORT BREACHES

Case 240/86, Commission v. Greece
[1988] ECR 1835

ADVOCATE GENERAL LENZ[83]

It follows from the second paragraph of Article 169 of the EEC Treaty that an action may be brought before the Court if the alleged breach of the Treaty is not discontinued within the period laid down in the reasoned opinion. . . .

Otherwise, in view of the length of the pre-litigation procedure, it would in many cases be impossible for the Court to exercise its jurisdiction with regard to breaches of the Treaty of short duration. Since the duration of conduct which is contrary to the Treaty is no indication of the

---

[81] Case 377/87, *Council* v. *Parliament* [1988] ECR 4017. The position, however, might be different if it were likely that some party might later wish to seek redress from the institution in question for loss caused by the illegal failure to act.
[82] N. 63 above, 334.   [83] [1988] ECR 1835, 1844.

gravity of the infringement it must be possible to bring proceedings even in relation to a breach of the Treaty which is limited in time.

However, if the effects of a specific infringement, which is the subject matter of Commission proceedings, have actually come to an end before the expiry of the period set out in the reasoned opinion, the action before the ECJ will be inadmissible even if the Commission fears that a similar breach is likely to occur again in the future.[84]

(c) ESTABLISHING THE LIABILITY OF A DEFAULTING MEMBER STATE

Case 240/86, Commission v. Greece
[1988] ECR 1835

THE ECJ

14. As the Court has consistently held (see most recently the judgment in Case 103/84, *Commission* v. *Italy* [1986] ECR 1759) the subject-matter of an action brought under Article 169 is established by the Commission's reasoned opinion and even where the default has been remedied after the period laid down pursuant to the second paragraph of that article has elapsed, an interest still subsists in pursuing the action. That interest may consist in establishing the basis for a liability which a Member State may incur, by reason of its failure to fulfil its obligations, towards those to whom rights accrue as a result of that failure.

Clearly, an individual's action for redress before the national courts could derive considerable assistance from a prior finding of the ECJ that the Member State in question had acted in violation of Community law. The *Francovich*[85] case law indicates that in certain circumstances where a state fails to implement a directive which was intended to benefit individuals, EC law will render the state liable in damages to those individuals who have suffered loss as a result. A prior finding by the ECJ of an infringement is likely to be an effective means, albeit not a necessary one, of showing the illegality of state action when damages are sought for loss caused by that action.[86]

7. TYPES OF BREACH BY MEMBER STATES OF COMMUNITY LAW

Article 226 (ex Article 169) is very general in its description of a Member State violation for the purposes of enforcement proceedings. The Commission must simply consider that a state 'has failed to fulfil an obligation under this Treaty'. Clearly this

---

[84] Case C–362/90, *Commission* v. *Italy* [1992] ECR I–2353.
[85] Cases C–6/90 & C–9/90, *Francovich and Bonifaci* v. *Italy* [1991] ECR I–5357. See Ch. 6.
[86] See the attempt made by the applicant in Case T–182/97, *Smanor* v. *Commission* [1998] ECR II–271 to obtain an enforcement ruling from the ECJ for this precise purpose.

may include actions as well as omissions on the part of states, failure to implement directives, breaches of specific Treaty provisions or of other secondary legislation, or of any rule or standard which is an effective part of Community law. Recently, some of the first cases involving a breach by Member States in the sphere of the Community's external competence reached the Court.[87] Certain kinds of breach are far more often the subject of infringement proceedings than others, and the following examples illustrate some of the sorts of breaches with which the cases are concerned.

(a) BREACH OF THE OBLIGATION OF CO-OPERATION UNDER ARTICLE 10 (EX ARTICLE 5) EC

Case 96/81, Commission v. Netherlands
[1982] ECR 1791

The Commission brought proceedings against The Netherlands alleging failure to implement certain bathing water directives and claiming that the Dutch Government had failed to provide information on its compliance with the provisions of one directive, as was required by the terms of directive itself. The Commission argued that due to the failure to supply this information, it was entitled to presume that the respondent state had failed to implement the necessary national measures. The breach identified in the application to Court by the Commission was not however 'failure to comply with the duty to provide information' but rather 'failure to fulfil the obligation to implement the directive'.

THE ECJ

6. It should be emphasized that, in proceedings under Article 169 of the EEC Treaty for failure to fulfil an obligation, it is incumbent upon the Commission to prove the allegation that the obligation has not been fulfilled. It is the Commission's responsibility to place before the Court the information needed to enable the Court to establish that the obligation has not been fulfilled, and in doing so the Commission may not rely on any presumption.

However, although the Commission cannot rely on a presumption of breach where a Member State fails to provide information on compliance, the ECJ has ruled that once the Commission has produced sufficient evidence to show that the Member State appeared to be violating Community law it is incumbent on the state not simply to deny the allegations, but to contest substantively the information produced.[88] In the bathing water case above, the EC went on to say that all Member States had, under Article 10 (ex Article 5) EC, an obligation to facilitate the achievement of the Commission's tasks, including that of monitoring compliance with the Treaty.

This particular mode of infringement is frequently invoked by the Commission in enforcement actions where Member State authorities refuse or fail to respond to its

---

[87] See Cases C–13/00, *Commission* v. *Ireland* [2002] ECR I–nyr, and C–466–476/98, *Commission* v. *UK et al.*, AG's Opinion of 31 Jan. 2002.

[88] Case 272/86, *Commission* v. *Greece* [1988] ECR 4875, para. 21.

requests for information.[89] Clearly, if a Member State is not willing to respond at the pre-litigation stage of an investigation by the Commission for the purposes of infringement proceedings, it will be very difficult for the Commission to ascertain whether or not there has been a breach by the state. The Commission's attempt to find a way around this is to initiate separate enforcement proceedings on the basis of a breach of the obligation of co-operation.[90]

The issue of the adequate discharge by the Commission of the burden of proof which it bears in infringement proceedings has regularly been raised by Member States, at times in order to challenge the Commission's reliance on the duty of co-operation. However, while the Court has emphasized strongly the duty on the Member States to co-operate fully with the Commission's investigations, it has also repeated that it is incumbent on the Commission to prove that an obligation has not been fulfilled,[91] and has at times dismissed complaints brought by the Commission for lack of proof or for reliance on presumptions.[92] However, even though the burden of proof lies with the Commission to show breach, where the complaint is of inadequate transposition of a directive, it is not necessary for the Commission to actually demonstrate the harmful effects of the transposing legislation.[93]

(b) INADEQUATE IMPLEMENTATION OF COMMUNITY LAW

In many cases, the cause of the Commission's complaint is not the complete failure to implement Community legislation, but rather its inadequate implementation.

Case 167/73, Commission v. France
[1974] ECR 359

[ToA renumbering: Art. 48 is now Art. 39]

The French legislature had failed to repeal a provision of the French Code du Travail Maritime under which a certain proportion (roughly 3:1) of the crew of a ship was required to be of French nationality. This nationality requirement was contrary to Community law, but the French Government claimed that directions had been given verbally to the naval authorities to treat Community nationals as French nationals, and that this was sufficient to comply with Community law.

THE ECJ

40. It appears both from the argument before the Court and from the position adopted during the parliamentary proceedings that the present state of affairs is that freedom of movement for

---

[89] Case 240/86, *Commission* v. *Greece* [1988] ECR 1835.

[90] For other cases on Art. 10 (ex Art. 5), see, e.g., Cases C–35/88, *Commission* v. *Greece* [1990] ECR I–3125; C–48/89, *Commission* v. *Italy* [1990] ECR I–2425; C–374/89, *Commission* v. *Belgium* [1991] ECR I–367, and 272/86, *Commission* v. *Greece* [1988] ECR 4875.

[91] See Case C–365/97, *Commission* v. *Italy* [1999] ECR I–7773.

[92] Case C–217/97, *Commission* v. *Germany* [1999] ECR I–5087.

[93] Case C–392/96, *Commission* v. *Ireland* [1999] ECR I–5901.

workers in the sector in question continues to be considered by the French authorities not as a matter of right but as dependent on their unilateral will.

41. It follows that although the objective legal position is clear, namely, that Article 48 and Regulation No 1612/68 are directly applicable in the territory of the French Republic, nevertheless the maintenance in these circumstances of the wording of the Code du Travail Maritime gives rise to an ambiguous state of affairs by maintaining, as regards those subject to the law who are concerned, a state of uncertainty as to the possibilities available to them of relying on Community law.

42. This uncertainty can only be reinforced by the internal and verbal character of the purely administrative directions to waive the application of the national law.

In the case of directives, which are not in themselves directly applicable, it is clearly incumbent on the Member States to implement them fully. Even where directives are vertically directly enforceable—i.e. against the state—or where they can be given indirect domestic effect in another way, this does not reduce the obligation on the state to implement them properly. Article 249 (ex Article 189) EC provides that the manner and form of implementation of directives are a matter for each Member State to decide, but this does not mean that the ECJ will not review the adequacy of the method of implementation chosen by a state.

Case 96/81, Commission v. Netherlands
[1982] ECR 1791

THE ECJ

12. It is true that each Member State is free to delegate powers to its domestic authorities as it considers fit and to implement the directive by means of measures adopted by regional or local authorities. That does not however release it from the obligation to give effect to the provisions of the directive by means of national provisions of a binding nature. The directive in question . . . is intended to approximate the applicable laws, regulations and administrative provisions in the Member States. Mere administrative practices, which by their nature may be altered at the whim of the administration, may not be considered as constituting the proper fulfilment of the obligation deriving from that directive.

In later proceedings, the ECJ outlined a further objection to a Member State's reliance on such 'whimsical' administrative practices, namely that, quite apart from their uncertainty and alterability, they lacked the appropriate publicity to constitute adequate implementation.[94] However, it has not always ruled against a Member State which has failed to adopt any specific measures to implement a directive.

---

[94] Case 160/82, *Commission v. Netherlands* [1982] ECR 4637.

Case 29/84, Commission v. Germany
[1985] ECR 1661

[ToA renumbering: Art. 189 is now Art. 249]

The Commission brought enforcement proceedings against Germany for failure to implement Directives 77/452 and 77/453 governing the right of establishment and freedom to provide services for nurses.

THE ECJ

17. The German Government does not deny that mere administrative practices, which by their nature can be modified as and when the administration pleases and which are not publicized widely enough, cannot be regarded as a proper fulfilment of the obligation imposed on the Member States by Article 189 of the Treaty, as the Court has consistently held. However, the government claims that that principle cannot be applied in this instance because the administrative practice in question cannot be changed as and when the administration pleases and it has been given sufficient publicity.

After summarizing the Commission's counter-argument, the ECJ ruled as follows:

22. Faced with those conflicting views, the Court considers it necessary to recall the wording of the third paragraph of Article 189 of the Treaty, according to which a directive is binding, as to the result to be achieved upon each Member State to which it is addressed, but leaves to the national authorities the choice of form and methods.

23. It follows from that provision that the implementation of a directive does not necessarily require legislative action in each Member State. In particular the existence of general principles of constitutional or administrative law may render implementation by specific legislation superfluous, provided however that those principles guarantee that the national authorities will in fact apply the directive fully and that, where the directive is intended to create rights for individuals, the persons concerned are made fully aware of their rights and, where appropriate, afforded the possibility of relying on them before the national courts.

In subsequent judgments the ECJ added to this by ruling that proper transposition was particularly important for individuals to know their rights when those on whom the Directive in question conferred rights were nationals of *other* Member States.[95]

However, in proceedings brought by the Commission against the United Kingdom for improper implementation of the Product Liability Directive 85/374, the ECJ made an interesting use of the 'indirect effect' of directives—i.e. the obligation on national courts to construe domestic law in accordance with a relevant directive[96]—to dismiss the Commission's application. Whereas the Commission argued that the United Kingdom was in breach of the Directive because national courts would be required to

---

[95] See Cases C–365/93, *Commission* v. *Greece* [1995] ECR I–499, para. 9, and C–96/95, *Commission* v. *Germany* [1997] ECR I–1653, paras. 34–35. See also Cases C–185/96, *Commission* v. *Greece* [1998] ECR I–6601 and C–162/99, *Commission* v. *Italy* [2001] ECR I–541.

[96] See Case C–300/95, *Commission* v. *UK* [1997] ECR I–2649.

interpret national law *contra legem* in order to conform with its requirements, the ECJ simply ruled that there was nothing to suggest that the UK courts would not, if called upon to do so, interpret the relevant national law—the Consumer Protection Act—in the light of the wording and purpose of the Directive so as to give effect to its aim.[97]

Finally, the Commission has at times used the infringement procedure to 'monitor' Member State implementation of a particular law or set of laws in an ongoing way, and in some cases to challenge relatively minor breaches where they are part of a pattern of inadequate implementation and compliance in practice.[98]

(c) FAILURE TO GIVE PROPER EFFECT TO COMMUNITY LAW

In furtherance of its policy of encouraging Member States to take steps to ensure the effectiveness of Community law, the Court has also stated that Article 10 (ex Article 5) EC will be breached if a Member State fails to penalize those who infringe Community law in the same way as it penalizes those who infringe national law.[99]

Case 68/88, Commission v. Greece
[1989] ECR 2979

THE ECJ

23. It should be observed that where Community legislation does not specifically provide any penalty for an infringement or refers for that purpose to national laws, regulations and administrative provisions, Article 5 of the Treaty requires the Member States to take all measures necessary to guarantee the application and effectiveness of Community law.

24. For that purpose, whilst the choice of penalties remains within their discretion, they must ensure in particular that infringements of Community law are penalised under conditions, both procedural and substantive, which are analogous to those applicable to infringements of national law of a similar nature and importance and which, in any event, make the penalty effective, proportionate and dissuasive.

Further, a Member State may be in breach of the Treaty where it fails to prevent action by other parties which is frustrating Community objectives, even if there is no 'discrimination' of the kind suggested in the case above. Thus in proceedings brought by the Commission against France, the ECJ found that in failing to take adequate steps to prevent violent and disruptive protests by French farmers which were hindering

---

[97] Contrast Case C–338/91, *Steenhorst-Neerings* v. *Bestuur van de Bedrijfsvereniging voor Detailhandel* [1993] ECR I–5475, in which the ECJ ruled that where a Member State had not implemented a dir. properly, the capacity of national courts to read apparently inconsistent national legislation in a way which conformed with the un-implemented dir. would not absolve the Member State from the obligation to implement properly.

[98] See Case C–365/97, *Commission* v. *Italy* [1999] ECR I–7773 and the comment by J.C. van Haersolte (2002) 39 *CMLRev*. 407.

[99] See also Case 143/83, *Commission* v. *Denmark* [1985] ECR 427, paras. 8–10 of the judgment.

the free movement of agricultural goods, the Member State was in breach of its obligations under the Treaty.[100]

(d) ACTION BY THE COURTS OF A MEMBER STATE

A failure of a Member State's judiciary to comply with Community law has never formed the basis of Article 226 (ex Article 169) proceedings against that state. Does this mean that a national court's judgment cannot be the subject of infringement proceedings by the Commission? Certainly, the Court has said that the Member State is responsible even for actions and inaction on the part of constitutionally independent organs of the state. And, given the central role played by national courts in the implementation and enforcement of Community law domestically, their failure to comply with Community obligations could have serious consequences for Community law. According to Rawlings, the Commission's avoidance of such potential breaches is part of its exercise of discetion, in particular by 'steering clear of certain highly sensitive areas'.[101] And although the ECJ has never addressed the question whether a national court could be the subject of infringement proceedings, an Advocate General has expressed a view on the matter:

Case 30/77, R. v. Bouchereau
[1977] ECR 1999

ADVOCATE GENERAL WARNER[102]

No doubt the constitutionally independent institution whose action, or rather inaction, in each of those cases lay at the root of the default of the Member State concerned was its Parliament, but the relevant principle, as there stated, is wide enough to apply also to the Judiciary of a Member State. Indeed it must logically do so. I am reminded that, in case 9/75 *Meyer-Burckhardt* v. *Commission* [1975] ECR 1171 at 1187, I felt no hesitation about that.

It is obvious on the other hand that a Member State cannot be held to have failed to fulfil an obligation under the Treaty simply because one of its courts has reached a wrong decision. Judicial error, whether due to the misapprehension of facts or to misapprehension of the law, is not a breach of the Treaty. In the judicial sphere, Article 169 could only come into play in the event of a court of a Member State deliberately ignoring or disregarding Community law.

8. STATE DEFENCES IN ENFORCEMENT PROCEEDINGS

Although Member States have not lacked ingenuity or resourcefulness in providing reasons to justify their failure to fulfil Treaty obligations,[103] the ECJ has not been particularly receptive to such arguments. There are a great many examples of

---

[100] Case C–265/95, *Commission* v. *France* [1997] ECR I–6959.
[101] See n. 17 above.   [102] [1977] ECR 1999, 2020.
[103] See, e.g., Case C–353/96, *Commission* v. *Ireland* [1998] ECR I–8565.

'defences' which have unsuccessfully been pleaded by the States in response to infringement proceedings. Having said that, there is nothing to prohibit Member States from springing surprise defences which they have not raised in the pre-litigation procedure, even though of course the Commission cannot spring surprise complaints in the same way.[104] Further, the fact that a Member State's infringement has arguably had 'no adverse effects' is not a defence to infringement proceedings.[105] In a recent interesting case, the Advcate General commented on the unusual fact that an intervening Member State which was not the subject of the infringement proceedings had put forward a defence of the State against which the proceedings had been brought, but the ECJ rejected the intervention as inadmissible (which in fact was a challenge to the jurisdiction of the Court) and found a breach of EC law.[106]

(a) FORCE MAJEURE

Case 77/69, Commission v. Belgium
[1970] ECR 237

[ToA renumbering: Arts. 95 and 169 are now Arts. 90 and 226]

Belgium had drafted and put before Parliament a law designed to amend a national tax provision to comply with EC requirements, but the draft legislation had lapsed owing to the dissolution of Parliament. In response to infringement proceedings against it, Belgium claimed *force majeure* and argued that the separation-of-powers doctrine in Belgian constitutional law prevented the Government from requiring the necessary measure to be passed.

THE ECJ

15. The obligations arising from Article 95 of the Treaty devolve upon States as such and the liability of a Member State under Article 169 arises whatever the agency of the State whose action or inaction is the cause of the failure to fulfil its obligations, even in the case of a constitutionally independent institution.

Similar arguments have been made many times, including in proceedings brought against Italy for breach of Article 228 (ex Article 171) in failing to comply with a previous judgment of the Court.[107] It argued that difficulties had been encountered in the parliamentary procedures which were required to abolish the offending measure, and which were outside its control. The ECJ, however, rejected this argument, ruling

---

[104] Case C–414/97, *Commission* v. *Spain* [1999] ECR I–5585.

[105] Case C–150/97, *Commission* v. *Portugal* [1999] ECR I–259.

[106] Case C–13/00, *Commission* v. *Ireland* [2002] ECR I–nyr, where the UK intervened to argue that the breach alleged constituted a violation of international law obligations and not of EC law.

[107] See Cases 48/71, *Commission* v. *Italy* [1972] ECR 527; and 7/68, *Commission* v. *Italy* [1968] ECR 423. For subsequent proceedings against Italy under Art. 228 (ex Art. 171) before the existence of the pecuniary penalty, see Case C–101/91, *Commission* v. *Italy* [1993] ECR I–191.

that any other conclusion would subject the application of Community law to the varying laws of the different Member States in this regard. The ECJ has repeatedly ruled in such cases that:

a Member State may not plead provisions, practices or circumstances existing in its internal legal system in order to justify a failure to comply with obligations and time limits laid down in Community directives.[108]

The overall responsibility of each state for any failure to comply with Community law thus precludes the argument that the breach was brought about by another organ or institution of the state which is independent of the government. One situation which the ECJ agreed could constitute *force majeure* was where a bomb attack presented 'insurmountable difficulties', rendering compliance with the Treaty impossible.[109]

(b) THERE WAS NO INERTIA OR OPPOSITION TO THE APPLICATION OF EC LAW

Case 301/81, Commission v. Belgium
[1983] ECR 467

The Commission brought proceedings against Belgium for failure to implement Directive 77/780 concerning credit institutions. Belgium emphasized the technical and political difficulties encountered in adopting the necessary national implementing legislation, and argued that the Commission's reasoned opinion contained no evidence of inertia or opposition to EC law by Belgium within the short time period prescribed.

THE ECJ

8. In that respect it must be observed that the admissibility of an action based on Article 169 of the Treaty depends only on an objective finding of a failure to fulfil obligations and not on proof of any inertia or opposition on the part of the Member State concerned.

9. Finally, the Directive allowed the Member States a period of twenty-four months for the adoption of implementing measures. The period of two months laid down in the reasoned opinion merely constitutes an additional period in which the Member State is invited to put an end to the failure with which it is charged. Further, the Commission waited almost two years after sending the reasoned opinion before bringing the matter before the Court. It is therefore futile for the Kingdom of Belgium in those circumstances to challenge the period of two months laid down in the reasoned opinion.

---

[108] See, e.g., Case 280/83, *Commission* v. *Italy* [1984] ECR 2361, para. 4. Also, e.g., Cases 160/82, *Commission* v. *Netherlands* [1982] ECR 4637; 215/83; *Commission* v. *Belgium* [1985] ECR 1039; C–298/97, *Commission* v. *Spain* [1998] ECR I–3301; C–326/97, *Commission* v. *Belgium* [1998] ECR I–6107.

[109] Case 33/69, *Commission* v. *Italy* [1970] ECR 93, para. 16 of the judgment. However, the Court was not satisfied in the case that the bomb attack did render compliance excessively difficult by the time proceedings were brought. See also Case 70/86, *Commission* v. *Greece* [1987] ECR 3545 and Case C–334/87, *Greece* v. *Commission* [1990] ECR I–2849, para. 11, for a definition of *force majeure* in other circumstances.

This further underlines the point emphasized in various rulings of the ECJ that Article 169 (now Article 226) proceedings are 'objective' in nature.[110] The Court looks only to see whether or not the infringement has taken place as alleged, and the breach in question need not involve deliberate infringement or moral wrongdoing on the part of the Member State.[111]

(c) THE COMMUNITY MEASURE ON WHICH THE INFRINGEMENT PROCEEDINGS ARE BASED IS ILLEGAL

Case 226/87, Commission v. Greece
[1988] ECR 3611

[ToA renumbering: Arts. 90, 169, 170, 173, and 175 are now Arts. 86, 226, 227, 230, and 232]

A year after adopting a decision under Article 90 EC declaring Greek legislation on public-sector insurance to be incompatible with the Treaty, when Greece had taken no action to amend the legislation, the Commission brought infringement proceedings before the ECJ. The Greek Government contested the lawfulness of the Commission's initial Article 90 decision.

THE ECJ

14. The system of remedies set up by the Treaty distinguishes between the remedies provided for in Articles 169 and 170, which permit a declaration that a Member State has failed to fulfil its obligations, and those contained in Articles 173 and 175, which permit judicial review of the lawfulness of measures adopted by the Community institutions, or the failure to adopt such measures. Those remedies have different objectives and are subject to different rules. In the absence of a provision of the Treaty expressly permitting it to do so, a Member State cannot therefore plead the unlawfulness of a decision addressed to it as a defence in an action for a declaration that it has failed to fulfil its obligations arising out of its failure to implement that decision.

It appears from this ruling that it is not possible for a Member State to plead the illegality of an earlier Community decision addressed to it, in order to resist judgment against it in Article 226 (ex Article 169) proceedings for failure to comply with that decision. The rationale seems to be that if the Member State truly objected to the decision, it had the opportunity at the time of bringing a direct action for its annulment under Article 230 (ex Article 173). It seems, however, that a plea of illegality might be a defence to an action under Article 226 where the earlier measure was not a decision addressed to the Member State in question, but a regulation the

---

[110] The ECJ has rejected as irrelevant the argument that a particular Member State breach was minor: see recently Case C–43/97, *Commission* v. *Italy* [1997] ECR I–4671.

[111] See, however, Case C–146/89, *Commission* v. *UK* [1991] ECR 3533, in which, although the Court rejected the UK's attempt to justify its breach by pointing to the failure by other Member States to fulfil their similar obligations, it was sufficiently impressed by the 'exemplary conduct' of the UK in later voluntarily remedying its breach to order each party to bear its own costs.

illegality of which might reasonably not have been apparent to the Member State until the Commission brought enforcement proceedings, or where the Community measure was so gravely flawed as to be legally 'non-existent'.[112] It may also be possible for the illegality of the decision to be pleaded in an extreme case where the decision infringes a principle of a constitutional nature.[113]

(d) OTHER MEMBER STATES ARE ALSO IN BREACH

This ground has been pleaded many times by Member States, without success. The idea that the obligation to comply with Community law is a reciprocal one, dependent on full compliance by other Member States, has long been rejected by the ECJ. The Court has been determined since *Van Gend en Loos*[114] to distinguish Community law from the traditional forms and principles of international law.[115] However, this has not deterred Member States from continuing to raise the concept of reciprocity in their defence in infringement proceedings.

Case C–146/89, Commission v. United Kingdom
[1991] ECR 3533

THE ECJ

47. It must first be pointed out in this regard that, according to the well-established case-law of the Court (see in particular the judgment of 26 February 1976 in Case 52/75 *Commission* v. *Italy* [1976] ECR 277) a Member State cannot justify its failure to fulfil obligations under the Treaty by pointing to the fact that other Member States have also failed, and continued to fail, to fulfil their own obligations. Under the legal order established by the Treaty, the implementation of Community law by Member States cannot be made subject to a condition of reciprocity. Article 169 and 170 of the Treaty provide a suitable means of redress for dealing with the failure by Member States to fulfil their obligations under the Treaty.

9. ARTICLE 227 (EX ARTICLE 170)

Apart from the enforcement action which the Commission may bring under Article 226 (ex Article 169), the EC Treaty also provides a means for any Member State to initiate an action against another state which it considers to be in breach of the Treaty.[116]

To that effect, Article 227 (ex Article 170) provides:

---

[112] See Mancini AG in Case 204/86, *Commission* v. *Greece* [1988] ECR 5323, 5343–5, and Case 226/87, *Commission* v. *Greece* [1988] ECR 3611, 3617. For an unsuccessful attempt to plead the illegality of a directive (rather than a decision addressed to it) which the state had failed to implement see Case C–74/91, *Commission* v. *Germany* [1992] ECR I–5437.

[113] Cases 6 & 11/69, *Commission* v. *France* [1969] ECR 523, 70/72; *Commission* v. *Germany* [1973] ECR 813; and 156/77, *Commission* v. *Belgium* [1978] ECR 1881.

[114] Case 26/62, *Van Gend en Loos* [1963] ECR 1.

[115] See Case 52/75, *Commission* v. *Italy* [1976] ECR 277, para. 11.   [116] See also Art. 142 Euratom.

A Member State which considers that another Member State has failed to fulfil an obligation under this Treaty may bring the matter before the Court of Justice.

Before a Member State brings an action against another Member State for an alleged infringement of an obligation under this Treaty, it shall bring the matter before the Commission.

The Commission shall deliver a reasoned opinion after each of the States concerned has been given the opportunity to submit its own case and its observations on the other party's case both orally and in writing.

If the Commission has not delivered an opinion within three months of the date on which the matter was brought before it, the absence of such opinion shall not prevent the matter from being brought before the Court.

Unlike under Article 226 (ex Article 169), the Member State bringing the action under Article 227 (ex Article 170) does not first have to contact the Member State which is the subject of the complaint. Rather, as can be seen, the matter must first be brought by the complainant state before the Commission. The procedure thereafter is similar to that under Article 226 except that both states in the case of Article 227 must be heard and given a chance to make oral and written submissions before the Commission gives its reasoned opinion. Given that Article 227 provides a mechanism for Member States rather than the Commission to bring another state before the ECJ, it appears that the complainant state may bring the case to the ECJ even where the Commission takes the view that there is no breach.

Article 227 has very rarely been used, no doubt because of the degree of political ill-will this would occasion between Member States.[117] In 1978 France, with the support of the Commission, successfully brought proceedings against the UK over a fishing dispute.[118] More recently Belgium, without the support of the Commission but with the support of four other Member States, brought an unsuccessful action against Spain in relation to its requirements concerning rules of origin for Rioja wine.[119]

10. INTERIM MEASURES

Under Articles 242 and 243 (ex Articles 185 and 186), the ECJ has the power to prescribe interim measures which it considers to be necessary in a case which has been brought before it.[120] Although they may be sought in any case before the ECJ,[121] they

---

[117] The procedure was set in motion by the Commission in response to a complaint from France against The Netherlands, which led to a reasoned opinion by the Commission: see Case 169/84, *Cofaz* v. *Commission* [1986] ECR 391, para. 6 of the judgment.

[118] Case 141/78, *France* v. *UK* [1979] ECR 2923.

[119] Case C–388/95, *Belgium* v. *Spain* [2000] ECR I–3121.

[120] See also Arts. 39 ECSC, 157–158 Euratom. See C. Gray, 'Interim Measures of Protection in the European Court' (1979) 4 *ELRev.* 80; G. Borchardt, 'The Award of Interim Measures by the ECJ' (1985) 22 *CMLRev.* 203; P. Oliver, 'Interim Measures: Some Recent Developments' (1992) 29 *CMLRev.* 7.

[121] See, e.g., the Court's dismissal of Greece's objection to an application for interim measures in the context of Art. 298 (ex Art. 225) enforcement proceedings against it: Case C–120/94R, n. 1 above. For a well-known example of interim measures in the UK, see Case 246/89R, *Commission* v. *UK* [1989] ECR 3125. This action was brought prior to the reference to the ECJ from the HL in the famous case arising from the same legislation, Case C–213/89, *R.* v. *Secretary of State for Transport, ex p. Factortame* [1990] ECR I–2433.

may be particularly useful for the Commission to seek at the same time as proceedings under Article 226 (ex Article 169).

When in Article 226 proceedings a breach is found, the Court simply declares that the Member State has failed to fulfil its obligations, and its ruling does not have any effect on the impugned national rule or provision. The Treaty makes clear that, in general, actions before the Court—and not only actions under Article 226 (ex Article 169)—do not have suspensory effect. Article 242 (ex Article 185) provides:

Actions brought before the Court of Justice shall not have suspensory effect. The Court of Justice may, however, if it considers that circumstances so require, order that application of the contested act be suspended.

Article 243 (ex Article 186) then provides:

The Court of Justice may in any cases before it prescribe any necessary interim measures.

The Court's Rules of Procedure specify that such interim measures may not be ordered unless there are circumstances giving rise to urgency, as well as factual and legal grounds which establish a *prima facie* justification for granting the measures sought. The effect of the urgency requirement is that the interim measures requested must be of such a nature as to prevent the injury which is alleged. Further, the Commission must display diligence in response to a complaint made against a Member State if it is seeking interim measures, given the requirement of urgency, and the ECJ may refuse to order such measures if it has not done so.[122]

11. CONCLUSIONS

   i. Dissatisfaction with the enforcement procedure has been expressed over the years, the main objections being to its alleged ineffectiveness, the lack of constraint on the Commission's discretion, and the inadequacy of the role provided for individual complainants.

   ii Some aspects of these criticisms have been addressed in amendments to Article 228 (ex Article 171) of the Treaty, and others have been addressed in response to pressure from the Ombudsman, but the nature and operation of the enforcement procedure remains essentially the same.

   iii. The effectiveness of the procedure has arguably been slightly enhanced by the penalty payment procedure which, although it has so far resulted in very few judgments by the ECJ, is actively used by the Commission in its enforcement strategy.

   iv. Following the Ombudsman's own-initiative report on the enforcement procedure and the steady trickle of individual complaints to him about the Commission's procedure, a number of other minor but practical reforms have been introduced by the Commission. These include a greater degree of transparency whereby many stages of the enforcement proceedings are now posted on the

---

[122] Case C–87/94R, *Commission v. Belgium* [1994] ECR I–1395.

Commission's website, there is greater use of press releases, and better communication with complainants when a decision to terminate an investigation has been taken. However, although the Commission is apparently in the course of codifying its administrative procedure, the status of complainants remains unchanged.

12. FURTHER READING

(a) Books

GIL IBÁÑEZ, A., *The Administrative Supervision and Enforcement of EC Law* (Hart, 1999)

HARTLEY, T. C., *The Foundations of European Community Law* (Oxford University Press, 4th edn., 1998)

SCHERMERS, H., *Judicial Protection in the European Union* (Kluwer, 6th edn., 2002)

(b) Articles

BORCHARDT, G., 'The Award of Interim Measures by the European Court' (1985) 22 *CMLRev.* 203

BORZSAK, L., 'Punishing Member States or Influencing Their Behaviour or *Iudex (non) calculat?*' (2001) 13 *JEL* 235

DASHWOOD, A., and WHITE, R., 'Enforcement Actions Under Articles 169 and 170 EEC' (1989) 14 *ELRev.* 388

EVANS, A., 'The Enforcement Procedure of Article 169 EEC: Commission Discretion' (1979) 4 *ELRev.* 442

GRAY, C., 'Interim Measures of Protection in the European Court' (1979) 4 *ELRev.* 80

KUNZLIK, P., 'The Enforcement of EU Environmental Law: Article 169, the Ombudsman and the Parliament' (1997) 6 *EELR* 46.

MASTROIANNI, R., 'The Enforcement Procedure under Article 169 of the EC Treaty and the powers of the European Commission: Quis Custodiet Custodes?' (1995) 1 *European Public Law* 535

RAWLINGS, R., 'Engaged Elites, Citizen Action and Institutional Attitudes in Commission Enforcement' (2000) 6 *ELJ* 4

11

PRELIMINARY RULINGS AND THE BUILDING OF A EUROPEAN JUDICIAL SYSTEM

1. INTRODUCTION

Article 234 EC (ex Article 177), which contains the preliminary ruling procedure, is one of the most interesting provisions of the EC Treaty. There would have been few, at the inception of the Treaty, who would have guessed the importance of this Article in shaping both Community law, and the relationship between the national and Community legal systems. Article 234 is very much the 'jewel in the Crown' of ECJ's jurisdiction. It reads as follows:

The Court of Justice shall have jurisdiction to give preliminary rulings concerning:

(a) the interpretation of the Treaty;

(b) the validity and interpretation of acts of the institutions of the Community and of the ECB;

(c) the interpretation of the statutes of bodies established by an act of the Council, where those statutes so provide.

Where such a question is raised before any court or tribunal of a Member State, that court or tribunal may, if it considers that a decision on the question is necessary to enable it to give judgment, request the Court of Justice to give a ruling thereon.

Where any such question is raised in a case pending before a court or tribunal of a Member State, against whose decision there is no judicial remedy under national law, that court or tribunal shall bring the matter before the Court of Justice.

Prior to the Nice Treaty only the ECJ could give preliminary rulings. Article 225(3) now accords the CFI jurisdiction to give such rulings in specific areas laid down by the Statute of the court of Justice. If the CFI feels that such a case raises issues of principle, which will affect the unity or consistency of EC law, it may refer the case to the ECJ. Where the CFI does give a preliminary ruling, its decision may exceptionally be subject to review by the ECJ, under the conditions laid down by the ECJ's Statute, where there is a serious risk that the unity or consistency of EC law will be affected.

The relationship between national courts and the ECJ is reference-based. It is not an appellate system. No individual has a right of appeal to the ECJ. It is for the national court to make the decision to refer. The ECJ will rule on the issues referred to it, and the case will then be sent back to the national courts, which will apply the Community law to the case at hand.

2. CENTRAL ISSUES

i. Article 234 (ex Article 177) has been of seminal importance for the *development of Community law*. It is through preliminary rulings that the ECJ has developed concepts such as direct effect and supremacy.[1] Individuals would assert in national courts that their *Member States* had broken a Community provision, which gave them rights that they could enforce in their national courts. The national court would seek a ruling from the ECJ whether the particular Community provision really did have direct effect, and the ECJ was thereby enabled to develop the concept. Article 234 is also an indirect way of testing the validity of *Community action* for conformity with EC law.[2]

ii. Article 234 has been the mechanism through which national courts and the ECJ have engaged in *a discourse on the appropriate reach of Community law when it has come into conflict with national legal norms*.

iii. Article 234 has been the principal vehicle through which the *relationship between the national and Community legal systems has been fashioned*. The *original* conception of the relationship was *horizontal* and *bilateral*. It was horizontal in that the ECJ and the national courts were separate but equal. They had differing functions, which each performed within its own appointed sphere. It was for the national court to decide whether to refer a matter to the ECJ, which the ECJ would then interpret. It was bilateral in the sense that, in principle, the ECJ's rulings were delivered to the particular national court that made the request. In this sense, there was a series of bilateral relationships between the ECJ and each of the national courts. The relationship has become steadily more *vertical* and *multilateral*. It has become more vertical in that developments have emphasized the fact that the ECJ sits in a superior position to that of the national courts. The verticality of the relationship also manifests itself in a less obvious, but equally important, manner. The ECJ has, in effect, enrolled the national courts as enforcers and appliers of Community law. They are perceived as a central part of a Community-wide judicial hierarchy,[3] with the ECJ sitting at the apex of this hierarchy. The relationship has become more multilateral, in that judgments given in response to the request for a ruling from one Member State are increasingly held to have either a *de facto* or *de jure* impact on all other national courts.

iv. There has been much discussion about *reform of the Community judicial system*.[4] This discourse has been driven by the increased workload on the ECJ and CFI, and by the prospects of enlargement of the EU.

3. THREE TYPES OF PRELIMINARY-RULING PROCEDURE

The changes introduced by the ToA mean that there are now three different types of preliminary-ruling procedure.

The first, general version of this procedure is contained in Article 234, set out

---

[1] F. Mancini and D. Keeling, 'From *CILFIT* to *ERT*: The Constitutional Challenge Facing the European Court' (1991) 11 *YBEL* 1, 2–3.

[2] See below, 435.

[3] *Report of the Court of Justice on Certain Aspects of the Application of the Treaty on European Union* (1995), paras. 11–15.

[4] See below, 473–9.

above, which is the re-numbered and unaltered Article 177. This version will continue to apply to all requests for preliminary rulings coming under Pillar 1, the EC Treaty itself, except for those arising under Articles 61–69 (ex Articles 73i–73q).

The second species of preliminary ruling operates in the context of Articles 61–69, the new Title IV of the EC Treaty, dealing with 'Visas, Asylum, Immigration and Other Policies Concerning the Free Movement of Persons'. These matters were, prior to the ToA, dealt with in Pillar 3, concerning Justice and Home Affairs (JHA). There were, as we have seen, criticisms voiced about treating such matters in this way.[5] The ToA brought many important Pillar 3 issues within Pillar 1, the EC Treaty itself. The Article 234 procedure has, however, been modified in its application in relation to Title IV. Article 68 (ex Article 73p) stipulates that a preliminary ruling can be sought only by a national court or tribunal against whose decisions there is no judicial remedy in national law. This is as opposed to the 'normal' position under Article 234 whereby any such court or tribunal has a discretion to seek a reference.[6]

The third species of preliminary ruling was introduced by Article 35 of the TEU as modified by the ToA (replacing the old Article K. 7). This covers the remodelled Pillar 3 which now deals with 'Police and Judicial Co-operation in Criminal Matters' (PJCC). Article 35 in effect provides that the ECJ shall have jurisdiction to give preliminary rulings on the interpretation and validity of certain measures adopted under this Pillar (although not, it seems, on the Treaty provisions themselves), but *only if* the Member State accepts the ECJ's jurisdiction by making a declaration. Article 35(3) further provides that a Member State has a choice whether a preliminary ruling can be sought by any court or tribunal or only by such a body against whose decisions there is no judicial remedy in national law.

4. THE PROVISIONS WHICH CAN BE REFERRED

A preliminary reference can be made in relation to three types of subject matter. References may be made concerning *the interpretation of the Treaty*: Article 234(1)(a).[7] This includes all Treaties amending or supplementing the EC Treaty. Particular subsidiary conventions may provide for references to be made to the ECJ. It should be noted, as stated above, that it is through Article 234(1)(a) that the Court has given many of its seminal judgments concerning direct effect. The 'interpretation' of the Treaty will, therefore, cover the issue of whether a Treaty Article is capable of generating rights for individuals. It should, however, be made clear that under Article 234

---

[5] See Ch. 1 above.

[6] Art. 68(3) also provides that the Council, Commission, or a Member State can request the ECJ to give a ruling on a question of interpretation arising under Title IV, or acts of the institutions based on this Title. Such rulings do not apply to judgments of national courts etc which have become *res judicata*.

[7] Rights and obligations arising from agreements concluded before the entry into force of the Treaty between a Member State and a third country are not affected by the provisions of the Treaty. For a Community provision to be deprived of effect such an agreement must have been concluded before the entry into force of the EC Treaty, and the third country must derive rights from it which it can require the Member State concerned to respect: Cases C–364 and 365/95, *T. Port GmbH & Co. v. Hauptzollamt Hamburg-Jonas* [1998] ECR I–1023.

the ECJ does not pass judgment on the validity as such of a national law. It interprets the Treaty. The consequence of such an interpretation may be that a provision of national law is incompatible with EC law, and the supremacy of EC law will mean that there is an obligation on, *inter alia*, national courts to redress the situation. This does not alter the fact that the ECJ itself is not directly making any judgment on the validity of national law.[8]

Article 234(1)(b) allows for preliminary references to be made which relate *to the validity and interpretation of acts of the institutions* of the Community. The former covers cases such as *ICC*[9] and *Foto-Frost*,[10] to be considered below, in which the validity of, for example, a Community decision or regulation arises in proceedings before a national court. The latter covers, *inter alia*, those cases in which an individual argues that a Community regulation is capable of giving rise to rights that can be enforced in national courts. However, it should be made clear that references can be made under Article 234(1)(b) irrespective of whether or not the Community provision is directly effective. A reference may be required in such circumstances in order to clarify the interpretation of the provision in question. References may also be made in relation to non-binding acts such as recommendations.[11] It has also been held that Article 234(1)(b) gives the ECJ jurisdiction to make a ruling in respect of certain agreements with non-member States.[12]

The precise ambit of Article 234(1)(c), which embraces *the interpretation of statutes of bodies established by an act of the Council*, is not so clear. The word 'statute' in Community law normally connotes an instrument which governs the operation of an institution, such as the statute of the ECJ. Such statutes will be acts of the Council, and will therefore fall within Article 234(1)(b). It may well be that, as Hartley suggests, Article 234(1)(c) is designed to limit the scope of Article 234(1)(b) in relation to such statutes.[13]

The ECJ has also held that a preliminary reference may be made in circumstances in which a provision of national law is based on or makes some reference to Community law, even if the consequence is that the ambit of Community law is extended by the national provisions.[14]

---

[8] See, e.g. Case C–167/94R, *Grau Gomis* [1995] ECR I–1023, [1996] 2 CMLR 129; Cases C–37 and 38/96, *Sodiprem SARL* v. *Direction Générale des Douanes* [1998] ECR I–2039; Cases C–10 and 22/97, *Ministero delle Finanze* v. *IN. CO. GE. '90 Srl* [1998] ECR I–6307; *The ECJ's Guidance on References by National Court for Preliminary Rulings* [1997] 1 CMLR 78, paras. 3 and 7.

[9] Case 66/80, *International Chemical Corporation* v. *Amministrazione delle Finanze dello Stato* [1981] ECR 1191.

[10] Case 314/85, *Firma Foto-Frost* v. *Hauptzollamt Lübeck-Ost* [1987] ECR 4199.

[11] Case 322/88, *Salvatore Grimaldi* v. *Fonds des Maladies Professionnelles* [1989] ECR 4407.

[12] Case 181/73, *Haegeman* v. *Belgium* [1974] ECR 449; Cases 267–269/81, *Amministrazione delle Finanze dello Stato* v. *Società Petrolifera Italiana SpA and SpA Michelin Italia* [1983] ECR 801; Case C–53/96, *Hermes International* v. *FHT Marketing Choice BV* [1998] ECR I–3603; Cases C–300 and 392/98, *Parfums Christian Dior* v. *Tuk Consultancy BV* [2000] ECR I–11307. For comment see T.C. Hartley, *The Foundations of European Community Law* (Clarendon Press, 4th edn., 1998), 262–5.

[13] *Ibid.*, 260.

[14] Cases C–297/88 and 197/89, *Dzodzi* v. *Belgium* [1990] ECR I–3763; Case C–231/89, *Gmurzynska-Bscher* v. *Oberfinanzdirektion Köln* [1990] ECR I–4003; Case C–384/89, *Tomatis and Fulchiron* [1991] ECR I–127; Case C–73/89, *Fournier* v. *Van Werven* [1992] ECR I–5621; Case C–88/91, *Federazione Italiana dei Consorzi Agrari* v. *Azienda di Stato per gli Interventi nel Mercato Agricolo* [1992] ECR I–4035; Case C–28/95, *Leur-Bloem* v. *Inspecteur der Belastingdienst/Ondernemingen Amsterdam 2* [1997] ECR I–4161; Case C–130/95, *Bernd Giloy* v. *Hauptzollamt Frankfurt am Main-Ost* [1997] ECR–I 4291.

There are specific subject-matter limits as to what can be referred under the modified Article 234 procedure which applies to Title IV, Articles 61–69,[15] and to that which operates in the context of Pillar 3.[16]

5. THE COURTS OR TRIBUNALS TO WHICH ARTICLE 234 APPLIES

Article 234(2) and (3) is framed in terms of courts or tribunals of a Member State, which may or must make a reference. It is clear that it is for the ECJ to decide whether a body is a court or tribunal for the purposes of this Article, and that the categorization of that body under national law is not conclusive.[17] The ECJ will take a number of factors into account when making this determination, including: whether the body is established by law, whether it is permanent, whether its jurisdiction is compulsory, whether its procedure is *inter partes*, whether it applies rules of law, and whether it is independent.[18] The *Broekmeulen* case provides a good example of the ECJ's reasoning on this issue:

Case 246/80, C. Broekmeulen v. Huisarts Registratie Commissie
[1981] ECR 2311

[Note ToA renumbering: Art. 177 is now 234]

The case concerned a Dutch body called the Appeals Committee for General Medicine. It heard appeals from another body, which was responsible for registering those who wished to practise medicine in the Netherlands. Both of these bodies were established under the auspices of the Royal Netherlands Society for the Promotion of Medicine. Although this was a private association, it was indirectly recognized in other parts of Dutch law, and in reality it was not possible to practise without registration. The Appeals Committee was not a court or tribunal under Dutch law, but it did follow an adversarial procedure and allow legal representation. Broekmeulen was of Dutch nationality, but had qualified in Belgium. He sought to establish himself as a doctor in The Netherlands and his application to be registered was refused. The question arose whether the Appeals Committee was a court or tribunal for the purposes of Article 177.

---

[15] Art. 68(2): the ECJ has no jurisdiction to rule on any measure, etc. made pursuant to Art. 62(1) concerning the maintenance of law and order, and the safeguarding of internal security.

[16] Art. 35(5) TEU: the ECJ has no jurisdiction to review the validity or proportionality of operations of the police or other law enforcement agencies, or the exercise of the Member States' responsibilities in relation to law and order and internal security.

[17] Case 43/71, *Politi* v. *Italy* [1971] ECR 1039; Case C–24/92, *Corbiau* v. *Administration des Contributions* [1993] ECR I–1277.

[18] Case C–54/96, *Dorsch Consult Ingenieurgesellschaft mbH* v. *Bundesbaugesellschaft Berlin mbH* [1997] ECR I–4961; Cases C–9 and 118/97, *Proceedings brought by Jokela and Pitkaranta* [1998] ECR I–6267; Case C–407/98, *Abrahamsson and Anderson* v. *Fogelqvist,* [2000] ECR I–5539; Case C–195/98, *Österreicher Gewerkschaftsbund, Gewerkschaft Öffentlicher Dienst* v. *Republik Österreich,* [2000] ECR I–10497.

14. A study of the Netherlands legislation and of the statutes and internal rules of the Society shows that a doctor who intends to establish himself in the Netherlands may not in fact practise either as a specialist, or as an expert in social medicine, or as a general practitioner, without being recognised and registered by the organs of the Society. In the same way it may be seen that the system thus established is the result of close cooperation between doctors who are members of the Society, the medical faculties and the departments of State responsible for higher education and health.

15. It is thus clear that . . . the Netherlands system of public health operates on the basis of the status accorded to doctors by the Society and that registration as a general practitioner is essential to every doctor wishing to establish himself in the Netherlands as a general practitioner.

16. Therefore a general practitioner who avails himself of the right of establishment and the freedom to provide services conferred upon him by Community law is faced with the necessity of applying to the Registration Committee established by the Society, and, in the event of his application's being refused, must appeal to the Appeals Committee. The Netherlands Government expressed the opinion that a doctor who is not a member of the Society would have the right to appeal against such a refusal to the ordinary courts, but stated that the point had never been decided by the Netherlands courts. Indeed all doctors, whether members of the Society or not, whose application to be registered as a general practitioner is refused, appeal to the Appeals Committee, whose decisions to the knowledge of the Netherlands Government have never been challenged in the ordinary courts.

17. [I]t should be noted that it is incumbent upon Member States to take the necessary steps to ensure that within their own territory the provisions adopted by the Community institutions are implemented in their entirety. If, under the legal system of a Member State, the task of implementing such provisions is assigned to a professional body acting under a degree of governmental supervision, and if that body, in conjunction with the public authorities concerned, creates appeal procedures which may affect the exercise of rights granted by Community law, it is imperative, in order to ensure the proper functioning of Community law, that the Court should have an opportunity of ruling on issues of interpretation and validity arising out of such proceedings.

18. As a result of all the foregoing considerations and in the absence, in practice, of any right of appeal to the ordinary courts, the Appeals Committee, which operates with the consent of the public authorities and with their cooperation, and which, after an adversarial procedure, delivers decisions which are recognised as final, must, in a matter involving the application of Community law, be considered as a court or tribunal of a Member State within the meaning of Article 177 of the Treaty. Therefore, the Court has jurisdiction to reply to the question asked.

It is necessary that the body making the reference be a court or tribunal of a Member State.[19] This can be problematic in, for example, the context of arbitration. Whether an arbitral court or tribunal can be regarded as an emanation of a Member State will depend on the nature of the arbitration in question. The fact that the arbitral body gives a judgment according to law, and that the award is binding between the parties, will not, however, be sufficient. There must be a closer link

[19] Case C–355/89, *DHSS (Isle of Man)* v. *Barr and Montrose Holdings Ltd.* [1991] ECR I–3479; Case C–100/89, *Kaefer and Procacci* v. *France* [1990] ECR I–4647.

between the arbitration procedure and the ordinary court system in order for the former to be considered as a court or tribunal of a Member State.[20]

Article 234 draws a distinction between courts or tribunals with a discretion to refer to the ECJ, which are covered by Article 234(2), and courts or tribunals 'against whose decisions there is no judicial remedy under national law', dealt with in Article 234(3). The latter are under an obligation to refer, provided that a decision on a question is necessary to enable judgment to be given.

There are two views about the type of bodies covered by Article 234(3). According to the abstract theory, the only bodies which come within this Article are those whose decisions are never subject to appeal. According to the concrete theory, the real test is whether the court or tribunal's decision is subject to appeal in the type of case in question.[21]

The case law is not entirely clear. The ruling in *Costa*[22] suggests that the ECJ favours the concrete theory. In that case the *giudice conciliatore*, (magistrate), made a reference to the ECJ. Although the decisions of the *giudice conciliatore* were appealable in some instances, there was no such right of appeal in the particular case, because the sum involved was relatively small. Notwithstanding this fact, the ECJ treated the national court as one against whose decision there was no judicial remedy in the actual case at hand.

If the concrete theory is correct, the application of that theory in the context of the United Kingdom might still be problematic. Court of Appeal decisions can normally be appealed to the House of Lords, but only if the leave of either the Court of Appeal or the House of Lords is granted. The issue was considered in the *Chiron* case. Balcombe LJ stated that:[23]

Except in those cases . . . where the Court of Appeal is the court of last resort, the Court of Appeal is not *obliged* to make a reference to the ECJ . . . If the Court of Appeal does not make a reference to the ECJ, and gives its final judgment on the appeal, then the House of Lords becomes the court of last resort. If either the Court of Appeal or the House of Lords grants leave to appeal, then there is no problem. If the Court of Appeal refuses leave to appeal, and the House of Lords is presented with an application for leave to appeal, before it refuses leave it should consider whether an issue of Community law arises which is necessary for its decision (whether to grant or refuse leave) and is not *acte clair*. If it considers that a reference is requisite, it will take such action as it may consider appropriate in the particular case.

The issue of whether national courts can be limited by national procedural rules on whether they can raise a matter of EC law appears to be as follows. In *Peterbroeck* the ECJ held that a national procedural rule, which prevented a national court from raising a matter of EC law of its own motion, concerning the compatibility of a

---

[20] Case 102/81, *Nordsee Deutsche Hochseefischerei GmbH* v. *Reederei Mond Hochseefischerei Nordstern AG and Co. KG* [1982] ECR 1095; Case C–126/97, *Eco Swiss China Time Ltd.* v. *Benetton International NV* [1999] ECR I–3055.

[21] Difficulties may also arise in circumstances where the judgment in question can be reconsidered in other proceedings. See Case 107/76, *Hoffmann-La Roche* v. *Centrafarm* [1977] ECR 957.

[22] Case 6/64, [1964] ECR 585, 592, [1964] CMLR 425.

[23] *Chiron Corporation* v. *Murex Diagnostics Ltd.* [1995] All ER (EC) 88, 93–4. Italics in the original. For more general discussion see Hartley, n. 12 above, 273–5; F. Jacobs, 'Which Courts and Tribunals are Bound to Refer to the European Court?' (1977) 2 *ELRev.* 119.

national law with EC law, even where it had not been raised by the person concerned within the specified time, was itself contrary to Community law. It was held that the domestic rule could not be justified on the ground of legal certainty or the proper conduct of procedure.[24] This case was distinguished in *Van Schijndel*.[25] The ECJ held that there was no such obligation on national courts if it would oblige the national court to abandon the passive role assigned to it by the domestic procedural rules by going beyond the ambit of the dispute as defined by the parties themselves.

The ECJ has made it clear that, unless they had been granted leave to intervene in the national proceedings, parties other than those mentioned in Article 20 of the Statute of the Court have no rights to intervene in Article 234 proceedings.[26]

6. THE EXISTENCE OF A QUESTION: THE DEVELOPMENT OF PRECEDENT

It is clear that Article 234 is designed to be used only if there is a question to be answered which falls into one of the categories mentioned in Article 234(1). There may be a number of reasons why a 'question' posed by the national court does not necessitate a ruling, the most obvious being that the ECJ has already ruled on the matter.

Cases 28–30/62, Da Costa en Schaake NV, Jacob Meijer NV and
Hoechst-Holland NV v. Nederlandse Belastingadministratie
[1963] ECR 31

[Note To A renumbering: Arts. 12 and 177 are now Arts. 25 and 234]

The facts in the case were materially identical to those in Case 26/62, *Van Gend en Loos*. The questions asked were also materially identical to those posed in the *Van Gend* case.

THE ECJ

The regularity of the procedure followed by the Tariefcommissie in requesting the Court for a preliminary ruling under Article 177 of the EEC Treaty has not been disputed and there is no ground for the Court to raise the matter of its own motion.

The Commission . . . urges that the request be dismissed for lack of substance, since the questions on which an interpretation is requested from the Court in the present cases have already been decided . . . in Case 26/62, which covered identical questions raised in a similar case.

This contention is not justified. A distinction should be made between the obligation imposed by

---

[24] Case C–312/93, *Peterbroeck, Van Campenhout & Cie SCS* v. *Belgium* [1995] ECR I–4599.
[25] Cases C–430–431/93, *Van Schijndel and Van Veen* v. *Stichting Pensioenfonds voor Fysiotherapeuten* [1995] ECR I–4705. See ch. 6 above for more general discussion of remedies, procedural autonomy, and EC law.
[26] Case C–181/95, *Biogen Inc.* v. *Smithkline Beecham Biologicals SA* [1997] ECR I–357.

the third paragraph of Article 177 upon national courts or tribunals of last instance and the power granted by the second paragraph of Article 177 to every national court or tribunal to refer to the Court of the Communities a question on the interpretation of the Treaty. Although the third paragraph of Article 177 unreservedly requires courts or tribunals of a Member State against whose decisions there is no judicial remedy under national law—like the Tariefcommissie—to refer to the Court every question of interpretation raised before them, the authority of an interpretation under Article 177 already given by the Court may deprive the obligation of its purpose and thus empty it of its substance. Such is the case especially when the question raised is materially identical with a question which has already been the subject of a preliminary ruling in a similar case.

When it gives an interpretation of the Treaty in a specific action pending before a national court, the Court limits itself to deducing the meaning of the Community rules from the wording and spirit of the Treaty, it being left to the national court to apply in the particular case the rules which are thus interpreted. Such an attitude conforms with the function assigned to the Court of ensuring unity of interpretation of Community law within the six Member States. . . .

It is no less true that Article 177 always allows a national court, if it considers it desirable, to refer questions of interpretation to the Court again. This follows from Article 20 of the Statute of the Court of Justice, under which the procedure laid down for the settlement of preliminary questions is automatically set in motion as soon as such a question is referred by a national court.

The Court must, therefore, give a judgment on the present application.

The interpretation of Article 12 of the EEC Treaty, which is here requested, was given in the Court's judgment . . . in Case 26/62.

[*The Court then repeated the judgment it had given in the case of* Van Gend en Loos. *It continued as follows.*]

The questions of interpretation posed in this case are identical with those settled as above and no new factor has been presented to the Court.

In these circumstances the Tariefcommissie must be referred to the previous judgment.

The ECJ's approach appears clearly in this extract. The national court is still able, in formal terms, to refer a matter to the ECJ, even where the ECJ has ruled on the issue. However, it is clear that such an application must raise some new factor or argument. If it does not do so, then the Court will be strongly inclined to restate the substance of the earlier case. The existence of an earlier ruling can deprive the national court's obligation to refer 'of its purpose and thus empty it of its substance'. The *Da Costa* case, therefore, initiated what is in effect a system of precedent. These seeds have been developed by the ECJ in later cases:

Case 283/81, Srl CILFIT and Lanificio di Gavardo SpA v. Ministry of Health
[1982] ECR 3415

[Note ToA renumbering: Art. 177 is now Art. 234]

The plaintiffs were textile firms who alleged that certain duties they were obliged to pay under Italian law were in breach of Regulation 827/68. The Italian Ministry of Health urged the Italian

Court of Cassation, against whose decisions there was no judicial remedy under national law, not to refer the matter to the ECJ, on the ground that the answer to the substantive question was so obvious as to obviate the need for a reference. The Court of Cassation decided that this contention was itself an issue of Community law. It therefore requested a ruling from the ECJ on whether the obligation to refer imposed in Article 177(3), was unconditional, or whether it was premised on the existence of reasonable interpretive doubt about the answer which should be given to a question. The ECJ's response to the *acte clair* point will be examined in detail below. The ECJ also gave guidance on the relevance of its prior decisions.

THE ECJ

8. In this connection, it is necessary to define the meaning for the purposes of Community law of the expression 'where any such question is raised' in order to determine the circumstances in which a national court or tribunal against whose decisions there is no judicial remedy under national law is obliged to bring a matter before the Court of Justice.

9. In this regard, it must in the first place be pointed out that Article 177 does not constitute a means of redress available to the parties to a case pending before a national court or tribunal. Therefore the mere fact that a party contends that the dispute gives rise to a question concerning the interpretation of Community law does not mean that the court or tribunal concerned is compelled to consider that a question has been raised within the meaning of Article 177. On the other hand, a national court or tribunal may, in an appropriate case, refer a matter to the Court of Justice of its own motion.

10. Secondly, it follows from the relationship between paragraphs (2) and (3) of Article 177 that the courts or tribunals referred to in paragraph (3) have the same discretion as any other national court or tribunal to ascertain whether a decision on a question of Community law is necessary to enable them to give judgment. Accordingly, those courts or tribunals are not obliged to refer to the Court of Justice a question concerning the interpretation of Community law raised before them if that question is not relevant, that is to say, if the answer to that question, regardless of what it may be, can in no way affect the outcome of the case.

11. If, however, those courts or tribunals consider that recourse to Community law is necessary to decide a case, Article 177 imposes an obligation on them to refer to the Court of Justice any question of interpretation which may arise.

12. The question submitted by the Corte di Cassazione seeks to ascertain whether, in certain circumstances, the obligation laid down by paragraph (3) of Article 177 might none the less be subject to certain restrictions.

13. It must be remembered in this connection that in its judgment of 27 March 1963 in Joined Cases 28–30/62 (*Da Costa*) the Court ruled that: 'Although paragraph (3) of Article 177 unreservedly requires courts or tribunals of a Member State against whose decision there is no judicial remedy under national law . . . to refer to the Court every question of interpretation raised before them, the authority of an interpretation under Article 177 already given by the Court may deprive the obligation of its purpose and thus empty it of its substance. Such is the case especially when the question raised is materially identical with a question which has already been the subject of a preliminary ruling in a similar case.'

14. The same effect, as regards the limits set to the obligation laid down by paragraph (3) of Article 177, may be produced where previous decisions of the Court have already dealt with the point of law in question, irrespective of the nature of the proceedings which led to those decisions, even though the questions at issue are not strictly identical.

15. However, it must not be forgotten that in all such circumstances national courts and tribunals, including those referred to in paragraph (3) of Article 177, remain entirely at liberty to bring a matter before the Court of Justice if they consider it appropriate to do so.

This extract contains a number of important observations concerning the relationship between national courts and the ECJ. It makes clear that a case can be relied on even if the ruling did not emerge from the same type of proceedings, and even though the questions at issue were not strictly identical. Provided that the point of law has already been determined by the ECJ, it can be relied on by a national court in a later case, thereby obviating the need for a reference. This is qualified in paragraph 15, in which the ECJ leaves it open to the national court to refer in such circumstances if it really wishes to do so. The message from the ECJ is none the less clear. There is a clear encouragement to national courts to rely on prior rulings of the ECJ, in instances where the substance of the legal point has already been adjudicated. Those earlier ECJ rulings will, in that sense, be regarded as precedents for the national courts.

This development of precedent has implications for the more general relationship between national courts and the ECJ. It modifies the original conception of a horizontal and bilateral relationship. The reasons are clear. In so far as ECJ rulings do have precedential value, they place the Court in a superior position to the national courts. The very existence of a system of precedent is indicative of a shift to a vertical hierarchy between the ECJ and national courts: the ECJ will lay down the legally authoritative interpretation, which will then be adopted by national courts. The creation of precedent serves also to render that relationship less bilateral, and more multilateral, since an earlier ECJ ruling can be relied on by any national court faced with the point of law that has already been decided by the ECJ.

The cases discussed thus far have concerned the impact of an earlier ECJ ruling when it has been Member State action which has been alleged to be in breach of the Treaty. The ECJ has been even more forceful when the impact of its previous decisions on the validity of Community legislation has been in issue. This is exemplified by the *ICC* case:

Case 66/80, International Chemical Corporation v. Amministrazione delle Finanze dello Stato
[1981] ECR 1191

Council Regulation 563/76 was designed to reduce the stocks of skimmed-milk powder. It made the grant of Community aid dependent on proof that the recipient had purchased a certain quantity of such skimmed milk held by an intervention agency. Compliance with this obligation was secured, *inter alia*, by the payment of security that was forfeited if the skimmed-milk was not in fact bought. The plaintiff received the Community aid and paid the security, but it did not comply with the obligation to buy the skimmed milk powder, and hence the national intervention agency did not release the security. In an earlier case the ECJ had found that Regulation 563/76 was invalid, because the price at which the milk powder was to be bought was regarded as disproportionately high.[27] The plaintiff, therefore, took the view that the security could not be forfeited, since it only served to ensure compliance with an obligation (to buy the milk powder) which was itself invalid. The Italian court requested a ruling on whether the earlier judgment, holding the regulation to be null and void, was effective in any subsequent litigation, or whether such a finding was only of relevance in relation to the court which had originally sought the ruling.

THE ECJ

11. The main purpose of the powers accorded to the Court by Article 177 is to ensure that Community law is applied uniformly by national courts. Uniform application of Community law is imperative not only when a national court is faced with a rule of Community law the meaning and scope of which is to be defined; it is just as imperative when the Court is confronted by a dispute as to the validity of an act of the institutions.

12. When the Court is moved under Article 177 to declare an act of one of the institutions to be void there are particularly imperative requirements concerning legal certainty in addition to those concerning the uniform application of Community law. It follows from the very nature of such a declaration that a national court may not apply the act declared to be void without once more creating serious uncertainty as to the Community law applicable.

13. It follows therefrom that although a judgment of the Court given under Article 177 of the Treaty declaring an act of an institution, in particular a Council or Commission regulation, to be void is directly addressed only to the national court which brought the matter before the Court, it is sufficient reason for any other national court to regard that act as void for the purposes of a judgment which it has to give.

14. That assertion does not however mean that national courts are deprived of the power given to them by Article 177 . . . and it rests with those courts to decide whether there is a need to raise once again a question which has already been settled by the Court where the Court has previously declared an act of a Community institution to be void. There may be such a need in particular if questions arise as to the grounds, the scope and possibly the consequences of the invalidity established earlier.

15. If that is not the case national courts are entirely justified in determining the effect on the cases brought before them of a judgment declaring an act void given by the Court in an action between other parties.

16. It should further be observed, as the Court acknowledged in its judgments . . . in Joined Cases 117/76 and 16/77, *Ruckdeschel and Diamalt*,[28] and Joined Cases 124/76 and 20/77, *Moulins de Pont-à-Mousson and Providence Agricole*,[29] that as those responsible for drafting regulations declared to be void the Council or the Commission are bound to determine from the Court's judgment the effect of that judgment.

17. In the light of the foregoing considerations and in view of the fact that by its second question the national court has asked, as it was free to do, whether Regulation 563/76 was void, the answer should be that that is in fact the case for the reasons already stated in the judgments of 5 July 1977.

[27] See Case 116/76, *Granaria v. Hoofdproduktschap voor Akkerbouwprodukten* [1977] ECR 1247.
[28] [1977] ECR 1753.
[29] [1977] ECR 1795.

The *ICC* case provides further evidence of the ECJ's attitude to precedent. The national court has discretion to refer a matter to the Court, even if the latter has already given judgment. However, the ECJ makes it patently clear that, although such a judgment is addressed primarily to the court which requests the original ruling, it can and should be relied on by other national courts before which the matter arises. The original ruling will, in this sense, have a multilateral and not merely a bilateral effect. A decision of the ECJ will, therefore, have a precedential impact on all national courts within the Community, and this serves to enhance the status of the ECJ as the supreme court within the Community system.

While an ECJ ruling on the validity of a Community regulation will have an *erga omnes* effect, the Court has made it clear that national courts cannot themselves find a Community norm to be invalid.

Case 314/85, Firma Foto-Frost v. Hauptzollamt Lübeck-Ost
[1987] ECR 4199[30]

A national court inquired whether it had the power to declare invalid a Commission decision, on the ground that it was in breach of a Community regulation on a certain issue.

THE ECJ

13. In enabling national courts against whose decisions there is a judicial remedy under national law to refer to the Court for a preliminary ruling questions on interpretation or validity, Article 177 did not settle the question whether those courts themselves may declare that acts of Community institutions are invalid.

14. Those courts may consider the validity of a Community act and, if they consider that the grounds put forward before them by the parties in support of invalidity are unfounded, they may reject them, concluding that the measure is completely valid. By taking that action they are not calling the existence of the Community measure into question.

15. On the other hand, those courts do not have the power to declare acts of the Community institutions invalid. As the Court emphasised in the judgment . . . (Case 66/80, *International Chemical Corporation* . . .), the main purpose of the powers accorded to the Court by Article 177 is to ensure that Community law is applied uniformly by national courts. That requirement of uniformity is particularly imperative when the validity of a Community act is in question. Divergences between courts in the Member States as to the validity of Community acts would be liable to place in jeopardy the very unity of the Community legal order and detract from the fundamental requirement of legal certainty.

. . .

17. Since Article 177 gives the Court exclusive jurisdiction to declare void an act of a Community institution, the coherence of the system requires that where the validity of a Community act is challenged before a national court the power to declare the act invalid must also be reserved to the Court of Justice.

18. It must also be emphasised that the Court of Justice is in the best position to decide on the

---

[30] See also, Case C–27/95, *Woodspring DC* v. *Bakers of Nailsea Ltd.* [1997] ECR I–1847.

validity of Community acts. Under Article 20 of the Protocol on the Statute of the Court of Justice of the EEC, Community institutions whose acts are challenged are entitled to participate in the proceedings in order to defend the validity of the acts in question. Furthermore, under the second paragraph of Article 21 of that Protocol the Court may require the Member States and institutions which are not participating in the proceedings to supply all information which it considers necessary for the purpose of the case before it. . . .

19. It should be added that the rule that national courts may not themselves declare Community acts to be invalid may have to be qualified in certain circumstances in the case of proceedings relating to an application for interim measures; however, that case is not referred to in the national court's question.

20. The answer to the first question must therefore be that national courts have no jurisdiction to declare that acts of Community institutions are invalid.

The ECJ, in *Atlanta*,[31] has provided guidance on the issue of interim relief raised in paragraph 19. Where a national measure is challenged, because of the alleged invalidity of the EC regulation on which it was based, the national court can grant interim relief. Certain conditions must however be met. The national court must have serious doubts about the validity of the EC measure, and must have referred the measure to the ECJ for a ruling. The interim relief must be necessary to prevent serious and irreparable damage to the applicant. The national court must take due account of the Community interest.[32] It must moreover respect any decision of the ECJ or CFI already given on the substance of the disputed measure.

7. THE EXISTENCE OF A QUESTION: THE '*ACTE CLAIR*' DOCTRINE

A national court may well feel that the answer to the issue is so clear that no reference to the ECJ is warranted. National courts have, in the past, refused to make a reference for this reason.[33] The conditions in which it is legitimate for a national court to take this course were considered in the *CILFIT* case:

---

[31] Case C–465/93, *Atlanta Fruchthandelsgesellschaft mbH* v. *Bundesamt für Ernährung und Forstwirtschaft* [1995] ECR I–3761; Cases C–143/88 and 92/89, *Zuckerfabrik Süderdithmarschen AG* v. *Hauptzollamt Itzehoe* [1991] ECR I–415; Case C–334/95, *Kruger GmbH & Co. KG* v. *Hauptzollamt Hamburg-Jonas* [1997] ECR I–4517.

[32] By considering whether, e.g., the EC measure would be deprived of all effectiveness if it were not implemented immediately.

[33] See, e.g., *Re Société des Pétroles Shell-Berre* [1964] CMLR 462.

Case 283/81, Srl CILFIT and Lanificio di Gavardo SpA v. Ministry of Health
[1982] ECR 3415

[Note ToA renumbering: Art. 177(3) is now Art. 234(3)]

The facts of this case have been set out above. In reading what follows, it is important to realize that the conditions which the ECJ stipulates may operate independently from the situation in which there is a precedent stemming from a prior ECJ decision. Where a precedent does exist, then the relationship of the ECJ and the national court is as set out in the preceding section. The *acte clair* doctrine may apply in circumstances where no such prior decision of the ECJ on the point currently exists. The extract follows on immediately from that given above.

THE ECJ

16. Finally, the correct application of Community law may be so obvious as to leave no scope for any reasonable doubt as to the manner in which the question raised is to be resolved. Before it comes to the conclusion that such is the case, the national court or tribunal must be convinced that the matter is equally obvious to the courts of the other Member States and to the Court of Justice. Only if those conditions are satisfied may the national court or tribunal refrain from submitting the question to the Court of Justice and take upon itself the responsibility for resolving it.

17. However, the existence of such a possibility must be assessed on the basis of the characteristic feature of Community law and the particular difficulties to which its interpretation gives rise.

18. To begin with, it must be borne in mind that Community legislation is drafted in several languages and that the different language versions are equally authentic. An interpretation of a provision of Community law thus involves a comparison of the different language versions.

19. It must also be borne in mind, even where the different language versions are entirely in accord with one another, that Community law uses terminology which is peculiar to it. Furthermore, it must be emphasised that legal concepts do not necessarily have the same meaning in Community law and in the law of the various Member States.

20. Finally, every provision of Community law must be placed in its context and interpreted in the light of the provisions of Community law as a whole, regard being had to the objectives thereof and to its state of evolution at the date on which the provision in question is to be applied.

21. In the light of all those considerations, the answer to the question submitted . . . must be that paragraph (3) of Article 177 of the EEC Treaty is to be interpreted as meaning that a court or tribunal against whose decisions there is no judicial remedy under national law is required, where a question of Community law is raised before it, to comply with its obligation to bring the matter before the Court of Justice, unless it has established that the question raised is irrelevant or that the Community provision in question has already been interpreted by the Court or that the correct application of Community law is so obvious as to leave no scope for any reasonable doubt. The existence of such a possibility must be assessed in the light of the specific characteristics of Community law, the particular difficulties to which its interpretation gives rise and the risk of divergences in judicial decisions within the Community.

(a) *CILFIT* AS PART OF A DISCOURSE WITH, AND CONSTRAINT ON, NATIONAL COURTS

The implications of the ECJ's decision in *CILFIT* have been considered by a number of commentators. Three different views of the case will be presented. Once again references to Article 177 should now be read as referring to Article 234.

G.F. Mancini and D.T. Keeling, From CILFIT to ERT: The Constitutional Challenge Facing the European Court[34]

CILFIT has many detractors. They accuse the Court of having capitulated in the face of the resistance that its role under Article 177 encountered in the late 1960s and early 1970s on the part of some of Europe's great courts. Like Shakespeare's shrew, Katherine, the Court surrendered, at the end of a long and painful taming process, having verified its evident inability to 'seek for rule, supremacy and sway'.

Such criticism is misconceived. It fails to appreciate the subtlety displayed by the Court in *CILFIT*, together with an acute understanding of judicial psychology. It is true that at least three supreme courts—the French Conseil d'Etat, the equivalent Greek organ, and the German Bundesfinanzhof—blatantly defied the authority of the Court of Justice. It is equally certain that, without reaching that extremity the supreme courts of all the other Member States simply ignored the obligation imposed by Article 177 on at least one or two occasions. But the Court of Justice was not 'tamed' by such conduct, nor can it be said to have rendered more than lip service to the argument—the so-called doctrine of *acte clair*—with which the national courts sought to justify their attitude. For proof of that one need only look at the most notorious instance of a breach of the third paragraph of Article 177: namely, the French Conseil d'Etat's refusal to make a reference in the *Cohn-Bendit* case. Such a refusal would clearly not have been justified under the *CILFIT* guidelines, no matter how liberally they are construed.

The correct analysis of *CILFIT* was given by a Danish scholar, Professor Hjalte Rasmussen,[35] who maintains that the judgment was based on an astute strategy of 'give and take'. The Court, recognizing that it could not in any case coerce the national courts into accepting its jurisdiction, concedes something—a great deal in fact, nothing less than the right not to refer if the Community measure is clear—to the professional or national pride of the municipal judge, but then, as we have just seen, restricts the circumstances in which the clarity of the provision may legitimately be sustained to cases so rare that the nucleus of its own authority is preserved intact (or rather consolidated because it voluntarily divested itself of a part of its exclusive jurisdiction). The objective of the Court is plain: by granting supreme courts the power to do lawfully that which they could in any case do unlawfully, but by subjecting that power to stringent conditions, the Court hoped to induce the supreme courts to use willingly the 'mechanism for judicial cooperation' provided by the Treaty. The result is to eliminate sterile and damaging conflicts and to reduce the risk that Community law might be the subject of divergent interpretations.

---

[34] N. 1 above, 4.
[35] H. Rasmussen, 'The European Court's *Acte Clair* Strategy in *CILFIT*' (1984) 9 *ELRev.* 242.

Mancini and Keeling then see *CILFIT* as a necessary dialogue between the ECJ and the national courts, with the intent being to rein in the latter. The 'give and take' of *CILFIT* involved the ECJ accepting the *acte clair* doctrine in principle, but placing significant constraints on its exercise in the hope that national courts would play the game and only refuse to refer when matters really were unequivocally clear.

(b) *CILFIT* AS A FLEXIBLE TOOL WHICH CAN BE MANIPULATED BY NATIONAL COURTS

Not all writers have, however, perceived the *CILFIT* ruling as a successful instance of the ECJ curbing the discretion of national courts. Compare the views of Mancini and Keeling with those of Arnull:

A. Arnull, The Use and Abuse of Article 177[36]

The effect of the *CILFIT* decision, it was argued,[37] would be to enable national judges to justify any reluctance they might feel to ask for a preliminary ruling by reference to a decision of the European Court. Of the factors to be borne in mind by national courts before they concluded that the meaning of a provision of Community law was clear, only the requirement that the different language versions be compared, it was submitted, had any teeth. However, even this requirement was less onerous than it seemed, as comparison of the different language versions would usually be carried out by reference to the version in the judge's own tongue. Moreover, the extension of the *da Costa* principle . . . risked opening the way for extensive examinations by national courts of the European Court's case law in order to elicit the answer to a particular question. In short, the over-all effect of *CILFIT* would be to encourage national courts to decide points of Community law for themselves. This could only jeopardise the uniform application of the Treaty.

[*Arnull then examined the practice of the United Kingdom courts that had cited the* CILFIT *decision. He concluded in the following vein.*[38]]

The English cases in which *CILFIT* has been cited and a reference made seem to support Rasmussen's view that the effect of that decision, despite appearances to the contrary, would be to make national courts wary of deciding points of Community law for themselves. However, the English cases where *CILFIT* was mentioned but no reference made show that sometimes the outcome of that ruling has been far less beneficial. They illustrate how it can be used to justify refusing to make a reference where the national court has formed a view as to how the points of Community law at issue should be resolved. Courts in the United Kingdom make far fewer references than courts in other Member States of comparable size and even some smaller ones, as the results of a project coordinated by the European University Institute in Florence show. It is therefore a serious matter when a decision of the European Court is used by the English Courts as a reason for failing to take a step which it might otherwise have been more difficult to avoid.

---

[36] (1989) 52 *MLR* 622, 626.

[37] Arnull is referring to an earlier piece, 'Reflections on Judicial Attitudes at the European Court' (1985) 34 *ICLQ* 168, 172.

[38] N. 36 above, 636–7.

(c) THE EXTENSION OF *CILFIT*

It has been argued that the conditions in *CILFIT* are in fact too restrictive, and that more discretion should be left to national courts. Advocate General Jacobs has, for example, argued that national judges should not have to consider all the official language versions of Community acts.[39] A loosening of the conditions has also been advocated by Rasmussen.

H. Rasmussen, Remedying the Crumbling EC Judicial System[40]

The thrust of a *CILFIT II* should be to give the initiative back to the judges of the Member States, trusting them to solve on their own far more questions of interpretation of Community law, including those which are not straightforward. In technical terms, a *CILFIT II* should operate so as to enlarge considerably the scope of the Community acts which are deemed to be *actes clairs*. The job to pin down on paper the demarcation line between those cases which will deserve EC judicial attention . . . and those classes of cases which the national judges ought to decide on their own responsibility will not be an easy one, but it is as indispensable as difficult.

8. THE EXISTENCE OF A QUESTION: THE DEVELOPMENT OF A MORE HIERARCHICAL JUDICIAL SYSTEM

Opinions will doubtless continue to differ on the rationale for, and success of, the ECJ's strategy in *CILFIT*. The doctrine of precedent, the *acte clair* concept, and sectoral delegation of functions to national courts do, however, have broader ramifications for the development of the judicial system in the Community as a whole, as the discussion within this section will show.

(a) PRECEDENT: NATIONAL COURTS AS COMMUNITY COURTS

Let us begin by considering precedent itself. The *Da Costa* decision, which introduced a *de facto* system of precedent into Community law, can be seen as a rational step for the ECJ to have taken. Rasmussen is surely correct in pointing out the advantages which this has for Community law.[41] The *authority* of the Court's decisions was thereby enhanced, in the sense that those decisions became authoritative rulings for national courts. The relationship between national courts and the ECJ was altered. It was no longer bilateral, where rulings were of relevance only to the national court which requested them. It became multilateral, in the sense that ECJ rulings had an impact on all national courts. This was to be expected, since it enabled the ECJ to construct a more truly authoritative system of Community law.

---

[39] Case C–338/95, *Wiener v. Hauptzollamt Emmerich* [1997] ECR I–6495.
[40] (2000) 37 *CMLRev.* 1071, 1109.   [41] N. 35 above, 249–50.

The decision in *CILFIT* to reinforce precedent was surely not unintentional. The ECJ would have been aware of the use made by national courts of the *Da Costa* ruling. The ECJ's determination to expand the precedential impact of past cases, notwithstanding this evidence, is also explicable: by expanding the precedential impact of past decisions, the ECJ thereby increased the authoritative scope of its past rulings. Those rulings were now to have authority for situations where the point of law was the same, even though the questions posed in earlier cases were different, and even though the proceedings in which the issue originally arose differed.

It might be objected that this legitimation of precedent leaves open the possibility that national courts may misinterpret past ECJ authority, and even refuse to make a reference, on mistaken assumptions about the existing state of Community law. There are two answers to this objection.

It can, on the one hand, be accepted that national courts may make such mistakes, but this does not undermine the rationality of having a system of precedent. The development of such a system is still perfectly sensible, provided that it leads *in aggregate* to a more effective regime of Community law. A system of precedent entails certain 'error costs': the possibility of mistakes by national courts. Precedent does, however, also have substantial and important 'benefits'. Most fundamentally, national courts now become enforcers of Community law in their own right. When the ECJ has decided an issue, national courts can then apply that ruling without further resort to the ECJ. The national courts are, in this sense, 'enrolled' as part of a network of courts adjudicating on Community law, with the ECJ at the apex of that network. National courts no longer apply only national law. They become 'delegates' in the enforcement of EC law, and part of a broader Community judicial hierarchy. The amount of work that can be processed through this enlarged judicial regime is thereby increased. The costs of precedent must therefore be weighed against the benefits. These include both the increased volume of Community law which can be litigated, mostly correctly, at any one time, and also the important symbolic advantage which flows from the recognition that the national courts are part of a real Community judicial hierarchy.

The legitimation of precedent can, on the other hand, be defended on the ground that there was not, in reality, any other choice for the ECJ. Let it be accepted that the original conception of the relationship between the ECJ and national courts really was bilateral; that ECJ rulings were meant to be of relevance only for the national court which requested them. This bilateral conception was certain to be placed under severe strain, precisely because it was always unrealistic. Taken literally it would mean that a ruling would have to be given, even if the inquiry sought by a national court replicated exactly that in an earlier decision made by the ECJ. The Court would be 'forced' solemnly to hear the matter, only to reach the same conclusion as it had done previously. A judicial system could not be supposed to exist on such terms. The ECJ would quickly tire of the waste of time and resources. The national courts would not see the sense of a system which placed pressure on them to allow issues to be litigated again, where the ECJ had already given a considered judgment.

(b) *ACTE CLAIR*: NATIONAL COURTS AS DELEGATES OF THE ECJ

Let us now move to *acte clair*. The ECJ's treatment of this concept fits with the preceding analysis. The Court in *CILFIT* was faced with a choice. It could have denied any place for the *acte clair* doctrine in EC law, the view espoused by Advocate General Capotorti.[42] The Court declined to follow this approach, and instead gave the doctrine limited support. Now it might be contended, as seen above, that the real objective was to deal it a death-blow, by hedging it around with a plethora of restrictions. Or, more moderately, that the Court's purpose was to convince national courts to be more responsible when using *acte clair*.

We must, however, distinguish purpose and effect. Even accepting the Mancini/Keeling thesis as to the Court's purpose, the effect of the decision is to leave cases which fall within these conditions to be decided by national courts. For such clear-cut cases, the national courts operate once again as the delegates of the ECJ for the application of Community law. The ECJ itself can then utilize its time in resolving more problematic cases. The strict conditions that the ECJ set help to ensure that national courts will not readily regard cases as coming within *acte clair* unless they really are free from interpretive doubt. Indeed, it has been argued, as seen above, that the conditions set in *CILFIT* are too limited and that they should be drafted in less restrictive terms.[43] It is doubtless true that national courts could still manipulate the existing criteria, should they be minded to do so, and thereby avoid the need to make a reference. Notwithstanding this possibility, the qualified approval given to the concept by the ECJ can still be regarded as rational.

This is in part because the cost/benefit analysis discussed in the context of precedent applies equally here. The fact that a national court might, on occasion, misapply the criteria, intentionally or unintentionally, does not render the exercise a failure. These costs have to be balanced against the benefits: straightforward cases can be disposed of expeditiously by national courts. Moreover, this method of dealing with such cases further emphasizes the role of national courts as but part of a broader judicial hierarchy, which has the ECJ at the apex.

The other reason why the qualified acceptance of *acte clair* can be regarded as rational is that there are 'safety' devices built into the system, quite independently of the conditions mentioned in *CILFIT*. The concern is that a national court might refuse to make a reference, even though the conditions in *CILFIT* were not present. However, even should this occur the matter might still come before the ECJ via a different legal system. Moreover, even if this should not transpire, it would still be open to the ECJ to correct aberrant interpretations by national courts, in the context of a case on a related point that has come before it. The danger of incorrect constructions made by national courts becoming embedded or ossified, while possible, should not, therefore, be over-stated.

---

[42] [1982] ECR 3415, 3439.   [43] See n. 39, 40 above.

(c) SECTORAL DELEGATION: SYSTEMATIC DELEGATION TO NATIONAL COURTS

This discussion would be incomplete if it did not take into account what is in effect *sectoral delegation of responsibility* to national courts. This phrase connotes a conscious choice made by the Community to devolve and delegate certain application and enforcement functions to the national courts, as in the context of competition policy.[44] The rationale for this devolution is instructive. The Commission is charged with the initial role in the enforcement of competition policy. It does not possess anything like the resources necessary for this task. It has therefore called on the national courts. These have always played a role in the enforcement of competition law, but this has been consciously generalized, so that straightforward competition violations are dealt with at national level. The Commission, the CFI, and the ECJ will deal with more difficult cases, or those which raise new issues of principle.

There is a very real connection between sectoral delegation, precedent, and the *acte clair* doctrine. Sectoral delegation is possible because of the accumulated weight of Community precedent in an area, and because, even where no precedent exists, the matter may none the less be evident within the sense of the *acte clair* doctrine.

It would, of course, be mistaken to pretend that there are no difficulties with the application of this regime.[45] But then few choices are ever problem-free. There may, of course, be mistakes made by the national courts, and in that sense error costs. The benefits are equally undeniable. Large numbers of cases can be disposed of more expeditiously, with a consequential improvement in the enforcement of Community principles. It does moreover facilitate the creation of a Community judicial system, in which the national courts play an increased role as Community, and not just national, judicial institutions. It is therefore unsurprising that the ECJ should have stated in its report for the 1996 IGC that 'national courts are called upon to play a central role as courts with general jurisdiction for Community law'.[46]

(d) SUMMARY

i. The relationship between national courts and the ECJ has been transformed by the development of precedent, *acte clair*, and sectoral delegation of responsibility.

ii. These developments have made national courts Community courts in their own right. They can dispose of cases without the need for a further reference to the ECJ. They can do so, where there is a Community precedent on the point, where the matter is so clear as to obviate the need for a reference, or where more general responsibility has been delegated to them in a particular area.

iii. The combined effect has been to render the relationship more vertical and multilateral than it was at the inception of the Community.

---

[44] See Ch. 25 below.   [45] *Ibid.*   [46] N. 3 above, para. 15.

9. THE DECISION TO REFER: THE NATIONAL COURT'S PERSPECTIVE

The discussion thus far has touched on factors which can influence the national court's decision whether to refer, in particular the existence of an ECJ ruling on the issue, and the *acte clair* doctrine. The more general factors, which a national court may take into account when making this decision, must now be considered. There are two criteria that must be satisfied before a reference may be made.

The first is that the question must be raised before the court or tribunal of the Member State. However, it has been seen that the *CILFIT* case held that a national court may raise a matter of its own motion, even if this has not been done by the parties.[47]

The second general criterion is that the national court must consider that a decision on the question is necessary to enable it to give judgment. *CILFIT* makes it clear that even a national court of last resort, covered by Article 234(3), must believe that this is so before it is obliged to make a reference. It should also be pointed out that Article 234 does not provide that the reference must be necessary, but that a decision on the question be necessary, to enable the national court to give judgment. The danger of confusing these two issues is brought out in the *Bulmer* case.

The *Bulmer* case shows the *early approach* of the UK courts to the exercise of the discretion accorded to them.

H.P. Bulmer Ltd. v. J. Bollinger SA
[1974] 2 WLR 202

Bollinger made champagne and claimed that the use of the word champagne by makers of cider, in the form of champagne cider, should be prohibited. As part of its claim, Bollinger alleged that the use of the word champagne to describe products other than those which came from the Champagne region in France was contrary to Community law. Bollinger asked that this question of Community law should be referred to the ECJ. The judge at first instance refused to make the reference, and Bollinger appealed to the Court of Appeal.

COURT OF APPEAL: LORD DENNING MR

The Condition Precedent to a Reference: It must be 'Necessary'

. . . An English court can only refer the matter to the European Court '*if it considers* that a decision on the question is necessary to enable it to give judgment'. Note the words '*if it considers*'. that is, 'if the *English court* considers'. On this point again the opinion of the English courts is final, just as it is on the matter of discretion . . .

. . .

---

[47] See also nn. 24 and 25 above.

(1) Guidelines as to whether a decision is necessary.

(i) The point must be conclusive.
The English court has to consider whether 'a decision on the question is *necessary* to enable it to give *judgment*' . . . In short, the point must be such that, whichever way the point is decided, it is conclusive of the case. Nothing more remains but to give judgment. . . .

(ii) Previous ruling.
In some cases, however, it may be found that the same point—or substantially the same point—has already been decided by the European Court in a previous case. In that event it is not necessary for the English court to decide it. It can follow the previous decision without troubling the European Court. But . . . the European Court is not bound by its previous decisions. So if the English court thinks that a previous decision of the European Court may have been wrong – or if there are new factors which ought to be brought to the notice of the European Court – the English court may consider it necessary to re-submit the point to the European Court. In that event, the European Court will consider the case again. It was so held . . . in the *Da Costa* case. . . .

(iii) Acte claire.
In other cases the English court may consider the point is reasonably clear and free from doubt. In that event there is no need to interpret the Treaty but only to apply it: and that is the task of the English court. . . .

(iv) Decide the facts first.
. . . As a general rule you cannot tell whether it is necessary to decide a point until all the facts are ascertained. So in general it is best to decide the facts first.

(2) Guidelines as to the exercise of discretion. Assuming that the condition about 'necessary' is fulfilled, there remains the matter of discretion. . . .

(i) The time to get a ruling. The length of time . . . before a ruling can be obtained from the European Court. This may take months and months. . . . Meanwhile, the whole action in the English court is stayed until the ruling is obtained. This may be very unfortunate, especially in a case where an injunction is sought or there are other reasons for expedition. . . .

(ii) Do not overload the Court. The importance of not overloading the European Court by references to it. If it were overloaded, it could not get through its work. . . .

(iii) Formulate the question clearly. The need to formulate the question clearly. It must be a question of *interpretation only* of the Treaty. It must not be mixed up with the facts. . . .

(iv) Difficulty and importance. The difficulty and importance of the point. Unless the point is really difficult and important, it would seem better for the English judge to decide it himself. For in so doing, much delay and expense will be saved. . . .

(v) Expense. The expense of getting a ruling from the European Court. . . .

(vi) Wishes of the parties. The wishes of the parties. If both parties want the point referred . . .

the English court should have regard to their wishes, but it should not give them undue weight. The English court should hesitate before making a reference against the wishes of one of the parties, seeing the expense and delay which it involves.

Lord Denning MR decided on the facts that a reference was not needed for a number of reasons.[48] Stephenson LJ, with whom Stamp LJ concurred, held that a reference should only be made if it was necessary, as opposed to being convenient or desirable, for the purposes of giving judgment, and found that there was, as yet, no such necessity.[49]

Lord Denning's judgment was not uncontroversial. The relevant issue is whether a decision on the question posed is necessary to enable the court to give judgment. It is not, as suggested at one stage in the judgment, whether a reference is necessary. Moreover, the guidelines themselves have been criticized. Francis Jacobs begins by critically considering Lord Denning's comments on cost and delay:

F.G. Jacobs, When to Refer to the European Court[50]

Lord Denning refers to these matters as grounds for refusing to exercise the discretion to refer; but there will be many situations . . . where both time and costs will be saved by an early reference. Indeed *Bulmer* v. *Bollinger* is the best illustration, since the time and costs incurred by a reference from the judge at first instance, resulting in a ruling from the European Court on the point at issue, will hardly be greater than those incurred by a fruitless appeal to the Court of Appeal against the refusal to make a reference. . . .

Closely connected with this is another factor mentioned by Lord Denning, the difficulty and importance of the point. . . . Clearly this is a matter which it is proper for the court to consider in exercising its discretion. But in Community law, as in English law, points of the first importance have often arisen in cases where little is at stake between the parties. *Costa* v. *ENEL* is the classic example, but there are many others.

The *Samex* case is more indicative of the *current approach* of the UK courts. While our courts have acknowledged the 'authority' of Lord Denning's approach, they have, none the less, been more ready to refer than he was.

Customs and Excise Commissioners v. ApS Samex (Hanil Fiber Industrial Co. Ltd., third party) [1983] 1 All ER 1042

An EC regulation allowed Member States to impose quantitative limits on the import of textiles from certain countries outside the Community. The implementation of the import scheme was left

---

[48] The time and expense involved; the facts had not been fully found; and the point was not a difficult one, [1974] 3 WLR 202, 216–17.

[49] [1974] 3 WLR 202, 218–19.   [50] (1974) 90 *LQR* 486, 492.

to the Member States, who were to issue import licences up to the quota for each year. The
defendant made a contract to buy goods from a non-Member State, which stipulated that the
goods had to be shipped by a certain date. The Customs authorities discovered that the goods had
been shipped outside the relevant dates, and imposed penalties on the defendant. The latter
responded by arguing that the Customs authorities were in breach of the Community regulation,
and sought a reference to the ECJ. Bingham J considered the guidelines set out by Lord Denning
MR in *Bulmer*. He then continued as follows.

HIGH COURT: BINGHAM J

In endeavouring to follow and respect these guidelines I find myself in some difficulty, because it
was submitted by counsel on behalf of the defendant that the issues raised by his client should be
resolved by the Court of Justice as the court best fitted to do so, and I find this a consideration
which does give me some pause for thought. Sitting as a judge in a national court, asked to decide
questions of Community law, I am very conscious of the advantages enjoyed by the Court of
Justice. It has a panoramic view of the Community and its institutions, a detailed knowledge of
the treaties and of much subordinate legislation made under them, and an intimate familiarity
with the functioning of the Common Market which no national judge denied the collective
experience of the Court of Justice could hope to achieve. Where questions of administrative
intention and practice arise the Court of Justice can receive submissions from the Community
institutions, as also where relations between the Community and non-Member States are in issue.
Where the interests of Member States are affected they can intervene to make their views
known. . . .

  Where comparison falls to be made between Community texts in different languages, all texts
being equally authentic, the multinational Court of Justice is equipped to carry out the task in a
way which no national judge, whatever his linguistic skills, could rival. The interpretation of
Community instruments involves very often not the process familiar to common lawyers of labori-
ously extracting the meaning from words used but the more creative process of supplying flesh to a
spare and loosely constructed skeleton. The choice between alternative submissions may turn not
on purely legal considerations, but on a broader view of what the orderly development of the
Community requires. These are matters which the Court of Justice is very much better placed to
assess and determine than a national court.

R. v. Plymouth Justices, ex parte Rogers
[1982] 3 WLR 1

The defendant was charged with using fishing nets which had a device to reduce the size of the
nets' mesh. This was contrary to Community and national law. The defendant admitted all the
evidence, except for the evidence that the device had in fact reduced the size of the nets. At the end
of the case the defendant claimed that the Community regulations and the national law were both
in breach of the Treaty, and sought a reference to the ECJ. The magistrates decided to make the
reference. The prosecution sought judicial review of the magistrates' decision, on the ground that
as there was an issue of fact still to be determined (*viz.* the issue whether the device had reduced
the size of the nets), therefore a reference was not necessary at this stage. In making this
argument, reliance was placed on Lord Denning MR in *Bulmer*, who had stressed that the facts
should be found before a reference was to be made.

QUEEN'S BENCH DIVISION DIVISIONAL COURT: LORD LANE CJ

Taking the argument of counsel for the applicant to its logical conclusion, it means that no court or tribunal can refer questions to the European Court under Article 177 unless all the facts have been admitted or found on all the issues in the case . . . This involves giving an extremely narrow interpretation to the word 'necessary' in Article 177.

Such an interpretation is not in accord with the general approach to Article 177 adopted by the European Court. . . .

[Lord Lane CJ then quoted from the Rheinmühlen case [1974] ECR 33, 38, and from the decision of the Court of Appeal in Polydor [1980] 2 CMLR 413, 426, 428.]

Having regard to these authorities, it is not right to say that the magistrates' court in this case had no jurisdiction to agree to refer questions to the European Court at the stage which the case which was then before them had reached. The validity of the regulations was the substantive issue before the court. As counsel for the respondent correctly pointed out, in a criminal case a defendant was entitled to have a decision whether there was a case to answer before he was called on to lead evidence in support of his defence. To rule on the submission, a decision on the questions of Community law raised by the respondent was necessary, since if the decision was in the respondent's favour he would be acquitted and if it was not, he would have to decide whether to contest further the one issue of fact which remained.

While United Kingdom courts do sometimes still refer to the guidelines in *Bulmer* they also tend to be more ready to make a reference. Sir Thomas Bingham MR encapsulates the more modern approach.[51]

[I]f the facts have been found and the Community law issue is critical to the court's final decision, the appropriate course is to refer the issue to the Court of Justice unless the national court can with complete confidence resolve the issue itself. In considering whether it can . . . the national court must be fully mindful of the differences between national and Community legislation, of the pitfalls which face a national court venturing into what may be an unfamiliar field, of the need for uniform interpretation throughout the Community and of the great advantages enjoyed by the Court of Justice in construing Community instruments. If the national court has any real doubt, it should obviously refer.

10. THE REFERENCE TO THE ECJ: THE INITIAL APPROACH, COME ONE, COME ALL

In the preceding section we considered the factors which the national court takes into account in deciding whether to refer a matter to the ECJ. This section, and the two which follow, will be concerned with the reverse side of the same coin: the way in

---

[51] *R. v. International Stock Exchange, ex p. Else* [1993] QB 534. See also *Polydor Ltd. v. Harlequin Record Shops Ltd.* [1980] 2 CMLR 413; *R. v. Pharmaceutical Society of Great Britain, ex p. The Association of Pharmaceutical Importers* [1987] 3 CMLR 951; *R. v. HM Treasury, ex p. Daily Mail and General Trust plc* [1987] 2 CMLR 1; *R. v. Secretary of State for the National Heritage, ex p. Continental Television BV* [1993] 2 CMLR 333; *R. v. Ministry of Agriculture, Fisheries and Food, ex p. Portman Agrochemicals Ltd.* [1994] 3 CMLR 18.

which the ECJ perceives its role when an issue is referred to it by a national court. On reading the materials it will become apparent that the ECJ's approach has altered since the inception of the Community.

(a) THE CORRECTION OF IMPROPERLY FRAMED REFERENCES

A not uncommon objection is that the questions framed by the national court are, in some sense, incorrect. The ECJ's approach, particularly in the early days of the Community, was, wherever possible, to read the references so as to preserve its ability to pass judgment on the case. This is exemplified by the *Schwarze* and *Costa* cases.

Case 16/65, Firma C. Schwarze v. Einfuhr und Vorratsstelle für Getreide und Futtermittel [1965] ECR 877

[Note ToA renumbering: Arts. 173 and 177 are now Arts. 230 and 234]

Schwarze obtained import licences from the EVSt to import barley. The EVSt fixed the rate of levy which should be paid, pursuant to a Council regulation. The rate of levy was fixed on the basis of a Commission decision. Schwarze argued that the levy rate was too high, and that the Commission decision was both procedurally and substantively illegal. The Finanzgericht therefore submitted a number of detailed questions to the ECJ. France argued that the questions being asked were concerned not with the interpretation of the Treaty, but rather with the validity of Community acts; and that the proper way of challenging such acts was via Article 173, and not via Article 177.

THE ECJ

It appears from the wording of the questions submitted that the Hessisches Finanzgericht is concerned not so much with the interpretation of the Treaty or of an act of a Community institution, as with a preliminary ruling on the validity of such an act under Article 177(1)(b). . . .

In its comments, the government of the French Republic complains that several of the questions submitted call for more than just an interpretation of the Treaty. The Court of Justice would, in answering these alleged questions of interpretation, actually be ruling on points involving not the interpretation of the Treaty but the validity of acts of the EEC institutions.

The contention of the French Republic that Article 177 cannot be used to obtain from the Court a ruling that such an act is null and void is pertinent. That provision does, however, expressly give the Court power to rule on the validity of such an act. Where it appears that the real object of the questions submitted by a national court is a review of the validity of Community acts rather than an interpretation thereof, the Court of Justice must nevertheless decide the questions immediately, instead of holding the referring court to a strict adherence to form which would only serve to prolong the Article 177 procedure and be incompatible with its true nature. Such a strict adherence to form is conceivable in actions between parties whose respective rights must be determined according to strict rules. It would not, however, be appropriate in the very special area of judicial cooperation provided for in Article 177, where the national court and the Court of Justice—each within its own jurisdiction and with the purpose of ensuring a uniform application of Community law—must together and directly contribute to the legal conclusions. Any other procedure would have the result of letting the national courts rule on the validity of acts of the Community.

Case 6/64, Costa v. ENEL
[1964] ECR 585

[Note ToA renumbering: Arts 169 and 170 are now Arts. 226 and 227]

The case has been considered above.[52] It will be remembered that Costa alleged that the nationalization of electricity in Italy infringed certain Articles of the Treaty. The Giudice Conciliatore in Milan sought a ruling on these arguments from the ECJ. The Italian Government objected that the questions posed by the Italian court were not confined to an interpretation of the Treaty, but also asked the ECJ to determine whether certain Italian laws were compatible with the Treaty; the Government argued that the only procedure by which this type of issue could be litigated was Articles 169 and 170.

THE ECJ

The complaint is made that the intention behind the question posed was to obtain, by means of Article 177, a ruling on the compatibility of a national law with the Treaty.

By the terms of this Article, however, national courts against whose decisions, as in the present case, there is no judicial remedy, must refer the matter to the Court of Justice so that a preliminary ruling may be given upon the 'interpretation of the Treaty' whenever a question of interpretation is raised before them. This provision gives the Court no jurisdiction to apply the Treaty to a specific case or to decide upon the validity of a provision of domestic law in relation to the Treaty, as it would be possible for it to do under Article 169.

Nevertheless, the Court has power to extract from a question imperfectly formulated by the national court those questions which alone pertain to the interpretation of the Treaty. Consequently a decision should be given by the Court not upon the validity of an Italian law in relation to the Treaty, but only upon the interpretation of the above mentioned Articles in the context of the points of law stated by the Giudice Conciliatore.

(b) CHALLENGING THE REASONS FOR MAKING A REFERENCE OR THE FACTS ON WHICH IT IS BASED

Litigants who do not wish the ECJ to make a ruling have often sought to argue that it should reassess the reason for making the reference, and/or the facts on which the reference was based. The ECJ held, in general, that it would not do so, and emphasized that this was the domain of the national court. Three examples can be given of this approach.

In *Costa* a further objection was that the ruling was not necessary for the solution of the dispute before the national court. The Court stated that Article 177 (now Article 234) 'is based on a clear separation of functions between national courts and the Court of Justice'. The ECJ was not empowered to 'investigate the facts of the case or to criticise the grounds and purpose of the request for interpretation'.[53]

In *Pierik*,[54] which was concerned with the application of social security schemes to

---

[52] See 277–8 above.   [53] N. 22 above, 593.
[54] Case 117/77, *Bestuur van het Algemeen Ziekenfonds, Drenthe-Platteland* v. *G. Pierik* [1978] ECR 825.

workers and their families within the Community, the Commission took the view that the question posed by the Dutch court was not relevant to the case at hand. The ECJ reiterated that Article 177 (now Article 234) was based on a clear division of function, and that this precluded it from judging the relevance of the questions asked, or from determining whether those concepts of Community law really were applicable to the case before the national court.

Case 35/76, Simmenthal SpA v. Ministero delle Finanze
[1976] ECR 1871

Simmenthal had imported meat into Italy from France. The meat was inspected at the border, and the costs of the inspection were levied on Simmenthal. It was argued by Simmenthal that the charges were equivalent to customs duties, that they were contrary to the Treaty and that it should be entitled to recover the money paid. Proceedings were begun in the Italian court, which referred certain questions to the ECJ.

THE ECJ

3. The Government of the Italian Republic has denied that the veterinary and public health inspections of the products referred to in the directives which it organised were carried out systematically and produces documents in support of its view that this is not the case. Consequently it has expressed doubts as to the relevance of the questions referred.

4. Article 177 of the EEC Treaty is based on a distinct separation of functions between national courts and tribunals on the one hand and the Court of Justice on the other hand and it does not give the Court jurisdiction to take cognisance of the facts of the case, or to criticise the reasons for the reference.

The ECJ's approach during the Community's early development was therefore an open and flexible one. The Court clearly did not wish to discourage litigants from having recourse to Community law. This was especially important precisely because, as we have seen, it was through Article 177 (now Article 234) that the Court was able to develop the fundamental doctrines of direct effect and supremacy. Nor did the ECJ wish to place obstacles in the path of national judiciaries who were minded to make use of Article 177 by refusing to answer questions unless they were perfectly framed. This would not have encouraged national judges to make use of novel legal machinery.

11. THE REFERENCE TO THE ECJ: THE FOUNDATIONS OF THE COURT'S AUTHORITY OVER THE CASES REFERRED TO IT

Notwithstanding the authorities considered in the previous section, the ECJ has, on occasion, considered the reasons for the making of a reference, and has also declined to give a ruling where it believed that it would be inappropriate to do so. The best known early example of this is the decision in the *Foglia* case.

Case 104/79, Pasquale Foglia v. Mariella Novello
[1980] ECR 745

[Note ToA renumbering: Arts. 95 and 177 are now Arts. 90 and 234]

Foglia made a contract to sell wine to Novello, and the contract stated that Novello would not be liable, *inter alia,* for any taxes levied by the French or Italian authorities which were contrary to EC law. The goods were carried by Danzas, a general transporter. The contract of carriage also contained a clause stipulating that Foglia would not be liable for charges which were contrary to EC law. Danzas in fact paid a French tax, and this was included in the bill submitted to Foglia, who paid the bill including the amount of the disputed tax, notwithstanding the clause in the contract of carriage which would have entitled him not to pay that portion of the total bill. Foglia then sought to recover this amount from Novello in an action before an Italian court. The latter refused to pay, relying on the clause in her contract with Foglia which stipulated that she would not be liable for any unlawful charge. Novello argued that the charge was contrary to Article 95. The Italian court sought a preliminary ruling whether the French tax was in fact contrary to Community law.

THE ECJ

9. In their written observations submitted to the Court of Justice the two parties to the main action have provided an essentially identical description of the tax discrimination which is a feature of the French legislation concerning the taxation of liqueur wines; the two parties consider that that legislation is incompatible with Community law. In the course of the oral procedure before the Court Foglia stated that he was participating in the procedure before the Court in the view of the interest of his undertaking as such and as an undertaking belonging to a certain category of Italian traders in the outcome of the legal issues involved in the dispute.

10. It thus appears that the parties to the main action are concerned to obtain a ruling that the French tax system is invalid for liqueur wines by the expedient of proceedings before an Italian court between two private individuals who are in agreement as to the result to be attained and who have inserted a clause in their contract in order to induce the Italian court to give a ruling on the point. The artificial nature of this expedient is underlined by the fact that Danzas did not exercise its rights under French law to institute proceedings over the consumption tax although it undoubtedly had an interest in doing so in view of the clause in the contract by which it was also bound and moreover of the fact that Foglia paid without protest that undertaking's bill which included a sum paid in respect of that tax.

11. The duty of the Court of Justice under Article 177 of the EEC Treaty is to supply all courts in the Community with the information on the interpretation of Community law which is necessary to enable them to settle genuine disputes which are brought before them. A situation in which the Court was obliged by the expedient of arrangements like those described above to give rulings would jeopardise the whole system of legal remedies available to private individuals to enable them to protect themselves against tax provisions which are contrary to the Treaty.

12. This means that the questions asked by the national court, having regard to the circumstances of this case, do not fall within the framework of the duties of the Court of Justice under Article 177 of the Treaty.

13. The Court of Justice accordingly has no jurisdiction to give a ruling on the questions asked by the national court.

The Italian judge then referred certain further questions to the ECJ. He asked, in effect, whether the preceding ruling was consistent with the principle that it was for the national judge to determine the facts and the need for a reference. These issues were dealt with by the ECJ in the second *Foglia* case.

Case 244/80, Pasquale Foglia v. Mariella Novello (No. 2)
[1981] ECR 3045

THE ECJ

12. In his first question the Pretore requested clarification of the limits of the power of appraisal reserved by the Treaty to the national court on the one hand and the Court of Justice on the other with regard to the wording of references for a preliminary ruling and of the appraisal of the circumstances of fact and law in the main action, in particular where the national court is requested to give a declaratory judgment.

. . .

14. With regard to the first question it should be recalled, as the Court of Justice has had occasion to emphasise in very varied contexts, that Article 177 is based on cooperation which entails a division of duties between the national courts and the Court of Justice in the interest of the proper application and uniform interpretation of Community law throughout all the Member States.

15. With this in view it is for the national court—by reason of the fact that it is seised of the substance of the dispute and that it must bear the responsibility for the decision to be taken—to assess, having regard to the facts of the case, the need to obtain a preliminary ruling to enable it to give judgment.

16. In exercising that power of appraisal the national court, in collaboration with the Court of Justice, fulfils a duty entrusted to them both of ensuring that in the interpretation and application of the Treaty the law is observed. Accordingly the problems which may be entailed in the exercise of its power of appraisal by the national court and the relations which it maintains within the framework of Article 177 with the Court of Justice are governed exclusively by the provisions of Community law.

17. In order that the Court of Justice may perform its task in accordance with the Treaty it is essential for national courts to explain, when the reasons do not emerge beyond any doubt from

the file, why they consider that a reply to their question is necessary to enable them to give judgment.

18. It must in fact be emphasised that the duty assigned to the Court by Article 177 is not that of delivering advisory opinions on general or hypothetical questions but of assisting in the administration of justice in the Member States. It accordingly does not have jurisdiction to reply to questions of interpretation which are submitted to it within the framework of procedural devices arranged by the parties in order to induce the Court to give its view on certain problems of Community law which do not correspond to an objective requirement inherent in the resolution of a dispute. A declaration by the Court that it has no jurisdiction in such circumstances does not in any way trespass upon the prerogatives of the national court but makes it possible to prevent the application of the procedure under Article 177 for purposes other than those appropriate for it.

19. Furthermore, it should be pointed out that, whilst the Court of Justice must be able to place as much reliance as possible upon the assessment by the national court of the extent to which the questions submitted to it are essential, it must be in a position to make any assessment inherent in the performance of its own duties in particular in order to check, as all courts must, whether it has jurisdiction. Thus the Court, taking into account the repercussions of its decisions in this matter, must have regard, in exercising the jurisdiction conferred upon it by Article 177, not only to the interests of the parties to the proceedings but also to those of the Community and of the Member States. Accordingly it cannot, without disregarding the duties assigned to it, remain indifferent to the assessments made by the courts of the Member States in the exceptional cases in which such assessments may affect the proper working of the procedure laid down by Article 177.

. . .

21. The reply to the first question must accordingly be that whilst, according to the intended role of Article 177, an assessment of the need to obtain an answer to the questions of interpretation raised, regard being had to the circumstances of fact and law involved in the main action, is a matter for the national court it is nevertheless for the Court of Justice, in order to confirm its own jurisdiction, to examine, where necessary, the conditions in which the case has been referred to it by the national court.

. . .

25. The reply to the fourth question must accordingly be that in the case of preliminary questions intended to permit the national court to determine whether provisions laid down by law or regulation in another Member State are in accordance with Community law the degree of legal protection may not differ according to whether such questions are raised in proceedings between individuals or in an action to which the State whose legislation is called in question is a party, but that in the first case the Court of Justice must take special care to ensure that the procedure under Article 177 is not employed for purposes which were not intended by the Treaty.

The important point of principle, indelibly imprinted on the law reports in *Foglia (No. 2)*, was that the ECJ would be the ultimate decider of the scope of its own jurisdiction. The reasoning is both subtle and dramatic. The judgment begins in orthodox fashion in demarcating the roles of national courts and the ECJ. A few paragraphs later this has been transformed: due regard was to be given to the national courts as to whether a response was required to a question, but the ultimate decision rested with the ECJ itself. If, in order to resolve this issue, further and better particulars were required from the national courts, then these must be forthcoming. When understood in this sense *Foglia* was not simply, or even primarily, about hypothetical cases and the like. It was about the primacy of control over the Article 177 (234) procedure. It was about the shape of the judicial hierarchy, involving Community and national courts, which operates through this Article. The original division of function between national courts and the ECJ may have been separate but equal, as manifested in the idea that the former decide whether to refer, while the latter gives the ruling on the matter placed before it. *Foglia* represented a reshaping of that conception. The ECJ was not simply to be a passive receptor, forced to adjudicate on whatever was placed before it. It was to assert some control over the suitability of the reference. The decision in the case itself, concerning the allegedly hypothetical nature of the proceedings, was simply one manifestation of this assertion of jurisdictional control. The ECJ would, in the future, 'make any assessment inherent in the performance of its own duties in particular in order to check, as all courts must, whether it has jurisdiction' (paragraph 19).

The *Foglia* case generated a considerable amount of comment when it first appeared. Bebr argued against the ruling. References to Article 177 should now be read as Article 234.

G. Bebr, The Existence of a Genuine Dispute: An Indispensable Precondition for the Jurisdiction of the Court under Article 177 EEC Treaty?[55]

In its well-established case law the Court of Justice has always viewed Article 177 as establishing a method of co-operation between the national courts and the Court, based on jurisdictional exclusivity rather than on a hierarchical superiority. Moreover it has systematically refused to review the grounds for questions raised and their relevance to the pending litigation, being obviously anxious to demonstrate that its function is limited to an interpretation of Community rules or to a review of validity of Community acts. . . .[56]

The Court refrained from reviewing the relevance of questions raised even in such instances in which a referring national court admitted that the question referred was not relevant to the litigation but that its clarification would be helpful for future cases. . . . Thus in *Rewe-Zentrale* v. *Hauptzollamt Emmerich*, the referring national court itself stated in its reference that one of the questions raised was not relevant to the litigation. Yet it considered the question appropriate because the litigation was a test case for a great number of similar forthcoming cases. . . .

. . . In this case it took note of several factors from which it inferred that the dispute was fabricated and that, therefore, it lacked jurisdiction. It is difficult to imagine how otherwise the Court could have reached such a conclusion. In a sense it went even further than merely reviewing the relevance of the questions raised. It reviewed the very nature of the dispute. Thus it noted the ambivalent stand of the plaintiff or, to cite another example, it viewed the failure of the carrier to challenge the legality of the imposed charges before the French courts as another indication of the fabricated nature of the litigation. . . .

The fabricated nature of a dispute as a precondition for the admissibility of a referral is a slippery concept, not without dangerous pitfalls. The French government which participated in the preliminary proceedings did not, it may be noted, even contest the jurisdiction of the Court. The

---

[55] (1980) 17 *CMLRev.* 525, 530–2.
[56] The author quotes examples of this approach including cases such as *Costa*.

Court did so of its own motion. Of course, there may be various shades and degrees to which litigation may appear fabricated. The situation may seldom be clear cut. Litigation in which a private party seeks to obtain a ruling in a test case in which it invokes a directly effective Community rule against a Member State before its own national courts may raise a similar problem; it may also lack the character of a genuine dispute. Who may say with any certainty that the plaintiff entertained the action seriously or whether he merely sought to obtain a decision in a test case which although of negligible interest to him, raised a question of principle? Of course, such litigation may, at first, appear less suspicious as to its genuine character than that which arises between private parties—simply because it may be easier in this instance to fabricate such a dispute.[57]

Not all were however opposed to the decision in *Foglia*. Wyatt argued in favour of the ruling.

D. Wyatt, Foglia (No. 2): The Court Denies it has Jurisdiction to Give Advisory Opinions[58]

Where Member States are alleged to have infringed the Treaty . . . actions may be initiated by the Commission or by other Member States to establish that fact under Articles 169 and 170 EEC. Both Articles contain pre-trial safeguards for Member States. Actions under either Article may be subjected to preliminary objections as to admissibility, which the Court will examine to consider whether or not the action in question is capable of securing its intended purpose, i. e. whether or not the Court's jurisdiction has been properly invoked.

. . . At bottom the controversy over the Court's decision in *Foglia* v. *Novello* . . . turns on the simple question whether or not references to the European Court from national courts are subject, before the European Court, to the same preliminary objections as to admissibility as any other claim upon the part of private parties, Member States, or Community institutions, to invoke the Court's jurisdiction. If they are not, then the guardians of the European Court's judicial functions, indeed of its very jurisdiction, within the framework of Article 177 EEC, are national courts, rather than the Court itself. It is not impossible that the draftsmen of the Treaty should have ordained such a thing. Simply improbable, in view of the departure from principle which it would involve: superior courts are invariably entrusted with the competence to determine their own jurisdiction.

[*Wyatt then demonstrates,* inter alia, *differing ways in which the ECJ would itself determine various jurisdictional issues, such as whether the body making the reference really was a court or not. At a later point in the article he refers to the reasoning in* Foglia (No. 2), *in which the ECJ emphasizes that it has no jurisdiction to give advisory opinions, and that it must not be compelled to answer questions which are only submitted to it as the result of procedural devices arranged between private parties. He then continues as follows:*]

While the Court must be able to place as much reliance as possible upon assessments by national courts of questions referred, it must, it insisted, be in a position to make *itself* any assessment inherent in the performance of its own duties, in particular in order to *check*, as all

---

[57] Bebr also objected to the *Foglia* ruling because of the difficulties which it would thereby create for the judge in the national courts, and for the implications which it might have for the ambit of direct effect.

[58] (1982) 7 *ELRev.* 186, 187–8, 190. Italics in the original.

courts must, whether it had jurisdiction. In exercising its *jurisdiction* under Article 177, the Court was bound to consider, not only the interests of the parties to the proceedings, but also the interests of the Community, and of the Member States. . . .

The Court's reasoning is convincing. It affirms its right to determine its own jurisdiction, and contrasts its own essentially judicial functions, with the delivery of advisory opinions. The distinction between a judgment and an advisory opinion is that the former affects the legal position of the parties to a dispute; the latter has no such effect. The capacity to give a *judgment* itself characterises the organ in question as a *court*. The capacity to give legal advice of course has no such corollary; indeed, the constitutional objection to courts giving advisory opinions in the United States has from early times been rationalised as a facet of the separation of powers between the executive and the judiciary. It will be noted that the preliminary rulings are binding on national courts which seek them—a feature rather at odds with the capacity to give advisory opinions (the International Court of Justice's jurisdiction to give Advisory Opinions is discretionary, and such Opinions—in contrast with its judgments in contentious proceedings—are not binding).

12. THE REFERENCE TO THE ECJ: DEVELOPING CONTROL OVER THE ARTICLE 234 PROCEDURE

(a) THE TYPES OF CASE WHERE THE ECJ WILL DECLINE JURISDICTION

The principle in *Foglia* lay dormant for some considerable time. Attempts to invoke it did not prove markedly successful.[59] This served to fuel the belief that the case was a one-off, justified by the particular circumstances, and unlikely to be repeated. It was business as usual, with the ECJ's 'come one, come all' strategy operating as before. The ECJ did however begin to make use of the *Foglia* principle,[60] and has been more willing to decline to take a case. These cases fall into a number of categories.

The *hypothetical nature of the question* provides one example. There are a number of reasons for refusing to give such rulings. They are, in part, practical, in the sense that it would be a waste of judicial resources to give a ruling in an hypothetical case, because the putative problem may never in fact transpire.[61] There are also problems of a more conceptual nature. If a case really is hypothetical it may be unclear precisely who should be the appropriate parties to the action, and there is the connected difficulty that the relevant arguments may not be put. Moreover, if the hypothetical problem does actually become 'concrete', it may not do so in exactly the form

---

[59] Case 261/81, *Walter Rau Lebensmittelwerke* v. *De Smedt Pvba* [1982] ECR 3961; Case 46/80, *Vinal SpA* v. *Orbat SpA* [1981] ECR 77; Case C–150/88, *Eau de Cologne and Parfumerie-Fabrik Glockengasse No. 4711 KG* v. *Provide Srl* [1989] ECR 3891.

[60] For earlier case law see Case 126/80, *Salonia* v. *Poidomani and Giglio* [1981] ECR 1563; Case C–368/89, *Crispoltini* v. *Fattoria Autonoma Tabacchi di Città di Castello* [1991] ECR I–3695.

[61] The wastage of resources argument will also be of relevance if the problem has become moot, in the sense that it has been resolved. Whether a problem has become moot can itself be contentious. Compare Cases C–422–424/93, *Zabala* v. *Instituto Nacional de Empleo* [1995] ECR I–1567 with Case C–194/94, *CIA Security International SA* v. *Signalson SA* [1996] ECR I–2201.

envisaged by the court's judgment, thereby giving rise to problems concerning the relevance of the original judgment in the light of what has subsequently transpired. While there may, therefore, be sound reasons for refusing to give opinions in hypothetical cases, there is also a fine line dividing that type of case from test cases.[62] One function of all legal systems is to enable people to plan their lives with knowledge of the legal implications of the choices they make. Test cases enable individuals to gain such knowledge. That the line between advisory opinions/hypothetical judgments and test cases can be a fine one is exemplified by the facts of the *Foglia* case itself.[63]

A second reason why the ECJ may not wish to give a ruling is that *the questions raised are not relevant to the resolution of the substantive action in the national court*. Given the complexity of Community law this may not be evident to the referring court. The *Meilicke*[64] case provides a good example of this. The action was brought by a German lawyer who sought to attack a particular theory of non-cash contributions of capital as it had been developed by the German courts. He held a single share in a German company and the company sought to raise capital. The German courts referred a question to the ECJ on the compatibility of the theory of disguised non-cash subscriptions with the Second Banking Directive. The ECJ declined to give a ruling. It referred to the duty of co-operation between national courts and the ECJ, accepting in principle that when the national court asked a question it should give an answer. However, it then went on to cite *Foglia (No. 2)*, drawing from that case the principle that the ECJ may, if necessary, have to examine the circumstances of the reference in order to determine whether the Court's jurisdiction had been properly invoked. The ECJ emphasized that the national court should find the facts first and then deal with any issues of national law. The ECJ declined to give a ruling, because it had not been shown that the issue of non-cash subscriptions was actually at stake in the main substantive action. This approach was apparent once again in the *Corsica Ferries* case.[65] The ECJ reiterated that it had no jurisdiction to rule on questions which

---

[62] Case C–412/93, *Leclerc-Siplec* v. *TFI Publicité and M6 Publicite*, Jacobs AG [1995] ECR I–179; Case C–200/98, *X AB and Y AB* v. *Rikssatteverket* [1999] ECR I–8261.

[63] It is far from self-evident that the *Foglia* case on its facts was a hypothetical case of the kind which the ECJ should have declined. The facts certainly did not represent a request for an advisory opinion concerning a hypothetical case, as that phrase is normally understood. The case was concerned with an actual seller of wine, whose business was being affected by a current French tax, which he believed to be contrary to Community law. The issues were sharply defined and current. The arguments utilized by the Court to suggest that the issue could and should have been resolved by a different route will not withstand examination. Danzas, the general carrier, would have no incentive to press the claim in France, even though it initially paid the tax. The company was a general carrier, and it would make no commercial sense for it to start an expensive suit which was of no specific concern to its business. There is also an explanation for Foglia's decision to pay Danzas, even though it could have resisted payment under the terms of its contract. If Foglia had resisted payment then one of two outcomes would have been likely. Either Danzas would have accepted this, swallowed the loss, and still not have pursued the claim in France because it would not be worthwhile; and/or it would have accepted this, but increased the cost of carriage by the amount of the tax for subsequent journeys and thence passed it on to Foglia. In either eventuality the legality of the tax under Community law might have remained uncontested, because both of the preceding outcomes would probably have been reached without formal litigation. Even if, contrary to the above, Danzas had resorted to formal litigation with Foglia, there is every reason to believe that this suit would have been initiated in Italy, since it would have been an ordinary contract suit the governing law of which would probably have been Italian. Compare *Foglia* to Case C–379/98, *PreussenElektra AG* v. *Schhleswag AG, in the presence of Windpark Reufenkoge III GmbH and Land Schleswig-Holstein* [2001] ECR I–2099, paras. 38–46.

[64] Case C–83/91, *Wienand Meilicke* v. *ADV/ORGA F. A. Meyer AG* [1992] ECR I–4871.

[65] Case C–18/93, *Corsica Ferries Italia Srl* v. *Corpo dei Piloti del Porto di Genova* [1994] ECR I–1783.

bore no relation to the facts or the subject-matter of the main action. It decided that only four of the possible eight questions met this criterion. The same concern with relevance was evident in the *Monin* case[66] where the ECJ held that it lacked jurisdiction to answer questions which did not involve an interpretation of Community law which was objectively required for the decision to be taken by the national court. It therefore declined to answer questions placed before it by an insolvency judge, given that this judge would not have to deal with these issues in the insolvency itself. The *Dias* case exemplifies the same general point.[67]

Case C–343/90, Lourenço Dias v. Director da Alfandega do Porto
[1992] ECR I–4673

[Note ToA renumbering: Art. 95 is now Art. 90]

Dias was a van driver who was prosecuted for modifying his imported vehicle in a manner which altered its categorization for tax purposes, without having paid the extra tax. The ECJ was presented with eight detailed questions from the national court concerning the compatibility of the relevant national rules with Article 95. The Portuguese government argued that the sole basis of the dispute was a narrow question concerning its tax system and that none of the questions actually referred dealt with that issue. The ECJ accepted that national courts were *prima facie* in the best position to decide on the need for a reference, and that therefore, in principle, the ECJ was bound to give a ruling when asked. It then qualified this obligation.

THE ECJ

17. Nevertheless, in Case 244/80 *Foglia (No. 2)* . . . paragraph 21, the Court considered that, in order to determine whether it has jurisdiction, it is a matter for the Court of Justice to examine the conditions in which the case has been referred to it by the national court. The spirit of cooperation which must prevail in the preliminary ruling procedure requires the national court to have regard to the function entrusted to the Court of Justice, which is to assist in the administration of justice in the Member States and not to deliver advisory opinions on general or hypothetical questions. . . .

18. In view of that task, the Court considers that it cannot give a preliminary ruling . . . where, *inter alia*, the interpretation requested relates to measures not yet adopted by the Community institutions (see Case 93/78, *Mattheus* . . .), the procedure before the court making the reference . . . has already been terminated (see Case 338/85 *Pardini* . . .) or the interpretation of Community law sought by the national court bears no relation to the actual nature of the case or to the subject-matter of the main action (Case 126/80 *Salonia* . . .).

19. It should also be borne in mind that . . . it is appropriate that, before making the reference to the Court, the national court should establish the facts of the case and settle the questions of purely national law. . . . By the same token, it is essential for the national court to explain the

---

[66] Case C–428/93, *Monin Automobiles-Maison du Deux-Roues* [1994] ECR I–1707.

[67] See also Case C–134/95, *Unità Socio-Sanitaria Locale No 47 di Biella (USSL)* v. *Istituto Nazionale per l'Assicurazione contro gli Infortuni sul Lavoro (INAIL)* [1997] ECR I–195; Cases C–320, 328, 329, 337, 338, and 339/94, *Reti Televisive Italiane SpA (RTI)* v. *Ministero delle Poste e Telecommunicazione* [1996] ECR I–6471.

reasons why it considers that a reply to its questions is necessary to enable it to give judgment. . . .

20. With this information in its possession, the Court is in a position to ascertain whether the interpretation of Community law which is sought is related to the actual nature and subject-matter of the main proceedings. If it should appear that the question raised is manifestly irrelevant for the purposes of deciding the case, the Court must declare that there is no need to proceed to judgment.

A third rationale for refusing to take a case may be that *the questions are not articulated clearly enough for the ECJ to be able to give any meaningful legal response*. It would not be a proper use of the ECJ's time to elicit the 'real' question from a reference which was very badly framed. This should be contrasted with the situation in which the ECJ does tease out the real question from a reference which has been imperfectly formulated.[68] The ECJ will not however alter the substance of the questions referred to it. Governments and the parties concerned are allowed to submit observations under Article 20 of the Statute of the Court. They are notified of the order of the referring court, and hence it would be wrong for the ECJ to alter the substance of the questions referred.[69]

Closely allied to this third rationale is a fourth, which covers the situation in which *the facts are insufficiently clear for the Court to be able to apply the relevant legal rules*. It is often thought that the ECJ merely responds in an abstract manner to very generally framed questions under Article 234. This is not so. The Court will normally only be able to characterize the nature of the relevant legal issue if it is presented with a reference which has an adequate factual foundation, as the following case makes clear.

Cases C–320–322/90, Telemarsicabruzzo SpA v. Circostel, Ministero delle Poste e Telecommunicazioni and Ministerio della Difesa[70] [1993] ECR I–393

An Italian court referred two questions to the ECJ concerning the compatibility of national provisions on the distribution of TV frequencies with EC competition law. The national court provided almost nothing by way of explanation for these questions.

THE ECJ

6. It must be pointed out that the need to provide an interpretation of Community law which will be of use to the national court makes it necessary that the national court define the factual

---

[68] Case C–88/99, *Roquette Frères SA* v. *Direction des Services Fiscaux du Pas-de-Calais*, [2000] ECR I–10465.
[69] Case C–235/95, *AGS Assedic Pas-de-Calais* v. *Dumon and Froment* [1998] ECR I–4531.
[70] See also Case C–157/92, *Banchero* [1993] ECR I–1085; Case C–386/92, *Monin Automobiles* v. *France* [1993] ECR I–2049; Case C–458/93, *Criminal Proceedings against Saddik* [1995] ECR I–511; Case C–167/94R, *Grau Gomis* [1995] ECR I–1023; Case C–2/96, *Criminal Proceedings against Sunino and Data* [1996] ECR I–1543; Case C–257/95, *Bresle* v. *Préfet de la Région Auvergne and Préfet du Puy-le-Dôme* [1996] ECR I–233.

and legislative context of the questions it is asking or, at the very least, explain the factual circumstances on which those questions are based.

7. Those requirements are of particular importance in the field of competition, which is characterized by complex factual and legal situations.[71]

8. The orders for reference contain no such details.

9. Although the Court has been provided with some information by the file submitted by the national court and the written observations . . ., and by the oral observations of the parties at the hearing, that information is fragmentary and does not enable the Court, in the absence of adequate knowledge of the facts underlying the main proceedings, to interpret the Community competition rules in the light of the situation at issue. . . .

10. In those circumstances, there is no need to give a decision on the questions submitted. . . .

The ECJ has now incorporated the results of its case law in its *Guidance on References by National Courts for Preliminary Rulings*.[72] Paragraph 6 states that the order for reference should contain a statement of reasons which is succinct but sufficiently complete to give the Court a clear understanding of the factual and legal context of the main action. It should include, in particular, a statement: of the essential facts; the relevant national law; the reasons why the national court referred the matter; and a summary of the parties' arguments where appropriate.

(b) THE LIMITS OF THE ECJ'S POWER TO DECLINE TO TAKE CASES

The ECJ has therefore exerted greater control over the admissibility of references than hitherto. It has however also made it clear that it will decline to give a ruling only if the issue of EC law on which an interpretation is sought is manifestly inapplicable to the dispute before the national court, or bears no relation to the subject-matter of that action.[73]

Case C–264/96, ICI Chemical Industries plc (ICI) v. Colmer (HM Inspector of Taxes) [1998] ECR I–4695

The case concerned the compatibility of UK tax legislation with the rules on freedom of establishment.

---

[71] These requirements are less pressing where the questions relate to specific technical points and the file contains sufficient information even though it does not provide an exhaustive description of the legal and factual situation: Case C–316/93, *Vaneetveld* v. *Le Foyer SA* [1994] ECR I–763.

[72] [1997] 1 CMLR 78.

[73] Case C–85/95, *Reisdorf* v. *Finanzamt Köln-West* [1996] ECR I–6257; Case C–118/94, *Associazione Italiana per il World Wildlife Fund* v. *Regione Veneto* [1996] ECR I–1223; Case C–129/94, *Criminal Proceedings against Bernaldez* [1996] ECR I–1829; Case C–446/93, *SEIM—Sociedade de Exportacoa de Materias, Ld* v. *Subdirector-Geral das Alfandegas* [1996] ECR I–73; Case C–266/96, *Corsica Ferries France SA* v. *Gruppo Antichi Ormeggiatori del Porto di Genova Coop. Arl* [1998] ECR–3949; Case C–355/97, *Landsgrundverkehrsreferent der Tiroler Landesregierung* v. *Beck mbH and Bergdorf GmbH, in liquidation* [1999] ECR I–4977; Cases C–215 and 216/96, *Bagnasco* v. *BPN and Carige* [1999] ECR I–135; Case C–379/98, *PreussenElektra AG*, n. 63 above, paras. 38–9.

THE ECJ

14. The United Kingdom Government has expressed doubts as to the relevance of the first question in determining the issue in the main proceedings. It argues that, even if the Act were found to entail a restriction on freedom of establishment, incompatible with Article 52 of the Treaty, this would have no bearing on the determination of the proceedings. ICI would in any event be denied the tax relief provided for under the Act, since the majority of the companies . . . are resident, not in other Member States, but in non-member countries.

15. According to established case law, it is solely for the national courts before which the proceedings are pending . . . to determine in the light of the particular circumstances of each case both the need for a preliminary ruling to enable them to give judgment, and the relevance of the questions which they submit to the Court . . . A request for a preliminary ruling from a national court may be rejected only if it manifest that the interpretation of Community law or the examination of the validity of a rule of Community law sought by that court bears no relation to the true facts or the subject matter of the main proceedings.

16. However, that is not the situation in the present case. The House of Lords observes that opinion differs as to the proper construction of section 258(5) . . . one interpretation of which makes it necessary to determine whether the Act is compatible with Article 52 of the Treaty.

(c) SUMMARY

i. The ECJ will decline to take a case under Article 234 in a number of situations. These are where the question referred is hypothetical, where it is not relevant to the substance of the dispute, where the question is not sufficiently clear for any meaningful legal response, and where the facts are insufficiently clear for the application of the legal rules.

ii. It will, however, only decline to give a ruling if the issue of EC law on which an interpretation is sought is manifestly inapplicable to the dispute before the national court, or bears no relation to the subject-matter of that action.

iii. The rhetoric in Article 234 cases will often be phrased in traditional terms: the judgment will speak of the co-operation between national courts and the ECJ and of the fact that it is for the national court to decide whether to refer or not.[74] This form of language *is* still meaningful. The relationship under Article 234 is a co-operative one. It is, however, now common for the traditional formula to be supplemented by appropriately drawn caveats which make it clear that the ECJ will not adjudicate if the questions are not relevant, or if they are hypothetical, etc.[75] With changes in the rhetoric have come changes in reality. The co-operation between national courts and the ECJ still exists, but the latter is no longer the passive receptor of anything thrust before it. It has begun to exercise more positive control over its own jurisdiction in the manner redolent of most other superior courts.

---

[74] See, e.g., Case C–435/97, *World Wildlife Fund (WWF)* v. *Autonome Provinz Bozen* [1999] ECR I–5613.
[75] See, e.g., Cases C–332, 333, and 335/92, *Eurico Italia Srl* v. *Ente Nazionale Risi* [1994] ECR I–711.

13. THE REFERENCE TO THE ECJ: INTERPRETATION VERSUS APPLICATION

Article 234 gives the ECJ power to interpret the Treaty, but does not specifically empower it to apply the Treaty to the facts of a particular case. Indeed the very distinction between interpretation and application is meant to be one of the characteristic features of the division of authority between the ECJ and national courts: the former interprets the Treaty, the latter apply that interpretation to the facts of a particular case. This distinction is, moreover, perceived to be a further reason for differentiating the relationship between national courts and the ECJ from that which exists in a more truly federal, appellate system where the superior court may well decide the actual case.

Theory and reality have not, however, always marched hand in hand. The dividing line between interpretation and application can be perilously thin. The more detailed is the interpretation provided by the ECJ, the closer does it approximate to application. The line between the two is rendered more problematic by the fact that many of the questions submitted to the Court are, by their nature, very detailed, and are capable of being answered only by a specific response.

Litigants have often argued that the Court should decline to give a ruling because the question posed was not seeking an interpretation, but rather an application, of the Treaty. The ECJ has not been deterred by such objections. Thus in *Van Gend en Loos*[76] it was argued that the question presented concerning the tariff classification of urea-formaldehyde required, not an interpretation of the Treaty, but rather an application of the relevant Dutch customs legislation. The Court rejected the argument, stating that the question did relate to interpretation: the meaning to be attributed to the notion of duties existing before the coming into force of the Treaty.

A willingness to respond in detail can be perceived in other cases. *Cristini* v. *SNCF*[77] was concerned with the meaning of Article 7(2) of Regulation 1612/68, which provides that a Community worker who is working in another Member State should be entitled to the same 'social advantages' as workers of that State. The question put by the French court was whether this meant that a provision which allowed large French families to have reduced rail fares was a social advantage within the ambit of Article 7(2). Although the ECJ denied that it had power to determine the actual case, in reality it did just that, and responded to the question by stating that the concept of a social advantage did indeed include the very type of fare reduction offered by the French rail authorities.[78] Another example of the detailed nature of the ECJ's rulings can be found in *Marleasing*.[79] The ECJ produced a detailed response to the question whether Article 11 of Directive 68/151 was exhaustive of the types of case in which the annulment of the registration of a company could be ordered. The judgment

---

[76] Case 26/62, [1963] ECR 1.   [77] Case 32/75, [1975] ECR 1085.   [78] *Ibid.*, para. 19.
[79] Case C–106/89, *Marleasing SA* v. *La Comercial Internacional de Alimentacion SA* [1990] ECR 4135.

furnished the national court with a very specific answer to this question, and one which required no more of the Spanish court than that it execute the ECJ's ruling.

The willingness of the ECJ to provide very specific answers to questions serves to blur the line between interpretation and application. It also serves to render the idea of the ECJ and the national courts being separate but equal, each having their own assigned roles, more illusory. The more detailed the ruling given by the ECJ, the less there is for the national court to do, other than literally apply that ruling to the case at hand, in the sense of executing an issue-specific judgment of the Court. It is, moreover, clear that the ECJ will be particularly motivated to provide 'the answer' in those cases where it wishes to maintain maximum control over the development of an area of the law. This is exemplified by cases concerning damages liability of Member States. The ECJ has furnished 'guidance' to the national court on whether there has been a serious breach for the purposes of the test.[80] It has also gone further, and stated that it has sufficient information to dispose of this aspect of the case in its entirety.[81]

There is much, however, which is of interest even in those situations where the ECJ does leave an important issue of application to national courts. It is clear that in many such cases the ECJ is delegating an aspect of Community law to the national courts. One of many examples will suffice for the present. The ECJ might decide that, as a matter of principle, the idea of collective dominance can apply within Article 82 (formerly Article 86).[82] It will lay down the general criteria by which the existence of this is to be judged. It will then pass the matter back to the national courts to determine whether these criteria exist on the facts of the case. In such cases it is misguided to perceive the national courts as simply applying Community law, in the sense of executing a decision which has already been arrived at by the ECJ. Their role is more important and creative than this. They will be helping in the articulation, development, and application of Community law itself under the guidance of the principles set out by the ECJ itself.

14. REFORM OF THE PRELIMINARY-RULING PROCEDURE

The 1961 volume of the European Court Reports had 350 pages. The 1999 volume contained in excess of 9,000 pages for the ECJ, and more than 3,500 for the CFI. It does not take a mathematical wizard to realize that the 'come one, come all' strategy would lead to practical problems of work-load for the ECJ. This is without the additional burdens which flow from increased membership of the Community, and from the expansion of its competence after the SEA, the TEU, and the ToA. The establishment of the CFI has done something to alleviate the workload, but not enough in the longer term.

The catalyst for discussion of reform was the IGC that led to the Nice Treaty. This

---

[80] Cases C–46 and 48/93, *Brasserie du Pêcheur SA* v. *Germany, R.* v. *Secretary of State for Transport, ex p. Factortame Ltd.* [1996] ECR I–1029.
[81] Case C–392/93, *R.* v. *HM Treasury, ex p. British Telecommunications plc* [1996] ECR I–1631.
[82] See Ch. 23 below.

was directly concerned with the institutional implications of enlargement, including the effect on the Community courts. Two important papers were produced which addressed the future shape of the Community's judicial architecture. One was written by those currently in the ECJ and CFI,[83] and will be referred to hereafter as the Courts' paper. The other was produced by a Working Party composed largely of former judges of the ECJ at the behest of the Commission.[84] The Chairman was Ole Due and it will be referred to as the Due Report.

The steep rise in the number of Article 234 references was of particular concern. These have increased by 85 per cent since 1990,[85] and account for more than half of the new cases brought before the ECJ, 264 references out of 485 cases. It was noted in the Courts' paper that 'the constant growth in the number of references for preliminary rulings emanating from courts and tribunals of the Member States carries with it a serious risk that the Court of Justice will be overwhelmed by its case-load'.[86] Both the Courts' paper and the Due Report consider different ways in which this problem could be tackled.[87]

(a) LIMITATION OF THE NATIONAL COURTS EMPOWERED TO MAKE A REFERENCE

There is a 'precedent' for a reform of this kind in Articles 61–69, the new Title IV of the EC Treaty. Article 68 stipulates that a preliminary ruling can be sought only by a national court or tribunal against whose decisions there is no judicial remedy in national law. Notwithstanding this the Courts' paper and the Due Report came down firmly against any general extension of this idea as a method of limiting preliminary rulings.[88] Nor is this surprising. The ability of any national court or tribunal to refer a question to the ECJ has been central to the development of Community law in both practical and conceptual terms.

In practical terms, it has been common for cases raising important points of EC law to have arisen on references from lower level national courts. To limit the ability to refer would result in cases being fought to the apex of national judicial systems merely to seek a reference to the ECJ. The ability to refer by any national court is also a safeguard against the possibility that the court of final resort may be 'conservative or recalcitrant' and hence reluctant to refer.

In conceptual terms, the ability of any national court or tribunal to refer has been

---

[83] *The Future of the Judicial System of the European Union (Proposals and Reflections)* (May 1999). Hereafter *FJS*.

[84] *Report by the Working Party on the Future of the European Communities' Court System* (Jan. 2000). Hereafter *WP*.

[85] *FJS*, n. 83 above, 5.

[86] *Ibid.*, 22. See also T. Kennedy, 'First Steps Towards a European Certiorari?' (1993) 18 *ELRev*.121.

[87] H. Rasmussen, n. 40 above; P. Craig, 'The Jurisdiction of the Community Courts Reconsidered', in G. de Búrca and J.H.H. Weiler (eds.), *The European Court of Justice* (Oxford University Press, 2001), ch. 6; J. Weiler, 'Epilogue: The Judicial Apres Nice', *ibid.*, 215; C. Turner and R. Munoz, 'Revising the Judicial Architecture of the European Union' (1999–2000) 19 *YBEL* 1; A. Arnull, 'Judicial Architecture or Judicial Folly? The Challenge Facing the European Union' (1999) 24 *ELRev*. 516; A. Dashwood and A. Johnston (eds.), *The Future of the Judicial System of the European Union* (Hart, 2001).

[88] *FJS*, n. 83 above, 23–4; *WP*, n. 84 above, 12–13.

of importance in emphasizing the penetration of EC law to all points of the national legal system. It is of course true that even if references were limited to courts of last resort, lower courts would still have the ability to apply existing precedent of the Community courts. The fact that any national court can refer does however emphasize that individuals can rely on their directly effective Community rights at any point in the national legal system.

(b) A FILTERING MECHANISM BASED ON THE NOVELTY, COMPLEXITY, OR IMPORTANCE OF THE QUESTION

A reform of this kind would allow the ECJ 'to concentrate wholly upon questions which are fundamental from the point of view of the uniformity and development of Community law'.[89] The Due Report advocated some constraints of this kind.[90] It suggested that national courts of final resort should be obliged to refer only questions which are 'sufficiently important for Community law', and where there is still 'reasonable doubt' after examination by lower courts. There are two problems with this suggestion.

One is that 'national courts and tribunals might well refrain from referring questions to the Court of Justice, in order to avoid the risk of their references being rejected for lack of interest'.[91] This could jeopardize the machinery for ensuring that Community law is interpreted uniformly throughout the Member States.

There is another problem that is not mentioned in the Courts' paper or in the Due Report. Those who are in favour commonly point to the USA where the Supreme Court will decide which cases it is willing to hear. It is however mistaken to believe that this can be directly copied in the EC. The crucial difference is that the US is an appellate system, and the EC is a referral system. In the USA if the Supreme Court declines to hear a case there will be a decision on the point of law from a lower tier federal court or state court. The situation in the EC is markedly different. The national court has not decided the case. It has referred a question for resolution by the ECJ. If the ECJ declines to answer the question because it is not sufficiently important or novel there is no decision by a Community court at all. This places the national court in a difficult position. It could attempt to decide the matter of EC law for itself. The national court could alternatively decline to decide the EC point one way or the other. The effect would be that the party who sought to rely on the EC point would be unable to do so, and the case would be decided on the assumption that this point was unproven.

(c) THE NATIONAL COURT PROPOSES AN ANSWER TO THE QUESTION

The national court could include in its reference a proposed reply to the question referred. The advantages were said, in the Courts' paper, to be that it would 'lessen the

---

[89] FJS, n. 83 above, 25. See also Case C–338/95, *Wiener v. Hauptzollamt Emmerich* [1997] ECR I–6495, Jacobs AG.

[90] WP, n. 84 above, 14–15.   [91] FJS, n. 83 above, 25.

adverse effect of the filtering mechanism on the co-operation between the national court and the Court of Justice, while the proposed reply could at the same time serve as the basis for deciding which questions need to be answered by the Court of Justice and which can be answered in the terms indicated'.[92] A similar proposal was advanced in the Due Report: national courts should be encouraged, though not obliged, to include in the preliminary questions reasoned grounds for the answers which the national court considers to be most appropriate. Where the ECJ concurred with the national court it could reply, specifying its reasoning by reference to the reasons given by the national court.[93]

There are however difficulties with this proposal. Most national courts are not specialists in EC law. It is one thing for the national court to identify a question that is necessary for the resolution of the case. It is another thing entirely to be able to provide an answer to that question, since many national courts will be ill-equipped for this inquiry. Higher level national courts may well be able to furnish some answer to the question posed. This proposal would none the less transform the task of such courts. There would have to be detailed argument before the national court of the EC issues in order to provide the judge with the requisite material from which to give an answer to the question posed.

Nor is it clear that this proposal would in reality relieve the case-load on the ECJ. Even if national courts are required or encouraged to provide an answer to the question posed, the ECJ will still have to give the matter some detailed consideration. This will be necessary in order to decide whether the question really can be answered in the terms indicated by the national court, or whether it needs to be answered afresh by the ECJ.

(d) TOWARDS AN APPELLATE SYSTEM

A more radical option considered in the Courts' paper would transform the system from one which is reference based, to one which is more appellate in nature.[94]

A more radical variant of the system would be to alter the preliminary ruling procedure so that national courts which are not bound to refer questions to the Court of Justice would be required, before making any reference, first to give judgment in cases raising questions concerning the interpretation of Community law. It would then be open to any party to the proceedings to request the national court to forward its judgment to the Court of Justice and to make a reference for a ruling on those points of Community law in respect of which that party contests the validity of the judgment given. This would give the Court of Justice the opportunity of assessing, at the filtering stage, whether it needed to give its own ruling on the interpretation of Community law arrived at in the contested judgment.

This proposal is interesting and has far-reaching implications. The Due Report was strongly opposed to this change, stating that 'such a proposal would debase the entire system of co-operation established by the Treaties between national courts and the Court of Justice'.[95]

---

[92] *FJS*, n. 83 above, 25–6. [93] *WP*, n. 84 above, 18.
[94] *FJS*, n. 83 above, 26. [95] *WP*, n. 84 above, 13.

If this proposal were to be adopted it would fundamentally alter the regime encapsulated in Article 234. This is not an objection in and of itself, but we should none the less be cognizant of the change thereby entailed. It would in effect change the regime from a reference system to an appellate one. The national court would give a decision on the case, and it would then be for the parties to 'require' the national court to make a reference to the ECJ. This was acknowledged in the Courts' paper.[96]

[S]uch a procedure would involve a fundamental change in the way in which the preliminary ruling system currently operates. Judicial co-operation between the national courts and the Court of Justice would be transformed into a hierarchical system, in which it would be for the parties to an action to decide whether to require the national court to make a reference to the Court of Justice, and in which the national court would be bound, depending on the circumstances, to revise its earlier judgment so as to bring it into line with a ruling by the Court of Justice. From the point of view of national procedural law this aspect of the system would doubtless raise problems which could not easily be resolved.

There are a number of *difficulties* with this proposal. To require national courts to decide the point of EC law would be to impose a burden on them which many lower tier courts would find difficult to discharge. It would be unlikely to relieve the ECJ's case-load, since there would always be an incentive on the losing party to seek a reference to the ECJ.[97] It would seem to involve the overruling of *Foto-Frost*,[98] since the national court might well be adjudicating on the validity of a Community law norm. It is, moreover, unclear in the Court's paper whether the losing party can request or require the national court to refer the matter to the ECJ.[99]

We should also consider the *possible advantages* of this proposal. An appellate system is more characteristic of a developed federal or confederal legal system, and it could be argued that the EC is ready for such a change. National courts have become more familiar with EC law, and it may be time to move towards an appellate regime where the national court gives judgment on the case, subject to appeal to the ECJ. We should not however go down this road on the assumption that it will thereby radically limit the case-load of the ECJ. It will not do so for the reason given above: there will always be an incentive for the loser before the national court to appeal to the ECJ.

(e) THE CREATION OF DECENTRALIZED JUDICIAL BODIES

The ECJ's burden would be eased if decentralized courts were created. This would also bring legal redress physically closer to citizens, who could obtain a preliminary ruling without the necessity of travelling to Luxembourg. The Courts' paper and the Due Report were however concerned that such decentralized courts would jeopardize the uniformity of Community law,[100] and the Due Report was against this option largely for this reason.[101] The Courts' paper sought to meet this concern by allowing a case to go to the ECJ from one of the decentralized courts.

---

[96] *FJS*, n. 83 above, 26.   [97] *FJS*, n. 83 above, 26.
[98] Case 314/85, *Firma Foto-Frost v. Hauptzollamt Lübeck-Ost* [1987] ECR 4199.
[99] *FJS*, n. 83 above, 26 is ambiguous in this respect.   [100] *FJS*, n. 83 above, 28; *WP*, n. 84 above, 21.
[101] *WP*, n. 84 above, 21–2.

The creation of some form of regional courts to supplement the existing judicial architecture of the Community has been advocated in the past,[102] but has generally been opposed by the CFI.[103] The suggestion was not taken up in the Nice Treaty. It may however be inevitable if the Community really does expand to encompass twenty-seven states. If such courts were to be created they should be part of the Community judicial machinery operating at national or regional level.

(f) CONFERMENT ON THE CFI OF JURISDICTION TO GIVE PRELIMINARY RULINGS: THE OPTION CHOSEN AT NICE

Prior to the Nice Treaty all requests for a preliminary ruling had to go to the ECJ. The ECJ's work-load would be reduced by allowing the CFI to give preliminary rulings. The possibility of conferring such jurisdiction on the CFI was canvassed positively, albeit cautiously, in the Courts' paper.[104] The Due Report was however opposed to this change, except in a limited number of special areas.[105]

There is none the less much to be said for the idea that the CFI should be able to give preliminary rulings. Many of the cases heard by the ECJ under Article 234 involve indirect challenge to the validity of Community norms where the non-privileged applicants cannot satisfy the standing criteria under Article 230. These cases are therefore concerned with the very issues that would be heard by the CFI in a direct action under Article 230. It is therefore difficult to argue that the CFI should not be able to hear such cases if they emerge indirectly via national courts as requests for preliminary rulings. There are moreover many Article 234 cases that involve no broad issue of principle at all. They are concerned with the detailed interpretation of a particular provision of a regulation or directive. These cases require judicial resolution. They do not require resolution by the ECJ.

The fact that the Nice Treaty modified Article 225 is therefore to be welcomed. Article 225(1) now provides that the CFI can hear actions covered by Articles 230, 232, 235, 236, and 238, with the exception of those cases assigned to a judicial panel and those reserved in the Statute for the ECJ itself. Article 225(3) accords the CFI power for the first time to hear preliminary rulings in specific areas laid down by the Statute of the Court of Justice. Where the CFI believes that the case requires a decision of principle, likely to affect the unity or consistency of Community law, it may refer the case to the ECJ. Preliminary rulings given by the CFI can, exceptionally, be subject to review by the ECJ, under the conditions laid down in the Statute, where there is a serious risk to the unity or consistency of Community law being affected.[106] A Declaration was attached to the modified Article 225 urging the ECJ and the Commission to give overall consideration to the division of competence between the ECJ and

---

[102] J-P. Jacque and J. Weiler, 'On the Road to European Union—A New Judicial Architecture: An Agenda for the Intergovernmental Conference' (1990) 27 *CML Rev.* 185.

[103] *Report of the Court of Justice on Certain Aspects of the Application of the Treaty on European Union— Contribution of the Court of First Instance for the Purposes of the 1996 Intergovernmental Conference*, May 1995.

[104] *FJS*, n. 83 above, 27.

[105] *WP*, n. 84 above, 22.

[106] See Art. 62 of the Statute of the Court of Justice.

CFI, and to submit proposals as soon as the revised Treaty enters into force.[107] There are further Declarations concerning the nature of the review procedure that is to operate under Articles 225(2) and 225(3), the practical operation of which is to be evaluated after three years.

15. CONCLUSION

i. The ECJ is not a fully developed federal, supreme court, either procedurally or institutionally. In procedural terms, individuals have no right of appeal to the ECJ. The ECJ will not actually decide the case, but rule on the point referred to it. In institutional terms, notwithstanding the creation of the CFI, the EC does not yet have the judicial hierarchy characteristic of federal systems. In countries such as the United States, there is a system of federal courts existing below the Supreme Court, which exercise jurisdiction over a particular area of the country.

ii. The original conception of the relationship between national courts and the ECJ does not however capture reality. Many of the developments have transformed this from a *horizontal* and *bilateral*, to a *vertical* and *multilateral*, relationship. These include: the assertion of Community law supremacy; the development of precedent; the *acte clair* doctrine; the sectoral devolution of responsibility to national courts; the ECJ's exercise of control over the cases that it will hear; and the blurring of the line between interpretation and application. These changes serve to emphasize the evolution of a Community judicial hierarchy in which the ECJ sits at the apex, as the ultimate Constitutional Court for the Community. It is assisted by national courts, which apply and interpret Community law.

iii. Reform of the Community's judicial architecture will remain on the agenda, notwithstanding the changes made by the Nice Treaty. There will be two crucial issues in an EC of twenty-seven states. The first will be whether there is a shift from a reference to an appellate system, in which the national courts make a decision in the case subject to appeal to a Community court. The second will be whether regional Community courts should be created on the model of federal judicial regimes elsewhere.

---

[107] It seems that the ECJ has submitted a working paper dealing with some aspects of the division of responsibilities between the ECJ and CFI. The criterion is the nature of the parties, rather than the subject matter. Thus the proposal is for the ECJ to retain jurisdiction in cases based on Arts. 230 and 232 brought by a Member State, a Community institution, or the ECB against an act or failure to act by the EP or Council, or both institutions acting jointly. It is also proposed that the ECJ should hear cases brought under the same Arts. by a Community institution or the ECB against an act or failure to act by the Commission.

16. FURTHER READING

(a) *Books*

ANDENAS, M. (ed.), *Article 177 References to the European Court—Policy and Practice* (Butterworths, 1994)

ANDERSON, D., *Preliminary Rulings* (Sweet & Maxwell, 1995)

DASHWOOD, A., and JOHNSTON, A. (eds.), *The Future of the Judicial System of the European Union* (Hart, 2001)

DE BÚRCA, G., and WEILER, J.H.H. (eds.), *The European Court of Justice* (Oxford University Press, 2001)

SCHERMERS, H., TIMMERMANS, C., KELLERMAN, A., and STEWART WATSON, J., *Article 177 EEC: Experiences and Problems* (North Holland, 1987)

(b) *Articles*

ANDERSON, D., 'The Admissibility of Preliminary References' (1994) 14 *YBEL* 179

ARNULL, A., 'The Use and Abuse of Article 177 EEC' (1989) 52 *MLR* 622

—— 'Does the Court of Justice Have Inherent Jurisdiction? ' (1990) 27 *CMLRev.* 683

—— 'The Evolution of the Court's Jurisdiction under Article 177 EEC' (1993) 18 *ELRev.* 129

—— 'Judicial Architecture or Judicial Folly? The Challenge Facing the European Union' (1999) 24 *ELRev.* 516

BARAV, A., 'Preliminary Censorship? The Judgment of the European Court in *Foglia* v. *Novello*' (1980) 5 *ELRev.* 443

BARNARD, C., and SHARPSTON, E., 'The Changing Face of Article 177 References' (1997) 34 *CMLRev.* 1113

BEBR, G., 'The Possible Implications of *Foglia* v. *Novello* II' (1982) 19 *CMLRev.* 421

—— 'Arbitration Tribunals and Article 177 of the EEC Treaty' (1985) 22 *CMLRev.* 489

CRAIG, P., 'The Jurisdiction of the Community Courts Reconsidered', in G. de Búrca and J.H.H. Weiler (eds.), *The European Court of Justice* (Oxford University Press, 2001), ch. 6

JACOBS, F.G., 'When to Refer to the European Court' (1974) 90 *LQR* 486

JACQUE, J.P., and WEILER, J., 'On the Road to European Union—A New Judicial Architecture: An Agenda for the Intergovernmental Conference' (1990) 27 *CMLRev.* 185

KENNEDY, T., 'First Steps Towards a European *Certiorari*?' (1993) 18 *ELRev.* 121

KOOPMANS, T., 'The Future of the Court of Justice of the European Communities' (1991) 11 *YBEL* 15

MAHER, I., 'National Courts as European Community Courts' (1994) 14 *LS* 226

MANCINI, F., and KEELING, D., 'From *CILFIT* to *ERT*: The Constitutional Challenge Facing the European Court' (1991) 11 *YBEL* 1

MATTLI, W., and SLAUGHTER, A.-M., 'Constructing the European Community Legal System from the Ground Up: The Role of Individual Litigants and National Courts', Harvard Jean Monnet Working Paper 6/96

RASMUSSEN, H., 'The European Court's *Acte Clair* Strategy in *CILFIT*' (1984) 9 *ELRev.* 242

—— 'Remedying the Crumbling EC Judicial System' (2000) 37 *CMLRev.* 1071

STRASSER, S., 'Evolution and Effort: The Development of a Strategy of Docket Control for the European Court of Justice & The Question of Preliminary References', Harvard Jean Monnet Working Paper 3/95

TURNER, C., and MUNOZ, R., 'Revising the Judicial Architecture of the European Union' (1999–2000) 19 *YBEL* 1

VAN GERVEN, W., 'The Role and Structure of the European Judiciary Now and in the Future' (1996) 21 *ELRev.* 211

WEILER, J., 'Epilogue: The Judicial Après Nice', in G. de Búrca and J.H.H. Weiler (eds.), *The European Court of Justice* (Oxford University Press, 2001), 215

WYATT, D., '*Foglia (No. 2)*: The Court Denies it has Jurisdiction to give Advisory Opinions' (1982) 7 *ELRev.* 186

12

REVIEW OF LEGALITY

1. INTRODUCTION

It is readily apparent from the materials considered thus far that the Community has power to advance policy through the promulgation of regulations, directives, and decisions. Any developed legal system must have a mechanism for testing the procedural and substantive legality of such measures. This topic is, therefore, concerned with access to justice and review of legality by the Community courts.

There are, as will be seen, a number of ways in which Community norms can be challenged, but the principal Treaty provision is Article 230 (ex Article 173):

The Court of Justice shall review the legality of acts adopted jointly by the European Parliament and the Council, of acts of the Council, of the Commission, and of the ECB other than recommendations and opinions, and acts of the European Parliament intended to produce legal effects *vis-à-vis* third parties.

It shall for this purpose have jurisdiction in actions brought by a Member State, the European Parliament, the Council or the Commission on the grounds of lack of competence, infringement of an essential procedural requirement, infringement of this Treaty or of any rule of law relating to its application, or misuse of powers.

The Court shall have jurisdiction under the same conditions in actions brought by the Court of Auditors and by the ECB for the purpose of protecting their prerogatives.

Any natural or legal person may, under the same conditions, institute proceedings against a decision addressed to that person or against a decision which, although in the form of a regulation or decision addressed to another person, is of direct and individual concern to the former.

The proceedings provided for in this Article shall be instituted within two months of the publication of the measure, or of its notification to the plaintiff, or, in the absence thereof, of the day on which it came to the knowledge of the latter, as the case may be.

It is evident that four broad conditions have to be satisfied before an act can successfully be challenged. The act has to be of a kind which is open to challenge at all; the institution or person making the challenge must have standing to do so; there must be a procedural or substantive illegality of a type mentioned in Article 230(1); and the challenge must be brought within the time limit indicated in Article 230(5).[1]

---

[1] Discussion of time limits can be found in A. Ward, *Judicial Review and the Rights of Private Parties in EC Law* (Oxford University Press, 2000), 205–9.

2. CENTRAL ISSUES

i. The judicial interpretation of Article 230 has been problematic, particularly the extent to which private individuals have standing to contest the legality of Community acts.

ii. The inter-relationship between direct challenge under Article 230, and indirect challenge, particularly under Article 234 (ex Article 177), is of importance.

iii. The connection between standing to seek judicial review and other aspects of citizen-involvement in the decision-making process is also significant. The link between participation in the making of the original decision or regulation and standing to challenge the resultant act before the Court is an important, albeit neglected, issue.

iv. It is important to be aware not only of the grounds of review available to a person accorded standing, *but also* the intensity of this review. The latter will determine the extent to which the CFI and ECJ are willing to review determinations made by the Community institutions, especially those of a discretionary nature.

3. THE RANGE OF REVIEWABLE ACTS

It is apparent that Article 230 (ex Article 173) allows the Court to review the legality of acts other than recommendations and opinions. This clearly covers regulations, decisions, and directives, which are listed in Article 249 (ex Article 189). The ECJ has, however, also held that this list is not exhaustive, and that other acts which are *sui generis* can also be reviewed, provided that they have binding force or produce legal effects.[2]

Case 22/70, Commission v. Council
[1971] ECR 263

[Note ToA renumbering: Arts. 173 and 228 are now Arts. 230 and 300]

The Member States acting through the Council adopted a Resolution on 20 March 1970, the object of which was to co-ordinate their approach to the negotiations for a European Road Transport Agreement (ERTA/AETR). The Commission disliked the negotiating procedure established in the Resolution, and sought to challenge it before the ECJ under Article 173.

THE ECJ

48. As regards negotiating, the Council decided, in accordance with the course of action decided upon at its previous meetings, that the negotiations should be carried on and concluded by the six Member States, which would become contracting parties to the AETR.

49. Throughout the negotiations and at the conclusion of the agreement, the States would act

---

[2] See also Case C–57/95, *France* v. *Commission (Re Pension Funds Communication)* [1997] 2 CMLR 935.

in common and would constantly coordinate their positions according to the usual procedure in close association with the Community institutions, the delegation of the Member State currently occupying the Presidency of the Council acting as spokesman.

50. It does not appear from the minutes that the Commission raised any objections to the definition by the Council of the objective of the negotiations.

51. On the other hand, it did lodge an express reservation regarding the negotiating procedure, declaring that it considered that the position adopted by the Council was not in accordance with the Treaty, and more particularly with Article 228.

52. It follows from the foregoing that the Council's proceedings dealt with a matter falling within the power of the Community, and that the Member States could not therefore act outside the framework of the common institutions.

53. It thus seems that in so far as they concerned the objective of the negotiations as defined by the Council, the proceedings of 20 March 1970 could not have been simply the expression or the recognition of a voluntary coordination, but were designed to lay down a course of action binding on both the institutions and the Member States, and destined ultimately to be reflected in the tenor of the regulation.

54. In the part of its conclusions relating to the negotiating procedure, the Council adopted provisions which were capable of derogating in certain circumstances from the procedure laid down by the Treaty regarding negotiations with third countries and the conclusion of agreements.

55. Hence, the proceedings of 20 March 1970 had definite legal effects both on relations between the Community and the Member States and on the relationship between institutions.

Whether a particular act does produce legal effects may sometimes be controversial,[3] as shown by the *IBM* case:

Case 60/81, International Business Machines Corporation v. Commission
[1981] ECR 2639

[Note ToA renumbering: Arts. 86 and 173 are now Arts. 82 and 230]

IBM sought the annulment of a Commission letter notifying it of the fact that the Commission had initiated competition proceedings against it, in order to determine whether it was in breach of Article 86. The letter was accompanied by a statement of objections, with a request that the company reply to it within a specified time. The Commission objected that the impugned letter was not an act challengeable for the purposes of Article 173.

THE ECJ

9. In order to ascertain whether the measures in question are acts within the meaning of Article 173 it is necessary, therefore, to look to their substance. According to the consistent case-law of the Court any measure the legal effects of which are binding on, and capable of affecting

---

[3] T.C. Hartley, *The Foundations of European Community Law* (Oxford University Press, 4th edn., 1998), 333–41.

the legal interests of, the applicant by bringing about a distinct change in his legal position is an act or decision which may be the subject of an action under Article 173 for a declaration that it is void. However, the form in which such acts or decisions are cast is, in principle, immaterial as regards the question whether they are open to challenge under that article.

10. In the case of acts or decisions adopted by a procedure involving several stages, in particular where they are the culmination of an internal procedure, it is clear from the case-law that in principle an act is open to review only if it is a measure definitively laying down the position of the Commission or the Council on the conclusion of that procedure, and not a provisional measure intended to pave the way for the final decision.

11. It would be otherwise only if acts or decisions adopted in the course of the preparatory proceedings not only bore all the legal characteristics referred to above but in addition were themselves the culmination of a special procedure distinct from that intended to permit the Commission or the Council to take a decision on the substance of the case.

12. Furthermore, it must be noted that whilst measures of a purely preparatory character may not themselves be the subject of an application for a declaration that they are void, any legal defects therein may be relied upon in an action directed against the definitive act for which they represent a preparatory step.

The applicant failed.[4] The letter was merely the initiation of the competition procedure, a preparatory step leading to the real decision at a later stage. The statement of objections did not, in itself, alter the legal position of IBM, although it might indicate, as a matter of fact, that it was in danger of being fined later.[5] This may be contrasted with the *SFEI* case.[6] It was held that in an area, such as competition policy, where the Commission has power to investigate and impose fines pursuant to a complaint from an individual, a letter from the Commission indicating that it did not intend to pursue the matter was reviewable as an act producing legal consequences.[7]

Article 230 now refers to review of the legality of: acts adopted jointly by the European Parliament and the Council; acts of the Council;[8] acts of the Commission; acts of the European Central Bank; and acts of the European Parliament intended to have legal effects for third parties. Prior to the TEU, Article 173 as it then was only formally applied to the Council and the Commission, but the ECJ held that the acts of

---

[4] See also Cases C–133 and 150/87, *Nashua Corporation* v. *Commission and Council* [1990] ECR I–719; Case C–282/95P, *Guérin Automobiles* v. *Commission* [1997] ECR I–503; Case T–554/93, *Saint* v. *Council* [1997] ECR II–563; Case T–81/97, *Regione Toscana* v. *Commission* [1998] ECR II–2889; Case C–159/96, *Portuguese Republic* v. *Commission* [1998] ECR I–7379; Case C–180/96, *United Kingdom* v. *Commission* [1998] ECR I–2265.

[5] Compare Case 53/85, *AKZO Chemie BV* v. *Commission* [1986] ECR 1965.

[6] Case C–39/93P, *Syndicat Français de l'Express International (SFEI)* v. *Commission* [1994] ECR I–2681.

[7] See also Cases T–10–12, 15/92, *SA Cimenteries CBR* [1992] ECR II–2667; Case C–25/92R, *Miethke* v. *European Parliament* [1993] ECR I–473; Case C–480/93, *Zunis Holding SA, Finan Srl and Massinvest SA* v. *Commission* [1996] ECR I–1; Case T–120/96, *Lilly Industries Ltd.* v. *Commission* [1998] ECR II–2571.

[8] The Court may review acts of the Council which are intended to have legal effects irrespective of whether they have been passed pursuant to Treaty provisions: Case C–316/91, *European Parliament* v. *Council* [1994] ECR I–625. However, decisions adopted by representatives of the Member States acting not as the Council, but as representatives of their governments, and thus collectively exercising the powers of the Member States, are not reviewable under Art. 230: Cases C–181 and 248/91, *European Parliament* v. *Council and Commission* [1993] ECR I–3685. It will be for the Court to decide whether a measure really was an act of the institutions or whether it was an act of the Member States acting independently: *ibid.*

the European Parliament were also susceptible to review by the ECJ.[9] Moreover, as Hartley states, if a Community institution which has the power to take reviewable decisions delegates that power to another institution, the Court will not be prevented from reviewing the acts of such a delegate.[10]

The general principle is that an act which is reviewable will have legal effect until it is set aside by the ECJ or the CFI,[11] and the challenge must be brought within the time limit specified in Article 230(5). The exception to this general rule is for acts which are tainted by particularly serious illegality, which are deemed to be 'non-existent'. Three consequences flow from the ascription of this label. First, the normal time limits for challenge do not apply, since such an act can never be cloaked with legality by the effluxion of time. A second is that such acts do not have any provisional legal effects. The final consequence is that, odd though it may seem, non-existent acts are not actually susceptible to annulment as such, because there is no 'act' to annul. A judicial finding that an act is non-existent will, however, have the same effect in practice as if it had been annulled. Thus in the *BASF* case[12] the CFI found that a decision of the Commission in competition proceedings against the PVC cartel was non-existent on the grounds that: the Commission could not locate an original copy of the decision which had been duly authenticated in the manner required by the Rules of Procedure; it appeared that the Commissioners had not agreed on the precise text of the decision; and it had been altered after it had been formally adopted. The non-existence of a measure should, said the CFI, be raised by the Court of its own motion at any time during the proceedings. The matter was appealed from the CFI to the ECJ,[13] which took a different view. It held that the defects were not so serious as to make the act non-existent, but it did, however, find that the decision was tainted by sufficient irregularity for it to be annulled.

The ECJ has, since the ToA, now been given limited power under Article 35 TEU (ex Article K. 7) to review the legality of framework decisions and decisions made pursuant to the re-modelled Third Pillar dealing with Police and Judicial Co-operation in Criminal Matters (PJCC). Actions can brought by the Commission or a Member State within two months of the publication of the measure.[14]

4. ARTICLE 230: STANDING FOR PRIVILEGED APPLICANTS

Article 230(2) (ex Article 173(2)) states that the action may be brought by a Member State, the European Parliament, the Council, or the Commission. It appears from this that these applicants are always allowed to bring an action, even where the decision is in fact addressed to some other person or body.

---

[9] Case 294/83, *Parti Ecologiste 'Les Verts' v. European Parliament* [1986] ECR 1339.

[10] Hartley, n. 3 above, 346–7. This assumes that the delegation itself is legal.

[11] Case C–137/92P, *Commission v. BASF AG* [1994] ECR I–2555.

[12] Cases T–79, 84–86, 89, 91–92, 94, 96, 98, 102, 104/89, *BASF AG v. Commission* [1992] ECR II–315.

[13] 13. Case C–137/92P, n. 11 above.

[14] The ECJ can also review acts made under the TEU where it is claimed that they should have been passed under the EC pillar: Case C–170/96, *Commission v. Council (Airport Transit Visas)* [1998] ECR I–2763.

The status accorded to the European Parliament in review proceedings has altered over time. Prior to the TEU it was not accorded any formal privileged status. In the 'Comitology' case[15] the ECJ rejected the Parliament's argument that it should have the same unlimited standing as other privileged applicants. The issue was considered again in the 'Chernobyl' case,[16] where the ECJ took a different view, and held that the EP could have a quasi-privileged status so as to protect its own prerogatives. Article 173(3) was re-drafted in the TEU so as to reflect the legal position in the Chernobyl judgment: the Parliament had standing to defend its own prerogatives.[17] The Nice Treaty has now added the European Parliament to the list of privileged applicants.

The Court of Auditors and the European Central Bank (ECB) remain covered by Article 230(3), so that they only have standing to defend their own prerogatives.[18]

5. ARTICLE 230(4): A CRITICAL ANALYSIS OF THE GENERAL STANDING RULES FOR NON-PRIVILEGED APPLICANTS

In many of the cases considered below the Court may refer to Article 173(2) EC, which was the provision on standing for non-privileged applicants prior to the TEU, or Article 173(4) which was the relevant provision after the TEU. The matter is now governed by Article 230(4), but there has been no change in the wording of this part of the Article. Article 230(4) clearly does not give non-privileged applicants unfettered access to the ECJ. Review proceedings can only be brought in three types of case.

The first is straightforward: the addressee of a decision can challenge it before the ECJ or CFI. The second type of case is where there is a decision addressed to another person, and the applicant claims that it is of direct and individual concern to him or her. The third type of case is where there is a decision in the form of a regulation, and the applicant claims that it is of direct and individual concern to him or her. Litigation has, not surprisingly, been primarily concerned with categories two and three.

Article 230 does not on its face allow any challenge by non-privileged applicants to directives. It has none the less been held that the mere fact that the measure is a directive will not in itself render the action inadmissible. The Community institutions cannot, by their choice of legal instrument, deprive the applicant of the judicial protection afforded by the Treaties. It is therefore possible for an applicant to argue that the directive was not in substance a directive, but was in reality a decision which

[15] Case 302/87, European Parliament v. Council [1988] ECR 5615.
[16] Case C–70/88, European Parliament v. Council [1990] ECR I–2041. See also Case C–156/93, European Parliament v. Commission [1995] ECR I–2019; Case C–187/93, European Parliament v. Council [1994] ECR I–2855; Case C–360/93, European Parliament v. Council [1996] ECR I–1195.
[17] For discussion of the scope of this phrase, see K. Bradley, 'Sense and Sensibility: Parliament v. Council Continued' (1991) 16 ELRev. 245; J. Weiler, 'Pride and Prejudice—Parliament v. Council' (1989) 14 ELRev. 334; G. Bebr, 'The Standing of the European Parliament in the Community System of Legal Remedies: A Thorny Jurisprudential Development' (1990) 10 YBEL 171.
[18] For discussion of what this means in the context of the ECB, see, P. Craig, 'EMU, the European Central Bank and Judicial Review', in P. Beaumont and N. Walker (eds.), Legal Framework of the Single European Currency (Hart, 1999), 112–15.

was of direct and individual concern. It is however clear that any applicant will have an uphill struggle to convince the CFI or ECJ that this is so.[19]

(a) CHALLENGES TO DECISIONS ADDRESSED TO ANOTHER PERSON

The seminal case on this type of situation is the decision in *Plaumann*:

Case 25/62, Plaumann & Co. v. Commission
[1963] ECR 95

In 1961 the German Government requested the Commission to authorize it to suspend the collection of duties on clementines imported from non-member countries. The Commission refused the request, and addressed its answer to the German Government. The applicant in the case was an importer of clementines, who sought to contest the legality of the Commission's decision. The ECJ adopted the following test to determine whether the applicant was individually concerned by the decision addressed to the German Government. The ECJ stated that the right of interested parties to bring an action should not be interpreted restrictively. It then set out the following test for individual concern.

THE ECJ

Persons other than those to whom a decision is addressed may only claim to be individually concerned if that decision affects them by reason of certain attributes which are peculiar to them or by reason of circumstances in which they are differentiated from all other persons and by virtue of these factors distinguishes them individually just as in the case of the person addressed. In the present case the applicant is affected by the disputed Decision as an importer of clementines, that is to say, by reason of a commercial activity which may at any time be practised by any person and is not therefore such as to distinguish the applicant in relation to the contested Decision as in the case of the addressee.

For these reasons the present action for annulment must be declared inadmissible.

The test in *Plaumann* has been cited in many later cases, and is still the leading authority on the point. It is therefore worth dwelling on the test itself, and its application to the facts of the case. It is then possible to understand why private applicants have found it so difficult to succeed under the *Plaumann* formula.

The *test itself* is encompassed in the first sentence in the paragraph. This serves to emphasize that applicants who claim to be individually concerned by a decision addressed to another can do so only if they are in some way differentiated from all other persons, and by reason of these distinguishing features singled out in the same way as the initial addressee. The test does, however, recognize that it is perfectly

---

[19] Case C–298/89, *Gibraltar v. Council* [1993] ECR I–3605; Case T–99/94, *Asociacion Espanalo de Empresas de la Carne (ASOCARNE) v. Council* [1994] ECR II–871; upheld on appeal, Case C–10/95P, [1995] ECR I–4149; Case T–135/96, *UEAPME v. Council* [1998] ECR II–2335, para. 63; Cases T–172, 175, and 177/98, *Salamander AG v. Parliament and Council* [2000] 2 CMLR 1099.

possible for there to be more than one applicant who is individually concerned in the above sense.

The *application of the test* to the facts of the case is contained in the second sentence of the quotation: the applicant in the instant case failed because it practised a commercial activity which could be carried on by any person at any time. The reason for rejecting the claim can be criticized on both pragmatic and conceptual grounds.

In *pragmatic terms* the application of the test can be criticized as being economically unrealistic. If there are, for example, only a very limited number of firms pursuing a certain trade this is not fortuitous, nor is the number of those firms likely to rise overnight. The presently existing range of firms is established by the ordinary principles of supply and demand: if there are two or three firms in the industry this is because they can satisfy the current market demand. Even if there should be a sudden surge of desire for clementines, the result will normally be that the existing firms will import more of the produce. The argument that the activity of importing clementines can be undertaken by any person, that the number might alter significantly, and that therefore the applicant is not individually concerned is thus unconvincing.

The ECJ's reasoning is also open to criticism in *conceptual terms*, since it renders it literally impossible for an applicant *ever* to succeed, except in a very limited category of retrospective cases. This can be demonstrated as follows. The test in the first sentence of the quotation has to be applied at some point in time. There are only three choices. The relevant question could be asked when the contested determination was made, when the application for review was lodged, or at some future, undefined date. It has been held that the test for standing must be judged when the application was lodged.[20] This is indeed sensible. However it is scant comfort to the applicant in a *Plaumann*-type case to be told that standing will be judged at the time the application is lodged, but then to be told the application fails because the activity of clementine-importing could be carried out by anyone at any time. On this reasoning the applicant would fail even if there were only one such importer at the time the challenged decision was made, since it would always be open to the Court to contend that others could enter the industry. On this reasoning no applicant could ever succeed, subject to the caveat considered below, since it could *always* be argued that others might engage in the trade at some juncture. This serves, in reality, to shift the focus to choice three: some future, ill-defined date. The 'possibility' of *locus standi* would be like a mirage in the desert, ever receding and never capable of being grasped. Even if our sole trader were to return to the Court and protest that it was still the only firm affected by the decision, it would still be greeted by the same reasoning as on its first foray into the judicial arena. It would still be argued that it had not demonstrated the necessary individuality because others might engage in the activity in question.[21] It must, as Advocate General Roemer stated, be mistaken to take account of the future effect of a decision. This is because it would never be possible to claim individual concern in

---

[20] Case T–16/96, *Cityflyer Express Ltd.* v. *Commission* [1998] ECR II–757, para. 30.
[21] In reality such reported forays would not be possible since there would be time-limit problems.

relation to a measure which had a permanent effect, even though at the time it was made the decision affected only one firm.[22]

The argument advanced in the previous paragraph might be opposed by contending that the applicant in the *Plaumann* case was properly rejected, since he was a member of an open rather than closed category of applicants, and hence was not individually concerned. Thus Hartley remarks that since anyone can import fruit, and the measure would apply to anyone who commenced operations after the decision came into effect, the category was an open one and the applicant was not individually concerned by it.[23] Open categories are regarded as those in which the membership is not fixed at the time of the decision; a closed category is one in which it is thus fixed. This reasoning serves however to reinforce, rather than dispel, the concerns. There are two problems with this reasoning.

On the one hand, in practical terms, the language of open categories is employed to rule out standing for any applicant, even if there is only a very limited number presently engaged in that trade, on the ground that others might undertake the trade thereafter. If the presence of such notional, future traders renders the category open, this ignores the practical economics that determine the number of those who supply a particular commodity.

On the other hand, in conceptual terms, the sense in which a category is said to be open at the time of the contested decision is questionable. To regard any category as open merely because others might notionally undertake the trade in issue is not self-evident. It would mean, of course, that any decision with a future impact would be unchallengeable because the category would be regarded as open. The test in *Plaumann* is based on the assumption that some people have attributes which distinguish them from others, and that they possess these attributes at the time the contested decision is made. The fact that others may acquire these attributes *later*, by joining that trade, does not, of course, mean that they are presently part of the same category as those who already do work in that sphere. Nor does it mean that they should somehow be regarded retrospectively as part of the limited group which initially operated in that area. The matter can be put quite simply. The fact that I may wish to become striker for England, a great pianist, or a clementine importer does not mean that I currently have the attributes associated with any of these roles in life.

The argument that the Court's test is unduly restrictive is reinforced when one realizes the reality of the situation in cases such as *Plaumann*. The applicants in this case were in effect objecting to a decision which affected them directly. The reason this was so was due to the structure of decision-making within this area of Community law: traders would request that a certain duty should be lowered, the request would be dealt with initially by the national authorities, who would then pass it on to the Commission. The Commission decision would then be given to the German Government, but the real addressees were the clementine importers themselves. The same point can be made about the *Piraiki-Patraiki* case: the decision to allow France

---

[22] Cases 10 and 18/68, *Società 'Eridania' Zuccherifici Nazionali* v. *Commission* [1969] ECR 459, 492. Roemer AG did not believe that the *Plaumann* test intended to limit applicants in this manner, but it is difficult to read the application of the test in *Plaumann* itself and in later cases in any other way.

[23] Hartley, n. 3 above, 356, 362–4.

to impose a quota on yarn coming from Greece was in reality also a decision prohibiting the Greek yarn producers from exporting to France during the relevant period.

Case 11/82, A.E. Piraiki-Patraiki v. Commission
[1985] ECR 207

The applicants were seven Greek cotton undertakings who sought to challenge a decision authorizing the French government to impose a quota system on imports into France of yarn from Greece between November 1981 and January 1982. Some of the undertakings had already entered into contracts to export cotton yarn to France, which were to be fulfilled during the quota period and which were for amounts of yarn in excess of that allowed by the quota. The Court quoted the test from the *Plaumann* case, and then reasoned as follows.

THE ECJ

12. The applicants argue that they fulfil the conditions set out above since they are the main Greek undertakings which produce and export cotton yarn to France. They argue that they therefore belong to a class of traders individually identifiable on the basis of criteria having to do with the product in question, the business activities carried on and the length of time during which they have been carried on. In that regard the applicants emphasize that the production and export to France of cotton yarn of Greek origin requires an industrial and commercial organization which cannot be established from one day to the next, and certainly not during the short period of application of the decision in question.

13. That proposition cannot be accepted. It must first be pointed out that the applicants are affected by the decision at issue only in their capacity as exporters to France of cotton yarn of Greek origin. The decision is not intended to limit the production of those products in any way, nor does it have such a result.

14. As for the exportation of those products to France, that is clearly a commercial activity which can be carried on at any time by any undertaking whatever. It follows that the decision at issue concerns the applicants in the same way as any other trader actually or potentially finding himself in the same position. The mere fact that the applicants export goods to France is not therefore sufficient to establish that they are individually concerned by the contested decision.

Certain of the applicants were given standing, because they had entered into contracts of sale with French customers before the date of the contested decision, which were to be performed during the time that it was in force.[24] Notwithstanding this fact the decision in *Piraiki-Patraiki* provides a good example of the difficulties which applicants face in this area. The applicants contended that they should be regarded as individually concerned, being those firms which would be affected by the quota introduced by the contested decision. Let us ignore the basic economics of supply and demand. Let us assume, even though there was no evidence whatsoever for the

---

[24] Case 11/82, [1985] ECR 207, paras. 15–19. The *Piraiki* case was however distinguished in Case C–209/94P, *Buralux SA v. Council* [1996] ECR I–615.

assumption, that there may be an incentive for new yarn traders to enter the market. None the less, it was quite clear that no other firm could plausibly set up production in this area during the limited period of the decision in question. It would take considerably longer than three months to adapt any factory to this line of business, let alone establish any new factory. The applicants' argument that they were a limited group was therefore forceful, albeit rejected by the ECJ.[25]

Applicants have been successful where the decision concerns a completed set of past events, as in *Toepfer*.

Cases 106 and 107/63, Alfred Toepfer and Getreide-Import Gesellschaft v. Commission[26]
[1965] ECR 405

The applicants were dealers in grain who applied for import licences from the German authorities on 1 October 1963. On that date the levy for the relevant imports was zero. Because of changes in market conditions the German authorities realized that the dealers would make large profits, and therefore rejected their applications until the levy had been increased. The importers were told that their applications would be rejected, and the Commission was asked to confirm this decision. The Commission then raised the levy from 2 October, and on 3 October confirmed the ban with regard to the period from 1–4 October inclusive. The dealers sought to have this decision annulled.

THE ECJ

It is clear from the fact that on 1 October 1963 the Commission took a decision fixing new free-at-frontier prices for maize imported into the Federal Republic as from 2 October, that the danger which the protective measures retained by the Commission were to guard against no longer existed as from this latter date.

Therefore the only persons concerned by the said measures were importers who had applied for an import licence during the course of the day of 1 October 1963. The number and identity of these importers had already become fixed and ascertainable before 4 October, when the contested decision was made. The Commission was in a position to know that its decision affected the interests and the position of the said importers alone.

The factual situation thus created differentiates the said importers, including the applicants from all other persons and distinguishes them individually just as in the case of the person addressed.

Therefore the objection of inadmissibility which has been raised is unfounded and the applications are admissible.

---

[25] Other restrictive examples of the application of *Plaumann* can be found in Case 1/64, *Glucoseries Réunies* v. *Commission* [1964] CMLR 596; Case 38/64, *Getreide-Import Gesellschaft* v. *Commission* [1965] CMLR 276; Case 97/85, *Union Deutsche Lebensmittelswerke GmbH* v. *Commission* [1987] ECR 2265; Case 34/88, *CEVAP* v. *Council* [1988] ECR 6265; Case 191/88, *Co-Frutta SARL* v. *Commission* [1989] ECR 793; Case 206/87, *Lefebvre Frère et Soeur SA* v. *Commission* [1989] ECR 275; Case T–398/94, *Kahn Scheepvaart* v. *Commission* [1996] ECR II–477; Case T–86/96, *Arbeitsgemeinschaft Deutscher Luftfahrt-Unternehmen and Hapag-Lloyd Fluggesellschaft mbH* v. *Commission* [1999] ECR II–179.

[26] See also Case 62/70, *Bock* v. *Commission* [1971] ECR 897; Case 11/82, *Piraiki-Patraiki*, n. 24 above.

(b) CHALLENGES TO REGULATIONS: THE TRADITIONAL APPROACH

The other type of problematic case is where an individual asserts that, although the challenged measure is in the form of a regulation, it is in reality a decision which is of direct and individual concern to him or her. Applications of this type have not proven to be notably successful, and the ECJ has not always adopted the same approach to the issue. There were initially two tests in the case law: the closed category test and the abstract terminology test. The latter is stricter than the former, and it is this test which until recently constituted the general rule applied by the Court. The *Calpak* case is one of the best examples of the abstract terminology test in operation, and the test has been used in many other judgments:[27]

Cases 789 and 790/79, Calpak SpA and Società Emiliana Lavorazione Frutta SpA v. Commission
[1980] ECR 1949

[Note ToA renumbering: Arts. 173 and 189 are now Arts. 230 and 249]

The applicants were producers of William pears, and they complained that the calculation of production aid granted to them was void. Under the terms of an earlier regulation, production aid was to be calculated on the basis of the average production over the previous three years, in order to avoid the risk of over-production. The applicants alleged that the Commission had in fact abandoned this method of assessing aid, and had based its aid calculation on one marketing year, in which production was atypically low. The applicants also claimed that they were a closed and definable group, the members of which were known to, or identifiable by, the Commission.

THE ECJ

6. The Commission's main contention is that as the disputed provisions were adopted in the form of regulations their annulment may only be sought if their content shows them to be, in fact, decisions. But in the Commission's view the provisions in question, which lay down rules of general application, are truly in the nature of regulations within the meaning of Article 189 of the Treaty
. . .

7. The second paragraph of Article 173 empowers individuals to contest, *inter alia*, any decision which, although in the form of a regulation, is of direct and individual concern to them. The objective of that provision is in particular to prevent the Community institutions from being in a position, merely by choosing the form of a regulation, to exclude an application by an individual against a decision which concerns him directly and individually; it therefore stipulates that the choice of form cannot change the nature of the measure.

8. By virtue of the second paragraph of Article 189 of the Treaty the criterion for

---

[27] See also Cases 103–109/78, *Beauport v. Council and Commission* [1979] ECR 17; Case 162/78, *Wagner v. Commission* [1979] ECR 3467; Case 45/81, *Alexander Moksel Import-Export GmbH & Co. Handels KG v. Commission* [1982] ECR 1129; Cases 97, 99, 193, & 215/86, *Asteris AE and Greece v. Commission* [1988] ECR 2181; Case 160/88R, *Fédération Européenne de la Santé Animale v. Council* [1988] ECR 4121; Case C–298/89, *Gibraltar v. Council* [1993] ECR I–3605; Case C–309/89, *Codorniu SA v. Council* [1994] ECR I–1853.

distinguishing between a regulation and a decision is whether the measure is of general application or not. . . .

9. A provision which limits the granting of production aid for all producers in respect of a particular product to a uniform percentage of the quantity produced by them during a uniform period is by nature a measure of general application within the meaning of Article 189 of the Treaty. In fact the measure applies to objectively determined situations and produces legal effects with regard to categories of persons described in a generalized and abstract manner. The nature of the measure as a regulation is not called in question by the mere fact that it is possible to determine the number or even identity of the producers to be granted the aid which is limited thereby.

10. Nor is the fact that the choice of reference period is particularly important for the applicants, whose production is subject to considerable variation from one marketing year to another as a result of their own programme of production, sufficient to entitle them to an individual remedy. Moreover, the applicants have not established the existence of circumstances such as to justify describing that choice . . . as a decision adopted specifically in relation to them and, as such, entitling them to institute proceedings under the second paragraph of Article 173.

11. It follows that the objection raised by the Commission must be accepted as regards the applications for the annulment of the provisions in the two regulations in question.

The abstract terminology test placed those who challenged an act in the form of a regulation in a difficult position. The purpose of allowing such challenge is, as the ECJ stated in *Calpak*, to prevent the Community institutions from immunizing matters from attack by the form of their classification. Thus, if regulations were never open to challenge the institutions could classify matters in this way, safe in the knowledge that private individuals could never contest them. Article 230(4) seeks to prevent this by permitting a challenge when the regulation is in reality a decision which is of direct and individual concern to the applicant. This requires, as acknowledged in *Calpak*, the Court to look behind the *form* of the measure, in order to determine whether in *substance* it really is a regulation or not.

The problem with the abstract terminology test is that, rather than looking behind form to substance, it comes perilously close to looking behind form to form. The reason is the nature of the test. A regulation will be accepted as a true regulation if, as stated in *Calpak*, it applies to 'objectively determined situations and produces legal effects with regard to categories of persons described in a generalized and abstract manner'. However, it is always possible to draft norms in this manner, and thus to immunize them from attack, more especially as the Court makes it clear that knowledge of the number or identity of those affected will not prevent the norm from being regarded as a true regulation. If the Commission wishes, therefore, to ensure that its measures are rendered safe from challenge under Article 230(4), it can frame them as regulations drafted in the abstract and generalized manner described above.

It is, moreover, quite clear that many measures which are regarded as 'true' regulations, and are in this sense characterized as 'legislative' in nature, are short-lived in terms of time and apply only to a very limited group. They do not differ from many measures, which in domestic legal systems would be classified as administrative in nature.

The Court has, however, adopted a closed-category approach in cases which deal with a completed set of past events, where the regulation relates to a fixed, closed category of traders. The category is closed in the sense that the disputed regulation applies to past events, and does not have a future impact. Thus in *International Fruit*[28] importers of apples from non-Member States applied in advance to the relevant national authorities for an import licence. The national authorities passed the information to the Commission, and the Commission enacted a regulation that laid down the criteria for these applications. The regulation applied to a closed category of persons, those who had made import applications in the previous week. The Court held that an action to challenge the regulation was admissible, and it characterized the measure as being a bundle of individual decisions.[29]

The abstract terminology test then provided the general criterion applied by the ECJ, with the closed-category test being used when the case concerned a completed set of past events.

(c) CHALLENGES TO REGULATIONS AND DECISIONS: THE MORE MODERN JURISPRUDENCE, THE SIGNIFICANCE OF *CODORNIU*

When the abstract terminology test was applied by the ECJ it was normally the sole criterion employed: if a regulation was a 'true' regulation as judged by this test then the Court would stop the inquiry, and conclude that the applicants did not have standing. There are, however, indications that the ECJ and CFI now view matters rather differently. They are willing to admit that a regulation may well be a 'true' regulation as judged by the abstract terminology test, *but* to admit that none the less such a regulation may well be of individual concern to certain applicants. This approach was initially employed in the context of anti-dumping,[30] but has now been used more generally, as shown by the *Codorniu* case.

Case C–309/89, Codorniu SA v. Council
[1994] ECR I–1853

The applicant challenged a regulation which stipulated that the term *crémant* should be reserved for sparkling wines of a particular quality coming from France or Luxembourg. The applicant made sparkling wine in Spain and held a trade mark which contained the word *crémant*. However, other Spanish producers also used this term. The Council argued vigorously that the measure was a regulation within the *Calpak* test, and that it could not be challenged irrespective of whether it was possible to identify the number or identity of those affected by it.

THE ECJ

18. As the Court has already held, the general applicability, and thus the legislative nature, of a measure is not called in question by the fact that it is possible to determine more or less exactly

---

[28] Cases 41–44/70, *International Fruit Company BV* v. *Commission* [1971] ECR 411.

[29] See also Case 100/74, *Société CAM SA* v. *Commission* [1975] ECR 1393; Case C–354/87, *Weddel* v. *Commission* [1990] ECR I–3487.

[30] Case C–358/89, *Extramet Industrie SA* v. *Council* [1991] ECR I–2501.

the number or even identity of the persons to whom it applies at any given time, so long as it is established that it applies to them by virtue of objective legal or factual situation defined by the measure in question in relation to its purpose. . . .

19. Although it is true that according to the criteria in the second paragraph of Article 173 of the Treaty the contested provision is, by nature and by virtue of its sphere of application, of a legislative nature in that it applies to the traders concerned in general, that does not prevent it from being of individual concern to some of them.

20. Natural or legal persons may claim that a contested provision is of individual concern to them only if it affects them by reason of certain attributes which are peculiar to them or by reason of circumstances in which they are differentiated from all other persons (. . . *Plaumann* . . .).

21. Codorniu registered the graphic trade mark 'Gran Cremant de Codorniu' in Spain in 1924. . . . By reserving the right to use the term 'crémant' to French and Luxembourg producers, the contested provision prevents Codorniu from using its graphic trade mark.

22. It follows that Codorniu has established the existence of a situation which from the point of view of the contested provision differentiates it from all other traders.

The willingness to accept that a norm could be a true regulation as judged by the abstract terminology test, and yet that it could be of individual concern, was certainly a liberalizing move. Under the earlier approach, the finding that a norm was a true regulation effectively ruled out standing for all applicants.

It would be rash, however, to assume that this has revolutionized Article 230(4) for private applicants. An applicant will still have to show individual concern, and *Plaumann* is the criterion, as is made clear from paragraph 20 of the judgment. We have already seen the difficulties with satisfying this test. If therefore the change in the Court's approach to regulations is to be meaningful it will have to be accompanied by a more liberal interpretation of the *Plaumann* test. If this does not occur then individuals will be no better off than they were before: they will, in principle, be able to challenge real regulations, but they will find it impossible to satisfy the requirement of individual concern. This would simply be 'déjà-vu all over again'. It is, therefore, crucially important to determine the meaning given to individual concern in this more recent jurisprudence. It may come as no surprise that differing interpretations can be detected in the case law. Three approaches can be distinguished.

(d) CHALLENGES TO REGULATIONS AND DECISIONS: THE MODERN JURISPRUDENCE POST-*CODORNIU*

The first may be termed the 'infringement of rights or breach of duty' approach. *Codorniu* itself exemplifies the former. The applicant was held to be individually concerned because it possessed a trade mark right which would have been over-ridden by the contested regulation.[31] An example of the latter is to be found in *Antillean Rice*.[32] The applicants challenged a decision fixing a minimum import price

---

[31] The argument failed in Case T–158/95, *Eridania Zuccherifici Nazionali SpA v. Council* [1999] ECR II–2219, para. 61.

[32] Cases T–480 and 483/93, *Antillean Rice Mills NV v. Commission* [1995] ECR II–2305.

for certain goods. The CFI held that the contested measure was in reality of a legislative nature,[33] but that the applicants were none the less individually concerned. This was because the relevant Article on which the contested decision was based meant that the Commission was under a duty to take account of the negative effects of such a decision introducing safeguard measures on the position of those such as the applicants.[34]

The second may be termed the 'degree of factual injury' approach. On this view the existence of individual concern will be determined by a largely factual inquiry into the significance of the contested regulation for the applicant. This is exemplified by *Extramet*,[35] where the ECJ allowed the applicant to challenge an anti-dumping regulation. The Court held that the applicant was individually concerned. It reached this conclusion because the applicant was the largest importer of the product on which the dumping duty was imposed. It was the end user of the product, its business activities depended to a very large extent on the imports, and it would be very difficult for it to obtain alternative sources of supply of the relevant product.

The third approach may be termed 'pure *Plaumann*'. Applicants will be denied standing by applying the *Plaumann* test *in the same manner* as in *Plaumann* itself. The fact that the applicant operates a trade which could, *in the sense considered above*, be engaged in by any other person will serve to deny individual concern. The existence of particular factual injury to the applicant will not be relevant, unless the case can be brought within the narrow exception for completed past events. Most cases have adopted this approach. In *Buralux*[36] the applicants were linked companies which sought to challenge a regulation concerning the shipment of waste within the EC. The ECJ held that the mere fact that it was possible to determine the number or even identity of those affected did not mean that the regulation was of individual concern to them, so long as the measure was abstractly formulated.[37] Individual concern was to be determined by the *Plaumann* test.[38] The applicants failed to satisfy this test since they were affected only as 'economic operators in the business of waste transfer between Member States, in the same way as any other operator in that business'.[39] The applicants' contention[40] that the CFI had erred by paying insufficient attention to the factual circumstances of their position was rejected by the ECJ. The ECJ held that the fact that the applicants were the only companies engaged in shipment of waste between France and Germany was not relevant, since the regulation applied to all waste shipments in the EC.[41] In *Campo Ebro*[42] the applicants sought to challenge a regulation concerned with sugar prices on the Spanish market. Their application was denied by the CFI. It held that even on the assumption that the applicants were the

---

[33] *Ibid.*, para. 65.

[34] *Ibid.*, paras. 70, 76; Cases T–32 and 41/98, *Government of the Netherlands Antilles* v. *Commission* [2000] ECR II–20. The argument failed in Cases T–38 and 50/99, *Sociedade Agricola dos Arinhos* v. *Commission*, 7 Feb. 2001.

[35] Case C–358/89, n. 30 above, para. 17; Case T–164/94, *Ferchimex SA* v. *Council* [1995] ECR II–2681.

[36] Case C–209/94P, n. 24 above.

[37] *Ibid.*, para. 24.   [38] *Ibid.*, para. 25.   [39] *Ibid.*, para. 28.   [40] *Ibid.*, para. 14.

[41] *Ibid.*, para. 29. The ECJ was, moreover, unwilling to accord the applicant standing on the ground that it had concluded contracts for the shipment of waste before the passage of the reg.: paras. 30–36. The Court distinguished *Piraiki-Patraiki*, n. 24 above.

[42] Case T–472/93, *Campo Ebro Industrial SA* v. *Council* [1995] ECR II–421.

only producers of isoglucose in Spain, they were only affected in 'their objective capacity as isoglucose producers in the same way as any other trader in the sugar sector who actually or *potentially*, is in an identical situation'.[43] The same reasoning is apparent in *Unifruit Hellas*.[44] The applicant's challenge to a regulation imposing countervailing charges on the import of apples from Chile failed. The CFI accepted that a regulation might be of individual concern to a trader, but then applied the *Plaumann* test in the same manner as in that case. The regulations concerned the applicant 'only in its objective capacity as an importer of Chilean apples in the same way as any other trader in an identical situation'.[45] Other cases on regulations exhibit the same reasoning.[46] The force of this third approach is also evident in more recent challenges to decisions as exemplified by the *Greenpeace* case.[47]

Case T–585/93, Stichting Greenpeace Council
(Greenpeace International) v. Commission
[1995] ECR II–2205

The applicants sought the annulment of a Commission decision granting financial assistance from the European Regional Development Fund for the construction of two power stations in the Canary Islands. The applicants were individual fishermen, farmers, and residents concerned by the impact of the development on tourism and the environment, and also environmental interest groups. The CFI began by reiterating the *Plaumann* test. The applicants expressly argued that the CFI should adopt a more liberal approach and accord standing based solely on the fact that loss or detriment would be suffered from the harmful environmental effects of the Commission's unlawful conduct. The CFI held that the *Plaumann* test was applicable irrespective of the nature, economic or otherwise, of the applicant's interest which was affected. It then continued as follows.

THE CFI

51. Consequently, the criterion which the applicants seek to have applied, restricted merely to the existence of harm suffered or to be suffered, cannot alone suffice to confer *locus standi* on an applicant, since such harm may affect, generally and in the abstract, a large number of persons who cannot be determined in advance in a way which distinguishes them individually in the same way as the addressee of a decision, in accordance with the case-law cited above [*Plaumann* etc]. That conclusion cannot be affected by the fact, put forward by the applicants, that in the practice of national courts in matters relating to environmental protection *locus standi* may depend merely

---

[43] *Ibid.*, para. 33. Emphasis added.
[44] Case T–489/93, *Unifruit Hellas EPE* v. *Commission* [1994] ECR II–1201.
[45] *Ibid.*, para. 23. The fact that the applicant had goods in transit did not suffice to single it out, and the CFI distinguished Case C–152/88, *Sofrimport Sàrl* v. *Commission* [1990] ECR I–2477.
[46] See, e.g., Case T–116/94, *Cassa Nazionale di Previdenza a Favore degli Avvocati e Procuratori* v. *Council* [1995] ECR II–1; Case T–122/96, *Federolio* v. *Commission* [1997] ECR II–1559; Case T–158/95, *Eridania*, n. 31 above; Case T–138/98, *Armement Coopératif Artisanal Vendéen (ACAV)* v. *Council* [2000] ECR II–341.
[47] Upheld on appeal: Case C–321/95P, *Stichting Greenpeace Council (Greenpeace International)* v. *Commission* [1998] ECR I–1651. See also Case T–117/94, *Associazione Agricoltori della Provincia di Rovigo* v. *Commission* [1995] ECR II–455; Case T–60/96, *Merck & Co. Inc.* v. *Commission* [1997] ECR II–849; Case T–192/95R, *Danielsson* v. *Commission* [1995] ECR II–3051; Case T–86/96, n. 25 above.

on their having a 'sufficient interest', since *locus standi* under the fourth paragraph of Article 173 of the Treaty depends on meeting the conditions relating to the applicants's being directly and individually affected by the contested decision.

[*The CFI then considered whether the applicants had standing judged by the* Plaumann *test.*]

54. The applicants are 16 private individuals who rely either on their objective status as 'local resident', 'fishermen' or 'farmer' or on their position as persons concerned by the consequences which the building of the two power stations might have on local tourism, on the health of Canary Island residents and on the environment. They do not, therefore, rely on any attribute substantially distinct from those of all the people who live or pursue an activity in the areas concerned and so for them the contested decision, in so far as it grants financial assistance for the construction of two power stations. . ., is a measure whose effects are likely to impinge on, objectively, generally and in the abstract, various categories of person and in fact any person residing or staying temporarily in the areas concerned.

55. The applicants thus cannot be affected by the contested decision other than in the same manner as any other local resident, fisherman, farmer or tourist who is, or might be in the future, in the same situation (Case 231/82, *Spijker* . . . Case T–117/94, *Rovigo* . . .).

56. Nor can the fact that the second, fifth and sixth applicants have submitted a complaint to the Commission constitute a special circumstance distinguishing them individually from all other persons and thereby giving them *locus standi*. . . . No specific procedures are provided for whereby individuals may be associated with the adoption, implementation and monitoring of decisions taken in the field of financial assistance granted by the ERDF. Merely submitting a complaint and subsequently exchanging correspondence with the Commission cannot therefore give a complainant *locus standi* . . .

[*The CFI then considered whether the applicant associations such as Greenpeace could have standing.*]

59. It has consistently been held that an association formed for the protection of the collective interests of a category of persons cannot be considered to be directly and individually concerned . . . by a measure affecting the general interests of that category, and is therefore not entitled to bring an action for annulment where its members may not do so individually (Cases 19 to 22/62, *Fédération Nationale* . . . ; Case 72/74, *Union Syndicale* . . ., Case 282/85, *DFH* . . . ; Cases T–447–449/93, *AITEC* . . .). Furthermore, special circumstances such as the role played by an association in a procedure which led to the adoption of an act within the meaning of Article 173 . . . may justify holding admissible an action brought by an association whose members are not directly and individually concerned by the contested measure (Cases 67, 68 and 70/85, *Van der Kooy* . . . and Case 313/90, *CIRFS* . . .).

60. The three applicant associations, Greenpeace, TEA and CIC, claim that they represent the general interest, in the matter of environmental protection, of people residing on Gran Canaria and Tenerife and that their members are affected by the contested decision; they do not, however, adduce any special circumstances to demonstrate the individual interest of their members as opposed to any other person residing in those areas. The possible effect on the legal position of the members of the applicant associations cannot, therefore, be any different from that alleged by the applicants who are private individuals. Consequently, in so far as the applicants . . . who are private individuals cannot . . . be considered to be individually concerned . . . nor can the members of the applicant associations. . . .

[*The CFI then examined whether the associations could come within the exception mentioned in the second part of paragraph 59 and decided on the facts that they could not.*]

Certain provisional conclusions can be drawn from the case law. It is clear that approaches one and two are more 'applicant friendly' than the third. It is clear also that when the ECJ or the CFI does employ the third approach the chances of the applicant being accorded standing are limited, to say the very least. The third approach does, moreover, appear to be the 'default position': it will be applied unless the applicant can bring itself within one of the other two. The laudable hope[48] that *Codorniu* might have led to a test for standing based on adverse impact, judged on the facts of the case, has not therefore been realised.[49]

(e) A RAY OF HOPE: A TEST OF SUBSTANTIAL ADVERSE EFFECT

Legal rules can always change. This is a trite proposition. It is also true and serves to make legal study especially interesting. Just when many legal commentators were giving up hope that the ECJ would alter its restrictive approach to standing, Advocate General Jacobs has produced a bold Opinion. He suggested a test whereby an applicant would have standing if the measure had, or was liable to have, a substantial adverse effect on his or her interests. Whether his suggestions are accepted by the ECJ remains to be seen. If they are, then the standing rules will be transformed. If they are not, then his Opinion will still remain as a principled critique of the existing law.

Case C-50/00 P, Unión de Pequeños Agricultores v. Council
unreported, March 2002

An association of farmers, UPA, sought the annulment of Regulation 1638/98, which amended substantially the common organisation of the olive oil market. The CFI dismissed the application because the members of the association were not individually concerned by the Regulation under Article 230(4). The UPA argued, *inter alia*, that it was denied effective judicial protection because it could not readily attack the measure via Article 234. The following extract contains the Advocate General's own summary of his Opinion.

ADVOCATE GENERAL JACOBS

102. . . .

(1) The Court's fundamental assumption that the possibility for an individual applicant to trigger a reference for a preliminary ruling provides full and effective judicial protection against general measures is open to serious objections:

— under the preliminary ruling procedure the applicant has no right to decide whether a reference is made, which measures are referred for review or what grounds of invalidity are raised and thus no right of access to the Court of Justice; on the other hand, the national court cannot itself grant the desired remedy to declare the general measure in issue invalid;

---

[48] A. Arnull, 'Private Applicants and the Action for Annulment under Article 173 of the EC Treaty' (1995) 32 *CMLRev.* 7.

[49] A. Arnull, 'Private Applicants and the Action for Annulment since *Codorniu*' (2001) 38 *CMLRev.* 7, 51–2.

— there may be a denial of justice in cases where it is difficult or impossible for an applicant to challenge a general measure indirectly (e.g. where there are no challengeable implementing measures or where the applicant would have to break the law in order to be able to challenge ensuing sanctions);

— legal certainty pleads in favour of allowing a general measure to be reviewed as soon as possible and not only after implementing measures have been adopted;

— indirect challenges to general measures through references on validity under Article 234 present a number of procedural disadvantages in comparison to direct challenges under Article 230 before the Court of First Instance as regards for example the participation of the institution(s) which adopted the measure, the delays and costs involved, the award of interim measures or the possibility of third party intervention.

(2) Those objections cannot be overcome by granting standing by way of exception in those cases where an applicant has under national law no way of triggering a reference for a preliminary ruling on the validity of the contested measure. Such an approach

— has no basis in the wording of the Treaty;

— would inevitably oblige the Community Courts to interpret and apply rules of national law, a task for which they are neither well prepared nor even competent;

— would lead to inequality between operators from different Member States and to a further loss of legal certainty.

(3) Nor can those objections be overcome by postulating an obligation for the legal orders of the Member States to ensure that references on the validity of general Community measures are available in their legal systems. Such an approach would

— leave unresolved most of the problems of the current situation such as the absence of remedy as a matter of right, unnecessary delays and costs for the applicant or the award of interim measures;

— be difficult to monitor and enforce; and

— require far-reaching interference with national procedural autonomy.

(4) The only satisfactory solution is therefore to recognise that **an applicant is individually concerned by a Community measure where the measure has, or is liable to have, a substantial adverse effect on his interests.** That solution has the following advantages:

— it resolves all the problems set out above: applicants are granted a true right of direct access to a court which can grant a remedy, cases of possible denial of justice are avoided, and judicial protection is improved in various ways;

— it also removes the anomaly under the current case-law that the greater the number of persons affected the less likely it is that effective judicial review is available;

— the increasingly complex and unpredictable rules on standing are replaced by a much simpler test which would shift the emphasis in cases before the Community Courts from purely formal questions of admissibility to questions of substance;

— such a re-interpretation is in line with the general tendency of the case-law to extend the scope of judicial protection in response to the growth of powers of the Community institutions (*ERTA, Les Verts, Chernobyl*);

(5) The objections to enlarging standing are unconvincing. In particular:

— the wording of Article 230 does not preclude it;
— to insulate potentially unlawful measures from judicial scrutiny cannot be justified on grounds of administrative or legislative efficiency: protection of the legislative process must be achieved through appropriate substantive standards of review;
.— the fears of over-loading the Court of First Instance seem exaggerated since the time-limit in Article 230(5) and the requirement of direct concern will prevent an insuperable increase of the case-load; there are procedural means to deal with a more limited increase of cases.

(6)   The chief objection may be that the case-law has stood for many years. There are however a number of reasons why the time is now ripe for change. In particular:

— the case-law in many borderline cases is not stable, and has been in any event relaxed in recent years, with the result that decisions on admissibility have become increasingly complex and unpredictable;
— the case-law is increasingly out of line with more liberal developments in the laws of the Member States;
— the establishment of the Court of First Instance, and the progressive transfer to that Court of all actions brought by individuals, make it increasingly appropriate to enlarge the standing of individuals to challenge general measures;
— the Court's case-law on the principle of effective judicial protection in the national courts makes it increasingly difficult to justify narrow restrictions on standing before the Community Courts.

The CFI has provided added momentum for change in the standing rules. In *Jego-Quere*[50] the CFI found that there were real difficulties in challenging the Community norm indirectly. It held that, in order to ensure effective legal protection, a person should be regarded as individually concerned by a Community measure of general application that concerns him directly, if the measure affects his legal position, in a manner which is both definite and immediate, by restricting his rights or by imposing obligations.

(f) SUMMARY OF THE CASE LAW

i. The ECJ and CFI are now willing to find that a regulation can be a true regulation in substance as well as form, as judged by the abstract terminology test, but that it is also of individual concern to a particular applicant.

ii. The central issue is therefore whether the applicant can show that he or she is individually concerned. This is so whether the challenged measure is a decision addressed to a third party, or a regulation which the applicant claims is in reality a decision.

iii. *Plaumann* is still the test for individual concern. The applicant must show that

---

[50] Case T–177/01, *Jego-Quere et Cie SA* v. *Commission*, 3 May 2002.

she has attributes or characteristics which distinguish her from all other persons and mark her out in the same manner as the addressee.

iv. This will normally be interpreted in the same manner as in *Plaumann* itself. The fact that the applicant operates a trade which could be engaged in by any other person will serve to deny individual concern. It is this interpretation of the *Plaumann* test which makes it almost impossible for most applicants to succeed. The existence of particular factual injury to the applicant will not usually be relevant.

v. *Plaumann* can, exceptionally, be interpreted more favourably to the applicant. This will be so where it can be shown that the challenged measure either infringed the applicant's right, or was in breach of a duty owed to the applicant. It will be rare for the CFI or ECJ to allow a claim merely because of the factual injury suffered by the applicant.

vi. Interest groups will not, in general, be in any better position than a private individual.

vii. The case law will of course take a very different turn if the ECJ follows the opinion of Advocate General Jacobs in the *UPA* case.

6. ARTICLE 230: STANDING FOR NON-PRIVILEGED APPLICANTS IN PARTICULAR AREAS

It has, in the past, been common to treat separately standing for non-privileged applicants in certain areas where it was clear that the ECJ had been more liberal. It could be argued that the changes post-*Codorniu* have brought the two bodies of law into line, and that the same test of individual concern will apply irrespective of the nature of the subject matter being challenged. There is some force in this view. This section will, none the less, continue to give a separate account of standing for antidumping, competition, and state aids for two reasons. First, the relevant Treaty Articles and regulations which apply in these areas have a marked impact on judicial decisions. Secondly, the interpretation accorded to the key criterion of individual concern is still arguably more liberal in these areas than it is in others.

(a) ANTI-DUMPING CASES

The Community may pass anti-dumping regulations to prevent those outside the Community from selling goods within the Community at too low a price, to the detriment of traders within the EC. The Community response is to impose an antidumping duty on the firm or firms in question. Whether a firm is in fact dumping, and the consequential issues concerning the calculation of its 'normal' production costs and prices of sale, are often very controversial.

Three types of applicant may wish to challenge an anti-dumping duty: the firm which initiated the complaint about dumping, the producers of the product which is subject to the anti-dumping duty, and the importers of the product on which the duty is imposed.[51] In deciding whether to accord standing to such applicants the Court is placed in a difficult position since anti-dumping duties must be imposed by regulation, as opposed to decision. If, therefore, the Court holds that the regulation is not in fact a regulation at all, then it is arguable that the Commission had no power to impose the measure.

The *Timex* case provides an example of the first category of applicant: a company which initiated the complaint, but is unhappy with the resultant regulation.

Case 264/82, Timex Corporation v. Council and Commission
[1985] ECR 849

The Community had imposed, through a regulation, an anti-dumping duty on watches from the USSR. It had done so at the instigation of Timex, which had initiated the proceedings, and the duty had explicitly stated that it had taken account of the injury caused to Timex by the dumped imports. However, Timex sought to challenge the regulation, arguing that the duty was too low, and thus that it was still being injured by the imports. An initial issue was whether Timex had standing to challenge the regulation. The Council and Commission argued that Timex was not named in the regulation, and that it was not individually concerned by it, since it affected all watchmakers in the Community alike. Timex argued by way of response that the regulation was in reality a decision which was of individual concern to it, since it had initiated the proceedings, and since the duty was fixed with reference to its economic situation.

THE ECJ

12. Article 13(1) of Regulation 3017/79 provides that 'Anti-dumping or countervailing duties, whether provisional or definitive, shall be imposed by regulation'. In the light of the criteria set out in Article 173(2) the measures in question are, in fact, legislative in nature and scope, inasmuch as they apply to traders in general; nevertheless, their provisions may be of direct and individual concern to some of those traders. In this regard it is necessary to consider in particular the part played by the applicant in the anti-dumping proceeding and its position on the market to which the contested legislation applies.

. . .

14. The complaint which led to the opening of the investigation procedure . . . owes its origin to the complaints originally made by Timex. Moreover, it is clear from the preamble to Council Regulation 1882/82 that Timex's views were heard during that procedure.

15. It must also be remembered that Timex is the leading manufacturer of mechanical watches and watch movements in the Community and the only remaining manufacturer of those products in the United Kingdom. Furthermore, as is also clear from the preambles to Regulation 84/82 and 1882/82, the conduct of the investigation procedure was largely determined by Timex's observations and the anti-dumping duty was fixed in the light of the effect of the dumping on Timex. More specifically, the preamble to Regulation 1882/82 makes it clear that the definitive anti-dumping duty was made equal to the dumping margin which was found to exist 'taking into account the extent of the injury caused to Timex by the dumped imports'. The contested regulation is therefore based on the applicant's own situation.

[51] A. Arnull, 'Challenging EC Anti-Dumping Regulations: The Problem of Admissibility' [1992] *ECLR* 73.

16. It follows that the contested regulation constitutes a decision which is of direct and individual concern to Timex within the meaning of Article 173(2) of the EEC Treaty. As the Court held in . . . Case 191/82, *EEC Seed Crushers' and Oil Processors' Federation (Fediol)* v. *Commission*, the applicant is therefore entitled to put before the Court any matters which would facilitate a review as to whether the Commission has observed the procedural guarantees granted to complainants by Regulation 3017/79 and whether or not it has committed manifest errors in its assessment of the facts, has omitted to take any essential matters into consideration or has based the reason for its decision on considerations amounting to a misuse of its powers. In that respect, the Court is required to exercise its normal powers of review over a discretion granted to a public authority, even though it has no jurisdiction to intervene in the exercise of the discretion reserved to the Community authorities by the aforementioned regulation.

17. Since the action is therefore admissible, the objection of inadmissibility raised by the Council and the Commission must be dismissed.

In the *Timex* case it was the complainant who was accorded standing. In the *Allied Corporation* case[52] the ECJ confirmed that the producers and exporters who were charged with dumping could also be regarded as individually concerned, at least in so far as they were identified in the measure adopted by the Commission or involved in the preliminary investigation.

The third category of applicant who may wish to contest the legality of an anti-dumping regulation is the importer of the product against which the anti-dumping duty has been imposed. The position here is rather more complex, and in rejecting some applications by importers the ECJ has been influenced by the fact that they might be able to challenge the measure indirectly under Article 234 EC (ex Article 177) in a legal action against the national agency which collects the duty. The *Extramet* case now provides an indication of when an importer will be held to have standing.[53]

Case C–358/89, Extramet Industrie SA v. Council
[1991] ECR I–2501

Extramet (E) imported calcium from outside the EC, which it then processed itself. There was only one Community producer of calcium, P, which refused to supply the raw material to E. P also claimed that E's supplies from outside the EC were being dumped in the EC and a dumping duty was imposed. It was this duty which E then sought to have annulled.

THE ECJ

13. . . . although in the light of the criteria set out in the second paragraph of Article 173(2)

---

[52] Cases 239 and 275/82, *Allied Corporation* v. *Commission* [1984] ECR 1005; Case T–155/94, *Climax Paper Converters Ltd.* v. *Council* [1996] ECR II–873; Case T–147/97, *Champion Stationery Mfg Co. Ltd.* v. *Council* [1998] ECR II–4137.

[53] Cases 239 and 275/82, *Allied*, n. 52 above, para. 15; Cases C–133 and 150/87, *Nashua*, n. 4 above; Case T–161/94, *Sinochem Heilongjiang* v. *Commission* [1996] ECR II–695; Case T–2/95, *Industrie des Poudres Sphériques* v. *Council* [1998] ECR II–3939.

regulations imposing anti-dumping duties are in fact, as regards their nature and scope, of a legislative character, inasmuch as they apply to all the traders concerned, taken as a whole, their provisions may none the less be of individual concern to certain traders (see . . . *Allied* . . .)

14. It follows that measures imposing anti-dumping duties may, without losing their character as regulations, be of individual concern in certain circumstances to certain traders who therefore have standing to bring an action for annulment.

15. The Court has acknowledged that this was the case, in general, with regard to producers and exporters who were able to establish that they were identified in the measures adopted by the Commission or the Council or were concerned by the preliminary measures (see *Allied* . . . *Nashua* . . .), and with regard to importers whose retail prices for the goods in question have been used as a basis for establishing the export prices (see, most recently, *Enital* . . . *Neotype* . . .).

16. Such recognition . . . cannot, however, prevent other traders from also claiming to be individually concerned by such a regulation by reason of attributes which are peculiar to them and which differentiate them from all other persons (see *Plaumann*).

17. The applicant has established the existence of factors constituting such a situation . . . The applicant is the largest importer of the product forming the subject-matter of the anti-dumping measure and, at the same time, the end-user of the product. In addition, its business activities depend to a very large extent on those imports and are seriously affected by the contested regulation in view of the limited number of manufacturers of the product concerned and of the difficulties which it encounters in obtaining supplies from the sole Community producer, which, moreover, is its main competitor for the processed product.

(b) COMPETITION CASES

A second area in which the ECJ has been liberal in according standing is competition policy, regulated by Articles 81 and 82 EC (ex Articles 85 and 86). Under Article 3(2) of Regulation 17, a Member State, or any natural or legal person who claims to have a legitimate interest, can make an application to the Commission, putting forward evidence of a breach of Articles 81 and 82.[54] The Commission is also empowered to investigate matters of its own initiative.

Case 26/76, Metro-SB-Großmärkte GmbH & Co KG v. Commission
[1977] ECR 1875

[Note ToA renumbering: Arts. 85, 86, and 173 are now Arts. 81, 82, and 230]

Metro argued that the distribution system operated by SABA was in breach of Article 85 of the Treaty. It initiated a complaint under Article 3(2) of Regulation 17. The Commission decided that certain aspects of the distribution system were not in fact in breach of Article 85, and it was this decision, addressed to SABA, that Metro sought to annul. The question arose whether Metro could claim to be individually concerned by a decision addressed to another.

---

[54] The regime for the enforcement of competition policy is about to change: see *Proposal for a Council Regulation on the Implementation of the Rules Laid Down in Articles 81 and 82 of the Treaty*, COM(2000)582 final, Art. 7.

The contested decision was adopted in particular as the result of a complaint submitted by Metro and it relates to the provisions of SABA's distribution system, on which SABA relied and continues to rely as against Metro in order to justify its refusal to sell to the latter or to appoint it as a wholesaler, and which the applicant had for this reason impugned in its complaint.

It is in the interests of a satisfactory administration of justice and of the proper application of Articles 85 and 86 that natural or legal persons who are entitled, pursuant to Article 3(2)(b) of Regulation No 17, to request the Commission to find an infringement of Articles 85 and 86 should be able, if their request is not complied with wholly or in part, to institute proceedings in order to protect their legitimate interests.

In those circumstances the applicant must be considered to be directly and individually concerned, within the meaning of the second paragraph of Article 173, by the contested decision and the application is accordingly admissible.

The more liberal attitude in this case is apparent by contrasting it with the approach of the case law interpreting the *Plaumann* test. If the 'normal' interpretation of individual concern had been adopted then Metro would almost certainly have failed. The decision addressed to SABA would have been held to affect an open category: those who were self-service wholesalers and who wished to handle the products of SABA. Given the special circumstances of competition policy, the Court was, however, willing to accord standing to Metro. The result will be different where the applicant has not taken part in the administrative procedure.[55]

The willingness of the Court to review competition decisions pursuant to a complaint under Article 3 of Regulation 17 is further exemplified by the *BEUC* case.[56] A number of public-interest groups submitted a complaint to the Commission about an agreement between British and Japanese motor manufacturers which sought to restrict imports of Japanese cars into the Community. The Commission declined to take up the complaint for a number of reasons. The CFI reviewed and annulled the Commission's decision. In *Vittel*[57] the CFI held that representatives of employees could be regarded as individually concerned so as to challenge a merger ruling. This was because the merger regulation expressly mentioned them among the third parties which had a sufficient interest to be heard during the procedure for investigating the planned concentration. This was so irrespective of whether they had taken part in that procedure.[58]

(c) STATE AIDS

The provision of state aid to industry is regulated by Articles 87 to 89 EC (ex Articles 92 to 94). The principal objective is to prevent the conditions of competition from

---

[55] Case C–70/97, *Kruidvart BVBA* v. *Commission* [1998] ECR I–7183.

[56] Case T–37/92, *Bureau Européen des Unions des Consommateurs* v. *Commission* [1994] ECR II–285.

[57] Case T–12/93, *Comité Central d'Entreprise de la Société Anonyme Vittel* v. *Commission* [1995] ECR II–1247; Case T–96/92, *Comité Central d'Entreprise de la Société Générale des Grands Sources* v. *Commission* [1995] ECR II–1213; Cases T–528, 542, 543, 546/93, *Métropole Télévision SA* v. *Commission* [1996] ECR II–649.

[58] See also Cases C–68/94 and C–30/95, *France* v. *Commission* [1998] ECR I–1375.

being distorted, which would be the case if the firms in one State could obtain aid or subsidies from their government.[59] The Commission will determine whether the aid is compatible with the Treaty, and will address a decision to the relevant State. The State could clearly challenge the decision under Article 230 (ex Article 173), but the Treaty is less clear on whether a complainant may also do so. Such complainants are not afforded the same recognition as in the context of competition proceedings, but the ECJ has shown itself to be liberal in its construction of standing in this area.

Case 169/84, Compagnie Française de l'Azote (COFAZ) SA v. Commission
[1986] ECR 391[60]

[Note ToA renumbering: Arts. 93 and 173 are now Arts. 88 and 230]

Three French fertilizer companies complained to the Commission that the Netherlands was granting a preferential tariff for the supply of natural gas to its own Dutch producers of fertilizer. The Commission instituted an investigation under Article 93(2), in which the applicant companies played a full part. The Dutch Government then modified its pricing policy for gas, and the Commission decided that the procedure under Article 93(2) could be halted. The applicants disagreed and sought to have the decision of the Commission annulled. Did they have standing to challenge it? The Court quoted the *Plaumann* test and then proceeded as follows.

THE ECJ

23. More particularly, as regards the circumstances referred to in that judgment, the Court has repeatedly held that where a regulation accords applicant undertakings procedural guarantees entitling them to request the Commission to find an infringement of Community rules, those undertakings should be able to institute proceedings in order to protect their legitimate interests (judgments in Cases 26/76, *Metro* . . ., 181/82, *Fediol* . . ., and 210/81, *Demo-Studio Schmidt* . . .).

24. In its judgment in Case 264/82 (*Timex* . . .) the Court pointed out that it was necessary to examine in that regard the part played by the undertaking in the administrative proceedings. The Court accepted as evidence that the measure in question was of concern to the undertaking, within the meaning of Article 173(2) EEC, the fact that the undertaking was at the origin of the complaint which led to the opening of the investigation procedure, the fact that its views were heard during that procedure and the fact that the conduct of the procedure was largely determined by its observations.

25. The same conclusions apply to undertakings which have played a comparable role in the procedure referred to in Article 93 EEC provided, however, that their position on the market is significantly affected by the aid which is the subject of the contested decision. Article 93(2) recognises in general terms that the undertakings concerned are entitled to submit their comments to the Commission but does not provide any further details.

---

[59] See Ch. 27 below.
[60] See also Case T–435/93, *ASPEC* v. *Commission* [1995] ECR II–1281; Case T–380/94, *AIUFFASS* v. *Commission* [1997] 3 CMLR 542.

The status of a competitor of the recipient of the aid is however not sufficient in itself to secure standing. The applicant must have played a part in the administrative procedure, and have been affected by the aid which is the subject of the decision in issue.[61]

(d) REINFORCING THE DEMOCRATIC NATURE OF THE COMMUNITY

The last type of case in which there is evidence of a more lenient approach to standing concerns the institutional structure of the Community itself, and the extent to which this can be perceived as a democratic community open to all parties across the political spectrum.

Case 294/83, Parti Ecologiste 'Les Verts' v. Parliament
[1986] ECR 1339

The Parliament made an allocation of funds to cover the costs incurred by political parties who had participated in the 1984 European elections. The manner of allocating the funds was biased towards those parties which had been represented in Parliament before the election, and was less favourable to those seeking representation for the first time. The allocation was challenged by a party in this latter category.

THE ECJ

35. This action concerns a situation which has never before come before the Court. Because they had representatives in the institution, certain political groupings took part in the adoption of a decision which deals both with their own treatment and with that accorded to rival groupings which were not represented. In view of this, and in view of the fact that the contested measure concerns the allocation of public funds for the purpose of preparing for elections and it is alleged that those funds were allocated unequally, it cannot be considered that only groupings which were represented and which were therefore identifiable at the date of the adoption of the contested measure are individually concerned by it.

36. Such an interpretation would give rise to inequality in the protection afforded by the Court to the various groupings competing in the same elections. Groupings not represented could not prevent the allocation of the appropriations at issue before the beginning of the election campaign because they would be unable to plead the illegality of the basic decision except in support of an action against the individual decisions refusing to reimburse sums greater than those provided for. It would therefore be impossible for them to bring an action for annulment before the Court prior to the decisions or to obtain an order from the Court under Article 185 of the Treaty suspending application of the contested basic decision.

37. Consequently, it must be concluded that the applicant association, which was in existence at the time when the 1982 Decision was adopted and which was able to present candidates at the 1984 elections, is individually concerned by the contested measures.

---

[61] Case C–106/98, *CGT, CFDT, CFE–CGC* v. *Commission* [2000] ECR I–3659.

38. In the light of all those considerations, it must be concluded that the application is admissible.

7. ARTICLE 230: THE POLICY ARGUMENTS CONCERNING STANDING OF NON-PRIVILEGED APPLICANTS

Commentators have given differing answers to why the ECJ has taken, in general, a restrictive view of standing.

(a) THE APPELLATE COURT ARGUMENT

H. Rasmussen, Why is Article 173 Interpreted against Private Plaintiffs?[62]

It is the contention of this paper that . . . a comprehensive pattern does exist. The suggestion is that the Court arguably has a long term interest in reshaping the judiciary of the Community to allow itself to act more like a high court of appeals of Community law, with the courts and tribunals of the Member States, and any administrative and other Community courts which might be established, acting as courts of first instance. This interest outweighs the citizen's interest in direct access to the Court. The remaining part of this paper is concerned with relating the empirical evidence which supports this hypothesis.

[Three types of evidence are adduced by Rasmussen to support his argument.]

First, the Court not only restricts the citizen's access to judicial review of administrative acts. It also restricts the right of private individuals under Article 175(3), to seek an injunction against an institution which disregards an obligation to act under Community law. Several individuals have sought such an injunction, but the Court has dismissed the actions, primarily on the ground that the parties did not satisfy the Article's requirements on standing. . . .

For many years the Court was equally unsympathetic to actions for damages brought under Article 178, generally on the ground that they attempted to circumvent Article 173's narrow standing requirements. In the early 1970s the Court ostensibly shifted its position, interpreting more liberally the provisions that allow private persons to sue the Community for damages. Despite this apparent shift, the Court has, for two reasons, clearly disappointed the expectations of private plaintiffs. First, the Court defined the conditions for Community liability so narrowly that no private party has yet been awarded damages. Secondly, the Court has found alternative means to inhibit private actions. . . .

The denial of a remedy under Article 173 is thus paralleled by the unavailability of remedies under Articles 175 and 178. This parallelism strongly supports, in my opinion, the validity of the hypothesis that these denials are but elements of the Court's policy to establish itself as . . . a high appellate Court on matters of Community law.

[The second piece of evidence adduced by Rasmussen is the existence of a Court memorandum from 1978, in which the ECJ sought to persuade the Council of the need for changes in the ECJ's structure, through the introduction of a Court of First Instance. The object was to relieve the ECJ itself of certain cases, such as those concerning staff, and more generally to allow it to

---

[62] (1980) 5 ELRev. 112, 122–7. References to Arts. 173, 175, 177, and 178 should now be read as to Arts. 230, 232, 234, and 235.

concentrate on matters of law. The third strand of the argument draws on the development of direct effect. On this Rasmussen argues as follows.]

A last brick should be put into place. It is this. If the restriction of the citizen's access to the Court was not to amount to a pure denial of justice or rather a denial of remedies, it was necessary simultaneously to enlarge the responsibility of the national courts and tribunals to provide the citizen with an effective protection of his Community rights. . . . If the framers of the EEC Treaty intended the law of the Community to be directly applicable (and there are indications in the Treaty that they did), it is fair to say that in the hands of the Court direct applicability has been extended far beyond their intentions.

In sum, injured parties have no choice but to bring actions before the national courts. In turn, these courts should, in the opinion of the European Court, seek preliminary rulings under Article 177 in all instances where an interpretation of Community law is desirable or required by law, or where doubt about its validity is aired before the national judge.

In theory, then, the national courts will try the cases on their merits with the European Court serving as the ultimate arbiter of questions of interpretation of Community law and its validity. It is no secret, however, that in practice, when making preliminary rulings the Court has often transgressed the theoretical borderline between mere interpretation and fact evaluation. The court does so when it provides the national judge with an answer in which questions of law and of fact are sufficiently interwoven as to leave the national judge with only little discretion and flexibility in making his final decision. . . . It should not, therefore, be a surprise that one commentator has seen the Court's way of going about its business as a '[demonstration of] the ease with which Article 177 could be turned into a vehicle of appellate review'.

Rasmussen's thesis is interesting, and may well have played some part in the approach of the Court. There are, however, two difficulties in accepting it as the main motivating force behind the Court's case law.

First, as Harding has argued,[63] it is hard to explain the early, restrictive case law as being based on a desire by the ECJ to assert itself as an appellate court. This case law was developed in the 1960s at a time when the Court was not faced with severe work-load problems.

Secondly, the ECJ may well have aspirations to become an 'appellate court' for the Community. The contention that this is the prime reason it has 'closed down' Article 230 EC (ex Article 173), with the objective of forcing applicants to proceed via Article 234 (ex Article 177) instead, is problematic for the following reason. The ECJ clearly wished to limit the range of applicants who can, in general, challenge decisions or regulations within Article 230. However, under Article 234 references can be made at the behest of a wide range of individuals who are affected by a Community norm, even if the norm is substantively a true regulation. The individual will base the claim on the fact that, for example, the norm in question is contrary to a directly effective Treaty Article, which gives the applicant rights which can be utilized in national courts.[64] The idea, then, that the ECJ intended to limit Article 230 very restrictively, with the intention of forcing claims through Article 234, when it would have very little control over the range of applicants using the latter Article, *or* the types of norm

---

[63] C. Harding, 'The Private Interest in Challenging Community Action' (1980) 5 *ELRev.* 354, 355.
[64] See 528–32 below.

challenged thereby, is not wholly convincing. The 'causality' in this area may well have been otherwise: the ECJ restricted Article 230 for reasons to be considered below, and applicants who sought to challenge Community norms were forced to do so through the mechanism of Article 234.

(b) RESTRICTIVE ACCESS AND THE LANGUAGE OF THE TREATY

A different explanation for the ECJ's case law is that it is explicable simply on the ground that the Treaty itself did not countenance any broader grounds of challenge.

C. Harding, The Private Interest In Challenging Community Action[65]

It has perhaps been easy, amid the welter of technical and difficult discussion of 'direct and individual concern' under Article 173(2), to lose sight of a relatively simple message that is forcefully sent out from some of the earlier instances of private challenge of the legality of Community action: that Article 173(2) itself, taken together with Article 189, does not, and was probably never intended to hold out much hope to private plaintiffs in the case of measures not actually addressed to them. From the Treaty, it is unequivocally clear that true regulations cannot be challenged by individuals, that there is a difference between regulations and decisions and that decisions not addressed to the complainant can only be challenged by him if he has a special interest in the matter—that is he is directly and individually concerned. The purport of Article 173(2) would appear to be that in practice only rarely should a private party be able to challenge directly a Community measure which is more than an administrative act concerned simply with the person's case. More specifically, regulations and decisions addressed to Member States ought not in principle to be susceptible to private challenge. . . . If an explanation is sought for this apparently restrictive view of Article 173(2), the answer is perhaps disarmingly simple: that provision is based on the assumption that it would not be a good policy to allow private parties to challenge measures such as regulations and decisions addressed to Member States. It should also be remembered that the Court . . . emphasised that for private persons the action under Article 173(2) was in some respects more restrictive than the corresponding earlier procedure under Article 33 of the Coal and Steel Community Treaty. This difference could be justified on account of the wider legislative competence of the Community institutions under the EEC Treaty, which may be viewed as a 'traité-cadre' rather than a 'traité-loi'.

While it is true that the Treaty clearly imposes limits on the extent to which individuals may contest legality under Article 230(4), the explanation proffered by Harding is, none the less, contestable. It is, of course, the case that the Treaty does not readily countenance challenges by private applicants. However, it is equally the case that the Treaty does contemplate some such challenges. The crucial issue is, therefore, not whether the Treaty imposes limits on standing, but whether the interpretation of those limits could be considered to be overly restrictive. Until recently challenges to decisions addressed to another, and to regulations, were virtually impossible unless

---

[65] N. 63 above, 355. References to Arts. 173 and 189 should now be read as to Arts. 230 and 249.

the case concerned a completed set of past events. The judicial reasoning used to reach such conclusions is, as seen above, open to criticism, *even given* the language of Article 230(4) itself. The case law post-*Codorniu* holds out some greater hope for applicants, but the interpretation accorded to individual concern will bar most applicants. The idea that the Court's case law in this area is simply an application of the intent of the Treaty, and that this renders further evaluation of the policy issues underlying this case law unnecessary, does not, therefore, suffice.

Moreover, whatever the intent of the original framers of the Treaty, we have now moved on. The control of illegality by and through individual actions is as important in the Community context as it is within any national legal system. The Court has shown itself quite capable of fashioning Treaty Articles to meet the current needs of the Community, even where it had considerably less to work with than in the case of Article 230(4).

(c) THE NATURE OF THE SUBJECT MATTER: DISCRETIONARY DETERMINATIONS AND THE CAP

The Court's reluctance to accord individuals standing in the mainline cases may be more readily understood by focusing on the subject matter involved. Hartley has correctly observed that the ECJ appears to be more reluctant to afford standing where the norm is discretionary.[66] The reason can be appreciated by considering more closely the subject matter in such cases.

Virtually all the cases considered in section 5 above concern challenges to norms made pursuant to the Common Agricultural Policy (CAP). The substantive challenge is, for example, that there has been a breach of Article 34(3) EC (formerly Article 40(3)). This Article provides that the common organization of agricultural markets shall be limited to pursuit of the objectives contained in Article 33 (formerly Article 39), and shall exclude discrimination between producers or consumers within the Community. An allegation of a breach of Article 34(3) will often require the Court to consider whether Article 33 has itself been breached. Article 33 is the foundational provision of the CAP, and is of a broad discretionary nature. The Article sets out a broad range of general objectives for the CAP. They include the increase in agricultural productivity, with the object, *inter alia*, of ensuring a fair standard of living for the agricultural community; the stabilization of markets; assuring the availability of supplies; and reasonable prices for consumers. It is readily apparent that these objectives can clash with each other.[67] The Commission and Council will therefore have to make difficult discretionary choices. Whether the resultant choices discriminate between producers may be contentious. The ECJ has, not surprisingly, accepted that the Community institutions have a considerable degree of choice as to how to balance the objectives which are to be pursued.[68]

---

[66] N. 3 above, 357.

[67] See, e.g., Case 34/62, *Germany* v. *Commission* [1963] ECR 131; Case 5/67, *Beus* v. *Hauptzollamt München* [1968] ECR 83.

[68] See, e.g., Cases 197–200, 243, 245, 247/80, *Ludwigshafener Walzmühle Erling KG* v. *Council* [1981] ECR 3211; Case 8/82, *KG in der Firma Hans-Otto Wagner GmbH Agrarhandel* v. *Bundesanstalt für Landwirtschaftliche Marktordnung* [1983] ECR 371; Case 283/83, *Firma A. Racke* v. *Hauptzollamt Mainz* [1984] ECR 3791.

The regulations or decisions will not always please all those concerned. The choices made pursuant to Articles 33, 34, and 37 EC will often mean that there are winners and losers from the regulatory process. Certain groups will be content with, for example, the aid or subsidies granted to them; others will feel that they have been harshly treated. Countless claims of this kind are possible, given the plethora of regulations and decisions made by the Community in the context of the CAP.

The ECJ does not wish to be placed in a position whereby it is being constantly asked to second-guess the discretionary choices made by the other Community institutions. The Court would be swamped by such cases. It would be wrong for the Court simply to substitute its view on the 'correct' balance between the objectives in Article 33 for that of the Commission and the Council. The ECJ has two techniques to prevent it being placed in this position.

It could, on the one hand, adopt a restrictive standard of review. The Court would overturn choices reached by the original decision-makers only if there was some manifest error. This is indeed the general approach taken by the ECJ when it does engage in substantive review in this area.[69]

It could, on the other hand, use strict tests of standing to limit the number of such cases heard under Article 230. This is far less demanding on the Court's time. The first technique of limited review still requires the Court to hear the substance of the case, even if it ultimately finds that the applicant has failed to show the level of error to justify annulment. If the applicant is excluded at the standing level, then an in-depth analysis of the substantive claim is obviated.

This may serve to explain the strict requirements for standing in the mainline cases. The Court does not wish to become enmeshed in large numbers of cases where the applicants seek to challenge the way that the Commission and Council have exercised their discretion to make policy choices in the CAP. It is not therefore surprising that in the post-*Codorniu* case law the strictest interpretation of the *Plaumann* test of individual concern has been in CAP cases, or other areas where discretionary choices are being made.[70]

The way in which applicants have sought to circumvent these limits, by channelling their actions through Article 234 (ex Article 177), will be considered below.

(d) THE NATURE OF THE SUBJECT MATTER: QUASI-JUDICIAL DETERMINATIONS AND THE MORE LIBERAL CASE LAW

There are two features which help to explain the more liberal case law in the context of dumping, state aids, and competition.

The first is that the *procedure* in these areas does explicitly or implicitly envisage a role for the individual complainant, who can alert the Commission to the breach of Community law. The complainant may then play a prominent role in the assessment

---

[69] D. Wyatt and A. Dashwood, *The Substantive Law of the EC* (Sweet & Maxwell, 2nd edn., 1987), 301. The topic is not dealt with in later editions of this work. For a discussion of the way in which the Court limits the intensity of its review in such instances, see 537–40 below.

[70] See, e.g., Case C–480/93, *Zunis Holding*, n. 7 above; Case T–585/93, *Stichting Greenpeace Council (Greenpeace International)* v. *Commission* [1995] ECR II–2205.

of whether the alleged breach has actually occurred. The nature of this assessment has been properly described as quasi-judicial.[71]

The second distinguishing feature relates to the *substantive* nature of the subject-matter. A common feature in the areas where the ECJ has been more liberal is that the interests of the Community can be stated less equivocally.[72] State aids can be taken as an example. The provision of such aid is contrary to the Community's interest, since it places the recipient firm at a competitive advantage as compared with its rivals. The Court is, therefore, likely to be receptive to an argument, such as that in *COFAZ*, that the Commission has been mistaken in thinking that the transgressing State has corrected its past illegal behaviour.[73] A similar point can be made about dumping. The Community has a clear interest in ensuring that goods from outside the Community are not sold within it at too low a price. The Court is, therefore, once again likely to be willing to listen to an argument, put forward in *Timex*, that the Commission has set the dumping duty too low, with the consequence that firms within the Community are still being harmed. This is particularly so when the applicant firm is well placed to make an assessment of the pricing and cost issues which are involved.[74]

The situation in these areas can be contrasted with that in the mainline cases on the CAP. In these cases the paradigm is one in which there are conflicting claims within the Community. Discretionary choices will be made and it may not be possible to satisfy all those affected. For the reasons given above, the ECJ is reluctant to become engaged in second-guessing the precise nature of the discretionary choice made in a particular instance.[75]

It might be helpful by way of conclusion to this discussion to consider two central issues concerning standing which affect the entire topic.

(e) TWO CENTRAL ISSUES CONCERNING STANDING (I): THE MEANING TO BE GIVEN TO INDIVIDUAL CONCERN

The central issue in the post-*Codorniu/Extramet* case law is the meaning to be accorded to individual concern. It is of course true, in one sense, that this will be dependent on the facts of the particular case. This should not, however, serve to conceal the fact that the *test itself* is being given different meanings in various cases. We have already seen the three approaches in the case law.[76] It is important to

---

[71] Hartley, n. 3 above, 364–9.

[72] This does not, of course, mean that there may not be difficult factual issues involved in such cases.

[73] It should, however, be noted that the Court will not normally engage in intensive review of Commission decisions in the field of state aids: see Ch. 27 below.

[74] The rationale for allowing the firms on which the dumping duty is imposed to have standing is obviously different. There are two explanations for this. First, while the dumping duty must be imposed by regulation, it is in reality often closer to a decision addressed to specific firms. The second is that the existence of dumping, and the calculation of the costing and pricing factors, is very controversial. To allow the affected firms to contest the regulation may well, therefore, be a political judgement on the part of the Court.

[75] The rationale for the more liberal approach in the *Les Verts* case must be sought on yet other grounds. The most likely explanation is that the Court wished to emphasize the fact that the Community was open to all shades of political party, and in that sense representative of European opinion. It did not wish to be seen supporting a regime in which those currently represented within the Parliament could weight the financial system in their own favour. To borrow from the language of Ely, the Court was willing to use its own power to ensure that the democratic system was not used by the 'ins' to exclude or prejudice the 'outs': J. H. Ely, *Democracy and Distrust: A Theory of Judicial Review* (Harvard University Press, 1980); Case 294/83, *Partie Ecologiste 'Les Verts' v. Parliament* [1986] ECR 1339.   [76] See 496–500 above.

emphasize the real differences which exist between them. The second approach is based on a showing of some factual injury to the applicant that marks it out. This is very different from the third, the pure *Plaumann* approach, which excludes such factual considerations, so that standing is denied if the category of applicants is open in the sense exemplified by *Plaumann* itself and many subsequent cases. Under this approach it will not suffice for a particular trader to show particular harm, unless the case comes within the narrow exception for completed past events. Nor will the fact that all present traders may be seriously affected by a regulation suffice for them to be accorded standing. While this attitude persists many cases are doomed to failure.

The Community courts are faced with a policy choice which cannot be avoided, and should not be masked. In many cases an applicant' will have suffered serious adverse impact from a contested norm. In many other cases all the relevant applicants may be in the same position, in the sense that all may have been seriously harmed by the challenged provision. The policy choice is whether to accord such applicants standing. If we believe that they should not have standing, then we can continue to interpret individual concern in pure *Plaumann* terms, approach three. If we believe the contrary, then approach three has to be modified, along the lines suggested by Advocate General Jacobs in the *UPA* case. The choice is there to be made. If we persist with the former, negative response, let us not, however, pretend that we have really liberalized standing. Let us be truthful and recognize that 'one *Codorniu*, does not an applicant's summer make'.

(f) TWO CENTRAL ISSUES CONCERNING STANDING (II): STANDING, PARTICIPATION, AND INTERVENTION

Public lawyers will immediately recognize that there is a connection between three related matters. These are standing to seek judicial review; participation in the making of the original decision now being challenged; and intervention rights for third parties, whether before the body which made the initial decision, or before the reviewing court itself.[77] The nature of this connection can be explained quite simply in both legal and political terms.

In legal terms, the greater the participation or intervention rights afforded to parties when the initial decision was made, the greater the likelihood that such parties should also be granted standing to challenge the resultant decision before the Court via judicial review. The reason is obvious. If parties are allowed to participate in the making of the initial decision, then it makes sense for them to be able to challenge that decision in judicial review proceedings. They might wish to argue, for example, that their views, although listened to in a formal sense, were in fact disregarded; that the decision-maker had in effect reached a decision which was biased towards certain interests; and that the substantive decision should therefore be overturned. Intervention rights in judicial review actions can also be important as a means of facilitating public-interest litigation before the ECJ.[78] Intervention rights

---

[77] R. Stewart, 'The Reformation of American Administrative Law' (1975) 88 *Harv. LR* 1667.

[78] C. Harlow, 'Towards a Theory of Access for the European Court of Justice' (1992) 12 *YBEL* 213.

are governed by Article 40[79] of the Statute of the Court of Justice: Member States and Community institutions can intervene as of right; private parties can do so only in cases between private parties and only where they can establish an interest.[80] Intervention rights clearly cannot be a substitute for standing: someone must be granted standing before others can intervene. There is, however, much to be said for using such rights to enable interest groups to make their views known when a case does come before the Court. It obviates the need for separate action on the same point; facilitates class actions; and makes it easier for interest groups to proffer their opinions.

In political terms, participation is recognized as one way of imbuing decisions with greater legitimacy. It is clear from the institutional reports leading to the 1996 IGC that the Community institutions were very concerned about the EC's overall legitimacy.[81] Participation is perceived as a valuable way of making decision-making more accessible to those affected, and of enabling them to have direct participatory input into the decision reached. There is, moreover, as Shapiro correctly notes, a connection between transparency and participation: 'full transparency can only be achieved through participation or through dialogue as a form of participation'.[82]

It is therefore important to see how far the connection between standing, participation, and intervention has been recognized judicially and politically.

There is some evidence of this link in the *ECJ's jurisprudence*. We have seen that the Court's willingness to accord standing in areas such as competition and state aids was premised on the fact that the applicant was afforded a role in the initial decision-making of, or complaint to, the Commission. The ECJ's general approach is, however, to resist a connection between the *fact* of participation in the making of a legislative measure and standing. Such participation does not lead to standing where the relevant Treaty Article does not provide for any intervention *rights* in the making of the original measure.[83] The ECJ has also resisted the grant of any general right to be heard before the adoption of Community legislation. Where a Community act is based on a Treaty Article, the only obligations to consult are those laid down in that Article.[84]

There has been some *political recognition* of the connection between standing, participation, and intervention in the European Council's 1993 Inter-institutional Declaration on Democracy, Transparency, and Subsidiarity. This laid the foundation for greater access to Community documentation. It also proposed the creation of a notification procedure, in which the Commission would publish a brief summary of the draft measure in the Official Journal. There would then be a deadline by which interested parties could submit their comments. The implications of this reform could have been far-reaching. There is a clear analogy between this formulation, and the

[79] This was Art. 37 of the ECJ Statute. Art. 40 is the new number after the modification to the Statute by the TN.

[80] See Case T–138/98, *Armement Coopératif Artisanal Vendéen (ACAV)* v. *Council* [1999] ECR II–1797, for intervention rights of local and regional bodies.

[81] P. Craig, 'Democracy and Rule-making within the EC: An Empirical and Normative Assessment' (1997) 3 *ELJ* 105; G. de Búrca, 'The Quest for Legitimacy in the European Union' (1996) 59 *MLR* 349.

[82] M. Shapiro, 'The Giving Reasons Requirement' [1992] *U Chic. Legal Forum* 179, 205.

[83] Case T–99/94, *ASOCARNE*, n. 19 above, para. 19, upheld on appeal, Case C–10/95P, n. 19 above; Case T–135/96, *UEAPME*, n. 19 above; Case T–583/93, *Greenpeace*, n. 70 above, para. 56.

[84] Case C–104/97P, *Atlanta AG* v. *European Community* [1999] ECR I–6983, paras. 31–40.

United States' Administrative Procedure Act 1946 (APA). The APA established a notice and comment procedure whereby rules have to be published in the Federal Register, and the agency has to allow a period of time for notice and comment. The 1993 Declaration appeared to have borrowed directly from the American experience. Those familiar with this topic will know that US courts have regularly been faced with actions in which participants in the notice and comment procedure have been granted standing to seek judicial review.[85] The Commission's response to this aspect of the 1993 Declaration was, however, limited. It did not bring forward any general measure for the EC akin to the APA, and the discussion of participation rights in its report for the 1996 IGC was exiguous to say the least.[86] It has, however, broadened consultation through the increasing use of Green and White Papers when important areas of EC policy are being developed.

8. ARTICLE 230: DIRECT CONCERN

If an applicant proves individual concern, it will still have to show that the decision was of direct concern, if it is to be accorded standing. The general principle applied by the ECJ is that a measure will be of direct concern where it directly affects the legal situation of the applicant and leaves no discretion to the addressees of the measure, who are entrusted with its implementation. This implementation must be automatic and result from Community rules without the application of other intermediate rules.[87] It can be difficult to determine whether there is some autonomous exercise of will interposed between the original decision and its implementation.[88]

Cases 41–44/70, NV International Fruit Company v. Commission
[1971] ECR 411

The case was concerned with the importation of apples from non-member countries. The Community had adopted a regulation which limited the import of such apples from third countries during the period from 1 April 1970 to 30 June 1970. The regulation provided for a system of import licences, which were granted to the extent to which the Community market allowed. Under this system, a Member State would notify the Commission, at the end of each week, of the quantities for which import licences had been requested during the preceding week. The Commission would then decide on the issue of licences in the light of this information. The challenge was to a regulation applying this scheme to a particular week. The ECJ held that the applicant was individually concerned: the number of those applications affected by this regulation was fixed and

---

[85] A. Aman, *Administrative Law and Process* (Matthew Bender, 1993), chs. 4 and 6.

[86] P. Craig, 'Democracy and Rule-making within the EC: An Empirical and Normative Assessment' (1997) 3 *ELJ* 105.

[87] Case C–386/96, *Société Louis Dreyfus & Cie v. Commission* [1998] ECR I–2309; Case T–54/96, *Oleifici Italiana SpA and Fratelli Rubino Industrie Olearie SpA v. Commission* [1998] ECR II–3377; Case T–69/99, *Danish Satellite TV (DSTV) A/S (Eurotica Rendez-vous Television) v. Commission* [2000] ECR II–4039.

[88] See also, e.g., Case T–96/92, *Comité Général*, n. 57 above; Case T–12/93, *Vittel*, n. 57 above; Case T–509/93, *Richco Commodities Ltd. v. Commission* [1996] ECR II–1181; Cases T–172, 175, and 177/98, *Salamander*, n. 19 above.

known when the regulation was adopted, and the Court held that the Regulation should be treated as a bundle of individual decisions. Was it of direct concern to the applicant?

THE ECJ

23. Moreover, it is clear from the system introduced by Regulation No 459/70, and particularly from Article 2(2) thereof, that the decision on the grant of import licences is a matter for the Commission.

24. According to this provision, the Commission alone is competent to assess the economic situation in the light of which the grant of import licences must be justified.

25. Article 1(2) of Regulation No 459/70, by providing that the 'Member States shall in accordance with the conditions laid down in Article 2, issue the licence to any interested party applying for it', makes it clear that the national authorities do not enjoy any discretion in the matter of the issue of licences and the conditions on which applications by the parties concerned should be granted.

26. The duty of such authorities is merely to collect the data necessary in order that the Commission may take its decision in accordance with Article 2(2) of that regulation, and subsequently adopt the national measures needed to give effect to that decision.

27. In these circumstances as far as the interested parties are concerned, the issue of or refusal to issue the import licences must be bound up with this decision.

28. The measure whereby the Commission decides on the issues of the import licences thus directly affects the legal position of the parties concerned.

29. The applications thus fulfil the requirements of the second paragraph of Article 173 of the Treaty, and are therefore admissible.

The decision in the *International Fruit* case can be compared to the following judgment by the Court.[89]

Case 222/83, Municipality of Differdange v. Commission
[1984] ECR 2889

The Commission authorized Luxembourg to grant aid to steel firms, on the condition that they undertook reductions in capacity. The applicant municipality argued that it was directly and individually concerned by this decision, *inter alia*, on the ground that the reduction in production capacity and closure of factories would lead to a reduction in local taxes.

THE ECJ

10. In this case the contested measure, which is addressed to the Grand Duchy of Luxembourg, authorizes it to grant certain aids to the undertakings named therein provided that they reduce their production capacity by a specified amount. However, it neither identifies the establishments

---

[89] See also, e.g., Case 69/69, *Alcan Alumininium Raeren* v. *Commission* [1970] ECR 385; Case 62/70, *Bock* v. *Commission* [1971] ECR 897.

in which the production must be reduced or terminated nor the factories which must be closed as a result of the termination of production. In addition, the Decision states that the Commission was to be notified of the closure dates only by 31 January 1984 so that the undertakings affected were free until that date to fix, where necessary with the agreement of the Luxembourg government, the detailed rules for the restructuring necessary to comply with the conditions laid down in the Decision.

11. That conclusion is, moreover, confirmed by Article 2 of the Decision according to which the capacity reductions may also be carried out by other undertakings.

12. It follows that the contested Decision left to the national authorities and under-takings concerned such a margin of discretion with regard to the manner of its implementation and in particular with regard to the choice of factories to be closed, that the Decision cannot be regarded as being of direct and individual concern to the municipalities with which the undertakings affected, by virtue of the location of their factories, are connected.

13. Since the action is therefore inadmissible also to the extent to which it is based on the provisions of the EEC Treaty, it must be dismissed.

9. ARTICLE 232: FAILURE TO ACT

The Community Treaties provide an action for a wrongful failure to act in Article 232 (formerly Article 175):

Should the European Parliament, the Council or the Commission, in infringement of this Treaty, fail to act, the Member States and the other institutions of the Community may bring an action before the Court of Justice to have the infringement established.

The action shall be admissible only if the institution concerned has first been called upon to act. If, within two months of being so called upon, the institution concerned has not defined its position the action may be brought within a further period of two months.

Any natural or legal person may, under the conditions laid down in the preceding paragraphs, complain to the Court of Justice that an institution of the Community has failed to address to that person any act other than a recommendation or an opinion.

The Court of Justice shall have jurisdiction, under the same conditions, in actions or proceedings brought by the ECB in the areas falling within the latter's field of competence and in actions or proceedings brought against the latter.

(a) THE RANGE OF REVIEWABLE OMISSIONS

There is clearly a close relationship between Articles 230 and 232 of the EC Treaty. This should be reflected in the range of omissions which are reviewable under Article 232. It seems, in principle, that the only failures to act which should come within Article 232 are failures to adopt a reviewable act, in the sense of an act which has legal effects. Article 232 does, however, simply refer to failure to act. An argument could, therefore, be made that this allows the action to be used in relation to the failure to adopt a non-binding act, such as a recommendation or an opinion.[90] There are, however, conceptual and practical objections to this view, which would serve to create

---

[90] A.G. Toth, 'The Law as it Stands on the Appeal for Failure to Act' (1975) 2 *LIEI* 65, 79–80.

an odd distinction between the action for annulment and that for failure to act.[91] Notwithstanding this the Court stated in the *Comitology* case[92] that the Parliament could bring an Article 232 action for failure to adopt a measure that was not itself a reviewable act. If this is indeed so it will apply only in the context of Article 232(1), since Article 232(3) makes it clear that the action cannot be brought by private individuals with respect to recommendations or opinions.

Article 232 will be available only if the applicant can show that there was an obligation to act. The existence of wide discretionary powers on the part of the Commission will, therefore, normally preclude such a finding.[93] It is also important to note that Article 232 has been held to refer to a failure to act in the sense of a failure to take a decision or to define a position. It does not refer to the adoption of a measure different from that desired by the applicant.[94]

The interrelationship between Articles 230 and 232, and the scope of reviewable omissions, is also evident in the *Eridania* case considered below.

Cases 10 and 18/68, Società 'Eridania' Zuccherifici Nazionali v. Commission [1969] ECR 459

[Note ToA renumbering: Arts. 173, 175 and 176 are now Arts. 230, 232, and 233]

The applicants sought the annulment of Commission decisions granting aid to certain sugar refineries in Italy. They claimed that their competitive position on the sugar market would be deleteriously affected by the grant of such aid. The Court rejected this action on the ground that the applicants were not individually concerned by the decision in question: the fact that their competitive position on the relevant market might be affected was not sufficient to show individual concern. The same applicants also brought an action under Article 175, arguing that there had been a failure to act, this being the failure to revoke the decisions in question.

THE ECJ

15. This application concerns the annulment of the implied decision of rejection resulting from the silence maintained by the Commission in respect of the request addressed to it by the applicants seeking the annulment or revocation of the three disputed decisions for illegality or otherwise because they are inappropriate.

16. The action provided for in Article 175 is intended to establish an illegal omission as appears from that Article, which refers to a failure to act 'in infringement of this Treaty' and from Article 176 which refers to a failure to act declared to be 'contrary to this Treaty'.

Without stating under which provision of Community law the Commission was required to annul or revoke the said decisions, the applicants have confined themselves to alleging that those

---

[91] Hartley, n. 3 above, 384–6.   [92] Case 302/87, n. 15 above.

[93] Case 247/87, *Star Fruit Company* v. *Commission* [1989] ECR 291; Case C–301/87, *France* v. *Commission* [1990] ECR I–307; Case T–277/94, *Associazone Italiana Tecnico Economica del Cemento (AITEC)* v. *Commission* [1996] ECR II–351.

[94] Cases 166 and 220/86, *Irish Cement* v. *Commission* [1988] ECR 6473; Case T–387/94, *Asia Motor France SA* v. *Commission* [1996] ECR II–961.

decisions were adopted in infringement of the Treaty and that this fact alone would thus suffice to make the Commission's failure to act subject to the provisions of Article 175.

17. The Treaty provides, however, particularly in Article 173, other methods of recourse by which an allegedly illegal Community measure may be disputed and if necessary annulled on the application of a duly qualified party.

To admit, as the applicants wish to do, that the parties concerned could ask the institution from which the measure came to revoke it and, in the event of the Commission's failing to act, refer such failure to the Court as an illegal omission to deal with the matter would amount to providing them with a method of recourse parallel to that of Article 173, which would not be subject to the conditions laid down by the Treaty.

18. This application does not therefore satisfy the requirements of Article 175 of the Treaty and must thus be held to be inadmissible.

The ECJ's reference to the use of Article 175 (ex Article 232), to evade limits placed on Article 173 (ex Article 230), includes, *inter alia*, the ability to bypass the time limits for contesting an action under Article 230.[95] It was indeed argued in *Eridania* that the applicants were out of time for challenging the legality of two of the relevant decisions under Article 173. The Court preferred however to rule out the nullity action because the applicants were not individually concerned.

(b) THE PROCEDURE

Article 232 requires the applicant to call upon the institution to act. This special procedure is because it may not be easy, in the context of an omission, to say when it came into existence and its content. Thus the omission is deemed to have taken place at the end of the first two-month period and its content is defined by the terms of the request.[96]

The Treaties do not specify any time limit within which the procedure for failure to act should be initiated. The Court has, however, specified that this procedure must be initiated within a reasonable time.[97] Once the request to act has been made, the institution has a period of two months within which to define its position. If it has not done this, the applicant has a further two months within which to bring the action under Article 232.[98]

(c) STANDING

Article 232 EC, like Article 230, draws a distinction between privileged and non-privileged applicants. The former are identified in Article 232(1): the Member States and other institutions of the Community. This has been held to cover the European

---

[95] See also Cases 21–26/61, *Meroni* v. *High Authority* [1962] ECR 73, 78.

[96] Hartley, n. 3 above, 392.

[97] Case 59/70, *Netherlands* v. *Commission* [1971] ECR 639. For a critique of the reasoning therein see Hartley, n. 3 above, 393–4.

[98] The construction of these provisions is contestable. Contrast the views of Toth, n. 90 above, 81–2, with those of Hartley, n. 3 above, 391–2.

Parliament.[99] The latter are covered by Article 232(3). The wording of this Article allows a natural or legal person to complain of a failure to address an act, other than a recommendation or an opinion, to that person. Whether this places the individual in a worse position under Article 232 than under Article 230 is unclear, as the following discussion reveals:

A.G. Toth, The Law as it Stands on the Appeal for Failure to Act[100]

As regards the destination of the measure, two different opinions have been put forward . . . The first view is based on the assumption that unlike the E.C.S.C. Treaty, the E.E.C./Euratom Treaties created two distinct legal remedies in the form of action for annulment and action for failure to act. While a private party can bring annulment proceedings against measures which, although adopted in the form of a regulation or a decision addressed to another person, affect him directly and individually, he can use the action for failure to act only to obtain an act which by its very nature and destination must be addressed to him. . . . According to a second view, the action for annulment and action for failure to act form one and the same legal remedy and, therefore, the concept of an 'act' that can be the subject of an appeal is necessarily the same for the purposes of both actions. An action for failure to act is, therefore, available in respect of all acts which are subject to annulment, even if not formally addressed (if taken) to the person bringing the action provided they concern him directly and individually. Should this not be so, the undesirable situation might arise in certain cases that the existence or absence of a judicial remedy would depend on the (arbitrary) conduct of the institution to which a request was submitted.

The matter has now been decided by the *ENU* case.[101] The ECJ held that standing under Article 148 of the Euratom Treaty, the equivalent of Article 232, would be available to an applicant provided that it would be directly and individually concerned: it was not necessary for the applicant to be the actual addressee of the decision.[102] This test, is, however, applied in the same restrictive manner as under Article 230.[103]

---

[99] Case 13/83, *European Parliament* v. *Council* [1985] ECR 1513. For discussion of the issues involved see Bebr, n. 17 above, 173–81.

[100] N. 90 above, 85–6.

[101] Case C–107/91, *ENU* v. *Commission* [1993] ECR I–599; Case T–95/96, *Gestevision Telecinco SA* v. *Commission* [1998] ECR II–3407, para 58; Cases T–79/96, 260/97, and 117/98, *Camar Srl and Tico Srl* v. *Commission* [2000] ECR II–2193, para. 79. See, however, Case T–277/94, *AITEC*, n. 93 above, para. 58, where the CFI was more guarded, holding that the applicant must show that he is the potential addressee of a measure which the Commission was obliged to take in relation to him. The CFI was, however, undoubtedly influenced by the fact that the failure to act concerned the exercise of Commission prosecutorial discretion in the context of state aids. The CFI did, moreover, consider the possibility of a broader reading of standing under Art. 175 (now Art. 232): para. 62.

[102] Normally it will not be possible to use Art. 232(3) to challenge a failure to act where the act in question was a reg. or a dir., since this would not be addressed to him at all. This will be possible only if the individual can show that the act which was omitted, although it might have taken the form of a reg., would have been of individual concern to him; or would have been a decision which directly and individually concerned him: Cases T–79/96 etc., *Camar*, n. 101 above, paras. 72–84.

[103] See, e.g., Case T–398/94, *Kahn Scheepvart BV* v. *Commission* [1996] ECR II–477.

10. ARTICLE 241:
THE PLEA OF ILLEGALITY

Article 241 (formerly Article 184) provides:

Notwithstanding the expiry of the period laid down in the fifth paragraph of Article 230, any party may, in proceedings in which a regulation adopted jointly by the European Parliament and the Council, or a regulation of the Council, of the Commission or of the ECB is at issue, plead the grounds specified in the second paragraph of Article 230, in order to invoke before the Court of Justice the inapplicability of that regulation.

(a) THE RANGE OF ACTS WHICH CAN BE CHALLENGED

The essence of Article 241 is as follows. An individual may wish, in the course of proceedings which have been initiated for a different principal reason, to call into question the legality of some other measure. Thus, for example, the principal foundation for the action may be a challenge to a decision, in the course of which the applicant wishes to raise the legality of a more general measure on which the particular decision is based. Article 241 does not therefore constitute an independent cause of action.[104]

Only the legality of regulations can be contested in this way. There must, moreover, be some real connection between the individual decision which is the subject matter of the action, and the general measure the legality of which is being contested.[105] However, in this, as in other areas of Community law, it is the substance of the measure, and not its form, which is decisive. The mere fact that an act is expressed to be in the form of a decision will not, therefore, preclude a challenge if the Court decides that in substance it is a regulation. This is demonstrated by the *Simmenthal* case:

Case 92/78, Simmenthal SpA v. Commission
[1979] ECR 777

[Note ToA renumbering: Arts. 173 and 184 are now Arts. 230 and 241]

The applicant sought to annul a Commission Decision concerning the minimum selling prices for frozen beef. In support of its claim, the applicant wished to use Article 184 to challenge the legality of certain regulations and notices which formed the legal basis of the contested decision. The ECJ held that the applicant was directly and individually concerned by the primary decision, even though it was actually addressed to the Member State. The Court then considered the arguments concerning Article 184.

---

[104] Case 33/80, *Albini* v. *Council* [1981] ECR 2141; Case T–154/94, *Comité des Salines de France* v. *Commission* [1996] ECR II–1377.

[105] A. Barav, 'The Exception of Illegality in Community Law: A Critical Analysis' (1974) 11 *CMLRev.* 366, 373–4.

34. While the applicant formally challenges Commission Decision No 78/258 it has at the same time criticized, in reliance on Article 184 of the EEC Treaty, certain aspects of the 'linking' system in the form in which it has been implemented pursuant to the new Article 14 of Regulation No 805/68, by Regulation No 2900/77 and No 2901/77 and also by the notices of invitations to tender of 13 January 1978.

. . .

36. There is no doubt that this provision (Article 184) enables the applicant to challenge indirectly during the proceedings, with a view to obtaining the annulment of the contested decision, the validity of the measures laid down by Regulation which form the legal basis of the latter.

37. On the other hand there are grounds for questioning whether Article 184 applies to the notices of invitations to tender of 13 January 1978 when according to its wording it only provides for the calling in question of 'regulations'.

38. These notices are general acts which determine in advance and objectively the rights and obligations of the traders who wish to participate in the invitations to tender which these notices make public.

39. As the Court in its judgment . . . in Case 15/57, *Compagnie des Hauts Fourneaux de Chasse* . . ., and in its judgment . . . in Case 9/56, *Meroni* . . ., has already held in connexion with Article 36 of the ECSC Treaty, Article 184 of the EEC Treaty gives expression to a general principle conferring upon any party to proceedings the right to challenge, for the purpose of obtaining the annulment of a decision of direct and individual concern to that party, the validity of previous acts of the institutions which form the legal basis of the decision which is being attacked, if that party was not entitled under Article 173 of the Treaty to bring a direct action challenging those acts by which it was thus affected without having been in a position to ask that they be declared void.

40. The field of application of the said article must therefore include acts of the institutions which, although they are not in the form of a Regulation, nevertheless produce similar effects and on those grounds may not be challenged under Article 173 by natural or legal persons other than Community institutions and Member States.

41. This wide interpretation of Article 184 derives from the need to provide those persons who are precluded by the second paragraph of Article 173 from instituting proceedings directly in respect of general acts with the benefit of judicial review of them at the time when they are affected by implementing decisions which are of direct and individual concern to them.

42. The notices of invitations to tender of 13 January 1978 in respect of which the applicant was unable to initiate proceedings are a case in point, seeing that only the decision taken in consequence of the tender which it had submitted in answer to a specific invitation to tender could be of direct and individual concern to it.

43. There are therefore good grounds for declaring that the applicant's challenge during the proceedings under Article 184, which relates not only to the above-mentioned regulations but also to the notices of invitations to tender of 13 January 1978, is admissible, although the latter are not in the strict sense measures laid down by Regulation.

The ECJ's reasoning in the *Simmenthal* case could also lead to the conclusion that individuals should be able to use Article 241 to challenge individual acts which would not be challengeable under Article 230. This would be so where the absence of relief under Article 230 is because the individual could not show direct and individual concern.

By way of contrast, it now appears to be the case that where it is clear that the individual would be able to bring a direct challenge under Article 230, then an indirect action seeking to use Article 241 will not be possible.[106] This aspect of the matter will be considered more fully below.[107]

(b) THE FORUM IN WHICH ARTICLE 241 CAN BE USED

Article 241 does not specify the court in which the plea of illegality may be raised. The ECJ has, however, held that Article 241 cannot be used in proceedings before a national court, but can only be raised in proceedings before the ECJ itself.

Cases 31 and 33/62, Milchwerke Heinz Wohrmann & Sohn KG and Alfons Lütticke GmbH v. Commission [1962] ECR 501

[Note ToA renumbering: Arts. 173, 177, and 184 are now Arts. 230, 234, and 241]

The applicants wished to challenge a decision by which the Commission had authorized Germany to impose certain duties on the import of powdered milk. They could not use Article 173 itself, since they were out of time. The question which arose was whether they could invoke Article 184 before the ECJ as an ancillary device to the action placing in issue a regulation before a national court.

THE ECJ

Before examining the question whether the contested measures are of their nature decisions or regulations, it is necessary to examine whether Article 184 empowers the Court to adjudicate upon the inapplicability of a regulation when this is invoked in proceedings—as in the present case—before a national court or tribunal.

Article 184 enables any party, notwithstanding the expiry of the period laid down in the third paragraph of Article 173, to invoke before the Court of Justice, for the purpose of making an application for annulment, the inapplicability of a regulation in proceedings in which it is at issue and to plead the grounds specified in the first paragraph of Article 173.

Because Article 184 does not specify before which court or tribunal the proceedings in which the regulation is at issue must be brought, the applicants conclude that the inapplicability of that regulation may in any event be invoked before the Court of Justice. This would mean that there would exist a method of recourse running concurrently with that available under Article 173.

This is however not the meaning of Article 184. It is clear from the wording and the general scheme of this Article that a declaration of the inapplicability of a regulation is only contemplated in proceedings brought before the Court of Justice itself under some other provision of the Treaty, and then only incidentally and with limited effect.

---

[106] Case C–188/92, *TWD Textilwerke Deggendorf GmbH* v. *Germany* [1994] ECR I–833; Case C–310/97P, *Commission* v. *AssiDomän Kraft Products AB* [1999] ECR I–5363, para. 60.

[107] See 527–8 below.

More particularly, it is clear from the reference to the time limit laid down in Article 173 that Article 184 is applicable only in the context of proceedings brought before the Court of Justice and that it does not permit the said time limit to be avoided.

The sole object of Article 184 is thus to protect an interested party against the application of an illegal regulation, without thereby in any way calling in issue the regulation itself, which can no longer be challenged because of the expiry of the time limit laid down in Article 173.

. . .

Although, therefore, Article 184 does not provide sufficient grounds to enable the Court of Justice to give a decision at the present stage, Article 177 does empower the Court to give a ruling if a national court or tribunal were to refer proceedings instituted before it to the Court.

In the light of all these considerations, the Court must declare that it has no jurisdiction to consider the present applications, both insofar as they seek the annulment of the contested measures and insofar as they seek to have them declared inapplicable. It is unnecessary therefore to decide upon the question of the Court's jurisdiction with regard to the exact nature of the measures of the Commission which are challenged by the applicants.

It is clear therefore that Article 241 can only be used before the ECJ itself, and then only when the primary challenge is based on some other provision of the Treaty. The nature of the proceedings in which the Article 184 plea can be raised must, therefore, be considered.

(c) THE TYPES OF PROCEEDINGS IN WHICH ARTICLE 241 CAN BE RAISED[108]

The most common usage of Article 241 (ex Article 184) is an additional, incidental challenge in an annulment action brought under Article 230 (ex Article 173), as exemplified by the *Simmenthal* case.

It is less clear whether Article 241 can be used as an incident to enforcement proceedings brought under Article 226 (ex Article 169) against a Member State. This will not be possible where the Member State has not challenged the measure within the time limits allowed for annulment.[109] To allow the State to rely on Article 241 in such circumstances would mean that it could circumvent the time limits laid down under Article 230.[110]

(d) THE PARTIES WHO ARE ALLOWED TO USE ARTICLE 241

It is clear that private parties can use Article 241. More contentious is the issue whether it can be used by privileged applicants, the Community institutions, and the Member States. Bebr is against privileged applicants being able to use Article 241, on the ground, *inter alia*, that such applicants can challenge any binding act of

---

[108] Barav, n. 105 above, 375–81.   [109] Case C–310/97P, *Kraft Products*, n. 106 above.
[110] Barav, n. 105 above, 378–9.

Community law under Article 230 within the time limit.[111] However, as Barav has noted,[112] the irregularities in a general act may appear only after the relevant implementation measures have been adopted, and hence the State may not have realized the necessity for challenging the general act until after the time limit under Article 230 has passed. The observations of Advocate General Roemer suggest that Article 230 should be available to Member States,[113] both for the reason advanced by Barav, and because the wording of the Article refers to 'any party'. The ECJ did not deal with the point, deciding the case on other grounds.

11. ARTICLE 234: PRELIMINARY RULINGS AS A MECHANISM FOR CONTESTING THE LEGALITY OF COMMUNITY MEASURES

(a) THE RATIONALE FOR USING ARTICLE 234

Preliminary rulings are important as a method of indirect challenge to the legality of Community action. Article 234(1)(b) EC (ex Article 177(1)(b)) allows national courts to refer to the ECJ questions concerning the 'validity and interpretation of acts of the institutions of the Community'. This provision has assumed an increased importance for private applicants because of the Court's narrow construction of the standing criteria under Article 230. Often a reference under Article 234 is the only mechanism whereby such parties may contest the legality of Community norms. The following extract provides a succinct summary of the reasons why individuals wish to use Article 234.

C. Harding, The Impact of Article 177 of the EEC Treaty on the Review of Community Action[114]

It should perhaps be borne in mind at this point why a request for a ruling under Article 177(b) is likely to take place in certain kinds of case rather than a direct action. . . . A direct claim may not be a feasible course for a number of reasons. Firstly, the time limit (two months) may well have passed before the alleged illegality or indeed the private party's wish or need to litigate has become apparent. In the second place, the individual may lack locus standi . . . which itself presents an insurmountable hurdle in many cases. There is, finally, a related point. It would be misleading to picture the private plaintiff as a disinterested legal watchdog, alert to identify as soon as may be any possibly illegal Community activity. In practice, the individual's interest is likely to arise when his own activities are affected by Community action—usually through the instrumentality of Member State authorities and not necessarily very soon after the inception of the Community measure. If the individual's interest is seen in this light, then Article 177(b) appears as an equally if not more natural avenue of review than Article 173.

---

[111] G. Bebr, 'Judicial Remedy of Private Parties against Normative Acts of the European Communities: The Role of the Exception of Illegality' (1966) 4 *CMLRev.* 7.

[112] N. 105 above, 371.   [113] Case 32/65, *Italy* v. *Commission* [1966] ECR 389, 414.

[114] (1981) 1 *YBEL* 93, 96. See also C. Harding, 'Who Goes to Court in Europe? An Analysis of Litigation against the European Community' (1992) 17 *ELRev.* 105.

(b) THE MECHANISM FOR TESTING COMMUNITY LEGALITY VIA THE NATIONAL COURTS

It is important to understand how Article 234 (ex Article 177) is used in this context. A common situation is of a Common Agricultural Policy (CAP) regulation which cannot be contested under Article 230, either because the applicant lacks standing or because it is outside the time limit. These regulations will normally be applied at national level by a national intervention agency. This provides the factual setting for the Article 234 action. The national intervention agency will apply the Community regulation. This may, for example, require in certain circumstances the forfeiture of a deposit which has been given by a trader. The trader believes that this forfeiture, and the regulation on which it is based, are contrary to Community law. The allegation may be that it is disproportionate, or discriminatory. If the security is forfeited the trader may then institute judicial review proceedings in the national court, claiming that the regulation is invalid. It will be for the national court to decide whether to refer the matter to the ECJ under Article 234(1)(b). In other instances the matter may arise somewhat differently. A regulation might demand a levy which the trader believes to be in breach of Community law. The trader's strategy might be to resist payment, be sued by the national agency, and then raise the alleged invalidity of the regulation on which the demand is based by way of defence. Once again, it would then be for the national court to decide whether to refer the matter to the ECJ.[115]

(c) THE ACTS WHICH CAN BE CHALLENGED UNDER ARTICLE 234

Article 234(1)(b) allows a challenge to be made to the validity of acts of the Community institutions. This enables challenges to regulations via the national courts.

The situation with respect to individual decisions is more complex. A person who is *not* the addressee of an individual decision may, it seems, contest this decision through the national courts, in much the same way as with a regulation. Thus, if a decision is addressed to a Member State or state agency which requires that certain action should be taken, then an individual affected by this can contest the validity of the decision on which the action is based through the national courts.[116] This is exemplified by the *Universität Hamburg* case.[117] In that case the Commission had issued a decision to all Member States refusing to allow an exemption from customs duty in relation to scientific equipment which had been imported from the United States.[118] The German authorities applied this decision, refusing the customs exemption, and the applicant sought to contest this before the national court. The ECJ held that the case could be brought via Article 177 (now Article 234). It was influenced by

---

[115] For examples, among many, see Case 181/84, *R. v. Intervention Board for Agricultural Produce, ex p. E. D. & F. Man (Sugar) Ltd.* [1985] ECR 2889; Case C–66/80, *ICC* [1981] ECR 1191.

[116] See Case C–188/92, *TWD*, n. 106 above.

[117] Case 216/82, *Universität Hamburg v. Hauptzollamt Hamburg-Kehrwieder* [1983] ECR 2771.

[118] The rationale being that the Commission claimed that equipment of equivalent scientific value was being manufactured in the Community itself.

the fact that the Commission decision did not have to be published, and that it did not have to be notified to the person applying for the tax exemption. Both of these factors would have rendered any challenge within the time limit under Article 230 virtually impossible. The Court pronounced more generally on the point in *Rau*.[119] It held that the applicants, who were margarine producers, could contest in the national courts the legality of a scheme whereby the Community sold cheap butter on the German market to test consumer reaction. There was no need to ascertain whether or not the applicants had the possibility of challenging the Community decision directly before the ECJ.

This decision must, however, be seen in the light of the *TWD* case.[120] The Commission declared aid which Germany had granted to a firm to be incompatible with the common market. The aid had, therefore, to be repaid. The German Government informed the company, and told it also that the Commission's decision could be challenged under Article 230. The company did not do so, but instead sought to raise the legality of the Commission's decision in an action in the German courts. The ECJ held that no indirect challenge was possible in this instance, given that the company had been informed of its right to challenge under Article 230, and given also that it would 'without any doubt'[121] have had standing to do so.[122] It seems therefore that a challenge under Article 234 will not be possible if the matter could have been raised by a person who had standing under Article 230, and who knew of the matter within the time limits for a direct action.

Where it is unclear whether the applicant would have had standing under Article 230 the ECJ is more willing to admit the indirect action. Thus in the *Accrington Beef* case[123] the ECJ distinguished *TWD*, and held that the failure to challenge a regulation under Article 230 was no bar to an Article 234 action, since it was not obvious that the Article 230 action would have been admissible. In *Eurotunnel* the ECJ held that a private party could challenge the validity of provisions of a directive in a national court, since the directive was addressed to Member States and it was not obvious that an action would have been possible under Article 230.[124] The ECJ is also likely to be more receptive to actions under Article 234 where the applicant would not have known of the relevant measure in time to challenge it under Article 230.[125]

---

[119] Cases 133–136/85, *Walter Rau Lebensmittelwerke* v. *Bundesanstalt für Landwirtschaftliche Marktordnung* [1987] ECR 2289.

[120] Case C–188/92, *TWD*, n. 106 above. See also Case C–178/95, *Wiljo NV* v. *Belgium* [1997] ECR I–585, [1997] 1 CMLR 627.

[121] *Ibid.*, para. 24.

[122] The ECJ distinguished *Rau* on the ground that the applicants in that case had in fact brought an annulment action before the ECJ, and that therefore the issue of the time bar under Art. 173 (now Art. 230) and the effect of this on a possible Art. 177 (now Art. 234) action did not arise.

[123] Case C–241/95, *R.* v. *Intervention Board for Agricultural Produce, ex p. Accrington Beef Co. Ltd.* [1996] ECR I–6691.

[124] Case C–408/95, *Eurotunnel SA* v. *Sea France* [1997] ECR I–6315.

[125] See the ground on which the Court distinguished the *Universität Hamburg* case in *TWD*, n. 106 above, para. 23.

(d) THE LIMITATIONS AND DRAWBACKS OF INDIRECT CHALLENGE

It is common for the ECJ, when denying the possibility of a direct action under Article 230, to advert to the possibility of indirect challenge through Article 234. We should, however, be mindful of the problems which indirect challenge can pose for applicants. These have been addressed recently by Advocate General Jacobs in the *UPA* case,[126] and earlier in *Extramet*. The most obvious is that this is dependent on the national court being willing to make a reference. This is particularly important because the national court has no jurisdiction to invalidate a Community norm.[127] The applicant will also, by definition, have to fight the case through at least two courts,[128] the national court and the ECJ. It may in addition be difficult to find an appropriate defendant in the national arena. Advocate General Jacobs brings out clearly other difficulties with the indirect action.

Case C–358/89, Extramet Industrie SA v. Council
[1991] ECR I-2501

[Note ToA renumbering: Arts. 173 and 177 are now 230 and 234]

The case was concerned with anti-dumping. Advocate General Jacobs' comments are however of more general application.

ADVOCATE GENERAL JACOBS

70. ... Article 173 contains no suggestion that the availability of the action for annulment depends on the absence of an alternative means of redress in the national courts of the Member States. If it did, the result would be far from satisfactory, for the existence and scope of any domestic remedy will depend on national law.

71. In any event, as an alternative to a direct action before this Court, proceedings before the national courts present serious disadvantages to an importer in the anti-dumping context. National courts, without special expertise in the subject and without the benefit of the partici-pation of the Council and Commission, are not the most appropriate forum for dealing with challenges to anti-dumping regulations. Their decisions are likely to lack the uniform character which could be achieved by this Court . . . Even with the use of Article 177, the decision of this Court is available only on the specific points which are referred to it. It is true that this Court has the advantage, in deciding such cases, of obtaining the views of the Community institutions and the Member States if they choose to take part, but the final disposition of the case rests with the national court.

72. Proceedings in the national courts, with the additional stage of a reference under Article 177, are likely to involve substantial delays and extra costs. In addition the national courts

---

[126] Case C–50/00P, *Unión de Pequeños Agricultores* v. *Council*, March 2002. See also Arnull, n. 48 above, 41–2; Arnull, n. 49 above, 48–51.

[127] Case 314/85, *Foto-Frost* [1987] ECR 4199.

[128] It could be more depending on whether the first national court before which the case comes is willing to make the reference, or whether the applicant has to take the case on appeal within the national legal system.

have no jurisdiction to declare the Community regulations invalid, since, according to . . . *Foto-Frost* . . . a ruling to that effect can be given only by this Court. The potential for delay inherent in proceedings before domestic courts, with the possibility of appeals within the national system, makes it likely that interim measures will be necessary in anti-dumping cases, but the national courts do not seem the appropriate forum for granting such measures. . . .

73. Moreover, a reference from a national court on the validity of regulation does not always give the Court as full an opportunity to investigate the matter as a direct action against the adopting institution. . . .

74. . . . [E]ven if the issues were fully identified in the order for reference, proceedings under Article 177 might not provide an effective remedy in anti-dumping cases because of the nature of the procedure. Where complex issues of law and fact are raised, only a full exchange of pleadings, as in a direct action, is likely to be adequate, if those issues are to be properly considered. Moreover, it is only in a direct action before the Court that all the parties concerned by the imposition of the duty, including the Community industry, will be able to participate.

(e) SUMMARY

i. Private parties who are not able to challenge Community action under Article 230 because they do not have standing may be able to do so indirectly under Article 234.

ii. Where this is possible, they will be able to challenge the validity of regulations, directives, and decisions under Article 234.

iii. They will not be able to challenge decisions in this manner where it is clear that they would have standing for a direct action under Article 230.

iv. The effectiveness of the indirect challenge is however limited in a number of ways. It is dependent upon the national court being willing to make a reference to the ECJ. It requires an action in at least two courts. It presupposes that the applicant can find an appropriate defendant at national level. It can lead to difficulties where there are references from different national courts asking different questions about the same issue. It is also subject to the difficulties mentioned by Advocate General Jacobs in the preceding extract.

12. THE GROUNDS OF REVIEW

If the applicant has standing, and is within the time limits for the bringing of a direct action, it will still have to show the existence of some reason for the Community act to be annulled or declared invalid. Four grounds are specified in Article 230: lack of competence; infringement of an essential procedural requirement; infringement of the Treaty or any rule of law relating to its application; and misuse of power. The same grounds are relevant for indirect actions under Article 234.[129]

---

[129] Hartley, n. 3 above, 402, 410.

(a) LACK OF COMPETENCE

The Community institutions must be able to point to a power within the Treaty which authorizes their action. If they are not able to do so then the act in question will be declared void for lack of competence. This ground of review has in the past been used relatively rarely. There are two connected reasons for this.

It is in part because the ECJ has interpreted the powers of the Community institutions broadly and purposively, in order to achieve the Community's objectives. This approach to Treaty interpretation has itself been complemented by the implied-powers doctrine, under which the Commission has been held impliedly to have the powers which are necessary to enable it to carry out the tasks expressly conferred on it by the Treaty.[130] It is in part because there are Treaty provisions that confer broader legislative power, notably Articles 94 and 308 EC (previously Articles 100 and 235).[131] Thus, it has been rare for the Community's action to be struck down on this ground.

This ground of challenge may be used where the claimant alleges that there has been an unlawful delegation of power. This is exemplified by the *Meroni* case,[132] in which the High Authority had delegated certain powers to outside agencies in connection with the administration of a scrap equalization scheme. The Court held that it was legitimate to delegate clearly defined executive powers which were subject to objective criteria set by the delegating authority. It was not, however, permissible to delegate broad, discretionary powers which entailed the exercise of considerable freedom of judgement for the delegee.

It might also be argued that the Community lacked competence because of subsidiarity. A claim that Community legislation had infringed the subsidiarity principle could be framed in terms of the Community's lack of competence to adopt the measure. However, as we have seen,[133] the case law thus far does not hold out much hope for claims of this nature.

In more general terms it remains to be seen how far the *Tobacco* case[134] signals tighter judicial controls over the assertion of legislative competence to act under broad Treaty provisions such as Articles 308 and 95.[135]

(b) INFRINGEMENT OF AN ESSENTIAL PROCEDURAL REQUIREMENT

Not all failures to comply with procedural requirements will lead to annulment. The defect must relate to an essential procedural requirement. What counts as essential is a matter of construction for the ECJ. The following are examples of procedural requirements which have been held to be essential for these purposes:

---

[130] Cases 281, 283–285, 287/85, *Germany v. Commission* [1987] ECR 3203, [1988] 1 CMLR 11.
[131] See Ch. 3 above.
[132] Case 9/56, *Meroni and Co. Industrie Metallurgiche SpA v. ECSC* [1957–8] ECR 133.
[133] See Ch. 3 above.
[134] Case C–376/98, *Germany v. European Parliament and Council* [2000] ECR I–8419.
[135] See Ch. 3 above.

the requirement to give a hearing;[136] the duty to provide reasons;[137] access to documents;[138] and the duty to consult. The following case provides an example of the Court's reasoning in this context.

Case 138/79, Roquette Frères SA v. Council
[1980] ECR 3333

[Note ToA renumbering: Art. 43 is now Art. 37]

The applicant and the Parliament claimed that a regulation had been adopted without regard to the consultation procedure of Article 43(2) of the Treaty.

THE ECJ

32. The applicant and the Parliament in its intervention maintain that since Regulation No 1111/77 as amended was adopted by the Council without regard to the consultation procedure provided for in the second paragraph of Article 43 of the Treaty it must be treated as void for infringement of essential procedural requirements.

33. The consultation provided for in the third subparagraph of Article 43(2), as in other similar provisions of the Treaty, is the means which allows the Parliament to play an actual part in the legislative process of the Community. Such power represents an essential factor in the institutional balance intended by the Treaty. Although limited, it reflects at Community level the fundamental democratic principle that the peoples should take part in the exercise of power through the intermediary of a representative assembly. Due consultation of the Parliament in the cases provided for by the Treaty therefore constitutes an essential formality disregard of which means that the measure concerned is void.

34. In that respect it is pertinent to point out that observance of that requirement implies that the Parliament has expressed its opinion. It is impossible to take the view that the requirement is satisfied by the Council's simply asking for the opinion. The Council is, therefore, wrong to conclude in the references in the preamble to Regulation No. 1293/79 a statement to the effect that the Parliament has been consulted.

(c) INFRINGEMENT OF THE TREATY OR OF ANY RULE OF LAW RELATING TO ITS APPLICATION

It is readily apparent that this third ground of review is capable of overlapping with the other grounds mentioned above. It is, therefore, not surprisingly pleaded in almost all cases.

Infringement of the Treaty embraces all the provisions of the constitutive treaties as well as Treaties which amend or supplement these.

---

[136] Case 17/74, *Transocean Marine Paint* v. *Commission* [1974] ECR 1063.
[137] Case 24/62, *Germany* v. *Commission* [1963] ECR 63; Case 5/67, *Beus GmbH & Co.* v. *Hauptzollamt München* [1968] ECR 83; Case C–143/95P, *Commission* v. *Sociedade de Curtumes a Sul do Tejo Ld (Socurte)* [1997] ECR I–1; Case T–83/96, *Gerard van der Wal* v. *Commission* [1998] ECR II–545.
[138] Case T–124/96, *Interporc Im- und Export GmbH* v. *Commission* [1998] ECR II–231.

The phrase 'any rule of law relating to its application' covers all those rules of Community law other than those in the Treaties themselves. This includes general principles of Community law,[139] and the fact that one Community act is in breach of another Community act which is hierarchically superior to it. These two categories of illegality are exemplified in the following cases.

Case 4/73, Nold KG v. Commission
[1974] ECR 491

The full facts of the case have been set out above.[140] It will be remembered that Nold sought the annulment of a Commission decision which meant that it could only purchase coal from a supplier on conditions which were burdensome. As a result it suffered loss because it could no longer buy direct from its supplier.

THE ECJ

12. The applicant asserts finally that certain of its fundamental rights have been violated, in that the restrictions introduced by the new trading rules authorized by the Commission have the effect, by depriving it of direct supplies, of jeopardizing both the profitability of the under-taking and the free development of its business activity, to the point of endangering its very existence.

In this way, the Decision is said to violate, in respect of the applicant, a right akin to a proprietary right, as well as its right to the free pursuit of business activity, as protected by the Grundgesetz of the Federal Republic of Germany and by the Constitutions of other Member States and various international treaties, including in particular the Convention for the Protection of Human Rights and Fundamental Freedoms of 4 November 1950 and the Protocol to that Convention of 20 March 1952.

13. As the Court has already stated, fundamental rights form an integral part of the general principles of law, the observance of which it ensures.

In safeguarding these rights, the Court is bound to draw inspiration from constitutional traditions common to the Member States, and it cannot therefore uphold measures which are incompatible with fundamental rights recognized and protected by the Constitutions of those States.

Similarly, international treaties for the protection of human rights on which the Member States have collaborated or of which they are signatories, can supply guidelines which should be followed within the framework of Community law.

The submissions of the applicant must be examined in the light of these principles.

14. If rights of ownership are protected by the constitutional laws of all the Member States and if similar guarantees are given in respect of their right freely to choose and practise their trade or profession, the rights thereby guaranteed, far from constituting unfettered prerogatives, must be viewed in the light of the social function of the property and activities protected thereunder.

For this reason, rights of this nature are protected by law subject always to limitations laid down in accordance with the public interest.

[139] See Chs. 8 and 9 above.   [140] See Ch. 8 above.

Within the Community legal order it likewise seems legitimate that these rights should, if necessary, be subject to certain limits justified by the overall objectives pursued by the Community, on condition that the substance of these rights is left untouched.

As regards the guarantees accorded to a particular undertaking, they can in no respect be extended to protect mere commercial interests or opportunities, the uncertainties of which are part of the very essence of economic activity.

15. The disadvantages claimed by the applicant are in fact the result of economic change and not of the contested Decision.

It was for the applicant, confronted by the economic changes brought about by the recession in coal production, to acknowledge the situation and itself carry out the necessary adaptations.

16. This submission must be dismissed for all the reasons outlined above.

The decision in *CNTA*[141] provides a good example of an attempt to found the illegality of one Community norm on the fact that it was in breach of a more basic, but still secondary, norm of Community law.[142] The applicant argued that the withdrawal of monetary compensatory amounts (MCAs), designed to compensate traders for fluctuations in exchange rates, was in breach of the basic regulation governing the payment of such sums. The applicant contended that this basic regulation did not allow the withdrawal of MCAs once instituted, and that, in any event, if this were to be done it could only be done on the basis of monetary factors, to the exclusion of broader economic factors. This claim was rejected on the construction of the relevant basic regulation, but claims of this type are commonplace.

The phrase 'any rule of law relating to its application' can also cover other matters in addition to infringement of general principles of Community law and breach of higher Community secondary norms. Thus, as we have seen,[143] an individual can base a claim on a breach of an international agreement with non-Member States, provided that the agreement is binding on the Community and provided also that it has direct effect.[144]

(d) MISUSE OF POWERS

The concept of misuse of powers covers adoption by a Community institution of a measure with the exclusive or main purpose of achieving an end other than that stated, or evading a procedure specifically prescribed by the Treaty for dealing with the circumstances of the case.[145] All systems of public law possess a doctrine similar, if not identical, to this. Challenges of this sort are less common in the EC, principally because applicants base their claims on another head of review. There is, moreover, a

---

[141] Case 74/74, *CNTA SA* v. *Commission* [1975] ECR 533.
[142] The case will be more fully considered in the context of a damages action, at 550–1 below.
[143] See Ch. 5 above.
[144] For the possibility of using a subsidiary convention to attack a Community act see Hartley, n. 3 above, 415.
[145] Case C–156/93, n. 16 above; Case C–84/94, *United Kingdom* v. *Council (Re Working Time Directive)* [1996] ECR I–5755; Case T–72/97, *Proderec-Formacao e Desinvolvimento de Recursos Humanos, ACE* v. *Commission* [1998] ECR II–2847; Case C–48/96P, *Windpark Groosthusen GmbH & Co. Betriebs KG* v. *Commission* [1998] ECR I–2873.

close connection between claims based on misuse of powers and those based on proportionality. The distinguishing feature, in principle, is that in the former instance the object or purpose which is sought to be achieved will itself be improper, whereas in the latter instance the objective will be legitimate, and the issue will be whether it was achieved in a disproportionate manner.

There are, however, successful claims for misuse of power, as exemplified by *Franco Giuffrida v. Council*.[146] The applicant sought the annulment of a decision appointing Martino to a higher grade in the Community service, pursuant to a competition in which he and Martino were the two contestants for the post. He claimed that the competition was in reality an exercise to appoint Martino to the job, the rationale being that Martino had already been performing the duties associated with the higher grade. The Court quashed the appointment, stating that the pursuit of such a specific objective was contrary to the aims of the recruitment procedure and was, therefore, a misuse of power. Internal promotions should be based on selecting the best person for the job, rather than pre-selecting a particular candidate to whom the job would be given.

(e) THE INTENSITY OF REVIEW

The discussion thus far has concentrated on the heads of review which are available under the Treaty. To stop there would, however, be to give only an incomplete view of the subject. Those familiar with public law will be aware of another issue which is relevant to the enquiry. This concerns the intensity of the review. The issue is how far the ECJ will go in reassessing decisions, particularly those involving discretion, made by the Commission and Council. The ECSC Treaty contained explicit dictates on the matter.[147] There is no directly analogous provision in the EC Treaty. However, the intensity of review has, not surprisingly, always been an issue under the EC Treaty. Many of the cases in which applicants seek to have Community acts annulled or declared illegal concern determinations made pursuant to the CAP. The intensity of the Court's review has arisen at different levels.

First, it has arisen in the context of a challenge to the *very choice of objective to be pursued, and the appropriate means by which this should be done*. We have already seen that the foundational provisions of the CAP, Articles 33, 34, and 37 (previously Articles 39, 40, and 43), contain a number of objectives which are set out at a relatively high level of generality.[148] This necessitates the making of discretionary choices by the Commission and the Council. In evaluating the chosen option the Court has held that the competent Community institutions enjoy wide discretionary power concerning, *inter alia*, the definition of the objectives to be pursued and the choice of the appropriate means of action.[149] The *Biovilac* case provides a good illustration.[150] The applicant argued that Community regulations on skimmed-milk powder were illegal, *inter alia*, because they disregarded the object of stabilizing markets set out in Article 33(1)(c). The Court rejected the claim. It held that even if the object of stabilizing markets and that of ensuring a fair return to the agricultural community

---

[146] Case 105/75, [1976] ECR 1395.
[147] Art. 33 ECSC.   [148] See 513–14 above.   [149] Case 105/75, [1976] ECR 1395.
[150] Case 59/83, *SA Biovilac NV v. European Economic Community* [1984] ECR 4057.

were only partially reconciled by the regulation, it could not be said that these were in breach of Article 33. The legality of such measures could be affected only if they were *manifestly unsuitable* for achieving the aim pursued.

A second context in which the intensity of review has arisen concerns the *interpretation of regulations or decisions* made pursuant to the CAP. These may often contain terms which premise Community action on the basis that there are 'serious disturbances' on the relevant market, or where 'economic difficulties' may be caused by a certain change in prices or currency values. There is no doubt that the Court could undertake an extensive re-evaluation of the factual and legal issues, in order to determine whether such circumstances existed, and that on occasion it has engaged in quite close scrutiny of the data.[151] To adopt this approach on a broad scale would, however, be time-consuming; it would encourage applicants to ask the Court to second-guess evaluations made by the Community institutions; and it would involve intensive review of measures which are often adopted under severe time constraints, or in situations where there is an urgent need for measures to combat a temporary problem in the market. These reasons for less intensive review are evident in the following extract. Lord Mackenzie Stuart considers the problems posed for the Community and the Court by the currency fluctuations of the 1970s.

Lord Mackenzie Stuart, The European Communities and the Rule of Law[152]

It is difficult to give a short and up-to-date account of the various currency crises since 1971 and I make no attempt. It would, I fear, be out of date before the ink dried on the page and of only antiquarian interest by the time these lectures are delivered.

In any case, you might ask, what is the relevance of this to the work of the Court? It could be said that I have just described a series of economic emergencies requiring a political rather than a legal solution. This is true. Nonetheless commerce continues and must continue in good times as in bad. Moreover, economic storms can sometimes bring fortune to those who can ride with them provided they can still steer a course when driven under bare poles. At any rate, the economic climate of the Community is ever reflected in the disputes, claims and grievances of those whose commercial transactions have been affected. Accordingly the Court has been compelled, in spite of the obvious difficulties, to apply the discipline of legal analysis to measures whose impetus has been the necessity of finding an immediate response to unacceptable economic pressures.

That is to say, the Court has had to consider the actions of the Community institutions taken, of necessity, at speed against a background of rapidly changing pressures, when almost every aspect has been under fire from those whose interests have been affected.

Lord Mackenzie Stuart illustrated these problems by reference to a number of cases, including *Balkan-Import-Export*[153] and *Merkur*, the latter of which will be considered more fully below. He then continued as follows.

---

[151] See, e.g., Cases 106 and 107/63, *Alfred Toepfer and Getreide-Import Gesellschaft* v. *Commission* [1965] ECR 405.

[152] (Stevens, 1977), 91, 96.   [153] Case 5/73, n. 149 above.

What do these instances demonstrate? First, I think, that the Court has had and is having to deal with a series of cases . . . arising in circumstances not only never envisaged by the Treaty of Rome but in circumstances running counter to one of its basic premises. Secondly, they show that the Court appreciates that in moments of economic stress when contingency measures have to be taken the Community authorities must be allowed some lee-way. That with hindsight it may appear that the measures chosen were not necessarily the best is not sufficient to annul what has been done. Even so, and this is the third and most important point, 'the law' must be applied to protect the administered if, no doubt with the best motives imaginable, the Council or Commission, as the case may be, has failed to protect their legitimate interest.

The ECJ's predominant approach has, therefore, not been one of complete substitution of judgment, or of a complete rehearing of issues of fact or mixed fact and law, at least in CAP cases. These account for many of the actions brought against the Community under Article 230 or Article 234.

The ECJ's approach can be exemplified by the following cases. In *CNTA*[154] the applicant complained of the withdrawal of monetary compensatory amounts (MCAs), and also contested the criteria on which such sums should be given. MCAs can be given to compensate for certain exchange-rate movements, in circumstances where those movements might otherwise disturb trade in agricultural products. The Court held that the Commission possessed a large degree of discretion in determining whether alterations in monetary values as a result of exchange-rate movements might lead to such disturbances in trade and, therefore, whether MCAs were warranted. The Court also held that the Commission could properly take account of broader economic factors, and was not confined to considering only monetary values. A similar approach can be perceived in the *Deuka* case.[155] The applicant sought, through Article 234, to test the legality of a particular regulation under which premiums payable on wheat were modified. It was argued that this was illegal, on the ground that the basic regulation on these matters permitted adjustments only 'where the balance of the market in cereals is likely to be disturbed'. The Court rejected the claim. It stated that the Commission had a 'significant freedom of evaluation' in deciding on both the existence of a disturbance and the method of dealing with it. The ECJ would intervene only if there were a patent error or a misuse of power.[156]

The third context in which the intensity of review has arisen concerns the *application of principles such as legitimate expectations, proportionality, and non-discrimination.*[157] It is clear that these principles can be used to strike down CAP regulations or decisions. It is also clear that the Court will not readily find that these principles have been violated in the agricultural sphere. For example, in the *Merkur* case[158] the applicant complained that the Commission had failed to fix compensatory payments for certain products in line with a basic regulation on this issue, and that this constituted discrimination since others in a similar position had received such payments. The Court rejected the claim. It was influenced by the fact that the basic

---

154 Case 74/74, *CNTA*, n. 141 above.

155 Case 78/74, *Deuka, Deutsche Kraftfutter GmbH, B.J. Stolp* v. *Einfuhr- und Vorratsstelle für Getreide und Futtermittel* [1975] ECR 421.

156 *Ibid.*, 432. See also Case 57/72, *Westzucker GmbH* v. *Einfuhr- und Vorratsstelle für Zucker* [1973] ECR 321; Case 98/78, *Firma A. Racke* v. *Hauptzollamt Mainz* [1979] ECR 69.

157 See Ch. 9 above.   158 Case 43/72, *Merkur GmbH* v. *Commission* [1973] ECR 1055, 1074.

Community regulation was an emergency measure, and that the rules for its implementation to particular product categories had to be devised within a very short space of time. The Commission assessment was perforce an overall one. The possibility that some of the decisions might subsequently appear to be debatable on economic grounds would not in itself be sufficient to prove discrimination, provided that the considerations adopted by the Commission were not manifestly erroneous.

Space precludes any detailed analysis of these principles in the agricultural sphere. It is, however, clear that the Court will be similarly reluctant to find, for example, a breach of the proportionality principle unless there was some manifest disproportionality in the challenged decision.[159] This is borne out by the secondary literature which attests to the difficulty of successfully utilizing such principles. Thus, Vajda comments that the Court's reluctance to involve itself in economic-policy considerations makes it hesitant to question the Commission's exercise of discretion on the grounds of proportionality, unless the charge in question was really disproportionate.[160] Sharpston is equally clear on the difficulties facing applicants who wish to plead legitimate expectations. Few such cases succeed in the agricultural sphere. The 'general rule appears to be that the European Court will usually be prepared to back the Council and/or the Commission and to hold that they are entitled to have a fairly wide margin of manoeuvre in market management, even where the chosen scheme has been subjected to fairly heavy criticism'.[161]

It should not be thought that the intensity of judicial review is only of relevance in the context of the CAP. That would be mistaken. A similar judicial reluctance to engage in intensive review is also apparent in other areas in which the Commission is possessed of discretionary power requiring it to make complex evaluative choices, as in the case of state aids,[162] dumping,[163] safeguard measures,[164] and mergers.[165]

13. THE CONSEQUENCES OF ILLEGALITY AND INVALIDITY

It should be noted at the outset that where the addressee has not challenged a decision within the time limits in Article 230, it is then definitive as against that person.[166]

Where there has been a successful challenge,[167] the Treaty has two principal

---

[159] Case C–331/88, *R. v. Minister of Agriculture, Fisheries and Food and the Secretary of State for Health, ex p. FEDESA* [1990] ECR I–4023, 4061; Case C–8/89, *Vincenzo Zardi v. Consorzio Agrario Provinciale di Ferrara* [1990] ECR I–2515, 2532–3.

[160] C. Vajda, 'Some Aspects of Judicial Review within the Common Agricultural Policy—Part II' (1979) 4 *ELRev.* 341, 347–8.

[161] E. Sharpston, 'Legitimate Expectations and Economic Reality' (1990) 15 *ELRev.* 103, 108.

[162] See Ch. 27 below. See Case T–380/94, *AIUFFASS v. Commission* [1996] ECR II–2169; Case T–358/94, *Compagnie Nationale Air France v. Commission* [1996] ECR II–2109.

[163] Case T–118/96, *Thai Bicycle Industry Co. Ltd. v. Council* [1998] ECR II–2991; Case T–2/95, *Industrie des Poudres*, n. 53 above.

[164] Case C–390/95P, *Antillean Rice Mills NV v. Commission* [1999] ECR I–769, para. 48.

[165] See Ch. 24 below.   [166] Case C–310/97P, *Kraft Products*, n. 106 above, para. 57.

[167] The Commission cannot avoid a challenge by withdrawing the contested measure when it is challenged before the ECJ, while seeking to preserve the effects it has produced: Case C–89/96, *Portuguese Republic v. Commission* [1999] ECR I–8377.

provisions which determine the consequences of illegality.[168] Article 231 (ex Article 174) provides that if the action under Article 230 (ex Article 173) is well founded, the Court shall declare the act void. This is then modified by Article 231(2) which states that, in the case of a regulation, the Court shall, if it considers it necessary, state which of the effects of the regulation declared void shall be considered as definitive. Article 233 (ex Article 176) complements this by stating that the institution whose act has been declared void, or whose failure to act has been declared contrary to the Treaty, shall be required to take the necessary measures to comply with the ECJ's judgment. This may involve, for example, eradicating the effects of the measure found to be void, and/or refraining from adopting an identical measure.[169] It does not however require the Commission, at the request of interested parties, to re-examine identical or similar decisions allegedly affected by the same irregularity, addressed to persons other than the applicant.[170]

The general principle of Community law is that nullity is retroactive: once the act is annulled under Article 230 it is void *ab initio*. Such a ruling has an effect *erga omnes*. In general terms, it is true, as Toth argues,[171] that it is only the annulment of law-making measures that can produce genuine *erga omnes* effects, affecting the public at large. The meaning of the phrase can however be more limited, particularly where decisions are in issue, as is clear from the *Kraft Products* case.[172] The ECJ held that the scope of any annulment could not go further than that sought by the applicants. The *erga omnes* authority of its annulment ruling did attach to both the operative part and the ratio decidendi of its judgment.[173] It did not however entail annulment of an act not challenged before the ECJ, even where it was alleged to be vitiated by the same illegality.

Normally an act will have to be challenged for its invalidity to be established. There are, however, certain limited instances in which the act will be treated as absolutely void or non-existent, where the act may be treated as if it were never adopted.[174] In general, however, proceedings will be required to establish the illegality of the act.

The principle of retroactive nullity can cause hardship, particularly in those instances where the measure is a regulation, which has been relied on by many, and which may be the basis of other measures adopted later. This is the rationale for Article 231(2), which allows the Court to qualify the extent of the nullity.[175] This

---

[168] The ECJ has power to prescribe interim measures under Art. 243 (ex Art. 186): see Case C–149/95P(R), *Commission* v. *Atlantic Container Line AB* [1995] ECR I–2165, and it also has power to order the suspension of the contested act: Art. 242 (ex Art. 185).

[169] Cases T–480 and 483/93, *Antillean Rice*, n. 32 above. Where the applicant is dissatisfied with the measures taken pursuant to an act being found to be void there may be a further Art. 230 or 232 action: Case T–387/94, *Asia Motor*, n. 94 above.

[170] Case C–310/97P, n. 106 above, para. 56.

[171] A.G. Toth, 'The Authority of Judgments of the European Court of Justice: Binding Force and Legal Effects' (1984) 4 *YBEL* 1, 49.

[172] Case 310/97P, n. 106 above, paras. 52–54.

[173] Case 3/54, *ASSIDER* v. *High Authority* [1955] ECR 63; Case 2/54, *Italy* v. *High Authority* [1954–6] ECR 37, 55.

[174] See 485–6 above.

[175] The ECJ has extended the principle of Art. 231(2) to dir.: Case C–295/90, *European Parliament* v. *Council* [1992] ECR I–4193, and to decisions, Case C–22/96, *European Parliament* v. *Council (Telematic Networks)* [1998] ECR I–3231.

Article has been used to limit the temporal effect of the Court's ruling. Thus, in *Commission* v. *Council*[176] the Court annulled part of a regulation concerning staff salaries. However, if the regulation had been annulled retroactively then the staff would not have been entitled to any salary increases until a new regulation had been adopted. The Court, therefore, used Article 231(2), ruling that the regulation should continue to have effect until a new regulation, in accord with the Court's judgment, had been promulgated. In addition to the power to limit the temporal effect of its rulings, the Court may also find that the illegality affects only part of the measure in question.

A finding of invalidity pursuant to Article 234 EC is, in theory, different from a decision made pursuant to Article 230. The former is addressed only to the national court which requested the ruling. However, as we have seen,[177] the Court has held that its rulings on Article 234 references concerning validity do have an *erga omnes* effect. These rulings provide a sufficient reason for any other national court to treat that act as void.[178] Moreover, the Court has applied the principles of Articles 231 and 233 (formerly 174 and 176), which technically only operate in the context of Articles 230 and 232 (formerly 173 and 175), by analogy to cases arising under Article 234. This has further eroded any distinction between the effects of a judgment given under Articles 230 and 234. This is exemplified by the following case.[179]

Case 112/83, Société de Produits de Maïs v. Administration des Douanes
[1985] ECR 719

[Note ToA renumbering: Arts. 173, 174, 176, and 177 are now Arts. 230, 231, 233, and 234]

The case concerned the effects of a ruling by the ECJ on the validity of a regulation, following a reference from the French courts under Article 177.

THE ECJ

16. It should in the first place be recalled that the Court has already held in its judgment . . . (Case 66/80, *International Chemical Corporation* . . .) that although a judgment of the Court given under Article 177 of the Treaty declaring an act of an institution, in particular a Council or Commission Regulation, to be void is directly addressed only to the national court which brought the matter before the Court, it is sufficient reason for any other national court to regard that act as void for the purposes of a judgment which it has to give.

17. Secondly, it must be emphasised that the Court's power to impose temporal limits on the effects of a declaration that a legislative act is invalid, in the context of preliminary rulings under

---

[176] Case 81/72, [1973] ECR 575, [1973] CMLR 639.

[177] See 442–4 above.

[178] Case 66/80, *International Chemical Corporation* v. *Amministrazione delle Finanze dello Stato* [1981] ECR 1191. The national court may make a reference on the same point if it is unclear about the scope, grounds, or consequences of the original ruling.

[179] See also Cases C–38, 151/90, *R.* v. *Lomas* [1992] ECR I–1781.

indent (b) of the first paragraph of Article 177, is justified by the interpretation of Article 174 of the Treaty having regard to the necessary consistency between the preliminary ruling procedure and the action for annulment provided for in Articles 173, 174 and 176 of the Treaty, which are two mechanisms provided by the Treaty for reviewing the legality of acts of the Community institutions. The possibility of imposing temporal limits on the effects of the invalidity of a Community Regulation, whether under Article 173 or Article 177, is a power conferred on the Court by the Treaty in the interest of the uniform application of Community law throughout the Community. . . .

18. It must be pointed out that where it is justified by overriding considerations the second paragraph of Article 174 gives the Court discretion to decide, in each particular case, which specific effects of a Regulation which has been declared void must be maintained. It is therefore for the Court, where it makes use of the possibility of limiting the effect of past events of a declaration in proceedings under Article 177 that a measure is void, to decide whether an exception to that temporal limitation of the effect of its judgment may be made in favour of the party which brought the action before the national court or of any other trader which took similar steps before the declaration of invalidity or whether, conversely, a declaration of invalidity applicable only to the future constitutes an adequate remedy even for traders who took action at the appropriate time with a view to protecting their rights.

In addition to the discretion to limit the temporal effects of a ruling given under Article 234, the Court has held that the principle underlying Article 233 is also applicable in the context of Article 234. This enables the Court to order remedial action which it considers to be appropriate instead of a simple declaration of invalidity.[180]

It is also necessary to consider the effect of a preliminary ruling concerning the interpretation of EC law, which calls into question the compatibility of national law with EC law. The general principle is that the ruling defines the legal position as it must have been understood from the time when the relevant EC norm came into force.[181] The Community norm must, therefore, be applied by national courts to situations which occurred before the actual ruling of the ECJ was given, provided that the conditions enabling an action relating to that rule to be brought before the courts having jurisdiction are satisfied. This proposition will only be qualified in exceptional circumstances.[182]

---

[180] See Cases 4, 109, 145/79, *Société Co-opérative 'Providence Agricole de la Champagne' v. ONIC* [1980] ECR 2823.

[181] Cases 66, 127 and 128/79, *Salumi v. Amministrazione delle Finanze* [1980] ECR 1237, paras. 9–10; Case C–50/96, *Deutsche Telekom AG v. Schröder* [2000] ECR I–743, para. 43.

[182] E.g., where there is a risk of serious economic repercussions owing to the large number of legal relationships entered into in good faith on the basis of the rules considered to be validly in force and where the individuals and national authorities have adopted practices which do not comply with EC law because of uncertainty about what EC law requires, to which the conduct of the Commission may even have contributed: Cases C–197 and 252/94, *Société Bautiaa v. Directeur des Services Fiscaux des Landes* [1996] ECR I–505; Case 61/79, *Denkavit Italiana* [1980] ECR 1205; Case C–137/94, *R. v. Secretary of State for Health, ex p. Richardson* [1995] ECR I–3407.

14. CONCLUSION

i. There are a number of avenues through which to test the legality of Community action. Direct challenge is through Article 230, indirect challenge is primarily via Article 234. These are intended to provide an integrated route through which the legality of Community action can be tested.

ii. It is, however, very difficult for non-privileged applicants to sustain a direct action, because of the limitations on standing. While this leaves open the possibility of an indirect action, this is dependent on the willingness of the national court to refer the matter to the ECJ. There are, moreover other difficulties with the indirect action, which have been set out above. It is to be hoped that the suggestions of Advocate General Jacobs are adopted by the ECJ.

iii. If the case does come before the Community courts, they do have a considerable range of powers to ensure the legality of Community action. There is no 'gap' in the powers of the CFI and ECJ.

iv. The interpretation of these review powers leaves a considerable discretion to the CFI and ECJ in deciding whether in fact to strike down a Community norm. In reaching this decision the nature of the subject-matter under scrutiny will play an important part in determining the standard or intensity of review adopted. We must therefore always be aware of the substantive issues that come before the Court. In this way a richer understanding can be gained of the Court's decisions concerning review of legality, whether these relate to matters of procedure or substance.

15. FURTHER READING

(a) *On* Locus Standi

ARNULL, A., 'Challenging EC Anti-Dumping Regulations: The Problem of Admissibility' [1992] *ECLR* 73

—— 'Private Applicants and the Action for Annulment under Article 173 of the EC Treaty' (1995) 32 *CMLRev.* 7

—— 'Private Applicants and the Action for Annulment since *Codorniu*' (2001) 38 *CMLRev.* 7

BARAV, A., 'Direct and Individual Concern: An Almost Insurmountable Barrier to the Admissibility of Individual Appeal to the EEC Court' (1974) 11 *CMLRev.* 191

BEBR, G., 'The Standing of the European Parliament in the Community System of Legal Remedies: A Thorny Jurisprudential Development' (1990) 10 *YBEL* 170

BRADLEY, K., 'Sense and Sensibility: *Parliament* v. *Council* Continued' (1991) 16 *ELRev.* 245

COOKE, J., '*Locus Standi* of Private Parties under Article 173(4)' (1997) *Irish Jnl. of European Law* 4

CRAIG, P.P., 'Legality, Standing and Substantive Review in Community Law' (1994) 14 *OJLS* 507

DINNAGE, J., 'Locus Standi and Article 173 EEC' (1979) 4 ELRev. 15

GREAVES, R.M., 'Locus Standi under Article 173 EEC when Seeking Annulment of a Regulation' (1986) 11 ELRev. 119

HARDING, C., 'The Private Interest in Challenging Community Action' (1980) 5 ELRev. 354

HARLOW, C., 'Towards a Theory of Access for the European Court of Justice' (1992) 12 YBEL 213

HEDEMANN-ROBINSON, M., 'Article 173 EC, General Community Measures and Locus Standi for Private Persons: Still a cause for Individual Concern?' (1996) 2 EPL 127

NEUWAHL, N., 'Article 173 Paragraph 4 EC: Past, Present and Possible Future' (1996) 21 ELRev. 17

RASMUSSEN. H., 'Why is Article 173 Interpreted against Private Plaintiffs?' (1980) 5 ELRev. 112

SCHERMERS, H., 'The Law as it Stands on the Appeal for Annulment' (1975) 2 LIEI 92

STEIN, P., and VINNING, J., 'Citizen Access to Judicial Review of Administrative Action in a Transnational and Federal Context' (1976) 70 Am. J Comp. L 219

WEILER, J., 'Pride and Prejudice—Parliament v. Council' (1989) 14 ELRev. 334

WARD, A., Judicial Review and the Rights of Private Parties in EC Law (Oxford University Press, 2000), ch. 6

(b) On Failure to Act

TOTH, A.G., 'The Law as it Stands on the Appeal for Failure to Act' (1975) 2 LIEI 65

(c) On the Exception of Illegality

BARAV, A., 'The Exception of Illegality in Community Law: A Critical Analysis' (1974) 11 CMLRev. 366

BEBR, G., 'Judicial Remedy of Private Parties against Normative Acts of the European Communities: The Role of the Exception of Illegality' (1966) 4 CMLRev. 7

(d) On Procedural Rights

LENAERTS, K., and VANHAMME, J., 'Procedural Rights of Private Parties in the Community Administrative Process' (1997) 34 CMLRev. 531

(e) On the Use of Article 234 (ex Article 177)

BEBR, G., 'Preliminary Rulings of the Court of Justice: Their Authority and Temporal Effect' (1981) 18 CMLRev. 475

—— 'The Reinforcement of the Constitutional Review of Community Acts Under Article 177 EEC Treaty' (1988) 25 CMLRev. 667

HARDING, C., 'The Impact of Article 177 of the EEC Treaty on the Review of Community Action' (1981) 1 YBEL 93

WYATT, D., 'The Relationship between Actions for Annulment and References on Validity after TWD Deggendorf', in J. Lombay and A. Biondi (eds.), Remedies for Breach of EC Law (Wiley, 1996), ch. 6.

(f) *On the Consequences of Illegality*

BEBR, G., 'Preliminary Rulings of the Court of Justice: Their Authority and Temporal Effect' (1981) 18 *CMLRev.* 475

HARDING, C., 'The Impact of Article 177 of the EEC Treaty on the Review of Community Action' (1981) 1 *YBEL* 93

TOTH, A.G., 'The Authority of Judgments of the European Court of Justice: Binding Force and Legal Effects' (1984) 4 *YBEL* 1

WAELBROECK, M., 'May the Court of Justice Limit the Retrospective Operation of its Judgments?' (1981) 1 *YBEL* 115

13

DAMAGES ACTIONS AND MONEY CLAIMS

1. INTRODUCTION

In any developed legal system there must be a mechanism whereby losses caused by governmental action may be recovered in an action brought by an individual. Compensation within the EC is governed by Article 288 (ex Article 215(2)):

In the case of non-contractual liability, the Community shall, in accordance with the general principles common to the laws of the Member States, make good any damage caused by its institutions or by its servants in the performance of their duties.

The Article leaves the ECJ with considerable room for interpretation,[1] and directs it to consider the general principles common to the laws of the Member States.

2. CENTRAL ISSUES

i. The key issue is as to the test for liability where losses are caused by Community acts that are illegal.

ii. It will be seen that the ECJ has fashioned different tests for cases where the challenged act is of a discretionary nature, and for those where it is not.

iii. In doing so it has drawn on its jurisprudence on state liability in damages.

3. LIABILITY FOR LEGISLATIVE AND NON-LEGISLATIVE DISCRETIONARY ACTS

(a) THE GENERAL TEST

The cases considered here are those where the decision-maker has a significant element of discretion. The norms challenged will normally be legislative in nature. It will however become clear from the subsequent discussion that an individualized norm, which contains a significant element of discretion, will also be subject to the

---

[1] Liability under Art. 288 cannot be founded on the primary Treaty Arts. themselves, since these do not constitute 'acts of the institutions' but are international agreements, Case T–113/96, *Edouard Dubois et Fils* v. *Council & Commission* [1998] ECR II–125.

legal test discussed in this section. The norm may not have been annulled, because of the restrictive interpretation of *locus standi*.

The early approach of the ECJ did not augur well for individuals, for it was held in *Plaumann*[2] that annulment of the norm was a necessary condition precedent to using Article 288 EC (ex Article 215). If this requirement had been adhered to Article 288 would have been of little use, given the difficulty an individual faces in proving *locus standi* for annulment. The necessity for annulment was, however, generally discarded in later cases, and the action for damages came to be regarded as an independent, autonomous cause of action.[3] This is clear from *Schöppenstedt*.

Case 5/71, Aktien-Zuckerfabrik Schöppenstedt v. Council
[1971] ECR 975

[Note ToA renumbering: Arts. 40 and 215 are now Arts. 34 and 288]

The applicant claimed that Regulation 769/68, concerning the sugar market, was in breach of Article 40(3), in that it was discriminatory in the way in which it established the pricing policy for the product.

THE ECJ

11. In the present case the non-contractual liability of the Community presupposes at the very least the unlawful nature of the act alleged to be the cause of the damage. Where legislative action involving measures of economic policy is concerned, the Community does not incur non-contractual liability for damage suffered by individuals as a consequence of that action, by virtue of the provisions contained in Article 215, second paragraph, of the Treaty, unless a sufficiently flagrant violation of a superior rule of law for the protection of the individual has occurred. For that reason the Court, in the present case, must first consider whether such a violation has occurred.

The ECJ decided that no breach of a superior rule of law could be proven on the facts. The test laid down has been taken to establish the general conditions for liability in this area.

---

[2] Case 25/62, *Plaumann* v. *Commission* [1963] ECR 95.
[3] Case 5/71, *Aktien-Zuckerfabrik Schöppenstedt* v. *Council* [1971] ECR 975; Cases 9 and 11/71, *Compagnie d'Approvisionnement de Transport et de Crédit SA et Grands Moulins de Paris SA* v. *Commission* [1972] ECR 391; Case T-178/98, *Fresh Marine Company SA* v. *Commission*, 24 Oct. 2000, paras. 45–50. There may, however, be instances where the failure to proceed with an Art. 230 action will have consequences for an Art. 288(2) action where the individual was directly and individually concerned by the offending norm and could have successfully challenged it under Art. 230, but either failed to do so entirely or failed to do so within the period for challenge laid down in Art. 230: Cases C–199 and 200/94, *Pesqueria Vasco-Montanesa SA (Pevasa) and Compania Internacional de Pesca y Derivados SA (Inpesca)* v. *Commission* [1995] ECR I–3709; Case T–93/95, *Laga* v. *Commission* [1998] ECR II–195; Case C–310/97P, *Commission* v. *AssiDomän Kraft Products AB* [1999] ECR I–5363, para. 59. See, generally, P. Mead, 'The Relationship between an Action for Damages and an Action for Annulment: The Return of *Plaumann*', in T. Heukels and A. McDonnell (eds.), *The Action for Damages in Community Law* (Kluwer, 1997), ch. 13.

(b) LEGISLATIVE AND NON-LEGISLATIVE DISCRETIONARY ACTS

The fact that it is the element of discretion that is crucial to the application of the *Schöppenstedt* test was brought out clearly in *Bergaderm*,[4] and *Antillean Rice*.[5] The cases will be examined more fully below. Suffice it to say for the present that the ECJ held that the crucial factor in determining the applicability of the test set out above was the degree of discretion possessed by the institution in relation to the challenged measure. The general or individual nature of the measure was not a decisive criterion for identifying the limits of the discretion enjoyed by the institution in question.

This means that the *Schöppenstedt* test can apply to individualized acts which entail a significant element of discretion. It will also apply to legislative acts which involve an element of discretionary choice on the part of the Community authorities. Many legislative acts will have this feature, but there is no logical reason why this should be so for all acts of a legislative nature.

It is clear both in principle and on authority, that whether an act is legislative for the purposes of the *Schöppenstedt* test will be dependent upon the substance of the measure, and not the legal form in which it is expressed.[6] This means that it is always open to an applicant in an Article 288(2) action to claim that the measure, although called a regulation, was in reality an administrative decision.[7] The converse is also true: it is possible for a measure to be a decision for some purposes, but to be a legislative act for the purposes of Article 288(2).[8] Moreover, the mere fact that an applicant has a sufficient interest for a challenge under Article 230 will not necessarily mean that the measure is not legislative for the purposes of the Article 288(2) action.[9]

(c) THE MEANING OF SUPERIOR RULE OF LAW

The case law of the ECJ has indicated that three differing types of norms can, in principle, qualify as superior rules of law for the protection of the individual.

First, it is clear that many Treaty provisions fall within this category. One of the most commonly cited grounds in cases under Article 288(2) is the ban on discrimination contained in Article 34(3) (ex Article 40(3)), in the context of the Common Agricultural Policy (CAP). This is not surprising, given that many of the damages actions are brought pursuant to regulations made under the CAP.[10]

A second ground of claim is that a regulation is in breach of a hierarchically

---

[4] Case C–352/98, *Laboratoires Pharmaceutiques Bergaderm SA and Goupil v. Commission* [2000] ECR I–5291, para. 46.

[5] Case C–390/95P, *Antillean Rice Mills NV v. Commission* [1999] ECR I–769, paras. 56–62.

[6] *Ibid.*, para. 60; A. Arnull, 'Liability for Legislative Acts under Article 215(2) EC', in *The Action for Damages in Community Law*, n. 3 above, 131–6.

[7] Case C–119/88, *Aerpo and Others v. Commission* [1990] ECR I–2189; Case T–472/93, *Campo Ebro and Others v. Commission* [1995] ECR II–421.

[8] Cases T–481/93 and 484/93, *Vereniging van Exporteurs in Levende Varkens v. Commission (Live Pigs)* [1995] ECR II–2941; Case C–390/95P, *Antillean Rice*, n. 5 above, para. 62.

[9] Cases T–480 and 483/93, *Antillean Rice Mills v. Commission* [1995] ECR II–2305; Case C–390/95P, *Antillean Rice*, n. 5, para. 62.

[10] See, e.g., Case 43/72, *Merkur-Aussenhandels-GmbH v. Commission* [1973] ECR 1055; Case 153/73, *Holtz und Willemsen GmbH v. Commission* [1974] ECR 675.

superior regulation.[11] The regulations which are made pursuant to, for example, the CAP, may be 'one-off' provisions, but they may also relate to a prior network of regulations on the same topic. There may therefore be regulations which are made pursuant to more general regulations on the same topic.

A third ground which has been held capable of sustaining the claim in damages is where the Community legislation is held to infringe certain general principles of law such as proportionality, legal certainty, or legitimate expectations.[12]

The ECJ does not articulate *why* the above might constitute superior rules of law, nor *what* other matters might be added to the list. It is clear that rules of the World Trade Organization (WTO) cannot be relied on in this context.[13] It is often left to the Advocate General to question the wisdom of adding to the list of such rules.[14] Superior sometimes seems to be equated with 'important', and sometimes with a more formalistic conception of one rule being higher than another, as in the case of the regulation being in breach of a parent regulation. These various possible grounds of claim can be exemplified by considering the *CNTA* case.

Case 74/74, Comptoir National Technique Agricole (CNTA) SA v. Commission [1975] ECR 533

The applicant claimed that it had suffered loss by the withdrawal of monetary compensatory amounts (MCAs) by Regulation 189/72. The system of MCAs was designed to compensate traders for fluctuations in exchange rates. Regulation 189/72, which entered into force on 1 February 1972, abolished these MCAs in so far as they had been applicable to colza and rape seeds, because the Commission decided that the market situation had altered, thereby rendering the MCAs unnecessary. The applicant had, however, entered into contracts before the Regulation was passed, even though these contracts were to be performed after the ending of the scheme. It argued that it had made these contracts on the assumption that the MCAs would still be payable, and that it had set the price on that hypothesis. The sudden termination of the system in this area, without warning, was said by the applicant, to have caused it loss. The ECJ began by citing the general principle from the *Schöppenstedt* case and then continued in the following vein.

THE ECJ

17. In this connexion the applicant contends in the first place that by abolishing the compensatory amounts by Regulation 189/72 the Commission has infringed basic Regulation 974/71 of the Council.

18. That Regulation, it contends, while conferring on the Commission the power to ascertain that the conditions for the application of the compensatory amounts are met, does not allow it to

---

[11] Case 74/74, *Comptoir National Technique Agricole (CNTA) SA* v. *Commission* [1975] ECR 533.

[12] The duty to give reasons does not appear to qualify as a superior rule of law for these purposes: Case 106/81, *Julius Kind KG* v. *EEC* [1982] ECR 2885; Case C–119/88, n. 7 above; Cases T–466, 469, 473, 474, 477/93, *O'Dwyer* v. *Council* [1996] 2 CMLR 148.

[13] Case C–149/96, *Portugal* v. *Council* [1999] ECR I–8395; Case T–18/99, *Cordis Obst und Gemüse Grosshandel GmbH* v. *Commission* [2001] ECR II–913.

[14] See, e.g., Trabbuchi AG in the *CNTA* case, n. 11 above, 560–1.

take a decision withdrawing compensatory amounts once instituted and it requires in any event that the Commission's decision be taken on the basis of an assessment of solely monetary factors to the exclusion of economic factors which in this case the Commission has taken into consideration.

19. It follows from the last sentence of Article 1(2) of Regulation No 974/71 that the option for Member States to apply compensatory amounts may only be exercised where the monetary measures in question would lead to disturbances to trade in agricultural products.

20. As the application of compensatory amounts is a measure of an exceptional nature, this provision must be understood as enunciating a condition not only of the introduction but also of the maintenance of compensatory amounts for a specific product.

21. The Commission has a large measure of discretion for judging whether the monetary measure concerned might lead to disturbances to trade in the product in question.

22. In order to judge the risk of such disturbances, it is permissible for the Commission to take into account market conditions as well as monetary factors.

23. It has not been established that the Commission exceeded the limits of its power thus defined when it considered towards the end of January 1972 that the situation on the market in colza and rape seeds was such that the application of compensatory amounts for those products was no longer necessary.

[*The ECJ then considered whether the withdrawal of the compensatory amounts violated certain general principles of law. It held that Regulation 189/72 was not retroactive, as had been claimed by the applicants. The Court then proceeded to consider whether this withdrawal had violated the principle of legitimate expectations. It held that the object of the regime for the fixing of refunds in advance on export orders could not be regarded as tantamount to a guarantee for traders against the risk of movements in exchange rates. It continued as follows.*]

41. Nevertheless the application of the compensatory amounts in practice avoids the exchange risk, so that a trader, even a prudent one, might be induced to omit to cover himself against such a risk.

42. In these circumstances, a trader may legitimately expect that for transactions irrevocably undertaken by him because he has obtained, subject to a deposit, export licences fixing the amount of the refund in advance, no unforeseeable alteration will occur which could have the effect of causing him inevitable loss, by re-exposing him to the exchange risk.

43. The Community is therefore liable if, in the absence of an overriding matter of public interest, the Commission abolished with immediate effect and without warning the application of compensatory amounts in a specific sector without adopting transitional measures which would at least permit traders either to avoid the loss which would have been suffered in the performance of export contracts, the existence and irrevocability of which are established by the advance fixing of the refunds, or to be compensated for such loss.

44. In the absence of an overriding matter of public interest, the Commission has violated a superior rule of law, thus rendering the Community liable, by failing to include in Regulation 189/72 transitional measures for the protection of the confidence which a trader might legitimately have had in the Community rules.

The ECJ stated, however, that the Community was not liable to pay the full cost of the relevant mcas which would have been applicable to the transactions, but rather that the extent of the applicant's legitimate expectation was merely that of not suffering loss by reason of the withdrawal of the MCAs. In later proceedings it was held that the applicant had not in fact suffered such losses.[15]

(d) THE MEANING OF FLAGRANT VIOLATION/SERIOUS BREACH: THE EARLY CASE LAW

It is evident from *Schöppenstedt* that the individual must prove not only that there has been a breach of a superior rule of law for the protection of the individual, but also that the breach was flagrant. The meaning of this term will now be considered.

Cases 83, 94/76, 4, 15, 40/77, Bayerische HNL Vermehrungsbetriebe GmbH & Co KG v. Council and Commission [1978] ECR 1209

[Note ToA renumbering: Arts. 40 and 215 are now Arts. 34 and 288]

The Community was experiencing a surplus of milk which took the form of large stocks of skimmed-milk powder. In order to reduce these stocks Council Regulation 563/76 was passed. This Regulation imposed an obligation to purchase skimmed-milk powder for use in certain feed-ingstuffs. The applicant claimed that this had rendered the costs of feeding its animals more expensive. In earlier cases the ECJ had held that the Regulation was null and void. The ECJ held that the Regulation imposed the obligation to purchase at such a disproportionate price that it was equivalent to a discriminatory distribution of the burden of the costs between the various agricultural sectors, which was not justified by the objective in view, namely the disposal of stocks of skimmed-milk powder.[16] The present action was concerned with the applicants' claim for damages.

THE ECJ

3. The finding that a legislative measure such as the Regulation in question is null and void is however insufficient by itself for the Community to incur non-contractual liability for damage caused to individuals under the second paragraph of Article 215 of the EEC Treaty. The Court of Justice has consistently stated that the Community does not incur liability on account of a legislative measure which involves choices of economic policy unless a sufficiently serious breach of a superior rule of law for the protection of the individual has occurred.

[*The ECJ held that a breach of Article 40(3) was such a superior rule of law, and that it had been broken in this case. The Court stated, however, that more was required before the Community could be liable, and that the laws of the Member States indicated that it was only 'exceptionally and in special circumstances' that a public authority would be liable for losses resulting from a legislative measure which involved choices of economic policy. The Court continued as follows:*]

4. . . . This restrictive view is explained by the consideration that the legislative authority, even where the validity of its measures is subject to judicial review, cannot always be hindered in making its decisions by the prospect of applications for damages whenever it has occasion to

---

[15] Case 74/74, [1976] ECR 797.
[16] See, e.g., Case 116/76, *Granaria BV v. Hoofdproduktschap voor Akkerbouwprodukten* [1977] ECR 1247.

adopt legislative measures in the public interest which may adversely affect the interests of individuals.

5. It follows from these considerations that individuals may be required, in the sectors coming within the economic policy of the Community, to accept within reasonable limits certain harmful effects on their economic interests as a result of a legislative measure without being able to obtain compensation from public funds, even if that measure has been declared null and void. In a field such as the one in question, in which one of the chief features is the exercise of a wide discretion essential for the implementation of the Common Agricultural Policy, the Community does not therefore incur liability unless the institution concerned has manifestly and gravely disregarded the limits on the exercise of its powers.

6. This is not so in the case of a measure of economic policy such as that in the present case, in view of its special features. In this connection it is necessary to observe first that this measure affected very wide categories of traders, in other words all buyers of compound feeding-stuffs, so that its effects on individual undertakings were considerably lessened. Moreover, the effects of the Regulation on the price of feeding-stuffs as a factor in the production costs of those buyers were only limited since that price rose by little more than 2 per cent. This price increase was particularly small in comparison with the price increases resulting, during the period of application of the Regulation, from the variations in the world market prices of feeding-stuffs containing protein, which were three or four times higher than the increase resulting from the obligation to purchase skimmed-milk powder introduced by the Regulation. The effects of the Regulation on the profit-earning capacity of the undertakings did not ultimately exceed the bounds of economic risks inherent in the activities of the agricultural sectors concerned.

It is apparent that the breach was held not to be manifest and grave because its *effects* were not regarded as serious enough to warrant recovery under Article 215 (now Article 288). In the *Amylum* case this condition was read in a rather different way.

Cases 116 and 124/77, Amylum NV and Tunnel Refineries Ltd. v. Council and Commission [1979] ECR 3497

[Note ToA renumbering: Arts. 39, 40, and 177 are now Arts. 33, 34, and 234]

The applicants were manufacturers of isoglucose, a sweetener made from starch. The product could not, at the time, be crystallized. It could be used in liquid form, and in this form it was in competition with sugar. There was a surplus of sugar on the market, and it was subject to production constraints. The producers of isoglucose were therefore perceived as having an economic advantage, and it was decided that they too should be subject to a production levy. The system for levies was introduced by Council Regulation 1111/77 and Commission Regulation 1468/77. In an earlier case arising under Article 177 the ECJ had held that Regulation 1111/77 was invalid because the particular production levy imposed was in breach of Article 40(3). The Court added that the Council could none the less devise appropriate measures to ensure that the market in sweeteners functioned properly.[17] The applicants sought

---

[17] Cases 103 & 145/77, *Royal Scholten-Honig (Holdings) Ltd.* v. *Intervention Board for Agricultural Produce*; *Tunnel Refineries Ltd.* v. *Intervention Board for Agricultural Produce* [1978] ECR 2037.

compensation for losses suffered, as a result of the reduction in profits due to the fact that the companies replaced sales of isoglucose with less profitable sales of starch, and because of lost production in their factories. The Court began its judgment in the damages action by quoting the principle laid down in the *Bayerische* case set out above. It then proceeded to consider whether there had been a manifest and grave disregard of the limits of their power by the Council and Commission.

THE ECJ

17. In this respect it must be recalled that the Court did not declare invalid any isoglucose production levy, but only the method of calculation adopted and the fact that the levy applied to the whole of the isoglucose production. Having regard to the fact that the production of isoglucose was playing a part in increasing sugar surpluses, it was permissible for the Council to impose restrictive measures on such production.

. . .

19. In fact, even though the fixing of the isoglucose production levy at 5 units of account per 100 kg. of dry matter was vitiated by errors, it must nevertheless be pointed out that, having regard to the fact that an appropriate levy was fully justified, these errors were not of such gravity that it may be said that the conduct of the institutions in this respect was verging on the arbitrary and was thus of such a kind as to involve the Community in non-contractual liability.

20. It must also be pointed out that Regulation No 1111/77 was adopted in particular to deal with an emergency situation characterized by growing sugar surpluses and in circumstances which, in accordance with the principles set out in Article 39 of the Treaty, permitted a certain preference to be given to sugar beet, Community production of which was in surplus, while Community production of maize was in deficit.

It is readily apparent that the reasons for the applicants' failure in *Amylum* were not the same as in *Bayerische*. In the *Amylum* case the applicants did not lose because the *effects* of the breach were insufficiently serious: the losses were severe. The ECJ's reasoning focused rather upon the *manner* of the breach. This was said not to be arbitrary, for the following reason. The general aim of stabilizing the market in sweeteners was a legitimate one for the Community to pursue. Mistakes had occurred in the *particular way* in which this was achieved, namely in the calculation of the levy. This was not, however, enough to render the decision arbitrary, especially given the fact that this was an emergency situation.

The result of *Bayerische* and *Amylum* was that an applicant would have to show both that the *effects* of the breach were serious, in terms of the quantum of loss suffered, and also that the *manner* of the breach was arbitrary. These hurdles were not easy to surmount, particularly the second. It will be rare for the Community institutions to promulgate a regulation which is wholly unrelated to the general ends they are entitled to advance under their powers in, for example, the agricultural sphere. The mistakes are likely to be made precisely in the carrying out of general, legitimate policies in an erroneous manner. Claimants did however occasionally win.[18]

---

[18] Cases 64, 113/76, 167, 239/78, 27, 28, 45/79, *Dumortier Frères SA* v. *Council* [1979] ECR 3091.

(e) THE MEANING OF FLAGRANT VIOLATION/SERIOUS BREACH: MORE RECENT DEVELOPMENTS

More recent cases have evinced a less restrictive interpretation of the term flagrant violation. They have done so in two ways.

First, the ECJ has modified its position in relation to the *manner of the breach*. In *Stahlwerke*[19] it held that fault in the nature of arbitrariness was not required for liability.[20] This did not mean that illegality *per se* would suffice for liability. The CFI, whose decision in *Stahlwerke* was being reviewed by the ECJ, had found fault, examined whether this fault was the result of an excusable or an inexcusable error, and decided on the facts that there was fault of such a nature as to render the Community liable.

This approach fits neatly with that in *Bergaderm*. It has already been seen that when discussing state liability in damages the ECJ, in *Brasserie du Pêcheur*,[21] gave its judgment on the premise that the test should not be different for the liability of the Community itself under Article 288(2).[22] It follows that the ECJ's interpretation of the term 'serious breach' in *Brasserie du Pêcheur* will be of importance in the Article 288(2) jurisprudence. This has been confirmed by *Bergaderm*, where the ECJ completed the circle by explicitly drawing on the factors mentioned in *Brasserie du Pêcheur* to determine the meaning of flagrant violation for the purposes of liability under Article 288(2).[23] This means that under Article 288(2) the seriousness of the breach will be dependent upon factors such as: the relative clarity of the rule which has been breached; the measure of discretion left to the relevant authorities; whether the error of law was excusable or not; and whether the breach was intentional or voluntary.

Case C–352/98, Laboratoires Pharmaceutiques Bergaderm SA and Goupil v. Commission [2000] ECR I–5291

[Note ToA renumbering: Art. 215 is now Art. 288]

This was an appeal from the CFI to the ECJ. The applicant sought damages for losses suffered by the passage of a directive, which prohibited the use of certain substances in cosmetics. It claimed, *inter alia*, that the directive should be regarded as an administrative act, since it only concerned the applicant. The purpose of this argument was to maintain that a showing of illegality *per se* would suffice, rather than having to prove a sufficiently serious breach.

---

[19] Case C–220/91P, *Stahlwerke Peine-Salzgitter AG v. Commission* [1993] ECR I–2393. See also Case T–120/89, *Stahlwerke Peine-Salzgitter v. Commission* [1991] ECR II–279. However, compare Cases T–481 and 484/93, *Live Pigs*, n. 8 above, para. 128, where the CFI used the language of arbitrariness in deciding upon the liability of the Commission.

[20] See also Case C–282/90, *Industrie- en Handelsonderneming Vreugdenhil BV v. Commission* [1992] ECR I–1937, paras. 17–19.

[21] Cases C–46 & 48/93, *Brasserie du Pêcheur SA v. Germany; R. v. Secretary of State for Transport, ex p. Factortame Ltd.* [1996] ECR I–1029.

[22] See Ch. 6 above.

[23] T. Tridimas, 'Liability for Breach of Community Law: Growing Up and Mellowing Down?' (2001) 38 *CMLRev.* 301.

40. The system of rules which the Court has worked out with regard to [Article 215] takes into account, *inter alia*, the complexity of situations to be regulated, difficulties in the application or interpretation of the texts and, more particularly, the margin of discretion available to the author of the act in question (*Brasserie du Pêcheur*, para. 43).

41. The Court has stated that the conditions under which the State may incur liability for damage caused to individuals by a breach of Community law cannot, in the absence of particular justification, differ from those governing the liability of the Community in like circumstances. The protection of the rights which individuals derive from Community law cannot vary depending on whether a national authority or a Community authority is responsible for the damage (*Brasserie du Pêcheur*, para. 42).

42. As regards Member State liability for damage caused to individuals, the Court has held that Community law confers a right to reparation where three conditions are met: the rule of law infringed must be intended to confer rights on individuals; the breach must be sufficiently serious; and there must be a direct causal link between the breach of the obligation resting on the State and the damage sustained by the injured parties (*Brasserie du Pêcheur*, para. 51).

43. As to the second condition, as regards both Community liability under Article 215 . . . and Member State liability for breaches of Community law, the decisive test for finding that a breach of Community law is sufficiently serious is whether the Member State or the Community institution concerned manifestly and gravely disregarded the limits on its discretion (*Brasserie du Pêcheur*, para. 55 . . .).

44. Where the Member State or the institution in question has only considerably reduced, or even no discretion, the mere infringement of Community law may be sufficient to establish the existence of a sufficiently serious breach (*Hedley Lomas*, para. 28).

45. It is therefore necessary to examine whether . . . the Court of First Instance erred in law in its examination of the way in which the Commission exercised its discretion when it adopted the Adaptation Directive.

46. In that regard, the Court finds that the general or individual nature of a measure taken by an institution is not a decisive criterion for identifying the limits of the discretion enjoyed by the institution in question.

47. It follows that the first ground of the appeal, which is based exclusively on the categorisation of the Adaptation Directive as an individual measure, has in any event no bearing on the issue and must be rejected.

The second way in which the ECJ has become more liberal relates to the *effects of the breach*. The possibility of a large number of claimants will not, in itself, rule out an Article 288(2) action. This is evident from the *Mulder* case.[24] This was a sequel to the earlier *Mulder* case,[25] where the ECJ held that a Community regulation, which precluded Mulder and many others in the same position from being qualified for a milk quota, violated their legitimate expectations and was invalid. With reference to the regulation which totally denied the farmers any quota at all, a damages action could lie. This regulation constituted a breach of the farmers' legitimate expectations, and

[24] Cases C–104/89 & 37/90, *Mulder* v. *Council and Commission* [1992] ECR I–3061.
[25] Case 120/86, *Mulder* v. *Minister van Landbouw en Visserij* [1988] ECR 2321.

there was no countervailing, higher public interest justifying this action.[26] With reference to the illegality of a later regulation imposing a 60 per cent quota, the ECJ reached the opposite conclusion. The Court accepted that this, too, infringed the legitimate expectations of the applicants, but this illegality was not sufficiently serious. It was not sufficiently serious *because* there was a higher public interest at stake here. The 60 per cent quota was a choice of economic policy made by the Council, seeking to balance the need to avoid excess production in this area with the interest of the farmers who had entered the earlier scheme.

(f) THE PRESENT LAW: SUMMARY

i. For an applicant to succeed it will be necessary to show that there has been a violation of a superior rule of law for the protection of individuals, that it was manifest and grave, or sufficiently serious, and that it has caused the damage.

ii. The key criterion as to whether it is necessary to show that the breach was sufficiently serious is the margin of discretion accorded to the author of the act in question. Where such discretion exists it will be necessary for the applicant to prove such a breach. This is so irrespective of whether the measure is general/legislative or individual/administrative in nature.

iii. The factors mentioned in *Brasserie du Pêcheur* and *Bergaderm*, which go to the issue of whether the breach was sufficiently serious, will be determinative in the Article 288(2) case law.

iv. The applicant should not have to show that the loss suffered was serious. It is not part of the *Brasserie du Pêcheur* test, and should not, as a matter of principle be required.

v. It is no longer fatal to a claim that there is a large number of potential applicants.

(g) THE PRESENT LAW: AN ASSESSMENT

The initial question must be whether there are valid reasons for limiting liability under Article 288(2). Views on this issue will undoubtedly differ, but we believe that there are good arguments for doing so. Most of the major cases arise out of the CAP, under which the Community institutions have to make difficult discretionary choices of a legislative nature. This will often entail a complex process designed to balance the conflicting variables identified in Article 33 (ex Article 39). A finding of illegality *per se* should not suffice as the basis for a damages action. Such a strict standard of liability would render the decision-makers susceptible to a potentially wide liability, and would run the risk that the Court might be 'second-guessing' the decisions made by the Council and Commission on how the variables within Article 33 should be balanced in any particular instance.[27] Directly analogous considerations have influenced UK courts in similar

---

[26] See also Case C–152/88, *Sofrimport Sàrl* v. *Commission* [1990] ECR I–2477.

[27] *Cf.* Capotorti AG in Cases 83 and 94/76, 4, 15, and 40/77, *Bayerische HNL Vermehrungsbetriebe GmbH & Co. KG* v. *Council and Commission* [1978] ECR 1209, 1223–4.

types of case.[28] The only circumstances in which it would be feasible to regard illegality *per se* as the appropriate test under Article 288(2) would be if such illegality were to be taken as proven only where the conduct of the Community institutions was particularly flagrant. Such a test would, in effect, be building an element of serious breach into the definition of illegality which was to operate in this area.[29]

Secondly, if this is accepted the crucial issue is then how to interpret the phrase 'flagrant violation' or 'serious breach'. In the past this has been interpreted very restrictively to require something akin to arbitrary action by the EC authorities. This is too restrictive a test. The approach in *Brasserie du Pêcheur* and *Bergaderm* is far more nuanced in this regard, and is to be welcomed. The existence of such a serious breach requires attention to the very type of factors which the ECJ identified in those cases. The mere fact that the general aim being pursued by the EC was legitimate should not, in and of itself, serve to shield it from liability if it can be shown that there was a serious breach in the manner of attaining this end, when judged by the *Brasserie du Pêcheur* criteria.

Thirdly, where loss has been caused by sufficiently serious illegal action the applicant should not have to prove that the loss was particularly serious. The applicant will have to show that the illegality *caused* the loss, but there should be no requirement over and above this.[30] The ordinary 'economics of litigation' should ensure that claims are, in general, only pursued when it is economically worthwhile to do so.

4. LIABILITY FOR NON-DISCRETIONARY ACTS

(a) THE GENERAL PRINCIPLE: ILLEGALITY, CAUSATION, DAMAGE

The discussion thus far has focused upon liability in damages for legislative and non-legislative which involve an element of discretion. Where a legislative act does not entail any meaningful discretionary choice then it will normally suffice to show the existence of illegality, causation, and damage.[31] This test of illegality, causation, and damage will also be that which normally applies to administrative acts. These may be defined as 'acts by which the administration applies general rules in individual cases or otherwise exercises its powers in an individual manner'.[32] Van der Woude has helpfully grouped such cases into four categories: failure to exercise supervisory powers; factual conduct; problems arising from public procurement; and those arising from funding operations.[33] Successful claims are rare.[34] While the test of illegality,

---

[28] P. Craig, 'Once More Unto the Breach: The Community, the State and Damages Liability' (1997) 113 *LQR* 67.

[29] *Cf.* Capotorti AG, n. 27 above, 1233.   [30] *Ibid.*, 1233–4.

[31] Cases 44–51/77, *Union Malt* v. *Commission* [1978] ECR 57; Cases T–481 and 484/93, *Live Pigs*, n. 8 above; Case 26/81, *Oleifici Mediterranei* v. *EEC* [1982] ECR 3057, para. 16; Case C–146/91, *KYDEP* v. *Council and Commission* [1994] ECR I–4199; Cases C–258 & 259/90, *Pesquerias de Bermeo SA and Naviera Laida SA* v. *Commission* [1992] ECR I–2901; Case T–175/94, *International procurement Services* v. *Commission* [1996] ECR II–729, para. 44; Case T–178/98, *Fresh Marine*, above n. 3, para. 54; Cases T–79/96, 260/97, 117/98, *Camar Srl and Tico Srl* v. *Commission* [2000] ECR II–2193, paras. 204–5.

[32] M. van der Woude, 'Liability for Administrative Acts under Article 215(2)', in *The Action for Damages in Community Law*, n. 3 above, ch. 6, 112.

[33] *Ibid.*, 117–25.   [34] *Ibid.*, 126.

causation, and damage will be that which is normally applied in such instances, this still leaves open three issues of more general importance.

(b) QUALIFICATIONS TO THE GENERAL PRINCIPLE

The first is that the *Schöppenstedt* test discussed in the previous section will and should apply to administrative acts which contain a significant element of discretion. *Bergaderm*[35] and *Antillean Rice*[36] have confirmed that the general or individual nature of the measure is not a decisive criterion when identifying the limits of discretion possessed by an institution, and this echoes earlier statements in *Brasserie du Pêcheur*.[37] This must be correct in principle. Many administrative measures involve discretionary choices which are just as difficult as those which have to be made in the context of legislative action.[38] The very line between the two is difficult to draw in substantive terms.

The second important point is that the Court will inevitably have to decide whether the challenged measure falls to be determined by the *Schöppenstedt* formula, or whether it will suffice for the claimant to show illegality, causation and damage. This is exemplified by *Schröder*.[39] The CFI held that in the context of administrative action any infringement of law constitutes illegality giving rise to damages liability. The CFI was however willing to consider whether the challenged norms, which were Commission *decisions*, really were administrative or legislative. The Commission decisions were made pursuant to a directive dealing with veterinary checks applicable to live trade in animals. These decisions imposed a ban on the export of pigs from Germany because of swine fever. The CFI decided that they were legislative because of their generalized application, their discretionary nature, and the need to balance the free movement of animals with the protection of health. Liability could therefore only be incurred if there was a manifest and serious breach of a superior rule of law. This approach was confirmed by the ECJ in the following case.

Case C–390/95P, Antillean Rice Mills NV v. Commission
[1999] ECR I–769

The applicants challenged, *inter alia*, aspects of the basic Council Decision which governed the relationship between the overseas countries and territories (OCTs) and the EC. They also challenged a Commission Decision, which introduced safeguard measures for rice originating in the Dutch Antilles, for breach of the Council Decision. The CFI dismissed most of the claim. On

---

[35] Case C–352/98, n. 4 above, para. 46; Case T–178/98, *Fresh Marine*, n. 3 above, para. 57.

[36] Case C–390/95P, *Antillean Rice*, n. 5 above, paras. 56–62.

[37] N. 21 above, para. 43; Cases C–178, 179, 188–190/94, *Dillenkofer* v. *Germany* [1996] ECR I–4845.

[38] See, e.g., in the context of the UK, *X (Minors)* v. *Bedfordshire CC* [1995] 2 AC 633.

[39] Case T–390/94, *Aloys Schröder* v. *Commission* [1997] ECR II–501. See also Cases T–458 and 523/93, *ENU* v. *Commission* [1995] ECR II–2459; Case T–178/98, *Fresh Marine*, above n. 3, para. 57; Case 79/96, *Camar Srl*, above n. 31, para. 206; Case C–64/98, *Petrides Co. Inc.* v. *Commission* [1999] ECR I–5187, paras. 26–8.

appeal to the ECJ the applicants argued, *inter alia,* the CFI was wrong to have required proof of a sufficiently serious breach, since the contested measures were decisions.

THE ECJ

57. It must be noted, first, that it is settled case-law that in a legislative context involving the exercise of a wide discretion, the Community cannot incur liability unless the institution concerned has manifestly and gravely disregarded the limits on the exercise of its powers. . . .

58. Second, . . . the CFI proceeded on the basis that the Commission enjoyed a wide discretion in the field of economic policy, which means that the stricter criterion of liability must be applied, namely the requirements of a sufficiently serious breach of a superior rule of law for the protection of the individual.

59. It follows that the CFI correctly applied the stricter criterion of liability.

60. The fact that the contested measure is in the form of a decision, and hence in principle capable of being the subject of an action for annulment, is not sufficient to preclude its being legislative in character. In the context of an action for damages, that character depends on the nature of the measure in question, not its form.

. . .

62. . . . [I]t must be stated that the fact they are individually concerned has no effect on the character of the measure in the context of an action for damages, since that action is an independent remedy. . . .

The third important issue concerns the meaning to be attributed to 'illegality' in this context. In one sense any infringement of law can constitute illegality.[40] It is possible to list a variety of errors which *might* lead to liability. These will include: failure to gather the facts before reaching a decision, taking a decision based on irrelevant factors, failure to accord appropriate procedural rights to certain individuals before making a decision, and inadequate supervision of bodies to whom power has been delegated. The mere proof of such an error will not however always ensure success in a damages action. It is always open to a court to construe illegality narrowly, or to define it so as to preclude liability unless there has been some error, or something equivalent thereto.[41] The point is exemplified by the following cases.

Cases 19, 20, 25, 30/69, Denise Richez-Parise and Others v. Commission
[1970] ECR 325

The applicants were Community officials who had been given incorrect information concerning their pensions. This information was supplied as a consequence of a request by the Commission to the officials concerned that they should contact the relevant department in order to obtain

---

[40] Case T–79/96, *Camar Srl*, above n. 31, para. 205.

[41] Many of those who do argue that a different test from that in *Bayerische* should be applied outside the discretionary, economic sphere also make it clear that they are not advocating liability being based on illegality alone: see, e.g., Darmon AG in *Vreugdenhil*, n. 20 above, 821–2.

information concerning their financial provisions on termination of employment. The information which was given was based on an interpretation of the relevant regulation, which was believed to be correct at the time at which it was given. The department which gave the information later had reason to believe that its interpretation of the regulation was incorrect, but no immediate steps were taken to inform the applicants of this. This was done only at a later stage, by which time the applicants had already committed themselves as to the way in which they would take their pension entitlements. The applicants sought, *inter alia*, to obtain compensation for losses which they had suffered.

THE ECJ

36. Apart from the exceptional instance, the adoption of an incorrect interpretation does not constitute in itself a wrongful act.

37. Even the fact that the authorities request those concerned to obtain information from the competent departments does not necessarily involve those authorities in an obligation to guarantee the correctness of the information supplied and does not therefore make them liable for any injury which may be occasioned by incorrect information.

38. However, whilst it may be possible to doubt the existence of a wrongful act concerning the supply of incorrect information, the same cannot be said of the department's delay in rectifying the information.

39. Although such rectification was possible as early as April 1968 it was deferred without any justification until the end of 1968.

. . .

41. A correction made shortly before or after 16 April, that is to say, before the time when those concerned had to make their decision, would have certainly enabled the defendant to avoid all liability for the consequences of the wrong information. The failure to make such a correction is, on the other hand, a matter of such a nature as to render the Communities liable.

Case 145/83, Stanley George Adams v. Commission
[1985] ECR 3539

In 1973 Adams sent a letter to the Commission indicating that his employer in Switzerland was engaged in a number of anti-competitive practices. He stated in the letter that he was about to leave the company, and that he would then be prepared to give evidence in court. The Commission investigated the company and made a decision against it. The company believed that Adams was the informant and had him arrested for economic espionage when he returned to Switzerland in 1974. He was held in solitary confinement and not allowed to communicate with his family. His wife committed suicide. Early in 1975 the Commission confirmed that he was the informant. Adams was eventually given a one year suspended sentence. He claimed damages on the ground that the Commission had wronged him by disclosing his identity to the company. The Court stated that information supplied in circumstances such as these did give rise to a duty of confidentiality, more especially since the informant had requested that his identity should be kept secret. It continued as follows.

35. As regards the case before the Court, it is quite clear from the applicant's letter of 25 February 1973 that he requested the Commission not to reveal his identity. It cannot therefore be denied that the Commission was bound by a duty of confidentiality to the applicant in that respect. In fact the parties disagree not so much as to the existence of such a duty but as to whether the Commission was bound by a duty of confidentiality after the applicant had left his employment with Roche.

36. In that respect it must be pointed out that the applicant did not qualify his request by indicating a period upon the expiry of which the Commission would be released from its duty of confidentiality regarding the identity of its informant. No such indication can be inferred from the fact that the applicant was prepared to appear before any court after he had left Roche. . . .

37. It must therefore be inferred that the Commission was under a duty to keep the applicant's identity secret even after he had left his employer.

. . .

53. It must therefore be concluded that in principle the Community is bound to make good the damage resulting from the discovery of the applicant's identity by means of the documents handed over to Roche by the Commission. It must however be recognised that the extent of the Commission's liability is diminished by reason of the applicant's own negligence.

Thus in *Richez-Parise* the ECJ construed the requisite illegality for the purposes of damages liability so as to exclude a mere incorrect interpretation of a regulation. Such regulations are often complex, and are open to more than one construction. To render the Communities liable in damages whenever such a construction proved to be incorrect would be too harsh. It would, in effect, open the Community to a form of strict liability, where the only condition for recovery would be proof that the interpretation adopted was incorrect, even if that interpretation was plausible, and even if the decision-maker had taken due care in reaching it.[42] In *Adams* one might choose to characterize the liability which was imposed as being based on illegality *per se*, but it was quite clear from the facts that the relevant Community officials had been negligent. We see the same general point in *Fresh Marine*.[43] The applicant sought damages because the Commission had erroneously decided that the company was in breach of an undertaking it had given in relation to the dumping of salmon. The CFI held that it was not necessary for the applicant to prove a sufficiently serious breach, since the alleged error did not involve complex discretionary choices by the Commission. A mere infringement of EC law would suffice. However it then defined the relevant error leading to illegality to be lack of ordinary care and diligence by the Commission, and took account of the applicant's contributory negligence.[44]

---

[42] See the similar reasoning in relation to state liability in Case C–392/93, *R. v. HM Treasury, ex p. British Telecommunications plc* [1996] ECR I–1631. The same type of problem can occur in domestic law, where an agency construes a statute incorrectly and losses are caused to individuals: see P.P. Craig, *Administrative Law* (Sweet & Maxwell, 4th edn., 1994), ch. 26.

[43] Case T–178/98, above n. 3, para. 61.

[44] *Ibid.*, paras. 57–61.

(c) PRESENT LAW: A SUMMARY

i. The test for liability for non-discretionary acts is proof of illegality, causation, and damage.

ii. The CFI and ECJ will necessarily have to make a judgment as to whether an act, general or individual, falls to be judged by this test, rather than the test discussed in the previous section.

iii. The CFI and ECJ will also have to decide what constitutes illegality for the purposes of liability for non-discretionary acts.

5. LIABILITY FOR OFFICIAL ACTS OF COMMUNITY SERVANTS

Article 288 (ex Article 215) allows for loss to be claimed where it has been caused either by the Community institutions or by the acts of its servants 'in the performance of their duties'. It is clear that not every act performed by a servant will be deemed to be an act in the performance of his or her duties. The matter is rendered more complex by the fact that Article 12 of the Protocol on the Privileges and Immunities of the European Communities states that: 'officials and other servants of the Community shall . . . be immune from legal proceedings in respect of acts performed by them in their official capacity'. The interrelationship between these provisions will be considered below. Before we do so the leading case in this area must be analysed:

Case 9/69, Sayag v. Leduc
[1969] ECR 329

Sayag was an engineer employed by Euratom. He was instructed to take Leduc, a representative of a private firm, on a visit to certain installations. He decided to drive him there in his own car, and he obtained a travel order which enabled him to claim the expenses for the trip from the Community. An accident occurred and Leduc claimed in the Belgian courts damages against Sayag for the injuries which he had suffered. It was argued that Sayag was driving the car in the performance of his duties, and that therefore the action should have been brought against the Community. The Belgian Cour de Cassation sought a preliminary ruling on the meaning of the phrase 'in the performance of their duties' in Article 188(2) of the Euratom Treaty, which is equivalent to 215(2) of the EC Treaty.

THE ECJ

By referring at one and the same time to damage caused by the institutions and to that caused by the servants of the Community, Article 188 indicates that the Community is only liable for those acts of its servants which, by virtue of an internal and direct relationship, are the necessary extension of the tasks entrusted to the institutions.

In the light of the special nature of this legal system, it would not therefore be lawful to extend it to categories of acts other than those referred to above.

A servant's use of his private car for transport during the course of his duties does not satisfy the conditions set out above.

A reference to a servant's private car in a travel order does not bring the driving of such car within the performance of his duties, but is basically intended to enable any necessary reimbursement of the travel expenses involved in this means of transport to be made in accordance with the standards laid down for this purpose.

Only in the rare case of *force majeure* or in exceptional circumstances of such overriding importance that without the servant's using private means of transport the Community would have been unable to carry out the tasks entrusted to it, could such use be considered to form part of the servant's performance of his duties, within the meaning of the second paragraph of Article 188 of the Treaty.

It follows from the above that the driving of a private car by a servant cannot in principle constitute the performance of his duties within the meaning of the second paragraph of Article 188 of the EAEC Treaty.

The range of acts done by its servants for which the Community will accept responsibility is therefore narrow, and more limited than that which exists in the laws of most of the Member States. No real justification for the limited nature of this liability is provided by the ECJ.

If the Community is not liable then an action can be brought against the servant in his or her personal capacity, and any such action is brought in national courts and is governed by national law. However, as seen above, the Protocol on the Privileges and Immunities of the European Communities provides that servants have immunity from suit in national courts in relation to 'acts performed in their official capacity'. The language of this provision differs from that of Article 288(2), which speaks in terms of servants acting in 'performance of their duties'. Normally one would expect that where the Community is liable under Article 288(2), because the servant was acting in the performance of his or her duties, then it would also follow that the servant would not be personally liable, since he or she would be deemed to be acting in an official capacity. The interrelationship between these two provisions may, none the less, be more problematic, and the ECJ has held that the servant's personal immunity and the scope of the Community's liability for the acts of the servant are separate issues.[45] The matter is considered by Schermers and Swaak, who address the relationship between the two provisions in the following way.

H.G. Schermers and R.A. Swaak, Official Acts of Community Servants and Article 215(4)[46]

Claiming immunity involves liability. Whenever the Community invokes immunity of jurisdiction for a particular act of a servant it implicitly accepts that the act is an act of the Community, because it has no right to invoke immunity for any other act. The Community can then be held liable. The reverse is not necessarily true. By waiving the immunity, the Community may indicate that it holds the civil servant liable, it cannot so exclude its own liability. To what extent it is jointly

---

[45] Case 5/68, *Sayag v. Leduc* [1968] ECR 395, 408.
[46] *The Action for Damages in Community Law*, n. 3 above, 177.

or severally liable will depend on the circumstances of the case and is to be decided by the Community's courts. Neither does the Community's acceptance of liability for an act of one of its servants necessarily imply that the act is a Community act. There is no legal prohibition denying the Community the right to accept liability for private acts of its servants. In practice, however, the Community will accept liability only for acts which it considers as official acts.

It is not entirely clear to what extent acts 'in the performance of their duties' are the same as acts 'in their official capacity'. Probably the drafters of the texts intended the latter wording to be more restrictive. . . . We submit that acts of servants 'in the performance of their duties (leading to the Communities' liability) *include but are not limited* to acts 'performed by them in their official capacity (leading to the servants' immunity).

It has been assumed thus far that the Community will be liable for the acts of its institutions, and for the acts of its servants, subject to the limitations of the *Sayag* case. Hartley points out that there may in fact be a third category of acts for which the Community is also responsible. This category covers acts performed by bodies to which the Communities have delegated certain governmental functions. Drawing on case law concerning the ECSC,[47] Hartley states:[48]

From this it may be concluded that, where a Community institution delegates governmental powers to some other body, the acts of that body in the exercise of those powers may be imputed to the Community; but where such a body carries out functions which are not of a governmental nature, its acts will not be imputable to the Community.

6. LIABILITY FOR VALID LEGISLATIVE ACTS

(a) THE NATURE OF THE PROBLEM

Individuals may well suffer loss flowing from lawful acts of the Community, as well as from acts which are tainted with some form of illegality. This problem can occur in any legal system, but the potential for its occurrence in the Community is particularly marked.

H.J. Bronkhorst, The Valid Legislative Act as a Cause of Liability of the Communities[49]

There are many reasons why private individuals may have a particular interest in the existence of a clearly defined principle concerning Community liability for legal acts which result in damage for them. In the first place, the Common Agricultural Policy, which in the beginning mainly existed as a price support mechanism, has been transformed for several sectors into an instrument imposing quantitative production limits. In this respect, the Community has had recourse to various instruments, including production quotas. At the same time, other instruments have been applied to reduce over-production: in the field of common fisheries, the Council has reduced the length of

---

[47] Case 18/60, *Worms* v. *High Authority* [1962] ECR 195.
[48] T.C. Hartley, *The Foundations of European Community Law* (Clarendon Press, 4th edn., 1998), 455.
[49] *The Action for Damages in Community Law*, n. 3 above, ch. 8, 153–4.

beams to be used for catching certain species of fish in defined fishery zones. Does a fisherman, who, on very short notice, has to make very important changes to his vessel, thus incurring substantial financial costs, have an action for compensation even if the Community measures as such cannot be challenged on the ground of illegality?

In the second place, private individuals, operating in the field of the Common Agricultural Policy, may easily suffer financial injury because of the fact that competing producers are favoured by Community measures. Producers of vegetable fats may very well undergo the effects of (uneven) competition if producers of butter or milk powder are able to dispose of large quantities of their products on the European markets with the help of Community subsidies.

The problem of loss being caused by lawful governmental action is not peculiar to the Community. Thus, French law recognizes a principle of *égalité devant les charges publiques*, and German law has the concept of *Sonderöpfer*. Under these principles loss caused by lawful governmental action can be recovered, albeit in limited circumstances.[50] While there is hardship for individuals in the situations postulated by Bronkhorst, the difficulties of deciding when to grant such compensation should not be underestimated.

P.P. Craig, Compensation in Public Law[51]

Legislation is constantly being passed which is explicitly or implicitly aimed at benefiting one section of the population at the expense of another. It is a matter of conscious legislative policy. This may be in the form of tax changes or in a decision to grant selective assistance to one particular type of industry rather than another. Any incorporation of state liability arising out of legislation as part of a risk theory would necessitate the drawing of a difficult line. It would be between cases where the deleterious effect on a firm or group was the aim of the legislation or a necessary correlative of it, and where legislation is passed which incidentally affects a particular firm in a serious manner, but where there is no legislative objection to compensating the firm for the loss suffered.

The drawing of such a line in the context of the EC is particularly problematic, given that within, for example, the Common Agricultural Policy (CAP) there will often be 'winners and losers' as the result of the institutions' attempts to give effect to the often conflicting objectives which lie at the heart of that policy.[52] At the very least, it serves to explain why the Community is reluctant to admit such claims.

---

[50] *Ibid.*, 155–9.
[51] (1980) 96 *LQR* 413, 450. See also Case T–113/96, n. 1 above, for a good example of this in the Community context.
[52] See Ch. 12 above for discussion of this issue.

(b) THE CASE LAW

Claims to recover for lawfully caused loss have been advanced before the Community courts on a number of occasions, and have been rejected.[53] The leading case is now *Dorsch Consult*.

Case T–184/95, Dorsch Consult Ingenieurgesellschaft mbH v. Council
[1998] ECR II–667[54]

The case arose out of the Gulf war. The EC, acting pursuant to a resolution of the United Nations Security Council, passed a regulation banning trade with Iraq. The Iraqi government retaliated with a law which froze all assets and rights of companies doing business in Iraq, where those companies were based in countries which had imposed the embargo. The applicant was such a company. It argued, *inter alia*, that it should be compensated by the EC for the loss it had incurred, even if the EC had acted lawfully.

THE CFI

59. At the outset, the Court would point out that if the Community is to incur non-contractual liability as the result of a lawful or unlawful act, it is necessary in any event to prove that the alleged damage is real and the existence of a causal link between that act and the alleged damage. . . .

. . .

80. It is clear from the . . . case law of the Court of Justice that, in the event of the principle of Community liability for a lawful act being recognised in Community law, such liability can be incurred only if the damage alleged, if deemed to constitute a 'still subsisting injury', affects a particular circle of economic operators in a disproportionate manner in comparison with others (unusual damage) and exceeds the economic risks inherent in operating in the sector concerned (special damage), without the legislative measure that gave rise to the alleged damage being justified by a general economic interest (*De Boer Buizen, Compagnie d'Approvisionnement, Biovilac*).

81. As regards the unusual nature of the alleged damage . . . [N]ot only the applicant's claims . . . were affected but also those of all Community undertakings which . . . had not yet been paid. . . .

82. . . . It cannot therefore claim to have suffered special damage or to have made exceptional sacrifice. . . .

83. . . . It is common ground that Iraq . . . was already regarded . . . as a 'high risk country'. In those circumstances, the economic and commercial risks deriving from the possible involvement of Iraq in renewed warfare . . . and the suspension of payment of its debts . . . constituted foreseeable risks inherent in any provision of services in Iraq. . . .

. . .

---

[53] Cases 9 & 11/71, *Compagnie d'Approvisionnement de Transport et de Crédit SA and Grands Moulins de Paris SA* v. *Commission* [1972] ECR 391, para. 45; Cases 54–60/76, *Compagnie Industrielle et Agricole du Comté de Loheac* v. *Council and Commission* [1977] ECR 645, para. 19; Case 59/83, *SA Biovilac NV* v. *EEC* [1984] ECR 4057, 4080–1; Case 265/85, *Van den Bergh & Jurgens BV and Van Dijk Food Products (Lopik) BV* v. *EEC* [1987] ECR 1155; Case 81/86, *De Boer Buizen* v. *Council and Commission* [1987] ECR 3677.

[54] The decision was upheld on appeal: Case C–237/98, *Dorsch Consult Ingenieurgesellschaft mbH* v. *Council* [2000] ECR I–4549.

85. It follows that the risks involved in the applicant's providing services in Iraq formed part of the risks inherent in operating in the sector concerned.

7. CAUSATION AND DAMAGE

(a) CAUSATION

A.G. Toth, The Concepts of Damage and Causality as Elements of Non-Contractual Liability[55]

... [T]he establishment of the necessary causality may give rise to difficult problems in practice. This is particularly so in the field of economic and commercial relations where the cause of an event can usually be traced back to a number of factors, objective as well as subjective, operating simultaneously or successively and producing direct as well as indirect effects. Broadly speaking, it may be said that there is no causality involving liability where the same result would have occurred in the same way even in the absence of the wrongful Community act or omission in question. The converse proposition, i.e., that the requisite causality exists whenever it can be shown that the damage would not have occurred without the Community action, is, however not always correct. Although in theory it is true that any circumstance, near or remote, without which an injury would not have been produced may be considered to be its cause, the fact that a Community act or omission is one only of several such circumstances may not in itself be sufficient to establish a causal connection entailing non-contractual liability. For that purpose, the causality must be 'direct, immediate and exclusive' which it can be only if the damage arises directly from the conduct of the institutions and does not depend on the intervention of other causes, whether positive or negative.

The difficulties of proving that it was the Community's action which caused the loss can be exemplified by the *Dumortier* case.

Cases 64, 113/76, 167, 239/78, 27, 28, 45/79, Dumortier Frères SA v. Council [1979] ECR 3091

Certain Council regulations provided that production refunds should be payable for maize starch, but that they should be abolished in the case of maize groats and meal (gritz), which were used in the production of beer. This differential treatment had been held to be in breach of Articles 39 and 40,[56] and the applicants now claimed damages for the losses suffered. The subsidies had been restored in the light of the ECJ's decision, but only for the future, and therefore losses had still

---

[55] *The Action for Damages in Community Law*, n. 3 above, 192.

[56] Cases 124/76, 20/77, *SA Moulins et Huileries de Pont-à-Mousson and Société Coopérative 'Providence Agricole de la Champagne'* v. *Office National Interprofessionnel des Céréales* [1977] ECR 1795.

been suffered in the intervening period. The Court cited the principle from the *Bayerische* case, and found that there had been a manifest and grave breach by the Community. Some of the applicants claimed that they should be compensated because they were forced to close their factories.

THE ECJ

21. ... The Council argued that the origin of the difficulties experienced by those undertakings is to be found in the circumstances peculiar to each of them, such as the obsolescence of their plant and managerial or financial problems. The data supplied by the parties in the course of the proceedings are not such as to establish the true cause of the further damage alleged. However, it is sufficient to state that even if it were assumed that the abolition of the refunds exacerbated the difficulties encountered by those applicants, those difficulties would not be a sufficiently direct consequence of the unlawful conduct of the Council to render the Community liable to make good the damage.

It will be necessary for an applicant to show not only that the Community action caused the loss being claimed, but also that the chain of causation has not been broken by the action either of the Member State or of the applicant himself. The ECJ has held that where the loss arises from an independent/autonomous act by the Member State, the Community is no longer liable.[57] If, however, this conduct has been made possible by an illegal failure of the Commission to exercise its supervisory powers, then it will be this failure which will be considered to be the cause of the damage.[58] There may be instances where both the Community and the Member State are responsible. This complex issue will be considered below.

Precisely what type of conduct by the individual will serve to break the chain of causation is not entirely clear. Negligence, or contributory negligence, will suffice either to defeat the claim or to reduce the award of damages.[59] It has also been held, as seen above, that if the individual ought to have foreseen the possibility of certain events which might cause loss, then the possibility of claiming damages will be diminished or lost.[60] Moreover, an individual who believes that a wrongful act of the Community has caused loss has been encouraged by the Court to challenge the measure in proceedings under Article 177 (now Article 234). Thus, in the *Amylum* case the ECJ stated that this was open to an individual, particularly in those areas where implementation was in the hands of national authorities.[61]

[57] Case 132/77, *Société pour l'Exportation des Sucres SA* v. *Commission* [1978] ECR 1061, 1072–3.

[58] Cases 9 & 12/60, *Vloeberghs* v. *High Authority* [1961] ECR 197, 240; Case 4/69, *Alfons Lütticke GmbH* v. *Commission* [1971] ECR 325, 336–8.

[59] Case 145/83, *Adams* v. *Commission* [1985] ECR 3539, 3592; Case T–178/98, *Fresh Marine*, above n. 3.

[60] Case 59/83, *Biovilac*, n. 53 above; Case T–514/93, *Cobrecaf* v. *Commission* [1995] ECR II–621, 643; Case T–572/93, *Odigitria* v. *Council and Commission* [1995] ECR II–2025, 2051–2; Case T–184/95, *Dorsch Consult* [1998] ECR II–667.

[61] Cases 116, 124/77, *Amylum NV and Tunnel Refineries Ltd.* v. *Council and Commission* [1979] ECR 3497.

(b) DAMAGE

Although Article 288 (ex Article 215) speaks of the duty of the Community to make good 'any damage', it is clear that losses will only be recoverable if they are certain and specific, proven and quantifiable.[62] These requirements will be examined in turn.

While the damage claimed must in general be *certain*, the Court held in *Kampff-meyer* that it is possible to maintain an action 'for imminent damage foreseeable with sufficient certainty even if the damage cannot yet be precisely assessed'.[63] The rationale was that it might be necessary to pursue an action immediately in order to prevent even greater damage.

The idea that the damage suffered must be *specific*, in the sense that it affects the applicant's interests in a special and individual way, is to be found in various guises in ECJ decisions. Thus, in the *Bayerische* case, considered above, it will be noted that, in denying recovery to the applicants, the Court emphasized that the effects of the regulation did not exceed the bounds of economic risk inherent in the activity in question.[64] Similar themes concerning the special nature of the burden imposed on a particular trader, or group of traders, can be found in the case law concerning the possible recovery for lawful governmental action.[65] The question whether an applicant should have to prove abnormal or special damage in a case concerning unlawful Community action has already been discussed.

The injured party will have the onus of *proving* that the damage occurred. In general the individual will have to show that the injury was actually sustained.[66] This may not be easy, and it is not uncommon for cases to fail for this reason.[67]

The damage must also be *quantifiable* if the applicant is to succeed. In order to decide whether the loss is indeed quantifiable, one needs to know what *types* of damage are recoverable. Advocate General Capotorti has put the matter in the following way:[68]

It is well known that the legal concept of 'damage' covers both a material loss *stricto sensu*, that is to say, a reduction in a person's assets, and also the loss of an increase in those assets which would have occurred if the harmful act had not taken place (these two alternatives are known respectively as *damnum emergens* and *lucrum cessans*). . . . The object of compensation is to restore the assets of the victim to the condition in which they would have been apart from the unlawful act, or at least to the condition closest to that which would have been produced if the unlawful nature of the act had not taken place: the hypothetical nature of that restoration often entails a certain degree of approximation. . . . These general remarks are not limited to the field of private law, but apply also to the liability of public authorities, and more especially to the non-contractual liability of the Community.

---

[62] Toth, n. 55 above, 180–91.

[63] Cases 56–60/74, *Kampffmeyer* v. *Commission and Council* [1976] ECR 711, 741; Case T–79/96, *Camar Srl*, above n. 31, para. 207.

[64] See 553 above.   [65] See 567 above.

[66] Case 26/74, *Roquette Frères* v. *Commission* [1976] ECR 677, 694, Trabucchi AG.

[67] See, e.g., Case 26/68, *Fux* v. *Commission* [1969] ECR 145, 156; Case T–1/99, *T. Port GmbH & Co. KG* v. *Commission* [2001] ECR II–465.

[68] Case 238/78, *Ireks-Arkady* v. *Council and Commission* [1979] ECR 2955, 2998–9.

While the ECJ has been prepared to grant damages for losses actually sustained, and while it is willing in principle to give damages for lost profits, recovery of the latter sums will often prove more difficult than of the former. Thus, in the *Kampffmeyer* case, while the Court admitted that lost profit was recoverable, it did not grant such damages to traders who had abandoned their intended transactions because of the unlawful act of the Community, even though these transactions would have produced profits.[69] In the *CNTA* case it was held that lost profits were not recoverable where the claim was based on the concept of legitimate expectations, the argument being that that concept only served to ensure that losses were not suffered owing to an unexpected change in the legal position; it did not serve to ensure that profits would be made.[70] However, in *Mulder*[71] the ECJ was prepared to compensate for lost profit, although it held that any such sum must take into account the income which could have been earned from alternative activities, applying the principle that there is a duty to mitigate loss.

In quantifying the loss suffered by the applicant the Community institutions have argued that damages should not be recoverable if the loss has been passed on to the consumers. This was accepted in principle by the ECJ in the *Quellmehl and Gritz* litigation.[72] Toth has justly criticized this reasoning. He points out that whether a firm could pass on a cost increase to consumers would depend upon many variables, which might operate differently for different firms, and which would be difficult to assess. He argues, moreover, that such an idea is wrong in principle, since it would mean that losses would be borne by consumers, rather than by the institutions which had committed the wrongful act.[73]

8. JOINT LIABILITY OF THE COMMUNITY AND MEMBER STATES

The joint liability of the Community and the Member States gives rise to complex problems which can be dealt with only in outline.[74] The approach of Oliver, which distinguishes between procedural and substantive issues, will be adopted here.[75]

(a) PROCEDURAL ISSUES

In procedural terms it is not possible for Community non-contractual liability to be decided by national courts. Article 235 (ex Article 178) confers this jurisdiction on the

---

[69] Cases 5, 7, 13–24/66, *Kampffmeyer v. Commission* [1967] ECR 245, 266–7.

[70] Case 74/74, n. 11 above, 550.   [71] Cases C–104/89 and 37/90, [1992] ECR I–3061.

[72] See Case 238/78, n. 68 above, 2974.   [73] See n. 55 above, 189–90.

[74] For more detailed treatment see, e.g., A. Durand, 'Restitution or Damages: National Court or European Court?' (1975–6) 1 *ELRev.* 431; Hartley, n. 48 above, 476–83; T.C. Hartley, 'Concurrent Liability in EEC Law: A Critical Review of the Cases' (1977) 2 *ELRev.* 249; W. Wils, 'Concurrent Liability of the Community and a Member State' (1992) 17 *ELRev.* 191.

[75] P. Oliver, 'Joint Liability of the Community and the Member States', in *The Action for Damages in Community Law*, n. 3 above, ch. 16.

ECJ and, while it does not state that this jurisdiction is exclusive, this is implied by Article 240 (ex Article 183).[76] Conversely, it is not possible for an individual to bring an action against a Member State before the ECJ, since there is no provision for this in the Treaty.

When an action is brought before the ECJ under Article 288(2), it is clear that Community law is applied. An action brought against a Member State in the national court will be governed by national law. This will, however, include Community law. The national courts are under an obligation to provide an effective remedy for the enforcement of directly effective Community provisions; and the rights against the state in such suits must be no less favourable than those which exist in domestic matters.[77]

(b) SUBSTANTIVE ISSUES

Joint liability of the Community and the Member States can arise in different situations. Two will be explored here.

The *first is where the Community has taken inadequate steps to prevent a breach of Community law by national authorities.* This issue arose in the *Lütticke* case where the Court appeared to accept that, in principle, such an action was possible.[78] However, there are considerable obstacles in the path of any such action. It is, for example, doubtful whether the Commission has a duty to bring an action under Article 226 (ex Article 169) against a Member State which is in breach of Community law.[79] The position may well be different where the Commission has adopted a more formal measure, which approves of the illegal national action, as in the *Kampffmeyer* case.

Cases 5, 7, 13–24/66, Kampffmeyer v. Commission
[1967] ECR 245

The case arose from the gradual establishment of a common market in cereals. On 1 October 1963 the German intervention board issued a notice stating that the levy for the import of such products would be set at zero. On that same day, the applicants applied for import licences for the import of maize from France, with the levy having been set at zero for January 1964. Some of the applicants had actually bought maize from France. The German government on the same day, 1 October 1963, then suspended the zero-rated import licences for maize. Under Article 22 of Regulation 19 the German Government could refuse such applications only if there was a threat of a serious disturbance to the market in question. Such a decision had to be confirmed by the Commission, and the Commission on 3 October duly authorized this to remain in force until 4 October. This decision was annulled in an action before the ECJ.[80] The applicants then sought compensation from the Commission under Article 215. Some of them had paid the duties imposed

---

[76] Art. 240: 'save where jurisdiction is conferred on the Court of Justice by this Treaty, disputes to which the Community is a party shall not on that ground be excluded from the jurisdiction of the courts or tribunals of the Member States': Cases 106–120/87, *Asteris* v. *Greece and EEC* [1988] ECR 5515; Case T–18/99, *Cordis*, above n. 13, para. 27.

[77] See Oliver, n. 75 above, 289.

[78] Case 4/69, *Alfons Lütticke GmbH* v. *Commission* [1971] ECR 325.

[79] See Ch. 10.

[80] Cases 106 & 107/63, *Toepfer* v. *Commission* [1965] ECR 405.

by the German authorities and imported the maize on these terms; others had repudiated their contracts to buy the maize, after the German Government had refused to issue the zero-rated licences. These are the two categories of applicants referred to by the ECJ in the following extract. Referring to the Commission decision authorizing the protective measures, the ECJ reasoned as follows.

THE ECJ

As is clear, moreover, from the judgment of the Court of 1 July, 1965, this decision constituted an improper application of Article 22 of Regulation No 19 . . . On October 3 1963 the Commission applied Article 22(2) of Regulation No 19 in circumstances which did not justify protective measures in order to restore the situation resulting from the fixing by it of a zero levy. As it was aware of the existence of applications for licences, it caused damage to the interests of importers who had acted in reliance on the information provided in accordance with Community rules. The Commission's conduct constituted a wrongful act or omission capable of giving rise to liability on the part of the Community.

In trying to justify itself by the assertion that in view of the economic data at its disposal on 3 October 1963 a threat of serious disturbance was not to be excluded and that consequently its mistaken evaluation of the data is excusable, the defendant misjudges the nature of the wrongful act or omission attributed to it, which is not to be found in a mistaken evaluation of the facts but in its general conduct which is shown clearly by the improper use made of Article 22, certain provisions of which, of a crucial nature, were ignored.

[*The ECJ then proceeded to determine the appropriate forum in which the issue of compensation should be decided.*]

However, with regard to any injury suffered by the applicants belonging to the first and second categories above-mentioned, those applicants have informed the Court that the injury alleged is the subject of two actions for damages, one against the Federal Republic of Germany before a German court and the other against the Community before the Court of Justice. It is necessary to avoid the applicants' being insufficiently or excessively compensated for the same damage by the different assessment of two different courts applying different rules of law. Before determining the damage for which the Community should be held liable, it is necessary for the national court to have the opportunity to give judgment on any liability on the part of the Federal Republic of Germany. This being the case, final judgment cannot be given before the applicants have produced the decision of the national court on this matter, which may be done independently of the evidence asked of the applicant in the first category to the effect that they have exhausted all possible methods of recovery of the amounts improperly paid by way of levy. Furthermore, if it were established that such recovery was possible, this fact might have consequences bearing upon the calculation of the damages concerning the second category. However, the decisive nature of the said evidence required does not prevent the applicants from producing the other evidence previously indicated in the meantime.

It is clear from the *Kampffmeyer* case that the Community can, therefore, be liable when it has wrongfully authorized a measure taken by a national body. The procedural aspect of the case has, however, been the subject of widespread criticism. It has been argued that there was no reason to require the applicants to proceed initially in the German courts, and that the ECJ's rationale for doing so was based implicitly on the assumption that the German authorities were primarily liable, with the Community bearing only a residual liability.[81]

This criticism may be overstated, and it may be necessary to distinguish the claim for the return of the levies paid from the more general tort action. As regards the former, the idea that the primary liability rested with Germany may well have substance, given that it was Germany which imposed the levy and it was Germany to which the funds were paid. As regards the latter, there is no particular reason why the liability of the Community should be seen as somehow secondary to that of the Member State.

The *second situation in which the issue of joint liability may arise is where the Member State applies unlawful Community legislation.* This can arise, for example, in the context of the CAP, where Community regulations will often be applied by national intervention boards. The general rule here is that it is the national intervention boards, and not the Commission, which are responsible for the application of the CAP, and that an action must normally be commenced in the national courts. The next case illustrates this in relation to the recovery of charges which an individual believes to have been wrongfully levied.

Case 96/71, R. and V. Haegeman Sprl v. Commission
[1972] ECR 1005

[Note ToA renumbering: Art. 177 is now Art. 234]

Haegeman was a Belgian company which imported wine from Greece which was at the time outside the Community. It alleged that it had suffered loss because of a countervailing charge which was imposed on the import of wine from Greece to Belgium. This charge was imposed by a Council regulation and was levied by the Belgian authorities.

THE ECJ

7. Disputes concerning the levying on individuals of the charges and levies referred to by this provision must be resolved, applying Community law, by the national authorities and following the practices laid down by the law of the Member States.

8. Issues, therefore, which are raised during a procedure as to the interpretation and validity of regulations establishing the Communities' own resources must be brought before the national courts which have at their disposal the procedure under Article 177 of the Treaty in order to ensure the uniform application of Community law.

. . .

14. The applicant maintains further that by reason of the defendant's behaviour it has suffered exceptional damage as a result of loss of profit, unforeseen financial outlay and losses on existing contracts.

15. The question of the possible liability of the Community is in the first place linked with that of the legality of the levying of the charge in question.

---

[81] See Oliver, n. 75 above.

16. It has just been found that, in the context of the relationship between individuals and the taxation authority which has levied the charge in dispute, the latter question comes under the jurisdiction of the national courts.

17. Accordingly, at the present stage the claim for compensation for possible damage must be dismissed.

The decision in *Haegman* can be criticized since the money levied went into the Community's funds. The mere fact that the sums were collected by national authorities should make no difference, given that these sums were imposed by the Community and were collected on behalf of the Community by the Member State.[82] It does, however, appear to be the case that an action to recover such a charge must be commenced in the national courts and that this is also so where a trader is seeking payment of a sum to which he believes himself to be entitled under Community law.[83] It has also been held that this principle applies even where the Commission has sent telexes to the national board setting out its interpretation of the relevant regulations.[84] The authorities of a Member State may, however, be able to recover from Community funds where they have paid for losses which are the responsibility of the Community.[85]

There are, however, a number of situations in which it is possible to proceed against the Community directly. First, if the Commission sends a telex which is interpreted, in the context of the relevant legislation, as an instruction to the national agency to act in a particular manner, then an action may be brought against the Commission for damages.[86] A second situation in which it is possible to proceed against the Community is where no action could conceivably be brought against any national authority and hence there would be no remedy available in the national courts. Thus, in the *Unifrex* case, an applicant sought damages before the ECJ by reason of the failure of the Commission to pass a regulation which would have granted the applicant a subsidy for exports to Italy when the Italian lira was devalued. It was held that the action could proceed before the ECJ, since proceedings in the national court would not have helped the applicant: even if the relevant Community rules had been declared illegal pursuant to Article 234 (ex Article 177), 'that annulment could not have required the national authorities to pay higher monetary compensatory amounts to the applicant, without the prior intervention of the Community legislature'.[87] The third situation in which it is possible to bring a claim in the ECJ is where the substance of the claim is that the Community has committed a

[82] See Hartley, n. 48 above, 479.

[83] Case 99/74, *Société des Grands Moulins des Antilles* v. *Commission* [1975] ECR 1531.

[84] Case 133/79, *Sucrimex SA and Westzucker GmbH* v. *Commission* [1980] ECR 1299; Case 217/81, *Compagnie Interagra SA* v. *Commission* [1982] ECR 2233.

[85] This may be possible in the context of the CAP. The basis for shifting the loss to the Community is to be found in Council Reg. 729/70, and is bound up with the operation of the EAGGF. For discussion of this issue see Oliver, n. 75 above, 306–8; J.A. Usher, *Legal Aspects of Agriculture in the European Community* (Oxford University Press, 1988), 104–6, 150–2.

[86] Case 175/84, *Krohn & Co. Import-Export GmbH & Co. KG* v. *Commission* [1986] ECR 753.

[87] Case 281/82, *Unifrex* v. *Commission and Council* [1984] ECR 1969; Case T–167/94, *Nolle* v. *Council and Commission* [1995] ECR II–2589; Case T–18/99, *Cordis*, above n. 13, para. 28.

tortious wrong to the applicant. This is exemplified by the *Dietz* case[88] in which the essence of the claim was that the Community authorities had introduced a levy without transitional provisions and had thereby caused loss to the applicant in breach of its legitimate expectations. This claim could be pursued in the ECJ since the wrong alleged was entirely directed towards the Community's behaviour, and not that of the Member State.

9. LIABILITY IN CONTRACT

The discussion thus far has focused on the liability of the Community arising under Article 288(2) which deals with non-contractual liability. The Community will obviously also make contracts,[89] and Article 288(1), (ex Article 215(1)), provides that contractual liability shall be governed by the law applicable to the contract in question.

The meaning of this phrase requires explanation. Contracts are often made between parties in different countries, and therefore it is necessary to determine which law should govern the contract. The answer will often be of considerable importance, since the contractual rules in different countries may differ significantly as regards matters such as the place of formation of the contract, and the types of damages which are recoverable. The body of law which deals with this issue is known as the conflict of laws or private international law. Contracts often have choice-of-law clauses, specifying the law to be applied. The Commission always inserts such a clause in its contracts. It has been held that this clause prevails, and cannot be displaced by arguments that the contract was more closely connected with a different country from that specified in the choice-of-law clause.[90]

It would of course be possible in principle for a choice-of-law clause to specify Community law as that which is applicable to the contract. It is true that Article 288(1), in contrast to Article 288(2), does not state that the Community is to develop a system of law by drawing on the relevant general principles which are common to the laws of the Member States. The implication of this might be that the Community is not to develop its own Community contract law. However, such a development may well be necessary in the future, as an adjunct of the expansion of Community competence into novel areas.

Such a development can be seen, albeit indirectly, in staff cases. The Court has characterized contracts of employment of certain Community officials as public-law contracts, emphasizing that the work performed was of a governmental nature, with the consequence that the contracts were governed by administrative law. The Court did not state that any system of national administrative law was to be applied.[91]

---

[88] Case 126/76, *Dietz* v. *Commission* [1977] ECR 2431; Case T–18/99, *Cordis*, above n. 13, para. 26. The application of the principle in the *Dietz* case, which allows the action to proceed in the ECJ, may not operate if the national authorities themselves were partially to blame for the loss caused to the individual: see, e.g., the first *Kampffmeyer* case, 573 above.

[89] T. Heukels, 'The Contractual Liability of the European Community Revisited', in *The Action for Damages in Community Law*, n. 3 above, ch. 5.

[90] Case 318/81, *Commission* v. *CODEMI* [1985] ECR 3693.

[91] Case 1/55, *Kergall* v. *Common Assembly* [1955] ECR 151; Cases 43, 45, 48/59, *Von Lachmüller* v. *Commission* [1960] ECR 463.

Even if the parties to a contract choose a particular legal system to govern the substance of their contractual obligations, this still leaves open the issue of which court will have jurisdiction to try the dispute. The ECJ is empowered by Article 238 (ex Article 181), which states that the Court of Justice shall have jurisdiction to give judgment pursuant to any arbitration clause contained in a contract concluded by or on behalf of the Community, whether that contract be governed by public or private law.[92]

10. LIABILITY TO MAKE RESTITUTION

Most legal systems recognize some species of liability in restitution or quasi-contract, in addition to that based on contract or tort. The precise nature of this liability continues to divide academics, but the better view is that it is distinct from both contract and tort. The essence of the argument is that restitution is not based upon a promise, but rather on the existence of unjust enrichment by the defendant: hence its difference from contractual liability. Restitution does not normally require the proof of a wrongful act by the defendant, in the sense of fault or a breach of a duty of care, and the measure of recovery is normally determined by the extent of the defendant's unjust enrichment rather than the extent of the loss to the plaintiff: hence its difference from most forms of tort liability.

A common restitutionary claim arises from payments made to public bodies in circumstances where they have no right to the money. This species of claim is of considerable importance in the context of the EC. It can arise in two types of situation. On the one hand, there can be cases where a Member State has, for example, imposed a levy which is illegal under EC law, as exemplified by *Van Gend en Loos* itself. In such cases, the matter will be remitted to the national court, once the ECJ has found that the levy was in breach of Community law. It will then be for the national court to devise a remedy which gives effect to the Community right, and this will often take the form of a return of the sum which has been paid over to the national authority.[93] On the other hand, there may be instances under, for example, the CAP in which money is paid into Community funds, pursuant to an obligation imposed by Community law, where there may be no legal obligation to pay the sum in question. It is this latter issue which concerns us here.

The ECJ has applied restitutionary principles in cases where there has been unjust enrichment by an individual against the Community.[94] It is clearly correct in principle that a remedy should be available in favour of an individual, where the Community has been unjustly enriched at his or her expense, as where the EC has imposed an unlawful charge. If a levy imposed by a Member State, which is unlawful because it is in breach of the Treaty, is recoverable, so too should be an

---

[92] Although Art. 181 (now Art. 238) talks of the ECJ giving judgment pursuant to an arbitration clause, it is clearly not simply an arbitrator in the normal sense of that term: Hartley, above n. 48, 440–1.

[93] See Ch. 6 above.

[94] See, e.g., Case 18/63, *Wollast v. EEC* [1964] ECR 85; Case 110/63, *Willame v. Commission* [1965] ECR 649.

illegal charge levied by the Community. The matter is, however, complicated in two different ways.

First, there is case law of the ECJ, outlined above, which has insisted that, in many such instances, the action should be commenced in the national court against the national collecting agency, even where the funds are treated as Community funds.[95]

Secondly, there is the difficulty of locating restitutionary claims within the Treaty itself. It could be argued that such claims may be based on Article 288(2), but, as has been pointed out,[96] the wording of the Article, which requires the Community to 'make good any damage caused' by its institutions, does not fit perfectly with the idea of a restitutionary action. The Article is, however, framed in terms of 'non-contractual liability', and this is clearly wide enough to cover restitutionary relief. Moreover, if the ECJ were to find that it had no jurisdiction over such actions, then Article 240 (ex Article 183) would mean that relief could be sought in an action against the Community in national courts. It is doubtful whether the ECJ would wish to be in a position where it had 'no control' over the development of appropriate restitutionary principles involving Community liability.

11. CONCLUSION

i. The ECJ's jurisprudence under Article 288 has, in the past, been criticized for being overly restrictive. The case law was, until recently, unclear about the precise criterion for the application of the *Schöppenstedt* test.

ii. More recent developments have clarified the law. It is now clear that the crucial issue concerns the discretionary or non-discretionary nature of the act. Discretionary acts will be subject to the *Schöppenstedt* test. This requires proof of a breach of a superior rule of law for the protection of the individual, the breach must be sufficiently serious, there must be causation and damage. It is clear also that the factors laid down in the case law on state liability in damages will be directly relevant when deciding whether there has been a sufficiently serious breach under Article 288.

iii. Where the challenged act is not discretionary it will, subject to what was said above, suffice to show illegality, causation and damage.

12. FURTHER READING

(a) *Books*

HEUKELS, T., and MCDONNELL, A. (eds.), *The Action for Damages in Community Law* (Kluwer, 1997)

SCHERMERS, H.G., HEUKELS, T., and MEAD, P. (eds.), *The Non-Contractual Liability of the European Communities* (Martinus Nijhoff, 1988)

---

[95] See 572–4 above.   [96] Hartley, n. 48 above, 445–6.

(b) *Articles*

DURAND, A., 'Restitution or Damages: National Court or European Court?' (1975–6) 1 *ELRev.* 431

HARDING, C., 'The Choice of Court Problem in Cases of Non-Contractual Liability under EEC Law' (1979) 16 *CMLRev.* 389

HARTLEY, T.C., 'Concurrent Liability in EEC Law: A Critical Review of the Cases' (1977) 2 *ELRev.* 249

JONES, M.L., 'The Non-Contractual Liability of the EEC and the Availability of an Alternative Remedy in the National Courts' (1981) 1 *LIEI* 1

LEWIS, A.D.E., 'Joint and Several Liability of the European Communities and National Authorities' [1980] *CLP* 99

OLIVER, P., 'Enforcing Community Rights in the English Courts' (1987) 50 *MLR* 881

TRIDIMAS, T., 'Liability for Breach of Community Law: Growing Up and Mellowing Down?' (2001) 38 *CMLRev.* 301

WILS, W., 'Concurrent Liability of the Community and a Member State' (1992) 17 *ELRev.* 191

14

FREE MOVEMENT OF GOODS: DUTIES, CHARGES, AND TAXES

1. INTRODUCTION: FORMS OF ECONOMIC INTEGRATION

The discussion in the previous chapters has focused on the institutional law of the EC. The remainder of the book will be concerned with EC substantive law. We will, however, be stressing the links between the two parts of Community law, as we have done in the preceding discussion.

This Chapter and that which follows are concerned with the free movement of goods. This is one of the 'four freedoms' guaranteed by the original Rome Treaty, the others being free movement of workers, freedom of establishment and the provision of services, and free movement of capital. To realize the importance of these provisions we need to understand what a common market actually is, and how it differs from other forms of economic integration. Swann provides a succinct description of the different forms of economic integration.

D. Swann, The Economics of the Common Market[1]

Economic integration can take various forms and these can be ranged in a spectrum in which the degree of involvement of participating economies, one with another, becomes greater and greater. The *free trade area* is the least onerous in terms of involvement. It consists in an arrangement between states in which they agree to remove all customs duties (and quotas) on trade passing between them. Each party is free, however, to determine unilaterally the level of customs duty on imports coming from outside the area. The next stage is the *customs union*. Here tariffs and quotas on trade between members are also removed but members agree to apply a *common* level of tariff on goods entering the union from without. The latter is called the common customs, or common external, tariff. Next comes the *common market* and this technical term implies that to the free movement of *goods* within the customs union is added the free movement of the *factors of production*—labour, capital and enterprise. Finally there is the *economic union*. This is a common market in which there is also a complete unification of monetary and fiscal policy. There would be a common currency which would be controlled by a central authority and in effect the member states would become regions within the union.

---

[1] (Penguin, 7th edn., 1992), 11–12, italics in the original.

Part Three of the EC Treaty contains many of the fundamental principles which are of importance in the establishment of a *customs union and common market*.[2] This part of the Treaty sets out, *inter alia*, the 'four freedoms' which are of central importance in realizing the goals of the Community.

Title I of Part Three is concerned with the Free Movement of Goods. This is designed to ensure the removal of duties, quotas, and other quantitative restrictions on the movement of goods within the Community: Articles 25 and 28–31 (ex Articles 12 and 30–37). Articles 26–27 deal with the Common Customs Tariff.[3] The fundamental objective of these provisions is to ensure that competition between goods coming from different Member States is neither prevented nor distorted by the existence of government provisions which limit the amount of such goods which can be imported (quotas), or increase their price (tariffs). Other Treaty Articles contained within Title III of Part Three specify the rules for the free movement of labour, capital, and enterprise. A brief explanation will be of help in understanding the economic objectives of these Articles taken as a whole.

The provisions on the free movement of goods are designed to establish the basic principles of a customs union: the prohibition of tariffs etc. on trade between Member States and the existence of a common tariff. The object is to ensure that goods themselves can move freely, with the consequence that those which are most favoured by consumers will be most successful, irrespective of the country of origin. This will also serve to maximize wealth-creation in the Community as a whole.

The provisions of Title III, which are concerned with free movement of workers, establishment, services, and capital, reflect the same idea. These Articles have, as will be seen below,[4] social as well as economic objectives. It is with the basic economic aims that we are concerned here. Labour and capital are two of the economic factors of production, the elements that are used to make a product. The basic object is to ensure the optimal allocation of resources within the Community, by enabling factors of production to move to the area where they are most valued. This is not a complex idea. Labour is one of the factors of production. It may be that this factor of production is valued more highly in some areas than in others. This would be so if, for example, there were an excess of supply over demand for labour in southern Italy, and an excess of demand over supply in certain parts of Germany. In this situation labour is worth more in Germany than it is in Italy. The value of labour within the Community as a whole is, therefore, maximized if workers are free to move within the Community to the area where they are most valued. The same idea is applicable to freedom of establishment. If a firm established in Holland believes that it could

[2] Prior to the TEU the provisions on free movement of goods were contained within what was labelled Part Two of the Treaty, entitled Foundations of the Community. After the TEU Part Two of the Treaty deals with Citizenship of the Union, and Part Three of the Treaty now has the name Community Policies. The provisions on free movement of goods constitute one such policy of the Community.

[3] The ToA has repealed a number of Arts. which were, in essence, concerned with transitional arrangements attendant upon the establishment of the customs union and common customs tariff. The old Arts. which have been thus repealed are 13–27.

[4] See Chs. 16–18 below.

capture part of the French market if it were allowed to set up in business there, then it should not be prevented from so doing by rules of French law which discriminate on grounds of nationality.[5]

2. THE STRUCTURE OF THE PROVISIONS CONCERNING FREE MOVEMENT OF GOODS

In this and the following chapters we shall consider the ECJ's jurisprudence on the free movement of goods. A moment's reflection will cause the reader to realize that this can be impeded in a number of different ways.

The most obvious form of protectionism will occur through customs duties or charges which have an equivalent effect, with the object of rendering foreign goods more expensive than their domestic counterparts. This is dealt with by Articles 23 to 25 (ex Articles 9 to 12). A State may also attempt to benefit domestic goods by taxes that discriminate against imports. This is covered by Articles 90 to 93 (ex Articles 95 to 99). These issues will be considered within this Chapter.

A State may, however, seek to preserve advantages for its own goods by imposing quotas or measures which have an equivalent effect on imports, thereby reducing the quantum of imported products. This aspect of free movement is dealt with in Articles 28 to 31 (ex Articles 30 to 37), and is addressed in the next chapter.

The third of the chapters that deals directly with free movement of goods concerns the legislative and judicial techniques for the completion of the single market. This discussion will, however, be delayed until the end of the book, since it has ramifications for topics other than free movement of goods.[6]

This and the following chapters are concerned with State action that creates barriers to trade. Such action can also result from aid granted by a Member State to a specific industry. This will obviously disadvantage competing products from other Member States, and Community law therefore closely regulates the granting of such aid through Articles 87 to 89 (ex Articles 92 to 94).[7]

Private parties may also take action that partitions the market along national lines, and hence impedes the realization of the Single Market. This can occur when private parties use industrial property rights to divide the Community on the basis of national divisions, or when firms agree among themselves not to compete in each other's markets. Community law has to address both of these issues in order to prevent private action from recreating barriers to trade analogous in their effect to duties or quotas.[8]

---

[5] The discussion in the text is a simplified one. There may, e.g., be cogent reasons why a political system wishes to preserve domestic industry in a particular region, and there may also be circumstances in which the firm which 'wins' is not unequivocally the more efficient.

[6] See Ch. 28 below.   [7] See Ch. 27 below.   [8] See Chs. 21, 26 below.

3. CENTRAL ISSUES

i. The abolition of customs duties and charges having an equivalent effect is central to the idea of a customs union and a single market. The ECJ has therefore interpreted Articles 23–25 strictly in order to ensure that this fundamental aim is fulfilled. It has made it clear that it will look to the effect of a duty, and not its purpose, and has given a broad reading to 'charges having equivalent effect' to a customs duty. It has allowed only very limited exceptions to these Articles, and any breach will be unlawful *per se*.

ii. The prohibition of taxes that discriminate against imports is equally central to the single market ideal. Customs duties apply when goods cross the border, and are caught by Articles 23–25. A State may however discriminate against imports through differential taxes once the goods are in its country. Articles 90–93 proscribe such conduct.

iii. The case law concerning Articles 90–93 can be controversial. This is in part because the Treaty language requires the ECJ to make decisions about difficult matters, such as whether goods are similar to each other, or whether a differential tax regime is protective of home State products. It is also in part because tax rules may be used to foster national preferences in relation to matters such as the environment. The ECJ has to adjudicate on whether such rules are compatible with Articles 90–93.

iv. It is essential when reading the materials in this chapter to have some idea of the broader context into which they fit. The discussion of the legal materials will therefore be placed within the context of the more general issues concerning the customs union and taxation respectively.

4. ARTICLES 23–25: DUTIES AND CHARGES

Article 23(1)[9] (ex Article 9(1)) is the foundational provision of this part of the Treaty:

The Community shall be based upon a customs union which shall cover all trade in goods and which shall involve the prohibition between Member States[10] of customs duties on imports and exports and of all charges having an equivalent effect, and the adoption of a common customs tariff in their relation with third countries.[11]

It is important to understand the structure of the other provisions in this part of the Treaty. The old Article 12 prohibited the imposition of *new* customs duties and

---

[9] Art. 23 will almost always be used in conjunction with one of the other Treaty Arts. in this area. When it is employed in this manner it will have direct effect: see, e.g., Case 18/71, *Eunomia di Porro & Co.* v. *Italian Ministry of Education* [1971] ECR 811.

[10] The ECJ has interpreted Art. 9 (now Art. 23) to prohibit customs duties, etc., even when they are applied within a Member State and are imposed on goods which enter one particular region of that State: Cases C–363, 407, 409, 411/93, *René Lancry SA* v. *Direction Générale des Douanes* [1994] ECR I–3957.

[11] The goods which benefit from the provisions on free movement contained in Arts. 23–25 and 28–31 are those which originate in a Member State and those which come from outside the Community, but are in free circulation within the Member States: Art. 23(2). The criteria for goods which come from outside the Community to be in free circulation within the Community are contained in Art. 24 (ex Art. 10): the goods must have complied with import formalities, and any customs duties and charges must have been paid by the trader and not have been reimbursed.

charges equivalent thereto,[12] while the old Article 13 obliged Member States to abolish *existing* duties within the transitional period, in accordance with Articles 13–15; the old Article 16 concerned the abolition of duties on exports. The passage of time has rendered redundant the distinction between new and existing duties. The previous Articles 12–17 have thus been repealed. Article 25 (ex Article 12) now relates to any customs duties and charges equivalent thereto, whether concerning imports or exports, with no distinction being drawn as to when such duties were imposed:

Customs duties on imports and exports and charges having equivalent effect shall be prohibited between Member States. This prohibition shall also apply to customs duties of a fiscal nature.

(a) DUTIES AND CHARGES: EFFECT, NOT PURPOSE

In its early case law the Court made it clear that whether the old Article 12 would bite would depend upon the effect of the duty or charge, and not on its purpose. This comes out clearly from the *Italian Art* case. There is no doubt that this approach will be equally applicable to Article 25.

Case 7/68, Commission v. Italy
[1968] ECR 423

[Note ToA renumbering: Art. 169 is now 226; Art. 16 has been repealed, but the substance of this Art. is now covered by the amended Art. 25]

Italy imposed a tax on the export of artistic, historical, and archæological items. The Commission brought an action under Article 169 alleging that this was in breach of Article 16 which prohibited duties and charges on exports. Italy argued that the items should not be regarded as goods for the purpose of the rules on the customs union and that the purpose of the tax in question was not to raise revenue, but to protect the artistic etc. heritage of the country. The Court rejected these arguments in the following terms.

THE ECJ

1. *The Scope of the Disputed Tax*
. . .
Under Article 9 of the Treaty the Community is based on a customs union 'which shall cover all trade in goods'. By goods, within the meaning of that provision, there must be understood products which can be valued in money and which are capable, as such, of forming the subject of commercial transactions.

The articles covered by the Italian law, whatever may be the characteristics which distinguish them from other types of merchandise, nevertheless resemble the latter, inasmuch as they can be

[12] It was Art. 12 (now Art. 25) which was in issue in the famous *Van Gend* case which laid the foundations for the concept of direct effect within Community law. See Ch. 5 above.

valued in money and so be the subject of commercial transactions. That view corresponds with the scheme of the Italian law itself, which fixes the tax in question in proportion to the value of the articles concerned.

- It follows from the above that the rules of the Common Market apply to these goods subject only to the exceptions expressly provided by the Treaty.

2. *The Classification of the Disputed Tax Having Regard to Article 16 of the Treaty*

In the opinion of the Commission the tax in dispute constitutes a tax having an effect equivalent to a customs duty on exports and therefore the tax should have been abolished, under Article 16 of the Treaty, no later than the end of the first stage of the common market, that is to say, from 1 January 1962. The defendant argues that the disputed tax does not come within the category, as it has its own particular purpose which is to ensure the protection and safety of the artistic, historic and archaeological heritage which exists in the national territory. Consequently, the tax does not in any respect have a fiscal nature, and its contribution to the budget is insignificant.

Article 16 of the Treaty prohibits the collection in dealings between Member States of any customs duty on exports and of any charge having an equivalent effect, that is to say, any charge which, by altering the price of an article exported, has the same restrictive effect on the free circulation of that article as a customs duty. That provision makes no distinction based on the purpose of the duties and charges the abolition of which it requires.

It is not necessary to analyse the concept of the nature of the fiscal system on which the defendant bases its argument upon this point, for the provisions of the section of the Treaty concerning the elimination of customs duties between the Member States exclude the retention of customs duties and charges having an equivalent effect without distinguishing in that respect between those which are and those which are not of a fiscal nature.

The disputed tax falls within Article 16 by reason of the fact that export trade in the goods in question is hindered by the pecuniary burden which it imposes on the price of the exported articles.

When a tax is caught by Article 25 as a duty or charge that is of equivalent effect then it is in effect *per se* unlawful. Thus, attempts by Italy to argue that its tax could be defended on the basis of Article 36 (now Article 30) were rejected by the Court. Article 36 can only be used as a defence in relation to quantitative restrictions which are caught by Article 30 (now 28). It cannot validate fiscal measures which are prohibited by Articles 9–12 (now Articles 23–25).

The emphasis in the *Italian Art* case on effect as opposed to purpose is clearly justifiable. The peremptory force of what is now Article 25 would be significantly weakened if it were open to a State to argue that a duty or charge should not be prohibited because its purpose was in some sense non-fiscal in nature. Had the Court proved receptive to this argument it would, moreover, have meant that the judiciary would have had to adjudicate on which types of social policy should be regarded as possessing a legitimate purpose sufficient to take them outside the Treaty.

The ECJ has reaffirmed its emphasis on effect rather than purpose in other cases. It has also made it clear that the Treaty provisions can be applicable even if the State measure was not designed with protectionism in mind. Thus in *Diamantarbeiders*[13] the Court considered the legality of a Belgian law requiring 0.33 per cent of the value of imported diamonds to be paid into a social fund for workers in the industry. The fact that the purpose of the fund was neither to raise money for the exchequer nor to protect domestic industry[14] did not save the charge in question. It was sufficient that the charge was imposed on goods by reason of the fact that they had crossed a border.

(b) CHARGES HAVING AN EQUIVALENT EFFECT: GENERAL PRINCIPLES[15]

Article 25 prohibits not only customs duties, but also charges having an equivalent effect (CEE). The reason is obvious. It is designed to catch protectionist measures that create a similar barrier to trade as customs duties *stricto sensu*. It is therefore unsurprising that the ECJ should have interpreted the term expansively.

Case 24/68, Commission v. Italy
[1969] ECR 193

[Note ToA renumbering: Arts. 9 and 12 are now Arts. 23 and 25.
Arts. 13 and 16 have been repealed]

Italy imposed a levy on goods which were exported to other Member States with the ostensible purpose of collecting statistical material for use in discerning trade patterns. The Court reiterated its holding that customs duties were prohibited irrespective of the purpose for which the duties were imposed, and irrespective of the destination of the revenues which were collected. It then continued as follows.

THE ECJ

8. The extension of the prohibition of customs duties to charges having an equivalent effect is intended to supplement the prohibition against obstacles to trade created by such duties by increasing its efficiency.

The use of these two complementary concepts thus tends, in trade between Member States, to avoid the imposition of any pecuniary charge on goods circulating within the Community by virtue of the fact that they cross a national border.

9. Thus, in order to ascribe to a charge an effect equivalent to a customs duty, it is important to consider this effect in the light of the objectives of the Treaty, in the Parts, Titles and Chapters in which Articles 9, 12, 13 and 16 are to be found, particularly in relation to the free movement of goods.

---

[13] Cases 2 and 3/69, *Sociaal Fonds voor de Diamantarbeiders* v. *SA Ch. Brachfeld & Sons* [1969] ECR 211. See also Cases 485 and 486/93, *Maria Simitzi* v. *Municipality of Kos* [1995] ECR I–2655; Cases C–441 and 442/98, *Michailidis AE* v. *IKA* [2000] ECR I–7145.

[14] Belgium did not produce diamonds.

[15] R. Barents, 'Charges Having an Equivalent Effect to Customs Duties' (1978) 15 *CMLRev.* 415.

Consequently, any pecuniary charge, however small and whatever its designation and mode of application, which is imposed unilaterally on domestic or foreign goods by reason of the fact that they cross a frontier, and which is not a customs duty in the strict sense, constitutes a charge having equivalent effect within the meaning of Articles 9, 12, 13 and 16 of the Treaty, even if it is not imposed for the benefit of the State, is not discriminatory or protective in effect and if the product on which the charge is imposed is not in competition with any domestic product.

10. It follows . . . that the prohibition of new customs duties or charges having equivalent effect, linked to the principle of the free movement of goods, constitutes a fundamental rule which, without prejudice to the other provisions of the Treaty, does not permit of any exceptions.

This clear message was repeated once again in *Diamantarbeiders*.[16] The ECJ reiterated the broad definition of a CEE. It made it clear that this would bite whether those affected by the charge were all Community citizens, those from the importing State, or only the nationals from the State that was responsible for passing the measure under scrutiny.

These decisions signalled the Court's intent that the Articles of the Treaty concerned with customs duties and CEEs were to be taken seriously.[17] They were not to be circumvented by the form in which the charge was imposed. They were applicable whether the duty/charge discriminated or not. They had an impact irrespective of whether the product on which the charge was imposed was in competition with domestic goods; and they admitted of no exceptions.

This strident approach by the ECJ was unsurprising and warranted, given the centrality of abolishing customs duties and CEEs to the very notion of a single Community market. The abolition of such measures goes to the very heart of this Community ideal. It was a necessary first step in the attainment of market integration. Eradicating customs duties and the like was vital if the broader aims of the common market were to be fulfilled.

(c) CHARGES HAVING AN EQUIVALENT EFFECT: INSPECTIONS AND THE 'EXCHANGE EXCEPTION'

A common defence is that the charge imposed on imported goods is justified because it is merely payment for a service which the State has rendered to the importer, and that therefore it should not be regarded as a CEE. The Court has been willing to accept this argument in principle. It has however been equally alert to the fact that a State might present a charge in this way, when in reality it was seeking to impede imports, or in circumstances where there was no commercial exchange at all. The Court has

---

[16] Cases 2 and 3/69, n. 13 above.

[17] See also Case 29/72, *Marimex SpA* v. *Italian Finance Administration* [1972] ECR 1309; Case 39/73, *Rewe-Zentralfinanz* v. *Direktor der Landwirtschaftskammer Westfalen-Lippe* [1973] ECR 1039; Case C–130/93, *Lamaire NV* v. *Nationale Dienst voor Afzet van Land- en Tuinbouwprodukten* [1994] ECR I–3215; Case C–16/94, *Edouard Dubois et Fils SA* v. *Garonor Exploitation SA* [1995] ECR I–2421.

therefore closely scrutinized such claims from States and has not readily accepted them.

Thus in *Commission* v. *Italy*,[18] considered above, the Italian Government argued that the charge should be seen as the consideration for the statistical information which it collected. The government contended that this information 'affords importers a better competitive position in the Italian market whilst exporters enjoy a similar advantage abroad';[19] and that therefore the charge should be viewed as consideration for a service rendered, as a *quid pro quo*, and not as a CEE. The Court was unconvinced. It held that the statistical information was beneficial to the whole economy and to the administrative authorities. It then continued in the following vein:[20]

Even if the competitive position of importers and exporters were to be particularly improved as a result, the statistics still constitute an advantage so general, and so difficult to assess, that the disputed charge cannot be regarded as the consideration for a specific benefit actually conferred.

The same theme is to be found in other ECJ decisions.[21] Even when the charge *is* more directly related to some action taken by the State with respect to specific imported goods, the Court has still been reluctant to accept that the charge can be characterized as consideration for a service rendered. This is apparent from the *Bresciani* case.

Case 87/75, Bresciani v. Amministrazione Italiana delle Finanze [1976] ECR 129

The Italian authorities imposed a charge for the compulsory veterinary and public-health inspections which were carried out on imported raw cowhides. Was this to be regarded as a CEE or not?

THE ECJ

6. The national court requests that the three following considerations be taken into account:
First, the fact that the charge is proportionate to the quantity of the goods and not to their value distinguishes a duty of the type at issue from charges which fall within the prohibition under Article 13 of the EEC Treaty. Second, a pecuniary charge of the type at issue is no more than the consideration required from individuals who, through their own action in importing products of animal origin, cause a service to be rendered. In the third place, although there may be differences in the method and time of its application, the duty at issue is also levied on similar products of domestic origin.

. . .

8. The justification for the obligation progressively to abolish customs duties is based on the

---

[18] Case 24/68, [1969] ECR 193, paras. 15–16.
[19] *Ibid.*, para. 15.   [20] *Ibid.*, para. 16.
[21] Case 63/74, *W. Cadsky SpA v. Istituto Nazionale per il Commercio Estero* [1975] ECR 281.

fact that any pecuniary charge, however small, imposed on goods by reason of the fact that they cross a frontier constitutes an obstacle to the free movement of such goods.

The obligation progressively to abolish customs duties is supplemented by the obligation to abolish charges having equivalent effect in order to prevent the fundamental principle of the free movement of goods within the common market from being circumvented by the imposition of pecuniary charges of various kinds by a Member State.

The use of these two complementary concepts thus tends, in trade between Member States, to avoid the imposition of any pecuniary charge on goods circulating within the Community by virtue of the fact that they cross a national frontier.

9. Consequently, any pecuniary charge, whatever its designation and mode of application, which is unilaterally imposed on goods imported from another Member State by reason of the fact that they cross a frontier, constitutes a charge having an effect equivalent to a customs duty. In appraising a duty of the type at issue it is, consequently, of no importance that it is proportionate to the quantity of the imported goods and not to their value.

10. Nor, in determining the effects of the duty on the free movement of goods, is it of any importance that a duty of the type at issue is proportionate to the costs of a compulsory public health inspection carried out on entry of the goods. The activity of the administration of the State intended to maintain a public health inspection system imposed in the general interest cannot be regarded as a service rendered to the importer such as to justify the imposition of a pecuniary charge. If, accordingly, public health inspections are still justified at the end of the transitional period, the costs which they occasion must be met by the general public which, as a whole benefits from the free movement of Community goods.

11. The fact that the domestic production is, through other charges, subjected to a similar burden matters little unless those charges and the duty in question are applied according to the same criteria and at the same stage of production, thus making it possible for them to be regarded as falling within a general system of internal taxation applying systematically and in the same way to domestic and imported products.

The ECJ's judgment in *Bresciani* indicates clearly its reluctance to accede to arguments which will take pecuniary charges outside the reach of the Treaty. In paragraph 9 it rejected the *first* of the Italian arguments: the fact that the charge was proportionate to the quantity of imported goods made no difference, since Article 12 (now Article 25 as amended) prohibited *any* charge imposed by reason of the fact that goods crossed a frontier.[22] The rejection of the *second* of the Italian arguments in paragraph 10 was equally significant. The State's argument had some plausibility: if you wish to import a product that requires health inspection, then you, the importer, should bear the cost. The Court's response was, however, unequivocal: the cost of inspections to maintain public health should be borne by the general public. It is doubtful whether this makes sense in micro-economic terms.[23] The ECJ's conclusion was, however, designed to limit the ambit of any exceptions to Articles 9–12 (now Articles 23–25). This is equally apparent in the way in which the Court disposed of the

[22] A charge will be deemed to be a CEE if it is a flat-rate charge which is based on the value of the goods: Case 170/88, *Ford España* v. *Spain* [1989] ECR 2305.

[23] By placing the cost on the general public it means that the importer of the product will not have to bear what is in reality one of the costs of making that product.

State's *third* contention. The ECJ's response is to be found in paragraph 11 of its judgment and required a strict equivalence between the charges levied on domestic and imported goods. Other attempts to employ the exchange argument have not generally proven successful.[24]

(d) CHARGES HAVING AN EQUIVALENT EFFECT: INSPECTIONS AND FULFILMENT OF MANDATORY LEGAL REQUIREMENTS

Where Community legislation *permits* an inspection to be undertaken by a State, the national authorities cannot recover any fees charged from the traders.[25] The Court has, however, accepted that a charge imposed by a State will escape the prohibition contained in Articles 9–12 (now Articles 23–25) when it is levied to cover the cost of a *mandatory* inspection required by Community law.[26]

Case 18/87, Commission v. Germany
[1988] ECR 5427

[Note ToA renumbering: Arts. 9–12, 36, are now Arts. 23–25, 30]

German regional authorities charged certain fees on live animals imported into the country. These charges were to cover the cost of inspections undertaken pursuant to Directive 81/389. The question arose whether they should be regarded as CEEs. The ECJ began by stating the now orthodox proposition that any pecuniary charge imposed as a result of goods crossing a frontier was caught by the Treaty, either as a customs duty or as a CEE. It then recognized an exception to this basic principle.

THE ECJ

6. However, the Court has held that such a charge escapes that classification if it relates to a general system of internal dues applied systematically and in accordance with the same criteria to domestic products and imported products alike (. . . Case 132/78, *Denkavit* v. *France* . . .), if it constitutes payment for a service in fact rendered to the economic operator of a sum in proportion to the service (. . . Case 158/82, *Commission* v. *Denmark* . . .), or again, subject to certain conditions, if it attaches to inspections carried out to fulfil obligations imposed by Community law (. . . Case 46/76, *Bauhuis* v. *Netherlands* . . .).

7. The contested fee, which is payable on importation and transit, cannot be regarded as relating to a general system of internal dues. Nor does it constitute payment for a service rendered

---

[24] See, e.g., Case 43/71, *Politi SAS* v. *Italian Ministry of Finance* [1971] ECR 1039; Case 132/82, *Commission* v. *Belgium* [1983] ECR 1649; Case 340/87, *Commission* v. *Italy* [1989] ECR 1483; Case C–209/89, *Commission* v. *Italy* [1991] ECR I–3533; Case C–272/95, *Bundesantalt für Landwirtschaft und Ernährung* v. *Deutsches Milch-Kontor GmbH* [1997] ECR I–1905.

[25] Case 314/82, *Commission* v. *Belgium* [1984] ECR 1543.

[26] Case 46/76, *Bauhuis* v. *Netherlands* [1977] ECR 5; Case 1/83, *IFG* v. *Freistaat Bayern* [1984] ECR 349, [1985] 1 CMLR 453. The costs of checks carried out pursuant to mandatory obligations imposed by international conventions to which all the Member States are party are treated in the same way: Case 89/76, *Commission* v. *Netherlands* [1977] ECR 1355.

to the operator, because this condition is satisfied only if the operator in question obtains a definite specific benefit . . ., which is not the case if the inspection serves to guarantee, in the public interest, the health and life of animals in international transport. . . .

8. Since the contested fee was charged in connection with inspections carried out pursuant to a Community provision, it should be noted that according to the case law of the Court . . . such fees may not be classified as charges having an effect equivalent to a customs duty if the following conditions are satisfied:

(a) they do not exceed the actual costs of the inspections in connection with which they are charged;

(b) the inspections in question are obligatory and uniform for all the products concerned in the Community;

(c) they are prescribed by Community law in the general interest of the Community;

(d) they promote the free movement of goods, in particular by neutralizing obstacles which could arise from unilateral measures of inspection adopted in accordance with Article 36 of the Treaty.

9. In this instance these conditions are satisfied by the contested fee. In the first place it has not been contested that it does not exceed the real cost of the inspections in connection with which it is charged.

10. Moreover, all the Member States of transit and destination are required, under, *inter alia*, Article 2(1) of Directive 81/389/EEC . . . to carry out the veterinary inspections in question when the animals are brought into their territories, and therefore the inspections are obligatory and uniform for all the animals concerned in the Community.

11. Those inspections are prescribed by Directive 81/389/EEC, which establishes the measures necessary . . . for the protection of live animals during international transport, with a view to the protection of live animals, an objective which is pursued in the general interest of the Community and not a specific interest of individual states.

12. Finally, it appears in the preambles to the . . . directives that they are intended to harmonize the laws of the Member States regarding the protection of animals in international transport in order to eliminate technical barriers resulting from disparities in the national laws. . . . In addition, failing such harmonization, each Member State was entitled to maintain or introduce, under the conditions laid down in Article 36 of the Treaty, measures restricting trade which were justified on grounds of the protection of the health and life of animals. It follows that the standardization of the inspections in question is such as to promote the free movement of goods.

13. The Commission has claimed, however, that the contested fee is to be regarded as a charge having equivalent effect to a customs duty because, in so far as fees of this type have not been harmonized, such harmonization, moreover, being unattainable in practice – their negative effect on the free movement of goods could not be compensated or, consequently, justified by the positive effects of the Community standardization of inspections.

14. In this respect, it should be noted that since the fee in question is intended solely as the financially and economically justified compensation for an obligation imposed in equal measure on all the Member States by Community law, it cannot be regarded as equivalent to a customs duty; nor, consequently, can it fall within the ambit of the prohibition laid down in Articles 9 and 12 of the Treaty.

15. The negative effects which such a fee may have on the free movement of goods in the Community can be eliminated only by virtue of Community provisions providing for the harmonization of fees, or imposing the obligation on the Member States to bear the costs entailed in the inspections or, finally, establishing that the costs in question are to be paid out of the Community budget.

(e) RECOVERY OF UNLAWFUL CHARGES[27]

The general principle is that a Member State must repay charges that have been unlawfully levied.[28] The procedural conditions for such repayment may be less favourable than those applying in actions between private individuals, provided that they apply in the same way to actions based on Community law and national law, and provided also that they do not make recovery impossible or excessively difficult.[29] There is, however, an exception to this general rule for circumstances in which the trader has passed on the loss to customers, since reimbursement could lead to the trader being unjustly enriched. This very exception may itself be qualified where the trader can, none the less, show that it has suffered loss.[30] The burden of proving that the duties have not been passed on to others cannot however be placed on the taxpayer.[31]

(f) THE CUSTOMS UNION: THE BROADER PERSPECTIVE

The discussion thus far has focused on the important legal issues surrounding Articles 23–25, and the limits placed on the capacity of Member States to impose duties or charges when goods cross a frontier. It would, however, be mistaken to believe that this constitutes the entirety of EC law in this area.

The *substantive importance of* customs law is far greater than this.[32] The very fact that customs barriers between Member States have been broken down means that once goods are in the EC they move freely. The consequence is that 'the ring fence around the single market is only as strong as its weakest link', and that there is no 'second chance' to impose limits on goods coming from a third country.[33] The maintenance of effective customs control for goods coming from outside the Community is important for a number of reasons. Such goods will be subject to a tariff, which is a significant part of the Community's own resources. The EC has, therefore, a strong interest in combating fraud. The fact that there is in effect only ever one customs barrier for goods to enter the EC also has implications for the battle against organized crime, counterfeit goods, and the like.

This has led to *organizational initiatives* designed to meet these new challenges. There is no Community customs service. The EC works through and with the customs authorities in the Member States. Much time has been spent on implementing the Customs 2002 Programme,[34] the object of which is that the customs administrations of the Member States should operate as efficiently and as effectively as would

---

[27] For more general discussion of remedies see Ch. 6 above.

[28] Case 199/82, *Amministrazione delle Finanze dello Stato* v. *San Giorgio* [1983] ECR 3595.

[29] Case C–343/96, *Dilexport Srl* v. *Amministrazione delle Finanze dello Stato* [1999] ECR I–579.

[30] Cases C–192–218/95, *Société Comateb* v. *Directeur Général des Douanes et Droits Indirects* [1997] ECR I–165.

[31] Case C–343/96, *Dilexport*, n. 29 above, para. 52; Cases C–441 & 442/98, *Michailidis*, n. 13 above, para. 38.

[32] Communication from the Commission to the Council, the European Parliament, and the Economic and Social Committee, *Concerning a Strategy for the Customs Union*, COM(2001) 51 final.

[33] Commission, *The Changing Role of Customs* (EC Commission 2000), 1.

[34] Dec. 210/97 [1996] OJ L33/24.

a single administration.[35] This is especially important with enlargement on the horizon. The difficulties of preventing fraud and the import of illegal goods will be all the greater with the advent of new Member States, whose customs authorities will be less used to the Community rules, and may be poorly financed.

5. ARTICLES 90–93:
DISCRIMINATORY TAX PROVISIONS

The preceding discussion has focused on Articles 23–25. It is necessary now to shift our focus to the provisions on discriminatory taxes to understand the importance of these Articles and the way in which they relate to those concerning customs duties and charges having an equivalent effect.

Article 90 (ex Article 95) is the central provision in this area. It has been directly effective since 1 January 1962.[36]

No Member State shall impose, directly or indirectly, on the products of other Member States any internal taxation of any kind in excess of that imposed directly or indirectly on similar domestic products.

Furthermore, no Member State shall impose on the products of other Member States any internal taxation of such a nature as to afford indirect protection to other products.

(a) THE PURPOSE OF ARTICLE 90

The aim of Article 90 can be stated quite simply: it is to prevent the objectives of Articles 23 to 25 from being undermined by discriminatory internal taxation. We have already seen that Articles 23 to 25 are designed to prevent customs duties, or charges equivalent thereto, from impeding the free flow of goods. The Treaty outlaws such measures, whatever legal form they assume, when they are imposed as a result of a product *crossing a frontier*. These provisions would, however, be to little avail if it were open to a State to prejudice foreign products once they were *inside* its own territory by levying discriminatory taxes, thereby disadvantaging those imported products in competition with domestic goods. Article 90 is designed to prevent this from happening, and this has been recognized by the ECJ.[37]

(b) ARTICLE 90(1): DIRECT DISCRIMINATION

Article 90(1) (ex Article 95(1)) does not stipulate that a Member State must adopt any particular regime of internal taxation. It requires only that whatever system is chosen should be applied without discrimination to similar imported products.

---

[35] Commission Report to the European Parliament and the Council, *On the Implementation of the Customs 2000 Programme*, Doc. XXI/1065/98 EN, para. 2.1.

[36] Case 57/65, *Alfons Lütticke GmbH* v. *Hauptzollamt Saarlouis* [1966] ECR 205; Case 28/67, *Mölkerei-Zentrale Westfalen/Lippe GmbH* v. *Hauptzollamt Paderborn* [1968] ECR 143; Case 74/76, *Ianelli & Volpi* v. *Meroni* [1977] ECR 557.

[37] Cases 2 and 3/62, *Commission* v. *Belgium and Luxembourg* [1962] ECR 425, 431; Case 252/86, *Gabriel Bergandi* v. *Directeur Général des Impôts* [1988] ECR 1343, 1374.

Thus in *Commission* v. *Italy*[38] the Italian Government charged lower taxes on regenerated oil than on ordinary oil. The policy was motivated by ecological considerations, but imported regenerated oil did not benefit from the same advantage. In its defence Italy argued that it was not possible to determine whether imported oil was regenerated or not. This argument was rejected by the ECJ which held that it was for the importers to show that their oil came within the relevant category, subject to reasonable standards of proof, and that a certificate from the State of export could be employed to identify the nature of the oil. Similarly in the *Hansen* case[39] the ECJ insisted that a German rule making tax relief available to spirits made from fruit by small businesses and collective farms must be equally applicable to spirits which were in the same category coming from elsewhere in the Community.[40]

The rules relating to non-discrimination with respect to the payment of taxes will also be broken if the procedure for collection of the tax treats domestic goods and those which come from another Member State unequally. This is demonstrated by *Commission* v. *Ireland*.[41] In this case, although the tax itself applied to all goods irrespective of origin, domestic producers were treated more leniently as regards payment, being allowed a number of weeks before payment was actually demanded, whereas importers had to pay the duty directly on importation.

(c) ARTICLE 90(1): INDIRECT DISCRIMINATION

The discussion thus far has focused on cases of direct discrimination under Article 90(1). The measures in question explicitly treated domestic goods and imports differently to the detriment of the latter. It is, however, clear that indirect discrimination may equally be caught by this Article. There may well be tax rules which do not on their face differentiate between the tax liability of goods based on the country of origin, but which none the less do place a greater burden on commodities coming from another Member State. The ECJ has emphasized that a tax system will be compatible with Article 90 only if it excludes 'any possibility' of imported products being taxed more heavily than similar domestic goods.[42]

---

[38] Case 21/79, [1980] ECR 1.

[39] Case 148/77, *H. Hansen* v. *Hauptzollamt Flensburg* [1978] ECR 1787.

[40] See also Case 196/85, *Commission* v. *France* [1987] ECR 1597; Case C–327/90, *Commission* v. *Greece* [1992] ECR I–3033; Case C–375/95, *Commission* v. *Greece* [1997] ECR I–5981.

[41] Case 55/79, [1980] ECR 481; Case C–68/96, *Grundig Italiana SpA* v. *Ministero delle Finanze* [1998] ECR I–3775.

[42] Case C–228/98, *Dounias* v. *Oikonomikon* [2000] ECR I–577, para. 41; Case C–265/99, *Commission* v. *French Republic*, 15 Mar. 2001, para. 40.

Case 112/84, Humblot v. Directeur des Services Fiscaux
[1985] ECR 1367

[Note ToA renumbering: Art. 95 is now Art. 90]

French law imposed an annual car tax. The criterion for the amount of tax to be paid was the power rating of the car. Below a 16CV rating the tax increased gradually to a maximum of 1,100 francs. For cars above 16CV in power there was a flat rate of 5,000 francs. There was no French car which was rated above 16CV, and therefore the higher charge was borne only by those who had imported cars. Humblot was charged the 5,000 francs on a 36CV imported vehicle, and argued that this tax violated Article 95 (now Article 90).

THE ECJ

12. It is appropriate in the first place to stress that as Community law stands at present the Member States are at liberty to subject products such as cars to a system of road tax which increases progressively in amount depending on an objective criterion, such as the power rating for tax purposes, which may be determined in various ways.

13. Such a system of domestic taxation is, however, compatible with Article 95 only in so far as it is free from any discriminatory or protective effect.

14. That is not true of a system like the one at issue in the main proceedings. Under that system there are two distinct taxes: a differential tax which increases progressively and is charged on cars not exceeding a given power rating for tax purposes and a fixed tax on cars exceeding that rating which is almost five times as high as the highest rate of the differential tax. Although the system embodies no formal distinction based on the origin of the products it manifestly exhibits discriminatory or protective features contrary to Article 95, since the power rating determining liability to the special tax has been fixed at a level such that only imported cars, in particular from other Member States, are subject to the special tax whereas all cars of domestic manufacture are liable to the distinctly more advantageous differential tax.

15. In the absence of considerations relating to the amount of the special tax, consumers seeking comparable cars as regards such matters as size, comfort, actual power, maintenance costs, durability, fuel consumption and price would naturally choose from among cars above and below the critical power rating laid down by French law. However, liability to the special tax entails a much larger increase in taxation than passing from one category of car to another in a system of progressive taxation embodying balanced differentials like the system on which the differential tax is based. The resultant additional taxation is liable to cancel out the advantages which certain cars imported from other Member States might have in consumers' eyes over comparable cars of domestic manufacture, particularly since the special tax continues to be payable for several years. In that respect the special tax reduces the amount of competition to which cars of domestic manufacture are subject and hence is contrary to the principle of neutrality with which domestic taxation must comply.

16. In the light of the foregoing considerations the question raised by the national court for a preliminary ruling should be answered as follows: Article 95 of the EEC Treaty prohibits the charging on cars exceeding a given power rating for tax purposes of a special fixed tax the amount of which is several times the highest amount of the progressive tax payable on cars of less than the said power rating for tax purposes, where the only cars subject to the special tax are imported, in particular from other Member States.

The *Humblot* case provides a good example of the ECJ's determination to catch indirect as well as direct discrimination. The reasoning of the Court is cogent, demonstrating as it does the way in which such tax provisions can distort the competitive process in the car market. The French authorities duly revised the tax rules in the light of the Court's decision, but the new scheme was challenged and found to be in breach of Community law. Under this new regime the French authorities replaced the 5,000 franc tax for cars above 16CV with nine more specific tax bands, the application of which was dependent on the power of the car. Although this scheme was less obviously discriminatory than that condemned in *Humblot*, it was still the case that the tax rate increased sharply above 16CV. This new tax system was therefore condemned in *Feldain*.[43]

(d) ARTICLE 90: NATIONAL AUTONOMY AND FISCAL CHOICES

While the Treaty prohibits indirect as well as direct discrimination under Article 90(1) (ex Article 95(1)) it may be necessary to determine which species of partiality is in issue in any particular case. The reason for care in this respect is that, while direct discrimination on the grounds of nationality cannot be justified, tax rules of a Member State which tend none the less to favour the national producers may be saved if there is some *objective justification* for the conduct complained of. This idea of objective justification is, as we shall see, one which recurs in relation to other Articles concerning free movement of goods, or those which regulate free movement of workers or competition policy.[44] The essential idea is that the Court will allow the defence to plead that there was some objective policy reason, which is acceptable to the Community, to justify the State's action. In this way such Treaty Articles are prevented from becoming too harsh or draconian in their application. The *Chemial* case exemplifies this judicial approach.

Case 140/79, Chemial Farmaceutici v. DAF SpA [1981] ECR 1[45]

Italy taxed synthetic ethyl alcohol more highly than ethyl alcohol obtained from fermentation. This was so even though the products could be used interchangeably. Italy was not a major producer of the synthetic product. The object was to favour the manufacture of ethyl alcohol from agricultural products, and to restrain the processing into alcohol of ethylene, a petroleum derivative, in order to reserve that raw material for more important economic uses. The Court made the following observations on this policy choice.

---

[43] Case 433/85, *Feldain v. Directeur des Services Fiscaux* [1987] ECR 3536; Case 76/87, *Seguela* v. *Administration des Impôts* [1988] ECR 2397; Case C–265/99, n. 42 above.

[44] See Chs. 15, 17, 18, and 21 below.

[45] See also Case 46/80, *Vinal SpA v. Orbat SpA* [1981] ECR 77.

13. .... It accordingly constitutes a legitimate choice of economic policy to which effect is given by fiscal means. The implementation of that policy does not lead to any discrimination since although it results in discouraging imports of synthetic alcohol into Italy, it also has the consequence of hampering the development in Italy itself of production of alcohol from ethylene, that production being technically perfectly feasible.

14. As the Court has stated on many occasions ... in its present stage of development Community law does not restrict the freedom of each Member State to lay down tax arrangements which differentiate between certain products on the basis of objective criteria, such as the nature of the raw materials used or the production process employed. Such differentiation is compatible with Community law if it pursues economic policy objectives which are themselves compatible with the requirements of the Treaty and its secondary law and if the detailed rules are such as to avoid any form of discrimination, direct or indirect, in regard to imports from other Member States or any form of protection of competing domestic products.

15. Differential taxation such as that which exists in Italy for denatured synthetic alcohol on the one hand and denatured alcohol obtained by fermentation on the other satisfies these requirements. It appears in fact that that system of taxation pursues an objective of legitimate industrial policy in that it is such as to promote the distillation of agricultural products as against the manufacture of alcohol from petroleum derivatives. That choice does not conflict with the rules of Community law or the requirements of a policy decided within the framework of the Community.

16. The detailed provisions of the legislation at issue before the national court cannot be considered as discriminatory since, on the one hand, it is not disputed that imports from other Member States of alcohol by fermentation qualify for the same tax treatment as Italian alcohol produced by fermentation and, on the other hand, although the rate of tax prescribed for synthetic alcohol results in restraining the importation of synthetic alcohol originating in other Member States, it has an equivalent economic effect in the national territory in that it also hampers the establishment of profitable production of the same product in Italian industry.

It is true that the Court in the *Chemial* case predicates its acceptance of the Italian policy on the basis that it does not result in any discrimination, whether direct or indirect. Notwithstanding this the ECJ's reasoning bears testimony to its willingness to accept objective justifications where the national policy is acceptable from the Community's perspective, even if this benefits domestic traders more than importers. It is clear, as the Court points out, that the Italian policy would hamper an Italian producer that wished to make synthetic ethylene alcohol. However, there was little domestic production of that product, and therefore the Italian tax rule hit importers harder than firms that were based in Italy. The same reasoning can be seen in other decisions.

Thus in *Commission* v. *France*[46] the Commission alleged that a French rule which taxed sweet wines produced in a traditional manner at a lower rate than liqueur wines was contrary to Article 95 (now Article 90). The Court disagreed. It found that there

---

[46] Case 196/85, [1987] ECR 1597.

was no direct discrimination on grounds of origin or nationality. Sweet wines made in the natural manner tended to be produced in areas where the growing conditions were less than optimal; there would often be poor soil and low rainfall. The rationale for the French policy was to provide some fiscal incentives for production in these areas. The Court was willing to accept that this could constitute an objective justification which was legitimate under this Article. In *Outokumpu Oy*[47] the EC held that it was legitimate for a Member State to tax the same or similar product differentially, provided that this was done on the basis of objective criteria, such as the nature of the raw materials used or the production process employed. Article 95 did not preclude differential tax rates on electricity, where they were based on environmental considerations, provided that there was no discrimination against imports.[48]

It is, moreover, possible for differential tax rates on cars, the *Humblot* case notwithstanding, to escape the prohibition of this Article. This could be so if the differential rates were to encourage the use of more environmentally friendly models, provided that they did not discriminate against imports. This is exemplified by *Commission* v. *Greece*.[49] The ECJ was once again faced with a national fiscal measure that imposed a progressively higher tax based on the cylinder capacity of the car. It held that this would not constitute a breach of Article 95 (now Article 90) unless it was discriminatory, and this would not be the case unless it both discouraged customers from buying highly taxed imported cars and encouraged them to buy domestic cars instead. The mere fact that all cars in the highest tax bracket were imported was not sufficient to establish a violation of this Article. EC law did not therefore prohibit the use of tax policy to attain social ends, provided that the tax was based on an objective criterion, was not discriminatory, and did not have a protective effect.

(e) THE RELATIONSHIP BETWEEN ARTICLE 90(1) AND 90(2)

Article 90(1) prohibits the imposition of internal taxes on products from other Member States in excess of those levied on *similar* domestic products. Thus once the two relevant products are judged to be similar then Article 90(1) bites, with the consequence that excessive taxes levied on the imported goods are banned. The dividing line between Article 90(1) and 90(2) (ex Article 95(2)) may be problematic since it will obviously be a contestable issue whether goods are deemed to be similar or not. This issue will be addressed below.

Article 90(2) is designed to catch national tax provisions that apply unequal tax ratings to goods which may not be strictly similar, but which may none the less be in competition with each other. The object is to prevent these differential tax ratings from affording indirect protection to the domestic goods. An example will serve to make this idea clearer. Wine and beer may not be adjudged to be similar goods as

[47] Case C–213/96, [1998] ECR I–1777.
[48] For a discussion of tensions within the case law see A. Easson, 'Fiscal Discrimination: New Perspectives on Article 95 of the EEC Treaty' (1981) 18 *CMLRev.* 521.
[49] Case C–132/88, [1990] ECR I–1567; Case C–421/97, *Tarantik* v. *Direction des Services Fiscaux de Seine-et-Marne* [1999] ECR I–3633.

such, but there may, notwithstanding this fact, be a degree of competition between them. Economists term this relationship cross-elasticity of demand. As the price of one product rises in relation to another, so consumers will switch to the lower-priced product. The extent to which they switch will depend on factors such as the price difference between the two products, and the degree to which consumers perceive them to be interchangeable. Thus, if a State which produces little wine but much beer chooses to tax the former at a considerably higher rate than the latter, then it is clear that wine sellers will be relatively disadvantaged and beer producers afforded a measure of indirect protection. Article 90(2) is designed to catch such situations. This relationship between Articles 90(1) and (2) is brought out in the following case.

Case 168/78, Commission v. France
[1980] ECR 347

[Note ToA renumbering: Arts. 9 to 17 have been replaced by Arts. 23 to 25; Art. 95 is now 90; Art. 169 is now 226]

France had higher tax rates for spirits which were based on grain, such as whisky, rum, gin, and vodka, than those which were based on wine or fruit, such as cognac, calvados, and armagnac. France produced very little of the former category of drinks, but was a major producer of fruit-based spirits. The Commission brought an Article 169 action alleging that the French tax regime violated Article 95. The ECJ began by emphasizing the connection between Article 95 and Articles 9 to 17 as they then were: Article 95 was to supplement the provisions on customs duties and charges by prohibiting internal taxation which discriminated against imported products. It continued as follows.

THE ECJ

5. The first paragraph of Article 95, which is based on a comparison of the tax burdens imposed on domestic products and on imported products which may be classified as 'similar', is the basic rule in this respect. This provision, as the Court has had occasion to emphasize in its judgment . . . in Case 148/77, *H. Hansen* v. *Haupzollamt Flensburg* [1978] ECR 1787, must be interpreted widely so as to cover all taxation procedures which conflict with the principle of the equality of treatment of domestic products and imported products; it is therefore necessary to interpret the concept of 'similar products' with sufficient flexibility. The Court specified in the judgment . . . in the *Rewe* case (Case 45/75 [1976] ECR 181) that it is necessary to consider as similar products those which 'have similar characteristics and meet the same needs from the point of view of consumers'. It is therefore necessary to determine the scope of the first paragraph of Article 95 on the basis not of the criterion of the strictly identical nature of the products but on that of their similar and comparable use.

6. The function of the second paragraph of Article 95 is to cover, in addition, all forms of indirect tax protection in the case of products which, without being similar within the meaning of the first paragraph, are nevertheless in competition, even partial, indirect or potential, with certain products of the importing country. The Court has already emphasized certain aspects of that provision in . . . Case 27/77, *Firma Fink-Frucht GmbH* . . . [1978] ECR 223, in which it

stated that for the purposes of the application of the first paragraph of Article 95 it is sufficient for the imported product to be in competition with the protected domestic production by reason of one of several economic uses to which it may be put, even though the condition of similarity for the purposes of the first paragraph of Article 95 is not fulfilled.

7. Whilst the criterion indicated in the first paragraph of Article 95 consists in the comparison of tax burdens, whether in terms of the rate, the mode of assessment or other detailed rules for the application thereof, in view of the difficulty of making sufficiently precise comparisons between the products in question, the second paragraph of that Article is based upon a more general criterion, in other words the protective nature of the system of internal taxation.

(f) ARTICLE 90(1) AND (2): THE DETERMINATION OF SIMILARITY

It is clear from the preceding discussion that the first step is therefore to determine whether the products are similar. If they are then Article 90(1) applies; if they are not then the tax rules may still be caught by Article 90(2). This issue has arisen in a number of cases. In an early judgment the ECJ held that products would be regarded as similar if they came within the same tax classification.[50] However, in some cases the ECJ has condemned the tax without too detailed an analysis of whether this was because of Article 95(1) or (2) (now Article 90(1) or (2)). This approach is particularly apparent in the early 'spirits cases', in which the Commission brought a number of Article 169 (now Article 226) actions against Member States, alleging that their tax rules on spirits infringed what was Article 95.[51] The reason the ECJ did not trouble unduly whether the condemnation should be based on the old Article 95(1) or (2) is apparent in the following extract:

Case 168/78, Commission v. France
[1980] ECR 347

[Note ToA renumbering: Art. 95 is now 90.]

The facts have been set out above. The Commission argued that all spirits constituted a single market. France responded by contending that they should be broken down into a number of more specific markets, depending on their composition, physical characteristics and consumer usages. The ECJ, having considered the characteristics of the spirits, decided, on the one hand, that they possessed certain generic features (such as high alcohol content); and on the other hand, that they were made from differing materials, and were consumed in different ways.

THE ECJ

12. Two conclusions follow from this analysis of the market in spirits. First, there is, in the case of spirits considered as a whole, an indeterminate number of beverages which must be

---

[50] Case 27/67, *Fink-Frucht GmbH v. Hauptzollamt München-Landsbergerstrasse* [1968] ECR 327.

[51] See also Case 169/78, *Commission v. Italy* [1980] ECR 385; Case 171/78, *Commission v. Denmark* [1980] ECR 447.

classified as 'similar products' within the meaning of the first paragraph of Article 95, although it may be difficult to decide this in specific cases, in view of the nature of the factors implied by distinguishing criteria such as flavour and consumer habits. Secondly, even in cases in which it is impossible to recognize a sufficient degree of similarity between the products concerned, there are nevertheless, in the case of all spirits, common characteristics which are sufficiently pronounced to accept that in all cases there is at least partial or potential competition. It follows that the application of the second paragraph of Article 95 may come into consideration in cases in which the relationship of similarity between the specific varieties of spirits remains doubtful or contested.

13. It appears from the foregoing that Article 95, taken as a whole, may apply without distinction to all the products concerned. It is sufficient therefore to examine whether the application of a given national tax system is discriminatory or, as the case may be, protective, in other words whether there is a difference in the rate or the detailed rules for levying the tax and whether that difference is likely to favour a given national production.

[*The Court then considered various arguments adduced by the French authorities which were designed to show that the spirits in question differed in terms of taste, use, and the like.*]

39. After considering all these factors the Court deems it unnecessary for the purposes of solving this dispute to give a ruling on the question whether or not the spiritous beverages concerned are wholly or partially similar products within the meaning of the first paragraph of Article 95 when it is impossible reasonably to contest that without exception they are in at least partial competition with the domestic products to which the application refers and that it is impossible to deny the protective nature of the French tax system within the second paragraph of Article 95.

40. In fact, as indicated above, spirits obtained from cereals have, as products obtained from distillation, sufficient characteristics in common with other spirits to constitute at least in certain circumstances an alternative choice for consumers. . . .

41. As the competitive and substitution relationships between the beverages in question are such, the protective nature of the tax system criticized by the Commission is clear. A characteristic of that system is in fact that an essential part of domestic production, . . . spirits obtained from wine and fruit, come within the most favourable tax category whereas at least two types of product, almost all of which are imported from other Member States, are subject to higher taxation under the 'manufacturing tax'.

These early 'spirits' cases demonstrate that the Court will not be overly concerned whether a case is characterized as relating to Article 95(1) or (2) (now Article 90(1) or (2)) if the nature of the products renders such classification difficult (paragraph 12 above); and if the Court feels that the tax should be condemned because the goods are in competition and the tax is protective (paragraph 39 above).

This approach can however be problematic. The consequence of 'globalizing'[52] Article 90(1) and (2) in this manner is that it obscures the appropriate response of the infringing State. A breach of Article 90(1) means that the offending State has to equalize the taxes on domestic and imported goods. Breach of Article 90(2) requires

---

[52] A. Easson, n. 48 above, 521, 535.

the State to remove the protective effect, but this may not entail equalization of the tax burdens on the respective goods.

Later courts have been more careful to determine whether the analysis should proceed under Article 90(1) or (2), as exemplified by *John Walker* v. *Ministeriet for Skatter*.[53] The issue was whether liqueur fruit wine was similar to whisky for the purposes of the old Article 95(1). The ECJ analysed the objective characteristics of the products, their alcohol content and method of manufacture, and consumer perceptions of the product. It decided that the goods were not similar: they did not possess the same alcohol content, nor was the process of manufacture the same. Further scrutiny of the tax would therefore have to be pursuant to the old Article 95(2).[54] The same approach can be perceived in *Commission* v. *Italy*.[55] The Commission brought an action against Italy claiming that its consumption tax on fruit was discriminatory under Article 95. Italy produced large amounts of fruit, such as apples, pears, peaches, plums, and oranges, but almost no bananas which were imported from France. Italy imposed a consumption tax on bananas which amounted to almost half the import price; other fruit was not subject to the tax. The Court considered whether bananas and other fruit were similar for the purposes of Article 95(1) (now Article 90(1)). It found that they were not, taking account of the objective characteristics of the products, including their organoleptic properties and the extent to which they could satisfy the same consumer need.[56] Further examination of the Italian tax would have to be under Article 95(2) (now Article 90(2)).

(g) ARTICLE 90(2): THE DETERMINATION OF PROTECTIVE EFFECT

One of the original 'spirits' cases brought by the Commission was against the United Kingdom for discriminatory taxation of wine with respect to beer. This was clearly a more difficult case than the others within this category, since there is undoubtedly a greater difference between wine and beer than between two spirits. It is for this reason that the ECJ initially declined to rule that the United Kingdom provisions were in breach of Article 95 (now Article 90), and required further information on the nature of the competitive relationship between the two products. Its judgment was finally delivered some years later, and provides insights in to the way in which the Court approaches the difficult adjudicatory problems presented by this Article.

---

[53] Case 243/84, [1986] ECR 875.
[54] *Cf.* Case 106/84, *Commission* v. *Denmark* [1986] ECR 833.
[55] Case 184/85, [1987] ECR 2013.
[56] Bananas do not have the same water content as other fruit, and therefore their thirst-quenching qualities are not the same; and bananas were perceived to have a nutritional value in excess of other fruit: *ibid.*, para. 10.

Case 170/78, Commission v. United Kingdom
[1983] ECR 2265

[Note ToA renumbering: Arts. 95 and 169 are now 90 and 226 respectively]

The United Kingdom levied an excise tax on certain wines which was roughly five times that which was levied on beer. The tax on wine represented about 38 per cent of the sale price of the product, as compared to the tax on beer which was 25 per cent of the product's price. The United Kingdom produces considerable amounts of beer, but very little wine. The Commission brought an Article 169 action, claiming that the differential excise tax was in breach of Article 95.

THE ECJ

8. As regards the question of competition between wine and beer, the Court considered that, to a certain extent at least, the two beverages in question were capable of meeting identical needs, so that it had to be acknowledged that there was a degree of substitution for one another. It pointed out that, for the purpose of measuring the possible degree of substitution, attention should not be confined to consumer habits in a Member State or in a given region. Those habits, which were essentially variable in time and space, could not be considered to be immutable; the tax policy of a Member State must not therefore crystallize given consumer habits so as to consolidate an advantage acquired by national industries concerned to respond to them.

9. The Court nonetheless recognized that, in view of the substantial differences between wine and beer, it was difficult to compare the manufacturing processes and the natural properties of those beverages, as the Government of the United Kingdom had rightly observed. For that reason, the Court requested the parties to provide additional information with a view to dispelling the doubts which existed concerning the nature of the competitive relationship between the two products.

. . .

11. The Italian Government contended in that connection that it was inappropriate to compare beer with wines of average alcoholic strength or, *a fortiori*, with wines of greater alcoholic strength. In its opinion, it was the lightest wines with an alcoholic strength in the region of 9, that is to say the most popular and cheapest wines, which were genuinely in competition with beer. . . .

12. The Court considers that observation by the Italian Government to be pertinent. In view of the substantial differences in the quality and, therefore, in the price of wines, the decisive competitive relationship between beer, a popular and widely consumed beverage, and wine must be established by reference to those wines which are the most accessible to the public at large, that is to say, generally speaking the lightest and cheapest varieties. Accordingly, that is the appropriate basis for making fiscal comparisons by reference to the alcoholic strength or to the price of the two beverages in question.

[*The Commission, Italy, and the United Kingdom differed as regards the criteria which should be used to determine whether the tax on the two products was discriminatory. The Commission argued that assessment of the tax burden should be based on volume plus alcohol content; Italy contended that volume alone should be determinative; while the United Kingdom argued that the true basis of comparison was product price net of tax. The ECJ held that none of these tests was sufficient in itself, but that all three could provide 'significant information for the assessment of the contested tax system'.*]

19. It is not disputed that comparison of the taxation of beer and wine by reference to the

volume of the two beverages reveals that wine is taxed more heavily than beer in both relative and absolute terms . . . the taxation of wine was, on average, five times higher, by reference to volume, than the taxation of beer; in other words wine was subject to an additional tax of 400% in round figures.

20. As regards the criterion for comparison based on alcoholic strength. . . .

21. In the light of the indices which the Court has already accepted, it is clear that in the United Kingdom . . . wine bore a tax burden which, by reference to alcoholic strength, was more than twice as heavy as that borne by beer, that is to say an additional tax burden of at least 100%.

22. As regards the criterion of the incidence of taxation on the price net of tax, the Court experienced considerable difficulty in forming an opinion, in view of the disparate nature of the information provided by the parties. . . .

26. After considering the information provided by the parties, the Court has come to the conclusion that, if a comparison is made on the basis of those wines which are cheaper than the types of wine selected by the United Kingdom and of which several varieties are sold in significant quantities on the United Kingdom market, it becomes apparent that precisely those wines which, in view of their price, are most directly in competition with domestic beer production are subject to a considerably higher tax burden.

27. It is clear, therefore, . . . —whatever criterion for comparison is used, there being no need to express a preference for one or the other—that the United Kingdom's tax system has the effect of subjecting wine imported from other Member States to an additional burden so as to afford protection to domestic beer production . . . Since such protection is most marked in the case of the most popular wines, the effect of the United Kingdom tax system is to stamp wine with the hallmarks of a luxury product which, in view of the tax burden which it bears, can scarcely constitute in the eyes of the consumer a genuine alternative to the typically produced domestic beverage.

28. It follows . . . that, by levying excise duty on still light wines made from fresh grapes at a higher rate, in relative terms, than on beer, the United Kingdom has failed to fulfil its obligations under the second paragraph of Article 95 of the EEC Treaty.

The decision in the United Kingdom *Wine/Beer* case throws interesting light on the Court's methodology when adjudicating on Article 95(2) (now Article 90(2)). Its judgment proceeds in two stages.

At the first stage the ECJ is concerned to establish that there is some competitive relationship between the two products in order to render Article 95(2) applicable at all (paragraphs 8 to 12). Product substitutability is central when determining the existence of this relationship. However, the degree to which consumers currently perceive the two products to be substitutable will not be regarded as fixed for all time (paragraph 8). This is because consumer preferences are not immutable, and because the very shape of those preferences will be affected by, *inter alia*, the relative tax rates of the two products. If the varying taxes levied on the commodities serve to place them artificially within separate categories in consumers' eyes, this will correspondingly reduce the extent to which the buying public perceives the products to be substitutable. It is this which the Court has in mind when castigating the United Kingdom tax policy for stamping wine with the hallmark of being a luxury product which is in a different category from beer (paragraph 27). This part of the ECJ's judgment also attests to the importance of accurately defining the nature of the two allegedly competing products. It would not have been plausible to suggest meaningful competition between beer and expensive wine. Hence the Court's acceptance of the Italian Government's contention that the real comparison was between beer and the cheaper end of the wine market.

Having established that there is some competitive relationship between the respective goods, the Court then moves on to determine whether the tax system was in fact protective of beer. Its judgment demonstrates its willingness to apply varying criteria suggested by the parties in order to decide whether a protective effect has been established or not. The criteria used by the Court may or may not be of relevance when dealing with two different products. On the facts of the actual dispute it is, however, difficult to contest the conclusion that the United Kingdom tax was indeed discriminatory. In circumstances where the disparity in tax rates between the two products is less dramatic than that between wine and beer, more finely tuned analysis may be required to determine whether there is any protective effect. Thus it may, for example, be necessary to determine the degree of cross-elasticity between the two products. If this is low, then only a 'large difference in tax burdens will have a protective tendency'.[57] Similarly, if the level of tax is low with respect to the final selling price of the goods, then it will take a very significant tax differential to have any protective impact.[58]

The same two stages can be perceived in other ECJ decisions under Article 95(2) (now Article 90(2)). Thus in *Commission* v. *Italy*[59] the ECJ considered whether the Italian consumption tax imposed on bananas was protective or not. It began by noting that, although bananas and other fruit were not similar, they were in partial competition, since bananas did afford consumers some further choice in the fruit market. This was, however, only the case with respect to fresh and not dried bananas, since there was no competitive relation between the latter and table fruit. Having established the existence of some competition between the two products, the Court moved to the second stage of deciding whether the Italian tax had a protective effect. It found that it did. The imposition of a consumption tax equivalent to half the import price of bananas, while no such tax applied to most Italian table fruit, was clear evidence of protectionism.[60]

The existence of Community harmonization will not preclude the application of Article 90 where it is only minimum harmonization. Thus in *Socridis*[61] Community legislation was held to require only that Member States imposed a minimum duty on beer. It did not preclude the application of Article 90 to determine whether a State was being protectionist in its treatment of beer as opposed to wine.

[57] Easson, n. 48 above, 539.   [58] *Ibid.*   [59] Case 184/85, n. 55 above, paras. 11–15.

[60] The existence of a tax differential between a domestic and an imported product will not, however, always suffice to establish protectionism for the purposes of Art. 95(2) (now Art. 90(2)). Thus, where the tax differential was small and the cost of the two products was substantially different, no breach of Art. 95(2) was found: Case 356/85, *Commission* v. *Belgium* [1987] ECR 3299.

[61] Case C–166/98, *Société Critouridienne de Distribution (Socridis)* v. *Receveur Principal des Douanes* [1999] ECR I–3791.

(h) TAXATION: THE BROADER PERSPECTIVE

The discussion thus far has concentrated on the legal constraints imposed by the Treaty on the taxation policies of the Member States, in order to prevent discrimination against imports. It is important, as in the case of the customs union, to place this material in a broader perspective.

Taxation can be direct or indirect. The paradigm of direct taxation is income tax, the paradigm of indirect taxation is a tax on sales. The EC does not exercise any general control over direct taxation. This is regarded as central to sovereignty. EC law will be of relevance only to prevent cross-border discrimination, interference with free movement, and the like. The sensitivity of tax matters is reflected in the requirement of unanimity that still prevails even after the Nice Treaty. EC law has a much greater impact on indirect taxation. Value Added Tax (VAT) was the first such tax to be harmonized in 1977. This was because the 'proper functioning of the internal market requires VAT and excise systems that are efficient and fully reflect the needs of EU businesses and consumers'.[62]

The Community is now striving for a more coherent tax policy.[63] In the context of indirect taxation, this is manifest in proposed improvements to the existing regimes governing VAT, excise duty, and the like. In the context of indirect and direct taxation, there is the growing realization of the extent to which national tax policy can impact on other policies, over which the Community does have competence. These include employment, the environment, economic and monetary union, health, and consumer protection.[64]

The tension this produces is readily apparent in the Commission's language. It recognized that there is no need for 'across the board harmonization of Member States' tax systems', that Member States are free to choose the 'tax systems they consider most appropriate and according to their preferences'.[65] It cautioned, however, that the level of public expenditure was a matter for national preference, so long as the budget remained in balance. It emphasized that Member States' choices did not take place in isolation and that international aspects should be taken into account. It reaffirmed the need for a high degree of harmonization in relation to indirect taxation. It admitted also that some harmonization of the tax treatment accorded to pay might be necessary, in order to remove obstacles to free movement, as in the case of occupational pensions.[66]

The Commission was candid about the difficulties of securing the passage of Community legislation, given the obstacle of unanimity. There are sixteen directives before the Council. It is unsurprising that the Commission has always advocated a shift to qualified-majority voting. What is particularly interesting is the Commission's

---

[62] Communication from the Commission to the Council, the European Parliament, and the Economic and Social Committee, *Tax Policy in the European Union—Priorities for the Years Ahead*, COM(2001) 260 final, para. 3.1.

[63] *Ibid.*, para. 1.

[64] Commission, *Tax Policy in the European Union* (2000), 8–9; *The Key, Taxation and Customs Union*, No. 15, Mar. 2001.

[65] *Tax Policy in the European Union*, n. 62 above, para. 2.4.   [66] *Ibid.*, para. 2.4.

willingness to talk openly about other mechanisms for achieving its objectives, given the difficulties of securing agreement in the Council.[67] The Commission considered in detail a range of options including greater use of Article 226, resort to soft law, and use of the enhanced co-operation procedure.

6. THE BOUNDARY BETWEEN ARTICLES 23–25 AND 90–93

The relationship between Articles 23 to 25 and Articles 90 to 93 has been touched on in the preceding analysis. It is now time to consider this in more detail.

The general principle is that the two sets of Articles are mutually exclusive.[68] They both concern the imposition of fiscal charges by the State. Articles 23 to 25 bite on those duties or charges levied as a result of goods crossing a border. The duty or charge is exacted at the time of, or on account of, the importation, and is borne specifically by the imported product to the exclusion of similar domestic products.[69] Articles 90 to 93, by way of contrast, are designed to catch fiscal policy which is internal to the State: they prevent discrimination against goods once they have entered a particular Member State. The Court has construed both sets of provisions so as to ensure that there is no gap between them.

The decision on which set of Treaty Articles is at stake is however of importance, since the result of this characterization can be of significance for the legal test to be applied.[70] If a State fiscal measure is caught by Article 25 then it will be unlawful. This reflects the importance of breaking down trade barriers. Customs duties or charges are the quintessential barriers to the establishment of a customs union, and hence the Treaty's insistence that they should be removed. If, by way of contrast, a fiscal measure falls within Article 90 then the obligation on the State is different. The taxation levels set by the State are not unlawful under the Treaty, and thus the inquiry will be whether the tax discriminates against the importer under Article 90(1), or has a protective effect under Article 90(2).

In most circumstances there will be little difficulty in determining whether the issue should fall under Article 25 or under Article 90. Certain situations are however more difficult. Three are worthy of mention here.

The *first type of case* which may present problems of characterization is that in which a State imposes a levy on an importer. Such a case would normally be decided on the basis of Article 25, and the levy would be deemed to be a CEE. The State would be condemned unless it could show that the levy was consideration for a service which it had given to the importer, or that it was imposed pursuant to mandatory require-ments of Community law.[71] Attempts to argue that the levy should instead be

---

[67] *Ibid.*, paras. 4.1–4.4.

[68] Case 10/65, *Deutschmann* v. *Federal Republic of Germany* [1965] ECR 469; Case 57/65, *Lütticke*, n. 36 above; Case 105/76, *Interzuccheri SpA* v. *Ditta Rezzano e Cavassa* [1977] ECR 1029.

[69] Case 193/85, *Cooperative Co-Frutta Srl* v. *Amministrazione delle Finanze dello Stato* [1987] ECR 2085, para. 8.

[70] Case 105/76, *Interzuccheri*, n. 68 above, para. 9.   [71] See 590–1 above.

considered under Article 90, because domestic producers also had to pay, have not been notably successful, as the *Bresciani* case demonstrates.[72] In exceptional circumstances the Court may, however, decide that although the charge or levy is taken at the border it is not to be characterized as a CEE within Article 25, but as a tax, the legality of which will be tested under Article 90. In *Denkavit*[73] the applicant was an importer of feedingstuffs from Holland into Denmark. Danish law required, *inter alia*, that the importer obtain an authorization from the Ministry of Agriculture, *and* charged an annual levy to meet the costs of checking samples of the goods. The ECJ held that the requirement of an authorization was caught by Article 30 (now Article 28),[74] but that it could be justified under Article 36 (now Article 30).[75] The Court then considered whether the levy was itself lawful. This levy was imposed on all those engaged in the feedingstuffs trade, whether importers or domestic producers. The ECJ held that it related to a general system of internal dues applied systematically and in accordance with the same criteria to domestic products and imported products alike, and therefore came within Article 90.[76] The ECJ has however made it clear in *Michailidis*[77] that a charge levied at the border will be regarded as an internal tax, rather than a CEE, only where the comparable charge levied on national products is applied at the same rate, at the same marketing stage and on the basis of an identical chargeable event.

The *second type of case* in which there can be boundary-line problems between Articles 25 and 90 is that in which the importing State does not make the imported product, but imposes a tax on it none the less. Should this be considered to be a charge within Article 25 or a tax within Article 90? One might have thought that the ECJ would choose the former characterization, since there are no similar domestic goods. This will not always be so as demonstrated by *Co-Frutta*.

Case 193/85, Cooperative Co-Frutta Srl v. Amministrazione delle Finanze dello Stato [1987] ECR 2085

[Note ToA renumbering: Arts. 12, 95, and 177 are now Arts. 25, 90, and 234 respectively]

This was another case which arose from the imposition by Italy of a consumption tax on bananas, even though no such tax was levied on other fruit produced in Italy. It will be remembered from the earlier discussion that Italy produced only a negligible number of bananas itself. This action was brought by a banana importer via Article 177 to test the legality of the tax. One of the initial questions which the Court addressed was whether the tax should be viewed as a CEE within Article 12, or as a tax to be assessed under Article 95.

---

[72] See 588–9 above.

[73] Case 29/87, *Dansk Denkavit ApS v. Danish Ministry of Agriculture* [1988] ECR 2965.

[74] As a measure having equivalent effect to a quantitative restriction, on which see Ch. 15 below.

[75] On the basis that although there was a Community dir. relevant to the case, which would normally render recourse to Art. 36 (now Art. 30) impossible, the dir. did not extend to the situation in the instant case.

[76] *Denkavit*, n. 73 above, para. 33. See also Case C–130/93, *Lamaire*, n. 17 above; Case C–90/94, *Haahr Petroleum Ltd. v. Abenra Havn* [1997] ECR I–4085.

[77] Cases C–441 & 442/98, n. 13 above, para. 24.

THE ECJ

8. According to established case law of the Court, the prohibition laid down by Articles 9 and 12 of the Treaty in regard to charges having an equivalent effect covers any charge exacted at the time of or on account of importation which, being borne specifically by an imported product to the exclusion of the similar domestic product, has the result of altering the cost price of the imported product, thereby producing the same restrictive effect on the free movement of goods as a customs duty.

9. The essential feature of a charge having an effect equivalent to a customs duty which distinguishes it from an internal tax therefore resides in the fact that the former is borne solely by an imported product as such whilst the latter is borne both by imported and domestic products.

10. The Court has however recognized that even a charge which is borne by a product imported from another Member State, when there is no identical or similar domestic product, does not constitute a charge having equivalent effect but internal taxation within the meaning of Article 95 of the Treaty if it relates to a general system of internal dues applied systematically to categories of products in accordance with objective criteria irrespective of the origin of the products.

11. Those considerations demonstrate that even if it were necessary in some cases, for the purpose of classifying a charge borne by imported products, to equate extremely low domestic production with its non-existence, that would not mean that the levy in question would necessarily have to be regarded as a charge having an effect equivalent to a customs duty. In particular, that will not be so if the levy is part of a general system of internal dues applying systematically to categories of products according to the criteria indicated above.

12. A tax on consumption of the type at issue in the main proceedings does form part of a general system of internal dues. The 19 taxes on consumption are governed by common tax rules and are charged on categories of products irrespective of their origin in accordance with an objective criterion, namely the fact that the product falls into a specific category of goods. Some of those taxes are charged on products intended for human consumption, including the tax on the consumption of bananas. Whether those goods are produced at home or abroad does not seem to have a bearing on the rate, the basis of assessment or the manner in which the tax is levied. The revenue from those taxes is not earmarked for a specific purpose; it constitutes tax revenue identical to other tax revenue and, like it, helps to finance State expenditure generally in all sectors.

13. Consequently, the tax at issue must be regarded as being an integral part of a general system of internal dues within the meaning of Article 95 of the Treaty and its compatibility with Community law must be assessed on the basis of that Article rather than Articles 9 and 12 of the Treaty.

The reasoning of the ECJ makes good sense. If any charge imposed by a State on a product which it did not make at all, or only in negligible quantities, were to be classified as a CEE under Article 25 then two consequences would follow. The charge would be automatically unlawful,[78] and the importing State could not tax goods which it did not produce itself, since any such tax would be condemned under Article 25.

[78] Assuming of course that it could not be saved on the ground that it represented consideration for a service, etc.

This draconian conclusion would make little social, economic, or political sense, and it is not therefore surprising that the Court avoided this result.[79] There may be good reasons why a State should choose to tax, for example, a luxury product even if there is no domestic production of this item. The criterion adopted by the ECJ provides a sensible and workable resolution of this problem. If the test propounded by the ECJ is met the charge will not necessarily be regarded as lawful; it will still fall to be assessed under Article 90 of the Treaty. In the instant case the tax was in fact held to be in breach of Article 95(2) (now Article 90(2)), for the same reasons as were given in the action brought against Italy by the Commission.[80]

The *third type of case* arises when a State chooses to make a selective refund of a tax, or if it uses the money to benefit only a particular group. The position appears to be as follows. If the money from a tax flows into the national exchequer and is then used for the benefit of a particular domestic industry, this could be challenged as a State aid: Articles 87 to 89 (ex Articles 92 to 94).[81]

Classification problems as between Articles 25 and 90 arise when the money that has been refunded can be linked to that which has been levied pursuant to a specific tax. The correct classification will then depend upon whether the refund or other benefit to the national producers wholly or partially offsets the tax. If the former, then the tax will be treated under Article 25, the rationale being that what in effect exists is a charge levied only on the imported product.[82] If, however, the refund or benefit is only partial the matter will fall to be assessed under Article 90, the rationale here being that the partial refund in effect means that there could be a discriminatory tax.[83] Barents, summarizing the early case law,[84] identifies three conditions for a charge to be considered under Article 25 rather than Article 90:[85]

Firstly, the charge must be destined exclusively for financing activities which very largely benefit the taxed domestic product; secondly, there must exist identity between the taxed product and the domestic product benefiting from the charge; and thirdly, the charges imposed on the domestic product must be completely compensated.

This approach is exemplified by the decision in *Scharbatke*.[86] There was a challenge to mandatory contributions levied in Germany when slaughtered animals were presented for inspection. The contribution was applied under the same conditions to national and imported products, and the money was assigned to a marketing fund for agricultural, forestry, and food products. The ECJ held that the mandatory

---

[79] See also Case 90/79, *Commission* v. *France* [1981] ECR 283.

[80] See 605 above.

[81] Cases C–78–83/90, *Compagnie Commerciale de l'Ouest* v. *Receveur Principal des Douanes de la Pallice Port* [1992] ECR I–1847.

[82] Note in this respect that Art. 25 expressly includes customs duties of a fiscal nature.

[83] Where the benefits from the activities financed by the charge accrue to both domestic producers and importers, but the former obtain proportionately greater benefits, the charge will fall under Art. 25 or Art. 90, depending on whether the advantage accruing to domestic producers fully or partially offsets their burdens: Case C–28/96, *Fazenda Publica* v. *Fricarnes SA* [1997] ECR I–4939.

[84] Case 77/76, *Fratelli Cuchi* v. *Avez* [1977] ECR 987; Case 94/74, *Industria Gomma Articoli Vari* v. *Ente Nazionale per la Cellulosa e per la Carta* [1975] ECR 699; Case 105/76, *Interzuccheri*, n. 68 above.

[85] N. 15 above, 430.

[86] Case C–72/92, *H. Scharbatke GmbH* v. *Federal Republic of Germany* [1993] ECR I–5509. See also Cases C–78–83/90, *Compagnie Commerciale*, n. 81 above.

contribution constituted a parafiscal charge.[87] Where the resulting revenue benefited solely national products, so that the advantages accruing *wholly* offset the charge imposed on the products, then the charge would be regarded as a CEE within Article 12 (now Article 25).[88] If the advantages which accrued only *partially* offset the charges imposed on national products, then the charge would constitute discriminatory internal taxation under Article 95 (now Article 90).[89]

7. CONCLUSION

i. There is little doubt that the ECJ's decisions in relation to duties and taxation have made a significant contribution to the realization of a single market. The Court's jurisprudence has consistently looked behind the form of a disputed measure to its substance, and the ECJ has interpreted the relevant Articles in the manner best designed to ensure that the Treaty objectives are achieved.

ii. In relation to the customs union, the main challenges in the years ahead are concerned with the need to forge an efficient and effective customs force from the fifteen Member State authorities so as to be able to fight fraud, the import of illegal goods, and the like.

iii. In relation to taxation, the issues are more complex. The original Rome Treaty left a considerable degree of autonomy to Member States in the fiscal field, albeit subject to the constraints imposed by Articles 23 to 25 and 90. Many of the problems concerning divergences between national taxation systems could only ever be fully resolved if legislative harmonization occurred. Taxation is however regarded as central to national sovereignty, and hence any extension of Community competence over tax is a hotly contested issue.

iv. It should, however, be noted that in this area, as in many others, there is often a link between judicial doctrine and legislative initiatives. The very fact that a challenged national tax policy will, according to the ECJ's decisions in *Chemial* and the *French Sweet Wines* case,[90] be upheld only if the Court deems it to be compatible with the Treaty can lead to paradoxical results. It has been noted[91] that the absence of harmonization has led to the ironical result that the Commission, abetted by the European Court, has managed to wield perhaps more influence over Member State tax policies, and thus their economic and social policies, than would be the case if the Council had agreed on a uniform tax regime.

---

[87] The ECJ held that the charge which was levied might also constitute State aid under Art. 87.

[88] It is not entirely clear whether *Scharbatke* is intended to modify earlier cases, which had held that in order for the charge to be regarded as a CEE within Art. 25 there must, *inter alia*, be a strict coincidence between the product which was being taxed and that which was receiving the benefit: Case 105/76, *Interzuccheri*, n. 68 above.

[89] See also Case 73/79, *Commission* v. *Italy* [1980] ECR 1533; Case C–347/95, *Fazenda Publica* v. *Uniao das Cooperativas Abastecedoras de Leite de Lisboa, URCL (UCAL)* [1997] ECR I–4911.

[90] See 596–8 above.

[91] J. Lonbay, 'A Review of Recent Tax Cases' (1989) 14 *ELRev*. 48, 50.

8. FURTHER READING

BARENTS, R., 'Charges of Equivalent Effect to Customs Duties' (1978) 15 *CMLRev.* 415

—— 'Recent Case Law on the Prohibition of Fiscal Discrimination Under Article 95' (1986) 23 *CMLRev.* 641

DANUSSO, M., and DENTON, R., 'Does the European Court of Justice Look for a Protectionist Motive Under Article 95?' (1990) 1 *LIEI* 67

EASSON, A., 'The Spirits, Wine and Beer Judgments: A Legal Mickey Finn?' (1980) 5 *ELRev.* 318

—— 'Fiscal Discrimination: New Perspectives on Article 95 of the EEC Treaty' (1981) 18 *CMLRev.* 521

GRABITZ, E., and ZACKER, C., 'Scope for Action by the EC Member States for the Improvement of Environmental Protection Under EEC Law: The Example of Environmental Taxes and Subsidies' (1989) 26 *CMLRev.* 423

LONBAY, J., 'A Review of Recent Tax Cases' (1989) 14 *ELRev.* 48

SCHWARZE, J., 'The Member States' Discretionary Powers under the Tax Provisions of the EEC Treaty', in J. Schwarze (ed.), *Discretionary Powers of the Member States in the Field of Economic Policies and their Limits under the EEC Treaty* (Nomos, 1988)

15

FREE MOVEMENT OF GOODS: QUANTITATIVE RESTRICTIONS

1. INTRODUCTION

The discussion in the previous chapter focused on the limits placed by Community law on duties, taxes, and the like. This is, however, only part of the overall Community strategy for an integrated Single Market. The free movement of goods is dealt with in Articles 28 to 31 (ex Articles 30 to 36). The renumbering of the Treaty provisions pursuant to the ToA has meant that the old Article 30 is now Article 28, and the old Article 36 is now Article 30. Particular care is therefore required when reading case law based on the old numbering.[1] Article 28 is the central provision within this Chapter of the Treaty. It states that:

Quantitative restrictions on imports and all measures having equivalent effect shall be prohibited between Member States.

Article 29 contains similar provisions relating to exports, while Article 30 (ex Article 36) provides an exception for certain cases in which a State is allowed to place restrictions on the movement of goods. Before examining the case law it may be helpful to understand the central issues which underlie this area.

2. CENTRAL ISSUES

i. It is necessary to understand the *way in which Articles 28–31 (ex Articles 30–36) fit into the more general strategy concerning the free movement of goods*. Articles 23–27 lay the foundations for a customs union by providing for the elimination of customs duties between Member States and by establishing a Common Customs Tariff. If matters rested there free movement would be only imperfectly attained. It would still be open to States to place quotas on the amount of goods that could be imported, and to restrict the flow of goods by measures which have an equivalent effect to quotas. The object of Articles 28–31 is to prevent Member States from engaging in these strategies.

ii. *The ECJ's interpretation of Articles 28 to 31 has been very important in achieving single-market integration.* The ECJ has given a broad interpretation to the phrase 'measures having equivalent effect' to a quantitative restriction (MEQR). It has also held that Article 30 (now Article 28) can apply even where there is no discrimination. The ECJ made it clear, in the famous *Cassis de Dijon*

---

[1] The old Arts. 31 to 33 which concerned transitional measures have been repealed by the ToA.

case,[2] that this Article can bite, subject to certain exceptions, when the same rule applies to both domestic goods and imports, where the relevant rule can inhibit the free flow of goods within the Community. Discrimination is therefore a sufficient, but not necessary, condition for the invocation of Article 28.

iii. *This topic exemplifies the interconnection between judicial and legislative initiatives for attaining the Community's objectives.* This is a theme stressed throughout this book. One way of dealing with trade rules that differ between Member States is through legislative harmonization. The process of such harmonization was, however, slow. The Commission had great difficulty in getting legislation through the Council from the mid-1960s until the early 1980s, a difficulty exacerbated by the requirement of unanimity in the Council.[3] The ECJ's jurisprudence constituted an alternative means for ensuring the free flow of goods even in the absence of legislation which harmonized the relevant rules. The message was clear: attainment of this central part of Community policy was not to be held up indefinitely by the absence of harmonization legislation. The Court's approach to Article 30 (now Article 28) was welcomed by the Commission. It led the Commission to the view that harmonization through legislation was less necessary than hitherto. The Commission made it clear that its own scarce resources should be best directed towards achieving harmonization in respect of those rules which were still lawful under the *Cassis de Dijon* formula, on the grounds that, for example, they were necessary to protect consumers or safeguard public health. The judicial approach, therefore, caused the Commission to reorient its own legislative programme.

iv. There are, however, three central problems to be aware of in this area. *The first is that the ECJ's jurisprudence has led to difficult issues about where this branch of EC law 'stops'.* The ECJ's decision that Article 30 (now Article 28) is applicable to trade rules even where they do not discriminate between goods on the basis of country of origin has led to difficulties about the outer boundaries of this area of Community law.

v. *The second problem is the relationship between negative and positive harmonization.* The ECJ's approach in *Cassis de Dijon* leads to 'negative harmonization': indistinctly applicable rules will be rendered unenforceable when they hinder cross-border trade unless they come within one of the exceptions. Harmonization is essentially negative and deregulatory, in the sense that the result is that national rules are held not to apply. This can be contrasted with 'positive harmonization', which results from Community legislative measures, stipulating which rules can apply across the Community as a whole. There are, as will be seen, important consequences that flow from developing Community policy by these differing strategies.

vi. *The third problem is the tension between Community integration and national regulatory autonomy.* The impact of Article 28 will often be to render national regulatory measures on a particular subject inapplicable. The relationship between the desire for integration, and the need for governmental regulation, is brought out well by Wils. It should be remembered that the author is referring to the old Article 30, now Article 28.

---

[2] Case 120/78, *Rewe-Zentrale AG* v. *Bundesmonopolverwaltung für Branntwein* [1979] ECR 649.
[3] See Ch. 4 above.

W.P.J. Wils, The Search for the Rule in Article 30 EEC: Much Ado About Nothing?[4]

Article 30 is one of the Treaty articles concerning *the integration of national markets for goods*. This same purpose is served by the whole of Part I, Title I of the Treaty, and also, in part by Articles 100 and 100A.

Integration can best be looked at from the negative side. The Community's efforts to integrate national markets are basically attempts to limit the influence of national governments on production and consumption activities throughout the Community. The desire to limit the influence of national governments stems from economic as well as political concerns. National measures restrict people in their economic activities throughout the Community, often at the expense of common welfare. As national governments regulate according to the desires of their constituencies alone, many national measures contain some protectionist bias. But even in the absence of this problem, the mere existence of a geographical patchwork of different regulations may impose a substantial economic burden. . . .

Although integration constitutes the specific concern of Article 30, it is only one among society's many objectives, with which it has to be reconciled. Given society's various objectives of efficiency and distributional justice, *a need for government regulation* is felt in many instances. This regulation will often have to be national regulation, either for practical reasons, Community regulation being unavailable, or for reasons of principle. Differences in societal preferences, or divergent natural or cultural characteristics may militate in favour of national regulation. . . .

Partial integration is the pragmatic solution reconciling the desire for integration with the desire for government intervention, translated—for the reasons just mentioned—into a desire for national regulation. In the Community's partially integrated market, national governments can influence people's activities, but only to some limited extent.

Partial integration is inherently unstable, however. Over time, opinions on the desirable scope of integration (and thus, conversely, on the scope of national government) will fluctuate. . . . National governments are allowed, and supposed, to influence people's activities, but only to a limited extent. There is thus a continuous need to identify and police the border between legitimate and illegitimate national regulation. Inevitably, some national government measures will overstep that boundary. . . . Article 30 is the tool for *policing the borderline between legitimate and illegitimate national regulation.*

3. DIRECTIVE 70/50 AND *DASSONVILLE*

Article 28 will catch quantitative restrictions and all measures which have an equivalent effect (MEQR). It can apply to Community measures,[5] as well as those adopted by Member States. The notion of a quantitative restriction was defined broadly in the *Geddo* case[6] to mean 'measures which amount to a total or partial restraint of, according to the circumstances, imports, exports or goods in transit'. MEQRs are more difficult to define, and will, by their very nature, be more varied. Both the Commission and the Court have taken a broad view of such measures.

[4] (1993) 18 *ELRev.* 475, 476–8. Italics in the original. See also M. Maduro, *We the Court, the European Court of Justice and the European Economic Constitution* (Hart, 1998), 54–8.
[5] Case C–114/96, *Criminal Proceedings against Kieffer and Thill* [1997] ECR I–3629.
[6] Case 2/73, *Geddo* v. *Ente Nazionale Risi* [1973] ECR 865, [1974] 1 CMLR 13.

Guidance on the Commission's view on this issue can be found in Directive 70/50. This Directive was only formally applicable during the Community's transitional period, but it continues to furnish some idea of the scope of MEQRs. The list of matters which can constitute an MEQR are specified in Article 2 and include:[7] minimum or maximum prices specified for imported products; less favourable prices for imported products; lowering the value of the imported product by reducing its intrinsic value or increasing its costs; payment conditions for imported products which differ from those for domestic products; conditions in respect of packaging, composition, identification, size, weight, etc., which apply only to imported goods or which are different and more difficult to satisfy than in the case of domestic goods; the giving of a preference to the purchase of domestic goods as opposed to imports, or otherwise hindering the purchase of imports; limiting publicity in respect of imported goods as compared with domestic products; prescribing stocking requirements which are different from and more difficult to satisfy than those which apply to domestic goods; and making it mandatory for importers of goods to have an agent in the territory of the importing State. Article 2, therefore, lists a number of ways in which the importing State can discriminate against goods coming from outside. It should be noted that, even as early as 1970, the Commission was thinking of the potential reach of Article 28 to indistinctly applicable rules, since Article 3 of the Directive, which will be considered below, regulates such rules to some degree.

The seminal judicial decision on the interpretation of MEQRs is to be found in *Dassonville*.

Case 8/74, Procureur du Roi v. Dassonville
[1974] ECR 837

[Note ToA renumbering: Art. 36 is now Art. 30]

Belgian law provided that goods bearing a designation of origin could only be imported if they were accompanied by a certificate from the government of the exporting country certifying their right to such a designation. Dassonville imported Scotch whisky into Belgium from France without being in possession of the requisite certificate from the British authorities. Such a certificate would have been very difficult to obtain in respect of goods which were already in free circulation in a third country, as in this case. Dassonville was prosecuted in Belgium and argued by way of defence that the Belgian rule constituted a MEQR.

THE ECJ

5. All trading rules enacted by Member States which are capable of hindering, directly or indirectly, actually or potentially, intra-Community trade are to be considered as measures having an effect equivalent to quantitative restrictions.

6. In the absence of a Community system guaranteeing for consumers the authenticity of a product's designation of origin, if a Member State takes measures to prevent unfair practices in

---

[7] Dir. 70/50, [1970] OJ L13/29, Art. 2(3).

this connection, it is however subject to the condition that these measures should be reasonable and that the means of proof required should not act as a hindrance to trade between Member States and should, in consequence, be accessible to all Community nationals.

7. Even without having to examine whether such measures are covered by Article 36, they must not, in any case, by virtue of the principle expressed in the second sentence of that Article, constitute a means of arbitrary discrimination or a disguised restriction on trade between Member States.

8. That may be the case with formalities, required by a Member State for the purpose of proving the origin of a product, which only direct importers are really in a position to satisfy without facing serious difficulties.

9. Consequently, the requirement by a Member State of a certificate of authenticity which is less easily obtainable by importers of an authentic product which has been put into free circulation in a regular manner in another Member State than by importers of the same product coming directly from the country of origin constitutes a measure equivalent to a quantitative restriction as prohibited by the Treaty.

Two aspects of the ECJ's reasoning should be noted. First, it is clear from paragraph 5 that the crucial element in proving a MEQR is its *effect*: a discriminatory intent is not required. The ECJ signals that it will take a very broad view of measures that hinder the free flow of goods within the Community. Indeed on its face this definition does not even require that the rules actually discriminate between domestic and imported goods. In this sense *Dassonville* sowed the seeds which bore fruit in the later *Cassis de Dijon* case, where the ECJ decided that Article 30 (now Article 28) could apply to rules which were not in themselves discriminatory. Secondly, the ECJ indicates, in paragraph 6, that reasonable restraints may not be caught by Article 30 (now Article 28). Herein lies the origin of what has become known as the 'rule of reason'. The precise meaning of this concept will be examined more fully below.

We shall begin this analysis by considering examples of the breadth of Article 28 in cases involving discrimination.

4. DISCRIMINATORY BARRIERS TO TRADE

There are numerous examples of cases where the Court has struck down national rules which directly or indirectly discriminate between domestic and imported goods. It should be made clear that Article 28 can bite if the national rule favours domestic goods over imports, and this is so even if the case, on its facts, is confined to products and parties from one Member State.[8] Article 28 can also apply to a national measure preventing import from one to another part of a particular Member State.[9]

[8] Cases C–321–4/94, *Criminal Proceedings against Pistre* [1997] ECR I–2343; Case C–448/98, *Criminal Proceedings against Guimont* [2000] ECR I–10663.

[9] Case C–67/97, *Criminal Proceedings against Bluhme* [1998] ECR I–8033.

(a) IMPORT AND EXPORT RESTRICTIONS

A common scenario is where a State applies discriminatory rules in the form of import or export restrictions. The ECJ has always been particularly harsh on such measures. Thus import or export licences are caught by Article 28.[10] So, too, are provisions which subject imported goods to requirements that are not imposed on domestic products. This is exemplified by *Commission* v. *Italy*,[11] in which the ECJ held that procedures and data requirements for the registration of imported cars, making their registration longer, more complicated, and more costly than that of domestic vehicles, were prohibited by Article 30 (now Article 28). While in *Rewe*[12] phytosanitary inspections on imports of plants were caught by this Article where no similar examination was made of domestic products. The same approach is apparent with respect to discriminatory export rules. Thus in *Bouhelier*[13] a French rule which imposed quality checks on watches for export, but not on those intended for the domestic market, was in breach of Article 34 (now Article 29).

(b) PROMOTION OR FAVOURING OF DOMESTIC PRODUCTS

Article 28 prohibits action by a State that promotes or favours domestic products to the detriment of competing imports. This can occur in a number of different ways.

The most obvious is where a *State engages in a campaign to promote the purchase of domestic as opposed to imported goods.*

Case 249/81, Commission v. Ireland
[1982] ECR 4005

[Note ToA renumbering: Arts. 30, 92, 93, and 169 are now
Arts. 28, 87, 88, and 226 respectively]

The Irish government sought to promote sales of Irish goods, the object being to achieve a switch of 3 per cent in consumer spending from imports to domestic products. It adopted a number of measures including: an information service indicating to consumers which products were made in Ireland and where they could be obtained (the Shoplink Service); exhibition facilities for Irish goods; the encouragement of the use of the 'Buy Irish' symbol for goods made in Ireland; and the organization of a publicity campaign by the Irish Goods Council in favour of Irish products, designed to encourage consumers to buy Irish products. The first two of these activities were subsequently abandoned by the Irish Government, but the latter two strategies continued to be employed. The Commission brought Article 169 proceedings, alleging that the campaign was an MEQR. Ireland argued that it had never adopted 'measures' for the purpose of Article 30, and that any financial aid given to the Irish Goods Council should be judged in the light of Articles 92

---

[10] Cases 51–54/71, *International Fruit Company* v. *Produktschap voor Groenten en Fruit (No 2)* [1971] ECR 1107; Case 68/76, *Commission* v. *French Republic* [1977] ECR 515.
[11] Case 154/85, [1987] ECR 2717.
[12] Case 4/75, *Rewe-Zentralfinanz* v. *Landwirtschaftskammer* [1975] ECR 843.
[13] Case 53/76, *Procureur de la République Besançon* v. *Bouhelier* [1977] ECR 197.

to 93, and not Article 30. The members of the Irish Goods Council were appointed by an Irish Government minister and its activities were funded in proportions of about six to one by the Irish Government and private industry respectively.

THE ECJ

15. It is thus apparent that the Irish government appoints the members of the Management Committee of the Irish Goods Council, grants it public subsidies which cover the greater part of its expenses and, finally, defines the aims and the broad outline of the campaign conducted by that institution to promote the sale and purchase of Irish products. In the circumstances the Irish government cannot rely on the fact that the campaign was conducted by a private company in order to escape any liability it may have under the provisions of the Treaty.

. . .

21. The Irish government maintains that the prohibition against measures having an effect equivalent to quantitative restrictions in Article 30 is concerned only with 'measures', that is to say, binding provisions emanating from a public authority. However, no such provision has been adopted by the Irish government, which has confined itself to giving moral support and financial aid to the activities pursued by the Irish industries.

22. The Irish government goes on to emphasise that the campaign has had no restrictive effect on imports since the proportion of Irish goods to all goods sold on the Irish market fell from 49.2% in 1977 to 43.4% in 1980.

23. The first observation to be made is that the campaign cannot be likened to advertising by private or public undertakings . . . to encourage people to buy goods produced by those undertakings. Regardless of the means used to implement it, the campaign is a reflection of the Irish government's considered intention to substitute domestic products for imported products on the Irish market and thereby to check the flow of imports from other Member States.

24. It must be remembered here that a representative of the Irish government stated when the campaign was launched that it was a carefully thought-out set of initiatives constituting an integrated programme for promoting domestic products; that the Irish Goods Council was set up at the initiative of the Irish government a few months later; and that the task of implementing the integrated programme as it was envisaged by the government was entrusted, or left, to that Council.

25. Whilst it may be true that the two elements of the programme which have continued in effect, namely the advertising campaign and the use of the 'Guaranteed Irish' symbol, have not had any significant success in winning over the Irish market to domestic products, it is not possible to overlook the fact that, regardless of their efficacy, those two activities form part of a government programme which is designed to achieve the substitution of domestic products for imported products and is liable to affect the volume of trade between Member States.

. . .

27. In the circumstances the two activities in question amount to the establishment of a national practice, introduced by the Irish government and prosecuted with its assistance, the potential effect of which on imports from other Member States is comparable to that resulting from government measures of a binding nature.

28. Such a practice cannot escape the prohibition laid down by Article 30 of the Treaty solely because it is not based on decisions which are binding upon undertakings. Even measures adopted by the government of a Member State which do not have binding effect may be capable of influencing the conduct of traders and consumers in that State and thus of frustrating the aims of the Community as set out in Article 2 and enlarged upon in Article 3 of the Treaty.

29. That is the case where, as in this instance, such a restrictive practice represents the implementation of a programme defined by the government which affects the national economy as a whole and which is intended to check the flow of trade between Member States by encouraging the purchase of domestic products, by means of an advertising campaign on a national scale and the organization of special procedures applicable solely to domestic products, and where those activities are attributable as a whole to the government and are pursued in an organized fashion throughout the national territory.

30. Ireland has therefore failed to fulfil its obligations under the Treaty by organizing a campaign to promote the sale and purchase of Irish goods within its territory.

The ECJ's reasoning provides an excellent example of its more general strategy under Article 30 (now Article 28). It looks to substance, not form. This is manifested in the way in which it treats the involvement of the Irish government with the Irish Goods Council (paragraph 15); with the way in which it rebuts the Irish argument that only formally binding measures are caught by Article 30 (paragraphs 21 and 28); and in its rejection of the argument that, as the campaign appeared to have failed, therefore EC law should be unconcerned with it (paragraph 25).[14]

A second type of case caught by Article 28 is where *a State has rules on the origin-marking of certain goods.*

Case 207/83, Commission v. United Kingdom
[1985] ECR 1201

[Note ToA renumbering: Arts. 30 and 169 are now Arts. 28 and 226]

The Commission brought an Article 169 action, arguing that United Kingdom legislation which required that certain goods should not be sold in retail markets unless they were marked with their country of origin was in breach of Article 30, as an MEQR. The United Kingdom argued that the legislation applied equally to imported and national products, and that this information was of importance to consumers since they regarded origin as an indication of the quality of the goods. The following extract relates to the first of these arguments.

THE ECJ

17. . . . it has to be recognized that the purpose of indications of origin or origin-marking is to enable consumers to distinguish between domestic and imported products and that this enables them to assert any prejudices which they may have against foreign products. As the Court has had occasion to emphasise in various contexts, the Treaty, by establishing a common market . . . seeks to unite national markets in a single market having the characteristics of a domestic market. Within such a market, the origin-marking requirement not only makes the marketing in a Member

---

[14] The campaign may have had some impact, since the diminution in sales of Irish goods might have been even greater had the campaign not been mounted. Not all measures which promote domestic goods will, however, be caught by the Treaty: Case 222/82, *Apple and Pear Development Council* v. *K.J. Lewis Ltd.* [1983] ECR 4083.

State of goods produced in other Member States in the sectors in question more difficult; it also has the effect of slowing down economic interpenetration in the Community by handicapping the sale of goods produced as the result of a division of labour between Member States.

18. It follows from those considerations that the United Kingdom provisions in question are liable to have the effect of increasing the production costs of imported goods and making it more difficult to sell them on the United Kingdom market.[15]

Member State legislation which contains rules on origin-marking will normally be acceptable only on the following conditions. These are if the origin implies a certain quality in the goods, that they were made from certain materials or by a particular form of manufacturing, or where the origin is indicative of a special place in the folklore or tradition of the region in question.[16] Thus in the 'Irish Souvenirs' case[17] the Court held that Irish legislation which prohibited the importation of certain souvenirs such as shamrocks, wolfhounds, etc., unless they had an indication of the country of origin, or the word 'foreign' attached to them, was an MEQR within Article 30 (now Article 28). The origin-marking did not come within the acceptable criteria mentioned above, because the essential characteristic of the souvenirs was that they constituted a pictorial reminder of the place which had been visited. This did not mean that the souvenirs had to have been manufactured in the country of origin.

The Court's clear intent to stamp firmly on national measures which favour domestic over imported products is equally apparent in a third type of case: *public procurement* cannot be structured so as to favour domestic producers. In *Du Pont*[18] the ECJ held that the reservation by a Member State of a proportion of its public supplies to products which were processed in a particular depressed region of the country impeded imports contrary to Article 30 (now Article 28). In *Campus Oil*[19] an obligation on importers into Ireland to buy a certain proportion of their supplies of oil from a national supplier was held to fall within Article 30 (now Article 28). The insistence that public procurement should be decided without preference for domestic tenderers is clearly evident in the *Dundalk Water Supply* case.

---

[15] The ECJ also rejected the UK's argument that origin-marking was related to consumer protection. The Court held that the origin-marking rules were only equally applicable to domestic and imported products as a matter of form: in reality they were intended to enable consumers to give preference to national goods: *ibid.*, para. 20.

[16] Case 12/74, *Commission* v. *Germany* [1975] ECR 181; Case 113/80, *Commission* v. *Ireland* [1981] ECR 1625.

[17] *Ibid.*, para. 15.

[18] Case C–21/88, *Du Pont de Nemours Italiana SpA* v. *Unita Sanitaria Locale No. 2 Di Carrara* [1990] ECR I–889.

[19] Case 72/83, *Campus Oil Ltd.* v. *Minister for Industry and Energy* [1984] ECR 2727.

Case 45/87, Commission v. Ireland
[1988] ECR 4929

[Note ToA renumbering: Arts. 30 and 169 are now Arts. 28 and 226]

Dundalk Council put out to tender a contract for water supply. One of the contract clauses (4.29) was that tenderers had to submit bids based on the use of certain pipes which complied with a particular Irish standard (IS 188: 1975). One of the bids was based on the use of a piping which had not been certified by the Irish authorities, but which did comply with international standards. The Council refused to consider it for this reason. The Commission brought an Article 169 action claiming a breach of Article 30.

THE ECJ

19. . . . it must first be pointed out that the inclusion of such a clause (as 4.29) in an invitation to tender may cause economic operators who produce or utilize pipes equivalent to pipes certified with Irish standards to refrain from tendering.

20. It further appears . . . that only one undertaking has been certified by the IIRS[20] to IS 188: 1975 to apply the Irish Standard Mark to pipes of the type required for the purposes of the public works contract at issue. That undertaking is located in Ireland. Consequently, the inclusion of Clause 4.29 had the effect of restricting the supply of the pipes needed for the Dundalk scheme to Irish manufacturers alone.

21. The Irish government maintains that it is necessary to specify the standards to which materials must be manufactured, particularly in a case such as this where the pipes utilized must suit the existing network. Compliance with another standard, even an international standard such as ISO 160: 1980, would not suffice to eliminate technical difficulties.

22. That technical argument cannot be accepted. The Commission's complaint does not relate to compliance with technical requirements but to the refusal of the Irish authorities to verify whether those requirements are satisfied where the manufacturer of the materials has not been certified by the IIRS to IS 188. By incorporating in the notice in question the words 'or equivalent' after the reference to the Irish standard, as provided for by Directive 71/305 where it is applicable, the Irish authorities could have verified compliance with the technical conditions without from the outset restricting the contract to tenderers proposing to utilize Irish materials.

A fourth type of case is where *the discrimination in favour of domestic goods is evident in administrative practice*, as exemplified by *Commission* v. *France*.[21] French law had discriminated against imported postal franking machines. The law had been changed, but a British company claimed that, notwithstanding this formal change in the law, the French authorities had repeatedly refused to approve its machines. The ECJ held that consistent and general administrative discrimination against imports could be caught by Article 30 (now Article 28). The discrimination could, for example, take the form of delay in replying to applications for approval, or by refusing approval on the grounds of various alleged technical faults which prove to be inaccurate.

---

[20] Institute for Industrial Research and Standards.
[21] Case 21/84, *Commission* v. *France* [1985] ECR 1356.

(c) PRICE-FIXING

There are diverse ways in which a State can treat imported goods less favourably than domestic products. Price-fixing regulations may have this effect by rendering it more difficult for importers to market their goods within the territory of the State imposing the restrictions.

If the price fixing is discriminatory it is clearly caught by Article 28. Thus in the *Roussel* case[22] the ECJ held that maximum selling prices for certain drugs which were fixed according to different criteria for domestic and imported goods were discriminatory and infringed this Article.[23] However, Article 28 can catch pricing rules even where they are not, on their face, discriminatory.

Case 82/77, Openbaar Ministerie v. Van Tiggele
[1978] ECR 25[24]

Dutch legislation laid down minimum selling prices for certain spirits. A seller was accused in criminal proceedings of selling them below the stipulated price. The question before the ECJ was whether the minimum selling prices were a MEQR within Article 30 (28).

THE ECJ

12. For the purposes of this prohibition it is sufficient that the measures in question are likely to hinder, directly or indirectly, actually or potentially, imports between Member States.

13. Whilst national price-control rules applicable without distinction to domestic products and imported products cannot in general produce such an effect they may do so in certain specific cases.

14. Thus imports may be impeded in particular when a national authority fixes prices or profit margins at such a level that imported products are placed at a disadvantage in relation to identical domestic products either because they cannot profitably be marketed in the conditions laid down or because the competitive advantage conferred by lower cost prices is cancelled out.

The ECJ found that the Dutch rule did contravene Article 30 (now Article 28). It seems that rules that fix prices by reference to a maximum percentage profit will, by way of contrast, be found to be more readily compatible with this Article. Such rules may take account of differences in production cost between domestic goods and imports.[25]

---

22 Case 181/82, *Roussel Labaratoria BV* v. *The State of The Netherlands* [1983] ECR 3849.
23 See also Case 56/87, *Commission* v. *Italy* [1988] ECR 2919.
24 See also Case 65/75, *Riccardo Tasca* [1976] ECR 291.
25 Case 78/82, *Commission* v. *Italy* [1983] ECR 1955.

(d) MEASURES WHICH MAKE IMPORTS MORE DIFFICULT OR COSTLY

There are numerous ways in which a Member State can render it more difficult for importers to break into that market. We have touched upon this idea already in the preceding analysis. The ECJ has used Article 28 to prohibit such action. The *Schloh* case provides a good example of this.

Case 50/85, Schloh v. Auto Contrôle Technique
[1986] ECR 1855

[Note ToA renumbering: Arts. 30 and 36 are now Arts. 28 and 30]

Schloh bought a car in Germany and obtained from a Ford dealer in Belgium a certificate of conformity with vehicle types in Belgium. Under Belgian law he was required to submit his car to two roadworthiness tests; fees were charged for these tests. He challenged the tests, arguing that they were an MEQR. The extract concerns the first roadworthiness test.

THE ECJ

12. ... Roadworthiness testing is a formality which makes the registration of imported vehicles more difficult and more onerous and consequently is in the nature of a measure having an effect equivalent to a quantitative restriction.

13. Nevertheless, Article 36 may justify such a formality on grounds of the protection of human life and health, provided that it is established, first, that the test at issue is necessary for the attainment of that objective and, secondly, that it does not constitute a means of arbitrary discrimination or a disguised restriction on trade between Member States.

14. As far as the first condition is concerned, it must be acknowledged that roadworthiness testing required prior to the registration of an imported vehicle may ... be regarded as necessary for the protection of human health and life where the vehicle in question has already been put on the road. In such cases roadworthiness testing performs a useful function inasmuch as it makes it possible to check that the vehicle has not been damaged and is in a good state of repair. However such testing cannot be justified on those grounds where it relates to an imported vehicle carrying a certificate of conformity which has not been placed on the road before being registered in the importing Member State.

15. As far as the second condition is concerned, it must be stated that the roadworthiness testing of imported vehicles cannot, however, be justified under the second sentence of Article 36 of the Treaty if it is established that such testing is not required in the case of vehicles of national origin presented for registration in the same circumstances. If that were the case it would become apparent that the measure in question was not in fact inspired by a concern for the protection of human health and life but in reality constituted a means of arbitrary discrimination in trade between Member States. It is for the national court to verify that such non-discriminatory treatment is in fact ensured.

The ECJ held that the Belgian rule was contrary to Article 30 (now Article 28), save in relation to cars which were already on the road, provided that in this type of case the rules were applied in a non-discriminatory fashion.

(e) NATIONAL MEASURES VERSUS PRIVATE ACTION

It seems clear that Article 28 applies to measures taken by the State, as opposed to those taken by private parties. Other Treaty provisions, notably Articles 81 and 82 (ex Articles 85 and 86), will apply to actions by private parties which restrict competition and have an impact on inter-state trade.[26]

This means that the issue of what is a state entity will have to be addressed, and the ECJ has done so on a number of occasions. Thus in the *'Buy Irish'* case[27] we have already seen that the ECJ rejected the argument that the Irish Goods Council was a private body and therefore immune from the application of Article 30 (now Article 28). The Irish Government's involvement with the funding of the organization and the appointment of its members was sufficient to render it public for these purposes. While in the *Apple and Pear Development Council* case[28] the existence of a statutory obligation on fruit growers to pay certain levies to the Council sufficed to render the body public for these purposes.

It is clear that institutions such as those concerned with trade regulation may come within the definition of the State for these purposes, even if they are nominally private, provided that they receive a measure of state support or 'underpinning'. Thus in *R. v. The Pharmaceutical Society, ex parte API*[29] the Society was an independent body responsible for the regulation of standards among United Kingdom pharmacists. A pharmacist had to appear on its register in order to be able to practise. Certain functions were, however, conferred on the Society by statute; its disciplinary functions had a statutory basis in the Pharmacy Act 1954; and removal from its register would effectively prevent a pharmacist from continuing to practise. The Court held that the Society was bound by Article 30 (now Article 28) of the Treaty.

Article 30 (now Article 28) can also apply against the State even though private parties have taken the main role in restricting the free movement of goods, as exemplified by *Commission v. France*.[30] The Commission brought an Article 169 (now Article 226) action against the French government for breach of Article 30 combined with Article 5 (now Article 10), on the ground that the government had taken insufficient measures to prevent French farmers from disrupting imports of agricultural produce from other EC countries. The ECJ held that it was incumbent on a government to take all necessary and appropriate measures to ensure that free movement was respected in its territory, even where the obstacles were created by private parties.

(f) SUMMARY

i. If a polity decides to embrace a single-market, then discriminatory or protectionist measures will be at the top of the list of those to be caught, since they are directly opposed to the single market ideal.

---

26 See Chs. 21–22 below.
27 Case 249/81, *Commission v. Ireland* [1982] ECR 4005.
28 Case 222/82, n. 14 above.
29 Case 266/87, [1989] ECR 1295.
30 Case C–265/95, [1997] ECR I–6959.

ii. The court entrusted with policing such a regime must be mindful of the many different ways in which a State can seek to discriminate against imported goods.

iii. The ECJ has been aware of this, and has made sure that indirect as well as direct discrimination is caught by Article 28.

5. JUSTIFYING DISCRIMINATORY BARRIERS TO TRADE: ARTICLE 30

If trade rules are found to be discriminatory[31] they can be saved through Article 30 (ex Article 36):

The provisions of Articles 28 and 29 shall not preclude prohibitions or restrictions on imports, exports or goods in transit justified on grounds of public morality, public policy or public security; the protection of health and life of humans, animals or plants; the protection of national treasures possessing artistic, historic or archaeological value; or the protection of industrial and commercial property. Such prohibitions or restrictions shall not, however, constitute a means of arbitrary discrimination or a disguised restriction on trade between Member States.

It will come as no surprise to learn that the Court has construed Article 30 (ex Article 36) strictly. National rules that discriminate against imports will be closely scrutinized before the Court accepts that they can be saved by Article 30. The challenged rule will have to come within one of the listed categories. It must also pass a test of proportionality: the Court demands that the discriminatory measure must be the least restrictive possible to attain the end in view. The burden of proof under Article 30 rests with the Member State seeking to rely on it.[32]

(a) PUBLIC MORALITY

Two of the main precedents have emerged from the United Kingdom, and concern challenges to laws dealing with pornography.

In *Henn and Darby*[33] the defendants were convicted of fraudulently importing indecent and obscene articles, contrary to UK law.[34] They had imported pornography into England from Rotterdam, but argued that UK law was contrary to Article 30 (now Article 28). The United Kingdom Government relied on Article 36 (now Article 30). The ECJ found that the import ban was within Article 30, and then considered whether it could be saved by the public morality exception found in Article 36. It was, said the Court, for each Member State to determine the standards of public morality which prevailed in its territory. The ECJ then proceeded to consider whether such national laws could constitute a disguised restriction on trade within the terms of

---

[31] It may of course be debatable whether a rule really is discriminatory, and therefore whether it is caught by Art. 30 (now Art. 28), and requires justification under Art. 36 (now Art. 30). A good example is Case C–2/90, *Commission* v. *Belgium* [1992] ECR I–4431, noted by L. Hancher and H. Sevenster, (1993) 30 *CMLRev.* 351, and D. Geradin, (1993) 18 *ELRev.* 144.

[32] Case C–17/93, *Openbaar Ministerie* v. *Van der Veldt* [1994] ECR I–3537.

[33] Case 34/79, *R.* v. *Henn and Darby* [1979] ECR 3795.

[34] As contained in the Customs Consolidation Act 1876, s. 42 and the Customs and Excise Act 1952, s. 304.

Article 36 (now Article 30). This was because UK law imposed an absolute ban on the import of pornography, even though domestic law did not ban absolutely the possession of such material. The ECJ none the less found that the import ban was not a disguised restriction on trade or a means of arbitrary discrimination. It held that while domestic UK law was not absolute in this respect, its purpose, taken as a whole, was to restrain the manufacture and marketing of pornography. The ECJ concluded that there was, therefore, no lawful trade in such goods within the United Kingdom. The United Kingdom could rely on Article 36 with the consequence that the criminal convictions were upheld. However, a different result was reached in the *Conegate* case.

Case 121/85, Conegate Ltd. v. Commissioners of Customs and Excise
[1986] ECR 1007

[Note ToA renumbering: Arts. 30, 36, and 177 are now Arts. 28, 30, and 234]

Conegate imported life-size inflatable dolls from Germany into the United Kingdom. The invoice for the dolls claimed that they were for window displays, but the Customs officials were unconvinced, particularly when they found items described as 'love love dolls'. They seized the goods, and magistrates ordered them to be forfeit. Conegate argued that the seizure and forfeiture were in breach of Article 30. The national court asked whether a prohibition on imports could be justified even though the State did not ban the manufacture or marketing of the same goods within the national territory. The ECJ repeated its reasoning from *Henn and Darby* that it was for each Member State to decide upon the nature of public morality for its own territory. It continued as follows.

THE ECJ

15. However, although Community law leaves the Member States free to make their own assessments of the indecent or obscene character of certain articles, it must be pointed out that the fact that goods cause offence cannot be regarded as sufficiently serious to justify restrictions on the free movement of goods where the Member State concerned does not adopt, with respect to the same goods manufactured or marketed within its territory, penal measures or other serious and effective measures intended to prevent the distribution of such goods in its territory.

16. It follows that a Member State may not rely on grounds of public morality to prohibit the importation of goods from other Member States when its legislation contains no prohibition on the manufacture or marketing of the same goods on its territory.

17. It is not for the Court, within the framework of the powers conferred on it by Article 177 . . . to consider whether, and to what extent, the United Kingdom legislation contains such a prohibition. However, the question whether or not such a prohibition exists in a State comprised of different constituent parts which have their own internal legislation can be resolved only by taking into consideration all the relevant legislation. Although it is not necessary, for the purposes of the application of the above-mentioned rule, that the manufacture and marketing of the products whose importation has been prohibited should be prohibited in the territory of all the constituent parts, it must at least be possible to conclude from the applicable rules, taken as a whole, that their purpose is, in substance, to prohibit the manufacture and marketing of those products.

18. In this instance . . . the High Court took care to define the substance of the national legislation the compatibility of which with Community law is a question which it proposes to determine. Thus it refers to rules in the importing Member State under which the goods in question may be manufactured freely and marketed subject only to certain restrictions . . . namely an absolute prohibition on the transmission of such goods by post, a restriction on their public display and, in certain areas of the Member States concerned, a system of licensing of premises for the sale of those goods to customers aged 18 years and over. Such restrictions cannot however be regarded as equivalent in substance to a prohibition on manufacture and marketing.

The United Kingdom defence based on Article 36 (now Article 30) failed, and Conegate recovered its goods. It is interesting to reflect on the difference between *Conegate* and *Henn and Darby*. It is clear that the crucial distinction lies in the ECJ's evaluation of whether imported goods subject to an absolute ban were being treated more harshly than similar domestic goods in the United Kingdom. In *Henn and Darby* the ECJ was willing to find that UK law did restrain the manufacture and marketing of pornography sufficiently to enable it to conclude that there was no lawful trade in such goods within the United Kingdom. In *Conegate*, by way of contrast, the ECJ examined the relevant national rules more closely, and reached the opposite conclusion: the restrictions could not be said to amount to a prohibition on domestic manufacture or marketing.

It is clear, then, that while Member States are free to determine the sense of public morality which should pertain within their own territory, they cannot place markedly stricter burdens on goods coming from outside than those which are applied to equivalent domestic goods. This is in line with the ECJ's jurisprudence in other areas, such as free movement of workers. Claims that workers should be excluded on grounds of public policy have generally failed where there was no proscription on domestic workers undertaking the same job.[35]

(b) PUBLIC POLICY

Public policy constitutes a separate head of justification within Article 30 (ex Article 36). The phrase is potentially broad, but the ECJ has resisted attempts to interpret it too broadly. The Court has, for example, rejected arguments that the term 'public policy' can embrace consumer protection. The ECJ has reasoned that since Article 30 derogates from a fundamental rule of the Treaty enshrined in Article 28, it must be interpreted strictly, and cannot be extended to objectives not expressly mentioned therein.[36]

A public policy justification must, therefore, be made in its own terms, and cannot be used as a vehicle through which to advance what amounts to a separate ground for

---

[35] See Ch. 19 below.
[36] Case 113/80, *Commission* v. *Ireland* [1981] ECR 1625; Case 177/83, *Kohl* v. *Ringelhan* [1984] ECR 3651; Case 229/83, *Leclerc* v. *Au Blé Vert* [1985] ECR 1.

defence. It is for this reason that relatively few cases contain any detailed examination of the public policy argument. The issue is considered in *Centre Leclerc*:

Case 231/83, Cullet v. Centre Leclerc
[1985] ECR 305

[Note ToA renumbering: Arts. 30 and 36 are now Arts. 28 and 30]

French legislation imposed minimum retail prices for fuel fixed primarily on the basis of French refinery prices and costs. The Court found that this constituted an MEQR within Article 30, since imports could not benefit fully from lower cost prices in the country of origin. The French Government sought to justify its action on the basis, *inter alia*, of public policy within Article 36. It argued that, in the absence of the pricing rules, there would be civil disturbances, blockades, and violence. Both the Advocate General and the ECJ rejected this argument, but the reason for doing so differed.

ADVOCATE GENERAL VERLOREN VAN THEMAAT[37]

However, I would add that the acceptance of civil disturbances as justification for encroachments upon the free movement of goods would, as is apparent from experiences of last year (and before, during the Franco–Italian 'wine war') have unacceptably drastic consequences. If roadblocks and other effective weapons of interest groups which feel threatened by the importation and sale at competitive prices of certain cheap products or services, or by immigrant workers or foreign businesses, were accepted as justification, the existence of the four fundamental freedoms of the Treaty could no longer be relied upon. Private interest groups would then, in the place of the Treaty and Community (and, within the limits laid down by the Treaty, national) institutions, determine the scope of those freedoms. In such cases, the concept of public policy requires, rather, effective action on the part of the authorities to deal with such disturbances.

THE ECJ

32. For the purpose of applying Article 36, the French Government has invoked the disturbances to law and order (*ordre public*) and public security caused by violent reactions which should be expected from retailers affected by unrestricted competition.

33. On this point it is sufficient to observe that the French Government has not shown that an amendment of the regulations in question in conformity with the principles set out above would have consequences for law and order (*ordre public*) and public security which the French Government would be unable to meet with the resources available to it.

Thus, while the Advocate General rejected the French argument on principle, the ECJ appeared to accept that it could be pleaded under Article 36 (now Article 30), while rejecting it on the facts. The ECJ's approach might well have been simply a more

---

[37] [1985] 2 CMLR 524, 534.

diplomatic way of disposing of the point, but the analysis of the Advocate General is more convincing as a matter of principle. If interest-group pressure leading to potential violence could provide the grounds for justification under Article 36 then fundamental Community freedoms would be placed in jeopardy.[38] This is more particularly so given that certain issues, such as workers from Member States taking jobs within another country, can generate real tensions, especially during periods of recession and unemployment.

(c) PUBLIC SECURITY

The leading authority is the *Campus Oil* case.

Case 72/83, Campus Oil Ltd. v. Minister for Industry and Energy
[1984] ECR 2727

[Note ToA renumbering: Arts. 30 and 36 are now Arts. 28 and 30]

Irish law required importers of petrol into Ireland to buy 35 per cent of their requirements from a state-owned oil refinery at prices fixed by the Irish government. This rule was held to constitute a MEQR within Article 30. In defence Ireland relied on public policy and security within Article 36. It argued that it was vital for Ireland to be able to maintain its own oil refining capacity. The challenged rule was the means of ensuring that its refinery products could be marketed.[39] The ECJ held that recourse to Article 36 would not be possible if there were Community rules providing the necessary protection for oil supplies. Certain Community measures did exist, but they were not comprehensive. The Court continued as follows.

THE ECJ

31. Consequently, the existing Community rules give a Member State whose supplies of petroleum products depend totally or almost totally on deliveries from other countries certain guarantees that deliveries from other Member States will be maintained in the event of a serious shortfall in proportions which match those of supplies to the market of the supplying State. However, this does not mean that the Member State concerned has an unconditional assurance that supplies will in any event be maintained at least at a level sufficient to meet its minimum needs. In those circumstances, the possibility for a Member State to rely on Article 36 to justify appropriate complementary measures at national level cannot be excluded, even where there exist Community rules on the matter.

[*The Court then considered whether the term 'public security' could cover this situation.*]

---

[38] In Case C–265/95, *Commission* v. *France* [1997] ECR I–6959, the ECJ accepted that serious disruption to public order could justify non-intervention by the police in relation to a specific incident, but that it could not justify any general policy of this nature. See also *R.* v. *Chief Constable of Sussex, ex p. International Traders' Ferry Ltd.* [1997] 2 CMLR 164.

[39] The applicants who challenged the Irish system argued that the real issue was not whether Ireland should maintain an independent refining capacity, but whether such a refinery should operate at a profit or loss. They claimed that this was an economic issue which could not come within public policy or security.

34. It should be stated in this connection that petroleum products, because of their exceptional importance as an energy source in the modern economy, are of fundamental importance for a country's existence since not only its economy but above all its institutions, its essential public services and even the survival of the inhabitants depend upon them. An interruption of supplies of petroleum products, with the resultant dangers for the country's existence, could therefore seriously affect the public security that Article 36 allows States to protect.

35. It is true that, as the Court has held on a number of occasions, most recently in . . . (Case 95/81, *Commission* v. *Italy*), Article 36 refers to matters of a non-economic nature. A Member State cannot be allowed to avoid the effects of measures provided for in the Treaty by pleading the economic difficulties caused by elimination of barriers to intra-Community trade. However, in the light of the seriousness of the consequences that an interruption in supplies of petroleum products may have for a country's existence, the aim of ensuring a minimum supply of petroleum products at all times is to be regarded as transcending purely economic considerations and thus as capable of constituting an objective covered by the concept of public security.

36. It should be added that to come within the ambit of Article 36 the rules in question must be justified by objective circumstances corresponding to the needs of public security. . . .

37. As the Court has previously stated . . . Article 36, as an exception to a fundamental principle of the Treaty, must be interpreted in such a way that its scope is not extended any further than is necessary for the protection of the interests which it is intended to secure and the measures taken pursuant to that Article must not create obstacles to imports which are disproportionate to those objectives. Measures adopted on the basis of Article 36 can therefore be justified only if they are such as to serve the interest which that Article protects and if they do not restrict intra-Community trade more than is absolutely necessary.

While the ECJ, therefore, accepted the public-security argument in *Campus Oil*, the circumstances to which it will be applicable are likely to be factually limited.[40] There is little enthusiasm for extending the reasoning, and in *Centre Leclerc* Advocate General VerLoren van Themaat devoted time in his opinion to distinguishing *Campus Oil* from the situation in *Centre Leclerc*.[41]

It should not, however, be forgotten in this respect that Member States can take certain measures relating to national security pursuant to what are now Articles 296 to 298.

(d) PROTECTION OF HEALTH AND LIFE OF HUMANS, ANIMALS, OR PLANTS

There have been numerous cases in which States have attempted to defend measures on this ground. The ECJ will closely scrutinize such claims.

First, *the Court will determine whether the protection of public health is the real purpose behind the Member States' action, or whether it was designed to protect domestic producers.* This is exemplified by *Commission* v. *United Kingdom*.[42] The United Kingdom in effect banned poultrymeat imports from most other Member States, justifying

---

[40] See also Case C–367/89, *Richardt* [1991] ECR I–4621.
[41] [1985] 2 CMLR 524, 535–6.
[42] Case 40/82, [1982] ECR 2793.

this on the ground that it was necessary to protect public health, by preventing the spread of Newcastle disease that affected poultry. The ECJ rejected the argument. It found that imports of poultry into the United Kingdom from other States had increased markedly, and that this had resulted in pressure from domestic producers to protect their interests, especially in the run-up to Christmas. Moreover, the French authorities had imposed controls to prevent Newcastle disease. The Court concluded that the import ban was motivated more by commercial reasons, to block French poultry, than by considerations of public health.[43] The ECJ will also closely examine the cogency of arguments concerning public health to determine whether they make sense on the facts.[44]

Secondly, the *ECJ may have to decide whether a public-health claim is sustainable where there is no perfect consensus on the scientific or medical impact of particular substances.* The ECJ's approach is exemplified by the *Sandoz* decision.

Case 174/82, Officier van Justitie v. Sandoz BV
[1983] ECR 2445

Authorities in Holland refused to allow the sale of muesli bars that contained added vitamins, on the ground that the vitamins were dangerous to public health. The muesli bars were readily available in Germany and Belgium. It was accepted that vitamins could be beneficial to health, but it was also acknowledged that excessive consumption could be harmful to health. Scientific evidence was not, however, certain as regards the point at which consumption of vitamins became excessive, particularly because vitamins consumed in one source of food might be added to those eaten from a different food source. There had been some Community legislation which touched on the general issue of food additives.

THE ECJ

15. The above mentioned Community measures clearly show that the Community legislature accepts the principle that it is necessary to restrict the use of food additives to the substances specified, whilst leaving the Member States a certain discretion to adopt stricter rules. . . .

16. As the Court found in its judgment . . . in Case 272/80 (*Frans-Nederlandse Maatschappij voor Biologische Producten* [1981] ECR 3277), in so far as there are uncertainties at the present state of scientific research it is for the Member States, in the absence of harmonization, to decide what degree of protection of the health and life of humans they intend to assure, having regard however for the requirements of the free movement of goods within the Community.

17. Those principles also apply to substances such as vitamins which are not as a general rule harmful in themselves but may have special harmful effects solely if taken to excess as part of the general nutrition, the composition of which is unforeseeable and cannot be monitored. In view of the uncertainties inherent in the scientific assessment, national rules prohibiting, without prior authorization, the marketing of foodstuffs to which vitamins have been added are justified on

---

[43] The ECJ also noted that less stringent measures could have been taken to reach the same end as that desired by the UK government: *ibid.*, para. 41. See also Case 42/82, *Commission* v. *France* [1983] ECR 1013.
[44] Case 124/81, *Commission* v. *United Kingdom* [1983] ECR 203.

principle within the meaning of Article 36 of the Treaty on the grounds of the protection of human health.

18. Nevertheless the principle of proportionality which underlies the last sentence of Article 36 of the Treaty requires that the power of the Member States to prohibit imports of the products in question from other Member States should be restricted to what is necessary to attain the legitimate aim of protecting public health. . . .

19. Such an assessment is, however, difficult to make in relation to additives such as vitamins the above mentioned characteristics of which exclude the possibility of foreseeing or monitoring the quantities consumed as part of the general nutrition and the degree of harmfulness of which cannot be determined with sufficient certainty. Nevertheless, although in view of the present stage of harmonization of national laws at the Community level a wide discretion must be left to the Member States, they must, in order to observe the principle of proportionality, authorize marketing when the addition of vitamins to foodstuffs meets a real need, especially a technical or nutritional one.

20. The first question must therefore be answered to the effect that Community law permits national rules prohibiting without prior authorization the marketing of foodstuffs marketed in another Member State to which vitamins have been added, provided that the marketing is authorized when the addition of the vitamins meets a real need, especially a technical or nutritional one.

The ECJ's approach in *Sandoz* is finely tuned. It will decide whether the public-health claim is sustainable in principle. If there is uncertainty about the medical implications of some substance it will,[45] in the absence of Community harmonization measures, be for the Member State to decide upon the appropriate degree of protection for its citizens. This will, however, be subject to the principle of proportionality, as applied by the ECJ in paragraph 18 of its judgment. A similar approach is apparent in other cases on this topic.[46]

Thirdly, a Member State might not ban imports, but *it might subject them to checks that rendered import more difficult, and it might do so even though the goods were checked in the State of origin*. This problem of double-checking has arisen on a number of occasions, and the ECJ has become stricter in its more recent case law. The early approach in *Denkavit*[47] was to urge national authorities to co-operate to avoid dual burdens. National authorities had a duty to ascertain whether the documents from the State of export raised a presumption that the goods complied with the demands of the importing State. The Court admitted, however, that a second set of checks in the State of import might be lawful, provided that the requirements were necessary and proportionate. The Court's more recent case law exhibits a healthy scepticism regarding whether a second set of controls is really required. This is evident from the decision in *Commission* v. *United Kingdom*[48] concerning UHT milk. The ECJ held that

---

[45] See, however, Case 178/84, *Commission* v. *Germany* [1987] ECR 1227.

[46] Case 53/80, *Officier van Justitie* v. *Koniklijke Kaasfabriek Eyssen BV* [1981] ECR 409; Case 94/83, *Albert Heijin BV* [1984] ECR 3263; Case 304/84, *Ministère Public* v. *Muller* [1986] ECR 1511; Case C–62/90, *Commission* v. *Germany* [1992] ECR I–2575.

[47] Case 251/78, *Denkavit Futtermittel* v. *Minister für Ernährung, Landwirtschaft und Forsten des Landes* [1979] ECR 3369.

[48] Case 124/81, *Commission* v. *United Kingdom* [1983] ECR 203.

the United Kingdom's concerns about the product could be met by less restrictive means than the import ban and marketing system which it had instituted. The United Kingdom could, said the Court, lay down requirements that imported milk had to meet, and could demand certificates from the authorities of the exporting State.[49] However, if such certificates were produced then it would be for the authorities within the importing State to ascertain whether these certificates raised a presumption that the imported goods complied with the demands of domestic legislation. The ECJ concluded that the conditions for such a presumption existed in this case.[50] An unwillingness to subject goods to a second set of checks can also be seen in the *Biologische Producten* case.[51] Dual checks would not be lawful where they unnecessarily imposed technical tests that had already been done in the State of origin, nor where the practical effect of the tests in the exporting State met the demands of the importing State.[52]

(e) OTHER GROUNDS FOR VALIDATING DISCRIMINATORY MEASURES?

The traditional view was that a Member State could not justify a discriminatory measure on grounds other than those listed in Article 30 (ex Article 36). This was so, even if the justifications were in the list that could be invoked for indistinctly applicable measures.[53] It was questionable whether *Commission* v. *Belgium*[54] was an exception to this proposition. The Commission challenged a Belgian regional decree, the effect of which was to ban the importation of waste into that area. The decree could be seen as discriminatory, in that it did not cover disposal of locally produced waste. Notwithstanding this, the Court allowed environmental protection to be taken into account when considering the legality of the regional decree. The case could, therefore, be seen as allowing justifications to be pleaded which are not found in Article 30. However, the ECJ in effect held that the decree was not discriminatory, notwithstanding appearances to the contrary in the challenged instrument. This was because of the special nature of the subject matter, waste. There were strong arguments, the Court said, for disposing of such material locally, and each area had the responsibility for disposing of its own waste. Thus, although the decree applied only to imports it was not discriminatory.

More recent case law has cast doubt on whether the list in Article 30 really is exhaustive. In *PreussenElektra*[55] Advocate General Jacobs re-examined the issue. He argued that the approach in the *Walloon Waste* case was flawed, in the sense that whether a measure was discriminatory was logically distinct from whether it could be justified. He suggested however that there could be good reasons for allowing environmental protection to be pleaded as a justification, even in cases where there

---

[49] *Ibid.*, paras. 27–28.   [50] *Ibid.*, para. 30.
[51] Case 272/80, *Frans-Nederlandse Maatschappij voor Biologische Producten* [1981] ECR 3277.
[52] *Ibid.*, paras. 14–15.   [53] See 659–61 below.
[54] Case C–2/90, [1992] ECR I–4431.
[55] Case C–379/98, *PreussenElektra AG* v. *Schleswag AG* [2001] ECR I–2099, paras. 225–238.

was direct discrimination. He argued more generally for a relaxation in the distinction between the justifications that could be pleaded under Article 30 (ex Article 36), and the rule of reason exceptions to *Cassis*. The ECJ did not, as Advocate General Jacobs suggested, give general guidance on the relationship between Article 30, and the exceptions to *Cassis*. It did however allow the national measure to be justified on environmental grounds.[56]

The relationship between Article 30 (ex Article 36), and the list of exceptions in *Cassis* is further complicated by the fact that the dividing line between cases involving discrimination and those involving indistinctly applicable rules can be a fine one.

It will be argued below that the same justifications should be applicable, irrespective of whether the measure is discriminatory or not, although the application of the justification could be affected by this factor.[57]

(f) THE RELATIONSHIP BETWEEN HARMONIZATION AND ARTICLE 30

Community harmonization measures may make recourse to Article 30 (ex Article 36) inadmissible. This will be the case where the Community measure is intended to harmonize the area totally or exhaustively. Member State action is thereby pre-empted. Thus in *Moormann*[58] the ECJ held that the existence of harmonization measures for poultry health inspections meant that a State could no longer use Article 30 (ex Article 36) to legitimate national rules on the matter. In *Commission v. Germany*[59] it was held that Community directives had harmonized the measures that could be taken 'for the detection of a pronounced sexual odour in uncastrated male pigs', thereby preventing Germany from applying different measures.

Many Community measures are however not intended to harmonize an area totally. The objective will be minimum harmonization. It will be for the ECJ to decide, in the case of doubt, whether the harmonization measure covers the whole field, or whether it leaves room for national regulatory initiatives.[60] In the case of minimum harmonization, Member States are permitted to 'maintain and often to introduce more stringent regulatory standards than those prescribed by Community legislation, for the purposes of advancing a particular social or welfare interest, and provided that such additional requirements are compatible with the Treaty'.[61] Thus in *de Agostini* it was held that Community directives on 'Television without Frontiers' only partially harmonized the law in this area. They did not preclude national rules to control

---

[56] See also Case C–389/98, *Aher-Waggon GmbH* v. *Bundesrepublik Deutschland* [1998] ECR I–4473.

[57] See below, 659–61.

[58] Case 190/87, *Oberkreisdirektor* v. *Moormann BV* [1988] ECR 4689. See also Case 5/77, *Tedeschi* v. *Denkavit* [1977] ECR 1555; Cases C–277, 318, & 319/91, *Ligur Carni Srl* v. *Unità Sanitaria Locale No XV di Genova* [1993] ECR I–6621; Case C–294/92, *Commission* v. *Italy* [1994] ECR I–4311; Case C–5/94, *R.* v. *Ministry of Agriculture, Fisheries and Food, ex p. Hedley Lomas (Ireland) Ltd.* [1996] ECR I–2553; Case C–1/96, *R.* v. *Minister of Agriculture, Fisheries, and Food, ex p. Commission in World Farming Ltd.* [1998] ECR I–1251.

[59] Case C–102/96, [1998] ECR I–6871.

[60] See, e.g., Case C–1/96, *R.* v. *Minister of Agriculture, Fisheries and Food, ex p. Compassion in World Farming Ltd.* [1998] ECR I–1251.

[61] M. Doogan, 'Minimum Harmonization and the Internal Market' (2000) 37 *CMLRev.* 853, 855.

television advertising designed to protect consumers.[62] The ECJ will ensure that such national regulations are proportionate and do not constitute a means of arbitrary discrimination.[63] Difficult issues can however arise, even in the context of minimum harmonization, as to whether a Member State can impose more stringent welfare standards on goods entering its territory than those prescribed by the directive.[64]

6. INDISTINCTLY APPLICABLE RULES: *CASSIS DE DIJON*

If Article 28 had been confined to the cases considered above it would still have made a notable contribution to the creation of a single market. The removal of discriminatory trade barriers is undoubtedly a necessary condition for the attainment of single-market integration. It is not, however, sufficient. There are many rules which do not discriminate between goods dependent upon the country of origin, but which nevertheless can create real barriers to the passage of products between Member States.

The Commission appreciated this in Directive 70/50. Article 2 of this Directive was concerned with discriminatory measures. Article 3 provides that the Directive also covers measures governing the marketing of products which deal, *inter alia*, with shape, size, weight, composition, presentation, and identification, where the measures are equally applicable to domestic and imported products, and where the restrictive effect of such measures on the free movement of goods exceeds the effects intrinsic to such rules. The possibility that Article 28 could be applied to indistinctly applicable rules was also apparent in *Dassonville*. The definition of an MEQR in paragraph 5 did not require a measure to be discriminatory. The seeds that were sown in Directive 70/50 and in Dassonville came to fruition in the seminal *Cassis de Dijon* case.

Case 120/78, Rewe-Zentrale AG v. Bundesmonopolverwaltung für Branntwein
[1979] ECR 649

[Note ToA renumbering: Art. 30 is now Art. 28]

The applicant intended to import the liqueur 'Cassis de Dijon' into Germany from France. The German authorities refused to allow the importation because the French drink was not of sufficient alcoholic strength to be marketed in Germany. Under German law such liqueurs had to have an alcohol content of 25 per cent, whereas the French drink had an alcohol content of

---

[62] Cases C–34–36/95, *Konsumentombudsmannen (KO)* v. *De Agostini (Svenska) Forlag AB and TV-Shop i Sverige AB* [1997] ECR I–3843, paras. 32–5.

[63] Case 4/75, *Rewe-Zentralfinanz GmbH* v. *Landwirtschafskammer* [1975] ECR 843; Case C–317/92, *Commission* v. *Germany* [1994] ECR I–2039; Case 17/93, *Van der Veldt*, n. 32 above.

[64] Compare Case C–1/96, *Compassion in World Farming*, n. 60 above, with Case C–389/98, *Aher-Waggon*, n. 56 above; Doogan, n. 61 above, 868–84.

between 15 and 20 per cent. The applicant argued that the German rule was an MEQR, since it prevented the French version of the drink from being lawfully marketed in Germany.

THE ECJ

8. In the absence of common rules relating to the production and marketing of alcohol . . . it is for the Member States to regulate all matters relating to the production and marketing of alcohol and alcoholic beverages on their own territory.

Obstacles to movement within the Community resulting from disparities between the national laws relating to the marketing of the products in question must be accepted in so far as those provisions may be recognized as being necessary in order to satisfy mandatory requirements relating in particular to the effectiveness of fiscal supervision, the protection of public health, the fairness of commercial transactions and the defence of the consumer.

9. The Government of the Federal Republic of Germany . . . put forward various arguments which, in its view, justify the application of provisions relating to the minimum alcohol content of alcoholic beverages, adducing considerations relating on the one hand to the protection of public health and on the other to the protection of the consumer against unfair commercial practices.

10. As regards the protection of public health the German Government states that the purpose of the fixing of minimum alcohol contents by national legislation is to avoid the proliferation of alcoholic beverages on the national market, in particular alcoholic beverages with a low alcohol content, since, in its view, such products may more easily induce a tolerance towards alcohol than more highly alcoholic beverages.

11. Such considerations are not decisive since the consumer can obtain on the market an extremely wide range of weakly or moderately alcoholic products and furthermore a large proportion of alcoholic beverages with a high alcohol content freely sold on the German market is generally consumed in a diluted form.

12. The German Government also claims that the fixing of a lower limit for the alcohol content of certain liqueurs is designed to protect the consumer against unfair practices on the part of producers and distributors of alcoholic beverages.

This argument is based on the consideration that the lowering of the alcohol content secures a competitive advantage in relation to beverages with a higher alcohol content, since alcohol constitutes by far the most expensive constituent of beverages by reason of the high rate of tax to which it is subject.

Furthermore, according to the German Government, to allow alcoholic products into free circulation wherever, as regards their alcohol content, they comply with the rules laid down in the country of production would have the effect of imposing as a common standard within the Community the lowest alcohol content permitted in any of the Member States, and even of rendering any requirements in this field inoperative since a lower limit of this nature is foreign to the rules of several Member States.

13. As the Commission rightly observed, the fixing of limits to the alcohol content of beverages may lead to the standardization of products placed on the market and of their designations, in the interests of a greater transparency of commercial transactions and offers for sale to the public.

However, this line of argument cannot be taken so far as to regard the mandatory fixing of minimum alcohol contents as being an essential guarantee of the fairness of commercial transactions, since it is a simple matter to ensure that suitable information is conveyed to the purchaser by requiring the display of an indication of origin and of the alcohol content on the packaging of products.

14. It is clear from the foregoing that the requirements relating to the minimum alcohol content of alcoholic beverages do not serve a purpose which is in the general interest and such as to take precedence over the requirements of the free movement of goods, which constitutes one of the fundamental rules of the Community.

In practice, the principal effect of requirements of this nature is to promote alcoholic beverages having a high alcohol content by excluding from the national market products of other Member States which do not answer that description.

It therefore appears that the unilateral requirement imposed by the rules of a Member State of a minimum alcohol content for the purposes of the sale of alcoholic beverages constitutes an obstacle to trade which is incompatible with the provisions of Article 30 of the Treaty.

There is therefore no valid reason why, provided that they have been lawfully produced and marketed in one of the Member States, alcoholic beverages should not be introduced into any other Member State; the sale of such products may not be subject to a legal prohibition on the marketing of beverages with an alcohol content lower than the limits set by the national rules.

The significance of *Cassis de Dijon* can hardly be overstated, and it is therefore worth dwelling upon the result and the reasoning used by the Court.

In terms of *result* the Court's ruling in *Cassis* affirmed and developed the *Dassonville* judgment. It *affirmed* paragraph 5 of *Dassonville*: Article 30 (now Article 28) could apply to national rules which did not discriminate against imported products, but which inhibited trade because they were different from the trade rules applicable in the country of origin. The fundamental assumption was that, once goods had been lawfully marketed in one Member State, they should be admitted into any other State without restriction, unless the State of import could successfully invoke one of the mandatory requirements. The *Cassis* judgment encapsulated therefore a principle of *mutual recognition*: paragraph 14(4). Small wonder, then, that Lord Mackenzie Stuart regarded the *Cassis* case as the most important decision made by the Court during his tenure of office.[65] The *Cassis* ruling also *built* upon paragraph 6 of *Dassonville*, in which the ECJ had introduced the rule of reason: in the absence of Community harmonization reasonable measures could be taken by a State to prevent unfair trade practices. Paragraph 8 of *Cassis* developed this idea. Four matters (fiscal supervision, etc.) were listed that could prevent a trade rule which inhibited the free movement of goods from being caught by Article 30 (now Article 28). This list is not exhaustive; it can be and has been added to by the ECJ. The mandatory requirements that constitute the rule of reason are taken into account within the fabric of Article 30 (now Article 28), and are separate from Article 36 (now Article 30).

The *reasoning* in *Cassis* is as significant as the result. The core of the reasoning is to be found in paragraph 8 of the judgment. This is a paragraph to be savoured, and we can learn a lot about the Court's style of judicial discourse by focusing upon it. The ECJ began by affirming the right of the States to regulate all matters that had not yet been the subject of Community harmonization. Yet within half a dozen lines the whole balance shifted. State regulation of such areas must be accepted, together with any obstacles to trade which may follow from disparities in national laws, *but* only in

[65] Interview by one of the authors.

so far as these trade rules could be justified by one of the mandatory requirements listed in paragraph 8. What began by an assertion of States' rights was transformed into a legal conclusion which placed the State on the defensive, having to justify the indistinctly applicable rules under the rule of reason. The reasoning showed how closely the ECJ would scrutinize assertions that the mandatory requirements applied. Now to be sure the German Government's claim in paragraph 10 was risible, and the Court was more polite in its response than the argument warranted. The substance of the main claim in paragraph 12 was little better, and was countered in paragraph 13. The one point of real substance raised by the German Government was to be found in paragraph 12(3), and it elicited no direct response from the Court. This is a point touched upon in the introduction: the effect of *Cassis* was deregulatory, in the sense of rendering inapplicable trade rules that prevented goods lawfully marketed in one State from being imported into another State. The result may be to end up with no rules on a particular issue, or with a common standard which would reflect the rule pertaining in the country with the lowest rules on alcohol levels, what is often referred to as the 'regulatory race to the bottom'.[66] It might be felt that this is desirable, or that it is not something that we should be overly concerned about. This may be so on the facts of *Cassis*, but, as we shall see below, matters are not always so simple.

7. INDISTINCTLY APPLICABLE RULES: THE POST-*CASSIS* JURISPRUDENCE

There have been numerous cases applying *Cassis* to varying trade rules. In *Déserbais*[67] an importer of Edam cheese from Germany into France was prosecuted for unlawful use of a trade name. In Germany such cheese could be lawfully produced with a fat content of only 34.3 per cent, whereas in France the name Edam was restricted to cheese which had a fat content of 40 per cent. The importer relied on Article 30 (now Article 28) by way of defence to the criminal prosecution. The ECJ held that the French rule was incompatible with this Article, even though there was no Community harmonization on the issue. The French rule constituted a restriction on trade in relation to goods which had been lawfully marketed in another Member State. This rule could be saved only if it came within one of the mandatory requirements of *Cassis*. This was not so on the facts of the case, since the consumer could be provided with adequate information on the relative fat content of different Edam cheeses.[68]

In *Gilli and Andres*[69] the importers of apple vinegar from Germany into Italy were prosecuted for fraud, because they had sold vinegar in Italy which was not made from the fermentation of wine. Once again the importers relied on Article 30 (now Article

---

[66] This will not always be so: see Ch. 28.

[67] Case 286/86, *Ministère Public* v. *Déserbais* [1988] ECR 4907.

[68] The ECJ acknowledged that there might be cases where a product presented under a particular name was so different in terms of its content from products generally known by that name that it could not be regarded as falling within the same category. This was not so on the facts of the instant case.

[69] Case 788/79, *Italian State* v. *Gilli and Andres* [1980] ECR 2071. See also Case C–17/93, *Van der Veldt*, n. 32 above.

28) by way of defence. Once again there was no Community harmonization on the issue. The ECJ adopted the same reasoning as in *Cassis* itself: in the absence of harmonization the State could regulate the matter, *provided* that such regulation did not constitute an obstacle, actually or potentially, to intra-Community trade. The rule in this case hampered Community trade and could, therefore, be saved only if it came within one of the mandatory requirements. This defence failed, since the imported apple vinegar was not harmful to health, and proper labelling could alert consumers to the nature of the product, thereby avoiding any consumer confusion.

The same approach is apparent in *Rau*,[70] which was concerned with national rules on packaging rather than content. Belgian law required all margarine to be marketed in cube-shaped packages. This rule applied to all margarine, irrespective of where it had been made, but it was clearly more difficult for non-Belgian manufacturers to comply without incurring cost increases since they would not normally have packaged their goods in this way. The ECJ held that the Belgian rule was caught by Article 30 (now Article 28), and that it could not be justified on the basis of consumer protection. Consumer confusion could be avoided by means that were less inhibiting on intra-Community trade, such as by the obligation to label products clearly.

In *Commission* v. *Germany*[71] the Court held that a German rule restricting the expiry dates for medicinal products which could be shown on a package to two a year was caught by Article 30 (now Article 28), since it would require importers to alter the expiry dates on their products. In *Piagème*[72] a national law which required the exclusive use of a specific language for the labelling of foodstuffs infringed Article 30 (now Article 28). Such a rule would be lawful only if it allowed for the use of another language that would also be understood by purchasers, or left open the possibility that purchasers could be informed in some other way.

8. INDISTINCTLY APPLICABLE RULES AND ARTICLE 29

Article 29 (ex Article 34) prohibits quantitative restrictions and MEQRs in relation to exports in the same manner as does Article 28 in relation to imports. The ECJ has, however, held that there is a difference in the scope of the two provisions. Whereas Article 28 will apply to discriminatory provisions and also to indistinctly applicable measures, Article 29 will, it seems, apply only if there is discrimination. An exporter faced with a national rule on, for example, quality standards for a product to be marketed in that State, cannot use Article 29 to argue that compliance with such a rule renders it more difficult for that exporter to penetrate other Community markets. This was established in the *Groenveld* case.[73] Dutch legislation prohibited all

---

[70] Case 261/81, *Walter Rau Lebensmittelwerke* v. *de Smedt Pvba* [1982] ECR 3961.

[71] Case C–317/92, [1994] ECR I–2039.

[72] Case C–369/89, *Groupement des Producteurs, Importeurs et Agents Généraux d'Eaux Minérales Etrangères (Piagème) Asbl* v. *Peeters Pvba* [1991] ECR I–2971.

[73] Case 15/79, *P.B. Groenveld BV* v. *Produktschap voor Vee en Vlees* [1979] ECR 3409. See also Case 237/82, *Jongeneel Kaas* v. *The State (Netherlands) and Stichting Centraal Organ Zuivelcontrole* [1984] ECR 483; Case 98/86, *Ministère Public* v. *Mathot* [1987] ECR 809.

manufacturers of meat products from having in stock or processing horsemeat. The purpose was to safeguard the export of meat products to countries which prohibited the marketing of horseflesh. It was impossible to detect the presence of horsemeat within other meat products, and therefore the ban was designed to prevent its use by preventing meat processors from having such horsemeat in stock at all. The sale of horsemeat was not actually forbidden in the Netherlands. None the less the Court held that the Dutch rule did not infringe Article 34 (now Article 29). Article 34 was aimed at national measures which have as their specific object or effect the restriction of exports, in such a way as to provide a particular advantage for national production at the expense of the trade of other Member States. This was not the case here, said the Court, since the prohibition in the instant case applied to the production of goods of a certain kind without drawing a distinction depending on whether such goods were intended for the national market or for export.[74]

The rationale for making Article 28 applicable to measures which do not discriminate is that they impose a dual burden on the importer who will have to satisfy the relevant rules in his or her own State and also the State of import. This will not normally be so in relation to Article 29. Thus, in a case such as *Groenveld* the rule applied to all goods, those for both the domestic and the export market, and the goods were subject to no further rule at that stage of production or sale.[75] One could, however, imagine instances where a dual burden might exist. There are, moreover, indications from the ECJ's jurisprudence under Article 59 (now Article 49) that rules which apply to exporters will be caught even if they are not discriminatory.[76] We shall discuss this issue further below.[77]

9. INDISTINCTLY APPLICABLE RULES: THE LIMITS OF ARTICLE 28

(a) THE NATURE OF THE PROBLEM: *CINÉTHÈQUE* AND *TORFAEN*

There are many other cases in which *Cassis* has been applied.[78] It is, however, necessary at this juncture to focus on the limits of Article 28. *Cassis* signalled the ECJ's willingness to extend Article 28 to catch indistinctly applicable rules. The difficulty is that all rules that concern trade, directly or indirectly, could be said to affect the free movement of goods in various ways. Thus, as Weatherill and Beaumont note, it could be said that rules requiring the owner of a firearm to have a licence, or spending limits imposed on government departments, reduce the sales opportunities for imported

---

[74] N. 73 above, para. 7.

[75] R. Barents, 'New Developments in Measures Having Equivalent Effect' (1981) 18 *CMLRev.* 271.

[76] Case C–384/93, *Alpine Investments BV* v. *Minister van Financiën* [1995] ECR I–1141. Jacobs AG doubted whether *Groenveld*, n. 73 above, would apply to rules of the exporting State which concerned the marketing of goods: [1995] ECR I–1141, para. 55.

[77] See Ch. 18 below.

[78] See, e.g., Case 298/87, *Smanor* [1988] ECR 4489; Case 407/85, *Drei Glocken* v. *USL Centro-Sud* [1988] ECR 4233; Case C–362/88, *GB-INNO-BM* v. *Confédération du Commerce Luxembourgeois Asbl* [1990] ECR I–667.

products.[79] It would, as they say, seem absurd to bring such rules within Article 28, yet they could be caught by the *Dassonville* formula.[80]

A distinction can however be drawn, as Weatherill and Beaumont note,[81] between what may be termed dual-burden rules and equal-burden rules. *Cassis* is concerned with dual-burden rules. State A imposes rules on the content of goods. These are applied to goods imported from State B, even though such goods will already have complied with the trade rules in State B. *Cassis* prevents State A from imposing its rules in such instances, unless they can be saved by the mandatory requirements. Equal-burden rules are those applying to all goods, irrespective of origin, which regulate trade in some manner. They are not designed to be protectionist. These rules may have an impact on the overall volume of trade, but this will be no greater impact for imports than for domestic products. A key issue is whether rules of this latter nature should be held to fall within Article 28, subject to a possible justification, or whether they should be deemed to be outside Article 28 altogether. The result of these two strategies may be the same in a particular case, in that the rule may be held lawful. The choice is none the less of importance. If these rules are within Article 28 they are prima facie unlawful, and the burden will be on those seeking to uphold the rule to show that there is some objective justification for it.

The ECJ's approach was not always uniform. In some cases it held that rules which did not relate to the *characteristics* of the goods and did not impose a dual burden on the importer, but concerned only the conditions on which all goods were *sold*, were outside Article 30 (now Article 28). Thus in *Oebel*[82] the Court held that a rule which prohibited the delivery of bakery products to consumers and retailers (but not wholesalers) at night was not caught, since it applied in the same way to all producers wherever they were established. Similarly in *Forest*[83] the ECJ decided that a French law imposing quotas for the milling of flour for human consumption did not affect the possibility of importing flour from other Member States. In *Blesgen*[84] the ECJ considered that a national rule restricting the sale of drinks above certain strength on premises used for public consumption had no connection with the import of such products, and would not affect trade between Member States. In *Quietlynn*[85] the Court found that a rule of United Kingdom law that restricted the sale of lawful sex articles to licensed shops was not in breach of Article 30 (now Article 28), since it merely regulated the distribution of the products without discrimination against imported goods.

In a number of other cases the Court held, however, that the Article could apply to rules which were not dissimilar to those in the preceding paragraph. The *Cinéthèque* case provides a good illustration of the problem posed by equal-burden rules. More recently the ECJ in the *Keck* case[86] departed from some of its previous case law. It is,

[79] S. Weatherill and P. Beaumont, *EU Law* (Penguin, 3rd edn., 1999), 608.

[80] Case 8/74, [1974] ECR 837, para. 5.

[81] N. 79 above, 608–9.

[82] Case 155/80, [1981] ECR 1993, para. 20.

[83] Case 148/85, *Direction Générale des Impôts and Procureur de la République v. Forest* [1986] ECR 3449, para. 11.

[84] Case 75/81, *Belgian State v. Blesgen* [1982] ECR 1211.

[85] Case C–23/89, *Quietlynn Ltd. v. Southend-on-Sea BC* [1990] ECR I–3059.

[86] Cases C–267 & 268/91, *Criminal Proceedings against Keck and Mithouard* [1993] ECR I–6097.

however, impossible to understand the significance of this finding without an appreciation of the Court's earlier case law.

Cases 60 and 61/84, Cinéthèque SA v. Fédération Nationale des Cinémas Français [1985] ECR 2605

French law banned the sale or hire of videos of films during the first year in which the film was released, the objective being to encourage people to go to the cinema and hence protect the profitability of cinematographic production. The rule applied equally to domestic and imported videos. The law was challenged by a distributor of videos as being in breach of Article 30. The ECJ noted that most Member States had some provisions akin to those in France, that they had the same objective, and that the Treaty left it to the states to determine the need for and form of such a system. It continued as follows.

THE ECJ

21. In that connection it must be observed that such a system, if it applies without distinction to both video-cassettes manufactured in the national territory and to imported video-cassettes, does not have the purpose of regulating trade patterns; its effect is not to favour national production as against the production of other Member States, but to encourage cinematographic production as such.

22. Nevertheless, the application of such a system may create barriers to intra-Community trade in video-cassettes because of the disparities between the systems operated in the different Member States and between the conditions for the release of cinematographic works in the cinemas of those States. In those circumstances a prohibition of exploitation laid down by such a system is not compatible with the principle of free movement of goods provided for in the Treaty unless any obstacle to intra-Community trade thereby created does not exceed that which is necessary in order to ensure the attainment of the objective in view and unless that objective is justified with regard to Community law.

23. It must be conceded that a national system which, in order to encourage the creation of cinematographic works irrespective of their origin, gives priority, for a limited initial period, to the distribution of such works through the cinema, is so justified.

24. The reply to the questions referred to the Court is therefore that Article 30 of the EEC Treaty must be interpreted as meaning that it does not apply to national legislation which regulates the distribution of cinematographic works by imposing an interval between one mode of distributing such works and another by prohibiting their simultaneous exploitation in cinemas and in video-cassette form for a limited period, provided that the prohibition applies to domestically produced and imported cassettes alike and any barriers to intra-Community trade to which its implementation may give rise do not exceed what is necessary for ensuring that the exploitation in cinemas of cinematographic works of all origins retains priority over other means of distribution.

The Court's reasoning in *Cinéthèque* can be summarized in the following manner. The rule was *prima facie* within Article 30 (now Article 28), but it might be regarded as lawful if there was an objective justification for it which was acceptable with regard to Community law, and provided also that the method of attaining the objective was proportionate: paragraph 22. The ECJ accepted the objective of the French rule: paragraph 23. The decision regarded equal-burden rules as being within Article 30, and added to the *Cassis* list of mandatory requirements a further ground for objective justification based on the protection or enhancement of artistic works.

The ECJ's approach can be contrasted with that taken by Advocate General Slynn. He regarded indistinctly applicable rules as being those that imposed an additional requirement on importers, thereby rendering importation more difficult.[87] He argued that this should be distinguished from the type of case before the ECJ in *Cinéthèque*.[88] The French rule did not make it any more difficult for an importer to sell his products than a domestic producer. It should not therefore fall within Article 30 (now Article 28), even if it did in fact lead to a reduction in imports.

The difficult question of the outer limits of Article 28, and whether it should be interpreted to catch equal-burden rules, came before the ECJ once again in the *Sunday Trading* cases.

Case 145/88, Torfaen BC v. B & Q plc
[1989] ECR 3851

B & Q was prosecuted for violation of the Sunday trading laws which prohibited retail shops from selling on Sundays, subject to exceptions for certain types of products. B & Q claimed that these laws constituted an MEQR within Article 30. The effect of the laws was to reduce total turnover by about 10 per cent, with a corresponding diminution of imports from other Member States. But imported goods were, in this respect, in no worse a position than domestic goods: the reduction in total turnover affected all goods equally.

THE ECJ

11. The first point which must be made is that national rules prohibiting retailers from opening their premises on Sunday apply to imported and domestic products alike. In principle, the marketing of products imported from other Member States is not therefore made more difficult than the marketing of domestic products.

12. Next, it must be recalled that in its judgment . . . in Joined Cases 60 and 61/84 (*Cinéthèque*) the Court held, with regard to a prohibition of the hiring of video-cassettes applicable to domestic and imported products alike, that such a prohibition was not compatible with the principle of the free movement of goods provided for in the Treaty unless any obstacle to Community trade thereby created did not exceed what was necessary in order to ensure the attainment of the objective in view and unless that objective was justified with regard to Community law.

13. In those circumstances it is therefore necessary in a case such as this to consider first of all whether rules such as those at issue pursue an aim which is justified with regard to Community law. As far as this question is concerned the Court has already stated in its judgment . . . in Case 155/80 (*Oebel* [1981] ECR 1993) that national rules governing the hours of work, delivery and

---

[87] Cases 60 and 61/84, *Cinéthèque* [1985] ECR 2605, 2611.   [88] *Ibid.*

sale in the bread and confectionery industry constitute a legitimate part of economic and social policy, consistent with the objectives of public interest pursued by the Treaty.

14. The same consideration must apply as regards national rules governing the opening hours of retail premises. Such rules reflect certain political and economic choices in so far as their purpose is to ensure that working and non-working hours are so arranged as to accord with national or regional socio-cultural characteristics, and that, in the present state of Community law, is a matter for Member States. Furthermore such rules are not designed to govern the patterns of trade between Member States.

15. Secondly, it is necessary to ascertain whether the effects of such national rules exceed what is necessary to achieve the aim in view. As is indicated in Article 3 of Commission Directive 70/50 . . . the prohibition laid down in Article 30 covers national measures governing the marketing of products where the restrictive effect of such measures on the free movement of goods exceeds the effects intrinsic to trade rules.

16. The question whether the effects of specific national rules do in fact remain within that limit is a question to be determined by the national court.

17. The reply to the first question must therefore be that Article 30 of the Treaty must be interpreted as meaning that the prohibition which it lays down does not apply to national rules prohibiting retailers from opening their premises on Sunday where the restrictive effects on Community trade which may result therefrom do not exceed the effects intrinsic to rules of that kind.

The approach in *Torfaen* was conceptually identical to that in *Cinéthèque*. The rule was *prima facie* caught by Article 30 (now Article 28), but it could escape prohibition provided that the objective behind the rule was justified from the perspective of Community law, and provided also that the effects of the rule were proportionate. It was for national courts to determine whether the proportionality criterion was met or not. Subsequent case law within the United Kingdom attested to the difficulty felt by these courts in applying the test laid down by the ECJ. Some courts found that the Sunday trading laws were compatible with Article 30, while others reached the opposite conclusion.[89] Later decisions by the ECJ sought to resolve these difficulties, by making it clear that Sunday trading rules were proportionate.[90]

The fundamental approach none the less remained the same: such rules were *prima facie* within Article 30 (now Article 28), but could be upheld provided that the objective was justified under Community law, and provided also that they were proportionate. The post-*Torfaen* case law simply made things easier for national courts by providing guidance on the proportionality part of this test.

It is now clear that the ECJ has had second thoughts on whether this general strategy for dealing with equal burden rules was correct. The *Keck* case signalled a

[89] *Stoke City Council* v. *B & Q plc* [1990] 3 CMLR 31; *Wellingborough BC* v. *Payless* [1990] 1 CMLR 773; *B & Q plc* v. *Shrewsbury BC* [1990] 3 CMLR 535; *Payless* v. *Peterborough CC* [1990] 2 CMLR 577. See generally A. Arnull, 'What Shall We Do On Sunday?' (1991) 16 *ELRev.* 112.

[90] Case C–312/89, *Union Département des Syndicats CGT de l'Aisne* v. *SIDEF Conforama* [1991] ECR I–997; Case C–332/89, *Ministère Public* v. *Marchandise* [1991] ECR I–1027; Cases C–306/88, 304/90, & 169/91, *Stoke-on-Trent CC* v. *B & Q plc* [1992] ECR I–6457, 6493, 6635; Cases C–418–421, 460–462, & 464/93, 9–11, 14–15, 23–24, & 332/94, *Semeraro Casa Uno Srl* v. *Sindaco del Commune di Erbusco* [1996] ECR I–2975.

change of approach towards such rules, one more redolent of that taken by Advocate General Slynn in *Cinéthèque*.

(b) ACADEMIC OPINION PRIOR TO *KECK*

The ECJ's case law provided academics with a rich source of material for discussion concerning the proper boundaries of Article 30 (now Article 28). Not surprisingly opinions differed. Some saw little wrong with the ECJ's approach in *Cinéthèque* and *Torfaen*. The relevant measures were *prima facie* within Article 30, and it would then be for the parties to justify them. Others were less happy with the Court's approach. Steiner argued that the Court should focus on whether a challenged rule hindered trade.[91] White proposed a different test, distinguishing between the characteristics of the goods and selling arrangements.

E. White, In Search of the Limits to Article 30 of the EEC Treaty[92]

[A]s the judgment of the Court in *Cassis de Dijon* clearly shows, Member States are not entitled to require that imported products have the same characteristics as are required of, or are traditional in, domestic products unless this is strictly necessary for the protection of some legitimate interest. There is not, however, the same need to require the rules relating to the circumstances in which certain goods may be sold or used in the importing Member State to be overridden for this purpose as long as imported products enjoy equal access to the market of the importing Member State compared with national goods. In such a case the imported product is not deprived of any advantage it derives from the different legal and economic environment prevailing in the place of production. In fact, any reduction of total sales (and therefore imports) which may result from restrictions on the circumstances in which they may be sold does not arise from disparities between national rules but rather out of the existence of the rules in the importing Member State.

. . . The proposed definition of a measure of equivalent effect to a quantitative restriction on imports for indistinctly applicable measures based on *Cassis de Dijon* case law is therefore *the application by a Member State to products legally produced and marketed in another Member State of its national rules relating to the characteristics required of such products on its territory (which therefore prevents this product from benefiting in the importing Member State from the advantages arising out of its production in the different legal and economic environment prevailing in the other Member State)*. . . . State measures which are entirely neutral in their effect on goods legally produced and marketed in other Member States, because they only regulate the circumstances in which all goods of the same kind may be sold or used, should not be regarded as falling under Article 30.

---

[91] J. Steiner, 'Drawing the Line: Uses and Abuses of Art. 30 EEC' (1992) 29 *CMLRev.* 749.

[92] (1989) 26 *CMLRev.* 235, 246–7. Italics in the original. See also K. Mortelmans, 'Article 30 of the EEC Treaty and Legislation Relating to Market Circumstances: Time to Consider a New Definition' (1991) 28 *CMLRev.* 115, 130.

(c) THE JUDGMENT IN *KECK*

Cases C–267 and 268/91, Criminal Proceedings against Keck and Mithouard
[1993] ECR I–6097

[Note ToA renumbering: Arts. 30 and 177 are now Arts. 28 and 234]

Keck and Mithouard (K & M) were prosecuted in the French courts for selling goods at a price which was lower than their actual purchase price (resale at a loss), contrary to a French law of 1963 as amended in 1986. The law did not ban sales at a loss by the manufacturer. K & M claimed that the French law was contrary to Community law concerning, *inter alia,* free movement of goods.

THE ECJ

11. By virtue of Article 30, quantitative restrictions on imports and all measures having equivalent effect are prohibited between Member States. The Court has consistently held that any measure which is capable of directly or indirectly, actually or potentially, hindering intra-Community trade constitutes a measure having equivalent effect to a quantitative restriction.

12. It is not the purpose of national legislation imposing a general prohibition on resale at a loss to regulate trade in goods between Member States.

13. Such legislation may, admittedly, restrict the volume of sales, and hence the volume of sales of products from other Member States, in so far as it deprives traders of a method of sales promotion. But the question remains whether such a possibility is sufficient to characterize the legislation in question as a measure having equivalent effect to a quantitative restriction on imports.

14. In view of the increasing tendency of traders to invoke Article 30 of the Treaty as a means of challenging any rules whose effect is to limit their commercial freedom even where such rules are not aimed at products from other Member States, the Court considers it necessary to re-examine and clarify its case law on this matter.

15. In '*Cassis de Dijon*' . . . it was held that, in the absence of harmonization of legislation, measures of equivalent effect prohibited by Article 30 include obstacles to the free movement of goods where they are the consequence of applying rules that lay down requirements to be met by such goods (such as requirements as to designation, form, size, weight, composition, presentation, labelling, packaging) to goods from other Member States where they are lawfully manufactured and marketed, even if those rules apply without distinction to all products unless their application can be justified by a public-interest objective taking precedence over the free movement of goods.

16. However, contrary to what has previously been decided, the application to products from other Member States of national provisions restricting or prohibiting certain selling arrangements is not such as to hinder directly or indirectly, actually or potentially, trade between Member States within the meaning of the *Dassonville* judgment . . . provided that those provisions apply to all affected traders operating within the national territory and provided that they affect in the same manner, in law and fact, the marketing of domestic products and of those from other Member States.

17. Where those conditions are fulfilled, the application of such rules to the sale of products from another Member State is not by nature such as to prevent their access to the market or to

impede access any more than it impedes the access of domestic products. Such rules therefore fall outside the scope of Article 30 of the Treaty.

18. Accordingly, the reply to be given to the national court is that Article 30 of the EEC Treaty is to be interpreted as not applying to legislation of a Member State imposing a general prohibition on resale at a loss.

It is clear that the rationale for the decision was based in part upon the distinction between dual-burden rules and equal-burden rules, as is evident from the reasoning in paragraphs 15 to 17. The test adopted in *Keck* was very similar to that advocated by White set out above.

Cassis-type *rules relating to the goods themselves* were within Article 30 (now Article 28), in part because these rules would have to be satisfied by the importer *in addition* to any such provisions existing within his or her own State (paragraph 15). Such rules were by their very nature[93] likely to impede access to the market for imported goods.

Rules concerning selling arrangements, by way of contrast, simply imposed an equal burden on all those seeking to market goods in a particular territory (paragraph 17). They did not impose extra costs on the importer,[94] their purpose was not to regulate trade (paragraph 12), and they did not prevent access to the market. They were therefore not within Article 30 (now Article 28), *provided* that the conditions mentioned in the second part of paragraph 16 were met. If the selling rules discriminated in law or in fact they would be caught by Article 28 (ex Article 30).

The reference to the earlier case law that was being reassessed (paragraph 16) was unclear, because the Court did not name specific cases. The Court's re-thinking appears to encompass decisions such as *Torfaen* and probably *Cinéthèque*.[95] In both of these cases the challenged rule concerned selling arrangements, which affected importers no more than domestic producers. In both of these cases the effect on intra-Community trade consisted of a reduction in the total volume of sales.

(d) *KECK*: STATIC AND DYNAMIC SELLING ARRANGEMENTS

Later case law provided evidence of the ECJ's desire to exclude selling arrangements from the ambit of Article 28. In *Tankstation*[96] the Court held that national rules which provided for the compulsory closing of shops, in this instance petrol stations, were not caught by Article 30 (now Article 28). The ECJ repeated its ruling in *Keck*, and concluded that the rules related to selling arrangements that applied equally to all traders without distinguishing between the origin of the goods. In *Punto Casa*[97] and *Semeraro*[98] the Court reached the same conclusion in relation to Italian legislation on

---

[93] Cases C–401 & 402/92, *Criminal Proceedings against Tankstation 't Heustke vof and J. B. E. Boermans* [1994] ECR I–2199, 2220.
[94] *Ibid.*
[95] In Cases C–401 & 402/92, *Tankstation*, n. 93 above, van Gerven AG felt that *Cinéthèque* would be decided differently now in the light of *Keck*.
[96] *Ibid.*
[97] Cases C–69 & 258/93, *Punto Casa SpA* v. *Sindaco del Commune di Capena* [1994] ECR I–2355.
[98] N. 90 above.

the closure of retail outlets on Sundays. The rule applied equally to domestic and imported products, and therefore was outside the scope of Article 30 (now Article 28). The same theme is apparent in *Hunermund*,[99] where the ECJ held that a rule prohibiting pharmacists from advertising para-pharmaceutical products that they were allowed to sell was not caught by Article 30. The Court observed that the rule was not directed towards intra-Community trade, that it did not preclude traders other than pharmacists from advertising such goods, and that it applied evenly as between all traders. Although the rule might have some impact on the overall volume of sales this was not enough to render it an MEQR for the purpose of Article 30. The ECJ also held that national provisions restricting the number of outlets for a given product, or imposing a licensing requirement, were outside Article 30 (now Article 28). This was either because the rule related to selling arrangements, or because the impact was too indirect and uncertain.[100]

While one can appreciate the ECJ's desire to limit Article 30 (now Article 28), the distinction drawn in *Keck* between rules that go to the nature of the product itself and those which relate to the selling arrangements for that product is problematic. The problem resides ultimately in the ambiguity about the meaning of the term 'selling arrangements'. This could connote only what may be termed *static selling arrangements*: rules relating to the hours at which shops may be open, the length of time for which people may work, or the type of premises in which certain goods may be sold. *Non-static or dynamic selling arrangements* include the ways in which a manufacturer chooses *to market this specific product*, through a certain form of advertising, free offers, and the like. The objection to taking all these latter rules out of Article 30 (now Article 28) is that they may relate much more closely to the very definition of the product itself. Legislation that restricted certain forms of advertising or sales-promotion might limit intra-Community trade, even if the rules were indistinctly applicable. It might force a producer to adopt sales-promotion or advertising schemes which differed as between States, or to discontinue a scheme which was thought to be particularly effective.[101] Non-static selling arrangements may form an integral aspect of the goods, in much the same way as do rules relating to composition, labelling, or presentation. Yet it is clear from *Keck* that the Court regarded some such rules as selling arrangements and outside this Article. Thus in paragraph 13 of its judgment it admitted that a rule prohibiting sales at a loss deprived traders of a method of sales-promotion, and hence reduced the volume of sales, and yet treated this rule as a selling arrangement which was outside Article 30 (now Article 28). While in *Hunermund*[102] and *Leclerc-Siplec*[103] a limited ban on advertising was characterized as a method of sales-promotion and held to be outside Article 30.

---

[99] Case C–292/92, *R. Hunermund v. Landesapothekerkammer Baden-Württemberg* [1993] ECR I–6787.

[100] Case C–387/93, *Banchero* [1996] 1 CMLR 829; Case C–379/92, *Peralta* [1994] ECR I–3453; Cases C–140–142/94, *Dip SpA v. Commune di Bassano del Grappa* [1995] ECR I–3257.

[101] Case 286/81, *Oosthoek's Uitgeversmaatschappij BV* [1982] ECR 4575. See also Case 382/87, *Buet v. Minstère Public* [1989] ECR 1235; Cases C–34–36/95, *Konsumentombudsmannen (KO) v. De Agostini (Svenska) Forlag AB and TV-Shop i Sverige AB* [1997] ECR I–3843.

[102] Case C–292/92, n. 99 above.

[103] Case 412/93, *Société d'Importation Edouard Leclerc-Siplec v. TFI Publicité SA* [1995] ECR I–179.

(e) *KECK* AND SELLING ARRANGEMENTS:
TWO JUDICIAL QUALIFICATIONS

The exclusion of selling arrangements from the ambit of Article 28 is however subject to two important qualifications in *Keck* itself.

First, *it is open to the ECJ to characterize certain rules which affect selling in some manner as part of the nature of the product itself, and hence within the ambit of Article 28.* This is exemplified by *Familiapress*.

Case C–368/95, Vereinigte Familiapress Zeitungsverlags- und Vertreibs GmbH v.
Heinrich Bauer Verlag
[1997] ECR I-3689

[Note ToA renumbering: Art. 30 is now Art. 28]

Familiapress, an Austrian newspaper publisher, sought to restrain HBV, a German publisher, from publishing in Austria a magazine containing crossword puzzles for which the winning readers would receive prizes. Austrian legislation prohibited publishers from including such prize competitions in their papers. Austria argued that its legislation was not caught by Article 30, since the national law related to a method of sales promotion, and was therefore, according to *Keck*, outside Article 30.

THE ECJ

11. The Court finds that, even though the relevant national legislation is directed against a method of sales promotion, in this case it bears on the actual content of the products, in so far as the competitions in question form an integral part of the magazine in which they appear. As a result, the national legislation in question as applied to the facts of the case is not concerned with a selling arrangement within the meaning of the judgment in *Keck and Mithouard*.

12. Moreover, since it requires traders established in other Member States to alter the contents of the periodical, the prohibition at issue impairs access of the products concerned to the market of the Member State of importation and consequently hinders free movement of goods. It therefore constitutes in principle a measure having equivalent effect within the meaning of Article 30 of the Treaty.

In *Bluhme*[104] the ECJ followed *Familiapress* and held that a Danish rule prohibiting the keeping of certain bees on a particular island was not a selling arrangement, but concerned the intrinsic characteristics of the bees.

Secondly, *even if a rule is categorized as being about selling, it will still be within Article 28 (ex Article 30) if the rule has a differential impact, in law or fact, for domestic*

---

[104] See also Case C–67/97, *Bluhme*, n. 9 above, para. 21.

traders and importers. This is made clear in paragraph 16 of *Keck*, and is exemplified by the following cases.[105]

Cases C-34–36/95, Konsumentombudsmannen (KO) v. De Agostini (Svenska) Forlag AB and TV-Shop i Sverige AB [1997] ECR I-3843

[Note ToA renumbering: Arts. 30 and 36 are now Arts. 28 and 30]

The case was concerned with a Swedish ban on television advertising directed at children under 12 and a ban on commercials for skincare products. It was argued that this was in breach of Article 30, and hence could not be applied in relation to advertising broadcast from another Member State. The ECJ, following *Leclerc-Siplec*, characterized the Swedish law as one concerning selling arrangements. It then continued as follows.

THE ECJ

40. In . . . *Keck* . . . at paragraph 16, the Court held that national measures restricting or prohibiting certain selling arrangements are not covered by Article 30 . . . so long as they apply to all traders operating within the national territory and as long as they affect in the same manner, in law and fact, the marketing of domestic products and of those from other Member States.

41. The first condition is clearly fulfilled in the cases before the national court.

42. As regards the second condition, it cannot be excluded that an outright ban, applying in one Member State, of a type of promotion for a product which is lawfully sold there might have a greater impact on products from other Member States.

43. Although the efficacy of the various types of promotion is a question of fact to be determined in principle by the referring court, it is to be noted that . . . de Agostini stated that television advertising was the only effective form of promotion enabling it to penetrate the Swedish market since it had no other advertising methods for reaching children and their parents.

44. Consequently, an outright ban on advertising aimed at children less than 12 years of age and of misleading advertising . . . is not covered by Article 30 . . ., unless it can be shown that the ban does not affect in the same way, in fact and in law, the marketing of national products and of products from other Member States.

45. In the latter case, it is for the national court to determine whether the ban is necessary to satisfy overriding requirements of general public importance or one of the aims listed in Article 36 of the Treaty, if it is proportionate to that purpose and if those aims or requirements could not have been attained or fulfilled by measures less restrictive of intra-Community trade.

[105] P. Koutrakos, 'On Groceries, Alcohol and Olive Oil: More on Free Movement of Goods after *Keck*' (2001) 26 *ELRev.* 391

Case C-405/98, Konsumentombudsmannen (KO) v. Gourmet International Products AB (GIP)
[2001] ECR I-1795

[Note ToA renumbering: Art. 30 is now Art. 28]

The Swedish Consumer Ombudsman sought an injunction restraining GIP from placing advertisements for alcohol in magazines. Swedish law prohibited advertising of alcohol on radio and
television, and prohibited advertising of spirits, wines, and strong beer in periodicals other than
those distributed at the point of sale. The prohibition on advertising did not apply to periodicals
aimed at traders such as restaurateurs. GIP published a magazine containing advertisements for
alcohol. 90 per cent of the subscribers were traders, and 10 per cent were private individuals. GIP
argued that the advertising ban was contrary to, *inter alia*, Article 30. It contended that the
advertising ban had a greater effect on imported goods than on those produced in Sweden.

THE ECJ

18. It should be pointed out that, according to paragraph 17 of its judgment in *Keck and
Mithouard*, if national provisions restricting or prohibiting selling arrangements are to avoid being
caught by Article 30 of the Treaty, they must not be of such a kind to prevent access to the market
by products from another state or to impede access any more than they impede the access of
domestic products.

19. The Court has also held, in paragraph 42 of . . . *De Agostini* . . . that it cannot be excluded
that an outright prohibition, applying in one Member State, of a type of product which is lawfully
sold there might have a greater impact on products from other Member States.

20. It is apparent that a prohibition on advertising . . . not only prohibits a form of marketing a
product but in reality prohibits producers and importers from directing any advertising messages
at consumers, with a few insignificant exceptions.

21. Even without its being necessary to carry out a precise analysis of the facts characteristic
of the Swedish situation, which it is for the national court to do, the Court is able to conclude that,
in the case of products like alcoholic beverages, the consumption of which is linked to traditional
social practices and to local habits and customs, a prohibition of all advertisements in the
press, on the radio and on television, the direct mailing of unsolicited material or the placing of
posters on the public highway is liable to impede access to the market by products from other
Member States more than it impedes access by domestic products, with which consumers are
instantly more familiar.

. . .

25. A prohibition on advertising such as that in issue . . . must therefore be regarded as
affecting the marketing of products from other Member States more heavily than the marketing
of domestic products and as therefore constituting an obstacle to trade between Member States
caught by Article 30 of the Treaty.

In *de Agostini* and *Gourmet* the relevant advertising ban was total. However the ECJ
has also brought cases which impeded market access within Article 28. In *Franzen*
Swedish law required a licence for those, including importers, engaged in the making
of alcohol, or in wholesaling. This was held to infringe Article 28, since it imposed
additional costs on importers, and because most licences had been issued to Swedish

traders.[106] In *Heimdienst* the ECJ showed that it was willing to consider the proviso to paragraph 16 of *Keck* in relation to a selling arrangement that impeded, rather than prevented, access to the market.

Case C-254/98, Schutzverband gegen unlauteren Wettbewerb v. TK-Heimdienst Sass GmbH
[2000] ECR I-151

The case concerned an Austrian rule relating to bakers, butchers and grocers. They could make sales on rounds in a given administrative district only if they also traded from a permanent establishment in that district or an adjacent municipality where they offered for sale the same goods as they did on their rounds. The ECJ classified the rule as one relating to selling arrangements, since it specified the geographical areas in which such operators could sell their goods in this manner. The ECJ found that the legislation did have a differential impact on domestic traders and others. Local economic operators would be more likely to have a permanent establishment in the administrative district or an adjacent municipality, whereas others would have to set up such an establishment, thereby incurring additional costs.

THE ECJ

29. It follows that the application to all operators trading in the national territory of national legislation such as that in point in the main proceedings in fact impedes access to the market of the Member State of importation for products from other Member States more than it impedes access for domestic products (see to this effect . . . *Alpine Investments* . . .).

(f) JUDICIAL AND ACADEMIC OPINION CONCERNING *KECK*: EQUALITY AND MARKET ACCESS

Reaction to the *Keck* decision was not generally favourable.[107] While commentators acknowledged the problems in the pre-*Keck* case law, they were, none the less, critical of the ECJ. It was argued that *Keck* placed too much emphasis on factual and legal equality at the expense of market access. The approach in *Keck* was, as we have seen, to deny that rules relating to selling arrangements came within Article 30 (now Article 28), provided that such rules did not discriminate in law or fact between traders from different Member States. It was argued that this ignored the importance of market access: trading rules could be formally equal in the preceding sense, and still operate so as to inhibit market access. In so far as this might be so, it would, therefore, be misguided to exclude them from consideration under this Article. This line of argument has been advanced judicially and in the academic literature. They will be considered in turn.

[106] Case C-189/95, *Criminal Proceedings against Franzen* [1997] ECR I-5909.
[107] See, e.g., N. Reich, 'The "November Revolution" of the European Court of Justice: *Keck, Meng* and *Audi* Revisited' (1994) 31 *CMLRev.* 459; D. Chalmers, 'Repackaging the Internal Market—The Ramifications of the *Keck* Judgment' (1994) 19 *ELRev.* 385; L. Gormley, 'Reasoning Renounced? The Remarkable Judgment in *Keck & Mithouard*' [1994] *Euro. Bus. L. Rev.* 63; S. Weatherill, 'After *Keck*: Some Thoughts on how to Clarify the Clarification' (1996) 33 *CMLRev.* 885; Maduro, n. 4 above, 83–7; C. Barnard, 'Fitting the Remaining Pieces into the Goods and Persons Jigsaw?' (2001) 26 *ELRev.* 35.

The concern was voiced *judicially* by Advocate General Jacobs in *Leclerc-Siplec*.[108] The case concerned a prohibition on television advertising imposed by French law on the distribution sector, the purpose being to protect the regional press by forcing the sectors in question to advertise through that medium. He felt that advertising could play a very important part in breaking down barriers to inter-state trade, and was therefore unhappy that it should always be outside Article 30 (now Article 28). His preferred approach represented a subtle modification of the *Keck* formula. Advocate General Jacobs' starting point was that all undertakings engaged in legitimate economic activity should have unfettered access to the market. If there was a *substantial* restriction on that access then it should be caught by Article 30 (now Article 28). When the measure affected the goods themselves, as in *Cassis*-type cases, then it would be *presumed to have this* substantial impact. If, however, the contested measure affected selling arrangements and was not discriminatory, the substantiality of the impact would depend, *inter alia*, on: the range of goods affected, the nature of the restriction, whether the impact was direct or indirect, and the extent to which other selling arrangements were available. If there was no substantial impact, or the effect on trade was *de minimis*, then such measures would not be within Article 30 (now Article 28).[109] The ECJ however declined to follow the suggestions of the Advocate General and applied *Keck* in an unaltered way to the case. The approach suggested by Advocate General Jacobs has none the less influenced the ECJ in its more recent jurisprudence. The ECJ has, as seen from *de Agostini* and *Heimdienst,* been willing to consider market access more seriously. It has done so through consideration of whether the proviso to paragraph 16 of *Keck* should be applicable in these cases. It has considered in particular whether the selling rule could have the same factual impact for the importer. It was not fortuitous that Advocate General Jacobs wrote the Opinions in *de Agostini*[110] and *Gourmet International,*[111] and that the ECJ adopted much of his reasoning.

The *academic argument* for an approach based on market access was put forcefully by Weatherill.[112] He drew upon the reasoning of Advocate General Jacobs considered above, and on jurisprudence concerned with Articles 59 and 48 (now Articles 49 and 39).[113] Weatherill argued that the correct approach to Article 30 (now Article 28), and these other Treaty Articles was to focus upon market access, and not just factual and legal equality. The reason the applicants failed in *Keck* was that 'they were measures applying equally in law and in fact and exercising no direct impediment to the access to markets of a Member State'.[114] He proposed the following test.

---

[108] N. 103 above, paras. 38–45. There is an interesting analogy here with competition law which in effect treats certain types of cartel behaviour as unlawful in and of themselves, while other types of activity are subjected to a market analysis to determine whether they do impede competition: see Ch. 21 below.

[109] See also Jacobs AG in Case C–384/93, *Alpine Investments,* n. 76 above; Lenz AG in Case C–391/92, *Commission* v. *Greece* [1995] ECR I–1621, 1628–9.

[110] Cases C–34–36/95, *de Agostini* [1997] ECR I–3843, paras. 95–105.

[111] Case C–405/98, *Konsumentombudsmannen (KO)* v. *Gourmet International Products AB (GIP)* [2001] ECR I–1795.

[112] (1996) 33 *CMLRev.* 885.

[113] Case C–384/93, *Alpine Investments,* n. 76 above; Case C–415/93, *Union Royale Belge des Sociétés de Football Association ASBL* v. *Jean-Marc Bosman* [1995] ECR I–4921.

[114] N. 112 above, 895.

S. Weatherill, After Keck: Some Thoughts on how to Clarify the Clarification[115]

Measures introduced by authorities in a Member State which apply equally in law and in fact to all goods and services without reference to origin and which impose no direct or substantial hindrance to the access of imported goods or services to the market of that Member State escape the prohibition of Articles 30 and 59.[116]

[*Weatherill summarizes the argument in the following way*:]

Pre-*Keck*, the Court had lost sight of the link between Article 30 and internal market building by pushing it too far in the direction of general review of national market regulation disassociated from a need to show a hindrance to trading activities aimed at the realization of the internal market. The most notorious example was the 'Sunday Trading' saga. The subjection of *all* measures of national market regulation to supervision under Community law was beginning to damage the image and legitimacy of the European Court. *Keck* exploded the notion that there might be an individual 'right to trade' capable of vindication *via* EC internal market law, but *Keck* itself created a risk of toppling too far in the opposite direction, thereby imperilling the internal market, by focusing on factual and legal equality of application to the exclusion of questions of market access and obstruction to the construction of the cross-border commercial strategies. The principal significance of the post-*Keck* adjustment is the welcome confirmation that internal market law is not confined to supervision of measures that are legally or factually unequal in application. . . .

In *Keck*, *Leclerc-Siplec* and other similar cases, the limit on commercial freedom could not be directly connected to any cross-border aspect of the activity. In *Alpine Investments*, by contrast, the cross-border aspect was of direct significance; so too in *Bosman*, whose access to employment in another state was directly affected by the rules.

. . . The injection of an adequate cross-border element enables a claim not simply to an equality right, but instead to the dynamic protection of Community law on free movement, subject only to the capacity of the regulator to show justification for the restrictions. . . .

The academic argument in favour of market access was reinforced by Barnard who, like Weatherill, drew on case law from persons and services, as well as goods.

C. Barnard, Fitting the Remaining Pieces into the Goods and Persons Jigsaw?[117]

[A]n approach based on the access to the market provides us with a more sophisticated framework for analysing the goods and persons case law. . . . [T]his is the approach advocated by Advocate General Jacobs in *Leclerc*. Non-discriminatory measures which directly and substantially impede access to the market (including the extreme case of preventing access to the market altogether) breach the Treaty provision unless they can be justified under one of the public interest grounds or the express derogations and are proportionate (*Schindler*, *Alpine* and *Bosman*). In the case of non-discriminatory measures which do not substantially hinder access to the market the Court will say either that the impediment is too uncertain and remote and so does not breach the Treaty provision at all (*Graf*, *Krantz*), or that the measure has no effect whatsoever on

---

[115] *Ibid.*, 885, 896–7, 904–6. Italics in the original.   [116] Now Arts. 28 and 49.
[117] (2001) 26 *ELRev.* 35, 52.

inter-state trade and so is not caught by EC law at all—the outcome is the same. This means that national restrictions on, for example, planning or the green belt, which were introduced for a variety of environmental and social reasons not directly concerned with inter-state trade, can be dealt with adequately. They are not 'certain selling arrangements' in the formal sense, but they are not discriminatory and they do not substantially hinder access to the market. Similarly, national restrictions on the opening hours of shops do not substantially hinder access to the market but merely curtail the exercise of that freedom. However extreme limits on opening hours may well substantially hinder access to the market and so should breach Article 28 and need to be justified.

(g) *KECK*, ARTICLE 28, AND MARKET ACCESS: MEANING AND APPLICATION

Market access may well be the idea underlying the jurisprudence on free movement. It is, however, necessary to clarify the meaning and application of this concept.

First, it is important to be clear about the *meaning accorded to market access in the ECJ's case law on goods*. In *Keck* itself prevention or impediment to market access appeared to be simply the consequence of a national rule that applied differentially as between domestic traders and importers: paragraphs 16 and 17. The focus in the post-*Keck* case law was on the existence of such factual or legal differentiation. The ECJ has more recently subtly shifted its position, according greater status to market access in its own right. In *Gourmet International*[118] the ECJ stated that selling arrangements would be outside Article 30 (now Article 28) only if they did not prevent access to the market by imported products *or* impede access by imports more than they impeded access by domestic products.

Secondly, it is equally important to understand the *general meaning of market access*. Market access can be viewed from the perspective of both the producer and the consumer of the goods. From the perspective of the producer, free movement facilitates sales of goods into different national markets, with the primary objective of challenging existing producers in the country of import and the secondary objective of allowing any economies of scale to be reaped. Market access is a means to an end, the end being to maximize sales/profits for the individual producer, and to enhance the optimal allocation of resources for the Community as a whole. From the perspective of the consumer, free movement increases choice. If Germans are given the option of drinking Dutch beer then they may well prefer it to the domestic product.

Thirdly, *it is doubtful whether any rigid distinction can be drawn between dynamic and static selling arrangements so far as market access is concerned*. The market-access approach is normally thought to apply to dynamic selling arrangements. There is, however, a reluctance to apply the same reasoning to static selling arrangements, in the sense of shop hours, locations, and the like. Thus, Weatherill contends that the *Sunday Trading* cases could be explained on the ground that there was no obstruction to the realization of economies of scale or wider consumer choice in an integrating market.[119] The rationale appears to be that consumer choice was not constrained

---

[118] Case C–405/98, *Gourmet International*, n. 111 above, para. 18.
[119] Weatherill, n. 107 above, 895–6.

because consumers could still buy the relevant goods, albeit only at limited times or at limited locations. If, however, *limitations* on the mode of marketing/advertising are to be regarded as going to market access, then why should this not also be so in terms of *limitations* on points of sale? The success of the producer in penetrating new markets may be affected as much by limitations on where and when goods can be sold as by constraints on marketing.[120] It may be argued that restrictions on where and when goods can be sold would not have a direct and substantial impact on market access. This is, however, contingent on the factual circumstances of the particular case. It cannot be regarded as an *a priori* proposition. The distinction between rules going to access and those that merely affect the volume of sales is no more readily sustainable. A producer perceives rules that limit advertising as detrimental *because* they will lead to a reduction in sales. There is no difference between a rule prohibiting certain forms of marketing or advertising, with, say, a diminution in sales of 30 per cent, and a rule which limits the number or operating hours of shops, leading to the same sales reduction. Both rules in essence affect the volume of sales and penetration of the new market.

Finally, *we must be cognizant of the difficulties of applying a test based on direct and substantial impact of access to the market.* Proponents of the test recognize that this can be difficult to estimate.[121] A court may have to take into account the range of goods affected, the existence or not of alternative selling arrangements, and the nature of the restriction itself. This will not be an easy task for the ECJ. It will be even more difficult for national courts,[122] and they will normally have this task. However, the ECJ may provide guidance to the national court, as in *Agostini*,[123] or it may go further and state there has been an impediment to market access, as in *Gourmet International.*[124] It is true that the ECJ, CFI, and national courts have to face not dissimilar tasks in the context of competition law, when deciding whether an agreement has an effect on competition. There are, however, real differences between the two areas. In competition law the backdrop to the inquiry is a developed micro-economic theory about cartels which deviate from perfect or even imperfect competition; in free movement of goods there is no ready consensus on what does and does not come within the meaning of market access. In competition law private agreements are at stake; in free movement it is national regulations.

(h) SUMMARY AND CHOICES

i. The case law prior to *Keck* exemplified the difficulties in defining the outer boundaries of Article 30 (now Article 28). The ECJ in its pre-*Keck* jurisprudence was being asked to apply this Article to an ever-wider range of rules,

---

[120] This was the argument made, unsuccessfully, in Cases C–418–421, 460–462, & 464/93, 9–11, 14–15, 23–24, & 332/94, *Semeraro*, n. 90 above.

[121] Weatherill, n. 107 above, 898–901; Barnard, n. 117 above, 55–6.

[122] National courts are intended to apply Art. 28 and hence to disapply conflicting national law of their own initiative, subject always to the possibility of an Art. 177 (now Art. 234) reference: Case C–358/95, *Tommaso Morellato v. Unità Sanitairia Locale (USL) No. 11 di Pordenone* [1997] ECR I–1431.

[123] Cases C–34–36/95, n. 101 above.

[124] Case C–405/98, n. 111 above.

the effect of which on trade was marginal. Small wonder that the Court in *Keck* felt that the time was ripe for a reappraisal of the outer limits of this Article. We have seen, however, that *Keck* itself has been criticized for being overly formalistic, and for employing a distinction between rules which go to the characteristics of the product and those which go to selling arrangements, which is unsatisfactory. It is this dissatisfaction which has led to the call to focus on market access. There are in essence three choices concerning the approach to Article 28.

ii. The first choice is to *use prevention or direct and substantial hindrance of access to the market as the general criterion for the applicability of Article 28.* This would be beneficial in focusing attention on a key policy reason underlying free movement of goods, services, and persons. The need to consider whether there has been some substantial restriction of market access does, however, inevitably entail costs, both for the courts which have to apply the test and for private parties who may be uncertain about the legality of their planned conduct. This is all the more so given the very uncertainty about what market access itself entails in this context.

iii. The second choice is *for a test based on substantial hindrance to market access, subject to presumptions based on the type of case.* This was the approach of Advocate General Jacobs in *Leclerc-Siplec*.[125] When the measure affected the goods themselves, as in *Cassis*-type cases, then it would be presumed to have this substantial impact. If, however, the contested measure affected selling arrangements and was not discriminatory, the substantiality of the impact would depend on factors such as the range of goods affected, the nature of the restriction, whether the impact was direct or indirect, and the extent to which other selling arrangements were available. It would on this view still be necessary to distinguish between cases concerning product characteristics and those concerning selling arrangements.

iv. The third choice *would be to persist with the test in Keck as developed by later case law.* Selling arrangements are presumptively outside Article 28, but can be brought within it either by being reclassified as concerned with product characteristics or because they have a differential application in law or fact. The ECJ in *Keck* intended to draw a more formal line as to the types of rule caught by Article 28. It was hoped that public and private costs would thereby be reduced, and that there would be clearer guidance on the limits of legitimate trading activity. However the more the ECJ reclassifies cases, the more closely it inquires into whether a selling arrangement has a differential impact, and the more it places direct emphasis on market access, the less certain is the outcome in any particular case. The reduction in public and private costs thereby diminishes, and the guidance on the legitimate limits of trading activity becomes less clear.

v. The indications are that the ECJ is in reality moving away from the third test, and towards the second.

---

[125] N. 103 above.

10. INDISTINCTLY APPLICABLE RULES: THE MANDATORY REQUIREMENTS

(a) THE RATIONALE FOR THE MANDATORY REQUIREMENTS

The rationale for the mandatory requirements is that *many rules which regulate trade are also capable of restricting trade, yet some of these rules serve objectively justifiable purposes.* If a country stipulates that goods should be packed in a particular manner, or that they should have a prescribed content, then it will be more difficult for importers of such goods to compete. The production and marketing processes of importers will not have been geared up to meet such criteria, and the goods produced will already have had to comply with any rules prescribed by the country of origin. The fact that many rules which regulate trade may also inhibit it means that it would be inappropriate to render *all* such rules illegal *per se.* These trade rules can serve justifiable purposes, as exemplified by the list of mandatory requirements in the *Cassis* case. The 'list' of mandatory requirements mentioned in *Cassis* is sometimes referred to as the rule of reason, drawing upon the earlier hint in *Dassonville* that, in the absence of Community measures on an issue, reasonable trade rules would be accepted in certain circumstances. A similar approach is evident in other areas of Community law, such as those dealing with the freedom to provide services and of establishment. National rules limiting such freedoms have been upheld where they serve an objectively justifiable goal.[126] Thus Advocate General Verloren van Themaat[127] regarded the rule of reason as a general principle of interpretation designed to mitigate the effects of strict prohibitions laid down in the Treaty provisions on free movement.[128]

(b) THE RELATIONSHIP BETWEEN THE MANDATORY REQUIREMENTS AND ARTICLE 30: THE CASES

The traditional view has been that the *Cassis* mandatory requirements are separate from the justifications under Article 30 (ex article 36). The ECJ held that the *Cassis* exceptions could only be used only in respect of rules that were not discriminatory.[129] The *Cassis* list of mandatory requirements includes matters, such as the protection of consumers and the fairness of commercial transactions, which are not mentioned within Article 30 (ex Article 36). The *Cassis* list is also not exhaustive, and the Court has added other objective justifications which might have been difficult to fit within the framework of Article 30 (ex Article 36). The ECJ's willingness to create a broader category of justifications for indistinctly applicable rules is also explicable because discriminatory rules strike at the very heart of what the Community is intended to

---

126 See Ch. 18 below.   127 Case 286 /81, *Oosthoek*, n. 101 above.
128 See also the discussion of the rule of reason in competition law, in Ch. 21 below.
129 Case 788/79, n. 69 above, para. 6; Case 113/80, n. 16 above, paras. 5–8.

abolish. It is unsurprising that they are viewed with suspicion by the Court, and that any possible justifications should be narrowly confined. The extension of Article 28 (ex article 30) to catch indistinctly applicable rules was a bold move by the ECJ. Exceptions or defences were therefore required, and the Court was willing to cast these in broader terms than Article 36 (now Article 30) to reflect the differences between discriminatory and non-discriminatory rules.

The distinction between Article 30 (ex Article 36), and the mandatory requirements in *Cassis* has however come under increasing strain in recent years. This is so for three reasons.

First, there has, as we have seen, been discussion about whether the list in Article 30 (ex Article 36) should be regarded as exhaustive.[130] It has been argued that there might be instances where, for example, environmental considerations should be able to be pleaded even in cases of discrimination.

Secondly, the distinction has also become less tenable because of the difficulty of distinguishing between cases involving discrimination and those concerned with indistinctly applicable rules. This distinction is relatively easy to draw in the paradigm cases of direct discrimination as compared to a *Cassis*-type indistinctly applicable rule. It can be more difficult to apply in other cases. The ECJ may well treat a case as coming within the *Cassis* category because it wishes to allow the state to avail itself of one of the mandatory requirements, even though, as in *Aher-Waggon*,[131] the measure appears to be discriminatory or distinctly applicable.

Thirdly, the reasoning in *Keck* has contributed to confusion in this respect. Selling arrangements are outside Article 28 so long as they apply to all traders in the national territory, and so long as they affect in the same manner, in law and fact, the marketing of domestic products and those from Member States. Much of the attention in later cases has focused on the possible differential impact of national selling arrangements. If this is proven then Article 28 is applicable, subject to possible justifications raised by the State. In some instances it will not matter whether the justification is considered within the mandatory requirements, or under Article 30 (ex Article 36), since it is covered by both, as in the case of public health.[132] In other instances it will be of relevance, since the alleged justification falls within only the *Cassis* list, and not Article 30. The ECJ has equivocated in some such cases. Thus in *de Agostini*[133] the ECJ held that the advertising ban might be justified to satisfy one of the mandatory requirements *or* one of the aims listed in Article 30 (ex Article 36). Consumer protection and fair trading are in the former list, but not the latter.

---

[130] See above, 634–5.
[131] See Jacobs AG in Case C–379/98, *PreussenElektra*, n. 55 above, para. 227, commenting in this respect on Case C–389/96, *Aher-Waggon*, n. 56 above.
[132] See, e.g., Case C–189/95, *Franzen*, n. 106 above; Case C–405/98, *Gourmet International*, n. 111 above.
[133] Cases C–34–36/95, n. 62 above, paras. 45–47.

(c) THE RELATIONSHIP BETWEEN THE MANDATORY REQUIREMENTS AND ARTICLE 30: PRINCIPLES

There is much to be said for simplification in this area. It would be best for the same justifications to be available in principle, irrespective of whether the measure is discriminatory or indistinctly applicable. When the justifications are applied to the facts it should then be of relevance whether the national rule was discriminatory or not. Greater justification should be required for discriminatory measures.

It might be argued that this is not possible, given the present wording of Article 30 (ex Article 36). This objection is not convincing. There is no reason why phrases within Article 30, such as protection of the health and life of humans, could not be interpreted to include matters such as consumer protection and the environment. The ECJ has construed other Treaty provisions in a far more expansive manner when it wished to do so. The legitimacy of the ECJ construing Article 30 in this way is enhanced by the ECJ's creative endeavour within *Cassis* itself. If it is legitimate for the ECJ to create, as it did, an open-ended list of mandatory exceptions, not mentioned in the Treaty at all, then why would it not be legitimate for the ECJ to read Article 30 to include matters such as the environment or consumer protection?

(d) THE MANDATORY REQUIREMENTS: CONSUMER PROTECTION

Case 178/84, Commission v. Germany
[1987] ECR 1227

German law prohibited the marketing of beer which was lawfully manufactured in another Member State unless it complied with sections 9 and 10 of the Biersteuergesetz (Beer Duty Act 1952). Under this law only drinks which complied with the German Act could be sold as '*Bier*', and this meant that the term could be used only in relation to those drinks which were made from barley, hops, yeast, and water. The German Government argued that the reservation of the term '*Bier*' to beverages made only from the substances mentioned in the German legislation was necessary to protect consumers who associated the term '*Bier*' with beverages made from these ingredients. It also argued that its legislation was not protectionist in aim, in that any trader who made beer from such ingredients could market it freely in Germany. The ECJ cited the principles from *Dassonville* and *Cassis*; it found that the German rule did constitute an impediment to trade and then proceeded to consider whether the rule was necessary to protect consumers.

THE ECJ

31. The German Government's argument that section 10 of the Biersteuergesetz is essential in order to protect German consumers because, in their minds, the designation 'Bier' is inseparably linked to the beverage manufactured solely from the ingredients laid down in section 9 . . . must be rejected.

32. Firstly, consumers' conceptions which vary from one Member State to the other are also likely to evolve in the course of time within a Member State. The establishment of the Common

Market is, it should be added, one of the factors that may play a major contributory role in that development. Whereas rules protecting consumers against misleading practices enable such a development to be taken into account, legislation of the kind contained in section 10 . . . prevents it from taking place. As the Court has already held in another context (Case 170/78, *Commission v. United Kingdom*), the legislation of a Member State must not 'crystallize given consumer habits so as to consolidate an advantage acquired by national industries concerned to comply with them'.

33. Secondly, in the other Member States of the Community the designations corresponding to the German designation 'Bier' are generic designations for a fermented beverage manufactured from barley, whether malted barley on its own or with the addition of rice or maize. The same approach is taken in Community law as can be seen from heading 22.03 of the Common Customs Tariff. The German legislature itself utilises the designation 'Bier' in that way in section 9(7) and (8) of the Biersteuergesetz in order to refer to beverages not complying with the manufacturing rules laid down in section 9(1) and (2).

34. The German designation 'Bier' and its equivalents in the languages of the other Member States may therefore not be restricted to beers manufactured in accordance with the rules in force in the Federal Republic of Germany.

35. It is admittedly legitimate to seek to enable consumers who attribute specific qualities to beers manufactured from particular raw materials to make their choice in the light of that consideration. However, as the Court has already emphasised (Case 193/80, *Commission v. Italy*) that possibility may be ensured by means which do not prevent the importation of products which have been lawfully manufactured and marketed in other Member States and, in particular, 'by the compulsory affixing of suitable labels giving the nature of the product sold'. By indicating the raw materials utilised in the manufacture of beer 'such a course would enable the consumer to make his choice in full knowledge of the facts and would guarantee transparency in trading and in offers to the public'. It must be added that such a system of mandatory consumer information must not entail negative assessments for beers not complying with the requirements of section 9 of the Biersteuergesetz.

The ECJ therefore held the German law to be in breach of Article 30 (now Article 28). The way in which it dealt with the argument concerning consumer protection is instructive. The argument was closely scrutinized to determine whether it really 'worked' on the facts of the case. The ECJ then assessed whether the interests of consumers could be safeguarded by less restrictive means: paragraph 35.

The same approach is apparent in other cases.[134] The *De Kikvorsch* case[135] shows that arguments about beer cut both ways. Dutch law contained indistinctly applicable rules that impeded the import of beer from Germany, because German beer exceeded the level of acidity permitted by Dutch law. The purpose was to protect the 'sour' taste of beer to which the Dutch were accustomed. The ECJ dismissed the argument that the Dutch rule could be justified on the ground of consumer protection. Consumers should not be prevented from trying beers brewed according to a different tradition,

---

[134] See, e.g., Case 261/81, *Rau*, n. 70 above; Case C–470/93, *Verein gegen Unwesen in Handel und Gewerbe Köln eV v. Mars GmbH* [1995] ECR I–1923.

[135] Case 94/82, *De Kikvorsch Groothandel-Import-Export BV* [1983] ECR 947.

and proper labelling could alert them that the beer was different from that to which they were accustomed.[136] The import of German beer was also impeded by a Dutch law that prohibited the printing on the label of the original wort strength of the beer. Dutch law required the strength of the beer to be indicated on the bottle in terms of alcohol percentages, and the Dutch felt that the inclusion of references to the wort strength would confuse consumers. The ECJ accepted that national rules limiting the amount of information available to consumers might be defensible to prevent consumers from being misled, but it had to be shown that there really was a risk of consumer confusion. This was a matter for the national courts to determine.[137] A similar approach is evident in *Neeltje*.[138] The ECJ held that, while national legislation concerning the hallmarking of precious metals was in principle defensible in terms of consumer protection, a particular State had to accept the method of hallmarking in another State. This was so even if it differed in detail, provided that it was intelligible to consumers of the importing State.

It is apparent from the cases considered above that the ECJ has often rejected justifications based on consumer protection for rules relating to the content of goods, by stating that adequate labelling requirements can achieve the desired national aims with less impact on intra-Community trade. However, even labelling requirements themselves may not escape Article 28 (ex Article 30). Thus in *Fietje*[139] the ECJ held that the obligation to use a certain name on a label could make it more difficult to market goods coming from other Member States. Such a rule would therefore have to be justified on the ground of consumer protection. Labelling requirements which demanded that the purchaser was provided with sufficient information on the nature of the product, in order to prevent confusion with similar products, could, said the Court, be justified, even if the effect was to make it necessary to alter the labels of some imported goods.[140] However, such protection would not be necessary or justifiable if the details given on the original labels of the goods contained the same information as required by the State of import, and that information was just as capable of being understood by consumers. Whether there was such equivalence was for the national court to determine.[141] Similarly in the *Clinique* case[142] the ECJ held that a German law forbidding the use of the name 'Clinique' on cosmetic products imported from other States was caught. The ECJ rejected the argument that the rule was necessary to protect consumers from being misled into believing that the product had medicinal properties. The goods were sold only in perfumeries and cosmetic departments of stores, not in pharmacies, and there was no indication of consumer confusion in the countries where the goods were marketed under the name 'Clinique'.

---

[136] *Ibid.*, para. 8.   [137] *Ibid.*, para. 12.
[138] Case C–293/93, *Ludomira Neeltje v. Barbara Houtwipper* [1994] ECR I–429.
[139] Case 27/80, *Fietje* [1980] ECR 3839.   [140] *Ibid.*, para. 11.
[141] *Ibid.*, para. 12. See also Case 76/86, *Commission v. Germany* [1989] ECR 1021.
[142] Case C–315/92, *Verband Sozialer Wettbewerb eV v. Clinique Laboratoires SNC* [1994] ECR I–317.

(e) THE MANDATORY REQUIREMENTS: FAIRNESS OF COMMERCIAL TRANSACTIONS

There is clearly an overlap between consumer protection and the fairness of commercial transactions. This particular mandatory requirement has been used to justify national rules that seek to prevent unfair marketing practices, such as the selling of imported goods which constitute precise imitations of familiar domestic goods. It seems, however, that in order to be justified on this ground the national rule must not prohibit the marketing of goods which have been made according to fair and traditional practices in State A, merely because they are similar to goods which have been made in State B.[143]

(f) THE MANDATORY REQUIREMENTS: PUBLIC HEALTH

We have already noted that the traditional view was that only indistinctly applicable rules could take advantage of the mandatory requirements. However, the ECJ has, on occasion, not been too concerned about whether it treats a justification within Article 36 (now Article 30) or within the list of mandatory requirements, *provided* that the justification pleaded by the State comes within both lists. This may occur particularly where it is unclear whether the impugned rule is discriminatory or not. Public health finds a place both in the list of *Cassis* mandatory requirements and in Article 36 (now Article 30). The following extract from the *German Beer* case provides an apt example of this:[144]

Case 178/84, Commission v. Germany
[1987] ECR 1227

[Note ToA renumbering: Arts. 36 and 169 are now Arts. 30 and 226]

A second rule of German law was challenged in the *German Beer* case which was discussed above. Under the German Foodstuffs Act 1974 there was an absolute ban on the marketing of beer which contained additives. In essence this Act prohibited non-natural additives on public-health grounds. The Commission in an Article 169 action challenged this rule. It was accepted that the German rule did constitute a barrier to the import of beer lawfully marketed in other States which contained additives. The question before the ECJ was whether the rule could come within Article 36 on public-health grounds.

THE ECJ

41. The Court has consistently held (in particular in Case 174/82, *Criminal Proceedings Against Sandoz BV*) that 'in so far as there are uncertainties at the present state of scientific

---

[143] Case 58/80, *Dansk Supermarked* v. *Imerco* [1981] ECR 181; Case 16/83, *Karl Prantl* [1984] ECR 1299.
[144] See also Case 53/80, *Eyssen*, n. 46 above; Case 97/83, *Criminal Proceedings against Melkunie BV* [1984] ECR 2367.

research it is for the Member States, in the absence of harmonization, to decide what degree of protection of the health and life of humans they intend to assure, having regard to the requirements of the free movement of goods within the Community.'

42. As may also be seen from the decision of the Court (and especially the *Sandoz* case, cited above, in Case 247/84, *Motte*, and in Case 308/84, *Ministère Public* v. *Muller*), in such circumstances Community law does not preclude the adoption by Member States of legislation whereby the use of additives is subjected to prior authorisation granted by a measure of general application for specific additives, in respect of all products, for certain products only or for certain uses. Such legislation meets a genuine need of health policy, namely that of restricting the uncontrolled consumption of food additives.

43. However, the application to imported products of prohibitions on marketing products containing additives which are authorised in the Member State of production but prohibited in the Member State of importation is permissible only in so far as it complies with the requirements of Article 36 of the Treaty as it has been interpreted by the Court.

44. It must be borne in mind, in the first place, that in its judgments in *Sandoz, Motte* and *Muller*, the Court inferred from the principle of proportionality underlying the last sentence of Article 36 of the Treaty that prohibitions on the marketing of products containing additives authorised in the Member State of production but prohibited in the Member State of importation must be restricted to what is actually necessary to secure the protection of public health. The Court also concluded that the use of a specific additive which is authorised in another Member State must be authorised in the case of a product imported from that Member State where, in view, on the one hand, of the findings of international scientific research, and in particular the work of the Community's Scientific Committee for Food, the Codex Alimentarius Committee of the Food and Agriculture Organisation of the United Nations (FAO) and the World Health Organisation, and, on the other, of the eating habits prevailing in the importing Member State, the additive in question does not present a risk to public health and meets a real need, especially a technical one.

45. Secondly, it should be remembered that, as the Court held in *Muller*, by virtue of the principle of proportionality, traders must also be able to apply, under a procedure which is easily accessible to them and can be concluded within a reasonable time, for the use of specific additives to be authorised by a measure of general application.

[*The Court then pointed out that the German rule prohibited all additives; that there was no procedure whereby traders could obtain authorization for a specific additive; and that additives were permitted by German law in beverages other than beer. The German Government then argued that such additives would not be needed in the manufacture of beer if it were made in accordance with section 9 of the Biersteuergesetz. The ECJ responded as follows:*]

51. It must be emphasised that the mere reference to the fact that beer can be manufactured without additives if it is made from only the raw materials prescribed in the Federal Republic of Germany does not suffice to preclude the possibility that some additives may meet a technological need. Such an interpretation of the concept of technological need, which results in favouring national production methods, constitutes a disguised means of restricting trade between Member States.

52. The concept of technological need must be assessed in the light of the raw materials utilised and bearing in mind the assessment made by the authorities of the Member States where the product was lawfully manufactured and marketed. Account must also be taken of the findings of international scientific research and in particular the work of the Community's Scientific Committee for Food, the Codex Alimentarius Committee of the FAO and the World Health Organisation.

53. Consequently, in so far as the German rules on additives in beer entail a general ban on additives, their application to beers imported from other Member States is contrary to the requirements of Community law as laid down in the case law of the Court, since that prohibition is contrary to the principle of proportionality and is therefore not covered by Article 36 of the EEC Treaty.

(g) OTHER MANDATORY REQUIREMENTS

The list of mandatory requirements in *Cassis* is not exhaustive. This is evident from the case itself, in which the ECJ stated that the mandatory requirements included *in particular* those mentioned in the judgment.[145] The non-exhaustive character of the *Cassis* list has been confirmed by later cases. It can include the protection of the environment.

Case 302/86, Commission v. Denmark
[1988] ECR 4607

Danish law required that containers for beer and soft drinks should be returnable and that a certain proportion should be re-usable. A national environmental agency had to approve containers to ensure compliance with these criteria. There was also a deposit-and-return system for empty containers. The Danish government argued that the rule was justified by a mandatory requirement related to the protection of the environment.

THE ECJ

8. The Court has already held in . . . Case 240/83, *Procureur de la République* v. *Association de Défense des Brûleurs d'Huiles Usagées* . . . that the protection of the environment is 'one of the Community's essential objectives', which may as such justify certain limitations of the principle of free movement of goods. That view is moreover confirmed by the Single European Act.

9. In view of the foregoing, it must therefore be stated that the protection of the environment is a mandatory requirement which may limit the application of Article 30 of the Treaty.
[*The Commission argued that the Danish laws were disproportionate.*]

12. It is therefore necessary to examine whether all the restrictions which the contested rules impose on the free movement of goods are necessary to achieve the objectives pursued by those rules.

13. First of all, as regards the obligation to establish a deposit-and-return system for empty containers, it must be observed that this requirement is an indispensable element of a system intended to ensure the re-use of containers and therefore appears necessary to achieve the aims pursued by the contested rules. That being so, the restrictions which it imposes on the free movement of goods cannot be regarded as disproportionate.

14. Next it is necessary to consider the requirement that producers and importers must use only containers approved by the National Agency for the Protection of the Environment.
[*The Danish Government argued that the number of approved containers had to be limited*

---

145 [1979] ECR 649, para. 8.

because otherwise retailers would not take part in the system. This meant that a foreign producer might have to manufacture a type of container already approved, with consequent increases in costs. To overcome this problem the Danish law was amended to allow a producer to market up to 3,000 hectolitres a year in non-approved containers, provided that a deposit-and-return system was established. The Commission argued that the limit of 3,000 hectolitres was unnecessary to achieve the objectives of the scheme.]

20. It is undoubtedly true that the existing system for returning approved containers ensures a maximum rate of re-use and therefore a very considerable degree of protection of the environment since empty containers can be returned to any retailer of beverages. Non-approved containers, on the other hand, can be returned only to the retailer who sold the beverages, since it is impossible to set up such a comprehensive system for those containers as well.

21. Nevertheless, the system for returning non-approved containers is capable of protecting the environment and, as far as imports are concerned, affects only limited quantities of beverages compared with the quantity of beverages consumed in Denmark owing to the restrictive effect which the requirement that containers should be returnable has on imports. In those circumstances, a restriction of the quantity of products which may be marketed by importers is disproportionate to the objective pursued.

22. It must therefore be held that by restricting . . . the quantity of beer and soft drinks which may be marketed by a single producer in non-approved containers to 3,000 hectolitres a year, the Kingdom of Denmark has failed, as regards imports of those products from other Member States, to fulfil its obligations under Article 30 of the EEC Treaty.

23. The remainder of the application must be dismissed.

It is clear that in the absence of Community harmonization measures national provisions on environmental protection can constitute a further mandatory requirement to be added to the *Cassis* list.[146]

Environmental protection is not the only new addition to this catalogue. In *Familiapress*[147] the ECJ recognized pluralism of the press as a value that could legitimate a national measure which was in breach of Article 30 (now Article 28). The offering of prizes for games in magazines could drive out smaller papers which could not afford to make such offers. In *Cinéthèque*[148] the ECJ was willing to recognize that the fostering of certain forms of art could constitute a justifiable objective within the context of Community law. While in *Torfaen*[149] it accepted that rules governing the opening hours of premises pursued a justifiable aim, in that such rules reflected certain social and political choices which might differ between Member States.[150]

---

[146] See also Case C–379/98, *PreussenElektra*, n. 55 above.

[147] Case C–368/95, *Vereinigte Familiapress Zeitungsverlags- und vertriebs GmbH v. Heinrich Bauer Verlag* [1997] ECR I–368.

[148] Cases 60 and 61/84, [1985] ECR 2605.

[149] Case 145/88, [1989] ECR 3851.

[150] While *Cinéthèque* and *Torfaen* would probably now fall outside Art. 28 (ex Art. 30), the recognition of these grounds of objective justification could be of relevance in cases which do fall within the province of the Art. even after *Keck*.

(h) THE RELATIONSHIP BETWEEN THE MANDATORY REQUIREMENTS AND HARMONIZATION

A Community harmonization measure may render it impossible for a state to have recourse to the mandatory requirements as a defence to a breach of Article 28.[151] Whether it has this effect will depend upon whether the measure is directed at total or only a minimum harmonization. The previous discussion of this issue is applicable here.[152]

(i) SUMMARY

i. The ECJ was creative in *Cassis* when it set out the mandatory requirements, and it has shown similar flexibility since then, by adding new defences to the list. The Court has, not surprisingly, interpreted the requirements strictly, obliging Member States to satisfy it that a defence is really warranted in the circumstances. There are however two causes for concern.

ii. First, the dividing line between the mandatory requirements and Article 30 (ex Article 36) is problematic. It has been argued that the same public interest defences should be available irrespective of whether the measure is discriminatory or not. This would be of relevance in the application of the mandatory requirement to the facts of the particular case.

iii. Secondly, the decision on whether the mandatory requirements provide a defence for the Member State can involve difficult balancing exercises for the ECJ, and for the national courts, to which many such issues are delegated by the ECJ. This issue will be examined more fully in the following section.

11. BROADER PERSPECTIVES ON *CASSIS*

(a) THE ADVANTAGES OF THE ECJ'S JURISPRUDENCE AND THE COMMISSION'S RESPONSE TO *CASSIS*

The Court's judgment in *Cassis* was, in part, a response to the difficulties faced by the Commission in securing acceptance by the Member States of harmonization measures. These measures were technically complex, and the Member States often disagreed about their content. The ECJ's judgment in *Cassis* had the effect, as we have seen, of rendering indistinctly applicable rules which impeded trade incompatible with Article 30 (now Article 28), unless they could be saved by one of the mandatory requirements. This was so even in the absence of relevant harmonization provisions. *Cassis* therefore fostered single-market integration, and obviated the need for many Community harmonization provisions.

It was argued at the beginning of this Chapter that the ECJ's jurisprudence in this

---

[151] See, e.g., Case C–383/97, *Criminal Proceedings against Van der Laan* [1999] ECR I–731.
[152] See above, 635–6.

area could not be viewed in isolation. It had an impact upon how the other Community institutions perceived their role. The Commission was not slow to respond to the Court's initiative. It published a Communication setting out its interpretation of the *Cassis* decision, which also provided insights into how the Commission perceived its legislative role in this area.

Commission Communication 3 October 1980, [1980] OJ C256/2

Whereas Member States may, with respect to domestic products and in the absence of relevant Community provisions, regulate the terms on which such products are marketed, the case is different for products imported from other Member States.

Any product imported from another Member State must in principle be admitted to the territory of the importing Member State if it has been lawfully produced, that is, conforms to rules and processes of manufacture that are customarily and traditionally accepted in the exporting country, and marketed in the territory of the latter.

This principle implies that Member States, when drawing up commercial or technical rules liable to affect the free movement of goods, may not take an exclusively national viewpoint and take account only of requirements confined to domestic products. The proper functioning of the common market demands that each Member State also gives consideration to the legitimate requirements of the other Member States.

Only under very strict conditions does the Court accept exceptions to this principle; barriers to trade resulting from differences between commercial and technical rules are only admissible:

—if the rules are necessary, that is appropriate and not excessive, in order to satisfy mandatory requirements . . .;

—if the rules serve a purpose in the general interest which is compelling enough to justify an exception to a fundamental rule of the Treaty such as the free movement of goods;

—if the rules are essential for such a purpose to be attained, i. e. are the means which are the most appropriate and at the same time least hinder trade.

[*The Commission then set out a number of guidelines in the light of the Court's judgment.*]

—The principles deduced by the Court imply that a Member State may not in principle prohibit the sale in its territory of a product lawfully produced and marketed in another Member State even if the product is produced according to technical or quality requirements which differ from those imposed on its domestic products. Where a product 'suitably and satisfactorily' fulfils the legitimate objective of a Member State's own rules (public safety, protection of the consumer or the environment, etc.), the importing country cannot justify prohibiting its sale in its territory by claiming that the way it fulfils the objective is different from that imposed on domestic products.

In such a case, an absolute prohibition of sale could not be considered 'necessary' to satisfy a 'mandatory requirement' because it would not be an 'essential guarantee' in the sense defined in the Court's judgment.

The Commission will therefore have to tackle a whole body of commercial rules which lay down that products manufactured and marketed in one Member State must fulfil technical or qualitative conditions in order to be admitted to the market of another and specifically in all cases where the trade barriers occasioned by such rules are inadmissible according to the very strict criteria set out by the Court.

The Commission is referring in particular to rules covering the composition, designation, presentation and packaging as well as rules requiring compliance with certain technical standards.

—The Commission's work of harmonization will henceforth have to be directed mainly at national laws having an impact on the functioning of the common market where barriers to trade to be removed arise from national provisions which are admissible under the criteria set out by the Court.

The Commission will be concentrating on sectors deserving priority because of their economic relevance to the creation of a single internal market.

There are two themes in the Commission's Communication, both of which are important.

The first is what has become known as the principle of *mutual recognition*. Goods lawfully marketed in one Member State should, in principle, be admitted to the market of any other State. Provided that the product from State A 'suitably and satisfactorily' fulfilled the legitimate objectives of State B's own rules, the latter could not prohibit an import on the ground that the way State A fulfilled those objectives was different from that imposed on domestic goods by State B. This leads to competition among rules, or regulatory competition. A producer will normally only have to comply with the national rules of one State, in order that its goods can move freely in the EC. Firms are then able to choose between different national regulations. Consumers can choose between the products that comply with those rules. This creates a 'competitive process among the different national rules: the choice of producers of where to produce and of consumers of what to buy will determine the "best rules"'.[153]

The second theme concerns the Commission's enforcement and legislative strategy for trade rules post-*Cassis*. This was to be double-edged. It would tackle trade rules that were *inadmissible* in the light of *Cassis*, by using its powers under Article 169 (now Article 226) to bring Member States to the ECJ where they refused to abandon the application of such rules to imports. The harmonization process would be directed towards those trade rules which were *admissible* under the *Cassis* test. The effect of the *Cassis* doctrine was thus to induce the Commission to re-orient the direction of its own legislative programme, by causing it to concentrate on those national rules which were still valid under the Court's case law. This strategy was reinforced by a Decision[154] establishing a procedure for the exchange of information about national measures which derogated from the free movement of goods. A Member State which seeks to prevent free movement of goods that have been lawfully produced or marketed in another Member State must notify the Commission. This information will enable the Commission to decide whether such State action should be the subject of an Article 226 action, or whether harmonization measures will be necessary at Community level to obviate the concerns of the State which is impeding free movement.

The Commission's Communication was important not only for what it said, but because its publication ensured that the *Cassis* decision received more attention from the Member States than it might otherwise have done. The combined effect of *Cassis*

---

[153] Maduro, n. 4 above, 132.   [154] Dec. 3052/95, [1995] OJ L321/1.

and the Communication drew a variety of responses from States and interest groups within the Community.

K.J. Alter and S. Meunier-Aitsahalia, Judicial Politics in the European Community: European Integration and the Pathbreaking Cassis de Dijon Decision[155]

The Member States reacted with apprehension and discontent to the broad policy implications of the *Cassis* decision drawn by the Commission. As relatively high standard countries, France, Germany and Italy were the most vigorously opposed to the new policy. They repeated the German government's argument that the principle of mutual recognition of goods would lead to a lowering of safety and quality standards. Even the British government had some reservations, although the United Kingdom was generally favourable to the principle of market liberalization and opposed to the excess of legislation in the EC.

. . . The publication of the Communication also triggered the mobilization of various interest groups. Consumer groups were torn between welcoming and rejecting the Commission's interpretation of the *Cassis* ruling. Although looking forward to the greater diversity and lower prices of products implied by a common market, consumer groups were worried that trade liberalization could have negative consequences on consumer safety and jeopardize the gains previously made in consumer legislation on the national front. The EC consumer group argued that 'it is necessary to maintain a balance between the securing of free trade, which should afford consumers a broad range of products, and the need to protect the health, safety and economic interests of consumers. We are concerned that the Commission interpretation of the *Cassis* ruling may jeopardize that balance'. . . . Consumer groups also denounced the use of the judicial process rather than legislative harmonization because such a process prevents groups from having an impact on the eventual directives.

Notwithstanding its mixed reception, the *Cassis* decision had the advantage of fostering single-market integration, and facilitating the Commission's task in this area.

(b) PROBLEMS WITH THE REALIZATION OF THE ECJ'S AND COMMISSION'S STRATEGY

Mutual recognition is the core of the ECJ's and Commission's strategy. The general assumption is that this works just fine. We accept almost without question the self-executing nature of this proposition: producers of goods that cross borders will be able to rely on mutual recognition to avoid the imposition of national rules relating to product characteristics in the state of import. Matters are not so simple. The Commission's paper on *Mutual Recognition*[156] emphasized that it did not always operate effectively, and made a number of proposals to improve it.[157] There is to be increased

---

[155] (1994) 26 *Comparative Political Studies* 535, 542, 544.
[156] Commission Communication to the European Parliament and the Council, *Mutual Recognition in the Context of the Follow-up to the Action Plan for the Single Market*, 16 June 1999.
[157] *Ibid.*, 7–12.

monitoring of mutual recognition by the Commission itself. This is to be complemented by measures designed to improve awareness of mutual recognition by
producers of goods and services. Member States, which have the primary responsibility for mutual recognition, should deal with requests concerning the application of
the principle within a reasonable time. They must also include mutual recognition
clauses in national legislation.

We see here once again the inter-relationship of judicial and legislative strategies.
The obligation to insert such clauses derives from the *Foie Gras* case.[158] The French
imposed requirements on the composition of *foie gras*. The Commission argued that
the French Decree containing the requirements for *foie gras* must also contain a
mutual recognition clause in the legislation itself, permitting preparations for *foie gras*
which had been lawfully marketed in another Member State to be marketed in France.
The ECJ agreed.[159] Henceforth any State which imposes requirements as to product
characteristics and the like must also include a mutual-recognition clause in the
enabling legal instrument.

A range of inspection and control bodies at national level will apply mutual recognition. Their degree of awareness, and understanding, of Community law may vary
greatly. The obligation to include mutual-recognition clauses within the relevant
national legal instrument is one way to alleviate this problem. National bodies will,
other things being equal, be more likely to take cognizance of a principle that is
expressly laid down in such legislation. The Commission paid testimony to the
importance of this by stating that 'it is through such clauses that not only individuals,
but also the competent national authorities and the heads of inspection and control
bodies become aware of how mutual recognition has to be applied in a given area'.[160]

(c) PROBLEMS FLOWING FROM THE ECJ'S AND COMMISSION'S STRATEGY

Cassis represented a welcome development for the Commission. No longer would it
have to attempt to promulgate harmonization measures to cover all spheres of trade
policy. It could restrict its initiatives to those areas in which national rules were still
valid under *Cassis*. Community policy was to be developed through a mixture of
adjudication and rule-making. *Adjudication* pursuant to the *Cassis* principle would be
used to evaluate trade rules and declare them incompatible with Article 30 (now
Article 28), unless they could be saved by one of the mandatory requirements. *Rule-
making* would be used for those national rules which survived because of the mandatory requirements, and therefore still posed a problem for market integration. They
would be dealt with through harmonization, since the *Cassis* exceptions operated only
where there was no complete harmonization.[161]

The impact of the *adjudicative limb* of this overall strategy was essentially

---

[158] Case C–184/96, *Commission v. France* [1998] ECR I–6197.   [159] *Ibid.*, para. 28.
[160] *Mutual Recognition*, above n. 156, 11.
[161] The Commission has modified its approach to harmonization. Discussion of the New Approach to
Harmonization the Commission can be found in Ch. 28.

deregulatory or resulted in *negative regulation*: those trade rules which could not be legitimated under the *Cassis* doctrine would be declared incompatible with Article 30 (now Article 28), either totally or partially.[162] By way of contrast the impact of the *rule-making limb* of the general strategy resulted in *positive regulation*. Rules that survived the *Cassis* test because of the mandatory requirements could still constitute a barrier to intra-Community trade. The Commission would then use harmonization. Where a harmonization measure was enacted then the result would be positive regulation: there would be a Community set of rules with which all States would have to comply. There are, however, four problems with this general strategy.

The *first problem* is that the strategy is dependent upon agreement with the outcome of the adjudicative process. If the challenged rule failed the *Cassis* test then it would have to be removed from the national statute book, and, provided that this was done, the Commission would probably leave the matter there. This conclusion was fine, provided that one agreed that the rules ought to fall in this manner. The result was less satisfactory if one disagreed with the ECJ's judgment, on the ground that it should have found certain trade rules to be saved by one of the mandatory requirements. This point can be exemplified by focusing on the ECJ's judgments concerning food standards. We have already seen that the Court's general approach has been that such rules are not saved by the mandatory requirements, because it believes that the policy of the importing State can be met by less restrictive rules on product labelling.[163] Weatherill has argued forcefully that the ECJ often takes a robust view of consumers, and has given relatively little attention to the prospects of consumer confusion.[164] Lasa[165] noted that food standards have a dual purpose: to preclude economic adulteration of the product, by preventing the manufacturer substituting inferior ingredients; and to provide a yardstick against which inferior or superior quality can be measured. He then argues that labelling requirements, as opposed to food standards, may not adequately protect the consumer for the following reasons:

H.-C. von Heydebrand u. d. Lasa, Free Movement of Foodstuffs, Consumer Protection and Food Standards in the European Community: Has the Court of Justice Got it Wrong?[166]

First of all, the Court might simply not be right that consumers are adequately informed through labels. After all, the majority of the consumers apparently do not pay much attention to the information given on the label. How does the Court know that for example German consumers will not be misled by the traditional champagne-type bottles with a wired stopper which a French importer used for the marketing of partially fermented grape juice having an alcoholic strength below 3 per cent? . . .

---

[162] In the sense that the Court would conclude that the object of the importing State's policy could be met by a rule which was less restrictive on intra-Community trade than the one being challenged before the Court.

[163] See 662–3 above.

[164] S. Weatherill, 'Recent Case Law Concerning the Free Movement of Goods: Mapping the Frontiers of Market Deregulation' (1999) 36 *CMLRev.* 51.

[165] See n. 166 below.

[166] (1991) 16 *ELRev.* 391, 409–13. See also O. Brouwers, 'Free Movement of Foodstuffs and Quality Requirements: Has the Commision Got it Wrong?' (1988) 25 *CMLRev.* 237.

Secondly, the Court's approach can confer an unfair competitive advantage on the importer. For example, the use of the designation jenever by a Dutch importer for a beverage which does not meet the Dutch standard for jenever, the similarity of the French fermented grape juice bottles with the German sparkling wine bottles . . . amount to a marketing advantage for which the importer does not pay. The consumer associates with the name or presentation of the product a familiar domestic product of a certain quality which is not met by the imported product, and will therefore perhaps be misled. . . .

Fourthly, the Court's case law, if implemented strictly in the long run, may well result in a 'labelling jungle' which even judges would find difficult to penetrate. The yardstick function of food standards . . . is put at risk, if labelling is substituted for standards on a large scale. . . .

Fifthly, while administrative resources are saved by foregoing harmonization, authorities of the Member States have to struggle with the food standards of the various Member States, since the imported product must still be 'lawfully produced and marketed' in the Member States of export. Mutual recognition of official inspections has its difficulties too, especially where the product designated for export is not at all or less carefully examined than the product which is sold on the home market.

Sixthly, depending on the market of the foodstuff in question, mutual recognition can lead to discrimination against manufacturers situated in the importing Member State, if that Member State does not timely adjust the food standard. For example, an obligation on Member States to allow the importation of milk substitutes lawfully produced and marketed in another Member State does not affect the obligation of their domestic manufacturers to comply with the standard which bans or restricts the sale of these products. . . .

More important . . . the Member State of export can by way of the economic damage caused by inverse discrimination impose de facto its food standard or standard free food law on the Member State of import. Relocation of production to the exporting Member State in an effort to secure market share at home has already occurred in practice. . . .

Seventhly, the preference of the Court for labelling is not sufficiently responsive to the local needs of the people of the importing Member State to define and classify the food they eat according to their conceptions, expectations and habits. It is not clear why the creation of a common market should require the strong disregard of these needs as reflected in the case law of the Court of Justice. . . .

. . . The attitude of the Court of Justice towards food standards makes it de facto impossible for the people of a Member State to enforce requirements about the quality, composition, designation and presentation of their food when their views are not shared by the people in the Member State of export. . . .

The *second problem* relates to the balancing exercise performed pursuant to Article 30 (ex Article 36), and the mandatory requirements. The broader the remit of Article 28, the more often will the ECJ be faced with difficult issues concerning defences raised by Member States. The ECJ is forced to adjudicate on the balance between market integration and the attainment of other societal goals, when deciding on the legitimacy of such defences. This can also be problematic for national courts, to which the ECJ may delegate decisions on whether a national rule limiting trade is proportionate, or whether it could be attained in a less restrictive manner. We have already seen the difficulties that this caused in the *Sunday Trading* cases. More recent cases indicate that national courts are being asked once again to adjudicate on matters that are either factually difficult to estimate or involve complex balancing. Thus in *de Agostini*[167] it seemed to be for the national court to decide whether the advertising ban affected imported goods differentially from domestic goods. It then had to decide whether the ban might satisfy a mandatory requirement, or Article 30 (ex Article 36), and whether it was proportionate. In *Familiapress*[168] the task given to the national court was even more problematic. The ban on the import of newspapers offering prizes had been held to be in breach of Article 28. It was for the national court to decide whether the ban could be saved on the ground that it was a proportionate method of preserving press diversity, and whether that objective could be achieved by less restrictive means. The national court was, moreover, required to decide on the degree of competition between papers offering prizes and those small newspapers that could not afford to do so. It was then to estimate the extent to which sales of the latter would decline, if the former could be offered for sale. It should not be forgotten in this context that a reference can be made to the ECJ by any national court. The questions posed in the above cases would be daunting for any national court, let alone for those at the lower level.

The *third problem* with the strategy set out above concerns the balance between market integration and the protective function played by national rules. Community legislative initiatives may well be required in order to ensure that the protective function of many trade rules is not lost sight of in the desire to enhance single-market integration.[169] We have already seen in the earlier discussion the way in which Article 28 mediates between the objective of integration and the legitimate protective concerns underlying many national rules.[170] It is true that safety and the like can be taken into account under the *Cassis* mandatory requirements. There is, however, as Weatherill and Beaumont note, a risk inherent in the *Cassis* line of authority. The risk is 'that the Court has introduced a legal test that tends to tip the balance away from legitimate social protection towards a deregulated (perhaps unregulated) free market economy in which standards of, *inter alia*, consumer protection will be depressed'.[171] Even if one agrees that certain national trade rules should be regarded as incompatible with the Treaty, this species of negative regulation may still require supplementation with more positive regulation, which can only be produced through Community legislative action. The essence of this point is captured well by Weatherill and Beaumont:[172]

[T]he essential concern about *Cassis* resides in the fear that it has promoted free trade but that the terms on which such free trade will ensue are thoroughly uncertain. *Cassis* may have deregulated the market by eliminating many national technical barriers to trade, but it remains questionable whether the removal of national barriers without accompanying positive Community regulations is sufficient to secure the realization of a true common market. At a more fundamental level of policy, one must address the question of the extent to which the Community *ought* to regulate the market in a positive sense.

---

[167] Case C–34–36/95, n. 62 above.   [168] Case C–368/95, n. 147 above.
[169] See, however, Case C–320/93, *Lucien Ortscheit GmbH* v. *Eurim-Pharm Arzneimittel GmbH* [1994] ECR I–5243, for judicial recognition of this problem.
[170] See 615 above.   [171] N. 79 above, 600.
[172] *Ibid.*, 599. Italics in the original.

The *final problem* concerns the allocation of regulatory competence between the Community and the Member States. The interpretation of Article 28 serves to define the sphere of regulatory competence left to the Member States, and the extent to which Community harmonization is required. This entails important choices, as the following extract reveals. Article 30 should be read as Article 28.

M. Maduro, We the Court, the European Court of Justice and the European Economic Constitution[173]

The institutional choices, regarding the allocation of regulatory powers, that can be detected in different interpretations of Article 30 and its co-ordination with Treaty rules on harmonisation may be represented in three ideal constitutional models of the European Economic Constitution: the centralised constitutional model, the competitive constitutional model and the decentralised constitutional model. The centralised model reacts to the erosion of national regulatory powers through Article 30 by favouring a process of market integration by means of the replacement of national laws with Community legislation. The competitive model promotes 'competition among national rules', notably through the principle of mutual recognition of national legislation. In the decentralised model, States will retain regulatory powers, but are, at the same time, prevented from developing protectionist policies. These models are heuristic devices. They are all present— and compete with each other—in the European Union. . . . These, in turn, can be linked with three different visions of the European Economic Constitution and its legitimation.

The first argues that negative integration, deriving from the application of market integration rules, must be followed by positive integration which is legitimised through the development of traditional democratic mechanisms in the European Union.

The second argues for the constitutionalisation of negative integration. No traditional democratic developments are required for the European Union institutions since powers are left to the market. . . . This vision protects market freedom and individual rights against public power.

The third vision still sees the highest source of legitimacy in national democratic legitimacy. The legitimacy of the European Economic Constitution derives therefrom and is thus conditioned. . . .

The disputes over Article 30 and European regulation are basically disputes over these different economic constitutional models and the different legitimacy they presuppose.

12. CONCLUSION

i. The ECJ had certain fundamental choices open to it when interpreting what is now Article 28 of the Treaty. It could have limited the remit of this Article to measures that were discriminatory or protectionist. It chose not to do so, and extended Article 28 to cover indistinctly applicable rules. That choice was encapsulated in *Cassis*. Consequences flow from any choice, and this applies as much to those made by courts as other decision-makers.

ii. The *legislative consequence* of *Cassis* was far-reaching. The decision facilitated the creation of a single market. It obviated the need for Community measures

---

[173] (Hart, 1998), 108–9.

in relation to the national rules that did not survive scrutiny under *Cassis*. The Commission re-oriented its legislative strategy, to concentrate on the trade rules that were still lawful in the light of *Cassis*. These were the rules that could be justified by the mandatory requirements. There would be harmonization pursuant to Article 95 (ex Article 100a), albeit often only minimum harmonization.

iii. The *judicial consequence* of *Cassis* was equally significant. The ECJ 'reaped the burden of its own success'. Litigants sought to challenge all manner of national trade rules claiming that they constituted an impediment, direct or indirect, actual or potential, to Community trade. It was this that led the ECJ to re-think its own jurisprudence in *Keck* in an attempt to stem the tide. The distinction between rules going to the characteristics of the goods and those pertaining to selling arrangements has proven fragile. The ECJ has increasingly brought selling arrangements within Article 28 either by treating them as going to the character of the goods, or because they apply unevenly, in fact or law, to imports. Market access has come closer to centre stage in the ECJ's reasoning.

iv. *Cassis* also had a *second-order judicial consequence*. The ECJ had to decide whether a Member State could legitimately plead a mandatory requirement as a defence. It was forced to make difficult decisions between the imperatives of market integration, and the pursuit of other social goals. National courts are faced with complex empirical and normative issues. They will often be told to decide whether a mandatory requirement is proportionate, and whether another less restrictive measure would be possible. It is the national courts that are instructed to balance, for example, press diversity against market integration.

v. *Cassis* had significant *regulatory consequences*. Member States lost regulatory competence. They could no longer apply their trade rules to imported goods. These had to be admitted because of mutual recognition, unless they could be saved by invocation of the mandatory requirements. The EC acquired regulatory competence, since the existence of a proven mandatory requirement brought Article 95 (ex Article 100a) into play. Difficult choices had to be made about the balance between the imperatives of market integration, and the pursuit of other social objectives.

13. FURTHER READING

(a) *Books*

BARNARD, C., and SCOTT, J. (eds.), *The Law of the Single European Market* (Hart, 2002)

BURROWS, F., *Free Movement in European Community Law* (Oxford University Press, 1987)

GORMLEY, L.W., *Prohibiting Restrictions on Trade within the EEC* (Elsevier/North Holland, 1985)

GREEN, N., HARTLEY, T.C., and USHER, J.A., *The Legal Foundations of the Single European Market* (Oxford University Press, 1991)

JARVIS, M., *The Application of EC Law by National Courts: The Free Movement of Goods* (Oxford University Press, 1998)

MADURO, M.P., *We the Court, The European Court of Justice and the European Economic Constitution* (Hart, 1998)

OLIVER, P., *Free Movement of Goods in the EC* (Sweet & Maxwell, 3rd edn., 1996)

(b) *Articles*

ALTER, K.J., and MEUNER-AITSAHALIA, S., 'Judicial Politics in the European Community: European Integration and the Pathbreaking *Cassis de Dijon* Decision' (1994) 26 *Comparative Political Studies* 535

BARNARD, C., 'Fitting the Remaining Pieces into the Goods and Persons Jigsaw' (2001) 26 *ELRev.* 35

BERNARD, N., 'Discrimination and Free Movement in EC Law' [1996] *ICLQ* 82

CHALMERS, D., 'Repackaging the Internal Market—The Ramifications of the *Keck* Judgment' (1994) 19 *ELRev.* 385

DOOGAN, M., 'Minimum Harmonization and the Internal Market' (2000) 37 *CMLRev.* 853

GORMLEY, L.W., '*Cassis de Dijon* and the Communication from the Commission' (1981) 6 *ELRev.* 454

—— 'Actually or Potentially, Directly or Indirectly? Obstacles to the Free Movement of Goods' (1989) 9 *YBEL* 197

—— 'Reasoning Renounced? The Remarkable Judgment in *Keck & Mithouard*' [1994] *Euro. Bus. L. Rev.* 63

HILSON, C., 'Discrimination in Community Free Movement Law' (1999) 24 *ELRev.* 445

KOUTRAKOS, P., 'On Groceries, Alcohol and Olive Oil: More on Free Movement of Goods after *Keck*' (2001) 26 *ELRev.* 391

LASA, H.-C., and VON HEYDEBRAND, U.D., 'Free Movement of Foodstuffs, Consumer Protection and Food Standards in the European Community: Has the Court of Justice Got it Wrong?' (1991) 16 *ELRev.* 391

MATTERA, A., 'L'Arrêt "*Cassis de Dijon*": Une Nouvelle Approche pour la Réalisation et le Bon Fonctionnement du Marché Interieur' [1980] *Revue du Marché Commun* 505

MORTELMANS, K., 'Article 30 of the EEC Treaty and Legislation Relating to Market Circumstances: Time to Consider a New Definition?' (1991) 28 *CMLRev.* 115

—— 'The Common Market, the Internal Market and the Single Market, What's in a Market' (1998) 35 *CMLRev.* 101

OLIVER, P., 'Some Further Reflections on the Scope of Articles 28–30 (ex 30–36)' (1999) 36 *CMLRev.* 738

REICH, N., 'The 'November Revolution' of the European Court of Justice: *Keck*, *Meng* and *Audi* Revisited' (1994) 31 *CMLRev.* 459

STEINER, J., 'Drawing the Line: Uses and Abuses of Article 30 EEC' (1992) 29 *CMLRev.* 749

WEATHERILL, S., 'After *Keck*: Some Thoughts on how to Clarify the Clarification' (1996) 33 *CMLRev.* 885

—— 'Recent Case Law Concerning the Free Movement of Goods: Mapping the Frontiers of Market Deregulation' (1999) 36 *CMLRev.* 51

WHITE, E., 'In Search of the Limits to Article 30 of the EEC Treaty' (1989) 26 *CMLRev.* 235

WEILER, J.J., 'From *Dassonville* to *Keck* and Beyond: An Evolutionary Reflection on the Text and Context of the Free Movement of Goods', in P. Craig and G. de Búrca (eds.), *The Evolution of EU Law* (Oxford University Press, 1999), ch. 10

WILS, W.P.J., 'The Search for the Rule in Article 30 EEC: Much Ado About Nothing?' (1993) 18 *ELRev.* 475

16

FREE MOVEMENT OF CAPITAL AND ECONOMIC AND MONETARY UNION

1. CENTRAL ISSUES

i. This Chapter is concerned with free movement of capital and economic and monetary union (EMU).

ii. The initial discussion will focus on the free movement of capital. This is one of the four freedoms enshrined in the original Treaty of Rome. The Treaty Articles that apply in this area were, however, altered radically by the TEU. There is now a growing body of case law testing the scope of these provisions. This jurisprudence raises similar issues to those encountered in the context of goods, persons, establishment, and services.

iii. The remainder of the discussion will be devoted to EMU. There will be an analysis of the movement towards EMU, and the Treaty provisions in the TEU that set the legal framework for EMU. There will be consideration of the arguments for and against EMU. The position of the European Central Bank (ECB) will be analysed in detail. The discussion will conclude with an overview of the stresses and strains of EMU.

2. FREE MOVEMENT OF CAPITAL

(a) THE ORIGINAL TREATY PROVISIONS

While the original Rome Treaty contained provisions on the free movement of capital, they were drafted very differently from the Treaty Articles concerned with the other freedoms. The original Treaty Articles have now been superseded by those in the TEU, as renumbered by the ToA. Some brief idea of the approach to capital movements adopted in the Rome Treaty is none the less of importance in understanding the later provisions of the TEU.

The rules on free movement of capital were originally to be found in Articles 67–73 of the Treaty of Rome.[1] These provisions were less peremptory than those applicable to the free movement of goods, workers, services, and establishment. Thus while Article 67(1) imposed an obligation to abolish progressively restrictions on capital movements during the transitional period, this was only to the extent necessary to ensure the proper functioning of the common market. This same theme was carried over to Article 68(1) which required Member States to be as liberal as possible in

[1] J. Usher, *The Law of Money and Financial Services in the European Community* (Oxford University Press, 1994), 14–16.

granting exchange authorizations after the entry into force of the Treaty. Similarly, Article 71 required Member States to endeavour to avoid the introduction of new exchange restrictions on capital movements. The wording of these Treaty Articles necessarily had an impact on the way in which the ECJ approached this area.[2] The Council enacted various directives pursuant to these Treaty provisions, the most important being Council Directive 88/361,[3] which finally established the basic principle of free movement of capital as a matter of EC law, with effect from 1 July 1990.

(b) THE CURRENT PROVISIONS: THE BASIC PRINCIPLE

The TEU completely revised the provisions on free movement of capital with effect from 1 January 1994.[4] Article 56 (ex Article 73b) now provides:

1. Within the framework of the provisions set out in this Chapter, all restrictions on the movement of capital between Member States and between Member States and third countries shall be prohibited.
2. Within the framework of the provisions set out in this Chapter, all restrictions on payments between Member States and between Member States and third countries shall be prohibited.[5]

The Treaty provisions do not define movement of capital, but the ECJ has held that reference can be made to the non-exhaustive list in Directive 88/361.[6] It will be for the ECJ to decide, with the aid of the Directive, whether a measure constitutes a restriction on the movement of capital. Thus a national prohibition on the creation of a mortgage in a foreign currency was prohibited by Article 56.[7] Discriminatory restrictions on the acquisition and disposal of movable property, such as requirements of prior administrative authorization, are proscribed.[8] Measures taken by a Member State which are liable to dissuade its residents from obtaining loans or making investments in other Member States have been held to constitute restrictions on the movement of capital.[9] Moreover, while direct taxation remains within Member States' competence, they must exercise that competence consistently with EC law and avoid discrimination on the grounds of nationality.[10]

---

[2] Case 203/80, *Casati* [1981] ECR 2595.

[3] [1988] OJ L178/5.

[4] See, generally, S. Peers, 'Free Movement of Capital: Learning Lessons or Slipping on Spilt Milk?' in C. Barnard and J. Scott (eds.), *The Law of the Single European Market* (Hart, 2002).

[5] This does not cover national procedural rules governing actions by a creditor seeking payment from a recalcitrant debtor: Case C–412/97, *ED Srl* v. *Italo Fenocchio* [1999] ECR I–3845.

[6] Case C–222/97, *Proceedings brought by Trummer and Mayer* [1999] ECR I–1661, para. 21.

[7] *Ibid.*; Case C–464/98, *Westdeutsche Landesbank Girozentrale* v. *Stefan and Republik Österreich* [2001] ECR I–173.

[8] Case C–302/97, *Konle* v. *Austrian Republic* [1999] ECR I–3099; Case C–423/98, *Albore* [2000] ECR I–5965.

[9] Case C–439/97, *Sandoz GmbH* v. *Finanzlandesdirektion für Wien, Niederösterreich und Burgenland* [1999] ECR I–7041, para. 19; Case C–478/98, *Commission* v. *Belgium* [2000] ECR I–7587, para. 18.

[10] Case C–251/98, *Baars* v. *Inspecteur der Belastingen Particulieren/Ondernemingen Gorinchem* [2000] ECR I–2787, para. 17; Cases C–397 & 410/98, *Metallgesellschaft Ltd., Hoechst AG and Hoechst (UK) Ltd.* v. *Commissioners of the Inland Revenue and HM Attorney General* [2001] ECR I–1727, para. 37.

A bare reading of Article 56 gives the impression that capital movements within the EC, and between Member States and non-member countries, are to be treated in the same way. This is not in fact so, since other Treaty Articles qualify the application of Article 56 to non-member countries. Article 57(1) (ex Article 73c) in effect allows lawful restrictions on such capital movements which existed on 31 December 1993 to remain in being, and Article 57(2) requires the Council only to endeavour to achieve such free movement with non-member countries to the greatest extent possible. The Council is also empowered under Article 59 (ex Article 73f) to take safeguard measures in exceptional circumstances where capital movements to or from non-member countries cause, or threaten to cause, serious difficulties for the operation of economic and monetary union. Such measures cannot last longer than six months, and can be taken only where strictly necessary.[11]

Article 73b(1) (now Article 56) was held to have direct effect in *Sanz de Lera*.[12] The ECJ held that Article 73b(1) lays down a clear and unconditional prohibition for which no implementing measure is required. The existence of Member State discretion to take all measures necessary to prevent infringement of national law and regulations contained within Article 73d(1)(b) (now Article 58(1)(b)), did not, said the ECJ, prevent Article 73b(1) from having direct effect. This was because the exercise of such discretion was itself subject to judicial review. The ruling in this case concerned an action against the State. Treaty Articles will normally have both vertical and horizontal direct effect, and thus be capable of being used against both the State and private individuals, and there is nothing in *Sanz de Lera* to indicate the contrary here. It would not be difficult, as Usher states,[13] to envisage a situation in which the unilateral conduct of a financial institution could restrict payments between States. This interpretation of Article 73b(1) is reinforced by the fact that it does not, on its face, refer only to the State.[14] The argument to the contrary would be derived by way of analogy with Article 28 (ex Article 30) concerned with the free movement of goods, which has been largely confined to actions against the State itself.[15]

(c) THE CURRENT PROVISIONS: THE EXCEPTIONS

Article 58(1)(a) (ex Article 73d(1)(a)) concerns taxation and constitutes one of the main exceptions to Article 56. It provides that the provisions of Article 56 shall be without prejudice to the right of Member States:

to apply the relevant provisions of their tax law which distinguish between tax-payers who are not in the same situation with regard to their place of residence or with regard to the place where their capital is invested.

Article 58(1)(a) is expressly made subject to Article 58(3), which stipulates that the

---

[11] See also Art. 60 (ex Art. 73g).

[12] Cases C–163, 165, & 250/94, *Criminal Proceedings against Lucas Emilio Sanz de Lera* [1995] ECR I–4821, paras. 41–7.

[13] N. 1 above, 27.

[14] In Case C–464/98, *Westdeutsche Landesbank*, n. 7 above, it was a private defendant who relied on Art. 56.

[15] The rationale for this limitation on Art. 28 is, however, based in large part on the overlap which would otherwise occur between Art. 28 and Arts. 81 and 82 (ex Arts. 85 and 86 respectively).

measures taken must not constitute a means of arbitrary discrimination or a disguised restriction on the free movement of capital and payments. For a difference in treatment not to be regarded as arbitrary for the purposes of Article 58(3) it will have to be objectively justified.[16] This will require the Member State to show, for example, that the differential treatment was intended to protect the integrity of the tax system and was necessary to achieve this end. The ECJ will interpret this requirement strictly. Thus in *Verkooijen*[17] it was held that a national provision making the grant of exemption from income tax on dividends paid to shareholders conditional on the company having its seat in the Netherlands was contrary to EC law. The ECJ rejected the defence that the rule was justified to encourage investment in the Netherlands: such purely economic objectives could not justify a limit placed on a fundamental freedom. The ECJ also rejected arguments that the contested rule was justified on the ground that it was necessary to preserve the cohesion of the Netherlands' tax system.[18]

Article 58(1)(b) (ex Article 73d(1)(b)) provides that the provisions of Article 56 shall be without prejudice to the right of Member States:

to take all requisite measures to prevent infringements of national law and regulations, in particular in the field of taxation and the prudential supervision of financial institutions, or to lay down procedures for the declaration of capital movements for purposes of administrative or statistical information, or to take measures which are justified on grounds of public policy or public security.

Article 58(1)(b) is also made subject to Article 58(3): the restrictions cannot constitute a means of arbitrary discrimination etc. Article 58(1)(b) effectively divides into two parts.

The first part covers the whole of the Article apart from the reference to public policy and public security. It has been convincingly argued[19] that this 'relates to the effective administration and enforcement of the tax system and the effective supervision of, for example, banks and insurance companies, rather than to matters of underlying economic policy', the latter being dealt with under Articles 119 and 120 (ex Articles 109h and 109i). The ECJ will inquire closely before accepting this defence. In *Commission* v. *Belgium*[20] the ECJ held that a national rule forbidding Belgian residents from subscribing to securities of a loan on the Eurobond market was caught by Article 56. The Belgian government argued that the contested measure was justified under Article 58(1)(b) because it preserved fiscal coherence. This argument was rejected because there was no direct link between any fiscal advantage and disadvantage which should be preserved in order to ensure such coherence. The Belgian government argued moreover that the contested measure prevented tax evasion by Belgian residents, and ensured effective fiscal supervision. The ECJ did not agree, and held that the national rule was disproportionate. It held that a general presumption of tax evasion could not justify a measure that compromised a Treaty Article.

The second part of Article 58(1)(b) covers public policy and public security.

---

[16] Usher, n. 1 above, 34.
[17] Case C–35/98, *Staatssecretaris van Financiën* v. *Verkooijen* [2000] ECR I–4071.
[18] See also Case C–251/98, *Baars*, n. 10 above.   [19] Usher, n. 1 above, 36.
[20] Case C–478/98, n. 9 above.

The ECJ draws on its considerable jurisprudence from the other freedoms when interpreting these terms. It is clear therefore that this exception will be interpreted narrowly and that the Member State will have the burden of proof. It is clear also that the restrictions will be struck down if a less restrictive measure would have sufficed to reach the desired end. In *Scientology International*[21] the ECJ held that a national law requiring prior authorization for capital investments that threatened public policy or security could, in principle, come within Article 58(1)(b). However, the particular French rule, which did not specify further details about the threat to public security, was regarded as too imprecise, and hence could not come within this Article.[22]

Article 58(2) (ex Article 73d(2)) states that the provisions of this Chapter shall be without prejudice to the applicability of restrictions on the right of establishment which are compatible with the Treaty. This Article is once again made subject to Article 58(3). These restrictions therefore include the exception in the case of official activities contained in Article 45 (ex Article 55).

Articles 119 and 120 (ex Articles 109h and 109i) contain a qualification to Article 56 which is of a rather different nature. These Articles cease to operate from the third stage of EMU except for States with a derogation. Articles 119 and 120 deal with balance-of-payments crises. The 'strategy' is to look initially to a Community-sponsored solution to the problem via Article 119, and then to authorize unilateral action by the State if this is not forthcoming via Article 120. Article 119 covers the situation where a State is in difficulty with its balance of payments, or as a result of the type of currency at its disposal. Where these difficulties are liable to jeopardize the functioning of the common market or the implementation of the common commercial policy, the Commission must investigate the matter and recommend measures to the State. Assistance may be provided to the State, but if this is not forthcoming or is insufficient the Commission can authorize the State to take protective measures. Article 120 allows a State that has a sudden balance-of-payments crisis to take protective measures where no mutual assistance has been provided under Article 119(2). Such measures, which could include restriction of capital movements, must, however, cause the least possible disturbance to the functioning of the common market and must not be wider than is strictly necessary to remedy the sudden difficulties.[23]

---

[21] Case C–54/99, *Association Eglise de Scientologie de Paris and Scientology International Reserves Trust v. The Prime Minister* [2000] ECR I–1355.

[22] See also Case C–423/98, *Albore*, n. 8 above, paras. 17–24.

[23] The Council may decide that such measures should be suspended, abolished, or amended: Art. 120(2).

3. EARLY ATTEMPTS AT EMU AND THE EUROPEAN MONETARY SYSTEM

Discussion of Economic and Monetary Union (EMU) must be set in its historical context. As early as 1969 the Heads of State resolved that a plan should be drawn up in relation to economic and monetary union.[24] To this end a committee was established under the chairmanship of Werner, the Luxembourg Prime Minister, to report on the matter. The Committee concluded[25] that EMU would entail either the total and irreversible convertibility of the Community currencies, free from fluctuations in exchange rates, or that preferably such currencies would be replaced by a single Community currency. The report also recognized that EMU would entail the central-ization of monetary and credit policy, and that there would have to be some Com-munity system for the national central banks. The report was followed by a Council Resolution on the attainment of EMU by stages.[26] Progress was, however, halted as a result of changes in economic circumstance. The Werner Report had been premised on the assumption of fixed exchange rates, and this key assumption was undermined by developments in the early 1970s.[27] Largely as a result of problems with the US economy,[28] European currencies began to float and there was an urgent need to prevent them from floating too far apart. This was the catalyst for the initiation of the 'snake', which established the principle that the difference between the exchange rates of two Member States should not be greater than 2.25 per cent. Economic pressures on particular Member States resulted in a number of departures from the 'snake', such that by 1977 only half of the ten Member States remained within it. This early attempt to forge some form of EMU was furthered hampered by the lack of progress towards the co-ordination of national economic policies, a step seen as vital to the ultimate success of the enterprise.[29]

A more general attempt to engender monetary stability took shape in the late 1970s, through the establishment, by a Resolution of the European Council in 1978,[30] of the European Monetary System (EMS).[31] There was growing dissatisfaction with floating exchange rates, which were perceived to have a detrimental impact on cross-border investment. Foreign currency movements were, moreover, also having a destabilizing effect on European currencies.[32] The EMS instituted the Exchange Rate Mechanism (ERM), and the European Currency Unit (ECU). The ECU rate was determined against a basket of currencies of the Member States. The ERM operated by setting for each participating State a currency rate against the ECU. These values, once determined collectively, could only be altered in the same manner. Once the

---

[24] For earlier developments see F. Snyder, 'EMU Revisited: Are We Making a Constitution? What Constitution Are We Making', in P. Craig and G. de Búrca (eds.), *The Evolution of EU Law* (Oxford University Press, 1999), 421–4.

[25] Bull. EC Supplement 11–1970.　　[26] [1971] OJ C28/1.　　[27] Usher, n. 1 above, 138.

[28] D. Swann, *The Economics of Europe, From Common Market to European Union* (Penguin, 9th edn., 2000), 204–5.

[29] *Ibid.*, 208.

[30] Bull. EC 12–1978. This Resolution was reinforced by an Agreement between the national central banks.

[31] Snyder, n. 24 above, 428–33.　　[32] Swann, n. 28 above, 209–10.

value of each currency was specified in relation to the ECU it was then possible to determine the worth of any particular national currency as against all other national currencies. These relative values are known as the bilateral central rates. The central plank of the ERM is that any participant country will not allow its exchange rate to fluctuate by more than a given percentage above or below these bilateral central rates. The normal margin of fluctuation was 2.25 per cent, with an exceptional band of 6 per cent. When a currency reached its bilateral limits against another currency intervention was required by the relevant central banks to redress the matter. The normal workings of the ERM were, however, thrown into disarray by the currency crises of 1992–3. Currency dealers speculated that certain weaker currencies could not be sustained within the relatively narrow bands of the ERM. Central banks sought to preserve the integrity of the ERM, but could not ultimately resist market pressures. The lira and the pound were suspended from the ERM. Further market pressures led to the widening of the bilateral bands to 15 per cent,[33] and to the devaluation of certain currencies which stayed within the ERM. These measures preserved the ERM in formal terms, but served to undermine the primary rationale for its existence, since they significantly weakened the drive for exchange rate stability.

4. ECONOMIC AND MONETARY UNION: THE THREE STAGES[34]

(a) STAGE ONE AND THE DELORS REPORT

While the SEA did not contain any commitment to EMU, it did, in one of its preambles, recall that in 1972 the Heads of State had approved the objective of progressing towards EMU. This was the initial catalyst for bringing the issue back onto the political agenda at the Hanover Summit of 1988, which saw the European Council meeting at Madrid in 1989 as the setting for making a decision on the issue. A committee was established to assist the European Council in its deliberations, and this committee was chaired by Jacques Delors, the President of the Commission. The Delors Committee Report[35] recommended that EMU should be approached in three stages.[36]

The essential elements of Stage One were seen as the completion of the internal market, closer economic convergence, and the membership of all States in the ERM. This stage did not require new Treaty powers. In Stage Two a European System of Central Banks (ESCB) would be created, with the tasks of co-ordinating national monetary policies and formulating a common monetary policy for the Community. Stage Three would see the locking of exchange rates and the emergence of a single

[33] Subject to a special agreement between Germany and the Netherlands to retain the 2.25% fluctuation band.

[34] K. Dyson and K. Featherstone, *The Road to Maastricht: Negotiating Economic and Monetary Union* (Oxford University Press, 1999).

[35] *Report on Economic and Monetary Union in the European Community* (EC Commission, 1988).

[36] Snyder, n. 24 above, 432–5.

currency, the management of which would fall to the ESCB. The ESCB was to be independent and have price stability as a primary goal. The Delors Report also recognized that there would have to be central control over national fiscal policy, since otherwise the action of a particular State could have deleterious consequences for inflation or interest rates in all states.

(b) STAGE TWO: THE TREATY ON EUROPEAN UNION

It was the Treaty on European Union which laid the Treaty foundations for progress towards EMU, and stipulated that the second stage of EMU would begin on 1 January 1994.[37] The provisions on EMU are complex. The best way to understand the maze of relevant Treaty Articles is to divide them in the following manner.

First, and foremost, the TEU added a new Article 3a to Part 1 concerned with Principles underlying the Treaty. Since the ToA this is now Article 4 of the EC Treaty. Article 4(1) stipulates that the activities of the Member States and the Community shall include the adoption of an economic policy which is based on the close co-ordination of Member States' economic policies, on the internal market, and on the definition of the common objectives, conducted in accordance with the principle of an open market economy with free competition. Article 4(2) is of particular importance in the present context. It provides that the activities of the States and the Community shall include the irrevocable fixing of exchange rates leading to the introduction of a single currency, the ECU, and the definition of a single monetary and exchange-rate policy. The primary objective is to be the maintenance of price stability and the support of the Community's general economic policies, in accordance with the principle of an open market and free competition. Article 4(3) states that the preceding activities should comply with the following guidelines: stable prices, sound public finances and monetary conditions, and a sustainable balance of payments.

Secondly, there are provisions dealing with economic policy. We have already seen from the previous discussion the intimate connection between monetary union in terms of a single currency and broader issues of macro-economic policy. This connection was perceived by both the Werner and Delors Reports, and is supported by sound economic logic. Monetary union is not plausible without some measure of centralized control over fiscal policy, and in particular over budgetary matters. This is the rationale for the inclusion of Articles 98–104 (ex Articles 102a–104c).[38] Article 99 (ex Article 103) provides that the States are to regard their economic policies as a matter of common concern and shall co-ordinate them within the Council. To this end, it is intended that the Council, on the basis of reports from the Commission, shall monitor economic developments in each of the States and make recommendations where necessary. Articles 101 and 102 (ex Articles 104 and 104a) prohibit overdraft and related facilities by government and public bodies with national central banks. Article 104 (ex Article 104c) is of particular importance, since it concerns national budgets. Member States are under an obligation in the second stage to endeavour to avoid

---

[37] Art. 116(1) (ex Art. 109e(1)).
[38] Some of the provisions contained within these Arts. apply only at the third stage of EMU. This will become clear from the subsequent discussion.

excessive budget deficits.[39] The Commission is to monitor the development of the national budgetary situation with a view to identifying gross errors, and criteria are set out to determine whether an actual or predicted national deficit exceeds a certain reference value.[40] It is open to the Commission to make a report to the Council, and the Council may then issue recommendations to the State concerned.[41]

Thirdly, there are Treaty Articles dealing with monetary policy itself. A European Monetary Institute (EMI) was established.[42] This was the forerunner to the European Central Bank (ECB) which came into being at Stage Three of EMU. The EMI had various tasks, including: strengthening of co-operation with national central banks, strengthening of the co-ordination of national monetary policies, and monitoring the functioning of the EMS.[43] It also had a number of duties concerned with the transition to Stage Three of EMU, ranging from the technical preparation of bank-notes to the preparation of the instruments required for applying monetary policy in the third stage.[44] The EMI, by 31 December 1996 at the latest, had to specify the regulatory, organizational, and logistical framework necessary for the European System of Central Banks (ESCB) to perform its tasks in the third stage. This frame-work had to be submitted to the ECB at the date of its establishment.[45] The Member States had their own institutional obligations in Stage Two of EMU, the most signifi-cant of which was to begin the process of ensuring that their central bank was independent.[46] Each Member State was also instructed to treat its exchange rate policy as a matter of common interest and take account of experience acquired within the EMS.[47]

(c) STAGE THREE: THE BASIC LEGAL FRAMEWORK

The third stage of EMU had, according to the Treaty,[48] to start no later than 1 January 1999. The TEU contained detailed criteria concerning the shift from Stage Two to Stage Three of EMU, which are contained in Article 121 (ex Article 109j). The Commission and the EMI should report to the Council on the progress made by the States towards EMU. These reports would examine, *inter alia*, the extent to which the States had made their central banks independent, and, most importantly, whether the convergence criteria had been met. Meeting these criteria is a condition precedent for a State to adopt the single currency.[49] The four criteria were set out in Article 121(1), and were fleshed out by a Protocol attached to the TEU. Member States that do not fulfil the criteria are referred to as 'Member States with a derogation'.[50] Their position is reassessed at least once every two years to determine whether they now meet the conditions.[51] While they remain outside the single currency certain Treaty Articles do not apply to them.[52]

---

[39] Art. 116(4) (ex Art. 109e(4)).   [40] Art. 104(2).
[41] At the third stage of EMU the Council is empowered to take tougher measures: see 690–1 below.
[42] Art. 117 (ex Art. 109f).   [43] Art. 117(2).   [44] Art. 117(3).
[45] Art. 117(3).   [46] Arts. 109 and 116(5) (ex Arts. 108 and 109e(5)).
[47] Art. 124 (ex Art. 109m).   [48] Art. 121(4) (ex Art. 109j(4)).
[49] Art. 121(2).
[50] Art. 122(1).   [51] Art. 122(2).   [52] Art. 122(3).

(i) The achievement of a high degree of price stability. This is to be judged by an average rate of inflation, over a one year period prior to the examination, which does not exceed by more than 1.5 per cent the average of the three best-performing States.

(ii) The sustainability of the government's financial position. This is defined as the avoidance of an excessive government budgetary deficit: an annual budget deficit of less than 3 per cent of Gross Domestic Product (GDP), and an overall public debt ratio of not more than 60 per cent of GDP.

(iii) The observance of the normal fluctuation margins provided by the ERM for at least two years without severe tensions and without devaluation against the currency of any other Member State.

(iv) The durability of convergence achieved by the Member State as reflected in long-term interest rates. This is defined as meaning that over a period of one year prior to the examination, the Member State has had an average nominal long-term interest rate that does not exceed by more than 2 per cent that of the three best performing Member States in terms of price stability.

It was on the basis of these reports that the Council under Article 121(2), acting by qualified majority on a recommendation of the Commission, assessed whether each Member State fulfilled the conditions for the adoption of a single currency. It also had to assess whether a majority of the Member States fulfilled these conditions. There then followed a somewhat curious institutional provision whereby the Council recommended its findings to the Council meeting in the composition of the Heads of State or Government.[53] The rationale for this novel institutional format was, however, simple: only the formal Heads of State should make decisions of this magnitude. The Council, meeting as the Heads of State or Government, had to decide by qualified majority, in the light of the Council recommendation referred to above, not later than 31 December 1996 whether a majority of the Member States fulfilled the conditions for the adoption of a single currency. It also had to decide whether it was appropriate for the Community to enter the third stage, and, if so, to set a date for the beginning of the third stage.[54]

If the date for the beginning of the third stage had not been set by the end of 1997 then the third stage was deemed to start on 1 January 1999.[55] Prior to 1 July 1998 the Council, meeting as the Heads of State or Government, had to repeat the exercise contained in Article 121(1) and (2) of deciding whether individual States met the convergence criteria, but it no longer had to decide whether a majority of the States fulfilled these conditions. The Council, meeting in this form, had then to confirm which States met the conditions for the adoption of a single currency.

(d) THE LEGAL CONSEQUENCES OF MOVING TO STAGE THREE

The move to the third stage of EMU has important consequences concerning institutional structure, monetary policy, and economic policy. These will be considered in turn.

[53] The European Parliament must be consulted and forward its view to the Council meeting as the Heads of State, etc.
[54] Art. 121(3).   [55] Art. 121(4).

In *institutional terms*, immediately after the decision on the starting date for Stage Three was taken the ECB was brought into being,[56] and the EMI went into liquidation.[57] The ECB has legal personality.[58] It has an Executive Board and a Governing Council. The Executive Board is composed of a President, Vice-President, and four other members, who must be recognized experts in monetary or banking matters. They serve for eight years and the posts are non-renewable.[59] The Governing Council consists of the Executive Board plus the Governors of the national central banks.[60] The independence of the ECB is enshrined in Article 108 (ex Article 107), which stipulates that the ECB shall not take any instruction from Community institutions, Member States, or any other body. This independence is reflected in the decision-making structure of the ECB: the President of the Council and a member of the Commission may participate in meetings of the ECB's Governing Council, but they do not have the right to vote.[61] The ECB is given the power to make regulations and take decisions. It is also empowered to make recommendations and deliver opinions.[62] These terms have the same meaning as in Article 249 (ex Article 189). The ECB is entitled, subject to certain conditions, to impose fines or periodic penalty payments on undertakings for failure to comply with obligations contained in its regulations and decisions.[63] The ECB is part of the European System of Central Banks (ESCB), the other members being the national central banks.[64] The start of the third stage of EMU also saw the establishment of the Economic and Financial Committee, to be composed of no more than two members drawn from the Member States, the Commission, and the ECB. This Committee has a number of tasks, including:[65] delivering opinions to the Council or Commission; keeping under review the economic and financial situation of the Member States and the Community; examining the situation regarding free movement of capital; and contributing to the preparation of Council work.

The most important consequence in terms of *monetary policy* was of course the establishment of a single currency. At the start of the third stage the Council fixed the conversion rates for the Member States entering the single currency.[66] The ECU was then substituted for these currencies at this rate, and became a currency in its own right. The Council was instructed to take other measures necessary for the rapid introduction of the ECU as the single currency of those Member States.[67] The TEU also contains important provisions concerning the objectives of Community monetary policy. These are set out in Article 105 (ex Article 105). The primary objective of the ESCB is to maintain price stability. Without prejudice to this objective, the ESCB must support the general economic policies of the Community with a view to attaining the objectives set out in Article 2 (ex Article 2). The ESCB is to act in accordance with the principle of an open market economy with free competition, favouring the

---

[56] Art. 123(1) (ex Art. 109l(1)).   [57] Art. 123(2).   [58] Art. 107(2) (ex Art. 106(2)).
[59] Art. 112(2) (ex Art. 109a(2)).   [60] Art. 112(1).   [61] Art. 113(1) (ex Art. 109b(1)).
[62] Art. 110 (ex Art. 108a).   [63] Art. 110(3).   [64] Art. 107(1) (ex Art. 106(1)).
[65] Art. 114(2) (ex Art. 109c(2)).
[66] This decision is made unanimously by those States which do not have a derogation, on a proposal from the Commission and after consulting the ECB: Art. 123(4) (ex Art. 109l(4)).
[67] Art. 123(4). These measures are, after the TN, made by qualified majority.

efficient allocation of resources and in compliance with the principles set out in Article 4. The basic tasks of the ESCB are:[68] to define and implement the Community's monetary policy; to conduct foreign-exchange operations; to hold and manage the official foreign reserves of the Member States; and to promote the smooth operation of the payment system. The ECB must be consulted on any Community act in its fields of competence and, subject to certain conditions, by national authorities regarding any draft legislative provision in its fields of competence.[69] The ECB has the exclusive right to authorize the issue of banknotes within the EC.[70] The ESCB is to 'contribute' to the smooth conduct of policies pursued by other competent authorities relating to the prudential supervision of credit institutions and the stability of the financial system.[71]

The shift to Stage Three also signals *the application of more peremptory Treaty provisions concerning economic policy.* This is particularly noteworthy in relation to fiscal and budgetary matters. Member States now have the obligation to avoid excessive government deficit and not just to endeavour to avoid them.[72] The Council's powers to deal with States that do not adhere to its recommendations on excessive budgetary deficits are reinforced in the third stage of EMU.[73]

5. UNDERSTANDING EMU: THE ECONOMIC FOUNDATIONS

The economic arguments for and against a single currency are hotly debated. They are also complex.[74] It would be impossible within the scope of this Chapter to give anything like an exhaustive account of these arguments. It would, however, be equally mistaken to exclude such matters entirely from the scope of the analysis and to rest content with discussion of the bare Treaty provisions on EMU. What follows is therefore an outline of some of the main themes in this debate.

(a) THE CASE FOR EMU

The case for EMU rests essentially on two connected foundations. It is argued that EMU will foster economic growth and engender greater price stability through low inflation, both of which are central objectives of national economic policy. These will be considered in turn.

The argument that EMU will enhance *economic growth* is based on a number of factors, the most important of which are as follows.

---

[68] Art. 105(2).   [69] Art. 105(4).

[70] Art. 106 (ex Art. 105a). The ECB and the national banks can actually issue the banknotes.

[71] Art. 105(5).   [72] Art. 104(1) (ex Art. 104c(1)).

[73] Arts. 104(9) and (11). These Treaty obligations have been given added force by the Stability and Growth Pact [1997] OJ C236/1, Reg. 1466/97 [1997], OJ L209/1, and Reg. 1467/97, [1997] OJ L209/6.

[74] See generally P. De Grauwe, *Economics of Monetary Integration* (Oxford University Press, 4th edn., 2000).

The most obvious factor is the *saving of transaction costs*. The existence of a single currency will remove exchange-rate conversions when money moves across national boundaries within the Community. The costs of buying foreign currency when travelling within the Community will thereby be saved. The Commission calculated that the total transaction cost savings would be in the order of $25 billion for the EU as a whole.[75]

An equally important, albeit contested, factor is the *link between the single market and a single currency*. This is captured most vividly in the Commission's slogan of 'one market, one money'. While it is clearly possible to have a single market without a single currency it is argued that the single market will work better in economic terms with a single currency than without. This has certainly been the view of the Commission and the link between the completion of a single market and a single currency is explicitly drawn in a number of Commission publications.[76] By having a single currency it will be possible for businesses to save on 'menu costs', in the sense of not having to maintain a different set of prices for each market. From the perspective of the manufacturer, this will facilitate the development of marketing strategies for the Community as a whole. From the perspective of the consumer, it will enable direct price comparisons to be made as to the cost of the same or similar products in different countries. The existence of a single currency will, moreover, render it easier to develop a single market in the sphere of banking and the provision of financial services than hitherto.

The existence of a single currency will also protect against the *costs associated with large exchange-rate changes and competitive devaluation*. Large changes in exchange rates can 'distort the single market by unpredictable shifts of advantage between countries unrelated to fundamentals',[77] thereby distorting trade flows, and in this sense 'the single market needs a single currency not just to push it forwards, but to stop it sliding backwards'.[78] Currency fluctuations of this nature can slow down economic growth by creating uncertainty for business, which is not conducive to investment or rational planning.[79] The very existence of wide price differentials fuelled in part by different currencies, combined with exchange rate changes, serves moreover to fuel attempts by Member States to prevent parallel imports and impede intra-Community trade.

It is argued that a single currency will also foster growth by *lowering interest rates and stimulating investment*. Countries will no longer have to raise their interest rates above German levels in order to stop their currencies from falling in relation to the D-mark.[80] Investment projects 'will become economic which were not so when they had to earn higher returns to repay expensive borrowed money, compensate for exchange rate uncertainty, and hand out high dividends to share-holders'.[81]

---

[75] *One Market, One Money* (European Commission, 1990), ch. 3.
[76] See, e.g., *Commission's Work Programme for 1998* (EC Commission, 1997).
[77] C. Johnson, *In with the Euro, Out with the Pound* (Penguin, 1996), 47.
[78] *Ibid.*
[79] *The Impact of Currency Fluctuations on the Internal Market*, COM(95) 503 final.
[80] Johnson, n. 49.   [81] *Ibid.*, 55.

The case for EMU is also, as seen, based on the argument that it fosters *stable prices and low inflation*. Savers tend to gain from low inflation, since their money retains its purchasing power for longer. This is so notwithstanding the fact that price rises are often accompanied by higher interest rates, since such high rates do not normally fully compensate for price rises. Inflation makes it more difficult to maintain long-term business plans, and redistributes income in an arbitrary manner. Businesses incur 'menu costs' when inflation rates are high or constantly changing. This is so in relation to the determination of wage costs, and in relation to the assimilation of information concerning the costs of their inputs. The ERM exerted some discipline over inflation rates, by the very fact that countries, in effect, linked their exchange rates to the D-mark, and limited their use of devaluation. There has, however, been a tendency for some countries to end up with exchange rates which were overvalued, and this was in part the rationale for the currency crises in 1992 and 1993. It is argued then that EMU offers a better, cheaper, and more stable way of reducing inflation, particularly when monetary policy is run by an independent central bank which is not subject to short-term political pressures of the kind which so often sway governments.

(b) THE CASE AGAINST EMU

It is important to recognize that there are a number of differing types of argument made against EMU. These can for the sake of analysis be divided into 'contingent disapproval' and 'outright rejection'.

The essence of the *contingent disapproval argument* can be put quite simply: the Member States are not ready for EMU, since they cannot meet the convergence criteria, except by creative forms of accounting which throw the whole enterprise into disrepute. This was exemplified by the letter signed by 155 German University professors, arguing that the time was not yet ripe for a move to EMU.[82]

The *outright rejection argument* is more complex, and is part political, part symbolic, and part economic.

In political terms, it is argued by some that a single currency is a major step on the route to a European super State, whether intentionally or not.[83] Important features of economic policy are shifted from the domestic policy agenda and transferred to Community organs. National governments no longer have the ultimate option of devaluation. There would no longer be any point in having parliamentary debates on matters such as inflation, interest rates, unemployment, and the like, since the operative power over such matters would be taken from national polities and given to the ECB. This would, so it is said, exacerbate problems of democratic deficit within the EC, given that the demise of national parliamentary power over such matters would not be offset by any meaningful control through the European Parliament.[84]

---

[82] *Financial Times*, 9 Feb. 1998.   [83] J. Redwood, *The Single European Currency* (Tecla, 1995), 11–12.
[84] *Ibid.*, 19–20.

In symbolic terms, a national currency is felt by some to be part of the very idea of nationhood. This point is captured well by Johnson:[85]

Advocates of monetary and exchange rate autonomy argue that it may not be perfect, but it is preferable to the alternative. The dishonour of a national currency may seem better than its death. Monetary sovereignty is sometimes felt to be part of a national sovereignty, so that giving it up involves a loss of political independence, and ultimately political union. It is almost a case of 'my country, right or wrong'.

In economic terms, it is argued that a single currency would lead to a variety of undesirable consequences. Prices would increase, since businesses would take advantage of the change from national currencies to the Euro to raise the real costs of their products before consumers had become accustomed to the new money. There would be significant costs entailed by the transition from national currencies to the Euro. A further argument is that a single currency would lead to greater controls over national economic policy. We have already seen that the Treaty provides for more extensive Community control over budget deficits in the third stage of EMU. Opponents of EMU claim that 'it is a small step from saying that the European Community has the right, indeed the duty, to control the level of deficit to saying that it would also take an interest in the level of spending and taxation'.[86]

(c) EMU: ECONOMICS, POLITICS, AND LAW

It is readily apparent that the debates about EMU are only in part economic in nature. The economic dimension shades into the political, and these often manifest themselves in legal form. This is brought out in the following extract.

F. Snyder, EMU Revisited[87]

The legal aspects of EMU are sometimes extremely controversial, either in public or behind the closed doors of diplomatic and monetary negotiations. Legal and other technical debates often act as a kind of shorthand for political disagreement. Competing economic theories frequently play the same role. This was the case long before EMU was set as a priority European Union objective. This does not mean, of course, that all legal aspects of EMU have been or are politically controversial. But, in the future also, political conflicts about EMU are likely often to appear in legal camouflage. This dialectical relationship between politics and law, political discourse and monetary discourse, and political discourse and legal discourse should not be surprising. The driving force in EMU, including its main legal aspects, has always been politics.

---

[85] N. 77 above, 87.   [86] Redwood, n. 83 above, 22.   [87] Snyder, n. 24 above, 468.

6. UNDERSTANDING EMU: CENTRAL BANK INDEPENDENCE

We have seen that the Treaty places particular emphasis upon the independence of the ECB.[88] The degree of independence possessed by national central banks varies.[89] Gormley and de Haan[90] identified five criteria which shape the division of responsibilities between national governments and their central banks.[91]

The first is the ultimate objective of monetary policy, which in many countries is price stability. The second, and related, feature is the specification of inflation targets. In some countries such as New Zealand this is agreed by the central bank with the government; in other countries, such as Germany, there is no obligation as such on the Bundesbank to announce or agree to any such targets. The third criterion is the degree of independence possessed by the bank and the juridical basis on which this rests. There will, for example, often be a statute dealing with such matters, which stipulates the extent to which the government can or cannot give any instructions to its central bank. The fourth criterion is closely connected to the third: the extent to which the government can ever override the central bank's view. In Germany, for example, the government can suspend the taking of decisions by the Bundesbank for a maximum of two weeks, and it would require a change of legislation for the government to exercise any greater control. The final factor is the appointment of bank officials, and the extent to which the government has any real discretion over this matter.

When judged by these criteria the ECB has a high degree of independence. Its independence is enshrined in Article 108. It is further reinforced by the fact that the Statute of the ESCB was attached as a Protocol to the TEU, and most of its provisions can be altered only by an amendment of the Treaty itself. In this sense the Treaty has constitutionalized the position of the ESCB: the organic law governing its operation cannot be altered by the ordinary legislative process, but only by revising the very provisions of the Treaty themselves.[92] The Treaty establishes the primary and secondary objectives of the ESCB. There is no formal requirement for the ECB to agree with the other Community institutions on the specification of price stability in particular economic circumstances, or on inflation targets. Nor is there is any formal provision allowing the other Community institutions to override the choices made by the ECB.

There is little doubt that this degree of independence was influenced by German desires to have an ECB which mirrored quite closely the powers and status of the Bundesbank. This sentiment was further strengthened because the ECB would be

---

[88] C. Zilioli and M. Selmayr, *The Law of the European Central Bank* (Hart, 2001).

[89] F. Amtenbrink, *The Democratic Accountability of Central Banks* (Hart, 1999), ch. 4.

[90] L. Gormley and J. de Haan, 'The Democratic Deficit of the European Central Bank' (1996) 21 *ELRev.* 95, 97–9; Amtenbrink, n. 89 above, 17–22.

[91] See also R. Lastra, 'European Monetary Union and Central Bank Independence', in M. Andenas, L. Gormley, C. Hadjiemmanuil, and I. Harden (eds.), *European Economic and Monetary Union: The Institutional Framework* (Kluwer, 1997), ch. 15; T. Daintith, 'Between Domestic Democracy and an Alien Rule of Law? Some Thoughts on the 'Independence' of the Bank of England', *ibid.*, ch. 17.

[92] Gormley and de Haan, n. 90 above, 101.

considering price stability, etc., for the Community as a whole. It was therefore particularly important that the short-term interests of certain Member States, or even the Community institutions, could not sway the ECB. While political considerations, therefore, played a role in shaping the ESCB, there are also sound economic arguments for central bank independence, as the following extract reveals.

L. Gormley and J. de Haan, The Democratic Deficit of the European Central Bank[93]

The general conclusion . . . is that businesses and households perform poorly when inflation is high and unpredictable. It is widely believed that the success of monetary policy in achieving a stable and low rate of inflation depends very much on the credibility of the monetary authorities. It makes quite a difference whether economic agents believe policy announcements and behave accordingly, or not. If a central bank with a high level of credibility indicates, for instance, that inflation is too high and that it will strive for a reduction, trade unions will take this announcement seriously in bargaining about wage levels. If the credibility of the central bank is low, trade unions may not believe that inflation will come down and demand higher wages, thereby fuelling the inflationary process.

By delegating monetary policy to an independent Central Bank with a clear mandate for price stability the credibility of the monetary authorities can be enhanced. A Central Bank which is independent will not be exposed to the same incentives to create unexpected inflation. The public can assume that the Central Bank will strive for a low level of inflation. Trade unions will lower their wage demands and investors will ask for lower interest rates as their inflationary expectations are reduced. Due to lower inflationary expectations, actual inflation will also decline.

It should not, however, be thought that there is only one way to structure a central bank, even given acceptance of independence as an ideal worth striving for. The preceding discussion of national central banks has revealed the range of factors that can influence the precise degree of independence accorded to such an institution. Two considerations are of particular importance when deciding upon this.

The first is economic in nature. It has been argued, for example, that the relationship between a central bank and government should be conceived of in terms of an agent/principal contract. On this view the principal, the government, would establish inflation targets and make the agent, the leadership of the central bank, responsible for attaining these targets.[94]

The second consideration is of a more political nature. A fully independent central bank, with little or no provision for policy override by the political branch of government, may well do much for the attainment of price stability, but at the expense of any real measure of democratic control. Monetary policy is, in this sense, taken off the normal political agenda. This is a choice which can and has been made by political systems, but the corresponding diminution in democratic control must also be acknowledged.

[93] *Ibid.*, 110.   [94] *Ibid.*, 111–12.

L. Gormley and J. de Haan, The Democratic Deficit of the European Central Bank[95]

By now it is well-known that Central Bank independence may improve upon monetary policy. In that sense, the independence of the ESCB and its mandate to strive for price stability are to be applauded, given the virtues of a low and stable rate of inflation. An important problem is how Central Bank independence is related to democratic accountability. Some authors argue that monetary policy should be treated like other instruments of economic policy, like fiscal policy, and should be fully decided upon by democratically elected representatives. Such an approach implies, however, too much a direct involvement of politicians with monetary policy. . . . Nevertheless, it is respectfully submitted that monetary policy ultimately must be controlled by democratically elected politicians. . . . Some way or another, the Central bank has to be accountable, and in relation to the ECB, the European Parliament is undoubtedly the appropriate body. National parliaments are, of course, responsible for Central Bank legislation; so too, logically, should the European Parliament be responsible for the legislative framework of the ECB, at least by way of co-decision. In other words, the 'rules of the game' (i. e. the objective of monetary policy) are decided upon according to normal democratic procedures, but the 'game' (monetary policy) is delegated to the Central Bank.

7. THE TRANSITION TO EMU: THE REAL WORLD

The formal decision of the Council, meeting as the Heads of State or Governments, that the applicant States, apart from Greece, had met the convergence criteria was made on 2 May 1998. The third stage of EMU duly began on 1 January 1999. The exchange rates of the participating countries were irrevocably set, and the Euro became a currency in its own right. There are twelve states participating in the Euro, Greece joining in January 2001. Denmark, Sweden, and the UK are the States with a derogation. The UK negotiated an opt-out Protocol, which was appended to the TEU, the import of which is that it is not bound to move to the third stage of EMU even if it does meet the convergence criteria. On 1 January 2002 the new banknotes and coins were introduced, and national currencies were withdrawn from circulation towards the end of February 2002.

This was so notwithstanding those who doubted whether some States really would meet the convergence criteria,[96] given the high debt levels in Italy and Belgium, and whether there would be sufficient political will to take the project forward. The Commission continued none the less to remain positive about attainment of EMU within the Treaty deadlines, although how far its views were 'expectation' and how far 'hope' was not always easy to discern. The positive tone of the Commission's pronouncements received added support from the Luxembourg European Council.[97] This summit affirmed the move towards Stage Three of EMU, noted the progress

[95] *Ibid.*, 112. See Amtenbrink, n. 89 above, ch. 5 for suggestions on how democratic accountability could be improved.
[96] For discussion of the interpretative leeway in these criteria see Snyder, n. 24 above, 457–63.
[97] 12–13 Dec. 1997.

made towards monetary union, and emphasized the interconnectedness of monetary policy and economic policy.[98]

8. CONCLUSION

i. In terms of *free movement of capital*, recent years have seen a growing body of case law testing the boundaries of the provisions introduced by the TEU. This case law should be viewed alongside that dealing with goods, persons, establishment, and services.

ii. There are a number of stresses and strains on EMU.

iii. In *monetary terms*, the Euro has had a rocky introduction to the world of currency markets. It has, for a variety of reasons, fallen considerably in relation to other currencies such as the pound and the dollar.[99]

iv. In *institutional terms*, this has led to criticism of the ECB for its overall management of the Euro currency, and for individual decisions such as whether to cut interest rates, and by how much. There also continues to be debate about the optimum degree of democratic control over the issues dealt with by the ECB.

v. The relationship between *monetary policy and broader economic policy* remains problematic. The EC has far greater control over monetary policy, as encapsulated in the Euro and the attendant ECB, than it does over broader economic policy. This is so notwithstanding the stability and growth pact.[100] The EC is none the less caught in a conundrum in this respect. It is generally recognized that there is an intimate relationship between monetary policy and economic policy: if countries run long-term budgetary deficits then this will cause the currency markets to take a poor view of the value of the Euro. There are however political difficulties for the EC in extending control over national economic policy, or even in making full use of the existing regime, lest it be accused of excessive centralization of economic decision-making.

vi. In more practical terms the switch to the Euro *has implications for a range of Community policies*, such as the budget, agriculture, and the internal market, all of which are particularly affected by the introduction of the new currency.[101]

---

[98] On this latter issue see Annex 1 Luxembourg European Council, 12–13 Dec. 1997: *Resolution of the European Council on Economic Policy Co-ordination in Stage 3 of EMU and on Treaty Articles 109 and 109b*.

[99] K. Dyson, *The Politics of the Euro-Zone: Stability or Breakdown* (Oxford University Press, 2000).

[100] Snyder, n. 24 above, 448–62; I. Harden, 'The Fiscal Constitution of EMU', in P. Beaumont and N. Walker (eds.), *Legal Framework of the Single European Currency* (Hart, 1999), ch. 5; I. Harden, J. von Hagen, and R. Brookes, 'The European Constitutional Framework for Member States' Public Finances', in *European Economic and Monetary Union*, n. 91 above, ch. 9.

[101] Commission Communication, *The Impact of the Changeover to the Euro on Community Policies, Institutions and Legislation*, COM(97)560; Commission Communication, *Progress towards Implementing the Commission's Communication of November 1997*, 12 Apr. 1999.

9. FURTHER READING

(a) *Books*

AMTENBRINK, F., *The Democratic Accountability of Central Banks* (Hart, 1999)

ANDENAS, M., GORMLEY, L., HADJIEMMANUIL, C., and HARDEN, I. (eds.), *European Economic and Monetary Union: The Institutional Framework* (Kluwer, 1997)

BEAUMONT, P., and WALKER, N. (eds.), *The Legal Framework of the Single European Currency* (Hart, 1999)

BRITTON, A., and MAYES, D., *Achieving Monetary Union in Europe* (Sage, 1992)

DE GRAUWE, P., *Economics of Monetary Integration* (Oxford University Press, 4th edn., 2000)

—— (ed.), *The Political Economy of Monetary Union* (Elgar, 2001)

DYSON, K., *Elusive Union, The Process of Economic and Monetary Union in Europe* (Longman, 1994)

—— *The Politics of the Euro-Zone: Stability or Breakdown* (Oxford University Press, 2000)

—— and FEATHERSTONE, K., *The Road to Maastricht: Negotiating Economic and Monetary Union* (Oxford University Press, 1999)

JOHNSON, C., *In with the Euro, Out with the Pound* (Penguin, 1996)

—— and COLLINGTON, S. (eds.), *The Monetary Economics of Europe* (Pinter, 1994)

MASSON, P., and TAYLOR, M. (eds.), *Policy Issues in the Operation of Currency Unions* (Cambridge University Press, 1993)

REDWOOD, J., *The Single European Currency* (Tecla, 1995)

SWANN, D., *The Economics of Europe, From Common Market to European Union* (Penguin, 9th edn., 2000)

USHER, J., *The Law of Money and Financial Services in the European Community* (Oxford University Press, 1994)

ZILIOLI, C., and SELMAYR, M., *The Law of the European Central Bank* (Hart, 2001)

(b) *Articles*

CRAIG, P., 'EMU, the ECB and Judicial Review', in P. Beaumont and N. Walker (eds.), *The Legal Framework of the Single European Currency* (Hart, 1999), ch. 4

DAINTITH, T., 'Between Domestic Democracy and an Alien Rule of Law? Some Thoughts on the 'Independence' of the Bank of England', in M. Andenas, L. Gormley, C. Hadjiemmanuil, and I. Harden (eds.), *European Economic and Monetary Union: The Institutional Framework* (Kluwer, 1997), ch. 17

HARDEN, I., 'The Fiscal Constitution of EMU', in P. Beaumont and N. Walker (eds.), *Legal Framework of the Single European Currency* (Hart, 1999), ch. 5

LASTRA, R., 'European Monetary Union and Central Bank Independence', in M. Andenas, L. Gormley, C. Hadjiemmanuil, and I. Harden (eds.), *European Economic and Monetary Union: The Institutional Framework* (Kluwer, 1997), ch. 15

Peers, S., 'Free Movement of Capital: Learning Lessons or Slipping on Spilt Milk?', in C. Barnard and J. Scott (eds.), *The Legal Foundations of the Single Market* (Hart, 2000)

Snyder, F., 'EMU Revisited: Are We Making a Constitution? What Constitution Are We Making', in P. Craig and G. de Búrca (eds.), *The Evolution of EU Law* (Oxford University Press, 1999), ch. 12

17

FREE MOVEMENT OF WORKERS
AND BEYOND

1. CENTRAL ISSUES

i. The free movement of persons is *one of the four fundamental freedoms* of Community law, along with the free movement of goods, services, and capital. This chapter deals primarily with the free movement of employed persons, and the next chapter with the free movement of the self-employed and of companies.

ii. There are *several central legal issues* that arise in the context of free movement of workers. These include the direct effect of Article 39; the meaning accorded to 'worker'; the extent to which the State is able to reserve certain tasks for its own nationals on the ground that they are part of the 'public service'; and the extent to which family members are protected by Community legislation.

iii. It is important, when addressing these issues, to *be aware of the tensions and interplay between the economic and the social aspects of the provisions on free movement of persons*. There is the image of the Community worker as a mobile unit of production, contributing to the creation of a single market and to the economic prosperity of Europe. There is also the image of the worker as human being, exercising a personal right to live in another

state and to take up employment there without discrimination, to improve the standard of living of his or her family. The policy of furthering the free movement of workers has been linked with a broader notion of European solidarity, with the underlying aspiration of integration of the peoples of Europe.

iv. The TEU introduced *citizenship* into EC law. There will be consideration of the range of rights encompassed by Union citizenship, the interpretation accorded to it by the ECJ, and the way in which citizenship is affecting the development of the law in this area.

v. The Treaty of Amsterdam brought the position of *third country nationals* directly into EC law. It introduced a new EC Treaty title on 'visas, asylum, immigration and the free movement of persons', which has the effect of shifting much of the pre-Amsterdam Third Pillar into the Community pillar. This raises a host of important issues concerning the conditions imposed on entry of third-country nationals, and the fairness of treatment accorded to them when they are in the Community. The political climate post-September 11, combined with concerns about immigration and asylum, are having a marked impact on this area.

2. THE DIRECT EFFECT OF ARTICLE 39

The basic provision is set out in Article 39 (ex Article 48) of the Treaty, which provides as follows:[1]

1. Freedom of movement of workers shall be secured within the Community.

2. Such freedom of movement shall entail the abolition of any discrimination based on nationality between workers of the Member States as regards employment, remuneration and other conditions of work and employment.

3. It shall entail the right, subject to limitations justified on grounds of public policy, public security or public health:

(a) to accept offers of employment actually made;

(b) to move freely within the territory of Member States for this purpose;

(c) to stay in a Member State for the purpose of employment in accordance with the provisions governing the employment of nationals of that State laid down by law, regulation or administrative action;

(d) to remain in the territory of a Member State after having been employed in that State, subject to conditions which shall be embodied in implementing regulations to be drawn up by the Commission.

4. The provisions of this Article shall not apply to employment in the public service.

The Court has repeatedly emphasized the central importance of the principle of freedom of movement and non-discrimination on grounds of nationality. The Article represents an application, in the specific context of workers, of the general principle in Article 12 (ex Article 6) of the Treaty that 'within the scope of application of this Treaty ... any discrimination on grounds of nationality shall be prohibited'.

The ECJ in *Walrave*[2] held that Article 48 (now Article 39) would apply even where the work was done outside the Community, so long as the legal relationship of employment was entered within the Community. This was extended further in *Boukhalfa*, in which it ruled that the Article applied also to the employment relationship of a Member State national which was entered into and primarily performed in a non-member country in which the national resided, at least as regards all aspects of the employment relationship which were governed by the legislation of the employing Member State.[3]

The Court made it clear, in *Walrave and Koch*[4] and in *Bosman*,[5] that the provisions of the Article were not just of 'vertical' direct effect. The rules challenged in these cases

---

[1] The ToA amended para. (1) so as to delete the words 'by the end of the transitional period at the latest'.

[2] Case 36/74, *Walrave and Koch* v. *Association Union Cycliste Internationale* [1974] ECR 1405.

[3] Case C–214/95, *Boukhalfa* v. *BRD* [1996] ECR I–2253.

[4] Case 36/74, n. 2 above.

[5] Case C–415/93, *Union Royale Belge des Sociétés de Football Association and others* v. *Bosman* [1995] ECR I–4921, paras. 82–4; Case C–411/98, *Angelo Ferlini* v. *Centre Hospitalier de Luxembourg* [2000] ECR I–8081, para. 50.

were made by international sporting associations, concerning cycling and football respectively, which were neither public nor State bodies. However, the Court ruled that this did not exempt them from the application of Article 48 (now Article 39):

Prohibition of such discrimination does not only apply to the action of public authorities but extends likewise to rules of any other nature aimed at regulating in a collective manner gainful employment and the provision of services. . . .

Since, moreover, working conditions in the various Member States are governed sometimes by means of provisions laid down by law or regulations and sometimes by agreements and other acts concluded or adopted by private persons, to limit the prohibitions in question to acts of a public authority would risk creating inequality in their application.[6]

It was not clear from these cases whether Article 39 (ex Article 48) was more generally horizontally applicable to the actions of individuals who did not have the power to make rules regulating gainful employment, e.g. a single employer who refused to employ someone on the ground of their nationality.[7] This issue has now been clarified by *Angonese*.[8]

Case C–281/98, Roman Angonese v. Cassa di Riparmio di Bolzano SpA
[2000] ECR I–4139

[Note ToA renumbering: Arts. 48 and 119 are now Arts. 39 and 141]

Angonese was an Italian national whose mother tongue was German. He was resident in Bolzano in Italy, but studied in Austria between 1993–7. He applied to take part in a competition for a post with a private bank in Bolzano, the Cassa di Riparmio. A condition for entry to the competition imposed by the bank was a certificate of bilingualism (in Italian and German). The bank was allowed to impose requirement of this type by a collective agreement with national savings banks in Italy, but an individual bank was free whether to impose such conditions at all. The certificate was issued by the public authorities in Bolzano after an examination held only in that province. The national court found as a fact that Angonese was bilingual, and that there could be practical difficulties for non-residents of Bolzano to obtain the certificate in good time. Angonese did not obtain the certificate and the bank refused to admit him to the competition for the post. Angonese argued that the Bank's requirement for an applicant to have the certificate was contrary to Article 48.

THE ECJ

30. It should be noted at the outset that the principle of non-discrimination set out in Article 48 is drafted in general terms and is not specifically addressed to the Member States.

31. Thus, the Court has held that the prohibition of discrimination based on nationality applies

---

[6] *Walrave*, n. 2 above, paras. 17–19.

[7] Art. 7(4) of Reg. 1612/68, which is discussed further below, provides some support for such an interpretation since it stipulates that clauses in individual contracts of employment will be void in so far as they discriminate on grounds of nationality.

[8] Noted by R. Lane and N. Nic Shubhne (2000) 37 *CMLRev.* 1237.

not only to the actions of public authorities but also to rules of any other nature aimed at regulating in a collective manner gainful employment and the provision of services (see . . . *Walrave* . . .).

32. The Court has held that the abolition, as between Member States, of obstacles to freedom of movement would be compromised if the abolition of State barriers could be neutralised by obstacles resulting from the exercise of their legal autonomy by associations or organizations not governed by public law (see *Walrave*, paragraph 18 . . . and . . . *Bosman* . . . paragraph 83).

33. Since working conditions in the different Member States are governed sometimes by provisions laid down by law or regulation and sometimes by agrrements and other acts concluded or adopted by private persons, limiting application of the prohibition of discrimination based on nationality to acts of a public authority risks creating inequality in its application (see *Walrave*, paragraph 19, and *Bosman*, paragraph 84).

34. The Court has also ruled that the fact that certain provisions of the Treaty are formally addressed to the Member States does not prevent rights from being conferred at the same time on any individual who has an interest in compliance with the obligations thus laid down (see . . . *Defrenne* . . .). The Court accordingly held . . . that the prohibition of discrimination applied equally to all agreements intended to regulate paid labour collectively, as well as to contracts between individuals. . . .

35. Such considerations must, *a fortiori*, be applicable to Article 48 . . ., which lays down a fundamental freedom and which constitutes a specific application of the general prohibition of discrimination contained in Article 6 (now . . . Article 12 EC). In that respect, like Article 119 . . . it is designed to ensure that there is no discrimination on the labour market.

36. Consequently, the prohibition of discrimination on grounds of nationality laid down in Article 48 . . . must be regarded as applying to private persons as well.

3.　WHO IS PROTECTED BY ARTICLE 39

Article 40 (ex Article 49) of the Treaty provides for the making of secondary legislation by the Council to bring about the freedoms set out in Article 39. Several directives and regulations have been passed to this effect, governing the conditions of entry, residence, and treatment of EC workers and their families. The most important of these are Directive 64/221, which governs the main derogations or exceptions to the rules on free movement;[9] Directive 68/360, which regulates the formalities and conditions of entry and residence of workers and the self-employed; and Regulation 1612/68, which elaborates on the equal-treatment principle and sets out many of the substantive rights and entitlements of workers and their families. Regulation 1251/70 protects the right of the worker, and those members of the worker's family listed in Regulation 1612/68, to remain in the territory of a Member State, mainly in the event of retirement, permanent incapacity to work, or death, after having been employed in that state for a period of time and subject to certain conditions.[10]

Despite the various measures of secondary legislation, many of the basic terms which determine the scope of these provisions are not defined either in the Treaty or

---

[9] Dir. 64/221 is discussed in detail in Ch. 19.　　　[10] [1970] II OJ Spec. Ed. 402, [1970] JO L142/24.

in the legislation, but have been shaped by the ECJ, most importantly the meaning of 'worker'.

A fundamental issue which was not immediately apparent from Article 39 was whether 'workers of the Member States' in paragraph (2) covered only nationals of the Member States, or whether it included non-EC nationals resident and working within the Community.[11] One commentator drew on the contrast between Article 69 of the ECSC Treaty, which mentioned 'workers who are nationals of the Member States', and Article 39 of the EC Treaty, which makes no reference to nationality. Plender argued that this implied that 'the draftsmen of the EEC Treaty intended to establish a common policy for all workers in the Community, irrespective of their nationality'.[12] However, the secondary legislation subsequently passed to implement Article 39, in particular Regulation 1612/68, specifically restricts its application to workers who are nationals of the Member States, and that has been the interpretation adopted by the ECJ. The status of third-country nationals who reside and work within the Community will be discussed further below.

(a) DEFINITION OF 'WORKER': A COMMUNITY CONCEPT

It should be made clear at the outset that the definition of the term 'worker' has been held to be a matter for Community law. The issue arose early in the case of *Hoekstra*, in the context of the interpretation of a Council social security regulation.

Case 75/63, Hoekstra (née Unger) v. Bestuur der Bedrijfsvereniging voor Detailhandel en Ambachten
[1964] ECR 177

[Note ToA renumbering: Arts. 48 and 51 are now Arts. 39 and 42 respectively]

THE ECJ[13]

The establishment of as complete a freedom of movement for workers as possible, which thus forms part of the 'foundations' of the Community, therefore constitutes the principal objective of Article 51 and thereby conditions the interpretation of the regulations adopted in implementation of that Article.

Articles 48 to 51 of the Treaty, by the very fact of establishing freedom of movement for 'workers', have given Community scope to this term.

If the definition of this term were a matter for the competence of national law, it would therefore be possible for each Member State to modify the meaning of the concept of 'migrant worker' and to eliminate at will the protection afforded by the Treaty to certain categories of person.

---

[11] See F. Burrows, *Free Movement in European Community Law* (Clarendon Press, 1987), 124.

[12] R. Plender, 'Competence, European Community Law and Nationals of Non-Member States' (1990) 39 *ICLQ* 599.

[13] [1964] ECR 177, 184.

Moreover nothing in Articles 48 to 51 of the Treaty leads to the conclusion that these provisions have left the definition of the term 'worker' to national legislation.

On the contrary, the fact that Article 48(2) mentions certain elements of the concept of 'workers', such as employment and remuneration, shows that the Treaty attributes a Community meaning to that concept.

Articles 48 to 51 would therefore be deprived of all effect and the above-mentioned objectives of the Treaty would be frustrated if the meaning of such a term could be unilaterally fixed and modified by national law.

Two themes are apparent in this judgment. The first is that the ECJ requires the term worker to be a Community concept; and the Court claims ultimate authority to define its meaning and scope. In the words of Federico Mancini, formerly Advocate General and Judge of the Court, it conferred on itself a 'hermeneutic monopoly' to counteract possible unilateral restrictions of the application of the rules on freedom of movement by the different Member States.[14] Thus the ECJ has held that a spouse can be employed by the other spouse as a worker,[15] and it has also held that Article 39 can be relied on by the employer and not just by the employee.[16] The second theme is that the Court will construe the term broadly, given that the establishment of the freedom constitutes part of the 'foundations' of the Community. Any person who pursues activities which are effective and genuine, to the exclusion of activities on such a small scale as to be regarded as purely marginal and ancillary, will be treated as a worker.[17]

(b) DEFINITION OF 'WORKER': ECONOMIC AND SOCIAL ASPECTS

A number of cases have been concerned with the interplay between the economic aspect of free movement, as determined by the level of remuneration, and the social aspect underlying free-movement policy. This issue arose in *Levin*, in the context of part-time workers.

Case 53/81, Levin v. Staatssecretaris van Justitie
[1982] ECR 1035

The appellant was a British citizen who was married to a non-EC national and living in the Netherlands, but whose application for a residence permit had been refused. She argued that she had sufficient income for her and her husband's maintenance, and that she had also taken up part-time employment as a chambermaid. The Staatssecretaris van Justitie had submitted that she was not a 'favoured EC citizen' since her employment did not provide sufficient means

---

[14] See G.F. Mancini, 'The Free Movement of Workers in the Case-Law of the European Court of Justice', in D. Curtin and D. O'Keeffe (eds.), *Constitutional Adjudication in European Community and National Law* (Butterworths, 1992), 67.

[15] Case C–337/97, *C.P.M. Meeusen v. Hoofddirectie van de Informatie Beheer Groep* [1999] ECR I–3289.

[16] Case C–350/96, *Clean Car Autoservice GmbH v. Landeshauptmann von Wien* [1998] ECR I–2521.

[17] Case C–337/97, *Meeusen*, n. 15 above.

for her support, not being equal at least to the minimum legal wage prevailing in The Nether-lands. A reference was made from the Dutch court to the ECJ, where the appellant argued that this 'minimum-wage' argument would place other Member State nationals in a less favourable position than nationals of the host country who have the option of working part-time for an income below the subsistence level. The Court referred to the *Hoekstra* judgment and to its argument that Member States could not unilaterally restrict the scope and meaning of the term worker.

THE ECJ

12. Such would, in particular, be the case if the enjoyment of the rights conferred by the principle of freedom of movement for workers could be made subject to the criterion of what the legislation of the host State declares to be a minimum wage, so that the field of application *ratione personae* of the Community rules on this subject might vary from one Member State to another. The meaning and the scope of the terms 'worker' and 'activity as an employed person' should thus be clarified in the light of the principles of the legal order of the Community.

13. In this respect it must be stressed that these concepts define the field of application of one of the fundamental freedoms guaranteed by the Treaty and, as such, may not be interpreted restrictively.

14. In conformity with this view the recitals to Regulation No 1612/68 contain a general affirmation of the right of all workers in the Member States to pursue the activity of their choice within the Community, irrespective of whether they are permanent, seasonal or frontier workers or workers who pursue their activities for the purpose of providing services. Furthermore, although Article 4 of Directive 68/360 grants the right of residence to workers upon the mere production of the document on the basis of which they entered the territory and of a confirmation of engagement from the employer or a certificate of employment, it does not subject this right to any condition relating to the kind of employment or to the amount of income derived from it.

15. An interpretation which reflects the full scope of these concepts is also in conformity with the objectives of the Treaty which include, according to Articles 2 and 3, the abolition, as between Member States, of obstacles to freedom of movement for persons, with the purpose *inter alia* of promoting throughout the Community a harmonious development of economic activities and a raising of the standard of living. Since part-time employment, although it may provide an income lower than what is considered to be the minimum required for subsistence, constitutes for a large number of persons an effective means of improving their living conditions, the effectiveness of Community law would be impaired and the achievement of the objectives of the Treaty would be jeopardized if the enjoyment of rights conferred by the principle of freedom of movement for workers were reserved solely to persons engaged in full-time employment and earning, as a result, a wage at least equivalent to the guaranteed minimum wage in the sector under consideration.

. . .

17. It should however be Stated that whilst part-time employment is not excluded from the field of application of the rules on freedom of movement for workers, those rules cover only the pursuit of effective and genuine activities, to the exclusion of activities on such a small scale as to be regarded as purely marginal and ancillary. It follows both from the Statement of the principle of freedom of movement for workers and from the place occupied by the rules relating to that principle in the system of the Treaty as a whole that those rules guarantee only the free movement of persons who pursue or are desirous of pursuing a genuine economic activity.

There are a number of important aspects to this judgment. The ECJ begins by reaffirming that the rules on free movement of persons are fundamental to the Community, and must therefore be broadly and inclusively interpreted (paragraphs 13 and 14). The freedom to take up employment was important, not just as a means towards the creation of a single market for the benefit of the Member State economies, but as a right for the worker to raise her or his standard of living. This was so even if the worker did not reach the minimum level of subsistence in a particular State (paragraph 15). Moreover, in response to the suggestion that Levin may only have sought work in order to obtain a residence permit to remain in the country, the Court ruled that the purpose or motive of the worker was immaterial, once he or she was pursuing or wishing to pursue a genuine and effective economic activity (paragraph 17). The requirement that work be undertaken as a genuine economic activity was probably a response to Member State concerns that their social security schemes would become overburdened. This might be so as a result of migrants entering from other countries whose systems of social benefits are less generous, and who do not really intend to engage in effective work. Advocate General Slynn acknowledged this concern. However, he noted the increasing dependence on part-time work, especially in times of unemployment. He emphasized that the exclusion of part-time work from the protection of Article 48 (now Article 39) would exclude not only women, the elderly, and disabled who, for personal reasons, might wish only to work part-time, but also women and men who would prefer to work full-time but are obliged to accept part-time work. *Levin* thus clarified that part-time workers were covered by the Treaty provisions on free movement, and that it did not matter if workers chose to supplement their income from other private sources.

In *Kempf,*[18] the issue was taken a step further. A German national who was living and working in the Netherlands as a music teacher, giving approximately twelve lessons a week, was refused a residence permit. The Dutch and Danish governments argued that work providing an income below the minimum means of subsistence in the host State could not be regarded as genuine and effective work if the person doing the work claimed social assistance from *public* funds. The Court disagreed, ruling that when a genuine part-time worker sought to supplement earnings below the subsistence level, it was:

irrelevant whether those supplementary means of subsistence are derived from property or from the employment of a member of his family, as was the case in *Levin*, or whether, as in this instance, they are obtained from financial assistance drawn from the public funds of the Member State in which he resides.[19]

Member State concerns about the possible abuse of the Treaty provisions by those who were simply seeking a Member State with better social provision in which to reside did not, said Advocate General Slynn, justify the exclusion of part-time workers in Kempf's position from the scope of the Treaty. Thus 'if a person deliberately and for no good reason took a part-time job when he could do a full-time job, that might

[18] Case 139/85, *Kempf* v. *Staatsecretaris van Justitie* [1986] ECR 1741.
[19] *Ibid.*, para. 14.

under national law affect his rights to public funds. It does not prevent him from being a worker'.[20]

This fairly broad reading of the term 'worker' is also to be seen in other cases. The ECJ has ruled that the practice of sport may fall within Community law in so far as it constitutes an economic activity, although the composition of national teams could be a question of purely sporting and not of economic interest.[21] It has also ruled that fishermen who are paid a share of the proceeds of sale of their catches can be considered to be 'workers', despite the irregular nature of their remuneration.[22] Yet despite the guidance on the need for 'genuine and effective work' and the exclusion of 'marginal and ancillary activities', questions concerning the concrete application of these terms to specific cases have regularly arisen and been referred to the ECJ.

In *Lawrie-Blum*,[23] it was asked to rule on the compatibility of German measures restricting access for non-nationals to the preparatory service stage which was necessary for qualification as a secondary school teacher. Addressing the question whether a trainee teacher participating in the preparatory service course would qualify as a 'worker' for the purposes of the relevant Treaty provisions, the Court provided a more elaborate three-part definition of the term:

That concept must be defined in accordance with objective criteria which distinguish the employment relationship by reference to the rights and duties of the persons concerned. The essential feature of an employment relationship, however, is that for a certain period of time a person performs services for and under the direction of another person in return for which he receives remuneration.[24]

The Court ruled that a trainee teacher did qualify as a worker since, during the period of preparatory service, these three conditions would be fulfilled: she would perform services of economic value, under the direction of the school in question, and would receive a measure of remuneration in return. The fact that the pay was less than a full teacher's salary was immaterial, for the same sorts of reasons given in *Levin* and *Kempf*: what mattered was the genuinely economic nature of the work and the receipt of some remuneration, and not the amount of the pay. In the following case, the ECJ pushed the concept of remuneration, and hence of economic activity, a little further.

---

[20] [1986] ECR 1741, 1744. For a similarly broad reading of the working population in the context of EC legislation on sex discrimination see Case C–317/93, *Inge Nolte v. Landesversicherungsanstalt Hannover* [1995] ECR I–4625, discussed in Ch. 20.

[21] Case 36/74, *Walrave*, n. 2 above; Case C–415/93, *Bosman*, n. 5 above; Case 13/76, *Donà v. Mantero* [1976] ECR 1333. Compare *Bosman*, paras. 120–129.

[22] See Case 3/87, *R. v. Ministry of Agriculture, Fisheries and Food, ex p. Agegate Ltd.* [1989] ECR 4459, paras. 33–36.

[23] Case 66/85, *Lawrie-Blum v. Land Baden-Württemberg* [1986] ECR 2121.

[24] *Ibid.*, para. 17. See also Case C–3/90, *Bernini v. Minister van Onderwijs en Wetenschappen* [1992] ECR I–1071.

Case 196/87, Steymann v. Staatsecretaris van Justitie
[1988] ECR 6159

Steymann was a German national living in the Netherlands, where he had worked for a short time as a plumber. He then joined the Bhagwan Community, a religious community which provided for the material needs of its members. He participated in the life of the community by performing plumbing work, general household duties, and other commercial activity on the community's premises. His application for a residence permit to pursue an activity as an employed person was refused and, on his application for review of this, a reference was made to the Court.

THE ECJ

9. It must be observed *in limine* that, in view of the objectives of the European Economic Community, participation in a community based on religion or another form of philosophy falls within the field of application of Community law only in so far as it can be regarded as an economic activity within the meaning of Article 2 of the Treaty.

. . .

11. As regards the activities in question in this case, it appears from the documents before the Court that they consist of work carried out within and on behalf of the Bhagwan Community in connection with the Bhagwan Community's commercial activities. It appears that such work plays a relatively important role in the way of life of the Bhagwan Community and that only in special circumstances can the members of the community avoid taking part therein. In turn, the Bhagwan Community provides for the material needs of its members, including pocket-money, irrespective of the nature and the extent of the work which they do.

12. In a case such as the one before the national court it is impossible to rule out *a priori* the possibility that work carried out by members of the community in question constitutes an economic activity within the meaning of Article 2 of the Treaty. In so far as the work, which aims to ensure a measure of self-sufficiency for the Bhagwan Community, constitutes an essential part of participation in that community, the services which the latter provides to its members may be regarded as being an indirect *quid pro quo* for their work.

The fact that the work might be seen in conventional terms as being unpaid did not mean that it was not effective economic activity. He provided services of value to the religious community which would otherwise have to be performed by someone else, and in return for which his material needs were satisfied.

The ECJ's expansive approach is evident once again in *Raulin*.[25] The case concerned a French national, employed in the Netherlands, as a waitress under an on-call contract which gave no guarantee of the hours to be worked, but under which she had worked for sixty hours in all over an eight-month period. The ECJ held that she was not precluded, by virtue of the conditions of the on-call contract, from being considered a worker within Article 48 (now Article 39). The question whether she would

---

[25] Case C–357/89, *Raulin v. Minister van Onderwijs en Wetenschappen* [1992] ECR I–1027.

qualify as a worker was, with the aid of certain guidelines, ultimately left to the national court to determine as a matter of fact:

The national court may, however, when assessing the effective and genuine nature of the activity in question, take account of the irregular nature and limited duration of the services actually performed under a contract for occasional employment. The fact that the person concerned worked only a very limited number of hours in a labour relationship may be an indication that the activities exercised are purely marginal and ancillary. The national court may also take account, if appropriate, of the fact that the person must remain available to work if called upon to do so by the employer.[26]

(c) DEFINITION OF 'WORKER': THE RESIDUAL RELEVANCE OF THE PURPOSE OF EMPLOYMENT?

The general rule is that the purpose for which the employment is undertaken will not be relevant in determining whether a person is a worker. Provided that the employment is genuine and not marginal it will benefit from Article 39. There are, however, cases where some account has been taken of the purpose of the employment.

In *Bettray* the ECJ ruled on the application of Article 48 (now Article 39) to someone who was undertaking therapeutic work as part of a drug-rehabilitation programme under Dutch social employment law.[27] The aim of the programme was to reintegrate people who were temporarily incapacitated into the workforce. They would be paid a certain amount, and treated, in so far as possible, in accordance with normal conditions of paid employment. The ECJ began by noting that a job was being carried out under supervision and in return for remuneration, and that the low pay from public funds and the low productivity of the worker would not in themselves prevent the application of Article 48. However, unlike in its judgment in *Levin* where the reason for undertaking work was said not to be relevant to its genuineness, the ECJ went on to examine the purpose of the work performed:

However, work under the Social Employment Law cannot be regarded as an effective and genuine economic activity if it constitutes merely a means of rehabilitation or reintegration for the persons concerned and the purpose of the paid employment, which is adapted to the physical and mental possibilities of each person, is to enable those persons sooner or later to recover their capacity to take up ordinary employment or to lead as normal as possible a life.

It also appears from the order for reference that persons employed under the Social Employment Law are not selected on the basis of their capacity to perform a certain activity; on the contrary, it is the activities which are chosen in the light of the capabilities of the persons who are going to perform them in order to maintain, re-establish or develop their capacity for work. Finally, the activities involved are pursued in the framework of undertakings or work associations created solely for that purpose by local authorities.[28]

Clearly the purpose for undertaking the work was crucial to the decision which was reached by the Court here. The fact that the main or even sole purpose of the work

---

[26] [1992] ECR I–1027, para. 14.
[27] Case 344/87, *Bettray* v. *Staatssecretaris van Justitie* [1989] ECR 1621.
[28] *Ibid.*, paras. 17–19.

was to rehabilitate the person, to find work which would suit their requirements and capabilities rather than to meet a genuine economic need (as was the case in *Steymann*), resulted in a ruling against Bettray. The case is open to criticism, partly because ensuring the mobility of a well-trained workforce would seem to be an important part of the Treaty's aims, and the reintegration of people back into the workforce through sheltered employment is a part of this. Further, it is not clear whether the *Bettray* ruling would apply to the case of sheltered employment for disabled people, something which was mentioned by the Advocate General in the case. Is all sheltered employment now outside the scope of the Treaty rules on free movement of workers, or is it only when the *sole* purpose of the work is to reintegrate someone who is temporarily incapacitated back into employment? There are organizations in most states which create and support projects which provide sheltered employment for disabled people on a longer-term basis, and although productivity may be lower than that performed by able-bodied workers, the work generally is of some commercial value. Such workers should equally have the benefit of the Treaty rules on freedom of movement, and it may be that the fact that the activities would not be solely therapeutic, but partly for therapeutic and partly for commercial purposes, would be sufficient to distinguish them from the programme in *Bettray*.

The purpose behind the employment was also of relevance in *Brown*.[29] The ECJ indicated that, although someone who has engaged in genuine and effective work before leaving to begin a course of study will be considered to be a 'worker' within Article 48 (now Article 39), the fact that the work was undertaken purely in order to prepare for the course of study, rather than to prepare for an occupation or employment, would mean that not all of the advantages provided for workers within Community law may be claimed. This is an interesting notion introduced by the Court of a semi-status between worker and non-worker, which may be held when someone is engaged in genuine and effective work, but purely in order to become a student rather than to prepare for an occupation. Brown was a dual national relying on his French nationality in the UK, who had worked for nine months for a company in Scotland as a form of 'pre-university industrial training', before beginning an electrical engineering degree at Cambridge University. The Court ruled that although he was to be regarded as a 'worker' (since he had clearly engaged in eight months of effective, full-time economic activity, satisfying the three criteria of *Lawrie-Blum*), he was not entitled to the social advantage of a maintenance grant. This was because his employment was merely 'ancillary' to the course of study he wished to undertake. The issues raised by the case are difficult because the Court relies on rather fine distinctions based on the purpose for which work is undertaken. It seemed from earlier cases such as *Levin* that the purpose of undertaking work was irrelevant to the genuineness of the employment. The purpose of the work, to gain pre-University experience, was however taken into account in Brown's case, not to disqualify him as a worker, but to limit his rights. The conclusion can be seen as a response by the ECJ to concerns voiced by the Member States about the 'abuse' of the provisions on free movement of

---

[29] Case 197/86, *Brown v. Secretary of State for Scotland* [1988] ECR 3205.

workers by those who merely wished to avail themselves of the generous educational provision in a particular Member State.[30]

(d) DEFINITION OF 'WORKER': THOSE SEEKING WORK

The discussion thus far has been concerned with those who have a job of some kind. An important issue is how far those seeking work can benefit from Article 39. In *Levin*, the ECJ had referred in passing to the rules relating to freedom of movement for persons 'who wish to pursue an activity as an employed person',[31] and in *Royer* to the right 'to look for or pursue an occupation'.[32] The issue was addressed more directly in *Antonissen*,[33] where the ECJ held that those who are actively seeking work should have something like a 'semi-status' of worker. The formal status of worker protected under Article 48 (now Article 39) was separated from the bundle of material advantages which would normally attach to that status under Community legislation.

Case C–292/89, R. v. Immigration Appeal Tribunal, ex parte Antonissen
[1991] ECR I–745

[Note ToA renumbering: Art. 48 is now Art. 39]

Antonissen was a Belgian national who had arrived in the United Kingdom in 1984, and had attempted unsuccessfully to find work. Following his imprisonment for a drug-related offence, the Secretary of State decided to deport him. He applied for judicial review of the dismissal of his appeal against deportation, and the case was referred to the ECJ. One of the arguments made was that only Community nationals in possession of a confirmation of engagement of employment were entitled to a right of residence in another Member State.

THE ECJ

9. In that connection it has been argued that, according to the strict wording of Article 48 of the Treaty, Community nationals are given the right to move freely within the territory of the Member States for the purpose only of accepting offers of employment actually made (Article 48(3)(a) and (b)) whilst the right to stay in the territory of a Member State is stated to be for the purpose of employment (Article 48(3)(c)).

10. Such an interpretation would exclude the right of a national of a Member State to move freely and to stay in the territory of the other Member States in order to seek employment there, and cannot be upheld.

. . .

[30] The ruling in *Brown* can be contrasted to that in Case C–3/90, *Bernini*, n. 24 above. It should also be read in the light of Case C–184/99, *Rudy Grzelczyk v. Centre Public d'Aide Sociale d'Ottignes-Louvain-la-Neuve (CPAS)* [2001] ECR I–6193, paras. 34–35.

[31] Case 53/81, *Levin v. Staatssecretaris van Justitie* [1982] ECR 1035, para. 16.

[32] Case 48/75, *Royer* [1976] ECR 497, para. 31.

[33] Case C–292/89, *R. v. Immigration Appeal Tribunal, ex p. Antonissen* [1991] ECR I–745.

12. Moreover, a strict interpretation of Article 48(3) would jeopardize the actual chances that a national of a Member State who is seeking employment will find it in another Member State, and would, as a result, make that provision ineffective.

13. It follows that Article 48(3) must be interpreted as enumerating, in a non-exhaustive way, certain rights benefiting nationals of Member States in the context of the free movement of workers and that that freedom also entails the right for nationals of Member States to move freely within the territory of the other Member States and to stay there for the purposes of seeking employment.

Antonissen provides a clear example of the Court's purposive approach, in suggesting a wider scope for Article 48 (now Article 39) than the words of the Article themselves convey. The ECJ examined the Article and identified its purpose: in this case, to ensure the free movement of workers. It then concluded that a literal interpretation of its terms would hinder that purpose. If nationals could move to another Member State only when they already had an offer of employment, the number of people who could move would be small, and many workers who could well seek and find employment on arrival in a Member State would be prevented from so doing. A particularly interesting feature of the *Antonissen* ruling was the ECJ's statement that the rights expressly enumerated in Article 48 were not exhaustive. This open-ended approach leaves the Court with the power to adapt and even extend the scope of the Article through interpretation, in accordance with the changing social, economic, and political climate in the Community.

However, the ECJ was also clear that the status of an EC national searching for work was not the same as that of an EC national who was actually employed.[34] There may be provisions, such as unemployment insurance, that cannot be used by someone who has never participated in the employment market.[35] Moreover, Member States retained the power to expel a job-seeker who has not found work after a period of time, without needing to invoke one of the grounds of exception set out in Article 39(3).

---

[34] See Case 316/85, *Centre public d'aide sociale de Courcelles* v. *Lebon* [1987] ECR 2811, in which the Court held that many of the social and tax advantages guaranteed to workers within Community law were not available to those who were moving in search of work. But contrast Case C–57/96, *Meints* v. *Minister van Landbouw* [1997] ECR I–6689, on a one-off payment to agricultural workers who had been made redundant.

[35] Case C–278/94, *Commission* v. *Belgium* [1996] ECR I–4307. For the impact on women of the exclusion of domestic, caring, and family work from the EC conception of 'worker' see L. Ackers, 'Women, Citizenship and EC law: The Gender Implications of the Free Movement Provisions' (1995) 17 *JSWFL* 498.

4. DISCRIMINATION, MARKET ACCESS, AND JUSTIFICATION

It is clear that rules which directly discriminate on the grounds of nationality will be caught by Article 39.[36] It is equally clear that indirect discrimination and impediments to market access can also lead to infringement of Article 39.[37] Discrimination, whether direct or indirect, will, however, be found only where two groups which are comparable are treated differently, or where groups which are not comparable are treated in the same way.[38]

(a) DIRECT DISCRIMINATION

In proceedings brought by the Commission against France for failing to repeal provisions of the French Maritime Code, which had required a certain proportion of the crew of a ship to be of French nationality, the Court ruled that Article 48 was 'directly applicable in the legal system of every Member State' and would render inapplicable all contrary national law.[39] It is moreover clear that a State can be held in breach of Article 39, even though the discrimination is practised by, for example, a public university. Thus Italy was responsible for a discriminatory practice whereby certain public universities did not recognize the acquired rights of former foreign-language assistants.[40]

(b) INDIRECT DISCRIMINATION

Indirect as well as direct discrimination on grounds of nationality is prohibited by Article 39, so that a condition of eligibility for a benefit which is more easily satisfied by national than by non-national workers is likely to fall foul of the Treaty.

A common species of indirect discrimination is where benefits are made conditional, in law or fact, on *residency or place of origin requirements* that can more easily be satisfied by nationals as opposed to non-nationals.[41] In *Ugliola*, an Italian worker in Germany challenged a German law under which a worker's security of employment was protected by having periods of military service taken into account in calculating the length of employment.[42] The law in question applied only to those who had done

---

[36] This is so even where the benefit in question is granted to nationals of a State pursuant to a bilateral convention with a non-Member State. Such benefits must also be accorded to nationals of other Member States in comparable situations: Case C–55/00, *Elide Gottardo* v. *INPS*, 15 Jan. 2002.

[37] A. Castro Oliveira, 'Workers and Other Persons: Step-by-Step from Movement to Citizenship' (2002) 39 *CMLRev.* 77.

[38] Case C–391/97, *Frans Gschwind* v. *Finanzamt Aachen-Aussenstadt* [1999] ECR I–5451, para. 21; Case C–356/98, *Arben Kaba* v. *Home Secretary* [2000] ECR I–2623. See, for criticism of the *Kaba* case, S. Peers, 'Dazed and Confused: Family Members' Residence Rights and the Court of Justice' (2001) 26 *ELRev.* 76.

[39] Case 167/73, *Commission* v. *French Republic* [1974] ECR 359; Case C–185/96, *Commission* v. *Hellenic Republic* [1998] ECR I–6601.

[40] Case C–212/99, *Commission* v. *Italy* [2001] ECR I–4923.

[41] Case C–355/98, *Commission* v. *Belgium* [2000] ECR I–1221; Case C–350/96, *Clean Car*, n. 16 above.

[42] Case 15/69, *Württembergische Milchverwertung-Südmilch-AG* v. *Salvatore Ugliola* [1970] ECR 363.

their military service in the Bundeswehr, although the nationality of the worker was irrelevant. The Court stressed that Article 48 allowed for no restrictions on the principle of equal treatment other than as provided for in paragraph 3. It concluded that the German law had created an unjustifiable restriction by 'indirectly introducing discrimination in favour of their own nationals alone', since the requirement that the service be done in the Bundeswehr would clearly be satisfied by a far greater number of nationals than non-nationals.[43] In *Commission* v. *Belgium*[44] the ECJ held that a system of retirement pension points that could be more easily satisfied by workers possessing the nationality of that Member State than by workers from other Member States was indirectly discriminatory, and hence caught by Article 48. In *Zurstrassen*[45] the Court held that national rules, under which the joint assessment to tax of spouses was conditional on their both being resident on national territory, were incompatible with Article 48. In *Sotgiu* the German Post Office increased the separation allowance paid to workers employed away from their place of residence within Germany.[46] This increase was not paid to workers (whatever their nationality) whose residence at the time of their initial employment was situated abroad, and Sotgiu, an Italian employee, argued that this was in breach of Article 48 (now Article 39):

The rules regarding equality of treatment, both in the Treaty and in Article 7 of Regulation No 1612/68, forbid not only overt discrimination by reason of nationality but also all covert forms of discrimination which, by the application of other criteria of differentiation, lead in fact to the same result.

. . . It may therefore be that criteria such as place of origin or residence of a worker may, according to circumstances, be tantamount, as regards their practical effect, to discrimination on the grounds of nationality, such as is prohibited by the Treaty and the Regulation.[47]

Another obvious form of indirect discrimination is the imposition of a *language requirement* for certain posts, since it is likely that a far higher proportion of non-nationals than nationals will be affected by it. However, since such a requirement may well be legitimate, Article 3(1) of Regulation 1612/68 allows for the imposition of 'conditions relating to linguistic knowledge required by reason of the nature of the post to be filled'. The Court considered the scope of this exception in the following case.

---

[43] Case C–419/92, *Scholz* v. *Universitaria di Cagliari* [1994] ECR I–505; Case C–15/96, *Kalliope Schöning-Kougebetopoulou* v. *Freie und Hansestadt Hamburg* [1998] ECR I–47; Case C–187/96, *Commission* v. *Hellenic Republic* [1998] ECR I–1095.

[44] Case 35/97, [1998] ECR I–5325.

[45] Case C–87/99, *Patrick Zurstrassen* v. *Administration des Contributions Directes* [2000] ECR I–3337.

[46] Case 152/73, *Sotgiu* v. *Deutsche Bundespost* [1974] ECR 153.

[47] *Ibid.*, para. 11.

Case 379/87, Groener v. Minister for Education
[1989] ECR 3967

[Note ToA renumbering: Art. 48 is now Art. 39]

Groener was a Dutch national working in Ireland as a part-time art teacher at a State vocational college, who applied after two years for a permanent full-time post there. Despite being recommended for appointment, she was not appointed because she failed a special oral test in the Irish language. This was a requirement for appointment to the post which applied both to nationals and non-nationals, even though lessons would not have to be given in Irish. Her request to the Minister to waive the requirement was refused, on the ground that this could only be done where no other fully qualified applicants had applied for the post. She argued that these conditions were contrary to Article 48 of the Treaty and Article 3 of Regulation 1612/68, in particular since teaching was likely to be conducted exclusively in English and Irish was not required to carry out her duties.

THE ECJ

18. As is apparent from the documents before the Court, although Irish is not spoken by the whole Irish population, the policy followed by Irish governments for many years has been designed not only to maintain but also to promote the use of Irish as a means of expressing national identity and culture. It is for that reason that Irish courses are compulsory for children receiving primary education and optional for those receiving secondary education. The obligation imposed on lecturers in public vocational education schools to have a certain knowledge of the Irish language is one of the measures adopted by the Irish Government in furtherance of that policy.

19. The EEC Treaty does not prohibit the adoption of a policy for the protection and promotion of a language of a Member State which is both the national language and the first official language. However, the implementation of such a policy must not encroach upon a fundamental freedom such as that of the free movement of workers. Therefore, the requirements deriving from measures intended to implement such a policy must not in any circumstances be disproportionate in relation to the aim pursued and the manner in which they are applied must not bring about discrimination against nationals of other Member States.

The Court concluded that the role of teachers in the educational process was important in the implementation of this State policy. So long as the language requirement was not disproportionate (e.g., that knowledge of Irish had to be acquired within the State),[48] it could fall within the exception in Article 3(1). The ECJ here was clearly influenced by the wider policy concerns raised by the Commission, the intervening French Government, and the Advocate General about the importance of cultural diversity, identity, and the protection of minority languages within the Community.[49]

[48] Case C–281/98, *Roman Angonese* v. *Cassa di Risparmio di Bolzano SpA* [2000] ECR I–4139.

[49] For an example of indirect discrimination which was not justifiable see Cases C–259, 331–332/91, *Allué and Coonan* [1993] ECR I–4309, in which the Member State had imposed restrictions on the contracts of foreign-language teaching assistants. For a similar case involving direct discrimination see Case C–124/94, *Commission* v. *Greece* [1995] ECR I–1457. However, for a case in which the exclusion of foreign-language assistants from eligibility for temporary university teaching vacancies was held not to violate Art. 48 (now Art. 39) see Case C–90/96, *Petrie* v. *Università degli studi di Verona and Camilla Bettoni* [1997] ECR I–6527.

The ECJ has also taken an *expansive view of the proof requirements for indirect discrimination.* In *O'Flynn*, the court considered a UK rule which made the grant to a worker of a payment to cover funeral expenses conditional on the burial or cremation taking place within the UK. The ECJ ruled that in order for indirect discrimination to be established, it was not necessary to prove that a national measure in practice affected a higher proportion of foreign workers, but merely that the measure was 'intrinsically liable' to affect migrant workers more than nationals.[50] It is moreover clear from *Angonese* that a measure can be indirectly discriminatory on grounds of nationality, even if it also disadvantages some Italian nationals, as well as nationals from other Member States.

(c) ACCESS TO THE EMPLOYMENT MARKET

It was, until recently, unclear whether Article 39 applied to national measures which restricted the freedom of movement of EC workers, but which were neither directly nor indirectly discriminatory on grounds of nationality. This is an issue that has arisen in relation to goods and services: even non-discriminatory restrictions may breach the Treaty if they constitute an excessive obstacle to freedom of movement. It may well be difficult to distinguish between cases of indirect discrimination and those where the ECJ intervenes to protect access to the employment market. There can none the less be cases that fall clearly within the latter category.

The issue first emerged clearly in the context of free movement of workers in the famous *Bosman* ruling, in which the transfer system developed by national and transnational football associations was found to be in breach of Article 48.[51] In short, that system required a football club, which sought to engage a player whose contact with another club had come to an end, to pay a sum of money (often substantial) to the latter club. In the case of Bosman himself, who had been employed by a Belgian football club, this rule effectively prevented him from securing employment with a French club. The fact that the transfer system applied equally to players moving from one club to another within a Member State as to players moving between states, and that a player's nationality was entirely irrelevant, did not prevent the system, according to the ECJ, from falling foul of Article 48. This was so notwithstanding the reliance placed by the football associations on the *Keck* ruling,[52] which had narrowed the scope of the Treaty provisions on free movement of goods:

103. It is sufficient to note that, although the rules in issue in the main proceedings apply also to transfers between clubs belonging to different national associations within the same Member State and are similar to those governing transfers between clubs belonging to the same national association, they still directly affect players' access to the employment market in other Member States and are thus capable of impeding freedom of movement for workers. They cannot, thus, be

---

[50] Case C–237/94, *O'Flynn* v. *Adjudication Officer* [1996] ECR I–2617, and see also Case C–278/94, *Commission* v. *Belgium* [1996] ECR I–4307 on tideover allowances for young people who had completed their secondary education in a Belgian establishment.

[51] Case C–415/93, n. 5 above, paras. 98–103 (although see the earlier suggestion in Case 321/87, *Commission* v. *Belgium* [1989] ECR 997, para. 15); Case C–176/96, *Jyri Lehtonen, Castors Canada Dry Namur-Braine ASBL* v. *FRBSB* [2000] ECR I–2681.

[52] See Cases C–267 & 268/91, *Keck and Mithouard* [1993] ECR I–6097, discussed in Ch. 15.

deemed comparable to the rules on selling arrangements for goods which in *Keck and Mithouard* were held to fall outside the ambit of Article 30 of the Treaty (see also, with regard to the freedom to provide services, Case C–384/93 *Alpine Investments* v. *Minister van Financiën* [1995] ECR I–1141, paras. 36–38).

104. Consequently, the transfer rules constitute an obstacle to freedom of movement for workers prohibited in principle by Article 48 of the Treaty. It could only be otherwise if those rules pursued a legitimate aim compatible with the Treaty and were justified by pressing reasons of public interest. But even if that were so, application of those rules would still have to be such as to ensure achievement of the aim in question and not go beyond what is necessary for that purpose (see, *inter alia*, the judgment in *Kraus*, para. 32 and Case C–55/94 *Gebhard* [1995] ECR I–4165).

Thus the fact that there was no discrimination was irrelevant: the existence of an obstacle to the access of workers from one Member State to employment in another Member State was enough to attract the application of Article 48. National obstacles of this kind might be justified on various public interest grounds, but they nevertheless constituted a *prima facie* breach of that Article.[53]

The principle was reiterated in *Terhoeve*.[54] Provisions which could preclude or deter a national of a Member State from leaving his country of origin in order to exercise his free-movement rights constituted an obstacle to that freedom even if they applied without regard to the nationality of the workers concerned. A provision of national law requiring a worker to pay greater social contributions than if he continued to reside in the same Member State throughout the year, without any additional social benefits, was therefore prohibited by Article 39.

The fact that non-discriminatory provisions which impede market access can be caught, does, none the less, raise concerns about the outer boundaries of Article 39. The issue was thrown into sharp relief by *Graf*.[55] The applicant claimed that rules providing that compensation on termination of employment did not apply when the worker voluntarily ended the employment to take up employment elsewhere were in breach of Article 39. Advocate General Fennelly adverted to the dangers of regarding such rules as constituting a breach of Article 39. He argued that neutral national rules could be regarded as material barriers to market access only if it were established that they had actual effects on market actors akin to exclusion from the market.[56] The ECJ shared these concerns. It reiterated the principle from *Bosman* concerning market access. It held however on the facts that the challenged legislation did not offend this principle. The entitlement to compensation was not dependent on the worker's choosing whether or not to stay with his current employer. It was, rather, dependent on a future and hypothetical event, namely the subsequent termination of the contract without this being at his initiative. This was too uncertain and indirect a possibility for the legislation to be regarded as being in breach of Article 39.[57]

[53] For criticism see L. Daniele, 'Non-Discriminatory Restrictions to the Free Movement of Persons' (1997) 22 *ELRev.* 191.
[54] Case C–18/95, *F.C. Terhoeve* v. *Inspecteur van de Belastingdienst Particulieren/Ondernemingen Buitenland* [1999] ECR I–345, para. 39.
[55] Case C–190/98, *Volker Graf* v. *Filzmoser Mashinenbau GmbH* [2000] ECR I–493.
[56] *Ibid.*, para. 32 of the AG's Opinion.   [57] *Ibid.*, paras. 24–25 of the ECJ's judgment.

(d) INTERNAL SITUATIONS

Article 39 (ex Article 48) does not prohibit discrimination in a so-called 'wholly internal' situation. This has been described as a situation of 'reverse discrimination', since its effect is frequently that national workers cannot claim rights in their own Member State, which workers who are nationals of other Member States could claim there. In *Saunders* the ECJ held that since there was 'no factor connecting' the defendant 'to any of the situations envisaged by Community law', she could not rely on Article 48 to challenge an order which effectively excluded her from part of her own national territory.[58] Attempts have since been made to circumvent the 'internal situation' barrier by relying on the right to freedom of movement conferred by Article 16 (ex Article 8a) on European citizens, as something over and above the rights of movement of EC workers, but these have not succeeded before the ECJ.[59] It will be seen below that this 'internal situation' approach by the Court has given rise to some particularly invidious results in the context of the rights of workers and their families.[60]

It is none the less clear, as exemplified by *Terhoeve*,[61] that a worker will be able to use Article 39 against his or her own State, where the worker has been employed and resided in another Member State. Such a worker may then claim that he or she has been discriminated against in relation to, for example social security contributions, when returning to work in the worker's own Member State.

(e) OBJECTIVE JUSTIFICATION

The possible grounds for justifying indirect discrimination are broad, and not confined to the exceptions set out in the Treaty or in secondary legislation. This is exemplified in *Sotgiu*,[62] *O'Flynn*,[63] and in several decisions concerning provisions of Belgian tax law. In *Schumacker*, the Court ruled that indirect discrimination based on the residence of a worker, whereby an EC national employed but not resident in a particular Member State could not benefit from personal tax allowances, could in

---

[58] Case 175/78, *R. v. Saunders* [1979] ECR 1129. See also Case 298/84, *Pavlo Iorio v. Azienda Autonomo delle Ferrovie dello Stato* [1986] ECR 247; Cases C–225–227/95, *Kapasakalis, Skiathis and Kougiagkas v. Greek State* [1998] ECR I–4329.

[59] The issue was raised in the reference made by the UK Div. Ct. in Case C–229/94, *R. v. Secretary of State for the Home Department, ex p. Adams* [1995] All ER (EC) 177, but this was subsequently withdrawn. However, in Case C–299/95, *Kremzow v. Austria* [1997] ECR I–2629, involving a national imprisoned within his own Member State, the ECJ ruled that although any deprivation of liberty might impede someone from exercising the Community right to freedom of movement, the purely hypothetical possibility of doing so did not entail a sufficient connection with Community law. The Court cited its ruling in Case 180/83, *Hans Moser v. Land Baden-Württemberg* [1984] ECR 2539, where the prospect of being disadvantaged in a possible future search for employment abroad was deemed insufficient as a 'connecting factor' to attract the application of Art. 48 (now Art. 39). The implication of the ruling in *Kremzow* is that travel abroad in order to exercise one of the Treaty rights is still necessary as a connecting factor for the application of that Art.

[60] See in particular Cases 35 & 36/82, *Morson and Jhanjan v. Netherlands* [1982] ECR 3723 at n. 137 below.

[61] Case C–18/95, *Terhoeve*, n. 54 above.

[62] Case 152/73, *Sotgiu*, n. 46 above. The ECJ held that such indirect discrimination might be justified on the basis of objective differences, e.g. if the payment of the allowance to those resident in Germany was coupled with an obligation to transfer residence to the new place of work, whereas those resident outside Germany were not subject to such an obligation.

[63] Case C–237/94, *O'Flynn*, n. 50 above.

certain circumstances be justified.[64] This was because of the likely difference in position between workers from other Member States and resident workers, but such indirect discrimination could not be justified where, for example, the non-resident worker could not benefit from personal allowances in the Member State of residence either. Moreover, in *Commission* v. *Belgium*[65] and *Bachmann*,[66] the Court held that national rules, which allowed the deductibility from income tax of various insurance and pension contributions only if those contributions were paid in Belgium, were indirectly discriminatory contrary to Article 48, they could be justified. The rationale was the need to ensure the cohesion of the Belgian tax system. The ECJ accepted that contributions paid in Belgium were permitted to be deducted under the law because these deductions were offset by the tax imposed on sums paid out by insurers in Belgium. There could be no such certainty that the sums paid out by insurers not based in Belgium had been taxed.[67] These discriminatory measures were held by the Court to be justified, without the need for the state to invoke the special grounds of exception in Article 48(3), which are discussed in more detail below.

The ECJ will closely scrutinize claims that restrictions are justified. Thus in *Terhoeve*[68] the ECJ considered whether heavier social security contributions levied on a worker who transferred his residence from one Member State to another to take up work during the course of a year could be justified. The ECJ rejected justifications based on the need to simplify and co-ordinate the levying of such contributions, and technical difficulties preventing other methods of collection. In *Lehtonen*[69] it was held that rules establishing transfer deadlines in basketball could be justified, since late transfers could change the sporting strength of a team in the course of the championship. This could call into question the comparability of results between the teams taking part in the championship, and hence the proper functioning of the championship as a whole. There was, however, a different and later deadline date for transfers of players outside the European zone than for those within that zone. The ECJ held that there appeared to be no rationale for this distinction, and that therefore the rule on deadlines that applied within the European zone might go beyond what was necessary for achieving the aim pursued. This matter was left for the national court to decide.

---

[64] Case C–279/93, *Finanzamt Köln-Altstadt* v. *Roland Schumacker* [1995] ECR I–225. See F. Vanistendael, 'The Consequences of Schumacker and Wielockx: Two Steps Forward in the Tax Procession of Echternach' (1996) 33 *CMLRev.* 255.

[65] Case C–300/90, *Commission* v. *Belgium* [1992] ECR I–305.

[66] Case C–204/90, *Bachmann* v. *Belgium* [1992] ECR I–249.

[67] Contrast the Opinion of Mischo AG, *ibid.*, 260, who concluded that the Belgian legislation was disproportionately restrictive, since there were other means available to obviate the risk of tax evasion. See also Cases C–175/88, *Biehl* v. *Luxembourg* [1990] ECR I–1779, and C–151/94, *Commission* v. *Luxembourg* [1995] ECR I–3685.

[68] Case C–18/95, *Terhoeve*, n. 54 above, paras. 43–47.

[69] Case C–176/96, *Lehtonen*, n. 51 above, paras. 51–60.

5. THE PUBLIC-SERVICE EXCEPTION

It is evident from the preceding discussion that the ECJ's approach to the definition of worker has been a relatively expansive one. Its approach to the limiting clause in Article 39(4) (ex Article 48(4)), which provides that Article 39 shall not apply to 'employment in the public service', has not surprisingly been restrictive. The ECJ has been concerned to ensure that the scope of the exception does not go further than is necessary to fulfil the purpose for which it was put into the Treaty. This requires an analysis of why the exception is in the Treaty. The case law provides a good example of the contrast between a kind of 'original intent' interpretation argued for by the Member States, and the less historically rooted 'purposive' interpretation employed by the Court. The ECJ does not confine its 'hermeneutic monopoly' to the right-conferring terms such as 'worker', but extends it also to the public-service derogation: it is the Court and not the Member State which decides what constitutes employment in the public service. The battle over the scope of the public-service exception has been hard fought, perhaps even more strongly than that over the scope of the term worker. An explanation for this is offered by Mancini, who attributes it to 'the wide-spread view that the functioning of the public service is an exercise of full-State sovereignty'.[70] Certain fundamentals concerning the interpretation of Article 39(4) emerge from the case law.

(a) THE MEANING OF PUBLIC SERVICE IS TO BE DETERMINED BY THE ECJ, NOT THE MEMBER STATES

In *Sotgiu* the ECJ made it clear that it, and not the respective Member States, would define the scope of the exception:[71]

It is necessary to establish further whether the extent of the exception provided for by Article 48(4) can be determined in terms of the designation of the legal relationship between the employee and the employing administration.

In the absence of any distinction in the provision referred to, it is of no interest whether a worker is engaged as a workman (*ouvrier*), a clerk (*employé*), or an official (*fonctionnaire*) or even whether the terms on which he is employed come under public or private law.

These legal designations can be varied at the whim of national legislatures and cannot therefore provide a criterion for interpretation appropriate to the requirements of Community law.

Thus the Member States cannot deem a particular post to be 'in the public service' by the name or designation they give to that post, or by the mere fact that the terms of the post are regulated by public law. The German Government had argued that, because the Community was founded upon the State organizations of the Member States, the concept of the public service could only be interpreted in the light of these national concepts. The ECJ did not address this in *Sotgiu* since it had already decided that the derogation could not justify a pay differential, as opposed to limits on

---

[70] Mancini, n. 14 above, 77.   [71] Case 152/73, *Sotgiu*, n. 46 above, para. 5.

admission. The issue resurfaced, however, in a series of subsequent cases, in which the Commission brought infringement proceedings under Article 169 (now Article 226) against various Member States.

(b) THE ECJ'S TEST FOR PUBLIC SERVICE

In the case extracted below, the Belgian Government (supported by the UK, German, and French governments) argued that Article 48(4) differed from Article 55 (now Article 45). The latter provides a somewhat similar derogation in the context of freedom of establishment and freedom to provide services, when an activity involves the 'exercise of official authority'. This difference, according to the Belgian Government, was deliberately reflected in the respective wording of each. Article 55 specifically mentions the exercise of official authority, which implies a functional concept, whereas Article 48(4) refers to 'employment in the public service', which is an institutional concept. On the latter definition, what is important is the institution within which the worker is employed, rather than the nature of the work itself. The ECJ did now however accept this argument.

Case 149/79, Commission v. Belgium
[1980] ECR 3881

[Note ToA renumbering: Art. 48 is now Art. 39]

Possession of Belgian nationality was required as a condition of entry for posts with Belgian local authorities and public undertakings, regardless of the nature of the duties to be performed. Examples of such posts were those of unskilled railway workers, hospital nurses, and night-watchmen. The Commission argued to the ECJ that the scope of Article 48(4) could only cover posts implying actual participation in the exercise of official authority by those occupying them. The Belgian Government in response argued that, when the Treaties were drafted, there was no Community concept of the objectives and scope of public authorities and that the Member States' governments had wished the conditions of entry to public office to remain their preserve.

THE ECJ

10. That provision [Article 48(4)] removes from the ambit of Article 48(1) to (3) a series of posts which involve direct or indirect participation in the exercise of powers conferred by public law and duties designed to safeguard the general interests of the State or of other public authorities. Such posts in fact presume on the part of those occupying them the existence of a special relationship of allegiance to the State and reciprocity of rights and duties which form the foundation of the bond of nationality.

11. The scope of the derogation made by Article 48(4) to the principles of freedom of move-ment and equality of treatment laid down in the first three paragraphs of the article should therefore be determined on the basis of the aim pursued by that article. However, determining the sphere of application of Article 48(4) raises special difficulties since in the various Member States authorities acting under powers conferred by public law have assumed responsibilities of

an economic and social nature or are involved in activities which are not identifiable with the functions which are typical of the public service yet which by their nature still come under the sphere of application of the Treaty. In these circumstances the effect of extending the exception contained in Article 48(4) to posts which, whilst coming under the States or other organizations governed by public law, still do not involve any association with tasks belonging to the public service properly so called, would be to remove a considerable number of posts from the ambit of the principles set out in the Treaty and to create inequalities between Member States according to the different ways in which the State and certain sectors of economic life are organized.

Thus a state cannot bring certain activities, e.g., of an economic or social kind, within the Treaty derogation simply by including them in the scope of the public law of the state, and taking responsibility for their performance. The argument based on the states' intentions when the Treaty was drafted was ignored by the ECJ, which focused instead on the aim of the provision in the context of the Treaty and the Chapter as a whole. This was, in the ECJ's view, to permit Member States, should they so wish, to reserve for nationals those posts which would require a specific bond of allegiance and mutuality of rights and duties between state and employee. The Court's description of the posts that could be said to require such allegiance and to depend upon the bond of nationality was twofold. They must involve participation in the exercise of powers conferred by public law, and they must entail duties designed to safeguard the general interests of the state. The notion of 'powers conferred by public law' is rather a vague one, given the difficulties inherent in defining the scope of public law, but the idea of 'safeguarding the general interests of the State' is somewhat more concrete. Different views have been expressed on this point, but it seems that the two requirements are cumulative rather than alternative. A post will benefit from the derogation in Article 39(4) only if it involves *both* the exercise of power conferred by public law *and* the safeguarding of the general interests of the state.[72]

The Court dismissed the arguments of the French and Belgian Governments to the effect that the idea of nationality as a necessary condition for entry to any post in the public service of the state actually had constitutional status in certain states. Given the need for the 'unity and efficacy' of Community law, the ECJ repeated its view that the interpretation of limiting concepts such as public-service employment could not be left to the discretion of Member States, even if the state's rules were of a constitutional nature.[73]

(c) APPLICATION OF THE ECJ'S TEST

In the *Belgium* case[74] the ECJ ruled that it did not have enough information to be able to identify which of the specified posts fell outside the Treaty derogation. It

---

[72] Case 66/85, *Lawrie-Blum*, n. 23 above, para. 27 and Léger AG in Case C–473/93, *Commission* v. *Luxembourg* [1996] ECR I–3207, para. 18. See also D. O'Keeffe, 'Judicial Interpretation of the Public Service Exception to the Free Movement of Workers', in Curtin and O'Keeffe (eds.), n. 14 above, 89, 96.

[73] [1980] ECR 3881, paras. 18–19, and see Case C–473/93, *Commission* v. *Luxembourg* [1996] ECR I–3207, para. 38.

[74] Case 149/79, *Commission* v. *Belgium* [1980] ECR 3881.

invited Belgium and the Commission to re-examine and resolve the issue in the light of its judgment, and to report any solution to the ECJ. When they failed to agree on certain of the posts, the case came back to the ECJ two years later. The Court ruled that, with the exception of a limited number of posts, including certain supervisory posts, night watchman, and architect with the municipality of Brussels, none of the other posts satisfied the criteria for the application of the public-service exception.[75]

A further argument made by the four governments represented in the *Belgium* cases was that certain posts which may not at the outset involve participation in the powers conferred by public law require a certain flexibility of character. They argued that the duties and responsibilities of the post may change, or the holders of such initial posts may subsequently become eligible for careers at a higher grade with duties involving the exercise of public powers. This, too, was rejected as a reason for treating the initial post as being within the public-service exception, since that exception 'allows Member States to reserve to their nationals, by appropriate rules, entry to posts involving the exercise of such powers and such responsibilities within the same grade, the same branch, or the same class'.[76]

The point was made again by the ECJ in enforcement proceedings brought by the Commission against Italy, concerning laws protecting the security and tenure of researchers at the National Research Council (CNR) which were not applied to non-nationals.[77] Italy argued, first, that the work undertaken by the CNR involved satisfying the general interests of the state and was financed out of public funds. It argued, secondly, that if researchers became established members of staff, they could be promoted to higher managerial positions, which would entail participation in the exercise of public power. The ECJ rejected the first argument:[78]

Simply referring to the general tasks of the CNR and listing the duties of all its researchers is not sufficient to establish that the researchers are responsible for exercising powers conferred by public law or for safeguarding the general interests of the State. Only the duties of management or of advising the State on scientific and technical questions could be described as employment in the public service within the meaning of Article 48(4).

The second argument was equally summarily dismissed, with reference being made to the Court's ruling in the *Belgium* cases:[79]

It is sufficient to point out that Community law does not prohibit a Member State from reserving for its own nationals those posts within a career bracket which involve participation in the exercise of powers conferred by public law or the safeguarding of the general interests of the State.

Member States have attempted to use the exception in numerous other cases.[80] There is secondary legislation which attempts to clarify the concept. The Commission did once propose to draft legislation to clarify the derogation. That proposal

---

[75] Case 149/79, *Commission* v. *Belgium II* [1982] ECR 1845.   [76] *Ibid.*, para. 21.
[77] Case 225/85, *Commission* v. *Italy* [1987] ECR 2625.
[78] *Ibid.*, para. 9.   [79] *Ibid.*, para. 10.
[80] Case 66/85, *Lawrie-Blum*, n. 23 above, para. 28; Case 33/88, *Allué and Coonan* v. *Università degli Studi di Venezia* [1989] ECR 1591; Case C–213/90, *ASTI* v. *Chambre des Employés Privés* [1991] ECR I–3507; Case C–4/91, *Bleis* v. *Ministère de l'Education Nationale* [1991] ECR I–5627.

was, however, opposed by those who thought that the Member States might take advantage of detailed legislation to undermine the established case law, and also that such legislation could ossify the process of creating a 'citizens' Europe'.[81] The Commission instead, in 1988, published a document in the Official Journal on the scope of Article 48(4), providing some guidance on the sorts of State functions which it considered would or would not fall within that provision.[82] Those which probably would included the armed forces, police, judiciary, tax authorities, and certain public bodies engaged in preparing or monitoring legal acts, and those which probably would not included nursing, teaching, and non-military research in public establishments.

The issue is still one which is fraught with ideological tensions, the underlying debate being about the concept of nationality and when it is legitimate for the Member States to require nationality as a condition for employment. The efforts of the Member States to define the public-service derogation in terms of the 'public sector', the institutional approach, have repeatedly failed. The Court has adhered to a rather more difficult but narrower 'functional' approach, which examines closely the character of posts which might be said to require the reciprocal bond of allegiance which is said to be characteristic of nationality. The debate provides a clear example of the federal tensions, which emerge in many areas of Community law, over the proper scope of national as opposed to Community jurisdiction and competence, and in particular where the sensitive issue of nationality is concerned. Member State resistance to the ECJ's approach, and the judicial response thereto, is evident in Advocate General Mancini's critical and trenchant opinion in infringement proceedings involving public nursing posts in France:[83]

The decisions to which I have referred gave rise to severe criticisms from academic lawyers and, what is more important, they have not been 'taken in' by numerous governments. Such resistance is not surprising if it is borne in mind how deep-rooted is the conviction that the public service is an area in which the State should exercise full sovereignty and how wide-spread is the tendency, in times of high unemployment, to see the public service as a convenient reservoir of posts. Such resistance is a matter for concern and should be tackled head-on before cases similar to the present one multiply. . . .

. . . In short, in order to be made inaccessible to nationals of another State, it is not sufficient for the duties inherent in the post at issue to be directed specifically towards public objectives which influence the conduct and action of private individuals. Those who occupy the post must don full battle dress: in non-metaphorical terms, the duties must involve acts of will which affect private individuals by requiring their obedience or, in the event of disobedience, by compelling them to comply. To make a list . . . is practically impossible; but certainly the first examples which come to mind are posts relating to policing, defence of the State, the administration of justice and assessments to tax.

. . . It is a fact that an extremist disciple of Hegel might truly think that access to posts like the ones at issue here [nursing] should be denied to foreigners. But anyone who does not regard the State as 'the march of God in the world' must of necessity take the contrary view.

---

[81] Mancini, n. 14 above.   [82] [1988] OJ C72/2.

[83] Case 307/84, *Commission* v. *France* [1986] ECR 1725, 1727–33. For criticism of the Court's ruling in this case, see O'Keeffe, n. 72 above, 89, 101–3.

It was suggested, soon after the TEU was adopted, that the new provisions in the EC Treaty on citizenship might undermine the thinking behind, and reduce the importance of, the public service exception.

D. O'Keeffe, Judicial Interpretation of the Public Service Exception to the Free Movement of Workers[84]

There is an inherent conflict between Article 48(4) on the one hand and the creation of the internal market and increased European integration on the other. The public service exception is geared to a conception of the State performing certain essential activities related to its function as the State, where the legitimate interests of the State can best be served and protected by the recruitment of the State's own nationals to perform certain tasks on its behalf.

However, this view of the public service exception is founded on a conception of nationality which may face increasing strain. It is based on a very traditional notion of loyalty to the State and finds its parallel in the denial to foreigners of political rights. . . .

It is clear that these provisions [of the TEU on citizenship] will alter the perceptions of Member States concerning nationals of other Member States. They blur the distinction between the State's own nationals and nationals of other Member States in several ways which go to the heart of the concept of nationality. Previously, Community law, and in particular the case-law of the Court of Justice, had concentrated on the economic and social integration of Community migrants (viewed as economic actors by the Treaty) in order to create a Community citizenship. As Community nationals are now to enjoy political rights deriving from Community law, it will become progressively more difficult to justify a different treatment of them as regards employment in the public service, which is founded upon political considerations.

However, such optimism has not yet been shown to be justified, to judge by the recent set of infringement proceedings brought by the Commission which were, according to Advocate General Léger, in one of the cases 'vigorously defended' by the Member States.[85] It is clear from these cases that the provisions on citizenship were not the part of the TEU on which the Member States wished to focus in construing the scope of the public-service exception. The ECJ in the proceedings brought against Luxembourg was confronted with the argument that the public-service derogation was an important means for the Member States to preserve their national identities. But although it accepted that the preservation of such identities was a legitimate aim, and one which was acknowledged in Article F(1) (now Article 6(1)) TEU, the ECJ ruled that that interest could be safeguarded through other means than by generally excluding nationals of other Member States, for example by the imposition of language, experience, and training conditions.[86]

---

[84] In Curtin and O'Keeffe (eds.), n. 14 above, 105.

[85] See Cases C–473/93, *Commission* v. *Luxembourg* [1996] ECR I–3207; C–173/94, *Commission* v. *Belgium* [1996] ECR I–3265; and C–290/94, *Commission* v. *Greece* [1996] ECR I–3285, where the ECJ was asked once again to depart entirely from its previous case law.

[86] Case C–473/93, n. 73 above, para. 35.

(d) DISCRIMINATORY CONDITIONS OF EMPLOYMENT WITHIN THE PUBLIC SERVICE ARE PROHIBITED

It is in any event clear from *Sotgiu* that Article 39(4) cannot be used to justify discriminatory conditions for employment within the public service. Germany had invoked Article 48(4) (now Article 39(4)) in an attempt to justify its provisions on separation allowances for post office workers, which worked to the disadvantage of non-nationals, and the ECJ responded as follows:[87]

Taking account of the fundamental nature, in the scheme of the Treaty, of the principles of freedom of movement and equality of treatment of workers within the Community, the exceptions made by Article 48(4) cannot have a scope going beyond the aim in view of which this derogation was included.

The interests which this derogation allows Member States to protect are satisfied by the opportunity of restricting admission of foreign nationals to certain activities in the public service.

On the other hand this provision cannot justify discriminatory measures with regard to remuneration or other conditions of employment against workers once they have been admitted to the public service.

The very fact that they have been admitted shows indeed that those interests which justify the exceptions to the principle of non-discrimination permitted by Article 48(4) are not at issue.

Thus the Treaty derogation had to be confined to restricting the *admission* of non-nationals into the public service, but it did not permit discrimination in conditions once they were admitted. If they were deemed sufficiently loyal to the state to be admitted to such employment, there could be no grounds for paying them less on account of their nationality.

6. FORMAL REQUIREMENTS: DIRECTIVE 68/360

(a) FORMAL REQUIREMENTS FOR WORKERS

Directive 68/360 was adopted under Article 49 (now Article 40), so that, unlike Directive 64/221,[88] it is applicable only to the employed and not also to the self-employed. Directive 68/360 sets out to facilitate freedom of movement and the abolition of restrictions, in part by clarifying certain formal requirements relating to the right of entry and residence of non-nationals. This measure specifies what documents an EC worker will require on entering a Member State other than his or her own, and it provides for the issuing of residence permits to workers and their families. It should be noted that there is to be a new general Directive on free movement, which will replace Directive 68/360. It is considered below.[89]

Article 1 is a straightforward provision requiring the abolition of restrictions on movement and residence of nationals and their families. The family members covered

---

[87] Case 152/73, *Sotgiu*, n. 46 above, para. 4; Case C–195/98, *Österreicher Gewerkschaftsbund, Gewerkschaft Öffentlicher Dienst* v. *Republik Österreich* [2000] ECR I–10497, para. 37.
[88] Dir. 68/360 [1968] II OJ Spec. Ed. 485; Dir. 64/221 [1963–4] OJ Spec. Ed. 117.
[89] See below, at 761–2.

are those to whom Regulation 1612/68 applies, discussed in detail below. Article 2 requires Member States to grant such persons the right to leave their territory to go and work in other Member States, simply on producing an identity card or passport which their Member State must provide for them and which will be valid throughout the Community. No exit visa requirement may be imposed. Article 3 sets out similar conditions for the right to enter another Member State: all that is required is a valid identity card or passport and a visa requirement is impermissible, save for some third-country nationals.[90] Articles 4 and 9 provide for the issuing of five-year, automatically renewable, residence permits free of charge to those persons listed in Article 1, as proof of their right of residence. Article 6 provides for temporary residence permits for temporary and seasonal workers who work for more than three months but less than a year.[91] To obtain a permit, the worker must produce the document with which he or she entered the territory and proof of engagement from an employer. The Member States may not charge excessive fees for such permits, or fees which exceed in total what nationals must pay for their identity cards.[92] Family members must produce the document with which they entered the country, as well as proof of their relationship with the worker, and evidence of dependency or co-habitation if required under Regulation 1612/68. For family members who are non-EC nationals, a residence document coextensive with that of the worker must be issued.[93] The Directive makes clear in Article 5 that the rights to reside and work are not conditional upon initial satisfaction of the formalities for which it provides. Article 7 deals partly with unemployment, and Article 8 with those short-term (less than three months), seasonal, and so-called 'frontier' workers, whose right of residence must be recognized without the need for residence permits.[94] Article 10 ties in with Directive 64/221 by providing that Member States shall not derogate from the provisions of this Directive, 68/360, save on grounds of public policy, public security, or public health, and Article 11 distinguishes the provisions on workers of the ECSC and Euratom Treaties.

The Court has been at pains to point out that the provisions of Directive 68/360 are not limiting measures, in the sense that they are neither conditions which, if unfulfilled, will justify deporting the non-national, nor measures which confer rather than confirm the rights of the worker. Instead they elaborate on or give substance to existing rights that are inherent or express in the EC Treaty, and provide various formal and procedural protections to ensure the full exercise and benefit of those rights.

The case law provides many instances of Member States unsuccessfully attempting to impose additional requirements not provided for in the Directive, or attempting to use the non-fulfilment of one of the formal requirements for entry against a worker, either as a means of refusing entry or deporting that worker.

---

[90] Reg. 539/2001 [2001] OJ L81/1; Council Reg. 2414/2001 [2001] OJ L327/1.
[91] For clear breaches of these requirements see Case C–344/95, *Commission v. Belgium* [1997] ECR I–1035.
[92] *Ibid.*
[93] For an interpretation of this provision in the UK context by an English court see *Sahota* v. *Secretary of State for the Home Department* [1997] 3 CMLR 576.
[94] See Case C–344/95, n. 91 above, that although the State may require seasonal workers to report their presence, this does not allow the imposition of a residence-permit requirement.

Case 48/75, Royer

[1976] ECR 497

[Note ToA renumbering: Arts. 48 and 56 are now Arts. 39 and 46 respectively]

Royer, who was a French tradesman residing in Belgium with his wife, was told that he was unlawfully resident and ordered by the Belgian police to leave the country, since he had not completed the administrative formalities of entry on the population register when he first arrived. After complying with the order to leave, Royer subsequently re-entered the country in breach of the prohibition on returning. At a Tribunal hearing concerning his unauthorized residence, questions were referred to the ECJ asking whether the right of residence was independent of the possession of a permit, and whether failure to comply with administrative requirements for a permit could constitute a ground for deportation. The ECJ began by considering the rights conferred by the Treaty, and the relevant provisions of secondary legislation.

THE ECJ

28. These provisions show that the legislative authorities of the Community were aware that, while not creating new rights in favour of persons protected by Community law, the regulation and directives concerned determined the scope and detailed rules for the exercise of rights conferred directly by the Treaty.

29. It is therefore evident that the exception concerning the safeguard of public policy, security and public health contained in Articles 48(3) and 56 (1) of the Treaty must be regarded not as a condition precedent to the acquisition of the right of entry and residence but as providing the possibility, in individual cases where there is sufficient justification, of imposing restrictions on the exercise of a right derived directly from the Treaty.

. . .

33. The grant of this [residence] permit is therefore to be regarded not as a measure giving rise to rights but as a measure by a Member State serving to prove the individual position of a national of another Member State with regard to the provisions of Community law.

. . .

38. The logical consequence of the foregoing is that the mere failure by a national of a Member State to complete the legal formalities concerning access, movement and residence of aliens does not justify a decision ordering expulsion.

However, the ECJ also ruled that Community law would not prevent the states from adopting provisions to control non-nationals, backed up with appropriate sanctions other than expulsion. The principle of proportionality of sanctions for administrative breaches, which requires that sanctions should not impose excessive restrictions on freedom of movement, is central to the law in this area.

Case 118/75, Watson and Belmann
[1976] ECR 1185

A British national, who had stayed with an Italian family apparently as an *au pair*, was charged, along with one of the family, with failure to report the presence of a foreign national, within three days, to the Italian police. The penalty for such failure was a maximum of three months' detention or a fine of up to 80,000 lire, or, in the case of a foreign national, possible deportation from the state. A reference was made to the ECJ, which ruled that Member States were not prevented from adopting measures to allow for an exact knowledge of population movements within the territory, so that an obligation to report to the police did not infringe the rules on free movement of persons. However, unduly restrictive formalities could infringe those rules:

THE ECJ

19. In particular as regards the period within which the arrival of foreign nationals must be reported, the provisions of the Treaty are only infringed if the period fixed is unreasonable.

20. Among the penalties attaching to a failure to comply with the prescribed declaration and registration formalities, deportation, in relation to persons protected by Community law, is certainly incompatible with the provisions of the Treaty since, as the Court has already confirmed in other cases, such a measure negates the very right conferred and guaranteed by the Treaty.

21. As regards other penalties, such as fines and detention, whilst the national authorities are entitled to impose penalties in respect of a failure to comply with the terms of provisions requiring foreign nationals to notify their presence which are comparable to those attaching to infringement of provisions of equal importance by nationals, they are not justified in imposing a penalty so disproportionate that it becomes an obstacle to the free movement of persons.

In *Pieck* a Dutch worker in Britain was prosecuted for outstaying his leave. The Court ruled that the prohibition, in Article 3(2) of Directive 68/360, on Member States demanding an entry visa or similar requirement applied to the stamp of 'leave to enter for six months' which had been placed on his passport when re-entering the United Kingdom.[95] All that the states were permitted by the Directive to require was the production of a valid identity card or passport. Similarly in *Sagulo*, the ECJ ruled that no penalty could be imposed for failure to have a residence permit other than the permit provided for under Directive 68/360.[96] But it also ruled, perhaps surprisingly, that non-nationals who fail to show the documents required by that Directive need not be treated in the same way as nationals whose identity card has ceased to be valid:[97]

There is therefore no objection to such persons being subject to different penal provisions from those applying to nationals who infringe an obligation, possibly having its origin in a law or

[95] Case 157/79, *R. v. Pieck* [1980] ECR 2171.
[96] Case 8/77, *Sagulo, Brenca and Bakhouche* [1977] ECR 1495.
[97] *Ibid.*, paras. 10–11. See also Case C–265/88, *Lothar Messner* [1989] ECR 4209. See also Case C–363/89, *Roux* [1991] ECR I–273, where the Court ruled that the issuing of a residence permit could not be made dependent on prior registration with a social security scheme, or on any factor other than being engaged in effective economic activity.

regulation, to obtain certain identity documents. ... It is nevertheless to be observed that although Member States are entitled to impose reasonable penalties for infringement by persons subject to Community law of the obligation to obtain a valid identity card or passport, such penalties should by no means be so severe as to cause an obstacle to the freedom of entry and residence provided for in the Treaty.

However, in subsequent proceedings against Belgium concerning that state's practice of sometimes asking non-Belgian EC nationals at the border to produce their residence permit in addition to their passport or identity card, the ECJ seemed more concerned that any differences in treatment between nationals and non-nationals should, as far as possible, be minimized.[98] The ECJ ruled that the only precondition a state could impose on those covered by the Directives was the possession of a valid identity card or passport. Belgium could however check, within its territory, compliance with the obligation to carry a residence or establishment permit at all times, where an identical obligation was imposed upon Belgian nationals as regards their entry cards.[99] It is clear moreover that the penalty for failure to comply with this obligation must be comparable to those attaching to minor offences committed by a State's own nationals. Such penalties cannot be 'disproportionately different'.[100]

(b) FORMAL REQUIREMENTS FOR THOSE WHO SEARCH FOR WORK

It is clear that if a Community national has a Treaty-derived right of residence in a host Member State, failure to possess or produce a residence permit cannot justify expulsion by the Member State. It is less clear what the position is as regards a worker who leaves a job or otherwise becomes unemployed, or as regards a person of limited resources who has been seeking employment for a period of time, but who has not been able to find work.

The only mention of unemployment in Directive 68/360 is in Article 7(1). This provides that a residence permit cannot be withdrawn solely on the ground that the worker is unemployed either involuntarily, or through incapacity due to illness or accident, provided that the unemployment office confirms this. Article 7(2) provides that where involuntary unemployment has continued for more than twelve consecutive months the period of residence may be restricted, if the residence permit is being renewed for the first time, to not less than twelve months. The Directive says nothing about voluntary unemployment, or where it is due to something other than the stated causes of incapacity. The inference could be drawn that Member States are permitted to refuse to renew a residence permit, or perhaps to revoke a permit, in such circumstances. Yet if someone voluntarily leaves employment due to dissatisfaction with that post and is actively seeking other employment, this inference may well be unjustified.

This is suggested by *Antonissen*, which raised the question not of voluntary unemployment, but of the status of someone who is unemployed yet actively seeking work.[101] The Court ruled, as seen above, that Article 48 (now Article 39) also protects

---

[98] Case 321/87, *Commission* v. *Belgium* [1989] ECR 997.
[99] *Ibid.*, para. 12.
[100] Case C–24/97, *Commission* v. *Germany* [1998] ECR I–2133.
[101] Case C–292/89, n. 33 above.

the right to enter in *search* of work. However, the UK argued that this right was not unlimited, and that a Member State could, compatibly with that Article and with Directive 68/360, deport a non-national who had not yet found work after a certain period of time. It was argued that this period should be three months. This was the period provided for in a Council directive relating to the receipt of social security in a host Member State, and the minutes of a Council meeting revealed that it was the period intended by the Council when it adopted Directive 68/360.

Case C–292/89, Antonissen
[1991] ECR I–745

The facts are set out above.

THE ECJ

16. In that regard, it must be pointed out in the first place that the effectiveness of Article 48 is secured in so far as Community legislation or, in its absence, the legislation of a Member State gives persons concerned a reasonable time in which to apprise themselves, in the territory of the Member State concerned, of offers of employment corresponding to their occupational qualifications and to take, where appropriate, the necessary steps in order to be engaged.
[*The Court was dismissive of the declaration in the minutes of the Council meeting, demonstrating its preference for a broad purposive interpretation over one based even on the stated intention of the legislator which adopted the measure.*[102]]
18. However, such a declaration cannot be used for the purpose of interpreting a provision of secondary legislation where, as in this case, no reference is made to the content of the declaration in the wording of the provision in question. The declaration therefore has no legal significance.[103]
[*The ECJ concluded by ruling that a six-month period was probably not too short, but added a caveat which seemed to leave the period during which a non-national may search for work potentially open-ended.*[104]]
21. In the absence of a Community provision prescribing the period during which Community nationals seeking employment in a Member State may stay there, a period of six months, such as that laid down in the national legislation at issue in the main proceedings, does not appear in principle to be insufficient to enable the persons concerned to apprise themselves, in the host Member State, of offers of employment corresponding to their occupational qualifications and to take, where appropriate, the necessary steps in order to be engaged and, therefore, does not jeopardize the effectiveness of the principle of free movement. However, if after the expiry of that period the person concerned provides evidence that he is continuing to seek employment and

---

[102] The ECJ also rejected the argument that there was a connection between the right to unemployment benefit, which must be provided for 3 months under the relevant Dir., and the right to remain in a Member State.

[103] For a similar dismissal of the relevance of a declaration which preceded the adoption of a dir. see Case 306/89, *Commission* v. *Greece* [1991] ECR 5863, paras. 6 and 8. But contrast Case 136/78, *Ministère Public* v. *Auer* [1979] ECR 437, paras. 25–26.

[104] See, however, Case C–171/91, *Tsiotras* v. *Landeshauptstadt Stuttgart* [1993] ECR I–2925, for an example of a situation where the length of the period of unemployment would justify a decision by a Member State to deport.

that he has genuine chances of being engaged, he cannot be required to leave the territory of the host Member State.

Commenting on *Antonissen*, O'Keeffe has suggested that 'when confronted with the free movement of persons, which it sees as the way to an embryonic Community citizenship, the Court's vision is now informed by human rights principles, rather than by the strict imperatives of socio-economic law promoted by the Treaty'.[105] Whether or not this is the case may be open to argument, but certainly in so far as many third-country nationals are concerned, the ECJ is less generous in its interpretation of the rights to which they are entitled.[106]

7. SUBSTANTIVE RIGHTS AND SOCIAL ADVANTAGES: REGULATION 1612/68

(a) REGULATION 1612/68

The main focus thus far has been on the negative effects of Article 39 and the secondary legislation: the prohibition of discrimination and of barriers to freedom of movement, and the prohibition of entry visas or similar restrictions. The other side of the coin is that this Treaty Article confers positive, substantive rights of freedom of movement and equality of treatment on EC workers. The substantive nature of these rights is, to some extent, given flesh by the secondary legislation, and in particular by Regulation 1612/68.[107] The ECJ's approach to Regulation 1612/68 is similar to its approach to Directive 68/360, in so far as the legislation does not in itself create rights, rather than protecting and facilitating the exercise of the primary rights conferred by the Treaty. However, although the principle of equal treatment forms the backbone of the legislation, its degree of detail and specificity goes beyond what is express in the Treaty, and requires the Member States to ensure that Community workers enjoy a considerable range of the substantive benefits available to nationals. In particular, the Regulation covers the families of EC workers, which are nowhere mentioned in the Treaty. According to the Regulation's preamble, the elimination of obstacles to the free movement of workers will require ensuring 'the worker's right to be joined by his family and the conditions for the integration of that family into the host country'. It should be noted that there is to be a new general directive on free movement, which will replace parts of Regulation 1612/68. It is considered below.[108]

There are three titles within Part I of the Regulation, Title I (Articles 1 to 6) on eligibility for employment, Title II (Articles 7 to 9) on equality of treatment within employment, and Title III (Articles 10 to 12) on workers' families. Part II of the Regulation contains detailed provisions which require co-operation amongst the

---

[105] D. O'Keeffe, 'Trends in the Free Movement of Persons', in J. O'Reilly (ed.), *Human Rights and Constitutional Law* (Round Hall Press, 1992), 262, 274.
[106] Case C–171/95, *Recep Tetik* v. *Land Berlin* [1997] ECR I–329.
[107] [1968] OJ L257/2, [1968] OJ Spec. Ed. 475.   [108] See below, at 761–2.

relevant employment agencies of the Member States, and between the Member State agencies, the Commission, and the European Co-ordination Office, on applications for employment and the clearance of vacancies. Part III of the Regulation sets up an Advisory Committee and a Technical Committee made up of Member State representatives, to ensure close co-operation on matters concerning free movement of workers and employment. Parts II and III of the Regulation, which have been amended several times over the years, have attracted comparatively little legal attention. However, they may be very significant for a worker who is seeking to move to another Member State to find employment. The Member State authorities are required to provide detailed information on vacancies, working conditions, and the State of the national labour market, and to co-operate with the Commission in conducting studies on various matters.

However, it is Part I of the Regulation which has been the subject of most comment and analysis, and its provisions have generated a large amount of litigation. Article 1 of the Regulation sets out the right of Member State nationals to take up employment in another Member State under the same conditions as its nationals, and Article 2 prohibits discrimination against such workers or employees in concluding and performing contracts of employment. Articles 3 and 4 prohibit certain directly or indirectly discriminatory administrative practices, such as reserving a quota of posts for national workers, restricting advertising or applications, or setting special recruitment or registration procedures for other Member State nationals, but with an exception for genuine linguistic requirements. Article 5 guarantees the same assistance from employment offices to non-nationals as well as to nationals, and Article 6 prohibits discriminatory vocational or medical criteria for recruitment and appointment. Article 7 fleshes out Article 48(2) (now Article 39(2)) of the Treaty, providing in particular for the same social and tax advantages for nationals and non-nationals, for equal access to vocational training, and it declares void any discriminatory provisions of collective or individual employment agreements. Article 8 provides for equality of trade-union rights with nationals,[109] and Article 9 for the same access to all rights and benefits in matters of housing. Article 10 sets out the family members who have the right to install themselves with a worker who is employed in another Member State, so long as the worker has adequate housing available. These are the spouse and their descendants, who are either under 21 or dependent, and dependent relatives in the ascending line of the worker and spouse. Member States are also required to 'facilitate the admission' of other family members who are either dependent on the worker or living under the worker's roof in the Member State of origin.[110] Article 11 gives the spouse and children mentioned in Article 10 the right to take up activity as employed persons in the host Member State, and Article 12 provides for equal access for the children of a resident worker to the State's educational courses.

The Regulation has provoked a good deal of litigation. It will be seen that many of the cases, in particular those concerning the meaning of 'social advantages' in Article

---

[109] See Case C–213/90, *ASTI*, n. 80 above, and Case C–118/92, *Commission* v. *Luxembourg* [1994] ECR I–1891, on the right to vote and stand in elections in national occupational guilds.

[110] See, in general, n. 237 below.

7(2), are concerned also with distinguishing a social advantage under this Regulation from a social security benefit under Regulation 1408/71, since the latter is more restrictive than the concept of a social advantage in Article 7(2). Indeed, Article 7 has probably been the most fruitful provision for workers and their families, and it raises interesting questions about when, if at all, Member States are entitled to treat their own nationals more favourably than other EC nationals. Clearly, there are some advantages enjoyed by citizens of a state which are not available to others, for example political rights such as the right to vote in national elections,[111] and Article 7 of Regulation 1612/68 focuses attention on the permissible limits of these advantages. The evolving interpretation by the ECJ of this Article and its related provisions illustrates very well the inevitable social and political consequences of economic integration, and shows how the initial conferral of limited rights on economic actors has a tendency to develop into something more substantial.

(b) ARTICLE 7(2) OF REGULATION 1612/68

Initially, in *Michel S*, the Court read Article 7(2) in quite a limited way, ruling that it concerned only benefits connected with employment.[112] Thus the disabled son of an Italian employee who had worked in Belgium until he died could not invoke Article 7(2) to obtain specific benefits which were available under Belgian legislation to enable disabled Belgian nationals to recover their ability to work. The applicant, however, succeeded on other grounds. The Court, drawing on the references in the Regulation's preamble to freedom and dignity, ruled that the list of educational arrangements (general educational, apprenticeship, and vocational training courses) for workers' children in Article 12 was not exhaustive, so that it could also cover the Belgian disability benefit.[113] Subsequently in *Casagrande*, the Court continued its expansive reading of Article 12. It ruled that, although Article 12 specified only that the children of non-national workers should be 'admitted to courses', the fact that Member States are exhorted to encourage them to attend 'under the best possible conditions' meant that that provision would also cover any 'general measures intended to facilitate educational attendance', including an educational grant for secondary school in Germany.[114] This was a controversial interpretation, since strong submissions were made to the Court that the areas of educational and cultural policy in Germany were specifically reserved to the *Länder*, and that this would be viewed as an encroachment on those powers by Community law.[115]

In keeping with its wider approach to Article 12, the Court soon departed silently from its more restrictive interpretation of Article 7(2) in *Michel S*. In *Cristini v. SNCF*, the Italian widow of an Italian worker in France was refused a reduction card for rail

---

[111] See, however, the Commission's reference to the ECtHR decision in *Piermont* v. *France*, Series A no. 314 (1994), in its second report on citizenship of the Union, COM(97)230, which suggested that nationals of EU Member States should not be treated as 'aliens' for the purposes of restricting their political activities.

[112] Case 76/72, *Michel S* v. *Fonds National de Reclassement Handicapés* [1973] ECR 457.

[113] For a later ruling in which the ECJ gave a broader interpretation to the personal scope of Art. 12 than that of Art. 7 of the Dir. see Case C–7/94, *Landesamt für Ausbildungsförderung Nordrhein-Westfalen* v. *Lubor Gaal* [1996] ECR I–1031.

[114] Case 9/74, *Casagrande* v. *Landeshauptstadt München* [1974] ECR 773.

[115] Warner AG, *ibid.*, 783–4 (ECR).

fares for large families on the ground of her nationality.[116] It was argued that the benefits in Article 7 were restricted to those connected with the contract of employment itself, but the Court ruled that the term 'social advantages' in Article 7(2) could not be interpreted restrictively:[117]

It therefore follows that, in view of the equality of treatment which the provision seeks to achieve, the substantive area of application must be delineated so as to include all social and tax advantages, whether or not attached to the contract of employment, such as reductions in fares for large families.

The Court held that this right to equality of treatment was applicable not just to workers, but also, by virtue of Regulation 1251/70, which governs the right of workers and their families to remain in a Member State after having been employed there, to those surviving family members who had been residing with the deceased worker.

In *Inzirillo*, where an Italian worker in France was refused a disability allowance for his adult son, it was argued that Article 7 of the Regulation could not apply, since the allowance would be a social advantage to the son, rather than to the worker, as required by the Article.[118] The ECJ, however, ruled that dependent adult offspring were covered by Article 10(1) of the Regulation, and that an allowance for handicapped adults which a Member State awarded to its own nationals would indeed constitute a social advantage to a non-national worker. The notion of dependency in Article 10 is, according to the ECJ in *Lebon*, a matter of fact, in that it includes a member of the family who is in fact supported by the worker, whatever the reason for the support.[119]

Thus Article 7(2) covers all social and tax advantages, not just those which are linked to employment, and even when they are of indirect rather than of direct benefit to the worker herself or himself.[120] On the other hand, the ECJ has ruled that the provision can only be invoked where the advantage claimed is in fact of some direct or indirect benefit to the worker, and not just to a family member:[121]

[T] he members of a worker's family, within the meaning of Article 10 of Regulation No 1612/68 qualify only indirectly for the equal treatment accorded to the worker himself by Article 7 of Regulation No 1612/68. Social benefits such as the income guaranteed to old people by the legislation of a Member State (see . . . Case 261/83 *Castelli* v. *ONPTS* [1984] ECR 3199) or guaranteeing in general terms the minimum means of subsistence operate in favour of members of the worker's family only if such benefits may be regarded as a social advantage, within the meaning of Article 7(2) of Regulation No 1612/68, for the worker himself.

The limits to the rights which may be claimed by a worker under Article 7(2) were addressed in the following case.

---

[116] Case 32/75, *Fiorini (neé Cristini)* v. *Société Nationale des Chemins de Fer Français* [1975] ECR 1085.
[117] *Ibid.*, para. 13.
[118] Case 63/76, *Inzirillo* v. *Caisse d'Allocations Familiales de l'Arrondissement de Lyon* [1976] ECR 2057.
[119] Case 316/85, n. 34 above.
[120] See also Case 94/84, *Office National de l'Emploi* v. *Joszef Deak* [1985] ECR 1873.
[121] Case 316/85, *Lebon*, n. 34 above, para. 12.

Case 207/78, Ministère Public v. Even and ONPTS
[1979] ECR 2019

Even was a French worker in Belgium, who received an early retirement pension from the Belgian national pension office. A percentage reduction in the size of the pension per year of early payment was made for all workers except Belgian nationals who were in receipt of a Second World War service invalidity pension granted by an Allied nation. Even was in receipt of a war service pension under French legislation, and he pleaded the principle of equality of treatment to claim the benefit of an early retirement pension without any deduction. On a reference to the ECJ, Regulation 1612/68 was considered.

THE ECJ

22. It follows from all its provisions and from the objective pursued that the advantages which this regulation extends to workers who are nationals of other Member States are all those which, whether or not linked to a contract of employment, are generally granted to national workers primarily because of their objective status as workers or by virtue of the mere fact of their residence on the national territory and the extension of which to workers who are nationals of other Member States therefore seems suitable to facilitate their mobility within the Community.

23. . . . The main reason for a benefit such as that granted by the Belgian national legislation in question to certain categories of national workers is the services which those in receipt of the benefit have rendered in wartime to their own country and its essential objective is to give those nationals an advantage by reason of the hardships suffered for that country.

24. Such a benefit, which is based on a scheme of national recognition, cannot therefore be considered as an advantage granted to a national worker by reason primarily of his status of worker or resident on the national territory and for that reason does not fulfil the essential characteristics of the 'social advantages' referred to in Article 7(2) of Regulation No 1612/68.

The ECJ mentions three factors in determining whether workers are entitled, under Article 7(2), to a particular benefit in a host Member State: their status as workers, their residence on the national territory, and the suitability of the benefit in facilitating their mobility within the Community. Of course this is an inconclusive test, since arguably any kind of benefit available in a Member State, including indeed the right to vote, could be said to encourage workers from other Member States to move to the former state to reside and work there with their families.

The *Even* case is not very different on its facts from that of *Ugliola*,[122] yet the Court found that there was impermissible discrimination in the latter but not in the former case. *Ugliola* concerned the taking into account of military service in calculating seniority at work, as opposed to an exemption from deduction from an early retirement pension for those who were in receipt of a war-service invalidity pension. However, the distinction between the two cases cannot rest on the difference between wartime service and military service. This is because the ECJ has also ruled in *de Vos* that the statutory obligation on an employer to continue paying certain pension

---

[122] Case 15/69, n. 42 above.

insurance contributions on behalf of workers who were absent on military service was not a 'social advantage' to the worker within Article 7(2) of the Regulation, since it was an advantage provided by the state as partial compensation for the obligation to perform military service.[123] It was an advantage 'essentially linked to the performance of military service' rather than merely an advantage granted to workers by virtue of the fact of their residence in the Member State. The difference between the benefit which the employer was required to provide in *Ugliola* and that in *de Vos* is rather difficult to discern, since each was concerned with ensuring that workers who were away on military service would not be disadvantaged as a result. However, the ECJ seemed to treat the obligation to protect a worker's seniority and security of tenure as a condition of employment imposed by the state on employers in *Ugliola*, whereas the obligation on employers to continue paying pension contributions was treated as part of the state's mechanism for compensating those undergoing military service rather than as being linked to the employment contract.

The decision in *Even* also contrasts with the subsequent ruling in *Reina*, on the issue of what benefits could be said to flow from citizenship, so that they are excluded from the scope of Article 7(2) of Regulation 1612/68. In *Reina*, an interest-free 'child-birth loan' granted under German law to German nationals in order to stimulate the birth-rate of the population was held to be a social advantage within Article 7(2). Thus an Italian couple in Germany, one of whom was a worker, was also eligible for the loan.[124] The Court reached this conclusion despite the defendant bank's arguments that the refusal to grant a loan in no way hindered the mobility of workers within the Community, and that being principally a matter of demographic policy, such a discretionary loan fell within the area of political rights linked to nationality. The Court's response was to rule that the loan was a social advantage since its main aim was to alleviate the financial burden on low-income families. The fact that it touched on the Member State's pursuit of demographic policy did not rule out the application of Community law (presumably even if the demographic policy was to increase the birthrate of German nationals).[125]

(c) RIGHTS OF FAMILIES AS PARASITIC ON THE WORKERS' RIGHTS

However broad the interpretation of 'social advantages', it is only workers and those family members specifically listed in the Regulation who may avail themselves of them. This was clarified in *Lebon*, in which the ECJ ruled that once the child of a worker reached the age of 21, and was no longer dependent on the worker, benefits to that child could not be construed as an advantage to the worker.[126] The Court went on

---

[123] Case C–315/94, *De Vos* v. *Bielefeld* [1996] ECR I–1417, paras. 17–22. Contrast Case C–131/96, *Romero* v. *Landesversicherungsanstalt* [1997] ECR I–3659 dealing with Reg. 1408/71 on social security rather than Reg. 1612/68.

[124] Case 65/81, *Reina* v. *Landeskreditbank Baden-Württemberg* [1982] ECR 33. See also Case C–111/91, *Commission* v. *Luxembourg* [1993] ECR I–817.

[125] See also Case C–237/94, *O'Flynn* v. *Adjudication Officer* [1996] ECR I–2617, that a State payment to cover funeral expenses falls within Art. 7(2).

[126] Case 316/85, n. 34 above. For a restrictive reading of Art. 7(2) in relation to a spouse who was not an EC national see Case C–243/91, *Belgium* v. *Taghavi* [1992] ECR I–4401.

to consider the position of such an adult descendant, or indeed the position of any EC national, who was seeking work but not yet employed:[127]

It must be pointed out that the right to equal treatment with regard to social and tax advantages applies only to workers. Those who move in search of employment qualify for equal treatment only as regards access to employment in accordance with Article 48 of the EEC Treaty and Articles 2 and 5 of Regulation No 1612/68.

This ruling highlights the importance of being a full worker, or a specifically listed family member of such a worker, in order to benefit from the substantive rights described in the secondary legislation. Moreover, if the rights of someone who is unemployed but searching for work are limited as indicated in *Lebon*, so too, presumably, are the rights of the family members of such a person.[128] The Court has not had occasion to rule on what difference, if any, there may be between Article 10(1) and Article 10(2) of Regulation 1612/68. Article 10(2) provides that Member States shall 'facilitate the entry' of dependent relatives and those who were living under the same roof as the worker in the Member State of origin. This is more restrictively worded than Article 10(1), which guarantees to the worker the right to have specified family members installed with him or her, subject to the availability of suitable housing.[129] However, the difference may not be significant in the light of the broad reading the ECJ has given Article 7(2), by virtue of which a benefit to a dependent or co-resident relative of the worker may well be considered an advantage to the worker.

An inventive use of Article 7(2) can be seen in the case of *Reed*, in which the interpretation of the term 'spouse' arose.[130] The case concerned the denial of a right of residence to an unemployed British national who had come to The Netherlands to live with her long-term partner, who was a British national employed there. In contrast to its approach in giving a clear Community meaning to terms such as 'worker' and 'public service' in Article 48, the Court ruled that the term 'spouse' referred only to a marital relationship. A wider reading would be unjustifiable, in the ECJ's view, given the absence of consensus and the lack of a 'general social development' amongst all Member States towards treating unmarried companions as spouses. However, although the effect of this reasoning was to deny Reed an independent right of residence under Article 10(1), the Court followed the suggestion of the Commission and ruled that Article 7(2) could nevertheless be of assistance in the case. The Netherlands, as part of its policy on aliens, treated a person who had a stable relationship with a worker of Dutch nationality as that worker's spouse. Accordingly:

---

[127] *Ibid.*, para. 26.

[128] See, however, Case C–3/90, *Bernini*, n. 24 above, and Case C–357/89, *Raulin*, n. 25 above, which suggest that a worker who becomes involuntarily unemployed and takes up a course of study retains the right to educational benefits under Art. 7 of Reg. 1612/68. See similarly Case C–57/96, *Meints*, n. 34 above, on a benefit payable to agricultural workers who have been made redundant in certain circumstances. Compare Case C–43/99, *Ghislain Leclerc, Alina Deaconescu v. Caisse Nationale des Prestations Familiales* [2001] ECR I–4265.

[129] The Court has ruled that the housing requirement may only apply at the initial stage of entry of the family, and may not constitute a ground for refusing to renew residence permits if housing conditions subsequently deteriorate: Case 249/86, *Commission v. Germany* [1989] ECR 1263.

[130] Case 59/85, *Netherlands v. Reed* [1986] ECR 1283.

it must be recognised that the possibility for a migrant worker of obtaining permission for his unmarried companion to reside with him, where that companion is not a national of the host Member State, can assist his integration in the host State and thus contribute to the achievement of freedom of movement for workers. Consequently, that possibility must also be regarded as falling within the concept of a social advantage for the purposes of Article 7(2) of Regulation 1612/68.[131]

Cases such as *Lebon* and *Reed* highlight the derivative nature of families' rights, and make clear the importance of the requisite, traditionally defined, family link, whether it be that of a dependent child, a spouse, or as otherwise provided for in Regulation 1612/68. However, it has been argued that the lack of protection within Community law for less traditionally defined partners might violate the requirements of the ECHR.[132]

The current significance of a specific and continuing family link can be seen in the following case.

Case 267/83, Diatta v. Land Berlin
[1985] ECR 567

The applicant was a Senegalese national who had married a French national, and both were resident and working in Berlin. After some time together, she separated from her husband with the intention of divorcing him, and moved into separate accommodation. She was then refused an extension of her residence permit on the ground that she was no longer a family member of an EC national. The ECJ was asked whether a migrant worker's family must live permanently with that worker in order to qualify for a right of residence.

THE ECJ

18. In providing that a member of a migrant worker's family has the right to install himself with the worker, Article 10 of the Regulation does not require that the member of the family in question must live permanently with the worker, but, as is clear from Article 10(3), only that the accommodation which the worker has available must be such as may be considered normal for the purpose of accommodating his family. A requirement that the family must live under the same roof permanently cannot be implied.

19. In addition, such an interpretation corresponds to the spirit of Article 11 of the Regulation, which gives the member of the family the right to take up any activity as an employed person throughout the territory of the Member State concerned, even though that activity is exercised at a place some distance from the place where the migrant worker resides.

20. It must be added that the marital relationship cannot be regarded as dissolved so long as it has not been terminated by the competent authority. It is not dissolved merely because the spouses live separately, even where they intend to divorce at a later date.

---

[131] *Ibid.*, para. 28.
[132] See K. Lundström, 'Family Life and the Freedom of Movement of Workers in the EU' (1996) 10 *International Journal of Law, Policy and the Family* 250.

However, the ECJ made it clear that the worker's family did not have any independent right of residence, either under Article 11 of the Regulation or under any provision of the Treaty or otherwise.[133] Rather, the spouse's right of residence is conditional on the right of residence of the worker and on the satisfaction of the housing requirement in Article 10, although there is no obligation to live together.[134] The Court was probably influenced by the argument made on behalf of Mrs Diatta that, if cohabitation was mandatory, a worker could at any moment cause the expulsion of a spouse by depriving that spouse of a roof. However, although the ruling indicates that neither living apart nor the likelihood of divorce affects the rights of a spouse under Community law, the ECJ did not State what the position would be after divorce. The same question arose again in the case of *Singh*, where, despite the existence of a decree *nisi* of divorce, the Court ruled that the right of residence of a non-Community spouse was not affected.[135] The judgment suggests that the marriage must be *bona fide*, since the ECJ specifically commented that there was no suggestion of a sham.

(d) FAMILY MEMBERS IN AN 'INTERNAL SITUATION'

Like *Diatta*, the *Singh* case provides a good illustration of the importance of the requisite family link to a non-Community national or to a non-working Community national. However, the case also highlights some of the invidious results and curious distinctions which arise as a result of the ECJ's approach to the so-called 'wholly internal situation'. In *Saunders*[136] the ECJ ruled that a national could not rely on Article 48 (now Article 39) in his or her own Member State to challenge a restriction on freedom of movement, since there was no factor connecting the situation with Community law. This was rather more harshly illustrated in *Morson and Jhanjan*, where it was held that two Dutch nationals working in the Netherlands had no right under Community law to bring their parents, of Surinamese nationality, into the country to reside with them.[137] Had they been nationals of any other Member State working in the Netherlands, they would have been covered by Article 10 of Regulation 1612/68. However, because they were nationals working in their own Member State 'who had never exercised the right to freedom of movement within the Community', they had no rights under Community law.[138]

This was confirmed in *Uecker and Jacquet*, despite the referring German court's obvious invitation to the ECJ to depart from its previous position.[139] The case concerned two non-EC nationals who came to Germany to live with their spouses, both German nationals who resided and worked in Germany, and they sought to rely on Article 7 of Regulation 1612/68 in order to claim equal treatment with German

---

[133] For criticism of the case see J. Weiler, 'Thou Shalt not Oppress a Stranger: On the Judicial Protection of the Human Rights of Non-Community Nationals—a Critique' (1992) *EJIL* 65, 85.

[134] On the right of the spouse of a worker under Art. 11 of Reg. 1612/68 to access to employment see Case 131/85, *Gül v. Regierungspräsident Düsseldorf* [1986] ECR 1573.

[135] Case C–370/90, *R. v. Immigration Appeal Tribunal, ex p. Secretary of State for the Home Department* [1992] ECR I–4265.

[136] Case 175/78, n. 58 above.   [137] Cases 35 & 36/82, n. 60 above.

[138] *Ibid.*, para. 17.

[139] Cases C–64/96 & 65/96, *Land Nordrhein-Westfalen v. Uecker* and *Jacquet v. Land Nordrhein-Westfalen* [1997] ECR I–3171.

nationals in their employment. The ECJ ruled that they could not rely on this provision and reiterated its stance on wholly internal situations, despite the national court's suggestion that the sort of reverse discrimination brought about by that stance was in conflict with 'the fundamental principle of a Community moving towards European Union'.[140]

In *Singh*, however, the situation was slightly different. An Indian national had married a British national, and had travelled with her to Germany where they had both worked for some years before returning to the UK. The UK argued that the British spouse's right to re-enter the UK derived from national law and not from Community law. However, the ECJ clearly considered that the period of working activity in another Member State made all the difference, and enabled Singh now to claim rights as the spouse of a Community worker.

Case C–370/90, R. v. Immigration Appeal Tribunal and Surinder Singh, ex parte Secretary of State for the Home Department
[1992] ECR I–4265

THE ECJ

119. A national of a Member State might be deterred from leaving his country of origin in order to pursue an activity as an employed or self-employed person as envisaged by the Treaty in the territory of another Member State if, on returning to the Member State of which he is a national in order to pursue an activity there as an employed or self-employed person, the conditions of his entry and residence were not at least equivalent to those which he would enjoy under the Treaty or secondary law in the territory of another Member State.

20. He would in particular be deterred from so doing if his spouse and children were not also permitted to enter and reside in the territory of his Member State of origin under conditions at least equivalent to those granted them by Community law in the territory of another Member State.

The distinction between *Morson and Jhanjan* and *Singh* is a fine one. The latter ruling has also attracted criticism, since it is ambiguous as to whether the Community rights of nationals returning with their spouses to their own Member State remain dependent on the spouses' continued economic activity.[141] According to the Commission, the difference in the way a Member State may treat the non-EC spouse of a national of that state as compared with the non-EC spouse of a national of another Member State 'is regarded with disfavour', in view of 'the indivisible nature of citizenship of the Union'.[142] But it is not made clear to whom exactly this comment refers, whether Community citizens, certain Member States, or the Commission itself.

---

[140] *Ibid.*, para. 22.
[141] P. Watson, 'Free Movement of Workers: A One-way Ticket?' (1993) 22 *ILJ* 68.
[142] COM(97)230 para. 4.2. See Case C–60/2000, *Carpenter* v. *Home Secretary*, July 11, 2000.

8. EDUCATION

There was, until the TEU amendments, no reference in the EEC Treaty to education, but only to 'vocational training' in what was then Article 128. Following those amendments, Articles 3(p) and 149 of the EC Treaty (ex Articles 3(p) and 126) make specific reference to the development of education, bringing it expressly within the Community's competence. The Community, even before this, adopted legislation, with the ECJ's approval,[143] to establish Community schemes in areas such as vocational training, foreign languages, educational exchange, and educational mobility.[144]

There are three principal ways in which hard 'educational rights', as such, have been guaranteed as part of Community law.[145] Two of these are set out in the secondary legislation relating to workers, and the third was initially developed by the ECJ in the context of students who did not satisfy the criteria for workers, but who had moved to another Member State in order to study. Each of these three categories guarantees a slightly different range of educational rights.

(a) CHILDREN (AND FAMILY MEMBERS) OF WORKERS

The first and the most generous category covers a group not mentioned in the Treaty: the children of EC migrant workers. Article 12 of Regulation 1612/68 provides that 'the children of a national of a Member State, who is or has been employed in the territory of another Member State, shall be admitted to courses of general education, apprenticeship and vocational training under the same conditions as the nationals of that State, if those children reside in its territory'. Member States are to encourage 'steps allowing such children to follow the above mentioned courses under the best conditions'.[146]

It has been seen that Article 12 has been generously interpreted by the ECJ, both in the kinds of courses it covers,[147] and in terms of the broad meaning given to the phrase 'admitted to courses' so that grants and other such facilitative measures are included.[148] Essentially, Article 12 places the children of EC workers residing in a Member State in the same position as the children of nationals of that state in so far as any education is concerned. It has been held to protect the right to educational assistance even where the working parents have returned to their state of nationality, if the child is obliged by reason of the non-compatibility of educational systems to remain and to complete the education in the host state.[149] Article 12 has also been

---

[143] See, e.g., Cases C–51/89, 90/89, 94/89, *UK v. Council* [1991] ECR I–2757.

[144] J. Shaw, 'From the Margins to the Centre: Education and Training Law and Policy', in P. Craig and G. de Bùrca (eds.), *The Evolution of EU Law* (Oxford University Press, 1999), ch. 15.

[145] The Community has always had competence under Art. 47 (ex Art. 57) EC in relation to the mutual recognition of qualifications, discussed in Ch. 18.

[146] See also the provisions of Dir. 77/486 on language teaching for the children of migrant workers: see [1977] OJ L199/32.

[147] Case 76/72, *Michel S*, n. 112 above.   [148] Case 9/74, *Casagrande*, n. 114 above.

[149] Cases 389 & 390/87, *Echternach and Moritz* [1989] ECR 723.

held to require that, where grants are available to the children of nationals to study abroad, these must also be made available to the children of migrant EC workers, even if the studies abroad are to be in the Member State of the child's nationality.[150]

In *Gaal*, the ECJ ruled that the term children in Article 12 was wider than that in Article 10, so that Article 12 conferred educational rights on children who were over 21 and non-dependent, even though they were not covered by Article 10.[151] The ECJ held that the principle in Article 12 required the children of a migrant worker to be able to continue their studies in order to complete their education successfully, so long as the children had lived with a parent in the Member State at a time when that parent resided there as a worker and, possibly, although the ECJ does not actually say this, at a time when the child was either dependent or under 21.

Further, although Regulation 1612/68 does not make specific provision for the education of other family members of the worker, it is likely that the ECJ's interpretation of 'social advantages' to the worker in Article 7(2) includes at least some educational benefits for the protected family members of that worker, even if not the full range of benefits which are available to children.[152]

(b) WORKERS

The second category of persons who have been able to claim educational rights is that of workers themselves. These rights are set out in Article 7(3) of Regulation 1612/68, as part of the substantive equality of treatment to which EC workers are entitled. Article 7(3) provides that the worker shall 'by virtue of the same right and under the same conditions as national workers, have access to training in vocational schools and retraining centres'. The Article has been held to confer equal rights of access for non-national workers to all the advantages, grants, and facilities available to nationals. It has however been quite restrictively interpreted by the ECJ in relation to the sorts of institutions and courses covered:[153]

In that regard, it should be noted that in order for an educational institution to be regarded as a vocational school for the purposes of that provision, the fact that some vocational training is provided is not sufficient. The concept of a vocational school is a more limited one and refers exclusively to institutions which provide only instruction either alternating with or closely linked to an occupational activity, particularly during apprenticeship. That is not true of universities.

However, the ECJ went on to hold that workers could also invoke the 'social advantages' provision of Article 7(2) to claim entitlement to any advantage available to improve their professional qualifications and social advancement, such as a maintenance grant in an educational institution not covered by Article 7(3).[154] The

---

[150] Case C–308/89, *Di Leo* v. *Land Berlin* [1990] ECR I–4185.

[151] Case C–7/94, *Landesamt für Ausbildungsförderung Nordrhein-Westfalen* v. *Lubor Gaal* [1996] ECR I–1031. See N. Hopkins (1996) 18 *JSWFL* 114; R. White (1995) 20 *ELRev*. 501.

[152] See the argument made by S. Peers, n. 185 below, that such benefits may also be required to be available to members of the worker's family who are third-country nationals.

[153] Case 39/86, *Lair* [1988] ECR 3161.

[154] Case 235/87, *Matteucci* v. *Communauté Français de Belgique* [1988] ECR 5589; Case C–337/97, *Meeusen*, n. 15 above.

Court none the less imposed other limits on the ability of workers to invoke Article 7(2) in this way. It required that, although they did not have to be in the employment relationship just before or during the course of study, and although a fixed minimum period of employment cannot be required by a state,[155] there must be some continuity or link between the previous work and the purpose of the studies in question.[156] The one exception permitted was where a worker involuntarily became unemployed and was 'obliged by conditions on the job market to undertake occupational retraining in another field of activity'.[157]

The likely reason for the limitations imposed by the ECJ on Article 7(2) and (3) is that the status of worker carries with it a substantial range of social and other benefits, and the Member States wish to restrict those claiming such benefits to 'genuine' workers. If someone gives up work to pursue education or training, ceasing to be economically active, the states clearly fear that this could enable people to gain generous educational benefits after a short and purely instrumental period of employment. It is also clear from the ruling in *Brown*, above, that not only must there be a link between the previous employment and the subsequent studies, but the employment must not be 'ancillary' to the main purpose of pursuing a course of study.[158]

(c) STUDENTS

The third category of persons who have been permitted to claim educational rights under Community law was developed by the ECJ in the context of the original Articles 7 and 128 of the EEC Treaty (renumbered Articles 6 and 127 of the EC Treaty post-Maastricht and now Articles 12 and 150 post-Amsterdam). Article 7 contained the general prohibition on discrimination on grounds of nationality 'within the scope of application' of the Treaty, and Article 128 provided that the Council should 'lay down general principles for implementing a common vocational training policy'.

In *Forcheri*, the ECJ held that the Italian spouse of a migrant worker in Belgium was entitled, by virtue of these two provisions, to be admitted to the host state's vocational training courses without having to pay an enrolment fee which was not charged to nationals.[159] This ruling was developed in *Gravier*, in which a French student in Belgium challenged the requirement of an enrolment fee for non-Belgians. Unlike the applicant in *Forcheri*, Gravier had no family members in Belgium and thus no right of residence there, apart from her claim as a student to such a right.

---

[155] See Case 157/84, *Frascogna v. Caisse des Dépôts et Consignations* [1985] ECR 1739 on the requirement of a fixed period of residence; Case C–3/90, *Bernini*, n. 24 above, and Case C–357/89, *Raulin*, n. 25 above.
[156] Case 39/86, *Lair* [1988] ECR 3161, para. 37.
[157] *Ibid.*
[158] Case 197/86, n. 29 above.
[159] Case 152/82, *Forcheri v. Belgium* [1983] ECR 2323.

Case 293/83, Gravier v. City of Liège
[1985] ECR 593

[Note ToA renumbering: Arts. 7 and 128 are now Arts. 12 and 150 respectively]

Françoise Gravier was an art student of French nationality who was charged an enrolment fee (*minerval*) for a course in strip-cartoon art in Liège in Belgium, which Belgian nationals were not required to pay. She brought proceedings claiming exemption from the *minerval*, and the question whether Article 7 EEC prohibited Member States from treating their own nationals more favourably in the area of education was raised before the ECJ.

THE ECJ

15. Such unequal treatment based on nationality must be regarded as discrimination prohibited by Article 7 of the Treaty if it falls within the scope of the Treaty.

. . .

19. The first remark which must be made in that regard is that although educational organization and policy are not as such included in the spheres which the Treaty has entrusted to the Community institutions, access to and participation in courses of instruction and apprenticeship, in particular vocational training, are not unconnected with Community law.

. . .

21. With regard more particularly to vocational training, Article 128 of the Treaty provides that the Council is to lay down general principles for implementing a common vocational training policy capable of contributing to the harmonious development both of the national economies and of the common market. The first principle established in Council Decision 63/266 of 2 April 1963 laying down those general principles States that 'the general principles must enable every person to receive adequate training, with due regard for freedom of choice of occupation, place of training and place of work.'

. . .

23. The common vocational training policy referred to in Article 128 of the Treaty is thus gradually being established. It constitutes, moreover, an indispensable element of the activities of the Community, whose objectives include *inter alia* the free movement of persons, the mobility of labour, and the improvement of the living standards of workers.

24. Access to vocational training is in particular likely to promote free movement of persons throughout the Community, by enabling them to obtain a qualification in the Member State where they intend to work and by enabling them to complete their training and develop their particular talents in the Member State whose vocational training programmes include the special subject desired.

25. It follows from all the foregoing that the conditions of access to vocational training fall within the scope of the Treaty.

The imposition of a *minerval* only on non-national students as a condition of access to such training was found to be contrary to Article 7 of the Treaty.[160] Given the

---

[160] For subsequent litigation over continuing forms of discrimination in the Belgian higher education system see Case 42/87, *Commission* v. *Belgium* [1988] ECR 5445, and Case C–47/93, *Commission* v. *Belgium* [1994] ECR I–1593.

financial consequences for the Member States if they were required to treat all students of EC nationality on an equal footing with national students in conditions of access to vocational training, the *Gravier* ruling clearly had far-reaching potential. There were, however, two possible limits which the ECJ could place upon it: first, on what could constitute a course of 'vocational training', and secondly on what the 'conditions of access' were.

As regards the first, the ECJ actually interpreted 'vocational training' far more expansively than it had the 'vocational schools' for workers in Article 7(3) of Regulation 1612/68.[161] In *Gravier*, any form of education which prepared for a profession, trade, or employment was said to constitute vocational training, even if it included 'an element of general education'.[162] In *Blaizot*, the ECJ ruled that university education could constitute vocational training, unless the course was one intended for people to improve their general knowledge rather than to prepare themselves for an occupation.[163] A university course could prepare a person for a profession, not only where the final academic examination directly provided the required qualification for that particular profession, but also where the studies provided specific training and skills, even if there was no legislation making that knowledge necessary for that job.[164]

As regards the second possible limit, the 'conditions of access' to vocational training, the ECJ has been more cautious. In *Lair*, the Court was asked whether a maintenance and training grant provided by the state to pursue university study fell within the scope of the Treaty.[165] The Court ruled that only grants intended to cover charges relating specifically to access to vocational training, such as registration and tuition fees, were covered by the prohibition on discrimination.[166] In *Raulin*, the Court held that the principle of non-discrimination deriving from Articles 7 and 128 (now Articles 12 and 150) meant that an EC national, admitted to a vocational training course in another Member State, must have a right of residence in that state for the duration of the course.[167] Since it derived from the Treaty, that right was independent of the possession of a residence permit, but the Member States could legitimately impose conditions 'such as the covering of maintenance costs and health insurance'.[168] A dialogue between the legislative and judicial organs of the Community may be observed in this context. The Treaty-derived right of residence 'recognized' by the ECJ corresponds exactly with the right of residence for students to be found in Directive 90/366. This was adopted by the Council in 1990, but had not come into effect when the facts giving rise to the *Raulin* case first arose.[169] In defining the scope

---

[161] See Case 39/86, *Lair*, n. 153 above.

[162] Case 293/83, *Gravier* v. *City of Liège* [1985] ECR 59, para. 30. On this point see Case 263/86, *Belgium* v. *Humbel* [1988] ECR 5365. See also Case 242/87, *Commission* v. *Council* [1989] ECR 1425.

[163] Case 24/86, *Blaizot* v. *University of Liège* [1988] ECR 379, para. 20. The ECJ drew for support on Art. 10 of the Council of Europe's European Social Charter, which treats university education as a form of vocational training.

[164] *Ibid.*, para. 19. The ECJ limited the retroactivity of its ruling in *Blaizot*, because of Belgium's fear that it would throw the financing of university education into chaos.

[165] Case 39/86, n. 153 above.   [166] *Ibid.*, para. 15. See also Case 197/86, *Brown*, n. 29 above.

[167] Case C–357/89, n. 25 above.   [168] *Ibid.*, para. 39.

[169] Dir. 90/366, [1990] OJ L180/30, was annulled by the ECJ on procedural grounds in Case C–295/90, *European Parliament* v. *Council* [1992] ECR I–4193, but replaced in 1993 by a virtually identical measure, Dir. 93/96 [1993] OJ L317/59. See also Case C–424/98, *Commission* v. *Italy* [2000] ECR I–4001.

of the Treaty right of residence, the ECJ clearly took account of the conditions agreed by the Member States in the Directive, which in turn reflected the content of earlier ECJ rulings such as *Lair*.[170]

Although the TEU subsequently added Article 126 (now Article 149) of the EC Treaty, and amended Article 128 (renumbered as Article 127 and post-ToA as Article 150), Article C (now Article 3) TEU makes clear that the *acquis communautaire* must be respected.[171] This largely means that the existing law on vocational education was to be built upon rather than replaced. Certain results might flow from the combination of Articles 6 and 126 (now Articles 12 and 149 respectively). It may be argued that a claim for equal conditions of access to a host Member State's general educational courses can now be made by an EC national, without needing to show any vocational element in the course. In other words, the exclusion in *Blaizot* of courses which only improve 'general knowledge' may no longer exist. It has also been suggested that the Community has the power under Article 6 (now Article 12) to pass legislation governing the wider conditions under which education for Community nationals is to be provided, including formerly excluded areas such as maintenance grants and financing.[172] It should be noted in this respect that the ECJ's decision in *Grzelczyk*,[173] considered in detail below,[174] has implications for the extent to which Member States can discriminate in relation to the funding of students.

The new provisions are also carefully worded in such a way as to recognize the primary responsibility of the Member States for their own educational systems, and to indicate that the Community's role is to be supplementary and co-operative. Furthermore, Article 149 (ex Article 126) expressly provides that no attempt is to be made to harmonize or to jeopardize the diversity of the Member States in these areas.[175] Article 149 provides that the Council is to adopt 'incentive measures' under the co-decision procedure. It lists various projects at which Community action should be aimed, including the development of a European dimension in education, promoting co-operation between educational establishments, exchanges of information between Member States, and encouraging the mobility of students and teachers. Article 150 (ex Article 127) on vocational training contains its own list of objectives for Community action. The cautious tone, and the focus on subsidiarity, in these Treaty Articles is reflected in the soft measures and action programmes which the Commission has chosen to adopt since the time of Maastricht.[176] Moreover, both the cultural and the financial implications of a Community educational policy seem to be a major constraint on action.

---

[170] See also Case C–184/99, *Rudy Grzelczyk*, n. 30 above, paras. 37–40.

[171] K. Lenaerts, 'Education in European Community Law after "Maastricht"' (1994) 31 *CMLRev.* 7.

[172] *Ibid.*, 15–16.   [173] Case C–184/99, *Rudy Grzelczyk*, n. 30 above.   [174] See below, 758–9.

[175] Indeed Art. 128 (now Art. 151) as amended by the ToA further emphasizes the need for the Community to respect the diversity of Member State cultures in its actions under other parts of the Treaty.

[176] See, e.g., the Commission White Paper on Education and Training, 'Teaching and Learning: Towards the Learning Society', COM(95)590; Green Paper on Education, Training, Research, 'The Obstacles to Transnational Mobility', COM(96)462; 'Learning in the Information Society: Action Plan for a European Education Initiative', COM(96)471; Council Resolution on the Promotion of Linguistic Diversity [2002] OJ C50/1; Council Conclusions on the Report on Concrete Future Objectives of Education and Training Systems [2001] OJ C204/3. The open-method of co-ordination is now being used in the educational area.

S. O' Leary, The Evolving Concept of Community Citizenship[177]

The Community claims to exercise limited competence as regards education, excluding matters concerning the organisation, policy making and financing of education. In practice, however, its judgments have a considerable impact on these matters. . . . However, differences between Member States concerning public expenditure as percentages of the total national or education budget reflect national financial and social perspectives on higher education and explains the Member States' inability and unwillingness, in certain situations, to financially endorse the Community's perspectives on free movement and education. . . . The Court of Justice has actively developed the Community's competences in this area. However, if it is concluded that greater Community participation in education is a desirable or necessary consequence of the Community's action to date, or of the situation in Member States, Community legislative action may be preferable. . . .

The Community institutions have, until now, endorsed half-baked solutions in the field of education. Thus, equal treatment operates selectively with respect to certain conditions of access only and they unconvincingly deny competence in certain respects, in particular, with regard to the organising and financing of education. Free movement of students might be more suitably promoted by requiring Member States to finance the true economic cost of the education which their nationals receive in other Member States.

9. AMSTERDAM, BORDERS, AND THIRD-COUNTRY NATIONALS

(a) FROM THE SEA TO THE TOA

We have seen that while freedom of movement for EC workers is guaranteed by the Treaty and secondary legislation, this does not mean that Member States may no longer exercise control over population movements into and within their territories. Indeed some of the ECJ's case law on Directive 68/360 expressly recognized that Member States may have legitimate reasons for wishing to keep account of the flow of persons within their territories.[178]

However, attempts have been made for a number of years to create an area within the European Union which is genuinely free of frontiers, and in which the Member States would cease to impose internal border controls.[179]

In 1987 the Single European Act introduced into the EC Treaty Article 8a, which was renumbered Article 7a by the TEU (and since renumbered Article 14 by the Amsterdam Treaty). This Article provides that the Community shall progressively establish 'the internal market' (which was, optimistically, to be accomplished by the end of 1992 at the latest), which 'shall comprise an area without internal frontiers in which the free movement of goods, persons, services and capital' is to be ensured. However, the scope and meaning of this provision in relation to the free movement of

---

[177] (Kluwer, 1996), 188–9.
[178] Case 321/87, *Commission* v. *Belgium* [1989] ECR 997.
[179] See, for an early example, the Commission Communication on the abolition of controls of persons at intra-Community Borders, COM(88)640.

persons has been a matter for contention. In particular, given the concerns of Member States, and in particular Ireland and the UK,[180] over security and their desire to retain control over immigration policy in relation to third-country nationals, disagreement over the question of passport controls has persisted.[181]

The European Parliament forced the pace by bringing legal proceedings against the Commission for failure to present the necessary proposals for legislation under what was then Article 7a.[182] The case did not however go to judgment, because in 1995 the Commission adopted proposals for three Council Directives, two of which were based on this Article, one concerning the elimination of controls on crossing frontiers,[183] and another concerning the right of third-country nationals to travel within the Community.[184]

The question of border controls and unfettered freedom of movement within the EC is closely bound up with the position of non-EC nationals, whose rights of movement and residence under Community law are limited,[185] and with the attitude of the Member States towards their admission. The Commission has long made clear its view that the elimination of controls under Article 7a (now Article 14) applies 'to all persons, irrespective of their nationality'.[186]

However, given the lack of agreement on the meaning and implementation of Article 7a (now Article 14), five of the Member States initially agreed to co-operate, outside the Community structure, in abolishing checks at their shared borders and on matters of visa policy, by signing the Schengen Agreement of 1985 and the Schengen Implementing Convention of 1990.[187] By the end of 1996, thirteen of the fifteen Member States, excluding the UK and Ireland, were signatories.[188]

Following the coming into force of the TEU in 1993, matters of immigration from outside the Community were dealt with on an intergovernmental basis. This was under the Justice and Home Affairs 'third pillar'. To confuse matters, however, visa

---

[180] See R. v. Secretary of State for the Home Department, ex p. Flynn [1997] 3 CMLR 888 in which the English Court of Appeal ruled that what was then Art. 7a EC did not have direct effect and did not impose any obligation on Member States to abolish border controls. See now the Protocol on the application of Art. 7a (now Art. 14) EC to the UK and Ireland, attached by the ToA to the EC and EU Treaties.

[181] See Commission Communication of 6 May 1992 on the removal of border controls: Bull. EC 5–1992, 1.1.7.

[182] Case C–445/93, Parliament v. Council [1994] OJ C1/24, and the order of the ECJ of 11 July 1996.

[183] COM(95)347 [1995] OJ C289/16.

[184] COM(95)346 [1996] OJ C306/5. The third proposal was COM(95)348 to amend Dir. 68/360 and 73/148, based on Arts. 49, 54, and 63 EC (now Arts. 40, 44, and 52 after the ToA) as regards the formalities which Member States can request of non-EC national family members when they exercise their right to travel: [1995] OJ C307/18.

[185] S. Peers, 'Towards Equality: Actual and Potential Rights of Third Country Nationals in the European Union' (1996) 33 CMLRev. 7; M. Cremona, 'Citizens of Third Countries: Movement and the Employment of Migrant Workers Within the European Union' (1995) 2 LIEI 87; M. Hedemann-Robinson, 'An Overview of Recent Legal Developments at Community Level in relation to Third Country Nationals Resident within the European Union, with Particular Reference to the Case Law of the European Court of Justice' (2001) 38 CMLRev. 525.

[186] COM(97)230, para. 4.

[187] Further, all of the EC Member States signed the so-called Dublin Convention concerning asylum applications in 1990, which came into force on 1 Sept. 1997: see [1997] OJ C254 and C/268. Both the Schengen and Dublin Conventions made reference to EC law, but were not adopted within the Community framework.

[188] For comment see K. Hailbronner and C. Thiery, 'Schengen II and Dublin: Responsibility for Asylum Applications in Europe' (1997) 34 CMLRev. 957.

policy on non-Community nationals after the TEU fell within the scope of Community law, under what was then Article 100c of the EC Treaty.[189] A number of measures were adopted,[190] both under the provisions of the EC Treaty and under the third pillar of the TEU, concerning the movement of persons and in particular the movement of non-Community nationals into and within the EU.[191]

(b) THE TOA

The ToA introduced a new Title IV of Part III of the EC Treaty, incorporating a large part of the previous policy areas of the third pillar, with the consequential repeal of Articles 100c and 100d. The new EC Treaty title deals with most of the former third-pillar areas including visas, asylum, immigration, third-country nationals, judicial co-operation in civil matters, and administrative co-operation. This title cross-refers also to the policies of police and judicial co-operation in criminal matters under the amended Pillar 3, and its overall aim is said, in the new Article 61 EC, to be the progressive establishment of 'an area of freedom, justice and security'.

Ever since the Schengen and Dublin agreements were signed, the term 'fortress Europe' has been coined to describe the increasing preoccupation with the tightening up of entry to the EU from countries without, and the focus on policing and crime control (including the setting up of Europol[192]) within the EU. The aims and language of the new title tend to confirm this view.[193] There are nine Articles within the title, covering border controls, both internal and external, substantive and procedural rules on visas, the rights of third-country nationals including freedom to travel, and refugee and asylum measures, immigration policy, judicial co-operation in areas such as cross-border service of documents, co-operation in taking evidence, the recognition and enforcement of decisions, rules on the conflict of laws, and administrative co-operation.

The title is a curious amalgam of matters which have previously been dealt with under a range of different and fragmented instruments and frameworks: co-operation between some Member States within the Schengen framework; co-operation between all Member States under Pillar 3 of the TEU; various provisions and Conventions adopted under the EC Treaty; and international agreements such as the Dublin Convention adopted by all the Member States but at the time within neither the EC

---

[189] See also an earlier judgment touching on Community competence in matters touching on immigration policy in Cases 281, 283–5, 287/85, *Germany and Others* v. *Commission* [1987] ECR 3203.

[190] Reg. 1683/95 laying down a uniform format for visas [1996] OJ L164/1; Reg. 2317/95 to determine the third countries whose nationals must possess a visa when crossing the external borders of the Member States [1996] OJ L234/1. See K. Hailbronner, 'Visa Regulations and Third Country Nationals' (1994) 31 *CMLRev.* 969; Joint Actions on airport transit arrangements, and on a uniform format for residence permits of third country nationals, Joint Action 97/11/JHA, adopted under what was then Art. K. 3 TEU [1997] OJ L7/1.

[191] For an unofficial collection of many (often highly inaccessible) texts in these fields see T. Bunyan (ed.), *Key Texts on Justice and Home Affairs in the European Union: Volume 1 From Trevi to Maastricht* (Statewatch, 1997).

[192] See [1995] OJ C316/1.

[193] H. D'Oliveira has noted that despite the rhetoric of a citizen's Europe 'the European Community seems to fear its citizens as much as it fears uncontrolled migration': see 'Expanding External and Shrinking Internal Borders: Europe's Defence Mechanisms in the Areas of Free Movement, Immigration and Asylum', in D. O'Keeffe and P. Twomey (eds.), *Legal Issues of the Maastricht Treaty* (Chancery, 1994), 261, 278.

nor EU structure. There are features of the new title which differentiate it from the rest of the EC Treaty in quite significant ways.

First, like the Social Protocol before the ToA and like EMU, it is an area of what would now be called 'closer co-operation' since it did not apply to Ireland, the UK, or Denmark, given the protocols to the EC Treaty by the Amsterdam Treaty.

Secondly, the preliminary rulings jurisdiction which the ECJ has been granted is excluded in relation to certain measures or decisions relating to maintaining law and order or internal security. It is, moreover, only available from national courts from which there is no judicial remedy. It can however be invoked not only by a national court, but also by request of the Council, Commission, or a Member State.

There have been further moves to incorporate the Schengen Convention and its *acquis* officially and fully within the EC and EU framework, a process that has not been unproblematic.[194] A protocol attached by the Treaty of Amsterdam to both the EC and the EU Treaties provides for the integration of that body of law, and its allocation by decision of the Council to the relevant parts of the third pillar and the new EC title.[195] The protocol made special provision for the UK and Ireland, which were not parties to the Schengen agreement and Convention.[196] They were not bound by the Schengen *acquis*, but were permitted to opt in to some or all of it by availing of the new provisions on 'closer co-operation' added by the Amsterdam Treaty. There was an additional protocol excluding them from the application of the new EC Treaty title, but with the possibility either of *ad hoc* opting in or fuller opting in under the 'closer co-operation' provisions.[197] Another protocol on Article 14 (ex Article 7a) preserved the UK's right to maintain border controls with a similar right for Ireland so long as the passport union between the UK and Ireland continued.[198] The UK has now signed up to certain provisions of the Schengen acquis,[199] as has Ireland.[200]

It is important to understand that the treatment of third-country nationals has both an external and an internal dimension.[201]

The *external dimension* is concerned with 'getting into the EU'. The concentrated focus of the states and the EU institutions on immigration, border control,[202] and policing of movement draws attention to the vulnerability of third-country nationals *vis-à-vis* the European Union. Legislation has now been passed concerning important issues governed by Title IV. Regulations have, for example, been enacted amending the uniform format for visas,[203] and listing the third countries whose nationals must be in

---

[194] M. Den Boer [1997] *Maastricht Journal of European and Comparative Law* 310; P. Kuiper, 'Some Legal Problems Associated with the Communitarization of Policy on Visas, Asylum and Immigration under the Amsterdam Treaty and the Incorporation of the Schengen Acquis' (2000) 37 *CMLRev.* 345; S. Peers, 'Caveat Emptor?: Integrating the Schengen Acquis into the European Legal Order' (2000) 2 *CYELS* 87.

[195] ToA, Prot. No. 2.

[196] ToA, Prot. No. 2, Art. 4.

[197] ToA, Prot. No. 4.; M. Hedemann-Robinson, 'The Area of Freedom, Security and Justice with Regard to the UK, Ireland and Denmark: The 'opt-in opt-outs' under the Treaty of Amsterdam', in D. O'Keeffe and P. Twomey (eds.), *Legal Issues of the Amsterdam Treaty* (Wiley, 1999), ch. 17.

[198] ToA, Prot. No. 3. There was a further protocol on the position of Denmark, ToA, Prot. No. 5.

[199] Dec. 2000/365 [2000] OJ L131/43.

[200] Dec. 2002/192 [2002] OJ L64/20.

[201] See generally the Commission's Biannual Updates, COM(2001)278, and COM(2001)628.

[202] A Member State can still impose checks at a border, notwithstanding Art. 14: Case C–378/97, *Criminal Proceedings against Wijsenbeek* [1999] ECR I–6207.

[203] Reg. 334/2002 [2002] OJ L53/7.

possession of visas when crossing the external border.[204] There have been numerous Commission initiatives in relation to immigration and asylum.[205] This area is however especially prone to changes in the overall political climate. The emphasis post-September 11 has been on security. There has, moreover, been concern with certain Member States about immigration and the number of those seeking asylum. Both of these factors will render it more difficult for third-country nationals to gain access to the EU. Illegal immigration and the search for a common asylum policy were high on the agenda of the Seville European Council,[206] and there is already discussion of, for example, the return of illegal residents.[207]

There is also the *internal dimension*, the rights possessed by third-country nationals who reside within the EU. There is no coherent body of EC or EU law governing the position of third-country nationals. Such limited rights as they have are based on a number of different possible legal provisions and arrangements. These include their capacity as family members of certain EC nationals, or as employees of EC service-providers, or as subjects of one of the Community's Association, Co-operation, or other international Agreements with third countries.[208] The general range of EC rights and freedoms does not however apply to them. The introduction of a status of EU citizenship, which is conditional on the possession of Member State nationality, the invidious nature of many of the differences in treatment between EU residents who possess such nationality and those who do not is brought once more into focus.[209]

There has however been some change in this respect. The Tampere European Council called for the establishment of a set of uniform rights for third-country nationals, which are to be as near as possible to those enjoyed by EU citizens.[210] There is still a considerable gap between this aspiration and present reality. Community legislation has none the less been enacted, which deals with certain issues relating to residence of third-country nationals.[211] There is, moreover, important legislation about to be enacted, such as that concerned with the provision of cross-border services by third-country nationals established in the Community, and the posting of workers who are third-country nationals for the provision of cross-border services.[212] There is to be a directive concerning the status of third-country nationals who are long-term residents in a Member State, the aim being to give them equal status with Community nationals, in relation to matters such as access to employment, education, and social protection.[213] Another directive has been proposed concerning the

---

[204] Reg. 539/2001, [2001] OJ L81/1; Council Reg. 2414/2001 [2001] OJ L327/1.

[205] See, e.g., Communication from the Commission to the Council and the European Parliament, 'Towards a Common Asylum Procedure and a Uniform Status, Valid Throughout the Union, for Persons Granted Asylum', COM(2000)755; Communication from the Commission to the Council and European Parliament on a Community Immigration Policy, COM(2000)755; Proposal for a Council Directive on the Minimum Standards for the Qualification of and Status of Third Country Nationals and Stateless Persons as Refugees or as Persons who Otherwise Need International Protection, COM(2001)510; Proposal for a Council Directive Laying Down Minimum Standards on the Reception of Applicants for Asylum in Member States, COM(2001)91.

[206] 21–22 June 2002.   [207] COM(2002)175.   [208] For useful summaries, see n. 185 above.

[209] D'Oliveira, n. 193 above.   [210] 15–16 Oct. 1999.

[211] Reg. 1091/2001 [2001] OJ L150/4, dealing with freedom of movement for those with a national long-stay visa.

[212] COM(2000)271; COM(1999)3.   [213] COM(2001)127.

conditions of entry and residence for third-country nationals who seek employment, or self-employment, within the EU.[214] These initiatives are to be welcomed. The protections accorded to third-country nationals may be piecemeal, but the fact that Community legislation is now being enacted on such important issues is a step in the right direction. It should also be acknowledged that the passage of such measures is not proving to be easy, evidence of the reluctance of some Member States to liberalize the law in this area.

10. CITIZENSHIP

(a) THE INTRODUCTION OF CITIZENSHIP PROVISIONS

The symbolism of the move at Maastricht from European *Economic* Community to European Community, and from Community to Union, was evident also in a number of specific EC Treaty provisions, such as the introduction of the status of citizenship of the Union.[215] Although this represented the first formal constitutionalization of European citizenship, the idea of Community citizenship and the rhetoric of a 'People's Europe' had been in circulation for a long time.[216] The citizenship provisions are contained in Part Two of the EC Treaty, Articles 17–22 (ex Articles 8–8e). Article 17 provides that:

1. Citizenship of the Union is hereby established. Every person holding the nationality of a Member State shall be a citizen of the Union. Citizenship of the Union shall complement and not replace national citizenship.

2. Citizens of the Union shall enjoy the rights conferred by this Treaty and shall be subject to the duties imposed thereby.

(b) RIGHTS OF MOVEMENT AND RESIDENCE

Article 18 (ex Article 8a) provides that:

1. Every citizen of the Union shall have the right to move and reside freely within the territory of the Member States, subject to the limitations and conditions laid down in this Treaty and by the measures adopted to give it effect.

2. The Council may adopt provisions with a view to facilitating the exercise of the rights referred to in paragraph 1; save as otherwise provided in this Treaty, the Council shall act in accordance with the procedure referred to in Article 251. The Council shall act unanimously throughout this procedure.

---

[214] COM(2001)386.

[215] See C. Closa, 'The Concept of Citizenship in the Treaty on European Union' (1992) 29 *CMLRev.* 1137; S. O'Leary, 'Nationality Law and Community Citizenship: A Tale of Two Uneasy Bedfellows' (1992) 12 *YBEL* 353.

[216] See, e.g., 'Towards a Citizens' Europe', Bull. EC, Supp. 7–1975, 11, and the report on 'A People's Europe' following the Fontainebleau summit of the European Council, COM(84)446 final. See also D. O'Keeffe, 'Union Citizenship', in O'Keeffe and Twomey (eds.), n. 193 above, 87 and A. Wiener 'Assessing the Constructive Potential of Union Citizenship—A Socio-Historical Perspective', European Integration Online Papers, Vol. 1 (1997) No. 17.

The Nice Treaty has amended Article 18. Article 18(1) remains unaltered, but Article 18(2) has been changed, and Article 18(3) has been added.

2. If action by the Community should prove necessary to attain this objective [ie that in Article 18(1)] and this Treaty has not provided the necessary powers, the Council may adopt provisions with a view to facilitating the exercise of the rights referred to in paragraph 1. The Council shall act in accordance with the procedure referred to in Article 251.

3. Paragraph 2 shall not apply to provisions on passports, identity cards, residence permits or any other such document or to provisions on social security or social protection.

There are a number of points to be made about this important provision, which must, for the sake of clarity be distinguished.

First, the crucial restriction on the right to move and to reside in Article 18 is that *it is subject to such limits and conditions as are laid down in the Treaty and by the measures adopted to give it effect.* Where specific legislation has been enacted movement and residency rights will be subject to the conditions laid down therein. Thus two years before the TEU was signed, the Council had already adopted three directives granting rights of residence to categories of persons other than workers. Directive 90/366 (replaced later by Directive 93/96)[217] covered students exercising the right to vocational training. Directive 90/365 dealt with employed and self-employed people who had ceased to work, but without necessarily having moved to another Member State.[218] Directive 90/364 was a catch-all governing all those persons who did not already enjoy a right of residence under Community law.[219] These Directives require Member States to grant the right of residence, evidenced by a permit, to those persons and certain of their family members. This is, however, subject to the proviso that they have adequate resources not to become a burden on the social assistance schemes of the Member States and are all covered by sickness insurance. The Member States' financial interests were clearly taken into account in adopting these Directives, since, although the right of residence may no longer be dependent on the exercise of an economic activity, it is certainly dependent on the enjoyment of a degree of wealth or financial self-sufficiency. The 'limits and conditions' mentioned in Article 18 include the financial and other conditions set by these Directives, so that no rights of residence are conferred upon migrant EU citizens who lack sufficient financial resources.[220]

Secondly, *the crucial issue in legal terms is the extent to which rights can be derived from Articles 17 and 18, without thereby contravening the condition that the right to move and reside is subject to the limits laid down in the Treaty.* It was made clear in *Uecker*[221] that citizenship was not intended to extend the scope *ratione materiae* of the Treaty to cover internal situations with no link with Community law. In *Skanavi* the ECJ treated Article 8a (now Article 18) as residual and apparently secondary to other more specific Treaty rights.[222] The ECJ has, more recently, been willing to accord more substance to Article 18. The case of *Bickel & Franz*[223] was concerned with German and

217 [1993] OJ L317/59.   218 [1990] OJ L180/28.   219 [1990] OJ L180/26.
220 Case C–184/99, *Rudy Grzelczyk*, n. 30 above, paras. 37–40.
221 Cases C–64/96 & 65/96, *Uecker*, n. 139 above.
222 Case C–193/94, *Skanavi and Chyssanthakopoulos* [1996] ECR I–929.
223 Case C–274/96, [1998] ECR I–7637, para. 15.

Austrian nationals subject to criminal proceedings in Italy. They requested use of German in the proceedings, in accord with the rights granted to German-speaking Italians resident in that Italian province. The ECJ ruled that the principle of non-discrimination in Article 12 applied, and stressed that the accused were not only potential recipients of services, but also were exercising their right to free movement as European citizens based on Article 18. Citizenship also featured prominently in the following case.[224]

Case C–85/96, Maria Martinez Sala v. Freistaat Bayern
[1998] ECR I–2691

[Note ToA renumbering: Arts. 6, 8(2) and 8a are now Arts. 12, 17(2) and 18 respectively]

Martinez Sala was a Spanish national who had lived in Germany since 1968. She had undertaken work at various times, but since 1989 she had received social assistance. Until 1984 she had obtained residence permits from the German authorities, but thereafter she merely had documents saying that the extension of her permit had been applied for. She was issued with a residence permit in 1994. In 1993, when she did not possess a permit, she applied for a child-raising allowance. Her application was rejected because she did not have German nationality, a residence entitlement, or a residence permit. She argued that this was in breach of EC law. The ECJ found that the requirement of a residence permit for receipt of a benefit was discriminatory where a Member State's own nationals were not subject to the same condition, and was therefore prohibited under Article 6. The German government argued that even if this was so, the facts of the case did not come within the scope of the Treaty, and therefore the applicant could not rely on Article 6. The ECJ held that a child-raising allowance was within the scope *ratione materiae* of the Treaty, and that if she were found to be a worker she would be within the Treaty *ratione personae*. The Commission argued that, even if she was not a worker, she could come within the personal scope of the Treaty as a citizen because of Article 8a.

THE ECJ

60. It should, however, be pointed out that, in a case such as the present, it is not necessary to examine whether the person concerned can rely on Article 8a . . . in order to obtain recognition of a new right to reside in the territory of the Member State concerned, since it is common ground that she has already been authorised to reside there, although she has been refused a residence permit.

61. As a national of a member State lawfully residing in the territory of another Member State, the appellant . . . comes within the scope *ratione personae* of the provisions of the Treaty on European citizenship.

62. Article 8(2) . . . attaches to the status of citizen of the Union the rights and duties laid down by the Treaty, including the right, laid down in Article 6 . . . not to suffer discrimination on grounds of nationality within the scope *ratione materiae* of the Treaty.

---

[224] See also Case C–411/98, *Angelo Ferlini*, n. 5 above; Case C–135/99, *Ursula Elsen* v. *Bundesversicherungsanstalt* [2000] ECR I–10409, para. 34; Case C–224/98, *D'Hoop* v. *Office Nationale de l'Emploi*, July 11, 2002, paras. 27–40.

63. It follows that a citizen of the European Union . . . lawfully resident in the territory of the host Member State, can rely on Article 6 . . . in all situations which fall within the scope *ratione materiae* of Community law, including the situation where that member State delays or refuses to grant to that claimant a benefit that is provided to all persons lawfully resident in the territory of that State on the ground that the claimant is not in possession of a document which nationals of that same State are not required to have and the issue of which may be delayed or refused by the authorities of that State.

The ECJ applied the general principle of non-discrimination on grounds of nationality to Sala, and did so on the ground of citizenship. The ECJ was therefore willing to 'explode the linkages'[225] which had previously been required in order for the principle of non-discrimination to apply. It was not necessary for there to be involvement in an economic activity as a worker, or service provider, nor was it necessary to show preparation for a future economic activity as a student etc. The fact that the ECJ did not base Sala's right to reside on Article 18 (ex Article 8a), having found that Germany had authorized her residence, meant that the Court did not have to confront the limiting conditions within that Article. The ECJ could simply base itself on Article 17(2) (ex Article 8(2)): citizens of the Union have the rights granted by the Treaty. The Court developed citizenship further in *Grzelczyk*.

Case C–184/99, Rudy Grzelczyk v. Centre Public d'Aide Sociale
d'Ottignes-Louvain-la-Neuve (CPAS)
[2001] ECR I–6193

[Note ToA renumbering: Arts. 6 and 8a are now Arts. 12 and 18]

Grzelczyk (G) was a French national studying in Belgium. He worked part-time during his initial three years of study, but in his fourth year he applied to the CPAS for payment of the minimex, a non-contributory minimum subsistence allowance. The CPAS granted this, but then withdrew it after the Belgian minister decided that G was not entitled to it since he was not a Belgian national. The ECJ approached the case on the assumption that G was not a worker.

THE ECJ

29. It is clear . . . that a student of Belgian nationality, though not a worker . . ., who found himself in exactly the same circumstances as Mr Grzelczyk would satisfy the conditions for obtaining the minimex. The fact that Mr Grzelczyk is not of Belgian nationality is the only bar to its being granted to him. It is not therefore in dispute that the case is one of discrimination solely on the ground of nationality.

30. Within the sphere of application of the Treaty, such discrimination is, in principle, prohibited by Article 6. In the present case, Article 6 must be read in conjunction with the provisions of the Treaty concerning citizenship of the Union in order to determine its sphere of application.

---

[225] S. O' Leary, 'Putting Flesh on the Bones of European Union Citizenship' (1999) 24 *ELRev*. 68, 77–8. See also, H. Toner, 'Judicial Interpretation of European Union Citizenship—Consolidation or Transformation' (2000) 7 *MJ* 158.

31. Union citizenship is destined to be the fundamental status of nationals of the Member States, enabling those who find themselves in the same situation to enjoy the same treatment in law irrespective of their nationality, subject to such exceptions as are expressly provided for.

32. As the Court held in paragraph 63 . . . in *Martinez Sala* . . . a citizen of the European Union, lawfully resident in the territory of a host Member State, can rely on Article 6 . . . in all situations which fall within the scope *ratione materiae* of Community law.

33. Those situations include those involving the exercise of the fundamental freedoms guaranteed by the Treaty and those involving the exercise of the right to move and reside freely in another Member State, as conferred by Article 8a . . . (see . . . *Bickel & Franz* . . . paragraphs 15 and 16).

The ECJ's reasoning is similar in structure to that in the preceding case, but more far-reaching. It begins with a finding of discrimination on grounds of nationality (paragraph 29). The ECJ then uses citizenship to determine the sphere *ratione personae* for the application of Article 6 (now Article 12)(paragraph 30). It is because Grzelczyk is a Union citizen lawfully residing in Belgium that he can avail himself of Article 6, in all situations that come within the scope *ratione materiae* of Community law (paragraph 32). The final touch comes in paragraph 33: the very scope *ratione materiae* of Community law is defined in part by the right to move and reside freely in another Member State.

(c) POLITICAL RIGHTS

It is clear that the rights conferred by Union citizenship are in addition to, and do not replace, the rights enjoyed by Member State nationals by virtue of their own nationality and citizenship. This was emphasized by the ToA amendment, which added the last sentence to Article 17(1). The question of who is a Member State national remains for each Member State to decide.[226]

The remainder of Part Two dealing with citizenship confers a number of rights which, although limited in their range, are of some practical and symbolic importance. Article 19 (ex Article 8b) provides that citizens of the Union shall have the right in a Member State other than that of their nationality to vote and to stand as a candidate both in municipal and in European Parliament elections.[227] There was controversy about this Article because of its incompatibility with constitutional provisions in some Member States. Article 19 therefore allows for the possibility of derogations. Article 20 (ex Article 8c) provides that Union citizens have the right, in a third country where their own Member State is not represented, to the protection of the diplomatic authorities of any Member State. Article 21 (ex Article 8d) provides

[226] See Case C–369/90, *Micheletti v. Delegación del Gobierno en Cantabria* [1992] ECR I–4239; Case C–192/99, *R. v. Secretary of State for the Home Department, ex p. Kaur* [2001] ECR I–1237. See S. O'Leary, *The Evolving Concept of Community Citizenship* (Kluwer, 1996), ch. 2; S. Hall, 'Determining the Scope *Ratione Personae* of European Citizenship: Customary International Law Prevails for Now' (2001) 28 *LIEI* 355.

[227] See Council Dir. 93/109 on exercising the right to vote in European Parliament elections: [1993] OJ L329/34. See also the resolution of the European Parliament on the implementation of this Dir.: [1994] OJ C44/159. On the right to vote and stand in municipal elections see Dir. 94/80 [1994] OJ L368, modified by Dir 96/30 [1996] OJ L122/12.

that citizens have the right to petition the European Parliament, and apply to the Ombudsman.[228] EU citizens who write to any of the Community institutions in one of the official languages have the right to an answer in that language. Article 22 (ex Article 8e) requires the Commission to report every three years on the application of these provisions on citizenship, and thus far it has adopted three reports.[229] The Council is also empowered 'to adopt provisions to strengthen or to add to the rights laid down' in this part of the Treaty. However, the Council must act unanimously and Article 22 envisages that such action may require constitutional amendment at the national level.[230]

(d) CITIZENSHIP: CONCERNS AND POTENTIAL

The limits of EU citizenship as it has been formalized in the Treaty have been the subject of much adverse comment.[231] There has been concern at the symbolism of super-statehood inherent in the notion of EU citizenship. There has been criticism of the paucity of the rights created. Critics have focused on the absence of reciprocal duties which might give rise to a more active or participatory citizenship,[232] the subjection of the right of residence to the limiting conditions laid down in earlier directives, and the discrimination against resident third-country nationals. There has been concern over the Member States' reluctance to enforce the rights which have been created.[233] There is also a broader dimension to this critique. A meaningful idea of European citizenship requires not only concrete and practical measures on matters such as residence, travel, voting, etc., but is also connected with the need for broader institutional and political reform within the EU.[234]

However, it has also been argued that we can look at European citizenship in another way. We should consider not only the narrowly defined Treaty provisions on citizenship, but also the actual practice and experience of what might be called citizenship within the EU over many years. It is, moreover, possible to consider other, newer Treaty amendments as aspects of citizenship, such as the broadened non-discrimination clause in Article 13, and the right of access to documents of the European institutions in Article 255.[235] It is, as Shaw states, therefore essential to look

---

[228] Non-citizens resident in the EU can also do so: Arts. 194 and 195.

[229] COM(93)702, COM(97)230 and COM(2001)506.

[230] Denmark entered various reservations about the concept of Union citizenship in a 'Unilateral Declaration' at the 1992 Edinburgh summit, after the initial rejection by referendum in that Member State of the TEU.

[231] See, e.g., on the narrow and exclusionary nature of EU citizenship, M. Everson, 'The Legacy of the Market Citizen', in J. Shaw and G. More (eds.), New Legal Dynamics of European Union (OUP, 1995), 73; C. Lyons, 'Citizenship in the Constitution of the European Union: Rhetoric or Reality?', in R. Bellamy (ed.), Constitutionalism, Democracy, and Sovereignty: American and European Perspectives (Avebury, 1996), 96; H. D'Oliveira, 'European Citizenship: Its Meaning, Its Potential', in R. Dehousse (ed.), Europe after Maastricht (Munich, 1994).

[232] J. Weiler, 'Citizenship and Human Rights', in J. Winter et al. (eds.), Reforming the TEU: The Legal Debate (Kluwer, 1996).

[233] Ibid., and see also the Commission's comments to this effect in its second report: COM(97)230.

[234] See above Ch. 4.

[235] See, e.g., K. Armstrong, 'Citizenship of the Union? Lessons from Carvel and the Guardian' (1996) 59 MLR 582.

beyond the formal provisions on citizenship to see how and to what extent these 'citizens' are constituted as 'Members' having a stake in the European Union as a political entity.[236]

(e) CITIZENSHIP AND THE NEW LEGISLATION ON FREE MOVEMENT

There is, as mentioned in the preceding discussion, to be a new general directive on free movement for citizens of the Union and their family members.[237] It will replace much of the existing secondary legislation.[238]

The Commission consciously links the new legislation with broader concerns about Union citizenship. Its explanatory memorandum begins with statements about the need to bring the Community institutions closer to the people, and to make them more readily understandable.[239] The introduction of citizenship 'generalized for the benefit of all citizens, the right to enter and the right to reside in the territory of another Member State'.[240] It was therefore desirable to formalize the rights of Union citizens and to harmonize them into a single piece of legislation.[241] The basic premise was that Union citizens should be able to move between Member States on similar terms as a Member State national moving within her own country. Any additional administrative or legal obligations should be kept to a minimum.[242] A brief overview of some of the main provisions of the Directive can be given here.

The proposed Directive specifies the conditions governing the right to move and reside freely, and the right of permanent residence, within the Member States, by Union citizens and their family members, as well as the limits placed on those rights on grounds of public policy, public security, and public health.[243] Article 2 defines a Union citizen as a person who has the nationality of a Member State. The Directive also protects family members, the definition being broader and more uniform than hitherto.[244] Article 4 provides that Member States must give effect to the Directive without discrimination on a wide variety of grounds.[245]

Chapter II of the Directive provides a general right to move and reside for up to six months for Union citizens, and their family members, irrespective of their nationality. They must have a valid passport or identity card.[246]

Chapter III deals with rights of residence for more than six months. This right is accorded to the employed and self-employed, to those with sufficient resources to

---

[236] J. Shaw, 'European Union Citizenship: The IGC and Beyond' (1997) 3 *European Public Law* 413, 417.

[237] Proposal for a European Parliament and Council Dir. on the Right of Citizens of the Union and their Family Members to Move and Reside Freely within the Territory of the Member States, COM(2001)257 final.

[238] For background influences see Report from the Commission to the Parliament and the Council on the Implementation of Dir. 90/364, 90/365, and 93/96, and Communication from the Commission to the European Parliament and the Council on the Follow-Up to the Recommendations of the High-Level Panel of the Free-Movement of Persons, COM(1998)403.

[239] COM(2001)257, n. 237 above, para. 1.1.   [240] *Ibid.*, para. 1.2.   [241] *Ibid.*, para. 1.2.

[242] *Ibid.*, para. 1.3.   [243] *Ibid.*, Art. 1.

[244] *Ibid.*, Art. 2(2). This covers the spouse, and unmarried partners, provided that the host state treats unmarried couples as equivalent to married couples. It also covers direct descendants, and direct relatives in the ascending line.

[245] Sex, race, colour, ethnic or social origin, genetic characteristics, language, religion or beliefs, political or other opinion, membership of a minority, property, birth, disability, age or sexual orientation.

[246] *Ibid.*, Art. 6.

avoid becoming a burden on the host state, to students admitted to a course of vocational training, and to the family members of Union citizens who fall into one of these categories.[247] The host state can require Union citizens to register with the relevant authorities. They will be issued with a certificate of registration that provides evidence of the right of residence.[248] There are detailed provisions as to what should occur in the event of divorce and the like.[249]

Chapter IV introduces a new right of permanent residence where the Union citizen has resided legally and continuously for four years in the host state. The right, once gained, is lost only in the event of absence from the host state for four consecutive years.[250] The right of permanent residence can be gained earlier in certain circumstances.[251] Member States must issue permanent residence cards to those who have such residency rights.[252]

Chapter V lays down certain important provisions that are common to the right of residence and permanent residence. These include the right of family members, irrespective of nationality, to work, and the right to equal treatment.[253]

Chapter VI covers restrictions on the right of entry and right of residence on grounds of public policy, public security, and public health.

11. CONCLUSION

i. The free movement of workers is of central importance to the EU, in both economic and social terms. This is reflected in the Community legislation passed to flesh out the bare bones of Article 39. It is reflected also by the fact that the ECJ has read the enabling Treaty Articles and secondary legislation in a purposive manner designed to achieve the Community's objectives in this area.

ii. The addition of Union citizenship in the TEU did not, initially, have a significant impact on the law in this area. There are however now signs that the ECJ is making greater use of these provisions in order to expand the scope of Community protection. There are also indications that citizenship, over and beyond the specific Treaty rights, is becoming of greater importance in the passage of Community legislation in the area as a whole.

iii. The addition, by the ToA, of the new Title IV dealing with visas, asylum, immigration, and the like, is posing new challenges for the EU. The treatment of third-country nationals, in terms of the criteria for their entry, and their treatment once in the Community, raises difficult and important issues, legal and moral.

---

[247] *Ibid.*, Art. 7.   [248] *Ibid.*, Art. 8.   [249] *Ibid.*, Art. 13.   [250] *Ibid.*, Art. 14.
[251] *Ibid.*, Art. 15.   [252] *Ibid.*, Art. 17.   [253] *Ibid.*, Arts. 20–21.

12. FURTHER READING

(a) *Books*

GUILD, E. (ed.), *The Legal Framework and Social Consequences of Free Movement of Persons in the European Union* (Kluwer, 1999)

—— *Immigration Law in the European Community* (Kluwer, 2001)

—— and HARLOW, C., *Implementing Amsterdam: Immigration and Asylum Rights in EC Law* (Hart, 2001)

HANDOLL, J., *Free Movement of Persons in the European Union* (Chancery, 1995)

MEEHAN, E., *Citizenship and the European Community* (Sage, 1993)

O'LEARY, S., *The Evolving Concept of Community Citizenship* (Kluwer, 1996)

PEERS, S., *EU Justice and Home Affairs Law* (Longman, 2000)

SCHERMERS, H., *et al.* (eds.), *Free Movement of Persons in Europe* (Martinus Nijhoff, 1991)

STAPLES, H., *Legal Status of Third Country Nationals Resident in the EU* (Kluwer, 1999)

WEISS, F., and WOOLDRIDGE, F., *Free Movement of Persons within the European Community* (Kluwer, 2002)

(b) *Articles*

BERNARD, N., 'Discrimination and Free Movement in EC Law' (1996) 45 *ICLQ* 82

CASTRO OLIVEIRA, A., 'Workers and Other Persons: Step-by-Step from Movement to Citizenship' (2002) 39 *CMLRev.* 77

CREMONA, M., 'Citizens of Third Countries: Movement and the Employment of Migrant Workers Within the European Union' (1995) 2 *LIEI* 87

HAILBRONNER, K., and THIERY, C., 'Schengen II and Dublin: Responsibility for Asylum Applications in Europe' (1997) 34 *CMLRev.* 957

HEDEMANN-ROBINSON, M., 'An Overview of Recent Legal Developments at Community Level in relation to Third Country Nationals Resident within the European Union, with Particular Reference to the Case Law of the European Court of Justice' (2001) 38 *CMLRev.* 525

KKUIPER, P., 'Some Legal Problems Associated with the Communitarization of Policy on Visas, Asylum and Immigration under the Amsterdam Treaty and the Incorporation of the Schengen Acquis' (2000) 37 *CMLRev.* 345

LENAERTS, K., 'Education in European Community Law after "Maastricht"' (1994) 31 *CMLRev.* 7

LYONS, C., 'Citizenship in the Constitution of the European Union: Rhetoric or Reality?', in R. Bellamy (ed.), *Constitutionalism, Democracy, and Sovereignty: American and European Perspectives* (Avebury, 1996)

MANCINI, G.F., 'The Free Movement of Workers in the Case-Law of the European Court of Justice', in D. Curtin and D. O'Keeffe (eds.), *Constitutional Adjudication in European Community and National Law* (Butterworths Ireland, 1992)

O'Keeffe, D., 'Judicial Interpretation of the Public Service Exception to the Free Movement of Workers', in D. Curtin and D. O'Keeffe (eds.), *Constitutional Adjudication in European Community Law and National Law* (Butterworths Ireland, 1992)

—— 'Union Citizenship', in D. O'Keeffe and P. Twomey (eds.), *Legal Issues of the Maastricht Treaty* (Wiley, 1994)

O'Leary, S., 'The Free Movement of Persons and Services', in P. Craig and G. de Búrca (eds.), *The Evolution of EU Law* (Oxford University Press, 1999)

Peers, S., 'Towards Equality: Actual and Potential Rights of Third Country Nationals in the European Union' (1996) 33 *CMLRev.* 7

—— 'Dazed and Confused: Family Members' Residence Rights and the Court of Justice' (2001) 26 *ELRev.* 76

—— 'Caveat Emptor?: Integrating the Schengen Acquis into the European Legal Order' (2000) 2 *CYELS* 87

Shaw, J., 'European Union Citizenship: the IGC and Beyond' (1997) 3 *European Public Law* 413

—— 'The Many Pasts and Futures of Citizenship in the European Union' (1997) 60 *MLR* 554

—— 'From the Margins to the Centre: Education and Training Law and Policy', in P. Craig and G. de Búrca (eds.), *The Evolution of EU Law* (Oxford University Press, 1999)

Toner, H., 'Judicial Interpretation of European Union Citizenship—Consolidation or Transformation' (2000) 7 *MJ* 158.

18

FREEDOM OF ESTABLISHMENT AND TO PROVIDE SERVICES

1. CENTRAL ISSUES

i. In addition to the categories of workers, students, families, non-employed citizens, and others examined in the previous chapter, the Treaty provisions on the free movement of persons also cover also the self-employed who move on a temporary or permanent basis between Member States.

ii. The central principles governing the legal framework for freedom of establishment and the free movement of services are laid down in the EC Treaty and developed through ECJ case law. Important developments in the field of establishment and services have also been brought about through secondary legislation in fields such as insurance, financial services, telecommunications, and broadcasting. However, with the exception of some of the general secondary legislation relating to the recognition of professional qualifications, this chapter focuses mainly on the broad constitutional principles applicable to every sector.

iii. Articles 43 to 48 (ex Articles 52 to 58) EC on freedom of establishment require the removal of restrictions on the right of individuals and companies to maintain a permanent or settled place of business in a Member State. Establishment is defined as 'the actual pursuit of an economic activity through a fixed

establishment in another Member State for an indefinite period'.[1]

iv. Articles 49 to 55 (ex Articles 59 to 66) EC on the free movement of services require the removal of restrictions on the provision of services between Member States, whenever a cross-border element is present. This element can result from the fact that the provider is not established in the State where the services are supplied, or that the recipient has travelled to receive services in a Member State other than that in which he or she is established. A movement of services within the scope of Articles 49–50 (ex Articles 59–60) may also occur without the provider or the recipient moving, e.g., where the provision of the service takes place by telecommunication.[2]

v. While the Treaty provisions governing the free movement of services are residual, in that they apply only in so far as the provisions concerning capital,[3] persons, or goods do not apply, it is often difficult, in contexts such as broadcasting or telecommunications, to separate the issues concerning goods from those concerning services.[4]

vi. Although the principle of non-discrimination in Article 12 (ex Article 6) EC

---

[1] Case C–221/89, *R.* v. *Secretary of State for Transport, ex p. Factortame* [1991] ECR I–3905, para. 20.

[2] For another example see Case C–384/93, *Alpine Investments* [1995] ECR I–1141.

[3] See, e.g., Case C–423/98, *Albore* [2000] ECR I–5965.

[4] See, e.g., Case C–390/99, *Canal Satélite Digital* v. *Administración General del Estado* [2002] ECR I–nyr, paras. 31–33. For a case in which the ECJ treated the goods and services dimensions of a restriction on alcohol advertising separately, but reached the same conclusion in each case, see Case C–405/98, *Konsumentombuds-mannen* v. *Gourmet International Products* [2001] ECR I–1795. For fishing permits as services rather than goods, see Case C–97/98, *Jägerskiöld* v. *Gustafsson* [1999] ECR I–7319.

is an important aspect of these two Treaty chapters,[5] in that a non-national who is established in a Member State should in principle be treated in the same way as a national, and a non-established provider or recipient of services should be treated in the same way as a provider or recipient established in the Member State, the ECJ has gone further to declare that even non-discriminatory obstacles may be prohibited by the Treaty provisions. However, the concept of 'discriminatory measures' is not very sharply defined, and in the context of the free movement of goods the distinction between discriminatory and non-discriminatory measures is unclear.

vii. In addition to the Treaty-based exceptions to freedom of movement on grounds of public policy, security, and health, which are dealt with in Chapter 19, the ECJ has—as in the cases of goods and workers—acknowledged a range of public-interest justifications which Member States may invoke to restrict these freedoms.

2. PERSONS, SERVICES, AND ESTABLISHMENT: DIFFERENCES AND COMMONALITIES

(a) THE THREE CHAPTERS

The points of similarity between the various chapters on the free movement of persons and services have often been emphasized. Advocate General Mayras in *Van Binsbergen* pointed out that the principle of equal treatment on grounds of nationality (Article 12, ex Article 6) lay behind all three.[6] Articles 39 (ex Article 48) on workers and 43 (ex Article 52) on establishment are often compared on the basis that each requires equal treatment of persons who are *settled* in a Member State, having exercised their freedom of movement, the essential difference being whether they are working in an employed or a self-employed capacity.[7] The potential overlaps between workers (Article 39, ex Article 48) and temporary service providers (Article 49, ex Article 59) can be seen in a series of cases concerning posted workers in which the ECJ distinguished the two by ruling that 'workers employed by a business established in one Member State who are temporarily sent to another Member State to provide services do not, in any way, seek access to the labour market in that second State if they return to their country of origin or residence after completion of their work'.[8]

The similarities between establishment and services are evident when considering at what stage a self-employed person providing regular services into or within a Member State may be considered to be sufficiently connected with that State to be established, rather than merely providing services there.[9] The factors

---

[5] See Case 2/74, *Reyners* v. *Belgium* [1974] ECR 631, paras. 15–16.

[6] Case 33/74, *Van Binsbergen* v. *Bestuur van de Bedrijfsvereniging voor de Metaalnijverheid* [1974] ECR 1299.

[7] See Mayras AG in Case 2/74, *Reyners*, n. 5 above, and the ECJ in Case C–107/94, *Asscher* v. *Staatsecretaris van Financiën* [1996] ECR I–3089. See also Case C–268/99, *Jany* [2001] ECR I–8615, paras. 68–70, in the context of the EU–Poland Association Agreement.

[8] See most recently Case C–49/98, *Finalarte Sociedade Construçao Civil* v. *Urlaubs- und Lohnausgleichskasse der Bauwirtschaft* [2001] ECR I–7831, paras. 22–23.

[9] See Cases 205/84, *Commission* v. *Germany* [1986] ECR 3755, para. 22, and 33/74, *Van Binsbergen*, n. 6 above, para. 13. See also the Opinion of Jacobs AG in Case C–76/90, *Säger* v. *Dennemeyer & Co. Ltd* [1991] ECR I–4221.

which go to distinguish the temporary provision of services from the exercise of the right of establishment in a Member State were addressed by the ECJ in *Gebhard*:[10]

20. The situation of a Community national who moves to another Member State of the Community in order there to pursue an economic activity is governed by the chapter of the Treaty on the free movement of workers, or the chapter on the right to establishment or the chapter on services, these being mutually exclusive.

. . .

25. The concept of establishment within the meaning of the Treaty is therefore a very broad one, allowing a Community national to participate, on a stable and continuous basis, in the economic life of Member State other than his state of origin and to profit therefrom, so contributing to economic and social interpenetration within the Community in the sphere of activities as self-employed persons (see *Reyners* para. 21).

26. In contrast, where the provider of services moves to another Member State, the provision of the chapter on services, in particular the third paragraph of Article 60, envisage that he is to pursue his activity there on a temporary basis.

27. As the Advocate General has pointed out, the temporary nature of the activities in question has to be determined in the light, not only of the duration of the provision of the service, but also of its regularity, periodicity or continuity. The fact that the provision of services is temporary does not mean that the provider of services within the meaning of the Treaty may not equip himself with some form of infrastructure in the host Member State (including an office, chambers or consulting rooms) in so far as such infrastructure is necessary for the purposes of performing the services in question.

The crucial features of establishment are the 'stable and continuous basis' on which the economic or professional activity is carried on, and the fact that there is an established professional base within the host Member State. For the provision of services, the temporary nature of the activity is to be determined by reference to its 'periodicity, continuity and regularity',[11] and providers of services will not necessarily be deemed to be 'established' simply by virtue of the fact that they equip themselves with some form of infrastructure in the host Member State.[12] In its 2002 proposal for a directive to consolidate existing legislation on recognition of professional qualifications, the Commission suggested a further concretization of the case law to distinguish service provision from establishment, and proposed adopting a notional sixteen-week period to that effect.[13]

In the past, it was suggested that Article 49 (ex Article 59) was more obviously concerned with promoting the mobility of the services themselves and with setting up a single market,[14] by analogy with the Treaty provisions on free movement of

---

[10] Case C–55/94, *Gebhard* v. *Consiglio dell'Ordine degli Avvocati e Procuratori di Milano* [1995] ECR I–4165.

[11] Where a person or company establishes in a Member State to provide services to recipients there for an *indefinite* period, this does not fall within the Treaty provisions on freedom to provide services: Case C–70/95, *Sodemare* v. *Regione Lombardia* [1997] ECR I–3395.

[12] Further, providers of services cannot be made subject to a particular type of mandatory 'employment' relationship, since that would deprive them of their self-employed status: see Case C–398/95, *SETTG* v. *Ypourgos Ergasias* [1997] ECR I–3091.

[13] COM(2002)119, Art. 5 of the draft dir.

[14] See Warner AG in Case 52/79, *Procureur du Roi* v. *Debauve* [1980] ECR 833, 872.

goods,[15] rather than merely with the principle of non-discrimination on grounds of nationality which seemed to be the key underlying Articles 43 (ex Article 52) and 39 (ex Article 48) on workers and establishment. In more recent years, however, a robust approach to the right of establishment has also been adopted, with less emphasis on discrimination and more on liberalization.[16]

This theme of eliminating discrimination versus ensuring mobility, of equal treatment versus the creation of a single market, can be seen throughout the discussion in this chapter on freedom of establishment and freedom to provide services. It remains a highly salient theme, since it is clear that the extension of the Treaty rules to cover genuinely non-discriminatory restrictions reaches far into sensitive areas of national policy (and even into areas of private law), and sometimes in circumstances which appear to have little to do with abolishing barriers to the performance of economic activities by non-national companies and individuals. This can be seen in the case law on issues such as abortion, lotteries, health care, and the regulation of broadcasting.

(b) SECONDARY LEGISLATION GOVERNING ENTRY AND RESIDENCE

Directive 73/148,[17] adopted under the terms of Articles 44 and 52 (ex Articles 54 and 63) EC, is parallel to Directive 68/360 in the context of workers, in that it governs the terms and conditions of entry of other Member State nationals and their families into a host Member State. Article 1 covers those wishing to establish themselves or to provide or receive services and their families, listing the same family members as those in Regulation 1612/68 on workers. Directive 73/148 requires Member States to guarantee the right to enter and to leave a Member State for those purposes, without any visa requirements other than for non-EC nationals.[18] A right of permanent residence evidenced by a permit is granted to those who establish themselves in a self-employed activity, and a right of temporary residence for those providing or receiving services which is of equal duration with the length of the services.[19] The right of temporary residence is to be formalized by the issue of a 'right of abode' where the period during which services are provided or received exceeds three months.[20] All that is needed to apply for a residence permit or right of abode is an identity card or passport and proof of being one of the persons covered by the Directive.[21]

Directive 75/34 provides for the right of nationals of a Member State to remain in the territory of another Member State after having pursued an activity there in a self-employed capacity, and to be entitled to equality of treatment with nationals as under

---

[15] See Jacobs AG in Case C–76/90, *Säger*, n. 9 above, at 4234–5, and Gulmann AG in Case C–275/92, *HM Customs and Excise* v. *Schindler* [1994] ECR 1039, 1059. The close relationship between the free movement of goods and of services can be seen in an early case, Case 155/73, *Sacchi* [1974] ECR 409, where the ECJ ruled that the broadcasting of TV signals fell within the Treaty rules relating to services, whereas materials such as video or sound tapes were covered by the provisions on free movement of goods. For a recent in-depth analysis see J. Snell, *Goods and Services in EC Law* (Oxford University Press, 2002).

[16] See, e.g., Cases C–212/97, *Centros Ltd* v. *Erhvervs- og Selskabsstyrelsen* [1999] ECR I–1459 and C–55/94, *Gebhard* v. *Consiglio dell'Ordine degli Avvocati e Procuratori di Milano* [1995] ECR I–4165.

[17] Dir. 73/148 [1973] OJ L172/14.

[18] *Ibid.*, Arts. 2–3. See the AG's Opinion in C–60/00, *Carpenter* v. *Home Secretary*, 13 Sept. 2001.

[19] *Ibid.*, Art. 4(2).   [20] *Ibid.*   [21] *Ibid.*, Art. 6.

Directive 73/148.[22] The conditions which must be satisfied by the person in order to qualify for this right are very similar to those which apply to employed persons under Directive 1251/70, and like that Directive they apply also to the family members who are listed therein.[23]

In keeping with its programme of legislative consolidation, the Commission, as seen in the previous chapter, recently proposed an 'umbrella' directive on the free movement and residence of EU citizens, which would repeal and replace the provisions of Directives 73/148 and 75/34, along with several other key legislative measures in the area of free movement of persons.[24] The proposed Directive would incorporate some of the jurisprudential *acquis*, and would make certain amendments which include extending the range of family members who are covered, extending to six months the period during which an EU citizen may reside within the territory of another Member State without going through any formalities, and providing a permanent right of residence after four years of continual legal residence. At the time of writing, the proposal is making its way slowly through the legislative process, along with a number of related legislative proposals

(c) THE 'OFFICIAL AUTHORITY' EXCEPTION

Article 45 (ex Article 55) of the Treaty, which is extended by Article 55 (ex Article 66) to cover the chapter on services, states that the provisions of the chapter on freedom of establishment shall not apply 'so far as any given Member State is concerned, to activities which in that State are connected, even occasionally, with the exercise of official authority'. This provision has a similar role to that of the public-service derogation in Article 39(4) (ex Article 48(4)), but this time in the context of the self-employed. Advocate General Mayras defined it as follows:

Official authority is that which arises from the sovereignty and majesty of the State; for him who exercises it, it implies the power of enjoying the prerogatives outside the general law, privileges of official power and powers of coercion over citizens.[25]

The wording of Article 45 (ex Article 55) refers to those 'activities' which are connected with the use of official power, rather than to professions or vocations within which official authority might, under certain circumstances, be exercised. Questions over the interpretation of the provision first arose in the *Reyners* case, in which the Conseil d'Etat asked the ECJ whether, within the legal profession of *avocat*, only those activities which were connected with the exercise of official authority were excepted from the Treaty rules, or whether the whole of the profession was excepted by reason of the fact that it comprised activities connected with the exercise of such authority. According to the Luxembourg Government, the whole profession should be excepted because it was 'connected organically' with the public service of the administration of justice, in that it involved a set of strict conditions for admission and discipline, and participation by the *avocat* in the course of judicial procedures was largely obligatory.

---

[22] [1975] OJ L14/10. Dir. 75/35 [1975] OJ L14/14 made the provisions of Dir. 64/221 applicable also to these persons. See, further, Ch. 19 on Dir. 64/221.
[23] See Ch. 17.   [24] COM(2001)257 [2001] OJ C270/150.   [25] Case 2/74, n. 5 above, at 664.

Case 2/74, Reyners v. Belgium
[1974] ECR 63

[ToA renumbering: Arts. 52 and 55 are now Arts. 43 and 45 respectively]

THE ECJ

43. Having regard to the fundamental character of freedom of establishment and the rule on equal treatment with nationals in the system of the Treaty, the exceptions allowed by the first paragraph of Article 55 cannot be given a scope which would exceed the objective for which this exemption clause was inserted.

44. The first paragraph of Article 55 must enable Member States to exclude non-nationals from taking up functions involving the exercise of official authority which are connected with one of the activities of self-employed persons provided for in Article 52.

45. This need is fully satisfied when the exclusion of nationals is limited to those activities which, taken on their own, constitute a direct and specific connection with the exercise of official authority.

46. An extension of the exception allowed by Article 55 to a whole profession would be possible only in cases where such activities were linked with that profession in such a way that freedom of establishment would result in imposing on the Member State concerned the obligation to allow the exercise, even occasionally, by non-nationals of functions appertaining to official authority.

47. This extension is on the other hand not possible when, within the framework of an independent profession, the activities connected with the exercise of official authority are separable from the professional activity in question taken as a whole.

. . .

51. Professional activities involving contacts, even regular and organic, with the courts, including even compulsory cooperation in their functioning, do not constitute, as such, connection with the exercise of official authority.

52. The most typical activities of the profession of *avocat*, in particular, such as consultation and legal assistance and also representation and the defence of parties in court, even when the intervention or assistance of the *avocat* is compulsory or is a legal monopoly, cannot be considered as connected with the exercise of official authority.

53. The exercise of these activities leaves the discretion of judicial authority and the free exercise of judicial power intact.

The ECJ's reasoning is similar to that used in the context of the public-service derogation in the chapter on workers, in the sense that the exception must have a single Community definition and cannot be given a scope which would exceed its purpose. If specific activities which involve exercising official authority are severable from the rest of a profession, then Article 45 (ex Article 55) cannot apply to the profession as a whole.

In infringement proceedings brought by the Commission against Greece, the Greek

Government argued that the activity of traffic-accident expert was covered by Article 45 (ex Article 55).[26] The ECJ rejected the argument, pointing out that the reports of such experts did not bind the courts, and, repeating its ruling in *Reyners*, that they left intact the exercise of judicial power and discretion. Similarly in *Thijssen*, the Court ruled that the post of commissioner of insurance companies and undertakings was not covered by the exception in Article 45.[27] Although the post involved monitoring companies and reporting on possible infringements of the penal code, the power to prevent insurance companies from implementing certain decisions was not a definitive or final power. Similar rulings have been given by the ECJ in relation to transport consultants[28] and to private security activities.[29]

(d) ARE THE FREEDOMS HORIZONTALLY APPLICABLE?

We have seen in Chapter 17 that the ECJ has ruled that, unlike the Treaty provisions on free movement of goods, the provisions of Article 39 (ex Article 48) are binding not only on the State but also on private bodies.[30] Early on in the field of freedom of establishment and freedom to provide services, the ECJ had ruled in the case of *Walrave and Koch* that the Treaty prohibition on discrimination on grounds of nationality applied not only 'to the action of public authorities but extends likewise to rules of any other nature aimed at regulating in a collective manner gainful employment and the provision of services'.[31] It remains unclear however, even after the case of *Angonese* in the field of free movement of workers,[32] whether the Treaty freedoms are fully horizontally applicable, in the sense of imposing legal obligations on all individuals and not only on powerful collective actors such as sporting organizations which are effectively self-regulating and possess powers akin to public law. In the recent *Wouters* case concerning partnerships between barristers and accountants, the ECJ applied the *Walrave* ruling to a regulatory measure adopted by the Netherlands Bar Council, although without giving further guidance on whether the Treaty rules could apply to purely individual private conduct:

120. It should be observed at the outset that compliance with [Articles 43 and 49 (ex 52 and 59)] of the Treaty is also required in the case of rules which are not public in nature but which are designed to regulate, collectively, self-employment and the provision of services. The abolition, as between Member States, of obstacles to freedom of movement for persons would be compromised if the abolition of State barriers could be neutralised by obstacles resulting from the exercise of their legal autonomy by associations or organisations not governed by public law.[33]

---

[26] Case C–306/89, *Commission* v. *Greece* [1991] ECR I–5863. See also Case C–272/91, *Commission* v. *Italy* [1994] ECR I–1409 on operating a computerization system for a national lottery.

[27] Case C–42/92, *Thijssen* v. *Controledienst voor de Verzekeringen* [1993] ECR I–4047.

[28] Case C–263/99, *Commission* v. *Italy* [2001] ECR I–4195.

[29] Cases C–114/97, *Commission* v. *Spain* [1998] ECR I–6717; C–355/98, *Commission* v. *Belgium* [2000] ECR I–1221; and C–283/99, *Commission* v. *Italy* [2001] ECR I–4363.

[30] Cases C–415/93, *Bosman* [1995] ECR I–4921, paras. 83 and 84; and C–281/98, *Angonese* [2000] ECR I–4139, para. 32.

[31] Case 36/74, *Walrave and Koch* [1974] ECR 1405.

[32] Case C–281/98, n. 30 above.

[33] Case C–309/99, *Wouters* v. *Algemene Raad van de Nederlandse Orde van Advocaten* [2002] ECR I–nyr. See also C–411/98, *Ferlini* v. *CHL* [2000] ECR I–8081, para. 50.

3. THE RIGHT OF ESTABLISHMENT

Article 43 (ex Article 52) EC provides:

Within the framework of the provisions set out below, restrictions on the freedom of establishment of nationals of a Member State in the territory of another Member State shall be prohibited. Such prohibition shall also apply to restrictions on the setting up of agencies, branches, or subsidiaries by nationals of any Member State established in the territory of any Member State.

Freedom of establishment shall include the right to take up and pursue activities as self-employed persons and to set up and manage undertakings, in particular companies or firms within the meaning of the second paragraph of Article 48 (ex Article 58), under the conditions laid down for its own nationals by the law of the country where such establishment is effected, subject to the provisions of the chapter relating to capital.

The first paragraph of the Article is negatively worded, requiring the abolition of restrictions on freedom of primary and secondary establishment, and the second is positively worded, indicating that freedom of establishment entails the right for self-employed persons to pursue their activities on an equal footing with the nationals of the Member State in which they are established. The reference to capital acknowledges that there is a separate chapter on the free movement of capital, which has been subject to a different and more gradual regime of liberalization.[34]

The wording of Article 43 (ex Article 52) suggests two possible limits on its scope. In paragraph one, reference is made to the position of nationals in a Member State *other than that of their nationality*, which implies that Article 43 cannot be invoked by nationals against their own Member State. As far as agencies, branches, and subsidiaries are concerned, by contrast, the same paragraph refers to the setting up of these 'by nationals of any Member State established in the territory of any Member State'. The second possible limit appears in paragraph two, which refers to the right of establishment in a host Member State 'under the conditions laid down for its own nationals'. In other words, the Article seems to prohibit discrimination, and to imply that its requirements are satisfied if the person exercising the right of establishment is treated in the same way as a national. However, we shall see below that although this may initially have been the interpretation given to the Article, its scope since then has been given a wider reading than this part of the text might suggest.

Article 44 (ex Article 54) originally required the Council to draw up a general programme for the abolition of restrictions on establishment, which it did in 1961, and to issue directives to attain freedom for particular activities. Article 47 (ex Article 57) requires the Council to issue directives—by qualified majority other than where the existing principles governing professional training and access are being amended[35]—for the mutual recognition of diplomas and other qualifications, and

---

[34] See Ch. 16.

[35] For discussion of the different voting procedures, see the challenge brought to Directive 98/5 on establishment for lawyers [1998] OJ L77/36, in Case C–168/98, *Luxembourg* v. *Parliament and Council* [2000] ECR I–9131. For commentary, see P. Cabral (2002) 39 *CMLRev.* 129.

Article 48 (ex Article 58) places companies in the same position as natural persons for the purpose of the application of this chapter of the Treaty.

The 1961 General Programme made clear that discriminatory restrictions were the target of the Treaty provisions on establishment.[36] It required the elimination of restrictive laws and administrative practices which treat nationals of other Member States differently from nationals of the State concerned, and listed examples such as the attachment of licence conditions, periods of residence, tax burdens, etc., which make more difficult the exercise of activities by the self-employed or by companies. The Programme also required the elimination of restrictions on powers attaching to the exercise of such activities, such as the power to enter contracts, to acquire property, to have access to credit, and to receive state aids. Directly and indirectly discriminatory restrictions alike were mentioned, and a transitional system (which ultimately turned out to be a lengthy period of transition!) was permitted pending the subsequent mutual recognition of diplomas and qualifications by legislative means.

(a) THE EFFECT OF ARTICLE 43 (EX ARTICLE 52)

In *Reyners*, one of the earliest cases concerning freedom of establishment, the ECJ ruled that Article 43 (ex Article 52) of the Treaty was directly effective, despite the fact that the stringent conditions for direct effect which had been set out in *Van Gend en Loos* did not appear to have been met,[37] and despite the Council's failure to adopt all of the necessary implementing legislation envisaged under the Treaty provisions. Such legislation had not yet, by 1974, been adopted partly on account of the slow progress of legislative procedures in the Council in the aftermath of the Luxembourg Accords, and partly on account of the strong opposition within Member States to the process of opening the professions, and in particular the legal profession, to non-nationals.[38]

It will be remembered that Reyners was a Dutch national who had obtained his legal education in Belgium, and who was refused admission to the Belgian Bar solely on the ground that he lacked Belgian nationality. The ECJ ruled that, despite the Treaty requirement that directives should be adopted, Article 43 (ex Article 52) laid down a precise result which was to be achieved by the end of the transitional period, namely the requirement of non-discrimination on grounds of nationality. This was a result 'the fulfilment of which had to be made easier by, but not made dependent on, the implementation of a programme of progressive measures'.[39] Since no directive was required in Reyners' situation to remove the clearly discriminatory restriction which obstructed him, he could invoke Article 43 directly. The ECJ acknowledged, however, that the directives had 'not lost all interest since they preserve an important scope in the field of measures intended to make easier the effective exercise of the right of freedom of establishment'.[40]

The situation in which the direct effect of Article 43 (ex Article 52) would not be so effective in challenging a restriction on establishment, however, and where more

[36] OJ Spec. Ed., Second Ser., IX.
[37] Case 2/74, n. 5 above, and see Ch. 5.
[38] See the comments of Mayras AG in *Reyners* at [1974] ECR 631, 658.
[39] *Ibid.*, para. 26.   [40] *Ibid.*, para. 31.

detailed Community legislation was considered necessary, was that concerning educational, vocational, and other qualifications which differed considerably from state to state. If a doctor, qualified to practise medicine in Italy, sought to set up practice in the UK, would the refusal to recognize her qualification constitute an impermissible restriction on her freedom of establishment? Could she rely directly on Article 43 to require the UK authorities to permit her to practise even though the systems of medical training in the two countries were very different? In such circumstances, Community legislative intervention to attempt some kind of co-ordination of the varying requirements of different States for the same professional qualification seemed highly desirable, and even necessary.

However, even before such legislation was passed under Article 47 (ex Article 57), several cases came before the ECJ in which it was argued that, even in the absence of directives, and even where the restriction was not clearly based on nationality but on the adequacy of qualification, Article 43 (ex Article 52) could be relied on by an EC national seeking to practise a profession in another Member State. In *Thieffry*, a Belgian national, who obtained a doctorate in law in Belgium and practised as an advocate for some years in Brussels, subsequently obtained French university recognition of his qualifications as equivalent to a degree in French law, and obtained a certificate of aptitude for the profession of *avocat*.[41] However, he was refused admission to the training stage as an advocate at the Paris Bar on the ground that he lacked a degree in French law. According to the ECJ, the responsible professional bodies had a duty to ensure that their practices were in accordance with Treaty objectives:

Consequently, if the freedom of establishment provided for by Article 52 can be ensured in a Member State either under the provisions of the laws and regulations in force, or by virtue of the practices of the public service or of professional bodies, a person subject to Community law cannot be denied the practical benefit of that freedom solely by virtue of the fact that, for a particular profession, the directives provided for by Article 57 of the Treaty have not yet been adopted.[42]

Thus if Thieffry had already obtained what was recognized (both professionally and academically) to be an equivalent qualification, and had satisfied the necessary practical training requirements, the state authorities would not be justified in refusing him admission to the Bar solely on the ground that he did not possess a French qualification, despite the absence of EC directives in the field.[43]

The Court developed this argument further in subsequent decisions, ruling that Article 43 (ex Article 52) precluded the competent national authorities from simply refusing, without further explanation, to allow nationals of another Member State to practise their trade or profession on the ground that their qualification was not equivalent to the corresponding national qualification. On the contrary, the Treaty provisions imposed specific, positive obligations on national authorities and professional bodies to take steps to secure the free movement of workers and freedom of establishment, even in the absence of Community or national legislation providing

---

[41] Case 71/76, *Thieffry* v. *Conseil de l'Ordre des Avocats à la Cour de Paris* [1977] ECR 765.
[42] Ibid., para. 17.
[43] See also Case 11/77, *Patrick* v. *Ministre des Affairs Culturelles* [1977] ECR 1199.

for equivalence or for the recognition of qualifications. In *Heylens* the ECJ ruled, in the case of a Belgian football trainer working in France whose application for recognition of the equivalence of his Belgian diploma was refused by the French Ministry of Sport, that Member States were entitled, in the absence of harmonizing directives, to regulate the knowledge and qualifications necessary to pursue a particular occupation. However:

[T]he procedure for the recognition of equivalence must enable the national authorities to assure themselves, on an objective basis, that the foreign diploma certifies that its holder has knowledge and qualifications which are, if not identical, at least equivalent to those certified by the national diploma. That assessment of the equivalence of the foreign diploma must be effected exclusively in the light of the level of knowledge and qualifications which its holder can be assumed to possess in the light of that diploma, having regard to the nature and duration of the studies and practical training which the diploma certifies that he has carried out.[44]

Where employment was dependent on possession of a diploma, the ECJ ruled that it must be possible for a national of a Member State to obtain judicial review of a decision of the authorities of another Member State, and to ascertain the reasons for refusing to recognize the equivalence of a diploma.[45] This line of reasoning was continued in *Vlassopoulou*, which involved a Greek national who had obtained a Greek law degree and had practised German law for several years in Germany, but whose application for admission to the Bar and authorization to practice was rejected on the ground that she had not passed the relevant German examinations and so lacked the necessary qualifications:

Case 340/89, Vlassopoulou v. Ministerium für Justiz, Bundes und
Europaangelegenheiten Baden-Württemberg
[1991] ECR 2357

[ToA renumbering: Art. 52 is now Art. 43]

THE ECJ

15. It must be Stated in this regard that, even if applied without any discrimination on the basis of nationality, national requirements concerning qualifications may have the effect of hindering nationals of the other Member States in the exercise of their right of establishment guaranteed to them by Article 52 of the EEC Treaty. That could be the case if the national rules in question took no account of the knowledge and qualifications already acquired by the person concerned in another Member State.

16. Consequently, a Member State which receives a request to admit a person to a profession to which access, under national law, depends upon the possession of a diploma or a professional qualification must take into consideration the diplomas, certificates and other evidence of qualifications which the person concerned has acquired in order to exercise the same profession

---

[44] Case 222/86, *UNECTEF v. Heylens* [1987] ECR 4097, para. 13.
[45] See Ch. 6, n.16 and text, for discussion of this case in the context of remedies.

higher-education diplomas awarded on completion of professional education and training of at least three years' duration'.[54] The aim and content of this Directive were officially summarized shortly before the final adoption of the legislation:

The Directive differs from previous 'sectoral' directives in several respects. First, it is general in nature, in that the new system is intended to apply to all regulated professions for which university-level training of at least three years is required and which are not covered by a specific directive.

Second, recognition is to be based on the principle of mutual trust, without prior coordination of the preparatory educational and training courses for the various professions in question. As a basic principle, a host Member State may not refuse entry to a regulated profession to a national of a Member State who holds the qualifications necessary for exercise of that profession in another Member State.

Third, recognition is granted to the 'end product' i.e. to fully qualified professionals who have already received any professional training required in addition to their university diplomas. . . .

Fourth, where there are major differences in education and training, or in the structure of a profession, the draft Directive provides for compensation mechanisms, i. e. either an adaptation period or an aptitude test.[55]

By this single legislative measure a general system of recognition was established, avoiding the time-consuming and contentious process of securing agreement on a minimum harmonized standard for every specific trade or profession. However, there were obvious disadvantages to this approach, in that, unlike the earlier harmonization approach, it did not provide an automatic guarantee to those holding specified qualifications that they would be accepted by any Member State. Compliance with the criteria set out in Directive 89/48 guaranteed only a starting point for the person wishing to practise a trade or profession, and the qualification held by that person was to be subject to scrutiny and control by the authorities of the host Member State. The states remained free, where either the content of the education or training received is inadequate or the structure of the profession it represents is different, to impose the additional requirements of an aptitude test or an adaptation period.

The basic thrust of the Directive was that, if a Community national wished to pursue a regulated profession in any Member State, the competent authorities in the Member State could not refuse permission on the ground of inadequate qualifications if the person satisfied certain conditions.[56] Briefly, the conditions were that the person had pursued the equivalent of a three-year higher-education course in the Community, and had completed the necessary professional training in order to be qualified

---

[54] [1989] OJ L19/16. For cases involving non-implementation by Member States of Dir. 89/48, see, e.g., Cases C–216/94, *Commission* v. *Belgium* [1995] ECR I–2155; C–365/93, *Commission* v. *Greece* [1995] ECR I–499; and C–285/00, *Commission* v. *France* [2001] ECR I–3801.

[55] Bull. EC 6–1988, 11.

[56] A 'Community element' to the situation was, however, required: See Cases C–225–227/95, *Kapasakalis* v. *Greece* [1998] ECR I–4329 for a 'purely internal situation' in which the applicant could not rely on Dir. 89/48.

to take up the 'regulated profession' in question.[57] Satisfaction of these conditions did not mean that the person had to be given permission to pursue that profession, but it meant that the competent national authorities could not refuse permission solely on the ground of inadequate qualifications. If the qualifications were considered adequate, then permission to practise should be given. If the duration of the person's training and education was however at least one year less than that required in the host state, the Directive permitted Member States to require certain evidence of professional experience. If, on the other hand, the matters covered by the person's education and training differed substantially from those covered by the host-state qualification, or if the host-state profession comprised specific regulated activities which were not within the profession regulated in the Member State where the qualification was obtained, the Member State was permitted to require the completion of an adaptation period or that an aptitude test be taken.

Following Directive 89/48, the Council adopted Directive 92/51, which supplemented and followed the same approach as the system for recognition established by the former. The 1992 Directive covered education and training other than the three-year higher-education requirement of Directive 89/48. It covered *diplomas* awarded after a post-secondary course (other than higher-education courses covered by Directive 89/48) of at least one year in length, and which qualify the holder to take up a regulated profession. It also covered *certificates* awarded after educational or training courses other than these post-secondary courses of one year's duration, or after a probationary or professional practice period, or after vocational training, which qualify the holder to take up a regulated profession. A third general directive, Directive 99/42, was adopted in 1999 to replace the series of earlier liberalizing and transitional directives in a range of industrial and professional sectors, and using a similar mutual recognition approach, although one based on the recognition of periods of consecutive experience and possession of skills, and not just on the possession of formal qualifications or diplomas.[58]

Directives 89/48 and 92/51 were amended in 2001 along with most of the sectoral directives by a general Directive 2001/19/EC (the so-called SLIM Directive), which introduced a number of changes.[59] These include extending to the general system the concept of 'regulated education and training' which had been introduced by Directive 92/51; requiring host Member States to examine whether the professional experience gained by an applicant since obtaining her qualification(s) covers any gaps and differences between education or training in the state of qualification and the host state; simplifying the co-ordination procedure under the general directives; incorporating some of the ECJ case law on the relevance of recognition by a Member State of a third-country qualification and experience within another Member State; stipulating rights of appeal as well as the period within which Member State authorities must

---

[57] For an 'unregulated' profession, see Case C–164/94, *Arantis* v. *Land Berlin* [1996] ECR I–135 on geologists. For the Community definition of a 'regulated profession' in Dir. 89/48 [1989] OJ L19/16 and 92/51 [1992] OJ L208/25, which includes being governed by the terms of a collective agreement: see Case C–234/97, *Teresa Fernández de Bobadilla* v. *Museo Nacional del Prado* [1999] ECR I–4773, paras. 14–21.

[58] See [1999] OJ L201/77.

[59] [2001] OJ L206/1.

decide on applications for recognition, and making specific changes to some of the sectoral directives.

Although there are clearly many advantages to the system which is established by these measures, the move towards recognition which allows Member States to control and to supervise the process of recognition at each step, rather than the provision for automatic recognition in the earlier sectoral Directives, also has drawbacks, and is heavily reliant on mutual trust and on the adoption of a non-protectionist attitude by national competent authorities.[60] Despite such shortcomings, however, the strength of the mutual recognition approach is that almost anyone who has obtained some kind of professional qualification may rely on the Directives to prevent a Member State from simply refusing to permit that person to practise a regulated profession on grounds of inadequate qualifications. Nevertheless, the rulings in *Heylens* and *Vlassopoulou* on the direct effect of Article 43 (ex Article 52) in the context of mutual recognition have not lost their relevance, since there will still be cases in which the education or training received does not fall within the scope of either the three general directives or the earlier sectoral directives. Examples include persons who, as in the case of *Arantis*,[61] seek to pursue a profession which is unregulated in the host Member State. Other examples can be seen in the case of *Hocsman*, in which an EU national had obtained a basic diploma in a third country before continuing specialist studies and gaining practical experience within the EU,[62] and in *Dreessen*, in which the qualification held by the applicant was (apparently inadvertently) not included within the relevant sectoral directive and therefore could not benefit from legislative recognition.[63] In such cases, the basic principle underlying *Vlassopoulou* and *Heylens*, stemming directly from the Court's interpretation of Article 43 (ex Article 52), and imposing the requirement to examine the knowledge and qualifications already acquired or recognized in another Member State, to give proper reasons for the non-recognition of any qualification held, as well as access to a judicial remedy, are certainly of value to those who cannot rely on the directives.[64]

As with most of the Treaty provisions on free movement of persons, the directives in the field of recognition of qualifications do not themselves cover non-Community nationals.[65] Nor do they apply to qualifications obtained outside the Community, although, at the same time as the adoption of Directive 89/48, the Council passed a recommendation encouraging the Member States to recognize diplomas and other evidence of formal qualifications obtained in non-member countries by Community nationals.[66] And under the mutual recognition directives and the SLIM Directive, a diploma awarded within the Community (and which is therefore subject to the

---

[60] For an analysis see J. Pertek, 'Free Movement of Professionals and Recognition of Higher Education Diplomas' (1992) 12 *YBEL* 320–1.

[61] Case C–164/94, *Arantis* v. *Land Berlin* [1996] ECR I–135. See also Case C–234/97, *Teresa Fernández de Bobadilla* v. *Museo Nacional del Prado* [1999] ECR I–4773.

[62] Case C–238/98, *Hocsman* v. *Ministre de l'Emploi* [2000] ECR I–6623.

[63] Case C–31/00, *Conseil National de l'Ordre des Architectes* v. *Dreessen* [2002] ECR I–nyr.

[64] For those whose qualifications are covered by the Dirs., these requirements of reasoning and access to a judicial remedy are set out in the general directives and in the SLIM Dir.

[65] For their application to nationals of the EEA States, however, see Annex VII to the EEA Agreement.

[66] Council Recommendation 89/49 [1989] OJ L19/24.

mutual recognition rules of the directives) may in certain circumstances take into account education or training received outside the Community.

In *Tawil-Albertini*, a French national obtained in Lebanon a dental qualification, which was subsequently recognized by the Belgian authorities as equivalent to the corresponding Belgian qualification, and which authorized him to practise in Belgium.[67] He was also authorized to practise in two other Member States, but his application to the French authorities for permission to practise in France was refused. The qualifications listed in Council Directive 78/686 on mutual recognition of dental qualifications did not include any qualification obtained outside the Member States, but since his qualification had been recognized as equivalent to the Belgian diploma, he argued that it was also covered by the Directive. The ECJ ruled that the mutual recognition of qualifications in dentistry awarded by the Member States was based on the guarantees of specific minimum criteria set out in the co-ordination Directive. In the case of non-Member States, co-ordination of training could only be brought about by agreements between the states in question, so that although any Member State could recognize the equivalence of a non-member country's qualifications, this would not bring those qualifications within the scope of the Community directive on dentistry and could not bind other Member States which did not recognize those qualifications. In *Haim*, although the applicant did not hold one of the qualifications listed in the same Directive on dental qualifications, he was authorized to practise as a dentist in Germany.[68] When he applied to work on a social-security scheme in Germany, however, he was informed that he would have to complete a further two-year preparatory training period. He argued that his experience working for eight years as a dentist of a social-security scheme in Belgium should be taken into account, and the ECJ, citing *Vlassopoulou*, ruled in his favour:

The competent national authority, in order to verify whether the training period requirement prescribed by the national rules is met, must take into account the professional experience of the plaintiff in the main proceedings, including that which he has acquired during his appointment as a dental practitioner of a social security scheme in another Member State.[69]

Thus, although non-member-country qualifications are excluded from the general coverage of the directives, if a Member State chooses to recognize such a qualification, it must also take into account, in determining whether a national training period condition has been fulfilled, any practical training or professional experience obtained in another Member State.

The ruling of the ECJ in the *Hocsman* case was in even stronger terms, and appears to require national competent authorities to consider *all* diplomas or evidence of formal qualifications, and all relevant experience of an EU national seeking to exercise the right of establishment, whether or not they were obtained within the EU.[70] In this

---

[67] Case C–154/93, *Tawil-Albertini v. Ministre des Affairs Sociales* [1994] ECR I–451.

[68] Case C–319/92, *Haim v. Kassenzahnärtzliche Vereinigung Nordrhein* [1994] ECR I–425.

[69] *Ibid.*, para. 28. See, for a further unsuccessful challenge brought by Mr Haim to a language restriction imposed on his appointment as a social security scheme dental practitioner in Germany, Case C–424/97, *Haim v. Kassenzahnärtze Vereinigung Nordrhein* [2000] ECR I–5123.

[70] Case C–238/98, *Hocsman v. Ministre de l'Emploi* [2000] ECR I–6623. For comment see J. Prinssen (2001) 38 *CMLRev.* 1587.

case, while the applicant's basic medical diploma was obtained outside the EU and therefore his final qualification in urology was not covered by the relevant sectoral directive, he had obtained his specialist qualification within the EU and had subsequently practised lawfully for several years in the host Member State as a specialist before seeking to be registered with the professional medical association. In this case the ECJ affirmed again that the principles set out in *Vlassopoulou* and *Heylens* clearly applied so that the relevant competent authority would have to assess his application accordingly.[71]

Haim, Tawil-Albertini, and Hocsman were all Community nationals who had obtained non-member-country qualifications. However, apart from EEA nationals, nationals of non-member countries who are established in the Community have no general rights of mutual recognition or permission to practise in a self-employed capacity under Community law, even when they have undergone precisely the same education and training as Community nationals within a Member State, and they remain without any independent Community rights to recognition or establishment.

Following the trend towards legislative consolidation, the Commission in 2002 proposed a general draft directive on recognition of professional qualifications which would comprehensively revise and replace all of the earlier directives including the three mutual recognition directives and the array of sectoral measures (apart from those concerning lawyers' services and establishment).[72] Apart from its introductory and final provisions the proposed directive contains a title on freedom to provide services, a title on establishment (containing four chapters on a 'general system for the recognition of qualifications', 'recognition of professional experience', 'recognition on the basis of coordination of minimum training conditions', and 'common provisions' respectively), a title on arrangements for practising the profession, and a Title V on administrative co-operation and powers of implementation. The main aims of the proposed directive, apart from consolidating and streamlining the existing plethora of legislatives measures, are, in the Commission's words, to bring about greater liberalization in the field of freedom to provide services rather than the field of establishment, to seek to develop partnership between the public and private sectors through the professional bodies, and to provide a more central role for the competent national authorities. In fact it seems that the Commission wishes to strengthen its *own* role and to develop a more direct relationship with national professional bodies and educational establishments rather than having this mediated primarily through advisory committees of Member State representatives. The proposal is, at the time of writing, at a very early stage of the legislative process, and so it remains to be seen whether it will be adopted in the form desired by the Commission.

---

[71] Dir. 2001/19 [2001] OJ L206/1 applies the principles established in *Haim* and *Tawil-Albertini* to the sectoral directives. For a comment on this and comparison with the *Hocsman* case, see J. Prinssen (2001) 38 *CMLRev.* 1587, 1594–5.

[72] COM(2002)119.

(c) THE SCOPE OF ARTICLE 43 (EX ARTICLE 52)

(I) DOES IT COVER ONLY DISCRIMINATORY RESTRICTIONS?

It has been noted above that the wording of Article 43 (ex Article 52) might suggest that equal treatment of nationals and non-nationals is the primary requirement. Since Article 43 guarantees the right for nationals of a Member State to establish themselves in another Member State 'under the conditions laid down for its own nationals', it seems that EC nationals would have no ground for complaint under the Article if the same provisions were applied to them as to nationals of the host state. This interpretation was given support by some of the ECJ's Statements in its rulings on the Treaty Article. In *Commission* v. *Belgium*,[73] restrictions were placed on the provision of clinical biology services by laboratories. Although their effect appeared to be to require those engaged in clinical laboratory testing to maintain a primary establishment in Belgium, they did not actually refer to the nationality of the person or to the seat of the company providing the services. However, in response to the argument that the restrictions were in breach of Article 43 (ex Article 52) by hindering the right to *secondary* establishment, the Court ruled:

It is clear from [Article 52] and its context that, provided that such equality of treatment is respected, each Member State is, in the absence of Community rules in this area, free to lay down rules for its own territory governing the activities of laboratories providing clinical biology services.[74]

Other rulings lent support to this reading, including *Fearon*, in which Irish legislation provided that, in order for a company to benefit from an exemption from the compulsory purchase of its land, its members, and shareholders would have to reside on the land.[75] This residence requirement was imposed in pursuance of a national policy on rural agricultural holdings, and the ECJ ruled that so long as it was applied equally to nationals and non-nationals 'a residence requirement so delimited does not in fact amount to discrimination which might be found to offend against [Article 43 (ex 52)] of the Treaty'.[76]

However, in keeping with the pattern of its case law on the free movement of goods, services, and workers, the ECJ moved gradually away from the emphasis on unequal treatment. In *Klopp*, a German lawyer had been refused admission to the Paris Bar on the sole ground that he already maintained an office as a lawyer in another Member State.[77] The statutes of the Paris Bar, which applied equally to nationals and non-nationals, provided that a lawyer could have only one office, which must be within the district of the court at which that lawyer was admitted. Despite this apparently equal treatment the Court ruled that, although it was for the states to regulate the exercise of professions in their own territory, they could not require a lawyer who wished to

---

[73] Case 221/85, *Commission* v. *Belgium* [1987] ECR 719.

[74] *Ibid.*, para. 9.

[75] Case 182/83, *Robert Fearon and Co.* v. *Irish Land Commission* [1984] ECR 3677. For more recent cases concerning nationality and residence restrictions on land use see Cases 305/87, *Commission* v. *Greece* [1989] ECR 1461 and C–302/97, *Konle* v. *Austria* [1999] ECR I–2651.

[76] Case 182/83, n. 75 above, para. 10.

[77] Case 107/83, *Ordre des Avocats* v. *Klopp* [1984] ECR 2971.

practise there to have only one establishment throughout the Community, since Article 43 (ex Article 52) specifically guarantees the freedom to set up more than one place of work in the Community. There were less restrictive ways, given modern transport and telecommunications, of ensuring that lawyers maintain sufficient contact with their clients and the judicial authorities, and obey the rules of the profession. While *Klopp* was not of itself authority for a general proposition that even non-discriminatory rules may breach Article 43, given that Article 43 expressly guarantees the right to secondary establishment which was being denied in that case,[78] it did demonstrate that freedom of establishment requires more than equal treatment in certain circumstances. In *Wolf*,[79] *Stanton*,[80] and *Kemmler*,[81] the ECJ ruled that indistinctly applicable national rules on social-security exemptions for the self-employed were impermissible, because they were an unjustified and excessive impediment to the pursuit of occupational activities in more than one Member State, even though the rules contained no direct or indirect discrimination on grounds of nationality.[82]

The Court extended its interpretation further in cases which did not concern the right of secondary establishment, but where apparently non-discriminatory registration requirements were held to be in violation of Article 43 (ex Article 52) unless objectively justified.[83] The *Gebhard* ruling gave the clearest indication of the Court's broad interpretation of Article 43, where it indicated that the same principles underpin all of the Treaty provisions on freedom of movement, and stated that the provisions on goods, services, workers, and establishment should be similarly construed.[84] Certainly the Court can be seen to have adopted an increasingly common approach to the free movement rules, given the *Bosman* ruling on workers,[85] and *Alpine* and subsequent rulings on services.[86] These rulings adopt a robust approach, deeming non-discriminatory restrictions on access to be caught by the free movement rules, just as the ECJ had done many years previously in the context of free movement of goods in *Dassonville*[87] and *Cassis*,[88] and as it largely continues to do despite the confusion in that field since the *Keck* ruling.[89]

---

[78] See also Cases 96/85, *Commission* v. *France* [1986] ECR 1475, and C–351/90, *Commission* v. *Luxembourg* [1992] ECR I–3945, condemning other similar single-practice rules for doctors, dentists, and vets. Also Cases C–106/91, *Ramrath* v. *Ministre de la Justice* [1992] ECR I–3351, and C–162/99, *Commission* v. *Italy* [2001] ECR I–541.

[79] Cases 154–155/87, *RSVZ* v. *Wolf* [1988] ECR 3897.

[80] Case 143/87, *Stanton* v. *INASTI* [1988] ECR 3877.

[81] Case C–53/95, *INASTI* v. *Kemmler* [1996] ECR I–704. See also Case C–68/99, *Commission* v. *Germany* [2001] ECR I–1865, concerning social insurance law affecting artists.

[82] Case 143/87, *Stanton*, n. 80 above, para. 9.

[83] Case 292/86, *Gullung* v. *Conseil de l'Ordre des Avocats* [1988] ECR 111. Also Case 271/82, *Auer* v. *Ministère Public* [1983] ECR 2727, para. 18.

[84] Case C–55/94, *Gebhard* v. *Consiglio dell'Ordine degli Avvocati e Procuratori di Milano* [1995] ECR I–4165.

[85] Case C–415/93, *Union Royale Belge des Sociétés de Football Association and others* v. *Bosman* [1995] ECR I–4921, paras. 82–84.

[86] Cases C–384/93, *Alpine Investments* [1995] ECR I–1141, and C–369/96 and C–376/96, *Arblade* [1999] ECR I–8453.

[87] Case 8/74, *Procureur du Roi* v. *Dassonville* [1974] ECR 837.

[88] Case 120/78, *Rewe-Zentrale* v. *Bundesmonopolverwaltung für Branntwein* [1979] ECR 649.

[89] Cases C–267 & 268/91, *Keck and Mithouard* [1993] ECR I–6097. See however Cases C–34–36/95, *de Agostini* [1997] ECR I–3843 and C–254/98, *Schutzverband gegen unlauteren Wettbewerb* v. *TK-Heimdienst Sass GmbH* [2000] ECR I–151, and the discussion in Ch. 15.

Gebhard concerned a German national against whom disciplinary proceedings were brought by the Milan Bar Council for pursuing a professional activity as a lawyer in Italy on a permanent basis, in chambers set up by himself and using the title *avvocato*, although he had not been admitted as a member of the Milan Bar and his training, qualifications, and experience had not formally been recognized in Italy. Having established that in the absence of Community rules, Member States may justifiably subject the pursuit of self-employed activites to *bona fide* rules relating to organization, ethics, qualifications, titles, etc., the ECJ continued:

37. It follows, however, from the Court's case law that national measures liable to hinder or make less attractive the exercise of fundamental freedoms guaranteed by the Treaty must fulfil four conditions: they must be applied in a non-discriminatory manner; they must be justified by impera-tive requirements in the general interest; they must be suitable for securing the attainment of the objective which they pursue; and they must not go beyond what is necessary in order to attain it (Kraus, paragraph 32).

There is no mention in this paragraph of a requirement of discrimination, direct or indirect, but merely that the national rule be such as to hinder or make less attractive the exercise of the 'fundamental' freedom of establishment or any of the other fundamental freedoms.[90] It is certainly true that one of the reasons the Treaty prohibits 'equally applicable' rules and obstacles on freedom of establish-ment is that many such rules in fact bear more heavily on non-nationals than on nationals, although not all equally applicable rules are indirectly discriminatory in this way. And in fact in most of the cases in which the ECJ has included non-discriminatory restrictions within the scope of Article 43 (ex Article 52), the restrictions which seemed 'equally applicable' could in fact be categorized as indirectly discriminatory, in bearing more heavily on non-nationals than on nationals.[91] This was true of the *Clinical Biology Services* case discussed above,[92] where the legislation clearly had a more restrictive impact on clinical laboratories whose primary establishment was in a Member State other than Belgium. Similarly in *Fearon*, the residence requirement was more likely to restrict non-national than national shareholders who wished to participate in the formation of an Irish company. A more likely reason for the ECJ upholding the compatibility of the rules in each of these two cases with the Treaty was not that they were 'non-discriminatory' in effect, but rather that they were adopted in pursuit of legitimate public-interest aims, even if these were not fully articulated in the cases. The same could also be said of single-practice rules in cases like *Klopp*, which are likely to be indirectly discriminatory in their effect, in bearing more heavily on non-nationals with a primary practice in another Member State. Equally, in cases like *Stanton*, *Kemmler*, and *Wolf*, the legislation clearly disadvantaged those whose principal profes-sional activities were in a Member State other than Belgium. And neither single-practice rules nor such obstructive social security rules were adequately justified

[90] See also Case C–108/96, *MacQuen* [2001] ECR I–837, paras. 26–27.
[91] See G. Marenco, 'The Notion of a Restriction on the Freedom of Establishment and the Provisions of Services in the Case Law of the ECJ' (1991) 11 *YBEL* 111.
[92] Case 221/85, *Commission* v. *Belgium* [1987] ECR 719.

by reference to legitimate public interests, in accordance with the test set out in paragraph 37 of *Gebhard*, above.

In *Kraus*, which will be discussed further below, the ECJ ruled that a provision of national law requiring special permission for the use of a foreign academic title could be contrary to Article 43 (ex Article 52), on the ground that any national rule restricting the exercise of freedom of establishment of nationals or non-nationals would be contrary to that Article unless adequately justified.[93] Although it could be argued that the restriction in *Kraus* was in fact indirectly discriminatory, since a greater number of non-nationals are likely to hold foreign academic degrees, the judgment seems to imply that, even if as many or more German nationals than non-nationals established in Germany were obtaining LL.M degrees in other Member States, the restriction would still fall within the scope of Article 43. The fact that the complainant himself was a German national adds force to this suggestion.[94] The same could be said of *Gebhard*, since once again the contested rules were probably indirectly discriminatory in their effect, but what is more interesting for present purposes is that the ECJ in paragraph 37 moved beyond this by declaring that, even in the case of a rule which was not indirectly discriminatory, the very fact of a national rule which was sufficiently obstructive to constitute a hindrance to the freedom to establish in a Member State was enough to bring it within the scope of Article 43 and to require justification. The terms of this ruling have been affirmed on many occasions since.[95]

It should be noted, however, that the discriminatory nature of a restriction is by no means irrelevant, for several reasons. First, if a restriction on establishment discriminates directly on grounds of nationality, it will, without further question, fall within the scope of the Treaty prohibition (whereas not every non-discriminatory restriction is likely to constitute a sufficient hindrance, by analogy with the case law on goods[96] and on workers, as seen recently in *Graf*[97]). Secondly, it seems that, at least in certain contexts, if a restriction is directly or deliberately discriminatory, the Member State may rely for justification only on the express derogations on grounds of public policy, security, and health in Article 46 (ex Article 56) of the Treaty.[98] These derogations, it will be seen in the next chapter, have been more carefully circumscribed both by the ECJ and in secondary legislation.[99] On the other hand, when the obstacle stems from an equally applicable rule (whether indirectly discriminatory or not) which does not constitute deliberate discrimination, it seems that a wider and open-ended range of public-interest grounds (which are referred to *inter alia* as mandatory requirements, imperative requirements, objective justifications) may be relied upon to justify the restrictive measure. It should be noted, however, that the internal-market case law on

---

[93] Case C–19/92, *Kraus* v. *Land Baden-Württemberg* [1993] ECR I–1663.

[94] See also P. Stanley (1996) 33 *CMLRev.* 713, 719–21.

[95] See, e.g., Cases C–108/96, *MacQuen* [2001] ECR I–837 and C–212/97, *Centros Ltd.* v. *Erhvervs- og Selskabsstyrelsen* [1999] ECR I–1459, para. 34.

[96] See Cases 267–8/91, *Keck and Mithouard* [1993] ECR I–6097 and the discussion in Ch. 14.

[97] Case C–190/98, *Graf* v. *Filzmoser Maschinenbau* [2000] ECR I–493.

[98] Case 352/85, *Bond van Adverteerders* v. *Netherlands* [1988] ECR 2085, paras. 32–33. See also Cases C–17/92, *Federación de Distribuidores Cinematográficos* v. *Estado Español et Unión de Productores de Cine y Televisión* [1993] ECR I–2239, para. 16, and C–484/93, *Svensson and Gustavsson* v. *Ministre du Logement et de l'Urbanisme* [1995] ECR I–3955, para. 15.

[99] See, e.g., Case C–211/91, *Commission* v. *Belgium* [1992] ECR I–6757 on restricting access to cable TV networks.

what constitutes discrimination, whether direct or indirect, and on what kinds of justification are available, is highly confused.[100] This problem has been discussed in more detail in Chapter 15 in the context of the free movement of goods.[101]

(II) THE 'REVERSE DISCRIMINATION' QUESTION: CAN NATIONALS RELY ON ARTICLE 43 (EX ARTICLE 52) IN THEIR OWN MEMBER STATE?

The second potential limitation on the scope of Article 43, mentioned above, derives from the fact that the wording of the first sentence refers to the situation of nationals of a Member State wishing to establish themselves 'in the territory of another Member State'. This suggests that nationals setting up in a self-employed capacity in their own Member State cannot complain under Article 43 (ex Article 52) about the domestic regulation of those activities. A Member State is clearly obliged, under that Article and Directive 73/148, not to restrict its own nationals who wish to *leave* the territory in order to set up an establishment in another Member State,[102] but the situation involving nationals establishing themselves within their own Member State has been more complex, mirroring some of the issues regarding 'wholly internal' situations which have arisen in the context of the free movement of workers.

One obvious way in which such nationals may be disadvantaged is if the qualifications they have obtained in another Member State are not recognized by their own State. The *Knoors* case concerned a Dutch national who sought to practise as a plumber in the Netherlands, having obtained training and experience in Belgium.[103] The Dutch government took the view that he could not rely on Directive 64/427, even though it covered his qualifications, because as a national relying in his own Member State on qualifications obtained elsewhere he might simply be seeking to evade the application of legitimate national provisions. The ECJ however rejected this argument and ruled in relation to the Treaty provisions on free movement of persons, services, and establishment:

20. In fact these liberties, which are fundamental in the Community system, could not be fully realized if the Member States were in a position to refuse to grant the benefit of the provisions of Community law to those of their nationals who have taken advantage of the facilities existing in the matter of freedom of movement and establishment and who have acquired, by virtue of such facilities, the trade qualifications referred to by the Directive in a Member State other than that whose nationality they possess.

. . .

24. Although it is true that the provisions of the Treaty relating to establishment and the provision of services cannot be applied to situations which are purely internal to a Member State,

---

[100] See, e.g., C–204/90, *Bachmann* v. *Belgium* [1992] ECR I–249 in the context of free movement of workers, where the ECJ seemed to say that restrictions which appeared to be discriminatory could be justified without recourse to the specific Treaty exceptions. See also the range of justifications considered by the ECJ for the (arguably directly discriminatory) nationality restrictions in Case C–415/93, *Bosman* [1995] ECR I–4921. For a more general discussion of this confusion see 'Mandatory Requirements', by J. Scott in C. Barnard and J. Scott (eds.), *Law of the Single European Market* (Hart, 2002).

[101] See Ch. 15, nn. 54–57 and 130–132 and text.

[102] See Art. 2 of the Dir.

[103] Case 115/78, *Knoors* v. *Secretary of State for Economic Affairs* [1979] ECR 399. See also Case 246/80, *Broekmeulen* v. *Huisarts Registratie Commissie* [1981] ECR 2311.

the position nevertheless remains that the reference in Article 52 to 'nationals of a Member State' who wish to establish themselves 'in the territory of another Member State' cannot be interpreted in such a way as to exclude from the benefit of Community law a given Member State's own nationals when the latter, owing to the fact that they have lawfully resided on the territory of another Member State and have there acquired a trade qualification which is recognized by the provisions of Community law, are, with regard to their State of origin, in a situation which may be assimilated to that of any other persons enjoying the rights and liberties guaranteed by the Treaty.

Despite this flexible approach, however, subsequent rulings of the ECJ suggested that the existence of legislation giving Community recognition to the 'foreign' qualification of the Member State national was crucial, and that Article 43 (ex Article 52) did not, of itself, protect nationals established in the Member State of their nationality. In *Auer*,[104] a naturalized French citizen had obtained a veterinary qualification in Italy but was not permitted to practise in France because, in the absence of a Community directive on the subject, the Italian qualification was not deemed equivalent to that required in France. The ECJ chose to interpret Article 43 in a literal and rather restrictive manner, to the effect that:

Article 52 concerns only—and can concern only—in each Member State the nationals of other Member States, those of the host Member State coming already, by definition, under the rules in question.[105]

The ECJ agreed that the mere application of the rule of national treatment would not ensure complete freedom of establishment 'as such application retains all obstacles other than those resulting from the non-possession of the nationality of the host state, and in particular, those resulting from the disparity of the conditions laid down by the different national laws for the acquisition of an appropriate professional qualification'.[106] However, in the Court's view, what was needed to ensure complete freedom of establishment was the adoption of mutual recognition legislation by the Council, which would also cover nationals within their own Member States.

In *Bouchoucha*,[107] a French national who had obtained a diploma in osteopathy in the UK was prosecuted for practising as an osteopath in France, without being qualified as a doctor as required under French law. Council Directives 75/362 and 75/363 governed the harmonization and mutual recognition of medical qualifications, but did not define the activities of a 'doctor', and there were no Community measures specifically relating to osteopathy. The ECJ ruled that:

in the absence of Community legislation on the professional practice of osteopathy each Member State is free to regulate the exercise of that activity within its territory, without discriminating between its own nationals and those of the other Member States.[108]

The ECJ may have felt that this was an attempted 'abuse' situation, in which a Member State had a legitimate interest in preventing its own nationals from evading

---

[104] Case 136/78, *Ministère Public* v. *Auer* [1979] ECR 437.   [105] *Ibid.*, para. 20.
[106] *Ibid.*, para. 21. See however the successful outcome for the applicants in the second *Auer* case, brought after further EC harmonization directives had been adopted: Case 271/82, n. 83 above.
[107] Case C–61/89, *Bouchoucha* [1990] ECR I–3551, [1992] 1 CMLR 1033.
[108] *Ibid.*, para. 12.

the provisions of national legislation by attempting to use Article 43 (ex Article 52) to rely on a 'lesser' qualification obtained in another Member State. Its approach was markedly different from that in *Heylens* and *Vlassopoulou*, above, in which nationals of other Member States had sought to rely in a host Member State on their national qualifications, despite the fact that there was no EC directive governing those qualifications and therefore no Community mutual recognition.[109] In those cases, the ECJ required the host Member State at least to compare the nature and content of the qualification offered by the practitioner with that required under domestic law, and to give reasons for its lack of equivalence, if that was the result. In *Bouchoucha*, on the other hand, where a national attempted to rely on Article 43 (ex Article 52) in his own Member State, the Court simply held that, in the absence of Community recognition or of a directive in the field, Member States were free to regulate a profession in a non-discriminatory manner, without having to examine degrees of knowledge and training attested to by the 'foreign' qualification offered by the national.[110]

The situation in *Bouchoucha* is however much less likely to arise now, since a national who has obtained a qualification in another Member State and has returned to practise in his or her Member State of origin will probably be covered by one of the three general mutual recognition Directives.[111] However, even in situations not covered by any of the co-ordination or mutual recognition directives,[112] it seems in spite of the *Bouchoucha* ruling that the principles in *Heylens* and *Vlassopoulou* provide a partial answer. Thus in *Kraus*, the ECJ ruled that a national in his own Member State—a German national who had obtained a one-year postgraduate LL.M. degree in Edinburgh and had returned to Germany—could rely on Article 43 (ex Article 52) when there was no Community directive at the time covering his qualification.[113] The case did not concern a refusal to recognize the knowledge or qualification attested to by the degree, or a refusal to permit the practice of a profession, but simply a refusal of permission to use the title of such a foreign degree without having to obtain (at substantial cost) prior permission.[114] The ECJ ruled that freedom of movement for workers and the right of establishment under Articles 39 (ex Article 48) and 43 (ex Article 52) constituted fundamental liberties, which could not be fully implemented if Member States could refuse to allow their own nationals, who had availed themselves of their freedom of movement and had as a result acquired qualifications in another Member State, to benefit from them. None the less, in the absence of existing measures of harmonization or recognition, the Member State could regulate the conditions relating to the use of the degree title, so long as it was not done in an excessive or disproportionate manner, and so long as it was done compatibly with other Treaty requirements. *Kraus* therefore clearly indicates that nationals established in their own Member States may in certain circumstances rely on Article 43 even in the absence of

---

[109] See also Case C–108/96, *MacQuen* [2001] ECR I–837.

[110] See also Cases C–330–331/90, *Ministero Fiscal v. Lopez Brea* [1992] ECR I–323.

[111] Dir. 89/48, 92/51 n. 57 above, and 99/42, n. 58 above, discussed above.

[112] E.g. Case C–164/94, *Arantis v. Land Berlin* [1996] ECR I–135. See n. 61 above and also the discussion in Case C–234/97, *Fernández de Bobadilla v. Museo Nacional del Prado* [1999] ECR I–4773.

[113] Case C–19/92, *Kraus*, n. 93 above.

[114] See Art. 7 of Dir. 89/48 and Art. 11 of Dir. 92/51, both n. 57 above, on the right to use the lawful academic title from the Member State where the qualification was received.

any Community legislation providing for recognition, and this was more recently reinforced in the case of *Fernández de Bobadilla*.[115] Thus, the reasoning of the Court in the first *Auer* case seems no longer valid, and the scope of the ruling in *Bouchoucha* is probably limited to cases of so-called 'abuse', where an individual is unjustifiably seeking to evade legitimate national regulations in his or her own Member State.

The position none the less remains that nationals will only be permitted to rely on Article 43 (ex Article 52) to challenge a restriction on establishment in their own Member State where there is some 'Community element' present, such as the fact of having moved and obtained a vocational qualification in another Member State. Otherwise, the situation is likely to be a 'wholly internal' one, as was seen in the case law on free movement of workers.[116] In *Niño*, criminal proceedings were brought in Italy against four Italian nationals who, without having the required authorization to practise as medical doctors, had provided pranotherapy and biotherapy treatment.[117] They argued that they should not be refused the freedom to practise their profession solely on the ground that a directive relating to the practice of such therapy had not yet been adopted. The ECJ held that the situation was in a purely national setting, and that the Community provisions on freedom of establishment were not applicable.

However in *Werner*, the ECJ indicated that even if a national was resident in a Member State other than that of his nationality, so long as he maintained his place of establishment and professional practice in his own Member State, he could not rely on Article 43 to challenge tax provisions of his own State which favoured residents over non-residents.[118] As a national, established in his own Member State and paying tax there, and who was not being restricted from setting up a place of establishment in another Member State, he could not invoke Article 43 (ex Article 52). Rather than treating the case as one in which there was a certain restriction on the freedom to establish owing to the tax 'encouragement' to reside in the Member State of establishment, albeit a restriction which was justified for legitimate tax reasons, the ECJ simply ruled that the Article was inapplicable. By way of contrast, in *Asscher*, a Dutch national residing in Belgium who was a director of companies *both* in Belgium and in the Netherlands, and who, on account of his non-resident status and the level of his earnings outside the Netherlands, was subject within the Netherlands to a considerably higher rate of tax than residents of that State, was entitled to invoke Article 43 against his own Member State.[119] The ECJ ruled this was not an 'internal' situation because his exercise of his Treaty rights of establishment and his dual economic activities in Belgium and the Netherlands had resulted in this unfavourable tax

---

[115] Case C–234/97, *Teresa Fernández de Bobadilla* v. *Museo Nacional del Prado* [1999] ECR I–4773, paras. 30–34.

[116] E.g., Case 175/78, *R.* v. *Saunders* [1979] ECR 1129. See, however, the forthcoming judgment in Case C–60/00, *Carpenter* v. *Home Secretary*; AG's Opinion of 13.9.2001 on services.

[117] Cases 54 & 91/88 & 14/89, *Niño and others* [1990] ECR 3537. See also cases 204/87, *Bekaert* [1988] ECR 2029; C–152/94, *Openbaar Ministerie* v. *Geert van Buydner* [1995] ECR I–3981; C–134/94, *Esso Española SA* v. *Comunidad Autónoma de Canarias* [1995] ECR I–4223; C–17/94, *Criminal Proceedings against Gervais et al.* [1995] ECR I–4353; C–134/95, *Unità Socio-Sanitaria Locale no 47 de Biella* v. *INAIL* [1997] ECR I–195. Also Cases C–225–227/95, *Kapasakalis* v. *Greece* [1998] ECR I–4329 in which Dir. 89/48 N. 57 above was invoked. See for a discussion of the different issues arising, E. Cannizzaro, 'Producing 'Reverse Discrimination' through the Exercise of Competences' (1997) 17 *YBEL* 29.

[118] Case C–112/91, *Werner* v. *Finanzamt Aachen-Innenstadt* [1993] ECR I–429.

[119] Case C–107/94, *Asscher* v. *Staatsecretaris van Financiën* [1996] ECR I–3089.

situation. Although differential treatment of resident and non-resident taxpayers which constitutes *prima facie* discrimination under Article 43 could be justified by the state, given the possible objective differences between them, there can be no justification where such differences do not actually exist.[120]

It has been pointed out that, whatever the ECJ may say, cases like *Kraus* and *Asscher* are not instances of nationality-based discrimination, since they involve nationals established in their own Member States.[121] What these cases suggest is that Community law on freedom of establishment is not only about the elimination of unequal treatment of non-nationals and of protectionism, but rather the attempt to create a single market in order that, whatever their nationality, self-employed individuals and companies can set up business in various locations within that market without encountering 'unjustified' obstacles.

(iii) ARE RESTRICTIONS ON SOCIAL BENEFITS CONTRARY TO ARTICLE 43 (EX ARTICLE 52)?

We have seen that many different national rules and provisions may constitute impermissible restrictions on freedom of establishment under the Treaty. On the other hand, there has been no equivalent, within the law on freedom of establishment, of Regulation 1612/68 on the rights of workers and their families in the context of Article 39 (ex Article 48). In particular there is no provision like Article 7(2) of that Regulation guaranteeing the same social and tax advantages to non-nationals as are available to nationals, nor any mention of housing or educational rights for children. These issues will, however, be addressed in the same way for all categories of lawfully resident EU citizen, whether employed, self-employed, or other, if the Commission's recently proposed consolidation directive is adopted.[122]

Even in the absence of legislation, however, the ECJ had already interpreted Article 43 (ex Article 52) as prohibiting national measures which confer certain social advantages on nationals or companies maintaining their primary establishment in that Member State, to the exclusion of non-nationals or of companies maintaining a secondary establishment there. Taking what seemed initially a slightly less generous approach than that adopted under Article 7 of Regulation 1612/68 for workers, the ECJ ruled that the prohibition on discrimination under Article 43 was concerned with 'the rules relating to the various general facilities which are of assistance in the pursuit of [occupational] activities'.[123] In *Meeusen*, however, the ECJ ruled that the principle of equal treatment of self-employed persons under Article 43 precluded national legislation which imposed a residence requirement on the children of self-employed EU migrants, but not on the children of nationals, before they could obtain finance

---

[120] See also Cases C–80/94, *Wielockx* [1995] ECR I–2493 and C–279/93, *Finanzamt Köln-Altstadt* v. *Roland Schumacker* [1995] ECR I–225. In *Asscher*, the ECJ ruled that the 'coherence of the tax system' which was accepted as a justification in Cases C–300/90, *Commission* v. *Belgium* [1992] ECR I–305 and C–204/90, *Bachmann* v. *Belgium* [1992] ECR I–249, could not be pleaded here because the Netherlands was making an unjustified link between taxation and social security contributions. See also, in the context of services, Cases C–484/93, *Svensson and Gustavsson* v. *Ministre du Logement et de l'Urbaniseme* [1995] ECR I–3955 and C–294/97, *Eurowings Luftverkehrs AG* v. *Finanzamt Dortmund-Unna* [1999] ECR I–7447.

[121] Stanley, n. 94 above. See also C–60/00, *Carpenter*, n. 116, above.

[122] COM(2001)257. See Art. 21 of the draft dir.

[123] Case 63/86, *Commission* v. *Italy* [1988] ECR 29.

for their studies.[124] Further, in *Steinhauser*,[125] a restriction on renting premises for business purposes and, in *Stanton*,[126] the refusal of certain social-security exemptions were held to constitute restrictions on the right of establishment. And in infringement proceedings brought against Ireland and France concerning registration of vessels not used for an economic activity, the ECJ ruled that where a person moved to a Member State and set up residence there in order to pursue a self-employed activity, access to leisure activities available within that state was a corollary to that freedom of movement.[127]

We shall see below that the denial of tax advantages to companies whose primary establishment or registered office is not within the State may also infringe Article 43 (ex Article 52).[128] Such measures, although they may not directly regulate or curb the right of establishment, nevertheless constitute disadvantages for those exercising such Treaty rights. Unlike the restrictions on social advantages for workers which are pro- hibited by Article 39 (ex Article 48),[129] the link between the enjoyment of the social benefit and the ability to carry on the self-employed activity has at times been emphasized by the Court in the context of Article 43 and, as we shall see below, Article 49 (ex Article 59). In the Italian housing case, in which Italy argued that reduced-rate mortgage loans and social housing did not have to be provided for self-employed non-nationals on the same terms as for nationals, the Court ruled as follows:

Case 63/86, Commission v. Italy
[1988] ECR 29

16. If complete equality of competition is to be assured, the national of a Member State who wishes to pursue an activity as a self-employed person in another Member State must therefore be able to obtain housing in conditions equivalent to those enjoyed by those of his competitors who are nationals of the latter State. Accordingly any restriction placed not only on the right of access to housing but also on the various facilities granted to those nationals in order to alleviate the financial burden must be regarded as an obstacle to the pursuit of the occupation itself.

17. That being so, housing legislation, even where it concerns social housing, must be regarded as part of the legislation that is subject to the principle of national treatment which results from the provisions of the Treaty concerning activities as self-employed persons.

---

[124] Case C–337/97, *Meeusen v. Hofddirectie van de Informatie Beheer Groep* [1999] ECR I–3289.

[125] Case 197/84, *Steinhauser v. City of Biarritz* [1985] ECR 1819.

[126] Case 143/87, *Stanton*, n. 66 above, discussed above. See also Case 79/85, *Segers* [1986] ECR 2375 on the right of employees of a company to be affiliated to a social security scheme.

[127] Cases C–334/94, *Commission v. France* [1996] ECR I–1307, para. 21, and C–151/96, *Commission v. Ireland* [1997] ECR I–3327.

[128] Case 270/83, *Commission v. France* [1986] ECR 273. On indirect disadvantages to non-established credit institutions, due to the conditions imposed on subsidies for borrowers, see Case C–484/93, *Svensson and Gustavsson v. Ministre du Logement et de l'Urbanisme* [1995] ECR I–3955. See also Case C–410/96, *André Ambry* [1998] ECR I–7875 concerning restrictions imposed on travel agencies arranging security with a financial institution in another Member State to ensure a guarantee agreement is concluded with a credit institution situated in the host Member State.

[129] See, e.g., Cases 207/78, *Ministère Public v. Even and ONPTS* [1979] ECR 2019, and 65/81, *Reina v. Landeskreditbank Baden-Württemberg* [1982] ECR 33.

(d) ESTABLISHMENT OF COMPANIES

Article 48 (ex Article 58) of the Treaty provides:

Companies or firms formed in accordance with the law of a Member State and having their registered office, central administration or principal place of business within the Community shall, for the purposes of this Chapter, be treated in the same way as natural persons who are nationals of Member States.

'Companies or firms' means companies or firms constituted under civil or commercial law, including co-operative societies, and other legal persons governed by public or private law, save for those which are non-profit making.

Although this Article requires companies to be treated in the same way as nationals for the purposes of the Treaty provisions on freedom of establishment, this is not strictly possible, given the differences between natural and legal persons. It may be easier, for example, to recognize what is a primary as opposed to a secondary establishment in the case of the registered office of a company and one of its subsidiaries or branches, than it is in the case of a professional who has two places of practice in different Member States.[130] Further, despite the many company law directives which have been adopted, considerable differences in the way the various Member States regulate companies and their activities remain.

The definition of a company in Article 48 (ex Article 58) is wide, referring to 'legal persons governed by private or public law', but it excludes non-profit-making companies, although non-profit-making economic activities can be covered by Article 43 (ex Article 52).[131] The exclusion of non-profit-making companies may to some extent be considered alongside the exclusion from the scope of the Treaty of workers who are not remunerated, and services which are not provided for remuneration, and it reflects in part what is still, despite the changes made in other areas by the TEU and the increasing focus on 'citizenship' as a category to cover most of the free movement chapters of the Treaty, the commercial focus of these provisions.[132]

It is clear that, so long as a company is formed in accordance with the law of a Member State and has its registered office there and its principal place of business *somewhere* in the Community, it will be established in the first Member State within the meaning of the Treaty. The ECJ made it clear in *Segers* that this would hold true even if the company conducted no business of any kind in that Member State, but instead conducted its business through one of the various forms of secondary establishment—such as a subsidiary, branch, or agency—in another Member State.[133] This was affirmed in *Centros*, where the ECJ ruled that a company was lawfully established in the UK even though it had never traded there, and that the Danish

---

[130] See V. Edwards, 'Secondary Establishment of Companies—The Case Law of the Court of Justice' (1998) 18 *YBEL* 221.

[131] See Case C–70/95, *Sodemare* v. *Regione Lombardia* [1997] ECR I–3395.

[132] The fact that a company is non-profit-making does not however mean that it is not engaged in economic activity. For an illustration of this point in a different context see Case C–382/92, *Commission* v. *UK* [1994] ECR I–2435, para. 45, and see the cases on cross-border access to health care in the context of services, n. 183 below.

[133] Case 79/85, *Segers*, n. 126 above, para. 16.

authorities were not justified in restricting its right to establish a branch in Denmark.[134] In the *Insurance Services* case, the Court held that even an office managed for a company by an independent person on a permanent basis would amount to establishment in that Member State.[135] This latter form of establishment would amount to a secondary establishment, since the registered office or seat of the company and its principal place of business would presumably be elsewhere in the Community. A company has a right of secondary establishment only if it already has its principal place of business or central or registered office within the Community.

Many of the cases which have come before the ECJ have concerned restrictions or disadvantages imposed by Member States on companies whose registered offices were in another Member State. In *Commission* v. *France*, the Court drew an analogy between the location of the registered office of a company and the place of residence of a natural person.[136] It ruled that discrimination in tax laws against branches or agencies in a Member State by taxing them on the same basis as companies whose registered office is in that state yet not giving them the same tax advantages as such companies was an infringement of Article 43 (ex Article 52). Neither the lack of harmonization of the tax laws of the different Member States nor the risk of tax avoidance by companies could justify the restriction. According to the ECJ, Article 43 'expressly leaves traders free to choose the appropriate legal form in which to pursue their activities in another Member State and that freedom of choice must not be limited by discriminatory tax provisions'.[137] According to the Court, 'it is their corporate seat ... that serves as the connecting factor with the legal system of a Member State, like nationality in the case of natural persons'.[138] Nevertheless, the ECJ has accepted that a distinction based on the location of the registered office of a company or the place of residence of a natural person may, under certain conditions, be justified in an area such as tax law.[139] In *Futura*, it was permissible for a Member State to impose conditions as regards the keeping of accounts and the location where losses were incurred on a non-resident company (which had a branch but not a main establishment in the state) for the purposes of assessing liability to tax and allowable losses, although the specific restrictions imposed by Luxembourg in the case were closely scrutinized for proportionality, and the accounting requirement—even in the

---

[134] Case C–212/97, *Centros Ltd.* v. *Erhvervs- og Selskabsstyrelsen* [1999] ECR I–1459. For some useful commentaries see W.-H. Roth (2000) 37 *CMLRev.* 147 and P. Cabral and P. Cunha (2000) 25 *ELRev.* 157.

[135] Case 205/84, n. 9 above, para. 21.

[136] Case 270/83, n. 139 above, para. 18.

[137] *Ibid.*, para. 22. See also Case C–330/91, *R.* v. *Inland Revenue Commissioners, ex p. Commerzbank AG* [1993] ECR I–4017, in which the ECJ held that tax disadvantages imposed on a company not on the basis of its seat, but on the basis of its fiscal residence, were indirectly discriminatory, since in practice most companies are fiscally resident in the State in which they have their seat. See also Case C–1/93, *Halliburton Services BV* v. *Staatssecretaris van Financiën* [1994] ECR I–1137.

[138] Case C–330/91, para. 18, n. 137 above. See also Cases C–264/96, *ICI* v. *Colmer* [1998] ECR I–4695, para. 20; C–307/97, *Compagnie de Saint-Gobain* v. *Finanzamt Aachen-Innenstadt* [1999] ECR I–6161, para. 35; and C–397/98 & C–410/98, *Metallgesellschaft Ltd.* v. *Internal Revenue* [2001] ECR I–4727, para. 42.

[139] Case 270/83, *Commission* v. *France* [1986] ECR 273, para. 19. See also Cases C–279/93, *Finanzamt Köln-Altstadt* v. *Roland Schumacker* [1995] ECR I–225; C–80/94, *Wielockx* [1995] ECR I–2493; C–107/94, *Asscher* [1996] ECR I–3089; and C–311/97, *Royal Bank of Scotland* v. *Greece* [1999] ECR I–2651. Compare Cases C–264/96, C–307/97, & C–397/98, n. 138 above, and C–200/98, *X and Y* v. *Riksskatteverket* [1999] ECR I–8261.

absence of harmonized Community rules in this area—was found to be excessively restrictive.[140]

In *Segers*, the ECJ ruled that where a company had exercised its right of establishment under the Treaty, the Member States were prohibited from excluding the company's director from a national sickness-insurance benefit scheme solely on the ground that the company was formed in accordance with the law of another Member State where it also had its registered office but did not carry on any business.[141] The discrimination was therefore on the ground that the registered office of the company was not within the Member State.[142] Although the discrimination was practised against the manager rather than the company, the Court ruled that 'discrimination against employees in connection with social security protection indirectly restricts the freedom of companies of another Member State to establish themselves through an agency, branch or subsidiary'.[143] Nor was the discrimination justified under Article 46 (ex Article 56) on the ground of the need to combat fraud, because the refusal of sickness benefit was not an appropriate means of preventing fraud. In proceedings brought against Italy for providing that only companies in which the state owned a majority of the shares could obtain state contracts for developing data-processing systems for public authorities, the ECJ ruled that such indirect discrimination in favour of Italian companies was contrary to the Treaty, and was a disproportionate and inappropriate way of protecting the confidentiality of data.[144]

While companies are not covered by Directive 73/148, Article 2 of which guarantees to natural persons the right to leave their Member State, they have, according to the *Daily Mail* case, similar rights under the provisions of the Treaty.[145] However, that case also made clear that the provisions on freedom of establishment do not give companies the right, without any restriction or impediment from the Member State in which they are registered, to move their registered office or their central management and control to another Member State, whilst retaining an establishment in the first Member State. This is not to say that a company may not under Community law move its registered office or its central place of administration, for example, to a state in which the tax position would be more favourable, but simply that it cannot derive from Article 43 a right to do so, and that it may, if it does seek to move its seat, be subject to certain conditions laid down by the Member State from which it wishes to move. The reason for this is that the laws of the Member States on what constitutes

[140] Case C–250/95, *Futura Participations SA Singer* v. *Administration des Contributions* [1997] ECR I–2471. For indirect tax discrimination against companies having their principal place of business in other Member States, see Case C–254/97, *Société Baxter* v. *Premier Ministre* [1999] ECR I–4809.

[141] Case 79/85, n. 126 above, para. 19.

[142] In Case 93/89, *Commission* v. *Ireland* [1991] ECR I–4569, Art. 43 (ex Art. 52) was breached by the requirement that nationals of other Member States who owned a vessel registered in Ireland must establish a company in Ireland. However, this is really a restriction on individuals, rather than a restriction on a company established in another Member State. For similar vessel registration cases, see Cases C–221/89, *R.* v. *Secretary of State for Transport, ex p. Factortame* [1991] ECR I–3905; C–246/89, *Commission* v. *UK* [1991] ECR I–4585; C–334/94, *Commission* v. *France* [1996] ECR I–1307; and C–151/96, *Commission* v. *Ireland,* [1997] ECR I–3327.

[143] [1986] ECR 2375, para. 15. Contrast however the Clinical Biology Services case 221/85, n. 73 above.

[144] Case 3/88, *Commission* v. *Italy* [1989] ECR 4035. See also Cases C–272/91, *Commission* v. *Italy*, n. 26 above and C–101/94, *Commission* v. *Italy* [1996] ECR I–2691.

[145] Case 81/87, *R.* v. *HM Treasury and Commissioners of Inland Revenue, ex p. Daily Mail and General Trust PLC* [1988] ECR 5483.

the place of incorporation or the real head office of the company are not harmonized so that different Member States may legitimately have different views and different ways of regulating how a transfer of head office may be effected.[146]

In the *Daily Mail* case, a company which was resident in the UK but wished to transfer its residence to The Netherlands and to set up a subsidiary or branch in the UK instead, had to seek permission from the Treasury, which could require the company first to liquidate some of its assets.[147] The company argued that the requirement to obtain permission constituted an impermissible restriction on its freedom of establishment, but the Court ruled that Articles 43 (ex Article 52) and 48 (ex Article 58) did not apply in this situation, given the wide variation in national laws as to the required factor connecting a company to the national territory for the purposes of incorporation, and also the wide variation in national laws concerning transfer of a company's head office from one state to another.[148] In the absence of greater harmonization in this field, whether by convention or by legislation, the company could not rely on Articles 43 and 48.

The *Daily Mail* case thus indicated that, apart from the 'wholly internal situation' context, there were other situations in which Article 43 (ex Article 52) would not avail a company, e.g. where it sought to move its primary establishment freely from one Member State to another. There was no mention by the ECJ in *Daily Mail* of a possible 'abuse' of Article 43 by the company in its attempt to derive full benefit from the differences in company law as between the UK and the Netherlands, by moving residence unhindered. The Court simply declared that Article 43 did not, in view of the relatively unharmonized state of relevant company laws at the time, give the company such a right. However, the question of when a company which sought to benefit from the Treaty provisions on freedom of establishment might be considered to be 'abusing' those rights or seeking to evade legitimate national restrictions was raised directly in the *Centros* case.[149] The case concerned a company which was registered in the UK (and therefore had its primary establishment in the UK) but which had never traded there. It had chosen the UK in which to register because UK law imposed no requirements on limited liability companies as to the provision for, or the paying-up of, a minimum share capital. However, the actual purpose of establishing in the UK was to conduct business in Denmark (whose minimum capital requirement laws were considerably stricter) through a branch. The Danish Board of Trade and Companies refused to register the branch on the ground that Centros was not in fact seeking to establish a branch in Denmark—whose laws follow what is known as the 'incorporation theory' rather than the 'seat theory'—but rather a principal establishment, while circumventing legitimate national rules including those on

---

[146] Art. 220 (ex Art. 293) EC recognized the need for the adoption of agreements for the mutual recognition of companies and the retention of legal personality in the event of transfer of their seat from one country to another, but the Convention on the Mutual Recognition of Companies, which was adopted pursuant to this Art. in 1968, did not come into force. For a recent discussion of this and related matters, see J. Wouters 'European Company Law: Quo Vadis?' (2000) 37 *CMLRev.* 257.

[147] Case 81/87, *R. v. HM Treasury and Commissioners of Inland Revenue, ex p. Daily Mail* [1988] ECR 5483.

[148] *Ibid.*, para 23.

[149] Case C–212/97, *Centros Ltd. v. Erhvervs- og Selskabsstyrelsen* [1999] ECR I–1459.

the paying-up of minimum capital. The Board claimed that, had the establishment in the UK been genuine, in the sense that the company was actually trading there, it would not have refused to register a branch in Denmark. The questions for the ECJ were therefore whether the company could rely on Article 43 (ex Article 52) to plead infringement of the right to secondary establishment and, if so, whether the Danish Board could none the less justify the restriction.

C–212/97, Centros Ltd. v. Erhvervs- og Selskabsstyrelsen
[1999] ECR I–1459

[ToA renumbering: Art. 52, 54, and 58 are now Art. 43, 44, and 48 EC]

21. Where it is the practice of a Member State, in certain circumstances, to refuse to register a branch of a company having its registered office in another Member State, the result is that companies formed in accordance with the law of that other Member State are prevented from exercising the freedom of establishment conferred on them by Articles 52 and 58 of the Treaty.

22. Consequently, that practice constitutes an obstacle to the exercise of the freedoms guaranteed by those provisions.

23. According to the Danish authorities, however, Mr and Mrs Bryde cannot rely on those provisions, since the sole purpose of the company formation which they have in mind is to circumvent the application of the national law governing formation of private limited companies and therefore constitutes abuse of the freedom of establishment. In their submission, the Kingdom of Denmark is therefore entitled to take steps to prevent such abuse by refusing to register the branch.

24. It is true that according to the case-law of the Court a Member State is entitled to take measures designed to prevent certain of its nationals from attempting, undercover of the rights created by the Treaty, improperly to circumvent their national legislation or to prevent individuals from improperly or fraudulently taking advantage of provisions of Community law. . . .

25. However, although, in such circumstances, the national courts may, case by case, take account—on the basis of objective evidence—of abuse or fraudulent conduct on the part of the persons concerned in order, where appropriate, to deny them the benefit of the provisions of Community law on which they seek to rely, they must nevertheless assess such conduct in the light of the objectives pursued by those provisions. . . .

26. In the present case, the provisions of national law, application of which the parties concerned have sought to avoid, are rules governing the formation of companies and not rules concerning the carrying on of certain trades, professions or businesses. The provisions of the Treaty on freedom of establishment are intended specifically to enable companies formed in accordance with the law of a Member State and having their registered office, central administration or principal place of business within the Community to pursue activities in other Member States through an agency, branch or subsidiary.

27. That being so, the fact that a national of a Member State who wishes to set up a company chooses to form it in the Member State whose rules of company law seem to him the least restrictive and to set up branches in other Member States cannot, in itself, constitute an abuse of the right of establishment. The right to form a company in accordance with the law of a Member

State and to set up branches in other Member States is inherent in the exercise, in a single market, of the freedom of establishment guaranteed by the Treaty.

28. In this connection, the fact that company law is not completely harmonised in the Community is of little consequence. Moreover, it is always open to the Council, on the basis of the powers conferred upon it by Article 54(3)(g) of the EC Treaty, to achieve complete harmonisation.

29. In addition, it is clear from paragraph 16 of *Segers* that the fact that a company does not conduct any business in the Member State in which it has its registered office and pursues its activities only in the Member State where its branch is established is not sufficient to prove the existence of abuse or fraudulent conduct which would entitle the latter Member State to deny that company the benefit of the provisions of Community law relating to the right of establishment.

30. Accordingly, the refusal of a Member State to register a branch of a company formed in accordance with the law of another Member State in which it has its registered office on the grounds that the branch is intended to enable the company to carry on all its economic activity in the host State, with the result that the secondary establishment escapes national rules on the provision for and the paying-up of a minimum capital, is incompatible with Articles 52 and 58 of the Treaty, in so far as it prevents any exercise of the right freely to set up a secondary establishment which Articles 52 and 58 are specifically intended to guarantee.

The Court went on to rule that the refusal to register a branch of *Centros* was not justified in the interests of protecting creditors or preventing fraud, in part because there were other ways of countering fraud and protecting creditors (including through the existence of EC legislation governing corporate accounting and disclosure) which were less restrictive of freedom of establishment.

While the principles of law expressed in the case were familiar principles long announced by the ECJ in the context of freedom of establishment, their application to this factual situation and with this outcome caused considerable surprise, in particular amongst company lawyers.[150] The fact that the particular manœuvre engaged in by the Centros company was not caught by the 'abuse' or 'avoidance' exception was unexpected, and there has been very extensive commentary on the case. Far from constituting an *abuse* of Article 43, the ECJ ruled that deliberate choice of a Member State with lenient legislative requirements concerning incorporation in order to enjoy the right of secondary establishment more freely in a Member State with stricter incorporation requirements was simply an exercise of the rights inherent in the notion of freedom of establishment. Further, the absence of legislative harmonization, which had been used by the ECJ in *Daily Mail* as a reason for declaring Article 43 to be inapplicable to the facts of that case, was deemed in paragraph 28 of *Centros* to be irrelevant (and indeed gave the Court occasion to point to the availability to Member States of the option of adopting EC harmonizing legislation in this area of company law). There were other options open to Member States seeking to counter fraud or unjustified corporate evasion of *legitimate* regulatory requirements, which would be less restrictive than imposing the full range of its company law requirements on a branch whose primary establishment was lawfully in another Member State. However,

---

[150] The Celex database shows over 70 notes and commentaries on the case.

apart from mentioning the possibility of measures to enable public creditors to secure sufficient guarantees, the ECJ did not indicate what other sorts of restrictions would be acceptable and proportionate.

The case has been described as reflecting a judicial 'willingness to break down the remaining constraints to the free movement of companies in the Community' and as 'opening the door to competition among national rules as an alternative approach to ensure the completion of the internal market',[151] while others have noted that it none the less left the ruling in *Daily Mail* for the moment untouched.[152]

(e) SUMMARY

i. Despite restrictive early case law on the point, it appears that Article 43 may now be invoked by a national in his or her Member State of establishment, so long as there is a Community element present. This element consists normally of the fact that the individual has obtained a qualification or professional training in another Member State, so long as the situation involves no attempted 'abuse' of Community rights. The notion of abuse or evasion of legitimate control remains somewhat undefined.

ii. After years of pursuing a painstaking sectoral strategy of legislative harmonization of professional qualifications, there has been a change of approach since the late 1980s to one of mutual recognition. There are now three fairly comprehensive general mutual-recognition directives together with an amending directive which 'simplifies' the earlier sectoral directives. Most recently the Commission has made a proposal to reform and consolidate all of the legislation in one measure.

iii. Despite the emphasis for many years on equal treatment and non-discrimination in the field of establishment, the ECJ has gradually moved towards an approach which is similar to that in other areas of free movement, whereby any 'impediment' (whether differential in its impact or not) to freedom of establishment is caught by Article 43 unless it can be justified.

iv. The law governing establishment of companies is more complex than that governing natural persons, mainly because of the remaining differences between national company laws, and in particular relating to the 'incorporation theory' versus the 'seat theory'. The rights attaching to forms of 'secondary establishment' have been the subject of more extensive litigation and liberalization.

---

[151] See P. Cabral and P. Cunha, '"Presumed innocent": Companies and the Exercise of the Right of Establishment under Community Law' (2000) 25 *ELRev.* 157. See also S. Deakin, 'Two Types of Regulatory Competition: Competitive Federalism versus Reflexive Harmonisation. A Law and Econmoics Perspective on *Centros*' (1999) 2 *CYELS* 231.

[152] W. Roth (2000) 37 *CMLRev.* 147, 153–5.

4. FREE MOVEMENT OF SERVICES

If the right of establishment entails the pursuit of an economic activity from a fixed base in a Member State for an indefinite period, the freedom to provide services by contrast entails the carrying out of an economic activity for a temporary period in a Member State in which either the provider or the recipient of the service is not established. According to the *Insurance Services* case, if a person or an undertaking maintains a *permanent* base in a Member State, even if only an office, it cannot avail itself of the right to provide services in that state but will be governed by the law on freedom of establishment.[153] In *Gebhard*, however, we saw that the ECJ acknowledged that the provision of services did not necessarily cease to be *temporary* simply because the provider might need to equip herself with the necessary infrastructure—e.g., an office or chambers—to perform those services.[154] Thus what is relevant in order to determine whether a self-employed person is covered by the Treaty provisions on establishment or services is not the mere existence of an office in a Member State, but rather the temporary or permanent nature of the economic activities carried on there.

Further, the Court has ruled that if someone directs most or all of his or her services at the territory of a particular Member State but maintains his or her place of establishment outside that state in order to evade its professional rules (the abuse/evasion theory), that person may in certain circumstances be treated as being established within the Member State, and thus covered not by Article 49 (ex Article 59) but by Article 43 (ex Article 52).[155] In such a case the professional rules which that person was attempting to evade by maintaining an establishment in a different Member State could be applied as though they were established in the regulating state. However, in a statement which anticipated a similar ruling of the ECJ in the context of establishment in *Centros*,[156] Advocate General Léger in *Gebhard* declared that the fact that someone opened an office or chambers in order to provide occasional services within a Member State, while having their permanent establishment in another Member State, could not of itself give rise to an irrebuttable presumption of fraud or evasion of national requirements by that person: instead, the onus was on the state in each case to prove the existence of such fraud.[157]

Article 49 (ex Article 59) provides:

Within the framework of the provisions set out below, restrictions on freedom to provide services within the Community shall be prohibited in respect of nationals of Member States who are

---

[153] Case 205/84, n. 9 above, para. 21. The earlier decision in Case 39/75, *Coenen* v. *Sociaal-Economische Raad* [1975] ECR 1547, was somewhat contradictory on this point.

[154] Case C–55/94, *Gebhard* [1995] ECR I–4165, para. 27.

[155] Case 33/74, *Van Binsbergen*, n. 6 above, para. 13. See also Case 205/84, *Commission* v. *Germany*, n. 9 above, para. 22. For an example of a justified state restriction to prevent an abuse where a provider of services was established outside the Netherlands in order to evade broadcasting regulations, yet was directing its services at the Netherlands, see Cases C–148/91, *Vereniging Veronica Omroep Organisatie* v. *Commissariaat voor de Media* [1993] ECR I–487 and C–23/93, *TV10 SA* v. *Commissariaat voor de Media* [1994] ECR I–4795. Contrast Cases C–369/96 & C–376/96, *Arblade* [1999] ECR I–8453, para. 32.

[156] N. 149 above, para. 29.

[157] Case C–55/94, para. 84 of his Opinion.

established in a State of the Community other than that of the person for whom the services are intended.

The Council may, acting by a qualified majority on a proposal from the Commission, extend the provisions of the Chapter to nationals of a third country who provide services and who are established within the Community.

In order to benefit from the right to provide services, this provision indicates that the person in question, natural or legal, must already have a place of establishment within the Community. The General Programme on freedom to provide services specified in more detail that the right to provide services was available only to nationals established in the Community, or to companies formed under the laws of a Member State and having their seat, centre of administration, or main establishment within the Community.[158] If only the seat of a company is situated within the Community, then its activity must have a 'real and continuous link' with the economy of a Member State, other than a link of nationality. Without that economic foothold within the Community, there is no right under EC law for a company or a Community national established *outside* the Community to provide temporary services *within* the Community. A permanent economic base must first be established within a Member State, and from that base the person may provide temporary services in other Member States.

Article 50 (ex Article 60) provides:

Services shall be considered to be 'services' within the meaning of this Treaty where they are normally provided for remuneration, insofar as they are not governed by the provisions relating to freedom of movement for goods, capital and persons.

'Services' shall in particular include

(a) activities of an industrial character;

(b) activities of a commercial character;

(c) activities of craftsmen;

(d) activities of the professions.

Without prejudice to the provisions of the Chapter relating to the right of establishment, the person providing a service may, in order to do so, temporarily pursue his activity in the State where the service is to be provided, under the same conditions as are imposed by that State on its own nationals.

Article 50 (ex Article 60) specifies that the provisions on free movement of services will apply only in so far as a particular restriction is not covered by the provisions on free movement of goods, persons, or capital. Article 51 (ex Article 61) also excludes transport services from the chapter on services since transport is dealt with elsewhere in the Treaty,[159] and provides that banking and insurance services connected with capital movements are to be dealt with in line with the Treaty provisions on movement of capital.[160] The 'official authority' exception and the public policy, security, and health derogations provided for in Articles 45 and 46 (ex Articles 55 and 56) in

---

[158] See the 1961 General Programme, n. 36 above.
[159] See Arts. 70–80 (ex Arts. 74–84) EC.   [160] See Ch. 16.

the context of establishment are made applicable to the free movement of services by Article 55 (ex Article 66). These derogations, as in the case of workers and establishment, are currently regulated by the provisions of Directive 64/221,[161] which is one of the legislative measures which will be abolished and incorporated into a new directive on free movement of EU citizens, if the Commission's 2001 proposal is adopted.[162]

As in the chapter on establishment, Article 52 (ex Article 63) provided for a General Programme to be drawn up, and for directives to be issued by the Council so as to liberalize specific services. The General Programme which was drawn up was similar in many respects to that adopted on establishment, with an emphasis on the abolition of discrimination, and we can see this emphasis on equal treatment in the terms of Article 50 (ex Article 60) above also.

(a) THE EFFECT OF ARTICLE 49 (EX ARTICLE 59)

In many ways, then, the chapter on the provision of services is very similar to that on establishment, except that the activity in question is pursued on a temporary rather than a permanent basis in a Member State. Shortly after the *Reyners* ruling first established that Article 43 (ex Article 52) was directly effective, the *Van Binsbergen* case on the direct effect of Article 49 (ex Article 59) came before the Court.[163] The UK and Irish Governments intervened to argue that, despite the ECJ's ruling in *Reyners*, the area of provision of services was subject to even greater problems of control and discipline than that of establishment, that Articles 49 and 50 (ex Articles 59 and 60) should not be found to have direct effect, and that the only satisfactory solution was the adoption of directives as provided for by the Treaty.

Case 33/74, Van Binsbergen v. Bestuur van de Bedrijfsvereniging voor de Metaalnijverheid
[1974] ECR 1299

[ToA renumbering: Arts. 59, 60, 63, and 66 are now Arts. 49, 50, 52, and 55 respectively]

A Dutch national acting as legal adviser to Van Binsbergen, in respect of proceedings before a Dutch social security court, transferred his place of residence from the Netherlands to Belgium during the course of the proceedings. He was told that he could no longer represent his client since, under Dutch law, only persons established in the Netherlands could act as legal advisers. A reference was made to the ECJ to determine whether Article 59 had direct effect, and whether the Dutch rule was compatible with it.

THE ECJ

20. With a view to the progressive abolition during the transitional period of the restrictions referred to in Article 59, Article 63 has provided for the drawing up of a 'general programme'— laid down by Council Decision of 18 December 1961—to be implemented by a series of directives.

---

[161] See Ch. 19.   [162] See n. 24 above.   [163] Case 33/74, n. 6 above.

21. Within the scheme of the chapter relating to the provision of services, these directives are intended to accomplish different functions, the first being to abolish, during the transitional period, restrictions on freedom to provide services, the second being to introduce into the law of Member States a set of provisions intended to facilitate the effective exercise of this freedom, in particular by the mutual recognition of qualifications and the coordination of laws with regard to the pursuit of activities as self-employed persons.

22. These directives also have the task of resolving the specific problems resulting from the fact that where the person providing the service is not established, on a habitual basis, in the State where the service is performed he may not be fully subject to the professional rules of conduct in force in that State.

. . .

24. The provisions of Article 59, the application of which was to be prepared by directives issued during the transitional period, therefore became unconditional on the expiry of that period.

25. The provisions of that article abolish all discrimination against the person providing the service by reason of his nationality or the fact that he is established in a Member State other than that in which the service is to be provided.

26. Therefore, at least as regards the specific requirement of nationality or of residence, Articles 59 and 60 impose a well-defined obligation, the fulfilment of which by the Member States cannot be delayed or jeopardized by the absence of provisions which were to be adopted in pursuance of powers conferred under Articles 63 and 66.

The Court here identified two reasons for the Treaty provisions on the adoption of directives: first, to abolish restrictions and, secondly, to facilitate the freedom to provide services. An example of the latter would be the adoption of directives to harmonize or provide for mutual recognition of qualifications. In so far as the first was concerned, where the restriction was a straightforward restriction on the ground of nationality or place of establishment, the ECJ considered that no directive was necessary and the provisions of Article 49 (ex Article 59) could be relied on directly by the end of the transitional period. The residence requirement in issue in the case was a particularly straightforward infringement of that Treaty provision, given that the precise aim of the provision was to abolish state restrictions on the freedom to provide services which were imposed on non-resident providers.

Although the lawyer in this case was a national who sought to rely, in the Member State of his own nationality, on the provisions of Article 49 (ex Article 59), this did not present a possible 'internal situation' problem since that Article, by contrast with Article 43 (ex Article 52), does not expressly restrict its coverage to the situation of a national in a Member State other than that of her nationality. Instead the relevant factor for the application of Article 49 is that the provider must be established in a Member State other than that of the person for whom the service is to be provided. The provider may rely on Article 49 as against the State he or she is established in, so long as the services are provided for persons established in another Member

State.[164] The ECJ has ruled on several occasions since *Van Binsbergen* that restrictions imposed on the basis of residence are liable to operate mainly to the detriment of nationals of other Member States, since non-residents are in the majority of cases foreigners.[165]

(b) THE SCOPE OF ARTICLE 49 (EX ARTICLE 59)

(i) THE NEED FOR AN INTER-STATE ELEMENT

As in the context of workers and establishment, the 'wholly internal situation' restriction also applies to the chapter on services. In *Debauve*, criminal proceedings were brought against Belgian cable television companies for infringing a prohibition on the transmission of broadcasts of commercial advertisements in Belgium,[166] and the ECJ held that 'the provisions of the Treaty on freedom to provide services cannot be applied to activities whose relevant elements are confined within a single Member State'.[167] A different outcome was reached in *Koestler*, which concerned a bank in France carrying out certain stock-exchange orders and account transactions for a customer established in France.[168] Despite the fact that both the provider and the recipient of services were established in the same Member State, the ECJ ruled that there was a provision of services within the meaning of Article 50 (ex Article 60) because the customer moved, before the contractual relationship with the bank was terminated, to establish himself in Germany.

In *Coditel*[169] and *Bond van Adverteerders*,[170] which, like *Debauve*, concerned the provision of broadcasting services, the ECJ was asked whether there could be a provision of services within the meaning of the Treaty where the providers and recipients were firmly established within the same Member State. It will be remembered that Article 59 (now Article 49) refers to a provider who is established 'in a State of the Community other than that of the person for whom the services are intended'. This requirement did not appear to be fulfilled on the facts as presented in these two cases, but there was a certain inter-state element, in that the substance of the services, the cable television broadcasts, originated in a different Member State. The ECJ did not answer the question in *Coditel*, because it held that, even if the Treaty provisions did apply, the restriction could be justified by reference to the legitimate protection of industrial property rights.[171] Another opportunity to address the question arose in *Bond van Adverteerders*, but the Court again avoided it by identifying a provider and

---

[164] See, e.g., Cases C–18/93, *Corsica Ferries* [1994] ECR I–1783, para. 30; C–379/92, *Peralta* [1994] ECR I–3453, para. 40. For a 'wholly internal situation' in the services context see Case C–108/98, *RI.SAN* v. *Comune di Ischia* [1999] ECR I–5219.

[165] Case C–350/96, *Clean Car Autoservice* v. *Landeshauptmann von Wien* [1998] ECR I–2521 and C–224/97, *Ciola* v. *Land Vorarlberg* [1999] ECR I–2517.

[166] Case 52/79, n. 14 above.   [167] *Ibid.*, para. 9.

[168] Case 15/78, *Société Générale Alsacienne de Banque SA* v. *Koestler* [1978] ECR 1971.

[169] Case 62/79, *Compagnie Générale pour la Diffusion de la Télévision, Coditel* v. *SA Ciné Vog Films* [1980] ECR 881.

[170] Case 352/85, n. 98 above.   [171] Case 62/79, [1980] ECR 881, paras. 10 and 15.

recipient of services established in two different Member States.[172] And in *Deliège*, in which a Belgian sportswoman had challenged the selection rules of the Belgian Judo Federation, the ECJ rejected the argument that this was a wholly internal situation, relying on the fact that 'a degree of extraneity may derive in particular from the fact that an athlete participates in a competition in a Member State other than that in which he is established'.[173] Arguably, the ECJ—just as in the context of free movement of goods—is focusing increasingly on the mobility and availability of the service in question rather than emphasizing the *person*, i.e., the provider or the recipient, who is involved.[174]

(II) THE FREEDOM TO RECEIVE SERVICES

Article 49 (ex Article 59) expressly refers to the freedom to *provide* services, and Article 50 (ex Article 60) to the rights of the *provider* of services, and does not mention the recipient of the services. However, Article 1 of Directive 64/221, which regulates the public-policy, security, and health derogations provided for in the Treaty, protects the position of a recipient of services who resides in or travels to another Member State for that purpose.[175] Article 1(b) of Directive 73/148 also requires the abolition of restrictions on the movement and residence of 'nationals wishing to go to another Member State as recipients of services'. It was not until *Luisi and Carbone*, however, which concerned the export of currency to pay for medical services, that the ECJ confirmed that the Treaty Articles themselves cover the situation of recipients as well as providers of services, and ruled that the freedom for the recipient to move was the necessary corollary of the freedom for the provider:

16. It follows that the freedom to provide services includes the freedom, for the recipients of services, to go to another Member State in order to receive a service there, without being obstructed by restrictions, even in relation to payments, and that tourists, persons receiving medical treatment and persons travelling for the purposes of education or business are to be regarded as recipients of services.[176]

This holding was confirmed in several later judgments,[177] most notably in *Cowan*, in which the ECJ held that the refusal, under the French criminal compensation scheme, to compensate a British tourist who had been attacked while in Paris was a restriction within the meaning of Article 49 (ex Article 59), without the ECJ specifying exactly what service he had received.[178]

---

[172] Case 352/85, n. 98 above, paras. 14–15. See, however, the Opinion of the AG in the case, arguing that certain services, such as broadcasting, were neither domestic nor transfrontier but actually 'without frontiers': [1988] ECR 2085, 2114. See the subsequent 'TV without frontiers' Broadcasting Directive 89/552 [1989] OJ L298/23.

[173] Cases C–51/96 & C–191/97, *Deliège* v. *Ligue Francophone de Judi et Disciplines Associées ASBL* [2000] ECR I–2549, para. 59. See S. van den Bogaert (2000) 25 *ELRev.* 554.

[174] See the discussion on the cases concerning cross-border access to health care, below. For more general discussion see V. Hatzopoulos 'Recent Developments of the Case Law of the ECJ in the Field of Services' (2000) 37 *CMLRev.* 43, and J. Snell, *Goods and Services in EC Law* (Oxford University Press, 2002).

[175] [1963–4] OJ Spec.Ed. 117. See Ch. 19.

[176] Cases 286/82 & 26/83, *Luisi and Carbone* v. *Ministero del Tesoro* [1984] ECR 377.

[177] See, e.g., Cases C–17/00, *De Coster* v. *Collège des Bourgmestre et échevins de Watermael-Boitsford* [2001] ECR I–9445, C–294/97, *Eurowings Luftverkehrs AG* v. *Finanzamt Dortmund-Unna* [1999] ECR I–7447; and C–158/96, *Kohll* v. *Union des Caisses de Maladie* [1998] ECR I–1931.

[178] Case 186/87, *Cowan* v. *Le Trésor Public* [1989] ECR 195.

(iii) THE ECONOMIC NATURE OF THE SERVICES: REMUNERATION

Whether a provision of services falls within Articles 49 to 50 (ex Articles 59 to 60) of the Treaty depends not just on the inter-state element, but also on the services being economic in nature, in that they must be provided for remuneration. The ECJ has ruled that remunerated services do not lose their economic nature either because of an 'element of chance' inherent in the return, or because of the recreational or sporting nature of the services.[179] In *Deliège* the ECJ ruled further that 'that the mere fact that a sports association or federation unilaterally classifies its members as amateur athletes does not in itself mean that those members do not engage in economic activities'[180] and in *Bond van Adverteerders* the Court specified that the remuneration did not have to come from the recipient of the services, so long as there was remuneration from some party.[181] This was elaborated upon further in *Deliège* where the ECJ drew on its case law in the field of free movement of workers concerning economic activity which was not 'marginal or ancillary' and ruled:

56. In that connection, it must be Stated that sporting activities and, in particular, a high-ranking athlete's participation in an international competition are capable of involving the provision of a number of separate, but closely related, services which may fall within the scope of Article 59 of the Treaty even if some of those services are not paid for by those for whom they are performed. . .

57. For example, an organiser of such a competition may offer athletes an opportunity of engaging in their sporting activity in competition with others and, at the same time, the athletes, by participating in the competition, enable the organiser to put on a sports event which the public may attend, which television broadcasters may retransmit and which may be of interest to advertisers and sponsors. Moreover, the athletes provide their sponsors with publicity the basis for which is the sporting activity itself.[182]

But what if the remuneration for the service is provided by the state? This issue has been highlighted recently following a series of cases concerning cross-border access to medical and health-care services, which have threatened to disrupt the operation of national welfare systems.[183] The question first arose in the educational context in *Gravier*, where the ECJ was asked whether students receiving vocational training in a Member State other than that of their nationality were recipients of services within the meaning of Article 59 (now Article 49).[184] Although the Court did not address the

---

[179] Case C–275/92, *Schindler*, n. 15 above, paras. 33–4. See the similar rulings on the concept of an economic activity under Art. 39 (ex Art. 48) in Cases 36/74, *Walrave and Koch* v. *Association Union Cycliste Internationale* [1974] ECR 1405; C–415/93, *Bosman* [1995] ECR I–4921; C–51/96 & C–191/97, *Deliège* v. *Ligue Francophone de Judi et Disciplines Associées ASBL* [2000] ECR I–2549; and C–176/96, *Lehtonen* v. *FRBSB* [2000] ECR I–2681.

[180] Cases C–51/96 & C–191/97, n. 179 above.

[181] Case 352/85, n. 98 above. See also Case C–159/90, *SPUC* v. *Grogan* [1991] ECR I–4685 where student distributors of information in Ireland concerning abortion services in the UK received no payment or other remuneration from the providers of the actual service in the second Member State, and, in the absence of such an economic link between the information ban and the freedom to provide the service, the connection between them was 'too tenuous' to attract the application of Art. 49 (ex Art. 59) of the Treaty.

[182] N. 180 above.

[183] Cases C–120/95, *Decker* [1998] ECR I–1831 (albeit dealing with goods rather than services); C–158/96, *Kohll* v. *Union des Caisses de Maladie* [1998] ECR I–1931; C–368/98, *Vanbraekel* v. *ANMC* [2001] ECR I–5363; and C–157/99, *Geraets-Smits* v. *Stichting Ziekenfonds, Peerbooms* v. *Stichting CZ Groep Zorgverzekeringen* [2001] ECR I–5473.

[184] Case 293/83, *Gravier* v. *City of Liège* [1985] ECR 593, 603, [1985] 3 CMLR 1.

question, Advocate General Slynn considered that educational services were not remunerated within the meaning of Article 60 (now Article 50) if the remuneration came from the state through public taxes. The ECJ in the later *Humbel* case concerning a course taught under the national educational system, adopted a similar view.

Case 263/86, Belgium v. Humbel
[1988] ECR 5365

17. The essential characteristic of remuneration thus lies in the fact that it constitutes consideration for the service in question, and is normally agreed upon between the provider and the recipient of the service.

18. That characteristic is, however, absent in the case of courses provided under the national education system. First of all, the State, in establishing and maintaining such a system, is not seeking to engage in gainful activity but is fulfilling its duties towards its own population in the social, cultural and educational fields. Secondly, the system in question is, as a general rule, funded from the public purse and not by pupils or their parents.

19. The nature of the activity is not affected by the fact that pupils or their parents must sometimes pay teaching or enrolment fees in order to make a certain contribution to the operating expenses of the system.

Following the logic of this decision, the ECJ in *Wirth* ruled that, although most institutions of higher education were financed from public funds, those which sought to make a profit and were financed mainly out of private funds, for example by students or their parents, could constitute providers of services within Articles 49 and 50 (ex Articles 59 and 60).[185] The distinction between publicly and privately remunerated services on which these cases are based is however a difficult one, as a series of subsequent cases concerning access to cross-border health-care demonstrate.

In *Kohll*,[186] which was decided on the same day as the parallel *Decker*[187] case concerning free movement of goods, the ECJ took the view that treatment provided by an orthodontist established in a different Member State from the applicant amounted to a service provided for remuneration, and that the requirement to obtain prior authorization from the competent social-security institution in the applicant's home state before the cost would be reimbursed constituted an unjustified restriction on the

---

[185] Case C–109/92, *Wirth* v. *Landeshauptstadt Hannover* [1993] ECR I–6447. See also Cases C–159/90, *SPUC* v. *Grogan* [1991] ECR I–4685 and the comment by S. O'Leary (1992) 17 *ELRev.* 138; and C–70/95, *Sodemare* v. *Regione Lombardia* [1997] ECR I–3395, in which the ECJ considered the applicability of Art. 49 (ex Art. 59) to Italian conditions on the involvement of economic operators in the provision of the state's social-welfare services, such as the running of old people's homes.

[186] Case C–158/96, *Kohll* v. *Union des Caisses de Maladie* [1998] ECR I–1931. For a note on *Decker* and *Kohll* see P. Cabral (1999) 24 *ELRev.* 387. For a case concerning non-discriminatory access to medical care under Article 6 EC, see C–411 *Ferlini* v. *CHL*, n. 33, above.

[187] Case C–120/95, *Decker* [1998] ECR I–1831, which concerned a prior authorization requirement from the competent social-security institution before reimbursement of spectacles purchased in another Member State could be made.

freedom to receive cross-border services. Because the individual concerned in *Kohll* had actually paid in another Member State for the service received, there was no real argument about the commercial nature of the service nor about whether Article 49 (ex Article 59) was applicable. Further, in both the *Decker* and *Kohll* cases, the ECJ rejected justificatory arguments to the effect that the financial balance of the social security scheme would be upset, since the expenses were to be reimbursed at exactly the same rate as that applicable in the home state.

The cases of *Geraets-Smits/Peerbooms*[188] and *Vanbraekel*,[189] however, involved a more complex situation in which the financial balance of the national social-insurance systems would certainly have been affected. The cases therefore demonstrate more vividly the potentially disruptive effects on national welfare systems of the decision to bring essential and publicly organized services within the scope of the Treaty's free movement provisions. In *Geraets-Smits/Peerbooms*, the two applicants were insured for their medical costs under a Dutch social-insurance scheme for persons whose income is below a certain level. Some of the funding in this scheme was derived from individual premiums, some from the state and some from subsidization by other private insurance funds. Each of the applicants received medical treatment outside the Netherlands without having obtained prior authorization from the fund, apparently because of the restrictive conditions under which such authorization would be granted. The first condition was that the treatment must be regarded as 'normal in the professional circles concerned' and the second that the treatment must be 'necessary' for the person in question, in the sense that adequate care could not be provided without undue delay by a care provider which had entered into an agreement with the sickness-insurance fund in the home state. The question referred to the ECJ was whether this particular kind of prior authorization requirement was prohibited by Articles 49 and 50 (ex Articles 59 and 60). The Court began by reaffirming that Member States retain the power to organize their social-security systems, subject to compliance with the rules of EC law, and went on to consider the argument made by several governments, in reliance on the *Humbel* case, that hospital services did not constitute an economic activity when provided free of charge under a sickness insurance scheme.

> C–157/99, Geraets-Smits v. Stichting Ziekenfonds,
> Peerbooms v. Stichting CZ Groep Zorgverzekeringen
> [2001] ECR I–5473

53. It is settled case-law that medical activities fall within the scope of Article 60 of the Treaty, there being no need to distinguish in that regard between care provided in a hospital environment and care provided outside such an environment. . . .

54. It is also settled case-law that the special nature of certain services does not remove them from the ambit of the fundamental principle of freedom of movement (Case 279/80 *Webb* [1981] ECR 3305, paragraph 10, and *Kohll*, paragraph 20), so that the fact that the national rules at

---

[188] For commentaries, see E. Steyger (2002) 29 *LIEI* 97, and G. Davies (2002) 29 *LIEI* 27.
[189] Case C–368/98, *Vanbraekel* v. *ANMC* [2001] ECR I–5363.

issue in the main proceedings are social security rules cannot exclude application of Articles 59 and 60 of the Treaty (*Kohll*, paragraph 21).

55. With regard more particularly to the argument that hospital services provided in the context of a sickness insurance scheme providing benefits in kind, such as that governed by the ZFW, should not be classified as services within the meaning of Article 60 of the Treaty, it should be noted that, far from falling under such a scheme, the medical treatment at issue in the main proceedings, which was provided in Member States other than those in which the persons concerned were insured, did lead to the establishments providing the treatment being paid directly by the patients. It must be accepted that a medical service provided in one Member State and paid for by the patient should not cease to fall within the scope of the freedom to provide services guaranteed by the Treaty merely because reimbursement of the costs of the treatment involved is applied for under another Member State's sickness insurance legislation which is essentially of the type which provides for benefits in kind.

56. Furthermore, the fact that hospital medical treatment is financed directly by the sickness insurance funds on the basis of agreements and pre-set scales of fees is not in any event such as to remove such treatment from the sphere of services within the meaning of Article 60 of the Treaty.

57. First, it should be borne in mind that Article 60 of the Treaty does not require that the service be paid for by those for whom it is performed. . .

58. Second, Article 60 of the Treaty states that it applies to services normally provided for remuneration and it has been held that, for the purposes of that provision, the essential characteristic of remuneration lies in the fact that it constitutes consideration for the service in question (*Humbel*, paragraph 17). In the present cases, the payments made by the sickness insurance funds under the contractual arrangements provided for by the ZFW, albeit set at a flat rate, are indeed the consideration for the hospital services and unquestionably represent remuneration for the hospital which receives them and which is engaged in an activity of an economic character.

The Court then went on to conclude that the requirement of authorization subject to the conditions of necessity and 'normality' was indeed a barrier to the freedom to provide and receive services, but that in this context, unlike in the cases of *Decker* and *Kohll*, the restriction was in principle capable of being 'objectively justified' in the interests of maintaining a balanced medical and hospital service open to all, or of preventing the risk of the social-security system's financial balance being seriously undermined, or for essential public-health reasons under Article 46 (ex Article 56). However, the Court clearly indicated that the two conditions must be applied fairly in a non-discriminatory manner, so that the condition that the treatment sought should be 'normal' must, for example, take into account the findings of international medical science, and the condition concerning the 'necessity' should be applied to refuse authorization only if the same or equally effective treatment cannot be obtained without undue delay from an establishment with which the insured person's sickness insurance fund has contractual arrangements.

The *Vanbraekel* judgment which was given shortly afterwards was very similar, except that it involved also an interpretation of Regulation 1408/71.[190] The ECJ ruled

[190] *Ibid.*

that national legislation which failed to guarantee a person covered by its social insurance scheme, and who obtained prior authorization to receive hospital treatment in another Member State in accordance with Regulation 1408/71, a level of payment equivalent to that to which he would have been entitled if he had received hospital treatment in the Member State in which he was insured, was contrary to Article 49 (ex Article 59) EC. Such legislation could not be justified on the basis that it was intended to prevent the financing of the social-security system from being undermined, since the reimbursement at an equivalent level would not impose any additional financial burden on the sickness-insurance scheme of that state by comparison with the reimbursement to be made if hospital treatment had been provided in that latter state.

While the outcomes of these cases, and the *Geraets-Smits* case in particular, are not in themselves alarming, since they acknowledge the importance of the stable financing of national social-insurance systems and the justifiability of measures which seek to maintain a balanced and manageable national health-care system, they also undoubtedly open up to the rigours of the Treaty rules and to cross-border economic activity, some of the core aspects of national welfare systems. Articles 49–50 (ex Articles 59–60) apply to any service, however essential, which is 'provided for remuneration', and the line between publicly and privately remunerated services remains uncertain. Health services funded through a sickness-insurance fund of the kind at issue in the *Kohll*, *Geraets-Smits*, and *Vanbraekel* cases clearly do not fall within the *Humbel* exception for public-service provision where the state was described as 'not seeking to engage in gainful activity but is fulfilling its duties towards its own population in the social, cultural and educational field'. It remains to be seen to what extent other systems of mixed public and private financing of welfare and social services will come within the scope of the Treaty rules.

G. Davies, 'Welfare as a Service' (2002) 29 LIEI 27, 35–6

To summarise, the provision of essential welfare services is not privileged to be excluded from the Treaty, *Humbel* comments about duty notwithstanding. This would neither be a legally clear, nor a logical approach, nor would it fit with the other cases, which emphasise how even very important services can be included. Rather, whether welfare is a service depends how it is organised, and the most convincing defining element to emerge from the cases is the separateness of the paying and providing institutions. It makes sense that this should be a defining factor, since it creates a potential market-like system. The payer and recipient are not confined to a particular provider or providers by the very nature of the system, but rather by contingent elements of it, such as their own decision, or government rules. There is a structural potential for choice. Given that, it is logical that the Treaty should then begin to supervise whether such choice is unfairly restricted. Put another way, the Court will accept the essential nature of the systems Member States devise, but will police their operation.

. . .

There is no separate requirement of 'commercialism'. This is rather something that follows from the commerce-like organisation of the service. The motivations of the parties, in particular the presence of a profit-motive, and their formal public or private status are also not definitive, or even important. The State is quite capable of being a market actor, even in areas where it also has a responsibility.

(IV) CAN ILLEGAL ACTIVITIES CONSTITUTE SERVICES WITHIN ARTICLES 49–50 (EX ARTICLES 59–60)?

Several cases have raised the question of 'illegal' or 'immoral' services, concerning activities which are lawful in certain States but not in others. Clearly if someone established in a Member State in which a particular activity is lawful wishes to provide services in another Member State in which it is not lawful, the second state may have very good reasons for restricting the provision of that service. The first question in this context is whether such activities, on the legality of which the Member States cannot agree, can constitute 'services' at all within Community law.

In *Koestler*, the ECJ ruled that Germany's refusal to allow a French bank which had provided services for a German national, including a stock-exchange transaction which was treated as an illegal wagering contract in Germany but not in France, to recover from that client was not contrary to Article 49 (ex Article 59) if the same refusal would apply to banks established in Germany.[191] Despite the fact that the services were considered illegal in Germany, the ECJ ruled that the conclusion of the wagering contract could constitute a service, although the Member State was justified in restricting that service by refusing to allow the bank to sue for recovery. In *Grogan*, the Court considered whether the provision of abortion was a service within the meaning of the Treaty, in order to determine whether the restriction in one Member State on information about the provision of abortion in another state was contrary to Article 49.[192] In response to the argument that abortion could not be categorized as a service on the ground that it was immoral, the ECJ ruled that it was not for it 'to substitute its assessment for that of the legislature in those Member States where the activities are practiced legally'.[193] However, the fact that abortion constitutes a service within Article 49 does not mean that a Member State in which that activity is illegal may not prohibit or restrict the provision of such services in its territory from providers who are established in another Member State, as was made clear in *Koestler*. Less clear, even after *Grogan*, is whether a Member State can restrict the access of its citizens to services in another Member State, where those services are prohibited or restricted within the regulating State.[194]

In *Schindler*, the defendants were acting as agents on behalf of a German public lottery, seeking to promote that lottery by post and otherwise within the UK, and they were charged with an office under the UK lotteries legislation.[195] When the case was referred to the ECJ, several Member States argued that lotteries were not an 'economic activity' within the meaning of the Treaty, since they were traditionally prohibited or operated by public authorities in the public interest. The Court rejected this argument, ruling that lotteries were services provided for remuneration (the price of

---

[191] Case 15/78, n. 168 above.   [192] Case C–159/90, n. 181 above.   [193] *Ibid.*, para. 20.

[194] The AG in *Grogan*, n. 181 above, took the view that the restriction on information in the case in question was disproportionate. For an interesting example of an indirect restriction on access to artificial insemination services in another Member State which arose in the UK but was not referred to the ECJ, see *R. v. Human Fertilisation and Embryology Authority, ex p. Diane Blood* [1997] 2 CMLR 591.

[195] Case C–275/92, *Customs and Excise v. Schindler* [1994] ECR I–1039.

the lottery ticket), and that, although they were closely regulated in some Member States, they were not totally prohibited in any:

32. In these circumstances, lotteries cannot be regarded as activities whose harmful nature causes them to be prohibited in all the Member States and whose position under Community law may be likened to that of activities involving illegal products (see, in relation to drugs, the judgment in Case 294/82, *Einberger* v. *Hauptzollamt Freiburg* [1984] ECR 1177) even though, as the Belgian and Luxembourg Governments point out, the law of certain Member States treats gaming contracts as void. Even if the morality of lotteries is at least questionable, it is not for the Court to substitute its assessment for that of the legislatures of the Member States where the activity is practised legally.

Similarly in *Jany*, the ECJ ruled that the relevant provisions of the EU's Association Agreement with Poland on freedom of establishment and services were to have the same meaning and scope as those under the EC Treaty, so that 'the activitiy of prostitution pursued in a self-employed capacity can be regarded as a service provided for remuneration'.[196] In response to arguments based on the immoral nature of the services, the Court cited its rulings in *Grogan* and *Schindler*, and declared that 'far from being prohibited in all Member States, prostitution is tolerated, even regulated, by most of those States'.[197] The result of these rulings appears to be that provided it is lawful in some Member States (*quaere* whether one Member State would be sufficient), a remunerated activity constitutes a service within the meaning of Articles 49–50 (ex Articles 59–60) EC, although other Member States remain free to regulate and restrict it, so long as they do so proportionately and without arbitrary discrimination on grounds of nationality or place of establishment.[198]

(V) ARE RESTRICTIONS ON SOCIAL BENEFITS CONTRARY TO ARTICLE 49 (EX ARTICLE 59)?

We saw in the context of establishment that, despite the absence of secondary legislation such as Regulation 1612/68 for workers, restrictions on certain social advantages and benefits which are linked to the exercise of the self-employed activity may fall within the prohibition in the Treaty. The same is true of the free movement of services. In the Italian housing case, discussed also in the establishment context above, the ECJ ruled that a nationality requirement for access to reduced-rate mortgage loans and to social housing was contrary to Article 43 (ex Article 52) on freedom of establishment, but the Italian Government argued that access to publicly built housing could not possibly be relevant to the exercise of the right to provide services, which was precisely the right to provide services without having to have a place of residence in that state.

---

[196] Case C–268/99, *Jany* v. *Staatsecretaris van Justitie* [2001] ECR I–8615.

[197] *Ibid.*, para. 57.

[198] The ECJ's conclusion in *Schindler* that the UK legislation was justified on public-policy grounds had been criticized for ignoring the discrimination practised in favour of national small-scale lotteries, and for applying the proportionality test excessively loosely: see the comment by G. Straetmans (2000) 37 *CMLRev.* 991 on the subsequent gaming cases, Cases C–124/97, *Läärä* [1999] ECR I–6067 and C–67/98, *Zenatti* [1999] ECR I–7289.

Case 63/86, Commission v. Italy
[1988] ECR 29

18. It is true, as the Italian Government has contended, that in practice not all instances of establishment give rise to the same need to find permanent housing and that as a rule that need is not felt in the case of the provision of services. It is also true that in most cases the provider of services will not satisfy the conditions, of a non-discriminatory nature, bound up with the objectives of the legislation on social housing.

19. However, it cannot be held to be *a priori* out of the question that a person, whilst retaining his principal place of establishment in one Member State, may be led to pursue his occupational activities in another Member State for such an extended period that he needs to have permanent housing there and that he may satisfy the conditions of a non-discriminatory nature for access to social housing. It follows that no distinction can be drawn between different forms of establishment and that providers of services cannot be excluded from the benefit of the fundamental principle of national treatment.

Thus, even if temporary providers of services would be unlikely to satisfy the eligibility criteria for social housing, the ECJ ruled that they must in principle be given the benefit of access to such on the same terms as nationals. As in the case of establishment, however, if a restriction on social benefits is to be covered by the Treaty, the benefit must be in some way connected with facilitating the exercise of the occupation.

In *Cowan*, a British tourist in France was refused State compensation for victims of violent crime which was available to nationals and to residents.[199] The ECJ cited the general prohibition on discrimination 'within the scope of application of this Treaty' in Article 12 (ex Article 6),[200] and referred to its ruling in *Luisi and Carbone*, to the effect that tourists were covered by Article 49 (ex Article 59) as recipients of services:

When Community law guarantees a natural person the freedom to go to another Member State, the protection of that person from harm in the Member State in question, on the same basis as that of nationals and persons residing there, is a corollary of that freedom of movement. It follows that the prohibition of discrimination is applicable to recipients of services within the meaning of the Treaty as regards protection against the risk of assault and the right to obtain financial compensation provided for by national law when that risk materialises. The fact that the compensation at issue is financed by the Public Treasury cannot alter the rules regarding the protection of the rights guaranteed by the Treaty.[201]

And in proceedings against Spain, the Court ruled that a system under which Spanish nationals and residents were entitled to free admission into national museums, while other Member State nationals over 21 had to pay an entrance fee, was

[199] Case 186/87, *Cowan*, n.178 above.
[200] For cases in which the ECJ ruled that Art. 12 (ex Art. 6, originally Art. 7) EC could be the sole basis for a claim of discrimination in treatment, without being linked to another specific Treaty provision, see Cases C–92/92 & C–326/92, *Phil Collins v. Imtrat Handelsgesellschaft* [1993] ECR I–5145, C–274/96, *Bickel and Franz* [1998] ECR I–7637, and C–411/98, *Ferlini*, n. 33 above. That Art. will not however apply where another specific Treaty provision such as Art. 43 (ex Art. 52) applies: see Case C–1/93, *Halliburton*, n. 137 above.
[201] [1989] ECR 195, para. 17.

contrary to Articles 12 and 49 (ex Articles 6 and 59) of the Treaty.[202] At first sight, cases like this and like *Cowan* seem to be at odds with *Humbel*, where the Court ruled that Article 49 did not cover the receipt of state-funded services within the educational, social, and cultural fields. Since the state would pay the compensation in *Cowan*, and would presumably fund the museum in the Spanish case, why does a refusal of such benefits constitute a restriction on the freedom to receive services under the Treaty? The answer would appear to be that the compensation in *Cowan* and the entrance fee in the Spanish case do not in themselves consitute the 'service' being received. Instead the relevant services in these cases, although not specifically identified by the ECJ, must be other services (such as hotels, restaurants, etc.) for which, as tourists, the recipients provide remuneration. If, whilst in the course of a temporary stay in a Member State in order to avail themselves of remunerated services of this nature, such tourists are denied equal treatment with nationals in matters such as compensation for assault and entry fees to museums, they may be able to invoke Article 59 (now Article 49) of the Treaty.[203] The denial of such benefits can be seen to be at least loosely linked with the enjoyment of services as a tourist, although in the case of *Cowan* in particular, the link may seem rather tenuous.[204] However, to take a different example, it seems unlikely that if, during the course of a two-month holiday as a tourist in another Member State, a Community national invoked Article 49 (ex Article 59) to challenge the refusal of admission on equal terms to a three-week educational course which was free for nationals, the Court would find any breach of that provision.

(c) JUSTIFYING RESTRICTIONS ON THE FREE MOVEMENT OF SERVICES

As in the case of workers and establishment, once a suspect restriction on the free movement of services is found to exist, it is open to the Member States to try to justify it either under the Treaty exceptions or under a broader category of Court-developed exceptions. However, despite the broad approach adopted by the ECJ towards the notion of a 'restriction' in the field of free movement of services, not every rule which has been challenged under Article 49 (ex Article 59) has been found by it to constitute a restriction within the meaning of that provision.[205]

---

[202] Case C–45/93, *Commission* v. *Spain* [1994] ECR I–911.

[203] For cases which did not concern tourists, but others who may be seeking or providing inter-State services, see Cases C–43/95, *Data Delecta and Forsberg* v. *MSL Dynamics* [1996] ECR I–4661; C–323/95, *Hayes* v. *Kronenberger* [1997] ECR I–1171; and C–122/96, *Saldanha and MTS Securities Corporation* v. *Hiross Holdings* [1997] ECR I–5325 on national procedures requiring non-residents to provide security for costs in litigation, which the ECJ held to be capable of having an effect, even though indirect, on trade in goods and services between Member States.

[204] See also Case C–177/94, *Perfili* [1996] ECR I–161, in which the ECJ could not see how an Italian rule which required someone bringing civil litigation through a representative to grant that person a special power of attorney could be in breach of Art. 43 or 49 (ex Art. 52 or 59).

[205] In Cases C–51/96 & C–191/97, *Deliège*, n. 179 above, for example, the Judo Federation selection rules for competitions did not determine access to the labour market and were 'inherent in the conduct of a high-level international sports event'; therefore they did not amount to a restriction under Art. 49 (ex Art. 59) and did not require justification. See also Case C–190/98, *Graf* v. *Filzmoser Maschinenbau* [2000] ECR I–493 in the context of workers.

The three grounds of exception set out in Article 46 (ex Article 56), which permit Member States to discriminate on grounds of public policy, security, and health, are made applicable to the field of services by Article 55 (ex Article 66) EC. The nature of these exceptions and the secondary legislation relating to them are discussed in more detail in the next chapter. However, alongside these limited express exceptions, the ECJ has also developed a justificatory test for workers, services, and establishment alike which is similar to the *Cassis de Dijon* 'rule of reason' in the free movement of goods context.[206] Although in the area of goods, these open-ended exceptions have generally been referred to as 'mandatory requirements', we see that in the field of services the term 'imperative requirements' or the generic term 'objective justification' is more often used. The origins of this approach in the services context can be found in the case of *Van Binsbergen*.[207]

We have seen in that case that the Member States had argued there were greater dangers in the area of freedom to provide services than in the area of establishment, since the evasion of national regulation and control would be easier where the providers of services were not resident, or only temporarily rather than permanently present, within the state where the service was provided. These concerns—which indeed are to some extent reflected in the distinction between establishment and services in the Commission's proposed consolidation directive on professional qualifications[208]—were acknowledged by Advocate General Mayras in *Van Binsbergen*:

A fundamental aspect of the difference between, on the one hand, mere occasional provision of services, even temporary activities and, on the other hand, establishment, is that the person providing services falls outside the competence and control of the national authorities of the country where the services are provided.[209]

The ECJ addressed the issue by indicating that, although a residence requirement would probably be excessive in this case, it might not always be so:[210]

12. However, taking into account the particular nature of the services to be provided, specific requirements imposed on the person providing the service cannot be considered incompatible with the Treaty where they have as their purpose the application of professional rules justified by the general good—in particular rules relating to the organization, qualifications, professional ethics, supervision and liability—which are binding upon any person established in the State in which the service is provided, where the person providing the service would escape from the ambit of those rules being established in another Member State.

. . .

14. In accordance with those principles, the requirement that persons whose functions are to assist the administration of justice must be permanently established for professional purposes within the jurisdiction of certain courts or tribunals cannot be considered incompatible with the provisions of Article 59 and 60, where such requirement is objectively justified by the need

---

[206] See Ch. 15.　　[207] Case 33/74, n. 6 above.
[208] COM(2002)119. See n. 13 above and text.
[209] [1974] ECR 1299, 1317.
[210] See also Case 39/75, *Coenen*, n. 153 above, para. 9, in which the ECJ ruled that a residence requirement could be justified only where no other less restrictive rule would suffice.

to ensure observance of professional rules of conduct connected, in particular, with the administration of justice and with respect for professional ethics.[211]

Several conditions were laid down by the ECJ in these passages to be satisfied if a restriction on the freedom to provide services is to be compatible with Article 49 (ex Article 59). In the *first* place, the restriction must be adopted in pursuance of a legitimate public interest which is not incompatible with Community aims. In this context, the ECJ has ruled—mirroring one of the restrictions imposed on the scope of the Treaty derogations by Directive 64/221—that the purpose of a non-discriminatory national rule will be not legitimate if it pursues an *economic* aim. Thus the aim of protecting a particular economic sector within the Member State has been held not to be legitimate in this context,[212] whereas on the other hand the mainten-ance of the financial balance of the social-security system was a legitimate aim.[213] In *Finalarte* the ECJ ruled that that the aim of a measure is something to be determined 'objectively' by the national court,[214] although obviously the ECJ retains the ultimate role of pronouncing on the legitimacy of the aim.

The *second* condition is that the restriction must be one which is equally applicable to persons established within the state, and which must be applied without dis-crimination. In a series of cases concerning broadcasting restrictions, for example, the Court held that, although the promotion of cultural policy through ensuring a balance of programmes and restricting the content and frequency of advertisements was a legitimate aim, it must not be pursued in a discriminatory or protectionist manner.[215]

The *third* condition for 'objective justification' is that the restriction imposed on the provider of services must be proportionate to the need to observe the legitimate rules in question. The proportionality test entails examining whether the rule is 'suitable' or 'appropriate' in achieving its (legitimate) aim, and whether that aim could not be satisfied by other, less restrictive means. In *Van Binsbergen* itself, the Court ruled that the public interest in the proper administration of justice could be ensured by requiring an address for service to be maintained within the state, rather than a residence there. This test for objective justification was also seen above in paragraph 37 of the ruling in *Gebhard* in relation to freedom of establishment,[216]

---

[211] Case 33/74, n. 6 above. For a case in which the protection of creditors (and the 'sound administra-tion of justice') was held to be an important objective justifying the imposition of restrictions on the practice of debt-collection, see Case C–3/95, *Reisebüro Broede* v. *Sandker* [1996] ECR I–6511. See more recently, on restrictions preventing legal advocates from practising in partnership with accountants, Case C–309/99, *Wouters* v. *Algemene Raad van de Nederlandse Orde van Advocaten* [2002] ECR I–nyr, paras. 97–99,122.

[212] Case C–398/95, *SETTG* v. *Ypourgos Ergasias* [1997] ECR I–3091, paras. 22–23. See also Case C–49/98, *Finalarte Sociedade Construçao Civil* v. *Urlaubs- und Lohnausgleichskasse der Bauwirtschaft* [2001] ECR I–7831, para 39.

[213] Case C–158/96, *Kohll* v. *Union des Caisses de Maladie* [1998] ECR I–1931, para. 41.

[214] Case C–49/98, n. 212 above, paras. 40–41.

[215] See Cases 352/85, n. 98 above; C–288/89, *Stichting Collectiëve Antennevoorsiening Gouda* v. *Commis-sariaat voor de Media* [1991] ECR I–4007; and C–353/89, *Commission* v. *Netherlands* [1991] ECR I–4069. The subsequent adoption of the Broadcasting Dir. 89/552 [1989] OJ L298/23, which was enacted with the aim of ensuring freedom to provide services and freedom of establishment in the sphere of television, generated a further spate of litigation: e.g., Cases C–222/94, *Commission* v. *UK* [1996] ECR I–4025; C–11/95, *Commission* v. *Belgium* [1996] ECR I–4115; C–14/96, *Criminal Proceedings against Denuit* [1997] ECR I–2785.

[216] N. 10 above.

although it had been developed considerably earlier in the context of services in cases such as *Webb* and *Van Wesemael*:[217]

In *Webb*, the manager of a company established and licensed in the UK to supply manpower, which provided staff on a temporary basis for businesses located in the Netherlands, was prosecuted for doing so in the absence of a licence issued by the Dutch authorities. The ECJ ruled that the freedom to provide services:

may be restricted only by provisions which are justified by the general good and which are imposed on all persons or undertakings operating in the said State in so far as that interest is not safeguarded by the provisions to which the provider of the service is subject in the Member State of his establishment.[218]

A crucial factor in determining the proportionality and legitimacy of a restriction is therefore whether the provider is subject to similar regulation in the Member State in which that person is established.[219] If the requirement duplicates a condition already satisfied, it imposes a double burden on the provider of a service, and it therefore cannot be justified. Applying the objective justification test to the licence requirement in *Webb*, the ECJ held that the provision of manpower was sensitive from an occupational and a social point of view, so that the aims of preserving the interests of the workforce and of ensuring good relations on the labour market were part of a legitimate State policy.[220] Thus the *aim* of the licence requirement was legitimate, and the obligation imposed would be proportionate so long as it was applied equally to nationals and non-nationals, its requirements did not coincide with those in the state of establishment, and the host Member State took into account the relevant evidence and guarantees already furnished by the service provider in the Member State of his establishment.

A further condition of the test for justification which has not been frequently expressed by the ECJ is the requirement that the restrictive measure should respect the fundamental rights which are part of Community law and a condition for its legality.[221] Although this position has been affirmed by the ECJ in its case law on freedom of establishment and the free movement of goods[222] we have seen in Chapter 8 that not all members of the Court support it.[223]

[217] Cases 110–111/78, *Ministère Public* v. *Van Wesemael* [1979] ECR 35 and 279/80, *Criminal proceedings against Webb* [1981] ECR 3305.
[218] *Ibid.*, para. 17.
[219] See Case C–272/95, *Guiot and Climatec* [1996] ECR I–1905, C–369/96 & 376/96, *Jean-Claude Arblade*. [1999] ECR I–8453.
[220] Contrast Case C–113/89, *Rush Portuguesa* v. *Office National d'Immigration* [1990] ECR I–1417, where the ECJ ruled that the requirement of work permits for members of staff who were non-member State nationals of a company providing temporary services in a Member State other than that in which it was established was incompatible with Art. 59 (now Art. 49). Also Case C–43/93, *Raymond Vander Elst* v. *Office des Migrations Internationales* [1994] ECR I–3803. In both cases, however, it was permissible for the host Member State to apply its own labour legislation to these workers. See further Cases C–369/96 & C–376/96, *Arblade* [1999] ECR I–8453; C–493/99, *Commission* v. *Germany* [2001] ECR I–8163; C–165/98, *Mazzoleni, Guillame and others* [2001] ECR I–2189; and C–164/99, *Portugaia Construções* [2002] ECR I–nyr.
[221] *Opinion 2/94 on Accession by the Community to the ECHR* [1996] ECR I–1759, para. 34.
[222] See Cases C–260/89, *ERT* v. *DEP* [1991] ECR 2925, para. 42 in the context of the Treaty derogations, and C–368/95, *Vereinigte Familiapress Zeitungsverlags und Vertriebs-GmbH* v. *Heinrich Bauer Verlag* [1997] ECR I–3689 in the context of 'mandatory requirements' concerning the free movement of goods.
[223] See F. Jacobs, 'Human Rights in the EU: The Role of the Court of Justice' (2001) 26 *ELRev.* 331, discussed in Ch. 8, n. 110 and text. See, more recently, however, C–60/00, *Carpenter*, n. 18 above.

Although the proportionality test in principle is for the national court to apply to the restriction on the facts of the case, the ECJ frequently indicates which requirements or restrictions may be unnecessary/disproportionate in the context of the preliminary reference procedure,[224] or more directly in the context of infringement proceedings under Article 226 (ex Article 169),[225] such as the series of insurance services cases.[226] In the insurance cases the ECJ ruled that certain authorization requirements which were imposed on insurance undertakings which sought to provide particular kinds of direct insurance services through intermediaries or agents served a public-interest aim (which was not covered by existing EC insurance directives), they were non-discriminatory in application and, provided they did not duplicate the conditions of the state of establishment, they could be justified.[227] As regards the establishment condition, however, the ECJ ruled that a residence requirement had not been shown to be 'indispensable for attaining the objective pursued'.[228]

In the 'tourist guide' cases, the Court found licence requirements to be disproportionate, although they did not necessarily duplicate conditions already satisfied, and although the general interest in consumer protection and in the conservation of the national historical and artistic heritage could constitute a legitimate aim.[229] However, the licence requirement might not be to the benefit of the tourists since the inevitable bias towards local tour guides could mean they might be 'deprived of a guide familiar with their language, their interests and their expectations',[230] while freer competition could be more likely to improve the quality of tour guides to protect the interests of tourists.

In other cases the ECJ has rejected attempts to justify national restrictions by pointing to the fact that the purported aim of such restrictive measures may already be satisfied by the existence of EC legislation. Thus in Kohll[231] the ECJ rejected the Member States' invocation of the Treaty's public-health derogation to justify refusals to reimburse unauthorized dental treatment obtained in another Member State, indicating that the existence of EC directives harmonizing or co-ordinating the relevant professional qualifications provided sufficient guarantees in this respect. However, the ECJ has also indicated that in the absence of co-ordination of Member State

---

[224] See, e.g., Cases 16/78, *Choquet* [1978] ECR 2293 and C–193/94, *Skanavi and Chyssanthakopoulos* [1996] ECR I–929 on driving-licence requirements. In Case C–49/98, *Finalarte Sociedade Construçao Civil* v. *Urlaubs- und Lohnausgleichskasse der Bauwirtschaft* [2001] ECR I–7831, paras. 49–52, the Court gave a very directional set of guidelines on how the national court should assess whether the rules are a proportionate restriction. See also Case C–390/99, *Canal Satélite Digital* v. *Administracíon General del Estado* [2002] ECR I–nyr, paras. 34–42.

[225] See, e.g., the Lawyers' Services case, Case 427/85, *Commission* v. *Germany* [1988] ECR 1123, para. 26.

[226] Cases 205/84, *Commission* v. *Germany* [1986] ECR 3755, 206/84, *Commission* v. *Ireland* [1986] ECR 3817, 220/83, *Commission* v. *France* [1986] ECR 3663, and 252/83, *Commission* v. *Denmark* [1986] ECR 3713.

[227] For a case in which authorization procedures were held to go beyond what was necessary to maintain the quality of services provided, see Case C–58/98, *Josef Corsten* [2000] ECR I–7919.

[228] Case 205/84, [1986] ECR 3755, paras. 52–55.

[229] See Cases C–180/89, *Commission* v. *Italy* [1991] ECR I–709; C–154/89, *Commission* v. *France* [1991] ECR I–659; C–198/89, *Commission* v. *Greece* [1991] ECR I–727; and C–375/92, *Commission* v. *Spain* [1994] ECR I–923.

[230] Case C–180/89, *Commission* v. *Italy* [1991] ECR I–709, para. 22.

[231] Case C–158/96, *Kohll* v. *Union des Caisses de Maladie* [1998] ECR I–1931, paras. 45–49.

regulations on a given issue, a national rule will not be deemed to be disproportionate simply because it is stricter than rules which apply in other Member States.[232]

Finally, secondary legislation which implements the provisions on free movement of services in particular sectors or for particular activities must, according to the ECJ, be interpreted in the light of the fundamental principles laid down in the Treaty and in the case law, including the principles relating to the scope of permissible exceptions and imperative requirements.[233]

(d) ARE NON-DISCRIMINATORY RESTRICTIONS COVERED BY ARTICLE 49 (EX ARTICLE 59)?

A final question, which was discussed above in relation to establishment, is whether truly non-discriminatory restrictions (as opposed to indirectly discriminatory restrictions) come within the scope of Article 49 (ex Article 59), and therefore must satisfy the 'objective justification' test. It seems increasingly clear in recent years that the answer is in the affirmative.

Initially, however, while a great many of the cases on services have concerned the equal application of apparently non-discriminatory rules to those established within the Member State and to those established elsewhere, it seemed on examination that those rules did in fact impose a heavier burden—or a dual burden—on the non-national or the person who is established in another Member State than on the national or the person domestically established. Such restrictions or regulations, while not intended to be discriminatory, none the less inadvertently burdened non-nationals and non-established persons more heavily than nationals or established persons, or had a protectionist effect.[234] However, there were also a number of cases involving rules which could not be said to have burdened established providers of services any less than non-established providers, and yet which were found to be incompatible with Article 49 (ex Article 59), thus providing evidence that the ECJ considered that genuinely non-discriminatory measures could fall within the scope of that Article. Most significantly in recent years, however, the express language of the Court, and its increasing tendency to refer to all of the Treaty freedoms as being based on the same principles,[235] suggest that it is no longer necessary for any kind of direct or indirect discrimination to be established, but merely an impediment to free movement or a restriction on access to the market of another Member State.

In the *Lawyers' Services* case, concerning the implementation by Germany of Directive 77/249 on the exercise by lawyers of freedom to provide services, one of the complaints of the Commission concerned a rule of territorial exclusivity, which

---

[232] See Cases C–108/96, *MacQuen* [2001] ECR I–837 and C–67/98, *Zenatti* [1999] ECR I–7289.

[233] See, e.g., Case C–205/99, *Analir v. Administración General de l'Estado* [2001] ECR I–1271.

[234] See G. Marenco, 'The Notion of a Restriction on the Freedom of Establishment and the Provisions of Services in the Case Law of the Court' (1991) 11 *YBEL* 111. See Case C–379/92, *Peralta* [1994] ECR I–3453, para. 51, where, in the absence of any direct or indirect discrimination or any advantage for domestic interests, Art. 49 (ex Art. 59) was held not to apply to a prohibition on discharging harmful chemicals at sea.

[235] See Case C–55/94, *Gebhard*, n. 10 above, para. 37, and more recently Case C–390/99, *Canal Satélite Digital*, n. 4, in which the case law on goods and services was treated as being the same. On the convergence of the freedoms, see also C. Barnard, 'Fitting the Remaining Pieces into the Goods and Persons Jigsaw' (2001) 26 *ELRev.* 35.

provided that, in order to practise before certain of the higher German courts, a lawyer must first be admitted to practise before that judicial authority.[236] The Commission argued that this rule could not be applied to lawyers established in other Member States who were merely providing temporary services in Germany, and the ECJ agreed. Unlike in the cases of *Webb*,[237] *Van Wesemael*,[238] and *Choquet*,[239] the territoriality rule in question could not necessarily be said to burden a lawyer established in another Member State more heavily than a lawyer established in Germany, since it did not, for example, duplicate the conditions of a licence requirement already satisfied in the state of establishment. While the ECJ based its reasoning on the fact that a lawyer established in another state was in a less favourable position, in not having the advantages of a place of establishment in Germany, yet being required to go through the procedures for admission to practise there, the Advocate General argued that the rule had an equal impact on lawyers established within and outside Germany.

The case of *Säger* v. *Dennemeyer* concerned German legislation which reserved activites relating to the maintenance of industrial property rights to patent agents.[240] Reference had been made, in an intervention by the UK government, to the decision in *Koestler*,[241] in support of its argument that, in the absence of discrimination or unequal application, a restriction on the provision of services would not breach Article 49 (ex Article 59). Advocate General Jacobs considered the debate over whether a truly non-discriminatory restriction was covered by that provision:

It does not seem unreasonable that a person establishing himself in a Member State should as a general rule be required to comply with the law of that State in all respects. In contrast, it is less easy to see why a person who is established in one Member State and who provides services in other Member States should be required to comply with all the detailed regulations in force in each of those States. To accept such a proposition would be to render the notion of a single market unattainable in the field of services.

For this reason, it may be thought that services should rather be treated by analogy with goods, and that non-discriminatory restrictions on the free movement of services should be approached in the same way as non-discriminatory restrictions on the free movement of goods under the 'Cassis de Dijon' line of case-law. That analogy seems particularly appropriate where, as in the present case, the nature of the service is such as not to involve the provider of the service in moving physically between Member States but where instead it is transmitted by post or telecommunications. . . .

. . . I do not think that it can be right to state as a general rule that a measure lies wholly outside the scope of Article 59 simply because it does not in any way discriminate between domestic undertakings and those established in other Member States. Nor is such a view supported by the terms of Article 59: its expressed scope is much broader. If such a view were accepted, it would

---

[236] [1977] OJ L78/17. Case 427/85, *Commission* v. *Germany* [1988] ECR 1123. See also Case 292/86, *Gullung*, n. 83 above, for discussion of the Dir.'s requirements concerning professional ethics; and Case C–294/89, *Commission* v. *France* [1991] ECR I–3591.

[237] Case 279/80, n. 217 above.   [238] Cases 110–111/78, n. 217 above.

[239] Case 16/78, n. 224 above.   [240] Case C–76/90, n. 9 above.

[241] Case 15/78, n. 168 above, and text. See also the discussion in the Opinion of Gulman AG in Case C–275/92, *Schindler*, n. 15 above.

mean that restrictions on the freedom to provide services would have to be tolerated, even if they lacked any objective justification, on condition that they did not lead to discrimination against foreign undertakings. There might be a variety of restrictions in different Member States, none of them intrinsically justified, which collectively might wholly frustrate the aims of Article 59 and render impossible the attainment of a single market in services. The principle should, I think, be that if an undertaking complies with the legislation of the Member State in which it is established it may provide services in another Member State, even though the provision of such services would not normally be lawful under the laws of the second Member State. Restrictions imposed by those laws can only be applied against the foreign undertaking if they are justified by some requirement that is compatible with the aims of the Community.[242]

The approach recommended here clearly could be a very powerfully liberalizing one, since almost any national law which regulates the domestic market even in pursuance of important national policies would be subjected to rigorous scrutiny by the ECJ for justification. Further, as we saw in Chapter 15, the ECJ in *Keck* appeared to narrow its approach to the scope of Article 28 (ex Article 30) so that genuinely non-discriminatory selling arrangements would not so readily be caught.[243] However, cases subsequent to *Keck* have suggested that the scope of Article 28 is not limited only to directly or indirectly discriminatory measures, and that non-discriminatory measures which impede access to the market are also caught.[244]

Is this true also in the field of services, and are the 'four freedoms' converging around the notion of non-discriminatory restrictions on market access, as various commentators have claimed? Unquestionably, the suggestion which was made in earlier cases such as the *Lawyers' Services* case and *Schindler*[245] that genuinely non-discriminatory restrictions are caught by the Treaty provisions on services was confirmed by the ruling in *Alpine Investments*.[246] The case concerned a Dutch prohibition on cold-calling, i.e., on the making of unsolicited telephone calls without the prior written consent of the individuals concerned in order to offer financial services, and the prohibition applied both to calls made within the Netherlands and to calls made to other Member States. According to the ECJ:

28. However, such a prohibition deprives the operators concerned of a rapid and direct technique for marketing and for contacting potential clients in other Member States. It can therefore constitute a restriction on the freedom to provide cross border services.

. . .

35. Although a prohibition such as the one at issue in the main proceedings is general and non-discriminatory and neither its object nor its effect is to put the national market at an

---

[242] [1991] ECR I–4221, 4234–5.

[243] See Cases C–267–268/91, *Keck and Mithouard* [1993] ECR I–6097.

[244] Case C–254/98, *Schutzverband gegen unlauteren Wettbewerb* v. *TK-Heimdienst Sass GmbH* [2000] ECR I–151 and the discussion in Ch. 15.

[245] Case C–275/92, n. 15 above, para. 43. See J. Art, 'Legislative Lacunae, The Court of Justice and Freedom to Provide Services', in D. Curtin and D. O'Keeffe (eds.), *Constitutional Adjudication in European Community Law and National Law* (Butterworths Ireland, 1992), 121, and contrast G. Marenco, n. 91 above, 142–7.

[246] Case C–384/93, *Alpine Investments* [1995] ECR I–1141, n. 86 above. For criticism of the case, see L. Daniele, 'Non-discriminatory Restrictions on the Free Movement of Persons' (1997) 22 *ELRev.* 191 and C. Hilson, 'Discrimination in Community Free Movement Law' (1999) 24 *ELRev.* 445.

advantage over providers of services from other Member States, it can, none the less, as has been held (paragraph 28) constitute a restriction on the freedom to provide services.

36. Such a prohibition is not analogous to the legislation concerning selling arrangements held in *Keck and Mithouard* to fall outside the scope of Article 30 of the Treaty.

37. According to that judgment, the application to products from other Member States of national provisions restricting or prohibiting, within the Member State of importation, certain selling arrangements is not such as to hinder trade between Member States so long as, first, those provisions apply to all relevant traders operating within the national territory and, secondly, they affect in the same manner, in law and in fact, the marketing of domestic products and of those from other Member States. The reason is that the application of such provisions is not such as to prevent access by the latter to the market of the Member State of importation or to impede such access more than it impedes access by domestic products.

38. A prohibition such as that at issue is imposed by the Member State in which the provider of services is established and affects not only offers made by him to addressees who are established in that State or move there in order to receive services but also offers made to potential recipients in another Member State. It therefore directly affects access to the market in services in the other Member States and is thus capable of hindering intra-Community trade in services.

Although the reasoning was not altogether clear, the effect of paragraphs 37 and 38 is that a Member State's restriction will not fall outside the scope of Article 49 (ex Article 59) or 28 (ex Article 30) simply because it is genuinely non-discriminatory in law and in fact, unless it is *also* a restriction which does not in any way affect the 'access' of the person in question to the market in goods or services of another Member State. If an effect on an individual's access to the market of another Member State can be shown, then, regardless of the equally restrictive marketing effect on situations wholly internal to a Member State, the restriction in question will fall within the scope of Community law and require objective justification.

Further, the ruling in *Gebhard* in the context of freedom of establishment, which suggested that the same rules were applicable to all four freedoms, and that discrimination is not necessary for a national rule to constitute an impediment to freedom of movement under the Treaty, has since been repeated in several cases concerning the free movement of services. In a paragraph in *Arblade*, which has been repeated in a number of other rulings,[247] the ECJ declared:

It is settled case-law that Article 59 of the Treaty requires not only the elimination of all discrimination on grounds of nationality against providers of services who are established in another Member State but also the abolition of any restriction, even if it applies without distinction to national providers of services and to those of other Member States, which is liable to prohibit, impede or render less advantageous the activities of a provider of services established in another Member State where he lawfully provides similar services.[248]

---

[247] Cases C–165/98, *Mazzoleni and ISA* [2001] ECR I–2189, para. 22 and C–49/98, *Finalarte Sociedade Construçao Civil* v. *Urlaubs- und Lohnausgleichskasse der Bauwirtschaft* [2001] ECR I–7831, para. 28.
[248] Cases C–369/96 & C–376/96, *Arblade* [1999] ECR I–8453, para. 33.

Thus there appears, following the rulings in *Keck, Heimdienst, Bosman, Gebhard, Alpine, Arblade,* and others, to be an emergent harmony of rules relating to freedom of movement and the internal market, which is rather different from the earlier emphasis on discrimination and protectionism in these areas of EC law. The emphasis instead is on the creation of a genuinely 'single' Community market, so that any national rules, whether discriminatory or not, which may impede inter-state trade and movement by affecting the access of goods, persons, or services from one national market to another is in principle caught by Community law and must be justified by the regulating State.

5. CONCLUSIONS

i. The ECJ increasingly appears to adopt a similar approach to all of the Treaty freedoms, including the free movement of services and establishment, such that any national rule which constitutes an inter-state impediment to market access falls within the scope of the free movement rules and requires justification

ii. However, relevant differences remain between temporary service provision on the one hand and establishment on the other. These differences are reflected partly in the more extensive case law on objective justification in the field of services, partly in the greater concern about possible 'abuse' in the context of services, and partly in the distinction drawn in the recent proposal for consolidating the directives on recognition of professional qualifications.

iii. Apart from the proposed consolidation in the field of professional qualifications, there have been other recent moves towards legislative consolidation in the field of free movement, with the drafting of a single proposed directive to cover the rights of residence and free movement of all EU citizens, including the employed and the self-employed.

iv. While it is not clear whether the Treaty provisions on establishment and services are fully horizontally applicable, they have been applied to private organizations which adopt their own collective rules or which are largely responsible for the organization of a particular economic sector.

v. Although EC law on establishment and services applies only to economic activity, recent developments have indicated that important or 'special' public services such as health, welfare, and education will not escape the Treaty rules if they are organized and provided through a market-like system.

6. FURTHER READING

(a) *Books*

MEI, A.P., VAN DER, *Free Movement of Persons within the EC: Cross-Border Access to Public Benefits* (Hart, 2002)

SNELL, J., *Goods and Services in EC Law* (Oxford University Press, 2002)

(b) *Articles*

ART, J., 'Legislative Lacunae, The Court of Justice and Freedom to Provide Services', in D. Curtin and D. O'Keeffe (eds.), *Constitutional Adjudication in European Community Law and National Law* (Butterworths Ireland, 1992), 121

BIONDI, A., 'In and Out of the Internal Market: Recent Developments on the Principle of Free Movement' (1999/2000) 19 *YBEL* 469

DANIELE, L. 'Non-discriminatory Restrictions on the Free Movement of Persons' (1997) 22 *ELRev.* 191

DAVIES, G., 'Welfare as a Service' (2002) 29 *LIEI* 27

EDWARD, D., 'Establishment and Services: An Analysis of the Insurance Cases' (1987) 12 *ELRev.* 231

EDWARDS, V., 'Secondary Establishment of Companies—The Case Law of the Court of Justice' (1998) 18 *YBEL* 221

HATZOPOULOS, V., 'Recent Developments of the Case Law of the ECJ in the Field of Services' (2000) 37 *CMLRev.* 43

HILSON, C., 'Discrimination in Community Free Movement Law' (1999) 24 *ELRev.* 445.

LONBAY, J., 'Picking Over the Bones: Rights of Establishment Reviewed' (1991) 16 *ELRev.* 507

MARENCO, G., 'The Notion of a Restriction on the Freedom of Establishment and the Provisions of Services in the Case Law of the Court' (1991) 11 *YBEL* 111

O'LEARY, S., and FERNÁNDEZ-MARTÍN, J.M., 'Judicial Exceptions to the Free Provision of Services' (1995) 1 *ELJ* 303

19

THE PUBLIC POLICY, SECURITY, AND HEALTH DEROGATIONS: DIRECTIVE 64/221

1. CENTRAL ISSUES

i. Common grounds of derogation from the free movement of workers, freedom of establishment, and free movement of services alike, on grounds of public policy, public security, and public health, are provided for in the Treaty.

ii. Just as the ECJ has interpreted the three sets of freedoms fairly expansively, and the public-service and official-authority exceptions of Articles 39(4) and 45 (ex Articles 48(4) and 55) restrictively, the public policy, security, and health derogations under Articles 39(3) (ex Article 48(3)) and 46(1) (ex Article 56(1)) EC have been given a relatively narrow scope.[1]

iii. Unlike the public-service and official-authority exceptions, however, the scope of these derogations is not determined solely by the Court, but has been further defined in secondary legislation. Directive 64/221—which is soon to be replaced by the provisions of the new proposed directive on free movement and residence of EU citizens[2] seeks to 'co-ordinate' these national public policy, security, and health measures.[3] The Directive contains a number of substantive limitations on the kinds of derogations which Member States may adopt (e.g., that they must be non-economic, that they must be based on personal conduct), and it contains a range of procedural protections for the individuals concerned.

iv. Directive 64/221 applies only to natural persons, so that the application of the derogations to companies under the establishment and services chapters is governed only by Article 46 (ex Article 56) and by the general principles of Community law.[4] These include the principles of non-discrimination and of proportionality, which are also a part of the test for justifying public-interest restrictions on freedom of movement which the Court has developed alongside the Treaty derogations.[5] A

---

[1] The rights of workers under Art. 39(3) (ex Art. 48(3)) are 'subject to limitations justified on grounds of public policy, public security or public health'. Art. 46(1) (ex Art. 56(1)) on establishment and Art. 55 (ex Art. 66) on services specify that 'the provisions of this chapter and measures taken in pursuance thereof shall not prejudice the applicability of provisions laid down by law, regulation or administrative action providing for special treatment for foreign nationals on grounds of public policy, public security or public health'.

[2] COM(2001)257 [2001] OJ C270/150.   [3] [1963–4] OJ Spec. Ed. 117.

[4] For examples of the application of Arts. 46 and 55 (ex Arts. 56 and 66) to companies see Cases 3/88, *Commission* v. *Italy* [1989] ECR 4035; 352/85, *Bond van Adverteerders* v. *Netherlands* [1988] ECR 2085; C–114/97, *Commission* v. *Spain* [1998] ECR I–6717; and C–355/98, *Commission* v. *Belgium* [2000] ECR I–1221. Although Art. 46 (ex Art. 56) appears to permit only 'special treatment for foreign nationals', it is likely, since the Court has held that Arts. 43 and 49 (ex Arts. 52 and 59) protect also nationals in their own Member State and companies which have their primary establishment there, that the derogations may be invoked to permit special treatment for such companies and nationals in their own Member State.

[5] See Ch. 18. And see more generally on the role of EC law in a situation which was not covered by the Treaty's free-movement provisions, given the special geographical status of the British Channel islands, Case C–171/96, *Pereira Roque* v. *Governor of Jersey* [1998] ECR I–4607.

further important limit articulated by the Court is the requirement that Member States should respect the fundamental rights of the person when invoking one of the derogations.[6]

2. THE NATURE OF THE DEROGATIONS

We have seen in previous chapters that the public-service and official-authority exceptions relate to the nature of the work or activity to be undertaken, and that they allow for the exclusion of all non-nationals or foreign companies from certain kinds of work involving the exercise of public power or official authority. The public policy, security, and health derogations, by contrast, are concerned not with a certain kind of work or activity but with the specific characteristics of particular persons.[7] A final distinction between the two categories of exception or derogation is that, whereas the scope and content of the public-service and official-authority derogations have firmly been delimited by the ECJ, there is no single uniform interpretation of the public policy exception, and Member States retain a certain degree of discretion in defining its content. However, the limits to the exercise and scope of the public policy, security, and health exceptions are set by Community law—in particular by the general principles of law such as the principles of non-discrimination, proportionality, protection for fundamental rights, as well as by the various safeguards set out in Directive 64/221.

Directive 64/221 sets out to co-ordinate all measures relating to entry and deportation from their territory and issue or renewal of residence permits which Member States can adopt on grounds of public policy, security, and health, in relation to the employed, the self-employed, recipients of services, and the families of each. The first limit imposed in Article 2(1) is that none of the grounds shall be invoked 'to service economic ends'. In other words, a Member State cannot plead a ground such as high unemployment to justify deporting or refusing entry to another EC national who wishes to take up employment or an activity as a self-employed person in the state. This same limitation has already been seen in the context of the judicially-developed public-interest exceptions for non-discriminatory national measures which restrict the free movement of persons.[8] Article 3 places other limits on the use of the public policy and security exceptions, which will be examined in the cases below.

Article 4 concerns the public-health exception and refers to the illnesses listed in the Annex to the Directive, stating that diseases or disabilities occurring after the issue of a first residence permit shall not justify refusal to renew the permit or expulsion. The diseases listed in the Annex are under two main headings, the first concerning diseases which have been recognized to endanger public health, and the second, which includes drug-addiction and profound mental disturbance, concerning diseases and

---

[6] See Case C–260/89, *ERT* v. *DEP* [1991] ECR I–2925, and the earlier Case 36/75, *Rutili* v. *Minister for the Interior* [1975] ECR 1219. See S. Hall, 'The ECHR and Public Policy Exceptions to the Free Movement of Workers under the EEC Treaty' (1991) 16 *ELRev.* 466, and see Ch. 8 for a fuller discussion. A recent important case on these questions is pending before the ECJ: C–459/99, *MRAX* v. *Belgium*, AG's Opinion of 13.9.2001.

[7] See Cases C–114/97, *Commission* v. *Spain* [1998] ECR I–6717, paras. 40–42 and C–355/98, *Commission* v. *Belgium* [2000] ECR I–1221, para. 42.

[8] See, e.g., Case C–398/95, *SETTG* v. *Ypourgos Ergasias* [1997] ECR I–3091, paras. 22–3, discussed in Ch. 18 above, n. 212.

disabilities threatening public policy or security. Article 4 is a standstill clause, and Articles 5 to 9 set out a range of procedural protections for the person in relation to the way in which decisions concerning entry, residence permits, and expulsion must take place, and may be challenged. These provisions have given rise to a considerable amount of litigation, and it is notable that most of the cases concern the public policy exception, which is a less clearly defined and more amorphous concept than that of public security or public health. Genuine threats to public security from the personal conduct of one person appear to have been infrequent,[9] and the careful delimitation of the public-health exception leaves little scope for manœuvre beyond those limits by the Member States.

3. THE DISCRETION OF THE MEMBER STATES

(a) WHAT CONDUCT CAN JUSTIFY THE INVOCATION OF THE DEROGATIONS?

One of the early and well-known cases in which the ECJ was called upon to interpret the public policy exception and the provisions of Directive 64/221 indicates the degree of discretion which Member States retain in this context. The exception was invoked by the UK in an attempt to justify the refusal of permission to enter the state to a Dutchwoman who had come to work for the Church of Scientology, a quasi-religious organization which was considered by the State to be anti-social and harmful.

Case 41/74, Van Duyn v. Home Office
[1974] ECR 1337

[ToA renumbering: Art. 48(3) is now Art. 39(3)]

The facts are set out in Chapter 5.[10]

THE ECJ

10. It emerges from the order making the reference that the only provision of the Directive which is relevant is that contained in Article 3(1) which provides that 'measures taken on grounds of public policy or public security shall be based exclusively on the personal conduct of the individual concerned'.

. . .

---

[9] Note that Art. 296 (ex Art. 223) EC provides for a further exception to the rules of the Treaty (and not just to the free-movement rules) where a Member State considers that the essential interests of its security are at stake. For cases concerning Member State attempts to invoke the public-security exception in the context of free movement of capital and social policy respectively, see Cases C–423/98, *Albore* [2000] ECR I–5965, paras. 18–21; C–503/99, *Commission* v. *Belgium* [2002] ECR I–nyr, paras 45–48; C–54/99, *Association Eglise de Scientologie de Paris* v. *Prime Minister* [2000] ECR I–1335, and C–285/98, *Kreil* v. *Bundesrepublik Deutschland* [2000] ECR I–69, paras. 16–17.

[10] At 203 above.

17. It is necessary, first, to consider whether association with a body or an organization can in itself constitute personal conduct within the meaning of Article 3 of Directive No 64/221. Although a person's past association cannot, in general, justify a decision refusing him the right to move freely within the Community, it is nevertheless the case that present association, which reflects participation in the activities of the body or of the organization as well as identification with its aims or designs, may be considered a voluntary act of the person concerned and, consequently, as part of his personal conduct within the meaning of the provision cited.

18. This third question further raises the problem of what importance must be attributed to the fact that the activities of the organization in question, which are considered by the Member State as contrary to the public good are not however prohibited by national law. It should be emphasized that the concept of public policy in the context of the Community and where, in particular, it is used as a justification for derogating from the fundamental principle of freedom of movement for workers, must be interpreted strictly, so that its scope cannot be determined unilaterally by each Member State without being subject to control by the institutions of the Community. Nevertheless, the particular circumstances justifying recourse to the concept of public policy may vary from one country to another and from one period to another, and it is therefore necessary in this matter to allow the competent national authorities an area of discretion within the limits imposed by the Treaty.

19. It follows from the above that where the competent authorities of a Member State have clearly defined their standpoint as regards the activities of a particular organization and where, considering it to be socially harmful, they have taken administrative measures to counteract these activities, the Member State cannot be required, before it can rely on the concept of public policy, to make such activities unlawful, if recourse to such a measure is not thought appropriate in the circumstances.

20. The question raises finally the problem of whether a Member State is entitled, on grounds of public policy, to prevent a national of another Member State from taking gainful employment within its territory with a body or organization, it being the case that no similar restriction is placed upon its own nationals.

21. In this connection, the Treaty, while enshrining the principle of freedom of movement for workers without any discrimination on grounds of nationality, admits, in Article 48(3), limitations justified on grounds of public policy, public security or public health to the rights deriving from this principle. Under the terms of the provision cited above, the right to accept offers of employment actually made, the right to move freely within the territory of Member States for this purpose, and the right to stay in a Member State for the purpose of employment are, among others all subject to such limitations. Consequently, the effect of such limitations, when they apply, is that leave to enter the territory of a Member State and the right to reside there may be refused to a national of another Member State.

22. Furthermore it is a principle of international law, which the EEC Treaty cannot be assumed to disregard in the relations between Member States, that a State is precluded from refusing its own nationals the right of entry or residence.

The contrast with the lack of Member State discretion in determining the scope of the 'public-service' exception is evident in paragraph 18, where the Court accepts that the States retain a certain discretion as regards the public policy exception since 'the particular circumstances justifying recourse to the concept of public policy may vary from one country to another and from one period to another'. Or, as the ECJ phrased it more recently, no 'uniform code of values' is imposed by EC law.[11] Advocate General Mayras made a similar observation in relation to the concept of 'public security':

I did not think, contrary to the opinion of the Commission, that it is possible to deduce a Community concept of public security. That concept remains, at least for the present, national, and this conforms with reality inasmuch as the requirements of public security vary, in time and in space, from one State to another.[12]

The ECJ in its judgment also made clear that, although membership alone will not constitute personal conduct as required by Article 3 of the Directive, active participation and identification with the aims of an organization may do so.

(b) WHAT STEPS MAY MEMBER STATES TAKE AGAINST NON-NATIONALS?

A second important point made in *Van Duyn* is that, so long as the state adopts some administrative measures to counteract the activities of an organization, it is not required to criminalize or to ban that organization before it can rely on the public policy exception. Given that the UK could not deport its own nationals for working for the Church of Scientology, the ECJ seemed to accept that the deportation of a non-national for the same activity was an acceptable use of the public policy deroga-tion. However, the point made in paragraph 19 of the judgment is not elaborated further, so that it is not clear what a Member State must do in relation to a particular organization or activity before it can rely on the public policy concept against non-nationals. The background to the *Van Duyn* case in the UK was that there had been a ministerial statement during a debate in Parliament in 1968, expressing strong official disapproval of the activities of the Church of Scientology, but stating that there was no power to prohibit the practice of scientology. This was noted by Advocate General Mayras as 'one of the consequences of a liberal government', but which should not prevent the UK from refusing entry to non-nationals who intended to work for the organization.

The *Van Duyn* case attracted considerable critical comment in relation to the ECJ's acceptance of the disparity of treatment between nationals and non-nationals. If the activity really was contrary to public policy to such an extent that non-nationals could be refused entry or be deported, surely some measures had to be taken against nationals engaging in that activity other than a mere statement to Parliament con-demning the organization? The ECJ acknowledged that, despite the principle of non-discrimination expressed in the various Treaty Articles concerned, there is an inevitable discrimination between nationals and non-nationals, in that the latter can and the former cannot be deported.[13] However, the element of discrimination could be lessened by providing for more restrictive measures against the practice of the activity on the part of nationals. If it were thought undesirable to take any such restrictive measures in a liberal state, why would it be desirable to take the illiberal

---

[11] Case C–268/99, *Jany* v. *Staatssecretaris van Justitie* [2001] ECR I–08615.

[12] [1974] ECR 1337, 1357.

[13] See also Case C–171/96, *Pereira Roque* v. *Governor of Jersey* [1998] ECR I–4607, paras. 38 *et seq.*

measure of deporting otherwise lawfully resident non-nationals for engaging in similar conduct?

This issue arose in the *Adoui* case, and more recently in *Jany*,[14] where the ECJ addressed the question whether deportation in such circumstances could amount to unnecessary or arbitrary discrimination on grounds of nationality.

Cases 115 and 116/81, Adoui and Cornuaille v. Belgian State
[1982] ECR 1665

[Note ToA renumbering: Arts. 48 and 56 are now Arts. 39 and 46 respectively]

Adoui and Cornuaille were French nationals working in Belgium. Adoui's application to the City of Liège for a residence permit was refused on grounds of public policy, since she worked in a bar that was 'suspect from the point of view of morals' and she was subsequently ordered to leave the country. Cornuaille had similarly been contacted by the police, and a recommendation had been made by the Consultative Committee for Aliens that she be deported. When Adoui and Cornuaille challenged these decisions before Belgian courts, the ECJ was asked whether the Treaty permitted a Member State to deport a national of another Member State because of activities which, when carried out by the host State's own nationals, did not give rise to any repressive measures.

THE ECJ

6. Those questions are motivated by the fact that prostitution as such is not prohibited by Belgian legislation, although the Law does prohibit certain incidental activities, which are particularly harmful from the social point of view, such as the exploitation of prostitution by third parties and various forms of incitement to debauchery.

7. The reservations contained in Articles 48 and 56 of the EEC Treaty permit Member States to adopt, with respect to the nationals of other Member States and on the grounds specified in those provisions, in particular grounds justified by the requirements of public policy, measures which they cannot apply to their own nationals, inasmuch as they have no authority to expel the latter from the national territory or to deny them access thereto. Although that difference of treatment, which bears upon the nature of the measures available, must therefore be allowed, it must nevertheless be stressed that, in a Member State, the authority empowered to adopt such measures must not base the exercise of its powers on assessments of certain conduct which would have the effect of applying an arbitrary distinction to the detriment of nationals of other Member States.

8. . . . Although Community law does not impose upon the Member States a uniform scale of values as regards the assessment of conduct which may be considered as contrary to public policy, it should nevertheless be Stated that conduct may not be considered as being of a sufficiently serious nature to justify restrictions on the admission to or residence within the territory of a Member State of a national of another Member State in a case where the former Member State does not adopt, with respect to the same conduct on the part of its own nationals repressive measures or other genuine and effective measures intended to combat such conduct.

---

[14] Case C–268/99, *Jany* v. *Staatssecretaris van Justitie* [2001] ECR I–8615, paras. 59–62 in the context of the parallel free movement provisions of the Czech and Poland European Association Agreements.

The Court's emphasis here is on the need to take 'genuine and effective' repressive measures against the activities of nationals, if that same conduct is to be used as a reason for deporting or refusing entry to non-nationals. While that seems to represent a tighter reading of the public policy exception than in *Van Duyn*, the ECJ gave no examples of the kinds of repressive measures which a state might take. What other sufficiently repressive measures against nationals, short of prosecution for unlawful activity, could be taken? While the answer may remain unclear, the obligation to minimize discrimination in the treatment of nationals and non-nationals in the exercise of the exceptions has been emphasized in several rulings.

Case 36/75 Rutili v. Minister for the Interior
[1975] ECR 1219

[Note ToA renumbering: Arts. 7 and 48 EC are now Arts. 12 and 39]

The applicant was an Italian national who had been legally resident in France since his birth and was working there as a trade union official. In 1968 an order of the Minister for the Interior was made prohibiting him from residing in certain French territories (*départements*). The residence permit for an EC national which he was granted included a prohibition on residence in these territories, and he challenged this before the French courts, which referred the question to the ECJ.

THE ECJ

28. Accordingly, restrictions cannot be imposed on the right of a national of any Member State to enter the territory of another Member State, to stay there and to move within it unless his presence or conduct constitutes a genuine and sufficiently serious threat to public policy.

29. In this connection Article 3 of Directive No 64/221 imposes on Member States the duty to base their decision on the individual circumstances of any person under the protection of Community law and not on general considerations.

30. Moreover, Article 2 of the same directive provides that grounds of public policy shall not be put to improper use by being invoked to service economic ends.

31. Nor, under Article 8 of Regulation No 1612/68, which ensures equality of treatment as regards membership of trade unions and the exercise of rights attaching thereto, may the reservation relating to public policy be invoked on grounds arising from the exercise of those rights.

The ECJ ruled that the term 'measures' in Directive 64/221 should have a broad construction, covering not only national legislative measures but also individual decisions taken, which should therefore be subject to judicial control as required by the Directive:

46. Right of entry into the territory of Member States and the right to stay there and to move freely within it is defined in the Treaty by reference to the whole territory of those States and not by reference to its internal subdivisions.

47. The reservation contained in Article 48(3) concerning the protection of public policy has the same scope as the rights the exercise of which may, under that paragraph, be subject to limitations.

48. It follows that prohibitions on residence under the reservation inserted to this effect in Article 48(3) may be imposed only in respect of the whole of the national territory.

49. On the other hand, in the case of partial prohibitions on residence, limited to certain areas of the territory, persons covered by Community law must, under Article 7 of the Treaty and within the field of application of that provision, be treated on a footing of equality with the nationals of the Member State concerned.

On an initial reading of *Rutili*, it may seem odd that while the Treaty derogations and Directive 64/221 allow a Member State to take quite a drastic step—namely deportation—in relation to someone who is considered to be a threat to public policy, they do not allow a more restrained measure, such as a limited restriction order barring entry only to some parts of the territory. But the reasoning behind this conclusion is as follows: if the person in question poses a very serious threat to public policy, then the state should be able to justify a deportation order as required under Directive 64/221. But if the conduct in question is not so serious as to warrant expulsion, then any lesser restriction such as a partial territorial exclusion order can only be imposed on a non-national to the same extent to which it would be imposed on a national engaged in the same conduct.[15] In *Shingara and Radiom*, however, the ECJ did permit what might have appeared on its face to be discrimination between Member State nationals and other EC nationals.[16] The Court ruled that it was permissible for a Member State to provide only a remedy by way of judicial review to an EC national who was refused entry on grounds of public policy, even where there was a more substantial remedy by way of appeal for nationals whose immigration status was in question, because it considered that the two situations were not comparable.

(c) THE 'PERSONAL CONDUCT' REQUIREMENT

The only guidance given by Directive 64/221 on what may constitute 'personal conduct' serious enough to give grounds for invoking the public policy or security exception is negative, in that Article 3(2) provides that previous criminal convictions in themselves are not sufficient. A series of cases involving criminal convictions has fleshed out this provision.

---

[15] Compare the ruling in Case C–171/96, *Pereira Roque*, n. 13 above, in a context in which the Treaty free-movement provisions did not apply to Jersey, but a principle prohibiting arbitrarily unequal treatment was applicable.

[16] Cases C–65/95 & C–111/95, *R. v. Secretary of State for the Home Department, ex p. Shingara, and ex p. Radiom* [1997] ECR I–3341.

Case 67/74, Bonsignore v. Oberstadtdirektor der Stadt Köln
[1975] ECR 297

Bonsignore was an Italian national who came to Germany to work. Three years later, he fatally injured his younger brother in an accident while handling a pistol for which he had no firearms permit. Although he was convicted of causing death by negligence, no punishment was imposed by the court. However, a deportation order was subsequently made against him and, on appeal, a reference was made to the ECJ asking whether Community law permitted a Member State national to be deported for reasons of a general preventive nature, or whether the reasons had to be specific to the individual.

THE ECJ

5. According to Article 3(1) and (2) of Directive No 64/221, 'measures taken on grounds of public policy shall be based exclusively on the personal conduct of the individual concerned' and 'previous criminal convictions shall not in themselves constitute grounds for the taking of such measures'.

. . .

6. With this in view, Article 3 of the directive provides that measures adopted on grounds of public policy and for the maintenance of public security against the nationals of Member States of the Community cannot be justified on grounds extraneous to the individual case, as is shown in particular by the requirement set out in paragraph (1) that 'only' the 'personal conduct' of those affected by the measures is to be regarded as determinative.

As departures from the rules concerning the free movement of persons constitute exceptions which must be strictly construed, the concept of 'personal conduct' expresses the requirement that a deportation order may only be made for breaches of the peace and public security which might be committed by the individual affected.

Accordingly, the ECJ ruled that deportation of a 'general preventive nature' was prohibited by Article 3 of the Directive. The combination of the 'personal-conduct' requirement and the condition that criminal convictions in themselves were insufficient as a ground led it to conclude that more would be required if Bonsignore, on whom the German sentencing court had obviously taken pity in view of the tragic killing of his brother, was to be deported. Advocate General Mayras went somewhat further in his criticism of such preventive use of the power to deport:

I am, for my part, rather sceptical as to the real deterrent effect of a deportation which is ordered 'to make an example' of the individual concerned . . .,

In point of fact, one cannot avoid the impression that the deportation of a foreign worker, even a national of the Common Market, satisfies the feeling of hostility, sometimes verging on xenophobia, which the commission of an offence by an alien generally causes or revives in the indigenous population.[17]

---

[17] [1975] ECR 297, 315.

However, the fact that past criminal convictions cannot in themselves justify the adoption of measures on grounds of public policy or security does not mean that criminal convictions can never be relevant to the reasons a Member State has for invoking one of the exceptions.

Case 30/77, R. v. Bouchereau
[1977] ECR 1999

Bouchereau was a French national working in England, who was twice convicted there of unlawful possession of drugs. After the second conviction, the national court wished to recommend to the Secretary of State that he be deported. A reference was made to the ECJ, asking whether such a judicial recommendation would be a 'measure' within Directive 64/221, and whether past conduct resulting in a criminal conviction could be taken into account, despite Article 3(2) of that Directive, in deciding to recommend deportation. The ECJ ruled that the concept of a 'measure' included a judicial recommendation, as an important step in the process.

THE ECJ

27. The terms of Article 3(2) of the directive, which States that 'previous criminal convictions shall not in themselves constitute grounds for the taking of such measures' must be understood as requiring the national authorities to carry out a specific appraisal from the point of view of the interests inherent in protecting the requirements of public policy, which does not necessarily coincide with the appraisals which formed the basis of the criminal conviction.

28. The existence of a previous criminal conviction can, therefore, only be taken into account in so far as the circumstances which gave rise to that conviction are evidence of personal conduct constituting a present threat to the requirements of public policy.

29. Although in general, a finding that such a threat exists implies the existence in the individual concerned of a propensity to act in the same way in the future, it is possible that past conduct alone may constitute such a threat to the requirements of public policy.

. . .

35. In so far as it may justify certain restrictions on the free movement of persons subject to Community law, recourse by a national authority to the concept of public policy presupposes, in any event, the existence, in addition to the perturbation of the social order which any infringement of the law involves, of a genuine and sufficiently serious threat to the requirements of public policy affecting one of the fundamental interests of society.

The judgment states that the relevance of a criminal conviction is in whether it reveals that person to be a *present* and not just a past danger to the requirements of public policy. The ECJ expressly ruled that past conduct alone might well be enough to indicate a present danger, although it did not seek to explain in what way someone who would not commit future offences might nevertheless be a present danger. The *Bouchereau* judgment also elaborated further on the 'genuine and sufficiently serious threat to public policy', which was referred to in *Rutili*: it must be something more than the disruption which any breach of the law causes, and the public policy which it threatens must affect one of society's 'fundamental interests'. This sent a clear message to the Member States that the exception should not be lightly invoked, and that very substantial grounds should be shown before conduct, whether or not of a criminal nature, could be accepted as a threat to public policy within the meaning of the Treaty exception. However, the ECJ's failure to suggest how past criminal conduct in itself, without any likelihood of reoffending, may constitute such a serious threat, to some extent subverts the provision in Article 3 of the Directive that previous convictions in themselves cannot constitute grounds for invoking one of the exceptions.[18]

The issue of past criminal convictions arose in *Santillo*.[19] After he had served a prison sentence for violent sexual offences, a decision to deport Santillo was based on a recommendation made several years earlier by the sentencing court. The ECJ ruled that it was 'indeed essential that the social danger resulting from a foreigner's presence should be assessed at the very time when the decision ordering expulsion is made against him as the factors to be taken into account, particularly those concerning his conduct, are likely to change in the course of time'.[20] In *Calfa*, the ECJ ruled that legislation under which expulsion for life followed automatically (except where there were strong family reasons) from the conviction of a non-national of a drugs offence, without any account being taken of the personal conduct of the offenders or of the possible danger they represent for the requirements of public policy, would breach the requirements of the Directive.[21] And in *Nazli*, which concerned the rights of persons under the terms of an EU–Turkey Association Council decision, the Court also adopted a similar approach in giving a restrictive interpretation to the parallel derogations from fundamental free-movement rules in that context, and ruled that the deportation of a Turkish national had been done for preventive reasons only and was therefore in violation of the Directive.[22]

(d) THE PROCEDURAL PROTECTIONS UNDER DIRECTIVE 64/221

It has been said that the aim of Directive 64/221 was 'substantially to reduce the discretionary power of the States . . . by requiring that the individual position of such workers should be given a thorough examination which is subject to review by the courts'.[23] Whereas the provisions in the first half of the Directive set limits to what can constitute a public policy, security, or health ground, the provisions in the latter part set out a framework of procedural rights which must be provided for a person against whom one of the grounds is being invoked.

---

[18] In a press release in late 2001, IP 01 1380, the Commission indicated that it was bringing proceedings before the ECJ against Germany for its regular practice—which had been drawn to the Commission's attention by over 80 petitions to the European Parliament—of expelling EU citizens on public policy grounds related to offences they had committed.

[19] Case 131/79, *R. v. Secretary of State for Home Affairs, ex p. Mario Santillo* [1980] ECR 1585.

[20] *Ibid.*, para. 18. For a UK case on a similar issue which was not referred to the ECJ see *R. v. Home Secretary, ex p. Marchon* [1993] 2 CMLR 132.

[21] Case C–348/96, *Criminal Proceedings against Calfa* [1999] ECR I–11.

[22] Case C–340/97, *Nazli* [2000] ECR I–957. See also Case C–257/99, *Barkoci and Malik* [2001] ECR I–6557, on the Europe Association Agreement with the Czech republic.

[23] Mayras AG in Case 67/74, *Bonsignore v. Oberstadtdirektor der Stadt Köln* [1975] ECR 297, 316.

Article 5 provides that a decision to grant or refuse a first residence permit should be made as soon as possible and not later than six months from the date of application, allowing for temporary residence pending the decision. The host country, in essential cases, may ask the Member State of origin for information regarding any previous police record.

Article 6 provides that the person is to be informed of the grounds of public policy, security, or health on which the decision is taken, unless this is contrary to the interests of state security. It was held in *Adoui*[24] that the reasons given for expulsion must be sufficiently detailed to enable the person to protect her or his interests.

Under *Article 7*, official notification to the person concerned of any decision of refusal or expulsion is required. A period of time to leave must be given in the notice, and except in cases of urgency it must be at least fifteen days where the person has not yet been granted a residence permit, and at least a month in all other cases.

Articles 8 and 9, which are discussed in the cases which follow, provide for the legal remedies against a decision of refusal of issue or renewal of a permit or an expulsion. In *Shingara and Radiom*, the ECJ considered the case of two EC nationals who had been refused entry to the UK and who were not permitted either to appeal against the decisions or to have their cases referred to a competent authority, but only to judicial review of the decisions, whereas a UK national whose immigration status was being questioned and whose right to enter was refused would be entitled to an appeal.[25] The applicants argued that this was in breach of Article 8 of the Directive, since the same remedies were not available to nationals and non-nationals, but the ECJ disagreed, ruling that the situation of a non-national who was refused entry on grounds of public policy (rather than for some other more procedural reason) was in no way comparable with that of a national whose immigration status was in question. Accordingly, there was no unnecessary discrimination and the general availability of judicial review of administrative acts to challenge the specific decision to refuse entry satisfied the obligation imposed on Member States by Article 8. The ECJ did not follow the bolder opinion of the Advocate General, who suggested that Article 9 of the Directive could—in view of the development in protection for fundamental rights within EC law since the 1960s—be in breach of the fundamental principles of EC law in tolerating the lack of an appeal against expulsion orders in such circumstances, subject only to the obtaining of a non-binding opinion from another authority.[26]

In *Royer*, the ECJ was asked whether a decision ordering expulsion or a refusal to issue a residence permit could give rise to immediate measures of execution, or whether that decision could take effect only after remedies before the national courts were exhausted.[27] The case thus concerned the relationship between Article 8, which requires the same remedies to be available in the event of an expulsion order as are available to nationals against acts of the administration, and Article 9, which guarantees that in the absence of an effective appeal against the administrative decision the

---

[24] Cases 115 & 116/81, Adoui and Cornuaille v. *Belgian State* [1982] ECR 1665.
[25] Cases C–65/95 & C–111/95, R. v. *Secretary of State for the Home Department, ex p. Shingara, and ex p. Radiom* [1997] ECR I–3341.
[26] *Ibid.*, at para. 77 of the Opinion.
[27] Case 48/75, *Royer* [1976] ECR 497.

worker must at least be able to exercise rights of defence before an independent 'competent authority'.

Case 48/75, Royer
[1976] ECR 497

The facts are set out in Chapter 17.[28]

56. However, this guarantee would become illusory if the Member States could, by the immediate execution of a decision ordering expulsion, deprive the person concerned of the opportunity of effectively making use of the remedies which he is guaranteed by Directive No 64/221.

57. In the case of the legal remedies referred to in Article 8 of Directive No 64/221, the party concerned must at least have the opportunity of lodging an appeal and thus obtaining a stay of execution before the expulsion order is carried out.

58. This conclusion also follows from the link established by the directive between Articles 8 and 9 thereof in view of the fact that the procedure set out in the latter provision is obligatory *inter alia* where the legal remedies referred to in Article 8 'cannot have suspensory effect'.

59. Under Article 9 the procedure of an appeal to a competent authority must precede the decision ordering expulsion except in cases of urgency.

60. Consequently, where a legal remedy referred to in Article 8 is available the decision ordering expulsion may not be executed before the party concerned is able to avail himself of the remedy.

61. Where no such remedy is available, or where it is available but cannot have suspensory effect, the decision cannot be taken—save in cases of urgency which have been properly justified—until the party concerned has had the opportunity of appealing to the authority designated in Article 9 of Directive 64/221 and until this authority has reached a decision.

The point was reiterated in *Gallagher*,[29] in which the ECJ ruled that in situations covered by Article 9(1) (where the person affected already has a residence permit) if the available remedies are limited in the ways specified in that subsection, the opinion of the relevant competent authority must be obtained *before* the decision to expel or revoke has been taken, whereas in situations covered by Article 9(2) (where the person affected has not yet obtained a residence permit) the Opinion is obtained *after* the decision has been taken and only at the request of the person concerned. The ability of the person concerned to make representations to a competent authority, whose opinion might lead the primary decision-making authority to reconsider its decision would not be sufficient to satisfy Article 9(1).

The concept of an 'opinion of a competent authority' in Article 9 of the Directive

---

[28] At 730 above.
[29] Case C–175/94, *R. v. Secretary of State for the Home Department, ex p. Gallagher* [1995] ECR I–4253. For comment see S. O' Leary (1996) 33 *CMLRev.* 777 and R. White (1996) 21 *ELRev.* 241.

was also elaborated further upon in *Gallagher*[30] and *Santillo*.[31] In *Santillo*, noting that Member States were left 'a margin of discretion in regard to the nature of the authority', the ECJ ruled that a recommendation for deportation made by a criminal court at the time of conviction could satisify this requirement, provided that:

all the factors to be taken into consideration by the administration are put before the competent authority, if the opinion of the competent authority is sufficiently proximate in time to the decision ordering expulsion to ensure that there are no new factors to be taken into consideration, and if both the administration and the person concerned are in a position to take cognizance of the reasons which led the 'competent authority' to give its opinion—save where grounds touching the security of the State referred to in Article 6 of the directive make this undesirable.[32]

In *Gallagher*, the question of the independence of the competent authority was raised, and the ECJ ruled that the essential requirements were:

that it be clearly established that the authority is to perform its duties in absolute independence and is not to be directly or indirectly subject, in the exercise of its duties, to any control by the authority empowered to take the measures provided for in the directive.[33]

Further, although the Advocate General noted that Gallagher was not given any particulars of the grounds for his exclusion, the ECJ was not directly called on to address the difficult question of the balance between the right to be given reasons and the interests of national security under Article 6 of the Directive. Ultimately the Court ruled as before that it was for the national court to determine in each case whether the competent authority was independent, and whether the procedure it followed was such as to enable the person concerned effectively to present his or her defence. However, the ECJ did go on to specify that it was unnecessary for the members of the authority to be identified to the person affected, and it was permissible for the authority to be appointed by the same body which made the decision ordering expulsion, so long as the former authority remained absolutely independent in its *operation*.

In *Pecastaing*, the ECJ ruled that Articles 8 and 9 did not require Member States to allow the non-national to remain in the country for the duration of appeal or review procedures, so long as it was nevertheless possible to obtain a fair hearing and to have an adequate defence presented.[34] As for cases of urgency, in which neither suspension of the decision to deport nor recourse, before expulsion, to the opinion of a competent authority is required, the ECJ ruled that the determination of the existence of urgency was not a judicial matter but one for the administrative authority to make.[35]

In *Yiadom*, the ECJ gave an interesting judgment on the procedural provisions of

---

[30] Case C–175/94, [1995] ECR I–4253.

[31] Case 131/79, n. 19 above. See also Cases 115 & 116/81, Adoui, n. 24 above, where the ECJ stressed the need for the absolute independence of the authority.

[32] [1980] ECR 1585, para. 14. These requirements apply also in the context of someone who has been properly expelled, but who after a time seeks permission to re-enter. See Cases 115 & 116/81, *Adoui* n. 24 above.

[33] [1995] ECR I–4253, para. 24 of the judgment.

[34] Case 98/79, *Pecastaing v. Belgium* [1980] ECR 691.

[35] For criticism of this judgment, in particular regarding the determination of 'urgency', see D. O'Keeffe, 'Practical Difficulties in the Application of Art. 48 of the EEC Treaty' (1982) 19 *CMLRev.* 35, 36–9.

the Directive in which it ruled that the legislation was to be interpreted in the light of the EC Treaty provisions on citizenship.[36] The ECJ had been asked to consider the citizenship provisions also in *Calfa*, but did not so.[37] In *Yiadom*, however, the ECJ took up the 'citizenship' approach which had been recommended by the Commission in its 1999 Communication on Directive 64/221.[38] Here the Court ruled that where an EC citizen had been temporarily admitted to another Member State (in this case for up to seven months), a subsequent decision refusing that person leave to enter on public policy grounds could not be classified as a 'decision concerning entry' under Article 8, but instead fell within Article 9 with its more substantial procedural protections.

Case C–357/98, R. v. Home Secretary, ex parte Yiadom
[2000] ECR I–9265

23. Article 8a of the EC Treaty (now, after amendment, Article 18 EC) provides that every citizen of the Union is to have the right to move and reside freely within the territory of the Member States, subject to the limitations and conditions laid down in the Treaty and by measures adopted to give it effect.

24. The Court has consistently held that the principle of freedom of movement of persons must be given a broad interpretation (see, to that effect, Case C–292/89 *Antonissen* [1991] ECR I–745, paragraph 11; and Case C–344/95 *Commission* v *Belgium* [1997] ECR I–1035, paragraph 14), whereas derogations from that principle must be interpreted strictly (see, to that effect, Case 41/74 *Van Duyn* v *Home Office* [1974] ECR 1337, paragraph 18; Case 67/74 *Bonsignore* v *Stadt Köln* [1975] ECR 297, paragraph 6; and Case 139/85 *Kempf* v *Staatssecretaris van Justitie* [1986] ECR 1741, paragraph 13).

25. In the same way, provisions protecting Community nationals who exercise that fundamental freedom must be interpreted in their favour.

. . .

36. The main proceedings concern a Community national who was temporarily admitted to the territory of the Member State many months previously and was therefore physically present there when the competent national authorities notified her of a decision prohibiting her from entering that territory for the purposes of national law.

37. By reason of a legal fiction under national law, according to which the national who is physically present in the territory of the host Member State is regarded as not yet having been the subject of a decision concerning entry, that national does not qualify for the procedural safeguards granted under Article 9 of the Directive to nationals regarded as lawfully present in the territory who are the subject of a decision refusing the issue or renewal of a residence permit, or ordering expulsion from the territory.

38. In the light of the principles for interpreting the Directive which are set out in paragraphs 24 to 26 above, it must be held that the measure determining the situation of such a national cannot be classified as a 'decision concerning entry' within the meaning of the Directive, but that the national must be entitled to the procedural safeguards laid down in Article 9 of the Directive.

[36] Case C–357/98, *R. v. Home Secretary, ex p. Yiadom* [2000] ECR I–9265.
[37] Case C–348/96, *Criminal Proceedings against Calfa* [1999] ECR I–11. See also the pending ruling in C–459/99, *MRAX*, n. 6 above, in which the AG interpreted the legislation also in the light of fundamental rights even where a non-EU citizen is concerned.
[38] COM(1999)372.

39. It should be added that, in the main proceedings, almost seven months elapsed between the physical admission to the territory and the decision refusing entry.

40. It is of course understandable that a Member State should take the time necessary to carry out an administrative investigation of a Community national's situation before taking a decision refusing her leave to enter its territory.

41. However, if that State has accepted the physical presence of that national in its territory for a period which is manifestly longer than is required for such an investigation, it can also accept that national's presence during the time needed for him to exercise the rights of appeal referred to in Article 9 of the Directive.

4. THE PROPOSED LEGISLATION

In its 1999 Communication, the Commission had identified a number of concerns relating to the practice of Member States and the application of Directive 64/221.[39] These included (1) undue delay in examining resident-permit applications, (2) the role played by previous convictions in assessing public-order threats, (3) the use of general preventative measures, (4) inadequacies in informing people about measures adopted against them, and (5) the expulsion of second-generation migrants, long-term residents, and third-country national family members of EU citizens.

A chapter of the proposed new legislation on the free movement and residence of EU citizens, which is intended soon to replace Directive 64/221, now addresses several of these concerns.[40] The proposed measure integrates many of the main rulings of the ECJ on the subject into its definitions—*Pieck, Bouchereau, Adoui, Rutili, Calfa*, etc.—as well as taking over most of the relevant provisions of Directive 64/221 itself. According to the explanatory memorandum, the new legislation sets out to provide 'a tighter definition' of the circumstances under which the right of residence of EU citizens and their family members may be restricted. The new provisions are said to 'draw on the concept of fundamental rights' and provide better procedural protections. The Commission proposes to give absolute protection to minors who have family ties in the host country, and to people who have acquired a right of permanent residence under the new legislation.[41] Further, expulsion decisions are to be required to take into account the degree of integration of any EU citizen into the host country.

The annex containing the relevant list of diseases for the exercise of the public-health exception is omitted and a narrower list retained, to reflect current medical conditions, and the circumstances in which the health exception can be invoked are defined. The proposal also introduces a new provision which was not in Directive 64/221 to provide protection for EU citizens not only against measures based on public policy, etc., but also against expulsion decisions based merely on administrative grounds. Other significant modifications to the procedural guarantees are proposed, including requirements of better reasoning and clearer procedures for informing invididuals, and a new provision is proposed to require national criminal courts and

---

[39] COM(1999)372.   [40] See n. 2 above.
[41] For further discussion of the new legislative proposal, see Ch. 17, sect. 10 (e).

administrative authorities to have regard to EC law before they order the expulsion of an EU citizen as a penal measure.

5. CONCLUSIONS

i. As in other areas of EC law, and free-movement law in particular, there is a move towards legislative consolidation in this field. Directive 64/221 should soon be replaced by a chapter of the new proposed legislation on EU citizens.

ii. While the ECJ has always interpreted the derogations from free movement quite restrictively, and has enhanced the procedural protections provided, its recent case law also reflects a willingness to integrate EU citizenship considerations into this area of law.

iii. In this respect, the Commission and the Court are pursuing a similar rights-based approach, but it remains to be seen whether the Member States and the Council, whose interests generally reflect security concerns rather than fundamental rights concerns, will share this.

6. FURTHER READING

GUILD, E., and MINDERHOUD, P. (eds.), *Security of Residence and Expulsion* (Kluwer, 2001)

HALL, S., 'The ECHR and Public Policy Exceptions to the Free Movement of Workers under the EEC Treaty' (1991) 16 *ELRev*. 466

O'KEEFFE, D., 'Practical Difficulties in the Application of Article 48 of the EEC Treaty' (1982) 19 *CMLRev*. 35

20

EQUAL TREATMENT OF WOMEN AND MEN

1. CENTRAL ISSUES

i. The Treaty provision on which this Chapter focuses is Article 141 (ex Article 119), which first established the principle of equal pay between the sexes. Following the Amsterdam Treaty, this provision was amended to impose a legislative obligation on the Community to adopt measures in the area of equal opportunities and equal treatment of men and women at work going beyond the field of pay, and permitting forms of 'positive action'. Article 137 (ex Article 118) makes equal treatment of men and women at work and in the labour market an area for supportive Community action, giving the Council power to adopt directives.

ii. Although such express competence was included within the EC Treaty only in 1999, the Community long before had adopted more general legislation in the field of sex equality. The principle of equal treatment on grounds of sex has been gradually developed over the years through legislation, judicial action, Treaty amendment, and other policy change. It is an area of law which illustrates clearly the competing priorities of the economic and the social objectives of the Community, and which illustrates the interaction and dialogue which takes place between the Community's political and judicial branches in the law-making process.

iii. The gender equality principle remained for a long time fairly limited in scope and confined largely to employment-related sex discrimination. However, recent years have brought an apparently more determined institutional commitment to 'mainstream' gender equality across all EU policies and activities.[1] This commitment was enshrined at Amsterdam in Article 3 of the EC Treaty.[2] The Charter on Fundamental Rights contains a number of provisions relating to gender equality (Articles 21, 23, and 33(2)), and there is some evidence that sex equality law is being influenced by the wider body of EU anti-discrimination law emerging at present.

iv. EC sex-discrimination law was originally divided principally into three parts: equal pay, equal treatment, and social security. While the basic principle of non-discrimination on grounds of sex is common to all three, each is governed by different legal provisions which vary somewhat in content. Pay is governed by Article 141 (ex Article 119) and Directive 75/117; equal treatment by Article 141 and Directives 76/207, 86/613 (for the self-employed), and 96/34 (parental leave), and by Directive 92/85 concerning pregnancy; and social security by Directives 79/7, 86/378, and 96/97. However, we shall

---

[1] See the 1996 Communication on mainstreaming, COM(96)67 and the follow-up document COM(1998)122. More recently see COM(2001)295 on mainstreaming gender equality in EC development co-operation, and on mainstreaming in the structual funds see COM(2000)698 and COM(2001)539. For academic commentary see M. Pollack and E. Hafner-Burton, 'Mainstreaming Gender in the EU' (2000) 7 *JEPP* 432 and S. Mazey, *Gender Mainstreaming in the EU: Principles and Practice* (Kogan Page, 2001).

[2] Art. 3 declares that in all of the activities listed 'the Community shall aim to eliminate inequalities, and to promote equality, between men and women'.

see below that the division between these three categories is complex and has become blurred in various ways, particularly by the case law of the ECJ on pay and social security. Further, there are various measures such as Directives 97/80 and 97/81 on the burden of proof in sex-discrimination cases and on part-time work, which straddle both pay and equal treatment.

v. There has also been a considerable amount of soft law in the area of equal treatment, with the adoption of memoranda, resolutions, and recommendations on a range of equal-opportunities issues.[3] Sometimes these have acted as a form of precursor to further, harder law, and sometimes they have remained as an alternative to legislation.[4] The Commission has also adopted a range of action programmes, and more recently a first Framework Strategy on gender equality.

2. THE LEGAL FRAMEWORK

This chapter thus focuses only on one specific but important aspect of EU social policy, that of gender equality, which has in recent years gained more prominent status both in legal and in policy terms, even as a broader body of EU anti-discrimination law is developing alongside.[5] EU 'social policy' is a loose term which lacks an agreed definition within EU law, being, for some, synonymous with labour and employment law, while for others implying a much wider field.[6] The main EC Treaty provisions grouped under this heading are those in Articles 136 to 148 (ex Articles 117–125) EC. These Articles, into which the provisions of the Maastricht Social Policy Agreement (SPA) were incorporated,[7] contain the basis for Community legislative action concerning improvement of working conditions and the living standard of workers, and equality between men and women with regard to the labour market and treatment at work. These are followed by other provisions on what could also broadly be called Community social policy, i.e., the Treaty Articles governing education, culture, and public health, as well as a later chapter dealing with economic and social cohesion. An important new chapter on employment policy, focusing on the promotion of high employment, was added by the ToA to Articles 125–130 of

[3] For earlier initiatives on sexual harassment before the amendment to Dir. 76/207 discussed below, see Commission Recommendation 92/131 and Code [1992] OJ L49/1, and Commission communications on the consultation of management and labour on the prevention of sexual harassment at work: COM(96)373 and SEC(97)568. On child care see Council Recommendation 92/241 [1992] OJ L123/16. On the balanced participation of men and women in decision-making, and in family and working life see Council Recommendation 96/694 [1996] OJ L319, and more recently [2000]OJ C218/5.

[4] An interesting hybrid is the Council's Decision 2000/228/EC (a hard legislative measure) containing the Employment Guidelines (soft legislative instruments) under Art. 128 EC, which provides for strengthening policies for equal opportunities for men and women: OJ [2000] L72/15.

[5] See Ch. 9 for discussion of the range of EC anti-discrimination policies and laws emerging under Art. 13 EC.

[6] For some of the English language texts on labour law see C. Barnard, *EC Employment Law* (2nd edn., Oxford University Press, 2000), E. Szyszczak, *EC Labour Law* (Longman, 2000), R. Blanpain (ed.), *Labour Law and Industrial Relations in the EU* (Kluwer, 1998). For recent books on the broader social policy dimension see T. Hervey, *European Social Law and Policy* (Longman, 1998) and J. Shaw (ed.), *Social Law and Policy in an Evolving EU* (Hart, 2000).

[7] The UK, at the time of the Maastricht TEU, was the only one of the Member States to exclude itself from the application of the Social Policy Agreement (SPA) and Protocol, but a change of government led to the reversal of this policy in 1997. As a result, the Treaty of Amsterdam incorporated the provisions of the annexed Agreement into the body of the EC Treaty: C. Barnard, 'The United Kingdom, the 'Social Chapter' and the Amsterdam Treaty' (1997) 26 *ILJ* 275.

the EC Treaty. Articles 146 to 148, (ex Articles 123 to 125) concern the European Social Fund, which was established to provide financial assistance for some of the Community's social-policy objectives.

It is evident that the type of legal basis used for Community action and the type of legislative instrument used normally influence the nature and content of the measure. In other words the legal nature of the measure adopted, whether a soft legal instrument, a Directive, or another harder legislative measure adopted under one of the consultation, co-operation, or co-decision procedures, or following the agreement of the social partners under Article 139 (ex Article 118b), is very likely to affect the substantive nature of the measure which emerges. In the past, the Treaty basis for secondary legislation in the equal-treatment field has varied, with the Pay Directive being adopted under Article 94 (ex Article 100), the Equal Treatment and State Social Security Directives under Article 308 (ex Article 235), the Pregnancy Directive under Article 138 (ex Article 118a), and the framework agreements on part-time work and parental leave under what was previously the Social Policy Protocol, while Article 137 (ex Article 118) now provides a more general legislative base for such action. More recently, the Council adopted a decision establishing an action programme on gender equality under Article 13 EC,[8] while the proposal to amend equal treatment Article 76/207 has been based on the expanded Article 141 (ex Article 119).[9]

In the area of softer law and policy, the Commission adopted a series of action programmes to promote equality in the workplace, culminating in the Fourth Action Programme for 1996–2000,[10] before the first 'framework strategy on gender equality' was adopted in 2000. The Commission also began the practice, in 1996 of adopting an Annual Report on Equal Opportunities for Women and Men in the EU.[11] The framework strategy on gender equality was announced by the Commission in 2000, as a comprehensive programme going beyond the compartmentalized approach of earlier action plans, and intended to 'embrace all Community policies in its efforts to promote gender equality'.[12] On the basis of this framework strategy the Council in 2001 established a four-year programme on gender equality for 2001–5,[13] and the Commission has already adopted annual work programmes for 2000 and 2001 respectively.[14] There are five listed fields of intervention under the framework strategy and the action programme, which are: (a) economic life, (b) equal participation and representation,[15] (c) social rights, (d) civil life, and (e) gender roles and stereotypes.

Apart from the various concrete regimes of sex equality law outlined above, the ECJ has frequently stated that the general principle of equal treatment between men and women is a fundamental one in the Community legal order.[16] The Court ruled,

---

[8] Dec. 2001/51 [2001] OJ L17/22.   [9] See COM(2000)334 and COM(2001)321 [2001] OJ C270/9.

[10] See Council Dec. 95/593 [1995] OJ L335/37 on this programme.

[11] See the reports for 2000 and 2001, COM(2001)179 and COM(2002)258 respectively.

[12] COM(2000)335.   [13] Decision 2001/51 [2001] OJ L17/22.

[14] See COM(2001)119, COM(2002)773.

[15] The Commission has also committed itself firmly to achieving gender balance in committees and expert groups, in Decision 2000/407/EC [2000] OJ L154/34, which sets a minimum target of 40%.

[16] In Cases 20/71, *Sabbatini* [1972] ECR 345; 21/74, *Airola* [1972] ECR 221; and 75, 117/82, *Razzouk and Beydoun* v. *Commission* [1984] ECR 1509, the Court held that the *Community* institutions were bound by the principle of non-discrimination on grounds of sex in the treatment of their staff.

originally in *Defrenne III*,[17] and more recently in the cases of *P* v. *S*[18] and *Schröder*,[19] that the elimination of sex discrimination was one of the fundamental personal human rights which had to be protected within Community law. However, in *Defrenne III* in 1978, this principle was held not to be directly applicable against Member States, since the Community had not yet assumed competence in the area of equal treatment at work and the Treaty at that stage only prohibited the states directly from maintaining unequal pay between the sexes.[20] Indeed it remains the case, despite the frequent judicial rulings on the fundamental status of the principle of equal treatment on grounds of sex, that this principle is not directly effective *per se* and requires the existence of further legislative implementation such as Directive 76/207 to be fully effective in challenging national law or employer practice.

Further, it appeared for a time after the *P* v. *S* case concerning discrimination against transsexuals under Directive 76/207,[21] that the notion of 'sex equality' in EC law would be given a broad interpretation. Having ruled in that case that sex discrimination under the Directive included discrimination arising from the gender reassignment of the employee,[22] the ECJ however backtracked in the equal-pay case of *Grant*. There the Court ruled, against the opinion of the Advocate General, that the prohibition against discrimination on grounds of sex within Article 141 (ex Article 119) did not cover discrimination on grounds of sexual orientation.[23] The Court confirmed this stance in *D* v. *Council*,[24] and in both *D* and *Grant* appeared to retreat from the judicial expansiveness of *P* v. *S*, by pointing to the new legislative powers in the field of equal treatment, and passing responsibility for the protection of fundamental personal rights within the sphere of employment discrimination back to the political institutions.[25]

3. EQUAL PAY

From the outset, the Treaty included the principle of equal pay firmly within the scope of Community competence, and made it applicable to the Member States, although it was at first unclear whether the principle applied not only to equal work but also to work of equal value. Later rulings of the ECJ, subsequent secondary legislation, and ultimately the Amsterdam Treaty (ToA) amendments to Article 141 (ex Article 119) indicated that work of equal value was also covered. The ToA also added paragraphs 3 and 4, and Article 141 now provides:

1. Each Member State shall ensure that the principle of equal pay for male and female workers for equal work or work of equal value is applied.

---

[17] Case 149/77, *Defrenne* v. *Sabena* [1978] ECR 1365, paras. 26–27.
[18] Case C–13/94, *P* v. *S and Cornwall County Council* [1996] ECR I–2143, para. 19.
[19] C–50/96, *Deutsche Telekom* v. *Schröder* [2000] ECR I–743, para. 56.
[20] Case 149/77, n. 17 above, para. 30.   [21] Case C–13/94, *P* v. *S*, n. 18 above.   [22] *Ibid.*, para. 20.
[23] Case C–249/96, *Grant* v. *South-West Trains* [1998] ECR I–621. For commentaries see M. Bell (1999) 5 *ELJ* 63, C. Barnard (1998) 57 *Camb.* LJ 352.
[24] C–125/99P, *D* v. *Council* [2001] ECR I–4319. For further discussion see Ch. 8, nn. 65, 128–130 and accompanying text, and Ch. 9, n. 92 and acccompanying text.
[25] Case C–249/96, n. 23 above, paras. 47–48.

2. For the purpose of this Article, 'pay' means the ordinary basic or minimum wage or salary and any other consideration, whether in cash or in kind, which the worker receives directly or indirectly, in respect of his employment from his employer.

Equal pay without discrimination based on sex means:

(a) that pay for the same work at piece rates shall be calculated on the basis of the same unit of measurement;

(b) that pay for work at time rates shall be the same for the same job.

3. The Council, acting in accordance with the procedure referred to in Article 251, and after consulting the Economic and Social Committee, shall adopt measures to ensure the application of the principle of equal opportunities and equal treatment of men and women in matters of employment and occupation, including the principle of equal pay for equal work or work of equal value.

4. With a view to ensuring full equality in practice between men and women in working life, the principle of equal treatment shall not prevent any Member State from maintaining or adopting measures providing for specific advantages in order to make it easier for the under-represented sex to pursue a vocational activity or to prevent or compensate for disadvantages in professional careers.

According to various writers, the historical explanation for the original Article 141 (ex Article 119), given the absence of any mention in the Treaty of equal treatment other than in the context of pay, was France's concern that it would be at a competitive disadvantage in observing the principle of equal pay for equal work more thoroughly than it was observed in other Member States.[26] In other words, concern over unfair treatment of women in the labour market was not the primary factor motivating the drafters of this Article. However, it can certainly now be said that Article 141 and the other provisions of Community sex-discrimination law are viewed and interpreted not primarily as an instrument of economic policy, but as an important part of Community social policy. This was underscored by the Court in the recent case of *Schröder*.[27]

Just as in the context of the free movement of workers, the mixed objectives of the Treaty provisions emerge clearly in the areas of equal pay and equal treatment. On the one hand, just as those free-movement provisions were intended to liberalize the market and to further the economic aims of creating a single trading entity in Europe, the equal-treatment provisions were intended to 'level the playing field', to ensure that employers in no one Member State would have this particular competitive advantage over those in another Member State. On the other hand, just as the free-movement provisions have been interpreted by the ECJ also as a means of enhancing the living standard of individuals and conferring rights directly on them and on their families, so the ECJ ruled that Article 141 (ex Article 119) has a social and not just an economic

---

[26] C. Barnard, 'The Economic Objectives of Article 119', in D. O'Keeffe and T. Hervey (eds.), *Sex Equality Law in the European Union*, (Wiley, 1996).

[27] N. 19 above.

aim. In the first of the *Defrenne* cases, the Belgian Government argued that its aim was economic only, namely 'to avoid discrepancies in cost prices due to the employment of female labour less well paid for the same work than male labour'.[28] The Court rejected this view in *Defrenne II.*

Case 43/75, Defrenne v. Sabena
[1976] ECR 455

[ToA renumbering: Art. 119 is now Art. 141]

THE ECJ

8. Article 119 pursues a double aim.

9. First, in the light of the different stages of the development of social legislation in the various Member States, the aim of Article 119 is to avoid a situation in which undertakings established in States which have actually implemented the principle of equal pay suffer a competitive disadvantage in intra-Community competition as compared with undertakings established in States which have not yet eliminated discrimination against women workers as regards pay.

10. Secondly, this provision forms part of the social objectives of the Community, which is not merely an economic union, but is at the same time intended, by common action, to ensure social progress and seek the constant improvement of the living and working conditions of their peoples, as is emphasized by the Preamble to the Treaty.

. . .

12. This double aim, which is at once economic and social, shows that the principle of equal pay forms part of the foundations of the Community.

We saw in Chapter 5, however, that various Member States had avoided the implementation of the equal-pay principle for years, eventually arguing unsuccessfully to the ECJ in *Defrenne* that Article 141 (ex Article 119) lacked direct effect. However, the Court ruled that it had been directly effective since the end of the first stage of the transitional period, and that its direct effectiveness could not be affected by any implementing provision either of the states or of the Community. Nevertheless, the ECJ was swayed by the arguments of the Member States on the serious financial consequences of such a ruling for them, and it declared that in view of the likely incorrect understanding of the Member States of the effects of Article 141, due in part to the fact that the Commission had not brought earlier infringement proceedings against them, its ruling should only have effect prospectively. This meant that only those who had already brought legal proceedings or made a claim could rely on the Article in respect of pay claims for periods prior to the date of judgment. Prospective overruling of this kind by the Court has not been frequent, and the cases tend to be

---

[28] See Case 80/70, *Defrenne v. Belgium (Defrenne I)* [1971] ECR 445.

those in which there are considerable financial implications for the Member States or their industries.[29]

In the more recent case of *Schröder*, the ECJ was confronted with a conflict posited between the social (ensuring fairness to individual women and men) and the economic (ensuring equal conditions for competing employers) aims of Article 141 (ex article 119).[30] If the social aim were to take priority, German law could apply the equal-pay principle retroactively so as to permit part-time workers access to an occupational pension scheme, whereas if the economic aim were to take priority, Germany—in order to ensure that its firms were not operating under less favourable conditions than those of other Member State competitors which were permitted by *Defrenne II* not to apply the equal-pay principle retroactively—should also not do so. The ECJ began by repeating the 'double aim' ruling in paragraphs 8–11 of *Defrenne II* (above) and continued:

> 56. However, in later decisions the Court has repeatedly held that the right not to be discrimi-
> nated against on grounds of sex is one of the fundamental human rights whose observance the
> Court has a duty to ensure (see, to that effect, Case 149/77 *Defrenne III* [1978] ECR 1365,
> paragraphs 26 and 27, Joined Cases 75/82 and 117/82 *Razzouk and Beydoun* v. *Commission*
> [1984] ECR 1509, paragraph 16, and Case C–13/94 *P.* v. *S. and Cornwall County Council*
> [1996] ECR I–2143, paragraph 19).
> 57. In view of that case-law, it must be concluded that the economic aim pursued by Article
> 119 of the Treaty, namely the elimination of distortions of competition between undertakings
> established in different Member States, is secondary to the social aim pursued by the same
> provision, which constitutes the expression of a fundamental human right.

Thus the social aim of Article 141, read in the light of the Court's case law on fundamental human rights over the years, has come to take precedence over its economic rationale. It should be noted, too, that while *Schröder* itself was an equal-pay case, the ECJ's ruling seems to apply to Article 141 and the equal treatment principle more generally.

(a) DIRECTIVE 75/117

Directive 75/117, which was mentioned by the ECJ in the context of situations which might require further legislation before Article 141 (ex Article 119) could be applied,[31] was based on Article 94 (ex Article 100) of the Treaty, which concerns the approximation of the laws of the Member States.[32] The twin aims of the equal-pay principle are reflected in the preamble to the measure, and its basic thrust is to require the elimination of sex discrimination in pay in cases involving the same work or work to

---

[29] See below Case 262/88, *Barber* v. *GRE* [1990] ECR 1889, and in Ch. 17, n. 164 Case 24/86, *Blaizot* [1988] ECR 379. Contrast cases C–200/90, *Dansk Denkavit and Poulsen* v. *Skatteministeriet* [1992] ECR I–2217; C–137/94, *R.* v. *Secretary of State for Health, ex p. Richardson* [1995] ECR I–3407, and more recently C–184/99, *Grzelczyk* v. *CPAS* [2001] ECR I–6193 and C–366/99, *Griesmar* v. *Ministre de l'Economie* [2001] ECR I–9383. See N. Hyland, 'Temporal Limitation of the Effects of the Judgments of the Court of Justice' (1995) 4 *IJEL* 208.

[30] N. 19 above. For comments on the case see L. Besselink (2001) 38 *CMLRev.* 437 and E. Ellis (2000) 25 *ELRev.* 564.

[31] [1976] ECR 455, para. 20.   [32] Dir. 75/117 [1975] OJ L45/19.

which equal value is attached, and to require job-classification schemes to be similarly free from discrimination.[33] Member States are required to abolish any such discrimination in legislative or administrative provisions[34] and to ensure that any breaches of the equal-pay principle in collective agreements or contracts are rendered void or amended.[35] The Directive also imposes a more positive obligation on the states to take effective measures to ensure that the equal-pay principle is observed.[36] Other provisions, which are similar to those to be found in the Equal Treatment and Social Security Directives, are the requirement that employees should be able to pursue their claims by judicial process,[37] that complainants should be protected against dismissal,[38] and that employees should be properly informed of their rights.[39]

The fact that Directive 75/117 was intended to apply the equal-pay principle not just to 'similar work' but also to 'work of equal value' does not mean that Article 141 (ex Article 119) as it then was did not of itself cover the latter. Although the Directive fleshed out the provisions of that Article, the right has always been said by the Court to stem directly from the Treaty, and the words in the Directive are to be given the same meaning as those in the Treaty.[40] Thus, even before the express inclusion of 'work of equal value' by the Amsterdam Treaty amendment, the direct effect of Article 141 could be invoked against a private employer in a case concerning work of equal value, avoiding arguments about the horizontal direct effect of the Directive. And the ToA amendment did not render the Directive redundant, since the detailed provisions of the latter were designed to render the implementation of the equal-pay principle more effective in concrete situations. The Directive was intended to address the problem of how to apply the equal-pay principle when the work performed by two employees is quite different, but is alleged to be of equal value, and its aim was to place the onus on the states of putting the principle into practice. However, the Commission was not satisfied with the steps taken by all of the Member States to implement the Directive, and proceedings were brought against the UK in the 1980s for failing to ensure an adequate job-classification system for assessing work of equal value.[41] The ECJ ruled that where there was disagreement on the application of the equal-pay principle, a worker had to have at least a right of access to an appropriate authority which could give a binding ruling on whether or not his or her work has the same value as other work.[42]

In *Brunnhofer*, the Court indicated that the personal qualities of the employee and the manner in which he or she performed the work could not simply be conflated and used retrospectively by an employer to argue that the employee was not carrying out similar work or work of equal value to other employees, for the purposes of

---

[33] Art. 1. See Case 237/85, *Rummler* [1986] ECR 2101 where the Court ruled that the use of criteria such as muscle-demand for the purpose of determining rates of pay was permitted by Dir. 75/117. For criticism of the judgment see S. Fredman, 'EC Discrimination Law: A Critique' (1992) 21 *ILJ* 119, 123. For a comparison of muscular strength and manual dexterity see Case C–400/93, *Royal Copenhagen, Specialarbejderforbundet i Danmark* v. *Dansk Industri* [1995] ECR I–1275. See also Case C–236/98, *JämO* [2000] ECR I–2189, para. 48.

[34] Art. 3.   [35] Art. 4.   [36] Art. 6.   [37] Art. 2.   [38] Art. 5.   [39] Art. 7.

[40] See most recently Case C–381/99, *Brunnhofer* v. *Bank der Österreichischen Postsparkasse* [2001] ECR I–4961, para. 29. See also Case C–309/97, *Angestelltenbetriebsrat der Wiener Gebietskrankenkasse* [1999] ECR I–2865 on 'same work'.

[41] Case 61/81, *Commission* v. *UK* [1982] ECR 2601.

[42] *Ibid.*, para. 9.

explaining a pay differential which existed from the outset.[43] This did not, the ECJ ruled, mean that individual work capacity should not be taken into account in other ways, e.g., in relation to an employee's career development as compared with that of a more effective colleague, and therefore in *subsequent* postings and pay. However, rather confusingly, the ECJ both in *Brunnhofer* and earlier in *Angestelltenbetriebsrat der Wiener Gebietskrankenkasse* stated that professional training could be a valid criterion for ascertaining whether or not employees were engaged in the 'same work'.[44] This has rightly been criticized on the basis that while a person's higher qualifications or training may certainly provide grounds for *justifying* a higher level of pay for work done, it does not render such work qualitatively different from that carried out by other employees with lower qualifications performing the same task.[45]

The difficulties of assessment and proof which frequently confront employees wishing to make an equal-pay claim are illustrated by *Danfoss*, in which the ECJ ruled that employers were not entitled to maintain 'opaque' pay practices:

Case 109/88, Handels- og Kontorfunktionærernes Forbund i Danmark v. Dansk Arbejdsgiverforening, acting on behalf of Danfoss
[1989] ECR 3199

Danfoss, an employer, paid the same basic wage to employees in the same wage group, but it also awarded individual pay supplements which were calculated on the basis of mobility, training, and seniority. A complaint was brought before the industrial arbitration board on behalf of two female employees, each of whom worked within a different wage group, and within these two wage groups it was shown that a man's average wage was higher than that of a woman. The Board referred several questions to the ECJ.

THE ECJ

10. It is apparent from the documents before the Court that the issue between the parties to the main proceedings has its origin in the fact that the system of individual supplements applied to basic pay is implemented in such a way that a woman is unable to identify the reasons for a difference between her pay and that of a man doing the same work. Employees do not know what criteria in the matter of supplements are applied to them and how they are applied. They know only the amount of their supplemented pay without being able to determine the effect of the individual criteria. Those who are in a particular wage group are thus unable to compare the various components of their pay with those of the pay of their colleagues who are in the same wage group.

11. In those circumstances the questions put by the national court must be understood as asking whether the Equal Pay Directive must be interpreted as meaning that where an undertaking applies a system of pay which is totally lacking in transparency, it is for the employer to

---

[43] N. 40 above.

[44] Cases C–381/99, n. 40 above, para. 78, and C–309/97, *Angestelltenbetriebsrat der Wiener Gebietskrankenkasse* [1999] ECR I–2865, para. 19.

[45] See E. Ellis, 'The Recent Jurisprudence of the Court of Justice in the Field of Sex Equality' (2000) 37 *CMLRev.* 1403.

prove that his practice in the matter of wages is not discriminatory, if a female worker establishes, in relation to a relatively large number of employees, that the average pay for women is less than for men.

12. In that respect, it must first be borne in mind that in its judgment of 20 June 1988 in Case 318/86 *Commission* v. *France* [1988] ECR 3559, paragraph 27, the Court condemned a system of recruitment, characterized by a lack of transparency, as being contrary to the principle of equal access to employment on the ground that the lack of transparency prevented any form of supervision by the national courts.

13. It should next be pointed out that in a situation where a system of individual pay supplements which is completely lacking in transparency is at issue, female employees can establish differences only in so far as average pay is concerned. They would be deprived of any effective means of enforcing the principle of equal pay before the national courts if the effect of adducing such evidence was not to impose upon the employer the burden of proving that his practice in the matter of wages is not in fact discriminatory.

14. Finally, it should be noted that under Article 6 of the Equal Pay Directive Member States must, in accordance with their national circumstances and legal systems, take the measures necessary to ensure that the principle of equal pay is applied and that effective means are available to ensure that it is observed. The concern for effectiveness which thus underlies the Directive means that it must be interpreted as implying adjustments to national rules on the burden of proof in special cases where such adjustments are necessary for the effective implementation of the principle of equality.

15. To show that his practice in the matter of wages does not systematically work to the disadvantage of female employees the employer will have to indicate how he has applied the criteria concerning supplements and will thus be forced to make his system of pay transparent.

Thus in *Danfoss*, the ECJ decided that the requirement of effectiveness could impose on the employer, in a reversal of the normal onus of proof, an obligation to show that a non-transparent pay policy (as far as supplements were concerned) did not discriminate on grounds of sex. If the normal burden of proof were to apply in such a situation, it would be excessively difficult or impossible for an affected employee to show that pay discrimination had actually occurred.

Prior to *Danfoss*, the Commission had in 1988 proposed a directive on reversing the burden of proof in sex-discrimination cases, but this was blocked in the Council.[46] Yet the ECJ, implicitly overriding the Member State objections reflected in the blocking of this proposal, achieved a similar result at least in the field of pay. Such an assertion by the Court of its authority in the face of opposition on the part of the states and within the Community legislative process in the field of sex discrimination is not uncommon, as we shall see in the occupational pensions context below. However, to portray the ECJ as being constantly at loggerheads with the legislative institutions in the equal-treatment field would not present a fair picture, since the policy process is a complex one which involves, amongst others, the Member States, the EC political institutions, the ECJ, and indeed the national courts, each exercising a different degree

---

[46] [1988] OJ C176/5. For comment on this aspect of *Danfoss* see J. Shaw, 'The Burden of Proof and the Legality of Supplementary Payments in Equal Pay Cases' (1990) 15 *ELRev.* 260, 263–4.

of influence and input into that process. The fact that in 1997, following a fresh proposal by the Commission for such a measure, the Council eventually adopted a directive on the burden of proof under the then Social Policy Agreement and Protocol indicates that the interaction between judicial and legislative branches can be fruitful rather than conflictual.[47] This means that all of the Member States now accept that the employer/respondent should bear the burden of proof, once the employee/plaintiff has established facts from which it may be presumed that there has been direct or indirect discrimination.[48] The Directive, which had to be implemented in 2001, contains a fairly broad definition of indirect discrimination,[49] and the measure applies to the Equal Pay, Equal Treatment, Pregnancy, and Parental Leave Directives, but not to social security, contrary to what the Commission had originally proposed.

(b) 'INDIRECT' DISCRIMINATION IN PAY AND OBJECTIVE JUSTIFICATION

(i) INDIRECT DISCRIMINATION

Indirect discrimination is a concept which has been discussed in Chapters 16, 17, and 18 in the context of discriminatory restrictions on freedom of movement in the Community. In the context of equal treatment of women and men, indirect discrimination is a concept well known in many jurisdictions as a means of confronting and redressing systemic discrimination. Thus, where a rule or a practice, although not framed in terms which apply only to one sex, has the effect of disadvantaging a considerably higher percentage of one sex, that rule or practice will be considered indirectly discriminatory.

According to the ECJ in *Defrenne II*, while Article 119 (now Article 141) could have direct effect in a situation of clear and direct pay discrimination, it could not in the case of indirect and disguised discrimination, since further legislation might be required in the latter context before such discrimination could be identified.[50] This analysis was subsequently confirmed by the ruling in *Macarthys Ltd.* v. *Smith*,[51] in which the ECJ stated that, for the purpose of determining sex discrimination in pay, comparisons were to be confined to parallels drawn between work actually done by employees of different sex within the same establishment or service,[52] although the employment need not be contemporaneous.[53] Comparisons with a *hypothetical* male worker would take the situation outside the direct effect of Article 141 (ex Article

---

[47] Council Dir. 97/80 [1997] OJ L14/6. See also Council Dir 98/52 on the extension of Dir 97/80 to the UK [1998] OJ L205/66.

[48] See Case C–381/99, *Brunnhofer* v. *Österreichischer Bank Postsparkasse* [2001] ECR I–4961, where the national court had apparently assumed that the employer had to show that two posts were not comparable, without the plaintiff having first to establish a *prima facie* case of discrimination on the facts.

[49] This differs from the definition of indirect discrimination subsequently adopted in the two new discrimination directives on race and employment under Art. 13 EC. See Ch. 9, nn. 88–9.

[50] N. 31 above, para. 18.

[51] Case 129/79, *Macarthys Ltd.* v. *Smith* [1980] ECR 1275, paras. 14–15.

[52] For an example of the difficulties which can be encountered with comparisons within the same establishment see Case C–400/93, *Royal Copenhagen* [1995] ECR I–1275, paras. 29–38.

[53] See also Case C–200/91, *Coloroll Pension Trustees Ltd.* v. *James Richard Russell* [1994] ECR I–4389, paras. 103–104.

119), since the identification of discrimination in such a situation implied 'comparative studies of entire branches of industry and therefore requires, as a prerequisite, the elaboration by the Community and national legislative bodies of criteria of assessment'.[54] However, even if a comparator doing the same work or work of equal value within the same establishment cannot be found, no legislation is needed and Article 141 (ex Article 119) has direct effect where a woman is paid less than a man who is doing work of *lower* value within the same establishment.[55] But the ECJ's ruling is not authority for the proposition that Article 141 of itself requires proportionate pay, so that, although a woman in such circumstances is entitled to at least the same pay as a man doing work of lower value, she cannot necessarily rely directly on the Treaty for payment of a higher wage to reflect the value of her work.

Subsequently, Advocate General Warner in *Worringham* pointed out that the language used by the ECJ in *Defrenne II* was puzzling, since it implied that Article 141 (ex Article 119) could not have direct effect where discrimination was 'indirect' or 'disguised'.[56] Confirming his view, case law since then has made clear that, despite the rulings in *Defrenne II* and *Macarthys*, the existence of indirect discrimination does not preclude the direct effect of the Article, when such discrimination can be identified on what the ECJ called a 'purely legal analysis' without the need for further legislation. This was first established in *Jenkins*.

Case 96/80, Jenkins v. Kingsgate (Clothing Productions) Ltd.
[1981] ECR 911

[ToA renumbering: Art. 119 EC is now Art. 141]

The complainant, a part-time female employee of Kingsgate, was paid a lower hourly rate than her full-time male colleagues performing the same work. She brought an action before the Industrial Tribunal claiming a breach of the equal-pay principle and the UK Equal Pay Act 1970, which provided for equal pay whenever a woman was employed on 'like work' with a man in the same employment. Her employer acknowledged that the work was 'like work' but argued that the different pay rates were, in accordance with section 1(3) of the Act, due to a material difference other than the difference of sex.

THE ECJ

9. It appears from the first three questions and the reasons stated in the order making the reference that the national court is principally concerned to know whether a difference in the level of pay for work carried out part-time and the same work carried out full-time may amount to discrimination of a kind prohibited by Article 119 of the Treaty when the category of part-time workers is exclusively or predominantly comprised of women.

---

[54] It is not clear after this judgment whether a woman complaining of unequal pay can point to a male comparator in a different establishment.
[55] Case 157/86, *Murphy* v. *Bord Telecom Eireann* [1988] ECR 673.
[56] See his argument in Case 69/80, *Worringham and Humphreys* v. *Lloyd's Bank Ltd.* [1981] ECR 767, 803, that it was inaccurate to say that Art. 141 (ex Art. [k1]119) could not have direct effect in the case of covert or indirect discrimination.

10. The answer to the questions thus understood is that the purpose of Article 119 is to ensure the application of the principle of equal pay for men and women for the same work. The differences in pay prohibited by that provision are therefore exclusively those based on the difference of the sex of the workers. Consequently, the fact that part-time work is paid at an hourly rate lower than pay for full-time work does not amount per se to discrimination prohibited by Article 119 provided that the hourly rates are applied to workers belonging to either category without distinction based on sex.

11. If there is no such distinction, therefore, the fact that work paid at time rates is remunerated at an hourly rate which varies according to the number of hours worked per week does not offend against the principle of equal pay laid down in Article 119 of the Treaty, in so far as the difference in pay between part-time work and full-time work is attributable to factors which are objectively justified and are in no way related to any discrimination based on sex.

12. Such may be the case, in particular, when by giving hourly rates of pay which are lower for part-time work than those for full-time work the employer is endeavouring, on economic grounds which may be objectively justified, to encourage full-time work irrespective of the sex of the worker.

13. By contrast, if it is established that a considerably smaller percentage of women than of men perform the minimum number of weekly working hours required in order to be able to claim the full-time hourly rate of pay, the inequality in pay will be contrary to Article 119 of the Treaty where, regard being had to the difficulties encountered by women in arranging to work that minimum number of hours per week, the pay policy of the undertaking in question cannot be explained by factors other than discrimination based on sex.

14. Where the hourly rate of pay differs according to whether the work is part-time or full-time it is for the national courts to decide in each individual case whether, regard being had to the facts of the case, its history and the employer's intention, a pay policy such as that which is at issue in the main proceedings although represented as a difference based on weekly working hours is or is not in reality discrimination based on the sex of the worker.

Although the ECJ states in paragraph 10 that the only differences in pay prohibited by the Treaty are those based on sex, it appears from the rest of the judgment that this does not mean that only pay differences which are deliberately or directly discriminatory on grounds of sex will breach that provision. On the contrary, the following paragraph indicates that, even where there is no direct sex-based distinction, the difference in hourly pay between part-time and full-time workers will be compatible with Article 141 (ex Article 119) only 'insofar as they are objectively justified'. In paragraph 12 the Court gives an example of what it appears to consider a legitimate policy which an employer may be pursuing by maintaining different pay rates for part- and full-time work, namely to encourage a greater number of full-time workers.[57] Advocate General Warner noted that women constituted 90 per cent of part-time workers in the Community, and the ECJ ruled that the issue of objective justification was for the national court to weigh, with the onus being on the employer to demonstrate that it was based on something legitimate other than the sex of the

---

[57] See also the decision of the ECJ in the context of equal treatment, rather than pay, where it ruled that the interests of the enterprise might justify discrimination against part-time workers: Case C–189/91, *Kirshammer-Hack* v. *Sidal* [1993] ECR I–6185; also C–322/98, *Kachelmann* v. *Bankhaus Hermann Lampe* [2000] ECR I–7505; and the cases on social security discussed below.

worker. The broadening of the formal criterion of direct sex-based discrimination in this case to include the less obvious but equally or even more pervasive forms of pay discrimination affecting women was an important development, but the parallel development of an equally broad concept of objective justification reduced its impact. Article 2(2) of the Directive on the burden of proof integrates the notion of 'objective justification' into the definition of indirect discrimination: 'indirect discrimination shall exist where an apparently neutral provision, criterion or practice disadvantages a substantially higher proportion of the members of one sex unless that provision is appropriate and necessary and can be justified by objective factors unrelated to sex', but this definition was criticized by the Social Affairs Commissioner and by a number of women's interest groups. The concept also appears in the Framework Agreement on part-time work concluded by the social partners under the SPA, which was implemented by a Council directive.[58] The Agreement declares that it is intended to help in the removal of discrimination against part-time workers (except in so far as social security is concerned, since this is left to the Member States to govern) and to facilitate the development of and improve the quality of part-time work. Clause 4(1) provides that:

In respect of employment conditions, part-time workers shall not be treated in a less favourable manner than comparable full-time workers solely because they work part time unless different treatment is justified on objective grounds.

Paragraph four of the same clause also specifies that Member States under certain circumstances may make access to particular conditions of employment subject to a period of service, time worked, or earnings qualification 'where justified by objective reasons', although these qualifications should be periodically reviewed. Thus, although the stated aim of the Agreement and the Directive implementing it is to facilitate the development of voluntary part-time employment and to encourage equal treatment of part-time and full-time workers, this remains always subject to the proviso that differential treatment may be justified on 'objective' grounds. The Race and Framework Employment Anti-discrimination Directives, too, incorporate the absence of objective justification into their definitions of indirect discrimination.[59]

Exactly what can constitute objective justification remains unclear. The ECJ often leaves the matter for the national court to decide, which raises the likelihood of differences amongst the tribunals of the various Member States on whether an indirectly discriminatory pay policy is justified. The ECJ however has also given some guidance by declaring certain grounds of justification to be too general and indicating that others may be sufficient. Problems of inconsistency and uncertainty none the less remain, contributing to the volume of expensive and possibly duplicated litigation in different Member States. Further, even if such disparity amongst the different national courts and authorities on the issue of objective justification may cause problems, it is also clear that the Article 234 (ex Article 177) reference procedure does not necessarily provide the best forum for assessing an employer's or a state's proffered justification,

---

[58] Council Dir. 97/81 concerning the Framework Agreement on part-time work concluded by UNICE, CEEP, and the ETUC [1997] OJ L14/9.

[59] Council Dirs. 2000/43 [2000] OJ L180/22 and 2000/78 [2000] OJ L303/16.

unless the factual information supplied to the ECJ is very thorough. Nevertheless, more guidance on this issue has gradually emerged.

In *Bilka*, concerning eligibility of part-time workers for an occupational pension scheme, the ECJ formulated a test for objective justification very similar to the three-part proportionality test developed when examining State justifications for restrictions on the free movement of goods and services.[60]

Case 170/84, Bilka-Kaufhaus GmbH v. Karin Weber von Hartz
[1986] ECR 1607

[Note ToA renumbering: Arts. 119 and 177 are now Arts. 141 and 234 respectively]

29. If, therefore, it should be found that a much lower proportion of women than men work full time, the exclusion of part-time workers from the occupational pension scheme would be contrary to Article 119 of the Treaty where, taking into account the difficulties encountered by women workers in working full-time, that measure could not be explained by factors which exclude any discrimination on grounds of sex.

30. However, if the undertaking is able to show that its pay practice may be explained by objectively justified factors unrelated to any discrimination on grounds of sex there is no breach of Article 119.

. . .

33. In its observations Bilka argues that the exclusion of part-time workers from the occupational pension scheme is intended solely to discourage part-time work, since in general part-time workers refuse to work in the late afternoon and on Saturdays. In order to ensure the presence of an adequate workforce during those periods it was therefore necessary to make full-time work more attractive than part-time work, by making the occupational pension scheme open only to full-time workers. Bilka concludes that on the basis of the judgment of 31 March 1981 it cannot be accused of having infringed Article 119.

. . .

36. It is for the national court, which has sole jurisdiction to make findings of fact, to determine whether and to what extent the grounds put forward by an employer to explain the adoption of a pay practice which applies independently of a worker's sex but in fact affects far more women than men may be regarded as objectively justified economic grounds. If the national court finds that the measures chosen by the employer correspond to a real need on the part of the undertaking, are appropriate with a view to achieving the objectives pursued and are necessary to that end, the fact that the measures affect a far greater number of women than men is not sufficient to show that they constitute an infringement of Article 119.

The proportionality requirement can be seen in paragraph 36. An indirectly discriminatory measure of this kind may be justified if, first, the measure answers a 'real need' of the employer; secondly, the measures are 'appropriate' to achieve the objectives they pursue; and, finally, the measures are 'necessary' to achieve those

---

[60] See in particular Chs. 16 and 18.

objectives. Phrased in slightly different language, this test corresponds broadly to the proportionality test in the context of restrictions on the free movement of goods and services. However, the ECJ in *Bilka*, while it appeared to accept that the encouragement of full-time workers was an acceptable policy, did not rule on whether this policy justified the pay disadvantage to women, and ultimately left the proportionality test for the national court to apply.

Some years later in *Rinner-Kühn*, the Court was faced with a similar case involving the exclusion of part-time workers from sick-pay provision.[61] On this occasion the indirectly discriminatory provisions were contained in national legislation, rather than in the act of an employer. The ECJ ruled that although the legislative provision was in principle contrary to the aim of Article 141 (ex Article 119), it was capable of objective justification. However, the justification offered by the government was inadequate:

13. In the course of the procedure, the German Government stated, in response to a question put by the Court, that workers whose period of work amounted to less than 10 hours a week or 45 hours a month were not as integrated in, or as dependent on, the undertaking employing them as other workers.

14. It should, however, be stated that those considerations, in so far as they are only generalizations about certain categories of workers, do not enable criteria which are both objective and unrelated to any discrimination on grounds of sex to be identified. However, if the Member State can show that the means chosen meet a necessary aim of social policy and that they are suitable and requisite for attaining that aim, the mere fact that the provision affects a much greater number of female workers than male workers cannot be regarded as constituting an infringement of Article 119.

The Advocate General in *Rinner-Kühn* had argued against the establishment of a presumption of indirect discrimination whenever a national legislative provision was seen to have an adverse impact on a far greater number of women than men. In his view, employer agreements such as that in *Bilka* were 'rules of law of modest status', whereas legislative provisions which might have taken into account many 'social, economic, and political' circumstances other than the adverse effects on women were of a different order and should not have to be justified simply on the ground of their adverse effects on women. The ECJ, however, applied the same analysis as it had done in *Bilka*.[62] Thus the onus was on the employee—save in a case like *Danfoss*, above, where the employer's system was insufficiently transparent—to show in the first instance that those receiving lower payments were predominantly or disproportionately women. The onus would then shift to the employer to justify such indirect discrimination, without the employee having to impute a discriminatory intent or to prove that the pay policy was in some way based on sex.[63] Now, under the Burden of Proof Directive, the employee must simply establish 'facts from which it may be presumed that there has been direct or indirect discrimination', leaving it for the

---

[61] Case 171/88, *Rinner-Kühn* v. *FWW Spezial-Gebäudereinigung GmbH* [1989] ECR 2743.

[62] See, however, n. 315 below and text, that in the context of *social security* legislation, the Court in fact applies the proportionality test loosely, leaving a considerable 'margin of discretion' to the States.

[63] See J. Shaw, 'Sick Pay for Cleaners' (1989) 14 *ELRev*. 428, for criticism of the AG's argument and the difficulties it would pose for employees.

employer to prove that there has been no such discrimination, or that any differential impact is objectively justified.[64]

The proportionality test was slightly differently phrased in *Rinner-Kühn*, where discrimination by the state rather than an employer was in issue. The 'real need of the employer' mentioned in *Bilka* was replaced in *Rinner-Kühn* by a 'necessary aim' of social policy and, rather than requiring the means chosen to achieve that aim to be 'appropriate and necessary', the ECJ in *Rinner-Kühn* said it must be 'suitable and requisite'. The thrust of the test, however, remains essentially the same, its aim being to require the responsible authority to demonstrate that any discrimination which does occur is effective in achieving a legitimate purpose and goes no further than is necessary to achieve that purpose. And although the Court declared that generalized considerations about the tendency of full-time as opposed to part-time workers to integrate more in the workplace could not constitute good grounds for indirect discrimination, it suggested that 'social policy' aims might do so.[65]

In *Bötel*,[66] *Lewark*,[67] and *Freers*,[68] the ECJ acknowledged that while the payment of compensation for attending training courses to full-time workers on a more favourable basis than that paid to part-time workers[69] was likely to discriminate indirectly against women, and to deter them from performing staff committee functions for which the training courses provided preparation, it was none the less possible that such discrimination was justified by reference to social-policy aims unrelated to sex. One social policy aim which was in principle accepted by the ECJ in *Freers* and *Lewark* was the government's desire to ensure the honorary nature and independence of staff committees in their promotion of harmonious labour relations, and to ensure that there would be no financial incentive to stand for election to a staff committee.[70]

Similarly in *Danfoss*, the ECJ considered what kinds of justification for indirect discrimination in the criteria for supplementary pay might be acceptable.[71] The pay criteria included factors such as mobility, training, and length of service of employees. 'Mobility'—a term used, somewhat oddly, apparently to describe characteristics such as enthusiasm and initiative—was, in the ECJ's view, a neutral criterion which should not disadvantage women unless the employer misapplied it. However, if mobility meant adaptability to hours and places of work, then the ECJ considered that it could disadvantage women because of family and household duties for which they so often bear responsibility. The criteria of training and length of service, too, although apparently 'neutral', could disadvantage women. However, while ultimately leaving

---

[64] Dir. 97/80, n. 47 above.

[65] In the UK, the House of Lords in *EOC* v. *Secretary of State for Employment* [1994] 1 WLR 409 concluded that, although the aim of increasing the availability of part-time work was a proper social-policy aim, discrimination against part-time workers in pay or in the requirement of qualifying periods for statutory protection was neither a suitable nor a requisite means of achieving that aim. Contrast the decision of the ECJ in Case C–189/91, n. 58 above.

[66] Case C–360/90, *Arbeiterwohlfahrt der Stadt Berlin* v. *Bötel* [1992] ECR I–3589.

[67] Case C–457/93, *Kuratorium für Dialyse und Nierentransplantation* v. *Lewark* [1996] ECR I–243.

[68] Case C–278/93, *Freers and Speckmann* v. *Deutsche Bundespost* [1996] ECR I–1165.

[69] Whether the basis for payment did in fact give preferential treatment to full-time workers was perhaps open to question, as Jacobs AG in *Lewark* considered: on this, see J. Shaw (1997) 22 *ELRev.* 256, 259.

[70] Contrast the view of Darmon AG in *Freers*, who concluded that the national rules were not in the circumstances objectively justifiable: [1996] ECR I–1165, 1179–80.

[71] Case 109/88, *Danfoss* [1989] ECR 3199.

the issue for the national court to decide, the ECJ took the view that they could be objectively justified if the employer could show, for example, that it was of importance for the performance of specific tasks that the employee could be adaptable and mobile, or had valuable experience due to the length of service.

In *Kowalska*,[72] indirect discrimination stemming not from legislative provisions nor from an occupational scheme established by an employer, but from a provision in a collective-bargaining agreement, was said to breach the Treaty unless objectively justified.[73] In *Nimz*, decided shortly after *Kowalska*, the ECJ considered whether an indirectly discriminatory term in a collective agreement, whereby only half of the period of service of certain part-time workers was taken into account in calculating their salary grade, could be justified on general grounds.

Case 184/89, Nimz v. Freie und Hansestadt Hamburg
[1991] ECR 297

13. In this regard, the City of Hamburg claimed during the procedure that full-time employees or those who work for three-quarters of normal working time acquire more quickly than others the abilities and skills relating to their particular job. The German Government also relied on their more extensive experience.

14. It should however, be stated that such considerations, in so far as they are no more than generalizations about certain categories of workers, do not make it possible to identify criteria which are both objective and unrelated to any discrimination on grounds of sex. . . . Although experience goes hand in hand with length of service, and experience enables the worker in principle to improve performance of the tasks allotted to him, the objectivity of such a criterion depends on all the circumstances in a particular case, and in particular on the relationship between the nature of the work performed and the experience gained from the performance of that work upon completion of a certain number of working hours. However, it is a matter for the national court, which alone is competent to evaluate the facts, to determine in the light of all the circumstances whether and to what extent a provision in a collective agreement such as that here at issue is based on objectively justified factors unrelated to any discrimination on grounds of sex.

This ruling underscores the point made in *Rinner-Kühn*, that general assumptions or assertions about the attributes of part-time workers are unlikely to constitute adequate grounds for justifying a measure which has a disproportionately adverse impact on one sex. Even the argument relating to the greater experience of full-time workers was not in itself sufficient as a justification, since the ECJ considered that it depended very much on the nature of the work performed. However, it seems clear that a criterion of seniority is likely to disadvantage women disproportionately, given the frequent interruption of their career patterns on account of family responsibilities.

---

[72] Case 33/89, *Kowalska* v. *Freie und Hansestadt Hamburg* [1990] ECR 2591.

[73] In Cases C–3/99, C–409, & C–425/92, C–34, C–50 & C–78/93, *Stadt Lengerich* v. *Helmig* [1994] ECR I–5727, the ECJ ruled that there was no indirect discrimination where collective agreements restricted payment of overtime supplements to cases where the normal working hours fixed for full-time workers were exceeded. See also Case C–236/98, *JämO* [2000] ECR I–2189, on an 'inconvenient hours' supplement.

Apart from discrimination as between part-time versus full-time workers, other forms of indirect sex discrimination potentially arise where certain professions are predominantly female while others—which are more highly paid—are predominantly male.

Case 127/92, Enderby v. Frenchay Health Authority and the Secretary
of State for Health
[1993] ECR 5535

Enderby, who was employed as a speech therapist by the defendant authority, complained of sex discrimination. She argued that members of her profession, which was overwhelmingly a female profession, were paid appreciably less well than members of comparable professions whose jobs were of equal value to hers. She cited the higher pay received by clinical psychologists and pharmacists, since these were professions in which, at an equivalent professional level, there were more men than women. The Court of Appeal referred a number of questions under Article 234 (ex Article 117), and having cited its rulings on the burden of proof in *Bilka*, *Kowalska*, and *Danfoss* (discussed above), the ECJ continued:

THE ECJ

15. In this case, as both the FHA and the United Kingdom observe, the circumstances are not exactly the same as in the cases just mentioned. First, it is not a question of *de facto* discrimination arising from a particular sort of arrangement such as may apply, for example, in the case of part-time workers. Secondly, there can be no complaint that the employer has applied a system of pay wholly lacking in transparency since the rates of pay of NHS speech therapists and pharmacists are decided by regular collective bargaining processes in which there is no evidence of discrimination as regards either of those two professions.

16. However, if the pay of speech therapists is significantly lower than that of pharmacists and if the former are almost exclusively women while the latter are predominantly men, there is a *prima facie* case of sex discrimination, at least where the two jobs in question are of equal value and the statistics describing that situation are valid.

17. It is for the national court to assess whether it may take into account those statistics, that is to say, whether they cover enough individuals, whether they illustrate purely fortuitous or short-term phenomena, and whether, in general, they appear to be significant.

18. Where there is a *prima facie* case of discrimination, it is for the employer to show that there are objective reasons for the difference in pay. Workers would be unable to enforce the principle of equal pay before national courts if evidence of a *prima facie* case of discrimination did not shift to the employer the onus of showing that the pay differential is not in fact discriminatory.

Although the reference had been made from the national court on the assumption that the two jobs were of equal value, *Enderby* illustrates the problem of establishing indirect discrimination in the sense of showing that work which is performed predominantly by women is undervalued in comparison to work which is performed predominantly by men.[74] In the case of part-time and full-time workers, it is clear that the actual tasks being done are the same, whereas in the case of two distinct types of work, and in the absence of a job-classification scheme, it is considerably more difficult to establish this.

The situation is more complex still in a situation where the average pay of several groups is compared, and where, although the highest-paid group consists principally of women, so also does the lowest-paid group. This arose in the *Royal Copenhagen* case, in which it was argued that the system of piece-work pay schemes, in which pay depends largely on the individual output of each worker, led to indirect discrimination against women.[75] The ECJ ruled that the mere finding that the average pay, within such a pay scheme, of a group of workers consisting predominantly of women was appreciably lower than the average pay of a group of predominantly male workers carrying out work of equal value would not be sufficient to establish indirect pay discrimination. This was because, so long as the same unit of measurement was used for the two groups—a matter which was for the national court to assess—the difference in pay received could be due to their different individual output. However, the Court went on to cite its reasoning in *Enderby* and *Danfoss* concerning the situations in which the burden of proof would shift to the employer to establish that there was no discrimination or that it was justified. On the facts of the *Royal Copenhagen* case, the burden of proof might indeed shift if the pay consisted in part of a variable element, depending on each worker's output, and it was not possible to identify the factors determining the unit of measurement used to calculate this variable element.[76] Arguably this situation is now governed by Article 4 of the Burden of Proof Directive, in the sense that the differential impact on different gender groups of a variable pay element would amount to the establishment of facts from which indirect discrimination could be presumed.

In *Seymour-Smith*, the question was what kind of statistical evidence would be necessary to establish 'unfavourable impact' such that indirect discrimination could be inferred.[77] The case concerned the two-years-employment requirement for eligibility for compensation for unfair dismissal, and the ECJ gave some guidelines for the national court to follow in determining whether the statistics were adequate and whether they established that 'a considerably smaller percentage of women than men' could meet the requirement imposed.[78] In *Schnorbus*, by contrast, the ECJ ruled that it was not necessary to rely on statistics to prove indirect discrimination in the case of preferential admission to practical legal training being given to those who had completed compulsory military or civilian service, since under the relevant German legislation, women were not required to do military or civilian service.[79] In *Gruber*,

---

[74] See Case C–236/98, *JämställdhetsOmbudsmannen v. Örebro läns landsting* [2000] ECR I–2189, where a comparison of the pay of midwives and clinical technicians was in issue.

[75] Case C–400/93, *Royal Copenhagen* [1995] ECR I–1275.

[76] *Ibid.*, paras. 24–27. The ECJ acknowledged that the employer could deny discrimination by showing that the pay differentials were due, e.g., to differences in the worker's choice concerning the rate of work.

[77] Case C–167/97, *Seymour-Smith and Perez* [1999] ECR I–623.

[78] *Ibid.*, paras. 54–65. See Case C–243/95, *Hill and Stapleton v. Revenue Commissioners* [1998] ECR I–3739, where statistical evidence showed that 99.2% of clerical assistants who job-shared and 98% of all civil servants who job-shared were women.

[79] Case C–79/99, *Schnorbus v. Land Hessen* [2000] ECR I–10997.

however, the ECJ rejected the argument that there was indirect discrimination against women in the context of national legislation which granted a lower termination payment to workers who end their employment relationship prematurely in order to take care of their children owing to a lack of child-care facilities than it did to workers who resigned for an important reason related to working conditions or to the employer's conduct.[80] These two situations, according to the ECJ, were relevantly different so that there was no inequality of treatment and no indirect discrimination. However, although workers who had taken parenting leave were held to be in a different situation from actively employed workers, so that the payment to the latter of a voluntary exceptional Christmas bonus would not in itself breach Article 141, the ECJ in *Lewen* ruled that there *would* on the other hand be unlawful indirect discrimination if the bonus was in fact a retrospective payment for work done during the year, since female workers were 'likely . . . to be on parenting leave when the bonus is awarded far more often than male workers'.[81]

(ii) OBJECTIVE JUSTIFICATION

Once indirect discrimination is established to have occurred, of course, the next difficulty is in showing that the justification offered for the pay differential between two different but equally valuable sorts of work is not adequate, given the adverse impact of that pay differential on one sex. The onus is on the employer to show justification, but it is often difficult for an employee to counter the justifications offered, when broad economic grounds are pleaded. Two grounds were offered by the employer in *Enderby*, and while the Court ruled that the separate bargaining processes could not of themselves justify the discrimination, since otherwise the employer could 'easily circumvent the principle of equal pay by using separate bargaining processes',[82] it stated that the needs of the market might constitute adequate justification, depending on whether the proportion of the increase in pay was in fact attributable to the need to attract suitable candidates to the less popular job. The case shows some of the weaknesses of the concept of indirect sex discrimination, and indeed of law, in addressing inequality within the labour market. The fact that women traditionally tend to pursue certain careers and professions which allow for flexibility, even if they offer less competitive salary rates than other professions which attract a greater number of men, means that women's pay is likely remain at lower levels than other work which is objectively equal in value.

Just as do the cases of *Nimz*[83] and *Kowalska*,[84] *Enderby* also shows that there may be a conflict between the principle of non-discrimination on grounds of sex and the collective-bargaining process, which was described by the Health Authority in its defence as 'a process of industrial democracy in which those affected by the terms and conditions of employment can participate', sometimes after many years of negotiation and comprehensive studies. The ECJ, however, made clear in these and

---

[80] In Case C–249/97, *Gruber* v. *Silhouette International Schmied* [1999] ECR I–5295.
[81] Case C–333/97, *Lewen* v. *Denda* [1999] ECR I–7243, para. 40.
[82] [1993] ECR I–5535, para. 22.
[83] Case C–184/89, *Nimz* v. *Freie und Hansestadt Hamburg* [1991] ECR I–297.
[84] Case C–33/89, *Kowalska* [1990] ECR I–2591.

other cases[85] that the prohibition on sex discrimination, direct or indirect, must take priority over the autonomy of the industrial-bargaining process. On the other hand, in *Royal Copenhagen*, the ECJ stated that the fact that rates of pay had been determined by collective bargaining or negotiation at local level could be taken into account by the national court as a factor in assessing whether differences between the average pay of two groups of workers were due to objective factors unrelated to sex.[86]

In *Schnorbus*, the ECJ considered that indirect discrimination against women in access to practical legal training could be objectively justified in order to compensate for the delay occasioned to the careers of men who had undergone compulsory military or civilian service, and the preferential treatment was not disproprotionate since it was limited to twelve months maximum.[87] In *JämO*, differences in working hours could constitute objective justification, although the employer would have to demonstrate that this was in fact the case.[88] In *Hill and Stapleton*, however, the Court gave a clear indication that discrimination against job-sharers (who were overwhelmingly women) in the method of determining pay progression could not be justified on a range of dubious grounds offered by the Revenue Commissioners,[89] which rather bizarrely included 'established practice', and an unsubstantiated assertion that this practice maintained staff morale and motivation. An economic justification based solely on the avoidance of increased costs was also held to be unacceptable. This ruling is particularly interesting for the fact that the ECJ drew attention to the specific type of indirect discrimination involved—i.e., against job-sharers—by noting that job-sharing was overwhelmingly chosen by women seeking to combine work and family responsibilities, and that the protection of women within family life and at work 'in the same way as for men' was a principle recognized by EC law as a 'natural corollary' of the equal-treatment principle. The implication in the context of this case seems to be that an even stronger onus to justify such indirect discrimination would therefore lie on the defendant whose practices undermined such a principle.

The shortcomings of the indirect discrimination/objective justification tests in the endeavour to promote equality in employment for women have been critically noted by many,[90] given the male norm on which the concept of discrimination used is based, and given the relative ease with which the commercial objectives of the undertaking or employer can defeat a claim of indirect discrimination.[91] However the ruling in *Hill and Stapleton*, together with that in *Seymour-Smith*, arguably shows the ECJ adopting a somewhat less deferential and more robust approach to scrutinizing the 'objective justifications' offered by states (rather than private employers) for

---

[85] See, e.g., Case C–281/97, *Krüger* v. *Kreiskrankenhaus Ebersberg* [1999] ECR I–5127.

[86] Case C–400/93, n. 75 above. Compare Case C–381/99, *Brunnhofer*, n. 40 above, paras. 44–47.

[87] Case C–79/99, *Schnorbus* v. *Land Hessen* [2000] ECR I–10997.

[88] Case C–236/98, n. 74 above, paras. 61–62.

[89] Case C–243/95, *Hill and Stapleton* v. *Revenue Commissioners* [1998] ECR I–3739. For comment see C. McGlynn and C. Farrelly, 'Equal Pay and the "Protection of Women within Family Life"' (1999) 24 *ELRev.* 202.

[90] S. Fredman, 'European Community Discrimination Law: A Critique' (1992) 21 *ILJ* 119, 125; G. More, 'Equal Treatment of the Sexes: What does "Equal" Mean?' (1993) 1 *Feminist Legal Studies* 45, 70; E. Szyszczak, 'L'Espace Social Européenne: Reality, Dreams or Nightmares?' [1990] *German Yearbook of International Law* 284, 296.

[91] See, e.g., Case C–189/91, n. 58 above, and T. Hervey, 'Small Business Exclusion in German Dismissal Law' [1994] *ILJ* 267. Also Case C–297/93, *Grau-Hupka* [1994] ECR I–5535.

indirectly discriminatory legislative measures. In *Seymour-Smith*, in which the UK had argued that legislation on protection against unfair dismissal which discriminated indirectly against women was designed to stimulate recruitment by employers, the ECJ accepted that this was a legitimate social-policy aim, and that the Member States in that respect had a margin of discretion.[92] But it went on to rule:

75. However, although social policy is essentially a matter for the Member States under Community law as it stands, the fact remains that the broad margin of discretion available to the Member States in that connection cannot have the effect of frustrating the implementation of a fundamental principle of Community law such as that of equal pay for men and women.

76. Mere generalisations concerning the capacity of a specific measure to encourage recruitment are not enough to show that the aim of the disputed rule is unrelated to any discrimination based on sex nor to provide evidence on the basis of which it could reasonably be considered that the means chosen were suitable for achieving that aim.

(iii) CAN 'DIRECT' PAY DISCRIMINATION BE JUSTIFIED?

A final question to be briefly addressed at this point is whether direct rather than indirect pay discrimination can ever be 'objectively justified'. While the ECJ has never actually ruled to this effect, it has none the less in a number of cases considered in more detail whether men and women who appear *prima facie* to be paid differently for performing similar work or work of equal value may actually be 'differently situated' such that the unequal pay does not in fact amount to discrimination. In *Birds Eye Walls*, discussed further below, the ECJ ruled that the payment of different bridging pensions to men and women did not constitute discrimination since they were not similarly situated in relevant respects.[93] And in *Abdoulaye*, the ECJ ruled that the situation of a male worker was not comparable to that of a female worker where the advantage granted specifically to the female is designed to offset the occupational disadvantages, inherent in maternity leave, which arise for female workers as a result of being away from work.[94] Finally in *Griesmar*, the ECJ considered in detail the argument that differential service credits for the calculation of retirement pensions for female (and not male) workers who had had children did not constitute discrimination, since the positions of male and female workers were not comparable in this respect.[95] Ultimately, the ECJ rejected the argument on the basis that their situations could indeed be comparable if the male worker had assumed the task of bringing up his children. However, the *Griesmar* ruling also drew attention to another possible basis for justifying apparently discriminatory pay practices, namely the 'positive action' provisions which appeared first in the Social Policy Agreement and are now contained in Article 141(4). Whether this paragraph, which permits Member States, *inter alia*, to adopt measures 'to compensate for disadvantages in professional careers', will be held by the ECJ to permit apparently differential pay for men and women remains to be seen.

[92] Case C–167/97, *Seymour-Smith and Perez* [1999] ECR I–623, paras. 71–73.

[93] Case C–132/92, *Roberts v. Birds Eye Walls Ltd.* [1993] ECR I–5579.

[94] Case C–218/98, *Abdoulaye and Others* [1999] ECR I–5723, paras. 18–20 in particular. See C. McGlynn (1999) 24 *ELRev.* 202.

[95] Case C–366/99, *Griesmar v. Ministre de l'Economie* [2001] ECR I–9383.

(c) THE BREADTH OF ARTICLE 141 (EX ARTICLE 119): WHAT CAN CONSTITUTE 'PAY'?

This relatively simple question has not given rise to simple answers, despite the guidance given in the Article itself on the meaning of the term 'pay'. The ECJ has given the term a very wide scope, which gave rise to some confusion as regards the apparent overlap between pay and social security. While some of the Court's rulings appeared to undermine measures adopted by the Community legislative institutions—and thus the bargains struck by the Member States in the Council when adopting those measures—at other times its rulings appeared responsive to the political context by retreating from earlier expansive positions in the face of obvious dissatisfaction from the Member States or the other institutions.

(I) 'SOCIAL SECURITY BENEFITS' ARE NOT PAY

In *Defrenne I*, which was brought against Belgium rather than against the employer, Sabena, the ECJ gave an early ruling on what subsequently became a very tangled relationship between pay and pensions.

Case 80/70, Defrenne v. Belgium
[1971] ECR 445

[ToA renumbering: Art. 119 is now Art. 141]

The ECJ was asked whether a Belgian law concerning retirement pensions, which excluded air hostesses from its scope, fell within the ambit of Article 119. The retirement pension was granted under the terms of a social security scheme financed by contributions from workers, employers, and state subsidy. Defrenne argued that there was a direct and necessary link between the retirement pension and salary, since certain conditions of the employment directly influenced the amount of the pension. The Commission argued that social security benefits in general and pensions in particular were excluded from the scope of Article 119.

THE ECJ

6. The provision in the second paragraph of the article extends the concept of pay to any other consideration, whether in cash or in kind, whether immediate or future, provided that the worker receives it, albeit indirectly, in respect of his employment from his employer.

7. Although consideration in the nature of social security benefits is not therefore in principle alien to the concept of pay, there cannot be brought within this concept, as defined in Article 119, social security schemes or benefits, in particular retirement pensions, directly governed by legislation without any element of agreement within the undertaking or the occupational branch concerned, which are obligatorily applicable to general categories of workers.

8. These schemes assure for the workers the benefit of a legal scheme, the financing of which workers, employers and possibly the public authorities contribute in a measure determined less by the employment relationship between the employer and the worker than by considerations of social policy.

9. Accordingly, the part due from the employers in the financing of such schemes does not constitute a direct or indirect payment to the worker.

10. Moreover the worker will normally receive the benefits legally prescribed not by reason of the employer's contribution but solely because the worker fulfils the legal conditions for the grant of benefits.

Although the ECJ stressed that 'consideration in the nature of social security benefits' was not in itself excluded from the concept of pay, the factors which went to exclude the employer's contributions to the retirement pension in this case from the scope of Article 119 (now Article 141) were threefold: first, the pension scheme was directly governed by legislation; secondly, there was no agreement on the scheme within the particular company or occupational branch concerned; and, thirdly, the retirement scheme was *obligatorily* applicable to *general* categories of workers. The determining role of the state and the lack of involvement of the particular employer are clearly crucial: in sum, that the pension scheme was set up essentially as a matter of social policy and not as a part of the employment relationship in question. The Court's definition of the difference between pay and social security is important, since equal treatment in social security is not covered by Article 141 (ex Article 119), but primarily by Directive 79/7, whereas occupational social security is covered in part by this Article and in part by Directive 86/378 and amending Directive 96/97.

(II) A WIDENING DEFINITION OF PAY

The wide interpretation of pay under Article 141 can be seen in cases such as *Garland* v. *British Rail Engineering*,[96] where the ECJ ruled that the fact that female employees could on retirement no longer enjoy travel facilities for their spouses and dependent children, whilst male employees continued to do so, constituted discrimination contrary to the Treaty.[97] Since they were *benefits conferred in respect of employment*, even if after retirement and irrespective of any specific contractual obligation, they were held to constitute pay.[98] Similarly in *Kowalska*, a severance grant was covered by Article 141 (ex Article 119) since it was compensation to which a worker was entitled by reason of her employment, even though it was not paid in the course of employment but rather on termination of the employment relationship.[99] And in *Seymour-Smith*, compensation for unfair dismissal was held to constitute pay, since it was designed to replace pay to which the employee would have been entitled had she not been unfairly dismissed.[100]

In *Worringham*, two female employees of Lloyds Bank challenged the payment to male staff under 25 years of a higher gross salary than to female staff of the same age

---

[96] Case 12/81, *Garland* v. *British Rail Engineering Ltd.* [1982] ECR 359.

[97] See also Case C–249/96, *Grant* v. *South-West Trains*, n. 23 above.

[98] On voluntary Christmas bonuses as pay see Case C–333/97, *Lewen* v. *Denda* [1999] ECR I–7243. However, an employee exercising a statutory right to parenting leave, carrying with it a parenting allowance, is in a special situation not comparable to that of a man or woman at work, so that Art. 141 is not breached where entitlement to a voluntary exceptional Christmas bonus (which does not constitute retroactive pay for work done during the year) is limited to those in active employment.

[99] Case C–33/89, n. 72 above, para. 10.   [100] Case C–167/97, n. 77 above.

engaged in the same work.[101] Contributions to a retirement scheme were compulsory for men under 25 but not for women under 25, and in order to cover their contribution, the bank added a sum equal to that amount to the gross salary for men. Since the calculation of various other benefits was linked to gross salary, the ECJ ruled that there was a breach of the equal-pay principle:

Although, where women are not required to pay contributions, the salary of men after deduction of the contributions is comparable to that of women who do not pay contributions, the inequality between the gross salaries of men and women is nevertheless a source of discrimination contrary to Article 119 of the Treaty since because of that inequality men receive benefits from which women engaged in the same work or work of equal value are excluded, or receive on that account greater benefits or social advantages than those to which women are entitled.[102]

In *Nimz*, the complainant was not challenging pay rates in themselves, but rather the rules governing the system of salary-classification into grades, and the Court confirmed that such rules fell within the concept of pay in Article 141 (ex Article 119) since they directly governed changes in employees' salaries.[103] In contrast, rules governing the calculation of the length of service of public servants for the purposes of determining eligibility for promotion, and thus indirectly determining the possibility of access to a higher level of remuneration, were a matter of equal treatment rather than equal pay.[104] Indeed, as early as *Defrenne II* the ECJ had ruled that the fact that the fixing of certain working conditions could have pecuniary consequences was not sufficient to bring such conditions within the scope of Article 141, and this point was confirmed again in *JämO*[105] and *Seymour-Smith*,[106] concerning a reduction in working time and the right not to be unfairly dismissed, respectively. Such conditions fell to be dealt with instead under Directive 76/207 on equal treatment.

In *Rinner-Kühn*, the Court ruled that statutory sick pay, i.e. wages which an employer is required by law to continue to pay an employee in the event of illness, fell within the meaning of pay in Article 141 (ex Article 119).[107] However, it is clearly difficult to distinguish this kind of pay from a social-security benefit. Although these wages were to be paid by the employer, 80 per cent of such payment, in the case of employees who worked a certain number of hours for a particular period of time, was thereafter to be reimbursed by the state. Given this fact, the wages seem to be paid more as a matter of 'social policy' as suggested in *Defrenne I*, than as pay as part of the contract of employment.[108] Clearly it is in the employee's interests that such sick pay is classified as pay rather than social security, given that Article 141, unlike Directive 79/7, is directly effective both against the state and against private employers, but the lack of clarity about precisely what it is that determines whether a benefit constitutes social security or pay is ultimately in no one's interests.

In *Gillespie*, whose facts arose prior to the adoption of the Pregnancy Directive

---

[101] Case 69/80, n. 56 above. See also Case 23/83, *Liefting* v. *Directie van het Academisch Ziekenhuis bij de Universiteit van Amsterdam* [1984] ECR 5225.

[102] Case 69/80, n. 56 above, para. 25.   [103] Case C–184/89, n. 84 above.

[104] Case C–1/95, *Gerster* v. *Freistaat Bayern* [1997] ECR I–5253.

[105] N. 34 above, paras. 59–60.   [106] N. 77 above, paras. 36–37.

[107] Case 171/88, *Rinner-Kühn* v. *FWW Spezial-Gebäudereinigung GmbH* [1989] ECR 2743, para. 7.

[108] Darmon AG did not take this view and emphasized the fact that the sick pay was directly related to the wages paid and to the hours and service of the employee. See J. Shaw, n. 63 above.

92/85 (discussed below), the ECJ ruled that since maternity benefit paid by an employer under legislation or collective agreements was based on the employment relationship, it constituted pay within Article 141 (ex Article 119).[109] Although this did not mean that women were required to receive full pay during maternity leave, they had to receive pay which was not so low as to undermine the purpose of such leave, and they must, like any other worker still linked to the employer by the contract of employment, benefit from any pay rise which is awarded during the period of maternity leave.[110] And in *Bötel*,[111] *Lewark*,[112] and *Freers*,[113] the ECJ ruled that statutorily required compensation payments to workers attending training courses which gave them the knowledge required for working on staff councils would constitute pay, since, even though it did not derive from the contract of employment, it was nevertheless paid by the employer by virtue of legislative provisions and under a contract of employment.

The ECJ in the famous case of *Barber* ruled that severance benefits, including statutory redundancy payments, would constitute pay under Article 141 (ex Article 119).

Case 262/88, Barber v. Guardian Royal Exchange
[1990] ECR 1889

13. As regards, in particular, the compensation granted to a worker in connection with his redundancy, it must be stated that such compensation constitutes a form of pay to which the worker is entitled in respect of his employment, which is paid to him upon termination of the employment relationship, which makes it possible to facilitate his adjustment to the new circumstances resulting from the loss of his employment and which provides him with a source of income during the period in which he is seeking employment.

14. It follows that compensation granted to a worker in connection with his redundancy falls in principle within the concept of pay for the purposes of Article 119 of the Treaty.

15. At the hearing, the United Kingdom argued that the statutory redundancy payment fell outside the scope of Article 119 because it constituted a social security benefit and not a form of pay.

16. In that regard it must be pointed out that a redundancy payment made by the employer, such as that which is at issue, cannot cease to constitute a form of pay on the sole ground that, rather than deriving from the contract of employment, it is a statutory or ex gratia payment.

17. In the case of statutory redundancy payments it must be borne in mind that, as the Court held in its judgment of 8 April 1976 in Case 43/75 *Defrenne* v. *Sabena* [1976] ECR 455 paragraph 40, Article 119 of the Treaty also applies to discrimination arising directly from legislative provisions. This means that benefits provided for by law may come within the concept of pay for the purposes of that provision.

18. Although it is true that many advantages granted by an employer also reflect considera-

---

[109] Case C–342/93, *Gillespie* v. *Northern Health and Social Services Boards* [1996] ECR I–475.

[110] *Ibid.*, paras. 20–22. See also Case C–411/96, *Boyle* v. *EOC* [1998] ECR I–6401.

[111] Case C–360/90, *Arbeiterwohlfahrt der Stadt Berlin* v. *Bötel* [1992] ECR I–3589.

[112] Case C–457/93, *Kuratorium für Dialyse und Nierentransplantation* v. *Lewark* [1996] ECR I–243.

[113] Case C–278/93, *Freers and Speckmann* v. *Deutsche Bundespost* [1996] ECR I–1165.

tions of social policy, the fact that a benefit is in the nature of pay cannot be called in question where the worker is entitled to receive the benefit in question from his employer by reason of the existence of the employment relationship.

The most significant developments in relation to the uncertain zone between pay and social security, however, were the rulings on *occupational pensions* in both *Barber* and *Bilka-Kaufhaus*,[114] along with the flood of litigation which followed *Barber*.[115]

(III) *BILKA* AND *BARBER*: MANY OCCUPATIONAL PENSIONS CONSTITUTE PAY

The ECJ first addressed the issue of occupational pension schemes directly in *Bilka-Kaufhaus*. At the time judgment was given, a proposal for what subsequently became Directive 86/378 on occupational social security, to supplement Directive 79/7 on statutory social security, was being considered by the Council of Ministers.

The terms of the 1986 Directive indicate that the institutions considered occupational pensions to be a matter of social security rather than pay, so that they were dealt with in a more gradual manner similar to matters covered by Directive 79/7, rather than under the strictures of Article 141 (ex Article 119). However, the ECJ in *Bilka* took a different view, in the context of a supplementary occupational pension scheme entirely financed by the employer.

Case 170/84 Bilka-Kaufhaus GmbH v. Karin Weber von Hartz
[1986] ECR 1607

[ToA renumbering: Art. 119 is now Art. 141]

The background is set out at 856 above.

THE ECJ

20. It should be noted that according to the documents before the Court the occupational pension scheme at issue in the main proceedings, although adopted in accordance with the provisions laid down by German legislation for such schemes, is based on an agreement between Bilka and the staff committee representing its employees and has the effect of supplementing the social benefits paid under national legislation of general application with benefits financed entirely by the employer.

21. The contractual rather than the statutory nature of the scheme in question is confirmed by the fact that, as has been pointed out above, the scheme and the rules governing it are regarded as an integral part of the contracts of employment between Bilka and its employers.

22. It must therefore be concluded that the scheme does not constitute a social security scheme governed directly by statute and thus does not fall outside the scope of Article 119. Benefits paid to employees under the scheme therefore constitute consideration received by the

---

[114] Case 170/84, *Bilka-Kaufhaus GmbH* v. *Karin Weber von Hartz* [1986] ECR 1607.
[115] See further below, nn. 133–56 and text.

worker from the employer in respect of his employment, as referred to in the second paragraph of Article 119.

By contrast with the statutory pension scheme in *Defrenne I*, the ECJ in this case highlighted three factors: (1) the contractual nature of the pension scheme, (2) the fact that it was not directly governed by statute but by the agreement between employer and employee, and (3) that it was not financed in part by the public authorities but entirely by the employer. The fact that the employer chose to arrange the scheme in a way which corresponded to the statutory social-security scheme was held to be irrelevant, and the benefits paid to employees under the occupational scheme thus constituted 'pay'. More recently the ECJ also added that the fact that affiliation to an occupational pension scheme was made compulsory by legislation for employees, not just for reasons of social policy but also relating to considerations of competition in a particular economic sector, was irrelevant to the application of Article 141 (ex Article 119).[116]

Although the ruling in *Bilka* should have warned the institutions which were in the process of adopting Directive 86/378 and treating occupational pensions as social security not subject to Article 141 (ex Article 119), the Directive was nevertheless adopted in 1986. This difference of view between the Member States in the Council, on the one hand, and the Court, on the other, was starkly highlighted in the *Barber* case set out below, where the ECJ once again asserted its authority over the legislative institutions by reading Article 141 in such a way as to render much of Directive 86/378 redundant.[117]

Subsequently in *Newstead*, the ECJ had to consider whether compulsory *contributions of employees* to a contracted-out occupational pension scheme constituted pay within Article 141 (ex Article 119).[118] It had ruled in *Bilka* that *payments to employees* from a supplementary occupational pension scheme constituted pay even though the scheme was adapted to correspond with the statutory social-security scheme, but in *Newstead* the ECJ reasoned that since the occupational pension scheme was in part a substitute for the statutory pension scheme, contributions were in the nature of a social-security benefit and would fall outside the scope of Article 141. It will become clear after examining the ruling in *Barber* and subsequent decisions below, that the authority of *Newstead* is extremely weak,[119] if indeed it has not been implicitly overruled.[120]

Perhaps because of the confusion over *Bilka* and *Newstead*, the *Barber* ruling, in which the issue of 'contracted-out' occupational pension schemes was directly

---

[116] Case C–435/93, *Dietz v. Stichting Thuiszorg Rotterdam* [1996] ECR I–5223.

[117] For another example of this Court/Member State dynamic, see the comment on *Danfoss*, n. 47 above and text.

[118] Case 192/85, *Newstead v. Department of Transport* [1987] ECR 4735.

[119] D. Curtin, 'Scalping the Community Legislator: Occupational Pensions and "Barber"' (1990) 27 *CMLRev.* 475, 480–1 has suggested that it may remain as authority for the narrow proposition that employee contributions to a widow's pension fund are a matter of social security, rather than pay.

[120] The payments in *Newstead* would have to be distinguished from the payments made in Case C–152/91, *Neath v. Hugh Steeper Ltd.* [1993] ECR I–6935, para. 31, which were held, following *Barber*, to constitute pay. See n. 156 and text below.

addressed, came as a shock. Many had assumed, in spite of the *Bilka* ruling, that if an occupational pension scheme was contracted out, i.e., was set up by an employer in direct substitution for and in fulfilment of the obligations of the statutory scheme, payments of benefits to employees (and also, according to *Newstead*, deductions from the net pay of employees) would, by analogy with that statutory scheme, be treated as social security rather than as pay.

Case C–262/88, Barber v. Guardian Royal Exchange Assurance Group
[1990] ECR I–1889

[Note ToA renumbering: Art. 119 is now Art. 141]

Barber was an employee of Guardian and was made redundant at the age of 52. He belonged to an occupational pension scheme set up and wholly financed by Guardian, which was a 'contracted-out' scheme under social-security legislation as a substitute for the earnings-related part of the state pension scheme. This meant that members of the contracted-out scheme would contractually waive that part of the state pension scheme. Barber claimed that the terms of redundancy relating to his entitlement to an early retirement pension were in breach of Article 119, since a woman would be entitled to an immediate pension on reaching 50, whereas for a man the relevant age was 55. The ECJ was asked whether redundancy-related benefits, including a private occupational pension, constituted pay within Article 119 or Directive 75/117.

THE ECJ

22. It must be pointed out in that regard that, in its judgment of 25 May 1971 in Case 80/70 *Defrenne* v. *Belgium* [1971] ECR 445, paragraphs 7 and 8, the Court stated that consideration in the nature of social security benefits is not in principle alien to the concept of pay. However, the Court pointed out that this concept, as defined in Article 119, cannot encompass social security schemes or benefits, in particular retirement pensions, directly governed by legislation without any element of agreement within the undertaking or the occupational branch concerned, which are compulsorily applicable to general categories of workers.

23. The Court noted that those schemes afford the workers the benefit of a statutory scheme, to the financing of which workers, employers and possibly the public authorities contribute in a measure determined less by the employment relationship than by considerations of social policy.

24. In order to answer the second question, therefore, it is necessary to ascertain whether those considerations also apply to contracted-out private occupational schemes such as that referred to in this case.

25. In that regard it must be pointed out first of all that the schemes in question are the result either of an agreement between workers and employers or of a unilateral decision taken by the employer. They are wholly financed by the employer or by both the employer and the workers without any contribution being made by the public authorities in any circumstances. Accordingly, such schemes form part of the consideration offered to workers by the employer.

26. Secondly, such schemes are not compulsorily applicable to general categories of workers. On the contrary, they apply only to workers employed by certain undertakings, with the result that affiliation to those schemes derives of necessity from the employment relationship with a given employer. Furthermore, even if the schemes in question are established in conformity with national

legislation and consequently satisfy the conditions laid down by it for recognition as contracted-out schemes, they are governed by their own rules.

27. Thirdly, it must be pointed out that, even if the contributions paid to those schemes and the benefits which they provide are in part a substitute for those of the general statutory scheme, that fact cannot preclude the application of Article 119. It is apparent from the documents before the Court that occupational schemes such as that referred to in this case may grant to their members benefits greater than those which would be paid by the statutory scheme, with the result that their economic function is similar to that of the supplementary schemes which exist in certain Member States, where affiliation and contribution to the statutory scheme is compulsory and no derogation is allowed. In its judgment of 13 May 1986 in Case 170/84 *Bilka-Kaufhaus* v. *Weber von Hartz* [1986] ECR 1607, the Court held that the benefits awarded under a supplementary pension scheme fell within the concept of pay, within the meaning of Article 119.

28. It must therefore be concluded that, unlike the benefits awarded by national statutory social security schemes, a pension paid under a contracted-out scheme constitutes consideration paid by the employer to the worker in respect of his employment and consequently falls within the scope of Article 119 of the Treaty.

29. That interpretation of Article 119 is not affected by the fact that the private occupational scheme in question has been set up in the form of a trust and is administered by trustees who are technically independent of the employer, since Article 119 also applies to consideration received indirectly from the employer.

The distinction between social security and pay, which is one of the central issues in *Barber*, was important in relation to pensions, because of the exceptions to the equal-treatment principle which are allowed under Social Security Directive 79/7 in relation to pensionable age and related benefits.[121] No such exception exists under Article 141 (ex Article 119), and companies which had operated contracted-out occupational pension schemes had, prior to *Barber*, proceeded on the assumption that they could maintain discriminatory pensionable ages as between men and women.

The question was, in essence, whether contracted-out occupational pension schemes were governed by the principle set out in *Defrenne I*,[122] in which case they were social security, or that in *Bilka*, in which case they were pay. The ECJ, mirroring its reasoning in *Bilka*, focused on three features of the contracted-out scheme: first, it was agreed and entirely financed by the employer, not imposed directly by statute;[123] secondly, unlike most social-security benefits the scheme was not compulsorily applicable to general categories of employees and, although in conformity with national legislation, was governed by its own rules; and finally, although it was in substitution for the statutory scheme, its provisions could also go further and provide additional benefits, thereby making it indistinguishable from supplementary schemes such as those in *Bilka*. The fact that the fund was administered by trustees did not prevent the benefits paid from constituting pay, and this point was underlined later in

[121] See further below, Sect. 4(a)(iv).   [122] Case 80/70, n. 28 above.
[123] The ECJ made it clear subsequently in Case C–200/91, *Coloroll*, n. 53 above, para. 88, that all benefits payable to an employee under an occupational pension scheme, whether the scheme was contributory or non-contributory—i.e., whether or not the employee also made contributions—constituted pay within the Treaty Art.

Coloroll[124] and again in *Menauer*,[125] where the Court held that Article 141 (ex Article 119) could be relied upon directly as against the trustees, who were bound in their duties by the equal treatment principle.

Having established that private 'contracted out' occupational pension schemes were covered by the equal-pay principle, the ECJ went on to consider whether the different pension entitlements on redundancy for men and women were in breach thereof, and whether equal pay had to be ensured with respect to each element of pay:[126]

32. In the case of the first of those two questions thus formulated, it is sufficient to point out that Article 119 prohibits any discrimination with regard to pay as between men and women, whatever the system which gives rise to such inequality. Accordingly, it is contrary to Article 119 to impose an age condition which differs according to sex in respect of pensions paid under a contracted-out scheme, even if the difference between the pensionable age for men and that for women is based on the one provided for by the national statutory scheme.

. . .

34. With regard to the means of verifying compliance with the principle of equal pay, it must be stated that if the national courts were under an obligation to make an assessment and a comparison of all the various types of consideration granted, according to the circumstances, to men and women, judicial review would be difficult and the effectiveness of Article 119 would be diminished as a result. It follows that genuine transparency, permitting an effective review, is assured only if the principle of equal pay applies to each of the elements of remuneration granted to men or women.

(IV) LIMITING *BARBER*

This conclusion had serious repercussions throughout the Community, and fundamentally changed the way pension schemes would henceforth have to be organized.

D. Curtin, Scalping the Community Legislator: Occupational Pensions and Barber[127]

One of the major points to emerge from the Court's decision in *Barber* is that the limitation originally imposed by the Court as to the scope of the direct effect of Article 119 is, to all intents and purposes, redundant. It has been consistently argued over the years that highly complex problems such as the different life expectancies of men and women, different retirement ages, putative pensionable service during maternity leave etc. all militated against direct effect being ascribed to Article 119 in the pensions sphere in the absence of implementing legislation. The view was that since pension benefits were not tangible and calculable in money terms, detailed criteria determining how equality had to be achieved would have to be established through appropriate measures at either Community level or national level. However the Court's judgment in *Barber* adopts the approach that once the question of deciding that occupational benefits fall within the

---

124 *Ibid.*, para. 24.
125 Case C–379/99, *Pensionskasse für die Angestellten der Barmer Ersatzkasse* v. *Menauer* [2001] ECR I–7275, where neither the legal independence of the funds nor their status as insurers were relevant arguments against this.
126 See more recently, Cases C–381/99, *Brunnhofer*, n. 40 above, and C–236/98, *JämO*, n. 42 above.
127 N. 119 above, 484.

scope of 'pay' in Article 119 has been answered, the national court will *ipso facto* be in a position to decide whether the litigant receives less pay than a member of the opposite sex engaged in the same work. What is radical about this approach is that it confirms that equal treatment in the pension context does not require that the total amount of a particular benefit be mathematically equal since neither the costs nor the value of total pension benefits received will ever be known in advance. What seems to be required is rather that the rate at which the benefit is enjoyed be equal.

The radical nature of *Barber*, unsurprisingly, met with criticism from Member States—who had argued strongly against the Court's conclusion in their submissions during the case—and from employers alike. Some of the criticisms are expressed in the argument of a defendant employer in the post-*Barber* case of *Moroni*:

The *Barber* judgment . . . did not take sufficient account of the requirements of social policy which underlie occupational pension schemes such as that involved in this case. . . .

The test of equality which the Court of Justice applies to the factual justification for differential provisions in occupational pension schemes is stricter than that which it applies to statutory pension schemes.

Community legislation had itself taken account of this unavoidable link between statutory and occupational pensions by providing for the gradual and parallel application of the principle of equal treatment (see Directive 86/378/EEC). However, it is very disturbing, from the point of view of social policy and the protection of legitimate expectations, when a decision of the Court of Justice bypasses the provisions of a directive by means of an interpretation of Article 119.[128]

It was clear that occupational pensions would henceforth have to be organized differently to comply with the *Barber* ruling, but there was also concern over the prospect of large numbers of claims being made by all those who had, in the past, been adversely affected by the discriminatory conditions of pension schemes. In response to some of these concerns, the ECJ decided, as it had done in *Defrenne I*, to limit the retroactivity of its ruling. The UK had made submissions concerning the serious financial consequences the ruling would have, given the number of workers affiliated to contracted-out schemes which had provided for different pensionable ages for men and women.[129] And while in later rulings such as *Griesmar* and *Grzelczyk*[130] the ECJ insisted that the financial consequences alone would not justify limiting the temporal effect of a ruling, in *Barber* it took the view that the Member States and others had reasonably been entitled, in light of the authorization in the two Social Security Directives to defer implementation of the equal-treatment principle in relation to pensionable ages, to consider that Article 141 (ex Article 119) did not apply to pensions paid under contracted-out schemes:

44. In those circumstances, overriding considerations of legal certainty preclude legal situations which have exhausted all their effects in the past from being called in question where that

---

[128] See Case C–110/91, *Moroni* v. *Collo* [1993] ECR I–6591.

[129] In particular, the UK argued that, unless the retroactive effect of the judgment was limited, the increase in cost would run to between £33 and £45 billion, with disastrous effects for the UK economy as a whole.

[130] Cases C–184/99, *Grzelczyk* v. *CPAS* [2001] ECR I–6193, paras. 50–54 and C–366/99, *Griesmar* v. *Ministre de l'Economie* [2001] ECR I–9383, paras. 73–78.

might upset retroactively the financial balance of many contracted-out pension schemes. It is appropriate, however, to provide for an exception in favour of individuals who have taken action in good time in order to safeguard their rights. Finally, it must be pointed out that no restriction on the effects of the aforesaid interpretation can be permitted as regards the acquisition of entitlement to a pension as from the date of this judgment.

45. It must therefore be held that the direct effect of Article 119 of the Treaty may not be relied upon in order to claim entitlement to a pension with effect from a date prior to that of this judgment, except in the case of workers or those claiming under them who have before that date initiated legal proceedings or raised an equivalent claim under the applicable national law.

Although intended to promote legal certainty, these paragraphs gave rise to a great deal of uncertainty about the precise limits which had been placed upon the ruling. Several questions remained unanswered, and these came before the ECJ in the course of litigation arising in different Member States. There was confusion in particular about whether Article 141 (ex Article 119) could be relied on in relation to *periods of service* completed before the date of the judgment when no pension payments in respect of those periods had yet been received, or whether it could only be relied on in relation to periods of service completed after the date of the judgment. Clearly the latter interpretation would have the least serious financial consequences for employers.

Before those cases were heard, however, the concern aroused by *Barber* in the Member States had prompted the annexation of an additional Protocol to the EC Treaty by the Maastricht TEU, purporting to limit the retroactive effect of the judgment in the way stated above. In other words, the Protocol stipulated that, with the exception of those who had already instituted a legal claim, only pay attributable to periods of service completed after 17 May 1990—the date of the *Barber* judgment— would constitute pay within Article 141 (ex Article 119). It is noteworthy how, in much of the subsequent litigation, the ECJ's explanation of paragraphs 44–45 of *Barber* managed, without necessarily mentioning the Protocol, to correspond with its terms, thus avoiding an awkward conflict of Community laws. A Protocol attached to the EC Treaty has Treaty status[131] and this Protocol would override any previously conflicting judgment of the ECJ on the scope of Article 141 as soon as the TEU came into effect. Undoubtedly the Protocol was intended by the Member States to ensure that their desired interpretation of the scope of Article 141 would prevail, in the event that the ECJ preferred a different and wider interpretation in that respect.[132]

---

[131] See Art. 311 (ex Art. 239) EC.

[132] See D. Curtin, 'The Constitutional Structure of the Union: A Europe of Bits and Pieces' (1992) 29 *CMLRev.* 17, 51. See, however, Van Gerven AG's assertion that the Protocol was not intended to call into question the ECJ's case law nor to restrict the scope of Art. 141 (ex Art. 119), at para. 23 of his Opinion in Cases C–109/91, *Ten Oever* v. *Stichting Bedrijfspensioenfonds voor het Glazenwasseren Schoonmaakerbedrijf* [1993] ECR I–4879; C–110/91, n. 128 above; C–152/91, n. 120 above; and C–200/91, n. 53 above. See, more generally, T. Hervey, 'Legal Issues concerning the Barber Protocol', in D. O'Keeffe and P. Twomey (eds.), *Legal Issues of the Maastricht Treaty* (Wiley, 1994), 329.

(v) THE POST-*BARBER* CASE LAW

However, although it adopted an approach to the retroactivity of *Barber* which was essentially the same as that in the Protocol, the ECJ in further case law reasserted its independence by limiting the potential *reach* of that Protocol, ruling in *Fisscher* and *Vroege* that it had to be read 'in conjunction with the *Barber* judgment and cannot have a scope wider than the limitation of its effects in time'.[133] This meant that the Protocol related only to *benefits* and not to the *right to join or belong* to an occupational pension scheme. Thus discriminatory conditions governing *membership* of an occupational scheme, such as a full-time requirement or the exclusion of married women, were governed by the ECJ's earlier ruling in *Bilka* on this issue, rather than by the Protocol. The ECJ found that the reasons for limiting the retroactivity of the *Barber* ruling—i.e., the fact that the discrimination in pension schemes could reasonably have been considered to be permissible under Directive 86/378—did not apply to the issue of discrimination in access to membership of a pension scheme in *Bilka*, which was decided before the Directive had been adopted. The same was true of the entitlement to receive a retirement pension in *Dietz*,[134] or entitlement to additional special benefits in *Magorrian*,[135] which were indissolubly linked to the right to join or the right fully to participate in an occupational scheme, and the same was equally true of indirect discrimination in access to an occupational pension scheme in *Schröder*.[136] Thus, subject to the application of national time limits for bringing an action,[137] Article 141 (ex Article 119) could be relied on to challenge a discriminatory exclusion from a pension scheme as from the date of the *Defrenne II* judgment, in which it had been held to be directly effective. However, the ECJ also ruled that the right retroactively to join a pension scheme did not mean that such workers could avoid paying the value of the past contributions.[138]

In *Ten Oever*, when the ECJ was called upon to interpret the limitation in paragraphs 44–45 of the *Barber* ruling, it took the same approach as that adopted in the Protocol.

---

[133] Cases C–128/93, *Fisscher v. Voorhuis Hengelo BV and Stichting Bedrijfspensioenfonds voor de Detailhandel* [1994] ECR I–4583, and C–57/93, *Vroege v. NCIV Institut voor Volkshuisvesting BV and Stichting Pensioenfonds NCIV* [1994] ECR I–4541. See also Case C–7/93, *Bestuur van het Algemeen Burgerlijk Pensioenfonds v. Beune* [1994] ECR I–4471.

[134] Case C–435/93, *Dietz v. Stichting Thuiszorg Rotterdam* [1996] ECR I–5223, [1997] 1 CMLR 199, paras. 23–25.

[135] Case C–246/96, *Magorrian and Cunningham v. Eastern Health and Social Services Board and Department of Health and Social Services* [1997] ECR I–7153.

[136] Case C–50/96, *Deutsche Telekom v. Schröder* [2000] ECR I–743. Also Cases C–270/97 & C–271/97, *Deutsche Post v. Sievers and Schrage* [2000] ECR I–929.

[137] As in the Court's general case law on remedies, the rules relating to national time limits must be no less favourable than for similar actions of a domestic nature and must not render impossible the exercise of the right. See, however, Case C–147/95, *Dimossia Epicheirissi Ilectrismou* (DEI) v. *Efthimios Evrenopoulos* [1997] ECR I–2057, in which the ECJ considered that a claim initiated before 17 May 1990 should be governed by the *Barber* ruling even if the action was declared inadmissible by the national court due to the claimant's prior failure to lodge an objection, since the time limit for making such an objection had then been extended by the national court.

[138] Case C–128/93, n. 133 above, para. 37.

Case C–109/91, Ten Oever v. Stichting Bedrijfspensioenfonds voor het
Glazenwassers- en Schoonmaakbedrijf
[1993] ECR I–4879

THE ECJ

16. The precise context in which that limitation was imposed was that of benefits (in particular, pensions) provided for by private occupational schemes which were treated as pay within the meaning of Article 119 of the Treaty.

17. The Court's ruling took account of the fact that it is a characteristic of this form of pay that there is a time-lag between the accrual of entitlement to the pension, which occurs gradually throughout the employee's working life, and its actual payment, which is deferred until a particular age.

18. The Court also took into consideration the way in which occupational pension funds are financed and thus of the accounting links existing in each individual case between the periodic contributions and the future amounts to be paid.

19. Given the reasons explained in paragraph 44 of the *Barber* judgment for limiting its effects in time, it must be made clear that equality of treatment in the matter of occupational pensions may be claimed only in relation to benefits payable in respect of periods of employment subsequent to 17 May 1990, the date of the *Barber* judgment, subject to the exception in favour of workers or those claiming under them who have, before that date, initiated legal proceedings or raised an equivalent claim under the applicable national law.

The *Barber* Protocol was applied directly in the later *Defreyn* (not Defrenne!) case, in relation to an additional pre-retirement payment under an occupational social security scheme.[139] While the ECJ acknowledged that this consituted 'pay' rather than social security, it ruled that a benefit of this kind which was attributable to periods of employment prior to 17 May 1990 was clearly governed by the terms of the protocol and therefore fell to be treated as occupational social security under Directive 86/378 as amended by Directive 96/97.

In *Ten Oever* the ECJ also ruled that Article 141 (ex Article 119) covered pension benefits payable not just to an employee, but also to the employee's survivor—in this case a widow's pension—since the crucial factor was that the pension was paid by reason of the employment relationship between the employee and employer.[140] Following from this, the ECJ ruled in *Coloroll*[141] and later in *Menauer*[142] that Article 141 could be invoked against the employer or the trustees of the pension scheme, not just by an employee under the scheme, but also by the employee's dependants.[143]

---

[139] Case C–166/99, *Defreyn* v. *Sabena* [2000] ECR I–6155.

[140] See also Cases C–147/95, *DEI* v. *Efthimios Evrenopoulos* [1997] ECR I–2057 and C–50/99, *Podesta* v. *CRICA* [2000] ECR I–4039.

[141] Case C–200/91, n. 53 above, paras. 17–19.

[142] Case C–379/99, *Pensionskasse für die Angestellten der Barmer Ersatzkasse* v. *Menauer* [2001] ECR I–7275.

[143] This was sharply criticized by the German government in the case, which argued that a survivor's pension benefit should be not regarded as pay, since it did not represent consideration for work performed, but reflected social-policy concerns connected to the traditional allocation of men's and women's roles: see [1993] ECR I–4879.

In *Moroni*, the ECJ was asked whether the ruling in *Barber* applied in the same way to supplementary pension schemes as it did to contracted-out schemes.[144] It might be thought that this had been decided in *Bilka*, but the issue in *Bilka* was the compatibility with Article 119 (now Article 141) of the exclusion of part-time workers from a supplementary pension scheme, whereas the issue in *Moroni* was whether discriminatory pensionable ages *within* such a scheme were contrary to that Article. Despite the German government's argument that this was a form of social welfare rather than pay, the ECJ cited the reasoning used in *Bilka*, ruling that sums paid out under a supplementary occupational pension scheme did constitute pay, and that the discriminatory effects of setting different retirement ages were just as much a feature of supplementary occupational pension schemes as they were of contracted-out schemes such as that in *Barber*.[145]

(VI) OTHER KINDS OF PENSION

In the case of *Beune*,[146] concerning civil service pensions, the ECJ reviewed the criteria it had developed in its case law from *Defrenne I* to *Ten Oever* for determining whether a pension scheme constituted pay under Article 141 (ex Article 119) or social security under Directive 79/7. Ultimately, having considered the criteria of (a) agreement between employer and employee rather than statutory origin, (b) the absence of public funding of a scheme, and (c) the provision of benefits supplementary to State social security benefits, the ECJ concluded that the 'decisive' though not the 'exclusive' criterion (which seems to mean 'necessary' but not 'sufficient') was (d) that set out in Article 119 (now Article 141) itself: i.e., that the pension is paid to the worker by reason of the employment relationship between the worker and the former employer.[147] Consequently, even if the civil service pension scheme was affected by 'considerations of social policy, of State organisation, or of ethics or even budgetary preoccupations'—i.e., factors which would normally point to its classification as a state social-security scheme rather than pay—these could not prevail if three other factors were also present: if the pension paid by a public employer (1) concerned only a particular category of workers rather than general categories, (2) was directly related to the period of service, and (3) was calculated, in its amount, by reference to the civil servant's last salary, then it was comparable to a pension paid by a private employer and would constitute pay.[148] These principles were applied by the ECJ in *Griesmar*[149] and *Mouflin*[150] where French retirement pensions for civil servants were held to be pay rather than social security.

---

[144] Case C–110/91, n. 129 above.

[145] See also Case C–173/91, *Commission* v. *Belgium* [1993] ECR I–673, in which redundancy supplements were held to consitute pay within Art. 119 (now Art. 141), despite the argument of the Belgian Government that, being like early state retirement pensions, they constituted a form of social security falling within the exception in Art. 7(1)(a) of Dir. 79/7. The *Barber* Protocol limiting the retroactive effect of Art. 141 (ex Art. 119) to such schemes was later applied to pay of this kind in Case C–166/99, *Defreyn* v. *Sabena* [2000] ECR I–6155.

[146] Case C–7/93, *Bestuur van het Algemeen Burgerlijk Pensioenfonds* v. *Beune* [1994] ECR I–4471. See also Case C–50/99, *Podesta* v. *CRICA* [2000] ECR I–4039.

[147] *Ibid.*, paras. 43–44.   [148] *Ibid.*, para. 45.

[149] Case C–366/99, *Griesmar* v. *Ministre de l'Economie, des Finances et de l'Industrie* [2001] ECR I–9383.

[150] Case C–206/00, *Mouflin* v. *Recteur de l'académie de Reims* [2001] ECR I–nyr.

In *Beune* and *Moroni*, and the ECJ ruled that, whenever the legal criteria of pay and equal work could be identified, an employee could rely directly on Article 141 (ex Article 119), thus effectively overriding Article 8 of the original Directive 86/378, which had purported to allow the postponement until 1993 of the establishment of equal pensionable ages in occupational schemes.[151] However, the *Coloroll* ruling made clear that the limitation on the retroactive effect of *Barber* applied to discriminatory age conditions in both non-contracted-out and contracted-out occupational schemes.[152]

(VII) A LIMITED RETREAT

Among the various other issues raised in the cases of *Coloroll* and *Neath*[153] was the question whether payments by an employer to a contracted-out occupational pension scheme (rather than payments to an *employee*, as in *Barber*) were covered by Article 119 (now Article 141). This question arose because actuarial calculations of the different life expectancies of men and women were used in determining the sums payable by an employer into the scheme. In both cases, a 'defined-benefit' pension scheme was in issue, under which employees would receive a pension the criteria for which were fixed in advance, e.g., by reference to a fraction of their final year's salary for each year of service. It was held that contributions of *employees* to the scheme must consist of an identical amount for men and women, since, according to *Worringham*,[154] employee contributions were pay within Article 141. However, in such defined-benefit schemes, *employers'* contributions varied over time and were adjusted to take account of the pensions which would have to be paid. As a consequence of using the sex-based actuarial factors in calculating such employers' contributions, the amount which a male employee would receive on redundancy either in the form of a capital sum, transfer benefits, or a deferred pension would be less than that which a woman would receive.

The Commission argued that such sums constituted pay, and that the differences in pay between men and women could not be justified by reference to the statistical data based on the average life expectancy of the two sexes, since the right to equal pay was given to employees individually, rather than as members of a class. Advocate General van Gerven agreed and took the view that, in so far as it gave rise to different employee contributions or to different employee benefits (such as lump sums or transfer value), the use of sex-based actuarial factors to ascertain the funding needed for a pension scheme was contrary to the Treaty Article.[155] The ECJ, however, did not follow this

---

[151] *Ibid.*, paras. 64–65, and Case C–110/91, n. 129 above, paras. 25–26.

[152] Case C–200/91, n. 53 above, para. 71. It had been argued that it was clear, since the ruling in *Bilka* in 1986, that supplementary occupational pension schemes were covered by Art. 119 (now Art. 141), but neither the AG nor the Court accepted this. In the case of a pension benefit payable not according to length of service, but e.g. on the happening of an event such as the death of the employee, the Court held that the limit on the retroactive effect of the *Barber* ruling applied if the event took place before 17 May 1990. Contrast *Fisscher, Vroege*, and *Beune*, n. 133 above.

[153] Case C–152/91, n. 120 above.   [154] Case 69/80, n. 56 above.

[155] The AG was impressed by the fact that many differences in risk factors other than life expectancy were ignored in calculating the financing of the pension scheme, e.g., risks associated with certain occupations, health risks, or smoking. He also noted that no state pension scheme, as opposed to private occupational schemes, found it necessary to use such sex-based actuarial calculation factors.

view. In a defined-benefit scheme, the ECJ ruled that the pension which was promised according to fixed criteria constituted pay, since it represented the employer's 'commitment' to the employee. However, the Court considered that employer contributions were paid in order to ensure the adequacy of the funds to cover the cost of the promised pension, and although the *pension* constituted 'pay' within Article 141 (ex Article 119), neither the contributions of the employer nor the value of those contributions as represented by a lump sum or transfer benefits would fall within Article 141.[156]

Thus, having gradually broadened the concept of pay, eroding the distinction between pay and occupational social security, and creating a distinction between the latter and State social security, the ECJ drew back somewhat in *Neath* and *Coloroll.* Despite the force of the Advocate General's submission, the ECJ ruled that employers' contributions to defined-benefit occupational pension schemes did not fall within that Article. The contrary argument of the Commission reflected the proposal it had originally put forward for what became Directive 86/378, excluding the possibility of relying on different actuarial factors for men and women based on life-expectancy,[157] but the Council had rejected this proposal in adopting the Directive. The ECJ in *Neath* took a similar view to the Council rather than the Commission, and this was subsequently followed by both the Commission and Council in Directive 96/97, which amended Directive 86/378 largely by enacting the case law of the Court since *Barber.*[158]

Neath and *Coloroll* left it unclear whether Article 141 (ex Article 119) applied to contributions paid by an employer into what is called a 'money-purchase' or 'defined-contribution' scheme, as opposed to a 'defined-benefit' scheme. In contrast with the latter scheme, in which the criteria for the pension to be paid are fixed in advance even though the employer's contributions to the funding of the scheme will vary, the pension is paid in a defined-contribution scheme by reference to the amount of the contributions which the employer has made to the scheme. However, Article 6 of Directive 96/97 in amending Directive 86/378 makes clear that Article 141 (ex Article 119) does also apply to money-purchase schemes, but permits the use of actuarial factors which differ according to sex, and the payment of unequal contributions if the aim is to equalize the amount of the final benefits for both sexes. The Directive also allows another 'exception' to the scope of the equal treatment principle in occupational pensions which was established by the ECJ in *Coloroll,* where it ruled that certain pension benefits purchased by voluntary *employee* contributions to an occupational scheme would not fall within Article 119 (now Article 141) and thus would not constitute pay.[159] Other exceptions to the scope of the Directive include individual contracts for self-employed workers, schemes for the self-employed having only one member, insurance contracts of salaried workers to which the employer is not a party, and individual optional additional benefits within an occupational scheme.

---

[156] Cases C–152/91, *Neath*, n. 120 above, paras. 31–32, and C–200/91, *Coloroll*, n. 53 above, paras. 80–81.

[157] See [1983] OJ C134/7.

[158] [1997] OJ L46/20. See Case C–457/98, *Commission* v. *Greece* [2000] ECR I–11481, where Greece was condemned for failing to implement the Dir. See also for various other breaches of EC sex equality law, Case C–187/98, *Commission* v. *Greece* [1999] ECR I–7713.

[159] Case C–200/91, n. 53 above, paras. 90–93. See Art. 2(2)(e) of Dir. 96/97.

(VIII) REDRESSING DISCRIMINATION IN OCCUPATIONAL PENSIONS

A major question which remained following *Barber* was how the discrimination identified was to be remedied. In *Coloroll*, the ECJ ruled that, between the date of the *Barber* ruling and the date of entry into force of measures designed to eliminate discrimination, 'correct implementation of the principle of equal pay requires that the disadvantaged employees should be granted the same advantages as those previous enjoyed by other employees'. In other words, until amending measures were adopted, pension schemes could only 'level up', by giving men the same advantages as women enjoyed. This principle was first enunciated in *Defrenne II*,[160] in which the ECJ ruled that compliance with the equal pay principle could not be achieved other than by raising the lowest salaries, since Article 141 (ex Article 119) appeared in the context of the harmonization of working conditions while maintaining an improvement in those conditions. However, the Court in *Coloroll* took a more limited approach than that implied in *Defrenne II*, and applied the 'levelling-up' or improvement in conditions of pay only to the transitional stage between the date of the *Barber* ruling and the date on which measures were adopted to comply with it. The ECJ further ruled that, during this transitional stage, it was not open to the pension scheme or the employer to plead that a levelling-down approach was objectively justified by reason of the financial difficulties for the pension scheme, since 'the space of time involved is relatively short and attributable in any event to the conduct of the scheme administrators themselves'.[161] However, once equalizing measures were adopted, 'Article 119 does not then preclude measures to achieve equal treatment by reducing the advantages of the persons previously favoured'.[162] With regard to the period before the date of the *Barber* ruling, however, during which the pensionable age for women under these occupational schemes was lower than that for men, the ECJ made clear that, since it had limited the retroactivity of its ruling in this respect, EC law provided no reason at all for 'equalizing' of the positions of men and women by retroactively reducing the advantages enjoyed by women during that period. In other words, EC law had nothing to say about the age discrimination between men and women in occupational pension schemes prior to 17 May 1990. The Court reiterated this point in *Smith* v. *Advel*, decided on the same day as *Coloroll*, and ruled further that once an employer took steps for the future to comply with Article 141 (ex Article 119), the achievement of equality could not be made partial or progressive:

The step of raising the retirement age for women to that for men, which an employer decides to take in order to remove discrimination in relation to occupational pensions as regards benefits payable in respect of future periods of service, cannot be accompanied by measures, even if only transitional, designed to limit the adverse consequences which such a step may have for women.[163]

It is noticeable that the Court uses the language of 'advantage' in the occupational pensions case law to describe the position of women, since the retirement age for

---

[160] Case 43/75, *Defrenne* v. *Sabena* [1976] ECR 455, para. 15.
[161] Case C–408/92, *Smith* v. *Advel Systems Ltd.* [1994] ECR I–4435, para. 30.
[162] *Coloroll*, n. 53 above, para. 33.
[163] Case C–408/92, n. 161 above, para. 27. See also Case C–28/93, *Van den Akker* v. *Stichting Shell Pensioenfonds* [1994] ECR I–4527, as regards the impermissibility of any advantages for women once a uniform retirement age for men and women is introduced.

women was generally, being linked to that of State pension schemes, lower than that for men. However, it has been pointed out that the language of 'advantage' or 'favoured group' is hardly appropriate to apply to women in this context:

It would be misleading to consider this matter of 'more' or 'less' favoured groups at a theoretical level. Unquestionably, the less favoured group is in reality composed of women, who have worked and contributed to the scheme but receive very low pensions because of the level of pay which they earned during their working life, itself frequently shorter than the men's.[164]

It is perhaps this perception of male workers as the disadvantaged group that led the ECJ to permit what may be seen as direct pay discrimination by an employer, so as to compensate for the relative disadvantage of men as opposed to women in the context of pensionable ages. Although the case was decided by the Court on the basis that there was no real discrimination, it can also be seen as a case where discrimination in pay was permitted to make up for what was perceived to be an existing inequality.

Case C–132/92, Roberts v. Birds Eye Walls Ltd.
[1993] ECR I—5579

Mrs Roberts, who was forced to retire on grounds of ill health before reaching the statutory retirement age, challenged the amount of the bridging pension paid to her under the occupational pension scheme to which she had been affiliated. The bridging pension was an *ex gratia* payment—entirely financed by the employer—to employees who were forced to retire on grounds of ill health before reaching the statutory retirement age. Its purpose was said to be both to place employees in the financial position they would have been in had they not been forced to retire early, and to place the overall financial treatment of men and women in identical situations on an equal footing. For male and female employees retiring before the age of 60, when neither had reached state pensionable age, the bridging pension included an amount corresponding to the proportion of the state pension attributable to periods of service. After 60, however, the amount of the bridging pension paid to a woman was reduced on the ground that she was in receipt of a state pension, whereas the bridging pension paid to a man was not reduced until the age of 65, when he would receive a state pension.

THE ECJ

17. It should be noted that the principle of equal treatment laid down by Article 119 of the Treaty, like the general principle of non-discrimination which it embodies in a specific form, presupposes that the men and women to whom it applies are in identical situations.

18. However, that would not appear to be so where the deferred payment which an employer makes to those of his employees who are compelled to take early retirement on grounds of ill-health is regarded as a supplement to the financial resources of the man or woman concerned.

19. It follows clearly from the mechanism for calculating the bridging pension that the assessment of the amount thereof is not frozen at a particular moment but necessarily varies on account of changes occurring in the financial position of the man or woman concerned with the passage of time.

---

[164] D. de Vos, 'Pensionable Age and Equal Treatment from Charybdis to Scylla' (1994) 23 *ILJ* 175, 179.

20. Accordingly, although until the age of 60 the financial position of a woman taking early retirement on grounds of ill-health is comparable to that of a man in the same situation, neither of them as yet entitled to payment of the state pension, that is no longer the case between the ages of 60 and 65 since that is when women, unlike men, start drawing that pension. That difference as regards the objective premise, which necessarily entails that the amount of the bridging pension is not the same for men and women, cannot be considered discriminatory.

21. What is more, given the purpose of the bridging pension, to maintain the amount for women at the same level as that which obtained before they received the state pension would give rise to unequal treatment to the detriment of men who do not receive the state pension until the age of 65.

Birds Eye Walls was a surprising judgment, since, although men and women under a private occupational scheme clearly received different bridging pensions after the age of 60, the ECJ held that this was not discriminatory within Article 141 (ex Article 119), but focused instead on the fact that men and women over 60 were differently situated, since women were generally in receipt of a state pension by then. However, this was a departure from its reasoning in earlier cases such as *Worringham*, where the difference in the actual gross sum paid by an employer to men as opposed to women was held to be discriminatory, regardless of the fact that men were paid the extra sum in order to compensate for a deduction from their earnings to which women were not subject—in other words, regardless of the fact that men and women were not 'similarly situated' in that case either.[165] On the other hand, it seems from more recently decided cases such as *Abdoulaye* and *Griesmar* that the ECJ has occasionally adopted a less formalistic approach to the question whether men and women are genuinely similarly situated, for the purposes of deciding whether formally unequal pay may actually be designed to redress existing inequalities.[166]

In other respects, however, the ruling in *Birds Eye Walls* also ran against the trend of the ECJ's judgments in its earlier cases such as *Roberts*, in which it was not permissible for employers to link the granting of voluntary redundancy pensions to the state social-security scheme where the state scheme still maintained discriminatory retirement ages for men and women.[167] Instead, the ECJ required equality of age limits for the grant of a voluntary redundancy pension on voluntary redundancy, ignoring the different state pensionable ages. By way of contrast, although the employer in *Birds Eye Walls* was not seeking to replicate the discrimination in the state system in its bridging pension scheme, it was introducing discrimination between men and women in its scheme in order to counterbalance the effects of the state system, rather than simply paying equal bridging pensions. The case was criticized for its sudden departure from the formal notion of equal treatment which had for so long been followed by the ECJ.

---

[165] Case 69/80, n. 56 above. See more recently however Case C–381/99, *Brunnhofer* v. *Österreichischer Bank Postsparkasse* [2001] ECR I–4961, where the *Birds Eye Walls* ruling was cited at para. 39 as authority for the proposition that in order for different treatment to constitute discrimination men and women must be relevantly 'differently situated'.

[166] See nn. 94 and 95 above.

[167] Case 151/84, *Roberts* v. *Tate & Lyle Industries* [1986] ECR 703.

B. Fitzpatrick, Equality in Occupational Pension Schemes[168]

How remarkable it is that, the Court having propounded equality irrespective of sex as a fundamental right in Community law for nearly 20 years, a three man chamber of the Court should now
discover 'equality of outcomes'—but not for women who, generally speaking, receive much lower
benefits in occupational pension schemes, but rather for men upon whose stereotyped working
lives the discriminatory structure of pension schemes is based?

. . .

  Although *Birds Eye Walls* was decided upon the concept of equality, these conclusions call
into question aspects of the Court's case law upon the concept of pay within Article 119. In
Barber, the Court concluded . . . that each component part of the payment package had to be
judged autonomously on grounds of equality. It was not permissible to set off parts of the
remuneration package against each other. Here we are suddenly told that, because of a payment's purpose, it can be set off against, not merely another part of the employer's remuneration
package, but rather a *State* benefit. And yet, the focus of the Court's judgment in *Barber* . . . has
been to break the links between pay and welfare which bedevilled cases such as *Burton* and
Newstead.

The criticism which the judgment attracted did not deter the political institutions
from incorporating it into the amended occupational pensions legislation, and Article
2(3) of Directive 86/378, as amended by Directive 96/97, now effectively summarizes
the *Birds Eye* ruling. For the legislature to follow the lead of the ECJ in this field may
seem surprising, given that social security is an area which has been seen in Community law as a complex matter requiring gradual legislative progress—in the shape
of political compromises such as those in Directives 79/7 and 86/378 to enable gradual financial adaptation–rather than judicial change. Article 141 (ex Article 119) on
the other hand embodied a straightforward principle of equal pay which appeared to
involve none of the complexities of adapting a pension scheme, and which was to be
'policed' by the ECJ through the cases which came before it. Yet it was precisely the
series of rulings of the Court expanding the concept of pay to include most forms of
occupational social security, with limited exceptions such as those for sex-based
actuarial calculations in certain employer contributions and for bridging pensions,
and permitting a levelling-down rather than requiring a levelling-up approach,
which was followed and enshrined by the legislative institutions in the amending
Directive.[169]

---

[168] (1994) 23 *ILJ* 155, 163.
[169] For criticism of the 'purely declaratory' approach of Dir. 96/97, and its failure to address certain
deficiencies in this field, see E. Cassell, 'The Revised Directive on Equal Treatment for Men and Women in
Occupational Social Security Schemes—The Dog that Didn't Bark' (1997) 26 *ILJ* 269.

4. EQUAL TREATMENT

(a) EQUAL TREATMENT AS A GENERAL PRINCIPLE

The terms of Article 141 (ex Article 119) quite clearly established the principle of equal pay, but until the amendments made by the ToA they did not expressly refer to the equal treatment of men and women other than in terms of pay. This was consistent with the historical explanation for the Article, suggested above, which was to ensure equal conditions of competition for businesses operating in the different Member States as regards the cost of labour. However, the social rather than the economic objective of the original Treaty provision would evidently be better achieved in the context of a general commitment to equality between women and men, at least in the workplace.

In *Defrenne III*, it was argued to the ECJ that the principle of equal treatment of men and women was a fundamental principle of Community law.[170] More specifically, it was argued, following the successful equal-pay claim in *Defrenne II*, that the discriminatory compulsory termination of the plaintiff's employment contract at age 40 was contrary to Article 141 (ex Article 119). But the ECJ ruled that although the two Treaty Articles preceding Article 141 contemplated the harmonization of national social systems and the improvement of the conditions of employment, they were of a programmatic character, unlike the special and precise equal-pay rule. It was not possible, in the Court's view, to extend the scope of Article 141 at that stage to elements of the employment relationship other than pay. However, the ECJ went on to say that the elimination of sex discrimination more generally was a fundamental personal human right, and thus part of the general principles of Community law whose observance it must ensure. In its previous rulings in *Sabbatini*[171] and *Airola*,[172] the Court had recognized that the Community had to ensure equality of working conditions as between men and women in respect of its own staff. However, this was to be contrasted with the position of the Member States, at the stage of development of Community law at the time of *Defrenne III*, when the Community had not yet assumed any responsibility 'for supervising and guaranteeing the observance of the principle of equality between men and women in working conditions other than remuneration'.[173] Since the time of the events giving rise to *Defrenne III*, Directive 76/207 on equal treatment in conditions of employment, based on Article 308 (ex Article 235) of the Treaty, had been adopted.[174]

The mixed legal basis of the directives on sex discrimination in the past highlights the uncertainty of the social-policy provisions of the Treaty, with Directive 75/117 on equal pay and the amending Directive 96/97 on occupational social security being based on Article 94 (ex Article 100), Directives 76/207 on equal treatment and 79/7 on state social security primarily on Article 308 (ex Article 235), and Directives 86/378 on occupational social security and 86/613 on equal treatment for the self-employed

---

170 Case 149/77, *Defrenne* v. *Sabena (No. 3)* [1978] ECR 1365.
171 Case 20/71, n. 16 above.   172 Case 21/74, n. 16 above.
173 Case 149/79, n. 170 above, para. 30.   174 [1976] OJ L39/40.

on those two Articles jointly. Since then, the Treaty's social-policy provisions have gradually been amended and strengthened, with the Pregnancy Directive 92/85 being adopted on the basis of the post-SEA Article 138 (ex Article 118a) and Directives 96/34 and 97/81 on the framework agreements concerning parental leave and part-time work respectively, as well as Directive 97/80 on the burden of proof, under the terms of the post-TEU Social Policy Agreement (SPA). The incorporation of the SPA into the body of the EC Treaty post-Amsterdam added further to the strength, if not the cohesiveness, of the social-policy provisions, and there are now explicit bases for legislation in the field of equal treatment and equal opportunities more generally in Articles 137 (ex Article 118), 139 (ex Article 118b), and 141 (ex Article 119) EC.

(b) DIRECTIVE 76/207

The aim of this Directive is to secure equal treatment between men and women in three broad, employment-related areas, namely access to employment and promotion, vocational training, and working conditions. More recently the ECJ has held that its protection extends to retaliatory measures adopted by an employer after the end of the employment relationship.[175] Matters of social security are not within its scope by virtue of Article 1(2), which provides for the Council to adopt legislation on equal treatment in social security.[176] The equal-treatment principle is defined in Article 2 to mean any discrimination 'on grounds of sex either directly or indirectly by reference in particular to marital or family status'. Many of its provisions are similar to those of Directive 75/117 on equal pay, in that the Member States are required to abolish all legislative and administrative provisions in those three areas which discriminate on grounds of sex, and to ensure that any provisions of measures such as collective agreements and individual employment contracts are similarly abolished.[177] There are also parallel provisions to the Equal Pay Directive on access to a legal remedy, protecting complainants and ensuring that those affected know of their rights.[178] A proposal to amend Directive 76/207 is currently making its way through the legislative process, and its contents will be discussed further below.

The 1976 Directive is distinctive, however, in that, unlike the equal-pay provisions, it permits several exceptions to the equal-treatment principle. As far as all measures which contravene the formal equal-treatment principle in access to employment or conditions of work are concerned, Member States are required to ensure their revision 'when the concern for protection which originally inspired them is no longer well founded'.[179]

(i) THE OCCUPATIONAL QUALIFICATION EXCEPTION

Article 2 sets out three matters which Member States may exclude: the first, in Article 2(2), relates to occupational activities, including training, in respect of which 'by reason of their nature or the context in which they are carried out' the sex of the

---

[175] Case C–185/97, *Coote* v. *Granada Hospitality Ltd.* [1998] ECR I–5199.
[176] This was subsequently done with the adoption of Dir. 79/7 [1979] OJ L6/24.
[177] Dir. 76/207, n. 174 above, Arts. 3, 4, and 5.
[178] *Ibid.*, Arts. 6, 7, and 8 respectively.   [179] *Ibid.*, Arts. 3(2)(c) and 5(2)(c).

worker constitutes a determining factor. An example might be an actor's occupation, in which it may be legitimate to require a person of a specified sex to perform a role.

The scope of Article 2(2) was considered in the *Male Midwives* case in the UK.[180] The Court found that legislation which limited access for men to the profession of midwife was in conformity with the exception in Article 2(2), in view of the fact that 'personal sensitivities' could play an important role in the relationship between midwife and patient. The arguments of the Commission and the Advocate General that this could be adequately catered for by giving the patient the choice of a male or female midwife were not addressed by the Court (nor indeed the fact that other presumably equally 'sensitive' relationships such as between gynaecologist and patient did not seem to necessitate such limited access), which ruled that the UK had not exceeded the limits of the power granted to states by the Directive.[181]

Article 2(2) was also considered in *Johnston* v. *Chief Constable of the RUC*, in which the RUC sought to justify its decision not to employ women as full-time members of the RUC Reserve.[182] It was argued that if women were permitted to carry and use firearms, they would be at greater risk of becoming targets for assassination. The Commission, however, argued that the occupational activity of an armed police officer could not be considered an activity for which the sex of the officer was a determining factor, and that if an exception were to be made in relation to specific duties, the principle of proportionality would have to be observed. The Court accepted the UK's argument that the carrying of firearms by policewomen might create additional risks of assassination, without requiring any evidence to support the implication that women could not be trained to use firearms just as safely and effectively as men.[183] Hence the Court accepted that the sex of police officers could constitute a 'determining factor' for carrying out certain policing activities.[184] The assessment of the proportionality of the decision was left to the national court, e.g., to consider 'whether the refusal to renew Mrs Johnston's contract could not have been avoided by allocating to women duties which, without jeopardizing the aims pursued, can be performed without firearms'.[185]

Similar questions came before the Court in the cases of *Sirdar* and *Kreil*.[186] In *Sirdar*, a woman who was refused employment as a chef with the UK Royal Marines challenged their policy of excluding women from service on the ground that their presence is incompatible with the requirement of 'interoperability', i.e., 'the need for every Marine, irrespective of his specialisation, to be capable of fighting in a commando unit'. The ECJ ruled that this could be justified under Article 2(2), on the basis that the Marine corps was an exceptional and small force intended to be in the first line of attack. In *Kreil*, on the other hand, the applicant was challenging a more

---

180 Case 165/82, *Commission* v. *UK* [1983] ECR 3431, [1984] 1 CMLR 44.

181 *Ibid.*, para. 20.   182 Case 222/84, [1986] ECR 1651.

183 See Fredman, n. 26 above, 128; More, n. 67 above, 52–3.

184 See also Case 318/86, *Commission* v. *France* [1988] ECR 3559, para. 27, where the Court accepted that certain police duties could involve sex-specific duties, but nevertheless condemned France's separate recruitment systems for men and women, since they lacked transparency and made it impossible for the Community to supervise the use of Art. 2(2) of the Dir.

185 [1986] ECR 1651, para. 39.

186 Cases C–273/97, *Sirdar* v. *Army Board* [1999] ECR I–7403, and C–285/98, *Kreil* v. *Bundesrepublik Deutschland* [2000] ECR I–69. For comment on both cases, see P. Koutrakos (2000) 25 *ELRev.* 433.

general prohibition under German law which barred women from military posts involving the use of arms, and allowed them access only to the medical and military-music services. Here the ECJ ruled that, since the Article 2(2) derogation was intended to apply only to specific activities, the scope and breadth of this prohibition exceeded even the discretion given to Member States when adopting measures they consider necessary to guarantee public security. It could also be seen to be disproportionately broad from the fact that basic training in the use of arms was already provided to women in the services of the Bundeswehr which remained accessible to them.

It seems from the case law that Article 2(2) has often been used to maintain stereotyped roles rather than genuinely necessary sex segregration, and it remains to be seen whether the new 'Framework Strategy for Gender' which has identified gender stereotyping as one of its five priority themes, will have any impact in this regard.

(ii) THE MATERNITY-PROTECTION EXCEPTION

A second area which may be excluded from the equal-treatment principle is set out in Article 2(3) and relates to provisions adopted by the Member States 'concerning the protection of women, particularly as regards pregnancy and maternity'.[187] In so far as matters such as maternity leave are concerned, the 1992 Pregnancy Directive now goes further than simply allowing Member States to maintain protective provisions and imposes a requirement to provide a minimum of employment protection for women who are pregnant, breast-feeding, or who have recently given birth.[188] However, the Directive specifically states that it provides no ground for Member States to reduce the existing levels of protection they provide, if these are higher than the requirements of the Directive.

(iii) THE POSITIVE-ACTION PROVISION

The third area of 'exception' to the principle of formal equality is in Article 2(4)—the 'positive-action' provision which permits measures designed to redress inequality between men and women and to 'promote equal opportunity for men and women, in particular by removing existing inequalities which affect women's opportunities' in the three areas covered by the Directive.[189] This provision was first narrowly read by the Court, so that a provision of French law which permitted collective agreements to provide special rights for women—including shorter working hours for older women, the obtaining of leave when a child was ill, the granting of extra days of leave in respect of children—was not justified under Article 2(4).[190] France had not adequately shown that 'the generalized preservation of special rights for women' would reduce actual instances of inequality in social life.[191] The Court's and the AG's assumption seemed to be that there was no inequality faced by women which required these

---

[187] For a warning to Member States against reading this over-broadly, see Cases 222/84, *Johnston* [1986] ECR 1651, para. 44, and C–285/98, *Kreil* v. *Bundesrepublik Deutschland* [2000] ECR I–69, para. 30.

[188] Dir. 92/85 [1992] OJ L348/1.

[189] There is another exception of sorts in Art. 4(c) of the Dir. which provides that equal treatment in access to vocational training is to be ensured 'without prejudice to the freedom granted in certain Member States to certain private training establishments'.

[190] Case 312/86, *Commission* v. *France* [1988] ECR 6315.   [191] *Ibid.*, para. 15.

advantages, whereas the Commission's ground for condemning the French law was that 'the evolution of society is such that in many cases working men, if they are fathers, must share the tasks previously performed by the wife as regards the care and organisation of the family'.[192] It has been pointed out, however, that there are difficulties with arguments which claim that measures which positively discriminate reinforce traditional assumptions, such as that the female is always the primary carer, or that the male is always the main breadwinner:

S. Fredman, European Community Discrimination Law: A Critique[193]

Such an argument correctly highlights the need for close examination of measures purporting to benefit women. Any measure giving advantages to a group defined according to gender runs the risk of over-or under-inclusiveness and may well perpetuate damaging stereotypes. However, this in itself does not imply that anti-discrimination legislation should aspire to neutrality and thereby ignore disadvantage. The risks referred to need to be balanced against the possible gains of such criteria in reducing gender disadvantage. It may well be that social security is too costly and administratively too complex to test each person on an individual basis. In that case, it may be more advantageous overall to define a group according to gender than not to offer the benefit at all. On the other hand, the perpetuation of a stereotype may be more damaging than the overall benefit. Thus, discriminatory criteria should not be rejected out of hand, but instead scrutinized closely to discover whether they perpetuate disadvantage, or go some way towards alleviating it.

And much later in the *Lommers* case,[194] indeed, the ECJ upheld the compatibility with Article 2(1) and (4) of a scheme set up within a national ministry to tackle the extensive under-representation of women, in a situation 'characterised by a proven insufficiency of proper, affordable child-care facilities'. Under the scheme, the ministry made available a limited number of subsidized nursery places to its staff, and reserved those for female staff alone, while permitting male officials access only in individual cases of emergency. The ECJ ruled that this scheme would be acceptable on condition that the emergency exception was construed as allowing any male officials who took care of their children by themselves to have access to the nursery places on the same conditions as female officials.

In a somewhat surprising ruling in *Kalanke*, in 1995, the ECJ took the view that Article 2(4) was a 'derogation' from the right to equal treatment, and thus must be strictly interpreted.[195] Consequently, a German regional law which provided that, where candidates of different sexes shortlisted for promotion were equally qualified, priority must to be given to women in sectors where they were under-represented (i.e., made up less than half of the staff) would breach the Directive. The fact that the Bremen system involved a 'soft' rather than a 'rigid' quota, and was intended to

---

[192] *Ibid.*, 6322. See the similar argument of Jacobs AG at para. 14 of his Opinion in Case 373/89, *Integrity* v. *Rouvroy* [1990] ECR 4243 concerning 'positive discrimination' in national social-security benefits in favour of women, where the Court found a breach of the equal-treatment principle in Dir. 79/7.

[193] N. 33 above, 129.   [194] Case C–476/99, *Lommers* [2002] ECR I–nyr.

[195] Case C–450/93, *Kalanke* v. *Freie Hansestadt Bremen* [1995] ECR I–3051.

overcome the disadvantages faced by women and the perpetuation of past inequalities, as a result of which few women held senior posts, was insufficient to bring it within Article 2(4):

22. National rules which guarantee women absolute and unconditional priority for appointment or promotion go beyond promoting equal opportunities and overstep the limits of the exception in Article 2(4) of the Directive.

23. Furthermore, in so far as it seeks to achieve equal representation of men and women in all grades and levels within a department, such a system substitutes for equality of opportunity as envisaged in Article 2(4) the result which is only to be arrived at by providing such equality of opportunity.

The *Kalanke* ruling prompted a flood of criticism and comment, not only from women's interest groups and from academic and practising lawyers,[196] but also from the European Commission itself, which issued a communication on the interpretation of the judgment.[197] The Commission took the view that not all quotas would be unlawful, and listed a range of positive-action measures which would, in its view, be acceptable despite the ruling. It proposed also to amend (by 'clarifying') the terms of Article 2(4) to provide that a soft quota such as that in issue in *Kalanke* would not be contrary to the Directive, so long as it did not automatically give preference to the under-represented sex, but permitted the assessment of an individual's specific circumstances in a given case.[198]

The terms of Tesauro AG's Opinion in *Kalanke* were broad, and he disapproved sharply of quotas as an unlawful and discriminatory way of remedying past disadvantage, commenting caustically that 'under-representation of women in a given segment of the employment market, albeit indicative of inequality, is not necessarily attributable to a consummate determination to marginalize women'. In the subsequent case of *Marschall*, Jacobs AG suggested that even if individual candidates' circumstances had to be taken into account, a national measure which gave priority to women over men in underrepresented sectors where the candidates were equally qualified would still breach the Equal Treatment Directive.[199] He criticized the Commission's proposed clarificatory amendment to Article 2(4) and referred to criticisms of the *Kalanke* ruling as 'misconceived'.[200] However, the ECJ did not follow his Opinion and it narrowed the potential scope of *Kalanke* along the lines of the Commission's proposal, by confirming that while a rule guaranteeing 'absolute and unconditional priority' for women was impermissible, a softer quota which allowed for individual consideration of circumstances would fall within the existing terms of Article 2(4).

Marschall concerned a German regional law which provided that where there were fewer men than women in a higher grade post in a career bracket, women were to be given priority for promotion in the event of equal suitability, competence, and professional performance unless reasons specific to an individual male candidate

---

[196] For some of the commentaries see L. Charpentier [1996] *RTDE* 281; S. Dagmar (1996) 25 *ILJ* 239; S. Moore (1996) 21 *ELRev.* 156; A. Peters (1996) 2 *ELJ* 177; S. Prechal (1996) 33 *CMLRev.* 45; D. Schiek (1996) 25 *ILJ* 239; L. Senden (1996) 3 *MJ* 146; E. Szyszczak (1996) 59 *MLR* 876; S. Fredman (1997) 113 *LQR* 575.

[197] COM(96)88.   [198] [1996] OJ C179/8.

[199] Case C–409/95, *Hellmut Marschall v. Land Nordrhein Westfalen* [1997] ECR I–6363.

[200] *Ibid.*, para. 47 of his Opinion.

tilted the balance in his favour. In contrast with the *Kalanke* proceedings, in which the only national intervention was from the UK government in support of the applicant, five governments intervened in the subsequent case to support the compatibility of the positive-action legislation with EC law, and only the UK and France opposed it. The ECJ distinguished the rule in *Kalanke* from the *Marschall* rule by reference to its 'saving clause',[201] but also adopted a more nuanced view of the 'equal' chances of men and women on the labour market.

Case C–409/95, Hellmut Marschall v. Land Nordrhein Westfalen
[1997] ECR I–6363

29. As the Land and several governments have pointed out, it appears that even where male and female candidates are equally qualified, male candidates tend to be promoted in preference to female candidates particularly because of prejudices and stereotypes concerning the role and capacities of women in working life and the fear, for example, that women will interrupt their careers more frequently, that owing to household and family duties they will be less flexible in their working hours, or that they will be absent from work more frequently because of pregnancy, childbirth and breastfeeding.

30. For these reasons, the mere fact that a male candidate and a female candidate are equally qualified does not mean that they have the same chances.

31. It follows that a national rule in terms of which, subject to the application of the saving clause, female candidates for promotion who are equally as qualified as the male candidates are to be treated preferentially in sectors where they are underrepresented may fall within the scope of Article 2(4) if such a rule may counteract the prejudicial effects on female candidates of the attitudes and behaviour described above and thus reduce actual instances of inequality which may exist in the real world.

32. However, since Article 2(4) constitutes a derogation from an individual right laid down by the Directive, such a national measure specifically favouring female candidates cannot guarantee absolute and unconditional priority for women in the event of a promotion without going beyond the limits of the exception laid down in that provision. (*Kalanke* paras 21 and 22)

33. Unlike the rules at issue in *Kalanke*, a national rule which, as in the case in point in the main proceedings, contains a saving clause does not exceed those limits, if, in each individual case, it provides for male candidates who are equally as qualified as the female candidates a guarantee that the candidatures will be the subject of an objective assessment which will take account of all criteria specific to the individual candidates and will override the priority accorded to female candidates where one or more of those criteria tilts the balance in favour of the male candidate. In this respect, however, it should be remembered that those criteria must not be such as to discriminate against female candidates.

A positive-action provision 'with a view to ensuring full equality in practice' was subsequently inserted by the Amsterdam Treaty into paragraph 4 of Article 141 (ex Article 119) EC, which is set out at 846 above. This represents a version of what

---

[201] See also the significant role of the 'exceptional clause' in *Lommers*, n. 194 above.

was previously in Article 6(3) of the Social Policy Agreement, but refers now in formally neutral terms to the permissibility of providing specific advantages for the 'under-represented sex' to pursue vocational training or to compensate for career disadvantages, rather than referring, as previously, to women only.[202]

Article 6(3) of the Social Policy Agreement was considered by the ECJ in *Griesmar* (in relation to pay rather than equal treatment),[203] and Article 141(4) of the Treaty in *Abrahamsson*, which is discussed below. In both *Badeck* and *Abrahamsson* the ECJ ruled, curiously, that Article 141(4) would come into play only if the Court first considered that national 'positive-action' legislation was prohibited under Article 2 of the Directive.[204] In other words, positive-action measures are first to be tested for compatibility with the Directive, and only subsequently with the Treaty—thus arguably implying that Article 141(4) may be broader and more permissive than the provision in Article 2(4) of the Directive.

In *Badeck*,[205] the ECJ followed its more permissive post-*Kalanke* approach in finding that a whole series of German public-service rules designed to give priority to women in promotion, access to training, and recruitment were compatible with Article 2(4), since they contained sufficient flexibility and non-rigidity to comply with the criteria it had articulated in *Marschall*. Some of the provisions in question in *Badeck* seemed quite strong and even rather strict forms of positive action—for example the quota for training places and the rule on calling women to interview—but the ECJ did not hesitate in exempting them under Article 2(4), finding none to be 'automatic or unconditional' priority rules. In the more difficult Swedish case of *Abrahamsson*, the ECJ was asked to consider a practice which, unlike the various German provisions in *Kalanke*, *Marschall*, and *Badeck*, enabled preference to be given to a candidate of the under-represented sex who, although sufficiently qualified, did not possess qualifications equal to those of other candidates of the opposite sex.[206] The question framed by the ECJ was whether Article 2(1) and (4) would permit legislation 'under which a candidate for a public post who belongs to the under-represented sex and possesses sufficient qualifications for that post must be chosen in preference to a candidate of the opposite sex who would otherwise have been appointed, where this is necessary to secure the appointment of a candidate of the under-represented sex and the difference between the respective merits of the candidates is not so great as to give rise to a breach of the requirement of objectivity in making appointments'.

---

[202] A declaration appended to the Amsterdam Treaty, however, stated that in adopting measures referred to in para. 4, the Member States should 'aim at improving the situation of women in working life'.

[203] Case C–366/99, *Griesmar* v. *Ministre de l'Economie* [2001] ECR I–9383. Here the ECJ ruled that Art. 6(3) of the Social Policy Agreement could not be used to justify pay discrimination which consisted of service credits for the calculation of retirement pensions only for female workers who had had children, since this discrimination would not itself offset the disadvantages to which the careers of female civil servants were exposed.

[204] Cases C–158/97, *Badeck* v. *Landesanwalt beim Staatsgerichtshof des Landes Hessen* [1999] ECR I–1875 and C–407/98, *Abrahamsson* v. *Fogelqvist* [2000] ECR I–5539.

[205] Case C–158/97, n. 204 above.

[206] Case C–407/98, *Abrahamsson*, n. 204 above.

C–407/98, Abrahamsson v. Fogelqvist
[2000] ECR I–5539

46. As a rule, a procedure for the selection of candidates for a post involves assessment of their qualifications by reference to the requirements of the vacant post or of the duties to be performed.

47. In paragraphs 31 and 32 of *Badeck*, cited above, the Court held that it is legitimate for the purposes of that assessment for certain positive and negative criteria to be taken into account which, although formulated in terms which are neutral as regards sex and thus capable of benefiting men too, in general favour women. Thus, it may be decided that seniority, age and the date of last promotion are to be taken into account only in so far as they are of importance for the suitability, qualifications and professional capability of candidates. Similarly, it may be prescribed that the family status or income of the partner is immaterial and that part-time work, leave and delays in completing training as a result of looking after children or dependants in need of care must not have a negative effect.

48. The clear aim of such criteria is to achieve substantive, rather than formal, equality by reducing *de facto* inequalities which may arise in society and, thus, in accordance with Article 141(4) EC, to prevent or compensate for disadvantages in the professional career of persons belonging to the under-represented sex.

49. It is important to emphasise in that connection that the application of criteria such as those mentioned in paragraph 47 above must be transparent and amenable to review in order to obviate any arbitrary assessment of the qualifications of candidates.

50. As regards the selection procedure at issue in the main proceedings, it does not appear from the relevant Swedish legislation that assessment of the qualifications of candidates by reference to the requirements of the vacant post is based on clear and unambiguous criteria such as to prevent or compensate for disadvantages in the professional career of members of the under-represented sex.

51. On the contrary, under that legislation, a candidate for a public post belonging to the under-represented sex and possessing sufficient qualifications for that post must be chosen in preference to a candidate of the opposite sex who would otherwise have been appointed, where that measure is necessary for a candidate belonging to the under-represented sex to be appointed.

52. It follows that the legislation at issue in the main proceedings automatically grants preference to candidates belonging to the under-represented sex, provided that they are sufficiently qualified, subject only to the proviso that the difference between the merits of the candidates of each sex is not so great as to result in a breach of the requirement of objectivity in making appointments.

53. The scope and effect of that condition cannot be precisely determined, with the result that the selection of a candidate from among those who are sufficiently qualified is ultimately based on the mere fact of belonging to the under-represented sex, and that this is so even if the merits of the candidate so selected are inferior to those of a candidate of the opposite sex. Moreover, candidatures are not subjected to an objective assessment taking account of the specific personal situations of all the candidates. It follows that such a method of selection is not such as to be permitted by Article 2(4) of the Directive.

54. In those circumstances, it is necessary to determine whether legislation such as that at issue in the main proceedings is justified by Article 141(4) EC.

55. In that connection, it is enough to point out that, even though Article 141(4) EC allows the Member States to maintain or adopt measures providing for special advantages intended to prevent or compensate for disadvantages in professional careers in order to ensure full equality between men and women in professional life, it cannot be inferred from this that it allows a

selection method of the kind at issue in the main proceedings which appears, on any view, to be disproportionate to the aim pursued.

Thus in order for acceptable positive-action measures such as job-qualification criteria which indirectly favour the underrepresented sex (normally women) to be compatible with EC law, they must first genuinely be designed to reduce *de facto* inequalities and compensate for career disadvantages, and secondly they must be based on transparent and objective criteria which can be reviewed. The ruling does not give a great deal of guidance on the scope of Article 141(4), other than to indicate that the particular job-selection method challenged in this case would be a clearly disproportionate way of attempting to compensate for past disadvantages and to ensure full equality in professional life between women and men.

(IV) OTHER EXCEPTIONS

The ECJ has also addressed the question whether there are exceptions to the principle of equal treatment other than those expressly set out in Directive 76/207. In *Gerster*, the Court ruled that it was not permissible for a Member State to exclude public-service employment from the scope of Article 141 (ex Article 119).[207] And in *Johnston* the Court rejected the argument that the Directive was subject to a general public-safety proviso which was applicable across the whole of the Treaty, similar to the specific derogations expressly provided in the context of free movement of persons, services, goods, and in serious military situations.[208] However, in *Levy*[209] and *Minne*,[210] the Court acknowledged that the Member States were entitled to maintain a provision which was in breach of the Equal Treatment Directive, if its adoption had been necessary to ensure performance by the Member State, under Article 307 (ex Article 234) of the Treaty, of obligations arising from agreements concluded with non-member countries before the entry into force of the EC Treaty. Those cases concerned Convention No. 89 of the International Labour Organization, which involved night-work of women employed in industry, and which was apparently incompatible with Article 5 of the Equal Treatment Directive. However, the ECJ limited the scope of the Article 307 exception by requiring the national court to ascertain the extent to which the Convention actually constituted an obstacle to the Directive's application, as well as the extent to which the national provisions breaching the Equal Treatment Directive were designed to implement the Convention.[211]

---

[207] Case C–1/95, *Gerster* v. *Freistaat Bayern* [1997] ECR I–5253.

[208] Case 222/84, n. 182 above. The specific derogations mentioned by the Court were those in Arts. 30, 39, 46, 296, and 297 (ex Arts. 36, 48, 56, 223, and 224) EC. See also Cases C–273/97, *Sirdar*, and C–285/98, *Kreil*, both n. 187 above.

[209] Case C–158/91, *Ministère Public and Direction du Travail et de l'Emploi* v. *Levy* [1993] ECR I–4287. Contrast the earlier Case C–345/89, *Ministère Public* v. *Stoeckel* [1991] ECR I–4047, and see more recently Case C–197/96, *Commission* v. *France* [1997] ECR I–1489.

[210] Case C–13/93, *Office Nationale de l'Emploi* v. *Minne* [1994] ECR I–371.

[211] The issue of this ILO Convention was addressed in COM(87)105, in which the Commission indicated that a ban on night-work for women was incompatible with the Equal Treatment Dir. Thus the Member States were required to denounce Convention no. 89 in 1992, when the opportunity to do so in accordance with the terms of ILO Conventions arose. See N. Wuiame, 'Night Work for Women—*Stoeckel* Revisited' (1994) 23 *ILJ* 95 and in Case C–197/96, *Commission* v. *France* [1997] ECR I–1489.

(v) THE PROPOSAL TO AMEND DIRECTIVE 76/207

A proposal to amend the Equal Treatment Directive based on Article 141(3), was made by the Commission in 2000, and it should be adopted during 2002.[212] The proposal was intended to update and supplement the Directive, to reflect some of the relevant case law of the ECJ, and to maintain consistency with the other new discrimination directives adopted under Article 13 EC on race and employment respectively.[213] The current proposal contains a new definition of indirect discrimination, as well as a definition of sexual harassment which is deemed to constitute sex discrimination. The more modern and broader language of 'gender equality' is used in various parts. The proposal also provides for stronger remedial provisions including compensation without a fixed upper limit in certain cases and effective sanctions, and provides for employers to introduce proactive preventive measures and to provide regular equality reports to employees. Member States are to establish Equality Bodies with a range of powers, and the rights of women who have taken maternity leave are strengthened, as are the rights of return of those who have taken paternity or adoption leave where national law recognizes such rights. 'Positive-action' provisions are also proposed, and protection against adverse treatment is required for those who support victims of sex discrimination and sexual harassment.

(c) THE DISTINCTION BETWEEN CONDITIONS OF WORK, PAY, AND SOCIAL SECURITY

We have seen above how the distinction between pay and social security has given rise to a considerable amount of confusion. Similarly, the distinction between equal pay and equal treatment in conditions of work,[214] as well as between the latter and equal treatment in social security, has not always been clear.

The distinction between pay and conditions of work arose in *Bilka*, in which the ECJ ruled that the exclusion of part-time workers from a supplementary occupational pension scheme constituted indirect pay discrimination.[215] The ECJ was also asked whether Article 141 (ex Article 119) imposed an obligation on employers to organize their occupational pension schemes in a way which took into account the fact that women's family responsibilities prevented them from fulfilling the pension requirements. The argument was based on Article 141, because Directive 76/207 does not appear to impose any 'horizontally effective' positive obligations on employers to promote equal opportunities. The Court denied that Article 119 at the time could have any such effect, pointing out that it was restricted to pay discrimination and that problems related to other conditions of work and employment were governed by other provisions of Community law, which envisaged the need for legislative

---

[212] See COM(2000)334 and amended proposal COM(2001)321 [2001] OJ C270/9.

[213] Council Dirs. 2000/43 [2000] OJ L180/22 and 2000/78 [2000] OJ L303/16.

[214] See Case C–1/95, *Gerster*, n. 207 above, in which the ECJ ruled that provisions governing the calculation of the length of service of employees, for the purpose of determining possible access to promotion and to higher remuneration was a not a matter of equal pay but of equal treatment under Dir. 76/207. See also Case C–476/99, *Lommers*, n. 194 above, and contrast Cases C–342/93, *Gillespie* [1996] ECR I–475, para. 24 and C–166/99, *Defreyn* v. *Sabena* [2000] ECR I–6155, para. 35.

[215] Case 170/84, n. 114 above.

harmonization and approximation of Member States' social-security and other systems.[216] Like the *Kalanke* ruling, *Bilka* illustrates the limits of law as a tool for ensuring equal conditions for men and women, given the differences in the existing social and material circumstances of women and men, which, although they are apparently not to be exploited by employers, impose no positive obligations on them either.[217] And indeed, although Article 141 was amended by the ToA to allow for the adoption of measures to ensure equal treatment more broadly, this merely gives an express Treaty basis for legislation in the area, so that there is no directly effective obligation on the states or on employers not to discriminate in their treatment of men and women in the labour market, other than in relation to pay.

The complex relationship between equal treatment in working conditions, equality in social security, and equal pay can be seen in a series of cases beginning with *Burton*.[218] The ECJ was asked whether the maintenance of different age conditions in access to voluntary redundancy was contrary to Directive 76/207, and ruled that it was not, since the reason was not to discriminate on grounds of sex, but simply because the terms of the redundancy scheme had been tied by the employer to the national statutory retirement scheme. The national scheme, which maintained different pensionable ages for men and women, was covered by the exception in Social Security Directive 79/7. Thus the voluntary redundancy scheme, although it was not statutory social security within Directive 79/7 and in principle constituted 'dismissal' within Directive 76/207, could be arranged so as to correspond with the statutory scheme, including different pensionable ages, without breaching the Equal Treatment Directive.

Subsequently in *Roberts*, the complainant belonged to an occupational pension scheme providing for compulsory retirement with a pension at age 65 for men and 60 for women.[219] At the time, since it was before the *Bilka* ruling,[220] the pension scheme was not thought to be pay within Article 141 (ex Article 119). Under its compulsory redundancy terms, the company provided that both men and women could receive an immediate early pension at age 55. Since Roberts was 53 when she was made redundant, she did not receive a pension. She argued that the scheme was in breach of the equal-treatment principle, since men could receive an early pension ten years before their normal retirement age, whereas women could receive one only five years before. This time, the Court decided the case on the basis of the Equal Treatment Directive, and appeared to narrow the scope of the exception in the Social Security Directive. The imposition of an age limit for compulsory redundancy was not about the terms on which an early pension was granted—even if it involved the grant of a pension— but about the terms of *dismissal*.

[216] *Ibid.*, paras. 41–42.   [217] See the AG's Opinion [1986] ECR 1607, 1618.
[218] Case 19/81, *Burton* v. *British Railways Board* [1982] ECR 555.
[219] Case 151/84, n. 167 above. See also Case 262/84, *Beets-Proper* v. *Van Lanschot Bankiers* [1986] ECR 773.
[220] Case 170/84, n. 114 above.

Case 151/84, Roberts v. Tate & Lyle Industries
[1986] ECR 703

THE ECJ

34. As the Court emphasized in its judgment in the *Burton* case, Article 7 of Directive No 79/7 expressly provides that the Directive does not prejudice the right of Member States to exclude from its scope the determination of pensionable age for the purposes of granting old-age and retirement pensions and the possible consequences thereof for other benefits falling within the statutory social security schemes. The Court thus acknowledged that benefits linked to a national scheme which lays down a different minimum pensionable age for men and women may lie outside the ambit of the aforementioned obligation.

35. However, in view of the fundamental importance of the principle of equality of treatment, which the Court has reaffirmed on numerous occasions, Article 1(2) of Directive No 76/207, which excludes social security matters from the scope of that directive, must be interpreted strictly. Consequently, whereas the exception to the prohibition of discrimination on grounds of sex provided for in Article 7(1)(a) of Directive No 79/7 concerns the consequences which pensionable age has for social security benefits, this case is concerned with dismissal within the meaning of Article 5 of Directive No 76/207. In those circumstances the grant of a pension to persons of the same age who are made redundant amounts merely to a collective measure adopted irrespective of the sex of those persons in order to guarantee them all the same rights.

The implication in paragraph 35 is that if Roberts' employer had done as Burton's had done, and had tied the age for receipt of an immediate pension on compulsory redundancy to the statutory social-security scheme, it would not have been able to gain the benefit of the exception in Directive 79/7 for pensionable ages in statutory social-security schemes. Since the redundancy was classified by the ECJ as dismissal, the receipt of a pension on redundancy was a condition of dismissal within the scope of Directive 76/207. The fact that the age conditions for men and women were identical meant that there was no breach of the equal-treatment principle in that Directive, whereas if they had been linked with statutory pensionable ages there would have been a breach. In *Burton*, on the other hand, the Court allowed the linking of age conditions for *voluntary* redundancy to the different pensionable ages in the statutory social-security scheme to benefit by association with the exception in Directive 79/7, and to avoid breaching the Equal Treatment Directive. According to the ECJ in *Roberts*, however, the exception in Article 7(1)(a) of Directive 79/7 concerned 'the consequences which pensionable age has for social security benefits', and the grant of a pension on compulsory rather than voluntary redundancy was not a 'social security benefit' within Directive 79/7 but a 'condition governing dismissal' within Directive 76/207. The precise scope of the Article 7(1)(a) exception will be examined further below, in considering Directive 79/7.

The narrowing of this exception continued in *Marshall I*.[221] In this case, the Court

---

[221] Case 152/84, *Marshall v. Southampton and South-West Hampshire Area Health Authority (Teaching)* [1986] ECR 723.

was dealing, not with voluntary or compulsory *redundancy*, but with a compulsory *retirement* provision which mirrored the different statutory pensionable ages for men and women. Marshall was required to retire some time after reaching the age of 60, which was the statutory pensionable age and the compulsory retirement age which the company had set for women. Following its ruling in *Roberts*, the ECJ treated the compulsory retirement as dismissal within the terms of the Equal Treatment Directive, rather than as a consequence of the different statutory pensionable ages falling within the exception in Article 7(1)(a) of Directive 79/7.

The further complication arising from these cases concerns the relationship between social security and pay. It became clear after the later rulings in *Bilka*, *Barber*, and *Moroni* that payments made on redundancy and under occupational social-security schemes constituted pay within Article 141 (ex Article 119) and that the discriminatory effects of setting different pensionable ages were in breach of this provision. Only state social-security schemes could benefit from the exception in Article 7(1)(a) of Directive 79/7. The approach in *Burton* would therefore no longer be possible. Despite later attempts to distinguish the case,[222] *Burton* appears to have been silently overruled.[223]

The distinction between conditions of work under Directive 76/207 and social security under Directive 79/7 arose also in *Jackson and Cresswell*, where the ECJ held that a scheme of benefits would not be excluded from the scope of Directive 76/207 solely because it was formally part of a national social-security system.[224] However, the subject matter of any scheme falling within Directive 76/207 must concern access to employment,[225] access to promotions, vocational training, or conditions of work. Consequently an income-support scheme, the purpose of which was to supplement the income of those with inadequate means of subsistence, would not be within the scope of the Directive solely because the method for calculating eligibility could affect a single mother's ability to take up vocational training or employment.[226] In *Meyers*, however, the ECJ ruled that family credit, which was an income-related benefit awarded under UK social-security legislation, would fall within the scope of Directive 76/207, since one of the conditions for its award was that the claimant should be engaged in remunerative work, and its function was to encourage unemployed workers to accept low-paid work, and to keep poorly paid workers in employment, thus concerning access to employment.[227] Since the benefit was 'necessarily linked to a contract of employment' it did not matter that it was not a condition set out in the contract of employment, nor that entitlement to the benefit would not be affected by loss of employment or a salary increase for a certain period.[228]

In sum, the disparities between the legal regimes governing pay, conditions of work, and social security—all of which are regulated by the Community but in different ways and to different degrees—and the fact that matters of social assistance are left to

[222] See van Gerven AG's Opinion in *Barber*, n. 29 above.   [223] Curtin, n. 119 above.
[224] Cases C–63–64/91, *Jackson v. Chief Adjudication Officer* [1992] ECR I–4737, para. 27.
[225] See, e.g., Case C–100/95, *Kording v. Senator für Finanzen* [1997] ECR I–5289.
[226] Cases C–63–64/91, n. 222 above, paras. 29–30.
[227] Case C–116/94, *Meyers v. Adjudication Officer* [1995] ECR I–2131, paras. 19–22.
[228] *Ibid.*, para. 23. Contrast the opinion of Jacobs AG in Case C–312/94, *Hoever and Zachow v. Land Nordrhein Westfalen* [1996] ECR I–4895.

be regulated by the Member States—mean that the categorizations within EC sex-discrimination law are important, and regularly give rise to complex litigation and disputes of this kind.

(d) EQUAL TREATMENT AND PREGNANCY

Article 2(3) of Directive 76/207 provides that the Directive is to be without prejudice to provisions concerning the protection of women, particularly as regards pregnancy and maternity. This was designed to prevent any challenge on grounds of equal treatment in EC law to national employment provisions granting leave or other special conditions to women who are pregnant or have given birth, rather than to impose any obligation to adopt such provisions.

In *Hofmann*, however, a challenge was brought under the Equal Treatment Directive against provisions of German law relating to maternity leave. The argument was that the Directive permitted derogation from the equal-treatment principle only in so far as this was done to protect women before and after childbirth, and if the provision of leave went beyond that function, e.g., to care for the child in the longer term, then it should be open on an equal basis to men and to women alike.

Case 184/83, Hofmann v. Barmer Ersatzkasse
[1984] ECR 3047

Hofmann obtained unpaid leave from his employer in order to care for his newborn child. The period of time he requested was that between the expiry of the statutory eight weeks following childbirth available to the mother, during which German legislation provided that women may not work, and the date the child reached six months of age. The law provided that mothers were entitled to maternity leave from the end of the mandatory eight-week 'protective period' until the child was six months old. Since the mother in this case had not taken maternity leave after the eight-week period, and Hofmann had cared for the child from that time on, he challenged the refusal to grant him payment during the period of maternity leave provided by law for women only. The case was referred to the ECJ for a ruling on the effect of the Equal Treatment Directive 76/207.

THE ECJ

24. It is apparent from the above analysis that the Directive is not designed to settle questions concerned with the organization of the family, or to alter the division of responsibility between parents.

25. It should further be added, with particular reference to paragraph (3), that, by reserving to Member States the right to retain, or introduce provisions which are intended to protect women in connection with 'pregnancy and maternity', the directive recognizes the legitimacy, in terms of the principle of equal treatment, of protecting a woman's needs in two respects. First, it is legitimate to ensure the protection of a woman's biological condition during pregnancy and thereafter until such time as her physiological and mental functions have returned to normal after childbirth; secondly, it is legitimate to protect the special relationship between a woman and her child over the

period which follows pregnancy and childbirth, by preventing that relationship from being disturbed by the multiple burdens which would result from the simultaneous pursuit of employment.

26. In principle, therefore, a measure such as maternity leave granted to a woman on expiry of the statutory protective period falls within the scope of Article 2(3) of Directive 76/207, inasmuch as it seeks to protect a woman in connection with the effects of pregnancy and motherhood. That being so, such leave may legitimately be reserved to the mother to the exclusion of any other person, in view of the fact that it is only the mother who may find herself subject to undesirable pressures to return to work prematurely.

27. Furthermore, it should be pointed out that the Directive leaves Member States with a discretion as to the social measures which they adopt in order to guarantee, within the framework laid down by the Directive, the protection of women in connection with pregnancy and maternity and to offset the disadvantages which women, by comparison with men, suffer with regard to the retention of employment. Such measures are, as the Government of the United Kingdom has rightly observed, closely linked to the general system of social protection in the various Member States. It must therefore be concluded that the Member States enjoy a reasonable margin of discretion as regards both the nature of the protective measures and the detailed arrangements for their implementation.

In conferring a 'margin of discretion' on the Member States with regard to the exception in Article 2(3), the Court dismissed the arguments of the plaintiff and the Commission that, if the father were given the option of taking care of the child and attending to the upkeep of the household by the provision of a period of non-discriminatory parental leave, that would be an equally effective means of relieving the mother of the burdens which might impair her health. Normally, exceptions to fundamental rules are strictly construed by the ECJ, but in the context of the derogation for pregnancy and maternity protection the Court applied a looser test than its usual examination of whether a derogating measure was strictly 'necessary' to achieve its aim. Arguably, despite its statement in paragraph 24, in choosing a broad interpretation of the exception in Article 2(3), the Court was supporting the continuation by the Member States of the traditional division of responsibility which entrenches the role of the mother as primary carer, and which, by protecting 'the special relationship between a woman and her child', deprives the father of the opportunity to develop such a relationship in the period after birth, by refusing to give the parents a choice of who shall take leave. Both the ECJ and the AG appeared to assume that, even after the eight-week protective period, a mother was in an objectively different position from a father, in bearing other burdens and responsibilities, yet if the extended period of leave were open to either father or mother, the father, if the parents so wished, could take on the multiple burdens of household and caring duties. On the other hand, if the ECJ had read the exception more restrictively, preventing Member States from providing special protection for women other than while this was necessary to protect women's biological condition during and after pregnancy and childbirth, the Member States would have been free to 'level down' as well as to 'level up', in other words to abolish the more extended maternity leave for women rather than providing it for men.

An even clearer example of the reinforcement, through the interpretation of Article 2(3), of the view that only the mother does or should develop a special relationship with a child after birth is in the case of *Commission* v. *Italy*, concerning national laws giving compulsory maternity leave to the mother of an adopted child under 6 years of age, but not to the father.[229] The ECJ accepted Italy's 'legitimate concern to assimilate as far as possible the conditions of entry of the child into the adoptive family to those of the arrival of a newborn child in the family during the very delicate initial period',[230] although it is difficult to see why the initial three-month period is not equally delicate for an adoptive father as for an adoptive mother, especially when the child is not newborn.

Legislation which actually required Member States to provide a period of maternity leave for women was not adopted until the 1992 Pregnancy Directive, and a Framework Agreement and Directive on parental leave—which provides for a minimum-level individual right to three months' parental leave—was finally adopted, following many unsuccessful earlier attempts by the Commission, under the Social Policy Agreement in 1996.[231]

The exception in Article 2(3) of the Equal Treatment Directive 76/207 clearly covers provisions for the protection of women in the case of pregnancy or maternity, but it was not clear whether it could also cover other protective measures. This arose in *Johnston*, in which the ECJ ruled that it was clear from the express reference to pregnancy and maternity in Article 2(3) that the Directive was intended to protect a woman's biological condition and the special relationship existing between a woman and her child, and could not be used to justify a policy of not recruiting women to the RUC Reserve simply because 'public opinion demands that women be given greater protection than men against risks which affect men and women in the same way'.[232] In *Stoeckel*, too, 'protective' treatment in the form of a prohibition on night-work for women but not for men was ruled impermissible by the ECJ.[233] *Stoeckel* was confirmed and extended in *Minne*, where the ECJ ruled that even if legislation prohibited night-work for men and women alike, it was nevertheless contrary to the Directive for such legislation to provide different derogations from the prohibition for men and for women.[234] Only in the context of pregnancy and maternity would a ban on night-work for women be acceptable.[235]

In enforcement proceedings brought against France for inadequate implementation of Directive 76/207, the ECJ ruled that legislation allowing for 'special rights' for women, unconnected with pregnancy or maternity, would not benefit from the exemption in Article 2(3).[236] Some of the special rights, such as sick days in the case of

---

[229] Case 163/82, *Commission* v. *Italy* [1983] ECR 3273.

[230] *Ibid.*, para. 16.

[231] Council Dir. 96/34 on the framework agreement on parental leave concluded by UNICE, CEEP, and the ETUC [1996] OJ L145/4.

[232] [1986] ECR 1651, para. 44. See also *Kreil*, n. 187 above.

[233] Case C–345/89, *Stoeckel* [1991] ECR I–4047. See also Case C–197/96, *Commission* v. *France* [1997] ECR I–1489.

[234] Case C–13/93, n. 210 above.

[235] See Case C–421/92, *Habermann-Beltermann* v. *Arbeiterwohlfahrt, Bezirksverband* [1994] ECR I–1657, below.

[236] Case 312/86, n. 190 above, and text. See also *Griesmar*, n. 95 above, paras. 52–54.

children's illness, days off at the beginning of the school year, and the shortening of working hours for older women, were relevant to categories to which both men and women could equally belong.

Although the exceptions in Directive 76/207 *permit* Member States to maintain protective provisions which favour women in relation to pregnancy and maternity, it was not clear for some years whether it also *prohibited* measures which discriminated against women on grounds of pregnancy.

Case C–177/88, Dekker v. Stichting Vormingscentrum voor Jong Volwassenen
[1990] ECR I–3941

Dekker applied for the post of instructor at the defendant's training centre (VJV) for young adults, indicating that she was three months pregnant. Although she was put forward by the applications committee as the most suitable candidate for the job, VJV informed her that she would not be appointed for the reason that VJV's insurer would not reimburse the benefits VJV would be obliged to pay her during her maternity leave, which meant that it would be financially unable to employ a replacement during her absence. The Dutch Supreme Court asked the ECJ whether the employer was in breach of the Equal Treatment Directive.

THE ECJ

11. The reason given by the employer for refusing to appoint Mrs Dekker is basically that it could not have obtained reimbursement from the Risicofonds of the daily benefits which it would have had to pay her for the duration of her absence due to pregnancy, and yet at the same time it would have been obliged to employ a replacement. . . .

12. In that regard it should be noted that only women can be refused employment on grounds of pregnancy and such a refusal therefore constitutes direct discrimination on grounds of sex. A refusal of employment on account of the financial consequences of absence due to pregnancy must be regarded as based, essentially, on the fact of pregnancy. Such discrimination cannot be justified on grounds relating to the financial loss which an employer who employed a pregnant woman would suffer for the duration of her maternity leave.

. . .

17. It should be stressed that the reply to the question whether the refusal to employ a woman constitutes direct or indirect discrimination depends on the reason for that refusal. If that reason is to be found in the fact that the person concerned is pregnant, then the decision is directly linked to the sex of the candidate. In those circumstances the absence of male candidates cannot affect the answer to the first question.

The reason given by the Court in *Dekker* for why such refusal of employment on grounds of pregnancy is direct sex discrimination is that pregnancy is a condition which applies to women only. Did this mean that if certain physical or medical conditions applied only to men, such refusal or dismissal on grounds of absence due to such a condition would be considered sex discrimination in breach of Directive 76/207? In the case of *Hertz*, the ECJ ruled that dismissal on grounds of sickness to which one sex only is susceptible would not constitute sex discrimination, since both sexes were equally exposed to illness.[237] Yet the reason given by the Court for why dismissal on grounds of pregnancy constitutes sex discrimination seems formal and inadequate, since its only basis is that, since pregnancy is a condition affecting women alone, such dismissal must constitute sex discrimination. A more plausible reason why pregnancy-related dismissal is seen as impermissible is not just that pregnancy affects women only, but that it is a unique condition which is also of social value. Protection against pregnancy-based dismissal should exist because the role women play in reproduction and childbirth is an important one in which employers, men, and society as a whole have an interest.[238] Indeed, this was acknowledged by Advocate General Tesauro, who commented that 'it would be paradoxical if recognition of the social function of maternity, and consequent protection of pregnant women, should come about through their exclusion from the labour market'.[239]

Dekker established that the refusal to employ a worker for financial reasons consequent upon her pregnancy constitutes sex discrimination, but would this also be true if the refusal were on grounds of other pregnancy-related factors, such as illness arising from pregnancy, or because of a legislative prohibition on women performing certain work during pregnancy, or because of unavailability for essential work while absent during pregnancy? These questions were addressed by the ECJ in *Hertz*,[240] *Larsson*,[241] *Habermann-Belterman*,[242] and *Webb*.[243]

Hertz concerned dismissal on account of absence owing to sickness originating in pregnancy, and the ECJ rejected the argument that the protection provided by the Directive against dismissal owing to illness caused by pregnancy was unlimited in time.

Case C–179/88, Handels- og Kontorfunktionærernes Forbund i Danmark v. Dansk Arbejdsgiverforening
[1990] ECR I–3979

THE ECJ

13. It follows from [Articles 1(1), 2(1), 2(3) and 5(1)] of the Directive quoted above that the dismissal of a female worker on account of pregnancy constitutes direct discrimination on grounds of sex, as is a refusal to appoint a pregnant woman (see . . . *Dekker*).

---

[237] Case C–179/88, *Handels- og Kontorfuntionærernes Forbund i Danmark* v. *Dansk Arbejdsgiverforening* [1990] ECR I–3979.

[238] See, generally, S. Fredman, 'A Difference with Distinction: Pregnancy and Parenthood Reassessed' (1994) 110 *LQR* 106.

[239] See his Opinion in Case C–421/92, *Habermann-Beltermann*, n. 235 above, 1664. See also Cases C–207/98, *Mahlburg* [2000] ECR I–549 and C–136/95, *Thibault* [1998] ECR I–2011.

[240] Case C–179/88, *Handels- og Kontorfunktionærernes Forbund i Danmark* v. *Dansk Arbejdsgiverforening* [1990] ECR I–3979.

[241] Case C–400/95, *Handels- og Kontorfunktionærernes Forbund i Danmark, acting on behalf of Larsson* v. *Dansk Handel & Services, acting on behalf of Føtex Supermarked A/S* [1997] ECR I–2757.

[242] Case C–421/92, n. 235 above.

[243] Case C–32/93, *Webb* v. *EMO Air Cargo (UK) Ltd.* [1994] ECR I–3567.

14. On the other hand, the dismissal of a female worker on account of repeated periods of sick leave which are not attributable to pregnancy or confinement does not constitute direct discrimination on grounds of sex, inasmuch as such periods of sick leave would lead to the dismissal of a male worker in the same circumstances.

15. The Directive does not envisage the case of an illness attributable to pregnancy or confinement. It does, however, admit of national provisions guaranteeing women specific rights on account of pregnancy and maternity, such as maternity leave. During the maternity leave accorded to her pursuant to national law, a woman is accordingly protected against dismissal due to absence. It is for every Member State to fix periods of maternity leave in such a way as to enable female workers to absent themselves during the period in which the disorders inherent in pregnancy and confinement occur.

16. In the case of an illness manifesting itself after the maternity leave, there is no reason to distinguish an illness attributable to pregnancy or confinement from any other illness. Such a pathological condition is therefore covered by the general rules applicable in the event of illness.

17. Male and female workers are equally exposed to illness. Although certain disorders are, it is true, specific to one or other sex, the only question is whether a woman is dismissed on account of absence due to illness in the same circumstances as a man; if that is the case, then there is no direct discrimination on grounds of sex.

How far protection against dismissal on grounds of pregnancy should go in the context of illness is a difficult question. Advocate General Darmon admitted that he was 'tempted to propose a solution whereby medical conditions which were directly, definitely and preponderantly due to pregnancy or confinement would enjoy a sort of 'immunity' in the sense that the principle of equality of treatment would restrain the employer from dismissing his employee for a reasonable period after the event in question',[244] but he decided ultimately that such a solution was a matter for legislation. The ECJ followed his compromise, making the extent of protection against dismissal for pregnant women depend on the varying periods of maternity leave granted by the national legislation of different states. In *Larsson*, the Court ruled that the equal-treatment principle did not prevent a woman being dismissed due to absence caused by continuing illness which began *during* the pregnancy, nor did it prevent account being taken of absences from work during the period of pregnancy and maternity leave when calculating the period providing grounds for dismissal.[245] However in one of its rare moves of this kind, the ECJ later in *Brown* v. *Rentokil* expressly departed from this second part of its ruling *Larsson* and ruled that where a woman was absent owing to illness resulting from pregnancy or childbirth, where the illness arose during pregnancy and persisted during and after maternity leave, her absence during maternity leave and during the period extending from the start of her pregnancy to the start of her maternity leave should not be taken into account for computation of the period justifying her dismissal under national law.[246] One of the factors which the Court in *Brown* took into account was the recent adoption of

---

[244] See para. 43 of his Opinion in *Hertz*. For criticism of the *Hertz* case for imposing a model of equality where women must be compared with men, save for the 'exceptional' case of pregnancy, see G. More, 'Reflections on Pregnancy Discrimination under European Community Law' [1992] *JSWFL* 48.

[245] Case C–400/95, n. 241 above.   [246] Case C–394/96, *Brown* v. *Rentokil* [1998] ECR I–4185.

the Pregnancy Directive 92/85 which, although not in issue in the case, was in the Court's view part of the general context which had to be taken into consideration. The Pregnancy Directive to some extent harmonizes provisions for the protection of pregnant women against dismissal.

In *Habermann-Beltermann*, the ECJ was asked whether it was compatible with Directive 76/207 for an employee who had chosen to work nights only to be dismissed on becoming pregnant, because of national legislation prohibiting the assignment of night-work to women who were pregnant or breast-feeding; and secondly whether it was compatible with the Directive for her contract of employment to be declared void for mistake—since her employer did not know that she was pregnant when she was hired—given that the legislation provided that any term in an employment contract breaching the prohibition on night-work would be void.

Case C–421/92, Habermann-Beltermann v. Arbeiterwohlfahrt, Bezirksverband [1994] ECR I–1657

THE ECJ

15. It is clear that the termination of an employment contract on account of the employee's pregnancy, whether by annulment or avoidance, concerns women alone and constitutes, therefore, direct discrimination on grounds of sex. . . .

16. However, the unequal treatment in a case such as this, unlike the *Dekker* case referred to by the national court, is not based directly on the woman's pregnancy but is the result of the statutory prohibition on night-time work during pregnancy.

17. The basis for that prohibition, laid down by section 8(1) of the Mutter-schutzgesetz, is Article 2(3) of the directive, according to which the directive is without prejudice to the provisions concerning the protection of women, particularly as regards pregnancy and maternity.

18. The question, therefore, is whether the Directive precludes compliance with the prohibition on night-time work by pregnant women, which is unquestionably compatible with Article 2(3), from rendering an employment contract invalid or allowing it to be avoided on the ground that the prohibition prevents the employee from doing the nighttime work for which she was engaged.

. . .

23. In this case, the questions submitted for a ruling relate to a contract without a fixed term and the prohibition on night-time work by pregnant women therefore takes effect only for a limited period in relation to the total length of the contract.

24. In the circumstances, to acknowledge that the contract may be held to be invalid or be avoided because of the temporary inability of the pregnant employee to perform the night-time work for which she was engaged would be contrary to the objective of protecting such persons pursued by Article 2(3) of the Directive, and would deprive the Directive of its effectiveness.

Thus, in contrast to *Levy* and *Minne*, where pregnancy was not in issue,[247] a prohibition on night-work by pregnant women is, by virtue of Article 2(3), perfectly

---

[247] See nn. 163 and 164 above.

compatible with the Equal Treatment Directive. However, termination of a woman's employment contract on account of such a prohibition would breach the Directive, since it would undermine the aim of Article 2(3), which is intended not just to protect women's physical condition but also to protect them against disadvantage in employment on account of the pregnancy. The ECJ specifically limited its ruling to the case of a woman working without a fixed-term contract.[248] This issue was important also in *Webb*, concerning the dismissal of a woman who discovered, shortly after being employed as replacement for another employee on maternity leave, that she herself was pregnant. In addressing whether this would breach the Equal Treatment Directive, the ECJ made extensive reference to the 1992 Pregnancy Directive which had not yet come into effect.

Case C–32/93, Webb v. EMO Air Cargo (UK) Ltd.
[1994] ECR I–3567

THE ECJ

21. In view of the harmful effects which the risk of dismissal may have on the physical and mental State of women who are pregnant, have recently given birth or are breast-feeding, including the particularly serious risk that pregnant women may be prompted voluntarily to terminate their pregnancy, the Community legislature subsequently provided, pursuant to Article 10 of Council Directive 92/85 on the introduction of measures to encourage improvements in the safety and health at work of pregnant workers and workers who have recently given birth or are breastfeeding, by prohibiting dismissal during the period from the beginning of their pregnancy to the end of their maternity leave.

22. Furthermore, Article 10 of Directive 92/85 provides that there is to be no exception to, or derogation from, the prohibition on the dismissal of pregnant women during that period, save in exceptional cases not connected with their condition.

23. The question submitted by the House of Lords, which concerns Directive 76/207, must take account of that general context.

24. First, in response to the House of Lords inquiry, there can be no question of comparing the situation of a woman who finds herself incapable, by reason of pregnancy discovered very shortly after the conclusion of the employment contract, of performing the task for which she was recruited with that of a man similarly incapable for medical or other reasons.

25. As Mrs Webb rightly argues, pregnancy is not in any way comparable with a pathological condition, and even less so with unavailability for work on non-medical grounds, both of which are situations that may justify the dismissal of a woman without discriminating on grounds of sex. Moreover, in *Hertz*, cited above, the Court drew a clear distinction between pregnancy and illness, even where the illness is attributable to pregnancy but manifests itself after the period of maternity leave. As the Court pointed out, in paragraph 16, there is no reason to distinguish such an illness from any other illness.

26. Furthermore, contrary to the submission of the United Kingdom, dismissal of a woman recruited for an indefinite period cannot be justified on grounds relating to her inability to fulfil a

---

[248] See also Case C–207/98, *Mahlburg* [2000] ECR I–549.

fundamental condition of her employment contract. The availability of an employee is necessarily, for the employer, a precondition for the proper performance of the employment contract. However, the protection afforded by Community law to a woman during pregnancy and after childbirth cannot be dependent on whether her presence at work during maternity is essential to the proper functioning of the under-taking in which she is employed. Any contrary interpretation would render ineffective the provisions of the Directive.

27. In circumstances such as those of Mrs Webb, termination of a contract for an indefinite period on grounds of the woman's pregnancy cannot be justified by the fact that she is prevented, on a purely temporary basis, from performing the work for which she has been engaged: see *Habermann-Beltermann*.

The case of women employed on fixed-term contracts who are dismissed owing to pregnancy was left undecided by the ECJ, but arose in the later cases of *Jiménez Melgar* and *Tele Danmark*. In these cases the Court ruled that both Directive 76/207 and the Pregnancy Directive 92/85 prohibited the dismissal of a woman on grounds of pregnancy also in the case of a fixed-term contract.[249] However, in *Jiménez Melgar* the ECJ accepted that where non-renewal of a fixed-term contract was concerned, this could not always be equated with dismissal, and so it was for the national court to decide whether a decision not to renew a fixed-term contract which had come to an end was motivated by the worker's pregnancy (thus being illegal) or not.[250] And in *Tele Danmark* the Court made two further observations: first, that the duration of an employment relationship was almost always uncertain, even where a worker was initially recruited for a fixed period, and secondly that the Equal Treatment and Pregnancy Directives themselves had chosen to make no distinctions based on the duration of the employment relationship, which suggested that the legislature had not intended to exclude all those on fixed-term contracts from the protective scope of their provisions.[251]

In many of the cases, it is noteworthy that the interpretation given by the ECJ of Directive 76/207 corresponded with the provisions of the Pregnancy Directive, in providing essentially that dismissal for any pregnancy related reason *during the period of maternity leave* is impermissible.[252]

(e) THE PREGNANCY DIRECTIVE

In a move away from the treatment of pregnancy as an issue of 'equal treatment between men and women', Directive 92/85 was expressly based at the time on Article 138 (ex Article 118a) EC concerning health and safety at work, under which legislation could be adopted by a qualified majority.[253] The preamble to the Directive refers

---

[249] Cases C–438/99, *Jiménez Melgar* v. *Ayuntamiento de Los Barrios* [2001] ECR I–6915 and C–109/00, *Tele Danmark A/S* v. *HK* [2001] ECR I–6993.

[250] Case C–438/99, *Melgar*, paras. 45–47.   [251] Case C–109/00, *Tele Danmark*, paras. 32–33.

[252] See, however, J. Jacqmain, 'Pregnancy as Grounds for Dismissal' (1994) 23 *ILJ* 355, 358, suggesting that there may be a conflict between Dir. 76/207 and Dir. 92/85 in a situation where a pregnant woman applies for a job for which she is fully qualified, but which necessarily entails exposure to risks which are listed in the latter Dir., when no alternative work is available.

[253] [1992] OJ L348/1. For a critical analysis of the Dir. and of the various possible explanations for its adoption see V. Cromack, 'The EC Pregnancy Dir.: Principle or Pragmatism?' [1993] *JSWFL* 261.

to the 1989 Charter of Fundamental Social Rights for Workers, which was signed in 1989 by eleven of the then twelve Member States, and which now appears in the recitals to the TEU and in Article 136 (ex Article 117) EC as amended by the ToA, providing the impetus for various legislative initiatives in the field of social policy.[254] The chosen legal basis met with objection from the UK which wished to confine 'health and safety' to narrower issues such as fencing of machinery and dangerous substances at work.The Directive was adopted after considerable negotiation and compromise, which included, again at the insistence of the UK, the setting of the minimum level of pay for workers on maternity leave at the level of sick pay, despite the arguments against drawing parallels between sickness and pregnancy.

The Directive introduced a requirement of minimum protection by the Member States for three categories of female workers: pregnant workers, workers who have recently given birth, and workers who are breast-feeding. It is expressly stated that the Directive cannot be used to justify any reduction in higher levels of protection already provided in Member States, since they have committed themselves under the Treaty 'to encouraging improvements while maintaining the improvements made'. Thus it is clear that this is not a fully harmonizing Directive, and it does not attempt to require uniform rights of maternity leave for women in all of the Member States.

The Directive provides for guidelines to be drawn up by the Commission on substances and processes which are considered hazardous or stressful to those three categories of workers. It requires employers to assess the extent to which such women are exposed to specified risks and, under Article 5, to take any appropriate action such as adjusting their working hours or conditions, moving them to another job, or granting leave. Article 7 provides that they cannot be obliged to perform night-work for a period to be set by national law, and the option of day-work or extended maternity leave must be possible. Article 6 provides that pregnant or breast-feeding workers cannot be required to carry out duties involving the risk of exposure to specified substances, and Article 9 stipulates that pregnant workers must be entitled, where necessary, to time off work without loss of pay to attend ante-natal examinations.

The core provision on maternity leave is contained in Article 8, which specifies that the three categories of workers are to be given a minimum of fourteen continuous weeks' maternity leave before and/or after confinement, including at least two weeks of compulsory maternity leave. This is bolstered by Article 10, which requires Member States to prohibit the dismissal of such workers during the period of maternity leave, other than in exceptional cases unconnected with pregnancy.[255] It has been pointed out, however, that the Directive does not cover the *Dekker* situation, i.e., that of refusal to employ a woman on grounds of pregnancy, and for this situation it will still be necessary to rely on the concept of discrimination under the Equal Treatment Directive with the problem of hypothetical male comparator to which that approach gives rise.[256] In *Boyle*, the ECJ ruled that it was not contrary to Article 8 for an employer

---

[254] COM(89)471.
[255] For an interpretation of the requirement of Member State consent in exceptional cases under Art. 10(1), see Case C–438/99, *Jiménez Melgar* v. *Ayuntamiento de Los Barrios* [2001] ECR I–6914.
[256] Cromack, n. 253 above.

to specify when the obligatory fourteen-week period of maternity leave should commence, even if the employee was on sick leave at the time of giving birth.[257]

The requirement of access to a judicial remedy which was seen in the Equal Pay and Equal Treatment Directives is to be found in Article 12 of the Pregnancy Directive. Under Article 11, the right to maintenance of payment and other employment rights must be protected in the case of those workers who are on leave in the circumstances provided in Articles 5, 6, and 7. Significantly, the same is not required in the case of workers who are on maternity leave as provided in Article 8.[258] Instead, Article 11 specifies that they must be entitled to an 'adequate allowance' of not less than the amount of statutory sick pay.[259] Eligibility for the allowance can be subjected by national legislation to conditions, other than a condition which requires previous employment of more than twelve months prior to confinement. In *Boyle*, the ECJ ruled that a contractual term under which a higher level of pay than the statutory maternity payments was made conditional on the worker undertaking to return to work after the birth for at least one month, was compatible with this provision and also with Article 141 and the Equal Pay Directive.[260] In other words, the Pregnancy Directive guarantees only a minimum level of maternity pay and not any higher amount that the employer may choose to pay. Similarly in the case of the period of maternity leave granted: the employer is only required under Article 8 to grant fourteen weeks' leave, and if supplementary leave is also granted, there is nothing in the Pregnancy Directive or in Directive 76/207 to prevent the employer from limiting the entitlement to accrual of annual leave to the period of fourteen weeks. However, accrual of annual leave and accrual of occupation pension rights are firmly protected during the fourteen-week period, as basic rights of the employment contract,[261] by Article 11(2)(a).[262]

(f) DIRECTIVE 86/613

Since Directive 76/207 deals with equal treatment in relation to employed persons, Directive 86/613 was adopted under Articles 94 and 308 (ex Articles 100 and 235) EC in order to apply the principle of equal treatment also to the self-employed.[263] Article 2

---

[257] Case C–411/96, *Boyle* v. *EOC* [1998] ECR I–6401. The employer could not, however, make the right to take sick leave during the period of maternity leave conditional on the employee first agreeing to return to work and terminate maternity leave, except in the case where the period of maternity leave in question was an additional period granted by the employer in excess of that required by statute.

[258] In Case C–342/93, *Gillespie* v. *Northern Health and Social Services Boards* [1996] ECR I–475, on facts which arose before the Dir. was applicable, the ECJ ruled that the Treaty did not require a woman on maternity leave to continue to receive full pay, although the amount payable could not be so low as to undermine the purpose of maternity leave in protecting women before and after birth. See also Case C–66/96, *Handels- og Kontorfunktionærernes Forbund i Danmark, acting on behalf of Berit Høj Pedersen* v. *Fællesforeningen for Danmarks Brugsforeninger, acting on behalf of Kvickly Skive* [1998] ECR I–7327.

[259] In Case C–333/97, *Lewen* v. *Denda* [1999] ECR I–7243, it was held that while a voluntary Christmas bonus given to employees undoubtedly constituted pay within Art. 141 (ex Art. 119) it did not fall within the special concept of pay under Art. 11(2)(b) of the Pregnancy Dir. in relation to maternity leave.

[260] Case C–411/96, *Boyle* v. *EOC* [1998] ECR I–6401.   [261] *Ibid.*, paras. 84–87.

[262] See also Case C–333/97, *Lewen* v. *Denda* [1999] ECR I–7243, para. 50, on the difference between periods of parenting leave and periods of leave required for the protection of mothers, in relation to the calculation of entitlement to an allowance.

[263] See [1986] OJ L359/56 and COM(94)163.

sets out the personal scope of the Directive, providing that it applies to the self-employed 'including farmers and members of the liberal professions' as well as their spouses who are not employees or partners, but who participate in the same activities. Article 3 sets out the principle of equal treatment in a similar way to that in the other Equal Treatment and Social Security Directives.[264] Articles 4 to 8 then set out the 'material scope' of the scheme, which requires Member States to take action to eliminate sex discrimination in a range of matters, such as establishing a business or activity, forming a company, and providing for social-security schemes for spouses of the self-employed. Member States are also to 'examine under what conditions' the recognition of the work of spouses may be encouraged, and under what conditions female self-employed workers or wives of such workers may be protected in the event of pregnancy or motherhood—specifically, the Directive mentions access to temporary replacements or national social services and entitlement to cash benefits under public social-security or social-protection schemes.

(g) PARENTAL LEAVE

Following a number of unsuccessful attempts by the Commission to introduce legislation on parental leave, in 1996 a Framework Agreement on parental leave was concluded by the main organizations representing confederations of European employers' and employees' representatives, and this was implemented by Council Directive 96/34, under the terms of the Social Policy Agreement which at the time was attached by a Protocol to the EC Treaty.[265]

The main provisions of the Framework Agreement grant men and women workers a minimum-level individual right to at least three months' parental leave on the grounds of the birth or adoption of a child in order to care for the child, until a given age (up to 8 years) to be specified by the Member State or the social partners. The right to parental leave is in principle to be granted on a non-transferable basis, but the specific conditions of access and rules governing the leave are left to the Member States to define, either by law or by collective agreement. The Framework Agreement sets out a number of permissible conditions on which Member States may decide, such as whether leave is to be granted on a full- or part-time basis, whether it is to be subject to a period of work qualification, what notice periods may be required, in what circumstances employers may postpone the grant of leave, and the making of special arrangements for small undertakings.

Workers are to be protected against dismissal on grounds of applying for or taking the permitted parental leave, and they shall have the right to return to the same or an equivalent or similar job at the end of the leave period, without any other of their acquired rights being affected by the leave. No provision is made in the agreement regarding pay or any other allowance, and clause 2(8) specifies that all matters relating to social security are to be determined by the Member States in accordance with

---

[264] For a case discussing the concept of indirect discrimination under this Dir. and Dir. 76/207, see Case C–226/98, *Jørgensen* v. *Foreningen af Speciallæger* [2000] ECR I–2447.

[265] Council Dir. 96/34 on the framework agreement on parental leave concluded by UNICE, CEEP, and the ETUC [1996] OJ L145/4. This was extended to the UK by Dir. 97/75 [1998] OJ L10/24.

national law.[266] The Agreement also provides, in a less detailed clause, that Member States or the social partners shall take 'the necessary measures' to entitle workers to time off work 'on grounds of *force majeure* for urgent family reasons in cases of sickness or accident'.

Since the right to leave granted by the Framework Agreement is a minimum-level right, the final provisions specify that Member States may introduce more favourable provisions, and that the provisions of the Agreement will not in themselves justify reducing the general level of protection afforded to workers in this field. The interpretation of provisions of the Agreement is to be referred in the first instance to the signatory parties, without prejudice to the role of the Commission, national courts, and the ECJ.

It should be noted too that in the recent proposal to amend Directive 76/207 provision is made for protection of the right to return to employment of those who have taken parental leave under national law.[267]

(h) SEXUAL HARASSMENT

In 1991, having commissioned a report on the dignity of women at work, the Commission adopted a recommendation on the protection of the dignity of employees at work, calling on Member States to encourage employees to implement its Code of Practice.[268] The recommendation—a form of soft law which is not without legal effect[269]—was annexed to the Code of Practice on measures to combat sexual harassment.[270]

According to the report commissioned, the Commission accepted that sexual harassment was, in principle, contrary to Equal Treatment Directive 76/207, and thus also contrary to any national provisions implementing the Directive.[271] In 1996 the Commission issued a communication concerning the consultation of labour and management on the prevention of sexual harassment at work, accompanied by an evaluation report on the observance by Member States of its 1991 Recommendation.[272] The Commission evidently wished to encourage the social partners to take specific action to combat sexual harassment, but without success.[273]

Finally in 2002, however, the proposal to amend Directive 76/207 seems likely soon to be in force, containing for the first time a definition of harassment (as indeed do the two new anti-discrimination directives adopted under Article 13 EC), and specifying clearly that sexual harassment constitutes sex discrimination.

---

[266] See, however, Case C–333/97, *Lewen* v. *Denda* [1999] ECR I–7243 on this issue.

[267] N. 212 above.

[268] Recommendation 92/131 [1992] OJ L49/1. See also the Council Res. on the protection of the dignity of men and women at work [1990] OJ C157/3.

[269] Case C–322/88, *Grimaldi* v. *Fonds des Maladies Professionelles* [1989] ECR 4407.

[270] On the impact of the Recommendation and Code see J. Dine and B. Watt, 'Sexual Harassment: Hardening the Soft Law' (1994) 19 *ELRev.* 104, and T. Lester, 'Some Reflections on the European Community's Code of Conduct on Sexual Harassment' [1994] *JSWFL* 354.

[271] See M. Rubenstein, (1992) 21 *ILJ* 70.   [272] COM(96)373.

[273] See its report on a further stage of consultation of the social partners: SEC(97)568.

5. SOCIAL SECURITY

The two main legislative provisions in the field of social security are Directive 79/7 on statutory social security,[274] and Directive 86/378 as amended by Directive 96/97[275] on occupational social security, which has been discussed above in the context of equal pay following the *Barber* ruling.

(a) DIRECTIVE 79/7

Directive 79/7, which was anticipated by Article 1(2) of Directive 76/207, was adopted on the basis of Article 308 (ex Article 235), and its purpose is said to be the progressive implementation of the principle of equal treatment for men and women in the field of social security.[276] Following the ToA amendments, directives and other measures on social security could be adopted unanimously by the Council under Article 137(3) (ex Article 118) of the EC Treaty. This provision has in fact been amended again by the Nice Treaty, but social security remains firmly subject to the unanimity requirement, even while many other areas are now subject to qualified-majority voting.

The term 'progressive implementation' in the Social Security Directive is significant since, unlike Directive 75/117 on equal pay, Directive 79/7 provides various exceptions to the equal-treatment principle, and has allowed Member States a considerably longer period of time to adapt their laws to its requirements than was allowed to them under the Equal Treatment Directive.

Article 2 establishes the personal scope of the Directive, setting out two broad categories of people to which it applies. First, it covers the 'working population', which is subdivided into three categories: (i) those who are employed or self-employed; (ii) those under (i) whose work is interrupted by illness, accident, or involuntary unemployment; and (iii) those who are seeking employment. Secondly, it covers employees and the self-employed who are retired or invalided-out. Thus, in keeping with the Equal Pay and Equal Treatment Directives, Directive 79/7 covers only *employment-related* social security.

Article 3, which sets out the material scope of the Directive, then indicates that it does not cover all forms of employment-related social security. Rather, it covers those statutory schemes which provide protection against five specified risks, as well as social assistance which is intended to supplement or replace those statutory schemes. The five categories of risk are sickness, invalidity, old age, accidents at work and occupational diseases, and finally unemployment. Article 3(2) specifies that the Directive will not apply to provisions concerning survivors' benefits or family bene-fits, except family benefits due in respect of one of the five listed risks. Article 3(3) indicates that occupational social security is not covered, and provides for the

---

[274] [1979] OJ L6/24.
[275] See [1986] OJ L225/40, [1986] OJ L283/27, and [1997] OJ L46/20.
[276] Dir. 79/7, Art. 1.

adoption of later legislation in that sphere—Directive 86/378, as amended by Directive 96/97, being the example of such later legislation.[277]

The basic principle of equal treatment is set out in Article 4(1), providing that there is to be no discrimination on ground of sex, either directly or indirectly, by reference in particular to marital or family status. Provisions concerning the protection of women on grounds of maternity are again specifically exempted.[278] The Member States are required, as in the other equality directives, to take the necessary measures to ensure that any provisions in breach of the equal-treatment principle are abolished, and they are required to provide an adequate remedy for those who feel aggrieved.[279]

The permissible exceptions to the scope of the Directive are set out in Article 7(1). Five specific matters are listed which the Member States may choose to exclude from the application of the Directive. The first, which was mentioned above in relation to the cases of *Marshall* and *Roberts* on the Equal Treatment Directive, relates to the 'determination of pensionable age for the purposes of granting old-age and retirement pensions and the possible consequences thereof for other benefits'.[280] This has been the subject of much litigation. The second exception concerns advantages in respect of old-age pension schemes for persons who have brought up children and the acquisition of benefit entitlements following periods of interruption of employment due to the bringing up of children. The third concerns the granting of old-age or invalidity benefit entitlements 'by virtue of the derived entitlements of a wife', the fourth the granting of increases in long-term invalidity, old-age, accidents-at-work, and occupational-disease benefits for a dependent wife, and the fifth the consequences of the exercise of a right of option not to acquire rights or incur obligations under a statutory scheme.[281] However, these areas of permissible exception are not to be static, since Article 7(2) requires Member States to examine periodically any areas they have excluded, to see whether the justification for exclusion has altered in the light of social developments. Further, Member States must communicate to the Commission the provisions adopted pursuant to Article 7(2) and inform it of their reasons for maintaining existing provisions under Article 7(1), as well as the possibilities for future review of such derogations. The Directive was required to be fully in force in the Member States at the end of 1984.

(i) DIRECT EFFECT OF DIRECTIVE 79/7

The direct effect of the equal-treatment principle in Article 4(1) was confirmed in *FNV*, in which the ECJ was asked whether it could be relied upon after the deadline for implementation, either if the Member States failed to implement it or if they implemented it only partially.

---

[277] A third draft dir. on social security was proposed by the Commission in 1987 to remove the exceptions provided for in Dirs. 79/7 and 86/378, but it was never adopted. See [1987] OJ C309/10.

[278] Art. 4(2).   [279] Arts. 5 and 6.

[280] Art. 7(1)(a).   [281] Art. 7(1)(b)–(e).

Case 71/85, Netherlands v. Federatie Nederlandse Vakbeweging
[1986] ECR 3855

THE ECJ

18. It must be pointed out that, standing by itself, and in the light of the objective and contents of Directive 79/7/EEC, Article 4(1) precludes, generally and unequivocally, all discrimination on grounds of sex. The provision is therefore sufficiently precise to be relied upon in legal proceedings by an individual and applied by the courts. However, it remains to be considered whether the prohibition of discrimination which it contains may be regarded as unconditional, having regard to the exceptions provided for in Article 7 and to the fact that according to the wording of Article 5, Member States are to take certain measures in order to ensure that the principle of equal treatment is applied in national legislation.

The Court ruled that Article 7 was not relevant, since it simply excluded certain clearly defined areas from the equal-treatment principle of Article 4. Nor could Article 5, which obliges Member States to adopt the measures necessary to abolish infringements of the equal-treatment principle, be seen as imposing conditions on the clear prohibition on discrimination:

21. Consequently, Article 4(1) of the Directive does not confer on Member States the power to make conditional or to limit the application of the principle of equal treatment within its field of application and it is sufficiently precise and unconditional to allow individuals, in the absence of implementing measures adopted within the prescribed period, to rely upon it before the national courts as from 2 December 1984 in order to preclude the application of any national provision inconsistent with that article.

. . .

25. . . . a Member State may not invoke its discretion with regard to the choice of methods for implementing the principle of equal treatment in the field of social security laid down in Directive 79/7/EEC in order to deny all effect to Article 4(1) thereof, which may be invoked in legal proceedings even though the said Directive has not been implemented in its entirety.

Subsequently, in *Borrie Clark*, the ECJ ruled that it was contrary to Article 4(1) of the Directive for a Member State, by means of legislation passed after the coming into effect of the Directive, to extend the discriminatory effects of an old benefit to the criteria for eligibility for a new benefit.[282] The case concerned an application for a severe-disablement allowance, which had been brought in to replace the earlier invalidity allowance. The invalidity allowance had discriminated against married women by requiring them not only to be incapable of continuing to work, but also 'incapable of performing normal household duties', and the new severe-disablement allowance effectively continued the discriminatory criteria for eligibility. This was not permissible, and Article 4(1) could be directly relied on by the affected applicant.[283]

---

[282] Case 384/85, *Borrie Clark* v. *Chief Adjudication Officer* [1987] ECR 2865.
[283] See also Case 80/87, *Dik* v. *College van Burgemeester en Wethouders* [1988] ECR 1601.

(II) PERSONAL SCOPE

The personal scope of the Directive was given a broad reading by the ECJ in *Drake*, in which a woman who had given up work in order to care for her disabled mother was refused an invalid care allowance under national legislation on the ground that such an allowance was not payable to a married woman who was living with her husband. No such restriction was imposed by the legislation on a married man who was living with his wife, and the question for the ECJ was whether the applicant fell within the personal scope of Directive 79/7.

Case 150/85, Drake v. Chief Adjudication Officer
[1986] ECR 1995

THE ECJ

21. According to Article 3(1), Directive 79/7 applies to statutory schemes which provide protection against, inter alia, the risk of invalidity . . . and social assistance in so far as it is intended to supplement or replace the invalidity scheme. . . . In order to fall within the scope of the Directive, therefore, a benefit must constitute the whole or part of a statutory scheme providing protection against one of the specified risks or a form of social assistance having the same objective.

22. Under Article 2, the term 'working population', which determines the scope of the directive, is defined broadly. . . . That provision is based on the idea that a person whose work has been interrupted by one of the risks referred to in Article 3 belongs to the working population. That is the case of Mrs. Drake, who has given up work solely because of one of the risks listed in Article 3, namely the invalidity of her mother. She must therefore be regarded as a member of the working population for the purposes of the Directive.

23. Furthermore, it is possible for the Member States to provide protection against the consequences of the risk of invalidity in various ways. For example, a Member State may, as the United Kingdom has done, provide for two separate allowances, one payable to the disabled person himself and the other payable to a person who provides care, while another Member State may arrive at the same result by paying an allowance to the disabled person at a rate equivalent to the sum of those two benefits. In order, therefore, to ensure that the progressive implementation of the principle of equal treatment referred to in Article 1 of Directive 79/7 and defined in Article 4 is carried out in a harmonious manner throughout the Community, Article 3(1) must be interpreted as including any benefit which in a broad sense forms part of one of the statutory schemes referred to or a social assistance provision intended to supplement or replace such a scheme.

24. Moreover the payment of the benefit to a person who provides care still depends on the existence of a situation of invalidity inasmuch as such a situation is a condition *sine qua non* for its payment, as the Adjudication Officer admitted during the oral procedure. It must also be emphasized that there is a clear economic link between the benefit and the disabled person, since the disabled person derives an advantage from the fact that an allowance is paid to the person caring for him.

25. It follows that the fact that a benefit which forms part of a statutory invalidity scheme is paid to a third party and not directly to the disabled person does not place it outside the scope of Directive 79/7. Otherwise, as the Commission emphasized in its observations, it would be possible,

by making formal changes to existing benefits covered by the directive, to remove them from its scope.

Thus the fact that Mrs Drake had given up work in order to care for someone else who had become an invalid was sufficient to bring her within the scope of the Directive. The care allowance was treated by the Court in the same way as the mother's severe-disablement allowance, being simply the legislature's way of dividing up the payment of social-security benefits consequent on invalidity.

Directive 79/7 is strictly employment-related, in that it does not cover someone who has never worked. This was established in the case of *Achterberg-te Riele*, in which the Court also ruled that persons who give up work for a reason other than one of the five listed in the Directive—e.g., to look after children—fall outside its scope.[284] Benefits such as old-age pensions and invalidity allowances, which are referred to in Article 3, will fall within the scope of the Directive only when they are claimed by someone who is within one of the categories of people in Article 2:

This interpretation is in conformity with the objectives of Community law and the wording of the other provisions in the same field as Directive 79/7. Article 119 . . . Directive 75/117 . . . and Directive 76/207 . . . implement equal treatment between men and women not generally but only in their capacity as workers.[285]

These conditions were tightened further in the case of *Johnson I* where the Court ruled that in order to be covered by the Directive not only must one of the risks listed in the Directive have materialized, but the person in question must have either given up employment, or been obliged to give up seeking employment *at the time of materialization of the risk*.[286] Johnson had given up work for some years in order to care for her child, and in the meantime had developed a serious back condition which rendered her unable to return to work. She was refused an invalidity pension or severe-disablement allowance because she was cohabiting with her partner, and since this restriction did not apply to men and thus was discriminatory, she argued that it was in breach of Directive 79/7. Despite the Commission's argument that, since those who give up work to look after children are largely women, who would be at a considerable disadvantage if they were excluded from the Social Security Directive on account of an illness or disability *subsequently* arising, the ECJ ruled that they would not be within the personal scope of the Directive, and shifted the responsibility for removing the disadvantage faced by women on to the Community legislature.[287]

---

[284] Cases 48, 106, and 107/88, *Achterberg-te Riele v. Sociale Versekeringsbank, Amsterdam* [1989] ECR 1963.
[285] *Ibid.*, para. 12.
[286] Case C–31/90, *Johnson v. Chief Adjudication Officer* [1991] ECR I–3723, paras. 18–23.
[287] See also Case C–297/93, *Grau-Hupka v. Stadtgemeinde Bremen* [1994] ECR I–5535, even where such disadvantage affects women's pay.

Case C–31/90 Johnson v. Chief Adjudication Officer
[1991] ECR I–3723

THE ECJ

25. It must be observed, however, that according to the first recital of the preamble to Directive 79/7/EEC and Article 1 thereof, the Directive has in view only the progressive implementation of the principle of equal treatment for men and women in matters of social security. As far as the social protection of mothers remaining at home is concerned, it follows from Article 7(1)(b) . . . that the acquisition of entitlement to benefits following periods of interruption of employment due to the upbringing of children is still a matter for the Member States to regulate.

26. In those circumstances, it is for the Community legislature to take such measures as it considers appropriate to remove the discrimination which still exists in this regard in some bodies of national legislation.

This narrower reading of the personal scope of the Directive firmly underlines its employment-related focus, in excluding someone who cannot seek employment on account of a disability or illness he or she has suffered. Where someone seeking a benefit does satisfy the conditions of the Directive, however, the Court has ruled that the right to rely on the Directive is not confined to that person. In *Verholen*, one of the applicants before the Dutch court was the husband of a woman who was claiming sex discrimination in the conditions for determining affiliation of an old-age pension scheme.[288] The national court, of its own motion, raised the question of the applicability of Directive 79/7, and among the questions referred to the Court was that whether someone other than the person entitled to the benefit could rely on the measure:

It should be pointed out straight away that the right to rely on the provisions of Directive 79/7 is not confined to individuals coming within the scope *ratione personae* of the Directive, in so far as the possibility cannot be ruled out that other persons may have a direct interest in ensuring that the principle of non-discrimination is respected as regards persons who are protected.[289]

Accordingly, because the claimant's husband had suffered the effects of the discriminatory national legislation concerning his spouse, in that his pension would also be reduced, he could invoke the provisions of the Directive so long as his spouse came within its personal scope, even though he himself did not.[290]

However, in *Züchner*, the ECJ applied the narrower reasoning of its earlier judgments in *Achterberg-te Riele* and *Johnson*, rather than the broader approach in *Drake* and *Verholen*,[291] ruling that a woman who provided special home care and therapeutic treatment for her disabled husband would not fall within the scope of Directive 79/7, even though she had had to undergo a form of occupational training in order to

---

[288] Cases C–87–89/90, *Verholen and Others v. Sociale Versekeringsbank* [1991] ECR I–3757.
[289] *Ibid.*, para. 22.
[290] See also Case C–200/91, n. 53 above, para. 19 on occupational social security.
[291] For criticism of this aspect of *Züchner*, see L. Waddington, (1997) 22 *ELRev.* 587.

because the link between these criteria and the purpose of the benefit—i.e., to provide for those whose income was inadequate to cover housing costs—was insufficiently strong to conclude that the housing benefit was intended to protect against the risks of old age or invalidity. Arguably, had this approach had been taken in *Drake*, looking strictly at the intended aim of the benefit, the conclusion might have been that the aim of the invalid care allowance was to provide a source of income to someone who had given up work to care for another. The conclusion of the ECJ in *Smithson* seems to be that the housing benefit was really a form of social assistance which was not intended to supplement or replace one of the listed social security benefits, and it suggests a stricter approach to determining the scope of the equal treatment principle in the sphere of social security under EC law.

Subsequently in *Jackson and Cresswell*, the question was whether a supplementary allowance or income support could, in certain circumstances, fall within the scope of the Directive as a form of protection against the risk of unemployment. The applicants argued that the reduction in their benefits breached Directive 79/7, since it was a consequence of their not being able to deduct child-minding expenses when calculating their income in order to determine the amount of benefit they should receive. The prohibition on deduction of child-minding expenses was argued to be indirectly discriminatory against women. However, despite the attempts of Advocate General van Gerven to distinguish the benefits at issue in *Smithson*, the ECJ ruled that the benefits here were not 'directly and effectively' linked to protection against the risk of unemployment.

Cases C–63–64/91, Jackson v. Chief Adjudication Officer

[1992] ECR I–4737

THE ECJ

17. ... Article 3(1)(a) of Directive 79/7 does not refer to a statutory scheme which, on certain conditions, provides persons with means below a legally defined limit with a special benefit designed to enable them to meet their needs.

18. That finding is not affected by the circumstance that the recipient of the benefit is in fact in one of the situations covered by Article 3(1) of the Directive.

19. Indeed in *Smithson*, cited above, the Court held with regard to a housing benefit that the fact that some of the risks listed in Article 3(1) of Directive 79/7 were taken into account in order to grant a higher benefit was not sufficient to bring that benefit within the scope of the Directive.

20. Consequently, exclusion from the scope of Directive 79/7 is justified *a fortiori* where, as in the case at issue in the main proceedings, the law sets the amount of the theoretical needs of the persons concerned, used to determine the benefit in question, independently of any consideration relating to the existence of any of the risks listed in Article 3(1) of the Directive.

21. Moreover, in certain situations, in particular those of the appellants in the main proceedings, the national schemes at issue exempt claimants from the obligation to be available for work. That shows that the benefits in question cannot be regarded as being directly and effectively linked to protection against the risk of unemployment.

Unlike the Advocate General's approach, which did not focus exclusively on the *intention* or aim of the statutory scheme but also on its overall *effect* in providing protection against one of the risks in the Directive, the Court concentrated on the need which the scheme was 'designed' to meet. One problem with an approach which is largely intention-oriented, however, is that it may enable the Member States to structure their social-security and assistance schemes so as to avoid the application of the equal-treatment principle to many benefits which do, in fact, provide protection against one or more of the risks set out in the Directive.[293]

In *Hoever and Zachow*, the ECJ was asked whether a child-raising allowance intended to secure the maintenance of the family while children were being raised fell within the material scope of the Directive.[294] Although one of the effects of the benefit could be said to be that it helps keep people in employment, the ECJ, focusing again on its intended aim, ruled that it did not provide direct and effective protection against one of the risks listed in the Directive, and noted indeed that Article 3(2) largely excludes family benefits from its scope. However, although certain benefits, such as survivors' benefits, may be excluded from the Directive's scope, if a benefit such as invalidity benefit which *was* within its scope were to be withdrawn on becoming entitled to a survivor's benefit, this situation would be governed by the Directive.[295]

In *Richardson*, the Court ruled that UK national health regulations, which exempted those who qualify for an old-age pension from prescription charges, came within the scope of Directive 79/7, since they were part of a statutory scheme affording direct and effective protection against the risk of sickness, even though they did not strictly form part of national social-security rules.[296] Similarly in *Taylor*, a winter-fuel payment was held to be directly linked to protection against the risk of old age.[297] By way of contrast in the case of *Atkins*, also referred from a UK court, the ECJ ruled that a system of concessionary fares on public transport for those who had reached pensionable age, operated on an optional basis under national statutory authority by a District Council, fell outside the material scope of the Directive.[298] This was because the purpose or aim of the benefit was to facilitate access to public transport for certain classes of person needing such transport who were less well off financially and, as in *Smithson*, old age and invalidity were merely two of the criteria which could be applied to define the classes of beneficiaries for the concessionary scheme. The ECJ rejected the Commission's argument that Directive 79/7 could extend to measures of 'social protection' of this kind, going beyond the scope of social security proper, so long as they were granted to persons affected by one of the risks listed in the Directive, and it reaffirmed that a scheme of benefits would fall within the scope of the

---

[293] See J. Sohrab, 'Women and Social Security Law: The Limits of EEC Equality Law' [1994] *JSWFL* 5.

[294] Cases C–245/94 & C–312/94, *Hoever and Zachow* v. *Land Nordrhein Westfalen* [1996] ECR I–4895. Compare Case C–116/94, *Meyers* v. *Adjudication Officer* [1995] ECR I–2131, n. 227 above, and text, in which family credit was held to fall within the scope of Dir. 76/207 concerning access to employment, since one of its effects was to help keep people in employment. The ECJ did not address Dir. 76/207 in its ruling in *Hoever and Zachow*.

[295] Case C–338/91, *Steenhorst-Neerings* v. *Bestuur van de Bedrijfsvereniging voor Detailhandel, Ambachten en Huisvrouwen* [1993] ECR I–5475.

[296] Case C–137/94, *R.* v. *Secretary of State for Health, ex p. Richardson* [1995] ECR I–3407.

[297] Case C–382/98, *R.* v. *Secretary of State for Social Security, ex p. Taylor* [1999] ECR I–8955.

[298] Case C–228/94, *Atkins* v. *Wrekin District Council and Department of Transport* [1996] ECR I–3633.

Directive only if it were intended to afford direct and effective protection against one of the risks listed in Article 3, or to supplement or replace such a scheme.

(IV) THE EXCEPTIONS IN ARTICLE 7

We have seen that the Council in adopting Directive 79/7 did not attempt to require Member States to bring about immediate equality between women and men in social security, but permitted the gradual introduction of equal treatment in areas which would require considerable financial restructuring of existing state schemes. The exact scope of these exceptions, however, is not clear from the provisions of the Directive, and has given rise to a considerable amount of litigation. The most frequently litigated point, which has briefly been considered above in relation to conditions of dismissal under the Equal Treatment Directive, is the derogation concerning the determination of pensionable age.

Case C–9/91, R. v. Secretary of State for Social Security,
ex p. Equal Opportunities Commission
[1992] ECR I–4927

The pensionable age in the UK was 65 for men and 60 for women. The Equal Opportunities Commission (EOC) claimed that the State pension discriminated against men on grounds of sex, by requiring them to pay contributions for 44 years and women for 39 years in order to qualify for a full basic pension. Further, men working between the ages of 60 and 64 paid pension contributions whereas women working between those ages did not. The UK Government argued that the differences in treatment could be justified under the derogation in Article 7(1)(a) of Directive 79/7.

THE ECJ

13. Since the text of the derogation refers to 'the determination of pensionable age for the purpose of granting old-age and retirement pensions', it is clear that it concerns the moment from which pensions become payable. The text does not, however, refer expressly to discrimination in respect of the extent of the obligation to contribute for the purposes of the pension or the amount thereof. Such forms of discrimination therefore fall within the scope of the derogation only if they are found to be necessary in order to achieve the objectives which the Directive is intended to pursue by allowing Member States to retain a different pensionable age for men and women.

. . .

15. Although the preamble to the Directive does not state the reasons for the derogations which it lays down, it can be deduced from the nature of the exceptions contained in Article 7(1) of the Directive that the Community legislature intended to allow Member States to maintain temporarily the advantages accorded to women with respect to retirement in order to enable them progressively to adapt their pension systems in this respect without disrupting the complex financial equilibrium of those systems, the importance of which could not be ignored. Those advantages include the possibility for female workers of qualifying for a pension earlier than male workers, as envisaged by Article 7(1)(a) of the directive.

16. In a system such as the one concerned in the main proceedings, whose financial equilibrium is based on men contributing for a longer period than women, a different pensionable age for men

and women cannot be maintained without altering the existing financial equilibrium, unless such inequality with respect to the length of contribution periods is also maintained.

Any more limited interpretation of the derogation, the ECJ ruled, would render it entirely ineffective, since the financial upheaval which the exception was intended to avoid by permitting states to readjust their financing of pension schemes over a period of years would have to be faced before the deadline for implementation of the Directive. Thus the maintenance of different pensionable ages was not the only form of discrimination permitted by Article 7(1)(a), but 'also forms of discrimination such as those described by the national court which are necessarily linked to [the difference in statutory pensionable ages]'.

The derogation in Article 7(1)(a) extends not just to the setting of different pensionable ages, but also, as has been seen in *Burton* and *Roberts*[299] above, to 'the possible consequences thereof for other benefits'. The case of *Thomas* questioned whether the scope of the derogation was exceeded where the cessation of entitlement to invalid-care and severe-disablement allowances was linked to the attainment of statutory retirement age, which was 65 for men and 60 for women.[300] Having considered its reasoning in the *EOC* case in relation to discrimination in contribution periods, the ECJ ruled that the same sort of link between the discrimination and the difference in pensionable ages would have to be shown when the complaint concerned discrimination as regards 'other benefits'. The requisite link did not exist in relation to the disablement and invalid-care allowances at issue, since:

the grant of benefits under non-contributory schemes, such as severe disablement allowance and invalid care allowance, to persons in respect of whom risks have materialised, regardless of the entitlement of such persons to an old-age pension by virtue of contribution periods completed by them, has no direct influence on the financial equilibrium of the contributory pension schemes.[301]

In the case of *Rose Graham*, the rate of invalidity pension payable to those who opted, on reaching pensionable age, to continue receiving an invalidity rather than a retirement pension was reduced by reference to the rate of retirement pension which they would have received.[302] Given the difference in pensionable ages between men and women, it was argued that such a reduction was discriminatory and in breach of Directive 79/7, but the ECJ ruled that the discrimination was objectively and necessarily linked to the setting of different pensionable ages, and so was covered by the exception in Article 7(1)(a). This was because the invalidity benefit was designed to replace income from occupational activity, and the Member State was quite entitled to cease the invalidity benefit and to replace it with a retirement pension at the time when the recipients would have ceased to work on reaching retirement age. To hold otherwise, in the Court's view, would undermine the legitimate coherence of the

---

[299] Cases 19/81, n. 218 above, and 151/84, n. 167 above. See also Cases 262/84, n. 219 above, and 152/84, n. 221 above.

[300] Case C–328/91, *Secretary of State for Social Security* v. *Thomas* [1993] ECR I–1247.

[301] *Ibid.*, para. 14.

[302] Case C–92/94, *Secretary of State for Social Security and Chief Adjudication Officer* v. *Rose Graham* [1995] ECR I–2521.

national retirement scheme and the invalidity benefit scheme. And in *De Vriendt* and *Wolfs* the ECJ ruled that discrimination in the method of *calculating* pensions was necessarily and objectively linked to the difference which had been maintained regarding the specification of pensionable age.[303]

Similarly in *Balestra*, the ECJ ruled that the link between sex discrimination in an early retirement-benefit scheme and the difference in pensionable ages was necessary to preserve the coherence between the retirement-pensions scheme and the early-retirement scheme in question.[304] On the other hand, in *Richardson* the Court ruled that the discrimination in the system of exemption from prescription charges was not necessarily linked to the difference in pensionable ages, that the grant of such health-related non-contributory benefits would have no direct influence on the financial equilibrium of contributory pension schemes, and thus the system could not avail of the exception in Article 7(1)(a).[305] And in *Taylor*, a winter-fuel payment could not benefit from the derogation, for similar reasons.[306] Finally, in *Buchner*, the ECJ ruled that there was no necessary link and therefore no need for the preservation of coherence between the early old-age pension on account of incapacity for work on the one hand, and the old-age pension on the other, so that Article 7(1)(a) could not apply.[307]

It has been noted above that, although Article 7(1) sets out derogations to the scope of application of the Directive, Article 7(2) encourages Member States to carry out periodical examinations of any areas excluded to see whether they are still justified in the light of social changes. Once the Member State has acted to abolish discrimination from a previously exempt area, however, it cannot rely on the derogation to continue discriminatory practices in that area. In *Van Cant*, the applicant was challenging the provisions of Belgian legislation which in 1990 had abolished discriminatory pensionable ages and had fixed entitlement to a retirement pension for both men and women at age 60.[308] However, the method for calculating the amount of the pension, which had been based on the forty most favourable years for women and forty-five for men, remained unchanged so that it now favoured women. The ECJ ruled that, once discriminatory retirement ages had been abolished, Article 7(1)(a) could no longer be relied on to justify maintaining a difference in calculating the retirement pension which was linked to that difference in retirement ages.

In *Bramhill*, however, a more progressive abolition of discrimination which was the subject of an exception in Article 7(1)(d) was found to be compatible with the Directive.[309] The case involved the scope of the derogation concerning increases in benefits for a 'dependent wife' in that provision. The applicant was refused an increase, in respect of her dependent husband, on the pension she had received when she retired

---

[303] Cases C–377/96–C–384/96, *De Vriendt* v. *Rijksdienst voor Pensioenen* [1998] ECR I–2105 and C–154/96, *Wolfs* v. *ONC* [1998] ECR I–6173.

[304] Case C–139/95, *Balestra* v. *Istituto Nazionale della Previdenza Sociale (IPNS)* [1997] ECR I–549.

[305] Case C–137/94, n. 296 above, paras. 18–25.

[306] Case C–382/98, *R.* v. *Secretary of State for Social Security, ex p. Taylor* [1999] ECR I–8955.

[307] Case C–104/98, *Buchner* v. *Sozialversicherungsanstalt der Bauern* [2000] ECR I–3625. Contrast Case C–196/98, *Hepple* v. *Adjudication Officer* [2000] ECR I–3701, in which the reduced earnings allowance was sufficiently linked, in terms of the coherence of the system, to the legislation governing old-age pensions to benefit from the derogation in Art. 7(1)(a).

[308] Case C–154/92, *Van Cant* v. *Rijksdienst voor Pensionen* [1993] ECR I–3811.

[309] Case C–420/92, *Bramhill* v. *Chief Adjudication Officer* [1994] ECR I–3191.

at 60, on the ground that she did not satisfy the conditions in the social-security legislation. The conditions, which required her to have been in receipt of certain benefits for adult dependents prior to retirement, were clearly discriminatory since they did not apply to a married man in similar circumstances, but the UK argued that the provision was covered by the derogation in Article 7(1)(d). According to Mrs Bramhill, the derogation applied to increases in benefit for a dependent *wife* only, and did not apply to an increase in pension like that in the present case, which had been made available by legislation in 1984 in respect of dependent husbands and wives alike. She argued that, since the benefit was made available for both, whereas before the amending legislation in 1984 it had been available for dependent wives only, it fell outside the scope of the exception and the discriminatory conditions were thus in breach of Article 4(1):

To interpret the Directive in the way contended for by Mrs Bramhill, which would mean that in the case of benefits which a Member State has excluded from the scope of the Directive pursuant to Article 7(1)(d) it could no longer rely on the derogation provided for by that provision if it adopted a measure which, like that in question in the main proceedings, has the effect of reducing the extent of unequal treatment based on sex, would therefore be incompatible with the purpose of the Directive and would be likely to jeopardize the implementation of the aforesaid principle of equal treatment.[310]

The difference between *Van Cant* and *Bramhill* seems to be that, once a Member State abolishes a discriminatory provision in an area which has previously been excepted under Article 7(1), it cannot retain other associated forms of discrimination which existed only because of the now-abolished provision. However, where the state chooses not to abolish the original discrimination, but to alleviate it progressively by means of gradually improving the position of the disadvantaged sex, this cannot be said to be outside the scope of the derogation.

Article 7(1)(c) permits the exclusion from the Directive of the granting of old-age benefits by virtue of the derived entitlements of a wife. This provision was interpreted in *Van Munster*, in which it was held that the principle of equal treatment in Directive 79/7 permitted a Member State to refuse a retired worker the higher rate of pension which its legislation provided for persons with dependent spouses, where that worker's spouse was entitled in her own right to a retirement pension in another Member State.[311]

(v) INDIRECT DISCRIMINATION IN SOCIAL SECURITY

We have seen above that in the context of pay, Article 141 (ex Article 119) prohibits both direct and indirect discrimination on grounds of sex. In the social-security context, this is provided for in Article 4(1) of Directive 79/7, and the ECJ has developed the concept of indirect discrimination and objective justification in a very similar way to that in the context of pay.

---

[310] *Ibid.*, para. 21.
[311] Case C–165/91, *Van Munster* v. *Rijksdienst voor Pensioenen* [1994] ECR I–4661.

Case 30/85, Teuling v. Bedrijfsvereniging voor de Chemische Industrie
[1987] ECR 2497

Under Dutch law, all employed persons suffering from an incapacity for work, regardless of sex or civil status, were entitled to a net minimum benefit equal to 70 per cent of the statutory minimum wage. That minimum could be increased under certain conditions by means of supplements to 100 per cent, but in practice this was only for beneficiaries having family responsibilities, such as a dependent spouse or children. Mrs Teuling claimed that this system of entitlement to benefits was indirectly discriminatory against women and incompatible with Article 4(1) of Directive 79/7.

THE ECJ

13. In that regard, it should be pointed out that a system of benefits in which, as in this case, supplements are provided for which are not directly based on the sex of the beneficiaries but take account of their marital status or family situation, and in respect of which it emerges that a considerably smaller proportion of women than of men are entitled to such supplements, is contrary to Article 4(1) of the Directive if that system of benefits cannot be justified by reasons which exclude discrimination on grounds of sex.

14. It appears from the documents before the Court that according to statistics provided to the Commission by the Netherlands Government a significantly greater number of married men than married women receive a supplement linked to family responsibilities. According to the plaintiff and the Commission, that results from the fact that in the Netherlands there are at present considerably more married men than married women who carry on occupational activities, and therefore considerably fewer women who have a dependent spouse.

15. In such circumstances a supplement linked to family responsibilities is contrary to Article 4(1) of the Directive if the grant thereof cannot be justified by reasons which exclude discrimination on grounds of sex.

16. In that regard, the supplements at issue must be considered. According to the Netherlands Government, the General Law does not link benefits to the salary previously earned by the beneficiaries but seeks to provide a minimum subsistence income to persons with no income from work. It must be observed that such a guarantee granted by Member States to persons who would otherwise be destitute is an integral part of the social policy of the Member States.

17. Consequently, if supplements to a minimum social security benefit are intended, where beneficiaries have no income from work, to prevent the benefit from falling below the minimum subsistence level for persons who, by virtue of the fact that they have a dependent spouse or children, bear heavier burdens than single persons, such supplements may be justified under the Directive.

18. If a national court, which has sole jurisdiction to assess the facts and interpret the national legislation, finds that supplements such as those in this case correspond to the greater burdens which beneficiaries having a dependent spouse or children must bear in comparison with persons living alone, serve to ensure an adequate minimum subsistence income for those beneficiaries and are necessary for that purpose, the fact that the supplements are paid to a significantly higher number of married men than of married women is not sufficient to support the conclusion that the grant of such supplements is contrary to the Directive.

While it was ultimately left to the national court to say whether the supplements actually corresponded to the additional burden borne by those with dependent

families, the ECJ evidently considered that the indirect discrimination could be justified on the grounds of social policy which were put forward.[312] In subsequent proceedings against Belgium, the ECJ seemed to widen the discretion left to the Member
States in justifying indirect discrimination in unemployment allowances in favour of
those with dependent family members, who were predominantly men.[313] Belgium
argued that the discrimination reflected a necessary social policy aim in recognizing
the greater burdens of unemployment for households with only one income. The
Commission in response argued that the scheme of benefits would comply with the
equal-treatment principle only if its aim was to provide minimum means of subsistence, rather than to award replacement income for a lost salary. Despite the implicit
earlier support for the Commission's argument in paragraph 16 of the ruling in
Teuling, above, the ECJ here ruled that the relevant criterion was whether the supplements corresponded to the greater burdens resulting from non-income-earning
dependents, and that taking previous income into account did not breach the equal-
treatment principle. The aims of the Belgian scheme were said to form 'part of a social
policy which in the current state of Community law is a matter for the Member States
which enjoy a reasonable margin of discretion as regards both the nature of the
protective measures and the detailed arrangements for their implementation'.[314]

In *De Weerd*, however, the Court ruled that although an indirectly discriminatory
national measure, such as a previous income requirement for eligibility for incapacity
benefits, could be justified on social-policy grounds, and although budgetary considerations could influence the nature or scope of a Member State's social policy,
budgetary policy and the state of the public finances could not *of themselves*
constitute adequate justification for such discrimination.[315] On the other hand, in
Posthuma-Van Damme, the ECJ confirmed that a similar income requirement laid
down in a national scheme concerning insurance against incapacity for work could be
justified by reference to the social-policy aim of restricting eligibility for a given
benefit to persons who lost income following materialization of the risk which the
benefit was intended to cover, even if the scheme was replacing a previous scheme of
pure national insurance unconnected with loss of income.[316]

The readiness with which the ECJ permits indirect discrimination in the grant of
social security benefits to be justified by reference to national social-policy aims can
be seen in the cases of *Nolte* and *Megner*,[317] which concerned the exclusion of persons
in minor or short-term employment from statutory social security schemes, and in

[312] See also Case 102/88, *Ruzius-Wilbrink* v. *Bestuur van de Bedrijfsvereniging voor Overheidsdiensten*
[1989] ECR 4311, where there was indirect discrimination against part-time workers in eligibility for invalidity benefits. The Court did not accept, as a justification, the claim that it would be unjust to grant such
workers benefits which would exceed the income they had previously received.

[313] Case C–229/89, *Commission* v. *Belgium* [1991] ECR I–2205.

[314] *Ibid.*, para. 22. See also Case C–221/91, *Molenbroek* v. *Bestuur van de Soziale Verzekeringsbank* [1992]
ECR I–5943 where the state was accorded a similar margin of discretion in justifying indirect discrimination
in the award of supplementary pensions for dependent spouses.

[315] Case C–343/92, *De Weerd (née Roks)* v. *Bestuur van de Bedrijfsvereniging voor de Gezondheid, Geestelijke
en Maatschappelijke Belangen* [1994] ECR I–571, paras. 35–36.

[316] Case C–280/94, *Posthuma Van Damme* v. *Bestuur van de Bedrijfsvereniging voor Detailhandel,
Ambachten en Huisvrouwen* and *Öztürk* v. *Bestuur van de Nieuwe Algemene Bedrijfsvereniging* [1996] ECR
I–179.

[317] N. 240 above.

the case of *Laperre*,[318] which concerned the imposition of conditions relating to age and previous employment on the grant of certain income-support benefits. Since the excluded groups in these three cases consisted predominantly of women, indirect discrimination was presumptively established, but in each case the ECJ suggested that the discrimination could be justified by reference to social-policy aims. In *Nolte* and *Megner*, it ruled that the Member States had a broad margin of discretion in pursuing their social and employment-policy aims, and that the desire to respond to the social demand for minor and short-term employment and to foster its supply was a legitimate policy aim unrelated to any discrimination on grounds of sex. And in *Laperre*, the Court found that the age- and employment-related conditions for access to specific income-support benefits could be justified by reference to the social aim of supporting the long-term unemployed who had little chance of further employment, even if these were predominantly men.

The same criticisms of indirect discrimination and objective justification are applicable in the context of social security as those which have been noted in the equal-pay and equal-treatment context, and in fact in the social security field the ECJ allows an even wider 'margin of discretion' to Member States as regards their reasons for such discrimination. Further, Directive 79/7 and the whole area of equal treatment in Community social security law have been the subject of a more wide-ranging critique on account of its narrow focus and, once again, its use of a male norm and pattern of working life against which to measure standards of treatment.

J. Sohrab, Women and Social Security Law: The Limits of EEC Equality Law[319]

EEC equality law has had an important impact on national social security systems. Many forms of direct discrimination have been eliminated. However, two outstanding problems with the Directive remain. The first is what kind of equality can the Directive promote and is this enough to produce equality of outcomes between men and women? We have seen that the Directive applies only to workers claiming broadly employment related, rather than social assistance, benefits. In so doing the Directive, it is argued, perpetuates a market/family dichotomy, which hinders progress towards equality of outcomes. Women are not situated similarly to men in relation to employment and to caring responsibilities. Women's situation in one of these spheres cannot be seen in isolation from their situation in the other.

This leads us to the second problem, how strong is the concept of indirect discrimination? Once rules have been formally equalised the crucial part of Article 4(1) of the Directive becomes the prohibition of indirect discrimination. We have seen, however, that in implementing the Directive Member States may easily create indirect discrimination. Since men and women are not similarly situated, in many instances formally equal benefit rules can only help those women gain access to benefits who most closely conform to underlying structures of benefit entitlement. . . . It is clear then that where the underlying structures do not fit closely with women's employment and life patterns, equality of outcomes will remain elusive. A strong concept of indirect discrimination

---

[318] Case C–8/94, *Laperre v. Bestuurscommissie Beroepszaken in de Provincie Zuid-Holland* [1996] ECR I–273.

[319] [1994] *JSWFL* 5, 16. See, more generally, J. Sohrab, *Sexing the Benefit* (Dartmouth, 1996).

could be used to challenge both levelling down and benefit rules which do not allow women in practice to gain benefits in their own right. In cases that do not directly concern workers, however, the Court seems reluctant to engage in such a radical enterprise. The real challenge to equality law in the future is to promote a social security system in which women are no longer penalised, in terms of a lack of financial independence, for not conforming to the 'typical (male) employment pattern.' This should also mean encouraging men to participate to a greater extent in caring.

(b) DIRECTIVE 86/378 AS AMENDED BY DIRECTIVE 96/97

Directive 86/378, which was based on Articles 94 and 308 (ex Articles 100 and 235) EC and had been anticipated in Article 4(3) of Directive 79/7, was intended—before the ruling in *Barber* had been given—to extend the principle of equal treatment from state social security schemes, which were covered in Directive 79/7, to those in private or occupational social security schemes. As we have seen above, following the *Barber* ruling and the subsequent stream of related case law, much of Directive 86/378 was effectively overridden by the ECJ, and Directive 96/97 was adopted at the end of 1996 to amend Directive 86/378 so as to reflect this case law.[320]

Occupational social security schemes are defined in the amended Directive 86/378 as schemes, whose membership is optional or compulsory, which are intended to provide workers or self-employed persons in an economic sector or undertaking with benefits intended to supplement or replace those provided by statutory social security schemes. Certain schemes are excluded by Article 2, such as individual contracts for self-employed workers, insurance contracts to which the employer is not a party, and individual options for additional benefits. Article 3 sets out the personal scope of the Directive, covering the working population in terms very similar to those of Article 2 of Directive 79/7, except that, in addition to covering those whose work is interrupted by illness, accident, or involuntary unemployment, it also covers interruption by maternity and it now covers persons who are claiming under those specified. Article 4 sets out the material scope of the Directive, and again the risks covered are almost exactly the same—sickness, invalidity, old-age including early retirement, industrial accidents and occupational diseases, and unemployment. Article 4(b) also provides that any other social benefits provided for in an occupational scheme, such as family or survivor's benefits, will fall within the scope of the Directive in so far as they constitute consideration for the worker by reason of the worker's employment. Article 5 sets out the principle of equal treatment in terms virtually identical to those of Article 4 of Directive 79/7, and Article 6, which has been amended to reflect cases such as *Coloroll* and *Neath*, above, and sets out ten examples of provisions which contravene the principle of equal treatment by discriminating on the basis of sex, or marital or family status.

Articles 7 and 8 impose specific obligations on Member States to take the necessary steps to ensure that provisions of schemes which contravene the equal-treatment principles will be annulled or amended, and, following the amending Directive 96/97, this must be by January 1993 at the latest in the case of self-employed workers. The

---

[320] See nn. 158–9 above and text, and n. 169 above and text.

The Commission, CFI, and ECJ have continued to take an *expansive view of the meaning of 'agreement'*. Thus, in *Polypropylene*,[15] the Commission held that there was a single agreement between firms in the petrochemical industry, which had continued over many years. It was willing to hold that there was such an overall agreement even though the agreement was oral, even though there were no sanctions for breach, and even though it was not legally binding. Moreover, the finding of a single overall agreement facilitated a finding of guilt against the fifteen firms involved, notwithstanding the fact that not all the firms had taken part in all aspects of the cartel. An agreement existed if the parties reached a consensus on a plan which limited, or was likely to limit, their commercial freedom by determining the lines of their mutual action or abstention from action in the market. The CFI upheld the Commission in this respect,[16] holding that the firms' pattern of conduct was in pursuit of a single economic aim, namely the distortion of the market in question. It would therefore be artificial to split up this continuous conduct into a number of separate infringements. The CFI has moreover held that for there to be an agreement within Article 85 (now Article 81) it was sufficient that the undertakings in question should have expressed their joint intention to conduct themselves on the market in a specific way. Such was the case where there were common intentions between undertakings to achieve price and sales-volume targets.[17] The CFI also decided[18] that if an undertaking participated[19] with others in the making of an agreement it is not open to that undertaking to argue that, because of its limited size, it could not have had a restrictive effect on competition. An agreement does, however, require the concurrence of will between at least two parties, as distinct from unilateral measures.[20]

The other way in which the Commission and CFI have tackled the problems flowing from complex cartels that extend over many years, with multiple participants, *is to frame the claim in terms of 'agreement and/or concerted practice'*. This strategy was upheld in *Limburgse Vinyl*.[21] The CFI stated that where there were complex infringements over many years, involving many parties, the Commission could not be expected to classify the infringement precisely for each undertaking at any given moment. The dual classification designated a complex whole, where some factual elements were relevant to an agreement, others to a concerted practice. This classification did not mean that the Commission had to prove that there was an agreement and a concerted practice throughout the whole period of the cartel.

---

[15] Dec. 86/398, [1986] OJ L230/1, [1988] 4 CMLR 347. See also Dec. 89/190, *PVC* [1989] OJ L74/1, [1990] 4 CMLR 345, reversed on other grounds in Case C–137/92P, *Commission v. BASF AG* [1994] ECR I–2555; *LdPE* [1989] OJ L74/21, [1990] 4 CMLR 382; *Italian Flat Glass* [1989] OJ L33/44, [1990] 4 CMLR 535.

[16] Case T–7/89, n. 4 above, paras. 262–264, upheld on appeal: Case C–51/92P, *Hercules Chemicals NV v. Commission* [1999] ECR I–4235; Case T–305/94, *NV Limburgse Vinyl Maatschappij v. Commission* [1999] ECR II–93, para. 773.

[17] Case T–9/89, *Huls AG v. Commission* [1992] ECR II–499; Case T–11/89, *Shell International Chemical Company Ltd. v. Commission* [1992] ECR II–757.

[18] Case T–143/89, *Ferriere Nord SpA v. Commission* [1995] ECR II–917; Case T–142/89, *Usines Gustave Boël SA v. Commission* [1995] ECR II–867.

[19] The participation need not be 'active'. It is sufficient if an undertaking attends the relevant meetings and does not publicly distance itself from what occurred, thereby giving the impression that it subscribes to the results of the meeting: Case T–142/89, n. 18 above.

[20] Case T–41/96, *Bayer AG v. Commission* [2000] ECR II–3383.

[21] Case T–305/94, *NV Limburgse Vinyl*, n. 16 above, paras. 695–698.

The ECJ, in *ANIC*,[22] has confirmed the approach set out in the preceding paragraphs. This is clearly correct. Any other interpretation would have allowed parties to such agreements to escape liability through the creation of impossible evidential barriers.[23]

(b) CONCERTED PRACTICES

Even if there is no agreement, the undertakings will still be caught by Article 81 if there is a concerted practice. Two principal factors have to be taken into account in deciding on the construction of such a term.

On the one hand, firms can be very devious. They may well have colluded, but they may have been astute enough to destroy all paper evidence. They may never have committed anything to paper at all, relying instead on understandings and verbal exchanges. The collusion may be real none the less, and the construction of a term such as concerted practice must be flexible enough to capture this 'fact' of business life.

On the other hand, if the term is interpreted too broadly it may catch, for example, parallel pricing that is a rational, natural response of firms in that type of market. In normal competitive markets, it is unlikely that firms will price at the same level without some species of collusion, because of differences in cost structures and the like. This may be different in oligopolistic markets, which have the following characteristics. There are relatively few sellers, and high barriers to entry, in the sense that it is difficult for new firms to enter the market. There is relatively little in the way of product-differentiation. There tends to be price transparency, in that price changes are easily detectable by competitors. It has been argued that firms in such markets will naturally end up pricing at the same level, not because of any collusion as such, but rather because each of the firms independently recognizes their mutual interdependence. If any firm attempted to increase its market share at the expense of another, by cutting prices, this would simply lead to a similar response from the others. There would be a downward spiral of prices, but no actual increase in market share for any of the firms involved. No firm could unilaterally increase price, because its customers would switch their trade to a competitor.[24] The relevance of this theory for the purposes of Article 81 is readily apparent. *If* price uniformity really is the result of rational, natural action in an oligopoly, and there is no actual collusion as such, then it is neither rational nor fair to penalize such parties through fines and the like for colluding. The problem is no longer *behavioural*, in the sense that the parties are engaging in behaviour different from that which would exist in normal circumstances

---

[22] Case C–49/92P, *Commission v. ANIC Partecipazioni SpA* [1999] ECR I–4125; Cases T–202, 204, 207/98, *Tate & Lyle plc, British Sugar plc and Napier Brown & Co. Ltd.* v. *Commission* [2001] ECR II–2035.

[23] See more generally the approach taken to the massive cement cartel in Cases T–25 etc/95, *Cimenteries CBR SA and others* v. *Commission* [2000] ECR II–491.

[24] Moreover, the uniformity of prices which is said to be expected in an oligopoly will, on this theory, arise even if the respective firms have differing cost structures, because the nature of the demand curve facing the industry assumes a peculiar 'kinked' form. See F. Scherer and Ross, n. 1 above, ch. 5; Sweezy, 'Demand under Conditions of Oligopoly' (1937) 47 *J Pol. Econ.* 568; G. Stigler, 'The Kinked Oligopoly Demand Curve' (1947) 55 *J Pol. Econ.* 431.

in that type of market. The problem is *structural*, in the sense that this type of market will naturally generate this type of response. On this view, if there is concern about the effects of oligopoly, then a structural solution should be sought to a structural problem.

The theory considered above has, however, been criticized. The following extract contains a succinct summary of this criticism.

R. Whish, Competition Law[25]

The theory of interdependence has attracted criticism. Four particular problems have been pointed out. The first is that the theory overstates the interdependence of oligopolists. Even in a symmetrical three-firm oligopoly one firm might be able to steal a march on its rivals by cutting its price if, for example, there would be a delay before the others discovered what it had done: in the meantime the price-cutter may make sufficient profit to offset the cost of any subsequent price-war. . . .

A second problem is that the theory of oligopoly presents too simplistic a picture of industrial market structures. In a symmetrical oligopoly where producers produce identical goods at the same costs interdependence may be strong, but in reality market conditions are more complex. The oligopolists themselves will almost inevitably have different cost levels; they may be producing differentiated goods and will usually command at least some consumer loyalty; and their market shares will not be equal. . . . Many other factors affect the competitive environment in which oligopolists operate. The concentration of the market on the buying side is also important: the more concentrated it is, the less the oligopolists might compete with one another since it will be relatively easy to detect attempts to attract the custom of particular customers. The transparency of price information is significant: the easier it is to conceal the price of goods from competitors, the less will be the interdependence or mutual awareness of the oligopolists. . . .

A third problem with the theory of interdependence is that it fails to explain why in some oligopolistic markets competition is intense. Firms quite clearly do compete with one another in some oligopolies. Such competition may take various forms. Open price competition may be limited, although price wars do break out periodically in some oligopolistic markets. . . . Where open price competition is restricted, this does not mean that secret price cutting does not occur. . . . Non-price competition may be particularly strong in oligopolistic markets. This may manifest itself in various ways: offering better quality products and after sales service; striving for a lead in technical innovation and research and development . . . ; and by making large investments in advertising to improve brand image. . . .

A fourth objection to the theory of oligopolistic interdependence is that it does not explain satisfactorily its central proposition, which is that oligopolists can earn supra-competitive profits without actually colluding. The interdependence theory says that they cannot increase price unilaterally because they will lose custom to their rivals, and yet to earn supra-competitive profits, prices must have been increased from time to time: how could this have been achieved without collusion? A possible answer to this is that a pattern of price leadership develops whereby one firm raises its price and this acts as a signal for the others to follow suit. Prices therefore remain parallel without conspiracy amongst the oligopolists, although this is not particularly convincing. . . .

[25] N. 6 above, 463–4.

Having analysed the economic problems with the term concerted practice we should now consider the leading ECJ decision.

Case 48/69, ICI v. Commission
[1972] ECR 619

[Note ToA renumbering: Art. 85 is now Art. 81]

The Court considered allegations that there had been concerted practices in the dyestuffs industry. As will be apparent from the extract which follows, the firms attempted to argue that any identity of price was the result of the oligopolistic nature of the market. The extract begins with the Court providing a definition of concerted practice.

THE ECJ

64. Article 85 draws a distinction between the concept of 'concerted practices' and that of 'agreements between undertakings' or of 'decisions by associations of undertakings'; the object is to bring within the prohibition of that Article a form of coordination between undertakings which, without having reached the stage where an agreement properly so-called has been concluded, knowingly substitutes practical cooperation between them for the risks of competition.

65. By its very nature, then, a concerted practice does not have all the elements of a contract but may inter alia arise out of coordination which becomes apparent from the behaviour of the participants.

66. Although parallel behaviour may not by itself be identified with a concerted practice, it may however amount to strong evidence of such practice if it leads to conditions of competition which do not correspond to the normal conditions of the market, having regard to the nature of the products, the size and number of the undertakings and the volume of the said market.

67. This is especially the case if the parallel conduct is such as to enable those concerned to attempt to stabilize prices at a level different from that to which competition would have led, and to consolidate established positions to the detriment of effective freedom of movement of the products in the Common Market and of the freedom of consumers to choose their suppliers.

68. Therefore the question whether there was concerted action in this case can only be correctly determined if the evidence upon which the contested decision is based is considered, not in isolation, but as a whole, account being taken of the specific features of the market in the products in question.

[The Court found that 80 per cent of the dyestuffs market was supplied by ten producers; that these firms possessed differing cost structures; that there were a large number of dyes produced by each firm; that while standard dyes could be replaced by other products relatively easily, this was not the case with specialist dyes; that the market for specialist dyes tended to be oligopolistic; that the Community market in dyestuffs consisted of five separate national markets which had different price levels; and that this division along national lines was in part due to the need to supply local assistance to users of the product, and also to ensure immediate delivery of quantities which were often small. The Court then considered price increases which occurred in 1964, 1965, and 1967. It found that the increases were factually connected, and then continued as follows:]

88. In 1964 all the undertakings in question announced their increases and immediately put them into effect, the initiative coming from Ciba-Italy which, on 7 January 1964, following instructions from Ciba-Switzerland, announced and immediately introduced an increase of 15 per cent. This initiative was followed by the other producers on the Italian market within two or three days.

89. On 9 January ICI Holland took the initiative in introducing the same increase in the Netherlands, whilst on the same day Bayer took the same initiative on the Belgo-Luxembourg market.

. . .

91. As regards the increase of 1965 certain undertakings announced in advance price increases amounting, for the German market, to an increase of 15 per cent for products whose prices had already been similarly increased on the other markets, and to 10 per cent for products whose prices had not yet been increased. These announcements were spread over the period between 14 October and 28 December 1964.

92. The first announcement was made by BASF, on 14 October 1964, followed by an announcement by Bayer on 30 October and by Casella on 5 November.

93. These increases were simultaneously applied on 1 January 1965 on all the markets except for the French market because of the price freeze in that State, and the Italian market where, as a result of the refusal by the principal Italian producer, ACNA, to increase its prices on the said market, the other producers also decided not to increase theirs.

. . .

95. Otherwise the increase was general, was simultaneously introduced by all the producers mentioned in the contested decision, and was applied without any differences concerning the range of products.

[*The Court then considered a similar pattern in relation to the 1967 price increases. It continued as follows:*]

99. Viewed as a whole, the three consecutive increases reveal progressive cooperation between the undertakings concerned.

100. In fact, after the experience of 1964, when the announcement of the increases and their application coincided, although with minor differences as regards the range of products affected, the increases of 1965 and 1967 indicate a different mode of operation. Here, the undertakings taking the initiative, BASF and Geigy respectively, announced their intentions of making an increase some time in advance, which allowed the undertakings to observe each other's reactions on the different markets, and to adapt themselves accordingly.

101. By means of these advance announcements the various undertakings eliminated all uncertainty between them as to their future conduct and, in doing so, also eliminated a large part of the risk usually inherent in any independent change of conduct on one or several markets.

102. This was all the more the case since these announcements, which led to the fixing of general and equal increases in prices for the markets in dyestuffs, rendered the market transparent as regard the percentage rates of increase.

. . .

104. The fact that this conduct was not spontaneous is corroborated by an examination of other aspects of the market.

105. In fact, from the number of producers concerned it is not possible to say that the European market in dyestuffs is, in the strict sense, an oligopoly in which price competition could no longer play a substantial role.

106. These producers are sufficiently powerful and numerous to create a considerable risk that in times of rising prices some of them might not follow the general movement but might instead try to increase their share of the market by behaving in an individual way.

107. Furthermore, the dividing up of the Common Market into five national markets with different price levels and structures makes it improbable that a spontaneous and equal price increase would occur on all the national markets.

. . .

109. Therefore, although parallel conduct in respect of prices may well have been an attractive and risk-free objective for the undertakings concerned, it is hardly conceivable that the same action could be taken spontaneously at the same time, on the same national markets and for the same range of products.

. . .

111. As regards the increases of 1965 and 1967 concertation took place openly, since all the announcements of the intention to increase prices with effect from a certain date and for a certain range of products made it possible for producers to decide on their conduct regarding the special cases of France and Italy.

112. In proceeding in this way, the undertakings mutually eliminated in advance any uncertainties concerning their reciprocal behaviour on the different markets and thereby also eliminated a large part of the risk inherent in any independent change of conduct on those markets.

113. The general and uniform increase on those different markets can only be explained by a common intention on the part of those undertakings, first, to adjust the level of prices and the situation resulting from competition in the form of discounts, and secondly, to avoid the risk, which is inherent in any price increase, of changing the conditions of competition.

The ECJ's approach emerges clearly in the above extract.[26] It is, moreover, clear from the *Sugar Cartel* case that there can be a concerted practice even though there is no actual 'plan' operative between the parties. The key idea was that each undertaking should operate independently on the market:[27]

Although it is correct to say that this requirement of independence does not deprive economic operators of the right to adapt themselves intelligently to the existing and anticipated conduct of their competitors, it does however strictly preclude any direct or indirect contact between such operators, the object or effect whereof is either to influence the conduct on the market of an actual or potential competitor or to disclose to such a competitor the course of conduct which they themselves have decided to adopt or contemplate adopting on the market.

Four points should be made about the concept of concerted practice and its application.

First, the formal burden of proving an infringement of Article 81 will rest with the Commission, and the mere existence of parallel conduct will not, in itself, be sufficient to prove the existence of a concerted practice. Thus, if the parties can show that,

---

[26] See also Case 172/80, *Gerhard Züchner* v. *Bayerische Vereinsbank AG* [1981] ECR 2021.

[27] Cases 40–48, etc./73, '*Suiker Unie*', n. 29 below, 1942; Cases T–202, 204, 207/98, *Tate & Lyle plc*, n. 22 above; Case IV/34.503, *Commission* v. *P & O European Ferries Ltd.* [1997] OJ L26/23, [1997] 4 CMLR 798.

although there is parallel behaviour, there are explanations for what has taken place other than the existence of concertation then they may be exonerated.[28] It is equally the case that the Court will investigate whether there really is 'room' for the competition rules to operate in a particular context.[29]

Secondly, the Court will not lightly accede to an argument that uniformity of price has been produced as the result of oligopolistic market structure. If the facts do not indicate that the market structure will naturally lead to price uniformity, *and* if there are other factors which are indicative of collusion, then the onus may effectively shift to the firms to suggest how the identity of price came about without some element of concertation.

Thirdly, there can, however, be differences of opinion on which side of the line a case falls. In *Wood Pulp*[30] the Commission considered allegations of concerted practices by a large number of producers of wood pulp. In reaching the conclusion that there was a concerted practice, the Commission was strongly influenced by the nature of the market. It felt that this was not oligopolistic in nature, since there were a large number of firms operating on the market. The fact that they charged similar prices, and made uniform alterations to them simultaneously, was itself *prima facie* evidence that they were acting in concert. A significant part of the Commission's findings was annulled by the ECJ.[31] It held that parallel conduct cannot be regarded as proof of concertation unless concertation constituted the only plausible explanation for the conduct. Article 85 (now Article 81) did not deprive firms of the ability to adapt their behaviour intelligently to that of their competitors.[32] It held, moreover, that the parallelism of the prices and the price trends could satisfactorily be explained by the oligopolistic tendencies of the market and the specific circumstances prevailing during the relevant period.[33] In the long term the Court's decision may be of most significance in its insistence that rigorous economic analysis may be required in order to determine whether there is another plausible explanation for the parties' conduct. In the absence of some form of overt communication between the parties, the Commission will have to be ready to defend its assumptions against experts who can suggest some innocent explanation for the challenged behaviour.[34]

The *Polypropylene* cases provide a good contrast to *Wood Pulp*. In a series of

---

[28] Cases 29 & 30/83, *Compagnie Royale Asturienne*, n. 13 above.

[29] Cases 40–48, 50, 54–56, 111, 113 & 114/73, *Cooperatiëve Vereniging 'Suiker Unie' UA* v. *Commission* [1975] ECR 1663, 1916–24, the ECJ found that the degree of state regulation of the Italian sugar market left no appreciable room in which Art. 85 (now Art. 81) could operate; in Case C–219/95P, *Ferriere Nord SpA* v. *Commission* [1997] ECR I–4411, and Cases T–202, 204, 207/98, *Tate & Lyle plc*, n. 22 above, an analogous argument was rejected.

[30] Dec. 85/202, [1985] OJ L85/1, [1985] 3 CMLR 474.

[31] Cases 89, 104, 114, 116–17, 125–9/85, *A. Ahlström Oy* v. *Commission* [1993] ECR I–1307. See also Case T–36/91, *Imperial Chemical Industries plc* v. *Commission* [1995] ECR II–1847.

[32] *Ibid.*, para. 71.

[33] *Ibid.*, paras. 126–127. It may have been no coincidence that the *juge rapporteur* in *Wood Pulp* was Joliet who had, a number of years earlier, expressed misgivings about the possible impact of the *Dyestuffs* case: R. Joliet, 'La Notion de Pratique Concertée et l'Arrêt dans une Perspective Comparative' [1974] CDE 251.

[34] G. van Gerven and E. N. Varona, 'The *Wood Pulp* Case and the Future of Concerted Practices' (1994) 31 *CMLRev.* 575; F. Alese, 'The Economic Theory of Non-Collusive Oligopoly and the Concept of Concerted Practice under Article 81' [1999] *ECLR* 379.

decisions the CFI cited the definition of concerted practice given in the *Sugar Cartel* case. It held that participation in meetings concerning the fixing of price and sales-volume targets during which information was exchanged between competitors about the prices which they intended to charge, their profitability thresholds, the sales volumes they judged to be necessary, or their sales figures constituted a concerted practice. This was because the participant undertakings could not fail to take account of the information thus disclosed in determining their conduct on the market.[35] The CFI took a similarly strident view in relation to a number of cases concerned with *Welded Steel Mesh*, holding that the exchange of information between competing undertakings that might be used to establish a cartel itself constituted a concerted practice.[36] This was particularly so in relation to exchange of information by parties to a cartel concerning their respective deliveries, since such information could be used to monitor the effective operation of the cartel.[37]

Fourthly, there is the interesting issue of whether a concerted practice must have been put into effect. If the answer were to be in the affirmative then the mere meeting of competitors to exchange information, without this producing any cognizable impact on the market, would not amount to a concerted practice. This issue was addressed in *Huls*.

Case C–199/92P, Huls AG v. Commission
[1999] ECR I–4287

[Note ToA renumbering: Art. 85 is now Art. 81]

This case was one of the appeals from the CFI to the ECJ resulting from the *Polypropylene* decision of the Commission. The Commission had found that there was a concerted practice of fixing prices on this market. Huls argued that there was a lack of proof of conduct on the market corresponding to a concerted practice. The ECJ set out the definition of concerted practice, and then continued as follows.

THE ECJ

161. It follows, first, that the concept of a concerted practice . . . implies, besides undertakings' concerting with each other, subsequent conduct on the market, and a relationship of cause and effect between the two.

162. However, subject to proof to the contrary, which the economic operators concerned must adduce, the presumption must be that the undertakings taking part in the concerted action and remaining active on the market take account of the information exchanged with their competitors

---

[35] Case T–11/89, *Shell International*, n. 17 above. See also Cases T–202, 204, 207/98, *Tate & Lyle plc*, n. 22 above.

[36] Case T–142/89, *Boël*, n. 18 above. See also Cases IV/33.126 and IV/33.322, *Cement Cartel*, n. 5 above.

[37] Case T–148/89, *Tréfilunion SA v. Commission* [1995] ECR II–1063.

for the purposes of determining their conduct on that market. This is all the more true where the undertakings concert together on a regular basis over a long period, as was the case here. . . .

163. Secondly, contrary to Huls's argument, a concerted practice . . . is caught by Article 81(1) EC, even in the absence of anti-competitive effects on the market.

164. . . . it follows from the actual text of that provision that . . . concerted practices are prohibited regardless of their effect, when they have an anti-competitive object.

165. . . . although the very concept of a concerted practice presupposes conduct by the participating undertakings on the market, it does not necessarily mean that that conduct should produce the specific effect of restricting, preventing or distorting competition.

. . .

166. Consequently, contrary to Huls's argument, the Court of First Instance was not in breach of the rules applying to the burden of proof when it considered that, since the Commission had established to the requisite legal standard that Huls had taken part polypropylene producers' concerting together for the purpose of restricting competition, it did not have to adduce evidence that their concerting together had manifested itself in conduct on the market or that it had effects restrictive of competition; on the contrary, it was for Huls to prove that that did not have any influence whatsoever on its own conduct on the market.

6. THE OBJECT OR EFFECT OF PREVENTING, RESTRICTING, OR DISTORTING COMPETITION

Article 81(1) requires that the agreement, decision, or concerted practice has the object or effect of preventing, restricting, or distorting competition in the Common Market. The interpretation of this phrase has generated a significant body of litera-ture, with rival views on what the Court is, and what it should be, doing under this Article.

(a) THE NATURE OF THE PROBLEM

Article 81(1) captures *all* agreements, concerted practices, etc., which have as their object or effect the prevention etc. of competition. This immediately presents us with two related problems.

The first is that all contracts concerning trade impose restraints in some manner, 'to bind, to restrain is of their very essence'.[38] Now one could in theory stipulate that every contract was caught by the rules on competition law, but this would be both absurd and impractical. The problem is therefore to find the best way of resolving this conundrum.

The second problem is that an agreement may have features that both enhance and restrict competition. Imagine that a supplier wishes to break into a new market, and decides to use Brown as its distributor for a particular area. Brown may only be willing to risk marketing the new product if she is given certain incentives and protec-tion. This may take the form of a commitment from the supplier that it will not supply any other firm in the same area. There is undoubtedly some restriction of

---

[38] *Chicago Board of Trade v. US*, 246 US 231 (1918).

competition, in the sense that the supplier has undertaken not to sell to any firm other than Brown in the designated area. However, the whole agreement may enhance competition, since there is now a new product being marketed in the relevant area, which could be marketed *only* under these conditions.

The appropriate response to these related problems is contentious. A central aspect of this debate has been the extent to which the EC should follow the approach in the United States, and utilize a distinction between a rule of reason and *per se* rules, as a method of tackling these problems. A brief glance at the US experience is, therefore, necessary in order to understand the diversity of opinion in the EC.

(b) THE EXPERIENCE IN THE UNITED STATES

The dilemmas identified above are evident in section 1 of the Sherman Act, which states that every contract, combination, or conspiracy in restraint of trade is illegal. Did section 1 really render illegal every restraint of trade, did this embrace ordinary contracts, and was it possible to make trade-offs between the pro- and anti-competitive effects of an agreement? There was a range of answers to these questions.

One response was to use the language of ancillary restraints. If the restraint was deemed to be merely ancillary to the main purpose of a lawful contract, as in the case of a covenant on sale which imposed reasonable limits on the freedom of action of the covenantee, then it would be lawful. If the restraint was solely to limit competition then it would be illegal.[39]

Another response was to use the rule of reason. In *Standard Oil* v. *US* White CJ stated that a standard of reason had to be applied in order to determine whether a restraint was within the Sherman Act, and that only undue or unreasonable restraints should be condemned.[40] The precise meaning of this emergent idea was contested, and this is still the case even today.[41] The analysis mandated by the concept does, however, appear to demand a broad inquiry into whether the restrictions in the agreement increase or decrease competition in the market as a whole. The pro- and anti-competitive effects of the agreement are weighed in order to determine whether the agreement suppresses or promotes competition.[42] There is still controversy on two related matters.

There is, as will be seen below,[43] continuing disagreement on what the effects of particular types of agreement actually are, and therefore whether they should be prohibited or not.

There is disagreement on the range of considerations which should be taken into account within this analysis. For some this should be restricted to factors of a strictly

---

[39] *US* v. *Addystone Pipe and Steel Co.*, 175 US 211 (1889).
[40] 221 US 1 (1911).
[41] R. Bork, 'The Rule of Reason and the Per Se Concept: Price Fixing and Market Division' (1965) 74 *Yale LJ* 775; T. Piraino, 'Reconciling the Per Se Rule and the Rule of Reason Approaches to Antitrust Analysis' (1991) 45 *So. Cal. L. Rev.* 689 and 'Making Sense of the Rule of Reason: A New Standard for Section 1 of the Sherman Act' (1994) 48 *Vand. L. Rev.* 1770; O. Black, 'Per Se Rules and Rules of Reason: What are They?' [1997] *ECLR* 145; T. Calvani, 'Some Thoughts on the Rule of Reason' [2001] *ECLR* 201.
[42] *National Society of Professional Engineers* v. *US*, 435 US 679, 691–2 (1978).
[43] See Ch. 22 below.

economic nature. Others advocate a more wide-ranging inquiry, or are willing to ascribe economic value to social factors.[44]

Properly understood, *per se* rules develop from a rule-of-reason analysis. The relationship is as follows. The type of market inquiry demanded by the rule of reason may be time-consuming and costly. With the passage of time the courts came to identify certain types of agreement which were conclusively presumed to be 'without redeeming virtue' and which had a 'pernicious effect on competition'. The courts condemned these without the need for any elaborate inquiry into whether they had an impact on the market. Not surprisingly the types of cases held to fall within this category were those which were most obviously anti-competitive, such as horizontal price-fixing[45] and market division.[46] In these instances proof of the agreement was sufficient to condemn it, obviating the need for more detailed market investigation.[47]

(c) THE ACADEMIC DEBATE IN THE EC

There is an interesting debate about whether we should resolve the problems outlined above by adopting a rule of reason within Community law. Two factors should be noted in order to understand the materials which follow.

The first is that the EC has a mechanism, Article 81(3) (ex Article 85(3)), whereby agreements that are held to restrict competition can be exempted following an economic analysis. No such provision exists in the United States, and this renders the need for some species of rule-of-reason analysis more necessary in that country.

The second point to note is that national courts are able to apply Article 81(1) (ex Article 85(1)), but they could not apply Article 81(3). The Commission initiative to modernize EC competition policy will alter this.[48] References to Article 85 within these extracts should now be read as to Article 81.

V. Korah, The Rise and Fall of Provisional Validity—The Need for a Rule of Reason in EEC Antitrust[49]

The Community Court and Commission have not developed the same theory of per se offences so brilliantly developed in the early cases under the Sherman Act. Naked restraints on pricing, market sharing, and some kinds of collective boycott . . . are likely to be condemned with fairly

---

[44] Compare R. Bork, *The Antitrust Paradox: A Policy at War with Itself* (Basic Books, 1978) with E. Fox, 'The Modernization of Antitrust: A New Equilibrium' (1981) 66 *Cornell L Rev.* 1140 and 'The Politics of Law and Economics' (1986) 61 *NYUL Rev.* 554.

[45] *US* v. *Trenton Potteries Co.*, 273 US 392 (1927).

[46] *US* v. *Topco Associates*, 405 US 596 (1972).

[47] Because classification as a price-fixing agreement can have these serious consequences the courts will, on occasion, strive to avoid characterizing a case in this way, if they believe that it has redeeming features, notwithstanding an element of price control: *National Collegiate Athletic Assn.* v. *Board of Regents of the University of Oklahoma*, 468 US 85 (1984); *Broadcast Music Inc.* v. *Columbia Broadcasting Systems Inc.*, 441 US 1 (1979).

[48] See Ch. 25 below.

[49] (1981) 3 *NW J Int. L and Bus.* 320, 354–5. See also I. Forrester and C. Norall, 'The Laicization of Community Law: Self-Help and the Rule of Reason: How Competition Law is and Could be Applied' (1984) 21 *CMLRev.* 11.

short reasoning if they are found capable of restricting trade between Member States, but more market analysis is required in the case of ancillary restraints. In *Consten & Grundig*, the Court seems to have developed a per se rule against absolute territorial protection conferred by export bans . . ., and this has been consistently applied by the Commission, despite mounting criticism. For all other restraints, however, the Court seems to be applying a rule of reason, requiring an analysis of the actual or intended effects in the light of market conditions.

The Commission, however, habitually analyzes agreements under Article 85(1) in the formalistic way developed by the German case law . . . and condemns any restriction on the conduct of the parties, or third parties, provided the restriction has, or may be expected to have, appreciable effects on the market. Only under Article 85(3) does the Commission usually try to balance any pro-and anti-competitive effects.

If national courts adopt the Commission's practice, it is feared that many desirable contracts which restrict only competition that could not take place without such an agreement, or which restrict competition less than they increase it, may not be made. The Commission grants few exemptions. . . . Important agreements are unlikely to be exempted unless certain clauses are altered. These alterations may help one party more than the other, and the whole contract may have to be renegotiated after the parties have been implementing it, when their relative bargaining power may have been altered as a result of the collaboration. This is a considerable disincentive to notification.

. . .

There is fear that European firms that may have to compete in world markets may fall behind technologically or have to merge completely, so as to reduce the risk of collaboration. Market analyses are difficult, especially for lawyers and bureaucrats. But if such analyses are not made, agreements that may have overall desirable consequences should not be controlled. This means that national courts will have to be strong in resisting claims that agreements are anti-competitive just because some competitor is harmed.

Calls for a rule of reason within Article 81(1) have come from a number of other sources.[50] In order for there to be a debate there must, of course, be an opposing view. The work of Whish and Sufrin represents the most complete statement of the contrasting view. There are a number of aspects to their argument. One is that the case law of the Court does not, properly understood, signify acceptance of a rule of reason in EC law; or that, at the least, differing labels express the essence of what the ECJ is doing better than the simple adoption of labels from the United States. This aspect of the matter will be considered below.[51] A second aspect of their thesis is that there are very real differences between the antitrust laws of the United States and the EC, which render any transfer of terminology of limited utility.[52]

---

[50] See, e.g., R. Joliet, *The Rule of Reason in Antitrust Law: American, German and Common Market Laws in Comparative Perspective* (Faculté de Droit, Liège, 1967); M. Schecter, 'The Rule of Reason in European Competition Law' [1982] 2 *LIEI* 1; V. Korah, 'EEC Competition Policy—Legal Form or Economic Efficiency' (1986) 39 *CLP* 85; Forrester and Norall, n. 49 above.

[51] See 954–61 below.

[52] (1987) 7 *YBEL* 12–20.

R. Whish and B. Sufrin, Article 85 and the Rule of Reason[53]

The call for the adoption of a US-style rule of reason should be resisted and, indeed, there is much to be said for dropping this term (and the terms 'ancillary restraint' and 'per se illegality') from EEC antitrust law altogether, on the basis that they do more to confuse than to clarify. EEC competition law requires its own vocabulary, carefully honed to express its own particular tensions.

One ground for jettisoning the term 'rule of reason' from the vocabulary of EEC competition law is that it is now used in other areas of the law, for example, in the provisions on free movement of goods. . . .

A different reason for abandoning this terminology in EEC competition law is that it invites misleading comparison with antitrust law analysis in the United States. We have suggested above that the context of US antitrust law is so dissimilar from that of the EEC that comparative analysis should be undertaken with great caution.

Quite apart from the issue of terminology, the writers have other doubts about the wisdom of analysing Article 85(1) in a way that relies on an approach similar to that of the Sherman Act. It would not help the cause of certainty.

. . .

The matter of certainty is, of course, important. It is in no one's interest to retard beneficial collaboration between firms striving to compete in a competitive international market. However, the best answer to this problem is for the Commission to continue to improve its procedures, to publish block exemptions where this is possible, and to develop such notions as objective necessity and potential competition. We also expect its sophistication in dealing with economics to continue to improve, but do not consider that this goes hand in hand with rule-of-reason analysis. This would stifle the proper application of Article 85 which, precisely because of its more ample wording, does not bear the same intellectual burden that the words 'restraint of trade' do in the Sherman Act. We doubt, too, that it would be helpful to draw the national courts further into the application of Article 85 by asking them to undertake extensive economic analysis under Article 85(1). We are happy for them to enforce the competition rules against blatant cartels and abuses of a dominant position. We do not consider them to be appropriate fora for deciding upon complex economic issues.

(d) THE CASE LAW IN THE EC

The academic debate provides a fitting framework within which to evaluate the case law of the ECJ. In reading the materials which follow two matters should be borne in mind. How far is the Court balancing the pro- and anti-competitive effects of an agreement to determine whether it is caught within Article 81(1) (ex Article 85(1)), and how far is the terminology of the rule of reason an apt way of describing this approach?

---

[53] *Ibid.*, 36–7.

Case 56/65, Société Technique Minière v. Maschinenbau Ulm GmbH
[1966] ECR 235

[Note ToA renumbering: Art. 85 is now Art. 81]

The case concerned an exclusive supply contract, whereby STM had the exclusive right to sell in France certain grading equipment produced by Maschinenbau Ulm (MBU), a German undertaking. The contract did not, however, insulate the French territory: STM could sell the goods outside France, and parallel imports could be obtained from other countries. A contract dispute between STM and MBU led the former to argue that this contract was invalid under Article 85.

THE ECJ

Finally, for the agreement at issue to be caught by the prohibition contained in Article 85(1) it must have as its 'object or effect the prevention, restriction or distortion of competition within the Common Market'.

The fact that these are not cumulative but alternative requirements, indicated by the conjunction 'or', leads first to the need to consider the precise purpose of the agreement, in the economic context in which it is to be applied. This interference with competition referred to in Article 85(1) must result from all or some of the clauses of the agreement itself. Where, however, an analysis of the said clauses does not reveal the effect on competition to be sufficiently deleterious, the consequences of the agreement should then be considered and for it to be caught by the prohibition it is then necessary to find that those factors are present which show that competition has in fact been prevented or restricted or distorted to an appreciable extent.

The competition in question must be understood within the actual context in which it would occur in the absence of the agreement in dispute. In particular it may be doubted whether there is an interference with competition if the said agreement seems really necessary for the penetration of a new area by an undertaking. Therefore, in order to decide whether an agreement containing a clause 'granting an exclusive right of sale' is to be considered as prohibited by reason of its object or its effect, it is appropriate to take into account in particular the nature and quantity, limited or otherwise, of the products covered by the agreement, the position and importance of the grantor and the concessionaire on the market for the products concerned, the isolated nature of the disputed agreement or, alternatively, its position in a series of agreements, the severity of the clauses intended to protect the exclusive dealership or, alternatively, the opportunities allowed for other commercial competitors in the same products by way of parallel re-exportation and importation.

Cases 56 and 58/64, Etablissements Consten SARL and
Grundig-Verkaufs-GmbH v. Commission
[1966] ECR 299

[Note ToA renumbering: Art. 85 is now Art. 81]

Grundig granted to Consten a sole distributorship for its electronic products in France. Consten had an obligation to take a minimum amount of the product; it had to provide publicity and after-sales service; and it undertook not to sell the products of competing manufacturers. Moreover, the

French territory was in effect insulated, in the sense that there was absolute territorial protection. Consten undertook not to sell the goods outside the contract territory. A similar prohibition existed on other Grundig distributors in other countries. Grundig assigned to Consten its trademark, GINT, which Consten could use against any unauthorized sales in France. In 1961 a company called UNEF bought Grundig goods from sellers in Germany and sold them in France more cheaply than Consten. The latter brought an action for infringement of its trademark, and UNEF contended that the whole agreement between Grundig and Consten violated Article 85.

THE ECJ

The applicants and the German Government maintain that since the Commission restricted its examination solely to Grundig products the decision was based upon a false concept of competition . . . contained in Article 85(1), since this concept applies particularly to competition between similar products of different makes; the Commission, before declaring Article 85(1) to be applicable, should, by basing itself upon the 'rule of reason', have considered the economic effects of the disputed contract upon competition between the different makes. There is a presumption that vertical sole distributorship agreements are not harmful to competition and in the present case there is nothing to invalidate that presumption. On the contrary, the contract in question has increased the competition between similar products of different makes.

The principle of freedom of competition concerns the various stages and manifestations of competition. Although competition between producers is generally more noticeable than that between distributors of products of the same make, it does not thereby follow that an agreement tending to restrict the latter kind of competition should escape the prohibition of Article 85(1) merely because it might increase the former.

Besides, for the purpose of applying Article 85(1), there is no need to take account of the concrete effects of an agreement once it appears that it has as its object the prevention, restriction or distortion of competition.

Therefore, the absence in the contested decision of any analysis of the effects of the agreement on competition between similar products of different makes does not, of itself, constitute a defect in the decision.

[The Court considered the system of absolute territorial protection established by the agreement between Consten and Grundig. It then continued as follows:]

The situation as ascertained above results in the isolation of the French market and makes it possible to charge for the products in question prices which are sheltered from all effective competition. . . . Because of the considerable impact of distribution costs on the aggregate cost price, it seems important that competition between dealers should also be stimulated. The efforts of the dealer are stimulated by competition between distributors of products of the same make. Since the agreement thus aims at isolating the French market for Grundig products and maintaining artificially, for products of a very-well known brand, separate national markets within the Community, it is therefore such as to distort competition in the Common Market.

It was therefore proper for the contested decision to hold that the agreement constitutes an infringement of Article 85(1). No further considerations, whether of economic data . . . or of the correctness of the criteria upon which the Commission relied in its comparisons between the situations of the French and German markets, and no possible favourable effects of the agreement in other respects, can in any way lead, in the face of the above-mentioned restrictions, to a different solution under Article 85(1).

The preceding case law of the ECJ on the meaning of the terms 'object or effect' can be summarized as follows.

It is clear from the *STM* case that the Court, even at this early date, accepted that the words of Article 85 (now Article 81) were to be read disjunctively: if the object or purpose of the agreement was anti-competitive then it could be condemned without pressing further.[54] Agreements that are particularly heinous and indefensible, such as horizontal price-fixing, market-division, collective boycotts, and the like would be condemned without any further analysis of the market circumstances.[55] If one were using the language of the United States courts, such agreements would be *per se* illegal. This reading of Article 85 (now Article 81) is confirmed by *Ferriere Nord*.[56]

Where the anti-competitive quality of an agreement is not evident from its object then one must press further and consider its effects,[57] as has been emphasized in the *Delimitis* case.[58] The contrast between *STM* and *Consten and Grundig* is instructive in this respect. It is clear that the *STM* case does countenance some species of economic analysis within Article 85(1) (now Article 81(1)). It is clear also that the ECJ took into account the fact that the exclusive-supply contract may have been a necessary step in allowing MBU to penetrate the French market; *and* that this was something to be encouraged. The response of the ECJ in *Consten and Grundig* to the argument concerning the rule of reason must be seen in the light of the facts of that case. The parties sought to use that doctrine as a basis for legitimating a scheme that gave absolute territorial protection to the French distributor. Now it might well be the case that if one were engaging in a pure economic analysis, which involved trade-offs between the pro- and anti-competitive effects of an agreement, then even absolute territorial protection might be warranted.[59] However, the Community rules on competition have been strongly influenced by the desire to create a single market. Agreements which contain provisions that have the effect of partitioning the market along national lines will, therefore, be treated harshly by the ECJ. The *Consten and Grundig* case should not be perceived as rejecting economic analysis within Article 85(1), but rather as indicating that such analysis cannot serve to validate absolute territorial protection. Economic analysis is apparent in a number of other ECJ decisions.[60] The *Nungesser* case furnishes a further example of this approach.

[54] O. Odudu, 'Interpreting Article 81(1): Object as Subjective Intention' (2001) 26 *ELRev*. 60.

[55] See also Case 45/85, *Verband der Sachversicherer eV* v. *Commission* [1987] ECR 405, para. 39; Case T–77/92, *Parker Pen Ltd.* v. *Commission* [1994] ECR II–549; Case T–66/92, *Herlitz AG* v. *Commission* [1994] ECR II–531; Cases T–374, 375, 384, 388/94, *European Night Services* v. *Commission* [1998] ECR II–3141, para. 136.

[56] Case C–219/95P, *Ferriere Nord SpA* v. *Commission* [1997] ECR I–4411.

[57] Case 23/67, *Brasserie de Haecht SA* v. *Wilkin* [1967] ECR 407; Case 5/69, *Völk* v. *Vervaecke* [1969] ECR 295; Case T–7/93, *Langnese-Iglo GmbH* v. *Commission* [1995] ECR II–1533. See O. Odudu, 'Interpreting Article 81(1): Demonstrating Restrictive Effect' (2001) 26 *ELRev*. 261.

[58] Case C–234/89, *Delimitis* v. *Henninger Bräu AG* [1991] ECR I–935.

[59] The protection might be necessary to enable the manufacturer to penetrate a new market, and any reduction in intra-brand competition (competition between distributors of the same product) would be more than offset by an increase in inter-brand competition (competition between those who distribute goods of the same kind, e.g., different brands of stereo equipment).

[60] Case 262/81, *Coditel SA* v. *Ciné-Vog Films SA* [1982] ECR 3381.

which have as their purpose to guarantee a uniform image corresponding to specified requirements.

. . .

21. Thanks to the control exercised by the franchisor over the selection of goods offered by the franchisee, the public can find at each franchisee's shop merchandise of the same quality. . . . A clause prescribing that the franchisee can only sell products provided by the franchisor or by suppliers selected by him must, in these circumstances, be considered necessary for the protection of the reputation of the network. It must not, however, operate to prevent the franchisee from obtaining the products from other franchisees.

There are other cases that take the same approach. Thus, in *Remia*[61] it was held that non-competition clauses included in the sale of an undertaking would not come within Article 85(1) (now Article 81(1)). Such clauses were necessary to give effect to the sale, since otherwise the vendor, with his specialist knowledge of the transferred undertaking, could simply win back the custom from the purchaser of that undertaking. Clauses of this type could, therefore, enhance competition by leading to an increase in the number of undertakings on the relevant market. This will, however, exclude only certain clauses from the operation of Article 85(1). Thus, in the *Remia* case the Court held that the non-competition clause must be limited in time and scope,[62] while in *Pronuptia*,[63] the Court decided that certain clauses were not necessary for the integrity of the franchise agreement and were restrictive of competition within Article 85(1).

Notwithstanding the above the CFI, in the clearest judgment to date, has denied that there is a rule of reason as such within Article 81(1).

Case T–112/99, Métropole Télévision (M6), Suez-Lyonnaise des Eaux, France Telecom, and Television Française 1 SA (TFI) v. Commission
September 18, 2001

[Note ToA renumbering: Art. 85 is now Art. 81]

The applicant companies sought to annul a Commission decision relating to the creation of TPS, a company providing digital satellite television for payment. The agreement had an exclusivity clause, whereby the general-interest channels provided by the applicants would be broadcast exclusively by TPS. The applicants argued, based on cases such as *Nungesser*, that the Commission should have applied Article 85(1), in the light of the rule of reason, to this clause. There were already strong companies on the pay TV market, into which TPS was seeking to gain entry.

---

[61] Case 42/84, *Remia BV and Verenigde Bedrijven Nutricia NV v. Commission* [1985] ECR 2545; Case C–250/92, *Gottrup-Klim Grovvareforeninger v. Dansk Landburgs Grovvareselskab AmbA* [1994] ECR I–5641.

[62] Case 42/84, n. 61 above.

[63] Case 161/84, [1986] ECR 353, 382–5. This was particularly the case for those clauses which partitioned the market between franchisor and franchisee, or between franchisees themselves. Thus, the obligation on the franchisor not to allow other franchisees to open shops outside their allotted territory was held to fall foul of the *Consten and Grundig* principle. The fact that such a clause might be necessary for any franchisee to make the initial investment was recognized by the Court, but was considered to be of relevance only within Art. 85(3).

72. According to the applicants, as a consequence of the existence of the rule of reason in Community competition law, when Article 85(1) . . . is applied it is necessary to weigh the pro- and anti-competitive effects of an agreement in order to determine whether it is caught by the prohibition laid down in that article. It should, however, be observed, first of all, that contrary to the applicants' assertions the existence of such a rule has not, as such, been confirmed by the Community courts. Quite the contrary, in various judgments the Court of Justice and Court of First Instance have been at pains to indicate that the existence of a rule of reason in Community law is doubtful (see Case C–235/92, *Montecatini* . . . [1999] ECR I–4539, paragraph 133 . . . Case T–148/89, *Tréfilunion* [1995] ECR II–1063, paragraph 109).

73. Next, it must be observed that an interpretation of Article 85(1) . . ., in the form suggested by the applicants, is difficult to reconcile with the rules prescribed by that provision.

74. Article 85 . . . expressly provides, in its third paragraph, for the possibility of exempting agreements that restrict competition where they satisfy a number of conditions. . . . It is only in the precise framework of that provision that the pro- and anti-competitive effects of a restriction may be weighed (see . . . *Pronuptia* paragraph 24 . . . and *European Night Services* paragraph 136). Article 85(3) would lose much of its effectiveness if such an examination had to be carried out already under Article 85(1). . . .

75. It is true that in a number of judgments the Court of Justice and the Court of First Instance have favoured a more flexible interpretation of the prohibition laid down in Article 85(1) (see . . . *STM* . . . *Nungesser* . . . *Coditel* . . . *Pronuptia* . . . *European Night Services* . . .).

76. Those judgments cannot, however, be interpreted as establishing the existence of a rule of reason in Community competition law. They are, rather, part of a broader trend in the case law according to which it is not necessary to hold, wholly abstractly and without drawing any distinction, that any agreement restricting the freedom of action of one or more of the parties is necessarily caught by . . . Article 85(1). . . . In assessing the applicability of Article 85(1) to an agreement, account should be taken of the actual conditions in which it functions, in particular the economic context in which the undertakings operate, the products or services covered by the agreement and the actual structure of the market concerned. . . .

77. . . . It must, however, be emphasized that such an approach does not mean that it is necessary to weigh the pro- and anti-competitive effects of an agreement when determining whether . . . Article 85(1) . . . applies.

(e) SUMMARY: ECONOMIC ANALYSIS WITHIN ARTICLE 81(1)

i. It is reasonably clear that the ECJ condemns certain types of agreement on the basis of their object or purpose without any extensive market analysis, and in this sense it effectively proscribes these agreements as *per se* illegal. It is also clear that the Court has engaged in some form of economic analysis within Article 85(1) (now Article 81(1)). While the Court has not employed the language of the rule of reason, there is evidence of a balancing of the pro- and anti-competitive effects of an agreement, subject to the caveats made above.

ii. The reasoning in *Métropole* is not convincing for two reasons. First, the CFI's rationalization of the prior case law does not withstand scrutiny. The ECJ and the CFI have considered the entire economic context precisely because it is only by doing so that it is possible to tell whether, for example, a clause restricting conduct should none the less be allowed, because it enables a party to break into the market. It is for this reason that such restrictions on freedom of action are not restrictive of competition. The Community courts have, in this sense, balanced the pro- and anti-competitive effects of the agreement. The exclusivity clause in *Métropole* was designed to give subscribers something attractive so as to enable TPS to break into a market where there was strong competition. Secondly, the reasoning assumes that a rule of reason is incompatible with the existence of Article 81(3). It is however perfectly possible to balance the pro- and anti-competitive effects of an agreement within Article 81(1), and still to preserve a role for Article 81(3).[64]

iii. The Commission has not been enthusiastic about economic analysis in the past, and it has been criticized for equating a restriction on conduct with a restriction on competition. This is clearly mistaken, since restriction of competition is an economic concept, which must be assessed in relation to a market. It is unclear how far its approach has changed. In the *White Paper on Modernization*[65] the Commission stated that it has adopted the ECJ's approach in *Nungesser*[66] and *Pronuptia*[67] and balanced the pro- and anti-competitive effects of an agreement within Article 81(1) in relation to some restrictive practices. It however went on to say that any more systematic use of such rule-of-reason analysis under Article 81(1) would mean that Article 81(3) would be 'cast aside'. The Commission said that this would be paradoxical, given that Article 81(3) contains all the elements of a rule of reason.[68] This reasoning, although it derives support from the CFI in *Métropole*, has been vigorously contested. It has been argued that a more thoroughgoing balancing of pro- and anti-competitive effects within Article 81(1) would be beneficial, and would still leave room for a distinctive role for Article 81(3).[69]

7. THE EFFECT ON TRADE BETWEEN MEMBER STATES

In order for Article 81(1) to apply, the agreement etc. must have an effect on trade between Member States. If this hurdle is not satisfied the matter will remain within the jurisdiction of the relevant Member State. The hurdle has not, however, proven difficult for the Court to surmount. It has adopted a broad test and applied it in a similar fashion. The ECJ held, in *STM*, that the test was whether it was possible to 'foresee with a sufficient degree of probability on the basis of a set of objective factors

---

[64] R. Wesseling, 'The Commission White Paper on Modernisation of EC Antitrust Law: Unspoken Consequences and Incomplete Alternative Options' [1999] *ECLR* 420

[65] *White Paper on the Modernisation of the Rules Implementing Articles 85 and 86 of the EC Treaty*, Comm. Programme 99/027, para. 57.

[66] Case 258/78, [1982] ECR 2015.   [67] Case 161/84, [1986] ECR 353.

[68] *White Paper*, n. 65 above, para. 57.   [69] Wesseling, n. 64 above.

of law or of fact that the agreement in question may have an influence, direct or indirect, actual or potential, on the pattern of trade between Member States'.[70] The latitude of the test is apparent from its principal parts. The ability to focus on potential or indirect effects on trade means that it will be very rare for the Community to lack jurisdiction. Proof that the agreement had an actual impact on trade is not necessary, provided that it was capable of having that effect.[71] Moreover, the mere fact that all the parties to the agreement are from one Member State will not preclude the application of Article 81(1). Such an agreement will be held to have increased the compartmentalization of the Community along national lines, and rendered it more difficult for firms from other States to penetrate that national market.[72] Nor will the Court's jurisdiction be barred merely because the agreement relates to trade outside the EC if it might have an impact on trade within the Community.[73]

8. THE *DE MINIMIS* DOCTRINE

An agreement will not be caught by Article 81(1) if it does not have an appreciable impact on competition or on inter-state trade.[74] This principle has been imbued with greater specificity by Commission notices. The basic test was that the parties' market shares did not exceed 5 per cent *and* the aggregate turnover did not exceed 300 million ECUs.[75] The Commission has recently issued a new *Notice on Agreements of Minor Importance.*[76] It will not institute proceedings in cases covered by the Notice, nor will it impose fines where the parties assume, in good faith, that the Notice covers the agreement.

The criterion is that agreements between undertakings do not appreciably restrict competition where the aggregate market share held by the parties to the agreement does not exceed 10 per cent on markets where the *parties are actual or potential competitors.* The relevant figure is 15 per cent for cases where the *parties are not competitors* on the relevant markets.[77] In cases where it is difficult to classify the

---

[70] Case 56/65, [1966] ECR 235, 249. Moreover, provided that the agreement has this effect, it is not necessary for each of the restrictions to do so: Case 193/83, *Windsurfing International Inc.* v. *Commission* [1986] ECR 611.

[71] Case 19/77, *Miller International Schallplatten GmbH* v. *Commission* [1978] ECR 131; Case C–219/95P, *Ferriere Nord* [1997] ECR I–4411. This extends to the situation where the relevant restriction has not been implemented, since the very existence of the restriction can still have a psychological effect which contributes to the partitioning of the market: Case T–77/92, *Parker Pen*, n. 55 above, Case T–66/92, *Herlitz*, n. 55 above.

[72] Case 8/72, *Vereeniging van Cementhandelaren* v. *Commission* [1972] ECR 977; Case 246/86, *Société Coopérative des Asphalteurs Belges (BELASCO)* v. *Commission* [1989] ECR 2117; Case T–66/89, *Publishers Association* v. *Commission (No. 2)* [1992] ECR II–1995.

[73] See, e.g., *Franco-Japanese Ballbearings Agreement* [1974] OJ L343/19, [1975] 1 CMLR D8; *French and Taiwanese Mushroom Packers* [1975] OJ L29/26, [1975] 1 CMLR D83.

[74] Case 5/69, *Völk*, n. 57 above; Case T–77/92, *Parker Pen*, n. 55 above; Case C–180/98, *Pavlov* v. *Stichting Pensioenfonds Medische Specialisten* [2001] 4 CMLR 30.

[75] *Notice on Agreements of Minor Importance* [1986] OJ C231/2, as amended by [1994] OJ C368/20.

[76] *Notice on Agreements of Minor Importance which do not Appreciably Restrict Competition under Article 81(1) (de minimis)* [2001] OJ C368/13, replacing *Notice on Agreements of Minor Importance* [1997] OJ C372/3, [1998] 4 CMLR 192.

[77] *Ibid.*, para. 7.

agreement then the 10 per cent threshold applies. Paragraph 8 of the Notice deals with vertical cases, in which competition may be restricted by the cumulative effect of agreements. In such instances, the threshold is reduced to 5 per cent for agreements between both competitors and non-competitors. The Notice further provides that individual suppliers or distributors with a market share not exceeding 5 per cent will, in general, not be considered to contribute significantly to a cumulative foreclosure effect. Moreover, such an effect will be unlikely to exist if parallel networks of agreements having similar effects cover less than 30 per cent of the relevant market. The Notice provides a further buffer, in stipulating that agreements will not be restrictive of competition where the preceding thresholds are not exceeded by more than 2 per cent in two successive years.[78]

However, the benefits of the Notice are excluded if the agreement contains hardcore restrictions listed in paragraph 11. Agreements between competitors cannot contain restrictions as to sale price, limitation of output, or allocation of markets or customers.[79] Agreements between non-competitors cannot, for example, contain restrictions on minimum resale price, or the territory into which, or the customers to whom, the buyer may sell the contract goods.[80] There are, however, exceptions for types of vertical restriction that are not regarded as hardcore. The remainder of paragraph 11 contains other limitations on the types of restriction that cause the benefits of the Notice to be lost.

9. EXEMPTION UNDER ARTICLE 81(3)

If an agreement is held to be within Article 81(1) (ex Article 85(1)) it can gain exemption under Article 81(3) (ex Article 85(3)). In order to do so it must satisfy four conditions: it must improve the production or distribution of goods or promote technical or economic progress; consumers must receive a fair share of the resulting benefit; it must contain only restrictions which are indispensable to the attainment of the agreement's objectives; and it cannot lead to the elimination of competition in respect of a substantial part of the products in question. Exemption can be granted on an individual basis, or there can be block exemptions which exempt categories of agreement. These will be examined in turn.

(a) INDIVIDUAL EXEMPTION

The Commission has had the sole power to grant exemptions under Article 81(3), subject to review by the Court. This is set to change as a result of the new scheme for enforcement of competition law, to be discussed below.[81] In making such decisions the Commission must respect the rights guaranteed by the Community legal order in

---

[78] *Ibid.*, para. 9.
[79] *Ibid.*, para. 11(1).
[80] *Ibid.*, paras. 11(2)(a),(b).
[81] See Ch. 25 below.

administrative procedures, and this includes a duty to consider all the relevant aspects of an individual case.[82] It is readily apparent that the precise factors which will lead the Commission to exempt an agreement will differ from case to case. The type of reasoning employed can, however, be exemplified by considering two cases, one involving a decision by the Commission, the other a review judgment of the Court:

Re Bayer and Gist-Brocades NV
[1976] OJ L30/13, [1976] 1 CMLR D98

Bayer and Gist-Brocades (GB) made a specialization agreement whereby the former made 6–APA, an intermediate penicillin product, and GB made raw penicillin. Prior to the agreement both firms had made both products. The specialization agreement was supported by reciprocal supply contracts, under which each firm agreed to supply the requirements of the other: Bayer would supply 6–APA to GB, and GB would supply raw penicillin to Bayer. There were a number of other clauses to the agreement, which are adverted to by the Commission in its decision. The agreement was found to be in breach of Article 85(1), and the Commission then turned its attention to Article 85(3).

THE COMMISSION

57. 1. For the agreements to contribute to the improvement of production or distribution, or to promote technical and economic progress, they must objectively constitute an improvement on the situation that would otherwise exist. The fundamental principle in this respect, established at the time the Common Market was formed, lays down that fair and undistorted competition is the best guarantee of regular supply on the best terms. Thus the question of contribution to economic progress within the meaning of Article 85(3) can only arise in those exceptional cases where the free play of competition is unable to produce the best result economically speaking.

. . .

59. Account must . . . be taken of the limitations on Bayer's ability to expand its raw penicillin plants to cover rising supply requirements. The quality and yield of Bayer's raw penicillin strain were very low, and an increase in yield could not be expected. In order to improve production of raw penicillin, Bayer had to obtain the aid of a firm experienced in fermentation techniques. . . . At the same time this arrangement with Gist made it possible for Bayer to change from raw penicillin to the manufacture of 6–APA in larger quantities and under modernised conditions. The agreements therefore contribute to the improvement of production.

60. 2. As a result of the agreements both firms have been able to expand their production to an extent which should allow the consumer to enjoy the resulting benefit. These benefits will stem from the improved production which the combined technical knowledge of the firms makes possible. . . . The greater number of end-products available on the market and the general trend to lower prices show that the consumer is receiving a fair share of the benefits of the agreement. However, in order that the Commission may follow developments on the market, certain obligations should be imposed upon the parties.

---

[82] Case C–269/90, *Hauptzollamt München-Mitte* v. *Technische Universität München* [1991] ECR I–5469; Cases T–528, 542, 543 & 546/93, *Métropole Télévision SA* v. *Commission* [1996] ECR II–649.

61. 3. All of the clauses to the agreement as amended are indispensable to the attainment of the stated objectives.

62. (a) The decision by each firm that for the duration of the agreement it will not manufacture the specialised product on which the other will concentrate is essential, as are the long-term mutual supply contracts. . . .

. . .

65. (c) The no-challenge clause in the licensing agreement has ... been removed as an unnecessary restriction. If Gist-Brocades and Bayer, two of the world's largest 6–APA manufacturers, had continued to agree not to contest the validity of each other's patents, the result might have been that third parties would have been prevented from exploiting freely for the benefit of the consumer processes which did not in fact merit the protection of a patent.

. . .

68. 4. The agreements do not afford the undertakings concerned the possibility of eliminating competition in respect of a substantial part of the products in question.
[*The Commission reached this conclusion after taking into account the market shares possessed by the two companies in respect both of raw penicillin and 6–APA.*]

The reasoning of the Court in the *Nungesser* case reinforces the importance of breaking down national barriers and creating a single market. The conditions of Article 81(3) will not be satisfied if the agreement contains terms which partition the Community market:

Case 258/78, L. C. Nungesser KG and Kurt Eisele v. Commission
[1982] ECR 2015

The facts of the case have been set out above. It will be remembered that the Court held that the clauses in the agreement that gave absolute territorial protection were caught by Article 85(1). The Commission had also refused an exemption under Article 85(3) for certain aspects of the agreement because of this territorial protection. The applicants argued that the Court should overturn this part of the Commission's decision.

THE ECJ

73 . . . . The decision states that Mr Eisele enjoyed absolute territorial protection in respect of the distribution in Germany of the seeds for which he had exclusive rights, and that by its absolute nature the sole and direct consequence of such protection was to prevent all imports through other channels of the original products, namely INRA seeds originating in France, despite a persistent demand for such seeds in Germany, which in itself is not capable of contributing to an improvement in the production or distribution of goods within the meaning of Article 85(3). . . .

. . .

76. It must be remembered that under the terms of Article 85(3) . . . an exemption from the prohibition contained in Article 85(1) may be granted in the case of an agreement between undertakings which contributes to improving the production or distribution of goods or to

promoting technical progress, and which does not impose on the undertakings concerned restrictions which are not indispensable to the attainment of those objectives.

77. As it is a question of seeds intended to be used by a large number of farmers for the production of maize, which is an important product for human and animal foodstuffs, absolute territorial protection manifestly goes beyond what is indispensable for the improvement of production or distribution or the promotion of technical progress, as is demonstrated . . . by the prohibition agreed to by both parties to the agreement, of any parallel imports of INRA maize seeds into Germany even if those seeds were bred by INRA itself and marketed in France.

78. It follows that the absolute territorial protection conferred on the licensee . . . constituted a sufficient reason for refusing to grant an exemption under Article 85(3). . . . It is therefore no longer necessary to examine the other grounds set out in the decision for refusing to grant such an exemption.

The following extract serves to give an overall impression of the approach under Article 81(3).

R. Whish, Competition Law[83]

A narrow view of Article 81(3) is that it permits improvements in economic efficiency to be invoked by the parties to an agreement so that they may obtain exemption notwithstanding the fact that their agreement restricts competition: according to this view, the very wording of Article 81(3), which speaks of improvement to production and distribution and to technical and economic progress, is suggestive of an efficiency standard. Article 81(3), therefore, allows a balancing of the restrictive effects of an agreement under Article 81(1) against the enhancement of efficiency under Article 81(3). . . . The Commission's *White Paper on Modernisation* explains Article 81(1) and 81(3) in this way.

However, an alternative, and broader view of Article 81(3) is possible: that it allows policies other than economic efficiency to be taken into account when deciding whether to allow agreements that are restrictive of competition. There are many important policies in the Community, for example on industry, the environment, employment, the regions and culture, which go beyond the simple enhancement of efficiency. According to a broad view of Article 81(3), a benefit in terms of any of these policies could 'trump' a restriction of competition under Article 81(1).

[*Whish reviews a number of decisions where such factors seem to have had some impact on the Commission's reasoning. He continues as follows:*]

It is clear . . . that a number of factors have been influential in decisions under Article 81(3), not all of which can be considered to be 'narrow' improvements in efficiency. There are significant proponents of the view that Article 81(3) does admit broad, non-competition considerations.

This discussion suggests that there is uncertainty—even confusion—as to the proper application of Article 81(3). However, it is necessary to achieve a resolution of the various approaches . . . because under the Commission's *White Paper* proposals, decisions under Article 81(3) will, in the future, be made by NCAs[84] and national courts as well as by the Commission itself. These institutions must know the limits of their discretion under Article 81(3); furthermore, they seem

---

[83] N. 6 above, 125–8.   [84] National Competition Authorities.

ill-placed to balance the restriction of competition that an agreement might entail against a broad range of Community policies; they would have less difficulty, however, in applying a 'narrow' interpretation of Article 81(3), limited to a consideration of economic efficiencies.

These considerations suggest that Article 81(3) ought to be interpreted in a narrow rather than a broad manner, according to standards and by reference to principles that can properly be regarded as justiciable in courts of law. . . .

(b) BLOCK EXEMPTION

Article 81(3) allows the Commission to declare the provisions of Article 81(1) inapplicable to a category of agreements. This is the foundation for the series of block exemptions made by the Commission, acting under delegated authority from the Council. The object of such exemptions is to exclude a generic type of agreement from the ambit of Article 81(1), thereby obviating the need for separate and time-consuming individual exemptions. In some ways the technique of block exemption is conceptually similar to the evolution of *per se* rules, although the result produced is to exclude rather than condemn the agreement: experience with individual agreements leads to the conclusion that certain types of agreement, which contain particular terms, warrant exemption. A block exemption encapsulates this conclusion. It serves also to give more definite guidance to firms and their legal advisers.

Although the contents of the block exemptions differ, they possess certain structural features in common. Agreements that come within the terms of a block exemption do not need to be notified to the Commission. The Regulation containing the block exemption will state the reasons it has been enacted for this area. It will then set out the substance of the exemption. The block exemptions will normally also contain provisions that limit the size of the firms which can take advantage of them.

Such exemptions have been made for a number of areas, including: specialization agreements;[85] research and development;[86] vertical restraints;[87] technology transfer;[88] and franchising.[89] The structure and operation of block exemptions will be examined more closely in the context of vertical restraints.

10. CONCLUSION

i. The Community courts have given a broad reading to Article 81, with the objectives of enhancing efficiency and preventing the single market programme from being hindered by private actors. To this end the ECJ and CFI have read key concepts such as agreement and concerted practice expansively.

ii. The interpretation of Article 81 has also been markedly affected by the extent to which an economic analysis is mandated within Article 81(1). The ECJ's approach has been consistent since the inception of the Community. Object

---

[85] Reg. 2658/2000 [2000] OJ L304/3.   [86] Reg. 2659/00 [2000] OJ L304/7.
[87] Reg. 2790/99 [1999] OJ L336/21.   [88] Reg. 240/96 [1996] OJ L31/2.
[89] Reg. 4087/88 [1988] OJ L359/46.

and effect should be read disjunctively. Certain agreements will be condemned merely because of proof of their existence. They will be illegal *per se*. Horizontal market division, horizontal price fixing, and boycotts are the classic examples of such infringements. In relation to many other agreements, a market analysis will be required to determine whether they are within Article 81(1). The Commission has been far more reluctant to embrace an economic analysis within this part of Article 81. It has more recently modified its position, but there is still a reluctance to do 'too much' within Article 81(1).

iii. The jury is still out on whether Article 81(3) should be interpreted according to the narrow or broad view. This issue has been thrown into sharp relief by the devolution of competence over Article 81(3) to national courts and competition authorities. It is likely that this will tilt the balance in favour of the narrow view.

iv. The reach of Community competition law has not been the work of the courts alone. The legislature has intervened through measures such as the Merger Regulation. The Commission itself has orchestrated developments in diverse ways, through the passage of block exemptions, the control of mergers, the increased attention paid to competition in the public sector, and the reform of the enforcement mechanisms.

11. FURTHER READING[90]

AMATO, G., *Antitrust and the Bounds of Power* (Hart, 1997)

AREEDA, P., TURNER, D., and HOVENKAMP, H., *Antitrust Law: An Analysis of Antitrust Principles and their Application* (Little Brown, 1978)

BELLAMY, C., and CHILD, G., *European Community Law of Competition* (Sweet & Maxwell, 5th edn., 2001)

BISHOP, S., and WALKER, M., *The Economics of EC Competition Law, Concepts, Application and Measurement* (Sweet & Maxwell, 1999)

BORK, R. H., The Antitrust *Paradox: A Policy at War with Itself* (Basic Books, 1978)

DEMSETZ, H., *Efficiency, Competition, and Policy* (Oxford University Press, 1989)

FAULL, J., and NIKPAY, A. (eds.), *The EC Law of Competition* (Oxford University Press, 1999)

FRAZER, T., *Monopoly, Competition and the Law* (Harvester, 2nd edn., 1992)

GERBER, D., *Law and Competition in Twentieth Century Europe* (Oxford University Press, 1998)

GOYDER, D., *EC Competition Law* (Oxford University Press, 3rd edn., 1998)

GREEN, N., and ROBERTSON, A., *Commercial Agreements and Competition Law: Practice and Procedure in UK and EEC* (Kluwer, 2nd edn., 1997)

JOLIET, R., *The Rule of Reason in Antitrust Law—American, German and Common Market Laws in Comparative Perspective* (Faculté de Droit, Liège, Hague, 1967)

---

[90] There is a voluminous literature on this topic. The references will therefore be confined to books.

JONES, A., and SUFRIN, B., *EC Competition Law, Text, Cases and Materials* (Oxford University Press, 2001)

JONES, C., LEWIS, X., and WOUDE, M., VAN DER, *EC Competition Law Handbook* (Sweet & Maxwell, 1999/2000 edn.)

KORAH, V., *An Introductory Guide to EC Competiton Law and Practice* (Hart, 7th edn., 2000)

—— *Cases and Materials on EC Competition Law* (Hart, 2nd edn., 2001)

—— *Vertical Agreements: Distribution under the EC Competition Rules* (Hart, 2001)

NEVEN, D., PAPANDROPOLOUS, P., and SEABRIGHT, P., *Trawling for Minnows: European Competition Policy and Agreements between Firms* (Centre for Economic Policy Research, 1998)

POSNER, R., *Antitrust Law* (Chicago University Press, 1976)

RODGER, B., and MACCULLOCH, A., *Competition Law and Policy in the EC and UK* (Cavendish, 2001)

SCHERER, F., and ROSS, D., *Industrial Market Structure and Economic Performance* (Houghton Mifflin, 3rd edn., 1991)

SULLIVAN, L., *Antitrust* (West, 1977)

WESSELING, R., *The Modernisation of EC Antitrust Law* (Hart, 2000)

WHISH, R., *Competition Law* (Butterworths, 4th edn., 2001)

22

COMPETITION LAW: VERTICAL RESTRAINTS

Space precludes a detailed analysis of all the varying types of restraint which competition authorities have to deal with. However, consideration of the general principles of EC competition law takes one only so far. This Chapter will, therefore, be devoted to an examination of one important area of competition policy, that of vertical restraints.

1. CENTRAL ISSUES

i. Vertical agreements are made between parties at differing levels of the production process, a typical example being a distribution agreement between a manufacturer of a product and a retailer. They are of considerable practical importance for the organization of business.

ii. There is greater controversy in this area than in many others about the extent to which these agreements are economically harmful, and hence disagreement about the 'correct' approach for competition policy. It is therefore important to understand the policy arguments in this area, and these will be considered within the following section.

iii. There are a number of differing types of vertical restraint. It must be determined whether these are caught by Article 81(1). We shall see that the criterion used by the ECJ and the Commission has not always been the same, and that the Commission has been strongly criticized for taking too formalistic an approach to vertical agreements.

iv. In terms of Article 81(3), the EC has primarily used block exemptions to deal with vertical restraints. The initial approach was to have different block exemptions for different types of vertical agreement. The law has now changed, and there is a new-style block exemption that covers the great majority of vertical agreements.

2. THE ECONOMIC DEBATE

There is considerable diversity of opinion on whether vertical restraints are economically harmful or not.[1] Some believe that this species of restraint is not harmful at all, or only where there is some real degree of market power at the production level. Others believe that vertical restraints may produce a variety of anti-competitive

---

[1] R. Whish, *Competition Law* (Butterworths, 4th edn., 2001), 540–5; D. Neven, P. Papandropolous, and P. Seabright, *Trawling for Minnows: European Competition Policy and Agreements between Firms* (Centre for Economic Policy Research, 1998); J. Lever and S. Neubauer, 'Vertical Restraints, Their Motivation and Justification' [2000] *ECLR* 7.

effects, and that therefore it is correct for competition policy to subject them to some scrutiny.

(a) THE FIRST VIEW OF VERTICAL RESTRAINTS

The essence of the former view can be presented as follows. A manufacturer of a product will have to decide how to market that product. A number of options are open to the firm. It may decide to establish its own retail outlets, or to establish a joint venture with a company that has expertise in the retailing area. It may simply sell its products through any outlet which is willing to stock them. A further option is to sell through certain specialized shops, on the basis that the product requires sales exper- tise in that area. It may conclude that the optimum marketing technique is to sell through certain retail outlets, each of which will be given exclusive rights to distribute the product in that geographical area, either because retailers will only take the goods on these terms, or because this will maximize total sales. This list of distributive techniques is by no means exhaustive. The argument of those who do not see vertical restraints as harmful has four parts.

The *first* is that the manufacturer will choose whichever of the above options is felt to be the most efficient way of marketing the product. It will, for example, only use independent retailers on the assumption that this is a more efficient marketing tech- nique than establishing its own outlets. It will only give such outlets exclusivity on the assumption that this will lead to greater sales than if it had not been given. Now, it may be wrong in its assumptions, but if this is so then the market will 'punish' it, through reduced sales or by the ultimate sanction of bankruptcy. In any event, it is not the function of competition authorities to play at management consultancy and to try and devise a better marketing strategy for the manufacturer. This is in part because it is not their function, and in part because they are in a less good position than the manufacturer itself to make this choice.

The *second* aspect of the argument in favour of the legality of vertical restraints is that a manufacturer which imposes such restraints will not be restricting output to any greater degree than it would otherwise be doing, and will not be taking any greater monopoly profit, if such is available in the circumstances, through the pres- ence of a vertical restraint than it would otherwise be able to extract from that market.

The *third* part of the argument develops from the preceding foundations. The manufacturer will be devising the marketing strategy which is conceived to be the most efficient. Any restraints which are imposed are either outweighed by the pro- competitive effects of the agreement, and/or are necessary to persuade the distributor to undertake the marketing of the goods at all. An example will serve to clarify this idea. Imagine that a producer wishes to enter a new geographical market. It does not have retailing expertise, and therefore wishes to use an independent retailer. If the product is to be noticed within this new market it may require expenditure on adver- tising, and also a commitment to provide both pre- and post-sales service. A retailer may well not be willing to undertake this expense unless it is accorded some exclusiv- ity in the sales process. If this is not forthcoming the retailer will encounter what is known as the free-rider problem: that retailer will expend money on advertising, pre-sales service, and the like, only to witness the sales being taken by a rival retailer who has not had to incur these costs. The grant of such exclusivity will necessarily restrict intra-brand competition between retailers of the same product. However, it is felt that in most markets this species of competition is relatively unimportant, in that prices will be controlled by the existence of inter-brand competition. A retailer of Sony stereos who has exclusivity in a certain area will not be able to raise prices significantly since there will be competition from other stereo brands.

The *final* part of the argument of those who contend that vertical restraints should be lawful is that they do not accept that these restraints produce anti-competitive effects. The nature of these effects will be considered in more detail below.

A prominent exponent of the preceding view is Bork, and the following extract provides a summary of the argument.

R. Bork, The Antitrust Paradox, A Policy at War with Itself[2]

We have seen that vertical price fixing (resale price maintenance), vertical market division (closed dealer territories), and, indeed, all vertical restraints are beneficial to consumers and should for that reason be completely lawful. Basic economic theory tells us that the manufacturer who imposes such restraints cannot intend to restrict and must (except in the rare case of price discrimination, which the law should regard as neutral) intend to create efficiency. The most common efficiency is the inducement or purchase by the manufacturer of extra reseller sales, service or promotional effort.

The proposal to legalize all truly vertical restraints is so much at variance with conventional thought on the topic that it will doubtless strike many readers as troublesome, if not bizarre. But I have never seen any economic analysis that shows how manufacturer-imposed resale price maintenance, closed dealer territories, customer allocation clauses, or the like can have the net effect of restricting output. We have too quickly assumed something that appears untrue.

Perhaps the ambiguity of the word 'restraint' accounts for some of our confusion on this topic. When the Supreme Court speaks of a restraint it often, or even usually, refers to the manufacturer's control of certain activities of his resellers or to the elimination by the manufacturer of some forms of rivalry among his resellers. There is, of course, nothing sinister or unusual about using 'restraint' in that sense. It is merely a form of vertical integration by contract, a less complete integration than that which would obtain if the manufacturer owned his outlets and directed their activities. It is merely one instance of the coordination of economic activities which is ubiquitous in the economic world and upon which our wealth depends. The important point is that such vertical control never creates 'restraint' in that other common meaning, restriction of output. Perhaps, if we are more careful about the ambiguity of the word and make it clear in which sense we use it, our reasoning about antitrust problems, including the problem of vertical restraints, will improve.[3]

---

[2] (Basic Books, 1978), 297–8. See also R. Bork, 'The Rule of Reason and the *Per Se* Concept in Price Fixing and Market Division II' (1966) 75 *Yale LJ* 373. For the debate on this issue see J. R. Gould and B. S. Yamey, 'Professor Bork on Vertical Price Fixing' (1967) 76 *Yale LJ* 722; R. Bork, 'A Reply to Professors Gould and Yamey' (1967) 76 *Yale LJ* 731; J. R. Gould and B. S. Yamey, 'Professor Bork on Vertical Price Fixing: A Rejoinder' (1968) 77 *Yale LJ* 936.

[3] See also F. Easterbrook, 'Vertical Arrangements and the Rule of Reason' (1984) 53 *Antitrust LJ* 135; B. Bok, 'An Economist Appraises Vertical Restraints' (1985) 30 *Antitrust B* 117.

(b) THE SECOND VIEW OF VERTICAL RESTRAINTS

The commentators who adopt a more wary approach to vertical agreements do so for a variety of reasons. They perceive a number of possible dangers to the competitive process flowing from such agreements. Four may be briefly considered here.

The first is *market foreclosure*. If a producer has made exclusive contracts with certain outlets to sell only its brand of a particular product, then it may be difficult for other producers to secure outlets for their own sales. This is especially the case in those instances where either the best outlets have already been taken or the number of outlets for distributing a particular product is limited by the nature of that product or by external factors such as planning laws.

A second concern is that *consumers will be harmed*, in particular by certain types of vertical restraint. Resale-price maintenance is one of the most commonly cited instances of this, although the existence of such harm has been vigorously contested.[4] Consumer harm is said to be apparent in other ways. Thus, it is argued that systems of selective or exclusive distribution force a 'package' on consumers, which includes the basic price of the product, plus advertising costs, after-sales service, and the like, even though some consumers would prefer to take the raw product itself and worry about maintenance, etc., themselves.

A third disadvantage said to attend vertical agreements is that they can serve as a *mask for cartels between producers or distributors*. A producer may grant an exclusive distribution right to a distributor in circumstances in which the latter has agreed with other distributors of competing products to divide the market horizontally: the consequence will be that inter- as well as intra-brand competition is reduced. The cogency of this objection has been strongly contested. It has been questioned whether this actually happens, and whether it is exacerbated by the existence of the vertical agreement. It has also been argued that the appropriate policy response is that if it did occur then the real problem should be addressed: the horizontal agreement, not the vertical one.[5]

A final cause for concern with vertical agreements is peculiar to the EC. Community competition law is not concerned solely with efficiency. The *creation of a single European market is also of prime importance*. Agreements which either explicitly or implicitly divide the market along national or regional lines will, therefore, be treated particularly severely by the competition authorities, as exemplified by the Court's continuing opposition to agreements which attempt to provide absolute territorial protection.

In the following extract Comanor expresses the concerns of this second, more cautious, school of thought. He reviews some of the arguments utilized by those such as Bork, but does not believe that vertical agreements should always be regarded as legal.

---

[4] See n. 2 above.   [5] See Bork, n. 2 above, ch. 14.

THE CRITIQUE OF THE COMMISSION

W. Comanor, Vertical Price-Fixing, Vertical Market Restrictions, and the New Antitrust Policy[6]

When vertical restraints are used to promote the provision of distribution services, the critical issue for antitrust purposes remains whether consumers are better served by lower prices and fewer services or by higher prices and more services. In its *Spray-Rite* brief, the Department of Justice suggested that pure vertical restraints always lead to increased consumer welfare. This position is unfounded, and a more hostile treatment of vertical restraints is appropriate.

Because vertical restraints can either enhance or diminish consumer welfare, depending upon the situation, it is tempting to apply the rule of reason on a case-by-case basis.

... Yet it is no easy task to determine whether particular restraints increase or decrease efficiency: the answer depends in each case largely on the relative preferences of different groups of consumers. In the interests of judicial economy, therefore, it may be more expeditious to set general policy standards, even though they will sometimes lead to improper results.

Vertical restraints that concern established products are more likely to reduce consumer welfare. Large numbers of consumers are already familiar with such products and are therefore unlikely to place much value on acquiring further information about them. In this context, stringent antitrust standards should be applied to vertical price and non-price restraints alike. This approach could take the form either of a direct *per se* prohibition, or of a modified rule of reason analysis under which the defendant would be required to demonstrate that the restraints have benefited consumers generally. By contrast, in the case of new products or products of new entrants into the market, vertical restraints are less likely to lessen consumer welfare, because their novelty should create greater demand for information. In these circumstances, the restraints should be permissible, or at the least should be treated more leniently in any modified rule of reason analysis.

3. THE CRITIQUE OF THE COMMISSION

The approach of the Community authorities towards vertical restraints has been strongly criticized, and it is important to understand the nature of this critique before considering particular types of vertical agreement. The main target of the criticism has been the Commission rather than the CFI or ECJ. References to Article 85 should now be read as to Article 81.

B. Hawk, System Failure: Vertical Restraints and EC Competition Law[7]

The most fundamental, and the most trenchant, criticism is that the Commission too broadly applies Article 85(1) to agreements having little or no anticompetitive effects. This criticism rests on three pillars: 1) an inadequate economic analysis under Article 85(1); 2) an unpersuasive rationale for this overbroad application of 85(1), notably the 'economic freedom' notion; and 3)

---

[6] (1985) 98 *Harv. L Rev.* 983, 1001–2.
[7] (1995) 32 *CMLRev.* 973, 974–5, 977–8, 982. See also C. Bright, 'EU Competition Policy: Rules, Objectives and Deregulation' (1996) 16 *OJLS* 535.

the Commission's historical and continuing resistance to Court judgments evidencing a more nuanced economics-based interpretation of 85(1).

Inadequate economic analysis under 85(1)
The majority of Commission decisions fail adequately to consider whether the restraint at issue harms competition in the welfare sense of economics, i.e., effect on price or output. Concomitantly, market power, which should be the threshold issue, frequently is hardly examined (let alone given a central role) or is simply found to exist in a conclusory fashion under the rubric of 'appreciability'.

. . .

The Commission's rationale under 85(1) is unpersuasive
The . . . explanation for the inadequate economic analysis under 85(1) lies in the Commission's stubborn (in the face of Court judgments) adherence to the definition of a restriction on competition as a restriction on the 'economic freedom' of operators in the marketplace. The principal weaknesses of the Freiburg School notion of restriction on economic freedom are (1) its failure to generate precise operable legal rules, (i.e. its failure to provide an analytical framework); (2) its distance from and tension with (micro) economics which does provide an analytical framework; (3) its tendency to favour traders/competitors over consumers and consumer welfare (efficiency); and (4) its capture under Article 85(1) of totally innocuous contract provisions having no anti-competitive effects in an economic sense.

. . .

Commission refusal to follow Community Courts
The Court of Justice and the Court of First Instance have taken a more nuanced approach toward vertical arrangements under Article 85(1). The Courts have increasingly required an analysis of economic effects, particularly the possibility of foreclosure. This approach has been largely ignored or distinguished by the Commission, which adheres to its non-economics based application of Article 85(1), i.e. restriction on economic freedom.

The Commission published a wide-ranging Green Paper on Vertical Restraints.[8] A number of important points emerged from this document.

First, the Commission accepted that the academic consensus on the economic effects of vertical restraints is that market structure is of prime importance. The fiercer is the inter-brand competition, the more likely will it be that the pro-competitive and efficiency aspects of the agreement outweigh any anti-competitive effects. This is even more so when market power at the production level is limited and barriers to entry are low.[9]

Secondly, the report made it clear that the desire to create a single market means that vertical restraints that seek to insulate markets through the grant of absolute territorial protection will not be tolerated, either under Article 85(1) or (3) (now Article 81(1) or (3)).[10]

Thirdly, the Commission accepted, sometimes explicitly[11] and sometimes

---

[8] COM(96)721 final, [1997] 4 CMLR 519.   [9] *Ibid.*, paras. 82–5.
[10] *Ibid.*, para. 276.   [11] *Ibid.*, paras. 193 and 216.

implicitly,[12] that it did not engage in meaningful economic analysis within Article 85(1) (now Article 81(1)), but rather reserved such matters for consideration under Article 85(3) (now Article 81(3)).[13] There was no real explanation provided to reconcile this approach with that of the Community courts. The latter clearly do apply an economic analysis within Article 81(1) itself in order to decide whether a vertical restraint should be caught or not, and this analysis is not confined to dealing with cases where any impact on competition is merely *de minimis*.[14]

Fourthly, the Commission set out a number of options on which it invited comment. Option 1 was to preserve the then present system, which seemed to mean a broad, formalistic interpretation of Article 85(1) (now Article 81(1)), coupled with the existing block exemptions.[15] Option 2 was to widen the block exemptions by, for example, rendering them applicable to agreements involving more than two parties, and broadening the range of allowable clauses.[16] Option 3 was to develop more focused block exemptions, placing emphasis on the EC's market-integration objectives.[17] The final option was to have some economic analysis within Article 85(1) (now Article 81(1)), coupled with block exemptions.[18] It is clear that the Commission faced a dilemma. It was aware that many vertical restraints do not have any net anti-competitive impact. It was probably also aware that logically they should not therefore be held to fall within Article 81(1). It was, however, also mindful of the costs of engaging in extensive economic analysis within this Article.[19]

The Commission presented more concrete proposals in the *Follow-up to the Green Paper on Vertical Restraints*.[20] It concluded that there should be a more economics-based approach to vertical restraints, and that there should also be one broad block exemption for all vertical agreements. The new Regulation was adopted on 22 December 1999, and came fully into force on 1 June 2000.[21] It will be analysed in detail below. Before doing so, we should consider the differing kinds of vertical restraint and the extent to which they are caught by Article 81(1).

4. EXCLUSIVE DISTRIBUTION

The essential idea behind an exclusive distribution agreement (EDA) is that the producer agrees to supply only to a particular distributor within a particular territory. This may be buttressed by attempts to prevent third parties from selling into the contract territory of the designated distributor. This can be done either by imposing contract terms to that effect in agreements which the producer has with other distributors, and/or by assigning to the designated distributor trade mark rights,

---

[12] *Ibid.*, para. 180.
[13] The Commission does not appear to notice the shift in its pattern of thought from the language of Art. 85(1) to that of Art. 85(3) within, for example, para. 180 of the report.
[14] See 954–61.   [15] N. 8 above, para. 281.   [16] *Ibid.*, paras. 282–285.
[17] *Ibid.*, paras. 286–292.   [18] *Ibid.*, paras. 293–298.
[19] See *ibid.*, para. 86 for an express statement to this effect.
[20] [1998] OJ C365/3, [1999] 4 CMLR 281.
[21] Reg. 2790/99, [1999] OJ L336/21, [2000] 4 CMLR 398.

which will enable the latter to stop such infringements. This type of agreement may be necessary to persuade a distributor to market a new product, or to market an existing product in a new area. An EDA may also be beneficial to the producer by facilitating the efficient distribution of its goods, in the sense that it will not have to incur transport costs, etc., to multiple sites.

The central issue is whether an EDA will be caught by Article 81(1), and whether it will be exempted under Article 81(3), either individually or pursuant to a block exemption.

The applicability of Article 81(1) to an EDA has been touched on in the earlier discussion. It is clear that such agreements can be caught by Article 81(1), and that, in the view of the Court, the vertical restraint must be considered in its factual, legal, and economic context in order to consider whether it is caught by that Article (*STM* and *Brasserie de Haecht*).[22] It is also reasonably clear that the Commission has often adopted a formalistic attitude, eschewing the more general contextual approach advocated by the Court. Notwithstanding the divergence of approach between Court and Commission, it is apparent from their combined jurisprudence that certain types of restrictions within an EDA are especially likely to fall within the ambit of Article 81(1) (ex Article 85(1)). Thus, export bans which prohibit a distributor from exporting the product outside a designated area will be judged particularly severely, as will any other attempt to establish absolute territorial protection for a distributor.[23] Indirect attempts to attain the same end will also be condemned, as in the case of customer guarantees which are available only if the product is bought from the distributor in that State.[24]

If an EDA is caught by Article 81(1) the parties may either seek individual exemption or try and bring themselves within the terms of the block exemption. The principles that govern individual exemption have been examined above.[25] There was and until recently a separate block exemption for EDAs.[26] This has now been replaced by the general block exemption for vertical restraints, which will be examined below.

5. SELECTIVE DISTRIBUTION

The approach of the Court and the Commission to selective distribution agreements (SDA) stands in marked contrast to that adopted towards EDAs. A selective distribution system is one in which the supplier chooses to distribute the goods only through

---

[22] Case 56/65, *Société Technique Minière* v. *Maschinenbau Ulm GmbH* [1966] ECR 235; Case 23/67, *Brasserie de Haecht SA* v. *Wilkin* [1967] ECR 407. See 955–7 above.

[23] Cases 56 & 58/64, *Consten and Grundig* [1966] ECR 299; Case 258/78, *Nungesser* [1982] ECR 2015; Case 19/77, *Miller International Schallplatten GmbH* v. *Commission* [1978] ECR 131; Case C–279/87, *Tipp-Ex GmbH & Co KG* v. *Commission* [1990] ECR I–261; Case T–77/92, *Parker Pen Ltd.* v. *Commission* [1994] ECR II–549; Case T–66/92, *Herlitz AG* v. *Commission* [1994] ECR II–531, 458.

[24] Case 31/85, *ETA Fabriques d'Ebauches* v. *DK Investments SA* [1985] ECR 3933, [1986] 2 CMLR 674.

[25] See 964–8 above.

[26] Reg. 1983/83, [1983] OJ L173/1.

certain outlets, normally those which fulfil certain criteria concerning expertise. The Court has held that such agreements do not necessarily fall within Article 85(1) (now Article 81(1)). *Metro* is the seminal case.

Case 26/76, Metro-SB-Großmärkte GmbH & Co KG v. Commission and SABA
[1977] ECR 1875

[Note ToA renumbering: Art. 85 is now Art. 81]

Metro was a wholesaler of goods in Germany. It operated a system of self-service wholesaling and a cash-and-carry service, which enabled it to undercut the prices charged by other wholesalers. Metro applied to SABA to be allowed to stock the electronic equipment produced by the latter, but SABA refused to supply it, claiming that it did not fulfil the conditions that SABA required before supplying its goods. Metro complained to the Commission that SABA's policy was in breach of Article 85(1), but the Commission found in favour of SABA after the latter had amended its terms of trade in certain respects. Metro then sought to have this decision of the Commission annulled.

THE ECJ

20. ... In the sector covering the production of high quality and technically advanced consumer durables, where a relatively small number of large and medium-scale producers offer a varied range of items which, or so consumers may consider, are readily inter-changeable, the structure of the market does not preclude the existence of a variety of channels of distribution adapted to the peculiar characteristics of the various producers and to the requirements of the various categories of consumers. On this view the Commission was justified in recognising that selective distribution systems constituted, together with others, an aspect of competition which accords with Article 85(1), provided that the resellers are chosen on the basis of objective criteria of a qualitative nature relating to the technical qualifications of the reseller and his staff and the suitability of his trading premises and that such conditions are laid down uniformly for all potential resellers and are not applied in a discriminatory fashion.

21. It is true that in such systems of distribution price competition is not generally emphasised either as an exclusive or indeed as a principal factor. ... However, although price competition is so important that it can never be eliminated, it does not constitute the only effective form of competition or that to which absolute priority must in all circumstances be accorded. ... For specialist wholesalers and retailers the desire to maintain a certain price level, which corresponds to the desire to preserve, in the interests of consumers, the possibility of the continued existence of this channel of distribution in conjunction with new methods of distribution based on a different type of competition policy, forms one of the objectives which may be pursued without necessarily falling under the prohibition of Article 85(1), and if it does fall thereunder, either wholly or in part, coming within the framework of Article 85(3). ...

The significance of *Metro* is that, when the conditions elaborated therein are ful-filled, the SDA is held not to be within Article 81(1) at all. The principle enunciated in that case has oft been cited since then.[27] There are, however, a number of limits to the application of that principle.

First and foremost, the product has to be of the kind in relation to which the Court and the Commission believe that it is justifiable to limit price competition and to operate the regime of selective distribution with an element of non-price competition. Such products tend to be those that require specialist sales staff who have expertise in that area,[28] or goods where brand image is of particular importance.[29] Plumbing fittings are, by way of contrast, not deemed to be a technically advanced product which necessitates a selective distribution system.[30]

A *second*, and equally important, facet of the *Metro* principle is that it operates to legitimate outlets which are chosen on the basis of qualitative criteria. It can be extremely difficult to determine whether a particular requirement for a distributor to be acceptable to a supplier should really be classified as qualitative or not.[31] Subject to this uncertainty, the *Metro* principle does not allow a supplier to impose quantitative limits on those who can distribute the product, or to discriminate as between distributors.[32]

The logic of the distinction drawn between qualitative and quantitative criteria for restrictions on distribution is questionable, to say the least. We have seen that producers will tend to choose the distribution method that they believe will best maximize their sales. Whether they believe that this is best achieved by qualitative or quantitative criteria, or a mixture of both, will vary depending upon the nature of the product etc. The pro- and anti-competitive effects of such distribution strategies will not, however, differ radically depending on which of these criteria is chosen, as the following extract reveals.

J.S. Chard, The Economics of the Application of Article 85 to Selective Distribution Systems[33]

It should be clear from this discussion of the economic effects of qualitative and quantitative selection criteria that the Commission's attempts to distinguish between the criteria is essentially arbitrary and confusing. To be meaningful, qualitative criteria must have a quantitative effect . . . while quantitative criteria may have qualitative implications. With regard to the latter aspect for

---

[27] See, e.g., Case 210/81, *Demo-Studio Schmidt* v. *Commission* [1983] ECR 3045; Case 107/82, *AEG-Telefunken AG* v. *Commission* [1983] ECR 3151; Case C–376/92, *Metro SB-Großmärkte GmbH & Co KG* v. *Cartier SA* [1994] ECR I–15.

[28] Such as electronic equipment: *AEG*; audiovisual equipment: *Demo-Studio Schmidt*; computers: Dec. 84/233, *IBM Personal Computers* [1984] OJ L118/24, [1984] 2 CMLR 342.

[29] Such as ceramic tableware: Dec. 85/616, *Villeroy & Boch* [1985] OJ L376/15, [1988] 4 CMLR 461; jewellery: Dec. 83/610, *Murat* [1983] OJ L348/20, [1984] 1 CMLR 219; luxury cosmetics: Case T–19/92, *Groupement d'Achat Edouard Leclerc* v. *Commission* [1996] ECR II–1851.

[30] Dec. 85/44, *Grohe* [1985] OJ L19/17, [1988] 4 CMLR 612.

[31] Whish, n. 1 above, 559.

[32] See Case 107/82, *AEG-Telefunken*, n. 27 above; Cases 25 & 26/84, *Ford* v. *Commission* [1985] ECR 2725, [1985] 3 CMLR 528; Case T–19/92, *Edouard Leclerc*, n. 29 above; Dec. 90/38, *Bayo-N-Ox* [1990] OJ L21/71, [1990] 4 CMLR 930.

[33] (1982) 7 *ELRev*. 83, 97, 100–1. See also C. Vajda, 'Selective Distribution in the European Community' (1979) 13 *JWTL* 409.

example, in *Omega,* the Commission recognised that the number of concessionaires needed to be limited otherwise no concessionaire could attain a sufficient turnover to be able to undertake service and guarantee commitments. Thus, qualitative and quantitative criteria should be subject to the same analytical procedure.

[*The author suggests that a proper economic analysis along the following lines is required:*]

First, the Commission should examine whether there is direct evidence of collusion between manufacturers and/or distributors of different brands or whether the restriction embraces so large a fraction of the market . . . as to make cartelisation a plausible motivation for the restriction. If it finds the answer is no . . . there should be a presumption that the restriction has pro-competitive effects. The parties to the agreements in question can be expected to indicate the alleged pro-competitive effects and the Commission should not query these too closely. It should not be tempted to second-guess business judgments as to what arrangements would or would not provide adequate means for achieving the pro-competitive effects and attach conditions to the granting of negative clearance or exemption under Article 85(3), as its record in this respect does not inspire confidence.

Secondly, if there is some evidence of restrictions in competition between manufacturers and/or distributors, but the evidence is not conclusive, . . . the Commission should carefully examine whether pro-competitive effects are being achieved, . . . the burden of justification being shifted firmly onto the defendant. . . .

What evidence there is seems to cast doubt on the likely importance of anti-competitive effects while pro-competitive effects seem likely to be more common. A more rigorous investigation by the Commission of the competitive effects of selective distribution systems along the lines suggested could, therefore, lead to more distribution arrangements with restrictions on cross supplies, quantitative selection criteria, and restrictions of like effect, resulting in the protection of distributors from competition by other distributors of the same manufacturer's brand, being allowed under EEC rules of competition. If anti-competitive effects are usually absent, then the greater freedom of manufacturers to choose the distribution arrangements which suit them best will tend to result in the most efficient forms of arrangements being used.

The link between Chard's analysis and Bork's thesis is evident in the preceding extract. It should, however, be noted that the greater leniency shown by the competition authorities to SDAs as opposed to EDAs may be partially explained by the importance which the Community attaches to the attainment of a single European market. EDAs are more likely to divide the Community along national lines than are SDAs and, as seen above, the EC is particularly antagonistic towards such forms of market division. In any event, the extent to which Community law is willing to exclude SDAs from the ambit of Article 85(1) (now Article 81(1)) now has to be seen in the light of *Metro II.*

Case 75/84, Metro-SB-Großmärkte GmbH & Co KG v. Commission (No. 2)
[1986] ECR 3021

[Note ToA renumbering: Art. 85 is now Art. 81]

The Commission had renewed an exemption for SABA's selective distribution system. Metro, the original objector, sought to contest the renewal of the SDA. In the original decision the Court had intimated that its view (that SDAs were compatible with Article 85(1)), might be different if, in a particular area, the existence of a large number of SDAs similar to that operated by SABA eliminated firms such as Metro from this part of the market. In this second case, Metro argued that this had now occurred, and that therefore the exemption for the SABA SDA should not be renewed.

THE ECJ

40. It must be borne in mind that, although the Court has held in previous decisions that 'simple' selective distribution systems are capable of constituting an aspect of competition compatible with Article 85(1), there may nevertheless be a restriction or elimination of competition where the existence of a certain number of such systems does not leave any room for other forms of distribution based on a different type of competition policy or results in a rigidity in price structure which is not counterbalanced by other aspects of competition between other products of the same brand and by the existence of effective competition between different brands.

41. Consequently, the existence of a large number of selective distribution systems for a particular product does not in itself permit the conclusion that competition is restricted or distorted. Nor is the existence of such systems decisive as regards the granting or refusal of exemption under Article 85(3), since the only factor to be taken into consideration in that regard is the effect which such systems actually have on the competitive situation. Therefore the coverage ratio of selective distribution systems for colour television sets, to which Metro refers, cannot in itself be regarded as a factor preventing an exemption from being granted.

42. It follows that an increase in the number of 'simple' selective distribution systems after an exemption has been granted must be taken into consideration, when application for renewal of that exemption is being considered, only in the special situation in which the relevant market was already so rigid and structured that the element of competition inherent in 'simple' systems is not sufficient to maintain workable competition. Metro has not been able to show that a special situation of that kind exists in the present case.

43. As regards the effect on the market of the existence of selective distribution systems other than 'simple' systems, the Commission in renewing the exemption based itself on the relatively small market share covered by the SABA system and on the fact that that system is distinguished from 'simple' systems only by the existence of obligations pertaining to the promotion of sales. By so doing, it did not misdirect itself in exercising its discretion to assess, within the framework of Article 85(3), the economic context in which the SABA system is situated.

The judgment in *Metro II* clearly builds upon the cautionary remarks in the earlier *Metro* case. The situations in which a market analysis will be required in order to determine whether an SDA is within Article 81(1) are, however, bound to render it more difficult to predict whether a particular SDA will be caught by that Article. Moreover, it would be unfair if the creation of one further SDA brought it, but not those already existing, within Article 81(1). It would be equally odd if the creation of the most recent SDA had the effect of retrospectively bringing the previous SDAs within the ambit of Article 85(1).[34]

The *third* limitation to the legality of SDAs is that the ECJ will not tolerate clauses or agreements as part of a SDA where they operate so as to confer absolute territorial protection. This is apparent from the *BMW* case.

Case C–70/93, Bayerische Motorenwerke AG v. ALD Autoleasing D GmbH
[1995] ECR I–3439

[Note ToA renumbering: Art. 85 is now Art. 81]

BMW sold its vehicles through a selective distribution system. There was an agreement between BMW and its dealers that the latter were not to deliver vehicles to independent leasing companies that made vehicles available to customers residing or having their seat outside the contract territory of the dealer in question. This was challenged by an independent leasing company, ALD, which had supplied BMW cars in the manner which the agreement was designed to prohibit. Was the agreement caught by Article 85(1)?

THE ECJ

6. BMW claims that the appearance of independent leasing companies . . . has created an imbalance in its commercial organisation. Those independent companies concentrate on purchasing from certain BMW dealers and lease the vehicles to customers established outside the contract territory of those dealers. Those customers then turn for the customer services and maintenance to the BMW dealer in the contract territory in which they are established. Since those dealers are not involved in the original sales transaction, they do not obtain any profit margin. They therefore complained to BMW about the activities of independent leasing companies which were disturbing the network.
[*As a result of these complaints BMW instituted the agreement which was the subject-matter of this action.*]
. . .

19. As regards the requirement that competition be restricted, it should be noted that, by virtue of the agreement in question BMW dealers are able to supply vehicles of the BMW mark to independent leasing companies only if the vehicles are to be made available to lessees having their seat in the contract territory of the dealer in question. Consequently, only the dealer in whose territory the lessee has its seat is authorised by the manufacturer to supply to ALD vehicles of the BMW mark, to the exclusion of all other BMW dealers. That amounts to absolute territorial protection for the BMW dealer on whose territory the customer of ALD is established. Furthermore, the agreement reduces each dealer's freedom of commercial action in so far as each individual dealer's choice of customer is confined exclusively to those leasing

---

[34] R. Whish, *Competition Law* (Butterworths, 3rd edn., 1993), 594.

companies which have concluded contracts with lessees established within that dealer's contract territory.

There was, until recently, no block exemption for SDAs as such. They can now come within the new block exemption for vertical restraints, provided that the conditions therein are met.

6. FRANCHISING

The essence of a franchise agreement differs from that of the other methods of distribution considered thus far. The franchisor will allow the franchisee to use certain intellectual-property rights that belong to the former, such as trade names, logos, and the like. The premises on which the goods are sold are owned by the franchisee, who pays a royalty to the franchisor for the use of the trade name, etc. Franchises, therefore, benefit both parties: the franchisor receives a payment for the use of its intellectual-property rights; the franchisee is enabled to start an independent business, but with the assurance that the product and sales methods have been tried and tested elsewhere.

It is of the essence of a franchise that the franchisor will require the franchisee to comply with certain standards and methods of sale for the product in question. Failure to meet such standards by any particular franchisee can harm both the franchisor and other franchisees by damaging the reputation of the product and trade name. It is also central to the franchising system that the franchisor be enabled to impose terms which serve to protect the intellectual-property rights which have been assigned to the franchisee. In the seminal *Pronuptia* case the Court held that terms which related to both of the above issues were not caught by Article 85(1) (now Article 81(1)). However, other restrictions in the agreement, such as those which could divide the market territorially, would have to be examined under Article 85(3) (now Article 81(3)).[35] In *Yves Rocher* the Commission held that a franchise agreement under which the franchisor appointed only one franchisee for a particular area, agreed not to compete with the latter in that area, and forbade franchisees from opening more than one shop resulted in a degree of market-sharing which brought the agreement within Article 85(1).[36] The Commission made other decisions that built upon the judgment in *Pronuptia*.[37]

A block exemption was passed to cover certain types of franchise agreements, Regulation 4087/88.[38] This has now been replaced by the new general block exemption for vertical restraints.

---

[35] Case 161/84, *Pronuptia de Paris GmbH* v. *Pronuptia de Paris Irmgard Schillgallis* [1986] ECR 353. The case is set out in the text, at 959–60 above. See J. Venit, '*Pronuptia*: Ancillary Restraints or Unholy Alliances' (1986) 11 *ELRev*. 213.

[36] Dec. 87/14, [1987] OJ L8/49, [1988] 4 CMLR 592, 607.

[37] See, e.g., Dec. 87/407, *Computerland* [1987] OJ L222/12, [1989] 4 CMLR 259; Dec. 88/604, *ServiceMaster Ltd.* [1988] OJ L332/38, [1989] 4 CMLR 581.

[38] [1988] OJ L359/46.

7. EXCLUSIVE PURCHASING

Exclusive purchasing agreements (EPAs) are those in which one party agrees to buy all it needs of a particular product from a particular supplier. Common examples include petrol stations, which stock only one brand of petrol, and public houses, which carry only one general brand of beer.

Whether EPAs are within the ambit of Article 81(1) requires a market analysis: if the agreement, considered in its legal, factual, and economic context, could have the effect of restricting, preventing, or distorting competition then it will be within the ambit of this Article.[39]

Case T–7/93, Langnese-Iglo GmbH v. Commission
[1995] ECR II–1533

[Note ToA renumbering: Art. 85 is now Art. 81]

The CFI considered whether a network of exclusive purchasing agreements was caught by Article 85(1). The Commission had argued that there was no need for any real market analysis to determine whether the agreements restricted competition since the market share covered by the contested agreements was more than 15 per cent of the relevant market and the turnover of the undertakings concerned was well in excess of the ceilings laid down by the Notice on Agreements of Minor Importance.

THE CFI

98. It must be borne in mind that the Notice is intended only to define those agreements which, in the Commission's view, do not have an appreciable effect on competition or trade between Member States. The Court considers that it cannot however be inferred with certainty that a network of exclusive purchasing agreements is automatically liable to prevent, restrict or distort competition appreciably merely because the ceilings laid down in it are exceeded. Moreover, it is apparent from the actual wording of paragraph 3 of that Notice that it is entirely possible, in the facts of the present case, that agreements . . . which exceed the ceilings indicated affect . . . competition only to an insignificant extent and consequently are not caught by Article 85(1). . . .

99. As to whether the exclusive purchasing agreements fall within . . . Article 85(1) . . ., it is appropriate, according to the case-law, to consider whether, taken together, all the similar agreements entered into in the relevant market and the other features of the economic and legal context of the agreements at issue show that those agreements cumulatively have the effect of denying access to that market for new domestic and foreign competitors. If . . . that is found not to be the case, the individual agreements making up the bundle of agreements as a whole cannot

---

[39] Case 23/67, *Brasserie de Haecht*; n. 22 above; Case C–234/89, *Delimitis* v. *Henninger Bräu AG* [1991] ECR I–935; Case C–393/92, *Municipality of Almelo* v. *NV Energiebedrijf Ijsselmij* [1994] ECR I–1477. In deciding whether this is so, the competition authorities will take account of clauses which, although not constituting an obligation as such on the reseller to purchase all its requirements of a particular product from a particular supplier, none the less constitute inducements to do so. Offering discounts to the reseller is one obvious example.

undermine competition within the meaning of Article 85(1). . . . If, on the other hand, such examination reveals that it is difficult to gain access to the market, it is necessary to assess the extent to which the contested agreements contribute to the cumulative effect produced, on the basis that only agreements which make a significant contribution to any partitioning of the market are prohibited (*Delimitis*, paragraphs 23 and 24).

100. It must then be borne in mind, that as the Court of Justice held in . . . *Brasserie de Haecht*, consideration of the effects of an exclusive agreement implied that regard must be had to the economic and legal context of the agreement, in which it might combine with others to have a cumulative effect on competition.

[*The CFI found that the agreements were liable to affect competition appreciably and therefore came within Article 85(1).*]

The parties to an EPA can seek exemption, either on an individual basis or pursuant to the block exemption. There was a specific block exemption covering exclusive purchasing, Regulation 1984/83.[40] This has now been replaced by the new block exemption for vertical restraints.

8. THE BLOCK EXEMPTION

(a) THE NEW-STYLE BLOCK EXEMPTION

We have already seen the impetus for reform of vertical restraints. Regulation 2790/99,[41] is properly regarded as a new-style block exemption.[42] It differs from the previous block exemptions in this area in a number of ways. It is less formalistic than its predecessors, and is more economics-oriented. It applies to all species of vertical restraints, with the exception of distribution agreements for motor vehicles. It is less prescriptive than the earlier regulations. These had generally followed a format of having a specific list of white clauses that were allowed, and black clauses that were forbidden. The new Regulation no longer contains a white list: if conduct is not prohibited it is therefore permitted. It must be read in tandem with Commission Guidelines.[43]

The recitals to Regulation 2790/99 state that it is possible to define a category of vertical agreements that will normally satisfy the conditions of Article 81(3). These agreements are said to improve economic efficiency by facilitating co-ordination and reducing distribution costs.[44]

---

[40] [1983] OJ L173/5.

[41] *Comm. Reg. 2790/99 on the Application of Article 81(3) of the Treaty to Categories of Vertical Agreements and Concerted Practices* [1999] OJ L336/21, [2000] 4 CMLR 398.

[42] R. Whish, 'Regulation 2790/99: The Commission's "New Style" Block Exemption for Vertical Agreements' (2000) 37 *CMLRev.* 887.

[43] *Guidelines on Vertical Restraints* [2000] OJ C291/1.

[44] Reg. 2790/99, n. 41 above, rec. 6.

(b) ARTICLE 1: DEFINITIONS

Article 1 of Regulation 2790/99 is a definitional section. It provides definitions of matters such as exclusive supply obligation, selective distribution system and the like. The definition of 'non-compete obligation' is worthy of note.

'Non-compete obligation' means any direct or indirect obligation causing the buyer not to manu-facture, purchase, sell or resell goods or services which compete with the contract goods or services, or any direct or indirect obligation on the buyer to purchase from the supplier or from another undertaking designated by the supplier more than 80 per cent of the buyer's total purchases of the contract goods or services on the relevant market. . . .

(c) ARTICLE 2: THE CORE OF THE BLOCK EXEMPTION

The core of the block exemption is to be found in Article 2. *Article 2(1)* provides that:

. . . Article 81(1) shall not apply to agreements or concerted practices entered into between two or more undertakings each of which operates, for the purposes of the agreement, at a different level of the production or distribution chain, and relating to the conditions under which the parties may purchase, sell, or resell certain goods or services ('vertical agreements').

This exemption shall apply to the extent to which such agreements contain restrictions of competition falling within the scope of Article 81(1) ('vertical restraints').

Certain key points about Article 2 should be noted. First, we have already seen that many vertical agreements do not infringe Article 81(1) at all. Such agreements will not therefore need to use the block exemption.

Secondly, the block exemption can apply to all types of vertical agreement, and the exempted agreement can be multilateral. Article 2(1) is framed in terms of *two or more undertakings*, whereas the old block exemptions applied only to bilateral agreements. It is, however, necessary for *each* of the undertakings to operate, for the purposes of the agreement, at a different level of the production or distribution chain. The fact that Article 2(1) includes the phrase *for the purposes of the agreement* means that it is possible, subject to the limits of Article 2(4), for two firms that are, for example, both cement manufacturers, to come within the Regulation. This would be so where one suppliers material to the other.

Article 2(2) applies the block exemption to vertical agreements between an association of undertakings and its members, or its suppliers. All members of the association must however be retailers, and no individual member must have an annual turnover in excess of 50 million Euros.

Article 2(3) makes the block exemption applicable where intellectual property rights are ancillary to the main purpose of the vertical agreement.[45]

Article 2(4) is designed to prevent the block exemption being used by competing undertakings to indulge in market division. Competing undertakings are actual or potential suppliers in the same product market.[46] Article 2(4) provides that

---

[45] See Whish, n. 42 above, 903–5, for analysis of this provision.
[46] Reg. 2790/99, n. 41 above, Art. 1(a); *Guidelines*, n. 43 above, para. 26.

Article 2(1) shall not apply to vertical agreements between competing undertakings. Article 2(4) then provides that the exemption can apply where such undertakings enter into a non-reciprocal vertical agreement. There are other conditions to be met. The buyer must have a turnover not greater than 100 million Euros. Or the supplier is a manufacturer and distributor of goods, while the buyer is a distributor not manufacturing goods that compete with the contract goods. Or the supplier is a provider of services at several levels of trade, while the buyer does not provide competing services at the level of trade where it purchases the contract goods.

Article 2(5) states that this block exemption shall not apply to vertical agreements the subject matter of which falls within the scope of any other block exemption.

(d) ARTICLE 3: THE MARKET SHARE CAP

The likelihood of efficiency gains from vertical agreements outweighing any anti-competitive effects is said in the recitals to be dependent on the market power of the undertakings concerned, and the Regulation therefore has limits as to the market share of the participating firms.[47] Article 3(1) states that the exemption contained in Article 2 only applies on the condition that the market share held by the supplier does not exceed 30 per cent of the relevant market on which it sells the contract goods or services. In the case of vertical agreements containing exclusive supply obligations, the condition is that the market share of the buyer must not exceed 30 per cent of the relevant market on which it purchases the contract goods or services, Article 3(2).[48] The method of calculating market share is laid down in Article 9.

(e) ARTICLE 4: THE BLACK LIST

The recitals make it clear that certain types of clauses that are regarded as especially anti-competitive will not benefit from the block exemption. These include clauses relating to vertical price fixing and territorial protection.[49] This issue is dealt with in Article 4. It excludes the Regulation for vertical agreements which, directly or indirectly, in isolation or combination with other factors under the control of the parties, have as their object any of the following restrictions.

Resale price maintenance is excluded. Maximum selling prices and recommendations as to selling prices are allowed, subject to the caveat that they do not amount to a fixed or minimum sale price, as a result of pressure from, or incentives offered by, any of the parties.[50]

Restrictions on the territory into which, or the customers to whom, the buyer can sell the goods or services are also precluded.[51] This is subject to a number of exceptions. It is permissible to have a restriction on active sales into the exclusive territory or to an exclusive customer group reserved to the supplier, or allocated by the supplier to another buyer, where such a restriction does not limit sales by the customers to the

---

[47] Reg. 2790/99, n. 41 above, recs. 7–8.   [48] *Guidelines*, n. 43 above, paras. 21–22.
[49] Reg. 2790/99, n. 41 above, rec. 10.   [50] *Ibid.*, Art. 4(a); *Guidelines*, n 43 above, para. 47.
[51] Reg. 2790/99, n. 41 above, Art. 4(b).

buyer.[52] It is permissible to restrict sales to end users by a buyer operating at the wholesale level of trade, and to restrict sales to unauthorized distributors by the members of a selective distribution system. The final exception is that it is possible to restrict the buyer of components for use from selling them to a customer who would use them to make goods that would compete with those of the supplier.

The restriction of active or passive sales to end users by members of a selective distribution system operating at the retail level is not allowed. This is without prejudice to the possibility of prohibiting a member of the system from operating out of an unauthorized place of establishment.[53] It is important to note that, subject to this condition, selective and exclusive distribution can be combined within one agreement. Such an agreement could still come within the block exemption, provided that it complied with the other conditions laid down therein.[54]

It is not possible to have restrictions of cross-supplies between distributors within a selective distribution system, including between distributors operating at different levels of trade.[55] A selected distributor must therefore be able to buy from any approved distributor.

The final black-listed provision relates to the supply of components. It is designed to allow end-users and independent service-providers to obtain spare parts.[56]

(f) ARTICLE 5: OBLIGATIONS THAT DO NOT BENEFIT FROM THE EXEMPTION

The restrictions in Article 4 prevent the entire vertical agreement from benefiting from the block exemption. Article 5 excludes the benefit of the block exemption from certain terms contained in such an agreement. The agreement itself may however still gain the benefit of the block exemption if the objectionable clause can be severed. There are three types of obligation listed in Article 5.

Non-compete obligations cannot be indefinite or last longer than five years. Obligations not to compete after the term of the agreement are also excluded. This is subject to a qualification allowing such an obligation for one year on sales of competing goods or services from the place of sale that the buyer operated from during the contract, provided that this is necessary to protect the supplier's know-how. The benefit of the block exemption is also excluded from an obligation causing the members of a selective distribution system from selling brands of particular competing suppliers.

(g) ARTICLES 6–8: WITHDRAWING THE BENEFIT OF THE REGULATION

Articles 6–8 provide certain limits to the application of the block exemption. *Article 6* allows the Commission to withdraw the benefit of the block exemption where it finds that vertical agreements to which the Regulation applies nevertheless have effects

---

[52] *Guidelines*, n. 43 above, para. 50.
[53] Reg. 2790/99, n. 41 above, Art. 4(c); *Guidelines*, n. 43 above, para. 53.
[54] Whish, n. 42 above, 916.
[55] Reg. 2790/99, n. 41 above, Art. 4(d).   [56] *Ibid.*, Art. 4(e).

incompatible with Article 81(3). This will apply in particular where access to the relevant market or competition therein is significantly restricted by the cumulative effect of parallel networks of similar vertical restraints by competing suppliers or buyers.[57] *Article 7* allows the competent authority of a Member State, where the State has the characteristics of a distinct geographic market, to withdraw the benefit of the block exemption for that State, under the same conditions as in Article 6. *Article 8* empowers the Commission to pass a regulation declaring that the block exemption is inapplicable where there are vertical restraints covering more than 50 per cent of that market.

9. CONCLUSION

i. There has been fierce debate about vertical agreements. There have been disagreements in the academic community about whether they are harmful, and if so when.

ii. There has been criticism of the Commission for not talking with the same voice as the ECJ, and for employing a test that equates a restriction of conduct with a restriction of competition.

iii. The degree of difference between the Community courts and the Commission has diminished more recently. It would however be premature to say that the Commission has fully adopted the ECJ's approach to Article 81(1). Moreover, the very approach of the Community courts has been thrown into some doubt as a result of the CFI's decision in *Métropole*.[58]

iv. The importance of this difference has been lessened by the passage of the new block exemption. This Regulation is undoubtedly less formalistic than its predecessors. It should not however be forgotten that the Regulation has a market share cap of 30 per cent. Some commentators feel that this is warranted, since economic theory tells us that it is only when there is some degree of market power that vertical agreements are dangerous.[59] This may well be accepted, but other commentators regard the existing cap as too low, and have characterized the new Regulation as little more than an extended *de minimis* provision.[60]

10. FURTHER READING

(a) *Books*

AMATO, G., *Antitrust and the Bounds of Power* (Hart, 1997)

BELLAMY, C., and CHILD, G., *European Community Law of Competition* (Sweet & Maxwell, 5th edn., 2001)

---

[57] *Guidelines*, n. 43 above, paras. 71–75.
[58] Case T–112/99, *Métropole Télévision (M6), Suez-Lyonnaise des Eaux, France Telecom, and Télévision Française 1 SA (TFI)* v. *Commission*, September 18, 2001. See 960–1 above.
[59] Whish, n. 42 above.
[60] M. Griffiths, 'A Glorification of De Minimis—The Regulation on Vertical Agreements' [2000] *ECLR* 241.

BISHOP, S., and WALKER, M., *The Economics of EC Competition Law, Concepts, Application and Measurement* (Sweet & Maxwell, 1999)

BORK, R.H., *The Antitrust Paradox: A Policy at War with Itself* (Basic Books, 1978)

FAULL, J., and NIKPAY, A. (eds.), *The EC Law of Competition* (Oxford University Press, 1999)

GERBER, D., *Law and Competition in Twentieth Century Europe* (Oxford University Press, 1998)

JONES, A., and SUFRIN, B., *EC Competition Law, Text, Cases and Materials* (Oxford University Press, 2001)

KORAH, V., *An Introductory Guide to EC Competiton Law and Practice* (Hart, 7th edn., 2000)

—— *Vertical Agreements: Distribution under the EC Competition Rules* (Hart, 2001)

NEVEN, D., PAPANDROPOLOUS, P., and SEABRIGHT, P., *Trawling for Minnows: European Competition Policy and Agreements between Firms* (Centre for Economic Policy Research, 1998)

RODGER, B., and MACCULLOCH, A., *Competition Law and Policy in the EC and UK* (Cavendish, 2001)

WHISH, R., *Competition Law* (Butterworths, 4th edn., 2001)

(b) *Articles*

BOK, B., 'An Economist Appraises Vertical Restraints' (1985) 30 *Antitrust B* 117.

BORK, R., 'The Rule of Reason and the *Per Se* Concept in Price Fixing and Market Division II' (1966) 75 *Yale LJ* 373

BRIGHT, C., 'EU Competition Policy: Rules, Objectives and Deregulation' (1996) 16 *OJLS* 535

CHARD, J.S., 'The Economics of the Application of Article 85 to Selective Distribution Systems' (1982) 7 *ELRev.* 83

EASTERBROOK, F., 'Vertical Arrangements and the Rule of Reason' (1984) 53 *Antitrust LJ* 135

GRIFFITHS, M., 'A Glorification of De Minimis—The Regulation on Vertical Agreements' [2000] *ECLR* 241

HAWK, B., 'System Failure: Vertical Restraints and EC Competition Law' (1995) 32 *CMLRev.* 973

LEVER, J., and NEUBAUER, S., 'Vertical Restraints, Their Motivation and Justification' [2000] *ECLR* 7

SCHAUB, A., 'Vertical Restraints: Key Points and Issues under the New EC Block Exemption', in B. Hawk (ed.), *Fordham Corporate Law Institute* (Fordham University, 2000), ch. 13

VAJDA, C., 'Selective Distribution in the European Community' (1979) 13 *JWTL* 409

VENIT, J., '*Pronuptia*: Ancillary Restraints or Unholy Alliances' (1986) 11 *ELRev.* 213

WHISH, R., 'Regulation 2790/99: The Commission's "New Style" Block Exemption for Vertical Agreements' (2000) 37 *CMLRev.* 887

23

COMPETITION LAW: ARTICLE 82

1. INTRODUCTION

In the previous chapter we considered the applicability of Article 81 (ex Article 85). We now focus attention upon the other principal provision concerned with competition policy: Article 82 (ex Article 86):

Any abuse by one or more undertakings of a dominant position within the common market or in a substantial part of it shall be prohibited as incompatible with the common market in so far as it may affect trade between Member States. Such abuse may, in particular, consist in:

(a) directly or indirectly imposing unfair purchase or selling prices or unfair trading conditions

(b) limiting production, markets or technical development to the prejudice of consumers

(c) applying dissimilar conditions to equivalent transactions with other trading parties, thereby placing them at a competitive disadvantage

(d) making the conclusion of contracts subject to acceptance by the other parties of supplementary obligations which, by their nature or according to commercial usage, have no connection with the subject of such contracts.

2. CENTRAL ISSUES

i. The essence of Article 82 is the control of market power. The paradigm instance for the application of the Article is the single, dominant firm which abuses its market power in one of the ways exemplified above, by, for example charging unfair selling prices. It is however clear that one or more undertakings may be held to have abused a dominant position, and that the list of abusive practices are examples. They do not exhaust the definition of abusive conduct.

ii. The constituent elements of Article 82, such as the existence of a dominant position, demand an economic analysis.

iii. Article 82 does not prohibit market power or monopoly *per se*. It proscribes the *abuse* of market power. Firms are encouraged to compete, to engage in a market 'race', with the objective, *inter alia*, of ensuring that the most efficient players will emerge successful at the end of the contest. This contest never actually ends, since even those who are the current winners will have to face the potential of competition from new market entrants. It would be odd, although not logically impossible, to state that those who do emerge as the winners from the race at any one point in time should, *from that fact alone*, face the possibility of legal penalty or proscription. This would have the effect of penalizing the winner, who may have attained a species of market power by dint of being more efficient than the rest of the field. It is for this reason that most systems of competition policy stop short of proscribing market power *per se*. The thrust of the policy is directed at the *behaviour* of the firm with market power, rather than the *existence* of the power in and of itself. This is reflected within Article 82 by the fact that the Treaty speaks of *abuse* of a dominant position being prohibited, as opposed to dominance *per se*.

iv. This distinction is, however, more difficult to maintain in practice than might initially be thought. For example, Article 82(a) prohibits unfair selling prices by those with a dominant position. This appears to be a classic form of abusive market behaviour: the firm with market power charges significantly too much. This seems straightforward. It may well be in some instances, but in others it will be more problematic. This is because the behaviour of a rational monopolist will be to market the goods at a price which is higher than that prevailing under ordinary competitive conditions. It is part of standard economic doctrine that a monopolist will behave in this manner, in order to maximize its profits.

v. There is then a choice for the competition authorities. They may categorize such behaviour as being in breach of Article 82(a) by denominating the selling price as unfair. This is clearly an option, but the effect of pursuing this line would be, in effect, to prohibit monopoly *per se*. It would be to categorize the standard, economically rational, pricing behaviour of the monopolist as illegal. The alternative would be to interpret the phrase 'unfair selling price' differently, and only to proscribe pricing behaviour which is in some way excessively high, or indeed low, even by the standard of the monopolist or one possessed of market power.

vi. It might be argued in the light of the above that we should indeed prohibit market power *per se*, given that those with such power are likely to price higher, and limit production to a greater extent, than in ordinary market conditions. There are however two problems with any such strategy.

vii. One is that such an approach would entail a very different type of control over market power than that commonly exercised by competition authorities. If the ordinary, rational pricing and output policies of the monopolist were to be controlled, then this would necessitate some species of continuing regulatory control over the policies of the relevant firms. Regulatory structures of this kind can be established, and do indeed exist for certain industries in the United Kingdom, most notably those operating in the post-privatization spheres such as gas, telecommunications, and electricity. This type of control is, however, different from that exercised by competition authorities.

viii. The other problem with the proscription of market power *per se* is that it may well be undesirable because the dominant firm may have attained this position through superior efficiency and lower costs. We would, therefore, be penalizing the winner of the competitive race even though the victory was achieved through legitimate means. Difficulties of the kind outlined above will be returned to in the course of the following analysis.

3. DOMINANT POSITION: THE PRODUCT MARKET

Article 82 (ex Article 86) requires that the undertaking[1] or undertakings be in a dominant position before the prohibitions on abusive behaviour are applicable. The

---

[1] The definition of an undertaking is the same as in the context of Art. 85 (ex Art. 81), on which see 939–40 above. It covers any entity engaged in economic activity, regardless of its legal status and the way it is financed: Case T-128/98, *Aéroports de Paris* v. *Commission* [2000] ECR II–3929, para. 107. For an example of a body which was deemed not to be an undertaking for the purposes of Art. 86 see Case C–364/92, *SAT Fluggesellschaft mbH* v. *Eurocontrol* [1994] ECR I–43, [1994] 5 CMLR 208. The problems of applying Art. 86 (now Art. 82) to joint dominance are dealt with at 1026–9 below.

Article does not provide any formalistic definition of what is to constitute dominance, and therefore the application of this term necessitates an economic analysis. An undertaking cannot be dominant in the abstract. Dominance can be assessed only in relation to three essential variables: the product market, the geographical market, and the temporal factor. The first of these factors will be examined in this section, the second and third in the sections which follow.

Any firm will only have market power in the context of the supply of particular goods or services. The determination of the relevant product market is, therefore, crucial. Other things being equal, the narrower the definition of the product market the easier it is to conclude that an undertaking is dominant for the purposes of Article 82. It is not, then, surprising to find that many cases have been fought on this terrain, with the firm contesting that the Commission has adopted a narrow and inaccurate definition of the relevant product.

The general approach of the Commission and the Court to the definition of the product market has been to focus upon *interchangeability*: the extent to which the goods or services under scrutiny are interchangeable with other products.[2] This issue is addressed by looking at both the demand and supply sides of the market.

From the *demand side* interchangeability requires investigation of cross-elasticities of the product in question. The basic idea here is simple. Cross-elasticity is high where an increase in the price of one product, for example beef, will lead buyers to switch in significant numbers to lamb or pork. The existence of high cross-elasticity indicates that the products are in reality part of the same market. It may, however, be difficult to obtain reliable data on the relative cross-elasticities of different products. In these circumstances the Commission and the Court may well look to related factors to determine whether the products really are inter-changeable. These factors will include the prices of the two products and their physical characteristics. For example, wines may vary significantly in price and quality. An increase in the price of a top-quality wine may not lead buyers to switch to 'plonk', although it may lead them to buy more of another high-grade wine which has not increased in price to such a degree. The relevance of the physical characteristics of the product is exemplified by the *United Brands* case, in which the Court took into account the taste, seedlessness, and softness of bananas in order to determine whether they constituted a separate market from other fruits.[3]

The degree of interchangeability between products may also be affected by factors on the *supply side*. Even if firms are producing differing products it may be relatively simple for one firm to adapt its machinery to make the goods produced by a rival. In these circumstances the two products may be thought to be part of the same market.[4]

The following cases provide a sense of how the Court goes about defining the relevant product market, and the problems that this can entail:

[2] See, e.g., Case 27/76, *United Brands Company and United Brands Continentaal BV* v. *Commission* [1978] ECR 207.

[3] *Ibid.*

[4] Case 6/72, *Europemballage Corporation and Continental Can Co. Inc.* v. *Commission* [1973] ECR 215; Case T–65/96, *Kish Glass & Co. Ltd.* v. *Commission* [2000] ECR II–1885, para. 68.

Case 27/76, United Brands Company and United Brands Continentaal BV v. Commission
[1978] ECR 207

[Note ToA renumbering: Art. 86 is now Art. 82]

United Brands produced bananas, and was accused of a variety of abusive practices which were said to infringe Article 86. These practices will be examined below. An initial issue concerned the definition of the relevant product market. UB argued that bananas were part of a larger market in fresh fruit, and produced studies designed to show that cross-elasticity between bananas and other fruits was high. The Commission contended that cross-elasticity was in fact low, and that bananas were a distinct market in part because they constituted an important part of the diet of certain sections of consumers, and in part because they had specific qualities which made other fruits unacceptable as substitutes.

THE ECJ

22. For the banana to be regarded as forming a market which is sufficiently differentiated from other fruits it must be possible for it to be singled out by such special features distinguishing it from other fruits that it is only to a limited extent interchangeable with them and is only exposed to their competition in a way that is hardly perceptible.

23. The ripening of bananas takes place the whole year round without any season having to be taken into account.

. . .

27. Since the banana is a fruit which is always available in sufficient quantities the question whether it can be replaced by other fruits must be determined over the whole of the year for the purpose of ascertaining the degree of competition between it and other fresh fruit.

28. The studies of the banana market on the Court's file show that on the latter market there is no significant long term cross-elasticity any more than . . . there is any seasonal substitutability in general between the banana and all the seasonal fruits, as this only exists between the banana and two fruits (peaches and table grapes) in one of the countries (West Germany) of the relevant geographical market.

29. As far as concerns the two fruits available throughout the year (oranges and apples) the first are not interchangeable and in the case of the second there is only a relative degree of substitutability.

30. This small degree of substitutability is accounted for by the specific features of the banana and all the factors which influence consumer choice.

31. The banana has certain characteristics, appearance, taste, softness, seedlessness, easy handling, a constant level of production which enable it to satisfy the constant needs of an important section of the population consisting of the very young, the old and the sick.

32. As far as prices are concerned two FAO studies show that the banana is only affected by the prices—falling prices—of other fruits (and only of peaches and table grapes) during the summer months and mainly in July and then by an amount not exceeding 20 per cent.

. . .

34. It follows from all these considerations that a very large number of consumers having a constant need for bananas are not noticeably or even appreciably enticed away from the consumption of this product by the arrival of fresh fruit on the market and that even the seasonal peak periods only affect it for a limited period of time from the point of view of substitutability.

35. Consequently the banana market is a market which is sufficiently distinct from the other fresh fruit market.

Case 322/81, Nederlandsche Banden-Industrie Michelin NV v. Commission
[1983] ECR 3461

[Note ToA renumbering: Art. 86 is now Art. 82]

The Commission brought an action under Article 86 against Michelin based on the practice of awarding discounts on tyre sales which were not related to objective differences in costs. The allegation was, therefore, that the discounts were granted so as to tie purchasers to Michelin. Michelin was held to have a dominant position in the market for new replacement tyres for lorries, buses and similar vehicles. Michelin argued that this definition of the product market was arbitrary and artificial, and that regard should also be had to tyres for cars and vans, and to retreads.

THE ECJ

37. As the Court has repeatedly emphasised . . . for the purposes of investigating the possibly dominant position of an undertaking on a given market, the possibilities of competition must be judged in the context of the market comprising the totality of the products which, with respect to their characteristics, are particularly suitable for satisfying constant needs and are only to a limited extent interchangeable with other products.

However, it must be noted that the determination of the relevant market is useful in assessing whether the undertaking concerned is in a position to prevent effective competition from being maintained and behave to an appreciable extent independently of its competitors and customers and consumers. For this purpose, therefore, an examination limited to the objective characteristics only of the relevant products cannot be sufficient: the competitive conditions and the structure of supply and demand must also be taken into consideration.

38. Moreover, it was for that reason that the Commission and Michelin NV agreed that new, original-equipment tyres should not be taken into consideration in the assessment of market shares. Owing to the particular structure of demand for such tyres characterised by direct orders from car manufacturers, competition in this sphere is in fact governed by completely different factors and rules.

39. As far as replacement tyres are concerned, the first point which must be made is that at the user level there is no interchangeability between car and van tyres on the one hand and heavy-vehicle tyres on the other. Car and van tyres therefore have no influence at all on competition on the market in heavy-vehicle tyres.

40. Furthermore, the structure of demand for each of these groups of products is different. Most buyers of heavy-vehicle tyres are trade users . . . for whom . . . the purchase of replacement tyres represents an item of considerable expenditure. . . . On the other hand, for the average buyer of car or van tyres the purchase of tyres is an occasional event. . . .

41. The final point which must be made is that there is no elasticity of supply between tyres for heavy vehicles and car tyres owing to significant differences in production techniques and in the plant and tools needed for their manufacture. The fact that time and considerable investment are required in order to modify production plant for the manufacture of light-vehicle tyres instead of

heavy-vehicle tyres or vice versa means that there is no discernible relationship between the two categories of tyre enabling production to be adapted to demand on the market.

. . .

45. In establishing that Michelin NV has a dominant position the Commission was therefore right to assess its market share with reference to replacement tyres for lorries, buses and similar vehicles and to exclude consideration of car and van tyres.

The nature of the product market may indeed be particularly narrow as the next case illustrates.[5]

Case 22/78, Hugin Kassaregister AB and Hugin Cash Registers Limited v. Commission
[1979] ECR 1869

[Note ToA renumbering: Art. 86 is now Art. 82]

Hugin was held by the Commission to be in breach of Article 86 by refusing to supply spare parts for its cash registers to Liptons, which competed with Hugin in servicing Hugin's machines. The Commission defined the relevant market as being spare parts for Hugin machines which were needed by independent repairers. Hugin argued that the proper product market was cash registers in general, which was very competitive. The Court found that users of cash registers would require the services of a specialist to service the machines. It continued as follows.

THE ECJ

7. . . . there exists a separate market for Hugin spare parts at another level, namely that of independent undertakings which specialize in the maintenance and repair of cash registers, in the reconditioning of used machines and in the sale of used machines and the renting out of machines. The role of those undertakings on the market is that of businesses which require spare parts for their various activities. They need such parts in order to provide services for cash register users in the form of maintenance and repairs and for the reconditioning of used machines and for re-sale and renting out. Finally, they require spare parts for the maintenance and repair of new or used machines belonging to them which are rented out to their clients. It is, moreover, established that there is a specific demand for Hugin spare parts, since those parts are not interchangeable with spare parts for cash registers of other makes.

8. Consequently the market thus constituted by Hugin spare parts required by independent undertakings must be regarded as the relevant market for the purposes of the application of Article 86 to the facts of the case. . . .

9. It is necessary to examine next whether Hugin occupies a dominant position on that market. In this respect Hugin admits that it has a monopoly in new spare parts. For commercial reasons any competing production of spare parts which could be used in Hugin cash registers is not conceivable in practice. Hugin argues nevertheless that another source of supply does exist, namely the purchase and dismantling of used machines. The value of that source is disputed by the parties.

[5] See also Case 26/75, *General Motors Continental NV* v. *Commission* [1975] ECR 1367.

Although the file appears to show that the practice of dismantling used machines is current in the cash register sector it cannot be regarded as constituting a sufficient alternative source of supply. . . .

10. On the market for its own spare parts, therefore, Hugin is in a position which enables it to determine its conduct without taking account of competing sources of supply. There is therefore nothing to invalidate the conclusion that it occupies, on that market, a dominant position within the meaning of Article 86.

That the definition of the appropriate product market can be contentious is demonstrated by the following comment on the *Hugin* case:[6]

E. Fox, Monopolization and Dominance in the US and the EC: Efficiency, Opportunity and Fairness[7]

In Hugin Liptons, the Court of Justice defined the market as spare parts for Hugin machines in view of the demand by independent servicers and renting agents. In doing so it ignored facts that US courts would deem material; namely that the independents could get spare parts for the other cash registers from their producers and that Liptons could be expected to shift its business to the servicing and renting of more cash registers produced by other firms. A healthy market of independents who serviced and rented cash registers (made by other producers) would have remained.

When one asks whether Hugin's termination of Liptons was an effort to monopolize, the misfit of the monopoly framework becomes plain. Hugin was not a dominant cash register firm. It surely could not get a monopoly by charging a supracompetitive price for spare parts, and it would undercut its competitive attractiveness as a supplier of new machines if it developed a reputation for overcharging for repairs. Only two hypotheses seem plausible. Either Hugin was charging a low price for service and was providing rapid reliable service itself or through its authorized distributors, so as to wage more effective competition against its highly aggressive competitors, or Hugin wanted to keep the servicing business for itself and its authorized distributors and they were providing at least as good a price/service package as Liptons.

4. DOMINANT POSITION: THE GEOGRAPHIC MARKET AND THE TEMPORAL FACTOR

In order to determine whether an undertaking is dominant for the purposes of Article 82 (ex Article 86) it is necessary to make some judgement concerning the geographic market. Some goods or services can be supplied without differentiation over a wide

---

[6] See also the contested definitions of the product market in Cases 6 & 7/73, *Istituto Chemioterapico Italiano SpA and Commercial Solvents* v. *Commission* [1974] ECR 223; Case 6/72, *Continental Can*, n. 4 above; Case 85/76, *Hoffmann-La Roche and Co. AG* v. *Commission* [1979] ECR 461; Case C–333/94P, *Tetra Pak International SA* v. *Commission* [1996] ECR I–5951.

[7] (1986) 61 *Notre Dame LRev.* 981, 1003–4.

area; others may be supplied within a narrower area, because of technical or practical reasons which render wider distribution problematic. Transport costs are a factor of obvious importance in this regard. In the absence of such special factors, the relevant geographic market has been held in *Hilti* to be the entire EC.[8] The *United Brands* case provides insights into this aspect of the Court's thinking:

Case 27/76, United Brands Company and United Brands Continentaal BV v. Commission [1978] ECR 207

The facts have been set out above. One of the grounds on which UB challenged the findings of the Commission was that the latter had misconstrued the nature of the geographic market. The Commission had excluded France, Italy, and the United Kingdom from the applicable market, because of particular trading conditions which existed there. The applicants accepted this, but contended that trading conditions were also different in each of the other countries which had been treated by the Commission as the relevant geographic market.

THE ECJ

44. The conditions for the application of Article 86 to an undertaking in a dominant position presuppose the clear delimitation of the substantial part of the Common Market in which it may be able to engage in abuses which hinder effective competition and this is an area where the objective conditions of competition applying to the product in question must be the same for all traders.

45. The Community has not established a common organisation of the agricultural market in bananas.

46. Consequently import arrangements vary considerably from one Member State to another and reflect a specific commercial policy to the States concerned.

[*The Court then examined the special arrangements for bananas in France, Italy, and the United Kingdom. These arrangements differed in detail, but in general entailed preferential treatment for bananas coming from overseas territories of the three countries, or from the Commonwealth. It continued as follows:*]

51. The effect of the national organisation of these three markets is that the applicant's bananas do not compete on equal terms with the other bananas sold in these States which benefit from a preferential system and the Commission was right to exclude these three national markets from the geographic market under consideration.

52. On the other hand the six other States are markets which are completely free, although the applicable tariff provisions and transport costs are of necessity different but not discriminatory, and in which the conditions of competition are the same for all.

53. From the standpoint of being able to engage in free competition these six States form an area which is sufficiently homogeneous to be considered in its entirety.

---

[8] Dec. 88/138, [1988] OJ L65/19, [1989] 4 CMLR 677, upheld on appeal: Case C–53/92P, *Hilti AG* v. *Commission* [1994] ECR I–667.

In some instances the scope of the geographical market will be relatively straight-forward. This was the case in *British Telecommunications*,[9] where the issue was whether BT had abused its dominant position with regard to message-forwarding agencies in the United Kingdom: the geographical market was the United Kingdom, within which BT had a monopoly in the provision of telecommunication services. In other instances the scope of the geographical market may be influenced by factors such as transport costs. This was so in *Napier Brown–British Sugar*.[10] The Commission held that in determining whether a United Kingdom company had a dominant position in the production and sale of sugar the relevant market was Great Britain, since imports were very limited and acted as a complement to British sugar, rather than an alternative.

Markets may, as stated above, also have a temporal quality or element to them. Thus, a firm may possess market power at a particular time of year, during which competition from other products is low because these other products are available only seasonally. It is equally important to note that the very definition of the product market will have a temporal dimension to it, in the sense that technological progress and changes in consumer habits will shift boundaries between markets.[11]

5. DOMINANT POSITION: THE COMMISSION NOTICE ON MARKET DEFINITION

The Commission has published a Notice on the Definition of the Relevant Market for the Purposes of Community Competition Law.[12] The object of the Notice is to furnish firms with guidance on how the Commission approaches matters of market definition, and in this sense to foster transparency. The Notice is important in three related ways.[13]

First, the Commission makes it clear that the definition of the relevant market will be viewed differently depending upon the nature of the competition inquiry: an investigation into a proposed concentration is essentially prospective, whereas other types of investigation may be concerned primarily with an analysis of past behaviour.

Secondly, the Notice does, in reality, entail a shift in Commission thinking on how market definition should be conducted.[14] This may not be readily apparent from the face of the document, but it is true none the less. The Notice begins in orthodox fashion, by stating that the Commission will inquire into demand substitutability, supply substitutability, and potential competition. These factors have, as we have seen, played a significant role in Commission and Court thinking on this topic. The novelty

---

[9] Dec. 82/861, [1982] OJ L360/36, [1983] 1 CMLR 457. On appeal see Case 41/83, *Italy v. Commission* [1985] ECR 873.

[10] Dec. 88/518, [1988] OJ L284/41, [1990] 4 CMLR 196.

[11] Dec. 92/163, *Elopak Italia Srl v. Tetra Pak (No. 2)* [1992] OJ L72/1, [1992] 4 CMLR 551.

[12] [1997] OJ C372/5, [1998] 4 CMLR 177. A revised version of the Notice is on the DG IV website www.europa.eu.int/comm/competition.

[13] W. Bishop, 'Editorial: The Modernization of DGIV' [1997] *ECLR* 481.

[14] We have benefited in this para. from a competition memo published by *Lexecon*, 4 June 1997.

of the Notice stems from the detailed indication provided by the Commission on how these principles will be applied. In essence, the Commission adopts what is known as the SSNIP test, originally developed in the USA. SSNIP stands for 'small but significant and non-transitory increase in prices'. On this test, a relevant market is the narrowest range of products such that a hypothetical permanent monopolist in the relevant product area would find it both possible and worthwhile to institute an SSNIP. If demand substitution would be enough to make the price increase unprofitable because of the resulting loss of sales, then additional product substitutes would be included in the relevant market.

Thirdly, while it is axiomatic that the Commission cannot overrule ECJ decisions, whether through a Notice or by any other means, it is clear none the less that the Commission is moving away from some of the benchmarks used by the ECJ when engaged in product definition. Thus the similarity of product characteristics and intended use, which have featured in Commission and ECJ thinking,[15] are regarded as insufficient to determine whether two products are demand substitutes. The same is true of functional interchangeability,[16] because the responsiveness of customers to price changes may be determined by other considerations. In positive terms, the Commission states that it will consider: evidence of substitution in the recent past or where there have been shocks in the market; the views of customers and competitors; quantitative econometric tests; evidence of consumer preferences where available; barriers and costs entailed in substitution; and whether there are distinct groups of customers for the product.

6. DOMINANT POSITION: MARKET POWER

When the Court has defined the relevant product, geographical, and temporal elements of the market, it then has to decide whether the undertaking is dominant within that sphere. Some measurement of the market power possessed by the undertaking is, therefore, necessary.[17] The legal test employed by the Court emerges in the following passage from the *United Brands* case:[18]

The dominant position referred to in this Article relates to a position of economic strength enjoyed by an undertaking which enables it to prevent effective competition being maintained on the relevant market by giving it the power to behave to an appreciable extent independently of its competitors, customers and ultimately of its consumers.

This test was quoted with approval in *Hoffmann-La Roche*, and the Court then added the following rider:[19]

---

[15] See *United Brands*, n. 2 above, and *Commercial Solvents*, n. 6 above.

[16] Used by the ECJ in *Continental Can*, 1008–9 below.

[17] D. Landes and R. Posner, 'Market Power in Antitrust Cases' (1981) 94 *Harvard LR* 937; R. Schmalensee, 'Another Look at Market Power' (1982) 95 *Harvard LR* 1789.

[18] Case 27/76, [1978] ECR 207, para. 65; Case T–128/98, *Aéroports de Paris*, n. 1 above, para. 147.

[19] Case 85/76, *Hoffmann-La Roche*, n. 6 above, para. 39.

Such a position does not preclude some competition, which it does where there is a monopoly or a quasi-monopoly, but enables the undertaking which profits by it, if not to determine, at least to have an appreciable influence on the conditions under which that competition will develop, and in any case to act largely in disregard of it so long as such conduct does not operate to its detriment. A dominant position must also be distinguished from parallel courses of conduct which are peculiar to oligopolies in that in an oligopoly the courses of conduct interact, while in the case of an undertaking occupying the dominant position the conduct of the undertaking which derives profits from that position is to a great extent determined unilaterally. The existence of a dominant position may derive from several factors which, taken separately, are not necessarily determinative but among these factors a highly important one is the existence of very large market shares.

It is apparent from the Court's case law that an undertaking which has a statutory monopoly may be dominant for the purposes of Article 86 (now Article 82). The grant of the statutory monopoly confers no immunity from EC competition law, subject to the application of Article 90(2) (now Article 86(2)).[20]

In the more common situation in which there is no statutory monopoly, the Court will consider two types of evidence to determine whether the firm has market power: the market share possessed by the undertaking, and the extent to which there are other factors which serve to reinforce its dominance.

The actual size of the *market share* possessed by the undertaking will be central to the determination of whether it has market power in the sense set out above. Precisely what market share will serve to render the undertaking liable to Article 86 (now Article 82) proceedings is impossible to state with absolute accuracy. Certain guidelines can, none the less, be articulated. Few firms, other than with a statutory monopoly, will have 100 per cent of the market. Nor is a market share of this size necessary in order for the Article to 'bite'. Indeed, undertakings with significantly less of a market share than is commonly understood by the layman's sense of monopoly may be deemed to have a sufficient share of the market for the purposes of this Article. Thus, in *United Brands* UBC's 40 to 45 per cent of the market was held to be sufficient, although the Court also considered other factors indicative of its dominance.[21] However, in *Hoffmann-La Roche* the Court overturned a Commission finding that the firm was dominant in the market for B3 vitamins, in which it had only 43 per cent. It was not satisfied that there were other factors sustaining the conclusion that the undertaking had dominance in this market.[22] In the same case the Court did, however, also make it clear that, save in exceptional circumstances, the existence of a very large market share, which was held for some time, would in itself be indicative of dominance. It would secure for the undertaking concerned the freedom of action which was the hallmark of a dominant position.[23] In the *Akzo* case[24] the ECJ held that a market share of 50 per cent could be said to be very large, and hence indicative of a dominant position, and this finding was repeated in *Irish Sugar*.[25] It seems moreover

---

[20]   Case 41/83, *Italy* v. *Commission*, n. 9 above.   [21]   Case 27/76, *United Brands*, n. 2 above.
[22]   Case 85/76, *Hoffmann-La Roche*, n. 6 above.
[23]   *Ibid.*, para. 41. Case T–30/89, *Hilti AG* v. *Commission* [1991] ECR II–1439, para. 92: a market share of 70% was, in itself, indicative of market dominance.
[24]   Case C–62/86, *Akzo Chemie BV* v. *Commission* [1991] ECR I–3359, para. 60.
[25]   Case T–228/97, *Irish Sugar plc* v. *Commission* [1999] ECR II–2969, para. 70, upheld on appeal: Case C–497/1999P, *Irish Sugar plc* v. *Commission*, July 10, 2001.

that there is a concept of 'super-dominance' emerging, held to be applicable to under-takings with very large market shares. The Commission and Court regard such bodies as having a particular responsibility towards the competitive process.[26]

The question which *other factors serve to indicate dominance* can be problematic.[27] It is clear that the Court should pay attention to factors other than market share in determining dominance, since, even if a firm does possess a relatively large market share, this may be fragile because of the possibilities of new entrants on to the market. An essential aspect of the analysis must, therefore, be how far there are *barriers to entry* which render it difficult for other firms to penetrate this market. There is, however, considerable controversy about the more particular meaning to be ascribed to the concept of barriers to entry.

For some, it is a broad idea, embracing almost anything which makes it particularly difficult for a new firm to enter the market. This construction places more firms at risk of being defined as dominant for the purposes of this Article. *For others* the term has, or should have, a much narrower construction. Those who are in this camp are particularly concerned at the possibility that matters will be characterized as barriers to entry when they are merely indicative of the superior efficiency of the incumbent firm. We see here one manifestation of the dilemma outlined earlier: the difficulty of drawing the boundary between legitimate competitive activity and winning by means which are in some way deemed to be unfair or illegitimate. The following extract from Bork exemplifies this aspect of the argument.

R. Bork, The Antitrust Paradox, A Policy at War with Itself[28]

The concept of barriers to entry is crucial to antitrust debate. Those who advocate extensive and increasing legal intervention in market processes cite the existence of entry barriers as a reason to believe that unassisted market forces very often fail to produce adequate results. . . . The ubiquity and potency of the concept are undeniable.

Yet it is demonstrable that barriers of the sort these commentators and jurists believe they see do not exist. They are the ghosts that inhabit antitrust theory. Until the concept of barriers to entry is thoroughly revised, it will remain impossible to make antitrust law more rational or, indeed, to restrain the growth of its powerful irrational elements.

We may begin by asking what a 'barrier to entry' is. There appears to be no precise definition, and in current usage a 'barrier' often seems to be anything that makes the entry of new firms into an industry more difficult. It is at once apparent that an ambiguity lurks in the concept, and it is

---

[26] Cases C–395 & 396/96P, *Compagnie Maritime Belge Transports SA v. Commission* [2000] ECR I–1365, Fennelly AG, para. 137; *1998 World Cup* [2000] OJ L5/55, [2000] 4 CMLR 963, para. 86; A. Jones and B. Sufrin, *EC Competition Law, Text, Cases and Materials* (Oxford University Press, 2001), 235, 323.

[27] R. Whish, *Competition Law* (Butterworths, 4th edn., 2001), 156–61; A. Jones and B. Sufrin, *EC Competition Law, Text, Cases and Materials* (Oxford University Press, 2001), 308–16.

[28] (Basic Books, 1978), 310–11. See also S. Turnbull, 'Barriers to Entry, Article 86 and the Abuse of a Dominant Position: An Economic Critique of European Community Competition Law' [1996] *ECLR* 96; D. Harbord and T. Hoehn, 'Barriers to Entry and Exit in European Competition Policy' (1994) 14 *International Review of Law and Economics* 422; P. Jebsen and R. Stevens, 'Assumptions, Goals and Dominant Undertakings: The Regulation of Competition under Article 86 of the European Union' (1995–6) 64 *Antitrust Law Journal* 443.

this ambiguity that causes the trouble. When existing firms are efficient and possess valuable plant, equipment, knowledge, skill, and reputation, potential entrants will find it correspondingly more difficult to enter the industry, since they must acquire those things. . . . But these difficulties are natural; they inhere in the nature of the tasks to be performed. There can be no objection to barriers of this sort. Their existence means only that when market power is achieved by means other than efficiency, entry will not dissipate the objectionable power instantaneously, and law may therefore have a role to play. If entry were instantaneous, market forces would break up cartels before a typist in the Antitrust Division could rap out a form complaint. . . .

The question for antitrust is whether there exist artificial entry barriers. These must be barriers that are not forms of superior efficiency and which yet prevent the forces of the market—entry or the growth of smaller firms already within the industry—from operating to erode market positions not based on efficiency. Care must be taken to distinguish between forms of efficiency and artificial barriers. Otherwise the law will find itself—indeed, it has found itself—attacking efficiency in the name of market freedom. Joe Bain, whose work has done much to popularize the concept, lists among entry barriers such things as economies of scale, capital requirements, and product differentiation.[29] There may be disagreement about two of these barriers, but it is clear that at least one of them, economies of scale, is a form of efficiency. Uncritical adapters of Bain's work have not sufficiently inquired whether the others may not also be efficiencies.

Before examining some claimed entry barriers to determine whether they are efficiencies or artificial clogs upon competition, it should be noted that . . . an artificial barrier is, of course, an exclusionary practice. . . . Every barrier will be either a form of efficiency deliberately created or an instance of deliberate predation. There is no 'intermediate case' of non-efficient and unintended exclusion. Failure to bear that in mind leads to serious policy mistakes.

The Court's actual approach can be gleaned from its case law, as exemplified by *Hoffmann-La Roche*.[30] The case was concerned with alleged abusive behaviour by the undertaking in relation to vitamins. Having defined the relevant markets, the Court then proceeded to consider whether HLR was dominant in these areas. Its market share was taken into account, and the ECJ then evaluated the relevance of other factors which might be indicative of market power. The Commission had listed a number of such factors, some of which were rejected by the Court, others of which it accepted. The ECJ rejected, for example, the fact that HLR had retained its market share, since this might have resulted from effective competitive behaviour.[31] The Court also rejected the fact that HLR produced a wider range of vitamins than other undertakings, since the Commission itself had found that each group of the vitamins constituted a separate market.[32] The following factors were, however, deemed to be of relevance:[33]

On the other hand the relationship between the market shares of the undertaking concerned and of its competitors, especially those of the next largest, the technological lead of an undertaking over

---

[29] The reference is to J. Bain, *Barriers to New Competition* (Harvard University Press, 1956), ch. 1.
[30] Case 85/76, n. 6 above.
[31] *Ibid.*, para. 44. The ECJ did, however, state that if there is a dominant position then its retention may be indicative that abusive behaviour within Art. 86 has been used to maintain this dominance.
[32] *Ibid.*, paras. 45–46.   [33] *Ibid.*, para. 48.

its competitors, the existence of a highly developed sales network and the absence of potential competition are relevant factors, the first because it enables the competitive strength of the undertaking in question to be assessed, the second and third because they represent in themselves technical and commercial advantages and the fourth because it is the consequence of the existence of obstacles preventing new competitors from having access to the market.

The ECJ has persisted in taking a relatively wide view of barriers to entry, which places more firms in danger of Article 86 proceedings. The following factors have been deemed to be indicative of dominance and market power. It is questionable whether a number of these factors ought to be regarded as barriers to entry in the light of the argument advanced by Bork.

Thus, *economies of scale* have been considered to be relevant in assessing the market power of a particular firm,[34] as have the capital strength of the undertaking and its access to capital markets.[35] However, as seen above, the former is almost certainly indicative of efficiency. As for the latter, many commentators contend that access to capital is not a barrier to entry. This is either because the capital markets are efficient, in the sense of accurately reflecting the cost of capital to a particular firm, or because any inefficiency in this regard is best dealt with through the reform of capital markets themselves.

It is equally questionable whether the existence of *vertical integration* should be regarded as a factor indicating dominance.[36] The motivation for a firm to become vertically integrated was considered in the previous chapter.[37] It was seen that the rational firm would normally choose to integrate vertically only if that was the most efficient method of marketing its product.[38]

It is also doubtful whether *superior technology* should be perceived as a barrier to entry, even though the Court has consistently regarded it in this manner.[39] Any new firm wishing to enter the market should expect to have to expend money on developing technology and know-how. These costs will not necessarily be any greater than for the incumbent firm. Moreover, the protection afforded to firms by industrial and intellectual-property rights is given precisely as a reward for, and incentive to, inventiveness. Given that this is so, it might be thought odd that the presence of superior technology should render a firm more likely to be caught by EC law.

Other factors which the Court has taken into account as indicative of dominance include *legal provisions* within Member States which render it more difficult for new firms to break into the market. This is exemplified by the *Hugin* case, where the Court was influenced in finding dominance in the making of spare parts by the fact that other firms would be wary of doing so lest they were in breach of the Design Copyright Act 1968.[40] Other forms of intellectual or industrial-property rights will also be of relevance in this respect.[41]

---

[34] Case 27/76, *United Brands*, n. 2 above.   [35] *Ibid.*
[36] *Ibid.* See also Case 85/76, *Hoffmann-La Roche*, n. 6 above.   [37] See 972–3 above.
[38] It is, moreover, doubtful whether the existence of vertical integration enables the firm with some dominance to achieve any greater monopoly profit than it would do without the vertical integration.
[39] See, e.g., *United Brands*, n. 2 above; *Hoffmann-La Roche*, n. 6 above; *Michelin*, n. 44 below.
[40] Case 22/78, [1979] ECR 1869.
[41] Case T–30/89, *Hilti*, n. 23 above, para. 93: patent and copyright protection were of relevance in securing dominance.

It is also clear that the Court can and will take into account, in determining dominance, the *conduct of the firm* which is alleged to be the abusive behaviour, notwithstanding the apparent circularity that this entails. Thus, in *Michelin* the Court took account of Michelin's price discrimination as an indication of its dominance, even though it noted the circularity thereby involved.[42]

It is difficult to regard the Court decisions in this area as satisfactory. It may be argued, by way of response, that it is perfectly legitimate for the Court to take account of the preceding factors, since it is only seeking to determine whether the firm has some dominance, not whether it has actually abused that dominance. However, a finding of dominance will lay the firm open to investigation with attendant costs for the company, and these costs may be very significant. The problem of drawing the line between healthy and legitimate competition and winning by illegitimate means is ever-present. This problem was highlighted at the inception of the discussion, and picked up again in the quotation from Bork.

7. ABUSE: GENERAL PRINCIPLES

(a) GENERAL ISSUES OF INTERPRETATION

An undertaking will be condemned under Article 82 (ex Article 86) only if it has *abused* its dominant position: dominance *per se* is, as stated at the beginning, no offence. The construction accorded to the concept of abuse is, however, particularly important, given that Article 82 has no analogue to Article 81(3) (ex Article 85(3)). There is, in other words, no form of exemption if an undertaking is held to have abused its power. Four important issues arise in deciding on the meaning to be ascribed to 'abuse'.

The first is to decide *who* the Article is intended to protect: is this consumers, competitors, or both? If the answer is 'both', then, as we shall see, there can be instances in which the interests of consumers and competitors clash. Behaviour by a dominant undertaking that injures a competitor will not necessarily be injurious to consumers.[43]

The second problem is that while the existence of a dominant position is not itself illegal, such a firm is regarded as having a *'special responsibility'* not to allow its conduct to impair genuine undistorted competition on the relevant market.[44] This means that the undertaking in a dominant position may be deprived of the right to adopt a course of conduct which is not itself abusive, and which would be unobjectionable if taken by a non-dominant undertaking.[45] The conclusion of a contract or the acquisition of a right by a dominant undertaking may therefore

---

[42] Case 322/81, [1983] ECR 3461.

[43] Case C–7/97, *Oscar Bronner GmbH & Co. KG v. Mediaprint Zeitungs- und Zeitschriftenverlag GmbH & Co. KG* [1998] ECR I–7791, Jacobs AG, para. 58.

[44] Case 322/81, *Nederlandsche Banden-Industrie Michelin NV v. Commission* [1983] ECR 3461, para. 57; Case T–228/97, *Irish Sugar plc*, n. 25 above, para. 112.

[45] Case 322/81, *Michelin*, n. 44 above, para. 57; Case T–51/89, *Tetra Pak v. Commission* [1990] ECR II–309, para. 23; Case T–111/96, *ITT Promedia NV v. Commission* [1998] ECR II–2937, para. 138.

constitute an abuse under Article 82. Thus, while it is accepted that a dominant undertaking can take steps to protect its own interests when they are attacked by competitors, it is not allowed to strengthen its dominant position, which will be held to be an abuse.[46] This divide is difficult to apply, more especially given that it has to be judged in the light of the specific circumstances of each case where competition has been weakened.[47]

The third problem relates to the *kinds* of behaviour held to be abusive. It should be remembered that such behaviour must be distinguished from normal competitive strategy, and that dominance *per se* is not forbidden. It would, therefore, be odd to conclude that the ordinary, rational pricing and output decisions of the dominant firm were themselves to be classified as abusive. To do so would, in reality, mean that we were proscribing those with dominant market power *per se*. Having said this, it is also clear that Article 82 (ex Article 86) does explicitly prohibit unfair pricing and limits on productive capacity, and that some meaning must, therefore, be ascribed to these terms. It might be thought that this problem could be overcome if the concept of abuse was confined to practices such as price discrimination, predation, tying, and the like, which looked 'bad' or 'abnormal', even for the firm with dominance. The problem is not so easily resolved since, as will be seen, there is considerable disagreement among economists, both on whether these activities are in fact harmful, and on how they are to be measured. The application of Article 82 can, therefore, be particularly controversial, as will be seen from the following analysis.

Fourthly, it is clear that abuse of a dominant position in one market may be censured because of the effects that it produces on a different market.[48] This is especially so where the dominant undertaking can control access to the other market. This is exemplified by *Aéroports de Paris*.[49] The airport authority controlled access to the supply of catering services and abused its dominant position by discriminatory pricing.

(b) EXPLOITATION AND ANTI-COMPETITIVE PRACTICES

It is common to subdivide the situations to which Article 82 (ex Article 86) can apply into exploitation and anti-competitiveness.[50] The former signifies behaviour harmful to consumers. The latter, generally, connotes conduct deleterious to competitors, actual or potential. This division should not, however, be treated too rigidly, and in any event the same conduct by the dominant firm may be both exploitative and anti-competitive.

Although it is now clear that Article 82 covers both exploitation and anti-competitive behaviour, this was not so apparent at the inception of the Treaty. Indeed some commentators, such as Joliet, argued strenuously that the Article should be

---

[46] Case 27/76, *United Brands*, n. 2 above, para. 189; Case T–228/97, *Irish Sugar plc*, n. 25 above, para. 112.
[47] Case C–333/94P, *Tetra Pak*, n. 6 above, para. 24; Cases C–395–396/96P, *Compagnie Maritimes Belge* n. 26 above, para. 114.
[48] Whish, n. 27 above, 173–5.
[49] Case 128/98, n. 1 above, paras. 164–165.
[50] See, e.g., Whish, n. 27 above, 168–70; J. Temple Lang, 'Monopolisation and the Definition of Abuse of a Dominant Position under Art. 86 EEC Treaty' (1979) 16 *CMLRev.* 345.

restricted to clear forms of exploitative behaviour which were harmful to consumers in particular, and that there should be some real link between the harm and the market power possessed by the dominant undertaking.[51] In reaching this conclusion Joliet was influenced in part by the wording of the Article itself, and in part by the need to avoid what he perceived as a danger in the United States' case law, where the courts had, on occasion, come close to outlawing market power *per se*. This construction of the Article was rendered untenable by the ECJ's decision in *Continental Can*, which will be considered in the next section.

8. ABUSE: PARTICULAR EXAMPLES

(a) ABUSE AND MERGERS

EC law relating to mergers will be considered in the next chapter. It will be apparent that the Community has waited a long time for a specific regulation concerning mergers. The ECJ made it clear in the *Continental Can* case that some mergers at least would be caught by Article 86 (now Article 82) itself. The case is also of more general importance for the interpretation of the meaning of abuse.

Case 6/72, Europemballage Corporation and Continental Can Co. Inc. v. Commission
[1973] ECR 215

[Note ToA renumbering: Arts. 3f, 85, and 86 are now Arts. 3(1)(g), 81, and 82 respectively.]

Continental Can (CC) was a United States manufacturer of metal packaging which had a presence in Europe through a German firm (SLW), which it acquired in 1969. In 1970 it sought to purchase, through its subsidiary Europemballage, a controlling interest in a Dutch company, TDV. The Commission found that CC had a dominant position in Europe for certain types of packaging through SLW, and that there had been an abuse of that position by the purchase of TDV. CC argued before the Court that there had been no abuse.

THE ECJ

20. ... The question is whether the word 'abuse' in Article 86 refers only to practices of undertakings which may directly affect the market and are detrimental to production or sales, to purchasers or consumers, or whether this word refers also to changes in the structure of an undertaking, which lead to competition being seriously disturbed in a substantial part of the Common Market.

21. The distinction between measures which concern the structure of the undertaking and practices which affect the market cannot be decisive, for any structural measure may influence market conditions, if it increases the size and the economic power of the undertaking.

---

[51] R. Joliet, *Monopolization and Abuse of a Dominant Position* (Martinus Nijhoff, 1970).

22. In order to answer this question one has to go back to the spirit, general scheme and wording of Article 86, as well as to the system and objectives of the Treaty. . . .

23. Article 86 is part of the chapter devoted to the common rules on the Community's policy in the field of competition. This policy is based on Article 3(f) of the Treaty according to which the Community's activity shall Include the institution of a system ensuring that competition in the Common Market is not distorted. . . .

24. But if Article 3(f) provides for the institution of a system ensuring that competition in the Common Market is not distorted, then it requires a fortiori that competition must not be eliminated. This requirement is so essential that without it numerous provisions of the Treaty would be pointless. Moreover, it corresponds to the precept of Article 2 of the Treaty according to which one of the tasks of the Community is 'to promote throughout the Community a harmonious development of economic activities'. Thus the restraints on competition, which the Treaty allows under certain conditions because of the need to harmonise the various objectives of the Treaty, are limited by the requirements of Articles 2 and 3. Going beyond this limit involves the risk that the weakening of competition would conflict with the aims of the Common Market.

25. . . . Articles 85 and 86 seek to achieve the same aim on different levels, viz. the maintenance of effective competition within the Common Market. The restraint on competition, which is prohibited if it is the result of behaviour falling under Article 85, cannot become permissible by the fact that such behaviour succeeds under the influence of a dominant undertaking and results in the merger of the undertakings concerned. In the absence of explicit provisions one cannot assume that the Treaty, which prohibits in Article 85 certain decisions of ordinary associations of undertakings restricting competition without eliminating it, permits in Article 86 that undertakings, after merging into an organic unity, should reach such a dominant position that any serious competition is practically rendered impossible. Such a diverse legal treatment would make a breach in the entire competition law which could jeopardise the proper functioning of the Common Market. If, in order to avoid the prohibitions in Article 85, it sufficed to establish such close connections between the undertakings that they escaped the prohibition of Article 85 without coming within the scope of Article 86, then, in contradiction to the basic principles of the Common Market, the partitioning of a substantial part of the Common Market would be allowed. . . .

26. It is in the light of these considerations that the condition imposed by Article 86 is to be interpreted whereby in order to come within the prohibition a dominant position must have been abused. The provision states a certain number of abusive practices which it prohibits. The list merely gives examples, not an exhaustive enumeration of the sort of abuses of a dominant position prohibited by the Treaty. As may further be seen from subparagraphs (c) and (d) of Article 86(2), the provision is not only aimed at practices which may cause damage to the consumer directly, but also at those which are detrimental to them through their impact on an effective competition structure, such as is mentioned in Article 3(f) of the Treaty. Abuse may therefore occur if an undertaking in a dominant position strengthens such position in such a way that the degree of dominance reached substantially fetters competition, i. e. that only undertakings remain in the market whose behaviour depends on the dominant one.

27. Such being the meaning and scope of Article 86 of the EEC Treaty, the question of the link of causality raised by the applicants which in their opinion has to exist between the dominant position and its abuse, is of no consequence, for the strengthening of the position of an undertaking may be an abuse and prohibited under Article 86 of the Treaty, regardless of the means and the procedure by which it is achieved, if it has the effects mentioned above.

The decision in *Continental Can* is of seminal importance for the construction of Article 86 (now Article 82), both in terms of the reasoning employed and the result.

The *reasoning* of the ECJ provides a clear example of the teleological approach encountered in other areas of Community law. Reference is made to, and reliance is placed on, the general principles in the Treaty as a guide to the appropriate construction of the more particular Articles. The competition provisions are read as a whole, and the interpretation accorded to Article 86 is strongly influenced by the desire to avoid any 'gap' in the coverage of this part of the Treaty.

The *result* of the case signals the intent of the ECJ that Article 86 (now Article 82) should be held to cover situations where the competitive market structure was placed in jeopardy. The Article certainly included classic forms of *behavioural* abuse, which operated directly to the detriment of consumers. It was now clear that it would also embrace *structural* abuse, in the sense of action that weakened the competitive market structure. It was *Continental Can* which made it apparent that the Article would be held to cover anti-competitiveness, where the primary and direct injury was to competitors. This construction was reinforced by the Court's negation of the need for any real causal link between the dominance and the impugned action. On the facts of the case there did not need to be any proof that it was CC's 'economic muscle' which had forced the merger on a reluctant undertaking. The fact that the merger did in fact result in damage to the competitive market structure sufficed.[52]

The decision in *Continental Can* received a mixed reception when it first appeared, with certain commentators being critical of the reasoning employed as well as the result. The Court has, however, persisted in its general approach[53] as the cases in the following sections will demonstrate.

(b) ABUSE AND REFUSAL TO SUPPLY

The obligation on a firm which occupies a dominant position to supply to other firms wishing to purchase its products is exemplified by the decision in the *Commercial Solvents* case:

---

[52] See, generally, P. Vogelenzang, 'Abuse of a Dominant Position in Article 86: The Problem of Causality and Some Applications' (1976) 13 *CMLRev.* 61.

[53] In Case C–393/92, *Municipality of Almelo* v. *NV Energiebedrijf Ijsselmij* [1994] ECR I–1477, the ECJ held that an exclusive-purchasing obligation constituted an abuse for the purposes of Art. 86, and that this was so without any need to find that the purchasing obligation had been forced on the firms by the dominant undertaking. However, in Case C–333/94P, *Tetra Pak*, n. 6 above, the ECJ held that Art. 86 does presuppose a link between the dominant position and the alleged abusive conduct which is normally not present where conduct on a market distinct from the dominated market produces effects on that distinct market. In the case of distinct, but associated, markets, the application of Art. 86 to conduct on the associated, non-dominated market and having effects on that associated market can only be justified by special circumstances.

Cases 6 and 7/73, Istituto Chemioterapico Italiano SpA and
Commercial Solvents v. Commission
[1974] ECR 223

[Note ToA renumbering: Arts. 3f, 85, and 86 are now Arts. 3(1)(g), 81, and 82]

Commercial Solvents Corporation (CSC) made raw materials, nitropropane and aminobutanol, which were then used to make ethambutol, a drug for tuberculosis. CSC acquired 51 per cent of an Italian company, Istituto, which bought the raw material from CSC and sold it to another Italian company, Zoja, the latter then using it to manufacture ethambutol-based products. Istituto sought to acquire Zoja, but the negotiations were unsuccessful. Istituto then increased its price to Zoja, and Zoja found an alternative source of supply from other customers of CSC. This alternative source of supply then dried up, principally because CSC instructed those to whom it sold the raw material not to sell it on to firms such as Zoja. CSC then stated that it was no longer going to sell the raw material, but that it would instead integrate vertically down-market, in the sense that it would use the raw material for its own production of the finished product. When Zoja sought to re-order the raw material from CSC the latter refused to supply.

THE ECJ

25. However, an undertaking being in a dominant position as regards the production of raw material and therefore able to control the supply to manufacturers of derivatives, cannot, just because it decides to start manufacturing these derivatives (in competition with its former customers) act in such a way as to eliminate their competition which, in the case in question, would amount to eliminating one of the principal manufacturers of ethambutol in the Common Market. Since such conduct is contrary to the objectives expressed in Article 3(f) of the Treaty and set out in greater detail in Article 85 and 86, it follows that an undertaking which has a dominant position in the market in raw materials and which, with the object of reserving such raw material for manufacturing its own derivatives, refuses to supply a customer, which is itself a manufacturer of these derivatives, and therefore risks eliminating all competition on the part of this customer, is abusing its dominant position within the meaning of Article 86. In this context it does not matter that the undertaking ceased to supply in the spring of 1970 because of the cancellation of the purchases by Zoja, because it appears from the applicants' own statement that, when the supplies provided for in the contract had been completed, the sale of aminobutanol would have stopped in any case.

This appears to be a classic case of abusive behaviour: CSC, the dominant firm, teaches Zoja a lesson by making it clear that if the latter seeks an alternative source of supply which later dries up, then Zoja cannot necessarily expect CSC to resume supplies. The case could well have been decided in this way, and this would probably have been justified on the facts. However, the reasoning of the Court is phrased in broader terms. It specifically addresses the situation where the refusal to supply is based on a desire by the dominant firm to integrate vertically down into the finished-product market: such a refusal is still deemed an abuse for the purpose of Article 86 (now Article 82).

This is more controversial for the reasons given when discussing vertical restraints in the previous chapter.[54] A rational firm will seek to enter a new phase of the market downstream only if it believes that it can produce the finished product more efficiently than the incumbent firms. If it is correct in this calculation then the consumer will benefit by the product being cheaper. If it is wrong then it will suffer accordingly. It may well be true that the effect is that existing firms making the finished product will no longer be able to do so, if the dominant firm does not have enough of the raw material for its own needs and those of its rivals.[55]

This type of case exemplifies the tension mentioned earlier as to whether Article 82 is intended to protect consumers or competitors/the competitive market structure. There may be situations where actions by a dominant firm may benefit consumers but be harmful to its competitors. *Commercial Solvents* signals the intent of the Court that, if forced to choose between these, it will opt to protect the latter.[56]

Notwithstanding the difficulties with the reasoning in *Commercial Solvents* the Commission and the Court have built upon the case, and have condemned refusals to supply existing customers unless there is some objective justification.[57] It has not been easy for dominant firms to satisfy the Court that such justification exists.[58] This is apparent from the decision in *United Brands*.

Case 27/76, United Brands Company and United Brands Continentaal BV v. Commission [1978] ECR 207

[Note ToA renumbering: Arts. 3f and 86 are now Arts. 3(1)(g) and 82]

One of the allegations of abusive behaviour by UB was that it had refused to supply to Olesen who was a distributor in Denmark. UB argued that it had refused to continue supplying Olesen because the latter, having failed to secure preferential treatment from UB for the Danish market, then started to sell a competitor's product and to neglect the sale of UB's produce.

---

[54] See 972–5 above.

[55] On the facts of the case the ECJ was not convinced that CSC could not meet its own needs and those of Zoja: [1974] ECR 223, para. 28.

[56] It may be possible to 'square this circle' by arguing that in the medium or long term the consumer will in fact be better off if there are more competitors at the finished-product-market level; and that if the dominant firm really is more efficient than a firm such as Zoja then the latter will not, in any event, survive. This reconciliation is, however, not perfect: the finished-product market may, for example, be of a nature that it can only support one firm.

[57] One case where the Court overturned the decision of the Commission was *BP* which arose out of the OPEC oil crisis in 1973: Case 77/77, *Benzine en Petroleum Handelsmaatschappij BV, British Petroleum Raffinerij Nederland NV and British Petroleum Maatschappij Nederland BV* v. *Commission* [1978] ECR 1513. The complainant company argued that BP had abused its dominant position by reducing supplies to it during the oil shortage to a greater extent than it had done in relation to other customers. The Commission found in favour of the complainant. This decision was overturned by the ECJ on the ground that the complainant was not a regular customer of BP. However, the Court also affirmed that it would be an abuse, even during a time of short supply due to external factors, for a dominant firm to reduce supplies to firms which were in a comparable situation in a way which placed them at a comparative disadvantage.

[58] Case T–65/89, *BPB Industries plc and British Gypsum Ltd.* v. *Commission* [1993] ECR II–389.

182. . . . it is advisable to assert positively from the outset that an undertaking in a dominant position for the purpose of marketing a product—which cashes in on the reputation of a brand name known to and valued by the consumers—cannot stop supplying a long standing customer who abides by regular commercial practice, if the orders placed by that customer are in no way out of the ordinary.

183. Such conduct is inconsistent with the objectives laid down in Article 3(f) of the Treaty, which are set out in greater detail in Article 86, especially in paragraphs (b) and (c), since the refusal to sell would limit markets to the prejudice of consumers and would amount to discrimination which might in the end eliminate a trading party from the relevant market.

[*The Court then reviewed the reasons given by UB for discontinuing supplies to Olesen. It continued as follows:*]

189. Although it is true, as the applicant points out, that the fact that an undertaking is in a dominant position cannot disentitle it from protecting its own commercial interests if they are attacked, and that such an undertaking must be conceded the right to take such reasonable steps as it deems appropriate to protect its said interests, such behaviour cannot be countenanced if its actual purpose is to strengthen this dominant position and abuse it.

190. Even if the possibility of counter-attack is acceptable that attack must still be proportionate to the threat taking into account the economic strength of the undertakings confronting each other.

191. The sanction consisting of refusal to supply by an undertaking in a dominant position was in excess of what might, if such a situation were to arise, reasonably be contemplated as a sanction for conduct similar to that for which UBC blamed Olesen.

192. In fact UBC could not be unaware of that fact that by acting in this way it would discourage other ripener/distributors from supporting the advertising of other brand names and that the deterrent effect of the sanction imposed upon one of them would make its position of strength on the relevant market that much more effective.

193. Such a course of conduct amounts therefore to a serious interference with the independence of small and medium sized firms in their commercial relations with the undertaking in a dominant position and this independence implies the right to give preference to a competitors' goods.

It is unclear from the case precisely what type of reaction by UB would have been considered to be proportionate and lawful in the light of Olesen's behaviour. Given that refusal to supply was held to be unlawful, what could UB have done in the circumstances?

It is also unclear whether the rules on refusal to supply will apply to new customers as opposed to existing customers. The case law has certainly come close to condemning such refusals. Thus in *Boosey & Hawkes*[59] the Commission found against B & H, which had refused to supply brass-band instruments to a customer which had begun manufacturing in competition with it. The fact that a customer of a dominant producer had become associated with a competitor of that manufacturer would not normally entitle the dominant producer to withdraw all supplies immediately or take

[59] Dec. 87/500, [1987] OJ L286/36, [1988] 4 CMLR 67.

reprisals against that customer. This was not, said the Commission, a proportionate response. In the *GVL* case[60] the ECJ held that it was an abuse of Article 86 (now Article 82) for a national copyright-collecting society to refuse to admit to its membership nationals of other Member States. The fact that the discrimination was based on nationality may, however, explain the Court's approach in this case. In the *BPB* case[61] the CFI held that, in deciding how to allocate supplies in times of shortage, a firm must use an objective criterion; and that favouring loyal customers, even marginally, over others did not meet this test.

What is also apparent is that Article 86 (now Article 82) can apply to a refusal to supply a product which is required by another party to produce a different product. This is so even if the second product is in competition with the first and even if the producer of the first product enjoys an intellectual property right. This is exemplified by the *RTE* case.

Cases T–69, 70, 76/89, RTE, ITP, BBC v. Commission
[1991] ECR II–485[62]

RTE was a statutory authority providing broadcasting services, and it reserved the exclusive right to publish a weekly schedule of TV programmes for its channels in Ireland. An Irish company, Magill, sought to publish a weekly guide which would have information on all the available channels. RTE wished to prevent this, claiming that it infringed its copyright in the weekly schedule for its channels. The Commission found this to be an abuse of Article 86 and RTE challenged this before the CFI. The CFI accepted that the specific subject matter[63] of a copyright would enjoy protection under Community law, and in that sense the exclusive right to reproduce the protected work would not be an abuse for the purposes of Article 86. However, the copyright owner would not be protected if the manner of the exercise of the right was contrary to Article 86. It then continued as follows.

THE CFI

73. In the present case, it must be noted that the applicant, by reserving the exclusive right to publish its weekly television programme listings, was preventing the emergence on the market of a new product, namely a general television magazine likely to compete with its own magazine, the RTE Guide. The applicant was thus using its copyright in the programme listings which it produced in order to secure a monopoly in the derivative market of weekly television guides. . . .

Conduct of that type—characterised by preventing the production and marketing of a new product, for which there is potential consumer demand, on the ancillary market of television magazines and thereby excluding all competition from that market solely in order to secure the

---

[60] Case 7/82, *GVL* v. *Commission* [1983] ECR 483.

[61] Case T–65/89, n. 58 above, upheld on appeal: Case C–310/93P, *BPB Industries plc and British Gypsum Ltd.* v. *Commission* [1995] ECR I–865.

[62] Upheld on appeal, Cases C–241 and 242/91P, *Radio Telefis Eireann (RTE) and Independent Television Publications Ltd. (ITP)* v. *Commission* [1995] ECR I–743. See also Case T–70/89, *British Broadcasting Corporation and British Broadcasting Corporation Enterprises Ltd.* v. *Commission* [1991] ECR II–535; Case 238/87, *Volvo AB* v. *Erik Veng (UK) Ltd.* [1988] ECR 6211, [1988] 4 CMLR 122.

[63] See Ch. 26 below for a discussion of this issue.

applicant's monopoly—clearly goes beyond what is necessary to fulfil the essential function of the copyright as permitted in Community law.

Cases such as *RTE* come close to endorsing what has been termed an 'essential facilities doctrine'. This is the idea that the owner of a facility which is not replicable by the ordinary process of innovation and investment, and without access to which competition on a market is impossible or seriously impeded, has to share it with a rival.[64] This idea is apparent in other cases. Thus in *London European Airways/ Sabena*[65] the Commission held that an airline's refusal to allow access to its computer reservation system without a tie-in constituted an abuse for the purposes of Article 86. In the *Sealink* case[66] the Commission pursued the same theme. Sealink was the owner of the port of Holyhead. It also operated a ferry service to Ireland. A rival ferry company claimed that Sealink had organized the sailing schedules from the port in a way which was most inconvenient for the rival company. The Commission held that it was an abuse of Article 86 for the owner of an essential facility to use its power in one market to strengthen its position on another related market. This would occur if it granted its competitors access to the related market on terms which were less favourable than those for its own services without any objective justification.[67] There are, however, dangers in the essential facilities doctrine.

D. Ridyard, Essential Facilities and the Obligation to Supply Competitors[68]

It will always be tempting for a liberal-minded competition authority to respond favourably to firms who complain about lack of access to new markets, and there are certain instances where the use of essential facilities can legitimately be used as an aid to market liberalisation. There are many other instances, however, in which an uncritical approach favouring market entry can threaten the incentives to dynamic efficiency that provide the engine for economic and technical progress in workably competitive markets.

. . . To achieve a better balance, some limiting principles need to be found. . . . The approach suggested in this article is to recognise that essential facilities, and the obligations on essential facilities owners that accompany them, should be identified only in circumstances where competition does not and cannot be expected to operate, and with assets that cannot reasonably be subject to effective competition. The fact that it may be inconvenient or costly for competitors to achieve market access by their own devices is not sufficient. Nor is the fact that the asset owner might be enjoying a high return from its policy of refusing to deal with competitors.

---

64 Whish, n. 27 above, 614–5.
65 Dec. 88/589, [1988] OJ L317/47, [1989] 4 CMLR 662.
66 [1992] 5 CMLR 255. See also Dec. 94/19, Case IV/34.689, *Sea Containers Ltd.* v. *Stena SeaLink Ports and Stena Sealink Line* [1994] OJ L15/8, [1995] 4 CMLR 84; Case IV/35.388, *Irish Continental Group* v. *CCI Morlaix* [1995] 5 CMLR 177.
67 [1992] 5 CMLR 255, para. 41.
68 [1996] *ECLR* 438, 451–2. See also J. Temple Lang, 'Defining Legitimate Competition: Companies' Duties to Supply Competitors and Access to Essential Facilities' (1994) 18 *Fordham International LJ* 437; P. Areeda, 'Essential Facilities: An Epithet in Need of Limiting Principles' (1990) 58 *Antitrust LJ* 841; B. Doherty, 'Just What Are Essential Facilities?' (2001) 38 *CMLRev.* 397; C. Stothers, 'Refusal to Supply as Abuse of a Dominant Position: Essential Facilities in the European Union' [2001] *ECLR* 256.

Later decisions have indeed taken a more limited view of the application of the essential facilities doctrine. In *Ladbroke* the CFI made it clear that an action for refusal to supply would only be plausible if the product or service being sought was essential for the exercise of the relevant activity. It held that the supply of TV broadcasts concerning horse racing was not essential for the applicant's business of running betting shops.[69] In *ENS*[70] the CFI held that a product or service could not be considered necessary or essential unless there was no real or potential substitute for it. The same cautionary approach is apparent in *Bronner*.[71]

Case C–7/97, Oscar Bronner GmbH & Co. KG v. Mediaprint Zeitungs- und Zeitschriftenverlag GmbH & Co. KG
[1998] ECR I–7791

Bronner published a newspaper that had a circulation of 3.6 per cent of the market. Mediaprint published newspapers that had 71 per cent of the market. Bronner claimed that Mediaprint had abused its dominant position by not including Bronner's paper in Mediaprint's home delivery service. Mediaprint argued that the establishment of the service was a considerable financial investment, and that, although it had a dominant position, it was not bound to subsidize competing companies. The ECJ held that the ruling in the *RTE* case turned on a number of factors. These included the fact that the information on the TV schedules was indispensable for the publication of the TV guide, the fact that this prevented the appearance of a new product, and the fact that there was no objective justification for the action. The ECJ then held that access to Mediaprint's home delivery service was not indispensable to Bronner's primary business of newspaper production.

THE ECJ

43. In the first place, it is undisputed that other methods of distributing daily newspapers, such as by post and through sale in shops and at kiosks, even though they may be less advantageous for the distribution of certain newspapers, exist and are used by the publishers of those daily newspapers.

44. Moreover, it does not appear that there are technical, legal or even economic obstacles capable of making it impossible, or even unreasonably difficult, for any other publisher of daily newspapers to establish . . . its own nationwide home-delivery scheme. . . .

45. It should be emphasized in that respect that, in order to demonstrate that the creation of such a system is not a realistic potential alternative and that access to the existing system is therefore indispensable, it is not enough to argue that it is not economically viable by reason of the small circulation of the daily newspaper. . . .

46. For such access to be capable of being regarded as indispensable, it would be necessary at the very least to establish, as the Advocate General has pointed out . . ., that it is not economically viable to create a second home delivery scheme for the distribution of daily newspapers with a circulation comparable to that of the daily newspapers distributed by the existing scheme.

---

[69] Case T–504/93, *Tiercé Ladbroke SA v. Commission* [1997] ECR II–923.
[70] Cases T–374, 375, 384 & 388/94, *European Night Services Ltd. (ENS) v. Commission* [1998] ECR II–3141, paras. 208–209.
[71] M. Bergman, 'Editorial: The Bronner Case—A Turning Point for Essential Facilities' [2000] *ECLR* 59.

(c) ABUSE AND PRICE DISCRIMINATION

Article 82(c) explicitly prohibits the application of dissimilar trading conditions to equivalent transactions. Before examining the Court's case law it is important to understand the rudiments of the economic ideas which underlie this area, since a failure to do so can lead to error and confusion.

There is price discrimination where goods are sold or purchased at prices which are not related to differences in costs. Thus, price discrimination can cover the situation in which the same product is sold at different, non-cost-related prices; *and* it can also cover the situation where the goods are sold at the same price, even though there are real cost differences entailed.

Discrimination can occur in a variety of ways. It may be *geographical*, whereby the undertaking prices at different levels for different local markets, and then seeks to insulate one from the other in order to prevent arbitrage (reselling) between them. It may assume the form of *discounts* or *rebates* which are not related to any differences in costs, but have the objective of tying customers closer to that producer, with the object of rendering it more difficult for others to penetrate that market. It may also, in theory at least, appear as *predatory pricing*. The dominant firm seeks to protect its dominance by dropping its prices below a certain level in order to deter a would-be entrant to the market, the idea being that it will then raise them again to reap monopoly profits when it has 'seen the other firm off'.

It is common also to distinguish price discrimination according to the nature of the injured party. *Primary-line injury* refers to harm suffered by a competitor at the same level of the market as the dominant firm. Loyalty rebates and the like provide the classic kind of price discrimination which produces primary-line injury, by making it more difficult for a competitor to break into the market. *Secondary-line injury*, by way of contrast, is concerned with harm to the purchaser of the product. This is exemplified by uniform delivered pricing, whereby goods are sold at the same price irrespective of the fact that, for example, one customer is closer to the factory than the other, and therefore transport costs are different in the two instances.

The term 'price discrimination' is, in some ways, an unfortunate and tendentious one: the very language suggests that differences in the price at which goods are offered are themselves 'bad'. It is, however, not self-evident that price discrimination is in fact 'bad' in economic terms; or the cure may turn out to be worse than the disease. There are three reasons why this is not so self-evident.

The first reason concerns *measurement* or *assessment*. All species of price discrimination are dependent upon an assessment of the relative costs of production in different instances, and this may be difficult to determine. This is particularly problematic in relation to certain kinds of discrimination, such as predatory pricing. If a new firm enters the market then one would expect the existing dominant firm to respond in some manner, for this is the essence of competition. It is difficult to decide when this response crosses the line between a 'proper' competitive strategy and 'improper' predation. The problem is especially acute in relation to predation. This is because commentators disagree on the test for predation,[72] its application, and upon the empirical likelihood that it will occur.[73] It is this problem which has led some to argue that legal intervention can be ineffective or worse than the disease.[74] The court may select the wrong criterion. It may choose the criterion which a particular commentator believes to be correct, but misapply it to the facts of the instant case. The very existence of the legal rule may, moreover, have an adverse, dampening effect on competition. The existence of a legal proscription against, for example, predatory pricing can be a weapon in the hands of a firm seeking to break into the market.[75]

The second reason price discrimination is not self-evidently bad relates to *allocative efficiency*. In economic theory monopoly is bad because the monopolist will restrict output to a greater extent than under more normal competitive conditions, with a consequential misallocation of resources within society.[76] The key issue is, therefore, whether this misallocation will be greater under a regime which requires the charging of a single price to all customers or under one which permits price discrimination. This depends upon whether the price discrimination would have the effect of further restricting output, or whether it might actually lead to an increase in output. The following extract takes up this theme.

W. Bishop, Price Discrimination under Article 86: Political Economy in the European Court[77]

If a monopolist were able to charge each customer exactly that customer's maximum price, then the monopolist would realise very large profits, but output would be identical to that under perfect competition with not a single sale being sacrificed because of higher price. This is called perfectly discriminating monopoly and is very rare, perhaps non-existent.

Much more important is imperfect price discrimination—different prices in a number of different markets or for different classes of customers. British Rail for example discriminates by offering special discounts to students for no reason other than that most of them would not travel by train otherwise, and a little more revenue is better than none at all when it costs virtually nothing to carry an extra passenger outside peak hours.

In *United Brands* the court condemned imperfect price discrimination when practised on a regional basis so as to divide the common market into a number of sub-markets with different, discriminatory prices. However it is not at all clear that imperfect price discrimination generally reduces output below the level that would prevail under simple monopoly. Whether output under imperfectly discriminating monopoly is nearer the perfectly competitive or further from it will

---

[72] See, e.g., P. Areeda and D. Turner, 'Predatory Pricing and Related Practices under Section 2 of the Sherman Act: A Comment' (1975) 88 *Harv. LRev.* 697; F. M. Scherer, 'Predatory Pricing and the Sherman Act: A Comment' (1976) 89 *Harv. LRev.* 869; O. Williamson, 'Predatory Pricing: A Strategic and Welfare Analysis' (1977) 87 *Yale LJ* 284; J. Brodley and G. Hay, 'Predatory Pricing: Competing Economic Theories and the Evolution of Legal Standards' (1981) 66 *Cornell LRev.* 738; E. Mastromanolis, 'Predatory Pricing Strategies in the European Union: A Case for Legal Reform' [1998] *ECLR* 211.

[73] Thus, commentators, such as Bork, n. 28 above, 144–59, are sceptical whether a dominant firm really could suffer losses in the short term, drive the new entrant out of the market, and then reap monopoly profits.

[74] *Ibid.*

[75] This may be particularly the case in legal systems which award the successful litigant treble damages, as is the case in the USA.

[76] See any basic work on economics, e.g., G. Stigler, *The Theory of Price* (Macmillan, 3rd edn., 1966).

[77] (1981) 44 *MLR* 282, 287–8. See also Bork, n. 28 above, 394–8.

depend upon the facts of each case. Unfortunately in any real case the facts are extremely difficult to ferret out—in practice usually impossible to ascertain at all.

Moreover, as several economists have demonstrated, it is conceivable that price discrimination in practice may reduce economic efficiency, i.e. increase the misallocation of money and resources, even if it increases output as compared with output in the absence of discrimination. Probably the best we can do is to adopt one general rule on price discrimination. Many economists guess that price discrimination is probably on balance efficient, assuming that there will be monopoly anyway. Certainly there is no reason to believe that a rule prohibiting it will promote more efficient allocation of resources. Furthermore it is clear that enforcing the prohibition will lead both enforcers and defendants to incur costs that consume real social resources.

The third reason rules against price discrimination may be undesirable, or the cure may be worse than the disease, relates to *fairness*. This may seem to be intuitively odd, for many may regard price discrimination as unfair. Economists often express agnosticism on this issue, on the basis that it is not for them to express any prescriptive opinion on the *income* and *distributive* effects of certain policies. Some do, however, point out that the argument that price discrimination is unfair is a good deal less self-evident than might normally be thought. Bishop provides a succinct formulation of the counter-argument.

W. Bishop, Price Discrimination under Article 86: Political Economy in the European Court[78]

The rule in *United Brands* requires any monopolist who hitherto has discriminated in price between national submarkets to discontinue this practice. Henceforth such a monopolist must charge the same price (with due allowance for cost differences). Generally speaking discriminating monopolists will find it profitable to charge higher prices in higher income countries . . . than in lower income countries. . . . Suppose these firms are now required to charge only one price. Almost certainly the profit maximising price will lie somewhere between the highest and lowest discriminatory prices that such a firm could charge . . . consider the effect on income distribution as between high and low income countries. German consumers of (say) bananas get them at a lower price than before. Also some German consumers who did not buy bananas before do buy them now. All these German consumers are better off. Some British consumers who bought before now drop out of the market because the price is too high. Remaining British consumers pay more. All these British consumers are worse off. So, though efficiency effects in this example are ambiguous, distributional effects are quite clear: income is redistributed away from Britain and toward Germany. The general effect of *United Brands* is clear—*it redistributes income away from consumers in the poorer regions of Europe and toward consumers in the richer regions.*

It may be argued that this analysis ignores the importance of the creation of a *single market*, a factor which is of considerable importance within Community law. This explains the Court's opposition to market behaviour which entails divisions along

---

[78] Bishop, n. 77 above, 288–9, italics in the original.

national lines. While the hostility of the Community authorities to such barriers is undoubtedly an important factor, it should not be viewed as a self-evident justification for any and every aspect of the ECJ's jurisprudence. This is because the argument may not 'really work' in certain instances. We can lose sight of substance by concentrating upon form or labels. The rationale for a single market in economic terms was to create greater efficiency:[79]

To that end striking down arrangements in which arbitrary national barriers are preserved is a goal of the Community institutions. But that is very different from charging different prices in geographically separated markets, simply because the markets happen to be different countries. It is also very different when the effect of prohibiting the practice is possibly to induce greater misallocation of resources and certainly to redistribute wealth from the poor to the rich. The common European market was set up *as a means to the opposite ends*, so a general appeal to those means cannot justify the decision.

Some of the seminal decisions of the ECJ concerning price discrimination can now be considered.

Case 27/76, United Brands Company and United Brands Continentaal BV v. Commission [1978] ECR 207

The general facts of the case were set out above. UB was accused of abusive behaviour for a number of different reasons. The present discussion will focus on price discrimination. UB shipped bananas from Central America to Europe. Some of these bananas bore the brand name 'Chiquita', and these tended to fetch a higher price. UB sold the goods to ripeners, who sold them to wholesalers, who in turn sold to retailers. The bananas were landed at two ports, but there were no real differences in unloading costs. The Commission alleged that UB sold the bananas at different prices in different Member States, and that it did so without objective justification. The essence of UB's response was to contend that the price differentials reflected market forces, *viz.* the average anticipated market price in each state; that the Community had not established a single banana market; and that, therefore, it was not possible to avoid differences in the individual supply/demand situations in the different countries.

THE ECJ

227. Although the responsibility for establishing the single banana market does not lie with the applicant, it can only endeavour to take 'what the market can bear' provided that it complies with the rules for the regulation and coordination of the market laid down by the Treaty.

228. Once it can be grasped that differences in transport costs, taxation, customs duties, the wages of the labour force, the conditions of marketing, the differences in the parity of the currencies, the density of competition may eventually culminate in different retail selling price levels according to the Member States, then it follows that those differences are factors which UBC only has to take into account to a limited extent since it sells a product which is always the same and at the same place to ripener/distributors who—alone—bear the risks of the consumers' market.

---

[79] *Ibid.*, 288–9, italics in the original.

229. The interplay of supply and demand should, owing to its nature, only be applied to each stage where it is really manifest.

230. The mechanisms of the market are adversely affected if the price is calculated by leaving out one stage of the market and taking into account the law of supply and demand as between the vendor and the ultimate consumer and not as between the vendor (UBC) and the purchaser (the ripener/distributor).

231. Thus, by reason of its dominant position UBC . . . was in fact able to impose its selling price on the intermediate purchaser. . . .

232. These discriminatory prices, which varied according to the circumstances of the Member States, were just so many obstacles to the free movement of goods and were intensified by the clause forbidding the resale of bananas while still green and by reducing the deliveries of the quantities ordered.

233. A rigid partitioning of national markets was thus created at price levels which were artificially different, placing certain distributor/ripeners at a competitive disadvantage, since compared with what it should have been competition had thereby been distorted.

There is much confusion in this extract, which does not represent the Court's most lucid reasoning. The judgment omits any consideration of the general issue whether price discrimination can be beneficial. The ECJ's reasoning is punctuated by the mistaken use of concepts. It is, for example, central to the ECJ's judgment that UB would only have to take account of the many factors which differentiated the various retail markets to a limited extent; and that the risks would instead be borne by the distributors/ripeners.[80] This is highly questionable. A manufacturer may well bear the risk of differing demand conditions at the retail level. UB almost certainly did bear these risks. If it had tried to shift these risks to the distributors, then it would have been necessary to have given financial inducements to the latter.[81] The Court's references to the markets in which supply and demand is really manifest are equally problematic.[82]

Another major decision dealing with price discrimination was the *Hoffmann-La Roche* case.

Case 85/76, Hoffmann-La Roche & Co. AG v. Commission
[1979] ECR 461

The case turned on certain abusive practices which were engaged in by HLR in the markets for vitamins. One aspect of this behaviour was concerned with HLR's practice of giving rebates.

---

[80] Para. 228.

[81] The mere fact that a manufacturer possesses some degree of market power does not somehow mean that it is immune to the conditions in particular retail markets, particularly where the *degree* of that power will be directly related to conditions in differing retail markets: see Bishop, n. 77 above, 285–6.

[82] *Ibid.*, 284–5. For an example of discrimination on geographical lines see *Elopak Italia Srl* v. *Tetra Pak (No. 2)*, n. 11 above, para. 154.

THE ECJ

89. An undertaking which is in a dominant position on a market and ties purchasers—even if it does so at their request—by an obligation or promise on their part to obtain all or most of their requirements exclusively from the said undertaking abuses its dominant position within the meaning of Article 86 of the Treaty, whether the obligation in question is stipulated without further qualification or whether it is undertaken in consideration of the grant of the rebate. The same applies if the said undertaking, without tying the purchasers by a formal obligation, applies, either under the terms of agreements concluded with these purchasers or unilaterally, a system of fidelity rebates, that is to say discounts conditional on the customer's obtaining all or most of its requirements—whether the quantity of its purchases be large or small—from the undertaking in the dominant position.

90. Obligations of this kind . . . are incompatible with the objective of undistorted competition within the Common Market, because . . . they are not based on an economic transaction which justifies this burden or benefit but are designed to deprive the purchaser of or restrict his possible choices of sources of supply and to deny other producers access to the market. The fidelity rebate, unlike quantity rebates exclusively linked with the volume of purchases from the producer concerned, is designed through the grant of a financial advantage to prevent customers from obtaining their supplies from competing producers. Furthermore, the effect of fidelity rebates is to apply dissimilar conditions to equivalent transactions with other trading parties in that two purchasers pay a different price for the same quantity of the same product depending on whether they obtain their supplies exclusively from the undertaking in a dominant position or have several sources of supply. . . .

91. For the purpose of rejecting the finding that there has been an abuse of a dominant position the interpretation suggested by the applicant that an abuse implies that the use of the economic power bestowed by the dominant position is the means whereby the abuse has been brought about cannot be accepted. The concept of abuse is an objective concept relating to the behaviour of an undertaking in a dominant position which is such as to influence the structure of the market where, as a result of the very presence of the undertaking in question, the degree of competition is weakened and which, through recourse to methods different from those which condition normal competition in products or services on the basis of the transactions of commercial operators, has the effect of hindering the maintenance of the degree of competition still existing in the market or the growth of that competition.

The ECJ's antipathy to price discrimination in the form of loyalty rebates emerges clearly in the above extract,[83] and other cases.[84] The Court, moreover, made it clear that the existence of the 'English clause', whereby a purchaser could buy elsewhere if the goods could be obtained on more favourable terms, did not serve to exonerate HLR. This was because, *inter alia*, such a clause could give valuable information to HLR on a competitor's prices.[85] The ECJ also reiterated the point which had been made in the *Continental Can* case: there was no need under Article 86 (now Article 82) to prove that the abuse had been brought about by means of the firm's market

---

[83] Waelbroeck, M., 'Price Discrimination and Rebate Policies under EU Competition Law', in B. Hawke (ed.), *Fordham Corporate Law Institute* (Fordham, 1995), 147.

[84] Case T–228/97, *Irish Sugar*, n. 25 above, paras. 111–114.

[85] Case 85/76, n. 6 above, para. 107.

power. The concept of abuse was 'objective', and could apply to any behaviour which influenced the *structure* of the market and weakened competition.[86] Later cases demonstrate the continued hostility of the competition authorities to rebate or discount schemes of this kind.[87]

(d) ABUSE AND PREDATORY PRICING

Predatory pricing has already been touched on when discussing price discrimination. It is now time to focus more specifically on this type of abusive behaviour. *Akzo* is the leading case.

Case C–62/86, Akzo Chemie BV v. Commission
[1991] ECR I–3359

[ToA renumbering: Art. 86 is now Art. 82]

Akzo, based in Holland, and ECS, a smaller United Kingdom firm, both made organic peroxides. Benzoyl peroxide could be used in both the flour and the plastics markets. ECS was initially engaged in the flour market, but then moved into the plastics market in 1979 and solicited some of Akzo's customers. Akzo had a meeting with ECS at which it threatened that it would take aggressive action on the flour market unless ECS withdrew from the plastics market. ECS ignored the threats, which Akzo then put into operation. Akzo targeted certain of ECS's customers in the flour market, and offered them prices which were below previous rates and below average total cost. Akzo subsidized these low prices by money drawn from the plastics sector. ECS's business fell significantly as a result of this action. The Court quoted the test of abuse from *Hoffmann-La Roche* which is set out above,[88] and then reasoned as follows.

THE ECJ

70. It follows that Article 86 prohibits a dominant undertaking from eliminating a competitor and thereby strengthening its position by using methods other than those which come within the scope of competition on the basis of quality. From that point of view, however, not all competition by means of price can be regarded as legitimate.

71. Prices below average variable costs (that is to say, those which vary depending on the quantities produced) by means of which a dominant undertaking seeks to eliminate a competitor must be regarded as abusive. A dominant undertaking has no interest in applying such prices except that of eliminating competitors so as to enable it subsequently to raise its prices by taking advantage of its monopolistic position, since each sale generates a loss, namely the total amount of the fixed costs (that is to say, those which remain constant regardless of the quantities produced) and, at least, part of the variable costs relating to the unit produced.

72. Moreover, prices below average total costs, that is to say, fixed costs plus variable costs,

---

[86] *Ibid.*, para. 91.
[87] Case 322/81, *Michelin*, n. 44 above; *Elopak (No. 2)*, n. 11 above, paras. 154, 160–161; *Eurofix-Bauco* v. *Hilti* [1988] OJ L65/19, [1989] 4 CMLR 677, on appeal, Case T–30/89, n. 23 above.
[88] See 1002 above.

but above average variable costs, must be regarded as abusive if they are determined as part of a plan for eliminating a competitor. Such prices can drive from the market undertakings which are perhaps as efficient as the dominant undertaking but which, because of their smaller financial resources, are incapable of withstanding the competition waged against them.

The ECJ found that Akzo was in breach of the principles set out above. It had at various times offered customers of ECS prices which were lower than Akzo's own average total or variable costs, and it had done so as part of a deliberate strategy to remove ECS from the plastics market. The behaviour of Akzo was particularly blatant in the circumstances of the case, and also ill-advised in business terms. If a firm is intending to drive another out of a sector of the market, then the last thing that a manager of the dominant firm should be doing is committing to paper this aggressive strategy, given that the Commission may gain access to such information. Yet this is exactly what a manager of Akzo did in this case. The unequivocally wrongful intent of Akzo should not, however, lead us to underestimate the difficulties which a rule against predatory pricing presents for a system of competition policy. A number of these difficulties were touched on in the discussion of price discrimination, but they should be borne in mind in this specific context.

First, there is continuing disagreement about the proper definition of predation in economic terms.[89]

Secondly, there is the fact that the existence of this ground of challenge may do more harm than good. It may be a potent weapon in the hands of a firm, which can use it against the incumbent dominant firm. The line between vigorous price competition and illegal predation may be a fine one. A dominant firm may feel that it should not pursue price competition as vigorously as it might otherwise have done, lest this should leave it open to allegations of predatory abuse. Even if these allegations are in the end regarded as unfounded the cost of defending an action may be high and may be a potent disincentive to risking legal proceedings. This is all the more so given that, on the test propounded in *Akzo*, intention becomes of crucial importance where prices are below average total costs but above average variable costs. It may be extremely difficult, in such circumstances, to distinguish between intent to compete energetically in the market and intent to eliminate a competitor.

Finally, there are those who continue to doubt whether a rational firm would engage in predation. The potential gains from successful predation appear to be straightforward: the dominant firm lowers its prices, takes a loss in the short term, drives out the smaller firm, and then reaps high monopoly profits in the relevant market. The economic reality is much less certain. In order for predation to be a successful and rational strategy the future flow of profits has to exceed the present losses incurred as a result of the drop in price. This is not theoretically impossible, but it is more difficult to achieve than may initially be thought. Predation is, in this sense, a war of attrition, with the outcome to be determined by the combatants' relative losses and reserves: the 'war will be a *Blitzkrieg* only if the predator has greatly

---

[89] See n. 72 above.

disproportionate reserves or is able to inflict very disproportionate losses'.[90] There are significant obstacles to a successful campaign. The losses during the battle will be higher for the predator than the victim. Any anticipated monopoly profits must be discounted at current interest rates. The predator will, moreover, have to gauge the likelihood of another competitor entering the market, should it seek to reap excessive monopoly profits having disposed of the original combatant.[91] The prospect that future entrants would be deterred from entry by witnessing the plight of the victim is often accorded undue weight. The greater the monopoly profits now being reaped by the predator, the greater the incentive for new entrants. For the predator to seek to engage in another battle to drive out this new entrant would lead it to incur ever more losses in the hope of obtaining the desired monopoly returns once it has the field to itself.

Whether Akzo was behaving rationally depends upon whether its present losses were outweighed by future gains.[92] The answer to this is unclear, but it is not self-evident that the future gains would have compensated for the money lost in the battle. It must, however, be said that while Akzo was inept by consigning its strategy to paper, it was, in one respect, more astute. The losses to the predator from the campaign will be lower if it can price discriminate, by charging higher prices to its traditional customers, while poaching ECS's customers by billing them at a lower price. It appears from the facts of the case that Akzo did in fact do this, though how long this strategy could have been maintained is more debatable.

Notwithstanding the difficulties associated with the detection of predatory pricing the competition authorities continue to use this ground under Article 86 (now Article 82). Thus in *Tetra Pak*[93] the ECJ held that Tetra Pak, a world leader in the manufacture of aseptic cartons for liquid and semi-liquid food, had abused its dominant position by its pricing policy on non-aseptic cartons. The company had a dominant position on the market for aseptic cartons, and it was held that it had used profits from this market to subsidize sales on the market for non-aseptic cartons, selling the latter at a loss below average variable cost in seven of the Member States. The ECJ reiterated the holding in paragraphs 72 and 73 of *Akzo*. It was argued that the Commission and CFI should have taken into account the issue whether Tetra Pak had any realistic chance of recouping its losses. This argument was rejected by the ECJ, which held that it must be possible to penalize predation whenever there was a risk that competitors would be eliminated, and that this objective ruled out waiting until such a strategy resulted in the actual elimination of competitors.[94]

(e) ABUSE AND SELECTIVE PRICING

It is moreover clear from cases such as *Irish Sugar*[95] that when judging the legality of a selective pricing policy the CFI and ECJ will take account of the fact that the practice

---

[90] Bork, n. 28 above, 147.   [91] *Ibid.*, 149–55.
[92] R. Rapp, 'Predatory Pricing and Entry Deterring Strategies: The Economics of *AKZO*' [1986] *ECLR* 233.
[93] Case C–333/94P, n. 6 above.   [94] *Ibid.*, para. 44.
[95] Case T–228/97, n. 25 above, para. 114.

was aimed at eliminating a competitor from the market. This is readily apparent from the following case.

Cases C–395–396/96P, Compagnie Maritimes Belge Transportes SA, Compagnie Maritime Belge SA, and Dafra Lines A/S v. Commission
[2000] ECR I–1365

The applicants were members of a liner conference that had a dominant position on certain shipping routes in Africa. They were charged, *inter alia*, with the lowering of their freight rates in order to drive the only competitor from the market.

THE ECJ

117. . . . where a liner conference in a dominant position selectively cuts its prices in order deliberately to match those of a competitor, it derives a dual benefit. First, it eliminates the principal, and possibly the only, means of competition open to the competing undertaking. Second, it can continue to require its users to pay higher prices for the services which are not threatened by that competition.

118. It is not necessary, in the present case, to rule generally on the circumstances in which a liner conference may legitimately . . . adopt lower prices than those of its advertised tariff in order to compete with a competitor who quotes lower prices. . . .

119. It is sufficient to recall that the conduct at issue here is that of a conference having a share of over 90% of the market in question and only one competitor. The appellants have, moreover, never seriously disputed, and indeed admitted at the hearing, that the purpose of the conduct complained of was to eliminate G & C from the market.

9. JOINT DOMINANCE

The discussion thus far has proceeded on the assumption that one firm occupies a dominant position on the market. However, Article 82 speaks of an abuse of a dominant position by *one or more undertakings*.

It is clear that it can cover the situation, presented by cases such as *Continental Can* and *Commercial Solvents*, where the dominant position is held by a number of firms which are part of the same corporate group or economic unit.[96]

What has been less clear is whether the phrase also brings within the ambit of the Article oligopolistic markets, in which a number of independent firms operate in a parallel manner.[97] The ECJ appeared to have rejected this view in the *Hoffmann-La Roche* case,[98] when it held that unilateral behaviour by a single firm occupying a dominant position had to be distinguished from interactive behaviour by a number of independent firms, which made up an oligopoly. It does, however, now appear to be the case that some species of oligopolistic behaviour can be caught by Article 82.

---

[96] Whish, n. 27 above, 473.   [97] *Ibid.*, 471–82.   [98] Case 85/76, n. 6 above, para. 39.

Cases T–68, 77–78/89, Re Italian Flat Glass: Società Italiana Vetro v. Commission
[1992] ECR I–1403[99]

[Note ToA renumbering: Arts. 85 and 86 are now Arts. 81 and 82]

A company, Cobelli, a wholesaler of glass, alleged that three producers of flat glass were in breach of the Treaty by maintaining agreed price lists and identical conditions of sale. It also alleged that two of these companies had engaged in practices which were designed to achieve full control, not only of the production of glass, but also of its distribution, by excluding from the market independent wholesaler-distributors. The Commission found that there had been a breach of Article 85, by the producers of the flat glass, and also a breach of Article 86. In relation to the latter, it held that the undertakings had a collective dominant position, that they were able to pursue a commercial policy which was independent of ordinary market conditions, and that they presented themselves on the market as a single entity, rather than as individual concerns. The CFI partially annulled the findings with respect to Article 85, holding that the Commission had failed to establish the requisite agreement or concerted practice between the three producers. It then proceeded to consider Article 86.

THE CFI

358. The Court considers that there is no legal or economic reason to suppose that the term 'undertaking' in Article 86 has a different meaning from the one given to it in the context of Article 85. There is nothing, in principle, to prevent two or more independent economic entities from being, on a specific market, united by such economic links that, by virtue of that fact, together they hold a dominant position *vis-à-vis* the other operators on the same market. This could be the case, for example, where two or more undertakings jointly have, through agreements or licences, a technological lead affording them the power to behave to an appreciable extent independently of their competitors, their customers and ultimately of their consumers (*Hoffmann-La Roche*).

. . .

360. However, it should be pointed out that for the purposes of establishing an infringement of Article 86 EEC, it is not sufficient, as the Commission's agent claimed at the hearing, to 'recycle' the facts constituting an infringement of Article 85, deducing from the finding that the parties to an agreement or to an unlawful practice jointly hold a substantial share of the market, that by virtue of that fact alone they hold a collective dominant position, and that their unlawful behaviour constitutes an abuse of that collective dominant position. Amongst other considerations, a finding of a dominant position, which is in any case not in itself a matter of reproach, presupposes that the market in question has been defined (Case 6/72, *Continental Can*, Case 322/81, *Michelin*). The Court must therefore examine, first the analysis of the market made in the decision and, secondly, the circumstances relied on in support of the finding of a collective dominant position.

The CFI annulled the Commission's decision on Article 86, on the ground that there were errors in its reasoning both with respect to the definition of the relevant

[99] M. Schodermeier, 'Collective Dominance Revisited: An Analysis of the EC Commission's New Concepts of Oligopoly Control' [1990] *ECLR* 28.

market and because it had not adduced the necessary proof of a collective dominant position.[100] Notwithstanding the reversal of the Commission, the CFI's decision was important for its affirmation of the existence of collective dominance.[101]

The ECJ has supported the idea of collective dominance. In *IJM*[102] it held that, while one could not automatically conclude that a body such as IJM, which held a non-exclusive concession in only one part of one Member State, occupied a dominant position for the purposes of this Article, a different assessment should apply where that undertaking belonged to a group of undertakings which collectively occupied a dominant position. The idea of collective dominance was also endorsed in the *DIP* case,[103] where the ECJ held that to find such a collective dominant position it must be necessary for the undertakings to be linked in such a way that they adopt the same conduct on the market. The ECJ gave further guidance on the meaning of collective dominance in the following case.

Cases C-395–396/96P, Compagnie Maritime Belge Transports SA, Compagnie Maritime
Belge SA, and Dafra Lines A/S v. Commission
[2000] ECR I–1365

[Note ToA renumbering: Article 85 is now Article 81]

The facts have been set out in the previous extract. The members of the liner conference also argued that it was wrong of the Commission and the CFI to have concluded that they occupied a collectively dominant position. They contended that the Commission and CFI had, in making this finding, merely 'recycled' facts relating to the existence of a concerted practice.

THE ECJ

41. In order to establish the existence of a collective entity . . . it is necessary to examine the economic links or factors which give rise to a connection between the undertakings concerned. . . .

42. In particular, it must be ascertained whether economic links exist between the undertakings concerned which enable them to act independently of their competitors, their customers and consumers (see *Michelin*).

43. The mere fact that two or more undertakings are linked by an agreement, a decision . . . or a concerted practice within the meaning of Article 85(1) . . . does not, of itself, constitute a sufficient basis for such a finding.

---

[100] There are difficulties with the reasoning of the CFI: see Whish, n. 27 above, 474–6.

[101] R. Whish and B. Sufrin, 'Oligopolistic Markets and EC Competition Law' (1992) 12 *YBEL* 59; D. Ridyard, 'Economic Analysis of Single Firm and Oligopolistic Dominance' [1994] *ECLR* 255; B. Rodger, 'Oligopolistic Market Failure: Collective Dominance versus Complex Monopoly' [1995] *ECLR* 21; C. Caffarra and K-U. Kuhn, 'Joint Dominance: The CFI Judgment on Gencor/Lonhro' [1999] *ECLR* 355; R. Whish, 'Collective Dominance', in D. O'Keefe and A. Bavasso (eds.), *Judicial Review in European Union Law* (Kluwer, 2000), ch. 37; G. Monti, 'The Scope of Collective Dominance under Article 82' (2001) 38 *CMLRev.* 131; G. Niels, 'Collective Dominance—More Than Just Oligopolistic Independence' [2001] *ECLR* 168; E. Kloosterhuis, 'Joint Dominance and the Interaction between Firms' [2001] *ECLR* 79; C. Withers and M. Jephcott, 'Where to Now for EC Oligopoly Control?' [2001] *ECLR* 295.

[102] Case C–393/92, n. 53 above.

[103] Cases C–140–142/94, *DIP SpA v. Commune di Bassano del Grappa* [1995] ECR I–3257, paras. 25–26.

44. On the other hand, an agreement, decision or concerted practice (whether or not covered by an exemption under Article 85(3) . . .) may undoubtedly, where it is implemented, result in the undertakings concerned being so linked as to their conduct on a particular market that they present themselves as a collective entity vis-à-vis their competitors, their trading partners and consumers.

45. The existence of a collective dominant position may therefore flow from the nature and terms of an agreement, from the way in which it is implemented and, consequently, from the links or factors which give rise to a connection between undertakings which result from it. Nevertheless, the existence of an agreement or of other links in law is not indispensable to a finding of a collective dominant position; such a finding may be based on other connecting factors and would depend on an economic assessment and, in particular, on an assessment of the structure of the market in question.

The same approach to collective dominance is apparent in the context of mergers. In *Gencor*[104] the CFI held that collective dominance within the Merger Regulation could catch oligopolistic collusion, and that the existence of structural links between the relevant firms was not a necessary condition for collective dominance to apply.

It is still necessary to find that there has been an abuse by those firms that occupy a collective dominant position. The meaning of abuse in this context is difficult. If there is a concerted practices by oligopolists this will in any event be caught by Article 81. For Article 82 to be of use collective dominance will have to embrace non-collusive behaviour. However, to condemn parallel pricing behaviour by oligopolists as an abuse under Article 82 would be tantamount to condemning oligopoly *per se*, since this is the rational behaviour of firms in such markets. There is none the less still room for the concept of abuse to apply. Thus, if those occupying a collective dominant position seek to drive a competitor from the market, as exemplified by *Compagnie Maritime Belge*, they should properly be caught by Article 82.

We shall see that under the Merger Regulation collective dominance can be caught because in oligopolistic markets firms might be able to gain benefits from tacit co-ordination.[105] The reason to condemn a concentration that created or strengthened a collective dominant position is that it could make it easier for the firms to benefit in this manner. However, as Whish states,[106] the fact that tacit co-ordination can be prevented through the prohibition of a concentration under the Merger Regulation does not mean that actual co-ordination should be condemned under Article 82.

---

[104] Case T–102/96, *Gencor Ltd. v. Commission* [1999] ECR II–753, paras. 276–277.
[105] See Ch. 24.
[106] Whish, n. 27 above, 479.

10. OBJECTIVE JUSTIFICATION AND PROPORTIONALITY

We have already seen that Article 82 has no equivalent to Article 81(3). This is partly explicable on the ground that classical monopolistic behaviour was felt to be inexcusable, and that therefore there was no need for any Article 81(3) (ex Article 85(3)). Subsequent developments have shaken this view. Commentators are now more circumspect than previously about whether conduct such as price discrimination should be regarded as unequivocally bad; and the Court has extended its jurisprudence to cover structural abuse and detriment to the competitive market process in the manner considered above.

It is for these reasons that the Court has developed the concepts of objective justification and proportionality in order to provide some flexibility in what would otherwise be too draconian an application of Article 82. We have seen similar ideas at work in the context of Article 28 (ex Article 30) and the free movement of goods.[107] With these concepts in play Article 82 can be applied to behaviour such as refusal to supply and price discrimination, while legitimate commercial behaviour can be distinguished from that which should properly be caught by the Treaty. Thus if there is an objective justification for the dominant firm's conduct, and it is proportionate, then the firm will escape condemnation under this Article. Issues relating to objective justification and proportionality have been considered in a number of cases that have been litigated under this Article.[108]

While the ideas of objective justification and proportionality, therefore, imbue the application of the Article with added flexibility, the application of these concepts to the facts of specific cases is not self-executing. The decision, for example, whether a refusal to supply is objectively justified and proportionate in a particular case will often depend upon and reflect certain assumptions concerning the relative importance of protecting competitors and consumers, or the relative significance of single-market integration and consumer welfare. In this sense concepts such as objective justification merely serve to press the inquiry into the appropriate reach and direction of Community policy in relation to dominant firms one stage further back. They do not in themselves resolve that inquiry.

11. CONCLUSION

i. It is clear that adjudication under Article 82 involves difficult problems.

ii. There are *inherent problems relating to market definition*. There will always be differences of opinion on whether the Commission and the Community Courts

---

[107] See Ch. 15 above.
[108] See, e.g., Case 27/76, *United Brands*, n. 2 above; Case T–65/89, *BPB*, n. 58 above; Case T–30/89, *Hilti*, n. 23 above; Case 311/84, *Centre Belge d'Etudes du Marché-Télémarketing (CBEM)* v. *CLT SA* [1985] ECR 3261.

have adopted the 'correct' definition of the product and geographical market in any particular case.

iii. There are also *problems relating to the meaning of abuse* as it applies within Article 82. Most, if not all, commentators agree that Article 82 does not condemn dominance *per se*. The more precise application of the particular examples listed in Article 82, and other types of 'abusive' conduct not listed therein, is none the less difficult. This difficulty affects not only the factual application of an agreed concept, but also the very meaning of the concept itself. Two important examples can be given.

iv. It is, as we have seen, unclear from the ECJ's jurisprudence whether Article 82 is intended to protect consumers or competitors. While the same conduct may be harmful to both, albeit in different ways, this will not always be the case.[109]

v. A further example of this difficulty concerns the 'special responsibility' incumbent on firms in a dominant position. This is in once sense self-evident, since only such firms are subject to Article 82. It is however clear that this phrase carries a broader meaning in the ECJ's jurisprudence. The boundaries of this special responsibility are not clear from that jurisprudence, and this can undoubtedly make it difficult for the firm in a dominant position to know in advance what it is allowed to do.

12. FURTHER READING

(a) *Books*

BELLAMY, C., and CHILD, G., *European Community Law of Competition* (Sweet & Maxwell, 5th edn., 2001)

BISHOP, S., and WALKER, M., *The Economics of EC Competition Law: Concepts, Application and Measurement* (Sweet & Maxwell, 1999)

DEMSETZ, H., *Efficiency, Competition, and Policy* (Oxford University Press, 1989)

FAULL, J., and NIKPAY, A. (eds.), *The EC Law of Competition* (Oxford University Press, 1999)

FRAZER, T., *Monopoly, Competition and the Law* (Harvester Wheatsheaf, 2nd edn., 1993)

GOYDER, D., *EC Competition Law* (Oxford University Press, 3rd edn., 1998)

JOLIET, R., *Monopolisation and Abuse of a Dominant Position: A Comparative Study of American and European Approaches to the Control of Economic Power* (Martinus Nijhoff, 1970)

JONES, A., and SUFRIN, B., *EC Competition Law, Text, Cases and Materials* (Oxford University Press, 2001)

RODGER, B., and MacCULLOCH, A., *Competition Law and Policy in the EC and UK* (Cavendish, 2001)

WHISH, R., *Competition Law* (Butterworths, 4th edn., 2001)

---

[109] Case C–7/97, *Bronner*, n. 43 above, Jacobs AG, para. 58; Mastromanolis, n. 72 above.

(b) *Articles*

AREEDA, P., 'Essential Facilities: An Epithet in Need of Limiting Principles' (1990) 58 *Antitrust LJ* 841

BADEN FULLER, C., 'Article 86: EEC Economic Analysis of the Existence of a Dominant Position' (1979) 4 *ELRev.* 423

BERGMAN, M., 'Editorial: The Bronner Case—A Turning Point for Essential Facilities' [2000] *ECLR* 59

BISHOP, W., 'Editorial: The Modernization of DGIV' [1997] *ECLR* 481

DOHERTY, B., 'Just What Are Essential Facilities?' (2001) 38 *CMLRev.* 397

FOX, E., 'Monopolisation and Dominance in the United States and the European Community: Efficiency, Opportunity and Fairness' (1986) 61 *Notre Dame LRev.* 981

GYSELEN, L., and KYRIAZIS, N., 'Article 86 EEC: The Monopoly Power Measurement Issue Revisited' (1986) 11 *ELRev.* 134

HARBORD, D., and HOEHN, T., 'Barriers to Entry and Exit in European Competition Policy' (1994) 14 *International Review of Law and Economics* 422

JEBSEN, P., and STEVENS, R., 'Assumptions, Goals and Dominant Undertakings: The Regulation of Competition under Article 86 of the European Union' (1995–6) 64 *Antitrust Law Journal* 443

KLOOSTERHUIS, E., 'Joint Dominance and the Interaction between Firms' [2001] *ECLR* 79

KORAH, V., 'The Concept of a Dominant Position within the Meaning of Article 86' (1980) 17 *CMLRev.* 395

LANDES, D., and POSNER, R., 'Market Power in Antitrust Cases' (1981) 94 *Harvard LR* 937

MASTROMANOLIS, E., 'Predatory Pricing Strategies in the European Union: A Case for Legal Reform' [1998] *ECLR* 211

MONTI, G., 'The Scope of Collective Dominance under Article 82' (2001) 38 *CMLRev.* 131

NIELS, G., 'Collective Dominance—More Than Just Oligopolistic Independence' [2001] *ECLR* 168

RAPP, R., 'Predatory Pricing and Entry Deterring Strategies: The Economics of *AKZO*' [1986] *ECLR* 233

RIDYARD, D., 'Economic Analysis of Single Firm and Oligopolistic Dominance' [1994] *ECLR* 255

—— 'Essential Facilities and the Obligation to Supply Competitors under UK and EC Competition Law' [1996] *ECLR* 438

RODGER, B., 'Oligopolistic Market Failure: Collective Dominance versus Complex Monopoly' [1995] *ECLR* 21

SCHMALENSEE, R., 'Another Look at Market Power' (1982) 95 *Harvard LR* 1789

STOTHERS, C., 'Refusal to Supply as Abuse of a Dominant Position: Essential Facilities in the European Union' [2001] *ECLR* 256

TEMPLE LANG, J., 'Defining Legitimate Competition: Companies' Duties to Supply Competitors and Access to Essential Facilities' (1994) 18 *Fordham International LJ* 437

TURNBULL, S., 'Barriers to Entry, Article 86 EC and the Abuse of a Dominant Position: An Economic Critique of European Community Competition Law' [1996] *ECLR* 96

WAELBROECK, M., 'Price Discrimination and Rebate Policies under EU Competition Law', in B. Hawk (ed.), *Fordham Corporate Law Institute* (Fordham University, 1995), 147

WHISH, R., 'Collective Dominance', in D. O'Keefe and A. Bavasso (eds.), *Judicial Review in European Union Law* (Kluwer, 2000), ch. 37

—— and SUFRIN, B., 'Oligopolistic Markets and EC Competition Law' (1992) 12 *YBEL* 59

WITHERS, C., and JEPHCOTT, M., 'Where to Now for EC Oligopoly Control?' [2001] *ECLR* 295

24

COMPETITION LAW: MERGERS

1. INTRODUCTION

Community regulation of mergers was a long time coming.[1] Neither Article 85 nor Article 86 (now Articles 81 and 82) made specific mention of mergers. The Commission attempted to fill this gap as early as 1973 when it proposed a regulation to deal with the subject.[2] Agreement between the Member States was not, however, forthcoming. While the Member States recognized that some species of merger control was necessary, they could not agree on its specific form. They were divided on central issues such as the boundary line between Community and national merger control. There was also disagreement on the more precise form which Community control should take. The failure to resolve these and other issues meant that successive draft merger regulations became part of the established order of things in Community law.[3] The possibility of a 'final' regulation on mergers came to resemble *Waiting for Godot*.

The ECJ did not remain idle during this period. It signalled, as in other areas where there has been difficulty in achieving results through the legislative process, that it would use its own power in interpreting the Treaty to fill the gap, in part at least. Article 86 (now Article 82) was invoked, as we have seen, in the *Continental Can* case[4] to catch mergers by a firm in a dominant position. The Court took longer to apply Article 85 (now Article 81) to mergers. The traditional orthodoxy was that this Article did not apply to agreements the purpose of which was the acquisition of ownership.[5] This effectively ruled out the use of the Article for merger control. However, this orthodoxy was shaken in 1987 when the Court in the *BAT* case indicated its willingness to consider the application of Article 85 to some instances of share acquisition.[6]

This uncertainty, coupled with the need for a comprehensive merger regulation in the light of the Single Market initiatives, led to the promulgation in December 1989 of Regulation 4064/89, which became operative in September of the following year.[7]

---

[1] A. Jones and B. Sufrin, *EC Competition Law, Text, Cases and Materials* (Oxford University Press, 2001), 707–12; R. Whish, *Competition Law* (Butterworths, 4th edn., 2001), 735–43.

[2] *Commission Proposal for a Regulation of the Council of Ministers on the Control of Concentrations between Undertakings* [1973] OJ C92/1.

[3] See, e.g., [1982] OJ C36/3; [1984] OJ C51/8; [1986] OJ C324/5.

[4] Case 6/72, [1973] ECR 215.

[5] *Commission Memorandum on the Concentration of Enterprises in the Common Market.*

[6] Cases 142 & 156/84, *British American Tobacco Co. Ltd. and R. J. Reynolds Industries Inc. v. Commission* [1987] ECR 4487.

[7] [1989] OJ L395/1, [1990] 4 CMLR 286. Reg. 4064/89 has now been amended by Reg. 1310/97 [1997] OJ L180/1, [1997] 5 CMLR 387.

Most mergers will now be dealt with under this Regulation, but it may still be possible to use Articles 81 and 82 in certain cases.

2. CENTRAL ISSUES

i. Legal control of mergers is an important component of any regime designed to regulate competition.

ii. It is important to understand the *policy reasons* underlying merger control, and these are addressed in the following section.

iii. There are *procedural and substantive aspects* to Community merger policy.

iv. *Procedural issues* cover matters such as the way in which notice of a proposed merger must be given, and the investigative powers possessed by the Commission.

v. There are a number of important *substantive aspects* of merger policy. These include matters such as the types of merger or concentration brought within the sphere of Community merger control, the test for determining whether a merger or concentration should be allowed, and the extent to which the Merger Regulation covers collective dominance.

3. THE POLICY REASONS FOR MERGER CONTROL

Mergers can be of three kinds. *Horizontal mergers* are those between companies which make the same products and operate at the same level of the market. *Vertical mergers* are those between companies which operate at different distributive levels of the same product market. *Conglomerate mergers* are those between firms which have no connection with each other in any product market. Horizontal mergers are potentially the most damaging to the competitive process.

(a) ARGUMENTS AGAINST MERGERS

A merger can have a *marked impact on competition*. A horizontal merger may enable the new entity to set price and output in the same manner as a single-firm monopolist, with the same consequences for consumer welfare. In some countries indices are used to measure the reduction of competition brought about by the merger.[8] The impact of vertical mergers on competition is more controversial. In essence a vertical merger is merely one form of vertical integration: a company may relate to those downmarket by a number of means ranging from ordinary contract, through exclusive-distribution arrangements, to vertical merger. We have seen that such vertical relationships can be potentially anti-competitive, through, for example, foreclosing of outlets to other manufacturers.[9] But we have also seen that commentators dispute whether such vertical relationships really do harm competition.[10] This same disagreement carries over into the field of vertical merger: such a merger may, for

---

[8] The best known of these is the Herfindahl-Hirschman Index which is used in the USA.
[9] G. Abbamonte and V. Rabassa, 'Foreclosure and Vertical Mergers' [2001] *ECLR* 214.
[10] See Ch. 22 above.

example, improve the distribution of a branded product and hence promote inter-brand competition. There is also disagreement on the impact of conglomerate mergers on competition. Thus, while some see them as dangerous, allowing, for example, a wealthy firm to cross-subsidize from one product to another in order to defeat new entrants, others are sceptical whether such mergers involve any detriment to competition.[11]

Another reason legal systems seek to regulate merger activity is that mergers have been used to strip the *assets of the acquired firm,* and although this may be in the short-term interests of some shareholders, it may not be in the longer-term public interest. Concerns of this nature have been indirectly fuelled by empirical research, which indicates that mergers often do not produce the gains which were expected of them.[12]

Regional policy constitutes a third rationale for control of merger activity. A merger may lead to the rationalization of existing plants, with consequential effects on unemployment and regional vitality. A government may choose to use merger policy as one means of maintaining a balanced distribution of wealth and job opportunities around the country.[13]

(b) ARGUMENTS IN FAVOUR OF MERGERS

It would, however, be mistaken to suppose that all mergers are a bad thing. There are a number of ways in which they can have a beneficial impact. The most important of these is the argument based on *economic efficiency.* There are a number of aspects to the efficiency argument, which should be differentiated.

One concerns *economies of scale.* It is axiomatic that firms will produce most efficiently when they can maximize economies of scale. These are economies that can be reaped by the firm which is at the optimum size for that type of industry. A certain product may, for example, be made most efficiently with a particular piece of machinery, but this machinery may require a turnover of a specific amount before it is economically viable. Mergers are one way in which scale economies can be reaped.

Another aspect of the efficiency argument relates to *distributional efficiency.* It may, for example, be more efficient for a manufacturing firm which is seeking to extend its operations downmarket into the distributional sphere to merge with an existing distributor, rather than attempt to learn the skills of this new area from scratch.

There is also a considerable literature on the relationship between mergers and *managerial efficiency.*[14] The argument, in brief, is that the threat of a takeover is a spur

---

[11] R. Bork, *The Antitrust Paradox* (Basic Books, 1978), ch. 12.

[12] G. Newbould, *Management and Merger Activity* (Cruthstead, 1970); G. Meeks, *Disappointing Marriage: A Study of the Gains from Mergers* (Cambridge University Press, 1977); A. Hughes, 'Mergers and Economic Performance in the UK: A Survey of the Empirical Evidence 1950–1990', in M. Bishop and J. Kay (eds.), *European Mergers and Merger Policy* (Oxford University Press, 1993), ch. 1.

[13] There may indeed be a conflict between regional policy and competition policy in this respect, particularly where the latter focuses exclusively on the impact of mergers on competition without taking into account other factors.

[14] See, e.g., F. Easterbrook and D. Fischel, 'The Proper Role of a Target's Management in Responding to a Tender Offer' (1991) 94 *Harv. L.Rev.* 1161.

for management to perform efficiently. On this view the 'market for corporate control' helps to promote economic efficiency: where the shareholders are satisfied with the performance of management they will not wish to sell to another.

The Merger Regulation recognizes the inevitability and desirability of mergers within the Community. Thus the third recital to the Regulation acknowledges that the dismantling of internal frontiers will result in major corporate reorganization; while the fourth recital states that this is to be welcomed as one means of increasing the competitiveness of European industry on world markets. The approach of the Merger Regulation itself can now be considered.

4. REGULATION 4064/89 AS AMENDED:[15] PROCEDURAL ISSUES

A Mergers Task Force (MTF) within the Competition Directorate administers the Merger Regulation. Appeals from its decisions are heard by the CFI. In order for merger control to be effective it is obviously necessary for the Commission to be informed about any such acquisition. This is covered by Article 4(1), which deals with *pre-notification*. It provides that concentrations with a Community dimension must be notified not more than one week after the conclusion of the agreement, or the announcement of the public bid, or the acquisition of the controlling interest. Article 4(3) imposes an obligation on the MTF to publish those notifications that it considers to fall within the ambit of the Regulation. Failure to comply with the duty to pre-notify can lead to fines under Article 14(1)(a). The MTF has devised a standard form, known as Form CO, which is to be used for the notification.[16] This form requires the parties to submit certain information to the Commission, including copies of the documentation bringing about the concentration, copies of the accounts of the parties involved, and copies of any reports which have been prepared for the purposes of the concentration.[17]

The effectiveness of merger control also demands that a proposed concentration shall not be completed pending investigation by the Commission. This is dealt with by Article 7(1). This provides for the *suspension* of a concentration before notification, or until it has been declared to be compatible with the Common Market pursuant to decision under Article 6(1)(b) or Article 8(2), or on the basis of the presumption in Article 10(6). Article 14(2) allows the Commission to impose heavy fines for breach of this obligation. The suspensive effect of notification is, however, qualified by Article 7(3), which allows the Commission to derogate from Article 7(1). The derogation may be made subject to conditions.[18]

Once the concentration has been notified the MTF can then begin its investigation. This investigation is, in effect, conducted in two stages.

At the first stage the MTF can decide pursuant to Article 6(1) that the concentration

---

[15] As amended by Reg. 1310/97, n. 7 above.
[16] Reg. 447/98 [1998] OJ L61/1, [1998] 4 CMLR 542.
[17] Details concerning notification, the running of time and hearings are to be found in *ibid.*
[18] See, e.g., Case IV/M42, *Kelt/American Express* [1991] 4 CMLR 740.

is outside the Regulation. It can decide that it is within the scope of the Regulation, but is not incompatible with the common market. It may also decide that it is within the scope of the Regulation, that there are serious doubts about its compatibility with the common market, and that therefore proceedings should be initiated.[19] Decisions under Article 6(1) must normally be made within one month of the date of notification.[20]

At the second stage, the Commission will investigate those concentrations, where there are serious doubts about their compatibility with the Common Market. The Commission has a number of options, listed in Article 8. It can decide that the concentration or concentrative joint venture is not in fact in breach of the substantive criteria by which such matters are judged. Modifications may be required to the original concentration plans before the Commission decides that this is so.[21] It may determine that the merger is incompatible with the common market, because it creates or strengthens a dominant position as a result of which competition will be significantly impeded. The Commission may, in the case of certain joint ventures, decide that they do not qualify for exemption under Article 85(3), (now Article 81(3)).[22] It may demand the reversal of a merger which has already occurred.[23] Article 10 stipulates the time limits within which such decisions must be made, the basic rule being that this must be within four months from the initiation of the proceedings.[24] If the MTF fails to comply with the time limits then the merger will be deemed to be compatible with the common market.[25] There are rights to be heard before decisions are made,[26] and the list of parties who can be involved in the proceedings is quite broad.[27] Before any decision is made under Article 8 (or Articles 14 and 15), the Commission must consult the Advisory Committee on Concentrations. This Committee consists of one or two representatives from the Member States, and the meetings are chaired by the Commission.[28]

The Commission is given broad powers to facilitate *investigation* and *enforcement.* Thus Article 11 enables it to request information, Article 13 gives the Commission

---

[19] Art. 6(1)(a) of Reg. 4064/89 n. 7 above, now enables the Commission to decide that a proposed concentration which has been modified no longer raises serious doubts about its compatibility with the Common Market, and that it therefore can be declared to be compatible with the common market. Conditions can be attached and the decision can be revoked if the conditions are not complied with; if this is so the time limits in Art. 10(1) do not apply: Art. 6(1)(c).

[20] Reg. 4064/89, Art. 10(1); Reg. 447/98, Arts. 6–10. There is a simplified procedure for concentrations that do not raise competition concerns: *Notice on a Simplified Procedure for Treatment of Certain Concentrations under Council Regulation 4064/89* [2000] OJ C217/32.

[21] Reg. 4064/89, n. 7 above, Art. 8(2). Examples of clearance given to mergers subject to conditions can be found in Case IV/M18, *Alcatel/Telettra* [1991] OJ L122/48, [1991] 4 CMLR 778; and Case IV/M190, *Nestlé/Perrier* [1992] OJ L356/1, [1993] 4 CMLR M17. A decision finding that the concentration is compatible with the common market may also cover restrictions which are directly related and necessary to the implementation of the concentration: Art. 8(2), on which see the Commission's Notice on Ancillary Restraints [1990] OJ C203/5.

[22] Art. 8(3).

[23] Art. 8(4).

[24] This period may be extended where the MTF has to obtain additional information owing to circumstances for which one of the parties is responsible: Art. 10(4). See also Reg. 447/98, n. 7 above, Arts. 9 and 10.

[25] Art. 10(6), subject to Art. 9.

[26] Art. 18. The hearing rights apply to decisions made pursuant to Arts. 7(4), 8(2) second para., 8(3) to (5), 14, and 15.

[27] Reg. 447/98, Art. 11; Case T–290/94, *Kayserberg SA v. Commission* [1997] ECR II–2137.

[28] Reg. 4064/89, n. 7 above, Art. 19.

power to conduct on-site investigations, while Article 14 contains a power to impose fines which can be considerable. A fine of up to 10 per cent of the aggregate turnover of the undertakings concerned may, for example, be imposed where the parties have proceeded with a concentration which has been declared to be incompatible with the common market pursuant to a decision made under Article 8(3).[29]

5. REGULATION 4064/89 AS AMENDED: SUBSTANTIVE ISSUES

(a) CONCENTRATION: GENERAL

The Regulation will be applicable only if there is a concentration. This important issue is dealt with in Article 3(1):

A concentration shall be deemed to arise where:

(a) two or more previously independent undertakings merge, or

(b) — one or more persons already controlling at least one undertaking, or
— one or more undertakings,

acquire, whether by purchase of securities or assets, by contract or by any other means, direct or indirect control of the whole or parts of one or more undertakings.

Article 3(1) must be read in conjunction with Article 3(3):

For the purposes of this Regulation, control shall be constituted by rights, contracts or any other means which, either separately or in combination and having regard to the considerations of fact or law involved, confer the possibility of exercising decisive influence on an undertaking, in particular by:

(a) ownership of the right to use all or part of the assets of an undertaking;

(b) rights or contracts which confer decisive influence on the composition, voting or decisions of the organs of an undertaking.

It is clear that a combination of Article 3(1) and (3) will bring a number of different situations within the ambit of the Regulation. It is clear also that the Regulation catches concentrations with a Community dimension, and this is so irrespective of whether the firms are based in the EU or not.[30] The Commission has, moreover, made it clear that the determination of whether or not a concentration exists will be based on qualitative rather than quantitative criteria, focusing on the notion of control, and that in making this determination it will take account of issues of law *and* fact.[31]

Article 3(1)(a) covers the case of a *complete merger*. Although the Regulation does not define the term merger, it implies the formation of one enterprise from undertakings that were previously distinct and separate. The Commission has, however,

---

[29] Art. 14(2)(c).
[30] Case T–102/96, *Gencor Ltd* v. *Commission* [1999] ECR II–753.
[31] *Commission Notice on the Concept of Concentration under Council Regulation 4064/89 on the Control of Concentrations between Undertakings* [1998] OJ C66/5, [1998] 4 CMLR 586, para. 4.

made it clear that Article 3(1)(a) can bite in some circumstances where the undertakings retain their separate legal personalities, but create none the less a single economic unit.[32]

Article 3(1)(b) captures cases of *change of control*. This is a complex topic, detailed treatment of which can be found elsewhere.[33] The essence of this Article can, however, be conveyed as follows. A change of control can result in the acquisition of *sole control* by a person or an undertaking. This is exemplified by *Arjomari-Prioux/Wiggins Teape*,[34] where the Commission held that the acquisition of a 39 per cent shareholding in a company was sufficient to give a buyer control, given that the remaining shares were widely dispersed. It is also possible for two or more undertakings to acquire *joint control* over another. All the circumstances will be taken into account in deciding whether joint control exists in any particular case. Thus in *Northern Telecom/ Matra Telecommunications*[35] both companies were held to have acquired joint control over Matra SA on the ground that the consent of both parents was necessary for all important business decisions and financial plans. Cases concerning joint control raise difficult questions of how far the Regulation captures joint ventures. It is to this issue that we should now turn.

(b) CONCENTRATION: JOINT VENTURES

Joint ventures are created for many purposes. The term is not one of art and covers a wide range of business arrangements, from the establishment of a new corporate entity by two competitors to a joint-purchasing scheme or joint research and development. It is this very breadth of coverage of joint ventures which causes problems for competition systems. There has been debate about whether they should be treated by analogy with cartels, and be regarded as essentially a 'behavioural' problem to be dealt with under Article 81, or as a 'structural' problem, to be dealt with under the Merger Regulation.

The *original* approach in the Merger Regulation under the old Article 3(2) was that a joint venture would only be caught if it resulted in the creation of an autonomous economic entity on a lasting basis which did *not* give rise to, or have as its object or effect, the co-ordination of the competitive behaviour of independent undertakings. This meant that structural/concentrative aspects of joint ventures would be dealt with under the Merger Regulation, while behavioural/co-operative aspects concerned with the impact on competition of co-ordination between independent undertakings, would be considered under Article 81. The difficulties of this approach are exemplified in the extract.

---

[32] *Ibid.*, para. 7.
[33] See the *Commission's Concentration Notice*, n. 31 above. See also J. Cook and C. Kerse, *EC Merger Control* (Sweet & Maxwell, 3rd edn., 2000), ch. 2; T. Anthony Downes and J. Ellison, *The Legal Control of Mergers in the European Communities* (Blackstone, 1991), ch. 2.
[34] Case IV/M25, [1991] 4 CMLR 854.
[35] Case IV/M249.

B. Hawk, Joint Ventures under EEC Law[36]

If war is too important to be left to the generals, then the allocation of jurisdiction over joint ventures is too important to be left to the theorists. Very important practical consequences flow from the concentrative–cooperative distinction. To over simplify somewhat, as a joint venture leaves the high-tech deadline driven world of the merger task force, one moves to the more leisurely, scarce resources of the operating divisions of DG IV. The solution is not to continue to engage in the metaphysics of refining and rerefining the cooperative–concentrative distinction. The best solution is to provide a unified analysis of joint ventures that include both behavioural and structural considerations. If this cannot be done under the existing legislation, which appears to be the case, then the second best solution is to eliminate administrative and procedural differences to the extent possible between an examination of an arrangement under the Merger Regulation and a joint venture under Article 85.

The approach of Regulation 4064/89 has now been *modified*.[37] The wording of the new Article 3(2), set out below, expands the definition of joint ventures caught by the Merger Regulation, by removing the negative condition relating to the co-ordination of competitive behaviour between independent undertakings. It is now possible for a joint venture to be a concentration under Article 3(2), provided that it constitutes an autonomous economic entity created on a lasting basis, and this is still the case even if it might result in the co-ordination of competitive behaviour between independent undertakings. Given that this is so, it is therefore necessary to deal with such co-ordination within the confines of the Merger Regulation. This is the rationale for the new Article 2(4), which allows such determinations of possible anti-competitive behaviour to be made according to the criteria in Article 85 (now Article 81), and these determinations are made within the confines of the overall Merger Regulation. Hence, the Commission's powers of decision contained in Article 8, and the time limits specified in Article 10, apply to determinations made under Article 2(4).

Article 3(2) of Regulation 4064/89 as amended now provides that:

The creation of a joint venture performing on a lasting basis all the functions of an autonomous economic entity shall constitute a concentration within the meaning of paragraph (1)(b).

Article 2(4) of the Regulation states that:

To the extent that the creation of a joint venture constituting a concentration pursuant to Article 3 has as its object or effect the co-ordination of the competitive behaviour of undertakings that remain independent, such co-ordination shall be appraised in accordance with the criteria of Article 85(1) and (3) of the Treaty, with a view to establishing whether or not the operation is compatible with the Common Market.

In making this appraisal, the Commission shall take into account in particular:

— whether two or more parent companies retain to a significant extent activities in the same market as the joint venture or in a market which is upstream or downstream from that of the joint venture or in a neighbouring market closely related to this market,

---

[36] B. Hawk (ed.), *Fordham Corporate Law Institute* (Fordham University, 1991), 575–6.
[37] See the new recital 23 derived from Reg. 1310/97.

— whether the co-ordination which is the direct consequence of the creation of the joint
   venture affords the undertakings concerned the possibility of eliminating competition in
   respect of a substantial part of the products or services in question.

The fact remains that a joint venture will only be caught by the Merger Regulation
if it results in the creation of an autonomous economic entity which performs functions on a lasting basis. Guidance on the interpretation of this provision is to be found
in the Commission Notice on *Full Function Joint Ventures*.[38] The notice is not binding
as such, but it does provide a useful indication of the Commission's thinking on this
issue.

Concentrative joint ventures will lead to the creation of the requisite autonomous
economic entity. These joint ventures must operate on a market in the same general
way as other undertakings on that market. This means that they must have sufficient
financial and other resources to function as a business on a lasting basis.[39] Such joint
ventures are known as 'full-function' joint ventures. These conditions will not be met
where the joint venture only takes over a specific function of the parents' business
activities without access to the market, as in the case of joint ventures relating to
research and development.[40] The impact of the parent companies' support on the
operational autonomy of the joint venture must be determined in the context of the
relevant market. It must be decided whether the joint venture carries out functions
normally performed by other undertakings on that market.[41]

A full-function joint venture may also have co-operative features, in the sense that
the object or effect of the joint venture is the co-ordination of the competitive
behaviour of independent undertakings. Prior to the amendment of Regulation 4064/
89 such co-operative features served to remove the joint venture from the ambit of the
Regulation, unless they were *de minimis*. This is, as we have seen, not now the case.
Provided that there is a full-function joint venture it will be within the Regulation.
Any co-operative features that threaten to restrict competition will be evaluated under
Article 2(4). The Commission Notice is of help in indicating when it believes that the
co-ordination of the competitive behaviour of the parent companies may appreciably
limit competition.[42] Such a limitation of competition will not occur if the parent
companies transfer their entire business activities to the joint venture. In the converse
situation where the parent companies retain their activities in the relevant product
and geographic market there is a high probability of such co-ordination.[43] Various
intermediate positions are also possible, such as where the parent companies operate
in a market upstream or down stream from that of the joint venture.[44]

It can none the less be difficult to distinguish those joint ventures which will be
treated as concentrations for the purposes of Article 3(2) from those which will not. It

---

[38] *Commission Notice on the Concept of Full-Function Joint Ventures under Council Regulation 4064/89 on
the Control of Concentrations between Undertakings* [1998] OJ C66/1, [1998] 4 CMLR 581.
[39] *Ibid.*, para. 12.   [40] *Ibid.*, para. 13.
[41] Case T–87/96, *Assicurazioni Generali SpA and Unicredito SpA v. Commission* [1999] ECR II–203,
para. 73.
[42] *Commission Notice on the Concept of Full-Function Joint Ventures*, n. 38 above, paras. 16–17.
[43] Case IV/M.088, *Elf Enterprise* [1991] OJ C203/14.
[44] N. 38 above, para. 18.

should be remembered that much of the case law decided prior to the amendment to Regulation 4064/89 was concerned with the divide between concentrative and co-operative joint ventures. If the joint venture had more than *de minimis* co-operative features then it would not come within the Merger Regulation, even if it was an autonomous economic entity created on a lasting basis. The revised Article 3(2), combined with Article 2(4), now provides that any full-function merger will be caught by Regulation 4064/89, even if it has features which lead to the co-ordination of the competitive behaviour of the parent undertakings, these features then being assessed under Article 2(4). It will still, however, be necessary to decide whether what has been created really is a full-function joint venture for the purposes of Article 3(2), and in this sense the case law remains of relevance.

Case IV/M72, Re the Concentration between Sanofi and Sterling Drug Inc.
[1992] 5 CMLR M1

Sanofi (S) and Sterling Drug (SD) are pharmaceutical companies which entered into a series of joint ventures in order to combine worldwide their prescription drug (ethical) activities, and also their European over-the-counter (OTC) activities. The Commission found that the joint ventures were concentrative for the following reasons, but cleared the merger because there was no dominance on the relevant markets.

THE COMMISSION

7. The proposed transaction is a concentration within the meaning of Article 3 of Regulation 4064/89. In arriving at this conclusion the Commission has taken into account the following elements:

— the parties merge, transfer or otherwise lease or license on a permanent basis to operating entities established by the parties their existing production, distribution and marketing assets. All material contracts, government permits and licences . . . will be licensed, transferred or assigned. Employees will be transferred to the operating entities.

— product ranges will be marketed under common trade names. . . .

— with regard to research and development, which is of crucial importance for the ethical business, the parties will continue to carry out their research activities . . . independently. However, they agree to enable each other to participate in the development of future products right from the initial stages of such development. . . .

To this effect a Development Committee is established, in which both parties are equally represented, which will monitor and coordinate all research efforts and which will decide whether or not development should be pursued jointly.

In the event that the committee decides against joint development the parties may not continue development individually, and instead may only assign or license such rights to third parties. With regard to the OTC business, the parties have the choice of carrying out research and development within the 'Alliance' or availing themselves of Sterling Drug's facilities outside the territory:

— new acquisitions will be carried out jointly by the parties, —the new management structure will be fully integrated. Each venture provides for a management entity, which includes a strategic management committee responsible for all strategic management decisions. . . .

. . .

8. The Commission considers that these elements taken together bring about a lasting change in the structure of the undertakings concerned. The operation implies their effective withdrawal from the markets concerned, as they place all their interests in the various joint ventures.

(c) CONCENTRATIONS WHICH HAVE A 'COMMUNITY DIMENSION'

In order for a concentration to be caught by the Merger Regulation it must have a Community dimension. This is defined by Article 1(2) of the Regulation:

For the purposes of this Regulation, a concentration has a Community dimension where:

(a) the combined aggregate world-wide turnover of all the undertakings concerned is more than ECU 5,000 million, and

(b) the aggregate Community-wide turnover of each of at least two of the undertakings concerned is more than ECU 250 million,

unless each of the undertakings concerned achieves more than two-thirds of its aggregate Community-wide turnover within one and the same Member State.

The amended Regulation 4064/89 has now expanded the reach of Community merger control by the addition of what is now Article 1(3). The rationale for the inclusion of this broadened definition of concentrations with a Community dimension is to be found in the new Recital 11A–C to the Regulation. It was felt that concentrations which fell below the thresholds in Article 1(2) could none the less be examined under the merger laws of particular Member States, and that this could be costly as well as leading to conflicting assessments in the different legal systems. By extending the reach of Community merger control to catch such concentrations which could have a significant impact in several Member States, it was hoped therefore to ensure that the competitive impact of such concentrations could be considered for the Community as a whole. Article 1(3) now provides:

For the purposes of this Regulation, a concentration that does not meet the thresholds laid down in paragraph 2 has a Community dimension where:

(a) the combined aggregate world-wide turnover of all the undertakings is more than 2,500 million ECUs;

(b) in each of at least three Member States, the combined aggregate turnover of all the undertakings concerned is more than 100 million ECUs;

(c) in each of at least three Member States included for the purposes of point (b), the aggregate turnover of each of at least two of the undertakings concerned is more than 25 million ECUs; and

(d) the aggregate Community-wide turnover of each of at least two of the undertakings concerned is more than 100 million ECUs;

unless each of the undertakings concerned achieves more than two-thirds of its aggregate Community-wide turnover within one and the same Member State.

Turnover is calculated in accordance with Article 5 of the Regulation.[45] It should be noted that the test encapsulated in Article 1(2) and (3) is purely quantitative:[46] it does

---

[45] See also the *Commission's Turnover Notice* [1998] OJ C66/25, [1998] 4 CMLR 613.
[46] The thresholds set in Art. 1(2) and (3) can be revised: see Art. 1(4) and (5).

not in itself indicate that a merger will be regarded as contrary to the Regulation. The substantive criterion is contained within Article 2, which will be considered in the next section. It should also be noted that these definitions could bring many non-EC undertakings within the ambit of the Regulation.[47]

(d) CONCENTRATIONS: THE SUBSTANTIVE CRITERIA

The test for determining whether a merger is compatible with the Common Market is to be found in Article 2 of the Regulation:

1. Concentrations within the scope of this Regulation shall be appraised in accordance with the following provisions with a view to establishing whether or not they are compatible with the Common Market. In making this appraisal, the Commission shall take into account:

(a) the need to maintain and develop effective competition within the Common Market in view of, among other things, the structure of all of the markets concerned and the actual or potential competition from undertakings located either within or outwith the Community;

(b) the market position of the undertakings concerned and their economic and financial power, the alternatives available to suppliers and users, their access to suppliers or markets, any legal or other barriers to entry, supply and demand trends for the relevant goods and services, the interests of the intermediate and ultimate consumers, and the development of technical and economic progress provided that it is to consumers' advantage and does not form an obstacle to competition.

2. A concentration which does not create or strengthen a dominant position as a result of which effective competition would be significantly impeded in the Common Market or in a substantial part of it shall be declared compatible with the Common Market.

3. A concentration which creates or strengthens a dominant position as a result of which effective competition would be significantly impeded in the Common Market or in a substantial part of it shall be declared incompatible with the Common Market.

Article 2(1)–(3) should be read in conjunction with the new Article 2(4) set out above. It is clear from the wording of Article 2 that many of the issues encountered in the discussion of Article 82 will be of relevance here, too. Thus, it will be necessary to define the relevant market in geographical and product terms, and also to determine whether there is a dominant position, which has been created or strengthened by the concentration.[48] It should come as no surprise that the Commission makes reference to some of the seminal decisions under this Article when adjudicating on the Merger Regulation. It should also be made clear that the Commission Notice on the definition of the relevant market for the purposes of EC competition law, which was considered earlier,[49] will apply to the Merger Regulation. There must be a causal link between the creation and strengthening of a dominant position and the impact on competition.[50]

---

[47] See, e.g., Case IV/M24, *Mitsubishi Corporation/Union Carbide Corporation* [1992] 4 CMLR M50; Case IV/M69, *Kyowa Bank Limited/Saitama Bank Limited* [1992] 4 CMLR M105.

[48] Jones and Sufrin, n. 1 above, 753–68.

[49] See 1000–1 above.

[50] Cases C–68/94 & 30/95, *France* v. *Commission* [1998] ECR I–1375, para. 110.

The Commission's approach can be conveyed by reviewing some of its decisions. We can begin by considering an instance in which it cleared the merger. In reading this extract pay particular attention to the way in which the Commission dealt with the dynamic nature of the market and the issue of barriers to entry.

Case IV/M57, Re the Concentration between Digital Equipment International and Mannesman Kienzle GmbH
[1992] 4 CMLR M99

Digital Equipment International (DEIL), a wholly-owned subsidiary of Digital Equipment Corporation (DEC), made an agreement with Mannesman Kienzle (MK) to establish a limited partnership under German law, Digital/Kienzle, which was to be owned as to 65 per cent by DEIL and 35 per cent by MK. The new company was to acquire the computer business of MK, which was then to withdraw from the computer industry (except for printers). MK also agreed not to compete with Digital/Kienzle. DEC possessed only a relatively small market share, less than 10 per cent, of the market for personal computers, and this market was, as a whole, relatively fragmented with few firms possessing more than 10 per cent. The proposed concentration did not therefore raise serious doubts about its compatibility with the common market in this sphere. DEC was one of the world's largest suppliers of networked computer systems, but MK was very much smaller. The extract which follows concerns the market for workstations. The merger was cleared under Article 6(1)(b).

THE COMMISSION

19. The workstation market is the smallest among the four markets mainly affected, but shows the highest annual growth rate (more than 30 per cent). It is also the most concentrated market with DEC, Hewlett Packard and Sun Microsystems holding an aggregate market share of about 80 per cent. DEC's market share has been in the last three years on average 22 per cent.

20. It is unlikely that the concentration will create or strengthen a dominant position because conditions of competition will not significantly change. The workstation market is a fairly new market which developed out of the PC and small computer market during the last 10 years. High market shares on a new developing market are not extraordinary, and they do not necessarily indicate market power. In fact the development of the market shares of the three leading companies over a period of time shows the dynamic nature of this market. There has been constant change including a change of market leadership.

21. DEC acquires with MK only a relatively small vendor and one which is rather insignificant for the maintenance of competition on this market. . . . Finally, barriers to entry are relatively low for other computer systems manufacturers, especially for those who sell PCs and small multi-user computers. Market entry seems to be feasible even for companies on adjacent markets. . . .

22. Thus, also with regard to the workstation market the concentration does not raise serious doubts as to its compatibility with the Common Market.

At the opposite end of the spectrum we can consider a decision in which the Commission found that the concentration was caught by Article 2(3) of the Merger Regulation.

Case IV/M53, Re the Concentration between Aérospatiale SNI and Alenia-Aeritalia e Selenia SpA and de Havilland
[1992] 4 CMLR M2

Aérospatiale and Alenia controlled the world's largest producer of turbo-prop regional aircraft, ATR, and sought to take over de Havilland, which was the world number two in this market. The Commission found that the product market was regional turbo-prop aeroplanes with between twenty and seventy seats, with sub-markets for aircraft with twenty to thirty-nine seats, forty to fifty-nine seats and sixty seats and over. The geographical market was the world, excluding China and Eastern Europe. It then considered the impact of the concentration.

THE COMMISSION

A. Effect on ATR's Position

27. The proposed concentration would significantly strengthen ATR's position on the commuter markets, for the following reasons in particular:
— high combined market share on the 40 to 59-seat market, and of the overall commuter market
— elimination of de Havilland as a competitor
— coverage of the whole range of commuter aircraft
— considerable extension of customer base.

(a) Increase in Market Shares

28. The proposed concentration would lead to an increase in market shares for ATR in the world market for commuters between 40 to 59 seats from 46 per cent. to 63 per cent. The nearest competitor (Fokker) would have 22 per cent. This market, together with the larger market of 60 seats and above where ATR has a world market share of 76 per cent, is of particular importance in the commuter industry since there is a general trend towards larger aircraft. . . .

29. ATR would increase its share of the overall worldwide commuter market of 20 to 70 seats from around 30 per cent. to around 50 per cent. The nearest competitor (Saab) would only have around 19 per cent. On the basis of this the new entity would have half the overall world market and more than two and half times the share of its nearest competitor.

30. The combined market share may further increase after the concentration. The higher market share could give ATR more flexibility to compete on price (including financing) than its smaller competitors. . . .

Following a concentration between ATR and de Havilland, the competitors would be faced with the combined strength of two large companies. This would mean that where an airline was considering placing a new order, the competitors would be in competition with the combined product range of ATR and de Havilland. . . .

(b) Elimination of de Havilland as a Competitor

31. In terms of aircraft sold, de Havilland is the most successful competitor of ATR. . . .
. . .

The parties argue that if the proposed concentration does not proceed, although de Havilland would not be immediately liquidated, its production might be phased out by Boeing so that de Havilland might in any case be eliminated as a competitor in the medium to long term. Without

prejudice as to whether such a consideration is relevant pursuant to Article 2 of the Merger
Regulation, the Commission considers that such elimination is not probable. . . .

. . .

(c) Coverage of the Whole Range of Commuter Aircraft

32. The new entity ATR/de Havilland would be the only commuter manufacturer present in all
the various commuter markets as defined above.

. . .

One of the stated main strategic objectives of the parties in acquiring de Havilland is to obtain
coverage of the whole range of commuter aircraft. The competitive advantages which would arise
from this would emerge over time.

. . .

(d) Broadening of Customer Base

33. ATR would significantly broaden its customer base after the concentration. On the basis
of deliveries to date, the parties state that ATR has currently delivered commuters to 44
customers world-wide and de Havilland has delivered commuters to 36 other customers, giving a
combination of 80 customers in all. . . .

The customer base is an important element of market power for aircraft manufacturers since
there is at least to some extent a lock-in effect for customers once their initial choice of aircraft is
made.

. . .

B. Assessment of the Strength of the Remaining Competition

34. In order to be able to assess whether the new combined entity would be able to act
independently of its competitors, in view of its strengthened position, it is necessary to assess the
current and expected future strength of the remaining competitors.
[*The Commission evaluated the strength of the other competitors and decided that it was
questionable whether they could provide effective competition in the medium to long term.*]

. . .

D. Summary of Effect of the Proposed Concentration on the Commuter Markets

51. The combined entity ATR/de Havilland will obtain a very strong position in the world and
Community commuter markets of 40 seats and over, and in the overall world and Community
market, as a result of the proposed concentration. The competitors in these markets are relatively
weak. The bargaining ability of the customers is limited. The combination of these factors leads to
the conclusion that the new entity could act to a significant extent independently of its competitors
and customers, and would thus have a dominant position on the commuter markets as defined.

. . .

E. Potential Entry into the Market

53. In general terms, a concentration which leads to the creation of a dominant position may
however be compatible with the Common Market within the meaning of Article 2(2) of the
Merger Regulation if there exists strong evidence that this position is only temporary and would be
quickly eroded because of high probability of strong market entry. With such market entry the
dominant position is not likely to significantly impede effective competition within the meaning of
Article 2(3) of the Merger Regulation. In order to assess whether the dominant position of ATR/

de Havilland is likely to significantly impede effective competition therefore, it is necessary to assess the likelihood of new entry into the market.

[*The Commission evaluated the possibility of new entrants and came to the conclusion that there was no realistic potential competition in the commuter markets in the foreseeable future.*]

The Commission's decision to block the merger in the above case was not accepted unreservedly by the Advisory Committee on Concentrations. The latter was divided in its opinion. The majority agreed with the Commission. The minority disagreed with the Commission's market analysis, expressing the view that the Commission 'is not so much protecting competition but rather the competitors to this proposed concentration'.[51] The decision in *Aérospatiale–Alenia/de Havilland* also came under fire from commentators. Fox considers that the Commission's reasoning was praiseworthy in a number of respects, but that it also had five weaknesses.

E. Fox, Merger Control in the EEC—Towards a European Merger Jurisprudence[52]

First, the Commission seemed to take an ungenerous view of economies likely to be achieved. While it counted economies of scale it seemed to disregard economies of scope; it disregarded the pro-consumer aspects of savings resulting from the merged firm's full line, of opportunities for package buying, and of buyers' opportunities to save costs by concentrating on one firm's technology ('lock-in' effect). The fact that they also yield foreclosing effects simply increases the problem's complexity but does not eliminate the economies' value.

Second, the Commission viewed low pricing, also, only in its anti-competitive light and not in its pro-competitive light. If the merged firm has the incentive to trigger price competition, consumers will, at least in the short run, get a better bargain. . . .

Third, the Commission quickly concluded that the remaining competition would shrink from confrontation, responding with fear and retreat to the new competitive advantages of the merged firm. Might the rivals, rather, have been so challenged as to seek new efficiencies and to respond more aggressively to buyers' needs . . . ?

Fourth, the Commission readily adopted a low pricing/monopolization scenario with no mention of a dominant firm/cooperative scenario. Would ATR really engage in all out warfare with the aim of devastating its rivals, or would it more likely engage in leadership conduct inviting cooperative behaviour, with a view towards enjoying less tumultuous life and confronting fewer risks? . . .

Fifth and finally, the commuter aircraft industry is heavily subsidized in Europe and Canada, and moreover, despite subsidies, De Havilland was in seriously weakened financial condition. The Commission did not grapple with the difficult issues raised by either situation.

The Commission has since then approved a joint venture between Aérospatiale, Alenia, and British Aerospace.[53]

---

[51] [1992] 4 CMLR M2, 35.
[52] B. Hawk (ed.), *Fordham Corporate Law Institute* (Fordham University, 1991), ch. 28, 738–9.
[53] [1995] 4 CMLR 377.

The third example is of a case in which the Commission cleared the merger, but only after imposing conditions.

Case IV/M190, Re the Concentration between Nestlé SA and Source Perrier SA
[1993] 4 CMLR M17

There were three major suppliers of bottled water in France: Nestlé, Perrier, and BSN. Nestlé sought to take over Perrier and also made an agreement with BSN under which it would sell the Volvic source of Perrier to BSN if it acquired control over Perrier. The Commission held that the merger between Nestlé and Perrier, and the subsequent sale of the Perrier source to BSN, would create a duopolistic dominant position (as between Nestlé and BSN), which would significantly impede competition in the French bottled water market. Nestlé and BSN argued that the Merger Regulation did not apply to oligopolistic dominance. Did, therefore, Article 2(3) cover market situations where competition was impeded by more than one firm which firms together have the power to behave independently of the market?

THE COMMISSION

[*Assuming that the sale of Volvic to BSN went ahead the Commission found that the resulting duopolistic dominance of Nestlé and BSN would be caught by Article 2(3) for the following reasons:*[54] *it would create a duopoly with a combined market share of 82 per cent; there was no viable Community competitor; the proposed deal would eliminate a major competitor, Perrier, from the market; this would render it easier for the remaining two parties to engage in anti-competitive parallel behaviour; prices of the goods were transparent and the duopolists monitored each other's behaviour, thereby facilitating tacit co-ordination; demand was relatively inelastic; there were high barriers to entry; and the duopolists had acted to deter the entry of a third party to the market. Even if the Volvic agreement was not implemented the Commission found that the acquisition of Perrier by Nestlé would create a dominant position for the new entity.*[55] *The Commission, none the less, cleared the merger on acceptance by Nestlé of the following conditions:*[56]]

136. Nestlé has offered to modify the original concentration plan as notified by entering into the following commitments:

. . .

In order to meet the requirements of the Commission to facilitate the entry of a viable competitor with adequate resources in the bottled mineral water market or the increase in the capacity of an existing competitor so that in either case such competitor could effectively compete on the French bottled water market with Nestlé and BSN, Nestlé has undertaken that it will make available for sale both brand names and sufficient capacity of water for bottling to such competitor as will permit that competitor to have not less than 3,000 million litres of water capacity per annum.

. . .

---

[54] [1993] 4 CMLR M17, paras. 119–131.   [55] *Ibid.*, paras. 132–134.
[56] The extract below contains the main condition imposed by the Commission on Nestlé. There were a number of other related conditions, e.g., that Nestlé would keep the assets of Perrier distinct pending completion of the divestiture required by the Commission.

Nestlé acknowledges that the approval of the purchaser by the Commission is of the essence for the acceptance of its undertaking by the Commission. The establishment of an effective competitor *vis-à-vis* Nestlé and BSN depends on the strength of the purchaser to develop the sources and brands which will be sold to it. The purchaser must in particular have:

— sufficient financial resources to develop a nation-wide distribution organization and to adequately promote the acquired brands;
and
— sufficient expertise in the field of branded beverage or food products.

. . .

Nestlé is enjoined and restrained from re-acquiring, directly or indirectly, any of the sources or brands which it divests pursuant to this undertaking, for a period of 10 years from the date of this Decision, without the prior written approval of the Commission.

Given that the parties agreed to the conditions set by the Commission there was no reason to appeal the decision to the CFI or the ECJ.[57]

(e) COLLECTIVE DOMINANCE

The discussion thus far has focused on the applicability of the Merger Regulation to single firm dominance: where the concentration created or strengthened a dominant position by the parties to the concentration. The Commission took the view that it also covered collective dominance: where the concentration created or strengthened a dominant position between the parties to the concentration and another party on that market.[58] This has now been confirmed by the ECJ and CFI.[59]

Cases C–68/94 and 30/95, France v. Commission
[1998] ECR I–1375

K + S and MdK were proposing to enter into a concentration. Both firms operated in the potash and rock salt markets. The Commission was concerned that as a result of this concentration two entities would enjoy a dominant position: K + S/MdK and another firm, SCPA. The applicants argued that the Merger Regulation did not cover such cases of collective dominance. They claimed that the wording of the Merger Regulation did not, by way of contrast to Article 82, speak in terms of 'one or more undertakings', and that the legislative history of the Regulation showed that it was not meant to cover such cases.

---

[57] The Commission's decision was challenged by representatives of employees' organizations, but the CFI never proceeded to consider the substance of the case: Case T–96/92, *Comité Central d'Entreprise de la Société Générale des Grands Sources* v. *Commission* [1995] ECR II–1213.

[58] Case IV/M190, *Nestlé SA/ Source Perrier SA* [1993] 4 CMLR M17, paras. 112–115.

[59] R. Whish and B. Sufrin, 'Oligopolistic Markets and EC Competition Law' (1992) 12 *YBEL* 59; A. Winckler and M. Hansen, 'Collective Dominance under the EC Merger Control Regulation' (1993) 30 *CMLRev.* 787; D. Ridyard, 'Economic Analysis of Single Firm and Oligopolistic Dominance' [1994] *ECLR* 255; C. Caffarra and K-U. Kuhn, 'Joint Dominance: The CFI Judgment on Gencor/Lonhro' [1999] *ECLR* 355; R. Whish, 'Collective Dominance', in D. O'Keefe and A. Bavasso (eds.), *Judicial Review in European Union Law* (Kluwer, 2000), ch. 37.

166. . . . . it cannot be deduced from the wording of Article 2 of the Regulation that only concentrations which create or strengthen an individual dominant position, that is a dominant position held by the parties to the concentration, come within the scope of the Regulation. Article 2 . . . does not in itself exclude the possibility of applying the Regulation to cases where the concentrations lead to the creation or strengthening of a collective dominant position, that is a dominant position held by the parties to the concentration together with an entity not a party thereto.

[The ECJ found that the legislative history was not conclusive, and therefore that the scope of Article 2 should be considered by reference to its purpose and general structure. It considered the recitals to the Regulation and concluded that all concentrations with a Community dimension that could affect the structure of competition within the EC should be within the ambit of the Regulation.]

171. A concentration which creates or strengthens a dominant position on the part of the parties concerned with an entity not involved in the concentration is liable to prove incompatible with the system of undistorted competition which the Treaty seeks to secure. Consequently, if it were accepted that only concentrations creating or strengthening a dominant position on the part of the parties to the concentration were covered by the Regulation, its purpose . . . would be partially frustrated. The Regulation would thus be deprived of a not insignificant aspect of its effectiveness, without that being necessary from the perspective of the general structure of the Community system of control of concentrations.

Case T–102/96, Gencor Ltd. v. Commission
[1999] ECR II–753

There was a proposed concentration between two firms in the platinum market. The Commission was concerned that this would lead to a collective dominant position as between these two firms and another firm, the latter being the leading world-wide supplier of platinum and the principal competitor of the two firms that were proposing to concentrate their activities in this market. The CFI followed the decision of the ECJ in Cases 68/94 and 30/95, set out above, and held that collective dominance could be caught by the Merger Regulation: paragraphs 123–157 of the CFI's judgment. The CFI then gave guidance on the factors that would be relevant in judging whether collective dominance existed.

163. In assessing whether there is a collective dominant position, the Commission is therefore obliged to establish, using a prospective analysis of the relevant market, whether the concentration in question would lead to a situation in which effective competition in the relevant market would be significantly impeded by the undertakings involved in the concentration and one or more undertakings which together, in particular because of factors giving rise to a connection between them, are able to adopt a common policy on the market and act to a considerable extent independently of their competitors, their customers and, ultimately, of consumers.

[The CFI held that the existence of a very large market share could, save for exceptional circumstances be indicative of dominance: paragraph 205.]

206. It is true that, in the context of an oligopoly, the fact that the parties hold large market shares does not necessarily have the same significance. . . . Nevertheless, particularly in the case of a duopoly, a large market share is, in the absence of evidence to the contrary, likewise a strong indication of the existence of a dominant position.

[*The applicants argued that the Commission had ignored the CFI's decision in* Italian Flat Glass.[60] *They claimed that in that case the CFI had required some structural links, through agreements, licences and the like, as a pre-condition for a finding of collective dominance. The CFI in* Gencor *rejected this argument: paragraphs 273–275. It held that in* Italian Flat Glass *the structural links were regarded as but one way in which collective dominance could be shown.*]

276. Furthermore, there is no reason whatsoever in legal or economic terms to exclude from the notion of economic links the relationship of interdependence existing between the parties to a tight oligopoly within which, in a market with the appropriate characteristics, in particular in terms of market concentration, transparency, and product homogeneity, those parties are in a position to anticipate one another's behaviour and are therefore strongly encouraged to align their conduct in the market, in particular in such a way as to maximise their joint profits by restricting production with a view to increasing prices. In such a context, each trader is aware that highly competitive action on its part designed to increase its market share (for example a price cut) would provoke identical action by the others, so that it would derive no benefit from its initiative. . . .

277. That conclusion is all the more pertinent with regard to the control of concentrations, whose objective is to prevent anti-competitive market structures from arising or being strengthened. Those structures may result from the existence of economic links in the strict sense argued by the applicant or from market structures of an oligopolistic kind where each undertaking may become aware of common interests and, in particular, cause prices to increase without having to enter into an agreement or resort to a concerted practice.

It is clear from *Gencor* that collective dominance within the Merger Regulation can catch oligopolistic collusion, and that the existence of structural links between the relevant firms is not a necessary condition for the concept to apply.

It can none the less be contestable whether the conditions for collective dominance are met in any particular case. The Commission's decision in *Airtours/First Choice*[61] has been criticized for applying collective dominance to a market that did not have the classic characteristics of an oligopoly. The product, foreign package holidays, was not homogenous, market shares were volatile, demand was not stable, and barriers to entry were low. It was moreover difficult to punish firms that deviated from the tacitly agreed norm.[62]

It is in more general terms important to be clear about what is being caught through the concept of collective dominance.

[60] See 1027 above.   [61] Case IV/M1524, [2000] OJ L93/1.
[62] Lexecon Competition Memo (Lexecon Ltd., Nov. 1999). *Cf.* M. Motta, 'EC Merger Policy and the Airtours Case' [2000] *ECLR* 199.

C. Caffarra and K-U. Kuhn, Joint Dominance: The CFI Judgment on Gencor/Lonhro[63]

A major contribution of the [*Gencor*] judgment is perceived to be its explicit identification of joint dominance with the economic concept of *tacit collusion*. The Court makes it clear that explicit collusion, as any other isntance of abuse which may materialise after the merger, would have to be dealt with under Articles 81 and 82. The focus of merger control should be instead on whether the merger will increase the feasibility of *co-ordination*, or tacit collusion.

Here is where it gets complicated. Economically no meaningful distinction can be drawn for purposes of prevention between explicit and tacit collusion because what sustains collusion is the same essential mechanism. . . . What matters is not the exact mechanism by which firms can agree on a price increase, but the existence of a *credible mechanism to keep prices at that level*.
. . .

There are two distinct elements to collusion in the economic sense. One is how firms come to an agreement. . . . This is usually referred to as 'co-ordination'. The second element is how to ensure that no one has an incentive to deviate from that price. This is what economists describe as the *credibility* of the co-ordination. Enforcement against explicit collusion is generally aimed at the co-ordinating mechanism—firms are punished for just 'trying' to talk. Merger policy, which is preventive, should be based firmly on the second—the credibility of sustaining collusive prices in the future.

The CFI judgment puts emphasis on the market becoming more concentrated, but is less explicit on the question of how difficult it would have been for the remaining firms in the market to *sustain* the collusive mechanism. . . .

(f) MODIFICATIONS TO CONCENTRATIONS

We have seen that the parties may offer commitments in order to pass the test laid down in the Merger Regulation. The Commission has published a Notice providing guidance on the commitments that it will find acceptable.[64] Thus, for example, where a proposed merger threatens to create or strengthen a dominant position, such as to impede effective competition, the most effective way to restore effective competition, apart from prohibition, is to create the conditions for new competition or to strengthen existing competitors via divestiture.[65]

(g) CONCENTRATIONS: REFLECTIONS ON THE SUBSTANTIVE CRITERIA

The substantive criteria contained in Article 2 of the Merger Regulation are open to varying interpretations, and their application to the facts of particular cases will often, as seen above, be contentious. There are, however, two more general issues of interpretation which should be touched on here: the scope of the competition inquiry, and the relevance or not of non-competition issues. These will be considered in turn.

The *scope of the competition inquiry* under Article 2 raises a number of interesting

---

    63 [1999] *ECLR* 355, 356, 357. Italics in the original.
    64 *Commission Notice on Remedies Acceptable under Council Regulation 4064/89 and Commission Regulation 447/98* [2001] OJ C68/3.
    65 *Ibid.*, para. 13.

issues, one of the most important of which is the meaning to be accorded to efficiency within this inquiry.[66] The nub of the problem can be stated as follows. The general objectives of competition policy are based on the idea that competition will secure to the consumer the desired goods at the lowest price with the sacrifice of the fewest resources. In this sense competition is a mechanism for promoting economic efficiency. Merger policy is but one part of this more general strategy. Under Article 2(3) a concentration will be condemned if it creates or strengthens a dominant position, as a result of which competition will be significantly impeded. But what if the merger does strengthen a dominant position, yet also entails economic-efficiency gains by reducing costs? Is this a factor which can or should be taken into account in the assessment under Article 2(3)? Jenny has concluded from a study of decisions that the Commission may in fact hold such efficiency gains *against* the parties:[67]

To date the record of the Commission in the merger control area is clear. The possibility that a merger might lead to static efficiency gains . . . or to dynamic efficiency gains . . . which other non-merging firms are unlikely to achieve is interpreted as prima facie evidence that the merger will enable the merging firms to acquire a dominant position incompatible with the common market.

It is debatable whether this should be so in terms of economic theory. Williamson has shown that relatively modest cost savings can outweigh the impact of price increases when considering allocative efficiency.[68] This still leaves unanswered the question whether such an inquiry is possible within the present framework of Article 2. Some commentators take the view that this is not possible within the framework of the Merger Regulation.[69] Others suggest that possible efficiency gains may be taken into account implicitly.[70] Yet others are equivocal on the point.[71]

The other general issue of interpretation concerns *the relevance of non-competition issues*.[72] The discussion thus far has focused principally on the competition inquiry within the framework of Article 2. But how far can other matters be taken into account? The thirteenth recital to the Regulation states that, in considering the compatibility of a concentration with the common market, the Commission should bear in mind the fundamental objectives of the EC, including the strengthening of the Community's economic and social cohesion. The Commission has, none the less, taken the view that competition is to be the prime objective of the Regulation.[73] The failure of the Commission to take account of broader concerns of industrial policy

---

[66] Whish, n. 1 above, 778–9; Jones and Sufrin, n. 1 above, 792–7.

[67] F. Jenny, 'EEC Merger Control: Economies as an Antitrust Defense or an Antitrust Attack?', in B. Hawk (ed.), *Fordham Corporate Law Institute* (Fordham University, 1992), 603.

[68] O. Williamson, 'Economics as an Antitrust Defense: The Welfare Tradeoffs' (1968) 58 *Am. Econ. Rev.* 18. It might be argued by way of response that any such calculus designed to weigh the advantages and disadvantages of a proposed merger in efficiency terms would be too difficult, particularly within the tight timetables imposed by the Merger Reg. This might be so, although the cogency of this argument would be dependent upon assessing the marginal increase of time that any such inquiry would take over and above that already taken on the issues which are presently considered by the Commission.

[69] J. Faull and A. Nikpay (eds.), *The EC Law of Competition* (Oxford University Press, 1999), para. 4.167.

[70] P. Camesasca, 'The Explicit Efficiency Defence in Merger Control: Does it Make the Difference?' [1999] *ECLR* 26.

[71] H. Colin Overbury, 'EEC Merger Regulation', n. 67 above, 615–16.

[72] Whish, n. 1 above, 780–1.

[73] *Twentieth Report on Competition Policy*, point 20.

was a cause for criticism in *Aérospatiale–Alenia/de Havilland*, but it did not shake the Commission's resolve in this respect.[74] In so far as such issues are taken into account this may be in the College of Commissioners.[75]

Some social considerations may however have to be taken into account in accordance with the CFI's decision in *Vittel*.[76] Trade Unions challenged the Commission's decision to clear the *Nestlé/Perrier* merger, on the ground that account should have been taken of the employment consequences of the merger. The CFI held that recital 13 to the Merger Regulation, combined with Article 2(1)(b), could require the Commission to have regard to social considerations. However, the CFI also emphasized Article 18(4) of the Regulation, which makes specific reference to the interests of employees' representatives.

6. RELATIONSHIP BETWEEN COMMUNITY AND MEMBER STATE MERGER CONTROL

(a) THE GENERAL PRINCIPLE: ONE-STOP MERGER CONTROL

It is obviously undesirable for the same merger to be subject to investigation under differing regimes at Community and national level, given the expense that this would entail and given that they may apply different substantive criteria. A central feature of the Merger Regulation is, therefore, the idea that mergers which have a Community dimension should, in general, be investigated only by the Commission. This policy finds expression in Article 21(1), which states that only the Commission may take the decisions covered by the Merger Regulation. This is reinforced by Article 21(2) which provides that, subject to Article 9, no Member State may apply its national legislation to a merger which has a Community dimension. This same policy underlies the expansion in the definition of concentrations which have a Community dimension, considered above.[77] There are, however, a number of exceptions to this general principle.

(b) ARTICLE 21(3)

Article 21(3) allows a Member State to take appropriate measures to protect legitimate interests other than those taken into consideration by the Regulation, provided that they are compatible with Community law. Public security, plurality of the media, and prudential rules are listed as legitimate interests for these purposes. Any other public interest must be notified to the Commission, which must inform the Member State of its decision within one month.

---

[74] E. Fox, 'Merger Control in the EEC—Towards a European Merger Jurisprudence', n. 52 above, 709–10.
[75] Jones and Sufrin, n. 1 above, 797–801.
[76] Case T–12/93, *Comité Central d'Enterprise de la Société Anonyme Vittel* v. *Commission* [1995] ECR II–1247, paras. 38–40.
[77] See 1044–5 above.

(c) REFERRAL TO THE COMPETENT AUTHORITIES OF THE MEMBER STATE: THE GERMAN CLAUSE

When the Regulation was being drafted there was some concern that a merger might not be regarded as harmful from the Community perspective, but that it could still be detrimental at national level. These concerns found expression in Article 9, which allows a Member State to request that the Commission take action, or that the national authorities be allowed to take action, in the following circumstances. There must be a concentration with a Community dimension which threatens to create or strengthen a dominant position as a result of which effective competition would be significantly impeded on a market within that State, where the market has all the characteristics of a distinct market. Or there must be a concentration affecting competition on a market within a State, which has all the characteristics of a distinct market and which does not constitute a substantial part of the common market.[78] It is up to the Commission to decide both whether such a distinct market exists, and also whether there is in reality the relevant threat to competition.[79] The Commission has rejected a number of such applications from Member States,[80] but accepted a request from the United Kingdom.[81]

(d) ARTICLE 22(3): THE DUTCH CLAUSE

Article 22(3) provides that a Member State or States may request the Commission to investigate a concentration which does not have a Community dimension, where that concentration creates or strengthens a dominant position as a result of which effective competition on the territory of that State is impeded. The request may come from the competition authority of the Member State.[82] The Commission can then take action provided that the concentration affects trade between Member States. The object of this provision was to provide a mechanism for merger control where none existed at national level. It will be rarely used, given that most States do now have their own systems of merger control. The Member State that makes a request under Article 22(3) cannot control, or define the scope of, the Commission's investigation.[83]

---

[78] Art. 9(2).

[79] Art. 9(3). If the Commission accepts that this is so it can then either deal with the case itself, or refer the whole or part of the case to the relevant national authorities, subject to the proviso that it shall so refer the case where it accepts that the concentration does not affect a substantial part of the common market.

[80] See, e.g., Case IV/M41, *Varta/Bosch* [1991] OJ L320/26; Case IV/M222, *Mannesman/Hoesch* [1993] OJ L114/34.

[81] Case IV/M180, *Streetley plc/Tarmac* [1992] 4 CMLR 343. For examples where the Commission has referred concentrations under Art. 9 see, e.g., *Rheinmetall/British Aerospace/STN Atlas* [1997] 4 CMLR 987; *REW/Thyssengas/Bayernwerk/Isarwerke* [1997] 4 CMLR 23.

[82] Case T–22/97, *Kesko Oy* v. *Commission* [1999] ECR II–3775.

[83] Case T–221/95, *Endemol Entertainment Holding BV* v. *Commission* [1999] ECR II–1299.

(e) THE RESIDUAL ROLE OF ARTICLES 81 AND 82

We have already seen how the ECJ used Articles 85 and 86 (now Articles 81 and 82) to impose some control on mergers in the absence of any regulation. A question which remains to be considered is the scope of application of these Articles now. This question must be addressed both as to the powers of the Commission and as to those of the national courts.[84]

As regards the powers of the Commission, Article 22(1) of the Merger Regulation provides some guidance, albeit of a limited nature. It provides that Regulation 4064/89 alone shall apply to mergers as defined by Article 3 of the Regulation, and that the main implementing regulations concerning Article 85 (now Article 81) shall not be applicable to concentrations as defined by Article 3. This is subject to an exception in relation to joint ventures which do not have a Community dimension and which have as their object or effect the co-ordination of the competitive behaviour of independent undertakings.[85] It is clear, therefore, that the Commission can no longer use the general regulations designed to implement Articles 85 and 86 (now Articles 81 and 82) to oppose mergers.[86]

More problematic is the impact of Article 22 on national courts.[87] Articles 81 and 82 have direct effect. It would therefore be possible, for example, for an undertaking opposed to a hostile takeover to raise the matter in the national courts, and seek a reference to the ECJ under Article 234 (ex Article 177), claiming that the takeover was in breach of Article 81 or 82. This strategy would, moreover, be available even though the takeover would not qualify as one with a Community dimension under the Merger Regulation. A possible answer would be that Article 81 does not have direct effect in the absence of more detailed implementing regulations,[88] but this answer would not apply to Article 82, the direct effect of which does not seem to be dependent on such implementing regulations.[89] Challenges in national courts of the type considered above may well therefore occur in the future.

7. JUDICIAL REVIEW

Commission decisions under the Merger Regulation are reviewable by the Community courts. Applicants who wish to challenge such decisions will, however, have to satisfy the normal criteria for annulment under Article 230 (ex Article 173).[90]

---

[84] It should be remembered that the new Art. 2(4) allows Art. 85 (now Art. 81) to be applied to those joint ventures caught by Art. 3(2).

[85] This is entirely possible, given that the definition in Art. 1 is couched in entirely quantitative terms.

[86] Although the Commission could use the more general power contained in Art. 89 (now Art. 85), on which see Whish, n. 1 above, 757.

[87] Jones and Sufrin, n. 1 above, 748–50.

[88] Whish, n. 1 above, 757–8.

[89] Case 66/86, *Ahmed Saeed Flugreisen and Silver Line Reisebüro GmbH* v. *Zentrale zur Bekämpfung Unlauteren Wettbewerbs eV* [1989] ECR 803.

[90] See Ch. 13 above.

They will therefore have to show that there is a decision that has legal consequences or legal effects; they will have to prove that they have been directly and individually concerned; and they must be able to attack the contested decision on substantive grounds.[91] The CFI will, however, take account of the discretionary nature of the economic determinations made by the Commission when exercising its powers of judicial review.[92]

8. CONCLUSION

i. Merger policy necessarily entails choices. These choices relate to all the important aspects of merger control.

ii. In *procedural terms*, the Merger Regulation reflects the need for prompt notification, coupled with adequate investigative powers, in order that the Community controls can be effective. There is also the need for promptness in the application of the Community's powers, since important business decisions hang in the balance. The time limits under the Merger Regulation serve this imperative.

iii. In *substantive terms*, the Merger Regulation, coupled with its interpretation by the Commission, CFI, and ECJ, encapsulates important social and political choices. A number of examples of this are evident from the preceding analysis.

iv. The turnover threshold before the Merger Regulation can bite was the result of hard battles fought between the Commission and the Member States, the latter being wary of what they feared to be too intrusive Community regulation in this area. The Commission is of the view that the existing thresholds allow concentrations that have significant cross-border effects to fall outside the Regulation.

v. The substantive coverage of the Merger Regulation is broad, in terms of the types of concentration that fall within its ambit. The Commission, CFI, and ECJ have moreover adopted a teleological approach, as exemplified by the jurisprudence on collective dominance.

vi. Primacy is accorded to competition, and this seems to exclude or limit the extent to which an efficiency defence can be pleaded.

vii. The primacy accorded to competition also manifests itself in the exclusion, in general, of other social considerations within merger analysis.

viii. The Commission is now engaged in a wide-ranging review of the Merger Regulation.[93] Jurisdictional, substantive, and procedural issues will be considered. The review of substantive issues includes whether to shift from a dominance test to one based on the substantial lessening of competition, and whether to include a specific efficiency defence.[94]

[91] See, e.g., Case T–83/92, *Zunis Holdings SA v. Commission* [1993] ECR II–1169; Case T–3/93, *Société Anonyme à Participation Ouvrière Compagnie Nationale Air France v. Commission* [1994] ECR II–121; Case T–96/92, *Comité Central*, n. 57 above.

[92] Case T–221/95, *Endemol*, n. 83 above; Case T–22/97, *Kesko Oy*, n. 82 above.

[93] *Green Paper on the Review of Council Regulation 4064/89*, COM(2001)745/6 final.

[94] *Ibid.*, paras. 159–172.

9. FURTHER READING

(a) *Books*

BISHOP, M., and KAY, J. (eds.), *European Mergers & Merger Policy* (Oxford University Press, 1993)

BROBERG, M., *The European Commission's Jurisdiction to Scrutinise Mergers* (Kluwer, 1998)

COOK, J., and KERSE, C., *EC Merger Control* (Sweet & Maxwell, 3rd edn., 2000)

DOWNES, T.A., and ELLISON, J., *The Legal Control of Mergers in the European Communities* (Blackstone, 1991)

FAULL, J., and NIKPAY, A. (eds.), *The EC Law of Competition* (Oxford University Press, 1999), ch. 4

GOYDER, D., *EC Competition Law* (Oxford University Press, 3rd edn., 1998), ch. 18

HAWK, B., and HUSER, H., *European Community Merger Control: A Practitioner's Guide* (Kluwer, 1996)

JONES, A., and SUFRIN, B., *EC Competition Law, Text, Cases and Materials* (Oxford University Press, 2001), ch. 12

WHISH, R., *Competition Law* (Butterwoths, 4th ed., 2001), ch. 21

(b) *Articles*

ABBAMONTE, G., and RABASSA, V., 'Foreclosure and Vertical Mergers' [2001] *ECLR* 214

BELLAMY, C., 'Mergers Outside the Scope of the New Merger Regulation—Implications of the *Philip Morris* Judgment', in B. Hawk (ed.), *Fordham Corporate Law Institute* (Fordham University, 1989), ch. 22

BISHOP, B., and CAFFARRA, C., 'Merger Control in "New Markets"' [2001] *ECLR* 31

BRITTAN, L., 'The Law and Policy of Merger Control in the EEC' (1990) 15 *ELRev.* 351

CAFFARRA, C., and KUHN, K-U., 'Joint Dominance: The CFI Judgment on Gencor/Lonhro' [1999] *ECLR* 355

CAMESASCA, P., 'The Explicit Efficiency Defence in Merger Control: Does it Make the Difference?' [1999] *ECLR* 26

FOX, E., 'Merger Control in the EEC—Towards a European Merger Jurisprudence', in B. Hawk (ed.), *Fordham Corporate Law Institute* (Fordham University, 1991), ch. 28

HAWK, B., 'Joint Ventures Under EC Law', in B. Hawk (ed.), *Fordham Corporate Law Institute* (Fordham University, 1991), ch. 23

—— and HUSER, H., 'A Bright Line Shareholding Test to End the Nightmare under the EEC Merger Regulation' (1993) 30 *CMLRev.* 1155

KASSAMALI, R., 'From Fiction to Fallacy: Reviewing the EC's Merger Regulation's Community-Dimension Thresholds in the Light of Economics and Experience in Merger Control' (1996) 21 *ELR* Checklist No. 2 CC/89

JENNY, F., 'EEC Merger Control: Economies as an Antitrust Defense or an Antitrust Attack?', in B. Hawk (ed.), *Fordham Corporate Law Institute* (Fordham University, 1992), ch. 23

LANGEHEINE, B., 'Substantive Review Under the EEC Merger Regulation', in B. Hawk (ed.), *Fordham Corporate Law Institute* (Fordham University, 1990), ch. 22

MOTTA, M., 'EC Merger Policy and the Airtours Case' [2000] *ECLR* 199

NOEL, P.-E., 'Efficiency Considerations in the Assessment of Horizontal Mergers under European and US Antitrust Law' [1997] *ECLR* 498

RIDYARD, D., 'Economic Analysis of Single Firm and Oligopolistic Dominance' [1994] *ECLR* 255

SIBREE, W., 'EEC Merger Control and Joint Ventures' (1992) 17 *ELRev.* 91

SIRAGUSA, M., and SUBIOTTO, R., 'The EEC Merger Control Regulation: The Commission's Evolving Case Law' (1991) 28 *CMLRev.* 877

VENIT, J., 'The "Merger" Control Regulation: Europe Comes of Age . . . Or Caliban's Dinner' (1990) 27 *CMLRev.* 7

WHISH, R., 'Collective Dominance', in D. O'Keefe and A. Bavasso (eds.), *Judicial Review in European Union Law* (Kluwer, 2000), ch. 37

—— and SUFFRIN, B., 'Oligopolistic Markets and EC Competition Law' (1992) 12 *YBEL* 59

WINCKLER, A., and HANSEN, M., 'Collective Dominance under the EC Merger Control Regulation' (1993) 30 *CMLRev.* 787

25

COMPETITION: ENFORCEMENT
AND PROCEDURE

1. CENTRAL ISSUES

i. Competition rules must be enforced if they are to be effective. The earlier discussion revealed the interplay between *public enforcement, through actions brought by the Commission*, and *private enforcement, through direct effect*.[1] Direct effect alleviated the burden that would otherwise be placed on the Commission if it were to be the sole enforcer of Community norms. This is especially important in this area, since the Commission is hopelessly short of the resources necessary to enforce the competition rules throughout the Community.[2] The balance between public and private enforcement has shifted as a result of recent reforms.

ii. The *traditional approach* was based on notification of certain types of agreements to the Commission, combined with a Commission monopoly over Article 81(3).

iii. The *modified approach* will remove notification and the Commission's monopoly over Article 81(3). National competition authorities (NCAs), and national courts will be able to apply Article 81 in its entirety, subject

to the possibility of making a preliminary reference under Article 234.

iv. The rationale for these changes was set out in the Commission's *White Paper on Modernization*,[3] the reasoning of which will be considered in the following section. The reforms are being implemented by legislation that will replace Regulation 17, which was the key to enforcement in this area.

v. This Chapter will chart the key issues concerning the enforcement of EC Competition law. It will begin with an analysis of the Commission *White Paper*. This will be followed by discussion of public enforcement through the Commission, which will integrate the changes to be made by the new draft Council Regulation. The focus will then shift to the public enforcement role to be played by national competition authorities under the new regime. The latter part of the chapter will consider private enforcement through national courts. The existing role of national courts will be contrasted with their more extensive powers under the modernization proposals.

2. THE WHITE PAPER ON MODERNIZATION

The *traditional approach* to the enforcement of EC competition law had two foundations. Agreements had, subject to certain exceptions, to be notified to the

---

[1] See Ch. 5 above.
[2] R. Whish, *Competition Law* (Butterworths, 4th edn., 2001), 217.
[3] *White Paper on Modernization of the Rules Implementing Articles 85 and 86 of the EC Treaty*, Commission Programme 99/27, 28 Apr. 1999.

Commission, and the Commission had a monopoly over the application of Article 81(3). The system was, in this sense, a centralized one. There were none the less decentralized aspects to this regime. Articles 81 and 82 had direct effect. National courts could therefore apply Article 81(1) in cases that came before them, but could not grant an individual exemption under Article 81(3). The traditional approach came under increasing strain. The Commission, for its part, did not have the resources to deal with all the agreements notified to it within a reasonable time, nor did it have the resources to adjudicate on anything but a handful of individual exemptions. The Commission had, for some time, encouraged national courts to apply Articles 81 and 82. However, in the *White Paper on Modernization* it went considerably further, and proposed a thorough overhaul of the enforcement regime.

The *new approach* is to be based on more radical decentralization. Notification is abolished, as is the Commission's monopoly over Article 81(3). National courts and national competition authorities (NCAs) are empowered to apply Article 81 in its entirety. The Commission argued that the centralized system was warranted at the inception of the EC, but not any longer. Many of the central precepts of EC competition law were now well established, and capable of being applied by national courts and NCAs. The decentralized regime would allow the Commission to concentrate its resources on novel problems, or especially egregious breaches of competition rules.

The detailed provisions of the new regime will be examined below. The core of the new approach is, however, contained in Article 1 of the new draft Council Regulation, designed to implement the Commission changes.[4] This provides that agreements, etc., caught by Article 81(1) which do not satisfy the conditions of Article 81(3) shall be prohibited, no prior decision to that effect being required. The same principle is applicable to abuse of a dominant position in Article 82. Article 3 of the new draft Council Regulation deals with the relationship between Articles 81 and 82 and national competition law. It states that where an agreement, etc., within the meaning of Article 81 or the abuse of a dominant position within the meaning of Article 82 may affect trade between Member States, Community competition law shall apply to the exclusion of national competition law.

There is a voluminous literature on the *White Paper*, which contains all shades of opinion.[5] Limits of space preclude detailed analysis of this literature. Suffice it to say

---

[4] *Proposal for a Council Regulation on the implementation of the Rules laid down in Articles 81 and 82 of the Treaty and Amending Regulations 1017/68, 2988/74 and 3975/87*, COM(2000)582 final, hereafter *Regulation Implementing Arts. 81 and 82*.

[5] J. Nazerali and D. Cowan, 'Modernising the Enforcement of EU Competition Rules—Can the Commission Claim to be Preaching to the Converted?' [1999] *ECLR* 442; R. Wesseling, 'The Commission White Paper on Modernisation of EC Antitrust Law: Unspoken Consequences and Incomplete Treatment of Alternative Options' [1999] *ECLR* 420; C.-D. Ehlermann, 'The Modernization of EC Antitrust Policy: A Legal and Cultural Revolution' (2000) 37 *CMLRev.* 537; A. Schaub, 'Modernisation of EC Competition Law: Reform of Regulation No. 17', in B. Hawk (ed.), *Fordham Corporate Law Institute* (Fordham University, 2000), ch. 10; I. Forrester, 'Modernisation of EC Competition Law', *ibid.*, ch. 12; M. Siragusa, 'A Critical Review of the White Paper on the Reform of the EC Competition Law Enforcement Rules', *ibid.*, ch. 15; R. Whish, and B. Sufrin, 'Community Competition Law: Notification and Exemption—Goodbye to All That', in D. Hayton (ed.), *Law's Future(s): British Legal Developments in the 21st Century* (Hart, 2000), ch. 8; D. Gerber, 'Modernising European Competition Law: A Developmental Perspective' [2001] *ECLR* 122; S. Kingston, 'A "New Division of Responsibilities" in the Proposed Regulation to Modernise the Rules Implementing Articles 81 and 82 EC? A Warning Call' [2001] *ECLR* 340; M. Monti, 'European Competition Law for the 21st Century',

for the present analysis that the arguments surrounding the *White Paper* cover all aspects of the reform. Some question whether the proposed reform is lawful, given the wording of Article 81 itself. Others question the conceptual underpinnings of the Commission's proposals. They argue that these are based on too formalistic an interpretation of Article 81(1). Yet others are concerned about the practical operation of the new regime. They are worried about the relationship between national courts and NCAs in different Member States, about the relationship between national courts and the NCA within the same State, and about the interaction of the Commission and national courts and NCAs.

3. PUBLIC ENFORCEMENT BY THE COMMISSION: FINDING THE VIOLATION

It is axiomatic that the Commission must know of the existence of a competition infringement in order to take appropriate action. There are, in essence, three ways in which it could become aware of a potential violation.

(a) INVESTIGATION/INSPECTION

Under Article 85 (ex Article 89) the Commission is charged with the duty of ensuring the application of Articles 81 and 82 (ex Articles 85 and 86), and of investigating suspected infringements of these Articles. The detailed investigative powers of the Commission were contained in Regulation 17.

The Commission is empowered to *request information* from governments, competent authorities of Member States, and undertakings. This power was contained in Article 11 of Regulation 17. It is now to be found in Article 18 of the new draft Council Regulation.[6] The Commission must state the legal basis for, and the purpose of, the request, as well as making clear the penalties for supplying incorrect information.[7] If the information is not supplied within the requisite period then the Commission makes a decision requiring the information to be supplied; there are penalties for non-compliance.[8] Decisions of this nature are reviewable before the CFI.[9]

The Commission can also carry out an *inspection*. This power was set out in Article 14 of Regulation 17.[10] A modified version of this power is now contained in Article 20 of the new draft Council Regulation. The officials authorized by the Commission to

---

in B. Hawk (ed.), *Fordham Corporate Law Institute* (Fordham University, 2001), ch. 15; W. Wils, 'The Modernisation of the Enforcement of Articles 81 and 82 EC: A Legal and Economic Analysis of the Commission's Proposal for a New Council Regulation Replacing Regulation No. 17', *ibid.*, ch. 18.

  [6] *Regulation Implementing Arts. 81 and 82*, n. 4 above, Art. 18.
  [7] *ibid.*, Art. 18(2); (Reg. 17 [1956–62] OJ Spec. Ed. 87, Art. 11(3)).
  [8] *ibid.*, Art. 18(4); (Reg. 17, Art. 11(5)).
  [9] Case 374/87, *Orkem SA* v. *Commission* and Case 27/88, *Solvay and Cie* v. *Commission*, both [1989] ECR 3283.
  [10] It has been held in the *Orkem* case that the powers in Arts. 11 and 14 are independent, and hence that the existence of a decision made pursuant to Art. 14 does not prevent the Commission from using its powers under Art. 11: Case 374/87, n. 9 above, para. 14.

conduct an inspection are empowered to enter any premises of the concerned undertakings. This includes the homes of directors, managers, and other staff members, in so far as it is suspected that business records are being kept there.[11] The officials can examine company books and business records, and take copies of, or of extracts from, the documents. They can seal any premises or business records during the inspection. They can moreover ask any staff member questions relating to the subject matter and purpose of the inspection.[12]

Inspections can be either voluntary or mandatory. Voluntary inspections are conducted under Article 20(3) of the new draft Council Regulation. The Commission officials must produce a written authorization, which specifies the subject matter and purpose of the investigation, and also the possible penalties under Article 22. Mandatory inspections are conducted under Article 20(4). These are based on a decision that orders the investigation. The decision must state the subject matter and purpose of the investigation, the susceptibility to penalties, and the right to have the decision reviewed by the ECJ. The national competition authority (NCA) is to be consulted before the Commission makes the decision. The NCA shall, at the request of the Commission or of that NCA, actively assist the Commission. When it does so the NCA itself has the powers set out in Article 20(2). The intent is therefore that the Commission can use NCAs as their 'agents' when carrying out inspections. The authorities of the Member State must under Article 20(6) afford the necessary assistance to the Commission in the event that the firm in question proves intractable. This can include police assistance. Commission decisions made under Article 20(4) can be reviewed by the ECJ.[13]

The use of the investigative powers contained in Article 14 of Regulation 17 gave rise to the important decision in the *Hoechst* case.

Cases 46/87 and 227/88, Hoechst AG v. Commission
[1989] ECR 2859

The Commission was of the opinion that Hoechst was taking part in an illegal cartel, and instigated a dawn raid. The company refused to admit the Commission officials and contended that it was entitled to refuse entry until a search warrant had been obtained through national procedures. The Commission did eventually obtain access in this way, but then fined Hoechst for non-compliance with the original decision under Article 14. Hoechst argued that, in so far as Article 14 purported to allow the Commission to carry out searches, it was unlawful, being incompatible with fundamental rights, in that such searches should only be carried out on the basis of a warrant issued in advance.

---

[11] This requires judicial authorization, *Regulation Implementing Articles 81 and 82*, n. 4 above, Art. 20(7).

[12] *Ibid.*, Art. 20(2).

[13] National courts cannot review the necessity for the inspection. They can only ensure that the Commission decision is authentic, and that it is not arbitrary or excessive: *ibid.*, Art. 20(8). This reflects the holding in Cases 46/87 & 227/88, *Hoechst AG v. Commission* [1989] ECR 2859, para. 35.

12. It should be noted before the nature and scope of the Commission's powers of investigation under Article 14 of Regulation 17 are examined, that that Article cannot be interpreted in such a way as to give rise to results which are incompatible with the general principles of Community law and in particular with fundamental rights.[14]

. . .

26. Both the purpose of Regulation 17 and the list of powers conferred on Commission officials by Article 14 thereof show that the scope of investigations may be very wide. In that regard, the right to enter any premises . . . is of particular importance inasmuch as it is intended to permit the Commission to obtain evidence of infringements of the competition rules in the places in which such evidence is normally to be found, that is to say, on the business premises of undertakings.

27. That right of access would serve no useful purpose if the Commission officials could do no more than ask for documents or files which they could identify in advance. On the contrary, such a right implies the power to search for various items of information which are not already known or fully identified. Without such a power, it would be impossible for the Commission to obtain the information necessary to carry out the investigation if the undertakings concerned refused to co-operate or adopted an obstructive attitude.

28. Although Article 14 of Regulation 17 thus confers wide powers of investigation on the Commission, the exercise of those powers is subject to conditions serving to ensure that the rights of the undertakings concerned are respected.

29. In that regard, it should be noted first that the Commission is required to specify the subject-matter and purpose of the investigation. . . .

30. It should also be pointed out that the conditions for the exercise of the Commission's investigative powers vary according to the procedure which the Commission has chosen, the attitude of the undertakings concerned and the intervention of the national authorities.

[*The Court then noted the different types of investigation which can be carried out under Article 14, and more particularly the difference between those instances where there is co-operation between Commission and undertakings and those where there is not. What follows refers to the situation where the undertaking resisted the Commission's investigation and the latter sought the assistance of the Member State under Article 14(6) of Regulation 17:*]

34. . . . if the Commission intends, with the assistance of the national authorities, to carry out an investigation other than with the co-operation of the undertakings concerned, it is required to respect the relevant procedural guarantees laid down by national law.

35. The Commission must make sure that the competent body under national law has all that it needs to exercise its own supervisory powers. It should be pointed out that that body, whether judicial or otherwise, cannot in this respect substitute its own assessment of the need for the investigations ordered for that of the Commission, the lawfulness of whose assessments of fact and law is subject only to review by the Court of Justice. On the other hand, it is within the powers of the national body, after satisfying itself that the decision ordering the investigation is authentic, to consider whether the measures of constraint envisaged are arbitrary or excessive having regard to the subject-matter of the investigation and to ensure that the rules of national law are complied with in the application of those measures.

36. In the light of the foregoing, it must be held that the measures which the contested decision

---

[14] For discussion of the issues relating to fundamental rights in this case see Ch. 8 above.

ordering the investigation permitted the Commission officials to take did not exceed their powers under Article 14 of Regulation 17.

In some cases parties have sought to resist the taking of certain documents on the ground that they are covered by legal professional privilege between lawyer and client. Regulation 17 said nothing on this issue, but in the *AM & S* case[15] the ECJ held that such a privilege was recognized by EC law to a limited extent at least.[16] The confidentiality of written communications between lawyer and client was protected, provided that the communications were made for the purposes of the client's right of defence and that they emanated from independent lawyers, meaning those not bound to the client by an employment relationship.

The ECJ has also concluded that there is a limited privilege against self-incrimination: an undertaking is not required to answer questions which would be an admission of the very offence which the Commission is investigating; but the undertaking cannot refuse to hand over documentation which could establish the offence.[17] There is no absolute right to silence in competition proceedings, except so far as compulsion to provide an answer would entail admission of an infringement.[18]

Inspections can lead to the Commission being in possession of business secrets.[19] Protection of such secrets is taken into account in Articles 26(2) and 27 of the new draft Council regulation. In the *Akzo* case[20] the ECJ held that such secrets should not be divulged. In circumstances where the disclosure of information to, for example, interveners in an action might reveal confidential business information of the complainants, the Court has power to order that documents should be withheld. In deciding on this issue the Court will balance the applicant's legitimate interest in the non-disclosure of business secrets with the interveners' legitimate concern to have the information which will enable it to state its case before the Court.[21]

Subject to protection for business secrets, there is a general principle of access to the file in order that the addressee of a statement of objections can express its views on the conclusions reached by the Commission.[22]

(b) NOTIFICATION

The second way in which the Commission could become aware of a potential competition violation was if the parties notified an agreement to it. Regulation 17,

[15] Case 155/79, *Australian Mining and Smelting Europe Ltd. (AM and S Europe Ltd.)* v. *Commission* [1982] ECR 1575, paras. 21–22, 23, 27, 34.

[16] On what should happen in the event of a dispute whether documents did come within these criteria see *ibid.*, paras. 30–32.

[17] Case 374/87, *Orkem SA*, n. 9 above, paras. 34–35; Case 27/88, *Solvay*, n. 9 above, paras. 31–32.

[18] Case T–112/98, *Mannesmannrohren-Werke AG* v. *Commission* [2001] ECR II–729, paras. 66–67.

[19] J. Joshua, 'Balancing the Public Interests: Confidentiality, Trade Secrets and Disclosure of Evidence in EC Competition Procedures' [1994] *ECLR* 68.

[20] Case 53/85, *AKZO Chemie BV* v. *Commission* [1986] ECR 1965.

[21] Case T–30/89A, *Hilti AG* v. *Commission* [1990] ECR II–163; Case T–57/91, *National Association of Licensed Opencast Operators* v. *Commission* [1993] 5 CMLR 124.

[22] Case T–36/91, *ICI* v. *Commission* [1995] ECR II–1847. See also the Commission's Access to the File (Antitrust) Notice [1997] OJ C23/3, [1997] 4 CMLR 490.

Article 4(1), provided that agreements etc. that came into existence after the entry into force of the Regulation had to be notified to the Commission if the parties sought individual exemption under Article 85(3) (now Article 81(3)). Until they had been notified no decision concerning Article 85(3) could be taken. Article 4(2) specified certain agreements that did not have to be notified to the Commission. Notification also carried a limited immunity from fines for notified agreements, prior to the decision being made on Article 81(3).

Notification is, as we have seen above, to be abolished pursuant to the strategy identified in the *White Paper on Modernization*.[23] The general theme of the new approach is that parties must make their own assessments of whether their agreements comply with the competition rules. However, Article 4(2) of the new draft Council Regulation empowers the Commission to enact regulations relating to certain types of agreement, etc., that are caught by Article 81(1), requiring them to be registered. Registration will not confer any entitlement on the registering undertakings.

(c) COMPLAINTS

The final way in which the Commission may become aware of a possible infringement of Article 81 or 82 is through a complaint from an aggrieved party. Member States and any natural or legal person with a legitimate interest may make a complaint.[24] The law on this issue is complex, but the main principles can be stated as follows.

It is clear that the Commission is under a duty *to consider* a complaint which has been submitted to it.[25] Failure to do so could lead to an action under Article 232 for failure to act.

If the Commission *does decide to conduct an investigation* then it must generally do so with the degree of care that will enable it to assess the factual and legal considerations submitted by the complainant.[26]

Complainants shall be 'associated closely' with the Commission proceedings leading to a decision that there has been a violation of Article 81 or 82.[27]

If the Commission or the NCA decides that it is necessary then it *may hear* other natural or legal persons. It *shall hear* such persons who have a sufficient interest.[28]

Where the Commission decides not to pursue a complaint made to it then it must *inform the complainant of its reasons*.[29] These must be sufficient to enable the Court to review the lawfulness of the decision and make clear to the parties concerned the circumstances in which the Commission has applied the Treaty. The Commission must also fix a time limit for the complainant to submit any further comments in writing.[30]

---

[23] N. 3 above.   [24] *Regulation Implementing Arts. 81 and 82*, Art. 7(2); (Reg. 17, Art. 3(2)(b)).

[25] Case 210/81, *Demo-Studio Schmidt* v. *Commission* [1983] ECR 3045.

[26] Case T–7/92, *Asia Motor France SA* v. *Commission (No. 2)* [1993] ECR II–669.

[27] *Regulation Implementing Arts. 81 and 82*, n. 4 above, Art. 26(1).

[28] *Ibid.*, Art. 26(3).

[29] Case T–77/95 RV, *Union Française de l'Express (Ufex), DHL International, Service CRIE and May Courier* v. *Commission* [2000] ECR II–2167, para. 42.

[30] Case T–575/93, *Koelman* v. *Commission* [1996] ECR II–1; Cases T–70–71/92, *Florimex BV* v. *Commission* [1997] 5 CMLR 769. A decision by the Commission not to pursue a complaint does not deprive the national courts of jurisdiction over the same issue: Case T–387/94, *Asia Motor France SA* v. *Commission* [1996] ECR II–961; Case C–282/95P, *Guérin Automobiles* v. *Commission* [1997] ECR I–1503.

The Commission has limited resources with which to pursue competition violations. A corollary of this is that it may well have to pick and choose which possible
infringements are worthy of its attention. This may, not surprisingly, cause upset to
the complainant whose claim is not then pursued. The *Automec* case provides a good
example of this tension.

Case T–24/90, Automec Srl v. Commission[31]
[1992] ECR II–2223

[Note ToA renumbering: Art. 85 is now Art. 81]

The applicant lodged a complaint with the Commission alleging that the car manufacturer BMW
had terminated its dealership in breach of Article 85(1). It sought a mandatory injunction compelling BMW to resume supply. The Commission rejected the application on the ground, *inter alia*,
that the Italian courts had already taken cognizance of the matter and that there was not
a sufficient Community interest to warrant the Commission continuing with the case. The
complainant appealed to the CFI.

THE CFI

75. . . . it is clear from the case law of the Court of Justice (*GEMA*)[32] that the rights conferred
upon complainants by Regulations 17 and 99/63 do not include a right to obtain a decision, within
the meaning of Article 189 EEC, as to the existence or otherwise of the alleged infringement.
It follows that the Commission cannot be required to give a ruling in that connection unless
the subject-matter of the complaint is within its exclusive remit, such as the withdrawal of an
exemption granted pursuant to Article 85(3) EEC.

76. As the Commission has no obligation to rule on the existence or otherwise of an infringement it cannot be compelled to conduct an investigation, because this could have no purpose other
than to seek evidence of the existence or otherwise of an infringement the existence of which it is
not required to establish. . . .

77. In this connection it should be observed that, for an institution performing a public-service
task, the power to take all the organizational measures necessary for the fulfilment of that task,
including settling priorities in the framework laid down by law, where those priorities have not
been settled by the legislature, is an inherent part of the work of administration. This must apply
particularly where an authority has been given a supervisory and regulatory function as general
and extensive as that assigned to the Commission in the field of competition. Therefore the fact
that the Commission allocates different degrees of priority to the matters referred to it in the field
of competition is compatible with its obligations under Community law.

. . .

---

[31] See also Case T–144/92, *Bureau Européen des Médias de l'Industrie Musicale (BEMIM)* v. *Commission*
[1995] ECR II–147; Case T–37/92, *Bureau Européen des Unions Consommateurs and National Consumer
Council* v. *Commission* [1994] ECR II–285; Cases C–359 & 379/95P, *Commission and France* v. *Ladbroke Racing
Ltd.* [1999] ECR I–6265; Cases T–185, 189, 190/96, *Riviera Auto Service Etablissements Dalmasso SA* v. *Commission* [1999] ECR II–93; Case T–77/95 RV, *Ufex*, n. 29 above; Case 449/98 P, *International Express Carriers
Conference (IECC)* v. *Commission, La Poste, UK and the Post Office* [2001] ECR I–3875.
[32] Case 125/78, *GEMA* v. *Commission* [1979] ECR 3173.

79. However, although the Commission cannot be compelled to conduct an investigation, the procedural safeguards provided for by Article 3 of Regulation 17 and Article 6 of Regulation 99/63 oblige it nevertheless to examine carefully the factual and legal aspects of which it is notified by the complainant in order to decide whether they indicate behaviour likely to distort competition in the Common Market and affect trade between Member States. . . .

80. Where, as in the present case, the Commission has decided to close the file relating to the case without conducting an investigation, the review to be made by the Court of the legality of that decision seeks to ascertain whether the contested decision is based on materially wrong facts, is flawed by a mistake in law or a manifest error of assessment or by a misuse of powers.

81. It is for the Court to verify, in the light of these principles, first, whether the Commission has carried out the examination of the complaint which it is required to do by evaluating with all the requisite care the factual and legal aspects adduced by the applicant in his complaint and, secondly, whether the Commission has given proper reasons for closing the file on the complaint on the basis of its power 'to accord different degrees of priority to pursuing the matters referred to it' on the one hand, and on the basis of the Community interest in the matter as a criterion of priority on the other.

82. In this connection the Court finds, first, that the Commission carried out a careful examination of the complaint. . . .

83. Secondly, concerning the reasons for the contested decision to close the file, the Court points out in the first place that the Commission is entitled to accord different degrees of priority to examining the complaints it receives.

84. The second point to be considered is whether it is legitimate, as the Commission contends, to refer to the Community interest of a matter as a criterion of priority.

85. In this connection it should be observed that, unlike the civil courts, whose task is to safeguard the subjective rights of private persons in their mutual relations, an administrative authority must act in the public interest. Consequently it is legitimate for the Commission to refer to the Community interest in order to determine the degree of priority to be accorded to the different matters before it. This does not mean removing the Commission's acts from judicial review: as Article 190 EEC requires the reasons on which decisions are based to be stated, the Commission cannot merely refer to the Community interest in isolation. . . . Thus by reviewing the legality of those reasons the Court can review the Commission's acts.

86. To assess the Community interest in pursuing the examination of a matter, the Commission must take account of the circumstances of the particular case. . . . It is for the Commission in particular to weigh up the importance of the alleged infringement for the functioning of the Common Market, the probability of being able to establish the existence of the infringement and the extent of the investigation measures necessary in order to fulfil successfully its task of securing compliance with Articles 85 and 86.

The CFI upheld the Commission's decision that it was not necessary to proceed with the matter. It held that the proceedings in the Italian courts were an appropriate way of resolving the issues. The CFI held further that the Italian courts could always refer a point to the ECJ under Article 177 (now Article 234) if they felt it necessary to do so. Although the national court could not impose fines, it could apply Article 85(2) (now Article 81(2)), which stipulated that agreements in breach of Article 85(1) (now Article 81(1)) were automatically void. Moreover, the existence of a block exemption covering the subject matter of the dispute made it easier for the national court to apply competition law in this instance.[33]

The CFI will review the way in which the Commission has exercised its discretion in relation to complaints, and may annul its decision if it finds that the reasons for not taking up a complaint were not sustainable.[34] Moreover, the Commission may not regard as excluded in principle from its purview certain situations that are entrusted to it by the Treaty. It must assess in each case the seriousness, persistence, and consequences of the alleged offences.[35]

The Commission issued a Notice on Co-operation between National Courts and the Commission in Applying Article 85 and 86.[36] It built on the Court's case law, and encouraged national courts to apply competition law more frequently than hitherto. The Notice further stated that the Commission intended to concentrate on notifications, complaints, and own-initiative proceedings which 'have a particular political, economic or legal significance for the Community'. Complainants were encouraged to go to national courts in cases where such courts could provide adequate redress. This regime of co-operation will be superseded by the scheme contained in the new draft Council Regulation described below.

4. PUBLIC ENFORCEMENT BY THE COMMISSION: COMPETITION DECISIONS

The Commission, having discovered a possible competition violation, is empowered to make a formal decision whether there has been an infringement of Article 81 or 82. However, because of its limited resources the Commission developed a technique for informal settlement.

(a) INFORMAL SETTLEMENT

The principal technique for informal settlement was the comfort letter.[37] When firms sought negative clearance or individual exemption, they would be asked whether they would be satisfied with a comfort letter. This was a letter in which the Commission stated that it was willing to close the file on the matter, subject to the removal of clauses that it regarded as objectionable. This device was attractive to firms, but it suffered from the drawback that these letters were not binding on national courts. It would therefore be open to a third party, or indeed one of the parties to the actual agreement itself, to challenge it before the national court. Firms have none the less normally been willing to accept comfort letters.[38]

---

[33] [1992] ECR II–2223, paras. 87–98.
[34] Case T–37/92, *BEUC*, n. 31 above; Case T–198/98, *Micro Leader Business* v. *Commission* [1999] ECR II–3989.
[35] Case C–119/97 P, *Union Française de l'Express (Ufex), formerly Syndicate de l'Express International (SFEI)* v. *Commission* [1999] ECR I–1341.
[36] [1993] OJ C39/6, [1993] 4 CMLR 12.
[37] D. Stevens, 'The "Comfort Letter": Old Problems, New Developments' [1994] *ECLR* 81.
[38] Whish, n. 2 above, 217–8.

The rationale for comfort letters developed from the requirement to notify, and the consequent burden that this imposed on the Commission. The abolition of notification, which is central to the Commission's modernization proposals, will end this rationale for such informal settlement.

(b) FORMAL DECISIONS: INTERIM ORDERS

Competition violations can cause considerable damage to a firm. It may be some time before the Commission is able to come to a final determination. It is for this reason that interim relief is given. Regulation 17 contained no explicit provisions on interim orders, but the ECJ in *Camera Care*[39] decided that such a power existed, based on Article 3(1) of Regulation 17. Such measures could however be taken only in cases of urgency, where there was likely to be irreparable damage, or where the public interest demanded it. They had, moreover, to be temporary. The Commission has not used this power on many occasions. Indeed on some occasions it has been for the ECJ or the CFI to take the Commission to task for applying too stringent a test in deciding whether to grant interim relief. Thus in *La Cinq*[40] the CFI held that the Commission could not make the adoption of interim measures conditional on proof of a clear, flagrant infringement of Article 85 or 86 (now Article 81 or 82). This standard was held to be too high for the adoption of interim relief.

The new draft Council Regulation contains an explicit power to award interim measures. Article 8 adopts the criteria from the *Camera Care* case. The Commission can, in cases of urgency due to the risk of serious and irreparable damage to competition, order such measures. The decision to impose such measures can apply only for a maximum of one year, but it can be renewed.

(c) FORMAL DECISIONS: NEGATIVE CLEARANCE

Article 2 of Regulation 17 allowed the Commission to grant a negative clearance: the Commission certified that, on the basis of the facts in its possession, there were no grounds for believing that the agreement or practice fell within Article 85 or 86 (now Article 81 or 82). The parties had to apply for such a negative clearance, various procedural conditions had to be satisfied, and relatively few were granted.

Negative clearances were one way of dealing with the burden of notified agreements. The abolition of notification, pursuant to the Commission's modernization proposals, will end the practice of negative clearances. The new draft Council Regulation does contain a Commission power to declare that Article 81 is inapplicable to certain agreements. The rationale behind this power will be examined below.

---

[39] Case 792/79R, *Camera Care Ltd.* v. *Commission* [1980] ECR 119.
[40] Case T–44/90, *La Cinq SA* v. *Commission* [1992] ECR II–1, paras. 60–61.

(d) FORMAL DECISIONS: A FINDING OF INFRINGEMENT

The *power to make formal decisions* was originally contained in Article 3(1) of Regulation 17. The modified version of this power is to be found in Article 7 of the new draft Council Regulation. It provides that where the Commission, acting on a complaint or its own initiative, finds that that there has been an infringement of Article 81 or 82 it may by decision require the undertakings to bring the infringement to an end. The Commission may impose obligations on the undertakings, including remedies of a structural nature. If there is a legitimate interest in doing so, it may also find that an infringement has been committed in the past.

Article 19(1) of Regulation 17 provided for *hearing rights*. This will now be dealt with in Article 26 of the new draft Council Regulation. Article 26(1) provides that, before taking a decision under Article 7, 8, 22, or 23(2), the Commission shall give the undertakings that are the subject of the proceedings the opportunity of being heard on the matters to which the Commission has taken objection. The Commission must base its decisions only on objections on which the parties have been able to comment. Failure to comply with these conditions will lead to the Commission's decision being quashed.[41] Complainants must be closely associated with the proceedings. If the Commission or NCAs consider it necessary, they may also hear other natural and legal persons. Applications to be heard by such persons shall be granted where they show sufficient interest.[42]

Article 26(2) of the new draft Council Regulation specifies that the *rights of defence* of the parties concerned must be fully respected in the proceedings. They are entitled to *access to the file*, subject to the legitimate interest of undertakings in the protection of their business secrets.[43] The right of access to the file does not extend to confidential information and internal documents of the Commission or NCAs.[44] These new provisions accord with the jurisprudence of the Community courts. The ECJ initially held in *VBVB*[45] that there was no legal obligation to disclose such files. The Commission chose not to stick to the legal letter of this judgment, and permitted access except where, for example, information covered by professional secrecy was involved. The CFI judgment in *SA Hercules*[46] gave legal force to this administrative practice. The Commission is obliged to make available all documents obtained in the course of the investigation, save where they involve business secrets of other undertakings,

---

[41] Cases C–89/85, etc., *A. Ahlström Oy v. Commission* [1993] ECR I–1307, paras. 152–154; Case T–11/89, *Shell International Chemical Company Ltd. v. Commission* [1992] ECR II–757; Case T–10/89, *Hoechst AG v. Commission* [1992] ECR II–629; Cases C–395–396/96P, *Compagnie Maritime Belge Transports SA, Compagnie Maritime Belge SA and Dafra Lines A/S v. Commission* [2000] ECR I–1365, paras. 142–143.

[42] *Ibid.*, Art. 26(3).

[43] *Regulation Implementing Arts. 81 and 82*, n. 4 above, Art. 26(2): that legitimate interest may not constitute an obstacle to the disclosure and use by the Commission of information necessary to prove an infringement.

[44] *Ibid.*, Art. 26(2).

[45] Cases 43, 63/82, *VBVB and VBBB v. Commission* [1985] ECR 19, para. 25.

[46] Case T–7/89, *SA Hercules Chemicals NV v. Commission* [1991] ECR II–1711, para. 54; Case T–65/89, *BPB Industries plc and British Gypsum Ltd. v. Commission* [1993] ECR II–389.

confidential information, or internal Commission documents.[47] This is regarded as part of a wider principle of equality of arms.[48] The Commission decision must contain reasons for the conclusion reached.[49]

When the hearing has been held the Commission may conclude that there has been an *infringement which should be terminated*.[50] A formal decision may still be made even if the parties have, by that stage, ended their violation.[51] The precise nature of the Commission order will depend upon the circumstances. The remedies may be structural in nature. It is clear that the decision can impose a positive as well as a negative obligation, such as an order to supply certain goods. However, the nature of the order will depend upon which Article of the Treaty has been broken.[52] Thus while an obligation to supply can be ordered for a breach of Article 86 (now Article 82),[53] the fact that an agreement is in breach of Article 85 (now Article 81) cannot lead to an order to, for example, supply cars of a certain make to a distributor.[54]

Article 9 of the new draft Council Regulation empowers the Commission to accept *commitments* from the undertakings in order to meet the Commission's objections. The Commission may, by decision, make these commitments binding on the under-takings. The Commission can reopen the proceedings if there is a material change in the facts on which the decision was based, where the undertakings act contrary to the commitments, or where the decision was based on incomplete, incorrect or misleading information.[55]

When an infringement has been found the Commission has power to *impose fines and periodic penalty payments*.[56] This power was contained in Articles 15 and 16 of Regulation 17. A modified version of this power is to be found in Articles 22 and 23 of the new draft Council Regulation.[57] Article 22(1) authorizes the Commission to impose fines not exceeding 1 per cent of total turnover in the preceding business year for intentional or negligent breaches of certain of the provisions concerning requests for information and inspection. Article 22(2) empowers the Commission to impose a fine of up to 10 per cent of total turnover of each of the undertakings participating in the infringement, where it negligently or intentionally infringes Article 81 or 82, contravenes a decision imposing interim measures, or fails to comply with a commitment. The gravity and duration of the infringement are to be taken into account in determining the amount of the fine.[58] The Commission has published

---

[47] *Commission Notice on Internal Rules of Procedure for Access to the File* [1997] OJ C23/3, [1997] 4 CMLR 490.

[48] Case T–30/91, *Solvay SA* v. *Commission* [1995] ECR II–1775; Case C–51/92P, *Hercules Chemicals NV* v. *Commission* [1999] ECR I–4235; Case T–175/95, *BASF Lacke & Farben AG* v. *Commission* [1999] ECR II–1581.

[49] Cases T–374, 375, 384 & 388/94, *European Night Services* v. *Commission* [1998] ECR II–3141.

[50] *Regulation Implementing Arts. 81 and 82*, n. 4 above, Art. 7(1).

[51] Case 7/82, *GVL* v. *Commission* [1983] ECR 483. See, however, the limit on the Commission's powers in Case T–7/93, *Langnese-Iglo GmbH* v. *Commission* [1995] ECR II–1533.

[52] Whish, n. 2 above, 236.

[53] Cases 6, 7/73, *Commercial Solvents Co.* v. *Commission* [1974] ECR 223.

[54] Case T–24/90, *Automec* [1992] ECR II–2223.

[55] *Regulation Implementing Arts. 81 and 82*, n. 4 above, Art. 9(3).

[56] W. Wils, 'EC Competition Fines: To Deter or not to Deter' [1995] *YBEL* 17; I. van Bael, 'Fining a la Carte: The Lottery of EU Competition Law' [1995] *ECLR* 237.

[57] *Regulation Implementing Arts. 81 and 82*, n. 4 above, Arts. 24–25 deal with limitation periods.

[58] *Ibid.*, Art. 22(3).

guidelines to guide its discretion in the setting of fines, indicating the factors that will exacerbate or reduce the gravity of the infringement.[59] There is a power, in Article 23, to impose periodic penalty payments not exceeding 5 per cent of the average daily turnover in order to compel the undertakings to put an end to an infringement of Article 81 or 82, in accordance with a decision taken under Article 7. This power can be used to enforce compliance with a decision ordering interim measures, commitments, and can also be used to compel the supply of information and submission to an inspection. The ECJ emphasized in the *Musique Diffusion Française* case[60] that fines should be capable of having a deterrent impact, particularly as regards those infringements that were very harmful to the attainment of the objectives of the Community.[61] Different levels of fine may be imposed upon the participants in the same agreement if there are reasons why one party is more blameworthy.[62] The Commission has published a notice the import of which is to encourage participants in a cartel to inform the Commission of its existence: 'whistle blowing'. The consequence is that the firm that informs the Commission will have its fine significantly reduced or it may even be totally exempted from the fine.[63]

An Advisory Committee on Restrictive Practices and Dominant Positions must be consulted prior to the taking of any decisions under Article 7, 9, 10, 22, or 23(2) of the new draft Council Regulation.[64] The Committee is composed of representatives of the competition authorities of the Member States. It is to be supplied with a summary of the case and the preliminary draft decision, on which it delivers an opinion. The Advisory Committee may recommend that its opinion be published, and the Commission may carry out the publication.

The procedure for determining competition violations has been attacked on more than one occasion. A general complaint has been that the Commission combines the function of prosecutor and judge.

Cases 100–103/80, Musique Diffusion Française v. Commission[65]
[1983] ECR 1825

The Commission had found a concerted practice operating between four companies, the essence of which was the division of the market for Pioneer electronic equipment so that distributors in

---

[59] *Commission Guidelines on the Method of Setting Fines* [1998] OJ C9/3, [1998] 4. CMLR 472; W. Wils, 'The Commission's New Method for Calculating Fines in Antitrust Cases' (1998) 23 *ELRev*. 252; R. Richardson, 'Guidance without Guidance—A European Revolution in Fining Policy?' [1999] *ECLR* 360.

[60] Cases 100–103/80, *Musique Diffusion Française SA* v. *Commission* [1983] ECR 1825. See also Case T–275/94, *Groupement des Cartes Bancaires 'CB'* v. *Commission* [1995] ECR II–2169; Case C–137/95P, *Vereniging van Samenwerkende Prijsregelende Organisaties in de Bouwnijverheid* v. *Commission* [1996] ECR I–1611.

[61] Cases 100–103/80, *MDF*, n. 60 above, paras. 106–107.

[62] *Ibid.*, para. 132.

[63] *Commission Notice on the Non-Imposition or Reduction of Fines in Cartel Cases* [1996] OJ C207/4, [1996] 5 CMLR 362. The Notice is to be fine-tuned: see *Notice of the Commission Relating to the Revision of the 1996 Notice on the Non-implementation or Reduction of Fines in Cartel Cases* [2001] OJ C205/5.

[64] *Regulation Implementing Arts. 81 and 82*, n. 4 above Art. 14(1).

[65] See also Case T–11/89, *Shell International*, n. 41 above.

different countries had exclusive rights and cross-border sales were prevented. The companies put forward a number of objections to the Commission decision, one of which was that it infringed essential procedural requirements.

THE ECJ

6. MDF (Musique Diffusion Française) maintains that the contested decision is unlawful by the mere fact that it was adopted under a system in which the Commission combines the functions of prosecutor and judge, which is contrary to Article 6(1) of the European Convention for the Protection of Human Rights.

7. That argument is without relevance. As the Court held in its judgments in Cases 209 etc/78 (*Van Landewyck* v. *Commission*), the Commission cannot be described as a 'tribunal' within the meaning of Article 6. . . .

8. It should however be added . . . that during the administrative procedure before the Commission, the Commission is bound to observe the procedural safeguards provided for by Community law.

[*The Court then set out the provisions of Regulation 17, Article 19, and Regulation 99/63, Article 4.*]

10. As the Court recalled in its judgment . . . in Case 85/76 (*Hoffmann-La Roche* v. *Commission*), the above mentioned principles are an application of the fundamental principle of Community law which requires the right to a fair hearing to be observed in all proceedings, even those of an administrative nature, and lays down in particular that the undertaking concerned must have been afforded the opportunity, during the administrative procedure, to make known its views on the truth and relevance of the facts and circumstances alleged and on the documents used by the Commission to support its claim that there has been an infringement of the Treaty.

11. It follows that, although the general submission put forward by MDF must be rejected as being based on a misunderstanding of the nature of the procedure before the Commission, Community law contains all the means necessary for examining, and in an appropriate case, upholding the following submissions based on alleged breaches of the applicants' right to a fair hearing.

The concerns voiced by the applicants in this case have had some impact. Since 1982 the Commission has appointed a Hearing Officer to preside over the hearing and to ensure that the rights of the defence are properly protected. Although the parties are not entitled to see his report, the Commission has decided to make it available to them at the time of the decision itself.[66] The Commission has moreover made a decision that strengthens the role of the hearing officer in the competition proceedings.[67] It acknowledged the importance of entrusting the administrative proceedings to an independent person experienced in competition matters. This independence is to be protected by attaching hearing officers to the Commissioner with responsibility for competition, rather than to the Directorate General for Competition.

---

[66] Whish, n. 2 above, 234.
[67] *Commission Decision on the Terms of Reference of Hearing Officers in Certain Competition Proceedings* [2001] OJ L162/21.

(e) FORMAL DECISIONS: A FINDING OF INAPPLICABILITY

Article 10 of the new draft Council Regulation empowers the Commission, for reasons of the Community public interest, acting on its own initiative, to make a decision either that Article 81(1) is inapplicable to an agreement or that the conditions of Article 81(3) are fulfilled. The Commission has an analogous power in relation to Article 82. The rationale for this provision is to enable the Commission to make decisions about the legality of new types of agreements. The decisions made under this Article are declaratory, but national courts and NCAs would be bound to take them into account when reaching their own decisions. This is because Article 16 requires national courts and NCAs to use every effort to avoid conflicts with Commission decisions.

(f) FORMAL DECISIONS: EXEMPTIONS

A central feature of Community competition policy was that the Commission had exclusive jurisdiction to grant *individual exemption* under Article 81(3). This power was reserved to the Commission by Article 9(1) of Regulation 17. The removal of this exclusive jurisdiction was, as we have seen, a central feature of the modernization reforms. When the new draft Council Regulation becomes law, then national courts and NCAs will be able to adjudicate on the entirety of Article 81. The methods for co-ordinating Commission and national adjudication will be considered below.

The Commission's power to make regulations containing *block exemptions* is contained in Article 28 of the new draft Council Regulation. The benefit of such block exemptions can be withdrawn where the Commission finds that an agreement, etc., has effects incompatible with Article 81(3).

(g) JUDICIAL REVIEW BY THE CFI

Commission Decisions may be reviewed and, since 1989, review has been undertaken initially by the CFI. Parties who wish to contest Commission action or inaction will bring proceedings under Article 230 or 232 respectively. The general principles concerning these actions have been considered above.[68]

A condition for bringing an annulment action under Article 230 is that the applicant has standing. This is, as we have seen, often problematic. However, as we have also seen, this hurdle is rather less of a problem in competition matters than it is in relation to other issues.[69] It is clear that the party against whom a competition decision has been made can seek to have that decision annulled. It is clear also from the *Metro* case[70] that a complainant will be accorded standing.[71]

---

[68] See Ch. 12 above.
[69] *Ibid.*
[70] Case 26/76, *Metro-SB-Großmärkte GmbH & Co KG* v. *Commission* [1977] ECR 1875.
[71] See also Cases 228, 229/82, *Ford Werke AG* v. *Commission* [1984] ECR 1129; Case T–12/93, *Comité Central d'Entreprise de la Société Anonyme Vittel* v. *Commission* [1995] ECR II–1247.

An important issue concerns the range of measures that may be annulled under Article 230. There is little difficulty with formal Commission decisions such as findings of infringement. More difficulty has been encountered with less formal measures. The judicial decisions in this respect do not always sit easily together. In the *Perfumes* cases[72] the ECJ held that comfort letters were not acts capable of being reviewed, classifying them as purely administrative. This should be contrasted with the approach taken in the *IBM* case.[73] The ECJ held that any act capable of affecting the interests of the applicant by bringing about a change in its legal position could be reviewed. It also held that a statement of objections could not be reviewed since it was merely a preliminary stage in the initiation of formal proceedings.[74] Moreover, letters that definitively reject a complaint and close a file are reviewable.[75]

The grounds of review are listed in Article 230(1). Thus, for example, failure to authenticate the decision taken by the College of Commissioners in the proper manner constitutes breach of an essential procedural requirement, and the decision will be annulled.[76] The intensity of the review process has increased since the task has been allocated to the CFI, and a number of high-profile decisions have been overturned on the facts.[77] However, the CFI has indicated that the intensity of review is limited in situations entailing complex economic assessments.[78] In such circumstances, review should be confined to verifying compliance with procedural rules and those relating to the statement of reasons, verifying the material accuracy of facts and checking to ensure that there has been no manifest error of assessment or misuse of power.

An action may also be brought against the Commission for failure to act under Article 232. This provision will be used, for example, where a complainant is dissatisfied with the Commission's response to its complaint. However, as we have seen,[79] the Commission is not obliged to proceed with a complaint, and it has discretion whether to use its scarce resources to proceed, taking account of the Community interest.

It is possible to appeal from the CFI to the ECJ. However, the ECJ will only review the legal characterisation of the facts found by the CFI and the conclusions it has drawn from them. The ECJ will not itself examine the facts or the evidence the CFI accepted in support of the facts.[80]

---

[72] An example of which is Case 99/79, *Lancôme* v. *Etos* [1980] ECR 2511. See V. Korah, 'Comfort Letters—Reflections on the *Perfumes* Cases' (1981) 6 *ELRev.* 14.

[73] Case 60/81, *IBM* v. *Commission* [1981] ECR 2639; Cases T–125 & 127/97, *The Coca-Cola Company and Coca-Cola Enterprises Inc.* v. *Commission* [2000] ECR II–1733. Compare the application of this test in Cases 142, 156/84, *British American Tobacco Co. Ltd. and R. J. Reynolds Inc.* v. *Commission* [1987] ECR 4487, and Case C–282/95P, *Guérin,* n. 30 above.

[74] See also Case T–9/97, *Elf Autochem SA* v. *Commission* [1997] 5 CMLR 844.

[75] Case T–241/97, *Stork Amsterdam BV* v. *Commission* [2000] ECR II–309, para. 53.

[76] Case C–286/95 P, *Commission* v. *Imperial Chemical Industries plc (ICI)* [2000] ECR I–2341, paras. 41–43; Cases C–287–288/95 P, *Commission* v. *Solvay SA* [2000] ECR I–2391, paras. 45–46.

[77] See, e.g., Cases T–79/89, etc., *BASF* v. *Commission* [1992] ECR II–315; Cases C–89/85 etc., *A. Ahlström Oy,* n. 41 above.

[78] Case T–44/90, *La Cinq,* n. 40 above; Case T–7/92, *Asia Motor,* n. 26 above, following Cases 142 and 156/84, *British American Tobacco,* n. 73 above.

[79] See 1069–70 above.

[80] Case C–8/95 P, *New Holland Ford Ltd.* v. *Commission* [1998] ECR I–3175.

5. PUBLIC ENFORCEMENT: NATIONAL COMPETITION AUTHORITIES

The Commission raised the possibility of using national competition authorities (NCAs) in 1996.[81] This idea has been developed and extended in the modernization initiative. It is for the Member States to designate the competition authorities responsible for the application of Articles 81 and 82.[82] The powers of NCAs are set out in the new draft Council Regulation. Article 5 provides that NCAs shall have the power in individual cases to apply Article 81(1) where the conditions in Article 81(3) are not fulfilled. They are also empowered to apply Article 82. The NCAs can act on their own initiative or on a compliant. They are authorized to take any decision requiring the termination of an infringement, the imposition of interim measures, the acceptance of commitments, or the imposition of fines, penalty payments, or any other penalty imposed by national law. The NCAs can decide that there are no grounds for taking action.

Article 11 of the new draft Council Regulation sets out a framework for co-operation between NCAs and the Commission. Article 11(1) provides that the Commission and NCAs shall apply the Community competition rules in close co-operation. The Commission is obliged by Article 11(2) to transmit to NCAs copies of the 'most important documents' it has collected with a view to applying Articles 7–10. Article 11(3) imposes a reciprocal obligation on NCAs to inform the Commission of proceedings begun in the Member States. The NCAs are also obliged, by Article 11(4), to consult the Commission before they adopt a decision requiring an infringement of Articles 81 or 82 to be brought to an end, before they accept commitments or withdraw the benefit of a block exemption. The NCAs must supply the Commission with a summary of the case and copies of the most important documents no later than one month before taking the decision. NCAs may also consult the Commission on any other matter relating to the application of Community law: Article 11(5). If the Commission initiates proceedings for the adoption of a decision under the new draft Council Regulation the NCAs are 'relieved of their competence' to apply Articles 81 and 82.

Article 12 states that the Commission and NCAs may provide each other with, and use in evidence, any matter of fact or law, including confidential information, notwithstanding any national provision to the contrary.

NCAs will, in general, have investigative powers in their own national legislation. Article 21 of the new draft Council Regulation deals with co-operation between NCAs, and between NCAs and the Commission, in relation to investigation of competition violations. Article 21(1) authorizes an NCA in one State to carry out fact-finding under its national law, on behalf of an NCA in a different State. Article

---

[81] *Preliminary Draft Notice on Co-operation between National Competition Authorities and the Commission in Handling Cases Falling within the Scope of Arts. 85 or 86 of the EC Treaty* [1996] OJ C262/5; C. Kerse, 'Enforcing Community Competition Policy under Articles 88 and 89 of the EC Treaty—New Powers for UK Competition Authorities' [1997] *ECLR* 17.

[82] *Regulation Implementing Arts. 81 and 82*, n. 4 above, Art. 36.

21(2) enables the Commission to use an NCA to undertake inspections pursuant to Article 20(1) or 20(4).

It is clearly possible, under the new regime, for the same issue to arise before more than one NCA. This issue is addressed in Article 13(1). It states that where two or more NCAs have received a complaint, or are acting on their own initiative, against the same agreement, etc., 'the fact that one authority is dealing with the case shall be sufficient grounds for the others to suspend proceedings before them or to reject the complaint'. The Commission may also reject a complaint on the ground that an NCA is dealing with the matter. Where a case has already been dealt with by an NCA, or by the Commission, any other NCA may reject it.

The Commission may, on its own initiative or at the request of a Member State, include a case dealt with by an NCA on the agenda of the Advisory Committee on Restrictive Practices and Dominant Positions for discussion before the final decision is taken.[83]

6. PRIVATE ENFORCEMENT: THE ROLE OF THE NATIONAL COURTS PRIOR TO THE MODERNIZATION REFORMS

(a) THE ADVANTAGES AND DISADVANTAGES OF ENFORCEMENT THROUGH NATIONAL COURTS

The use of national courts to enforce competition law[84] has *advantages* for both the Commission and private parties. From the former perspective, national actions ease the Commission's workload, by decentralizing law enforcement in this area. Public enforcement through the Commission is thus complemented by private enforcement through national courts. This feature is highlighted by the *Notice on Co-operation between National Courts and the Commission in Applying Articles 85 and 86 of the EEC Treaty*[85] (now Articles 81 and 82) produced by the Commission. The distinguishing feature of private enforcement is that a private party at the national level brings the action. The national court may make a reference to the ECJ if it feels that this is necessary, but it may instead follow previous ECJ or CFI decisions.[86] It is direct effect that gives rights to individuals which they may enforce through the national legal system. From the perspective of the private parties themselves, the ability to use national courts also has advantages: the action is not dependent on the approval of the Commission, and Community law claims can be combined with those of a domestic nature.

---

[83] *Ibid.*, Art. 14(6).

[84] Whish, n. 2 above, ch. 8; R. Whish, 'The Enforceability of Agreements under EC and UK Competition Law', in F. Rose (ed.), *Lex Mercatoria: Essays on International Commercial Law in Honour of Francis Reynolds*, (LLP, 2000), ch. 15; C. Kerse, *EC Antitrust Procedure* (Sweet & Maxwell, 4th edn., 1998), ch. 10; C. Jones, *Private Enforcement of Antitrust Law in the EU, UK and USA* (Oxford University Press, 1999).

[85] [1993] OJ C39/6, [1993] 4 CMLR 12.

[86] The UK courts have, moreover, made it clear that it would be an abuse of process to attempt to litigate in national courts matters which *have been* determined by the Commission: *Iberian UK Ltd.* v. *BPB Industries plc* [1996] 2 CMLR 601.

There are, however, also *disadvantages or problems* with enforcement by national courts. Plaintiffs suing in national courts may be faced with difficult obstacles concerning the burden of proof, the standard of proof, discovery, and the availability of interlocutory relief. Any such action will be more costly as compared to investigation by the Commission, and there can be jurisdictional difficulties in locating the suitable forum.[87] There may also be difficulties in relation to the use of confidential information secured in proceedings brought by the Commission when an action is then commenced in a national court and a party seeks to rely on such information.[88] There is, moreover, the more general concern about the capacity of the national courts to deal with the types of question raised by Articles 81 and 82. The resolution of the last of these problems may lie in the establishment of a specialist court at the national level to deal with competition issues.

The reform of EC competition law will have a profound effect on the role of national courts. Prior to these reforms, national courts could apply Article 81(1), but not Article 81(3). This led to a number of problems discussed below. Under the new regime, national courts are empowered to apply Article 81 in its entirety. The discussion within this section will therefore summarize the law prior to the modernization regime. The following section will deal with the modernization regime itself.

(b) ARTICLE 81: ENFORCEMENT OF AGREEMENTS

Articles 81 and 82 (ex Articles 85 and 86) have direct effect.[89] The national courts can, therefore, apply Articles 81(1), 82, and the block exemptions. However, national courts did not, prior to the modernization reforms, have authority to give rulings on Article 81(3). Agreements caught by Article 81(1) are automatically void under Article 81(2),[90] subject to the fact that exemption may be granted under Article 81(3). The role of the national courts in adjudicating on agreements within Article 81(1) was considered in detail in the *Delimitis* case.[91] The principles that emerged from this case can be summarized as follows.

Notification was a prerequisite for individual exemption under Article 81(3). If there was *no notification* the national courts had a number of options:

i. If the agreement was clearly not within Article 81(1) the national court could proceed and rule on the agreement.[92]

ii. The same was true if the agreement clearly infringed Article 81(1), and there was no real possibility of a block exemption applying.[93]

---

[87] J. Shaw, 'Decentralisation and Law Enforcement in EC Competition Law' (1995) 15 *Legal Studies* 128, 145–9; Whish, n. 116 below.

[88] Case T–353/94, *Postbank NV* v. *Commission* [1997] 4 CMLR 33.

[89] Case 127/73, *Belgische Radio en Televisie and Société Belge des Auteurs, Compositeurs et Editeurs (BRT) de Musique* v. *SV SABAM and NV Fonior* [1974] ECR 51.

[90] Case C–126/97, *Eco Swiss China Time Ltd.* v. *Benetton International NV* [1999] ECR I–3055.

[91] Case C–234/89, *Delimitis* v. *Henninger Bräu AG* [1991] ECR I–935.

[92] *Ibid.*, para. 50; *Notice on Co-operation*, n. 85 above, para. 23.

[93] Case C–234/89, *Delimitis*, n. 91 above, para. 50; *Notice on Co-operation*, n. 85 above, para. 28.

   iii. The national court could apply a block exemption.[94]

   iv. The national court could seek the assistance of the Commission.[95]

   v. It could request a preliminary ruling under Article 234.[96]

The position with respect to agreements which *had been notified or which did not require notification* was different. Individual exemption was available in such cases, but could not be given by the national court. National courts did however have the right and the duty to apply Article 81(1). The position was further complicated by the fact that new notified agreements, those coming into existence after the entry into force of Regulation 17, did not have the benefit of what was known as provisional validity. If such agreements were within Article 81(1) then Article 81(2) applied, even though any exemption would be retrospective to the date when the agreement was notified.[97] Old agreements, which existed at the date of entry into force of Regulation 17, did enjoy provisional validity, pending the outcome of the Commission's decision on Article 81(3). The force of Article 81(2) did not bite in relation to these agreements until that decision had been made.[98] The options open to the national courts were as follows:

   i. If the agreement did not appear to fall within Article 81(1) then the national court could rule on it.[99]

   ii. The national court could also rule on the agreement where it clearly did infringe Article 81(1), and there was no possibility of individual exemption being granted.[100]

   iii. Where there was a possibility of an individual exemption then the national court could stay the action or adopt interim measures.[101]

   iv. A decision of a national court on Article 81(1) or 82 did not bind the Commission, and the latter could make a decision that conflicted with that of the national court. This decision was then binding on the national courts. The national court could not, moreover, give judgment contrary to a prior Commission decision.[102]

   v. The national court could apply a block exemption.[103]

   vi. It could make a reference under Article 234.

(c) NATIONAL COURTS AND COMFORT LETTERS

We have already seen that a significant number of competition issues were settled informally and that comfort letters played a central role in this process. These letters

---

[94] Case C–234/89, *Delimitis*, n. 91 above, para. 46; *Notice on Co-operation*, n. 85 above, para. 26.
[95] Case C–234/89, *Delimitis*, n. 91 above, para. 53; *Notice on Co-operation*, n. 85 above, paras. 33–44.
[96] Case C–234/89, *Delimitis*, n. 91 above, para. 54.
[97] Reg. 17, Art. 6(1).
[98] Case 48/72, *Brasserie de Haecht SA v. Wilkin (No. 2)* [1973] ECR 77; Case 43/69, *Brauerei A. Bilger Söhne GmbH v. Jehle* [1970] ECR 127.
[99] Case C–234/89, *Delimitis*, n. 91 above, para. 50.
[100] *Ibid.*, para. 50.
[101] Case C–234/89, *Delimitis*, n. 91 above, para. 52; *Notice on Co-operation*, n. 85 above, paras. 32, 33–44; *MTV Europe v. BMG Records* [1997] 1 CMLR 867; *Philips Electronics v. Ingman Ltd.* [1998] 2 CMLR 839.
[102] Case C–344/98, *Masterfoods Ltd v. HB Ice Cream Ltd.* [2000] ECR I–11369.
[103] Case C–234/89, *Delimitis*, n. 91 above, para. 46.

did not bind national courts, and therefore in theory a national court could arrive at a conclusion at variance with the Commission's view. However, this was not a significant problem in practice. Moreover, national courts could take account of comfort letters stating that Article 81 or 82 did not apply.[104]

7. PRIVATE ENFORCEMENT: THE ROLE OF NATIONAL COURTS UNDER THE MODERNIZATION REFORMS

It should, for the sake of clarity, be emphasized that the role of national courts is as set out in the previous section until the new draft Council Regulation comes into force. When that occurs, the position of national courts will be transformed: they will be able to apply the entirety of Article 81. This is affirmed by Article 6 of the new draft Council Regulation, which states that national courts before which the prohibition of Article 81(1) is invoked shall also have the jurisdiction to apply Article 81(3). It will be open to national courts to seek a preliminary ruling.

We have already seen the provisions made for co-operation between NCAs and the Commission under the new regime. The new draft Council Regulation also contains provisions for co-operation with national courts. Article 15(1) provides that, in proceedings for the application of Articles 81 and 82, national courts may ask the Commission for information in its possession, or for its opinion on questions concerning the application of Community competition rules. National courts are obliged to send the Commission copies of judgments applying Article 81 or 82 within one month of the date on which the judgment is delivered.[105] The Commission may on its own initiative, for reasons of the Community public interest, submit observations to national courts in relation to cases concerning Articles 81 and 82. It may be represented by an NCA. The NCAs may also submit observations. The Commission and the NCAs may, to this end, request national courts to transmit to them any necessary documents.[106] Under Article 16 of the new draft Council Regulation, national courts must, in pursuance of Article 10 EC, use every effort to avoid any decision that conflicts with Commission decisions.

8. DAMAGES ACTIONS AND RECOVERY OF BENEFITS

An important issue concerns the availability of damages consequent on a breach of Article 81 or 82.[107] Liability in damages may flow from domestic case law or pursuant to the Community's own jurisprudence.

The leading *domestic* authority is the *Garden Cottage* case,[108] where the plaintiff

---

[104] *Notice on Co-operation*, n. 85 above, para. 20.
[105] *Regulation Implementing Art. 81 and 82*, n. 4 above, Art. 15(2).
[106] *Ibid.*, Art. 15(3).
[107] This discussion should be read in conjunction with Ch. 6; C. Jones, *Private Enforcement of Antitrust Law in the EU, UK and USA* (Oxford University Press, 1999).
[108] *Garden Cottage Foods* v. *Milk Marketing Board* [1984] AC 130.

brought an action against the Milk Marketing Board, claiming that its refusal to supply certain products was an abuse of Article 86 (now Article 82). In the course of the application for an interlocutory injunction Lord Diplock reasoned that an injunction was not necessary since damages could provide an adequate remedy. He also held that the action should be framed as one for breach of statutory duty, the statute being the European Communities Act 1972, section 2.[109] The damages issue was not finally resolved, although subsequent cases have assumed that damages are available.[110]

The ECJ's own case law has, in any event, developed since then,[111] primarily through the action for state liability in damages, and the Court has confirmed that this remedy is in principle available where a state entity is the defendant in an Article 82 action.[112] Whether damages are available as a matter of Community law where the defendant is a private party in such an action was uncertain. Advocate General van Gerven argued strongly that such relief should be available, but the ECJ did not deal with the point.[113] The matter was dealt with in *Crehan*.[114] The ECJ held that the full effectiveness of Article 81 would be put at risk if it were not open to any individual, even a party to the agreement, to claim damages for loss caused by a contract, or by conduct liable to distort competition. There should not therefore be any absolute bar in national law to such actions, even by parties to the agreement. It was however open to national law to prevent a party from being unjustly enriched or profiting from his unlawful conduct. The national court should take into account, *inter alia*, the respective bargaining strength of the contracting parties, and the extent to which a contracting party had responsibility for the breach of Article 81.

It is important to keep distinct the issue of whether there should be damages liability, and the proper standard of such liability. Assuming that such liability is imposed the central issue would be whether the requirement of serious breach derived from the jurisprudence on state liability would be required here. It might be argued that liability should not be conditional on such a finding. This might either be because the subject matter does not involve discretionary determinations of the kind in *Brasserie du Pêcheur*,[115] or because a finding of serious breach would automatically be satisfied in cases where there was an abuse of a dominant position. Opinions will doubtless differ on the first of these issues. It is, however, clear that no automatic equation can necessarily be made between serious breach and a finding of abuse for the purposes of Article 82, since, as Whish notes,[116] an undertaking may be found to have abused its dominant position without any intent or recklessness. It might then be preferable to construct the cause of action so as to allow the court to distinguish

[109] F. Jacobs, 'Damages for Breach of Article 86 EEC' (1983) 8 *ELRev*. 353.

[110] Whish, n. 2 above, 279–80.

[111] See Ch. 6 above.

[112] Case C–242/95, *GT-Link A/S* v. *De Danske Statsbaner (DSB)* [1997] ECR I–4449.

[113] Case C–128/92, *Banks & Co. Ltd.* v. *British Coal Corporation* [1994] ECR I–1209, 1245–9.

[114] Case C–453/99, *Courage Ltd.* v. *Crehan* [2001] ECR I–6297, paras. 26–36.

[115] Cases C–46 & 48/93, *Brasserie du Pêcheur and Factortame* [1996] ECR I–1029.

[116] N. 2 above, 280. See also R. Whish, 'The Enforcement of EC Competition Law in the Domestic Courts of Member States' [1994] *ECLR* 60.

reprehensible cases from those where any harm suffered by the plaintiff is an incidental effect of the defendant's infringement of the competition rules.[117]

The issue of how far benefits conferred under a contract which is illegal can be recovered is a complex topic, detailed treatment of which can be found elsewhere.[118] The relevant principles of EC law have been considered above,[119] and the ECJ has confirmed that these principles apply to recovery pursuant to an Article 81 or 82 action, at least where the defendant is a public undertaking.[120]

9. CONCLUSION

i. The enforcement regime for Community competition law is in transition, from the *traditional approach*, based on notification and the Commission's monopoly over Article 81(3), to the *new approach*, based on the direct applicability of Article 81 in its entirety.

ii. The *traditional approach was problematic*. The notification regime placed a strain on Commission resources, and this would be bound to increase with Community enlargement. The Commission's monopoly over Article 81(3) gave rise to difficult problems of co-ordination between national courts and the Commission.

iii. The *new approach will not be unproblematic*. There will be difficulties of securing uniformity in interpretation by the NCAs, and the national courts in the different Member States. There will also be problems of co-ordinating enforcement action at Community level by the Commission, and at national level by NCAs and national courts. It remains to be seen how adept are national courts at the type of analysis required of them under Article 81(3).

iv. The *new approach is none the less the best way forward*. Decentralization of enforcement is sensible, given the expansion of the Community, and the developed body of case law on Articles 81 and 82. This strategy enables the EC to make full use of NCAs, as well as national courts, in the enforcement of Community competition law. This bears analogy to the developments under Article 234, whereby national courts were 'recruited' to aid the ECJ in its enforcement of EC law.[121] There is moreover much in the new draft Council Regulation that is designed to promote co-ordination between the Commission and national authorities, and between the national authorities of different Member States. The national courts always have the option of making a reference under Article 234.

[117] Whish, n. 2 above, 280.
[118] A. Jones, 'Recovery of Benefits Conferred under Contractual Obligations Prohibited by Article 85 or 86 of the Treaty of Rome' (1996) 112 *LQR* 606.
[119] See Ch. 6 above.
[120] Case C–242/95, *GT-Link*, n. 112 above.
[121] See Ch. 11 above.

10. FURTHER READING

(a) *Books*

KERSE, C., *EC Antitrust Procedure* (Sweet & Maxwell, 4th edn., 1998)

JONES, A., and SUFRIN, B., *EC Competition Law, Text, Cases and Materials* (Oxford University Press, 2001), chs. 14–16

JONES, C., *Private Enforcement of Antitrust Law in the EU, UK and USA* (Oxford University Press, 1999)

WHISH, R., *Competition Law* (Butterworths, 4th edn., 2001), chs. 7–8

(b) *Articles*

BAEL, I., VAN, 'Fining a la Carte: The Lottery of EU Competition Law' [1995] *ECLR* 237

DOHERTY, B., 'Playing Poker with the Commission: Rights of Access to the Commission's File in Competition Cases' [1994] *ECLR* 8

EDWARD, D., 'Constitutional Rules of Community Law in EEC Competition Cases' (1989–90) 13 *Fordham Int. LJ* 111

EHLERMANN, C.-D., 'Implementation of EC Competition Law by National Anti-Trust Authorities' [1996] *ECLR* 88

—— 'The Modernization of EC Antitrust Policy: A Legal and Cultural Revolution' (2000) 37 *CMLRev.* 537

FORRESTER, I., 'Modernisation of EC Competition Law', in B. Hawk (ed.), *Fordham Corporate Law Institute* (Fordham University, 2000), ch. 12

GERBER, D., 'Modernising European Competition Law: A Developmental Perspective' [2001] *ECLR* 122

JONES, A., 'Recovery of Benefits Conferred under Contractual Obligations Prohibited by Article 85 or 86 of the Treaty of Rome' (1996) 112 *LQR* 606

JOSHUA, J., 'Balancing the Public Interests: Confidentiality, Trade Secrets and Disclosure of Evidence in EC Competition Procedures' [1994] *ECLR* 68

KERSE, C., 'Enforcing Community Competition Policy under Articles 88 and 89 of the EC Treaty—New Powers for UK Competition Authorities' [1997] *ECLR* 17

KINGSTON, S., 'A "New Division of Responsibilities" in the Proposed Regulation to Modernise the Rules Implementing Articles 81 and 82 EC? A Warning Call' [2001] *ECLR* 340

MONTI, M., 'European Competition Law for the 21st Century', in B. Hawk (ed.), *Fordham Corporate Law Institute* (Fordham University, 2001), ch. 15

NAZERALI, J., and COWAN, D., 'Modernising the Enforcement of EU Competition Rules—Can the Commission Claim to be Preaching to the Converted?' [1999] *ECLR* 442

RICHARDSON, R., 'Guidance without Guidance—A European Revolution in Fining Policy?' [1999] *ECLR* 360

RILEY, A., 'The European Cartel Office: A Guardian without Weapons?' [1997] *ECLR* 3

SCHAUB, A., 'Modernisation of EC Competition Law: Reform of Regulation No. 17', in B. Hawk (ed.), *Fordham Corporate Law Institute* (Fordham University, 2000), ch. 10

SHAW, J., 'Decentralization and Law Enforcement in EC Competition Law' (1995) 15 *Legal Studies* 128

SIRAGUSA, M., 'A Critical Review of the White Paper on the Reform of the EC Competition Law Enforcement Rules', in B. Hawk (ed.), *Fordham Corporate Law Institute* (Fordham University, 2000), ch. 15

STEVENS, D., 'The "Comfort Letter": Old Problems, New Developments' [1994] *ECLR* 81

WESSELING, R., 'The Commission White Paper on Modernisation of EC Antitrust Law: Unspoken Consequences and Incomplete Treatment of Alternative Options' [1999] *ECLR* 420

WHISH, R., 'The Enforcement of EC Competition Law in the Domestic Courts of Member States' [1994] *ECLR* 60

—— 'The Enforceability of Agreements under EC and UK Competition Law', in F. Rose (ed.), *Lex Mercatoria: Essays on International Commercial Law in Honour of Francis Reynolds* (LLP, 2000), ch. 15

—— and SUFRIN, B., 'Community Competition Law: Notification and Exemption— Goodbye to All That', in D. Hayton (ed.), *Law's Future(s): British Legal Developments in the 21st Century* (Hart, 2000), ch. 8

WILS, W., 'EC Competition Fines: To Deter or not to Deter' [1995] *YBEL* 17

—— 'The Commission's New Method for Calculating Fines in Antitrust Cases' (1998) 23 *ELRev.* 252

—— 'The Modernisation of the Enforcement of Articles 81 and 82 EC: A Legal and Economic Analysis of the Commission's Proposal for a New Council Regulation Replacing Regulation No. 17', in B. Hawk (ed.), *Fordham Corporate Law Institute* (Fordham University, 2001), ch. 18.

26

INTELLECTUAL PROPERTY

Intellectual property is a generic term which covers both industrial and artistic forms of property right. The more common species of right included within this generic term are patents, trade marks, copyright, trade names, and indications of origin.

1. CENTRAL ISSUES: PROPERTY RIGHTS VERSUS THE SINGLE MARKET

i. It is important to understand why intellectual property rights pose particular problems for Community law. A standard feature of such arrangements is that the licensee of, for example, a patent will possess an exclusive right to market the product in its area. It will often, under national systems of intellectual-property law, also have a proprietary right to prevent the import of the product into its own territory from elsewhere. In this way a series of patent licences can have the effect of dividing the Community into a number of self-contained areas within which trade and competition in the relevant goods are not possible. An essential element of the EC is a customs union. Articles 28 to 30 (ex Articles 30 to 36) have been one of the major instruments in ensuring that *Member States* do not impede intra-Community trade through tariffs, quotas, and the like. These efforts to ensure a single market shorn of trade barriers would be undermined if *private parties* could, through arrangements such as those mentioned above, effectively re-partition the Community along national lines, or indeed along any lines at all.

ii. The Community's legal response to this problem was constrained by the Treaty itself.

Article 30 (ex Article 36) provides that Articles 28 and 29 will not preclude prohibitions on imports or exports which are justified, *inter alia*, on grounds of the protection of industrial or commercial property. This is subject to the caveat that such prohibitions do not constitute a means of arbitrary discrimination or a disguised restriction on trade between Member States. The message from Article 30 was reinforced by Article 295 (ex Article 222), which states that the Treaty shall in *no way* prejudice the rules in Member States governing the system of property ownership.

iii. The judicial resolution of this problem provides a good example of the ECJ's teleological reasoning. The danger of market partitioning through intellectual-property rights had to be addressed. The wording of Articles 30 and 295 meant, however, that judicial room for manœuvre was limited. The answer provided by the ECJ was to draw a distinction between the *existence* of an intellectual property right and its *exercise*. The Treaty would protect the former, the latter would be subject to the rigours of Articles 28 and 29, and also Articles 81 and 82 (ex Articles 85 and 86).[1]

---

[1] Case 119/75, *Terrapin (Overseas) Ltd.* v. *Terranova Industrie C.A. Kapferer and Co.* [1976] ECR 1039, para. 5.

iv. The precise meaning of the existence/exercise dichotomy will be considered later. For the present it should be noted that, in analytical terms, the distinction is questionable. It is generally accepted that property as a legal concept is made up of a bundle of rights, powers, privileges, and duties. These constitute the very meaning of property. To say therefore that the Treaty serves to protect only the existence of a property right and not its exercise should not delude us into thinking that the bundle of rights, etc., which would normally comprise this type of property has survived unscathed. The licensee of an intellectual-property right would normally be able to use the right to prevent imports from outside the territory. If the ECJ states that this is no longer possible, the effect is to diminish the sum total of rights possessed by both the licensor and licensee of the right.

v. It should however also be noted that the precise degree of protection which national legal systems afford to intellectual-property rights is itself a policy decision, which varies from State to State. Viewed from this perspective the Community law approach to intellectual property appears less novel. Given that *any* legal system will have to decide on the precise steps in the chain of production which require the consent of the right owner, then EC law is simply making this determination in the context of the Community's own legal order. Given, moreover, that *many* legal systems do operate a concept of exhaustion of rights within a particular State, then it should not be considered odd for the Community to have done so within the context of the area covered by the EC. The following extract from Cornish helps to place the exhaustion of rights doctrine in perspective.

W. R. Cornish, Intellectual Property: Patents, Copyright, Trade Marks and Allied Rights[2]

The manner in which intellectual property can be deployed to divide markets varies with the kind of right held. . . . But one general concept can usefully be introduced here. In every intellectual property law it is necessary to decide which steps in the chain of production and distribution of goods require the licence of the right-owner: manufacture, first sale by the manufacturer, subsequent sales and other dealings, export and import, use. In the past, legislators have often left the answer to the courts. In many cases, both in British and foreign laws, the rights are 'exhausted' after first sale by the right-owner or with his consent. But often this is confined to first sales within the territory covered by the right—it amounts to a principle of domestic, rather than international, exhaustion. Accordingly, national rights that are subject to such limitation can still be used to prevent the importation of goods sold abroad by the national right-owner or goods which come from an associated enterprise.

2. ARTICLES 28–30: THE EXHAUSTION OF RIGHTS DOCTRINE

(a) PATENTS

Patents are a reward for inventiveness. When a company spends considerable time and money in developing a new product then it is given certain rights over the invention

---

[2] *Intellectual Property: Patents, Copyright, Trade Marks and Allied Rights* (Sweet & Maxwell, 4th edn., 1999), 41.

for a period of time. The leading decision on the application of the Treaty to patents is *Centrafarm*.

Case 15/74, Centrafarm BV v. Sterling Drug Inc.
[1974] ECR 1147

[Note ToA renumbering: Arts. 30 and 36 are now Arts. 28 and 30]

Sterling Drug was a company based in New York, which held patents in several countries, including Holland and Great Britain, covering the method of preparing a drug for the treatment of urinary-tract infections. Centrafarm imported this drug into Holland from England and Germany without the agreement of Sterling Drug. The drug was considerably cheaper in England than it was in Holland, and this was the motivation for Centrafarm's actions. The drugs had been placed on the market in England and Germany by subsidiaries of Sterling Drug. Could Sterling obtain injunctive relief against Centrafarm to prevent it from selling the drug in Holland? Dutch law said that it could. The ECJ quoted Article 30 and then continued as follows.

THE ECJ

6. By Article 36 these provisions shall nevertheless not include prohibitions or restrictions on imports justified on grounds of the protection of industrial or commercial property.

7. Nevertheless, it is clear from this same Article, in particular its second sentence, as well as from the context, that whilst the Treaty does not affect the existence of rights recognized by the legislation of a Member State in matters of industrial and commercial property, yet the exercise of these rights may nevertheless . . . be affected by the prohibitions of the Treaty.

8. Inasmuch as it provides an exception to one of the fundamental principles of the common market, Article 36 in fact only admits of derogations from the free movement of goods where such derogations are justified for the purpose of safeguarding rights which constitute the specific subject matter of this property.

9. As regards patents, the specific object of industrial property is inter alia to ensure to the holder, so as to recompense the creative effort of the inventor, the exclusive right to utilise an invention with a view to manufacture and first putting into circulation of industrial products, either directly or by the grant of licences to third parties, as well as the right to oppose any infringement.

10. The existence, in national law on industrial and commercial property, of provisions that the right of a patentee is not exhausted by the marketing in another Member State of the patented product, so that the patentee may oppose the import into his own State of the product marketed in another State, may constitute an obstacle to the free movement of goods.

11. While such an obstacle to free movement may be justifiable for reasons of protection of industrial property when the protection is invoked against a product coming from a Member State in which it is not patentable and has been manufactured by third parties without the consent of the patentee or where the original patentees are legally and economically independent of each other, the derogation to the principle of free movement of goods is not justified when the product has been lawfully put by the patentee himself or with his consent, on the market of the Member State from which it is being imported, e.g., in the case of the holder of parallel patents.

12. If a patentee could forbid the import of protected products which had been marketed in another Member State by him or with his consent he would be enabled to partition the national markets and thus to maintain a restriction on the trade between the Member States without such a restriction being necessary for him to enjoy the substance of the exclusive rights deriving from the parallel patents.

. . .

15. The question should therefore be answered to the effect that the exercise by a patentee of the right given him by the laws of a Member State to prohibit the marketing in that State of a product protected by the patent and put on the market in another Member State by such patentee or with his consent would be incompatible with the rules of the EEC Treaty relating to the free movement of goods in the Common Market.

The judgment therefore defined the *existence* or *specific subject-matter* of the patent as being the right of the patent-holder itself, or through its licensees, to market the product initially and, as a necessary corollary, the right to bring actions for any infringement of this right. This was the reward for inventiveness that the patent was designed to secure. Community law did not affect it.

Community law would however control the *exercise* of the right, once the product had initially been marketed in this manner. The *exhaustion of rights* doctrine gave expression to the limitations imposed on the exercise of the right. The patent holder's rights were exhausted, in the sense that it could not prevent the goods from being bought by a third party in a country where the patentee or its licensee had marketed the goods and sold into another country. It was irrelevant in this respect whether the patentee and licensee belonged to the same corporate group. The fact that a firm was a licensee, and hence selling with the consent of the patentee, sufficed to bring the exhaustion of rights doctrine into play.[3]

There were only two situations in which the patentee or its licensee could obtain injunctive relief of the type being sought here. This was where it was sought against goods coming from a State where they were not patentable, and had been manufactured by third parties without the consent of the patentee, or where the original patentees were legally and economically independent of each other (paragraph 11). Neither of these is in reality an exception to the exhaustion of rights doctrine, since in neither instance has the original patentee obtained the benefit of the initial marketing of the goods.

It is clear, moreover, that the ECJ will strictly construe any qualifications to the exhaustion of rights doctrine. We have seen that one such qualification operates where the goods are imported from a country where they are not patentable *and* they have been made by third parties without the consent of the patentee. It is clear that both conditions must be met. Thus, if the patentee chooses to market the goods in a State where there is no patent protection available, then it cannot use its patent rights in a different country to prevent the import of these products. This is evident from

---

[3] See paras. 16–20 of the ECJ's judgment. See, however, the discussion at 1103–8 below, concerning the position where intellectual-property rights are assigned rather than licensed.

Merck v. *Stephar*.[4] Merck held a patent in Holland for a certain drug. Stephar had imported the same goods into Holland from Italy where they were not patentable, but had been placed on the market by Merck none the less. Merck argued that *Centrafarm* should be distinguished, since in this case it had not been able to obtain patent protection in Italy, and hence its sales in that country did not secure it any monopoly return. The ECJ was unconvinced:[5]

It is for the proprietor of the patent to decide, in the light of all the circumstances, under what conditions he will market his product, including the possibility of marketing it in a Member State where the law does not provide patent protection for the product in question. If he decides to do so he must accept the consequences of his choice as regards the free movement of the product within the Common Market, which is a fundamental principle forming part of the legal and economic circumstances which must be taken into account by the proprietor of the patent in determining the manner in which his exclusive right will be exercised.

The patent holder therefore has a stark choice. It can choose not to market in a country such as Italy, in which patent protection is not available, with the consequence that it can use its Dutch patent rights to prevent the import of any such goods from Italy into Holland. It can choose to make any possible gains from the Italian market by consenting to the manufacture of its goods in that country, but then it cannot legally prevent the import of the goods into Holland. A more recent attempt to overturn the *Merck* case was unsuccessful.[6]

It is, then, as Advocate General Mancini stated in the *Pharmon* case,[7] the patentee or licensee's consent which 'opens the door of the common market to patented products'. It is not the actual realization of a monopoly profit. Where there is no such consent, then import of the goods can be prevented. This will be so where the goods were initially marketed by a third party without the consent of the patentee; where the initial sale was made because of a legal obligation imposed by national or Community law;[8] or where that sale was the result of a compulsory licence, as demonstrated by the *Pharmon* case itself.

Case 19/84, Pharmon BV v. Hoechst AG
[1985] ECR 2281

[Note ToA renumbering: Arts. 30 and 36 are now Arts. 28 and 30]

Hoechst owned patents for a certain drug in Holland and Great Britain. A company in the United Kingdom, DDSA, obtained a compulsory licence for the product pursuant to United Kingdom law; the licence prohibited exportation of the goods and was non-assignable. In breach of this condition

---

[4] Case 187/80 [1981] ECR 2063.
[5] *Ibid.*, 2081–2 (ECR).
[6] Cases C–267–268/95, *Merck & Co Ltd.* v. *Primecrown Ltd.* [1996] ECR I–6285.
[7] Case 19/84, *Pharmon BV* v. *Hoechst AG* [1985] ECR 2281, 2288. See also Case C–316/95, *Generics BV v. Smith Kline & French Laboratories Ltd.* [1997] ECR I–3929.
[8] Cases C–267–268/95, n. 6 above, para. 41, where the ECJ also affirmed the correctness of the ruling in *Pharmon*.

DDSA sold to Pharmon, a Dutch company, a large consignment of the drugs which it had made. Pharmon sought to market these in the Netherlands, and Hoechst sought an injunction to prevent Pharmon from infringing Hoechst's Dutch patent. So the key question was could Hoechst use its patent rights in the Netherlands to prevent the marketing of goods which had been obtained from a third party pursuant to a compulsory licence which that third party had been granted under a parallel patent? Pharmon argued that there was little difference between a licence freely granted and a compulsory licence: the existence of either served to exhaust the patentee's rights. The ECJ disagreed.

THE ECJ

22. It must be recalled that the Court has consistently held that Articles 30 and 36 of the EEC Treaty preclude the application of national provisions which enable a patent proprietor to prevent the importation and marketing of a product which has been lawfully marketed in another Member State by the patent proprietor himself, with his consent, or by a person economically or legally dependent on him.

23. If a patent proprietor could preclude the importation of protected products marketed in another Member State by him or with his consent, he would be able to partition the national markets and thus restrict trade between the Member States, although such a restriction is not necessary to protect the substance of the exclusive rights under the patents.

24. The Hoge Raad's question is therefore essentially intended to establish whether the same rules apply where the product imported and offered for sale has been manufactured in the exporting Member State by the holder of a compulsory licence granted in respect of a parallel patent held by the proprietor of the patent in the importing Member State.

25. It is necessary to point out that where, as in this instance, the competent authorities of a Member State grant a third party a compulsory licence which allows him to carry out manufacturing and marketing operations which the patentee would normally have the right to prevent, the patentee cannot be deemed to have consented to the operation of that third party.

26. As the Court most recently held in its judgment of 14 July 1981 (*Merck* ...), the substance of a patent lies essentially in according the inventor an exclusive right of first placing the product on the market so as to allow him to obtain the reward for his creative efforts. It is therefore necessary to allow the patent proprietor to prevent the importation and marketing of products manufactured under a compulsory licence in order to protect the substance of his exclusive rights under his patent.

(b) TRADE MARKS

Trade marks, such as Coca-Cola or Martini, serve two related ends. They ensure to the holder of the mark the goodwill associated with the marked product, which may entail considerable expenditure by the manufacturer. They also inform the customer that the product is of a specific kind, as opposed to a copy, thereby avoiding the risk of confusion.[9] The *Centrafarm* case laid the initial foundations of EC law in this area.

---

[9] Case C–317/91, *Deutsche Renault AG* v. *Audi AG* [1993] ECR I–6227; Case C–251/95, *SABEL BV* v. *Puma AG* [1997] ECR I–6191; Case C–39/97, *Canon Kabushiki Kaisha* v. *Metro-Goldwyn-Mayer Inc.* [1998] ECR I–5507; Case C–255/97, *Pfeiffer GroBshandel GmbH* v. *Lowa Warenhandel GmbH* [1999] ECR I–2835.

Case 16/74, Centrafarm BV v. Winthrop BV
[1974] ECR 1183

This case arose out of the same facts as *Centrafarm* v. *Sterling Drug*, considered above. Sterling Drug (SD) held a trade mark for its patented drug. The trade mark was 'Negram', and was held in the United Kingdom by Sterling-Winthrop Group Ltd. and in Holland by a subsidiary, Winthrop BV. Centrafarm imported the drugs into Holland from the United Kingdom and Germany where they had been placed on the market by subsidiaries of SD. Some of the goods imported bore the 'Negram' mark. Winthrop BV sought to prevent this as an infringement of the mark which it held in Holland; Dutch law afforded Winthrop BV the relief it claimed. The question for the ECJ was whether EC law forbade a trade-mark holder such as Winthrop BV from preventing the import of marked goods which originated in another country where they had been placed on the market of that other country by the trade-mark owner or with its consent. The ECJ repeated the general principles which it had enunciated in the related case on patents. It then proceeded to apply this reasoning to trade marks.

8. As regards trade marks, the specific object of commercial property is *inter alia* to ensure to the holder the exclusive right to utilise the mark for the first putting into circulation of a product, and to protect him thus against competitors who would take advantage of the position and reputation of the mark by selling goods improperly bearing that mark.

9. The existence, in national laws on industrial and commercial property, of provisions that the right of the trade mark holder is not exhausted by the marketing in another Member State of the product protected by the mark, so that the holder may oppose the import into his own State of the product marketed in another State, may constitute an obstacle to the free movement of goods.

10. Such an obstacle is not justified when the product has been lawfully put, by the holder himself or with his consent, on the market of the Member State from which it is imported in such a way that there can be no question of abuse or infringement of the mark.

11. If the holder of the mark could forbid the import of the protected products, which had been marketed in another State by him or with his consent, he would be enabled to partition the national markets and thus to maintain a restriction on the trade between the Member States without such a restriction being necessary for him to enjoy the substance of the exclusive right deriving from the mark.

12. The question should therefore be answered to the effect that the exercise by the holder of a mark of the right given him by the laws of a Member State to prohibit the marketing in that State of a product bearing the mark put on the market in another Member State by such holder or with his consent would be incompatible with the rules of the EEC Treaty relating to the free movement of goods in the Common Market.

The ECJ's reasoning followed closely that used in the related case on patents. The *specific object* of a trade mark, which would be protected by Community law, was the right to place the goods initially on the market. This, said the Court, would safeguard the holder of the mark against competitors who sought to take advantage of the reputation possessed by the marked goods by selling goods which improperly bore that mark. In this sense Community law would recognize and protect the *existence* of this property right.

The *exercise* of national trade-mark rights would be controlled by EC law. *Consent* was the key to the *exhaustion of rights*. It was the placing of the goods[10] on the market[11] by the trade-mark holder itself, or with its consent, which exhausted the rights of all those who derived their mark through its initial holder. It is, however, clear that the consent principle will only apply so as to exhaust rights where the owners of the trade mark in the importing and exporting States are the same, or where, even though they are separate, they are economically linked.[12]

This latter idea will cover products placed into circulation by the same undertaking, by a licensee, by a parent company, by a subsidiary of the same group, or by an exclusive distributor. It will not normally cover the situation where goods are placed on the market by an assignee of a trade mark, if there is no legal or economic link between the assignor and the assignee. The rationale for this will be considered more fully below.[13] The application of these principles can, however, be problematic, since the importer may alter the packaging of the goods. This occurred in the following case.

Case 102/77, Hoffmann-La Roche & Co. AG v. Centrafarm Vertriebsgesellschaft Pharmazeutischer Erzeugnisse mbH
[1978] ECR 1139[14]

[Note ToA renumbering: Art. 36 is now Art. 30]

Hoffmann-La Roche (HLR) manufactured a drug under the mark 'Valium Roche' in Germany in batches of twenty to fifty for individual use, and 100 to 250 for hospital use. The British subsidiary of HLR marketed the same product at lower prices than in Germany in batches of 100 to 500. Centrafarm bought supplies of the drug in England, which it put into packages of 1,000 tablets. Centrafarm affixed the HLR trade mark, together with a notice that the product had been marketed by Centrafarm. Centrafarm also stated that it intended to repack tablets into smaller packages for sale to individuals. HLR sought to prevent this and under German law would be able to do so. The ECJ repeated its view from *Centrafarm* v. *Winthrop*

---

[10] The exhaustion principle operates only in relation to individual items of the product placed on the market with the owner's consent. If there are other individual items in the product placed on the market without the owner's consent, then the trade mark can still be used: Case C–173/98, *Sebago Inc., and Ancienne Maison Dubois et Fils* v. *G-B Unic SA* [1999] ECR I–4103. On the meaning of consent, see Cases C–414–416/99, *Zino Davidoff SA* v. *A & G Imports Ltd.* [2001] ECR I–8691, paras. 33, 35, 47.

[11] This means the market of the Member States, including the EEA. It does not include goods placed on the market of other States: Case C–355/96, *Silhouette International Schmied GmbH & Co. KG* v. *Hartlauer Handelsgesellschaft mbH* [1998] ECR I–4799.

[12] Case C–9/93, *IHT Internationale Heiztechnik GmbH* v. *Ideal-Standard GmbH* [1994] ECR I–2789.

[13] See 1103–8 below.

[14] See also Case 1/81, *Pfizer* v. *Eurim-Pharm* [1981] ECR 2913; Cases C–427, 429, & 436/93, *Bristol-Myers Squibb* v. *Paranova A/S* [1996] ECR I–3457; Cases C–71–73/94, *Eurim-Pharm Arzneimittel GmbH* v. *Beiersdorf AG* [1996] ECR I–3603; Case C–337/95, *Parfums Christian Dior SA* v. *Evora BV* [1997] ECR I–6013; Case C–349/95, *Frits Loendersloot, trading as F. Loendersloot Internationale Expeditie* v. *George Ballantine & Son Ltd.* [1997] ECR I–6227; Case C–379/97, *Pharmacia & Upjohn SA, formerly Upjohn SA* v. *Paranova A/S* [1999] ECR I–6927.

(paragraph 8) on what constituted the specific subject-matter of a trade mark. It then continued as follows.

THE ECJ

7. . . . In order to answer the question whether that exclusive right involves the right to prevent the trade mark being affixed by a third person after the product has been repackaged, regard must be had to the essential function of the trade mark, which is to guarantee the identity of the origin of the trade-marked product to the consumer or ultimate user, by enabling him without any possibility of confusion to distinguish that product from products which have another origin. This guarantee of origin means that the consumer or ultimate user can be certain that a trade-marked product which is sold to him has not been subject at a previous stage of marketing to interference by a third person, without the authorisation of the proprietor of the trade mark, such as to affect the original condition of the product. The right attributed to the proprietor of preventing any use of the trade mark which is likely to impair the guarantee of origin so understood is therefore part of the specific subject-matter of the trade mark right.

8. It is accordingly justified under the first sentence of Article 36 to recognise that the proprietor of a trade mark right is entitled to prevent an importer of a trade-marked product, following repackaging of that product, from affixing the trade mark to the new packaging without the authorisation of the proprietor.

9. It is however necessary to consider whether the exercise of such a right may constitute a 'disguised restriction on trade between Member States' within the meaning of the second sentence of Article 36. Such a restriction might arise, *inter alia*, from the proprietor of the trade mark putting on to the market in various Member States an identical product in various packages while availing himself of the rights inherent in the trade mark to prevent repackaging by a third person even if it were done in such a way that the identity of origin of the trade-marked product and its original condition could not be affected. The question, therefore, in the present case is whether the repackaging of a trade-marked product such as that undertaken by Centrafarm is capable of affecting the original condition of the product.

10. In this respect the answer must vary according to the circumstances and in particular according to the nature of the product and the method of repackaging. Depending on the nature of the product, repackaging in many cases inevitably affects its condition, while in others repackaging involves a more or less obvious risk that the product might be interfered with or its original condition otherwise affected. Nevertheless, it is possible to conceive of the repackaging being undertaken in such a way that the original condition of the product cannot be affected. This may be so where, for example, the proprietor of the trade mark has marketed the product in double packaging and the repackaging affects only the external packaging, leaving the internal packaging intact, or where the repackaging is inspected by a public authority for the purpose of ensuring that the product is not adversely affected. Where the essential function of the trade mark to guarantee the origin of the product is thus protected, the exercise of his rights by the proprietor of the trade mark in order to fetter the free movement of goods between Member States may constitute a disguised restriction within the meaning of the second sentence of Article 36 of the Treaty if it is established that the use of the trade mark right by the proprietor, having regard to the marketing system which he has adopted, will contribute to the artificial partitioning of the markets between Member States.

A similar problem arose in *Centrafarm BV* v. *American Home Products Corporation*.[15] In this case American Home Products (AHP) owned trade marks for the same product in different Member States. Centrafarm was once again the hero or the villain of the piece, depending upon one's perspective. It bought the product which had been lawfully marketed in the United Kingdom under one trade mark, and then imported it into Holland, where it sold it under the mark used for the goods in that country. The product was unaltered. The ECJ held that importation under these circumstances *could be* prevented by AHP. The right to affix a particular trade mark to a product was, said the Court, part of the specific subject-matter of the trade mark; it went to the existence of the mark itself. AHP could therefore prevent Centrafarm from changing the mark, since this would thereby safeguard the guarantee of origin, which was one of the main purposes of a trade mark. This was so even where, as here, the goods had lawfully been placed on the market of a State under one trade mark.[16] The Court accepted that it was legitimate for a company to use varying marks in different States. It was however mindful of the possibility that a company might seek, in the light of the ECJ's reasoning, to use different marks in different States with the intention of partitioning the market. If this was so it would constitute a disguised restriction on trade within the meaning of Article 36 (now Article 30) and would be unlawful. It was for the national courts to decide in any particular case whether this was the object of the trade-mark holder.[17]

(c) COPYRIGHT

The ECJ has applied the same basic approach to copyright as it has to patents and trade marks. The application of these principles may, however, be more complex in this area. This is in part because of the variety of artistic work covered by copyright laws. Thus copyright law will apply, albeit in different ways, to literary, dramatic, and musical work; to artistic work; to sound recording; to film; and to broadcast or cablecast. This very diversity means that the purpose behind copyright protection may not always be the same. The basic root of copyright may well be to protect the ownership of a certain book, play, etc., from reproduction without the consent of the author. However, the form of this reproduction may differ significantly from, for example, the unauthorized reproduction of a song into a sound recording, to the illegal performance of a play on a number of occasions without the consent of the author. It is for these reasons that it may be difficult to state with exactitude what the 'specific subject-matter' of copyright protection actually is, with the consequence that the impact of EC law may not always be clear.

An early case on copyright was *Deutsche Grammophon* v. *Metro*.[18] As in the cases concerning patents and trade marks, price differentials lay at the heart of the matter. Deutsche Grammophon (DG) made records and sold them in Germany under a

---

[15] Case 3/78, [1978] ECR 1823.   [16] *Ibid.*, paras. 11–18.
[17] *Ibid.*, paras. 19–23.   [18] Case 78/70, [1971] ECR 487.

retail-price-maintenance scheme. It exported records to France where Polydor, a sub-sidiary of DG, marketed them. Metro obtained records sold by Polydor in France and resold them in Germany at prices below the established price. DG used its exclusive right of distribution under German law, which was a right similar to copyright, in order to prevent Metro's actions. The ECJ based its judgment on the notion of consent. DG had placed the records on the market through Polydor in France, and could not therefore complain when Metro sought to import them into Germany. National laws which allowed a firm such as DG to do this would be contrary to the principles of free movement of goods.

A more complete enunciation of Community law as it applies to copyright is to be found in the next case, which also concerned records.

Cases 55 and 57/80, Musik-Vertrieb Membran GmbH v. Gesellschaft für Musikalische Aufführungs- und Mechanische Vervielfältigungsrechte (GEMA) [1981] ECR 147

[Note ToA renumbering: Arts. 30 and 36 are now Arts. 28 and 30]

GEMA was the German copyright-management society. Certain records were imported into Germany from other Member States. These records had been manufactured and placed on those markets with the consent of the copyright owner, but the royalties had been calculated only on the basis of distribution in the country of manufacture. GEMA claimed that its members were entitled to an extra royalty when the goods were imported into Germany, which was to be calculated on the basis of the German royalty less the amount of the lower royalty which had already been paid in the country of manufacture. This claim was recognized in German national law. Was it compatible with Articles 30 to 36?

THE ECJ

10. It is apparent from the well-established case law of the Court and most recently from the judgment . . . in Case 119/75, *Terrapin Overseas Ltd.* that the proprietor of an industrial or commercial right protected by the law of a Member State cannot rely on that law to prevent the importation of a product which has been lawfully marketed in another Member State by the proprietor himself or with his consent.

. . .

16. GEMA has argued that such an interpretation of Articles 30–36 of the Treaty is not sufficient to resolve the problem facing the national court since GEMA's application to the German courts is not for the prohibition or restriction of the marketing of the gramophone records and tape cassettes in question on German territory but for equality in the royalties paid for any distribution of those sound recordings on the German market. The owner of a copyright in a recorded musical work has a legitimate interest in receiving and retaining the benefit of his intellectual or artistic effort regardless of the degree to which his work is distributed and consequently it is maintained that he should not lose the right to claim royalties equal to those paid in the country in which the recorded work is marketed.

17. It should first be observed that the question put by the national court is concerned with the legal consequences of infringement of copyright. . . . On any view its claims are in fact founded on

the copyright owner's exclusive right of exploitation, which enables him to prohibit or restrict the free movement of the products incorporating the protected musical work.

18. It should be observed next that no provision of national legislation may permit an under-taking which is responsible for the management of copyrights and has a monopoly on the territory of a Member State by virtue of that management to charge a levy on products imported from another Member State where they were put into circulation by or with the consent of the copyright owner and thereby cause the Common Market to be partitioned. Such a practice would amount to allowing a private undertaking to impose a charge on the importation of sound recordings which are already in free circulation in the Common Market on account of their crossing a frontier; it would have the effect of entrenching the isolation of national markets which the Treaty seeks to abolish.

19. It follows from those considerations that this argument must be rejected as being incompatible with the operation of the Common Market and with the aims of the Treaty.

. . .

25. It should further be observed that in a common market distinguished by free movement of goods and freedom to provide services an author . . . is free to choose the place, in any of the Member States, in which to put his work into circulation. He may make that choice according to his best interests, which involve not only the level of remuneration provided in the Member State in question but other factors such as, for example, the opportunities for distributing his work and the marketing facilities which are further enhanced by virtue of the free movement of goods within the Community. In those circumstances, a copyright management society may not be permitted to claim, on the importation of sound recordings into another Member State, payment of additional fees based on the difference in the rates of remuneration in the various Member States.

The ECJ's reasoning flowed neatly from its initial premise that consent was the controlling criterion. GEMA would have no right to prevent the import of goods that had been placed in free circulation with its consent in other States (paragraph 10). Any claim for the extra royalty would, in effect, be based on the continuing existence in the copyright holder of a right to control the movement of such goods when they had been placed on the market with its consent (paragraph 17). The continued exist-ence of this right and the consequent ability to levy the extra royalty were inconsistent with the principle that a consensual placing of the goods on the market exhausted the rights of the copyright-holder (paragraph 18). The message was clear, and it was the same as in the context of patents. If the copyright-holder wished to reap the benefits of placing the goods on the market in one State, then it would have to be content with the return it received in that State. It would not be able to 'top up' relatively low royalties in State A if and when the goods were imported into State B (paragraph 25).[19]

---

[19] The ECJ was not dissuaded from this conclusion by the fact that the effect of the UK Copyright Act 1956 was to place a relatively low ceiling on royalty levels. The resulting disparity between national laws was something which should be resolved through Community harmonization. It did not justify the proposition that, in the absence of harmonization, national laws on intellectual property were predominant over free movement of goods: [1981] ECR 147, paras. 14, 21–4.

The ECJ's decision in *GEMA* identified its general strategy towards conflicts between EC law and national regimes on copyright. This strategy can none the less be problematic.

The first problem revolves around the *meaning of consent*. This issue arose in *EMI Electrola*.[20] In this case EMI Electrola was a German company which was the assignee of rights to works by Cliff Richard. It objected to the import from Denmark of Cliff Richard records. The defendant argued that EMI's rights were exhausted, and that the records had been lawfully marketed in Denmark because the period of protection under Danish copyright law had expired. It was open to the Court to reach one of two conclusions. It could find for the defendant on the basis that the time for copyright protection had run out in Denmark, that the copyright holder had enjoyed his legitimate protection, and that therefore the goods could move freely from Denmark elsewhere. It could alternatively decide that the sale in Denmark was not with the consent of the copyright holder, but only because the copyright had run out, and that therefore this was not a consensual exhaustion of rights within the *GEMA* principle. The ECJ adopted the latter course and held that the plaintiff could prevent the import into Germany.

The second problem arises because of *the difficulty of deciding on the specific subject matter of a particular copyright*. This difficulty flows from the real differences between copyright claims. Cases such as *GEMA* centred on copyright, where the subject matter of the claim arose in connection with literary works. The placing of those works at the disposal of the public involved their actual circulation in the form of books or records. The ECJ decided that the specific subject matter of copyright was the right of the author to reproduce and distribute the work. Where the author has consented to that, either personally or through another, then these rights will generally be exhausted. The matter is more complex when the nature of the copyright differs. Films, for example, are made available through public cinema, one characteristic of which is repeated performances. Fees will be calculated on the basis of the actual or probable number of performances. In this type of case it may therefore be necessary to characterize the specific subject matter of the copyright differently from the case of the one-off sale. Two cases exemplify this problem.

In *Coditel*[21] Ciné Vog Films (CVF) brought an action for infringement of copyright for damage caused to it by the reception in Belgium of a broadcast from Germany of a Chabrol film, *Le Boucher*, for which CVF had the exclusive distribution rights in Belgium. The showing of the film on television had, said CVF, jeopardized the commercial future of the film at cinemas in Belgium. The action was brought against the company that gave CVF the exclusive right, and against Coditel, the Belgian cable company, which had transmitted the film from Germany to Belgium. The question before the Court was whether Articles 59 and 60 (now Article 49 and 50) prohibited an assignment of the copyright of a film which was limited to one Member State, the argument being that a series of such assignments could lead to the partitioning of the Community market.

---

[20] Case 341/87, *EMI Electrola GmbH* v. *Patricia Im- und Export* [1989] ECR 79.
[21] Case 62/79, *SA Compagnie Générale pour la Diffusion de la Télévision, Coditel* v. *SA Ciné Vog Films* [1980] ECR 881.

The ECJ held that there was no infringement of the Treaty. It accepted that, in the case of books or records, the specific subject-matter was the right of exclusive initial reproduction or distribution of the work. It was, said the Court, different where, as in the case of a film, it was meant to be repeated. In this type of case the specific subject-matter of the copyright was different: 'the right of a copyright owner and his assigns to require fees for any showing of a film is part of the essential function of copyright in this type of literary and artistic work'.[22] The realization of the copyright in films, and the fees attaching thereto, could not therefore be attained without considering the possibility of television broadcasts, since this would lessen any revenue obtainable from showings at the cinema. The ECJ concluded that CVF could rely on its exclusive assignment for the film in Belgium. This enabled it to seek compensation for the showing of the film by Coditel, even though Coditel transmitted the film after it was shown in Germany with the consent of the original copyright-holder.[23]

The next decision is more problematic and demonstrates that there may be real difficulties in actually characterizing the nature of the copyright subject matter which is at stake. In *Warner Brothers*[24] Warner owned the United Kingdom copyright in the film *Never Say Never Again*. It assigned the video production rights in Denmark to Metronome. The videocassette was on sale in London, and Christiansen bought it with a view to hiring it out in Denmark. Warner and Metronome sought to prevent this. Under Danish law this was possible, since the author of a work had to give his or her consent to a hiring out. Under United Kingdom law the author could control the initial sale of a work, but had no control over any subsequent hiring out.

Advocate General Mancini had no doubt that the case *was* covered by *GEMA*. He reasoned as follows. The *GEMA* case had applied the exhaustion principle to copyright, provided that the sale of the work was by the author, etc., or with its consent. Although hiring out was obviously different from sale, both involved making the product available to the consumer. The consensual principle from *GEMA* applied accordingly. The initial sale exhausted the proprietary rights of the original owner of the work. It could henceforth move freely within the EC. The author could not therefore maintain any residual right to control the hiring of the work.[25]

The ECJ by way of contrast was equally clear that this case *was not* covered by *GEMA*. Christiansen relied on *GEMA* to argue that the copyright owner made its own marketing choice; if it chose to sell the video in a country which then afforded the seller no control over hiring out, so be it. The seller's rights over subsequent sale or hire were exhausted irrespective of whether or not the country of import gave the author power over hiring out. The ECJ disagreed. An important factor for the Court was that royalties have traditionally been collected only on sales, not hiring out. This has made it impossible for the film maker to gain a satisfactory return from the rental market. It therefore held that national laws designed to provide specific protection for the film maker in the hiring market were justified in principle as a protection of

---

[22] *Ibid.*, para. 14.   [23] *Ibid.*, para. 18.
[24] Case 158/86, *Warner Brothers and Metronome Video ApS v. Christiansen* [1988] ECR 2605.
[25] *Ibid.*, 2623–4.

an industrial property right within Article 36 (now Article 30). The defendant's argument based on *GEMA* could not be accepted, since 'where national legislation confers on authors a specific right to hire out video-cassettes, that right would be rendered worthless if its owner were not in a position to authorize the operations for doing so'.[26]

The ECJ's reasoning is difficult to reconcile with that in *GEMA*. The key to the ECJ's analysis in *Warner Brothers* is its acceptance of the fact that the poor return to authors from the rental market justified laws, such as those in Denmark, which gave the author power over hiring out, and served to qualify the exhaustion of rights principle. Yet in *GEMA* it was unconvinced by the argument that the way in which the royalty system operated in some countries meant the returns to authors, etc., would always be lower from those countries, thereby justifying the extra fee which GEMA sought on import of the records into Germany. The Court was not willing to accept that this could qualify the exhaustion principle. Problems of this kind should, it said, be addressed by harmonization.

The only way to reconcile the two cases is to accept, as the Court did in *Warner Brothers*, that the nature of the copyright was different from that in *GEMA*. This was the essential reason for the difference between the Advocate General and the Court itself. The former simply treated any rights that the copyright owner might have over hire as but part of the rights that it might have over sale and subsequent distribution. The Court, in effect, disaggregated the two issues, and was willing to recognize that there was a valid and separate issue concerning copyright protection, which related to hire. Given this crucial step, it was then willing to accept national laws that protected the specific subject matter of *this* facet of copyright.[27] The ECJ has confirmed this approach in *Metronome*.[28]

Case C-200/96, Metronome Musik GmbH v. Music Point Hokamp GmbH
[1998] ECR I-1953

Metronome produced a compact disc, 'Planet Punk', and sought to restrain Hokamp from renting it out. Directive 92/100 on rental rights provided, in Article 1(4), that the initial sale of the item or other act of distribution did not exhaust the rental rights of the copyright owner. Hokamp argued that this provision of the Directive was contrary to EC law, in particular the right to pursue a trade. The ECJ disagreed. It repeated the standard formula that the right would be exhausted after the initial marketing by the owner, or with her consent. It then distinguished between exhaustion in relation to sale and rental.

THE ECJ

15. However, as the Court pointed out in Case 156/86, *Warner Brothers* . . ., literary and artistic works may be the subject of commercial exploitation by means other than the sale of the

---

[26] *Ibid.*, para. 18.
[27] This was the rationalization of the case in Cases C–267–268/95, *Merck*, n. 6 above, para. 42.
[28] See also Case C–61/97, *FDV* v. *Laserdisken* [1998] ECR I–5171.

recordings made of them. That applies, for example, to the rental of video-cassettes, which reach a different public from the market for their sale and constitutes an important potential source of revenue for makers of film.

16. In that connection, the Court observed that, by authorising the collection of royalties only on sales to private individuals and to persons hiring out video-cassettes, it is impossible to guarantee to makers of films a remuneration which reflects the number of occasions on which the video-cassettes are actually hired out and which secures for them a satisfactory share of the rental market. Laws which provide specific protection of the right to hire out video-cassettes are therefore clearly justified on grounds of the protection of industrial and commercial property . . . (*Warner* . . .).

17. In the same judgment, the Court rejected the argument that a maker of a film who has offered . . . that film for sale in a Member State whose legislation confers on him no exclusive right of hiring it out must accept the consequences of his choice and the exhaustion of his right to restrain the hiring-out . . . in any other Member State. Where national legislation confers on authors a specific right to hire out video-cassettes, that right would be worthless if the owner were not in a position to authorise the operations for doing so. . . .

. . .

20. The introduction by the Community legislation of an exclusive rental right cannot therefore constitute any breach of the principle of exhaustion of the distribution right, the purpose and scope of which are different.

3. THE LIMITS OF ARTICLES 28–30: THE DEMISE OF THE COMMON ORIGIN DOCTRINE AND THE LIMITS OF CONSENT

The discussion thus far has focused upon the application of Articles 28 to 30 to intellectual-property rights. We have noted the conceptual basis of the ECJ's jurisprudence, in the form of the exhaustion of rights doctrine, and the limits placed on this idea. The Court has, however, applied Community law to intellectual-property rights beyond the exhaustion of rights doctrine. It has held that trade marks can be caught by Community law on the basis of their common origin. The relevant ECJ decisions were much criticized and, as will be seen below, the Court has now departed from its own previous rulings. Some understanding of this case law is none the less important because of the light it sheds on the more general approach of the ECJ to the relationship between intellectual-property rights and the EC Treaty. The subsequent discussion will show why it is so important to delineate accurately the specific subject matter of a particular intellectual-property right.

The villain of the peace was the decision by the ECJ in *Hag*.[29] The trade mark for the decaffeinated coffee 'Hag' was originally owned by Hag AG, a German company. It registered the mark in Germany, Belgium, and Luxembourg. In 1927 the mark for the latter two countries was transferred to a subsidiary of Hag AG based in Belgium. After the war in 1944 German property in Belgium was sequestered, and the shares in the

---

[29] Case 192/73, *Van Zuylen Frères* v. *Hag AG* [1974] ECR 731.

subsidiary were sold to the Van Oevelen family. In 1971 this trade mark in Hag was further transferred to Van Zuylen Frères (VZF). The German Hag company then sought to sell coffee in Luxembourg and VZF sought an injunction to prevent this, arguing that the sale infringed its trade-mark rights for that country.

The ECJ considered whether the grant of an injunction would infringe Articles 30 to 36 (now Article 28 to 30). The ECJ held that it could, and that this was so even though there was no financial, legal, or economic connection between VZF and Hag AG, the German company. The ECJ reasoned that trade marks could have the effect of partitioning the common market, more particularly since they were not subject to any temporal limit.[30] It was therefore incompatible with Articles 30 to 36 to allow the owner of a mark in one State to prevent the import of goods bearing the same mark from another State, where the mark had the same origin. This was so notwithstanding the fact that there was no connection between the relevant firms.[31] The ECJ acknowledged that a trade mark performed the function of indicating the origin of the products, but said that this could be accomplished by other means, which would not have the same detrimental effect on the free movement of goods.[32] There are two particular problems with this reasoning.

On the one hand, the Court's reasoning reduced the specific subject matter of the trade mark to almost vanishing point. We have already noted that trade marks serve two related ends: protection of the manufacturer's goodwill and an indication for the consumer that the product was of a specific kind and quality. Yet the reasoning of the Court in *Hag* ignored the first of these arguments, and purported to address the second by the weak response that this objective could be met in some other ill-defined manner.

On the other hand, the ECJ considerably exaggerated the danger of market partitioning in this type of case. This danger is undoubtedly real where a holder of a trade mark in one State then licenses or assigns the right to firms in other Member States. If each of these undertakings could prevent the movement of goods into their area from outside, then the common market could be divided along national lines. This was the very rationale for the exhaustion of rights doctrine. Yet the facts of a case such as *Hag* mean that any *systematic* or *thoroughgoing* market division will simply not occur. This is precisely because the firms in question do not have any legal or economic links. They are merely separate holders of a mark that has the same origin. Any market-partitioning effect will therefore be limited.

The criticism of *Hag I* led the Court to attempt a more elaborate defence of the notion of common origin in the *Terrapin* case.[33] The ECJ accepted that Articles 30 to 36 (now Article 28 to 30) did not prohibit the use of a trade-mark right to prevent the import of goods bearing a different, but similar, trade mark, where there was no economic link between independent firms. However, the ECJ continued to accept the common origin principle from *Hag I*, and it responded to the argument that the effect of its judgment in *Hag I* was to undermine one of the functions of a trade mark: that of indicating the origin of the goods. The Court responded by stating that in cases

---

[30] *Ibid.*, para. 11. [31] *Ibid.*, para. 15.
[32] *Ibid.*, para. 14. [33] Case 119/75, n. 1 above, para. 6.

such as *Hag* the indication of origin was, in any event, undermined by the very subdivision of the original right. This response was clearly inadequate, as shown by Advocate General Jacobs in *Hag II*. The following extract is a comment on the ECJ's reasoning in *Terrapin*.

Case C–10/89, SA CNL-SUCAL NV v. Hag GF AG
[1990] ECR I–3711

ADVOCATE GENERAL JACOBS[34]

That is a valiant attempt to legitimize the doctrine of common origin, but the logic on which it is based is, I think, fallacious. It is true that the essential function of a trade mark is to 'guarantee to consumers that the product has the same origin'. But the word 'origin' in this context does not refer to the historical origin of the trade mark; it refers to the commercial origin of the goods. The consumer is not, I think, interested in the genealogy of trade marks; he is interested in knowing who made the goods that he purchases. The function of a trade mark is to signify to the consumer that all goods sold under that mark have been produced by, or under the control of, the same person and will, in all probability, be of uniform quality. . . . Once the owner of the mark is deprived of his exclusive right to its use, he loses the power to influence the goodwill associated with it and he loses the incentive to produce high-quality goods. Looking at matters from the consumer's point of view, the result of all this is thoroughly unsatisfactory because the trade mark no longer acts as a guarantee of origin. At best he is confused; at worst he is misled. In the circumstances, it is difficult not to conclude that the essential function of the mark, its specific subject-matter is affected and—most seriously of all—its very existence is jeopardized. But none of those consequences ensued from the fragmentation of the Hag trade mark in 1944; they ensued from the Court's judgment in *Hag I*.

It is clear that Advocate General Jacobs was strongly opposed to the common origin doctrine. His opinion in *Hag II* was a convincing analytical indictment, from which the Advocate General reached the 'unpalatable but inescapable conclusion'[35] that the doctrine of common origin was not a legitimate creature of Community law. Advocate General Jacobs urged the Court to overrule *Hag I* expressly for the sake of legal certainty. The ECJ obliged in *Hag II*.

Case C–10/89, SA CNL-SUCAL NV v. Hag GF AG
[1990] ECR I–3711

[Note ToA renumbering: Arts. 30 and 36 are now Arts. 28 and 30]

This case grew out of the same facts as *Hag I*. We noted earlier that the Hag mark for the Benelux countries was transferred to Van Zuylen Frères (VZF) in 1971. The company SA CNL–SUCAL

---

[34] At 3735.
[35] Case C–10/89, [1990] ECR I–3711, 3736.

NV was created as a result of changes in the constitution of VZF. CNL–SUCAL then sought to sell coffee in Germany under the Hag mark. The German company, Hag AG, tried to stop this, asserting that its coffee was superior to that sold by CNL–SUCAL. The ECJ stated explicitly that it was necessary to reconsider its earlier decision in *Hag I* (paragraph 10). The Court began by reiterating the general principles relating to exhaustion of rights as developed in cases such as *Centrafarm*. This approach requires, as we have seen, the Court to identify the specific subject matter of the property right. The ECJ addressed this point as it relates to trade marks in the following terms.

THE ECJ

13. Trade mark rights are, it should be noted, an essential element in the system of undistorted competition which the Treaty seeks to establish and maintain. Under such a system, an undertaking must be in a position to keep its customers by virtue of the quality of its products and services, something which is only possible if there are distinctive marks which enable customers to identify those products and services. For the trade mark to be able to fulfil this role, it must offer a guarantee that all goods bearing it have been produced under the control of a single undertaking which is accountable for their quality.

14. Consequently, as the Court has ruled on numerous occasions, the specific subject-matter of a trade mark is in particular to guarantee to the proprietor of the trade mark that he has the right to use that trade mark for the purpose of putting a product into circulation for the first time and therefore to protect him against competitors wishing to take advantage of the status and reputation of the trade mark by selling products illegally bearing that mark. In order to determine the exact scope of this right exclusively conferred on the owner of the trade mark, regard must be had to the essential function of the trade mark, which is to guarantee the identity of the origin of the marked products to the consumer or ultimate user by enabling him without any possibility of confusion to distinguish that product from products which have another origin. . . .

15. For the purpose of evaluating a situation such as that described by the national court in the light of the foregoing considerations, the determinant factor is the absence of any consent on the part of the proprietor of the trade mark protected by national legislation to the putting into circulation in another Member State of similar products bearing an identical mark or one liable to lead to confusion, which are manufactured and marketed by an undertaking which is economically and legally independent of the aforesaid trade mark proprietor.

16. In such circumstances the essential function of the trade mark would be jeopardized if the proprietor of the trade mark could not exercise the right conferred on him by national legislation to oppose the importation of imported goods bearing a designation liable to be confused with his own trade mark, because, in such a situation, consumers would no longer be able to identify for certain the origin of the marked goods and the proprietor of the trade mark could be held responsible for the poor quality of goods for which he was in no way accountable.

17. This analysis cannot be altered by the fact that the mark protected by national legislation and the similar mark borne by the imported goods by virtue of the legislation of their Member State of origin originally belonged to the same proprietor, who was divested of one of them following expropriation by one of the two states prior to the establishment of the Community.

18. From the date of expropriation and notwithstanding their common origin, each of the marks independently fulfilled its function, within its own territorial field of application, of guaranteeing that the marked products originated from one single source.

19. It follows from the foregoing that in a situation such as the present case, in which the mark

originally had one sole proprietor and the single ownership was broken as a result of expropriation, each of the trade mark proprietors must be able to oppose the importation and marketing, in the Member State in which the trade mark belongs to him, of goods originating from the other proprietor, in so far as they are similar products bearing an identical mark or one which is liable to lead to confusion.

The reasoning and result in *Hag II* stand in marked contrast to those in *Hag I*. The ECJ approached the matter from first principles, by inquiring what was the specific subject matter of a trade mark, and then applied this reasoning to the case at hand. The Court was aided in this respect by an excellent opinion from Advocate General Jacobs. The opinion demonstrated acuity and analytical rigour, and revealed a willingness to subject the Court's previous case law to close critical scrutiny.

The change of approach is also evident in *IHT*.[36] We have already seen that the exhaustion of rights doctrine will apply where goods are placed on the market by the right owner itself or with its consent. What happens, however, where the right owner has assigned it to a company in one Member State, and there is no economic or legal link between the assignor and the assignee? Could the assignee choose, for example, to sell into the assignor's territory? Prior to the decision in *Hag II* the answer would, of course, have been that it could. The common origin doctrine would have been applied to defeat any claim for injunctive relief by the assignor. If, while *Hag I* was still good law, an *involuntary* assignment of a trade mark still had the effect of allowing sales from one territory into another where the trade mark was held by separate entities, then the same must *a fortiori* have been so where the assignment was *voluntary*. The obvious question which had to be resolved following the demise of *Hag I* was whether the reasoning in *Hag II* would be applied in the same manner to voluntary assignments as well as involuntary assignments.

This question was addressed in the *IHT* case, and the ECJ extended *Hag II* to cover voluntary assignments. The facts in *IHT* raised the issue in perfect form. Until 1984 the trade mark for 'Ideal Standard' sanitary fittings and heating equipment was held by subsidiaries of an American company in France and Germany. In 1984 the French subsidiary assigned the trade mark for its area to a company called SGF. IHT sought to import into Germany heating equipment bearing the name 'Ideal Standard' which it had acquired in France. The German subsidiary of the American parent sought to use its trade mark in Germany to prevent this. The question before the Court was whether, after a voluntary assignment of a trade-mark right, one of the original trade-mark holders could prevent importation from an assignee with whom there was no economic or legal link.

The Court held that this would not entail any breach of Community law. The ECJ reiterated the exhaustion of rights doctrine. Once the goods had been placed on the market by the trade-mark owner or with its consent, they could circulate freely within the Community. The Court clarified the reach of this doctrine by stressing that it would apply either where the owners of the right in the exporting and importing

---

[36] Case C–9/93, n. 12 above.

States were the same, or where, even though they were separate, there was an economic link between them. The idea of an economic link would, said the Court, cover products placed into circulation by the same undertaking, by a licensee, by a parent company, by a subsidiary of the same group, or by an exclusive distributor. The position of an assignee was, however, different. The crucial difference perceived by the ECJ was that a contract of assignment, in the absence of any economic link between assignor and assignee, gave the assignor no control over the quality of the goods placed on the market by the assignee. The consent implicit in the assignment itself was not the consent required for the purposes of invoking the exhaustion of rights doctrine. For that doctrine to apply the owner of the right must be able to determine, directly or indirectly, the products to which the mark was affixed and to apply quality control. No such power existed in the case of an assignment where there was no economic link with the assignor. IHT specifically argued before the ECJ that *Hag II* should be distinguished on the ground that the assignment in that case was involuntary, whereas here it was voluntary. The Court rejected this contention. It reiterated the basis of its judgment in *Hag II* and held that this reasoning applied irrespective of whether the splitting of the trade mark originally held by the same owner was due to an act of a public authority or a contractual assignment.[37]

4. ARTICLES 81 AND 82

(a) GENERAL PRINCIPLES: THE EXISTENCE/EXERCISE DISTINCTION

Articles 28 to 30 (ex Articles 30 to 36) are not the only provisions of the Treaty which are of relevance to intellectual-property rights. Articles 81 and 82 (ex Articles 85 and 86) have also frequently been used. The ECJ has adopted the same basic criterion as it has in the context of Articles 28 to 30: it has held that the existence of intellectual-property rights cannot be said to infringe the competition rules, but that the exercise of these rights may in certain circumstances do so.

Case 24/67, Parke Davis & Co. v. Probel and Centrafarm
[1968] ECR 55

[Note ToA renumbering: Arts. 30, 36, 85, 86, and 222 are now 28, 30, 81, 82, and 295]

Parke Davis, an American company, held patents in Holland for certain drugs. It brought an action in Holland seeking relief against the defendants which had marketed the drugs there without its consent. The defendants had acquired the drugs in Italy where patent protection was not available. The question before the Court was whether the reliance by the plaintiff on its patent could be said

---

[37] The ECJ did, however, make it clear that where undertakings which were independent of each other made trade-mark assignments following a market-sharing agreement this would be caught by Art. 85 (now Art. 81), and the assignments which gave effect to the agreement would be void: *ibid.*, para. 59.

to infringe Articles 85 and 86 of the Treaty, (considered if necessary in conjunction with Articles 36 and 222), on the ground, *inter alia,* that the price of the patented product was greater than that of the non-patented version.

THE ECJ

3. . . . .

A patent taken by itself and independently of any agreement to which it may be subject . . . results from a legal status granted by a State to products meeting certain criteria, and thus avoids the elements of contract or concert mentioned in Article 85(1).

But it is not impossible for provisions of that Article to become applicable if the utilisation of one or more patents, in concert between undertakings, should lead to the creation of a situation liable to fall within the bounds of agreements between undertakings, decisions of associations of undertakings or concerted practices within the meaning of Article 85(1). . . .

4. . . . For an act to be prohibited (under Article 86) it is thus necessary to find the existence of three elements: the existence of a dominant position, an improper exploitation of it, and the possibility that trade between Member States may be affected by it.

Although a patent confers on its holder a special protection within the framework of a State, it does not follow that the exercise of the rights so conferred implies the existence of the three elements mentioned. It could only do so if the utilisation of the patent could degenerate into an improper exploitation of the protection.

Besides in a comparable field, Article 36 of the Treaty, after having provided that Articles 30 to 34 do not prevent restrictions on imports or exports which are justified by reasons of protection of industrial and commercial property, provides . . . that those restrictions 'shall not amount to a means of arbitrary discrimination nor to a disguised restriction on trade between Member States.'

Consequently, since the existence of the patent right depends solely at present on internal laws, only the use made of it could fall within the ambit of Community law where that use contributes to a dominant position the improper exploitation of which would be liable to affect trade between Member States.

. . .

6. It follows from all the above that, on the one hand, the rights granted by a Member State to the holder of a patent are not affected as regards their existence by the prohibitions of Articles 85(1) and 86 of the Treaty, and, on the other hand, the exercise of those rights would fall under neither Article 85(1), in the absence of any agreement, decision or concerted practice mentioned by that provision, nor Article 86, in the absence of any abuse of a dominant position, and, finally, the higher level of the sale price of the patented product as compared with that of the non-patented product coming from another Member State does not necessarily constitute an abuse.

(b) ARTICLE 81: ASSIGNMENTS

In accordance with the principles set out in *Parke Davis* we must therefore examine the potential application of Article 81 to intellectual-property rights. An initial issue is whether assignments of intellectual-property rights fall within Article 81.

This question arose in the *Sirena* case.[38] In 1937 an American company assigned its

---

[38] Case 40/70, *Sirena Srl* v. *Eda Srl* [1971] ECR 69.

trade-mark rights in Italy for a cosmetic cream to an Italian company. At a later date the American company allowed a German corporation to use its mark in Germany. This latter company then sold the goods into Italy at a price which under-cut that of the Italian trade-mark holder. The Italian holder of the mark sought to prevent this. The Court had to decide how far an assignment of a trade-mark right which, under national law, would enable the Italian company to exclude the goods coming from Germany, constituted a breach of Article 85 (now Article 81).

The ECJ reiterated its holding in *Parke Davis*, to the effect that trade-mark rights do not *per se* possess the characteristics of a contract or concerted practice such as to fall within Article 85(1). It then said that the exercise of such rights through an agreement might fall within Article 85(1) if this was the object, the means, or the consequence of the agreement. If this 'exercise occurs by virtue of assignments to enterprises in one or more Member States it must be ascertained in each case whether it gives rise to situations prohibited by Article 85' (now Article 81).[39] The Court was concerned in particular about the possibility of a trade-mark owner making a series of assignments to different assignees in different Member States, where these assignments were used to prevent imports of the goods from other Member States. This would re-establish rigid frontiers between the States to the detriment of the common market.[40] References to Article 85 should now be read as referring to Article 81:[41]

Article 85 therefore applies where, by virtue of trade mark rights, imports of products originating in other Member States, bearing the same trade mark because their owners have acquired the trade mark itself or the right to use it through agreements with one another or with third parties, are prevented. The fact that national legislation makes the trade mark rights dependent on circumstances of fact and law other than the aforementioned agreements, such as the registration of the trade mark or its undisturbed use, does not prevent the application of Article 85.

A difficulty in applying Article 85 to trade-mark assignments is that the contract between the assignor and the assignee will effectively be discharged by completion of the assignment. It is for this reason that the Court in *Sirena* was forced to frame the application of Article 85 in terms of agreements that continue to have consequences thereafter.

This issue came before the Court again in the *EMI* case.[42] The trade mark 'Columbia' originally belonged to an American company. In 1917 it transferred the mark for countries which now comprise the Community to its English subsidiary. In 1923 the United Kingdom subsidiary was sold with the trade mark. The United Kingdom trade mark was now held by EMI. CBS had the trade mark in the United States and attempted to sell under this mark in the Community through its European subsidiaries. EMI sought an injunction to prevent this.

The Court repeated orthodoxy that a trade-mark right would not *per se* come

---

[39] *Ibid.*, para. 9.
[40] The assignments had been concluded before the entry into force of the Treaty and the referring court asked whether this would make any difference to the application of Art. 85. The ECJ responded in somewhat cavalier fashion, stating that it was necessary and sufficient if the agreement continued to have an effect after the Treaty became operative: *ibid.*, para. 12.
[41] *Ibid.*, para. 11.
[42] Case 51/75, *EMI Records Ltd* v. *CBS United Kingdom Ltd.* [1976] ECR 811.

within Article 85, but could do so if the exercise of that right 'were to manifest itself as the subject, the means or the consequence of a restrictive practice'.[43] For example, a restrictive agreement between traders within the Community and competitors in a non-member country could have this effect if it were to bring about the isolation of the Community.[44] However, in the present case, where the agreements, in the sense of the assignments, were no longer in force it was sufficient that 'such agreements continue to produce their effects after they have formally ceased to be in force'.[45] The Court then gave more guidance on the meaning of this somewhat elliptical phrase:[46]

An agreement is only regarded as continuing to produce its effects if from the behaviour of the persons concerned there may be inferred the existence of elements of concerted practice and of coordination peculiar to the agreement and producing the same result as that envisaged by the agreement. This is not so when the said effects do not exceed those flowing from the mere exercise of the national trade mark rights.

The problem with this formulation is that if a concerted practice could be inferred, then this would itself be sufficient to bring the parties within the ambit of Article 81(1), and hence the precise role to be played by the assignment is not clear. The existence of the prior agreement might however render it easier to prove a concerted practice. If it could be shown that the parties' behaviour was the continuation of a practice evident in the initial agreement, then this would lead to a strong presumption that there was indeed now a concerted practice.

The application of Article 85 (now Article 81) to assignments was reaffirmed with qualifications in the *IHT* case.[47] We have already seen that the Court held that the reasoning of *Hag II* applied to voluntary as well as involuntary assignments. The ECJ also made some cautionary statements about the application of Article 85 to assignments. It confirmed that, where independent undertakings made reciprocal trademark assignments as part of a market-sharing agreement then this would be caught by Article 85(1). The market-sharing agreement and the assignment would both be void under Article 85(2). But the Court then added that this rule could not be mechanically applied to every assignment. Before a trade-mark assignment could be treated as giving effect to an agreement which would fall within Article 85, it was necessary to analyse the context, the commitments underlying the assignment, the intention of the parties, and the consideration for the assignment.

(c) ARTICLE 81: LICENSING

The other main area to which Article 85 (now Article 81) has been applied is the licensing of intellectual-property rights. An owner of such a right can grant a licence to another party to make and/or distribute a particular product, where it may not have the resources or know-how to make and/or market the product in all areas of the Community. A licensing system enables the holder of the right to reap rewards by authorizing others to do so instead.

---

[43] *Ibid.*, para. 27.   [44] *Ibid.*, paras. 28–29.
[45] *Ibid.*, para. 30.   [46] *Ibid.*, paras. 31–32.
[47] Case C–9/93, n. 12 above.

It is for this reason that the ECJ recognized in *Centrafarm*[48] that the right to place the product on the market through a licensee was part of the specific subject matter of the intellectual-property right, which would not be placed in jeopardy by Community law. Not surprisingly, the Court has adopted the same criterion here as in other parts of this topic. The existence of the right will not be affected by EC law; the exercise of the right can fall foul of Article 81. Thus, while the *grant* of a licence will not lead to any infringement of EC law, its *terms* may bring it within Article 81. This will be decided on a case-by-case basis, but certain general principles have emerged from the Court's case law.

The most important of these principles is that the ECJ will not allow terms in a licence to result in absolute territorial protection for the licensee. This has been a consistent theme in the Court's case law from early decisions such as *Consten and Grundig*,[49] through to cases such as *Nungesser*[50] and *Pronuptia*.[51] These cases have been discussed fully in the context of competition law and reference should be made to that discussion.[52] The general thrust of the Court's decisions can however be conveyed here by taking *Nungesser* as an example.

The case was concerned with a contract made between INRA, a French research institute specializing in the development of plant seeds, and Eisele, a German supplier of seeds. The contract gave Eisele, and through him Nungesser, absolute territorial protection: INRA would not sell the seed to any other undertaking in Germany, and would prevent third parties from doing so; Eisele could use the plant breeder's rights assigned to him by INRA to prevent third parties selling into Germany. The Commission found that the agreement was in violation of Article 85(1). The applicant argued, *inter alia*, that the exclusive licence was necessary to enable INRA to enter a new market, and compete in it with comparable products, since no trader would risk launching a new product unless it were given protection from competition by the licensor and other licensees.

The Court distinguished between an open exclusive licence, whereby the owner merely undertook not to compete himself, nor to grant licences to others in the same territory, and an exclusive licence with absolute territorial protection, under which all competition from third parties was eliminated. It accepted that an open exclusive licence was compatible with EC law. If such a licence could not be given then no licensee might be willing to take on the project,[53] and therefore such a licence was not in itself incompatible with Article 85(1) of the Treaty. In relation to those aspects of the agreement that conferred absolute territorial protection, the Court, however, continued to follow *Consten and Grundig*, and to hold that these were illegal. It was not possible to insulate a market wholly from any competition by way of parallel imports.

Clauses in licensing agreements which seek to insulate the licensees from any

---

48 Case 15/74 [1974] ECR 1147, para. 9.
49 Cases 56 & 58/64, *Consten and Grundig* v. *Commission* [1966] ECR 299.
50 Case 258/78, *L.C. Nungesser KG and Kurt Eisele* v. *Commission* [1982] ECR 2015.
51 Case 161/84, *Pronuptia de Paris GmbH* v. *Pronuptia de Paris Irmgard Schillgallis* [1986] ECR 353.
52 See Ch. 21 above.
53 Case 258/78, *Nungesser*, n. 50 above, para. 57.

competition whatsoever are not the only ones which may fall foul of Article 81. The *Windsurfing* case provides an excellent example of the way in which the ECJ approaches licensing terms in order to decide whether they infringe Article 85 (now Article 81).

Case 193/83, Windsurfing International Inc. v. Commission
[1986] ECR 611

[Note ToA renumbering: Art. 85 is now Art. 81]

Windsurfing International (WI) was an American company which had a patent for the rig used on a windsurfer. It licensed certain firms within the Community to sell the rigs, but imposed conditions in the licences. The Commission held that a number of these conditions infringed Article 85. WI then sought to have this decision annulled by the ECJ.

THE ECJ

38. The first of the clauses at issue . . . imposed on licensees the obligation to exploit the invention only for the purpose of mounting the patented rig on certain types of board specified in the agreement, and the obligation to submit for the licensor's approval, prior to their being placed on the market, any new board types on which the licensees intended to use the rigs.

. . .

45. It is necessary to determine whether quality controls on the sailboards are covered by the specific subject-matter of the patent. As the Commission rightly points out, such controls do not come within the specific subject-matter of the patent unless they relate to a product covered by the patent since their sole justification is that they ensure 'that the technical instructions as described in the patent and used by the licensee may be carried into effect.' In this case, however, it has been established that it may reasonably be considered that the German patent does not cover the board.

46. However, even on the assumption that the German patent covers the complete sailboard, and therefore includes the board, it cannot be accepted without more that controls such as those provided for in the licensing agreements are compatible with Article 85. Such controls must be affected according to quality and safety criteria agreed upon in advance and on the basis of objectively verifiable criteria. If it were otherwise, the discretionary nature of those controls would in effect enable a licensor to impose his own selection of models upon the licensees, which would be contrary to Article 85.

. . .

54. The second of the clauses at issue relates to the obligation on the licensees to sell the components covered by the German patent, and therefore in particular rigs, only in conjunction with the boards approved by the licensor, or in other words, as complete sail-boards.

55. Windsurfing International takes the view that in any event a contractual provision prohibiting the sale of rigs to unlicensed manufacturers was entirely justified in view of the fact that such sales would have enabled unlicensed manufacturers to combine the rigs with their boards, which would have constituted patent infringement. It further argues that such a restriction is covered by the specific subject-matter of the patent.

. . .

57. In that regard it must be borne in mind that . . . the patent must be regarded as confined to

the rig. That being the case, it cannot be accepted that the obligation arbitrarily placed on the licensee only to sell the patented product in conjunction with a product outside the scope of the patent is indispensable to the exploitation of the patent.

. . .

68. The fourth of the clauses at issue relates to the obligation on the licensees to affix to boards manufactured and marketed in Germany a notice stating 'licensed by Hoyle Schweitzer' or 'licensed by Windsurfing International.'

. . .

73. Despite Windsurfing International's contention that it was not the object of the clause to distort competition but merely to convey the information, by means of a notice affixed in a place where it was easily visible, that the product and sale were made possible by a licence from Windsurfing International, it is none the less true that by requiring such a notice Windsurfing International encouraged uncertainty as to whether or not the board too was covered by the patent and thereby diminished the consumer's confidence in the licensees so as to gain a competitive advantage for itself.

. . .

89. The seventh of the clauses which the Commission regards as incompatible with Article 85(1) relates to the obligation on the licensees not to challenge the validity of the licensed patents.

. . .

92. It must be stated that such a clause clearly does not fall within the specific subject-matter of the patent, which cannot be interpreted as also affording protection against actions brought in order to challenge the patent's validity, in view of the fact that it is in the public interest to eliminate any obstacle to economic activity which may arise where a patent was granted in error.

The approach in the *Windsurfing* case clearly exemplifies the Court's strategy in deciding whether terms in a licensing agreement fall within Article 81. The key criterion is whether the relevant term relates to the specific subject-matter of the intellectual-property right. If it does, then it will not be condemned. If, as in many of the examples in the *Windsurfing* case itself, the conditions in the licence do not relate to the specific subject matter of the property right then they will fall within Article 81. They will be lawful only if they can be exempted under Article 81(3) or a block exemption. Thus in the *Windsurfing* case the contested conditions imposed by the patent owners related to quality control,[54] tying,[55] licensed-by notices,[56] and no-challenge clauses.[57] The Court also considered the legality of the terms on which royalties were paid, and decided that these, too, were restrictive since they were calculated on the net selling price of the complete sailboard whereas the patent covered only the rig.[58]

[54] See also *Campari* [1978] OJ L70/69.
[55] *Ibid.*
[56] See also Dec. 72/26, *Burroughs/Geha* [1972] OJ L13/53, [1972] CMLR D72.
[57] See, however, Case 65/86, *Bayer* v. *Süllhöfer* [1988] ECR 5249.
[58] Case 193/83, [1986] ECR 611, paras. 60–67.

(d) ARTICLE 81: BLOCK EXEMPTION

Prior to 1996 there were separate block exemptions for patent licensing and know-how licensing.[59] These have been replaced by the Technology Transfer Regulation, which applies to both types of licensing, provided that only two undertakings are parties to the relevant agreement.[60] The block exemption has the following format: there is a list of the basic licensing conditions which will be entitled to exemption, a 'white list' of other permissible clauses, and a 'black list' of impermissible clauses.[61] The Commission is reviewing the operation of the Regulation.

Article 1 lists the conditions which benefit from the exemption: an obligation on the licensor not to license other undertakings to exploit the licensed technology in the licensed territory; a duty on the licensor not to exploit the licensed technology in the licensed territory; an obligation on the licensee not to exploit the licensed technology in the territory of the licensor within the Common Market; an obligation on the licensee not to manufacture or use the licensed product in the territory of another licensee within the Common Market, or to engage actively in selling there, in the sense of advertising or setting up a branch; an obligation on the licensee not to invade the territories of other licensees in response to unsolicited orders; a qualified obligation to use the licensor's trade mark; and an obligation on the licensee to limit production of the licensed product to the quantities required in manufacturing his own products.

Article 1(2) stipulates the duration of the allowed territorial protection. While the Regulation applies in general to technology transfer, Article 2 sets different time limits for pure patent licences, pure know-how licences, and mixed licences.

Article 2(1)[62] sets out the white list of permissible conditions, which include obligations on the *licensee* relating to: confidentiality of know-how; the impermissibility of granting sub-licences or assignments of the licence; the banning of the use of know-how or patents after the termination of the agreement, provided that the know-how is still secret or the patents are still in force; the grant, subject to certain conditions, by the licensee to the licensor of a licence in respect of improvements made by the licensee to the licensed technology; the observance of minimum quality specifications; and royalties and minimum royalty payments.

The blacklisted clauses are found in Article 3. They include: price restrictions; no-competition clauses, other than to the degree inherent in the provisions on exclusivity contained in Article 1 of the Regulation; maximum limits on the quantity of the goods which may be produced by the licensee; and an obligation on the licensee to assign to the licensor any improvements to or new applications of the licensed technology; and any obligations on either the licensor or the licensee which in effect seek to impede parallel imports or parallel exports.

Article 7 allows the Commission to withdraw the benefits of the block exemption from an agreement, even though it fulfils the conditions of the Regulation, if it

---

[59] See, respectively, Reg. 2349/84 [1984] OJ L219/15, and Reg. 556/89 [1989] OJ L61/1.
[60] Reg. 240/96, [1996] OJ L31/2, [1996] 4 CMLR 405.
[61] A. Robertson, 'Intellectual Property' (1995) 15 *YBEL* 409.
[62] See also the opposition procedure contained in Art. 4.

has effects which are not compatible with Article 81(3). The factors which the Commission will take into account in this context are: the lack of effective inter-brand competition; the refusal by the licensee to respond to unsolicited orders from the territories of other licensees where there is no objective reason for this; or action by the licensor or licensee which is designed to impede parallel exporters or parallel importers.

The Commission has produced a report evaluating the block exemption,[63] and it is very likely that it will be amended. The existing Regulation is regarded as too formalistic, and too focused on intra-brand competition. A modified form of the Regulation will follow more closely the approach of the block exemption for vertical restraints.[64]

(e) ARTICLE 82

The discussion thus far has concentrated on Article 81 (ex Article 85). We must now consider what constraints Article 82 (ex Article 86) imposes on intellectual property rights. We have already seen from the *Parke Davis* case that the ECJ employs the existence/exercise dichotomy in relation to Article 86 (now Article 82) as well as to Article 85 (now Article 81).[65] This means that the monopoly power attendant upon the grant of an intellectual-property right will not in itself constitute a breach of Article 86. Were this to be otherwise Article 86 would outlaw all intellectual property. It is for this reason that the Court in *Parke Davis* held that it was only the use of a patent which would bring it within Community law where that use contributed to a dominant position the improper exploitation of which would be liable to affect trade between Member States.[66] The way in which Article 86 is applied to intellectual-property rights emerges clearly in the *CICRA* case.

Case 53/87, Consorzio Italiano della Componentistica di Ricambio per Autoveicoli (CICRA) and Maxicar v. Régie Nationale des Usines Renault[67]
[1988] ECR 6039

[Note ToA renumbering: Art. 86 is now Art. 82]

An Italian trade association, the members of which made bodywork spare parts for cars, sought a declaration that the protective rights which Renault had for ornamental designs for spare car parts were void, as being in breach of Community law. The essence of its complaint was that these protective rights made it impossible for it to make non-original spare parts for these cars.

---

[63] *Commission Evaluation Report on the Transfer of Technology Block Exemption Regulation 240/96, Technology Transfer Agreements under Article 81* (2001).
[64] See 986–90 above.
[65] See 1108–9 above.
[66] Case 24/67, [1968] ECR 55, para. 4.
[67] See also Case 238/87, *AB Volvo v. Erik Veng (UK) Ltd.* [1988] ECR 6211.

THE ECJ

10. It must first be stated that, as the Court held in . . . Case 144/81 (*Keurkoop* v. *Nancy Kean Gifts* [1982] ECR 2853), with respect to the protection of designs and models, in the present state of Community law and in the absence of Community standardization or harmonization of laws the determination of the conditions and procedures under which such protection is granted is a matter for national rules. It is for the national legislature to determine which products qualify for protection, even if they form part of a unit already protected as such.

11. It should then be noted that the authority of a proprietor of a protective right in respect of an ornamental model to oppose the manufacture by third parties, for the purposes of sale on the internal market or export, of products incorporating the design or to prevent the import of such products manufactured without its consent in other Member States constitutes the substance of his exclusive right. To prevent the application of the national legislation in such circumstances would therefore be tantamount to challenging the very existence of that right.

. . .

14. . . . the national court wishes to establish, essentially, whether the obtaining of protective rights in respect of ornamental models for car bodywork components and the exercise of the resultant exclusive rights constitutes an abuse of a dominant position within the meaning of Article 86 of the Treaty.

15. It should be noted at the outset that the mere fact of securing the benefit of an exclusive right granted by law, the effect of which is to enable the manufacture and sale of protected products by unauthorized third parties to be prevented, cannot be regarded as an abusive method of eliminating competition.

16. Exercise of the exclusive right may be prohibited by Article 86 if it gives rise to certain abusive conduct on the part of the undertaking occupying a dominant position such as an arbitrary refusal to deliver spare parts to independent repairers, the fixing of prices for spare parts at an unfair level or a decision no longer to produce spare parts for a particular model even though many cars of that model remain in circulation, provided that such conduct is liable to affect trade between Member States.

17. With reference more particularly to the difference in prices between components sold by the manufacturer and those sold by independent producers, it should be noted that the Court has held (. . . in Case 24/67, *Parke Davis* . . .) that a higher price for the former than for the latter does not necessarily constitute an abuse, since the proprietor of protective rights in respect of an ornamental design may lawfully call for a return on the amounts which he has invested in order to perfect the protected design.

The principle which determines the application of Article 86 (now Article 82) to intellectual-property rights emerges clearly in the above case. The ability to prevent unauthorized sales of the car bodyparts constituted the specific subject matter of the intellectual-property right and was not contrary to Article 86. It was only where the owner of the right acted abusively in the sense mentioned in paragraph 16 that this Article would come into play.

Matters may not always be so clear-cut, as is apparent from the *RTE* case.[68] This

---

[68] Case T–69/89, *Radio Telefis Eireann* v. *Commission* [1991] ECR II–485. See also Case T–70/89, *British Broadcasting Corporation and British Broadcasting Corporation Enterprises Ltd.* v. *Commission* [1991] ECR II–535; Case 238/87, *Volvo*, n. 67 above.

decision has been discussed earlier in the general context of Article 82.[69] It will be remembered that RTE was a statutory authority providing broadcasting services, and it reserved the exclusive right to publish a weekly schedule of TV programmes for its channels in Ireland. An Irish company, Magill, sought to publish a weekly guide that would have information on all the available channels. RTE wished to prevent this, claiming that it infringed its copyright in the weekly schedule for its channels. The Commission found this to be an abuse of Article 86, and RTE challenged this before the CFI. The CFI accepted the basic principle that the specific subject matter of a copyright would enjoy protection under Community law, and in that sense the exclusive right to reproduce the protected work would not be an abuse for the purposes of Article 86. However, the copyright owner would not be protected if the manner of the exercise of the right were contrary to Article 86. The CFI then held that the case fell within the latter rather than the former category, on the ground that RTE was using its exclusive copyright to publish its weekly listings in order to prevent the emergence of a *new product*, namely a general guide for all TV channels. This was held to go beyond what was necessary to fulfil the essential function of RTE's copyright as permitted by EC law.[70]

The potential reach of Article 86 (now Article 82) to cases concerning intellectual property is further exemplified by the CFI's decision in *Tetra Pak*.[71] The CFI held that there could be a violation of Article 86 where a firm in a dominant position strengthened that position by taking over another firm and thereby acquired an exclusive licence to exploit intellectual property. In reaching this decision the CFI reasoned on the basis of the ECJ's earlier ruling in *Continental Can*[72] that a merger could be caught by Article 86. The nature of the ECJ's reasoning in this case has been explored above,[73] but the application of this reasoning to the facts of *Tetra Pak* is contentious, given that the licence in question came within the ambit of the block exemption. The response of the CFI was that, while there might be no objection to the licence as such, this did not mean that it was unobjectionable for a dominant firm to take over another company that possessed such rights.

5. ARTICLE 12 AND NON-DISCRIMINATION

The discussion thus far has focused on the use of Articles 28 to 30 and Articles 81 and 82 in the context of intellectual property. An individual can, however, also rely on Article 12 (ex Article 6), the general prohibition on discrimination on grounds of nationality, in its own right without the necessity of relying on other Treaty Articles. This follows from the *Phil Collins* case.[74] The applicant was the singer who sought to

---

[69] See 1014–15 above.
[70] The case was upheld on appeal: Cases C–241 & 242/91P, *Radio Telefis Eireann (RTE) and Independent Television Publications Ltd. (ITP)* v. *Commission* [1995] ECR I–743.
[71] Case T–51/89, *Tetra Pak Rausing* v. *Commission* [1990] ECR II–309.
[72] Case 6/72, [1973] ECR 215.
[73] See 1008–9 above.
[74] Case C–92/92, *Phil Collins* v. *Imtrat Handelsgesellschaft mbH* [1993] ECR I–5145.

prevent the sale in Germany of a bootleg recording of his concert in the United States. Under German law, German nationals would have been afforded relief in such circumstances, but this was not available for non-Germans. The ECJ held that this was discrimination on grounds of nationality and constituted a breach of Article 6(1). This Article was directly effective and could be relied on by the applicant in the national courts.[75]

6. INTELLECTUAL-PROPERTY RIGHTS AND HARMONIZATION

Many of the problems discussed above flow from the fact that intellectual-property rights have traditionally been granted by nation States. It is, therefore, unsurprising that principles of exhaustion of rights have hitherto been developed on the assumption that the State is the basic territorial unit. This approach could, for the reasons considered above, not be accepted with the advent of the EC, since it would have resulted in the partitioning of the Community along national lines. Attempts to secure a single market by removing tariffs, quotas, and the like would have been undermined by the continued existence of barriers to trade created by private parties through the use of devices such as intellectual-property rights. The ECJ's creative jurisprudence was an attempt to prevent this happening, while not denuding such property rights of all content. The judiciary cannot, however, fashion a long-term solution to the problem. This requires legislative initiatives designed both to harmonize relevant national laws, and also more radically to shift the basic territorial unit for the purpose of intellectual-property rights from the State to the EC itself. Such legislative initiatives have been forthcoming, but the process of securing agreement between the Member States has not proven either easy or quick.[76]

The position in relation to *patents* is as follows. A Community Patent Convention[77] was agreed to at an intergovernmental level in 1975 between the nine Member States of the Community. Its central aim was to provide for a Community-wide patent. The owner's rights would be exhausted by placing the patented product on the market in any of the Member States. The Convention was signed in 1975, but there have been serious obstacles to its successful implementation.[78] This was in part because of a separate instrument, the European Patent Convention. It was concluded in 1973, and a number of the signatory States were not part of the EC. It did not create a Community Patent as such, but rather a method through which a number of national patents could be granted at the same time, thereby obviating the need to go through separate procedures in each of the States. The Commission has, more recently, revived

---

[75] G. Dworkin and J. Sterling, 'Phil Collins and the Term Directive' [1994] *EIPR* 187.
[76] L. Bently and B. Sherman, *Intellectual Property Law* (Oxford University Press, 2001), 16–18; T. Vinje, 'Harmonising Intellectual Property Laws in the European Union: Past, Present and Future' [1995] *EIPR* 361.
[77] [1976] OJ L17/1.   [78] Vinje, n. 76 above, 373.

the idea of a Community patent. It would provide inventors with the option of obtaining a patent valid throughout the entire EC.[79]

Legislative initiatives have also been forthcoming in relation to *trade marks*.[80] There has been progress towards harmonization of national laws through Directive 89/104.[81] A Community trade mark has also been introduced, allowing an applicant to register a mark for the EC as a whole.[82] It is administered by the Office of Harmonization in the Internal Market, based in Spain.[83]

There have in addition been various legislative initiatives in the context of *copyright*.[84] There have been directives concerned with rental, cable and satellite, databases, duration, e-commerce, resale rights, and the information society.

7. CONCLUSION

i.   It has been the ECJ that has fashioned the relationship between intellectual-property rights and the other principles contained in the Treaty, notably free movement of goods and competition. The principal concern has been that such rights could be used to divide the market and impede the realization of the internal market.

ii. The ECJ has used the distinction between the existence of the property right and its exercise. The former is not affected by EC law; the latter is, in so far as the exercise of the rights hinders the movement of goods or constitutes a violation of the EC competition law. The divide between existence and manner of exercise is questionable, precisely because a right is constituted by the ways in which it can be exercised. This distinction has none the less provided a malleable tool whereby the ECJ has sought to reconcile intellectual-property rights with the other Treaty objectives.

iii. The consistent theme in the ECJ's jurisprudence is that once the property right owner has placed the goods on the EC market itself or has consented to such marketing, the goods can move freely throughout the EC. They cannot be opposed by the right owner or any other person legally or economically con-nected with the right owner. This covers products placed into circulation by the same undertaking, by a licensee, by a parent company, by a subsidiary of the same group, or by an exclusive distributor.

iv. The ECJ has also been mindful of the limits of its own jurisprudence. It has realized the fallacy of the common origin doctrine. It has recognized that voluntary as well as involuntary assignments do not amount to a placing of the goods on the market with the consent of the right owner. It has moreover been cognizant of the variety of intellectual property rights. The case law on

---

[79] *Proposal for a Council Regulation on the Community Patent*, COM(2000)412 final.
[80] A. Robertson, 'Recent Developments in EEC Intellectual Property Legislation' (1992) 12 *YBEL* 175.
[81] [1989] OJ L40/1.   [82] Reg. 40/94, [1994] OJ L11/1.
[83] Bently and Sherman, n. 76 above, 747–52.   [84] *Ibid.*, 40–8; Vinje, n. 76 above, 361–6.

copyright and rentals shows that the ECJ is aware of the distinguishing features of different forms of copyright.

v. Developments in all areas of EC law are a mix of the judicial, administrative, and legislative. Judicial doctrine laid the foundations for the initial directive on trade marks, and continues to provide the bedrock for later EC legislation. It is however only through such legislation that more ambitious objects, such as the Community Trade Mark and the moves towards a Community patent, can be realized.

8. FURTHER READING

(a) *Books*

BENTLY, L., and SHERMAN, B., *Intellectual Property Law* (Oxford University Press, 2001)

CORNISH, W.R., *Intellectual Property: Patents, Copyright, Trade Marks and Allied Rights* (Sweet & Maxwell, 4th edn., 1999)

WHISH, R., *Competition Law* (Butterworths, 4th edn., 2001), ch. 19

(b) *Articles*

BONET, G., 'Intellectual Property' (1989) 9 *YBEL* 315

CORNISH, W.R., 'Intellectual Property' (1990) 10 *YBEL* 469

MANN, F.A., 'Industrial Property and the EEC Treaty' [1975] *ICLQ* 31

MARENCO, G., and BANKS, K., 'Intellectual Property and the Community Rules on Free Movement: Discrimination Unearthed' (1990) 15 *ELRev.* 224

OLIVER, P., 'Of Split Trade Marks and Common Markets' (1991) 54 *MLR* 587

PARR, N., 'Avoiding Antitrust Pitfalls in Drafting and Enforcing Intellectual Property Agreements In the European Union' [1997] *EIPR* 43

SHEA, N., 'Parallel Importers' Use of Trade Marks. The European Court of Justice Confers Rights but also Imposes Responsibilities' [1997] *EIPR* 103

VINJE, T., 'Harmonising Intellectual Property Laws in the European Union: Past, Present and Future' [1995] *EIPR* 361

WEATHERILL, S., 'Recent Case Law Concerning the Free Movement of Goods: Mapping the Frontiers of Market Deregulation' (1999) 36 *CMLRev.* 51

27

THE STATE AND THE COMMON MARKET

1. CENTRAL ISSUES

i. This Chapter is concerned with the way in which the actions of the State itself can infringe the Treaty. The Treaty contains a number of relevant provisions, including Articles 10, 16, 28, 81, 82, 86, and 87 to 89 (ex Articles 5, 7d, 30, 85, 86, 90, and 92 to 94).

ii. There are valid reasons in principle for controlling state action. Thus, for example, Article 86 (ex Article 90) is designed to prevent a State from enacting or maintaining in force measures relating to public undertakings etc. which derogate from other obligations under the Treaty. Some such provision is clearly required in order to prevent a State from evading the proscriptions of the Treaty in so far as these relate to such undertakings. It is equally apparent that the Community must, for example, have some rules concerning the provision of state aids. The control of such aid forms an aspect of the Community's single-market

policy: if a State were able to give preferential treatment to its own firms then the very idea of a level playing field would be undermined.[1]

iii. While there are valid reasons for Community controls, the topics discussed within this Chapter raise important issues concerning the very nature of the Community. Thus it will be seen that the jurisprudence under Article 86 (ex Article 90) has prompted questions about the extent to which it is possible for a State to entrust certain activities to a public monopoly, or to a private firm which has exclusive rights. The case law concerning state aids, Articles 87–89 (ex Articles 92–94), raises a plethora of broader issues concerning the way in which Community policy is developed in a particular area, and the appropriate balance between market integration and the attainment of other goals, such as regional policy and Community cohesion.

2. THE STATE AND PARTICIPATION IN THE MARKET: GENERAL PRINCIPLES

In mixed economic systems it is common for the State to play some role in the market-place. The rationale for this intervention and its legal form may well vary. It has, for example, been common in the past for utilities either to be nationalized, or to have some privileged monopoly or quasi-monopoly status. Recent thinking has tended to favour a more confined role for the State, as manifested in the privatization of nationalized industries and in the deregulation of sectors of the economy. Notwithstanding these changes, there continue to be undertakings which

---

[1] C.–D. Ehlermann, 'The Contribution of EC Competition Policy to the Single Market' (1992) 29 *CMLRev.* 257, 259.

either remain within public ownership or possess a certain privileged status in the market-place.

The basic starting position is to be found in Article 295 (ex Article 222), which states that the Treaty shall in no way prejudice the rules in Member States governing the system of property ownership. The mere fact that certain activities are undertaken in the public or the private sphere is not, therefore, in itself contrary to the Treaty. Article 295 is, however, subject to judicial interpretation.[2] Moreover, Article 157 (ex Article 130) provides that the Community and the Member States shall ensure that the conditions necessary for the competitiveness of the Community's industry exist. The Article is explicitly framed in terms of open and competitive markets. Action to attain this end includes the encouragement of initiative and the development of undertakings throughout the Community, particularly small and medium-sized undertakings.

Thus, while Article 295 can be seen as providing support for Community agnosticism as to the regime of ownership within any particular State, the thrust of much else in the Treaty is against the type of dominance which can accompany public ownership. It is also against the grant of any special, beneficial position to firms, which may have the consequence of distorting the competitive mechanism within the common market. We shall see how far this is affected by the addition to the EC Treaty of Article 16 (ex Article 7d).

3. PUBLIC UNDERTAKINGS AND ARTICLE 86

The sentiment expressed in the preceding paragraph is readily apparent from Article 86 (ex Article 90):

1. In the case of public undertakings and undertakings to which Member States grant special or exclusive rights, Member States shall neither enact nor maintain in force any measure contrary to the rules contained in this Treaty, in particular to those rules provided for in Article 12 and Articles 81 to 89.

2. Undertakings entrusted with the operation of services of general economic interest or having the character of a revenue-producing monopoly shall be subject to the rules contained in this Treaty, in particular to the rules on competition, in so far as the application of such rules does not obstruct the performance, in law or in fact, of the particular task assigned to them. The development of trade must not be affected to such an extent as would be contrary to the interests of the Community.

3. The Commission shall ensure the application of the provisions of this Article and shall, where necessary, address appropriate directives or decisions to Member States.

---

[2] See Ch. 26 above for the interpretation of Art. 295 in the context of intellectual property.

(a) THE SCOPE OF ARTICLE 86(1):
GENERAL PRINCIPLES

It is clear that Article 86 (ex Article 90) covers two types of undertaking: public undertakings and those to which Member States have granted special or exclusive rights. These will be examined in turn.

The scope of the term *public undertaking* was addressed by the ECJ in the Transparency Directive case.

Cases 188–190/80, France, Italy, and the United Kingdom v. Commission
[1982] ECR 2545

[Note ToA renumbering: Art. 90 is now Art. 86]

The Commission, acting pursuant to Article 90(3), enacted Directive 80/723[3] on the transparency of financial relations between Member States and public undertakings. The object of the Directive was to make available information on public funds which had been given to public undertakings, and the use to which such money had been put. Such information was necessary in order to ensure, *inter alia*, the proper operation of the rules on state aid. Three Member States sought to have the Directive annulled on a number of grounds. In the course of its judgment the ECJ considered the definition of public undertaking contained in the Directive. The Court acknowledged that the Commission did not set out in the Directive to define 'public undertakings' for the purpose of Article 90, but it none the less approved of the definition.

THE ECJ

25. According to Article 2 of the Directive, the expression 'public undertakings' means any undertaking over which the public authorities may exercise directly or indirectly a dominant influence. According to the second paragraph, such influence is to be presumed when the public authorities directly or indirectly hold the major part of the undertaking's subscribed capital, control the majority of the votes, or can appoint more than half of the members of its administrative, managerial or supervisory body.

26. As the Court has already stated, the reason for the inclusion in the Treaty of the provisions of Article 90 is precisely the influence which the public authorities are able to exert over the commercial decisions of public undertakings. That influence may be exerted on the basis of financial participation or of rules governing the management of the undertaking. By choosing the same criteria to determine the financial relations on which it must be able to obtain information in order to perform its duty of surveillance under Article 90(3), the Commission has remained within the limits of the discretion conferred upon it by that provision.

The definition in the Transparency Directive is not conclusive. It was, however, approved by the ECJ. The existence of a state influence in one of the above ways will

---

[3] See now Comm. Dir. 2000/52 [2000] OJ L193/75.

therefore be a sufficient reason for an undertaking to be characterized as public.[4] Thus in *Sacchi*[5] the Italian Broadcasting Authority, RAI, was under the control of a State holding company, IRI; the State was represented in its organs and could intervene in its operations.

Even if an undertaking is not public in the above sense, it may still fall within Article 86(1) if it is one to which a Member State has granted *special or exclusive rights*. The rationale is that where the State has relieved an undertaking wholly or partially from the discipline of competition, it must bear responsibility for the consequences. An example would be a nationalized industry that had been privatized, but which continued to have a protected monopoly in the relevant area, or which was accorded certain advantages resulting from the terms on which it had been established.

It is perfectly possible for undertakings to be caught by both limbs of Article 86(1). Thus, in *Sacchi*[6] the RAI, as well as being controlled by the State, also possessed a statutory monopoly in relation to broadcasting. In *Muller*[7] the State had power to nominate half of the members of the management and supervisory board of a company which controlled port facilities in Luxembourg. The company itself had certain privileges, including that of being consulted before the development of any other port facilities within a particular area was undertaken.

Article 86(1) requires that a Member State *shall neither enact nor maintain in force* any measure that is contrary to the Treaty. This language serves to emphasize the peremptory force of the duty imposed on a Member State. It constitutes both a standstill obligation, in the sense of a duty not to enact any measure which is contrary to the Treaty, and a positive obligation to remove any such measure which currently exists. Thus, the State may be responsible even if it has failed to correct an infringement of the Treaty.

A breach of Article 86(1) presupposes that some other Article of the Treaty has been broken, as exemplified by the specific reference to Articles 12, and 81 to 89 (ex Articles 6, and 85 to 94). It would clearly be possible for a Member State to maintain in force a measure which constituted a breach of some other Treaty Article, such as Article 28 (ex Article 30). The way in which Article 86(1) operates can be seen from the *Bodson* case.

Case 30/87, Bodson v. Pompes Funèbres des Régions Libérées SA
[1988] ECR 2479

[Note ToA renumbering: Arts. 86 and 90 are now Arts. 82 and 86]

French legislation entrusted the provision of external services for funerals (the carriage of the body after it has been placed in the coffin, the provision of hearses, etc.), to local communes. The communes then granted concessions to private undertakings and Pompes Funèbres (PF) held many such concessions. Bodson offered external funeral services at a price significantly lower than

---

[4] In order for Art. 86 to apply there must be an undertaking: Case C–22/98, *Criminal Proceedings against Becu* [1999] ECR I–5665.
[5] Case 155/73, [1974] ECR 409.   [6] *Ibid.*
[7] Case 10/71, *Ministère Public of Luxembourg v. Muller* [1971] ECR 723.

that set by PF. PF sought an injunction in the French courts, claiming that Bodson was acting in breach of its exclusive rights resulting from the concession. Bodson responded by arguing that PF had abused its dominant position in breach of Article 86 by charging excessive prices. One of the issues before the Court concerned the responsibility of the commune itself under Article 90.

THE ECJ

33. In so far as the communes imposed a given level of prices on the concession holders, in the sense that they refrained from granting concessions for the 'external services' to undertakings if the latter did not agree to charge particularly high prices, the communes are covered by the situation referred to in Article 90(1) of the Treaty. That provision governs the obligations of the Member States—which includes, in this context, the public authorities at the regional, provincial or communal level—towards undertakings 'to which [they] grant special or exclusive rights'. That situation covers precisely the grant of an exclusive concession for the 'external services' for funerals.

34. It follows from that finding that public authorities may not, in circumstances such as those in this case, either enact or maintain in force any 'measure' contrary to the rules of the Treaty. . . . They may not therefore assist undertakings holding concessions to charge unfair prices by imposing such prices as a condition for concluding a contract for a concession.

(b) THE SCOPE OF ARTICLE 86(1): AGNOSTICISM AS TO THE ORGANIZATION OF ECONOMIC ACTIVITIES?

We began this discussion by noting that the Treaty, in formal terms, is agnostic as to whether economic activity is undertaken by the State itself, or those to whom it has granted special or exclusive rights, as opposed to allowing the free and unfettered interplay of market forces. A State can therefore choose to grant exclusive rights to a particular undertaking and the normal Treaty rules will apply. Provided that the State itself does not infringe Article 86 (ex Article 90), and provided that the undertaking does not exercise its exclusive rights so as to constitute an abuse of a dominant position under Article 82 (ex Article 86), then all will be well. The exclusivity will not, in and of itself, infringe Article 82. On this view Article 86 simply preserves parity. It does no more than ensure that public undertakings or those to whom exclusive rights are granted do not thereby infringe any Treaty provision.

We have, however, also seen that the thrust of the Treaty is more generally in favour of eradicating any impediment to the free movement of goods, and of ensuring that normal competitive principles apply to determine the winners and losers in the market place. The result of this contest may lead to a firm that is dominant because of its economic prowess. This is one of the reasons that the Treaty does not proscribe monopoly *per se*. The Treaty is, none the less, against what may be regarded as artificial barriers to the normal interplay of competition. This can produce tensions in relation to public undertakings, or those to whom the state has granted special or exclusive rights, because their privileged position is not the result of economic prowess but of state grant.

The formal way in which the ECJ resolves these tensions is to recognize that the *grant* of exclusive rights will not *per se* infringe, for example, Article 82, but that the *exercise* of such rights may do so if it can be said to be abusive. This is fine in principle, but much depends on the more precise meaning given to the idea of abuse. We have already seen the elasticity of this concept in the discussion of Article 82.[8] The interpretation accorded to the term is particularly important in this context. The point can be put quite simply: the closer the Court comes to regarding the grant of exclusive rights as abusive in and of itself, the more difficult does it become for a State to choose to organize its economic activities in this manner. While the Court has not yet reached the position whereby it can be said that exclusivity is abusive, its case law evidences movement in this direction. It also demonstrates the fragility of the dividing line between the legitimate and illegitimate grant of exclusive rights.

The *Höfner*[9] decision demonstrates these difficulties. The case concerned the legality of German rules on certain categories of persons who were seeking work. Under these rules those looking for work were placed in contact with potential employers through a state-licensed agency, and this agency was given exclusive powers in the relevant area. The effect of this monopoly was to suppress the activities of independent employment consultants. The ECJ decided that the agency was an undertaking for the purposes of Article 86 (now Article 82), and that any state rule that compelled an undertaking to breach Article 86 would be illegal under Article 90(1) (now Article 86(1)). The ECJ held that the grant of exclusive rights was not *per se* incompatible with Article 86.[10] However, it also decided that a State would violate Article 90(1) if it placed an undertaking in such a dominant position that the very exercise of these exclusive rights could *not avoid* being abusive. The ECJ concluded that the Member State had created such a situation because the undertaking to which it had granted the exclusive right was not in a position to satisfy market demand for activities of this kind. Private companies were not allowed to engage in such activities, and contracts they made would be void. Moreover, the exclusivity could affect the nationals of other Member States.[11]

The fine line between a lawful grant of exclusive rights and illegality under Articles 90 (now Article 86) and 86 (now Article 82) is further demonstrated by *ERT*.[12] The case, examined in more detail below, concerned the legality of a statutory radio and television monopoly held by ERT granted to it by the Greek State. Once again the ECJ stated that the existence of a statutory monopoly was not in and of itself abusive for the purposes of Article 86. But the Court then held that Articles 86 and 90 could be infringed where the grant of the exclusive right would *lead* the grantee to infringe Article 86. This would be so where an exclusive right to retransmit programmes was given to an undertaking, which had the exclusive right to transmit broadcasts, since the grantee would be likely to favour transmission of its own programmes, rather than retransmission of the programmes from other companies.

The willingness of the ECJ to characterize a grant of exclusive rights as abusive

---

[8] See Ch. 23 above.

[9] Case C–41/90, *Höfner and Elser* v. *Macrotron GmbH* [1991] ECR I–1979.

[10] *Ibid.*, para. 29.

[11] *Ibid.*, para. 34; Case C–55/96, *Job Centre coop. arl.* [1997] ECR I–7119; Case C–258/98, *Criminal Proceedings against Carra* [2000] ECR I–4217; cf. Case C–387/93, *Banchero* [1995] ECR I–4663.

[12] Case C–260/89, *Elliniki Radiophonia Tileorassi AE (ERT)* v. *Dimotiki Etairia Pliroforissis (DEP) and Sotirios Kouvelas* [1991] ECR I–2925.

within Article 86 is even more apparent in the following case which develops the reasoning in the preceding two decisions.

Case C–179/90, Merci Convenzionali Porto di Genova SpA v. Siderurgica Gabrielli SpA
[1991] ECR I–5889

[Note ToA renumbering: Arts. 30, 85, 86, and 90 are now Arts. 28, 81, 82, and 86]

Merci enjoyed the exclusive right to organize dock work in the Port of Genoa. It would call upon a dock-work company to unload ships. Siderurgica (S) applied to Merci to have a consignment of steel unloaded, even though the ship's own crew could have performed the task itself. Merci called upon the relevant Genoa dock-work company to do the job. Delays arose in the unloading as a result of strikes. As a consequence S demanded reimbursement for the charges paid to Merci, claiming that they were unfair in regard to the services performed. The Italian court asked the ECJ whether Article 90 in combination with Articles 30, 85, and 86 applied to the instant case. The ECJ reaffirmed that an undertaking having a statutory monopoly over a substantial part of the common market would be regarded as having a dominant position for the purposes of Article 86. It then continued as follows.

THE ECJ

16. It should next be stated that the simple fact of creating a dominant position by granting exclusive rights within the meaning of Article 90(1) EEC is not as such incompatible with Article 86.

17. However, the Court has had occasion to state, in this respect, that a Member State is in breach of the prohibition contained in these two provisions if the undertaking in question, merely by exercising the exclusive rights granted to it, cannot avoid abusing its dominant position (see Case C–41/90, *Höfner* . . .) or when such rights are liable to create a situation in which that undertaking is induced to commit such abuses (see Case C–260/89, *ERT* . . .).

18. According to Article 86(2)(a), (b) and (c) EEC, such abuse may in particular consist in imposing on the persons requiring the services in question unfair purchase prices or other unfair trading conditions, in limiting technical development, to the prejudice of consumers, or in the application of dissimilar conditions to equivalent transactions with other trading parties.

19. In that respect it appears from the circumstances described by the national court . . . that the undertakings enjoying exclusive rights in accordance with the procedures laid down by the national rules in question are, as a result, induced either to demand payment for services which have not been requested, to charge disproportionate prices, to refuse to have recourse to modern technology, which involves an increase in the cost of the operations and a prolongation of the time required for their performance, or to grant price reductions to certain consumers and at the same time to offset such reductions by an increase in the charges to other consumers.

20. In these circumstances it must be held that a Member State creates a situation contrary to Article 86 EEC where it adopts rules of such a kind as those at issue before the national court, which are capable of affecting trade between Member States as in the case of the main proceedings, regard being had . . . to the importance of traffic in the Port of Genoa.

21. As regards the interpretation of Article 30 requested by the national court, it is sufficient to recall that a national measure which has the effect of facilitating the abuse of a dominant

position capable of affecting trade between Member States will generally be incompatible with that Article, which prohibits quantitative restrictions on imports and all measures having equivalent effect (see Case 13/77, *GB-INNO-BM* v. *ATAB*) in so far as such a measure has the effect of making more difficult and hence of impeding imports of goods from other Member States.

22. In the main proceedings it may be seen from the national court's findings that the unloading of the goods could have been effected at a lesser cost by the ship's crew, so that compulsory recourse to the services of the two undertakings enjoying exclusive rights involved extra expense and was therefore capable, by reason of its effect on the prices of the goods, of affecting imports.

The ECJ's reasoning is instructive.[13] In paragraph 16 the Court reiterated the proposition that the creation of exclusive rights was not itself abusive within Article 90 (now Article 86). This was then qualified in paragraph 17. Exclusivity could entail a breach of Articles 90 and 86 (now Articles 86 and 82) either when the exercise of the exclusive rights could not avoid being abusive (*Höfner*), or where such rights were liable to create a situation in which the undertaking was induced to commit an abuse (*ERT*). In paragraph 19 the Court applied the latter of these two formulations to the instant case.

This comes perilously close to regarding the grant of exclusivity as abusive *per se*, albeit through the back door. The reason is to be found in the notion that an undertaking may be *induced* to commit an abuse in one of the ways identified in paragraph 19. It is, of course, true that an undertaking can be in breach of Article 86 (now Article 82) through charging excessive prices, discriminatory prices, and the like. Any firm with the market power attendant upon a dominant position has the *potential* to do this. Whether it actually chooses to behave in this manner is another matter. The message from the Court is, however, that the very grant of the exclusive rights can create a situation in which the undertaking is *induced* to commit such abuses.

The meaning of the word *induce* here is, however, crucial. The ECJ's reasoning comes close to stating that, because the holder of the exclusive right possessed market power which enabled it to price in an abusive manner, therefore it was induced to do so. On this hypothesis it could always be said that the grantee of exclusivity would be induced to price abusively, with the consequence that exclusive rights would, in effect, be rendered illegal *per se*. It might be countered that this is to misread the Court's reasoning, and that it ignores the fact, mentioned at the beginning of paragraph 19, that the holder of the exclusive right had in fact priced in an abusive manner. Yet if this was indeed so then Merci itself should have been condemned on this basis alone. On this view nothing was to be gained from the language of inducement.

The fact that the Court did employ the language of inducement was, however, not fortuitous. It did so because it wished to make a point about the consequence of forms of economic organization *adopted by the State*. What is distinctive about the grant of a

---

[13] See also Case C–18/93, *Corsica Ferries Italia SRL* v. *Corpo dei Piloti di Genova* [1994] ECR I–1783; Case C–242/95, *GT-Link A/S* v. *De Danske Statsbaner (DSB)* [1997] ECR I–4449. The ECJ upheld the grant of exclusive rights in Case C–323/93, *Société Civile Agricole du Centre d'Insémination de la Crespelle* v. *Coopérative d'Elevage et d'Insémination Artificielle du Départment de la Mayenne* [1994] ECR I–5077.

statutory monopoly is the very fact that the grantee obtains a protected sphere of activity, which is immune from the normal rigours of competition. This is by way of contrast to other firms with a dominant position. They must always be looking over their shoulder lest new entrants erode their market power. This is one of the important reasons why such a firm might decide *not* to price too high, since it will act as an incentive for others to enter the market. The holder of the statutory exclusive right does not have the same rationale for self-restraint.[14] It is for this reason that such firms might well be *induced* to charge disproportionate prices, secure in the knowledge that such excessive pricing cannot operate as a carrot to bring others into the market. It is for this reason that the ECJ was particularly concerned about monopoly power in this form. This is readily understandable when looked at from the Community's point of view, but does not alter the fact that the Court's reasoning comes close to regarding the grant of exclusive statutory rights as abusive *per se*.

The general issue came before the Court again in *Corbeau*.[15] Corbeau set up his own postal service for the City of Liège; for deliveries outside this area he collected the post but sent it on via the normal postal services. He was prosecuted for contravening Belgian laws which conferred a monopoly on the official postal service. The question was whether this constituted a breach of Article 90 (now Article 86). The ECJ reiterated orthodoxy to the effect that the mere creation of a dominant position by the State through the grant of exclusive rights was not in itself incompatible with Article 90. However, it also held that this Article affirmed the idea that the State must not enact or maintain in force measures which could eliminate the effectiveness of provisions such as Article 86 (now Article 82). The Court then went on to consider the application of Article 90(2), which will be analysed below. The effect of the case on the legality of exclusive rights was not entirely clear.

Hancher argued that the Court seemed to condemn the very existence of national rules conferring a dominant position on an undertaking, *unless* the monopoly or exclusive rights could be justified under Article 90(2) (now Article 86(2)).[16] Edward and Hoskins echoed the same approach. They concluded that the creation of a legal monopoly by national law was *prima facie* illegal under EC law, unless it could be justified by a legitimate national objective and satisfied the principle of proportionality.[17]

This reading fits with the Court's mode of analysis in later cases. It has, in many instances, readily found or assumed a breach of Article 86(1), and then decided whether the exclusivity could be justified under Article 86(2). In *Traco*[18] it was held that the grant to Poste Italiana of exclusive rights to carry the post violated Article 86(1). Poste Italiana charged any other postal operator charges equivalent to those paid by customers of Poste Italiana, even though it did not carry the mail. It could not therefore avoid abusing its dominant position, was caught by Article 86(1), and had to

---

[14] At any rate not to nearly the same extent.

[15] Case C–320/91P, *Procureur du Roi* v. *Paul Corbeau* [1993] ECR I–2533.

[16] Note, (1994) 31 *CMLRev.* 105, 111. See also L. Hancher, 'Community, State and Market', in P. Craig and G. de Búrca (eds.), *The Evolution of EU Law* (Oxford University Press, 1999), ch. 20.

[17] D. Edward and M. Hoskins, 'Article 90: Deregulation and EC Law, Reflections Arising from the XVI FIDE Conference' (1995) 32 *CMLRev.* 157. See also Ehlermann, n. 1 above, 273.

[18] Case C–340/99, *TNT Traco SpA* v. *Poste Italiane SpA* [2001] ECR I–4109.

seek justification under Article 86(2). In *Ambulanz Glockner*[19] a public body refused to renew the applicant's authorization to provide non-emergency transport services for patients. Two other companies had exclusive rights to provide emergency services for patients. The ECJ assumed that the grant of these exclusive rights could violate Article 82(b), limiting markets, in the sense that only these two companies were allowed to provide non-emergency, as well as emergency, transport services. There was therefore *prima facie* a breach of Article 86(1), and the ECJ moved on to consider justification under Article 86(2).[20]

The general thrust of these developments is that it is now more difficult than hitherto for a state to organize its economic activities by giving special or exclusive rights to particular firms. Agnosticism as to forms of economic organization has been replaced by a more strident belief in the operation of free markets in which the actors enjoy no specially privileged position.

(c) THE SCOPE OF ARTICLE 86(2): THE FIRST STEP

Article 86(2) (ex article 90(2)) effectively falls into three parts. It begins by emphasizing that undertakings entrusted with the operation of services of a general economic interest, or which have the character of a revenue-producing monopoly, are subject to the Treaty. It then excludes the application of these rules where the performance of the tasks assigned to such undertakings is liable to be obstructed. This exception is then subject to a proviso that the development of trade must not be affected to such an extent as would be contrary to the interests of the Community.

The first step, therefore, in the application of Article 86(2) is to determine whether an undertaking is of the kind mentioned. Not surprisingly the ECJ has stressed that the category of entrusted undertakings should be strictly defined, since the Article derogates from the rules of the Treaty.[21] It is, however, not relevant whether the undertaking is public or private, provided that the service entrusted to it has been assigned by an act of a public authority.[22] While it does not seem that this act has to be in any particular legal form, the State must have taken some definite steps to assign the service to the specific undertaking.[23] It has been accepted that undertakings such as utilities do serve the general economic interest, as required by Article 86(2). The ECJ has also accepted in *Ahmed Saeed* that this Article may apply to airlines obliged by public authorities to operate routes that are not commercially viable, but which it is necessary to operate in the general interest.[24] The Court will, however, subject claims that a service is of a general economic interest to searching scrutiny. Thus, in

---

[19] Case C–475/99, *Ambulanz Glockner* v. *Landkreis Sudwestpfalz* [2001] ECR I–8089.

[20] See also Case C–67/96, *Albany International BV* v. *Stichting Bedrijfspensioenfonds Textielindustrie* [1999] ECR I–5751; Cases 147–148/97, *Deutsche Post AG* v. *Gesellschaft für Zahlungssyteme mbH and Citicorp Kartenservice GmbH* [2000] ECR I–825.

[21] Case 127/73, *BRT* v. *SABAM* [1974] ECR 313; Case C–242/95, *GT-Link*, n. 13 above.

[22] *Ibid.*

[23] Case 7/82, *GVL* v. *Commission* [1983] ECR 483.

[24] Case 66/86, *Ahmed Saeed Flugreisen and Silver Line Reisebüro GmbH* v. *Zentrale zur Bekämpfung Unlauteren Wettbewerbs eV* [1989] ECR 803, para. 55.

the *Merci* case[25] the ECJ rejected the argument that dock work came within this category.

(d) THE SCOPE OF ARTICLE 86(2):
THE SECOND AND THIRD STEPS

The second step in the application of Article 86(2) is to determine whether the exception applies. The ECJ has in the past held that the exception will apply only if the relevant Treaty prohibitions are *incompatible* with the performance of the undertaking's assigned tasks.[26] This is, however, no longer the approach. In *Commission v. Netherlands*,[27] the ECJ held that for Article 90(2) (now Article 86(2)) to apply it was sufficient if the application of the Treaty rules *obstructed the performance, in law or in fact*, of the special obligations incumbent on the undertaking. It was not necessary for the survival of the undertaking itself to be under threat. The Court interpreted *Corbeau*[28] to mean that the conditions for Article 90(2) were met if the maintenance of the exclusive rights was necessary to enable the holder thereof to perform the tasks of general economic interest assigned to it under economically acceptable conditions. The ECJ held that the Commission had not proved its case, judged by these criteria. It also made it clear that a Member State did not have to prove that no other conceivable measure could enable the tasks to be performed under the same conditions.[29]

The ECJ will look closely at claims that the exception applies. In *Ahmed Saeed*[30] the Court held that, in order to take advantage of the exception, the national authorities responsible for the approval of airline tariffs, and the courts to which disputes relating thereto were submitted, must be able to determine the exact nature of the needs in question and their impact on the structure of the tariffs applied by the airlines. While in *Merci*[31] the ECJ decided that, even if dock work were to be regarded as of general economic interest, there was no evidence that this demanded the modification of the Treaty rules so as to prevent any obstruction in the performance of this task. The same approach is apparent in other cases. Thus in *British Telecom*[32] the Commission had made a decision holding certain practices relating to the transmission of messages to be in breach of Article 86 (now Article 82). This decision was challenged by Italy, which argued that the measures adopted by BT should be exempted from the competition rules because of Article 90(2) (now Article 86(2)). The ECJ disagreed. It found that Italy had failed to establish that the

---

[25] Case C–179/90, [1991] ECR I–5889, para. 27; Case C–242/95, *GT-Link*, n. 13 above.
[26] Case 155/73, *Sacchi* [1974] ECR 409; Case 311/84, *Centre Belge d'Etudes du Marché-Télémarketing SA v. Compagnie Luxembourgeoise de Télédiffusion SA and Information Publicité Benelux SA* [1985] ECR 3261.
[27] Case C–157/94, [1997] ECR I–5699.
[28] Case C–320/91P, *Corbeau*, n. 15 above.
[29] See also Case C–340/99, *TNT Traco*, n. 18 above, para. 54; Case C–67/96, *Albany*, n. 20 above, para. 107.
[30] Case 66/86, n. 24 above, para. 56.
[31] Case C–179/90, n. 25 above, para. 27.
[32] Case 41/83, *Re British Telecommunications: Italy v. Commission* [1985] ECR 873, para. 33.

application of these rules to BT would prejudice the accomplishment of the tasks assigned to it.[33]

The ECJ has been more receptive to use of the exception in other cases. The common element in these cases is that the undertaking granted exclusivity has universal service obligations requiring it to perform some tasks that are not in themselves profitable. The only way that it can do this is to have exclusive rights over those parts of the service that are profitable. The fear is that other undertakings will 'cream off' the profitable parts of the relevant business. Thus, in *Corbeau*[34] the ECJ accepted that the Belgian postal service was an entrusted undertaking, and that some restriction on competition might be necessary to enable it to fulfil the duties it was required to perform. If this were not so then other firms could simply 'cream off' the profitable areas of business, since they would have no corresponding obligation to perform loss-making activities. This did not serve to exclude all competition. There could, said the Court, be services which could be dissociated from the general public service, which could be offered by other undertakings without threatening the economic stability needed by the holder of the exclusive right. It was for the national court to determine whether the services in this case came within that category. In *Albany*[35] a company argued that a Dutch law making affiliation to a supplementary pension scheme compulsory was contrary to Article 86. The ECJ decided that the exclusivity was justified under Article 86(2). The compulsory pension scheme was obliged to accept all workers without a prior medical examination, and contributions did not reflect risk. If the exclusive right of the fund to manage the supplementary pension scheme were removed, then undertakings with young employees in good health engaged in non-dangerous activities would seek more advantageous terms from private insurers. The progressive departure of these 'good risks' would leave the pension fund with an increasing share of 'bad risks'. This would lead to an increase in premiums for these workers, since the fund would not be able to offer pensions at the previous cost. The same general approach to the applicability of the Article 86(2) exception is apparent in other cases.[36]

Even if the exception does come into play, we should not forget the *third step* in Article 86(2): that the development of trade must not be affected to such an extent as would be contrary to the interests of the Community. This proviso to the exception has the effect of subjugating Member State interests to those of the Community in the relevant area.

[33] See also Case C–203/96, *Chemische Afvalstoffen Dusseldorp BV* v. *Minister van Volkshuisvesting, Ruimtelijke Ordening en Milieubeheer* [1998] ECR I–4075.

[34] Case C–320/91P, n. 15 above. An analogous argument was unsuccessful in Case T–260/94, *Air Inter SA* v. *Commission* [1997] ECR II–997.

[35] Case C–67/96, *Albany*, n. 20 above, paras. 107–111.

[36] Cases C–115–117/97, *Brentjens' Handelsonderneming BV* v. *Stichting Bedrijfspensioenfonds voor de Handel in Bouwmaterialen* [1999] ECR I–6025, paras. 107–111; Case C–340/99, *Traco*, n. 18 above, paras. 54–63; Case C–475/99, *Ambulanz Glockner*, n. 19 above, paras. 57–66; Cases 147–148/97, *Deutsche Post*, n. 20 above, paras. 50–62; Case C–209/98, *Entreprenorforeningens Affalds/Miljosektion (FFAD)* v. *Kobenhavns Kommune* [2000] ECR I–3473, paras. 77–83.

(e) THE SCOPE OF ARTICLE 86(3)

Article 86(3) gives the Commission power to ensure the application of Article 86 through directives or decisions addressed to Member States. It is one of the relatively rare Treaty provisions which confers direct legislative competence on the Commission. It should not, however, be thought that this is the only way in which Article 86 can be enforced. Recourse may still be had to actions under Article 226 (ex Article 169), and the interpretation of Article 86 can be clarified through Article 234 (ex Article 177) references.

The occasions on which the Commission has chosen to use Article 90(3) (now Article 86(3)) to pass directives have been relatively rare. They have also been the cause of conflict with the Member States, which have challenged the competence of the Commission to proceed in this manner. Thus in the *Transparency Directive* case,[37] the facts of which have been set out above, the Member States argued that the Directive could not be enacted under Article 90(3), which, they said, was limited to dealing with a specific situation in one or more Member States. It did not give any more general legislative power to the Commission. The Court rejected this argument: there was no warrant for construing the term 'directive' in Article 90(3) any differently from the same term in Article 189 (now Article 249).[38] The parties also contended that the directive should have been adopted by the Council pursuant to Article 94 (now Article 89). The ECJ disagreed. The specific power to issue directives contained in Article 90(3) was in furtherance of the Commission's duty of surveillance provided for in Article 90. The fact that the rules might have been enacted by the Council under its general power in Article 94 did not preclude the Commission's exercise of power under Article 90(3).[39] The Court adopted the same approach in the *Telecommunications Terminal Equipment* case.[40] It held that Article 90(3) empowered the Commission to specify in general terms the obligations arising under Article 90(1) by adopting directives. The Commission exercised that power where, without taking into consideration the particular situation existing in the various Member States, it defined in concrete terms the obligations imposed on them under the Treaty. It is clear that the ECJ did not wish unduly to curtail the Commission's power to make directives under Article 90(3) (now Article 86(3)).

The same message is apparent in *Koninklijke PTT Nederland NV*[41] concerning the power to make decisions under Article 90(3). It held that the power under Article 90(3) to make decisions could be used to find that a particular Member State was in breach of Article 90 and the decision could specify the measures which had to be taken to comply with Community law. In the context of decisions, it is apparent, then, that the Commission can proceed by way of Article 90(3) rather than Article 226.

---

[37] Cases 188–90/80, *France, Italy and United Kingdom* v. *Commission* [1982] ECR 2545, paras. 4–15.
[38] *Ibid.*, para. 7.   [39] *Ibid.*, para. 14.
[40] Case C–202/88, *France* v. *Commission* [1991] ECR I–1223.
[41] Cases C–48 & 66/90, *Netherlands, Koninklijke PTT Nederland NV and PTT Post BV* v. *Commission* [1992] ECR I–565; Case C–107/95P, *Bundesverband der Bilanzbuchhalter eV* v. *Commission* [1997] ECR I–947; Case C–163/99, *Portuguese Republic* v. *Commission* [2001] ECR I–2613.

When it chooses to do so it must, however, give fair hearing rights to the affected parties.

(f) ARTICLE 86 AND NATIONAL COURTS

We must now consider how far the provisions of Article 86 (ex Article 90) are directly effective. A distinction in this respect must be drawn between Article 86(1) and (2).

The reason there is difficulty in determining whether Article 86(1) has direct effect is that the Article points to other provisions of the Treaty. It is in this sense a reference provision. Member States are under a duty not to enact or maintain in force measures which are *contrary to the rules contained in the Treaty*. A breach of Article 86 is dependent upon a breach of some other Treaty Article. The ability of individuals to invoke Article 86 will therefore turn on whether the other rule of the Treaty allegedly broken is directly effective. This is exemplified by the *Merci* case.[42] The ECJ held that Articles 30, 48, and 86 (now Articles 28, 39, and 82) have direct effect when they fall to be considered within the framework of Article 90 (now Article 86). National courts must therefore protect the rights of the relevant parties.

The position with respect to direct effect and Article 86(2) is complicated in a rather different way. We have already seen that this Article has three parts: the determination of whether a body is an entrusted undertaking, the application of the exception, and the proviso to the exception.

The ECJ has long recognized the competence of national courts to answer the first of these questions. In *SABAM*[43] the ECJ affirmed that a national court has the duty of investigating whether an undertaking which invokes the provisions of Article 90(2) (now Article 86(2)) has in fact been entrusted by the Member State with the operation of a service of general economic interest.

There has been considerably more uncertainty about whether a national court may apply the exception. The initial response of the ECJ was that Article 90(2) could not be invoked by individuals before national courts in this way; that it did not create rights for individuals.[44] Subsequent case law cast doubt on this proposition. The situation has now been clarified by the *ERT* case.[45] The ECJ reasoned that Article 90(2) subjects entrusted undertakings to the Treaty, except in so far as it can be shown that those rules are incompatible with the performance of their particular tasks. From this premise it concluded that it was open to a national court to determine whether the practices of such an undertaking were compatible with, for example, Article 86 (now Article 82). The national court could also decide whether those practices, if they were contrary to such a provision, could be justified by the needs of the particular task which had been given to the undertaking.[46] The difficulties that this presents for national courts should not, however, be underestimated.[47]

---

[42] Case C–179/90, [1991] ECR I–5889, para. 23; Case C–242/95, *GT-Link*, n. 13 above, para. 57; Case C–258/98, *Carra*, n. 11 above, para. 11.   [43] Case 127/73, n. 21 above.

[44] Case 10/71, *Muller*, n. 7 above.   [45] Case C–260/89, n. 12 above, paras. 33–34.

[46] The ECJ adopted the same approach to the tasks of the national courts in the cases mentioned in nn. 35 and 36, above.

[47] See, e.g., the task presented to the national courts in Case C–320/91P, *Corbeau*, n. 15 above, discussed by Hancher, (1994) 31 *CMLRev.* 105, 119–20.

Should an applicant succeed in bringing a case within the exception, the question remains whether a national court is competent to apply the proviso in Article 86(2) (ex Article 90(2)). It would be difficult for the national courts to perform this task, since they may not have the information on which to make the assessment. On this view it would require a Commission decision made under Article 86(3) to decide the issue.

(g) SUMMARY

i. Article 86, and especially Article 86(2), seeks to reconcile a Member State's interest in using certain undertakings as an instrument of social and/or economic policy with the Community's interest in ensuring compliance with the rules on competition and the internal market.

ii. It is clear that the mere grant of a monopoly, or exclusive rights, will not infringe Article 86(1). It will do so only when the exercise of the exclusive rights could not avoid being abusive, or where such rights were liable to create a situation in which the undertaking was induced to commit an abuse.

iii. It is equally clear that the ECJ has been ready to find that either of these conditions applies, and that therefore Article 86(1) is applicable.

iv. It is then for the State to provide a justification under Article 86(2). It must be shown that the Treaty rules should be excluded because they would obstruct the performance of the tasks assigned to the undertaking granted exclusive rights. The ECJ will subject such claims to close scrutiny, and it has rejected them on a number of occasions. However, there is also a significant body of case law in which the ECJ has held the exception to be applicable. It has recognized this in relation to bodies with universal service obligations or the equivalent thereto. Exclusivity in such instances has been held to be warranted in order that the profitable parts of an activity are not 'creamed off' by the private sector, with the consequence that the body granted exclusive rights is unable, financially, to fulfil its remit.

4. THE STATE, ARTICLES 10, 81, 82, AND 28[48]

The discussion thus far has focused on Article 86 (ex Article 90). This is not, however, the only Treaty provision relevant to state action and the Community. The Court has also made important decisions on the basis of Articles 5, 85, 86, and 30 (now Articles 10, 81, 82, and 28). The basic principle is that a State may not adopt or maintain in force any measure which would deprive, for example, Article 85 (now Article 81) of its effectiveness or prejudice its full and uniform application. A State can be in breach of this obligation either when it requires or encourages undertakings to conclude cartels

---

[48] P.J. Slot, 'The Application of Articles 3(f), 5 and 85 to 94 EEC' (1987) 12 *ELRev.* 179; L. Gyselen, 'State Action and the Effectiveness of the Treaty's Competition Provisions' (1989) 26 *CMLRev.* 33.

in violation of Article 85, or when it divests its national provisions of their public nature by, in effect, delegating to the firms the responsibility for taking decisions about the boundaries of competition.[49] In essence, this jurisprudence is the means whereby the ECJ has extended the type of obligation imposed on a State by Article 90 (now Article 86) to situations where the undertakings are neither public nor enjoy any specially privileged position. The following cases illustrate the Court's jurisprudence at work.

In *Vereniging van Vlaamse Reisbureaus* v. *Sociale Dienst van de Plaatselijke en Gewestelijke Overheidsdiensten*[50] a travel agent was prosecuted for violating a professional code of practice incorporated into Belgian law. The code involved horizontal price fixing, a blatant breach of Article 85 (now Article 81). The Court also found that the Belgian State was in breach of Article 5 (now Article 10), read together with Article 85, by supporting the cartel through its own legal regime. A similar theme is apparent in *Van Eycke*.[51] Holders of certain Belgian savings accounts had the benefit of a tax exemption, provided that the bank offered them interest rates below that set by the Minister in a Royal Decree. Those who held accounts at banks which gave higher interest rates than that stipulated by the Royal Decree lost the tax exemption, with the consequence that it was unattractive for the banks to offer these higher rates. The effect of this was to limit price competition between banks. The ECJ held that, although the duty in Articles 85 and 86 (now Articles 81 and 82) is directed towards undertakings, the State itself has an obligation, derived from Article 5 (now Article 10), not to introduce measures which render the competition Articles ineffective. This would be the case where, for example, national legislation reinforced the effects of existing agreements that were in breach of Article 85; or where the State deprived its own legislation of its official character by delegating to private traders responsibility for taking decisions affecting the economic sphere.[52] More recent attempts to invoke this principle have, however, not been notably successful.[53]

Where the State intervenes not to support an existing agreement which is itself illegal under Article 81, but through an independent measure which undertakings must follow, Article 28 (ex Article 30) would be the most appropriate provision to employ in the case of goods, and Article 49 (ex Article 59) in the case of services.[54]

---

[49] For recent affirmation of this principle see Case C–2/91, *Wolf Meng* [1993] ECR I–5751; Case C–245/91, *Ohra Schadeverzekeringen NV* [1993] ECR I–5851; Case C–153/93, *Germany v. Delta Schiffahrts- und Speditionsgesellschaft mbH* [1994] ECR I–2517; Case C–185/91, *Bundesanstalt für den Güterfernverkehr* v. *Gebrüder Reiff GmbH & Co. KG* [1993] ECR I–5801; Cases C–140–142/94, *DIP SpA* v. *Commune di Bassano del Grappa* [1995] ECR I–3257; Case C–70/95, *Sodemare SA, Anni Azzuri Holding SpA and Anni Azzuri Rezzato Srl* v. *Regione Lombardia* [1997] ECR I–3395. On the facts of these cases there was no breach of the principle set out in the text.

[50] Case 311/85, [1987] ECR 3801.

[51] Case 267/86, *Van Eycke* v. *NV ASPA* [1988] ECR 4769.

[52] See also Case 229/83, *Leclerc* v. *Au Blé Vert* [1985] ECR 1, [1985] 2 CMLR 286; Cases 209–213/84, *Ministère Public* v. *Asjes* [1986] ECR 1425.

[53] See the cases in n. 49 above.

[54] Case 229/83, *Leclerc*, n. 52 above.

5. STATE AIDS: THE SUBSTANTIVE RULES, AND ARTICLE 87

(a) THE COMMISSION AND THE DEVELOPMENT OF POLICY

Certain general points should be made clear before discussing the detail of the rules on state aids.

First, the Commission, as the initial decision-maker, will develop the *general substantive policy* in this area.[55] The Commission decisions are subject to judicial review, but the ECJ and CFI will be mindful of the fact that assessment of the exceptions may entail complex evaluations of social and economic data, and they will not, therefore, substitute their view for that of the Commission. The Commission possesses discretion as to the general approach to be taken to state aids. Thus the Commission has, for example, applied a principle of compensatory justification. Before it will approve aid, there must be some contribution by the beneficiary of the aid, over and above the normal play of market forces, to the attainment of Community objectives as contained in the derogations from Article 87(3).[56] In general terms, aid can be designed to restructure an undertaking, to rescue an undertaking, or to help it with operating costs. The Commission has provided guidelines on these.[57] The guidelines for restructuring aid stipulate, *inter alia*, that viability is restored, that aid is in proportion to the restructuring costs and benefits, that undue distortions of competition are avoided, and that the restructuring plan is fully implemented. Operating aid relieves an undertaking of expenses that it would normally bear in its day-to-day operations, with no technical or structural alteration in the character of the recipient. It is generally regarded as objectionable by the Commission[58] and the Court,[59] and is normally only authorized to cope with specific regional or sectoral problems.

Secondly, the Commission can also choose *how to develop its substantive policy, whether through formal legislation or through informal rule-making*. The Commission has made formal legislation in certain areas. The Council has, pursuant to Article 94, delegated power to the Commission to make regulations exempting types of aid from the requirement of notification, and stipulating that it shall be regarded as compatible with the common market.[60] The Commission has used this power to make formal regulations concerning small and medium-sized enterprises,[61] *de minimis* aid,[62] and

---

[55] Valuable guides to the various sectoral and horizontal aid frameworks used by the Commission are to be found in L. Hancher, T. Ottervanger, and P.J. Slot, *EC State Aids* (Sweet and Maxwell, 2nd edn., 1999); A. Evans, *EC Law of State Aid* (Oxford University Press, 1997).

[56] *Ibid.*, ch. 3.

[57] *Community Guidelines on State Aid for Rescuing and Restructuring Firms in Difficulty* [1999] OJ C288/2.

[58] Evans, n. 55 above, 131–8.

[59] Case T–459/93, *Siemens SA v. Commission* [1995] ECR II–1675, upheld on appeal in Case C–278/95P, *Siemens SA v. Commission* [1997] ECR I–2507; Case T–214/95, *Vlaams Gewest v. Commission* [1998] ECR II–717.

[60] Council Reg. 994/98, [1998] OJ L142/1.

[61] Comm. Reg. 70/2001, [2001] OJ L10/33.

[62] Comm. Reg. 69/2001, [2001] OJ L10/30.

training aid.[63] Formal legislation has also been made on procedural matters.[64] However, in most instances the Commission has developed policy through guidelines, communications, and the like, rather than formal legislation. In *Vlaams Gewest*[65] the CFI held that it was legitimate for the Commission to adopt guidelines to structure its discretion under Article 87(3)(c), provided that they were consistent with the Treaty.

Thirdly, the Commission can choose to *develop its substantive policy through individual decisions or informal rule-making.*[66] This choice is open to all administrators, whether operating at national or Community level. It is unsurprising that in the field of state aids the Commission has chosen to employ rules and policy guidelines, as well as individual decisions. These rules and policy frameworks have been made both in relation to particular industrial sectors, and also in relation to matters, such as regional aid,[67] environmental aid,[68] deprived areas,[69] and the like. The ECJ has held that it is lawful for the Commission to structure its discretion through such guidelines, provided that they do not depart from the Treaty rules.[70] The reasons for employing such policy documents are part practical and part conceptual. In practical terms such guidelines help an overburdened administration to cope with an increased work-load.[71] In conceptual terms they have the advantages generally associated with a rule-making system.[72] They 'reduce Member States' room for manœuvre in giving aid and the controller's margin of discretion, choice and possible arbitrariness';[73] and they facilitate 'the transparency, legal security and credibility which result from strict and consistent enforcement, to the benefit of governments and industry'.[74] The use of rule-making is not, however, unproblematic. If the benefits of giving effect to administrative policy in this way are familiar to public lawyers, so, too, are some of the problems.

One such problem is the very variety of instruments used by the Commission. Directives, policy guidelines, and statements of policy all jostle one another within the Commission's portfolio.[75] While the legal form of the instrument may not, from

[63] Comm. Reg. 68/2001, [2001] OJ L10/20.

[64] Council Reg. 659/99, [1999] OJ L83/1.

[65] Case T–214/95, n. 59 above, para. 89; Case T–149/95, *Ducros* v. *Commission* [1997] ECR II–2031, para. 61.

[66] EC Commission *Commission Vademecum: Community Rules on State Aid* (EC Commission, 1999).

[67] *Community Guidelines on National Regional Aids* [1998] OJ C74/9; *National Ceilings for Regional Aid under the Derogations Provided for in Art. 87(3)(a) and (c) for the Period 2000–06* [1999] OJ C16/5.

[68] *Community Guidelines on State Aid for Environmental Protection* [2001] OJ C37/3.

[69] *Guidelines on State Aid for Undertakings in Deprived Urban Areas* [1997] OJ C146/8.

[70] Case C–313/90, *CIRFS* v. *Commission* [1993] ECR I–1125, paras. 34–36; Case C–288/96, *Germany* v. *Commission* [2000] ECR I–8237, para. 62.

[71] F. Rawlinson, 'The Role of Policy Frameworks, Codes and Guidelines in the Control of State Aid', in I. Harden (ed.), *State Aid: Community Law and Policy* (Bundesanzeiger, 1993), 56; Evans, n. 55 above, 408–27.

[72] P.P. Craig, *Administrative Law* (Sweet & Maxwell, 4th edn., 1999), ch. 16.

[73] Rawlinson, n. 71 above, 55.

[74] *Ibid.*, 57.

[75] This problem has been recognized by the Commission: see *Guidelines on National Regional Aid* [1998] OJ C74/6, para. 1.

the Commission's perspective, affect its binding character,[76] matters may not always be so clear-cut from the perspective of those on the receiving end of the system.[77]

Another problem concerns the extent to which such guidelines may be binding. In *Deufil*[78] the ECJ refused to accept that the absence of mention of a certain form of aid in a particular sectoral guideline generated a legitimate expectation that such species of aid were in fact permissible. However, in *CIRFS*[79] the ECJ was willing to accept that in the instant case the Commission was bound by the terms of its policy framework, and in *Ijssel-Vliet*[80] it held that Commission guidelines which had been built into a Dutch aid scheme were binding upon the Dutch government. Moreover, in *Vlaams Gewest*[81] the CFI held that the guidelines adopted by the Commission had to be applied in accordance with the principle of equal treatment, with the implication that like cases, as defined in the guidelines, had to be treated alike.

A final difficulty arising from the Commission's use of policy guidelines is of a broader intra-institutional nature. It concerns the relationship between this mode of developing policy and the possibility of passing Council regulations pursuant to Article 89 (ex Article 94), which would thereby involve Member State participation and consent more fully than under the guideline procedure. Rawlinson, a principal administrator within the state aids directorate, was forthright in this respect: the 'Commission does not go to the Council because it, and not the Member States, is the guardian of the Treaties in the area of state aids'.[82] While accepting that the Commission should and does consult Member States, he is clear in his belief that greater use of Article 89 would not only be inappropriate for the reason just given, but also that particularistic Member State interests would make policy-making far more protracted. Others are less happy about the effective by-passing of Article 89. Thus Cananea has pointed to the lack of clarity of certain guidelines, and to the fact that the rights of individuals have not always been properly safeguarded. He has suggested that the time may now be ripe for the passage of a 'Council regulation to cope with the existing lacunae of Community law on state aids'.[83] Hancher has also noted a number of important instances where there is uncertainty, concluding that there is an 'urgent need for clearer procedural guidelines for all concerned'.[84] Attempts to use this Article to promulgate more formal regulations have, however, been opposed by a majority of the states and the Commission.[85]

---

[76] Rawlinson, n. 71 above, 59.
[77] G. della Cananea, 'Administration by Guidelines: The Policy Guidelines of the Commission in the Field of State Aids', in *State Aid: Community Law and Policy*, n. 71 above, 68–9.
[78] Case 310/85, *Deufil* v. *Commission* [1987] ECR 901.
[79] Case C–313/90, *CIRFS*, n. 70 above.
[80] Case C–311/94, *Ijssel-Vliet Combinatie BV* v. *Minister van Economische Zaken* [1996] ECR I–5023.
[81] Case T–214/95, n. 59 above, para. 89.
[82] N. 71 above, 60.
[83] Della Cananea, n. 77 above, 74–5.
[84] L. Hancher, 'State Aids and Judicial Control' [1994] *ECLR* 134, 150.
[85] Evans, n. 55 above, 405–8.

(b) ARTICLE 87(1)

Article 87 (ex Article 92) lays down the basic test for state aids. It covers aid given to public undertakings within Article 86 (ex Article 90), subject to the reservation in Article 86(2), as well as aid given to private firms.[86] The Article has three parts. Paragraph (1) establishes the general principle that state aids are incompatible with the common market. Paragraph (2) provides certain exceptions for situations where the aid *will be deemed* to be compatible with the common market. Paragraph (3) lists certain types of case where the aid *may be deemed* to be compatible with the common market. Let us then begin with the basic proscription of state aids set out in Article 87(1):

Save as otherwise provided in this Treaty, any aid granted by a Member State or through State resources in any form whatsoever which distorts or threatens to distort competition by favouring certain undertakings or the production of certain goods shall, in so far as it affects trade between Member States, be incompatible with the common market.

The obvious starting point is the *definition of state aid*.[87] Article 87(1) does not itself provide any such definition. The ECJ and the Commission have, as might be expected, adopted a broad view of what constitutes state aid. The rationale for the giving of aid is not relevant for the definitional task performed under Article 87(1).[88] Moreover, substance, not form, is the criterion when defining aid. The Commission has provided a full list of the varying types of aid. These include direct subsidies, tax exemptions,[89] exemptions from parafiscal charges, preferential interest rates, favourable loan guarantees, the provision of land or buildings on special terms, indemnities against losses, preferential terms for public ordering, the deferment of the collection of fiscal or social contributions, and dividend guarantees. This list is, of course, illustrative rather than exhaustive. The ECJ has also made it clear that the concept of aid covers not only positive benefits, such as subsidies, but also actions which mitigate the charges an undertaking would normally bear, such as the supply of goods or services at a preferential rate,[90] a reduction in social security contributions,[91] or tax exemptions.[92]

General measures of economic policy, such as an interest-rate reduction, while benefiting industrial sales, will not in themselves be classified as aid.[93] In this sense a non-sectoral measure of general taxation policy will remain within the area of state

---

[86] Case C–387/92, *Banco de Credito Industrial SA (Banco Exterior de Espana SA)* v. *Ayuntamiento de Valencia* [1994] ECR I–877; Case T–106/95, *Fédération Française des Sociétés d'Assurances (FFSA)* v. *Commission* [1997] ECR II–229.

[87] Evans, n. 55 above, 27–46.

[88] Case 173/73, *Italy* v. *Commission* [1974] ECR 709; Case C–241/94, *France* v. *Commission* [1996] ECR I–4187; Case C–251/97, *France* v. *Commission* [1999] ECR I–6639.

[89] Case C–387/92, *Banco de Credito*, n. 86 above.

[90] Case C–241/94, *France*, n. 88 above; Case C–387/92, *Banco de Credito*, n. 86 above; Case C–39/94, *Syndicat Français de l'Express International (SFEI)* v. *La Poste* [1996] ECR I–3547; Case C–143/99, *Adria-Wien Pipeline GmbH and Wietersdörfer & Peggauer Zementwerke GmbH* v. *Finanzlandesdirektion für Kärnten* [2001] ECR I–8365.

[91] Case C–75/97, *Belgium* v. *Commission* [1999] ECR I–3671.

[92] Case C–6/97, *Italy* v. *Commission* [1999] ECR I–2981.

[93] Case C–143/99, *Adria-Wien*, n. 90 above, para. 35.

fiscal sovereignty. It is, however, also clear that a measure will be classified as aid even if it benefits a whole range of undertakings, as in the case of a general export aid. An intent to extend a benefit to the whole economy will not prevent relief granted to particular undertakings from being classified as aid.[94] Moreover, the dividing line between general measures of economic policy and state aids may be a fine one as the following extract makes clear.

C. Quigley, The Notion of a State Aid in the EEC[95]

Although general measures of economic policy will not constitute aid, many measures taken by the state can produce benefits to undertakings or production of goods generally. Such measures may constitute aid and, if they fulfil the other criteria in Article 92(1), will be incompatible with the common market. A distinction lies between general measures of economic policy and specific measures within that policy. Those elements of infrastructure which are normally provided by the state, such as roads, bridges and tunnels, would usually form part of the transport and environmental policy of the state and would not be regarded as aid, even though particular undertakings or regions would benefit from the improvements.[96] On the other hand, if the development is carried out, not solely as part of the general transport and environmental policy but as part of a regional or sectoral plan within that policy, there may be an element of aid. Also, where the state normally insists on such infrastructure being built by private persons, such as the roads on a private industrial estate, any provision by the state of such facilities may constitute aid.

Whether the taking of a shareholding in a private company by the State should be considered as aid has given rise to particular difficulty, as demonstrated by the following cases.

Case 323/82, Intermills SA v. Commission
[1984] ECR 3809

The Belgian government had intervened to aid a paper-making firm which was in financial difficulty. The object was to restructure the operations of the company, so that it shifted its production from the making of bulk paper to the making of special paper with a high added value. To this end the Belgian government, through the Walloon Regional Executive, made loans to the company and also injected capital into the enterprise, which gave it a controlling interest in the firm. One of the questions which arose in the case was whether the capital injection, whereby the government acquired shares in the firm, could constitute state aid for the purposes of Article 92(1).

---

[94] Case C–75/97, *Belgium* v. *Commission*, n. 91 above.

[95] (1988) 13 *ELRev.* 242, 252–3. References to Art. 92 should now be read as to Art. 87. See also Evans, n. 55 above, 46–54.

[96] On this point see now Case C–225/91, *Matra* v. *Commission* [1993] ECR I–3203: aid for infrastructure did not fall within Art. 92 (now Art. 87) since it was not intended for the exclusive benefit of those partaking in a joint venture.

31. It is clear from the provisions cited that the Treaty applies to aid granted by a State or through State resources 'in any form whatsoever'. It follows that no distinction can be drawn between aid granted in the form of loans and aid granted in the form of a holding acquired in the capital of an undertaking. Aid taking either form falls within the prohibition in Article 92 where the conditions set out in that provision are fulfilled.

Case C–142/87, Re Tubemeuse: Belgium v. Commission[97]
[1990] ECR I–959

[Note ToA renumbering: Arts. 92 and 93 are now Arts. 87 and 88]

In 1979 the Belgian Government acquired 72 per cent of the capital holding of Tubemeuse (T), which was in severe financial difficulty following the withdrawal of private shareholders. In 1982 the Commission approved a series of aid measures, but these were not successful and the State then acquired the remaining shares in the firm. Between 1984 and 1986 Belgium initiated a series of measures designed to increase the capital of T. These measures were notified to the Commission, but the Government did not wait for the Commission's approval of them as required by Article 93(2). The Commission then made a decision that these measures constituted unlawful aid and instructed Belgium to recover the sums. The Belgian Government contested this Commission decision. One of the grounds of this challenge was that the measures in 1984–6 did not constitute State aid at all, but were rather the normal reaction of any investor whose initial investment (made in 1979 and then in 1982) was at risk.

25. It should be pointed out that, according to settled case law, investment by the public authorities in the capital of undertakings, in whatever form, may constitute State aid where the conditions set out in Article 92 are fulfilled (see Case 323/82, *Intermills* v. *Commission* and Joined Cases 296 & 318/82, *Netherlands and Leeuwarder Papierwarenfabriek* v. *Commission*)

26. In order to determine whether such measures are in the nature of State aid, the relevant criterion is that indicated in the Commission's decision, and not contested by the Belgian government, namely whether the undertaking could have obtained the amounts in question on the capital market.

27. In the event, it can be seen from the contested measure taken together with the other documents before the Court that, in addition to the technical difficulties of its plant, which made necessary the extensive modernisation programme in 1982 carried out with the help of the public authorities and authorised by the Commission, the company has, since 1979, had to face structural financial difficulties. Excessively high production costs, continual operating losses, poor liquidity and heavy indebtedness led to the withdrawal of almost all the private shareholders from the undertaking.

---

[97] See also Cases 296 & 318/82, *The Netherlands and Leeuwarder Papierwarenfabriek BV* v. *Commission* [1985] ECR 809; Case 40/85, *Re Boch: Belgium* v. *Commission* [1986] ECR 2321 2 CMLR 301; Case T–16/96, *Cityflyer Express Ltd.* v. *Commission* [1998] ECR II–757; Evans, n. 55 above, 56–70.

28. Moreover, it is not contested that the seamless steel tubes sector whose production was intended principally for use in oil exploration, was in a state of crisis, marked by considerable surplus capacity in the producing countries and new production capacity in the developing and State trading countries. Furthermore, the restrictions which the United States imposed on the importation of steel tubes into their territory and the fall in world oil prices, which contributed to a reduction in drilling, led to a fall in demand for the tubes in question and therefore to a substantial reduction in their price and in world production. That is the reason why other Member States sought to reduce their production capacity in that sector.

29. Under those circumstances, there is nothing which suggests any error in the Commission's assessment that Tubemeuse's prospects of profitability were not such as to induce private investors operating under normal market economy conditions to enter into the financial transactions in question, that it was unlikely that Tubemeuse could have obtained the amounts essential for its survival on the capital markets and that, for that reason, the Belgian government's support for Tubemeuse constituted State aid.

The ECJ has continued to apply the same test. It was argued that a private investor[98] might invest money in a company for reasons not directly related to profitability, such as the wish to maintain the company's public image. The ECJ's response was that when capital is invested by a public investor there must be some interest in profitability in the long term, otherwise the investment will be characterized as aid for the purposes of Article 92(1) (now Article 87(1)).[99]

The privatization of an undertaking may also give rise to questions concerning state aid, depending upon the terms of the privatization. The Commission has provided guidelines on this issue.[100]

A second important aspect of Article 87(1) (ex Article 92(1)) is that the aid should be granted by a '*Member State or through State resources*'. Only advantages granted directly or indirectly through state resources are regarded as aid.[101] It is clear, as we have already seen from the *Intermills* case, that this can include regional as well as central government. It can also include advantages granted by a public or private body designated or established by the State.

---

[98] It is necessary to distinguish between the obligations which a State must assume as owner of the share capital, and its obligations as a public authority. The latter cannot be included in the calculation: Cases C–278–280/92, *Spain* v. *Commission* [1994] ECR I–4103.

[99] Case C–303/88, *Italy* v. *Commission* [1991] ECR I–1433; Case C–305/89, *Italy* v. *Commission* [1991] ECR I–1635; Case C–42/93, *Re State Aid to the Merco Company: Spain* v. *Commission* [1994] ECR I–4175; L. Hancher, 'State Aids and Judicial Control in the European Community' [1994] *ECLR* 134, 135–6.

[100] *Twenty-third Report on Competition Policy*, 255–6; Evans, n. 55 above, 70–6.

[101] Cases C–52–54/97, *Viscido, Scandella and Terragnolo* v. *Ente Poste Italiane* [1998] ECR I–2629.

Cases 67, 68 and 70/85, Kwerkerij Gebroeders Van der Kooy BV v. Commission[102]
[1988] ECR 219

The Commission made a decision that the tariffs charged by Gasunie for gas to certain firms in the horticultural industry were preferential and constituted aid for the purposes of Article 92. Gasunie was a company incorporated under private law, but 50 per cent of its shares were held by the Dutch government, and the tariffs charged by Gasunie were subject to approval by a government minister. One of the grounds on which the decision was challenged was that the fixing of the tariff did not constitute action by the Dutch State.

THE ECJ

32. In the first place, the applicants maintain that . . . the contested tariff was not imposed by the Dutch State and cannot be regarded as 'aid granted by a Member State or through State resources'.

33. They argue that Gasunie is a company incorporated under private law in which the Dutch State holds only 50% of the share capital and that the tariff is the outcome of an agreement concluded under private law between Gasunie, Vegin and the Landbouwchap, to which the Dutch State is not a party.

34. Turning to the point noted by the Commission that the Minister for Economic Affairs has a right of approval over the tariffs charged by Gasunie, the Dutch Government claims that that is no more than a retrospective supervisory power which is solely concerned with whether the tariffs accord with the aims of Dutch energy policy.

35. As the Court has held . . ., there is no necessity to draw any distinction between cases where aid is granted directly by the State and where it is granted by public and or private bodies established or appointed by the State to administer the aid. In this instance, the documents before the Court provide considerable evidence to show that the fixing of the disputed tariff was the result of action by the Dutch State.

36. First of all, the shares in Gasunie are so distributed that the Dutch State directly or indirectly holds 50% of the shares and appoints half of the members of the supervisory board—a body whose powers include that of determining the tariffs to be applied. Secondly, the Minister for Economic Affairs is empowered to approve the tariffs applied by Gasunie, with the result that, regardless of how that power may be exercised, the Dutch Government can block any tariff which does not suit it. Lastly, Gasunie and the Landbouwschap have on two occasions given effect to the Commission's representations to the Dutch Government seeking an amendment of the horticultural tariff. . . .

37. Considered as a whole, these factors demonstrate that Gasunie in no way enjoys full autonomy in the fixing of gas tariffs but acts under the control and on the instructions of the public authorities. It is thus clear that Gasunie could not fix the tariff without taking account of the requirements of the public authorities.

---

[102] See also Case 78/76, *Firma Steinike und Weinlig* v. *Bundesamt für Ernährung und Forstwirtschaft* [1977] ECR 595; Case 290/83, *Re Grants to Poor Farmers: Commission* v. *France* [1985] ECR 439; Case 57/86, *Commission* v. *Greece* [1988] ECR 2855; Case T–358/94, *Compagnie Nationale Air France* v. *Commission* [1996] ECR II–2109. However, as is shown by Cases C–72–73/91, *Sloman Neptun Schiffahrts AG* v. *Seebetriebsrat Bodo Ziesmer der Sloman Neptun Schiffahrts* [1993] ECR I–887, there may well be difficult issues as to what constitutes a resource granted from the State.

38. It may therefore be concluded that the fixing of the contested tariff is the result of action by the Dutch State and thus falls within the meaning of the phrase 'aid granted by a Member State'. . . .

The third requirement of Article 87(1) is that the aid should *distort or threaten to distort competition by favouring certain undertakings or the production of certain goods.*[103] In many cases this will be unproblematic. The grant of, for example, a subsidy will indubitably place the recipient in a more advantageous position than it would have been in without this financial benefit. The Court will consider the position of the relevant company prior to the receipt of the aid, and if this has been improved then the Article will have been met.[104] It is no 'defence' for the State to argue that the aid is justified because its effect is to lower the costs of a sector of industry which has, in relative terms, higher costs than other industrial sectors.[105] Nor is it possible for a State to contend that its aid should be excused on the ground that other States made similar payments to firms within those countries.[106]

The final element in Article 87(1) is that there should be an *effect on inter-state trade.*[107] If aid strengthens the financial position of one undertaking as compared to others within the Community then inter-Community trade will be affected.[108] Moreover, the ECJ has made it clear that the relatively small amount of the aid, or the relatively small size of the recipient undertaking, does not as such exclude the possibility that Community trade may be affected.[109] It is not necessary for the Commission to prove that trade will be affected; it is sufficient to show that trade may be affected.[110] The need to find an impact on Community trade will not normally hinder the Court if it is minded to press forward with investigation of an issue.[111]

(c) ARTICLE 87(2)

Article 87(2) (ex Article 92(2)) lists three types of aid which are deemed to be compatible with the common market.

Article 87(2)(a) states that 'aid having a social character, granted to individual consumers, provided that such aid is granted without discrimination related to the origin of the products concerned' will be compatible with the common market. This Article legitimates aid only if there is no discrimination as to the goods' origin. This limits the number of occasions on which a State will be able to take advantage of this provision, since most state aid is directed exclusively to a particular firm within the Member State providing the aid.

---

[103] Evans, n. 55 above, 76–91.   [104] Case 173/73, n. 88 above.
[105] *Ibid.*   [106] Case 78/76, *Steinike*, n. 102 above.
[107] Evans, n. 55 above, 92–6.
[108] Case 730/79, *Philip Morris Holland BV* v. *Commission* [1980] ECR 2671.
[109] Case C–142/87, *Re Tubemeuse: Belgium* v. *Commission* [1990] ECR I–959, para. 43.
[110] Cases T–298, 312, 313, 315, 600–607/97, 1, 3–6, & 23/98, *Alzetta Mauro* v. *Commission* [2000] ECR II–2319, paras. 76–90.
[111] Case C–75/97, *Belgium* v. *Commission*, n. 91 above.

Article 87(2)(b) legitimates 'aid to make good damage caused by natural disasters or exceptional occurrences'. The rationale for this exception is self-evident. The limits of this Article are, however, somewhat unclear. While the notion of a natural disaster is reasonably apparent, the meaning of exceptional occurrence is open to a wider range of interpretation. It is, for example, contestable whether this would cover economic difficulties.

Article 87(2)(c) makes provision for the special position of Germany, resulting from the division of the country, in order to compensate for the economic disadvantage caused by that division. It does not however allow full compensation for the new *Länder*.[112]

(d) ARTICLE 87(3): PARTICULAR CATEGORIES

Whereas aid which comes within the exceptions mentioned in Article 87(2) will be deemed to be compatible with the common market, the exceptions listed in Article 87(3) (ex Article 92(3)) are discretionary: aid which comes within these categories *may* be deemed to be compatible with the common market.

Article 87(3)(a) (ex Article 92(3)(a)) states that 'aid to promote the economic development of areas where the standard of living is abnormally low or where there is serious under-employment' may be considered to be compatible with the common market. There is a connection between this provision and Article 87(3)(c), in that both relate in a general sense to regional development. The wording of Article 87(3)(a) makes it clear that it can, however, only be used where the problem in an area is especially serious. The Commission has taken the view, upheld by the Court, that the seriousness of the regional problem must be judged in a Community and not a national context. To this end the Commission has published criteria for deciding upon the relative development of different regions as compared to the Community average.[113] This point, as well as the general principles mentioned above, are exemplified by the *Philip Morris Holland* case.

Case 730/79, Philip Morris Holland BV v. Commission
[1980] ECR 2671

[Note ToA renumbering: Art. 92(3) is now Art. 87(3)]

The Dutch Government gave aid to a tobacco manufacturer. The Commission found that the aid did not come within Article 92(3)(a),(b), or (c). What follows is an extract from the ECJ's reasoning concerning the general approach to Article 92(3), and its findings on Article 92(3)(a).

---

112 Cases T–132 & 143/96, *Freistaat Sachsen v. Commission* [1999] ECR II–3663.

113 *Guidelines on National Regional Aid* [1998] OJ C74/6, para. 3.5; F. Wishlade, 'Competition Policy or Cohesion Policy by the Back Door? The Commission Guidelines on National Regional Aid' [1998] *ECLR* 343.

THE ECJ

16. According to the applicant it is wrong for the Commission to lay down as a general principle that aid granted by a Member State to undertakings only falls within the derogating provisions of Article 92(3) if the Commission can establish that the aid will contribute to the attainment of one of the objectives specified in the derogations, which under normal market conditions the recipient firms would not attain by their own actions. Aid is only permissible under Article 92(3) of the Treaty if the investment plan under consideration is in conformity with the objectives mentioned in subparagraphs (a), (b) and (c).

17. This argument cannot be upheld. On the one hand it disregards the fact that Article 92(3), unlike Article 92(2), gives the Commission a discretion by providing that the aid which it specifies 'may' be considered to be compatible with the Common Market. On the other hand it would result in Member States being permitted to make payments which would improve the financial situation of the recipient undertaking although they were not necessary for the attainment of the objectives specified in Article 92(3).

18. It should be noted in this connection that the disputed decision explicitly states that the Dutch Government has not been able to give nor has the Commission found any grounds establishing that the proposed aid meets the conditions laid down to enforce derogations pursuant to Article 92(3) of the EEC Treaty.

19. The applicant maintains that the Commission was wrong to hold that the standard of living in the Bergen-op-Zoom area is not 'abnormally low' and that this area does not suffer serious 'under employment' within the meaning of Article 92(3)(a). In fact in the Bergen-op-Zoom region the under-employment rate is higher and the per capita rate lower than the national average in the Netherlands.

. . .

24. These arguments put forward by the applicant cannot be upheld. It should be borne in mind that the Commission has a discretion the exercise of which involves economic and social assessments which must be made in a Community context.

25. That is the context in which the Commission has with good reason assessed the standard of living and serious under-employment in the Bergen-op-Zoom area, not with reference to the national average in the Netherlands but in relation to the Community level.

Article 87(3)(b) (ex Article 92(3)(b)) states that 'aid to promote the execution of an important project of European interest or to remedy a serious disturbance in the economy of a Member State' may be considered to be compatible with the common market. This provision clearly covers two separate types of case. The meaning of the first limb was considered in the *Glaverbel* case. Note the ECJ's more general observations concerning the discretion possessed by the Commission, and its impact on the ECJ's standard of review.

Cases 62 and 72/87, Executif Régional Wallon and Glaverbel SA v. Commission [1988] ECR 1573

The Belgian Government gave aid to certain glass producers. The Commission found that the aid did not come within Article 92(3). The applicants argued that the aid could come within Article

92(3)(b) on the ground that the new technology made possible by the investment aid would reduce European dependence on American and Japanese producers in the relevant markets.

THE ECJ

21. It should be observed that the categories of aid set out in Article 92(3) ... 'may' be considered by the Commission to be compatible with the Common Market. It follows that the Commission enjoys a discretion in the matter.

23. ... The Commission has based its policy with regard to aid on the view that a project may not be described as being of common European interest for the purposes of Article 92(3)(b) unless it forms part of a transnational European programme supported jointly by a number of governments of the Member States, or arises from concerted action by a number of Member States to combat a common threat such as environmental pollution.

In adopting that policy and in taking the view that the investments envisaged in this case did not fulfil the requisite conditions, the Commission did not commit a manifest error of judgment.

24. The two applicants further complain that the Commission failed to give any reasons in the contested decision for its negative assessment. ....

25. The Court considers that a statement of reasons which is based on a supposedly 'clear' fact must generally be regarded as insufficient. In this case, however, the applicants' arguments cannot be accepted. None of the documents laid before the Court lends any support whatever to the conclusion that the aid at issue might contribute to the implementation of an 'important' project of 'common' European interest. The mere fact that the investments enabled new technology to be used does not make the project one of common European interest; that certainly cannot be the case when, as in this instance, the products have to be sold on a saturated market.

The first limb of Article 87(3)(b) has been used in cases concerned with the development of a common standard for high-definition television and environmental protection.[114]

The second limb of this Article concerning serious disturbance to the economy of a Member State will only rarely be used, since the economic problem must afflict the whole of the national economy.[115] More specific problems are dealt with under Article 87(3)(a) or (c).

Article 87(3)(c) (ex Article 92(3)(c)) is in many ways the most significant and interesting of the discretionary exceptions. It provides that 'aid to facilitate the development of certain economic activities or of certain economic areas, where such aid does not adversely affect trading conditions to an extent contrary to the common interest' may be compatible with the common market.

The Article allows aid to be legitimated by reference to the needs of a particular industrial sector,[116] and by reference to economic areas,[117] which the Commission has recognized can have a national, and not just a Community, dimension.[118] Thus

---

[114] Hancher, Ottervanger, and Slot, n. 55 above, ch. 15.
[115] Cases T–132 & 143/96, *Freistaat Sachsen*, n. 112 above.
[116] Evans, n. 55 above, ch. 5.
[117] *Ibid.*, ch. 4.
[118] *Guidelines on National Regional Aid* [1998] OJ C74/6, para. 3.6.

Article 87(3)(c) is the provision through which a State can seek to justify aid to a particular depressed region as judged by national criteria. This nationally based criterion is not, however, unqualified. It is still necessary to consider the impact of the aid on Community trade, and its sectoral repercussions at Community level.[119] The Commission will consider a State's regional problems and place them in a Community context: the better the position of the Member State relative to the Community situation, the more difficult will it be to justify aid to one of its regions.[120] The measurement of internal regional disparity has however altered. Prior to 1998, the measurement in terms of internal regional disparities in gross domestic product per head and unemployment rates constituted the first stage in determining which regions could qualify for aid under Article 87(3)(c). Under the 1998 Guidelines a similar mechanism is used to decide on what share of the overall total of aid for such regions any particular Member State will be given.[121] The criteria to determine these allocations are complex.[122]

The Community courts and Commission have, moreover, made it clear that aid will not normally qualify under this Article unless it is linked to initial investment, to job creation,[123] and/or to a restructuring of the activities of the undertaking concerned.[124] The purpose of the aid must be to develop a particular sector or region and not merely a specific undertaking therein.[125] The ECJ has moreover held that for aid in the form of capital injection into an ailing state-owned company, the activities of which are necessary for a region's long term development, to qualify as regional aid under Article 92(3)(a) or (c) (now Article 87(3)(a) or (c)) the aid must re-establish the company's profitability.[126] The application of the conditions in Article 87(3)(c) are evident in the *Glaverbel* case.

Cases 62 and 72/87, Executif Régional Wallon and Glaverbel SA v. Commission [1988] ECR 1573

The facts of the case have been given in the earlier extract. It was argued that the Commission had misapplied Article 92(3)(c). The Commission had found that the aid in question, which was for periodic plant renovation, did not satisfy the requirements for the development of the relevant sector without adversely affecting trading conditions to an extent contrary to the common interest.

---

[119] Cases T–126–127/96, *BFM and EFIM* v. *Commission* [1998] ECR II–3437; Cases T–132 & 143/96, *Freistaat Sachsen*, n. 112 above.

[120] *Eighteenth Report on Competition Policy* (EC Commission, 1989), point 147.

[121] Wishlade, n. 113 above, 349–50.

[122] *Ibid.*, 350–4.

[123] Evans, n. 55 above, 176.

[124] Cases C–278–280/92, *Spain* v. *Commission*, n. 98 above; Cases T–126–127/96, *BFM*, n. 119 above.; *Guidelines on National Regional Aid* [1998] OJ C74/6, paras. 1, 4.15; Evans, n. 55 above, 186–8.

[125] Evans, n. 55 above, 181–4. The general approach of the Commission was approved by the ECJ in Case 248/84, *Germany* v. *Commission* [1987] ECR 4013.

[126] Case C–42/93, *Merco*, n. 99 above.

THE ECJ

31. It is apparent from the points made by the Commission that it based its decision on the view that the investment in question was intended to renovate a float line and that such renovation, which must be carried out periodically, cannot be regarded as designed to facilitate the development of certain economic activities, even if such renovation entails the introduction of new technology. The Commission goes on to consider that, even if such renovation could constitute a new technical development which could be regarded as economic development within the meaning of Article 92(3)(c), it could not warrant an exemption under that provision in the case of the float-glass industry because, in view of the unused capacity in that industry, the aid would affect the position of other undertakings and would thus be contrary to the common interest.

32. It must be stated first of all that that line of reasoning is comprehensible and enables those concerned to ascertain the reasons for the Commission's adverse decision and the Court to review them. The complaint of insufficient reasons must therefore be rejected.

33. As far as the application of Article 92(3)(c) is concerned, it should be observed first of all that the applicants did not challenge the facts on which the Commission relied. In particular, they acknowledged that a float line must be periodically renovated and that, in this instance, the plant in question had to be renovated. . . .

34. It should also be borne in mind that the Commission enjoys a power of appraisal in applying Article 92(3)(c) as well as in applying Article 92(3)(b). It is, in particular, for the Commission to determine whether trading conditions between the Member States are affected by aid 'to an extent contrary to the common interest'. The applicants have supplied no evidence to suggest that in making that assessment the Commission misused its powers or committed a manifest error.

35. It follows from the foregoing that the complaints concerning the alleged infringement of Article 92(3)(c) and the insufficiency of the reasons given in that regard must be rejected.

It should not, however, be thought that the ECJ always upholds the Commission.[127] It will take seriously allegations that the Commission's decision is contradictory or that it has provided insufficient justification for its findings. It will also overturn Commission decisions on points of principle where it believes that the Commission has erred. This is exemplified by the *Intermills* case.

Case 323/82, Intermills SA v. Commission[128]
[1984] ECR 3809

The facts of the case have been given in the previous extract. The applicants sought to have the Commission's decision annulled on the ground, *inter alia*, that it misapplied Article 92(3)(c). The Commission was content with the aid granted in the form of loans, but found that the aid granted by the Belgian Government in the form of shareholdings did not qualify for exemption. This aid was not directly linked to the restructuring of the undertaking, but was rather rescue aid, intended

---

[127] This is also true in relation to Art. 92(3)(a): see Cases C–278–280/92, *Spain* v. *Commission*, n. 98 above.
[128] See also Case 248/84, *Germany* v. *Commission*, n. 125 above; Cases 296 & 318/82, *Leeuwarder Papierwarenfabriek*, n. 97 above.

to allow the undertaking to meet its financial commitments. Aid of this kind could, said the Commission, do serious damage to competition in the Community since the free play of market forces normally demanded that such undertakings should close, allowing more competitive firms to develop. The applicants contested the finding that the aid in the form of shareholdings was rescue aid, and argued that it was used to finance the closure of unprofitable factories, combined with the conversion of others to products which had a better prospect of profitability.

THE ECJ

33. . . . the criticism raised by the applicants appears to be well founded, inasmuch as the contested decision does indeed contain contradictions and does not make clear the grounds for the Commission's action on certain vital points. Such doubts and contradictions relate both to the economic justification for the aid and the question whether the aid was likely to distort competition within the Common Market.

34. First, as regards the economic justification for the aid, the Commission concedes in the statement of reasons on which its decision is based that the restructuring aimed at by the applicants corresponds, as such, to the Commission's own objectives for the European paper industry. That factor seems to be the chief ground on which the Commission recognised the compatibility with the Treaty of the aid granted in the form of low interest loans and advances.

35. On the other hand, the Commission gave no verifiable reasons to justify its finding that the holding acquired by the public authorities in the capital of the recipient undertaking was not compatible with the Treaty. It merely stated that that holding was 'not directly linked to the restructuring operation' and in view of the losses suffered by the undertaking over several financial years, constituted purely financial 'rescue aid'; . . . In making those assessments without giving any indication of its reasons, other than the statements just referred to, the Commission did not properly explain why its assessment of the restructuring operation in question . . . called for such a clear-cut distinction between the effect of the aid granted in the form of subsidised loans and the effect of the aid granted in the form of capital holdings.

. . .

37. In relation to its claim that the contested aid damages competition in the Common Market, the Commission referred to the provisions of Article 92(1) and to the requirement in Article 92(3), according to which aid may be exempted only if it does not adversely affect trading conditions to an extent contrary to the common interest.

38. As regards the first part of that requirement, the relevant paragraphs of the preamble to the decision merely note the objections raised by the Governments of three Member States, two trade associations and an undertaking in the paper industry. Apart from that reference, the decision gives no concrete indication of the way in which the aid in question damages competition.

39. As regards the second part of the requirement, the Commission, having stated that the aid granted in the form of a capital holding is not directly linked to the restructuring of the undertaking but constitutes 'rescue aid', asserts that such aid 'threatens to do serious damage to the conditions of competition, as the free interplay of market forces would normally call for the closure of the undertaking, allowing more competitive firms to develop'. On that point it must be stated that the settlement of an undertaking's debts in order to ensure its survival does not necessarily adversely affect trading conditions to an extent contrary to the common interest, as provided in Article 92(3), where such an operation is, for example, accompanied by a restructuring plan. In this case, the Commission has not shown why the applicant's activities on the market, following the conversion of its production with the assistance of the aid granted, were likely to

have such an adverse effect on trading conditions that the undertaking's disappearance would have been preferable to its rescue.

40. On those grounds, the contested decision must be declared void.

Article 87(3)(d) (ex Article 92(3)(d)) was added by the TEU. It provides that aid to promote culture and heritage conservation may be compatible with the common market, where such aid does not affect trading conditions and competition in the Community to an extent that is contrary to the common interest.

Article 87(3)(e) (ex Article 92(3)(e)) constitutes a safety net by providing that such other categories of aid as may be specified by the decision of the Council acting by a qualified majority on a proposal from the Commission may be deemed to be compatible with the common market. A number of directives on aid to shipbuilding have been adopted pursuant to this Article.

6. STATE AIDS: THE PROCEDURAL RULES AND ARTICLES 88 AND 89

The procedural rules that apply in this area are derived from the relevant Treaty articles, the case law of the ECJ and CFI, and from Regulation 659/99.[129]

(a) REVIEW OF EXISTING STATE AIDS

It is readily apparent that the Community has an interest in keeping under review aids which have been granted by Member States, even if the Commission has given the green light to those aids under Article 87(3). Article 88(1) (ex Article 93(1)) provides that:

The Commission shall, in co-operation with Member States, keep under constant review all systems of aid existing in those states. It shall propose to the latter any appropriate measures required by the progressive development or by the functioning of the common market.

There are a number of categories of existing aid. These may be regarded as existing aid because of ECJ case law[130] and Regulation 659/99.[131]

(a) Aid which existed before the entry into force of the Treaty.

(b) Aid which has been given the green light under Article 87(3) (ex Article 92(3)).[132] Individual disbursement of aid pursuant to a general aid scheme that has been approved by the Commission counts as existing aid, provided that it comes properly within the general scheme.[133]

---

[129] Reg. 659/99 [1999] OJ L83/1.

[130] Case C–44/93, *Namur – Les Assurances du Crédit SA* v. *Office National du Ducroire and Belgian State* [1994] ECR I–3829.

[131] Art. 1.

[132] The Commission can review an existing aid scheme and decide that it is no longer compatible with the common market, Reg. 659/99, n. 129 above, Arts. 17–18.

[133] Case C–47/91, *Italy* v. *Commission* [1994] ECR I–4635.

(c) Aid which has been notified to the Commission pursuant to the obligation contained in Article 88(3) (ex Article 93(3)), but in relation to which the Commission has taken no action within the requisite time period.

(d) Aid that is not recoverable because the limitation period has expired.

(e) Aid deemed to be existing aid because at the time that it was put into effect it did not constitute aid, and only became so due to the evolution of the common market.[134] Where certain measures become aid following the liberalization of an activity by Community law, such measures are considered existing aid after the date fixed for the liberalization.

(b) THE PROCEDURE FOR NEW STATE AIDS: NOTIFICATION AND PRELIMINARY REVIEW

In order for Commission monitoring of state aids to be effective, it is essential for the Commission to be notified of the existence of any aid proposal. It is for this reason that Article 88 (ex Article 93) establishes a two-stage procedure for state aids.

Stage one concerns prior notification of any plan to grant aid and preliminary investigation by the Commission. This is provided for in Article 88(3) (ex Article 93(3)):

The Commission shall be informed, in sufficient time to enable it to submit its comments, of any plans to grant or alter aid. If it considers that any such plan is not compatible with the common market having regard to Article 87, it shall without delay initiate the procedure provided for in paragraph 2. The Member State concerned shall not put its proposed measures into effect until this procedure has resulted in a final decision.

Member States are therefore under a duty to notify the Commission of any aid prior to granting it.[135] The ECJ has interpreted this Article to impose a standstill obligation on Member States during the period in which the Commission undertakes its initial review of the proposed aid. They cannot implement the grant of aid during this time.[136] The ECJ has also held that the Commission must come to some preliminary view within two months. If it does not do so the State is entitled to carry through its aid proposal, after having notified the Commission that it intends to do so.[137] The Commission can request further information, if it believes that the information supplied is incomplete.[138]

The Commission will at this early stage engage in a preliminary review of the aid proposal.[139] It may decide to approve the aid at this juncture, in which case it will notify the relevant Member State and the latter will then implement the aid proposal.

---

[134] Cases T–298 etc/97, *Alzetta Mauro*, n. 110 above, para. 143.

[135] Reg. 659/99, n. 129 above, Art. 2.

[136] Case 120/73, *Gebrüder Lorenz GmbH* v. *Germany* [1973] ECR 1471; Case 84/82, *Germany* v. *Commission* [1984] ECR 1451; Reg. 659/99, n. 129 above, Art. 3. The Commission must also be notified of any amendment to the aid proposal: Cases 91 & 127/83, *Heineken Brouwerijen BV* v. *Inspecteur der Vennootschapsbelasting* [1984] ECR 3435.

[137] Case 84/82, *Germany* v. *Commission* [1984] ECR 1451; Reg. 659/99, n. 129 above, Art. 4(5).

[138] *Ibid.*, Art. 5.   [139] *Ibid.*, Art. 4.

The ECJ has emphasized that the preliminary-review procedure within Article 93(3) (now Article 88(3)) is 'meant to be just that'.[140] It is to take a short time, not more than two months, and if there are difficulties in reaching a decision within this time then the Commission should proceed to the more complete review provided for in Article 93(2) (now Article 88(2)). This is important since, as we shall see below, other parties are entitled to be consulted under Article 88(2), but have no such rights under Article 88(3). Thus the Court found in *Germany* v. *Commission*[141] that if the Commission did not move briskly to the second stage, but engaged in complex negotiations lasting sixteen months with the applicant Member State to the exclusion of other interested parties, the resultant decision could be annulled at the request of such a party. Nor can the Commission avoid this by keeping other Member States informed at multilateral meetings. Moreover, the Commission can resolve a case under Article 88(3) only where it is clear that the aid is compatible with the common market. Where there are serious difficulties in deciding whether aid is compatible with the common market, the fuller investigation under Article 88(2) should be used.[142]

(c) THE PROCEDURE FOR STATE AIDS: DETAILED INVESTIGATION AND ENFORCEMENT

Stage two of the investigative process is based on the assumption that the Commission has not been able to give the green light to the state-aid proposal under Article 88(3). In these circumstances Article 88(2) (ex Article 93(2)) comes into play:

If, after giving notice to the parties concerned to submit their comments, the Commission finds that aid granted by a State or through State resources is not compatible with the common market having regard to Article 87, or that such aid is being misused, it shall decide that the State concerned shall abolish or alter such aid within a period of time to be determined by the Commission.

If the State concerned does not comply with the decision within the prescribed time, the Commission or any other interested State may, in derogation from the provisions of Articles 226 and 227, refer the matter to the Court of Justice direct.

Article 88(2) applies both to existing aids in relation to which questions have been raised pursuant to Article 88(1) and to new aids which have not been given the green light pursuant to the preliminary investigation under Article 88(3). If an existing aid is found to be incompatible with the common market as the result of a review under Article 88(1) then it will be unlawful from the date set for compliance with that decision. In the case of a new aid, the effect of the decision made under Article 88(2) will be to render permanent, the temporary prohibition which flows from Article 88(3) unless the Member State can at some future date show that the circumstances

---

[140] Case 84/82, *Germany* v. *Commission*, n. 137 above.
[141] *Ibid.*; Case C–198/91, *William Cook plc* v. *Commission* [1993] ECR I–2486.
[142] Case C–367/95 P, *Commission* v. *Sytraval and Brink's France SARL* [1998] ECR I–1719, para. 39; Case C–204/97, *Portugal* v. *Commission* [2001] ECR I–3175, para. 33; Case T–73/98, *Société Chimique Prayon-Ruppel SA* v. *Commission* [2001] ECR II–867, paras. 42–52.

have changed. In either eventuality the procedure described in Article 88(2) comes into operation.

A notice will be placed in the Official Journal inviting parties concerned to submit their comments. The Commission will summarize the relevant issues of fact and law, setting out its doubts about the compatibility of the aid with the common market.[143] We have already seen that third parties have no right to be consulted under Article 88(3),[144] but the first sentence of Article 88(2) provides the foundation for such procedural rights in the event of the more detailed investigation being undertaken by the Commission.[145] The phrase 'parties concerned' covers the undertakings receiving aid and other persons or undertakings whose interests may be affected by the grant of the aid, in particular competing undertakings and trade associations.[146] The participation rights of such parties may, however, be more limited than those of the party against whom the formal investigation has been instituted.[147] The period for comment will, normally, not exceed one month.[148] Commission findings pursuant to formal investigations are made by decisions. The Commission may decide that the aid is compatible, or incompatible, with the common market. It may attach conditions to a positive decision.[149] The Commission can revoke its decision where it was based on incorrect information that was a determining factor in the decision.[150]

The rationale for the more expedited enforcement process contained in the second paragraph of Article 88(2) is that the Commission has already had the opportunity to make its views known, and because the parties themselves have already been heard.

While Article 88(2) does, therefore, provide a speedier method of enforcement against a recalcitrant State, the Court has set itself against any further modification of the enforcement process as suggested by the Commission. This is clear from the *British Aerospace* case.[151] The Commission had approved certain aid to the Rover group on condition, *inter alia*, that no further aid should be granted. It was later discovered that a further capital sum had been provided in the form of 'sweeteners'. The Commission then issued a decision requiring this sum to be recovered from the beneficiaries. This decision was challenged before the Court and annulled. The ECJ held that the Commission could have used the special procedure in the second paragraph of Article 93(2) (now Article 88(2)); or it could have chosen to treat the extra payment as a new aid in its own right. But it could not just seek to recover the further payments.[152]

---

[143] Reg. 659/99, n. 129 above, Art. 6.   [144] Cases 91 & 127/83, *Heineken*, n. 136 above.

[145] Reg. 659/99, n. 129 above, Art. 20(1).

[146] Case 323/82, *Intermills SA* [1984] ECR 3809, para. 16; Case C–198/91, *William Cook*, n. 141 above, para. 24.

[147] Cases T–371 & 394/94, *British Airways plc and British Midland Airways Ltd.* v. *Commission* [1998] ECR II–2405.

[148] Reg. 659/99, n. 129 above, Art. 6(1).   [149] *Ibid.*, Art. 7.

[150] *Ibid.*, Art. 9.

[151] Case C–292/90, *British Aerospace plc and Rover Group Holdings plc* v. *Commission* [1992] ECR I–493.

[152] The Court did, however, accept that the Commission could, when considering whether the aid was compatible with the common market, take account of a previous decision on the matter and any obligations which may have been imposed on the Member State.

(d) EXCEPTIONAL CIRCUMSTANCES: ARTICLE 88(2), PARAGRAPHS 3 AND 4

The third and fourth paragraphs of Article 88(2) make provision for aid to be granted in certain exceptional circumstances in derogation from the provisions of Article 87.

On application by a Member State, the Council may, acting unanimously, decide that aid which that State is granting or intends to grant shall be considered to be compatible with the common market, in derogation from the provisions of Article 87 or from the regulations provided for in Article 89, if such a decision is justified by exceptional circumstances. If, as regards the aid in question, the Commission has already initiated the procedure provided for in the first subparagraph of this paragraph, the fact that the State concerned made its application to the Council shall have the effect of suspending that procedure until the Council has made its attitude known.

If, however, the Council has not made its attitude known within three months of the said application being made, the Commission shall give its decision on the case.

(e) ARTICLE 89: IMPLEMENTING REGULATIONS

Article 89 (ex Article 94) empowers the Council, acting by qualified majority on a proposal from the Commission, and after consulting the Parliament, to make any appropriate regulations for the application of Articles 87 and 88, and in particular to determine the conditions under which Article 88(3) shall apply and the categories of aid exempted from this procedure. Article 89 has been used relatively rarely, and the Commission has sought to rely on soft law and adjudication to develop policy in this area.[153] Article 89 was, however, the basis for the Council regulation empowering the Commission to make regulations about certain categories of aid.[154]

(f) CHALLENGE TO COMMISSION DECISIONS

Challenges to Commission decisions will normally be brought under Article 230 (ex Article 173) to annul the decision.[155] The most common applicants are the State whose aid has been found to be incompatible with the common market, the undertakings that are the intended beneficiaries of this aid, and competitors. Applicants will have to satisfy the requirements of Article 230 in order to proceed.[156] They will have to show that the action complained of produces legal effects.[157] The time limit of two

---

[153] Evans, n. 55 above, 405–27.

[154] Council Reg. 994/98, [1998] OJ L142/1.

[155] Actions for failure to act under Art. 232 (ex Art. 175) will be difficult to sustain, since the applicant must show an obligation to act by the Commission: Case T–277/94, *Associazione Italiana Tecnico Economica del Cemento (AITEC)* v. *Commission* [1996] ECR II–351. The Commission must, however, consider diligently whether it should act on a complaint: Case T–95/96, *Gestevision Telecinco SA* v. *Commission* [1998] ECR II–3407. For the use of Art. 241 see, Case T–82/96, *Associacao dos Refinadores de Acucar Portugueses (ARAP)* v. *Commission* [1999] ECR II–1889.

[156] In Case C–47/90, *Italy* v. *Commission* [1992] ECR I–4145, the ECJ held that the Commission's decision to open the Art. 88(2) procedure was itself a reviewable act which could be challenged before the Court.

[157] Case C–400/99, *Italy* v. *Commission* [2001] ECR I–7303, para. 62.

months will, in general, run from the date when the decision was published in the Official Journal.[158]

The State will, of course, have standing, as will a regional body that set up an aid programme condemned by the Commission.[159] The intended recipient of the aid has been readily admitted to plead the case,[160] and the Court has afforded standing to interveners who have submitted comments to the Commission and who would be likely to suffer harm if the aid were to be given to the targeted firm.[161] Economic operators that played a significant role in the Article 88(2) procedure have been held to be individually concerned, when they have been affected in their capacity as negotiators.[162] The fact that a party has taken part in the Article 88(2) procedure will not, however, suffice to be accorded standing under Article 230.[163] Moreover, where an undertaking has not exercised its right to submit comments under Article 88(2), it must, in the context of an annulment action, prove that it is individually concerned within Article 230(4). The mere fact that the undertaking is in a competitive relationship with the beneficiary of the aid does not mean that it will be regarded as individually concerned.[164]

An important point concerning the availability of review was affirmed in *William Cook*.[165] We have already seen that interested parties do not have consultation rights under Article 88(3) during the preliminary examination phase, but do have such rights under Article 88(2). This may be problematic if the Commission finds that an aid is compatible with the Common Market under Article 88(3), but an interested party disagrees with this finding and believes that the more thorough investigation under Article 88(2) should have been initiated. In *William Cook* the Court held that the procedural guarantees contained in Article 93(2) (now Article 88(2)) could, in such a situation, be properly safeguarded only if such parties were able to challenge such a Commission decision before the Court.[166] However, in an annulment action, for the applicant to show that it is concerned within the meaning of Article 88(2) it will have to show that its competitive position has been affected.[167]

The substantive grounds for challenge are set out in Article 230 (ex Article 173). The legality of a measure is decided on the basis of the facts and law existing when the measure was adopted.[168] It is common for applicants to argue that the Commission's decision is in breach of one of the general principles of Community law, that the reasoning is defective, or that the Commission has misinterpreted the meaning of

---

[158] Case T–11/95, *BP Chemicals Ltd.* v. *Commission* [1998] ECR II–3235.

[159] Case T–288/97, *Regione Autonoma Friuli-Venezia Giulia* v. *Commission* [1999] ECR II–1871.

[160] Case 730/79, *Philip Morris*, n. 108 above; Case 323/82, *Intermills*, n. 146 above.

[161] Case 169/84, *COFAZ* v. *Commission* [1986] ECR 391; Case C–198/91, *William Cook*, n. 141 above; Case T–380/94, *AIUFFASS* v. *Commission* [1997] 3 CMLR 542. cf. Case T–398/94, *Kahn Scheepvart BV* v. *Commission* [1996] ECR II–477; Case T–11/95, *BP*, n. 158 above.

[162] Case C–313/90, *CIRFS*, n. 70 above.

[163] Case C–106/98, *SNRT-CGT, SURT-CFDT and SNEA-CFE-CGC* v. *Commission* [2000] ECR I–3659.

[164] Case T–11/95, *BP*, n. 158 above; *cf* Case T–16/96, *Cityflyer Express*, n. 97 above.

[165] Case C–198/91, *William Cook*, n. 141 above.

[166] See also Case C–225/91, n. 96 above, Case C–367/95 P, *Sytraval*, n. 142 above, paras. 40–41.

[167] Case T–188/95, *Waterleiding Maatschappij 'Noord-West Brabant' NV* v. *Commission* [1998] ECR II–3713, para. 62; Case T–69/96, *Hamburger Hafen- und Lagerhaus Aktiengesellschaft* v. *Commission* [2001] ECR II–1037, para. 41.

[168] Case T–110/97, *Kneissl Dachstein Sportartikel AG* v. *Commission* [1999] ECR II–2881.

one of the phrases in the relevant Treaty Articles. However, as we have seen when considering the general issue of substantive review,[169] the Court possesses considerable discretion as to the intensity with which it will apply the various grounds mentioned in Article 230. The ECJ will often make reference to the Commission's considerable discretion concerning state aids, and will normally overturn such a decision only if the applicant can show a procedural defect, deficiency of reasoning, factual inaccuracy, a manifest error in assessing the facts, or some misuse of power.[170] The complex assessments made by the Commission are judged on the information available to it when it made the decision.[171]

7. STATE AIDS: AID THAT HAS NOT BEEN NOTIFIED

The consequences of a failure by a Member State to notify in accordance with Article 88(3) must be separately evaluated in relation to the Commission and the national courts.

In *relation to the Commission*, the ECJ has held that failure to notify does not in itself render implementation of the aid unlawful.[172] It held that the Commission has the power, after giving the Member State the opportunity for comment, to issue an interim decision requiring the State to suspend immediately the payment of the aid, pending the outcome of the Commission's determination of whether the aid was compatible with the common market.[173] If in the light of this request for information the State still refused to supply the requisite material, the Commission could then make an assessment of the compatibility of the aid on the basis of the information available to it. This decision could demand the recovery of aid that had been paid. It was also suggested that the Commission should be able to require immediate repayment of the aid.[174]

These principles have been enshrined in Regulation 659/99. Where the Commission has information from any source regarding alleged unlawful aid, then it must examine it without delay.[175] It can request information from the relevant State. The Commission may, after allowing the State to comment, make a decision requiring the State to suspend the aid until the Commission has taken a decision on its compatibility with the common market. This is termed a 'suspension injunction'.[176] The Commission may, after allowing the State to comment, make a decision requiring the State to recover the aid, pending a decision by the Commission on its compatibility with the

---

[169] See Ch. 12 above.
[170] See, e.g., Case C–56/93, *Belgium* v. *Commission* [1996] ECR I–723; Cases T–244 & 486/93, *TWD Textilwerke Deggendorf GmbH* v. *Commission* [1995] ECR II–2265, upheld on appeal, Case C–355/95P, *TWD* v. *Commission* [1997] ECR I–2549; Case T–358/94, *Air France*, n. 102 above; Case T–277/94, *AITEC*, n. 155 above; Case T–380/94, *AIUFFASS*, n. 161 above; Cases T–298/97, *Alzetta Mauro*, n. 110 above, para. 130.
[171] Case T–110/97, *Kneissl Dachstein*, n. 168 above.
[172] Case C–301/87, *France* v. *Commission* [1990] ECR I–307.
[173] Case C–75/97, *Belgium* v. *Commission*, n. 91 above.
[174] Case C–42/93, *Merco*, n. 99 above, Jacobs AG; Evans, n. 55 above, 436.
[175] Reg. 659/99, n. 129 above, Art. 10(1). The Commission may also re-open a case where aid has been misused: Art. 16.
[176] *Ibid.*, Art. 11(1).

common market. This is known as a 'recovery injunction'.[177] These injunctions may be ordered only where it is clear that there is aid, it is a matter of urgency, and there is a serious risk of substantial and irreparable damage to a competitor. Non-compliance with either type of injunction can lead to an action before the ECJ.[178] The Commission can make its substantive decisions on such aid by way of preliminary review, or by means of the formal procedure. In either eventuality, the normal time limits do not apply.[179] If the Commission decides that the aid is not compatible with the common market, it can issue a 'recovery decision'. This obliges the Member State to take all necessary measures to recover the aid from the beneficiary. This shall not be required if it would be contrary to a general principle of Community law.[180]

The *position of the national court* in relation to aid that has not been notified is somewhat different. The Commission sees national courts and itself as having complementary roles in this area, and its Notice builds upon the ECJ's jurisprudence.[181] The ECJ has established that the duty not to implement aid before notification to the Commission, and before the Commission has undertaken its preliminary investigation in accordance with Article 93(3) (now Article 88(3)), is directly effective.[182] The ECJ has also held[183] that, although a national court which is enforcing Article 93(3) cannot rule on the compatibility of the aid with the common market, this being a matter for the Commission, the national court should, none the less, rule aid to be illegal when it has not been notified as required by this Article.[184] The direct effect of Article 93(3) demanded that the rights of the individual should be protected in this manner. Moreover any later Commission decision which found that the aid was compatible with Article 92 (now Article 87) would not be retrospective in effect.

8. STATE AIDS: RECOVERY OF UNLAWFUL AID

The Court has, not surprisingly, held that, as a matter of principle, illegal state aids should be repaid,[185] this being the logical consequence of a finding that the aid was unlawful.[186] The peremptory force of this obligation will not easily be deflected by claims that repayment of the aid entails difficulties for the recipient.

---

[177] *Ibid.*, Art. 11(2).   [178] *Ibid.*, Art. 12.
[179] *Ibid.*, Art. 13.   [180] *Ibid.*, Art. 14.
[181] *Notice on Co-operation between National Courts and the Commission in the State Aid Field* [1995] OJ C312/8.
[182] Case 120/73, *Lorenz*, Cases 91 & 127/83, *Heineken*, both n. 136 above; Case C–143/99, *Adria-Wien*, n. 90 above, paras. 26–27; Case C–295/97, *Industrie Aeronautiche e Meccaniche Rinaldo Piaggio SpA v. International Factors SpA* [1999] ECR I–3735.
[183] Case C–354/90, *Fédération Nationale du Commerce Exterieur des Produits Alimentaires v. France* [1991] ECR I–5505.
[184] Where a State implements the aid before the Commission has reached its final determination under Art. 88(3) the national court can continue to exercise jurisdiction over the matter, and interpret and apply the concept of aid. In case of doubt it can ask the Commission for clarification or make a reference under Art. 234. The national court may also order interim measures: Case C–39/94, *SFEI*, n. 90 above.
[185] For discussion of attempts by private parties to prevent the payment of the aid through the issue of an interim order by the Court see Hancher, n. 99 above, 145–6.
[186] Case 310/85, *Deufil*, n. 78 above.

Case 52/84, Commission v. Belgium
[1986] ECR 89

[Note ToA renumbering: Arts. 5 and 173 are now Arts. 10 and 230]

The Commission had found that the acquisition by a public regional holding company of shares in a firm manufacturing ceramic ware constituted state aid, and ordered that it should be withdrawn since it considered that it was incompatible with the common market. The Belgian Government did not contest this decision, but it did stress the serious social consequences of closing down the undertaking, and it stated that Belgian law did not allow share capital to be refunded except by way of withdrawal of company profits, and no such profits were available. The Government also requested clarification from the Commission of what it meant by 'withdrawal of aid'. The ECJ held that the Belgian Government was outside the time limit for challenging the validity of the decision under Article 173. It then proceeded as follows.

THE ECJ

14. In those circumstances the only defence left to the Belgian Government in opposing the Commission's application for a declaration that it failed to fulfil its Treaty obligations would be to plead that it was absolutely impossible for it to implement the decision properly. In this connection it should be noted that the decision demands the withdrawal from the undertaking of a capital holding of 475 million Bfr . . . ; that demand is sufficiently precise to be complied with. The fact that, on account of the undertaking's financial position, the Belgian authorities could not recover the sum paid does not constitute proof that implementation was impossible, because the Commission's objective was to abolish the aid and, as the Belgian Government itself admits, that objective could be attained by proceedings for winding up the company, which the Belgian authorities could institute in their capacity as shareholder or creditor.

. . .

16. It should be added that the fact that the only defence which a Member State to which a decision has been addressed can raise in legal proceedings such as these is that implementation of the decision is absolutely impossible does not prevent that State—if, in giving effect to the decision, it encounters unforeseen or unforeseeable difficulties or perceives consequences overlooked by the Commission—from submitting those problems for consideration by the Commission, together with proposals for suitable amendments. In such a case the Commission and the Member State concerned must respect the principle underlying Article 5 of the Treaty, which imposes a duty of genuine co-operation on the Member States and Community institutions; accordingly, they must work together in good faith with a view to overcoming difficulties whilst fully observing the Treaty provisions, and in particular the provisions on aid. However, in the present instance none of the difficulties referred to by the Belgian Government is of that nature, and that Government made no proposals whatever to the Commission for the adoption of other suitable measures.

The message from the Court was clear. The only exception to the primary obligation to obtain repayment of the illegal aid was where recovery was absolutely impossible, and this was narrowly defined. If the recipient company had to be wound up, so be it. Even where the exception to the primary obligation does come into play, the State is not let off the hook entirely. There is a secondary obligation derived from

Article 5 (now Article 10), requiring the State to enter into a serious dialogue
Commission to resolve the problem.

The same uncompromising approach is apparent in other cases. In *Tube*
the ECJ accepted that in the event that the recipient company was being wo
then the recovery of the unlawful aid would have to take its place alongside c
the company's assets by other creditors. This was in accord with the general p
that recovery of aid should take place in accordance with the relevant provi
national law, subject to the proviso that those provisions were not to be appl
way which made recovery practically impossible.[188] However, the ECJ rejeo
argument that recovery of the debt would be disproportionate to the objecti
down in Articles 92 and 93 (now Articles 87 and 88), on the ground that it
cause serious damage to other creditors. Since recovery of illegal aid was the
consequence of the finding that the aid was unlawful, it could not be rega
disproportionate to the objectives of the Treaty, notwithstanding the fact tha
creditors might suffer.

Nor have applicants fared any better by relying on the concept of legi
expectations. Thus in *Deufil*[189] the ECJ rejected the argument that the existen
Commission guideline setting out the policy which it intended to adopt in app
State aids in a certain area gave rise to a legitimate expectation that, if a produ
not included in the guideline, then aid in relation to that product would not
be approved. In *Bug-Alutechnik*[190] the ECJ accepted that, as part and parcel
idea that recovery of state aid was to be determined in accordance with the r
principles of national law, this could include the concept of legitimate expect
and legal certainty. It went on to hold, however, that recipients of aid could no
a legitimate expectation that the aid was lawful unless it had been gran
accordance with the procedure in Article 93 (now Article 88). A diligent bu
man should normally be able to determine whether that procedure had bee
lowed. Moreover, the Court emphasized that a Member State which had granto
contrary to the principles of Article 93 could not rely on any legitimate expect
of the recipients to justify refusal to recover the sums. Furthermore nationall
cepts such as legitimate expectations could not be relied upon if the effect
make it impossible to recover the aid, as where the national doctrine set time
for the revocation of administrative acts. The ECJ has none the less recognize
there might be exceptional circumstances where recovery of aid should no
ordered.[191]

[187] Case C–142/87, [1990] ECR I–959; Case C–378/98, *Commission* v. *Belgium* [2001] ECR I–5107
C–261/99, *Commission* v. *France* [2001] ECR I–2537; Case C–6/97, *Italy* v. *Commission*, n. 92 above.
[188] Case 94/87, *Commission* v. *Germany* [1989] ECR 175.
[189] Case 310/85, *Deufil*, n. 78 above.
[190] Case C–5/89, *Re State Aid to Bug-Alutechnik GmbH: Commission* v. *Germany* [1990] ECR I–3437
C–24/95, *Land Rheinland-Pfalz* v. *Alcan Deutschland GmbH* [1997] ECR I–1591; Cases 244 & 486/93,
n. 170 above.
[191] Case C–354/90, *Fédération Nationale*, n. 183 above; Case C–39/94, *SFEI*, n. 90 above.

9. THE RELATIONSHIP OF STATE AIDS TO OTHER PROVISIONS OF THE TREATY

The provisions concerning state aids do not exist within a legal or political vacuum. The ECJ has had to consider the relationship of these provisions to a number of other Treaty provisions.

There have, for example, been a series of cases concerned with the relationship between Article 90 (ex Article 95) and the rules on State aids. The ECJ has held that the use of receipts from a levy may constitute a State aid, which is incompatible with the common market, but that this is a matter to be decided by the Commission and not the national court.[192]

The most interesting point of interconnection is, however, the relationship between Articles 87 to 89 and Article 28 (ex Article 30). The approach of the ECJ has altered over the years. In *Ianelli & Volpi*[193] the ECJ held that if some aspects of aid which might contravene Treaty provisions other than Articles 92 to 94 (now Articles 87 to 89) were so closely linked to the latter, then it would not be possible to evaluate them separately. However, where certain aspects of an aid scheme were not necessary or integral to the operation of that scheme, then those aspects could be subject to scrutiny under other provisions of the Treaty. In this sense the Court articulated a severability test.

In its later case law the Court appears to have been more ready to apply Article 30 (now Article 28) without too delicate an inquiry into whether the measure caught by this Article was an integral part of the aid scheme or not. Thus, in the *Buy Irish* case[194] the Irish Government argued that its campaign to encourage consumers to buy Irish goods should be considered under Articles 92 to 94, and not under Article 30 (now Article 28). The Court rejected this argument, holding that the fact that Article 92 (now Article 87) might be of relevance to the financing of the campaign did not mean that the campaign itself escaped from the prohibition in Article 30. In *Commission v. France*[195] the Court examined the legality of a measure which gave newspaper publishers tax exemptions on the condition that the papers were printed in France. The Commission argued that this constituted a breach of Article 30. The French Government responded to the effect that if its measures did constitute aid they should be considered under Article 92 (now Article 87), since the tax provisions could not be separated from the general aid scheme for the newspaper industry. The ECJ was unconvinced. It noted that France had never notified such a scheme in accordance with Article 93(3) (now Article 88(3)). It then proffered the following strong statement of principle:[196]

---

[192] Cases C–149 & 150/91, *Sanders Adour et Guyomarc'h Nutrition Animale* [1992] ECR I–3899, subject to the existing competence of the national courts in relation to Art. 88(3).
[193] Case 74/76, *Ianelli and Volpi SpA v. Ditta Paolo Meroni* [1977] ECR 557.
[194] Case 249/81, *Commission v. Ireland* [1982] ECR 4005.
[195] Case 18/84, [1985] ECR 1339.
[196] *Ibid.*, para. 13. References to Arts. 30 and 92 to 94 should now be read as to Arts. 28 and 87 to 89.

[I]t should be pointed out that Articles 92 and 94 cannot, as is clear from a long line of cases decided by the Court, be used to frustrate the rules of the Treaty on the free movement of goods or the rules on the repeal of discriminatory tax provisions. According to those cases, the provisions relating to the free movement of goods, the repeal of discriminatory tax provisions and aid have a common objective, namely to ensure the free movement of goods between Member States under normal conditions of competition. . . . The mere fact that a national measure may possibly be defined as aid within the meaning of Article 92 is therefore not an adequate reason for exempting it from the prohibition contained in Article 30. The argument relating to the Community rules on aid, which the French Republic in any case raised only by way of hypothesis in reply to the observations of the Commission, therefore cannot be accepted.

The Court has persisted with this approach.[197] Thus in *Du Pont de Nemours Italiana*[198] the ECJ considered whether Italian legislation which required that all public bodies obtain at least 30 per cent of their supplies from undertakings established in the Mezzogiorno where the products concerned were processed was in breach of Article 30 (now Article 28). The referring court asked whether this constituted aid, with the consequence that Article 30 would not be applicable. The ECJ gave a negative response. It adopted the same 'unitary' view of Articles 30 and 92 (now Articles 28 and 87) as it had done in *Commission* v. *France*: both sets of provisions were designed to ensure the free movement of goods under normal conditions of competition. The fact that a national measure might be considered aid within the meaning of Article 92 did not, therefore, serve to take it outside Article 30. It was incumbent on the national court to ensure the full effectiveness of Article 30 (now Article 28). The rule of reason within Article 28 may however serve to legitimate the measure.[199]

10. STATE AIDS, MARKET INTEGRATION, AND REGIONAL POLICY

The Court's reasoning in the cases just discussed has force, but it is not unproblematic. It is true that Articles 28 and 87 have in general terms the same objective. Yet the very structure of Articles 87 to 89 attests to the different way in which fulfilment of this general aim is played out in the context of state aids. These Articles are characterized by the existence of Commission discretion, enabling it to weigh certain social and economic variables in deciding whether aid is compatible with the common market. It is for this very reason that the provisions on state aids are directly effective only to a limited extent. If, in the event of any overlap between Articles 28 and 87, the former is to predominate then it will rule out the type of social balancing which takes place

---

[197] In the preceding cases the States in question had not notified the aid in accordance with Art. 88(3). One of the explanations of the Court's reasoning in these cases was based on this fact. However, in the *Du Pont* case Italy had notified its scheme to the Commission, but this made no difference to the ECJ's reasoning.

[198] Case C–21/88, *Du Pont de Nemours Italiana SpA* v. *Unità Sanitaria Locale No. 2 di Carrara* [1990] ECR I–889; Case C–351/88, *Laboratori Bruneau Srl* v. *Unità Sanitaria Locale RM/24 de Monterotondo* [1991] ECR I–3641; Case C–156/98, *Germany* v. *Commission* [2000] ECR I–6857, para. 78.

[199] Case C–379/98, *PreussenElektra AG* v. *Schhleswag AG* [2001] ECR I–2099, paras. 70–81.

particularly in the context of Article 87(3). Concerns of this nature are apparent in the following extract. The case to which the authors refer is the *Du Pont* decision set out above. References to Articles 30, 92, and 93 should be read as referring to Articles 28, 87, and 88.

J.F.M. Martin and O. Stehmann, Product Market Integration versus Regional Cohesion in the Community[200]

First of all, one of the grounds on which the Court of Justice justifies its position is that both sets of rules have a common objective, that is to ensure the free movement of goods under normal conditions of competition. Although this is true, it is only partially so. One should not ignore that there is a second objective underlying Articles 92(3) and 93, namely to grant the Commission the possibility to declare compatible with the EEC Treaty those aids which are intended to close the economic, social and regional gaps existing inside the Community. Therefore, the fact that some competition distorting State aids may be permitted to operate proves that certain exceptions to the free movement of goods and to free competition principles are to be admitted. . . .

Secondly, the relation of both sets of rules . . . may have certain undesirable consequences. Whereas this position might be justifiable . . . in those cases in which no prior notification has taken place, applying Article 30 as interpreted in *Dassonville* without engaging in a deeper economic (or other) analysis risks obliterating Articles 92 and 93. After the *Dassonville* definition, almost anything would come under the 'imperium' of Article 30. State aids, by their nature, always have a negative effect on inter-state trade when they strengthen national industry or regions . . . If one follows strictly the Court's reasoning of giving priority to the application of Article 30 . . . Articles 92 and 93 would lose much of their sense.

Thirdly, from a procedural point of view the Court's reasoning may also bring difficulties. Article 30 is directly applicable while Articles 92 and 93 are not so. . . .

From an economic point of view the Court's position leads to favouring rapid market integration—represented by the free movement of goods provisions—to the detriment of regional cohesion—represented by the State aids provisions. In the context of the '1992' internal market this attitude is worrying. The transition from national market economies to an European one should be achieved smoothly so as to avoid the increase of regional economic divergences. The speed with which trade barriers are dismantled in the Community increases sharply the need for quick measures to balance adverse effects on disfavoured regions. . . . The whole picture is aggravated by the fact that measures undertaken at the European level to balance these effects are far from sufficient. . . .

While there may be concerns at the too-ready application of Article 28, one must be cautious about the more general relationship between national regional-aid policy and that undertaken at the Community level. We must be careful not to condemn the Community for paying insufficient attention to regional problems. This is in part because, as we have already seen, regional[201] and environmental[202] concerns are taken

---

[200] (1991) 16 *ELRev.* 216, 228–30.   [201] Wishlade, n. 113 above.
[202] H. Vedder, 'The New Community Guidelines on State Aid for Environmental Protection—Integrating Environment and Competition?' [2001] *ECLR* 365.

into account within the fabric of Article 87. It is in part because of the existence of Community schemes for regional assistance, and because the proper boundary of regional assistance is itself a contestable issue. The legitimate bounds of regional assistance are raised because of the inhibiting effect such aid can have on market integration. Efficiency considerations are not, however, the only ones to be borne in mind. Articles 158 and 159 (ex Articles 130a and 130b) place a priority on the achievement of greater cohesion within the Community. The attainment of this goal necessitates limits on the grant of aid by the richer Member States to regions that may be poor relative to those States, but not in relation to the Community as a whole. Only in this way will cohesion be possible. The following extract brings out this point forcefully:

A. Petersen, State Aid and the European Union: State Aid in the Light of Trade, Competition, Industrial and Cohesion Policies[203]

Surveys published by the Commission show that Member States spend around 36 BECU a year (1990) subsidising their manufacturing industries. Most of this money, 80%, is spent in the four largest Member States: Germany, France, UK and Italy. The EC–12 spent over 12 BECU annually on regional aid to companies during the period 1988–90, while the Community currently spends 700 MECU for the same purpose—a ratio of over 17: 1.

Despite the fact that we authorise high intensities of up to 75% for investment grants in the weakest regions, in recognition of the structural problems which they face, the practical reality is that the poorer countries cannot afford to pay such high levels and average around 25%—levels which are not much higher than those authorised in central regions in Germany, France and the Benelux. These few figures serve to underline a point which is gaining increasing acceptance: strict control of State aid in the central, more prosperous, regions is necessary in the interests of cohesion as well as of competition policy.

However, persuading the richer Member States to increase their contributions to EC spending in the weaker regions is one thing, getting them to refrain in the name of cohesion from spending so much of their own taxpayers' money locally is quite another.

11. ARTICLE 16 AND SERVICES OF GENERAL ECONOMIC INTEREST

The discussion within this Chapter would be incomplete if it did not include Article 16, introduced by the ToA:

Without prejudice to Articles 73, 86 and 87, and given the place occupied by services of general economic interest in the shared values of the Union as well as their role in promoting social and territorial cohesion, the Community and the Member States, each within their respective powers and within the scope of application of this Treaty, shall take care that such services operate on the basis of principles and conditions which enable them to fulfil their missions.

---

[203] Harden (ed.), n. 71 above, 25.

Moreover, Article 36 of the Charter of Fundamental Rights[204] provides that the Union recognizes and respects access to services of general economic interest as provided for in national laws and practices, in accordance with the EC Treaty, in order to promote social and territorial cohesion of the EU.

The precise import of Article 16 is open to debate. It is, however, important to distinguish three different ways in which it is of relevance.

First, it is clear that Article 16 has been of influence in defining the terms on which the EC will liberalize trade within certain sectors of the economy. Thus EC legislation designed to liberalize markets in energy, telecommunications, and the like is not concerned only with the introduction of competition. The relevant directives enable Member States to impose public-service obligations relating to the security, regularity, quality, and price of supply on suppliers of gas or electricity.[205]

Secondly, the addition of Article 16 by the ToA has lent weight to certain of the ECJ's case law under Article 86(2). We have already seen that the undertakings most likely to gain exemption under this Article are those that have universal service obligations. It is these that will benefit from the derogation contained within Article 86(2). The existence of the more positively worded[206] Article 16 is likely to reinforce this strand within the case law.

Thirdly, the existence of Article 16 may have an impact on state aid. The present law is that a state aid is defined by its effect, not its purpose. The fact that such aid is granted to offset the cost of public-service obligations incumbent on an undertaking does not therefore prevent it from being characterized as aid, although it may be relevant in deciding whether the aid is justified because of Article 86(2).[207] The Commission intends to improve legal certainty by producing guidelines on state aid granted to undertakings entrusted with the provision of services of general economic interest, and may, if the circumstances warrant, move towards an exemption regulation for this topic.[208]

12. CONCLUSION

i. The Treaty contains a number of Articles that are of especial relevance to the State, and to the way in which it organizes its economic activity. Articles 10, 16, 81, 82, 86, and 87 to 89 are particularly important in this respect.

ii. The Treaty does undoubtedly place constraints on state behaviour. Some of this is relatively uncontroversial, such as the control of state aids, and is justified by

---

[204] [2000] OJ C364/1.

[205] *Commission Communication on Services of General Interest in Europe*, COM(2000)580 final; *Report to the Laeken European Council, Services of General Interest*, COM(2001) 598 final, paras. 48–52.

[206] M. Ross, 'Article 16 EC and Services of General Interest: From Derogation to Obligation?' (2000) 25 *ELRev.* 22.

[207] Case T–106/95, *Fédération Francaise des Sociétés d'Assurances (FFSA)* v. *Commission* [1997] ECR II–229, paras. 178, 199, upheld on appeal: Case C–174/97P, *FFSA* v. *Commission* [1998] ECR I–1303, para. 33; Case T–46/97, *SIC-Sociedade Independente de Comunicacao SA* v. *Commission* [2000] ECR II–2125, para. 84.

[208] *Report to the Laeken European Council*, n. 205 above, paras. 27–29.

the need to ensure a level playing field between undertakings in the EC. In other areas the Community courts have had to strike a difficult balance between a State's freedom to organize its economic activities, and the impact that this might have on the market, as exemplified by the jurisprudence under Article 86. The Community courts have had to face equally problematic issues concerning the more general relationship between state aids, and other provisions of the Treaty, such as those on free movement of goods.

iii. The ECJ and CFI have given a broad reading to the relevant Treaty Articles, have enhanced the competitive process, and demanded a justification from the State for the grant of monopoly or privileged status under Article 86.

iv. However, they have also been more willing, in recent jurisprudence, to recognize the importance of public-service obligations, and to admit that this is a valid ground for invoking the derogation in Article 86(2). This is reflected in Community legislation on liberalization, which has allowed States to impose such obligations on those providing energy, telecommunications, and the like, and in the proposals for guidelines on state aid to compensate for these obligations. The introduction of Article 16 and the weight accorded to it by the European Council have been of importance in this respect.

13. FURTHER READING

(a) *Books*

BLUM, F., and LOGUE, A., *State Monopolies under EC Law* (Wiley, 1998)

EVANS, A., *EC Law of State Aid* (Oxford University Press, 1997)

HANCHER, L., OTTERVANGER, T., and SLOT, P.J., *EC State Aids* (Sweet and Maxwell, 2nd edn., 1999)

HARDEN, I. (ed.), *State Aid: Community Law and Policy* (Bundesanzeiger, 1993)

SAUTER, W., *Competition Law and Industrial Policy in the EU* (Clarendon, 1997)

SCHINA, D., *State Aids Under the EEC Treaty* (ESC Publishing, 1987)

(b) *Articles*

EDWARD, D., and HOSKINS, M., 'Article 90: Deregulation and EC Law, Reflections Arising from the XVI FIDE Conference' (1995) 32 *CMLRev.* 157

EHLERMANN, C.-D., 'The Contribution of EC Competition Policy to the Single Market' (1992) 29 *CMLRev.* 257

EVANS, A., and MARTIN, S., 'Socially Acceptable Distortion of Competition: Community Policy on State Aid' (1991) 16 *ELRev.* 79

GARCIA, E., 'Public Service, Public Services, Public Functions and Guarantees of the Rights of Citizens: Unchanging Needs in a Changed Context', in M. Freedland and S. Sciarra (eds.), *Public Services and Citizenship in European Law* (Clarendon, 1998), ch. 4

HANCHER, L., 'State Aids and Judicial Control in the European Community' [1994] ECLR 134

—— 'Community, State and Market', in P. Craig and G. de Búrca (eds.), *The Evolution of EU Law* (1999, Oxford University Press), ch. 20

MARTIN, J.M.F., and STEHMANN, O., 'Product Market Integration versus Regional Cohesion in the Community' (1991) 16 *ELRev.* 216

PAPPALARDO, A., 'State Measures and Public Undertakings: Article 90 of the EEC Treaty Revisited' [1991] *ECLR* 29

PRIESS, H.-J., 'Recovery of Illegal State Aid: An Overview of Recent Developments in the Case Law' (1996) 33 *CMLRev.* 69

QUIGLEY, C., 'The Notion of a State Aid in the EEC' (1988) 13 *ELRev.* 242

RODGER, B., 'State Aid—A Fully Level Playing Field?' [1999] *ECLR* 251

ROSS, M., 'State Aids: Maturing into a Constitutional Problem' (1995) 15 *YBEL* 79

—— 'Article 16 EC and Services of General Interest: From Derogation to Obligation?' (2000) 25 *ELRev.* 22

SLOTBOOM, M., 'State Aid in Community Law: A Broad or Narrow Definition?' (1995) 20 *ELRev.* 289

VEDDER, H., 'The New Community Guidelines on State Aid for Environmental Protection—Integrating Environment and Competition?' [2001] *ECLR* 365

WINTER, J.A., 'Supervision of State Aids: Article 93 in the Court of Justice' (1993) 30 *CMLRev.* 311

WISHLADE, F., 'Competition Policy or Cohesion Policy by the Back Door? The Commission Guidelines on National Regional Aid' [1998] *ECLR* 343

28

COMPLETION OF THE SINGLE MARKET

1. CENTRAL ISSUES

i. The completion of the single market is central to the ideals of the EC. It is still in many respects the central *raison d'être* of the EC.

ii. This Chapter considers the limits of integration prior to 1986 and the steps taken since then to complete the single market. There is both a substantive and an institutional dimension to this story.

iii. In substantive terms, it is important to understand the economic dimension to the creation of the single market. It is equally important to understand that the realization of the single market in economic terms necessarily raises issues about the inter-relationship of the economic and social dimensions of EC policy. We shall see that this has now come to the forefront of Community policy. The single market has been reconceptualized to take account of broader social, consumer and environmental issues.

iv. In institutional terms, a subtle mix of legislative, administrative, and judicial initiatives has furthered the evolution of the single market. The legislative procedures were changed to facilitate the passage of harmonization legislation. The focus of this legislation altered, as captured by the idea of the new approach to harmonization. These developments were themselves facilitated by judicial doctrine, founded on the ideal of mutual recognition, that framed the area within which legislative and administrative initiatives operated.

2. THE LIMITS OF INTEGRATION PRIOR TO 1986

In earlier chapters we saw the contribution made by the Court towards the attainment of a single market. The original Rome Treaty was, none the less, modified in 1986 by the passage of the Single European Act, one of the main objectives of which was to facilitate the completion of the single market. Prior to 1986 the process of single-market integration had been advanced both by legislative and judicial means.

The *legislative contribution* to the creation of a single Community market assumed many forms, one of the most important of which was harmonization of laws. We have already seen how the existence of divergences in national provisions can create real barriers to free trade within the Community. Article 100 (now Article Article 94) was the original Treaty provision through which this problem was addressed:

The Council shall, acting unanimously on a proposal from the Commission, issue directives for the approximation of such laws, regulations or administrative provisions of the Member States as directly affect the establishment of the common market.

There were, however, two difficulties with this legislative mechanism. In *procedural terms* the passage of directives under this Article requires unanimity. In *substantive terms* the type of directive which the Commission normally devised in the 1970s and early 1980s demanded agreement between the States on a *detailed measure* which was often difficult to attain. Thus a typical directive passed during this period would define with great specificity what was to be regulated: for example, the packaging and labelling of dangerous substances. There would then be an obligation on the Member State not to place such a substance on the market unless it was properly labelled. The directive would indicate the warning that had to be placed on the product, and the national authorities would be obliged to approve appropriate packaging which complied with the directive. The process of securing agreement between twelve States on provisions such as this was slow and cumbersome. Technical developments meant, moreover, that the Commission was, in a sense, fighting a losing battle. As fast as it succeeded in securing the passage of a directive to cover one technical problem, so ten more would emerge on the horizon. This was the result of technical innovation combined with the emergence of new types of market, such as that generated by the revolutionary changes in telecommunications or computers.

The *judicial contribution* to market integration has been examined in the chapters dealing with goods, persons, services, competition policy, and the like. The ECJ, through Article 169 (now Article 226) actions and direct effect, interpreted the relevant Treaty Articles in the manner best designed to give effect to the Treaty objectives. Judicial doctrines, such as that developed in *Cassis de Dijon*, were of particular importance in breaking down barriers to intra-Community trade.[1] However, as we have already noted,[2] there were limits to this judicially created form of integration. The effect of *Cassis* was essentially negative and deregulatory, serving to invalidate trade barriers which could not be justified under one of the mandatory requirements, but it did not ensure that any positive regulations would be put in place of the national measures which had been struck down.

By the early 1980s much therefore still remained to be done notwithstanding the efforts of the Commission and the Court. It was, moreover, this very sense that the Community was falling behind its agenda which generated a feeling of pessimism in the Community in the late 1970s and early 1980s. There seemed to be no ready way in which the Community would ever attain its goals, and the reality of single-market integration appeared to be as far away as ever. This problem was not lost on the European Council, which, in the early 1980s, considered various techniques for expediting the passage of Community initiatives. It was in one of these meetings that the seeds of the Single European Act (SEA) were sown. In 1985 the European Council called on the Commission to draw up a detailed programme with a specific timetable for achieving a single market by 1992. The Commission, under the leadership of Jacques Delors, was not slow to respond. It produced a White Paper which was to provide the foundations for the passage of the SEA.

---

[1] See Ch. 15 above.   [2] *Ibid.*

3. THE COMMISSION'S PAPER AND THE BENEFITS OF A SINGLE MARKET

The Commission's White Paper, from which the extracts below are taken, addressed the problem in strident tones. It set out to establish the 'essential and logical consequences'[3] of accepting the commitment to a single market. The Commission noted that the Community had lost momentum 'partly through recession, partly through a lack of confidence and vision',[4] but it said that the mood had now changed. The Commission was ready to take up the challenge: the 'time for talk has now passed. The time for action has come. That is what this White Paper is about'.[5]

Completing the Internal Market, COM(85) 310, 14 June 1985[6]

10. For convenience the measures that need to be taken have been classified in this Paper under three headings:
— Part One: the removal of physical barriers
— Part Two: the removal of technical barriers
— Part Three: the removal of fiscal barriers

11. The most obvious example of the first category are customs posts at frontiers. Indeed most of our citizens would regard the frontier posts as the most visible example of the continued division of the Community and their removal as the clearest sign of the integration of the Community into a single market. Yet they continue to exist mainly because of the technical and fiscal divisions between Member States. Once we have removed those barriers, and found alternative ways of dealing with other relevant problems such as public security, immigration and drug controls, the reasons for the existence of the physical barriers will have been eliminated.

12. The reason for getting rid entirely of physical and other controls between Member States is not one of theology or appearance, but the hard practical fact that the maintenance of any internal frontier controls will perpetuate the costs and disadvantages of a divided market. . . .

13. While the elimination of physical barriers provides benefits for traders . . . it is through the elimination of technical barriers that the Community will give the large market its economic and industrial dimension by enabling industries to make economies of scale and therefore to become more competitive. An example of this second category—technical barriers—are the different standards for individual products adopted in different Member States for health and safety reasons, or for environmental or consumer protection. . . . The general thrust of the Commission's approach in this area will be to move away from the concept of harmonization towards that of mutual recognition and equivalence. But there will be a continuing role for the approximation of Member States' laws and regulations as laid down in Article 100 of the Treaty. Clearly, action under this Article would be quicker and more effective if the Council were to agree not to allow the unanimity requirement to obstruct progress where it could otherwise be made.

14. The removal of fiscal barriers may well be contentious and this despite the fact that the

---

[3] COM (85) 310, para. 3.   [4] *Ibid.*, para. 5.   [5] *Ibid.*, para. 7.
[6] References to Arts. 30–36, and 100 should now be read as to Arts. 28–30, and 94.

goals laid down in the Treaty are quite explicit and that important steps have already been taken along the road of approximation. This being so, the reasons why approximation of fiscal legislation is an essential element in any programme for completing the internal market are explained in detail in Part Three.

The Commission then explained that the White Paper was not intended to cover every possible issue of relevance to the integration of the Member States' economies. Matters such as the co-ordination of economic polices and competition policy were relevant in this respect; while other important areas of Community action, such as transport, the environment, and consumer protection, interacted with, and would benefit from, the completion of the internal market. The next extract from the White Paper looks more closely at the Commission's reasoning in relation to the second type of barrier, that which arises from differing technical rules. In reading this section note the way in which the Commission's strategy builds upon what the ECJ had achieved in *Cassis de Dijon*:

57. The elimination of border controls, important as it is, does not of itself create a genuine common market. Goods and people moving within the Community should not find obstacles inside the different Member States as opposed to meeting them at the border.

58. This does not mean that there should be the same rules everywhere, but that goods as well as citizens and companies should be able to move freely within the Community. Subject to certain important constraints (see paragraph 65), the general principle should be approved that, if a product is lawfully manufactured and marketed in one Member State, there is no reason why it should not be sold freely throughout the Community. . . .

60. Whilst the physical barriers dealt with in Part One impede trade flows and add unacceptable administrative costs (ultimately paid by the consumer), barriers created by different national product regulations and standards have a double-edged effect: they not only add extra costs, but they also distort production patterns; increase unit costs; increase stock holding costs; discourage business cooperation; and fundamentally frustrate the creation of a common market for industrial products. Until such barriers are removed, Community manufacturers are forced to focus on national rather than continental markets and are unable to benefit from the economies of scale which a truly unified market offers. . . .

The Need for a New Strategy

61. The harmonization approach has been the cornerstone of Community action in the first 25 years and has produced unprecedented progress in the creation of common rules on a Community-wide basis. However, over the years, a number of shortcomings have been identified and it is clear that a genuine common market cannot be realised by 1992 if the Community relies exclusively on Article 100 of the EEC Treaty. There will certainly be a continuing need for action under Article 100; but its role will be reduced as new approaches, resulting in quicker and less troublesome progress, are agreed. . . . Where Article 100 is still considered the only appropriate instrument, ways of making it operate more flexibly will need to be found. Clearly, action under this Article would be quicker and more effective if the Council were to agree not to allow the unanimity requirement to obstruct progress where it could otherwise be made.

63. In principle, therefore ... mutual recognition could be an effective strategy for bringing about a common market in a trading sense. This strategy is supported in particular by Articles 30 to 36 of the EEC Treaty, which prohibit national measures which would have excessively and unjustifiably restrictive effects on free movement.

64. But while a strategy based on mutual recognition would remove barriers to trade and lead to the creation of a genuine common trading market, it might well prove inadequate for the purposes of the building-up of an expanding market based on the competitiveness which a continental-scale uniform market can generate. On the other hand experience has shown that the alternative of relying on a strategy based totally on harmonization would be over-regulatory, would take a long time to implement, would be inflexible and could stifle innovation. What is needed is a strategy that combines the best of both approaches but, that above all, allows for progress to be made more quickly than in the past.

The Chosen Strategy

65. The Commission takes into account the underlying reasons for the existence of barriers to trade, and recognises the essential equivalence of Member States' legislative objectives in the protection of health and safety, and of the environment. Its harmonization approach is based on the following principles:

— a clear distinction needs to be drawn in future internal market initiatives between what it is essential to harmonize, and what may be left to mutual recognition of national regulations and standards; this implies that, on the occasion of each harmonization initiative, the Commission will determine whether national regulations are excessive in relation to the mandatory requirements pursued and, thus, constitute unjustified barriers to trade according to Articles 30 to 36 of the EEC Treaty;

— legislative harmonization (Council Directives based on Article 100) will in future be restricted to laying down essential health and safety requirements which will be obligatory in all Member States. Conformity with this will entitle a product to free movement;

— Harmonization of industrial standards by the elaboration of European standards will be promoted to the maximum extent, but the absence of European standards should not be allowed to be used as a barrier to free movement. During the waiting period while European Standards are being developed, the mutual acceptance of national standards, with agreed procedures, should be the guiding principle.

The Commission's White Paper did not rest content with the enunciation of general strategies. The Annex to the Paper listed 279 legislative measures, together with a timetable for the promulgation of each measure. The object was to complete this legislative process by 31 December 1992. The momentum behind the proposals gathered further force with the realization of the cost savings which would be generated by the completion of the internal market. The following extract examines this issue, and the economic benefits foregone by having a market which is not fully integrated.

M. Emerson, M. Aujean, M. Catinat, P. Goybet, A. Jacquemin, The Economics of 1992,
The E.C. Commission's Assessment of the Economic Effects of Completing
the Internal Market[7]

2. *The Nature of the Community's Internal Market Barriers* Tariffs and quantitative restrictions on trade have been largely eliminated in the Community. The remaining barriers essentially
consist of:

(i) differences in technical regulations between countries, which impose extra costs on intra-
EC trade;

(ii) delays at frontiers for customs purposes, and related administrative burdens for companies
and public administration, which impose further costs on trade;

(iii) restrictions on competition for public purchases through excluding bids from other
Community suppliers, which often result in excessively high costs of purchase;

(iv) restrictions on freedom to engage in certain service transactions, or to become established
in certain service activities in other Community countries. . . .

3. *The Nature of the Economic Gains to be Measured* . . . The removal of the constraints and
the emergence of the new competitive incentives will lead to four principal types of effect:

(i) a significant reduction in costs due to a better exploitation of several kinds of economies of
scale associated with the size of production units and enterprises;

(ii) an improved efficiency in enterprises, a rationalization of industrial structures and a setting
of prices closer to costs of production, all resulting from more competitive markets;

(iii) adjustments between industries on the basis of a fuller play of comparative advantages in
an integrated market;

(iv) a flow of innovations, new processes and new products, stimulated by the dynamics of the
internal market.

. . .

4. *Empirical Estimates* Any estimates of the effects of complex action like completing the
internal market can only be regarded as very approximate. . . . With these strong reservations
to be kept in mind, some rough orders of magnitude can be suggested. For perspective, the
Community's total gross domestic product in 1985 . . . was 3300 billion ECU for the 12 Member
States. . . .

(i) The direct costs of frontier formalities, and associated administrative costs for the private
and public sector, may be of the order of 1.8% of the value of the goods traded within the
Community or around 9 billion ECU.

(ii) The total costs for industry of identifiable barriers in the internal market, including not only
frontier formalities as above but also technical regulations and other barriers, have been
estimated . . . to average a little under 2% of . . . companies' costs. This represents about
40 billion ECU, or 3.5% of industrial value-added.

. . .

(iv) . . . industries and service sector branches subject to market entry restrictions could
experience considerably bigger potential cost and price reductions. . . . For public procurement
alone the gains could amount to around 20 billion ECU. For financial services also a range around
20 billion ECU in potential savings has been proposed. . . .

. . .

---

[7] (Oxford University Press, 1988), 1–10. See also P. Cecchini, *The European Challenge 1992, The Benefits
of a Single Market* (Gower, 1988).

(vii) The totality of the foregoing effects could be reflected, in the new equilibrium situation in the economy after several years, in a downward convergence of presently disparate price levels. . . . Under one set of hypotheses, implying strong market integration but far from complete price convergence and with incomplete sectoral coverage, the gains amounted to about 140 billion ECU.

(viii) Overall these estimates offer a range, starting with around 70 billion ECU (2.5% of GDP) for a rather narrow conception of the benefits of removing the remaining internal market barriers, to around 125 to 190 billion ECU (4.25% to 6.5% of GDP) on the hypothesis of a much more competitive, integrated market. . . .

. . .

7. *Final Remarks* The study supports the following essential conclusions:

(i) In the present condition of the European economy the segmentation and weak competitiveness of many markets means that there is large potential for the rationalization of production and distribution structures, leading to improvements in productivity, and reductions in many costs and prices.

(ii) The completion of the internal market could, if strongly reinforced by the competition policies of both the Community and Member States, have a deep and extensive impact on economic structures and performance. The size of this impact . . . could be sufficient to transform the Community's macroeconomic performance from a mediocre to a very satisfactory one.

(iii) In order to achieve a prize of this magnitude, all the main features of the internal market programme would need to be implemented with sufficient speed and conviction. . . . Implementation of half of the actions proposed in the White Paper will deliver much less than half of the potential benefits.

(iv) In fact, more than full implementation of the White Paper is required in order to achieve the full potential benefits of an integrated European market. There must be a strong competition policy. . . . Macroeconomic policy has to be set on a coherent, growth-oriented strategy. . . .

4. THE REINVIGORATION OF EUROPE: THE POLITICS OF INTEGRATION

The force of the Commission's proposals should not, however, cause us to ignore a simple, but important, question lurking in the background. Why did this initiative succeed? Why were the Commission's proposals not left to languish, like other reforms which were posited during the late 1970s and early 1980s?[8] The success of reform is often dependent upon the desire for change, which is felt at the same time by the key players in any particular political system. But who were the key players and why were they willing to accept reform at this juncture? Not surprisingly views on this question differ. Exigencies of space mean that it is not possible to do justice to the wealth of literature on this topic,[9] but the discussion would be incomplete if it did not include some consideration of this important issue. What follows are two contrasting

---

[8] For a discussion of other such efforts see Ch. 1 above.

[9] For a more general overview of this literature, see P. Craig, 'Integration Theory and Democratic Theory: Two Discourses Passing in the Night', in P. Craig and G. de Búrca (eds.), *European Union Law: An Evolutionary Perspective* (Oxford University Press, 1999), ch. 1.

views, both of which seek to explain the success of the single-market initiative and subsequent passage of the SEA against the backdrop of the pessimism which beset the Community in the late 1970s and the early 1980s.

Sandholtz and Zysman offer one thesis.[10] They reject explanations based on neofunctionalist integration theories and on the domestic politics of the Member States, although they admit that certain elements of these theories have a continuing relevance even under their own preferred explanation.[11] They argue that the success of the 1992 initiative should instead be viewed in 'terms of elite bargains formulated in response to international structural change and the Commission's policy entre-preneurship'.[12] On this hypothesis there were three crucial factors which combined to promote the success of the Community's reinvigoration: the domestic political context, the Commission's initiative and the role of the business elite.

W. Sandholtz and J. Zysman, 1992: Recasting the European Bargain[13]

The question is why national government policies and perspectives have altered. Why, in the decade between the mid-1970s and the mid-1980s, did the European governments become open to European-level, market-oriented solutions? The answer has two parts: the failure of national strategies for economic growth and the transformation of the left in European politics. First, the traditional models of growth and economic management broke down. The old political strategies for the economy seemed to have run out. After the growth of the 1960s, the world economy entered a period of stagflation in the 1970s. As extensive industrialization reached its limits, the existing formulas for national economic development and the political bargains underpinning them had to be revised. . . .

. . . the second aspect of the changed political context was the shift in government coalitions in a number of EC Member States. Certainly the weakening of the left in some countries and a shift from the communist to the market-socialist left in others helped to make possible a debate about market solutions (including unified European markets) to Europe's dilemma. In Latin Europe, the communist parties weakened as the era of Eurocommunism waned. Spain saw the triumph of Gonzalez's socialists, and their unexpected emergence as advocates of market-led development and entry into the Common Market. . . . In France, Mitterand's victory displaced the communists from their primacy on the left. . . . After 1983, Mitterand embraced a more market-oriented approach and became a vigorous advocate of increased European cooperation. . . . In Britain and Germany, the Labour and Social Democratic parties lost power as well as influence on the national debate.

. . .

In an era when deregulation—the freeing of the market—became the fad, it made intuitive sense to extend the European market as a response to all ailments. . . .

This was the domestic political soil into which the Commission's initiatives fell. Traditional models of economic growth appeared to have played themselves out, and the left had been transformed in such a way that socialist parties began to seek market-oriented solutions to economic ills. In this setting, the European Community provided more than the mechanisms of

---

[10] '1992: Recasting the European Bargain' (1989) 42 *World Politics* 95.
[11] *Ibid.*, 97–100.   [12] *Ibid.*, 97.   [13] *Ibid.*, 108–9, 111–12, 113, 116.

intergovernmental negotiation. The Eurocracy was a standing constituency and a permanent advocate of European solutions and greater unity. Proposals from the European Commission transformed this new orientation into policy, and more importantly, into a policy perspective and direction. The Commission perceived the international structural changes and the failure of existing national strategies and seized the initiative.

. . .

The third actor in the story, besides the governments and the Commission, is the leadership of the European multinational corporations. The White Paper and the Single European Act gave the appearance that changes in the EC market were irreversible and politically unstoppable. Businesses have been acting on that belief. Politically, they have taken up the banner of 1992, collaborating with the Commission and exerting substantial influence on their governments. The significance of the role of business, and of its collaboration with the Commission, must not be underestimated. . . .

This view has not gone unchallenged. Moravcsik tells a different tale. He contests the thesis that the SEA was the result of an elite alliance between the Commission, Parliament, and supranational business groups. He argues that the success of the reforms was principally due to inter-state bargains between Britain, France, and Germany. This was made possible by the convergence of European economic-policy preferences in the early 1980s, combined with the bargaining leverage which France and Germany used against Britain by threatening a two-track Europe, or a Europe *à deux vitesses*, with Britain in the slow lane. Moravcsik believes that regime theory, which stresses traditional ideas of national interest and power politics, best explains the signing of the SEA.

A. Moravcsik, Negotiating the Single European Act: National Interests and Conventional Statecraft in the European Community[14]

An alternative approach to explaining the success of the 1992 initiative focuses on inter-state bargains between heads of government in the three larger Member States of the EC. This approach, which can be called 'intergovernmental institutionalism', stresses the central importance of power and interests, with the latter not simply dictated by position in the intergovernmental system. . . . Intergovernmental institutionalism is based on three principles: intergovernmentalism, lowest common denominator bargaining, and strict limits on future transfers of sovereignty.

Intergovernmentalism. From its inception, the EC has been based on inter-state bargains between its leading Member States. Heads of government, backed by a small group of ministers and advisers, initiate and negotiate major initiatives in the Council of Ministers or the European Council. Each government views the EC through the lens of its own policy preferences; EC politics is the continuation of domestic politics by other means. . . .

Lowest-common-denominator bargaining. Without a 'European hegemony' capable of providing universal incentives or threats to promote regime formation and without the widespread use of

---

[14] (1991) 45 *International Organization* 19, 25–7. Italics in the original.

linkages and logrolling, the bargains struck in the EC reflect the relative power positions of the Member States. Small states can be bought off with side-payments, but larger states exercise a de facto veto over fundamental changes in the scope or rules of the core element of the EC, which remains economic liberalization. Thus, bargaining tends to converge toward the lowest common denominator of large state interests. The bargains initially consisted of bilateral agreements between France and Germany; now they consist of trilateral agreements including Britain.

The only tool that can impel a state to accept an outcome on a major issue that it does not prefer to the status quo is the threat of exclusion. Once an international institution has been created, exclusion can be expensive both because the nonmember forfeits input into further decision making and because it forgoes whatever benefits result. If two major states can isolate the third and credibly threaten it with exclusion and if such exclusion undermines the substantive interests of the excluded state, the coercive threat may bring about an agreement at a level of integration above the lowest common denominator.

Protection of sovereignty. The decision to join a regime involves some sacrifice of national sovereignty in exchange for certain advantages. Policymakers safeguard their countries against the future erosion of sovereignty by demanding the unanimous consent of regime members to sovereignty-related reforms. They also avoid granting open-ended authority to central institutions that might infringe on their sovereignty, preferring instead to work through intergovernmental institutions such as the Council of Ministers, rather than through supranational bodies such as the Commission and Parliament.

There is no need to decide unequivocally between these two theories. Most would agree that there were two connected conditions for the success of the new initiatives. There had to be *legislative reform* to facilitate the passage of measures designed to complete the internal market. There had also to be a *new approach to harmonization* which would expedite the process of breaking down the technical barriers to intra-Community trade. These will be considered in turn.

5. COMPLETING THE INTERNAL MARKET:
LEGISLATIVE REFORM AND THE SEA

The European Council, which had been the immediate catalyst for the Commission's study, endorsed the White Paper in June 1985. Intergovernmental meetings which gave shape to the Single European Act followed. The SEA was signed on 17 February 1986 and entered into force after ratification by Member States on 1 July 1987. The Act contained new procedures designed to facilitate the passage of legislation for completion of the internal market. It should not, however, be thought that the SEA was uncontroversial, or that there was complete agreement between the major political players on the content of the new legislative norms. There was not. The Commission pressed for more far-reaching changes than the Member States were willing to accept. The importance of the political background should not therefore be 'left behind' once one has read the materials in the previous section.

The SEA introduced two major legislative innovations which were of prime importance for the single market project: Article 7a (now Article 14)[15] and Article 100a (now Article 95).

(a) ARTICLE 14: THE OBLIGATION STATED

1. The Community shall adopt measures with the aim of progressively establishing the internal market over a period expiring on 31 December 1992, in accordance with the provisions of this Article and of Articles 15, 26, 47(2), 49, 80, 93 and 95[16] and without prejudice to the other provisions of this Treaty.

2. The internal market shall comprise an area without internal frontiers in which the free movement of goods, persons, services and capital is ensured in accordance with the provisions of the Treaty.

3. The Council, acting by a qualified majority on a proposal from the Commission, shall determine the guidelines and conditions necessary to ensure balanced progress in all the sectors concerned.

We can begin by considering the *content of the obligation* contained in Article 14(1). The extent to which this is legally enforceable will be analysed in due course. The Community was obliged to attain the internal market by the specified date. This obligation was imposed on the Community institutions as such, but the Member States had a duty pursuant to Article 10 (ex Article 5) to co-operate in the endeavour. Article 14(1) indicated the specific Treaty provisions to be used to achieve the internal market. These provisions were either introduced or amended by the SEA, but Article 14(1) made it clear that this list was without prejudice to other provisions of the Treaty. This was in part because there were other Treaty provisions, such as Article 37 (ex Article 43), which might form the basis for measures designed to secure the internal market. It also ensured that Member States could still use provisions such as Article 30 (ex Article 36), or the mandatory requirements of *Cassis de Dijon*, to justify rules which might hamper intra-Community trade, pending the passage of the requisite Community measures which would render such national rules otiose.

Article 14(2) contained the *definition of the internal market*. This could be defined in a variety of ways, some broad, some narrow. The framers of the SEA chose a two-part formulation: it was to be an area without internal frontiers, in which there could be free movement of goods, persons, etc. The first of these is capable of more precise specification than the second. The attainment of an area without internal frontiers can be judged by whether any border controls still exist on the free movement of goods or persons etc. Such controls are essentially formal in nature. It is considerably more difficult to determine how freely goods, persons, and capital can move within the Community, *even when* border controls have been removed. There may, for example, be technical rules which render it difficult to market goods from State A in State B. It may therefore not be easy to decide when the internal market really has been completed. A criterion would be whether the Commission had completed the

---

[15] Prior to the passage of the TEU this was Art. 8a. What was Art. 7 stated that the common market should be progressively established during a transitional period of 12 years. This has been repealed by the ToA, since it is now otiose.

[16] Ex Arts. 7c, 28, 57(2), 59, 84, 99, and 100a respectively.

legislative programme outlined in the White Paper. This has, as will be seen below, been largely realized. It would, none the less, be mistaken to assume that attaining the internal market is a once-and-for-all, static objective. It is not. Continuing technological developments pose new challenges for the single market ideal.

We must now consider the *legal effect* of Article 14, and whether it has any such effect in its own right. In the first working paper which the Commission submitted to the Intergovernmental Conference from which the SEA emerged it seems that it intended what has now become Article 14 to have direct effect. The sting of this provision was given even greater force by reason of the further Commission pro-posal that, if national rules on free movement were not removed by the agreed date, then they would automatically be recognized as equivalent. These suggestions 'stunned the participants at the Intergovernmental Conference'.[17] This idea was too radical for the Member States and the Commission was forced to modify its sugges-tions. This it did in an amended working paper submitted to the Conference.[18] The Member States were still concerned at the possibility that the Article could produce legal consequences and therefore they attached a Declaration to the Article which stated:

The Conference wishes by means of the provisions in Article 7a to express its firm political will to take before January 1, 1993 the decisions necessary to complete the internal market defined in those provisions, and more particularly the decisions necessary to implement the Commission's programme described in the White Paper on the Internal Market.

Setting the date of December 31, 1992 does not create an automatic legal effect.

The possibility that Article 14 will have legal consequences cannot, however, be discounted. It is at the very least necessary to distinguish between the legal effect of the Article *vis-à-vis* the Community itself, and in relation to possible actions against the Member States via direct effect.

The possibility that Article 14 might have *legal effects against the Community itself*[19] is based in part on its mandatory wording and in part on the fact that the Declaration, whatever its precise legal status, seeks to preclude direct effect through the words 'does not create automatic legal effect'. The possibility of using Article 232 (ex Article 175), in the event of Commission or Council inaction, would depend on whether the criteria for actions of this kind were met.[20] It is necessary that the measures which it is claimed should have been enacted are defined with sufficient specificity for them to be identified individually, and adopted pursuant to Article 233 (ex Article 176).[21] This will not be so where the relevant institutions possess discretionary power, with consequential policy options, the content of which cannot be identified with precision. The application of this criterion to Article 14 depends, as Wyatt and Dashwood state,[22] upon the nature of the alleged failure to

---

[17] C.-D. Ehlermann, 'The Internal Market Following the Single European Act' (1987) 24 *CMLRev.* 361, 371.

[18] *Ibid.*, 371–2.

[19] *Ibid.*, 372. See also H.J. Glaesner, 'The Single European Act: Attempt at an Appraisal' (1987) 10 *Fordham Intl. LJ* 446.

[20] On Art. 232 (ex Art. 175), see Ch. 12 above.

[21] Case 13/83, *European Parliament v. Council* [1985] ECR 1513.

[22] Wyatt and Dashwood's *European Union Law* (Sweet & Maxwell, 4th edn., 2000), 504–5.

act. It would, for example, be difficult to maintain that the Article 232 criterion was met if the allegation was that the Commission had failed to promote measures designed to ensure the free movement of goods, persons, services, or capital. This is 'too general an objective, and its attainment too fraught with policy choices, to be the subject of proceedings under'[23] Article 232. There may, by way of contrast, be a greater possibility for such an action where the allegation is that the Council had failed to adopt a specific Commission proposal. Even in this instance much would depend upon the nature of the proposal. A damages claim will be even more difficult to prove.[24]

There is also the possibility that Article 14 may have *legal consequences for the Member States*. This could possibly mean that, even if the relevant Community measures had not been enacted, it would none the less be open to an individual to argue that Member States' rules which constituted a barrier to the completion of the internal market should not be applied if they were incompatible with Article 14 itself. Toth[25] argued that the Declaration set out above does not, in and of itself, prevent the Article from having direct effect. He contended that the Declaration is merely interpretive without binding force as such, and that the ECJ would be free to determine the legal consequences of Article 14. It must still be shown that Article 14 fulfils the conditions for direct effect,[26] the most problematic of which is that there must be no further action required before the norm can have direct effect. We have seen that the ECJ has been willing to accord direct effect to certain Treaty Articles, notwithstanding the fact that further action is clearly intended in order to flesh out the Article.[27] It would, however, be bold for the Court to hold that Article 14 is directly effective. This is especially so given that the Article does contemplate further Community action, and given also that, pending such action, national measures which are valid under, for example, *Cassis* will continue to be lawful. Moreover, even though the Declaration may not formally preclude direct effect, it does clearly signal Member State intent in this respect.[28] It is, moreover, clear that the Court has been reluctant to accord direct effect to Article 14. In *Wijsenbeek*[29] the applicant claimed that a Dutch penalty for failure to produce a passport when entering the country was invalid, *inter alia*, for breach of Article 14. He argued that the Article had direct effect from the end of December 1992, with the consequence that the Member States no longer had competence in this field. It could not therefore impose border controls, at least in relation to internal frontiers. The ECJ rejected the argument. It held that in the absence of Community measures requiring Member States to abolish controls of persons at the internal frontiers, Article 14 could not have direct effect notwithstanding the expiry of the December 1992 deadline. Any such obligation

[23] *Ibid.*, 505.
[24] Case T–113/96, *Edouard Dubois et Fils SA v. Council and Commission* [1998] ECR II-125.
[25] A.G. Toth, 'The Legal Status of the Declarations Annexed to the Single European Act' (1986) 23 *CMLRev.* 803.
[26] Ch. 5.   [27] *Ibid.*
[28] In Case C–378/97, *Criminal Proceedings against Wijsenbeek* [1999] ECR I–6207, para. 9 the ECJ referred to the Declaration attached to Art. 14 but did not comment on its legal effect.
[29] *Ibid.*

presupposed harmonization of the laws of the Member States governing the crossing of the external borders, immigration, the grant of visas, and asylum.[30] A similar reluctance to find that Article 14 has direct effect was also apparent in *Echirolles Distribution*.[31] The applicant argued that Article 14(2) rendered illegal a French law imposing resale price maintenance on books. In an earlier case[32] the ECJ had found the French law to be compatible with the Treaty, but the applicant argued that this had been overtaken by the SEA and the introduction of Article 14. The ECJ disagreed. In a terse judgment it held that while the internal market was one of the objectives of the Treaty, it had to be read in conjunction with other Treaty provisions designed to implement those objectives. Since Articles 28, 30, and 81 had not been amended the ECJ's interpretation of them in the earlier case could not be called in question.[33]

The question until now has been of the possibility of direct effect where relevant Community measures to implement the internal market have not been passed. Where, however, they have been promulgated matters are different. The Community measure adopted might itself have direct effect, and so, too, might Article 14 (ex Article 7a).

(b) ARTICLE 15: THE OBLIGATION QUALIFIED

Article 15 (ex Article 7c) qualifies Article 14 (ex Article 7a). It requires the Commission, when drawing up proposals pursuant to Article 14, to take into account the extent of the effort that certain economies showing differences in developments will have to sustain during the period of establishment of the internal market, and it may propose appropriate provisions. If the provisions take the form of derogations, they must be temporary and cause the least possible disturbance to the functioning of the common market. Ehlermann captures the purpose of Article 15:[34]

It makes allowance for the fact that the Community has become more heterogeneous through the accession of new Member States. If the objective laid down in Article 8A[35] appears rather ambitious for the original Member States, it is far more so for most of the new Member States, given their relative economic weakness compared with the old established members and the considerable risks which the complete opening up of their domestic markets would therefore entail.

---

[30] *Ibid.*, para. 40. Moreover, even if Art. 14 were to be regarded as according Community nationals an unconditional right to move freely within the Community, Member States would still be able to impose passport controls at internal frontiers in order to be able to check whether a person was in fact a Community national: para. 43.

[31] Case C–9/99, *Echirolles Distribution SA v. Association du Dauphine* [2000] ECR I–8207.

[32] Case 229/83, *Leclerc v. Au Blé Vert* [1985] ECR 1.

[33] Case C–9/99, n. 31 above, paras. 23–24.

[34] 'The Internal Market Following the Single European Act' (1987) 24 *CMLRev.* 361, 374.

[35] For which now read Art. 14.

(c) ARTICLE 95(1): FACILITATING THE PASSAGE OF HARMONIZATION MEASURES

We have already seen that one of the principal difficulties in ensuring the passage of harmonization measures was the requirement of unanimity. This problem was alleviated in part by the changes in the voting rules which applied to the specific Articles mentioned in Article 14. However, if matters had rested there, the attainment of the internal market would still have been difficult for the following reason. Many of the measures aimed at harmonizing laws prior to 1986 were promulgated under Article 100 (now Article 94). This Article gives a general power to pass directives for the approximation of laws of the Member States that affect the establishment or functioning of the common market, but unanimity is required. The framers of the SEA correctly appreciated that the passage of harmonizing measures would be facilitated if there were to be a general legislative power akin to Article 100, without the unanimity requirement. This was provided by Article 100a (now Article 95), which was introduced into the Treaty by the SEA. Article 95(1) reads as follows:

By way of derogation from Article 94 and save where otherwise provided in this Treaty, the following provisions shall apply for the achievement of the objectives set out in Article 14. The Council shall, acting in accordance with the procedure referred to in Article 251 and after consulting the Economic and Social Committee, adopt the measures for the approximation of the provisions laid down by law, regulation or administrative action in Member States which have as their object the establishing and functioning of the internal market.

There are a number of features of this Article which should be noted. One concerns the *range of measures* which can be taken. Article 94 (ex Article 100) authorizes only the passage of directives. Article 95 (ex Article 100a), by way of contrast, empowers the Council to pass measures, which obviously includes directives, but also legitimates the use of the Article for the passage of, for example, regulations.[36]

A second noteworthy feature concerns *the role of the European Parliament*. Whereas Article 94 merely requires that the European Parliament be consulted, Article 95(1) accords the Parliament a greater say by making the measures subject to the co-decision procedure of Article 251 (ex Article 189b).[37]

The third important point concerning Article 95 is that it is *a residual provision*. It operates only 'save where otherwise provided in this Treaty'. This means that other, more specific Treaty provisions, such as Articles 37, 44, 47, and 71, should be used for measures designed to attain the internal market where they fall within the subject matter areas of those Articles. This can generate boundary-dispute problems about the correct legal basis for Community legislation. Boundary disputes will, however, normally arise only where a party has good reason to raise the point. In the past this has normally been the European Parliament, which had differing rights to participate

---

[36] For an expansive interpretation of 'measures' see Case C–359/92, *Germany v. Council* [1994] ECR I–3681.

[37] Originally Art. 100a (now Art. 95) provided that the co-operation procedure contained within Art. 189c (now Article 252) should be used. The substitution of the Art. 189b (now Art. 251) procedure was done by the TEU.

in the legislative process, depending on the particular Article in the Treaty which was the basis for the enactment. It therefore had a strong interest in ensuring that its legislative rights under Article 95 were not by-passed by the enactment of legislation on the basis of a different Treaty Article giving it less extensive rights in the legislative process.[38] The general test propounded by the ECJ for the resolution of such boundary disputes was that regard should be had to the nature, aim, and content of the act in question.[39] Where these factors indicated that the measure was concerned with more than one area of the Treaty, then it might be necessary to satisfy the legal requirements of two Treaty Articles.[40] The ECJ also made it clear that this would not be insisted upon where the relevant legal bases under the two Articles prescribed procedures which are incompatible. Boundary disputes are less likely to occur after the Treaty of Amsterdam since the legislative procedure applicable for most Treaty Articles, including Article 95, is co-decision.

The final point of importance concerns *the outer boundaries of Article 95*. The provision is broadly framed, but the ECJ confirmed in the *Tobacco* case that there are limits to this Article.[41] The ECJ struck down a Directive[42] designed to harmonize the law relating to the advertising and sponsorship of tobacco products. The Directive had been passed pursuant to Articles 47, 55, and 95, but most of the argument focused on the applicability of Article 95 itself. The ECJ read Article 95 in the light of Articles 3(1)(c) and 14. It concluded that the measures referred to in Article 95 must be intended to improve the conditions for the establishment and functioning of the internal market. It did not, as argued by the Commission, Council, and EP,[43] give any general power of market regulation. This would, said the ECJ, be contrary to the wording of Articles 3(1)(c) and 14, and it would be incompatible with the principle contained in Article 5, that the powers of the Community were limited to those specifically conferred on it.[44] The ECJ held that a measure adopted on the basis of Article 95 must genuinely have as its object the improvement of the conditions for the establishment and functioning of the internal market. If mere disparities between the relevant national rules, and the abstract risk of obstacles to the exercise of fundamental freedoms, or distortions of competition, could justify the use of Article 95, then judicial review of compliance with the proper legal basis would be rendered 'nugatory'.[45] Any distortion of competition must, moreover, be appreciable. If this were not required then 'the powers of the Community legislature would be practically unlimited'.[46] This was because national laws often imposed different regulatory conditions on activities. These could impact indirectly on the conditions for competition as between undertakings. If the EC could rely on the smallest distortions of

---

[38] See, e.g., Case 68/86, *United Kingdom v. Council* [1988] ECR 855; Case 11/88, *Commission v. Council* [1989] ECR 3799; Case C–151/91, *Commission v. Council* [1993] ECR I–939; Case C–187/93, *European Parliament v. Council* [1994] ECR I–2857.

[39] Case C–300/89, *Commission v. Council* [1991] ECR I–2867; Case C–426/93, *Germany v. Council* [1995] ECR I–3723; Case C–271/94, *European Parliament v. Council* [1996] 2 CMLR 481.

[40] Case 165/87, *Commission v. Council* [1988] ECR 5545.

[41] Case C–376/98, *Germany v. European Parliament and Council* [2000] ECR I–8419.

[42] [1998] OJ L 213/9.

[43] Case C–376/98, n. 41 above, para. 45.   [44] *Ibid.*, para. 83.

[45] *Ibid.*, para. 84.   [46] *Ibid.*, para. 107.

competition to justify using Article 95 then this would contradict the principle in Article 5 that the Community has only the powers specifically conferred on it.[47] It followed that the ECJ must therefore verify whether a measure enacted under Article 95 in fact pursued the objectives stated by the Community legislature,[48] and whether the distortion of competition which the measure purported to eliminate was appreciable.[49] When viewed in this way the Directive had not been validly made under Article 95.

(d) ARTICLE 95(2)–(10): QUALIFICATIONS TO ARTICLE 95(1)

The remainder of Article 95 qualifies the powers given by Article 95(1). These qualifications differ in nature, and their presence in the Treaty is the result of the political negotiations which attended the passage of the SEA and later Treaty amendments.

Article 95(2) encapsulates a straightforward exception to Article 95(1), by providing that the latter shall not apply to fiscal provisions, to those relating to the free movement of persons, or to those relating to the rights and interests of employed persons. These areas were felt by the Member States to be particularly sensitive, hence their exclusion from the ambit of Article 95(1). Legislation for these areas will therefore have to be passed by using either Article 94 or a more specific provision of the Treaty where one exists.[50]

Article 95(3) instructs the Commission, when passing measures under Article 95(1) relating to health, safety, environmental protection, and consumer protection, to take as a base a high level of protection, taking into account in particular any new development based on scientific facts. The European Parliament and the Council are also to use their respective powers to achieve this objective. As Ehlermann has pointed out,[51] there is an analogy between this Article and Article 15. The latter was demanded by relatively under-developed economies to protect them from the possible rigours of free competition under a completed internal market; Article 95(3) was included to placate countries such as Germany and Denmark, which were concerned that the harmonization measures which emerged might not be stringent enough. The wording of Article 95(3) does not, however, compel the Commission to enact a measure in accordance with the standards pertaining in the countries with high levels of protection. It merely requires that a high level of protection should be taken as the base.

Article 95(4)–(9) is the qualification to Article 95(1) that received most critical attention. The provision is complex and therefore should be set out in full:

---

[47] *Ibid.*, para. 107.   [48] *Ibid.*, para. 85.   [49] *Ibid.*, para. 106.
[50] For fiscal provisions see Art. 93 (ex Art. 99), which requires unanimity in the Council and consultation with the EP; for free movement of persons see Art. 18(2) (ex Art. 8a(2)), which does now impose the Art. 251 procedure in this area, but stipulates that unanimity is none the less required by the Council when using this procedure; for the rights of employed persons see Arts. 44 and 47 (ex Arts. 54 and 57).
[51] N. 17 above, 375.

4. If, after the adoption by the Council or by the Commission of a harmonization measure, a Member State deems it necessary to maintain national provisions on grounds of major needs referred to in Article 30, or relating to protection of the environment or the working environment, it shall notify the Commission of these provisions as well as the grounds for maintaining them.

5. Moreover, without prejudice to paragraph 4, if, after the adoption by the Council or the Commission of a harmonization measure, a Member State deems it necessary to introduce national provisions based on new scientific evidence relating to the protection of the environment or the working environment on grounds of a problem specific to that Member State arising after the adoption of the harmonization measure, it shall notify the Commission of the envisaged provisions as well as the grounds for introducing them.

6. The Commission shall, within six months of the notifications as referred to in paragraphs 4 and 5, approve or reject the national provisions involved after having verified whether or not they are a means of arbitrary discrimination or a disguised restriction on trade between Member States and whether or not they shall constitute an obstacle to the functioning of the internal market.

In the absence of a decision by the Commission within this period the national provisions referred to in paragraphs 4 and 5 shall be deemed to have been approved. When justified by the complexity of the matter and in the absence of danger for human health, the Commission may notify the Member State concerned that the period referred to in this paragraph may be extended for a further period of up to six months.

7. When, pursuant to paragraph 6, a Member State is authorised to maintain or introduce a national provision derogating from a harmonization measure, the Commission shall immediately examine whether to propose an adaptation to that measure.

8. When a Member State raises a specific problem on public health in a field which has been the subject of prior harmonization measures, it shall bring it to the attention of the Commission which shall immediately examine whether to propose appropriate measures to the Council.

9. By way of derogation from the procedure laid down in Articles 226 and 227, the Commission and any Member State may bring the matter directly before the Court of Justice if it considers that another Member State is making improper use of the powers provided for in this Article.

For the sake of clarity it should be noted that Article 95(5), (7), and (8) were new provisions introduced by the ToA, whereas the remainder of the paragraphs are modifications of pre-existing provisions. The inclusion of Article 95(4) (ex Article 100a(4)) gave rise to much critical comment. It was one of the principal defects emphasized by those opposed to the SEA.[52] The genesis of this Article and its exceptional character are evident in the following extract.

C.-D. Ehlermann, The Internal Market Following the Single European Act[53]

Whereas paragraph 1[54] is the most significant provision of the Single European Act, paragraph 4 is the most problematic. Its purpose is the same as that of the preceding paragraph, namely to protect any Member State in a minority position from being forced to accept the majority line.

---

[52] P. Pescatore, 'Some Critical Remarks on the "Single European Act" ' (1987) 24 *CMLRev*. 9.
[53] N. 17 above, 389.
[54] Of Art. 100a as it then was, now Art. 95.

However, the method devised is completely different. Whereas paragraph 3 is in keeping with the approach followed by the Community in the past, paragraph 4 represents a radical new departure.

It goes back to the fact that the United Kingdom, and later Ireland, wished to safeguard certain special measures connected with their island status against the threat of majority voting. Neither country was satisfied with the safeguard offered by paragraph 3. But they both accepted that retention of the unanimity requirement would have emasculated Article 100a.

The way out of this dilemma was paragraph 4, which was drafted by the European Council itself. . . .

Any assessment of Article 95(4)–(10) must take into account legal and political issues.

In *legal terms* the Member State concerns which can legitimately trigger Article 95(4) are finite: the matters covered by Article 30 (ex Article 36), plus the environment and working environment.[55] Other state concerns, such as consumer protection, which can justify national measures under *Cassis*[56] pending adequate harmonization measures find no place in Article 95(4).[57] The ToA has, moreover, modified the wording of Article 95(4). Whereas it had previously spoken of a State 'applying' national provisions on one of the specified grounds, Article 95(4) is now framed in terms of 'maintaining' such provisions. This implies that a State cannot invoke the Article to justify *new* national provisions which derogate from the harmonization measure, but can only use it to justify the *retention* of existing provisions.[58] The Member State concerns which can trigger Article 95(5) are also limited: there must be new scientific evidence relating to the environment etc., and there must be a problem which is specific to that State. Where the conditions mentioned in Article 95(5) are met the State may 'introduce' national provisions. It is clear that Article 95(4) and (5) are exceptions that derogate from the principles of the Treaty. They will therefore be restrictively construed by the Commission and the ECJ, and this is so notwithstanding the subjective wording of the Article (the State 'deems it necessary', etc.). The Commission's powers of scrutiny have been reinforced by Article 95(6). Prior to the ToA, Article 100a(4) spoke in terms of the Commission 'confirming' the national provisions. Article 95(6) now speaks of the Commission 'approving or rejecting' them. This shift in emphasis has itself been reinforced by modifications to Article 95(4) by the ToA, requiring the State to explain the reasons for maintaining the national provisions.[59] The ECJ has, moreover, confirmed that it can judicially review the

[55] Art. 95(4) as modified by the ToA does not however restrict the application of this Art. to measures passed by qualified majority, as did Art. 100a(4). It would, therefore, technically be possible for a State to invoke Art. 95(4) either: where the measure was passed by unanimity pursuant to Art. 94, assuming that the phrase 'harmonization measure' covers measures passed under Art. 94; or where the measure was passed by qualified majority under Art. 95(1).

[56] See Ch. 5 above.

[57] It should not, however, be forgotten that Art. 95(4), by way of contrast to Art. 30 (ex Art. 36) and the *Cassis* mandatory requirements, can be invoked by a State even though a harmonization measure has been passed.

[58] This view is further reinforced by Art. 95(5) which is framed in terms of the 'introduction' of national provisions based on new scientific evidence.

[59] Art. 95(5) contains a similar reasoning requirement.

invocation of what is now Article 95(4).[60] The process under Article 95 should not, however, be thought of in overly adversarial terms. Articles 95(7) and (8), introduced by the ToA, are both designed to facilitate a negotiated solution to the problem.

In *political terms* many of the more dramatic fears about the impact of Article 95(4) have not been borne out by state practice. Concerns that Member States would routinely seek to invoke the Article to prevent the application of harmonization measures have proven to be unfounded.

Article 95(10) is the final qualification to Article 95(1). It provides that harmonization measures may include safeguard clauses authorizing Member States to take, for one of the non-economic reasons in Article 30 (ex Article 36), provisional measures subject to Community control procedures. Recourse to Article 30 is normally precluded when Community harmonization measures have been enacted. The purpose of Article 95(10) is to allow a Member State, subject to a Community control procedure, to adopt temporary measures in the event of a sudden and unforeseen danger to health, life, etc.

6. COMPLETING THE INTERNAL MARKET: THE NEW APPROACH TO HARMONIZATION

(a) THE RATIONALE FOR THE NEW APPROACH

We noted earlier that the completion of the single market was dependent upon two necessary conditions. There had to be reform of the legislative procedure to facilitate the passage of measures to complete the internal market. There had also to be a new approach to harmonization which would make it easier to draft and secure the passage of these measures.

Reforms in the legislative process would not have been sufficient to secure the internal market, even though harmonization measures could now be passed more easily. This was because traditional Community harmonization techniques had a number of disadvantages.[61] They were slow, and generated excessive uniformity. There was a failure to develop links between harmonization and standardization, thereby leading to inconsistencies and wastage of time. Problems of certification and testing were not sufficiently addressed, and implementation within Member States was imperfect. The Commission recognized these shortcomings in its White Paper.[62] Thus in its proposals to the Council and Parliament for a New Approach to Technical Harmonization and Standards,[63] the Commission acknowledged the advances which had been made through the directives which had been passed. However, it also accepted that eighteen years' experience had shown the delays and difficulties with such an approach, stemming from attempting to harmonize by means of detailed

---

[60] Case C–41/93, *France* v. *Commission* [1994] ECR I–1829.

[61] J. Pelkmans, 'The New Approach to Technical Harmonization and Standardization' (1987) 25 *JCMS* 249, 252–3.

[62] COM(85)310, para. 64.   [63] Bull. EC 1–1985.

technical specification. The Commission admitted that the results of harmonization had been negligible in certain industrial fields, given the multiplicity of national technical regulations and the speed of technological change.

(b) THE NEW APPROACH TO HARMONIZATION

The general direction of the new approach to harmonization is apparent in the extract from the Commission's White Paper on Completing the Internal Market. There was to be mutual recognition through the *Cassis de Dijon* principle. National rules which did not come within one of the mandatory requirements would be invalid; legislative harmonization was to be restricted to laying down health and safety standards; and there would be promotion of European standardization. This general description of the Community's new approach must be fleshed out if it is to be understood. Four elements can be identified in the Community's new strategy.

The *first building block* was the adoption of Directive 83/189[64] on the provision of information on technical standards and regulations. This measure, known as the mutual information or transparency directive, imposes an obligation on a State to inform the Commission before it adopts any legally binding regulation setting a technical specification. The Commission then notifies the other States, and may require that the adoption of the national measure be delayed by six months, in order that possible amendments can be considered. A year's delay can result if the Commission decides to push ahead with a harmonization directive on the issue.

A *second facet* of the new approach was the willing acceptance of the *Cassis* jurisprudence. A product which had been lawfully manufactured in a Member State should be capable of being bought and sold in any other Member State. Mutual recognition should be the norm. No harmonization measures were required with respect to those national measures that would be condemned under the *Cassis* reasoning. Harmonization efforts should therefore be concentrated on those measures which would still be lawful under the *Cassis* exceptions or under Article 30 (ex Article 36).

This leads naturally on to the *third aspect* of the new approach. Legislative harmonization was to be limited to laying down essential health and safety requirements. The essence of this is captured by Pelkmans.

J. Pelkmans, The New Approach to Technical Harmonization and Standardization[65]

— harmonization of legislation is limited to the adoption . . . of the essential safety requirements . . . with which the products brought on the market must comply in order to qualify for free movement in the Community;
— it is the task of the competent (private) standardization organs, given technical progress, to formulate the technical specifications, on the basis of which industry needs to manufacture and market products complying with the fundamental requirements of the directives;

---

[64] [1983] OJ L109/8. See Case C–194/94, *CIA Security International SA* v. *Signalson SA and Securitel SPRL* [1996] ECR I–2201.
[65] N. 61 above. Italics in the original.

— these technical specifications are not binding and retain their character of voluntary (European) standards;

— but, at the same time, the governments are *obliged to presume* that the products manufactured in accordance with the European standards comply with the 'fundamental requirements' stipulated in the directive. It is this presumption that guarantees business free market access.

When a standard has been approved by the Commission and published in the Official Journal all Member States must accept goods which conform to it. If a Member State disputes whether the standard conforms to the safety objectives set out in the directive, the burden of proof will be on the State to substantiate its contentions. An analogous reversal of the burden of proof operates in the case of producers in the following sense. It is open to producers to manufacture according to specifications other than those laid down. The burden of proof will, however, then be on the producer to show that the goods meet the essential requirements specified in the directive.

The *final element* of the new approach is the promotion of European standardization. Standardization is of importance both because it reduces barriers to intra-Community trade, and because it increases the competitiveness of European industry:[66]

Standards can have a market-creating effect or, in other words, the lack of a standard between adjoining countries can make the Euromarket (i. e. trade between Member States) impossible, as is for instance the case with car telephones. Standards can also have an anticipatory effect. For instance, sufficient investment in product development, process technology and further innovations takes place in some products only when compatibility is secured first.

The principal bodies are the European Committee for Standardization (CEN) and the European Committee for Technical Standardization (CENELEC). Other more specialized bodies exist for particular industrial sectors. They 'ensure that standardization processes take place in parallel with harmonization at Council level and are based on "essential requirements"'.[67] Provided that standardization does comply with these 'essential requirements' then it is very likely to be approved. Standardization initiatives will also be made in the context of newly emerging fields or those in which rapid technological change is taking place, in order to facilitate the emergence of a more truly European market for these goods. In order to expedite decision-making the Community standardization bodies have moved to qualified-majority voting.

It is important to be clear about the relationship between Community harmonization of essential requirements and the standardization process. A directive which is passed pursuant to the new approach will lay down in general terms the health and safety requirements which the goods must meet. The setting of standards is designed both to help manufacturers prove conformity to these essential requirements and to allow inspection to test for conformity with them. Promoting Community-wide standards in the manner described above is designed to foster this process by

---

[66] *Ibid.*, 260.   [67] *Ibid.*, 256.

encouraging the development of consensus on what the relevant standards in a particular area should be. Allowing a manufacturer to show that its goods comply with the essential safety requirements, even if they do not comply with the Community standard, provides flexibility.

The advantages of the new approach to harmonization are considerable and can be compared to the disadvantages of the traditional technique. Directives can be drafted more easily since they are less detailed. The excessive 'Euro-uniformity' of the traditional approach is avoided by combining stipulated safety objectives with flexibility as to the type of product which can comply with those safety requirements, and flexibility also as to the standards through which this compliance can be achieved. The need for unanimity in voting is obviated through Article 95 (ex Article 100a). Harmonization and standardization are related. More Community directives can be made, and hence the gap between Community harmonization and the volume of national technical regulations can be reduced. Finally, incentives for proper implementation of directives by the Member States have been increased through judicial doctrine such as that in *Francovich*.[68]

This is not to say that the new approach has been problem-free. The adequacy of the funding for standardization bodies, the sufficiency of the bodies able to undertake the certification process, and the representation of consumer interests have all been causes for concern.[69] The Commission recognized the need for improvements in these areas.[70] Notwithstanding these difficulties the new approach to harmonization offers an opportunity for Community progress in this important area, and one which is a good deal more realistic than would have been the case using the traditional techniques.

(c) THE NEW APPROACH TO HARMONIZATION: LEGISLATIVE FORMAT

The operation of the new approach to harmonization will be clearer by way of an example, such as Council Directive 89/392 on the approximation of the laws of the Member States relating to machinery.[71]

This Directive *does not* lay down detailed requirements for how to build machinery. It concentrates on the health and safety risks arising out of the use of machinery, and states explicitly that the Directive was passed within the framework of the new approach to harmonization.

The recitals to the Directive note that the Member States have different systems of accident prevention; that the disparities in the national rules can constitute barriers to trade; that approximation of these national laws is therefore necessary to ensure free movement of goods without prejudicing the protection of health and safety; that the Directive is designed to define the essential health and safety requirements; and that

---

[68] See Ch. 6 above.

[69] Pelkmans, n. 61 above, 263–5; K. Armstrong and S. Bulmer, *The Governance of the Single European Market* (Manchester University Press, 1998), 157–63.

[70] *Commission Green Paper on the Development of Standardization: Action for Faster Technical Integration in Europe*, COM(90)456 final; *The Broader Use of Standardization in Community Policy*, COM(95)412 final.

[71] See also, e.g., Dir. 88/378 on toy safety; Dir. 89/106 on construction products; Dir. 89/336 on electro-magnetic compatibility.

standards (generated in the manner described above) will enable manufacturers to prove conformity with the essential requirements and allow inspection to ensure conformity with these requirements.

The recitals also locate this Directive within the broader framework of the Treaty. Notice the way in which the following recital from the Directive places this Community initiative, and indeed the whole of the new harmonization approach, within the context of the *Cassis* jurisprudence. National technical rules which impede trade, even if not discriminatory, are contrary to Community law unless saved by one of the mandatory requirements or Article 36 (now Article 30). It is therefore only those national rules which survive the *Cassis* test which have to be harmonized:

Whereas Community law, in its present form, provides—by way of derogation from one of the fundamental rules of the Community, namely the free movement of goods—that obstacles to movement within the Community resulting from disparities in national legislation relating to the marketing of products must be accepted in so far as the provisions concerned can be recognized as being necessary to satisfy imperative requirements; *whereas,* therefore, the harmonization of laws in this case must be limited only to those requirements necessary to satisfy the imperative and essential health and safety requirements relating to machinery; *whereas* these requirements must replace the relevant national provisions because they are essential.

Article 1 of the Directive then defines its scope: it is to apply to machinery, which is further specified both inclusively and exclusively. The essential health and safety requirements for machinery are set out in Annex 1 at a relatively high level of generality. Article 2(1) imposes a duty on Member States to ensure that machinery is marketed only when it complies with the essential requirements. Article 2(2) makes it clear that the Member States may choose to lay down provisions designed to protect workers using the machines, provided that the machinery is not modified in a manner not specified in the Directive. Article 3 states that the machinery covered by the Directive shall satisfy the essential requirements set out in Annex 1. Under the terms of Article 4 Member States are not to restrict the placing on the market of machinery which complies with the Directive. Article 5 refers to standards. If machinery bears the 'EC mark' and is accompanied by a declaration that it conforms to the essential health and safety requirements, the Member States shall accept that it does so conform.[72] If there are no harmonized standards Member States shall apply existing national standards relevant to the proper implementation of the essential health and safety requirements. Where a national standard transposes a harmonized standard, then machinery constructed in accordance with this standard shall be presumed to comply with the essential requirements. Article 6 contains safeguards in the event that machinery bearing the EC mark is perceived to be dangerous. The provisions of Article 8 describe the procedure whereby a manufacturer can obtain a certificate that its goods conform to the Directive; an EC mark can then be affixed to the goods.

The Safety of Machinery Directive provides a good example of the legislative format used by the Community under the new approach to harmonization. It should not, however, be thought that the Community has only one legislative strategy for

---

[72] See more generally Dir. 93/68 [1993] OJ L220/1.

trade barriers which are lawful under the Treaty. The following extract distinguishes three such strategies open to the Community.

A. McGee and S. Weatherill, The Evolution of the Single Market-Harmonisation or Liberalisation[73]

1. It may pass legislation which covers the entire field in question, albeit in a very general way. This approach is referred to here as 'Exhaustive Regulation' because it involves Community rule-making which excludes Member States' competence to regulate the area. A good example of this is provided by product safety.

2. It may pass legislation which deals with some issues in the area under consideration, but leaves others to national law. This approach is referred to here as 'Partial Regulation'. Two good examples of this are provided by the Product Liability Directive and the Regulation creating the European Economic Interest Grouping. . . .

3. It may not act at all; there are numerous possible reasons for this. One is simply lack of resources, since there is much to be done in the pursuit of the Single Market, and some matters inevitably have higher priority than others. Another possibility is political difficulty in reaching an agreed position. This may in turn take either of two forms. There may be agreement that regulation is required, but no consensus about the form of the regulation, or there may be disagreement as to whether any form of regulation is called for. . . . Such failure to act, for whatever reason, is referred to here as 'No Regulation'.

If a Community harmonization measure is exhaustive in the above sense then it will pre-empt inconsistent national rules. Whether the harmonization measure is intended to preclude any national measures that differ from the Community directive may itself be a contentious issue. In *Ratti*[74] the ECJ had to decide whether Directive 73/173 on packaging and labelling of dangerous substances precluded a State from prescribing 'obligations and limitations which are more precise than, or at all events different from, those set out in the directive'. The disputed Italian rules required more information to be attached to the packaging than specified in the Directive. The Court held that the Directive enjoined this. The rules contained in the Directive were intended to prevent the State from laying down any specific, stricter rules of its own.

It may, by way of contrast, be apparent from the Directive itself that it only partially regulates the area in question. In *Grunert*[75] a French producer of food preservative containing lactic and citric acid was prosecuted for selling the food preservative for use in the making of certain pork meats. French law prohibited the use of preservatives unless authorized by the national authorities, and the acids used by the accused were not on the national list. Relevant Community Directives 64/54 and 70/357 did, however, list the two acids as among those that could be used to protect food against

---

[73] (1990) 53 *MLR* 578, 582.
[74] Case 148/78, *Pubblico Ministero v. Ratti* [1979] ECR 1629.
[75] Case 88/79, *Ministère Public v. Grunert* [1980] ECR 1827. See also Cases C–54 & 74/94, *Cacchiarelli* [1996] 2 CMLR 542; Cases C–320, 328–329, 337–379/94, *RTI v. Ministero delle Poste e Telecomunicazione* [1997] 1 CMLR 346.

deterioration. This was Grunert's defence. The Directives, however, went on to provide that they were not to affect provisions of national law specifying the foodstuffs to which the preservatives listed could be added. This was subject to the proviso that such national provisions did not have the effect of totally excluding the use in foodstuffs of any of the listed preservatives. The ECJ decided therefore that the Member States did have a discretion as to the foodstuffs to which listed preservatives could be added.

The general Community approach has shifted towards minimum, rather than total, harmonization. Total harmonization entailed exhaustive regulation of the given field, the corollary being the pre-emption of national action in that area. Minimum harmonization enables Member States to maintain more stringent regulatory standards than those prescribed by Community standards, provided that these are compatible with the Treaty. The Community legislation sets a floor, and the Treaty a ceiling, with Member States being free to pursue their own policies within these boundaries.[76]

7. COMPLETING THE INTERNAL MARKET: TENSIONS AND CONCERNS

The analysis thus far has shown the real advantages of the new approach to harmonization. It would, however, be wrong to imagine that these changes have been problem-free. Commentators have perceived a number of tensions and concerns inherent in the single-market strategy. We shall address three such concerns. They bring into focus the interrelationship between reforms of the trading process on the one hand, and broader socio-political considerations on the other.

(a) CONSUMER INTERESTS AND COMMERCIAL POWER

One concern is whether consumer interests are sufficiently protected in the process of attaining a single market. We should remember that many national rules that impede intra-Community trade are designed to protect consumers. This has been recognized in the Treaty itself, through provisions such as Article 30 (ex Article 36). It has been acknowledged in the ECJ's jurisprudence through the *Cassis* mandatory requirements. It has been accepted by the Commission: harmonization under the new approach will be necessary where Member States have legitimate health and safety interests. So far so good. No conflict between the realization of the single market and consumer protection. The latter will, where necessary, be addressed through Community measures which, at one and the same time, remove or reduce disparities between national rules, thereby easing barriers to trade, and ensure the continued protection of the consumer by appropriately framed Community directives or regulations. The problem is, however, whether the Community directives which emerge in

---

[76] S. Weatherill, 'Beyond Preemption? Shared Competence and Constitutional Change in the European Community', in D. O' Keefe and P. Twomey (eds.), *Legal Issues of the Maastricht Treaty* (Chancery Law Publishing, 1994), ch. 2; M. Dougan, 'Minimum Harmonization and the Internal Market' (2000) 37 *CMLRev*. 853, 855–6.

this way really will adequately balance consumer and manufacturing interests. Consider the following discussion by McGee and Weatherill.

A. McGee and S. Weatherill, The Evolution of the Single Market-Harmonisation or Liberalisation[77]

It is submitted that there are structural reasons why the New Approach might serve the European consumer ill. The difficulty lies in the privatisation of the standards making process which supports the New Approach. For financial reasons it is likely that business will capture the standardisation process within CEN. Consumer organisations lack resources to participate fully in CEN committee work; in any event, consumer representation is ill-organized and haphazard in several Member States. . . . If standards making becomes the province of business alone, the balance between consumer protection and free trade will be distorted, prejudicing overall public confidence in the Community.

[The authors return to the theme in their conclusion:]

This article has highlighted some of the major difficulties which currently beset the development of the Single Market. To some extent these may be regarded as technical problems caused by diversity of national tradition which are likely to be difficult even with the full-hearted cooperation of all those involved. What is also clear is that there are vested interests at work, which in many cases want either to delay the process or at least to manipulate it for their own purposes. . . .

Not surprisingly, national governments appear to be the most effective at controlling developments. . . . Business and commercial interests have proved less successful in blocking developments, but have been highly effective in getting control of the standard-setting process, as in the case of Toy Safety, and in ensuring that other provisions take the form which they want. Thus, the EEIG Regulation[78] excluded worker participation, the Product Liability Directive allowed for the inclusion of the development risks defence and the Merger Regulation ignores all considerations of social policy. Again, it is not surprising to find that the highly motivated, well organised and generously resourced interests at work here have proved effective. Far less successful have been the consumer and employee interests, whose concerns seem largely to have been overridden. This too need not be a cause for surprise, but it is important to ask the fundamental question, what sort of Single Market is being created here? The answer seems to be that it is a Market in which business flourishes, relatively free from protective regulation, but the legitimate interests of other social groups are at risk of being ignored.

These concerns should be taken seriously. They were addressed in part by the establishment in 1992 of ANEC, the European Association for the Co-ordination of Consumer Representation in Standardization, a body which is independent of the European standards agencies themselves. This has served to alleviate the concerns expressed above, but not to dispel them. Problems still remain concerning access of

---

[77] N. 73 above, 585, 595. See also N. Reich, 'Protection of Diffuse Interests in the EEC and the Perspective of Progressively Establishing an Internal Market' (1988) 11 *Jnl. Cons. Policy* 395.

[78] European Economic Interest Grouping.

ANEC to the CEN technical board, and also to the Commission's own standing committee.[79] As Amstrong and Bulmer note:[80]

the representation of consumer interests provides the third and linking part of the triangle between public legislative institutions on the one side and private standards-setters on the other. Whether that side of the triangle will serve to legitimate the actions of the other two sides will depend not only on its ability to harness technical resources, but also on its ability to increase its human and financial resources to enable it effectively to represent the consumer interest.

We should at the same time recognize that these concerns are also present when regulations about product safety and the like are made at national level. Tensions which result from the imbalance in power between consumer and commercial interests are not *created* by or because of harmonization measures being passed at Community rather than national level. They are endemic in most Western-style market economies. Given that this is so, whether consumer interests fare better in the regulatory process at national or Community level will depend upon a complex calculus in which a number of factors will be of relevance. These include the relative capacities of commercial and consumer interests to influence the legislative process within the Community and within the nation State, and the relative costs involved in operating within these differing polities. This does not mean that we should be complacent about the existence of interest-group power within the Community. Rather that we should take care when ascribing causality and be ready to address solutions which may help to redress the problem within the Community.

(b) THE SINGLE MARKET, MARKET FREEDOM, AND STRUCTURAL BALANCE

A second tension inherent in the single-market project is that between a Community-wide free market and its impact on the weaker economies of the Community. We have already seen that the SEA addressed this problem to some extent through Article 7c (now Article 15).[81] Whether this sufficed to meet the difficulty is more contestable. Consider the view of Dehousse.

R. Dehousse, Completing the Internal Market: Institutional Constraints and Challenges[82]

At some point . . . a major challenge will have to be faced, for the objective of market integration itself remains unacceptable, politically speaking, for some Member States if it is not accompanied by specific effort to improve the social and economic cohesion within the Community. It is worth recalling in this respect that economically weaker countries have been reluctant to accept majority voting, precisely because they are those who might suffer most in the short term from the creation of a single market. Of the many problems linked to the completion of the internal market,

---

[79] B. Farquhar, 'Consumer Representation in Standardisation' (1995) 3 *Consumer Law Journal* 56.
[80] N. 69 above, 165.   [81] See 1183 above.
[82] R. Bieber, R. Dehousse, J. Pinder, and J. Weiler (eds.), *1992: One European Market?* (Nomos, 1988), 336.

this one is perhaps the most difficult: unlike the concerns for a high level of health, consumer safety or the environment, this kind of fear cannot be allayed by derogatory measures alone. A parallel in the Community's allocative and redistributive policies has been strongly advocated by recent studies, both from a theoretical and from a practical viewpoint. The Single Act pledges the Community to reinforce its action in favour of backward areas; it even explicitly states that the completion of the internal market should be pursued taking into account the existence of different levels of development within the Community. . . .

However, it fails to give the Community additional means to reach that end. The crucial point is that, at a given stage, progress towards the single European market might be conditioned by the capacity to tackle the problem of structural imbalances: if the Community does not find a way to offer some compensation to those countries which feel they have more to lose, market integration could be severely hampered. More than institutional pragmatism will be needed in order to cut this Gordian knot.

Fulfilment of the single market project can generate macro-economic and social tensions between rich, poor, and middle-class economies within the Community. This should come as no surprise. Reflect on experience within nation States. A free-enterprise, market-driven, national economic policy will often create regional problems within a particular country. There will be areas in which there is high unemployment, decline of traditional industries, and relative poverty. There will be calls for assistance to be given to these areas.[83] It is not therefore surprising that a vigorous policy of increased competitiveness and breaking down Community trade barriers will produce similar tensions, albeit on a larger scale. Some countries will be concerned about their general ability to survive and prosper within this barrier-free, competitive environment. Dehousse is therefore quite right to point to the connections between the single market project and the need to tackle structural imbalances within the Community. Articles 158–162 (ex Article Articles 130a–e) provide the foundation for structural policies to deal with this problem. The balance between the single-market and structural intervention will, however, always be problematic.

(c) POLITICS, ECONOMICS, AND THE SINGLE MARKET ENTERPRISE

Conceptions of market freedom are not value-free. The meaning of this phrase, the manner in which such freedom is to be attained, and the appropriate limits to free markets are all matters on which there is considerable disagreement. These are key issues which have divided political parties. Let it be accepted that the Community has decided that removing barriers to intra-Community trade will bring economic benefits. There is, as we have seen, sound economic evidence for this decision. Yet even given this consensus, there is still room for considerable diversity of opinion about the necessary or desirable scope of protective Community measures. These differences of opinion are, moreover, perfectly possible among those of differing political persuasions all of whom are committed to the European ideal. The politicization which in

---

[83] It is, of course, the case that such calls will now be strictly constrained by the Community rules on state aids. That is not, however, of direct relevance here.

this sense accompanies the process of market integration has been noted by commentators. Thus, as Pelkmans notes, an internal-market strategy which cuts deeply into the regulatory environment, and which severely limits the options available to Member States, cannot pretend to be entirely apolitical.[84] Weiler develops the same theme.

J. Weiler, The Transformation of Europe[85]

It is an article of faith for European integration that the Commission is not meant to be a mere secretariat, but an autonomous force shaping the agenda and brokering the decisionmaking of the Community. And yet at the same time, the Commission, as broker, must be ideologically neutral, not favouring Christian Democrats, Social Democrats or others.

This neutralization of ideology has fostered the belief that an agenda could be set for the Community, and the Community could be led towards an ever closer union among its peoples, without having to face the normal political cleavages present in the Member States. In conclusion, the Community political culture which developed in the 1960s and 1970s led . . . to an habituation of all political forces to thinking of European integration as ideologically neutral in, or transcendent over, the normal debates on the left–right spectrum. It is easy to understand how this will have served the process of integration, allowing a nonpartisan coalition to emerge around its overall objectives.

1992 changes this in two ways. The first is a direct derivation from the turn to majority voting. Policies can be adopted now within the Council that run counter not simply to the perceived interests of a Member State, but more specifically to the ideology of the government in power. The debates about the European Social Charter and the shrill cries of 'Socialism through the back-door', as well as the emerging debate about Community adherence to the European Convention on Human Rights and abortion rights are harbingers of things to come. . . .

The second impact of 1992 on ideological neutrality is subtler. The entire program rests on two pivots: the single market plan encapsulated in the White Paper, and its operation through the instrumentalities of the Single European Act. . . . It is not simply a technocratic program to remove the remaining obstacles to the free movement of all factors of production. It is at the same time a highly politicized choice of ethos, ideology and political culture: the culture of 'the market'. It is also a philosophy, at least one version of which—the predominant version—seeks to remove barriers to the free movement of factors of production, and to remove distortion to competition as a means to maximize utility. The above is premised on the assumption of formal equality of individuals. It is an ideology the contours of which have been the subject of intense debate within the Member States in terms of their own political choices. . . . A successful single market requires widespread harmonization of standards and environmental protection, as well as the social package of employees. This need for a successful market not only accentuates the pressure for uniformity, but also manifests a social (and hence ideological) choice which prizes market efficiency and European-wide neutrality of competition above other competing values.

---

[84] J. Pelkmans, 'A Grand Design by the Piece? An Appraisal of the Internal Market Strategy', in Bieber, Dehousse, Pinder, and Weiler (eds.), n. 82 above, 371.

[85] (1991) 100 Yale LJ 2403, 2476–8.

8. THE RECONCEPTUALIZATION OF THE INTERNAL MARKET

The single-market project did not magically come to an end in December 1992. There was a continuing flow of internal market legislation post-1992. This was matched by a number of reports that addressed various aspects of the Community regulatory process. These reports can be broadly divided into groups. In the first, the Commission focused on completion of the internal market in a relatively narrow economic sense. In the second group, the focus shifted. The concern for economic integration *per se* is still evident, but the internal market is consciously conceptualized in a broader, more holistic, manner.[86] Consumer welfare, social policy, environmental policy, and the like are all regarded as important facets of the internal market strategy. This material is therefore of direct relevance for the concerns voiced in the previous section.

There have been *many reports focusing on attainment of the internal market in the economic sense of the term*. In 1993 the Commission produced its strategic programme on *Making the Most of the Internal Market*,[87] in which it reviewed macroissues such as the completion of the legal framework, and the management and development of the single market. In 1996 the Commission undertook a wide-ranging study on *The Impact and Effectiveness of the Single Market*.[88] The study measured the economic gains from the internal market in terms of increase in GDP, lower inflation, higher employment, etc. It also confirmed areas where further action was required, such as public procurement, tax harmonization, company law, and the transposition of directives. The Commission developed these themes in its *Single Market-Action Plan*,[89] in which it identified four principal strategic goals for the development of the single market. These were: making the rules more effective, dealing with market distortions, removing sectoral obstacles to market integration, and delivering a single market for the benefit of all citizens. The Amsterdam European Council officially endorsed these goals in 1997. The 1997 *Action Plan* led to further reports that focused on specific aspects of free movement. Particular attention was given to making the principle of mutual recognition more effective.[90] There have been specific initiatives directed towards services,[91] and more especially to financial services.[92] There have been improvements to mutual recognition of professional qualifications, and a

---

[86] P. Craig, 'The Evolution of the Single Market', in C. Barnard and J. Scott (eds.), *The Law of the Single European Market* (Hart, 2002), ch. 1.

[87] COM(93)632 final.

[88] COM(96)520 final.

[89] Communication of the Commission to the European Council, *Action Plan for the Single Market*, SEC(97) 1 final.

[90] Communication from the Commission to the European Parliament and the Council, *Mutual Recognition in the Context of the follow-up to the Action Plan for the Single Market*, 16 June 1999.

[91] *An Internal Market Strategy for Services*, COM(2000) 888.

[92] Commission Communication, *Financial Services—Implementing the Framework for Financial Markets: Action Plan*, COM(1999)232; *Institutional Arrangements for the Regulation and Supervision of the Financial Sector*, Jan. 2000; *Financial Services Priorities and Progress, Third Report*, COM(2000)692/2 final.

new simplified directive has been adopted.[93] This directive was part of the more general Commission initiative designed to consolidate, codify, and simplify EU legislation.[94]

A broader conception of the internal market is however also to be found in a number of the major papers emanating from the Commission and the European Council. The internal market is conceptualized in more holistic terms, to include not only economic integration, but also consumer safety, social rights, labour policy, and the environment. This shift did not occur at any single moment. It developed across time. None the less certain important steps in this progression can be identified.

The *1997 Action Plan* is significant in this respect. The fourth strategic target was to deliver a single market for the benefit of all citizens. The Commission's introduction to the *Action Plan* consciously stressed that 'the single market was not simply an economic structure', but included basic standards of health and safety, equal opportunities, and labour law measures.[95] This theme was carried over in the *1997 Action Plan* itself. The strategic target of delivering a single market for the benefit of all citizens was particularized through action directed towards, *inter alia*, the protection of social rights, consumer rights, health and the environment, and the right of residence.[96]

The Lisbon European Council constituted another important stage in the reconfiguration of the internal market agenda. The meeting, held in March 2000, focused on employment, economic reform, and social cohesion. It set a 'new' strategic goal: the Union was to become 'the most competitive and dynamic knowledge-based economy in the world, capable of sustainable economic growth with more and better jobs and greater social cohesion'.[97] Completion of the internal market was to be one way of achieving this strategy.[98] The modernization of the European social model through the building of an active welfare state was to be another. This was crucial to ensure that 'the emergence of this new economy does not compound the existing social problems of unemployment, social exclusion, and poverty'.[99] This objective was further particularized in terms of better education, an active employment policy, modernizing social protection, and promoting social inclusion.[100] These commitments were reiterated at the Feira European Council.[101] The same theme permeated the Nice European Council.[102] It considered a 'New Impetus for an Economic and Social Europe'. It approved the European Social Agenda developed by the Commission, which was characterized by the 'indissoluble link between economic performance and

---

[93] *Professional Qualifications: Commission Welcomes Adoption of Simplification Directive,* 26 Feb. 2001; Dir. 2001/19, [2001] OJ L206/1, *Directive of the European Parliament and of the Council on the General System of the Recognition of Professional Qualifications.*

[94] Commission Communication on *Simpler Legislation for the Internal Market (SLIM): A Pilot Programme,* COM(96)204 final; *Commission Report on the SLIM Pilot Project,* COM(96)559 final; Report from the Commission to the European Parliament and the Council, *Results of the Fourth Phase of SLIM,* COM(2000)56 final; T. Burns, 'Better Lawmaking? An Evaluation of Lawmaking in the European Community', in P. Craig and C. Harlow (eds.), *Lawmaking in the European Union* (Kluwer, 1998), ch. 21.

[95] *Single Market Action Plan sets Agenda,* 18 June 1997, 2.

[96] *Action Plan,* n. 89 above, 9–11.

[97] Lisbon European Council, 23–24 Mar. 2000, para. 5.

[98] *Ibid.,* paras. 5, 16–21.   [99] *Ibid.,* para. 24.   [100] *Ibid.,* paras. 25–34.

[101] Feira European Council, 19–20 June 2000, paras. 19–39, 44–49.

[102] Nice European Council, 7–9 Dec. 2000.

social progress'.[103] This link had been forged by the Commission and endorsed by the European Parliament.[104] Economic growth and social cohesion were seen as mutually reinforcing.[105] The Stockholm European Council echoed the same idea. There was 'full agreement that economic reform, employment and social policies were mutually reinforcing';[106] a 'dynamic Union should consist of active welfare states'.[107]

The principal Commission reports concerning the internal market in 2000 pick up and develop the ideas articulated by the European Council. Thus the *2000 Review of the Internal Market Strategy*[108] took the strategic remit of the Lisbon European Council as its starting point. The internal market should be made as effective as possible in economic terms, but it must also seek to foster job creation, social cohesion, and safety. This is reflected in the detailed list of legislative and non-legislative initiatives appended to the report, many of which deal specifically with issues of consumer health and safety and the like.[109] The same stress on the interconnection between the economic and social aspects of the internal market is to be found in the later report on the *Functioning of Community Product and Capital Markets*.[110] In economic terms, a properly functioning internal market was seen as the key to prosperity for Community citizens. This meant breaking down barriers to trade where they existed, especially in the services sector. In social terms, the internal market was seen as the guarantee of specific rights to safe, high-quality products.[111] The Commission accepted the conclusions of the Internal Market Council of March 2000, that high levels of consumer protection and consumer confidence were needed for a well-functioning internal market.[112] It acknowledged also that environmental concerns required a 'reinforced, symbiotic integration of environmental policy and economic reforms inside the Internal Market'.[113] The updated Commission Communication on *Services of General Interest*[114] consciously drew on the conclusions of the Lisbon and Feira European Councils, and stressed the economic and social aspects of such services.

9. CONCLUSION

i. The most significant contribution of the SEA and the single market project to the process of European integration might, in the long term, be that it jolted the Community out of the Euro-pessimism of the 1970s and early 1980s. If there had been no SEA, the new approach to harmonization might never have taken hold at all. The SEA laid the foundations for the institutional and substantive changes which have occurred since then. Causality in international affairs is

---

[103] *Ibid.*, para. 15.   [104] *Ibid.*, Annex 1, paras. 8–9.
[105] *Ibid.*, Annex 1, paras. 9, 11. [106] Stockholm European Council, para. 2.
[107] *Ibid.*, para. 25.   [108] COM(2000) 257 final. [109] *Ibid.*, 15–17.
[110] *Economic Reform: Report on the Functioning of Community Capital and Product Markets*, COM(2000)881 final.
[111] *Ibid.*, 3–4. [112] *Ibid.*, 5. [113] *Ibid.*, 5.
[114] *Services of General Interest in Europe*, COM(2000)580 final. These are services that public authorities decide should be provided even though ordinary market forces may not do so: para. 14.

difficult to determine. But it is doubtful whether the TEU would ever have been negotiated had the SEA not preceded it.

ii. The focus in the 1980s and early 1990s was, not unnaturally, on the economic dimensions of the single market. Legislative, administrative, and judicial initiatives contributed towards the breaking down of the economic barriers to the single market. This is still a central aspect of single-market policy, notwithstanding the fact that a decade has passed since the 1992 deadline.

iii. The focus from the mid-1990s onwards has shifted. The internal market is now felt to embrace broader concerns relating to social, environmental, and consumer policy. This has been a conscious shift by the EC, anxious to avoid the critique that pursuit of the single market has undercut social, etc., protections that exist within the Member States.

10. FURTHER READING

(a) *Books*

ARMSTRONG, K., *Regulation, Deregulation, Re-regulation* (Kogan Page, 2000)

—— BULMER, S., *The Governance of the Single European Market* (Manchester University Press, 1998)

BARNARD, C., and SCOTT, J. (eds.), *The Law of the Single European Market* (Hart, 2002)

BREALEY, M., and QUIGLEY, C., *Completing the Internal Market of the EC* (Graham & Trotman, 2nd edn., 1989)

BIEBER, R., DEHOUSSE, R., PINDER, J., and WEILER, J. (eds.), *1992: One European Market?* (Nomos, 1988)

CECCHINI, P., *The European Challenge—1992* (Gower, 1988)

DAINTITH, T. (ed.), *Implementing EC Law in the United Kingdom, Structures for Indirect Rule* (Wiley, 1995)

EMERSON, M., AUJEAN, M., CATINAT, M., GOYBET, P., and JACQUEMIN, A., *The Economics of 1992* (Oxford University Press, 1988)

MAJONE, G., *Regulating Europe* (Routledge, 1996)

SNYDER, F. (ed.), *Constitutional Dimensions of European Economic Integration* (Kluwer, 1996)

(b) *Articles*

ARMSTRONG, K., 'Governance and the Single European Market', in P. Craig and G. de Búrca (eds.), *The Evolution of EU Law* (Oxford University Press, 1999), ch. 21

BIEBER, R., 'Legislative Procedure for the Establishment of the Single Market' (1988) 25 *CMLRev.* 711

BURROWS, N., 'Harmonisation of Technical Standards: Reculer Pour Mieux Sauter?' (1990) 53 *MLR* 597

CRAIG, P., 'The Evolution of the Single Market', in C. Barnard and J. Scott (eds.), *The Law of the Single European Market* (Hart, 2002), ch.1

CROSBY, S., 'The Single Market and the Rule of Law' (1991) 16 *ELRev.* 451

DAINTITH, T., 'European Community Law and the Redistribution of Regulatory Power in the United Kingdom' (1995) 1 *ELJ* 134

DEHOUSSE, R., '1992 and Beyond: The Institutional Dimension of the Internal Market Programme' [1989] 1 *LIEI* 109

DOUGAN, M., 'Minimum Harmonization and the Internal Market' (2000) 37 *CMLRev.* 853

EDWARD, D., 'The Impact of the Single Act on the Institutions' (1987) 24 *CMLRev.* 19

EHLERMANN, C.-D., 'The Internal Market Following the Single European Act' (1987) 24 *CMLRev.* 361

FARQUHAR, B., 'Consumer Representation in Standardisation' (1995) 3 *Consumer Law Journal* 56

FORWOOD, N., and CLOUGH, M., 'The Single European Act and Free Movement' (1986) 11 *ELRev.* 383

GLAESNER, H.J., 'The Single European Act: Attempt at an Appraisal' (1987) 10 *Fordham Int. LJ* 446

McGEE, A., and WEATHERILL, S., 'The Evolution of the Single Market-Harmonisation or Liberalisation' (1990) 53 *MLR* 578

MORAVCSIK, A., 'Negotiating the Single European Act: National Interests and Conventional Statecraft in the European Community' (1991) 45 *International Organization* 19

PESCATORE, P., 'Some Critical Remarks on the "Single European Act" ' (1987) 24 *CMLRev.* 9

PELKMANS, J., 'The New Approach to Technical Harmonization and Standardization' (1987) 25 *JCMS* 249

SANDHOLTZ, W., and ZYSMAN, J., '1992: Recasting the European Bargain' (1989) 42 *World Politics* 95

SUN, J.-M., and PELKMANS, J., 'Regulatory Competition and the Single Market' (1995) 33 *JCMS* 67

STREIT, M., and MUSSLER, W., 'The Economic Constitution of the European Community: From "Rome" to "Maastricht" ' (1995) 1 *ELJ* 5

TOTH, A., 'The Legal Status of the Declarations Annexed to the Single European Act' (1986) 23 *CMLRev.* 803

VIGNES, D., 'The Harmonization of National Legislation and the EEC' (1990) 15 *ELRev.* 358

WEATHERILL, S., 'Beyond Preemption? Shared Competence and Constitutional Change in the European Community', in D. O'Keeffe and P. Twomey (eds.), *Legal Issues of the Maastricht Treaty* (Chancery Law Publishing, 1994), ch. 2

INDEX

W